CLASSIFICATION
AND INDEX
OF THE
WORLD'S LANGUAGES

Foundations of Linguistics Series

Editor:
Charles F. Hockett, *Cornell University*

Contributors:
Erwin A. Esper
Mentalism and Objectivism in Linguistics:
The Sources of Leonard Bloomfield's Psychology of Language, 1968

Robert A. Hall, Jr.
Comparative Romance Grammar:
External History of the Romance Languages, Volume I, 1974
Proto-Romance Phonology, Volume II, 1976

C. F. and F. M. Voegelin
Classification and Index of the World's Languages, 1977

CLASSIFICATION
AND INDEX
OF THE
WORLD'S LANGUAGES

C. F. and F. M. Voegelin

Department of Anthropology, Indiana University

ELSEVIER

NEW YORK   OXFORD   AMSTERDAM

ELSEVIER NORTH-HOLLAND, INC.
52 Vanderbilt Avenue, New York, NY 10017

ELSEVIER SCIENTIFIC PUBLISHING COMPANY
335 Jan Van Galenstraat, P.O. Box 211
Amsterdam, The Netherlands

Library of Congress Cataloging in Publication Data

Voegelin, Charles Frederick, 1906—
    Classification and index of the world's languages.

    (Foundations of linguistics series)
    Bibliography: p.
    1. Language and languages—Classification. I. Voege-
lin, Florence Marie Robinett, 1927—   joint author.
II. Title.
P203.V6   401'.2   74-19546
ISBN 0-444-00155-7

Printed in the United States of America

Dedicated to
Franz Boas, Edward Sapir, Leonard Bloomfield,
the founding fathers
of anthropological linguistics

CONTENTS

ACKNOWLEDGMENTS

This volume is based in part upon our earlier survey of the literature, *Languages of the World*, published as twenty separate numbers of the journal *Anthropological Linguistics* (1964-66). With the assistance of a further NDEA contract the earlier work was revised with the guidance of additional consultants and with a fresh review of literature and the incorporation of information volunteered by readers of the first survey. Further revisions have here been added to the NDEA contract report (1973), through the guidance of further readers and consultants.

We are indebted to Charles F. Hockett, not only for suggesting that we prepare this volume, but also for providing us with a model for its preparation.

Whatever is freshly insightful in the text we owe to the wisdom of the many consultants who provided us with information and advice in the preparation of both this volume and the previous *Report* and *Languages of the World* fascicles from which it grew: Joseph Applegate, Jack Berry, David Blood, Doris Blood, Nicholas C. Bodman, William Bright, Denzel Carr, Y.R. Chao, Samuel H. Elbert, Murray B. Emeneau, David Francis, George Grace, Joseph H. Greenberg, Mary R. Haas, Kenneth L. Hale, Eric Hamp, Robert K. Headley, Jr., Carleton T. Hodge, Vladimir Honsa, Fred W. Householder, M. Dale Kinkade, Harold L. Klagstad, Winfred P. Lehmann, Fang Kuei Li, Ian Maddieson, Howard McKaughan, Fred K. Meinecke, Robert Morse, Geoffrey N. O'Grady, J. Joseph Pia, Alo Raun, Albert J. Schütz, Laurence C. Thompson, Donald Topping, E.M. Uhlenbeck, Albert Valdman, Harry Velten, Erhard F.K. Voeltz, Calvert Watkins, William Welmers, Hans Wolff, Dean S. Worth, Stephen A. Wurm, Akira Yamamoto.

The preparation of this volume could not have been accomplished without the assistance of the many graduate students who worked with us in preparing the *Report* and the *Languages of the World* fascicles, and in particular Ernest Lee and Noel W. Schutz, nor without the assistance of Gloria Daily, who typed, keypunched and alphabetized our work in progress with admirable accuracy.

C.F. and F.M. Voegelin

INTRODUCTION

Almost two centuries have passed since the recognition of exact genetic correspondences between daughter languages in the Indo-European family; one century since the recognition that all the languages of the world could yield reconstructed proto languages, including the unwritten ones (i.e. not only those languages with written documents attesting earlier stages).

One property of natural languages is that such languages permit theoretically exhaustive matching between their phonologies, grammars, and lexicons. This is of course not the only property, but it is the only aspect of natural languages that has been investigated extensively enough to permit a world-wide survey. It is true that large numbers of languages have been surveyed in the examination of typological problems in phonology and syntax (e.g. the limits of phonological systems and their components; e.g. the order of subject and object in respect to the verb), and in the examination of sociolinguistic problems (e.g. the extent of bilingualism in particular populations and the social situations in which the different languages are used; the extent of writing and the purposes for which it is used). However, since data on such aspects are extremely limited for some language families and non-existent for most, it will be for the future to attempt any beyond a sampling of aspects of language other than genetic relationship.

This implies of course that no major area of the world today remains untouched or, rather, unsampled for genetic relationship classification—but this state of affairs is quite recent. A few decades ago, New Guinea was linguistically *terra incognita*, with a reputation, nonetheless, of representing greater linguistic diversity than any other commensurate area. Now almost every New Guinea language has been identified—at least sufficiently for classification of one sort or another.

But this is not the only implication of the fact that natural languages can be compared. Of the relatively few ancient languages on which linguistic information is available, and of the many natural languages subject to linguistic investigation today, no counter-example, based on empirical evidence, has been shown to weaken the claim that natural languages fall within a relatively narrow range of variety in phonology and grammar, even though some natural languages are spoken in societies with sophisticated technologies, and others in societies with underdeveloped or 'primitive' cultures. Southern Paiute, bereft of cultural elaboration and without agriculture, equals in phonological complexity and grammatical subtlety languages spoken in ceremonially complex subsistence farming societies (as Hopi which belongs in the same family as Southern Paiute); and languages like Japanese or English, spoken in societies with sophisticated technologies, are no more elaborate in their phonologies or grammatical subtleties than are Southern Paiute and Hopi. The only legitimate doubt about the non-existence of improving evolution of language lies in the realm of translation—indirectly related to the size of the lexicon—as does the only evidence supporting the doubt. The most cited example is the greater facility with which Greek could be translated into Latin in Augustan times than into the Latin spoken long before Augustan times—because in the transitional period Latin developed terms or borrowed terms and the culture associated with the terms that permitted straight translation rather than paraphrastic translation of Greek. What can be said with certainty is that there is much less range in typological complexity of languages than there is in the typological complexity of the societies in which they are spoken.

Some sociolinguists would add a caveat to this, or protest that all the creoles known in the world do in fact—like societies with underdeveloped cultures—show a reduction in phonological and grammatical complexity when compared to the languages from which they are lexically derived. This question is so far indeterminate—part of the problem is that fully adequate grammars of creole languages are not yet available; they are still in the category of forthcoming research and publication. Without such detailed grammars, we do not know whether a loss of inflection in a creole from the language(s) on which it is based lexically may be offset by an elaboration in syntax.

The question of the proto-language from which creoles are descended is also indeterminate, and perhaps will remain indeterminate; hence we list creoles in terms of their predominant lexical source, as English-based creoles, French-based creoles, and so on. A creole can be said to be like any other natural language, but with more derivative borrowing than is usual for other natural languages, which are of course both potential donors and borrowers in languages in contact situations (and words also diffuse across multiple language boundaries from a source language to distant languages which are not in contact with the source language).

It is obvious that inner stimuli (what Sapir called 'drift' and Meillet called 'tendencies'), such as changes of rules (or changes in scope of the same rules) from generation to generation, do not alone provoke changes from a proto-language; they combine with outer stimuli from factors affecting languages in external history. Knowledge of the external history of languages in a given family, where available, points to possible sources of past borrowing by languages in that family. Such external history is best documented for the INDO-EUROPEAN languages of Europe, as for example by Hall (1974), External History of the Romance Languages.

So far, work in synchronic or descriptive linguistics has been more directly contributory to the classification of languages than the other way around. Language relationships can be made well attested only when information supplied by descriptive linguistics has preceded their classification and reconstruction; work in synchronic linguistics that precedes work in diachronic linguistics serves to guarantee the accuracy of the latter.

But the number of languages separated by high barriers to understanding is so large—and the number of their varieties is even larger (i.e. for virtually every language spoken there are two or more dialects)—that a corresponding number of grammars for each language would be required to obtain a classification that is demonstrably accurate for all languages of the world. Hence, in the classification articles (entries) which follow, the lack of ideal attestation is frequently noted for languages postulated as belonging in the same genetic group.

The genetic group may include languages which are more or less closely related, or quite remotely related; the former is here called a 'language family', and the latter a 'phylum'. (Some classifiers prefer to speak of the superordinate genetic group of remotely related languages as a 'family' rather than as a 'phylum'.) Language families including more than two languages have as constituents smaller 'families', 'subfamilies' or 'branches'; thus GERMANIC is variously called a 'family', 'subfamily' or 'branch' of the INDO-EUROPEAN family. Some recognized language families (e.g. UTO-AZTECAN) are postulated to be remotely related to other recognized language families (e.g. TANOAN) in an uncertain, distant or phylum relationship; we designate AZTEC-TANOAN as a phylum that includes both language families mentioned in one genetic group on the basis of correspondences found between the two families which are however less rich and detailed than those observed within each family. For such remotely related languages it is to be expected that much less evidence of the lexicon and the phonological and syntactic systems of the remote parent language will remain in the documented daughter languages; hence the relationship is attestable in less elaborate detail. But to the extent that the persisting correspondences are plausible and cogent the relationship is no less certain.

The classification of the world's languages (in terms of common descent from many proto languages) is directly contributory to the global perspective in anthropology; it is potentially contributory to some questions asked in psychology and philosophy; but it is only indirectly contributory to the science of language (synchronic linguistics, for the most part).

Since the center of linguistic theory has moved from the description and comparison of its relevant phenomena to raising explanatory questions, the relationship of synchrony and diachrony is being freshly examined. As mentioned, the science of linguistics (synchrony) has for long offered the best attestation for the history of languages (diachrony); now the classification (genetic rather than typological) of the world's languages may come to be contributory to some controversies in linguistic theory, especially in generative phonology. Thus, internal reconstructions of languages which are made on the basis of 'morphophonemics'—now broadened to 'generative phonology'—without benefit of comparison with cognate languages can be interestingly explanatory especially when their results are checked against phonological reconstructions which summarize comparisons between related languages.

What has been said of on-going work in linguistic theory (Jakobson, 1974, pp. 18, 19):— '... attention [is] focused upon the antinomies which one meets...' —can also be said as soon as one tries to work with classifications and subclassifications (internal relationships) of the world's language families and phyla. Under the headings *GROUPING* and *AFFILIATION* in the classificatory articles which follow, contradictions in classification are often given. These differences in part serve to suggest the current state of progress for a given family or phyla in inferring past developments from comparisons of contemporary languages, and in part are a reflection of the different bases of classification used by different investigators of a particular genetic group. Antinomies—i.e. conflicting opinions—can be found between classifications based on lexical comparisons done by informed intuitive inspection of the vocabulary or some part of it, by mass comparisons, by statistical comparison of fixed lexical lists (lexicostatistics), by the development of the sound systems of the languages from that of the parent language as reflected in cognates and by cognate reflection with syntactic comparison.

Lists of how many languages belong to a particular genetic group are also frought with contradictions. Counting languages presupposes that it is possible unequivocally to distinguish language from dialect. A variety of not always compatible criteria are used by different investigators. Some distinctions of dialect versus language are based on ethnic considerations rather than linguistic factors: if societies are identified by different names, their members are supposed to speak different languages; if the members of a society say they speak the same or a different language than the members of another society, then their languages are said to be the same or different ('ask the informant'). But the members of two societies at different socio-economic levels may disagree: thus Luri speakers say they speak a dialect of Persian, but Persian speakers say Luri is a different language. It is also said that if the (spelling) orthographies used by two societies are different, their languages are different. Other criteria mix ethnic and linguistic factors, as for example the much invoked mutual intelligibility criterion.

In addition there is a question involved in neighbor intelligibility. Speakers of A understand the speech of their neighbors, B, who also understand the speech of their neighbors, C, who also understand the speech of their neighbors, D; but the speakers of A and D are totally unable to understand each other. Are A and D then the same language or separate languages?

Others propose more strictly linguistic criteria for the definition of separate languages within the same family, such as unshared innovations in phonology, syntax or lexicon.

(Since writing this introduction we have read Hendrik Birnbaum's perspicuous critique of the latest volume of *Current Trends* (*Diachronic, Areal, and Typological Lingusitics*) in *Foundations of Language*, **13**, 267–91 (1975). Birnbaum holds that the two salient classifications in linguistics are (1) genetic—called '*Diachronic*' in the title of volume XI of *Current Trends*—and (2) typological classification; and that areal linguistics is inevitably incorporated in or inseparable from (1) and/or (2). We concur: Birnbaum confirms the initial emphasis of our introduction—that a world-wide survey of languages is now possible for classification (1), but will remain impossible for classification (2) until preliminary typological classifications become available for the continents and islands of the world.)

Content and Arrangement of the Entries

The title of an entry article appears in boldface beginning at the left margin of the line above the body of the entry. In general, each entry is given for its title the name of a group of related languages (e.g. AUSTRONESIAN, GERMANIC, INDO-EUROPEAN). In the case of single languages which are not part of a group at the level of relationship being treated—as Albanian, which is the sole member of its branch of INDO-EUROPEAN, or Basque, for which no relationships have been demonstrated—the entries report only on that one language rather than on a group of languages. (Names of groups of languages are printed entirely in capital letters, as GERMANIC; names of single languages, as Albanian, are not.)

On the whole the groups of languages discussed in an entry represent genetic units—or purported genetic units. For genetic units it is claimed that the languages within the group are more closely related to each other than to those outside the group. But, occasionally, in such large families as AUSTRONESIAN where comparative work has not been done on all the languages, no claims have been made about the internal relations of certain subgroups. These can only be reported on a geographical basis; when they are clearly not attested as being genetic subgroups they are specified as being geographical in the titles of their entries, e.g., EAST INDONESIAN AUSTRONESIAN (GEOGRAPHIC).

The genetic unity of some proposed groups is in doubt; such groups (as SINO-TIBETAN) are, however, often treated in separate entries, and the doubts are discussed in the body of the entry.

At least one entry (PALEOSIBERIAN) treats a group of languages not believed to be genetically related, but mentioned in the literature as a group so frequently as to seem worthy of an article.

The scope of relationship of the languages included in a genetic entry depends in part on the size of the groups which comprise the lowest subdivisions of that particular genetic unit. An attempt was made to avoid overly long lists of languages in any one entry—in other words, to keep the number of languages discussed in each entry down to a size which would allow the reader to find information on a particular language with reasonably small effort. For example, there are hundreds of languages classified as belonging to AUSTRONESIAN; if these were presented in a single list in an article on AUSTRONESIAN, the reader might well become bogged down. Therefore, instead of presenting a single list of all such languages, names of AUSTRONESIAN languages are listed in a number of entries on smaller subgroups, as POLYNESIAN, WEST INDONESIAN, and LOYALTY ISLANDS. The entry on AUSTRONESIAN then refers the reader to the various subgroups of AUSTRONESIAN.

The attempt to limit the length of articles could be carried out in all but a few cases. Thus, dividing WEST INDONESIAN into smaller subgroups would have produced too many entries on small, not-well-agreed-upon groups. For a more conspicuous example, observe the long list of BANTU languages which appear together in a single entry; one possible alternative to this long BANTU list would have been to provide separate entries for all the geographic zones, which are labelled by letters, A, B, C, and so on, which would have greatly proliferated the number of entries labelled as BANTU.

The internal relationships of the members of the group covered by an entry are discussed in an initial paragraph or paragraphs under the heading *GROUPING*, after which the members of the group, or various subgroups within it, are listed. For a few groups upon which scholarship is limited and little comparative work has been done (as some of the subgroups of the AUSTRALIAN MACRO-PHYLUM) the co-ordinate members of the group covered by the entry are simply listed under *GROUPING* without discussion.

After the discussion of their internal *GROUPING*, the languages belonging to the group treated in an entry article are listed. A given language may be identified by a single name or by two or more alternate names. For the latter case, name is followed by an equal sign followed by another name, or by a succession of additional equal signs and names up to a period. Where it seemed clear from the literature that a particular name among several for a language is most frequently used, and where a particular spelling of that name is known to be preferred, that name is given first and other names or other spellings are given after equal signs as alternatives. Where alternate names differ from each other only by the presence or absence of an additional letter or two, the alternation is shown by giving the name in the longer form with parentheses around the letter or letters which may be omitted. (The number of alternate names or alternate spellings of the same names listed is in part a happenstance of the nature of the classificatory literature consulted on the languages of particular areas of the world.) For North America, Landar (1973) presents an extraordinarily extensive list of alternate names (e.g., 32 spellings of Potawatomi); for Australia alternate names are extensively listed by Greenway.

The name of the language with its alternates is followed by the names of its dialects where known. In cases where the language name is a cover-term for the names of its dialects the list of dialects is preceded by the abbreviation 'Ds.' (for 'Dialects'). Where the language name is the same as the name of one of its dialects, the list of other dialects is preceded by 'Ds. also' or 'D. also' (in the case of a single additional dialect). The convention followed here of labelling each language by a single word name wherever possible may seem awkward to Americanists who are familiar with the convention of naming languages by hyphenating the names of the tribes which speak that language; the familiar Fox-Sauk-Kickapoo is given here as 'Fox. Ds. also Kickapoo, Sauk' (with alternate spellings of these), and cross-references will list Kickapoo and Sauk as dialects of Fox.

Where the literature is unclear on the question of whether different groups of people speaking the same language are dialectally differentiated, we list names of presumptive dialects as dialects, even though some such names may be names of different tribes which might not be dialectically differentiated. But whenever the literature clearly identifies tribes and yet remains non-committal as to whether such tribes speak different dialects—as in many parts of Africa—the tribal or band names in question are identified as such by the abbreviation 'Tr.' (for 'Tribe') rather than by 'D.' (for 'Dialect').

The names of the dialects of a language (or the name of the language, if no dialects are listed) are followed by the number of speakers of the language and the location of those speakers, where such information is known to us. However, when all or most of the languages in a particular group are spoken in the same area, the location is usually given in the discussion under *GROUPING* rather than specified at the listing of each language.

An asterisk preceding the name of a language or dialect indicates that that language or dialect is no longer spoken.

A question mark after the name of a language or dialect indicates that the language or dialect is only doubtfully included in that group—i.e., that the name has appeared in the literature in conjunction with other names of languages or dialects of the group, but has not been sufficiently identified.

For each entry the relationship of the group as a whole to other groups of languages is given finally, under the heading *AFFILIATION*. Thus, in the entry for

GERMANIC, one learns from the *AFFILIATION* statement that GERMANIC is a branch of INDO-EUROPEAN. If the reader then consults the entry for INDO-EUROPEAN he will learn from its *GROUPING* statement what other branches have been ascribed to INDO-EUROPEAN, as well as how these branches may be inter-related; and, from its *AFFILIATION* statement, what distant relationships of INDO-EUROPEAN with other groups, as SEMITIC, have been proposed.

Alphabetical Ordering

Entry articles are given in alphabetical order, and within an article the members of that group are also listed in alphabetical order. Thus, when the languages of the group are not further subgrouped, the languages are listed in alphabetical order, but if the entry group is divided into named subgroups (as CENTRAL SUDANIC is divided into BAGIRMI, BONGO, KARA, MANBETU, MANGBUTU-EFE, MORU-MA'DI, and SARA), the subgroups are given in alphabetical order and the languages within each are separately alphabetized. So also, if the subgroups of an entry group are numbered rather than named (as subgroups I through IX of ADAMAWA), the subgroups are given in numerical order with the languages in each numbered subgroup separately alphabetized.

The names of many languages and language groups begin with directional, locational, or other modifiers. Such modifiers are ignored in the primary alphabetiza-tion, so that WEST ATLANTIC appears in the *A*'s, WEST INDONESIAN in the *I*'s; FORMOSAN AUSTRONESIAN appears in the *A*'s, CENTRAL SUDANIC in the *S*'s, MACRO-ALGONQUIAN in the *A*'s, and so on. When such words are the sole name of a group, or part of place names which serve to name language groups, they are alphabetized in the same way as other names; thus, AUSTRALIAN appears in the *A*'s, EASTERN (of ADAMAWA-EASTERN) in the *E*'s, NEW CALEDONIA in the *N*'s. Modifiers are, however, not ignored in secondary alphabetization so that FORMOSAN AUSTRONESIAN is followed by NORTHEAST NEW GUINEA AUSTRONESIAN, NORTHWEST AUSTRONESIAN, PAPUA AUSTRO-NESIAN, and so on.

References

The research for this volume centers in classification; hence, the references cited throughout are to works which discuss the classification of particular groups of langu-ages. The references cited are not intended to be a full bibliography of the field. Though many other sources than those cited were consulted in the course of the preparation of this volume, we list almost exclusively those specifically mentioned in the entries. Consulted but excluded from the bibliography were many works which provided only the names of a few additional languages, alternate names, locations, and the like, whether they dealt directly with classification or not. Some works are listed in the references which are not specifically mentioned in the entries for which they provided information in the form of alternate names, populations, locations and the like, since their scope encompassed many entries; e.g., Chafe's (1962) "Estimates Regarding the Present Speakers of North American Indian Languages" and Landar's (1973) "The Tribes and Languages of North America: A Check List." Since this volume treats the results of classificatory work rather than the evidence on which the classifications are based, many important sources were omitted because their results are summarized in other sources. Other sources were omitted inadvertently because they were not encountered or had not yet appeared at the time particular entries were written. It is intended that the bibliography should lead the reader not only to other sources on the classification of languages but also, incidentally, to descriptive material on the languages classified.

Where no references are cited in the *GROUPING* or *AFFILIATION* statements for a particular entry the reader can find the relevant references by looking at the *GROUPING* and *AFFILIATION* statements of the larger group to which it belongs.

For the most part no references are cited for population figures. Many of the figures are taken from the sources cited for the language classification (e.g., Wurm (1971c) for many INDO-PACIFIC groups). Where estimates are very divergent, sources are sometimes cited, as for the MUNDA languages for which the figures of the 1951 Census of India are compared with figures from more recent sources. None of the figures should be taken too literally as the actual number of speakers, except, perhaps, those for languages of which only a few speakers remain, as some North American Indian languages (where the picture is also changing since many Indians are now studying their 'native' languages in classes). At best, census data for languages are more difficult to interpret than other census data; ambiguity not infrequently exists, especially where bi- or multi-lingualism of minority populations is involved— i.e., as to whether the population figures refer to members of a given ethnic group or to speakers of the language associated with that group. When Wurm encounters a couple of hundred Amto near the Upper Sepik River in New Guinea he may safely conclude that they all speak Amto, but when one encounters a couple of hundred Tewa in Arizona, one can be much less certain how many actually speak Tewa. Even in the case of census questionnaires designed to elicit language information ambiguity is often introduced in the responses to questions about 'mother tongue'—ambiguity as to whether the response refers to the respondent's first language, whether or not still used, or to his mother's language, which he may or may not speak.

ADAMAWA

GROUPING. The first 53 African languages following are subgrouped under nine Roman numerals (I through IX), which in turn are followed by four languages numbered (54) through (57). Each of the latter (54, 55, 56, 57) is coordinate in classification with each group of languages listed under Roman numerals. This classification reflects that of Greenberg (1966) as modified by Samarin (1971) and Welmers (1971b).

I. Nigeria, Bauchi Province. Samarin (1971) adds Longuda (4), formerly classified as a separate group by Greenberg.
1. Awak.
2. Cham. D. also Mona.
3. Dadi(y)a. 2,300.
4. Longuda = Nunguda. Ds. Hill Longuda, Plains Longuda. 14,000. Nigeria.
5. Tula = Kotule. 19,000.
6. Waja.
Kamu ?

II. 20,000 to 50,000. Cameroon, Nigeria, Congo.
7. Boli = Ndagam. Possibly a dialect of Chamba (8, below).
8. Chamba = Dschamba = Tsamba = Samba = Jamba. Ds. also Dako, Nakeyare. 50,000. Nigeria, Cameroon.
9. Donga = Dongo. 5,000. Congo.
10. Lekon = Chamba Lekon = Lego = Leko ? 10,000. Nigeria, Cameroon.
11. Mumbake = Mubako = Nyognepa. Cameroon, Nigeria.
12. Wom = Pereba = Zagai. Cameroon, Nigeria.

III. 3,000. Cameroon, Nigeria, Adamawa Province.
13. Daka = Chamba Daka = Dekka. 53,000. Nigeria, Cameroon.
14. Taram. Cameroon, Nigeria ?

IV. Cameroon, Nigeria.
15. Doyãyo = Donyayo = Donyanyo. Cameroon.
16. Dupa = Nduupa. 5,000. Cameroon.
17. Dur(r)u = Dui = Duli. Ds. also Goom, Nabang, Paani, Panon. 32,000. Cameroon.
18. Kolbil(l)a = Kobilari. Cameroon. Perhaps a dialect of Chamba (8, above).
19. Koma. 2,000. Cameroon.
20. Kotopo = Kotofo = Kotpojo. Cameroon. Perhaps a dialect of the same language as Kutin (21, below).
21. Kutin(n) = Kutine. 400. Cameroon, Nigeria. Perhaps a dialect of the same language as Kotopo (20, above).
22. Namshi = Namji = Nam(t)chi = Namdji = Namci. 11,000. Cameroon, Nigeria.
23. Pape. 1,000. Cameroon.
24. Sari. Cameroon, Sari Massif.
25. Sewe. Cameroon, Nigeria.

26. Ver(r)e = Were = Yere. 11,000. Nigeria, Cameroon.
27. Woko = Voko = Boko. 1,000. Cameroon, Nigeria.

V. 80,000. Nigeria, Adamawa Province, and Cameroon.
  28. Gengle. Mayo Beleva District, Nigeria. Possibly a dialect of Yendang (33, below).
  29. Kumba = Kuseki = Sate = Yofo. Mayo Beleva District, Nigeria. Possibly a dialect of Yendang (33).
  30. Mumuye. Ds. also Bajama, Ding-ding, Gola, Pugu = Hill Mumuye, Yakoko, Zinna. 103,000. Cameroon, Nigeria.
  31. Teme. Mayo Beleva District, Nigeria. Possibly a dialect of Yendang (33).
  32. Waka. Bajama District, Nigeria. Possibly a dialect of Yendang (33).
  33. Yendang. Ds. also Bali, Kugama, Passam. 2,000. Nigeria.

VI. Cameroon, Chad, Central African Republic.
  34. Kari = Kar(r)e = Kali. Ds. also Gonge = Gunje, Mbum (including Babal, Dek, K(e)pere = Pere = Ripere = Byrre, Laka Mbere = Nger, Lakka, Mbere, Njal), Pana, Pani (?), Pondo, Tali = Tale. 40,000. Chad, Cameroon and Central African Republic.
  35. Kera. 15,000. Cameroon.
  36. Manbai = Mambai = Mangbei. 2,000. Cameroon, Chad. Perhaps more closely related to Fali (54, below) than to languages of this group (Samarin 1971).
  37. Mono. D. also Dama. Cameroon.
  38. Mundang = Móundan. Ds. also Gelama, Kæle, Kiziere, Lere. 45,000. Lere may be a separate language.
  39. Tupuri = Tuburi = Toubouri = Ndore. Ds. Fianga-Chola (in Chad), Mata, Yagoua (in Cameroon), 85,000. Cameroon, Chad. This language has also been classified as belonging to CHADIC.
  40. Yas(s)ing = Ja(s)sing = Djasing = Zazing. 25,000. Cameroon.

VII. Nigeria.
  41. Libo.
  42. Mboi.
  43. Yunger = Lala = Binna. D. also Roba. 30,000.

VIII. Nigeria.
  44. Jen = Njeng = Dza. D. also Gwomo ? 10,000.
  45. Munga.

IX. Chad and Central African Republic.
  46. Bolgo (Dugag). Chad.
  47. Bua = Boa = Boua. 5,000–11,000. Chad.
  48. Fanya(n) = Fagnia. 1,500. Chad.
  49. Gula. Ds. also Kulaal = Gula Iro (2,500; including Patool, Poŋaal, Tiala, Tiitaal), Moriil, Taataal = Gula Gera (including Bon, Chinguil, Iber, Zan). Chad.

50. Koke = Khoke. 1,000. Chad.
51. Mana. Chad.
52. Nielim = Niellim = Nyilem. 2,000. Chad.
53. Tunya. 800. Central African Republic.

54. Fali. Ds. Bonum, Tingelin. 50,000. Cameroons.
55. Kam. Nigeria, Cameroons.
56. Masa. D. also Budugum = Bugudum. Chad, Cameroons.
57. Nimbari. Chad, Cameroons.

AFFILIATION. Member of ADAMAWA-EASTERN.

ADAMAWA-EASTERN PHYLUM

GROUPING. This phylum consists of two groups of languages:

ADAMAWA (q. v.)
EASTERN (of ADAMAWA-EASTERN) (q. v.)

AFFILIATION. Member of NIGER-CONGO (Greenberg 1966).

ADMIRALTY-WESTERN ISLANDS (GEOGRAPHICAL)

GROUPING. Aua (1, below) and Wuvulu (2) constitute one subgroup (Grace 1955); and the many languages of the Hermit Islands, Manus and adjacent small islands constitute a second, as opposed to Ninigo (3), a single language (Capell 1962). Little or no linguistic information is available for these AUSTRONESIAN languages, which are being, or have been, replaced by Neo-Melanesian. The total population of the Admiralty Islands was 19,017 in 1964.

Group I
1. Aua. 230 (1938). 1°27'S 143°05'E.
2. Wuvulu. 251 (1938). 1°44'S 142°50'E.

3. Ninigo. 261 (1938). Ninigo (Western) Islands, 1°15'S 143°30'E, and formerly on the Anchorite Islands, 0°53'S 145°30'E.

Group II. On Manus, 2°05'S 147°00'E, adjacent small islands and the Hermit Islands, 1°30'S 145°05'E.
4. Andra. 1°55'S 147°00'E.
5. Baluan. Ds. also Lou, Pam. Baluan Island, 2°35'S 147°20'E.
6. Bipi. Ds. also Bundrahai, Gogo, Kabuli, Kali, Ndroliu, Salien, Sapondralis. Bipi, 2°06'S 146°25'E.
7. Buyang. Ds. also Kawaliap, Liap, Lowa, Tingou. Buyang, 2°05'S 147°00'E.
8. Hus. 1°56'S 147°07'E.
9. Lebei. Ds. also Babun, Lindrou, Malai, Ndrehet.
10. Luf. D. also Marun. Luf, 1°32'S 145°05'E.
11. Mok. Ds. also Bomsau, Bursu, Mbuge, Mbunai (2°11'S 147°14'E), Ndrihol, Patusi (Bay, 2°11'S 147°07'E), Peli (2°13'S 146°58'E), Tawi Island (2°13'S

146°59'E). Mok, 2°31'S 147°22'E.

12. Mokareng. Ds. also Bowat, Labahan, Loniu, Ndranggot, Papitalai (Harbor, 2°02'S 147°25'E). Mokareng, 2°00'S 147°25'E.

13. Mundrau. Ds. also Derambat, Kup, Sau. Mundrou, 2°00'S 147°00'E.

14. Ndrosun. Ds. also Bua (6°44'S 147°33'E), Bulihan, Kapo, Katin, Laues, Malai (5°52'S 147°57'E), Sira, Sonilu, Yiriw.

15. Nyada. Ds. also Aokuk, Buboi, Lesau = Lessau 2°11'S 147°44'E.

16. Pak. D. also Tong (2°00'S 147°45'E). Pak, 2°04'S 147°38'E.

17. Pityilu. 1°55'S 147°15'E.

18. Ponam. 1°55'S 146°55'E.

19. Rambutjo. D. also Nauna. Rambutyo, 2°15'S 147°50'E.

20. Sori. D. also Harengan (1°57'S 146°35'E). Sori, 2°00'S 146°40'E.

21. Tawi. Ds. also Hatwara, Loitja, Marawurei, Ndrabito, Ndramndrau, Uldrau. Tawi is spoken on Manus.

22. Tongo. Ds. also Lundret, Ndranu, Sabon, Warabei, Yiringo. Tong, 2°00'S 147°45'E.

23. Tulu. Ds. also Aran, Bowai, Kabanu, Lala (2°09'S 146°47'E), Leiwa, Loi, Lorengau, Lowakai, Ndrabwi, Yiri.

24. Waimdra. Ds. also Badlok, Munduburew, Pundru. Waimdra Island, 2°05'S 147°00'E.

AFFILIATION. Subgroup of OCEANIC subgroup of AUSTRONESIAN.

AFROASIATIC = HAMITO-SEMITIC = CHAMITO-SEMITIQUE = HAMITIC = ERYTHRAIC = LISRAMIC PHYLUM

GROUPING. *Egyptian-Coptic is listed below; other AFROASIATIC languages are listed separately under each of five families: BERBER, CHADIC, CUSHITIC, OMOTIC, and SEMITIC.

The recognition of genetic relationships among members of the phylum — beyond *Egyptian-Coptic and SEMITIC — was stated in Meillet and Cohen (1952) after Cohen (1947) to include also BERBER and CUSHITIC, yielding a sum of four coordinate members for their CHAMITO-SEMITIQUE.

A fifth coordinate member, CHADIC, was added by Greenberg (1966 and earlier), who renamed the phylum AFROASIATIC. Five coordinate members are also recognized by Tucker and Bryan (1966) for their ERYTHRAIC, which includes some of the languages —those classified as CHADO-HAMITIC—but not all of the languages that are classified under CHADIC (q.v.). Hodge (1968) summarizes the AFROASIATIC classification so far.

The sixth coordinate member, OMOTIC, postulated by Fleming (1969, 1972), does not represent the addition of languages previously regarded as non-AFROASIATIC; rather, it represents a split of one family (CUSHITIC), already recognized as belonging in AFROASIATIC, into two families: OMOTIC (q.v.) and CUSHITIC (q.v.).

The new name for the phylum as a whole (AFROASIATIC) has been widely accepted because it was felt that the previous compound name (HAMITO-SEMITIC) was misleading. It is not the case that SEMITIC forms a subgroup as opposed to a HAMITIC subgroup for the rest of AFROASIATIC languages; and the implication sometimes read into

HAMITIC—that it has racial classification value—is false, as Greenberg (1966) points out.

1. *Egyptian-Coptic. Ds. (of Coptic): Akhmimic = Akhmim, Asyūtic = Assuit= Sub-Akhmimic, Bohayric = Bohairic = Standard Coptic (Lower Egypt), Fayumic = Bashmuric, Sahidic = Standard Coptic (Upper Egypt). Dialects of Coptic, daughter language of Ancient Egyptian, flourished until the Arab conquest of Egypt (640 A.D.), after which it was gradually replaced by Arabic. Coptic is believed to have died out in the sixteenth century, though it has been reported in the twentieth century (Worrell-Vycichl 1942), as well as in the nineteenth century (Cramer 1962).

AFFILIATION. The four maximum independent classes of African languages in Greenberg (1966) are AFROASIATIC beside KHOISAN and NIGER-KORDOFANIAN and NILO-SAHARAN. However, the independence of AFROASIATIC as a maximum genetic class has been questioned, and other relationships with AFROASIATIC have been suggested: with INDO-EUROPEAN (Pedersen 1903; Möller 1911; Cuny 1943); with BANTU and with DRAVIDIAN (Homburger 1955).

AGÖB

GROUPING. Wurm (1971c) treats only Mikud (7, below), formerly classified as belonging to MOREHEAD RIVER, as closely related to Agöb (1). Mikud is not mentioned by Greenberg (1971b), who groups with Agöb the other languages listed below, none of which is mentioned by Wurm.

1. Agöb = Agobd = Paswam. 1,055. Central area south of the Fly River in Western District, Papua.
2. Bugi.
3. Dabu.
4. Dibolug.
5. Kibuli.
6. Mbayaka = Jindabira.
7. Mikud. 200.
8. Ngamai-iki = Tupadidi.

AFFILIATION. Member of CENTRAL AND SOUTH NEW GUINEA.

Ainu. Ds. Hokkaido = Ezo = Yezo, including several subgroups of divergent dialects, Sakhalin = Saghalin, including Sōya and a number of dialects on Sakhalin, *Kuril = Shikotan (Hattori and Chiri 1960). Less than 16,000. Hokkaido, Sakhalin, and formerly on the Kuril and Ryukyu Islands.

AFFILIATION. None generally accepted; Hattori (cited by Tamura 1967) suggests a relationship with Japanese; INDO-EUROPEAN affiliation has also been suggested, but rejected by Hamp (1969c).

CENTRAL AKOKO

GROUPING. Two recently discovered African languages are spoken in an area where Yoruba is the lingua franca; this seems to have impeded the recognition of their independent status. The names are those suggested by Williamson (1972).

1. Ibaram-Efifa = Akpes. Villages of Akpes (Akunnu), Ikeram, Ibaram, Iyani, Gedegede, Daja and Efifa, Akoko Division, Western State, Nigeria.
2. Kakumọ = Ukaan. Villages of Kakumọ-Akoko and Anyaran, Akoko-Edo Division, Mid-Western State and Kakumọ-Aworo, Auga and Ishe, Akoko Division. Western State, Nigeria.

AFFILIATION. Member of KWA.

Albanian = Arber = Arbresh = Arnaut = Škip = Šhqip = Zhgabë = Shqipēri (current standard, based on Tosk dialect) = Shqipní (pre-World War II standard, based on Geg dialect in Tirana region). Ds. Arbanasi (Zadar), Arbresh (isolated dialects of southern Italy), Arvanitika (dialects of southern Greece), G(h)eg = Guegue (north Albania), Greek Albanian, Italo-Albanian, including Sicily, Makedonnija, Mandrica (Bulgaria, near Edirne), Ship = Kosovë, Srem (Syrmia), Tosk (south Albania), Ukraine (near Melitopol). An early source of information on Albanian dialects is Pedersen in the last century; progress made on dialect studies is reflected in the discussion of them by Hamp (1972) who cites Pedersen. As the localization of dialects shows, Albanian is spoken not only in its native country, but also in neighboring countries, and more widely in the Balkan countries. Albania (2,000,000–3,000,000); Yugoslavia (600,000); Greece (200,000); Italy (more than 500,000); also Turkey, Bulgaria, and the United States.

AFFILIATION. Albanian is a language isolated within INDO-EUROPEAN; many sound correspondences are attested by features of a small number of examples (Hamp 1972). Due to the abundance of Albanian loanwords from Latin, Turkish, Greek, and Bulgarian, and to radical morphological changes, it was not until the latter decades of the nineteenth century that Albanian was established as INDO-EUROPEAN, after which it received detailed treatment by Pedersen (1900) and Jokl (1927). Hamp (1966) surveys the interrelations of Albanian with other extinct and extant INDO-EUROPEAN languages and subgroups. In this century, the correct placement of Albanian in its general INDO-EUROPEAN relationships and in its broader Balkan relationships, especially of loanwords, is based on Jokl (1911 ff); yet Hamp is able to adduce a bibliography of all work on Albanian extending over 27 printed pages. The interrelations of Albanian with other extinct and extant INDO-EUROPEAN languages and subgroups is given by Hamp (1966) who now (1972) adds a bibliographic discussion.

ALGONQUIAN = ALGONKIAN = ALGONKIN

GROUPING. A few competitive subgroupings of languages in the ALGONQUIAN family have been proposed, not to mention the much controverted proposal for including Beothuk as a member of this family. Beothuk is not listed among the members of the MACRO-ALGONQUIAN phylum because the classification question hinges upon whether it is or is not related to ALGONQUIAN — not upon the degree of remoteness of an apparent relationship. Current work by Hewson (1968) can be interpreted as showing that the fragmentary records of Beothuk are not sufficient to distinguish between possible loans from neighboring ALGONQUIAN languages and possible single-line descent from Proto-Algonquian.

Michelson (1912) grouped all ALGONQUIAN languages into four branches: Arapaho, Blackfoot, Cheyenne (1, 2, 3) beside all the rest (4–17, below) included in a branch called CENTRAL-EASTERN by Bloomfield (1946).

Sapir in his 1916 correspondence with Lowie (cited by Haas 1966) wrote "I now incline strongly to a single group of Algonkin..." — i.e., without counting recent innovations in Plains languages (1, 2, 3, below) as a basis for setting up coordinate but separate branches within ALGONQUIAN.

Hockett (1948) advised those engaged in subgrouping "to withhold judgment on the status of the eastern and Plains languages until a good deal more of descriptive and comparative work has been done" — this in reference to the distinction between Proto-Algonquian and Proto-Central Algonquian. Voegelin (1969) reviewed current debate on attesting Proto-Eastern Algonquian and rejecting the Michelson-Bloomfield branches in the Plains. In this debate, Teeter (1967) represents the latest subgrouping by a tree diagram, which places some languages (including 1, 2, 3) as directly connected with Proto-Algonquian at the apex node, but not others; the Eastern languages (5, 7, 10, 13, 14) are connected with Proto-Algonquian through an intermediate node (Proto-Eastern Algonquian).

1. Ar(r)apaho(e) = Arapoho(e). Ds. also Atsina = Ahahnelin = Ahenin = Fall Indians = Gros Ventre (less than 10, Wyoming), Nawathinehena = Nawunena = Nermonsinnansee = Southern Arapaho (885 in Oklahoma, 1906). 1,000–3,000. Oklahoma, Wyoming.

2. Blackfoot = Earchethinue = Pedum - Nigrorum = Pieds-Noirs = Sastica = Sastika(a) = Schwarzfüssige = Siksika. Ds. also Blood = Kainah, Piegan = Paegan. 5,000–6,000. Alberta, Montana, Saskatchewan.

3. Cheyenne = Chayenne = Scheyenne = Sheyenne = Shienne = Shiyan = Shyenne. Ds. Northern, Southern. 3,000–4,000 (Montana, Oklahoma). Formerly North Dakota, South Dakota. Nebraska, Wyoming, eastern Montana, Oklahoma.

4. Cree = Cri(e) = Kri(h) = Kristinaux = Cris(e) = Crianæ = Christeneaux = Clistenos = Ile à la Crosse = Iyiniwok = Kalisteno = Kenistenoag = Killisteno = Knisteneaux = Muskotawenewuk = Roundhead = Saskathewan = Têtes de Boule. Ds. East Cree (5,000), Moose Cree (2,500, Northern Cree, Plains Cree (21,000), Swampy Cree (24,000), Woods Cree (2,500 together with Northern Cree), Montagnais = Montagnar = Montagnards = Montagnie = Mountain Indians = Mountainee = Mountaineers = Mountainiers = Sheshapotosh = Sheshatapoosh(oish) (5,000; Quebec), Naskapi = Nascapee = Naskapee = Scoffie = Skoffi = Skoffie (2,500; Labrador, Quebec). About 62,000. Canada (British Columbia to Labrador; Alberta, Saskatchewan, Manitoba, Ontario, Quebec), Montana.

5. Delaware = Delewes = Assunpink = Opuhnarke = Sankhican = Sankikani = Sankihani = Sankitani = Webanaki. Ds. also *Lenape = Lenapee = Lenapi = Lennape = Lennappé = Lenni ([-]Lenape) = Linapi, Munsee (less than 10,

Ontario), *Unami, *Unalachtigo. Less than 100. Oklahoma, Ontario (formerly in the Delaware basin in Pennsylvania, New York, New Jersey and Delaware).

6. Fox = Musquakie. Ds. also Kickapoo = Ki(k)apoo = Kikapu = Kikkapoe (500, Kansas, Oklahoma; 500, Mexico in eastern Chihuahua), Sauk = Sac = Sack = Sahkey = Sakewi = Sakis = Sauki(e) = Sawk(ee). 1000, Iowa, Oklahoma, Kansas (Fox and Sauk), Mexico.

7. *Massachusett type. Ds. or trs. *Massachuset(t) (subdivisions include Cata, Chickataubut, Cutshamakin = Cutshamequin = Kutchamakin = Manatahqua = Nahaton, Nanaepashemet), Nar(r)aganset(t) = Nousaghauset, *Natick (perhaps not extinct) = Eastern Indians = Natik = Massachuset = Massachusett(s), Pennacook = Merrimac = Nechegansett = Owaragees (subdivisions also include Agawam, Wamesit, Nashua, Souhegan, Amoskeag, Winnipesaukee), *Saconnet, Wampanoag = Massasoits = Philip's Indians (1 or 2 speakers, Massachusetts). Seventeenth century in area around Massachusetts and Naragansett Bays, north to New Hampshire.

8. Menomini = Menomeni(e) = Menomene(e) = Mennomonie = Menomine(e) = Menomonee = Menomoni = Mnemones = Malhommes = Wild Rice Men = Folle Avoine. 300 to 500. Wisconsin, near (formerly on the shores of) Green Bay.

9. Miami type. Ds. or trs. Illinois(e) = Illinese = Illinice = Cahokia = Kaskaskia= Mascouten = Michigamea = Moingwena = Peoria = Tamaroa = Tamarois = Ylinesa (fewer than 10; Illinois, Ohio, Indiana, Arkansas), *Miami = Atchatchakangouen = Kalatika = Mengakonkia = Piankashaw = Pepicokia = Tawatawas = Twightwees = Wea (Wisconsin, Michigan, Indiana, Ohio, Kansas), Peoria (fewer than 10; Oklahoma). Formerly central and southern Illinois, Ohio, Indiana, Arkansas.

10. Micmac = Micmak = Micmacensi = Mik(e)mak = Mikmaque = Miquemaque = Sourikwos = Souriquois = Gaspésien. 3,000–5,000. Nova Scotia, Prince Edward Islands, New Brunswick, Quebec; formerly also Cape Breton Island, later Newfoundland. Language of the Wabanaki confederacy ?

11. *Mohegan type. Ds. or trs. Conoy = Chanawese = Piscataway, Mahican(n) = Mahikan = Macicani = Akochakanen = Brotherton = Hikanagi = Housatonic = Loup, Manhasset, Mohegan = Moheagan = Moheakakannsew = Moheakannuk = Mohican = Mohikan = Mahican = Muhekaneew = Muhheconnuk = Muhhekaneew = Muhhekaneok = Muhkekaneew = Stockbridge (subdivisions: Mahican, Mechkentowoon, Stockbridges, Wawyachtonoc, Westenhuck = Wiekagjok), Montauk = Montauckett = Patcheag = Patchogue = Unachog = Unquachog, Nanticoke = Doegs = Nanticok = Nentego = Taux = Toags = Unalachtigo = Unechtgo = Wiwash, Pequot = Sickenames, Shinnecock (subdivisions: Corchaug, Manhasset, Massapeque, Matinecock, Merric, Montauk, Nesquake, Patchogue = Unquachog = Unachog, Rockaway, Secatogue, Setauket, Shinnecock), Wappinger = Hammonasset(t) = Massaco(e) = Menunkatuk = Naugatuck = Nochpeem = Podunk = Quinnipiac = Guilford Indians = Quinnipiak = Quiripi (including also Potatuck, Tuxis =

Sepous). New York, Rhode Island, Connecticut, Maryland, Pennsylvania, Delaware, West Virginia, Vermont. Closely akin to Delaware ?

12. Ojibwa = Ojibway = Chippewa = Chipouais = Chippawa(y) = Cypawaís = Ochepwa = Ochippeway = Objibwa = Odjibway = Objibwe = Ojibwemowin = Odschibwa = Objeboa = Ojebwa = Ojibbewa = Ojibbeway = Ojibbwa = Ojibua = Ojibue = Ojibwauk = Ojipue = Otchilpwe = Algic = Bawichti-goutek = Pillager (40,000–50,000; Saskatchewan, Manitoba, Ontario, Quebec, Montana, North Dakota, Minnesota, Wisconsin, Michigan). Ds. also Algonquin = Algonkin(e) = Algonkinska = Algonquian = Algonquine = Old Algonkin (under 1550 in 1900; Quebec, Ontario), Ottawa = Odahwah = Ottawwaw = Ottowa = Outaouk = Tawa (fewer than 100; Michigan, Oklahoma; previously also in Ontario, Ohio, Illinois, Indiana, Wisconsin, Kansas), Salteaux = Saulteurs.

13. Passamaquoddy = Machias = Openango = Pasamaquoddice = Quaddie = Quoddy = Saint Croix = Scotuks = Unchechauge = Unquechauge. D. also Malecite = Malechite = Maliseet = Malisete = Malisít = Mareschet = Mareschit(e) = Meeleeceet = Melicete = Melicite = Milicete = Milicite = Millicete = St. Jean = St. John('s) = Abnaki = E(t)chemin = Etchimi = Etechemin(e) = Wlastukweek (600–700). 9,000–10,000. New Brunswick, Maine, and adjacent Quebec.

14. Penobscot = Penobscotice = Pentaguot (60; Maine, Quebec). D. also Abnake = Ab(e)naki = Abanaki = Abenakise = Abenaqui = Albinaquis = Caniba = St. Francis = St. John = Tarratine = Wawenoc = Wewenoc (fewer than 10, Maine).

15. Potawatomi = Pot(t)awot(t)ami(e) = Podawahdmih = Poodawahduhme = Potawatomie = Potawatomy = Potawotamic = Potewateme = Potewatemi = Potewatimi = Potewattomie = Potewotomi = Potiwattomie = Potowatom(i)e = Potowotomi(e) = Potrwatame = Potrwatome = Pottawatameh = Pottawa-tomi(e) = Pottawotomi(e) = Poutouatomi = Putawatomi = Fire Nation = Mascouten. Fewer than 1,000. Oklahoma, Kansas, Wisconsin, Michigan (and Ontario ?). Previously also Illinois, Indiana, Ohio.

16. *Powhat(t)an type. Ds. or trs. Accohanoc, Appomattoc, Chesapeake, Chicka-hominy, Nansemond, Mattapony, Upper Mattapony, Pamunkey, Potomac, Rappahannock, Werowocomoco, Wicocomoco. Seventeenth century, centering on coastal Virginia.

17. Shawnee = Shawan(n)(ee) = Shawanese = Shawan(n)o = Shawanoese = Shawnese = Shawni = Shawnoe = Shavannice = Schawanese = Sawano(u) = Savan(n)a = Sawanwan ? = Savanahice = Savanahica ? = Chawano. 300–400. Oklahoma (formerly in Tennessee; also ranging into Alabama, Georgia, Illinois, Indiana, Kansas, Kentucky, Maryland, Missouri, Ohio, Pennsylvania, South Carolina, Texas, Virginia, and, from 1850s and 1860s, Oklahoma).

AFFILIATION. Member of MACRO-ALGONQUIAN.

MACRO-ALGONQUIAN PHYLUM

GROUPING. The nucleus of MACRO-ALGONQUIAN is the ALGONQUIAN family.

Four language isolates in the 'Gulf' area, two in California, one in Texas, and one language family (MUSKOGEAN) are now associated with ALGONQUIAN in the MACRO-ALGONQUIAN phylum.

Sapir (1913) first found that two geographically discontinuous languages in California (Wiyot, Yurok) showed resemblances to ALGONQUIAN in lexicon and grammatical formatives. Subsequently, after the California languages were better described, Haas (1958a) was able to bring additional evidence to support their relationship to ALGONQUIAN, a grouping which was identified by Teeter (1967) as ALGIC.

Dixon and Kroeber (1913a) grouped Wiyot and Yurok together as 'Ritwan'. But since it turns out that the 'Ritwan' languages are no more closely related to each other than either is to ALGONQUIAN, the identifying name for the pair has fallen into disuse.

Haas (1958a and b, 1960) has shown that Tonkawa (4, below), a language isolate in Texas, and the four 'Gulf' isolates (1, 2, 3, 5) are not only remotely related to each other but also to both ALGONQUIAN and MUSKOGEAN. The name MACRO-ALGONQUIAN is now commonly used to refer to the remote genetic association of the California isolates (Wiyot, Yurok), the language isolate in Texas (Tonkawa), and the 'Gulf' isolates (Atakapa, Chitimacha, Natchez, Tunica) with two language families (MUSKOGEAN, ALGONQUIAN).

ALGONQUIAN (q. v.)

1. *A(t)takapa = A(t)tacapa = Akokisa = Han. Ds. Eastern, Western. Louisiana, Texas.
2. Chitamacha = Shetimasha = Chetimacha = Chetemacha. Fewer than 10. Louisiana.

MUSKOGEAN (q. v.)

3. *Natchez = Na'htchi = Natches. Ds. also Avoyel, Taensa. Formerly along St. Catherine's Creek, near Natchez, Mississippi.
4. Tonkawa = Tonkawe = Kádiko = Kariko = Komkomé = Konkoné = Maneaters. Fewer than 10. Oklahoma (formerly central Texas from Cibolo Creek in southwest to Trinity River in northeast).
5. *Tunica = Yuron. Formerly on the lower course of the Yazoo River, Mississippi.
6. Wiyot = Weeyot = Weiyot = Wiyok = Wischosk = Kowilth = Viard = Humbolt Bay. Fewer than 10. California (formerly on lower Mad River, Humbolt Bay, and the lower Eel River).
7. Yurok = Euroc = Weithspek = Weitspeh. On lower Klamath River, California.

AFFILIATION. In an earlier proposal by Sapir (1929), ALGONQUIAN was remotely related to two language isolates (Beothuk and Kutenai) and three language families (CHIMAKUAN, SALISH, and WAKASHAN), under the rubric 'MOSAN'.

ALTAIC

GROUPING. Languages that are sometimes designated as ALTAIC include Korean, given below (1); they are otherwise grouped in the following families, treated in separate articles (q.v.):

JAPANESE
MONGOL
TUNGUS
TURKIC

The first proposal to regard Korean as genetically related to the traditional ALTAIC groups was made in the last century (Klaproth 1823; Boller 1857). In turn, JAPANESE has been supposed to be related to Korean, and hence indirectly or more remotely related in ALTAIC to the three traditional groups (MONGOL, TUNGUS, TURKIC).

The linguistic evidence clearly reflects long and intimate historical connections between languages in the traditional groups, but it remains a matter of interpretation as to whether this evidence points either to a convergence through diffusion (from Proto-Mongol, Proto-Tungus, and Proto-Turkic), or else to common descent with subsequent divergence (from Proto-Altaic to the modern languages in the MONGOL, TUNGUS, and TURKIC groups). Those who favor the convergence interpretation, as Denis Sinor (1972), necessarily reject the hypothesis of genetic descent of Korean-JAPANESE from Proto-Altaic. Those who favor the common descent interpretation, as Poppe (1960), are inclined to include Korean-JAPANESE in the genetic picture; thus, Martin (1966), and more specifically Roy Miller (1971), who places Korean-JAPANESE in an EASTERN ALTAIC branch together with MONGOL and TUNGUS, thereby isolating TURKIC as the sole constituent of a WESTERN ALTAIC branch.

1. Korean = Corean = Hankul = Chosen· Ds. Čečuto (on Cheju = Quelpart Island), Cuŋčöndo, Jöllato, Kyöŋsaŋto, Namkyöŋto, Pyöŋanto, Seoul. 32,300,000 in Korea, 1,100,000 in China, and 600,000 in Japan. The dialect boundaries generally correspond to the provincial boundaries; there is sufficient divergence between some dialects that they are not immediately intelligible when first encountered by speakers from different regions.

AFFILIATION. Member of URAL-ALTAIC.

ANATOLIAN = HITTITE-LUWIAN

GROUPING. Sturtevant (1933) was a staunch supporter of the Indo-Hittite hypothesis according to which the ANATOLIAN languages have to be interpreted as coordinate with INDO-EUROPEAN (as descendants of a proto language earlier than Proto-Indo-European). Puhvel (1966) and others now regard the Indo-Hittite hypothesis to be unnecessary, since ANATOLIAN languages can be interpreted historically as constituents of yet another branch of INDO-EUROPEAN (as direct descendants of Proto-Indo-European).

1. *Hittite = Ha(t)ti = Nesian. Widely spoken throughout Asia Minor during the second millennium B.C. The capital city of the Hittites was Hattusas in north-central Anatolia (now Boğaz-Köy in Turkey).
2. *Luwian = West Luwian. Ds. also Hieroglyphic Hittite = East Luwian = Late Luwian, Lycian = Late West Luwian.
3. *Palaic.

4. *Lydian.

AFFILIATION. Member of INDO-EUROPEAN.

ANDAMANESE

GROUPING. Greenberg (1971b) questions the inclusion of Järawa (2, below) in either ANDAMANESE or a wider grouping including ANDAMANESE.

1. Great = Northern Andamanese. Ds. earlier Ba, Bale = Balwa = Akar-Bale, Beada = Biada = Bea = Aka-Beada = Bojigniji?, Bogijiab = Bojigyab, Cari, Chariar, Jeru = Yerewa, Junoi, Kede, Kol, Kora, Puchikwar; division into a northern versus a southern cluster agreed upon, but assignment of particular dialect names varies. Basu (1955) reports dialects had leveled. 25 (1951). Great Andaman Islands except southern end of South Andaman.

2. Järawa. D. also Önge. 200. Southern South Andaman, Rutland, and Little Andaman.

AFFILIATION. Member of INDO-PACIFIC (Greenberg).

ANDEAN

GROUPING. The single language which is numbered 16 below (Simacu) is coordinate in classification with four major groups in the ANDEAN division (Greenberg 1960a). These major groups include both single languages (listed alphabetically within ANDEAN as a whole) and language families (listed alphabetically with the single languages, and subalphabetized for languages listed under each family name). An index of the four major groups is:

I. Alacaluf (1), CHON family (7, 8), Puelche (12), and Yaghan (19).
II. QUECHUMARAN phylum (13, 14).
III. CAHUAPANAN family (2–5), ZAPAROAN family (20–24).
IV. Catacao (6), Colan (9), Culle (10), Leco (11), Sec (15), XIBITO-CHOLON family (17, 18).

1. Alacaluf = Alakaluf = Alikuluf. Ds. Aduipliin = Adwipliin, Caucahue = Caucawe, Chono, Enoo = Peshera, Lecheyal, Yequinahue = Yekinawe. Up to 400. Southern coast of Chile and adjacent islands.

CAHUAPANAN = KAHUAPANA = CAHUAPANAN MAINA FAMILY. This small family is bifurcated: Cahuapana (3), on the one hand, and the CHEBEROAN group (2, 4, 5), on the other. North central Peru, between Huallaga and Porto Rivers.

2. Ataguate.
3. Cahuapana. D. also *Concho = Chonzo.
4. Chayahuita = Chaui = Chawi = Chayavita. D. also Yamorai = Balsapuertino. 3,000–5,000.
5. Chebero = Xevero = Jebero = Xihuila. 1,000.

6. Catacao. Still spoken in western Ecuador inland from former Sec area. Perhaps a sister language of Sec (15) in a larger family.

CHON = ONA-CHON FAMILY. Swadesh (1963) would include also Moseten, which Greenberg (1960a) places in GE-PANO-CARIB (q.v.), and Stark (1970) in PENUTIAN.

7. Chon = Tehuelche = Tewelche. Ds. Inaquen = Inaken = Southern, Payniken = Northern, Teuex = Teuesh = Tä'uüshn. Formerly in Argentinian part of Patagonia from the Rio Colorado south to the Strait of Magellan (perhaps a few families still speak Chon in the region of Rio Gallegos and Lago Argentino).

8. Ona. Ds. Huash = Huax, Shelknam = Selcnam. No more than 50 in 1940s. Tierra del Fuego.

9. *Colan. Peru. Probably extinct.

10. *Culle. Peru. Probably extinct.

11. Leco = Leca(n) = Lapalapa = Chuncho = Aleniano. Two dozen. Bolivia, west of Lake Titicaca.

12. Puelche = Pampa = Northern Tehuelche. Possibly extinct (less than 10, 1940). The Pampas of Argentina.

QUECHUMARAN = KECHUMARAN. Quechua and Aymara were said to be genetically related as early as Steinthal (1890). Some solid morphological evidence exists (Uhle 1912; Jijón y Caamaño 1943; Suárez 1970), but there is debate whether the phonology can be reconstructed because of the paucity of lexical items not attributable to borrowing (Mason 1950, Ferrario 1956; Parker 1963; Torero 1964). Longacre (1968a and b) argues that it is possible to reconstruct Proto-QUECHUMARAN. Farfán (1964) sets the date of separation of Quechua and Aymara over three millennia ago. The Quechua-speaking people originally had their homeland in the northern highlands of Peru, where Quechua B has remained; speakers of another dialect migrated to the southern highlands of Peru and, with the expansion of the Inca Empire in the fifteenth century, the dialect spread to Bolivia and Chile in the south, and Ecuador to the north, supplanting related and unrelated languages in the Andes (including that of tribes formerly speaking Aymara, as the Caranga, Quillagua, and Omasuyo). Quechua A and Quechua B may be mutually unintelligible.

13. Aymará = Aimara = Oruro. Ds. = Trs. *Cana, *Canchi, Charca, *Colla = *Collao, *Collagua, Collahuaya, Jaqaru-Chauqui (a small remnant in Yauyos Province, Lima Department, Peru), Lupac(c)a (preferred literary dialect), Ubina. More than 600,000. Bolivia and Peru (southern part of the Titicaca plateau of the central Andes between the eastern Cordillera Real and the western Maritime Cordillera, and southward to Poopó Lake and the Uyani salt marshes). Aymara was formerly more widely distributed, but contracted as a consequence of Inca expansion in the fifteenth century.

14. Quechua = Kechua = Quichua. Ds. Northern Quechua = Quechua B, including Aija, Ambo, Arancay, Cajatambo, Caraz, Carhuaz, Cerro de Pasco, Chiquián, Corongo, Huancayo, Huánuco, Huaraz, Huari, Huaylas, Jauja, Junín, La Unión, Llamellín, Paucartambo, Picoy, Pomabamba, Recuay, Sihuas, Tarma, Yanahuanca, Yauyos (northern highlands of Peru), Yungay; Southern Quechua = Quechua A, including Agato (highland Quichua, Ecuador), Almaguero (Colombia), Arequipa = Costeño. Argen-

tino = Argentina, Boliviano (including Cochabamba, Sucre; highlands of
Peru, Bolivia, Chile, and Argentina), Calderon (highland Quichua, Ecuador),
Canelo = Loreto (Ecuador), Cavina, Chasutino (Peru), Chilque = Aco =
Cuyo = Papre, Colta (highland Quichua, Ecuador), Cuenca (highland
Quichua, Ecuador), Cuzc(o) = Aya(r)marca = Anta = Equeco = Huaroc
= Huayllacan = Inca = Mara = Mayo = Poque = Quehuar = Quillis-
cachi = Quispicanchis = Sanco = Tampo (standard dialect), Dos Rios
(lowland Quichua, Ecuador), Ingano = Inca (Colombia, Ecuador),
Lamanyo = Lamisto (Peru), Lare, Maina (Peru, Ecuador), Paucartambo,
Putomayo (Colombia), Puo Pongo (lowland Quichua, Ecuador), Quijo =
Napo (Ecuador), Quiteño (Colombia, Ecuador), Quito (Ecuador), Riob-
amba (Ecuador), Solasaca (highland Quichua, Ecuador), Santiago del Estero
(Argentina), Saraguro (highland Quichua, Ecuador), Tena (Ecuador),
Tuichi (Bolivia), Ucayoli (Peru), Vilcapampa, Yanahuara. Over 6,000,000;
more including bilinguals. Colombia, Ecuador, Peru, Bolivia, Argentina,
Chile.

15. *Sec = Tallán = Sečhura = Sečura. Western Ecuador. Ds. ? *Chira = Lachira,
Piura. A number of other tribes are sometimes listed with Sec, possibly speaking
dialects or sister languages in a larger family.

16. Simacu. Perhaps related to extinct *Itucale and *Urarina in a language family.

XIBITO-CHOLON FAMILY. The constituents (17–18) may have been differentiated
only dialectally.
  17. *Cholon.
  18. *Xibito = Hibito.

19. Yahgan. 40 (1933). Southern coast of Tierra del Fuego and smaller islands to
the south of it.

ZAPAROAN FAMILY. This represents numerous tribes of northern Peru and
adjacent Ecuador, nearly all extinct, with little information available on which to
identify groups as ZAPAROAN, or with which to draw language boundaries within
ZAPAROAN. Tribal names, usually divided into three to five groups, are listed below
as if they were separate languages.
  20. Andoa. Ds. = Trs. *Andoa, including Guallpayo, Guasaga; Asaruntoa,
      *Gae = Siaviri, Semigae = Shimigae and half a dozen other tribes, mostly
      extinct; Iquito (500, Amazon basin west of Iquitos, Peru), including Mara-
      cana and *Auve.
  21. *Coronado. Trs. Coronado, Oa.
  22. Omurano = Roamaina. Trs. Arasa = Arazo, Habitoa, Pava, Pinche, Uspa,
      Zapa (? perhaps an alternate name for Sharpa, a dialect of Candoshi).
  23. Sabela = Tuey = Auca = Huarani. Ds. Ashiri, Warani. A few hundred.
      Northern Ecuador.
  24. Zaparo. D. also perhaps Arabela. Still spoken by a few older people among
      a group living on the Arabela River, northern Peru. Bilingual in Quechua.

AFFILIATION. J. P. Harrington (1943) proposed an affiliation of QUECHUMARAN with 'HOKAN-SIOUAN' in North America, but ANDEAN as a whole is classified as a division of ANDEAN-EQUATORIAL (Greenberg 1960a).

ANDEAN-EQUATORIAL PHYLUM

GROUPING. Several groups of languages that Greenberg (1960a) places together as being genetically related were not so placed previously — e.g., QUECHUMARAN and ZAPAROAN under ANDEAN within ANDEAN-EQUATORIAL. So also, many single languages that were previously unclassified have now been classified within one or another of the four divisions of ANDEAN-EQUATORIAL. Each of the four divisions is treated as a separate article: ANDEAN, EQUATORIAL, JIVAROAN, MACRO-TUCANOAN.

AFFILIATION. None known for ANDEAN-EQUATORIAL as a whole; but a proposal of affiliation with a North American phylum has been suggested for one of the ANDEAN language groups, QUECHUMARAN.

ARANDIC

GROUPING. Lower Aranda (1) and Iliaura (2) form URTWA (O'Grady et al. 1966). The ARANDIC languages are spoken in east central Northern Territory, Australia.

1. Lower Aranda.
2. Iliaura = Illiaura = Iljaura = Ilyuarra = Illyowra = Alyawarra. Ds. also Akara, Andakerebina = Undekerebina = Walwallie = Williwille = Yanindo, Anmatjera = Unmatjera = Imatjera = Urmitchee, Eastern Aranda, Southern Aranda = Pirdima, Western Aranda, Jaroinga = Jarionga = Yaroinga = Yarroinga = Yorrowinga = Yarrowin.
3. Kaititj = Kaititja = Kaitije = Katitja = Katitcha = Katitya = Kaitish = Kaddakie = Artuya.

AFFILIATION. Member of PAMA-NYUNGAN.

ARAWAKAN

GROUPING. That the ramifications of ARAWAKAN classification exceed those of TUPI is quite certain; still, it is obvious that these two are by far the 'largest' of families in the EQUATORIAL division of the phylum as a whole. About a hundred languages in the ARAWAKAN family are found scattered from Honduras, British Honduras, and Guatemala in Central America to the Gran Chaco of Brazil in South America, where the east-west distribution is from the mouth of the Amazon to the Andean foothills.

The classification followed for ARAWAKAN as a whole is that proposed by Noble (1965), after Greenberg (1960a), except that CHIPAYAN is not treated here as a subgroup of ARAWAKAN, while CHAPACURA-WANHAMAN is; see also Matteson (1972). Of the ARAWAKAN languages, four single languages, besides the minor group ARAUAN, are listed here. The two major groups of ARAWAKAN are treated separately: CHAPACURA-WANHAMAN (q.v.) and MAIPURAN (q.v.).

1. Amuesha = Amuexa. 4,000–9,000. Peru, headwaters of the Pachitea and Ucayali Rivers.

2. *Apolista = Lapuchu = Lapacho. Formerly spoken in Bolivia.

ARAUAN. Mason (1950) groups languages numbered 5, 8, and 9 in a YAMMADI subgroup; they may represent dialects of a single language. Rivet (1924) considered the Bolivian languages, Tereno and Guana-Layana to form a subgroup within ARAUAN, but others, including Noble (1965), include these in SOUTHERN MAIPURAN. The list following (3–11) is of ARAUAN languages.

3. Arauá.
4. Culiña = Culino = Kulino = Kulina = Culinha = Curi(ana) = Curina = Cuniba. Brazil (500), Peru (75).
5. Madihá.
6. Pama = Pamana.
7. Purupurú. Ds. also Paumarí = Pam(m)arí = Curucuru = Uaiai.
8. Sewacu.
9. Sipó = Cipo.
10. Yamamadí. Ds. also Capaná, Capinamari, Colo.
11. Yuberi.

12. *Chamicuro = Chamicura. Formerly spoken in Peru.

CHAPACURA-WANHAMAN (q.v.).
MAIPURAN (q.v.).
13. *Taino. Formerly spoken in the Greater Antilles and the Bahamas.

AFFILIATION. Member of EQUATORIAL in ANDEAN-EQUATORIAL.

Aricapu = Arikapu = Maxubi. 50 to 100 speakers at the headwaters of the Branco River, a tributary on the right margin of the Guaporé, in the Territory of Rondônia, Brazil (Lorraine Bridgeman, personal communication).

AFFILIATION. Unknown.

Armenian. Ds. Eastern Armenian, including: Agulis, Astrachan, Eriwan, Dschugha = Dschulfa, Karabagh, Schamachi, Tiflis, Artwin Armenian, Choi-Salmst, and Urmia-Maragha in northern Iran; Western Armenian, including: Akn, Arabkir, Charberd = Erzenka, Ewdokia = Tokat, Hamschen on the Black Sea, Karen = Erzerum, Cilicia, Northern Komedia, Istanbul, Crimea, Malatia, Musch, Rodosto, Schabin-Karahissar, Sebaste, Izmir, Syrien, Tigranakert = Diarbekir, Trapezunt, Van = Wan, and the dialects of the old Austria-Hungarian Region, 3,500,000 (2,500,000 U.S.S.R.; 175,000, U.S.; 120,000, Syria; 100,000, Egypt; 100,000, Lebanon; 60,000, Turkey; 70,000, France; also in Iran, Iraq, India).

The traditional center of the Armenian language is in the eastern half of Modern Turkey, in the area of Asia Minor east of a line formed by a northward extension of the western coastline of Syria. Today the bulk of Armenian speakers are concentrated in the Armenian S.S.R., and the adjacant Georgian and Azerbaijan S.S.R. *Old Armenian is known from surviving documents (Winter 1966).

AFFILIATION. On the basis of ancient authorities (Herodatus and Endoxes), the Phrygians are often regarded as the lineal ancestors of the Armenians. Meillet and Cohen (1952) found no decisive evidence to establish a Phrygian and Armenian connection, but Jensen (1959) thought 'a close linguistic connection' could be established by comparative evidence. Member of INDO-EUROPEAN, within which it may be most closely related to Greek (a suggestion of Meillet's favored by, e.g., Hamp 1967b, 1969a).

ASMAT = KAMORO

GROUPING. Greenberg (1971b) adds the ASIENARA subgroup (languages numbered 2 and 4, below), which Wurm (1971c) includes in WEST PAPUAN. The ASMAT languages are spoken east and south of the narrow neck part of West Irian.

1. Angadi.
2. Asienara. 700.
3. Asmat. 33,840.
4. Iria = Kamrau = Kambrau. 900.
5. Kajakaja.
6. Kamoro. 7,000–8,000.
7. Mimika.
8. Nagramadu.
9. Neferipi.
10. Sempan. 400.

AFFILIATION. Subgroup of CENTRAL AND SOUTH NEW GUINEA (Wurm 1971c); probably belongs to WESTERN NEW GUINEA (Greenberg 1971b).

ATHAPASCAN-EYAK

GROUPING. The ATHAPASCAN-EYAK hypothesis is, in principle, like the old 'Indo-Hittite' hypothesis (before Hittite was classified as a daughter language of INDO-EUROPEAN). Eyak is equidistant, in cognate count, from all the present-day ATHAPASCAN languages, and not remotely distant from any of them. Krauss (1973b) has marshaled the evidence for classifying Eyak as a coordinate branch of ATHAPASCAN-EYAK; in effect, then, modern Eyak can be said to have descended directly from Proto-Eyak after Proto-Eyak had descended from Proto-Athapascan-Eyak.

ATHAPASCAN = ATHABASCAN = ATHABASKAN. The founder of comparative ATHAPASCAN studies was Edward Sapir, followed by Li (1930 ff), by Hoijer (1938 ff), by Krauss (1973b), and others. The ATHAPASCAN family is divided into three geographic subgroups: (1) Northern (languages numbered 1, 2, 4, 5, 6, 8, 10, 13, 14, 15, 20, 21, 22, 23, 24, 25, 26, 27); (2) Pacific Coast (languages numbered 3, 7, 9, 11, 17, 19, 28, 29); and (3) Southwestern = Apachean (languages numbered 12, 18); in addition there is an ungrouped language. *Kwalhioqua-Tlatskanai (16). The organization followed by Krauss (1973b) 'is simply one of convenience' (i.e., with five ATHAPASCAN subdivisions: 1, Alaska; 2, Canada; 3, Kwalhioqua-Tlatskanai as

well as Nicola; and 4, Pacific Coast, and 5, Apachean). Neither the three geographic
subgroups nor the five subdivisions mentioned represent linguistic branches of the
ATHAPASCAN family. One such branch, APACHEAN, coincides with one geographic
subgroup (Southwestern). The other two geographic subgroups, Pacific Coast and
Northern, include a few and several branches, respectively. (Eyak, 30, below; is listed
after the ATHABASCAN languages.)

1. Ahtena = Copper River Indians. Ds. Chistochina = Batzulnetas, Chitina =
   Tonsina = Copper Center = Tazlina = Louise-Tyone = Gulkana-Gakona =
   Denali-Cantwell, Mentasta. 250. Alaska.

2. Carrier. Ds. = Trs. Babines, including Nataotin, Hwotsotenne; Northern
   Carriers, including Nikozliautin, Stelatin, Tatshiautin. Tatshikotin; Southern
   Carriers, including Naskatin, Natliatin, Ntshaautin, Tanotenne, Tautin. 1,000 to
   2,000. British Columbia, formerly around Eutsuk, Francis, Babine, and Stuart
   Lakes, and the headwaters of the Fraser River south to Quesnel.

3. Chasta Costa = Smith River Athabascan. Ds. *Chasta Costa = Chastacosta
   (formerly along Rogue River), Chetco, *Coquille = Upper Coquille = Mishikhwutmetunee (formerly on upper Coquille River), Tolowa = Ágüstă =
   Lagoons = Lopas (about 15; formerly on Cresent Bay, Lake Earl and Smith
   River), Tututni = Dootoodn = (Lower) Rogue River Indians (about 10; for-
   merely on lower Rogue River and Pacific coast at mouth of Rogue River). About
   25. Oregon.

4. Chilcotin = Tsilkotin. Ds. = Trs. *Nicola, Stone Chilcotin = Stonies, Tlathenkotin, Tleskotin, Toosey. 500 to 1,000. British Columbia, formerly Valley of
   Chilcotin River.

5. Chipewyan. Ds. = Trs. Chipewyan = Montagnais = Mountaineers, including
   Athabasca, Desnedekenade, Etheneldeli = Caribou-eaters, Thilanottine (north of
   Churchill River between Great Slave Lake and the Slave and Athabasca Rivers);
   Slave(s) = Slavey = Etchaottine = Brushwood Indians, including Desnedeyare-
   lottine, Eleidlinottine, Etcheridiegottine, Etechesottine, Klodesseottine (valley of
   Mackenzie River between Great Slave Lake and Fort Norman); Yellow-knife =
   Red-knife = Copper Indians = Tatsanottine (northern shores and eastern bays
   of Great Slave Lake). 4,400 to 6,600.

6. Dogrib. Ds. = Trs. Bear Lake; Dogrib = Dog-Ribs = Thlingchadinne =
   Atticmospicayes = Attimospiquaies = Flancs-de-Chien = Plats-Côtes-de-
   Chien, including Lintchanre, Takfwelottine, Tsantieottine, Tseottine (between
   Great Bear Lake and Great Slave Lake); Hare = Kawchottine = Peaux-de-
   Lièvres = Rabbit skins, including Chintagottine, Etatchogottine, Kawchogottine,
   Kfwetragottine, Nellagottine, Nigottine, Satchotugottine. 1,400. West and north
   of Great Bear Lake.

7. *Galice. Ds. Galice = Taltushtuntude (perhaps 1 speaker remaining; formerly
   on Galice Creek), Applegate = Applegate River Indians = Dakubetede (formerly
   on Applegate River). Oregon.

8. Han. Ds. = Trs. Katshikotin = Eagle, Takon of Nuklado, Fetutlin ? 30. The
   Yukon River drainage.

9. Hupa. Ds. *Chilula = Tsulu-la (formerly on lower Redwood Creek), Hupa =

Trinity Indians = Nibiltse = Natinnoh-hoi (about 120; valley of the Trinity River), *Whilkut = Hoilkut-hoi = Redwood Indians (formerly on upper Redwood Creek above Chilula, and on Mad River). About 130. California.

10. Ingalit. Ds. Kuskokwim (nearly extinct), Yukon (including Anvik-Shageluk, Bonasila, Holy Cross-Georgetown, McGrath). 150. Between Anvik and Holy Cross on Lower Yukon River, including drainage of the Anvik River and south of Kuskokwim River.

11. Kato = Batem-da-kai-ee = Kai Po-mo = Tlokeang. Formerly on uppermost course of the South Fork of Eel River. Less than 10 ? California.

12. Kiowa Apache = Pacer Band = Prairie Apaches. Less than 10, now in Oklahoma.

13. Koyukon = Koyukukhotana. Ds. 'Inner' (including Tanana Village, Stevens Village, Beaver, some at Allakaket, Crossjacket, Manley, Roosevelt-Minchumina, Bearpaw); 'Outer' (Kaltag, Nalato, Koyukuk, Ruby, Galena, Kokrines, Allakaket, Huslia, Hughes, some at Rampont). 600. Alaska.

14. Kuchin = Kutchin = Kutcha-Kutchin = Yukon Flats Kutchin = Fort Indians = Ikkillin = Itchali = Itkalyarūin = Itkpe′līt = Itku′dliñ = Lowland = O-til′-tin. 2,000. Alaska, valley of the Yukon; Canada.

15. Upper Kuskokwim. 150. At Nikolai, Telida, McGrath in Alaska.

16. *Kwalhioqua = Aywē′lāpc = Gilī′q!ulawas. Ds. Suwal, Wela′pakote′li; also Tlatskanai = Clatskanie = A′látskiné-i = Clackstar = Klatskanai. Formerly, the Kwalhioqua were in Washington on the upper course of the Willopah river and the western headwaters of the Chehalis, while the Tlaskanai occupied the mountains about the Clatskanie River.

17. Mattole = Tul′bush. D. also *Bear River = Ni′ekeni′. California: formerly on Bear and Mottole Rivers. Less than 10 ?

18. Navajo = Navaho. D. Navajo (120,000; Arizona, New Mexico, Utah, Colorado), and all Apache groups except the Kiowa Apache: Jicarilla-Lipan (1,000–15,000 Jicarilla, less than 10 Lipan; New Mexico), San Carlos-Chiricahua-Mescalero, including Chiricahua-Mescalero (Gileños and Mescaleros groups: 100–1,000 Chiricahua, Arizona, New Mexico, Oklahoma; 1,000–1,500 Mescalero in New Mexico), San Carlos, including Cibecue, San Carlos proper, Northern Tonto, Southern Tonto, White Mountain (8,000–10,000 in Arizona). Hoijer, cited in Krauss (1973b), regards Navajo and Apache as dialects of one language.

19. *Nongatl. Ds. also *Lassik, *Sinkyone. California: formerly on the Eel and Mad rivers, extending to coastal area.

20. Sarsi = Sarcee = Susee = Sussekoon = Circee = Ciriés = Castors des Prairies = Tcō′kō = Tsô-Ottinè. Trs. Bloods = Klowanga, Big Plume's Band, Broad Grass = Tents Cut Down = Crow-Child's Band, Uterus, Young Buffalo Robe = Many Horses' Band. 50. Headwaters of Peace and Laird rivers.

21. Sekani-Beaver. Ds. = Trs. Beaver = Tsattine (prairies south of Peace River, upper part of Peace River, and east of Rocky Mountains), Sekani = Al-ta-tin = Lhaten = Rocky Mountain Indians = Sastotene = Thé-ké-né = Tsekenné = Tseloni, including Sasuchan = Sasuten, Tsekani, Tseloni, Yutuwichan (Headwaters of Peace and Laird rivers). 400–800.

22: Tahltan. Ds. also Kaska, Tagish. 300–1,500.

23. Tanaina = Knaiakhotana. Ds. Inner (including Eklutna, Knik, Susitna-Talkeetna, some Tyonek); Outer (including Iliamna, Kenai, Lime-Hungry-Stone, Ninilchik, Nondalton, Seldovia, some Tyonek). 400. Alaska.

20. Tanana. Ds. Central (including Minto-Tolovana, Nenana, Toklat, Wood River); 'Transitional' (including Chena, Goodpaster, and Healy Lake, Salcha, Tanacross). 300. Alaska.

25. Upper Tanana. 300. At Tetlin and Northway, Alaska.

26. *Tsetsaut. Formerly at Portland Canal, southernmost Alaska.

27. Tutchone. 1,000.

28. *Upper Umpqua = Etnémitane = Nahankhuotana. Oregon: formerly on the upper Umpqua River.

29. *Wailaki = Kak-wits. Formerly along Eel River, Kekawaka Creek. California. Perhaps some speakers remaining ?

30. Eyak = Ugalachmut = Ugalakmiut = Ugalensé = Ugalenzisch. 3 speakers. Cordova, Yakutat in Alaska.

AFFILIATION. Member of NA-DENE.

WEST ATLANTIC

GROUPING. Westermann (1928), Greenberg (1963b), Dalby (1965), and J. David Sapir (1971) agree on distinguishing at least two branches of WEST ATLANTIC, namely NORTHERN and SOUTHERN = MEL. In addition, Sapir recognizes Bijago (31) as constituting a third branch; Dalby emphasizes the genetic remoteness of SOUTHERN in WEST ATLANTIC by renaming this branch MEL; and Sapir expands the number of languages in the SOUTHERN branch by the inclusion of two languages, Limba (32) and Mansoanka (33).

NORTHERN BRANCH. The following subgroups are based on lexicostatistical evidence assembled by Sapir (1971): SÉNÉGAL languages (12, 29, 30); CANGIN languages (11, 20, 25, 26, 28); BAK languages (7, 10, 14, 15, 19; 21, 22, 27; 3, 13); EASTERN SÉNÉGAL-PORTUGUESE GUINEA languages (1, 4, 5, 6, 8, 9, 16, 17, 18); and a final group consisting of Baga Mboteni (2), Mbulungish (23), and Nalu (24). Some reservation is expressed about some of these languages; thus, within EASTERN SÉNÉGAL, languages numbered 5, 6, 8 may belong either together as a close-knit subgroup or as a group of dialects of a single 'Tenda' language.

1. Badyara = Badyar(e) = Badian = Badyaranke = Pajade = Pajadinca = Pajadinka = (Bi)Gola. 10,000. Guinea, Portuguese Guinea, Senegal. Perhaps a dialect of Tenda.

2. Baga Mboteni. Guinea.

3. Bal(l)anta = Bal(l)ante = Alante = Balant = Bulante = Belante = Brassa. Ds. 'Fora' (Balanta), Kəntɔhɛ, (Balanta) Mane, Naga. 167,000. Portuguese Guinea, Senegal.

4. Banyun = Bagnoun = Ba(n)hun = Banhum = Bainuk = Bainouk = Banyuk = Bʌnyung = Elomay = Elunay. Ds. Gujaaxet, Gunyamolo. 18,000. Portuguese Guinea, Senegal.

5. *Bapεη = Bapẽ. Senegal.
6. Basari = Tanda Basari = Onian = Ayan = Biyan = Wo. 11,500. Guinea, Senegal, Gambia. Perhaps a dialect of Tenda.
7. Bayot. Senegal, Gambia.
8. Bedik = Tenda Bande = Tendanke = Basari du Bandemba. Senegal.
9. Biafada = Beafade = Bedfola = Biafar = Bi-Dyola = Bidyola = Dfola = Fada. 12,000. Portuguese Guinea.
10. Diola = Dyola = Jola = Yola = Dyamate = Kudamuta. Ds. Bandial, Bliss, Buluf, Esulau, Fogny = Fony = Kajamat = Filham, F(u)lup = Felup(e), Her, Hulôn, Huluf, Kasa, Kombo. Kasa is a trade language; a kind of Kasa-Fogny pidgin is also emerging as a trade language. Over 200,000. Portuguese Guinea, Gambia.
11. Falor. Senegal.
12. Ful(a) = Fulani = Fulbe = Fulah = Fellani = Fulfulde = Fulfede = Futa = Peul = Toucouleur = Tukolor. Ds. (geographical) Bagirmi = Baghirmi, Borroro, Foufoude = Foubéré, Fouta Jalon = Fouta Dyalon = Futa Fula, Pular = Pulâr = Poular, Macina. Over 6,000,000. Senegal, Mauritania, Guinea, Sierra Leone, Upper Volta, Mali, Nigeria, Chad, northern Cameroon.
13. Ganja. Sometimes listed as a dialect of Balanta.
14. Gusilay. In town of Tionk Essil. Senegal.
15. Karon. Senegal.
16. Kas(s)anga = Cassanga = I-hadja. 420. Portuguese Guinea.
17. Kobiana = Cobiana = Uboi = U-bôi. 300. Portuguese Guinea.
18. Konyagi = Koniagi = Cogniagui = Coniagui = Tenda Duka. 85,000. Guinea. Perhaps a dialect of Tenda.
19. Kwaatay. Senegal.
20. Lehar. Senegal.
21. Manjaku = Mandyak(o) = Manjiak = Mandfaque = Manfaco = Manjaco = Mãdyak = Kanyop = Ndyak. Ds. Bok = Babok = Teixeira Pinto = Tsaan = Sarar, Likəs-utsia = Baraan Kalkus, Cu(u)r = Churo, Lund, Yu = Siis = Pəlhiʃh = Pecixe. 84,000. Senegal, Portuguese Guinea.
22. Mankanya = Mankanha = Bola = Brame = Bulama = Buram(a) = Mancagne = Mancanka. Ds. also Burama, Shadal = Sadar = Shadar. 16,300. Portuguese Guinea, and small colonies in Senegal.
23. Mbulungish = Baga Foré = Baga Monson = Black Baga. Guinea.
24. Nalu = Nalou. 10,000. Portuguese Guinea, Guinea.
25. Ndut = Ndoute. Senegal.
26. Non = None = Serer None = Dyoba. Senegal.
27. Papel = Papei = Pepel. 36,341. Guineas. (Apparently the southern link in the Manjaku dialect chain.)
28. Safen. Senegal.
29. Ser(r)er = Serère. Ds. Fadyut = Fadiout = Fajut-Palmerin, Ndoute, Nyominka = Nyomi (5,000), Sin = Sinsin = Serer Sin, including Baol, Ndyégem = Dyéguéme = Dyεgεm, Segum. 300,000. Senegal, Gambia.
30. Wolof = Ouolof = Volof = Walaf = Jolof = Yallof. Ds. Baol, Cayor =

Kayor, Dyolof = Djolof = Gambia, Jolof, Lebou, Ndyanger = Ndyandèr, Saloum; urbanized dialects of Bathurst, Dakar, and St. Louis. Over 1,200,000 (and by others as a lingua franca).

31. Bijago = Bidyogo = Bijogo = Bijougot = Bijuga = Budjago = Bugago. Ds. also Anhaqui, Orango. 10,000. Roxa, Bijago Islands off Portuguese Guinea coast.

SOUTHERN BRANCH. There are three subgroups within the SOUTHERN BRANCH, according to Sapir (1971): Mansoanka (33), MEL (34–47) and Limba (32); however, the position of Limba is tenuous; it might instead be an isolated language within WEST ATLANTIC.

    32. Limba = Yimbe. Ds. Biriwa, Kamuke, Keleng, Safroko, Sela, Tonko, Warawara. 174,000. Sierra Leone, Guinea.

    33. Mansoanka = Sua = Kunant(e). 6,000. Portuguese Guinea.

The subgroup MEL consists of one language, Gola (43), coordinate with two groups: the TEMNE = NORTHWEST group (34–39, 46, 47) and the BULLOM = CENTRAL group (40, 41, 42, 44, 45), according to Sapir (1971). Dalby (1965) had a MEL 'A' division consisting of TEMNE and BULLOM, and a MEL 'B' division consisting of Gola.

    34. Baga Binari. Guinea (on the coast east of the Nunez River in Cercle Boké).

    35. Baga Koga. Guinea (on coast between Pongo and Konkouré rivers, extending out to the Ile de Kito).

    36. Baga Maduri = Mandari. Guinea (seeral islands in the Nunez River delta).

    37. Baga Sitemu. Guinea (southern bank of the Nunez River in the Cercles Boké and Boffa).

    38. Baga Sobané. Guinea (between the Kapatchez and Pongo rivers).

    39. Banta. Sierra Leone.

    40. Bom(e) = Bum = Bomo. Sierra Leone (along Bome River).

    41. Northern Bullom = Bolom = Bulem = Bullun = Bulin = Mmani = Mandingi. Sierra Leone, extending into Guinea.

    42. Southern Bullom = Sherbro = Shiba = Amampa = Mampa = Mampwa. Ds. also Shenge Sherbro, Sitia Sherbro. Sierra Leone.

    43. Gola = Gula = (Mana)gobla = De(ŋ) = Kɔŋgbaa = Kpo = Sen(j)e = Te(g)e = Toldil = Toodii. 150,000. Liberia, Sierra Leone.

    44. Kis(s)i = Kissien = Gissi = G(h)izi. D. also Liaro. 250,000. Sierra Leone (almost 50,000), Liberia (about 25,000), Guinea (more than 150,000).

    45. Krim = Kirim = Kittim = Kim(i). Sierra Leone (along Krim River).

    46. Landuma = Landoma = Landouman. D. also Tiapi = Tyapi = Tapessi. 8,000 to 10,000. Guinea, Portuguese Guinea.

    47. Temen = Timne = Themne = Timene = Timmanne. Ds. Bombali, Eastern = Deep Kunike = Western Kunike, Western Temne, Yoni. Over 650,000. Sierra Leone.

AFFILIATION. Member of NIGER-CONGO.

AUSTRALIAN MACRO-PHYLUM

GROUPING. The earlier groupings of Australian languages appear to maximize the possible diversity of languages aboriginal to Australia. The motivation for this is derived largely from culture history, which gives abundant evidence of prehistorically early occupation in Australia; hence, the expectation that the aboriginal languages had plenty of time in which to differentiate. Those who looked at vocabulary, rather than morphology and syntax as a whole, found some evidence to confirm the expectation mentioned above, which is reflected in earlier classifications (reviewed below).

Recent groupings of Australian languages minimize such extreme diversity for the aboriginal languages. For example, one language, Kardutjara, is spoken by dozens of separately named small groups scattered over a 900 mile territory in western Australia. And one language family, PAMA-NYUNGAN, includes some 160 closely related languages widely distributed in most of Western Australia and in almost all the rest of Australia south and east of Arnhem Land and the Kimberley district. And this widespread family is related to all other language families in Australia, large and small, since all families on the continent are subunits of the AUSTRALIAN macro-phylum. Within this phylum, evidence for what little linguistic diversity can be claimed for aboriginal Australia is localized in a northern area (Arnhem Land) and in an area to the west of Arnhem Land (the Kimberley district). It is in these two northerly areas that diversification can be stated in terms of 28 different families or subunits of the single Australian phylum; most language varieties in the rest of the island-continent are affiliated in a twenty-ninth family of the single Australian phylum. This recent classification is provided by O'Grady, Wurm, and Hale (1966), by O'Grady, Voegelin, and Voegelin (1966) and by Wurm (1971b).

Earlier classifications, formulated between 1886 and 1963, represent the expectation that heterogeneity is to be looked for, despite the fact that most of Australia appears to be homogeneous. Curr (1886) divided the continent into Western, Central, and Eastern sectors on the basis of homogeneity of languages within each area. Schmidt (1919a, 1919b) divided Australian languages into a diversified northern group situated north of a line running from Cape York Peninsula to the west Australian coast south of the Kimberleys and Dampierland, and into a homogeneous southern group; Holmer's (1963) classification was based on Schmidt's findings for the southern group, but for Schmidt's northern group he distinguished the prefixing languages, which he further subdivided into four groups, from the suffixing languages, which he divided into nine groups. Capell (1937) proposed a typological classification yielding five groups. Several years later he divided Australia into 11 linguistic areas whose boundaries are largely determined by geography (Capell 1963). Most recently Capell is reported (by Wurm 1971b), to have classified the languages into prefixing languages that are nonclassifying, dual classifying, or multiple classifying, and into suffixing languages that include multiple classifying, pronominalized, and nonpronominalized grammars.

At present, perhaps 47,000 Aborigines have some knowledge of an Australian language. Around 200 languages may still have at least one native speaker, but very few have relatively large numbers, e.g., Kardutjara of PAMA-NYUNGAN with 4,000, Tiwi with 1,000.

BUNABAN (q. v.)

BURERAN (q. v.)
DALY (q. v.)
DJAMINDJUNGAN (q. v.)
DJERAGAN (q. v.)
GARAMAN (q. v.)

1. Groote Eylandt = Andilyaugwa = Ingura. On Groote Eylandt in the Gulf of Carpentaria.
2. Gunavidji = Gidjiya = Gunabidji. Mouth of the Liverpool River on northern coast of Arnhem Land.

GUNWINGGUAN (q.v.)
IWAIDJAN (q. v.)

3. Janjula = Yanyula = Yanula = Anyoola = Aniula = Anjula = Anula = Leeanuwa. On the coast of the Gulf of Carpentaria in the region of the Limmen Bight River.
4. Kakadu = Kakadju = Katata = Karkadoo = Gagadu = Abedal. East and South Alligator rivers in northern Arnhem Land.

KARWAN (q. v.)

5. Kungarakany.

LARAKIAN (q. v.)

6. Mangarai = Mungarai = Mungerry. South of the western Roper River, Northern Territory.

MANGERIAN (q.v.)
MARAN (q. v.)

7. Mingin = Minkin = Myngeen = Minikin. Burketown in eastern Queensland.
8. Nakara = Nagara = Kokori. North of the Tomkinson River on Arnhem Land coast.
9. Ngewin. (Known only by name; Wurm 1971b.)
10. Nunggubuju = Nunggubuyu = Nungubuju = Nungbuju = Nungabuyu = Nungabuya = Nugubuyu. On eastern coast of Arnhem Land in the Rose River area, opposite Groote Eylandt.

NYULNYULAN (q. v.)
PAMA-NYUNGAN (q. v.)

11. Tiwi = Wunuk. 1,000. Bathurst and Melville Islands, north of Darwin on north-western coast, Northern Territory.

TJINGILI-WAMBAYAN (q. v.)
12. Warrai. Adelaide River, Northern Territory.

WORORAN (q. v.)

AFFILIATION. None known or seriously proposed.

AUSTRO-ASIATIC PHYLUM

GROUPING. With increased information on the languages of South and Southeast Asia and increased attention to their comparison, the postulation of an AUSTRO-ASIATIC phylum has gained wider acceptance. Zide (1966) states that his volume of papers "reinforces the recognition that the languages are, in fact, genetically interrelated, and indicates what some of the relationships are," though "no new overall classification is offered" because the opinions of the contributors were "simply not unifiable into one consistent and comprehensive system." The same might be said for the opinions of the participants in the First International Conference on Austroasiatic Linguistics (1973), since most of their comparative work is being done on subgroups of much more closely related languages rather than on the relationships between such subgroups. Nevertheless, overall classifications have been proposed; that of Pinnow (1959) is supplemented by that of Thomas and Headley (1970), whose MON-KHMER is more inclusive than Pinnow's MON-KHMER.

MALACCA (q.v.)
MON-KHMER (q. v.)
MUNDA (q. v.)
NICOBARESE (q. v.)

AFFILIATION. Benedict (1973a) and Headley (1973a) reopen the question of a possible relationship between AUSTRO-ASIATIC and AUSTRONESIAN in an AUSTRIC phylum, proposed by Schmidt (1906).

AUSTRONESIAN = MALAYO-POLYNESIAN

GROUPING. Similarities between Indonesian languages (including Malay) and languages of islands farther to the east were recognized by the beginning of the eighteenth century. In the ensuing century and a half it was believed, partly on racial grounds, that the languages of the Indonesians and the Polynesians were related to each other but not to the languages of the Melanesians; the latter were considered to have either some single separate origin or multiple separate origins. In the mid-nineteenth century, von der Gabelentz (1861) proposed the common origin of Polynesian and Melanesian languages. In the twentieth century, Otto Dempwolff published a number of works on the reconstruction of Proto-Austronesian between 1920 and 1940; comparative work of various sorts has continued on the whole family, which was for long called 'Malayo-Polynesian,' but is now called 'Austronesian.'

Though AUSTRONESIAN languages are frequently spoken of in terms of the culture areas in which they are spoken — Polynesia, Micronesia, Melanesia, and Indonesia — the culture area groupings do not wholly correspond with the linguistic groups, which crosscut and subdivide the culture areas.

No single classification of AUSTRONESIAN languages has compared all the languages on the same basis; hence, agreement on subgrouping does not always exist. Using ten of the languages of Melanesia, Micronesia, and Polynesia, Dempwolff (1937) set up Ur-Melanesisch as the common parent language of the languages of Polynesia and Melanesia (including Micronesia, except Palau and Chamorro) on the basis of common phonological developments not found in Indonesian languages. Capell (1943), following Ray (1926), does not recognize the possibility that such a group — later labeled OCEANIC (q. v.) — could have common ancestry, on the basis of a belief that the AUSTRONESIAN languages of Melanesia are mixtures of Indonesian languages with substrata of languages that were not AUSTRONESIAN. Grace (1955) proposed that OCEANIC includes all the languages of Melanesia east of the boundary between West Irian and Australian New Guinea, as well as all the languages of Polynesia and of Micronesia (except Palau and Chamorro). Dyen (1964) argues that the setting up of OCEANIC has been largely by inspection, since "traditional comparative procedures have actually been applied superficially." Also Dyen (1965) points out that OCEANIC "contains many languages and groups of languages that are independent and cannot be united by a lexicostatistical argument." However, Grace (1970) argues that Dyen's lexicostatistical classification "appears to be fundamentally incompatible with any classification based upon the sound correspondences as they are now understood," and that grouping based on "similarity of grammatical structure is not always associated with a corresponding degree of lexical similarity." Dyen's comparisons of word lists from 317 AUSTRONESIAN languages yielded a division into one major branch, MALAYO-POLYNESIAN (q. v.) and over 40 other branches, many of which are single languages. Most of the 40 other branches, however, are grouped by other scholars with languages of various subgroups of Dyen's MALAYO-POLYNESIAN or within OCEANIC, and are treated herein in the discussion of those subgroups. Only the languages of SOUTH HALMAHERA–WEST NEW GUINEA (q. v.) remain as not clearly subgrouped with other AUSTRONESIAN languages by anyone. The AUSTRONESIAN languages, which Dyen and others estimate to number around 500, are spoken from Madagascar to Easter Island, and from Formosa and Hawaii to New Zealand.

AFFILIATION. Benedict (1973b and earlier) proposes a relationship between AUSTRONESIAN and KAM-TAI in 'AUSTRO-THAI.'

FORMOSAN AUSTRONESIAN

GROUPING. Dyen (1971), after Dyen (1963), concludes that on the basis of "a noticeable number of words in cognate sets with basic meanings restricted to Formosan languages . . . there is at least some evidence for a hypothesis that the Formosan languages constitute a single family" within AUSTRONESIAN. Dyen (1965) separates the languages into three groups, ATAYALIC, including Atayal (2, below) and Seediq (16); EAST FORMOSAN, including Ami (1), Bunun (4), Paiwan (9) and Thao (19); and TSOUIC, including Kanakanabu (6), Saaroa (14), and Tsou (20).

The EAST FORMOSAN languages belong to a larger group, PAIWANIC, including also Pazeh (11) and Puyuma (12), with Babuza (3) and Siraya (17) lexicostatistically closer to PAIWANIC than to either of the other two groups (Dyen 1966, 1971). Rukai (13) has also been grouped with PAIWANIC languages (Dyen 1963).

Kavalan (7) does not clearly belong to any one of these three groups. But new evidence now suggests two main subgroups on Formosa, ATAYALIC as opposed to a group including PAIWANIC and TSOUIC to which Kavalan would also belong (Dyen 1971).

Lexicostatistical comparisons have not been made for the remaining Formosan languages. Saisiyat (15) was grouped with the ATAYALIC languages by Nikigawa (1953), but classified by Loukotka and Lanyon-Orgill (1958) as a dialect of the same language as Pazeh (11), which belongs to Dyen's PAIWANIC.

1. Ami = Amis = Pangtsah. Ds. Baran = Maran = Falanao, Kibi = Kiwit, Sabari, Taparon = Tavalon, Tauran = Nataoran = Ami = Amis. 87,345. Eastern coastal plain from Sincheng to south of Taitung (Pinan).
2. Atayal = Ataiyal = Taiyal = Tayal. Ds. also Sqolyek, Taihyo = Mekbengetseq = Bonotsek, Takonan, Taroko, Yukan. 36,000 (1958). Northern mountains, south of the Ketagalan area.
3. *?Babuza = Babusa = Favorlang. D. also Poavosa (still spoken 1908). West coast around 24°N.
4. Bunun = Bunum = Vunun = Vonum. Ds. also Ibaho = Ivaxo = Southern Bunun,*?Kagi, Katoguran = Katongulan = Ketanganau = Central Bunun, Sivukun = Sibuku, Tamaroan = Tamado'wan = Tamaroau = Northern Bunun, *?Tsuihwan = Chibora. 21,440. East and south sides of the central plain, south of the Seediq. Are the Tsuihwan = Chibora speakers the same as those reported as speaking a dialect of Tsou, below ?
5. *?Hoanya. Ds. also *Baksa, *Kongana, Pepohwan (still spoken 1908). West coast south of 24°N.
6. Kanakanabu = Kanabu = Kanakanavu = Southern Tsou. Ds. also Nagisaru = Nagisaran, possibly Sekhwan. West central mountains south of the Tsou. Loukotka and Lanyon-Orgill (1958) include in Saaroa (14, below).
7. Kavalan = Kuwarawan = Kiwarawa = Kuvarawan. D. also Kareovan. Used only as a home language by 1930. Northeast.
8. *?Ketagalan. Across northern end of the island.
9. Paiwan. Ds. also Kachirai = Tsoa-qatsilai, Kapiyan = Kaviangan = Kapiangan = Kipiyan, Kunanau = Kulalau, Naibun = Tsa'ovo'ovol = Tsa'ova'ovul, Raisha = Tsala'avus, Rikiriki = Raokrik = Laliklik = Lilisha, Shimopaiwan = Ka-paiwan-an = Kapaiwanan, Tachaban = Patsavan = Patsaval, Tamari = Tsaovali, Tokubun = Tokovul = Tokuvul. 36,775. Southernmost mountains.
10. *?Papora. Northwest coast, south of the Taokas (18).
11. Pazeh = Pazzehe = Pazehe = Pazeh-Kahabu. Used only a as home language by 1930; spoken only by people in their sixties and seventies by 1969 (Ferrell 1968). Near the west coast just north of 24°N.
12. Puyuma = Pyuma = Pilam = Pelam. Ds. also Banga, Bantaurang, Chipon = Chipun = Tipun = Kata-tipol = Pyuma, Hinan, Kanagu, Katsausan, Pachien = Paichien, Pinan = Hinan = Pilam, Saprek, Semobi, Sibucoon, Tibolal. 8,687. East coast south of Taitung (Pinan) and inland.
13. Rukai = Dukai for one group of dialects = Tsarisen = Tsalisen for another. Dukai ds. Maga = Tordukana, Mantauran = Upunuhu = Opunoho, Tona = Kongadavanu; Tsarisen ds. Dainan = Taromak = Taromaki, Taramakau = Talamakau = Takamakau. 5,871. South central mountains, west of the Puyuma. Loukotka and Lanyon-Orgill (1958) and other sources list Tsarisen as a separate

　　language, but Lanyon-Orgill (1961) reassigns the earlier 'Tsarisen' dialects to Rukai, Puyuma, and Paiwan.

14. Saaroa = Saarua = La'alua = La'aroa = Sisyaban = Southern Tsou. Ds. also Haisen = Paitsiana = La'aluwa, possibly Sekhwan. West central mountains south of the Tsou.

15. Saisiyat = Saisiat = Saisiet = Saisett = Saiset = Saisat = Seisirat. Ds. also Arikun, Buiok, Taiai = Sairakis. 3,394. Western mountains, west of the Atayal. Loukotka and Lanyon-Orgill (1958) add Pazeh (11) and Taokas (18) as dialects.

16. Seediq = Seedik = Sediq = Sedik = Shedekka = Sazek. Ds. also Buhwan, Iboho = Ilutso = Tlukko, Paran, Tangao, Taroko, Wu = Hogo = Gungo = Gunu. 14,000. Northern mountains, south of the Atayal.

17. *?Siraya = Sideia = Sideis. Ds. Makatao, Sideia, *Sinkan, Siraya (still spoken 1908), *Tamsui. Southwest coast.

18. *?Taokas. Northwest coast.

19. Thao = Sao = Shao = Sau = Chuihwan. 160 in 1930 who used it as a home language only. In the center, near Lake Suisha.

20. Tsou = Tsoo = Tsu'u = Tsu-u = Tsuou = Northern Tsou. Ds. also Arisan = Alisan, *Iimutsu, Luhtu = Dufutu = Namakaban = Namahabana = Namakabau = Ruftu, Tapangû, Tfuea = Tufuja = Tfuya = Chibora = Tsuihwan. 3,223. West central mountains southeast of Kagi around Mt. Ali. Are the Chibora = Tsuihwan the same as those listed under Bunun, above ?

AFFILIATION. Member of MALAYO-POLYNESIAN group of AUSTRONESIAN.

NORTHEAST NEW GUINEA AUSTRONESIAN (Geographical)

　　GROUPING. Grace (1955) assigns the languages of northeast New Guinea, southwest New Britain, and the intervening islands to four subgroups: first, those of Manam Island and the Schouten Islands; second, those of the coast and other offshore islands of the Sepik District; third, those of the Astrolabe Bay area of the Madang District; and fourth, those of the Morobe District, of southwest New Britain, and of the islands between New Britain and New Guinea. Capell (1962a) lists and locates the languages of these areas.

　　Dyen's (1965) sample included ten languages from this area; seven of them (Acira, Blupblup, Hapa, Kairiru, Kilenge, Nubami, Tami) did not share sufficient cognates to be subgrouped with any of the other AUSTRONESIAN languages; the remaining three form a subgroup, which is not subgrouped with any other languages. To this WILLAUMEZ subgroup, consisting of Bakovi (7), Kapore (28), and Nakanai (42), Allen and Hurd (1963) link two more languages, Karua (29) and Mera Mera (39).

1. Acira = Atsera. D. also Amari. 4,901 and 2,915, respectively (1937). Morobe District.

2. Ali. Ali Island, close to Aitape, Sepik District.

3. Aramot. Aramot Island, Morobe District.

4. Arawe. Southwestern New Britain and adjacent offshore islands.

5. Arop = Waropu. Sepik District.

6. Ata. 912. Talasea Sub-District, New Britain.

7. Bakovi = Kove (= Kobe ?). Willaumez Peninsula, New Britain.

8. Bao. 45. Talasea Sub-District, New Britain.

9. Barai. Southwestern New Britain.

10. Barim. Umboi Island.

11. Bebeli. 510. Talasea Sub-District, New Britain.

12. Biliau. Astrolabe Bay area, Madang District.

13. Blublup. Schouten Islands.

14. Bola = Bolo. Willaumez Peninsula, New Britain.

15. Buang. 7,000 (1964). Along the Snake River, Mumeng Sub-District of the Morobe District.

16. Bukaua = Bukawa = Kawa. 2,535 (1937). Morobe District.

17. Bulu. Willaumez Peninsula, New Britain.

18. Galek. Astrolabe Bay area, Madang District.

19. Ganglau. Astrolabe Bay area, Madang District.

20. Graged. Over 6,000. Sek, Yabob, Karkar, and Bagabag Islands, Astrolabe Bay.

21. Ham. Astrolabe Bay area, Madang District.

22. Hapa = Labu'. Morobe District.

23. Iangla. Umboi Island.

24. Kai. Morobe District.

25. Kairiru. 1,906. Sepik District.

26. Kaiwa. 844 (1937). Morobe District.

27. Kalai. Southwestern New Britain.

28. Kapore. Willaumez Peninsula, New Britain.

29. Karua = Garua. 799. Talasea Sub-District, New Britain.

30. Kelana = Kela = Laukanu. Morobe District.

31. Kilenge = Kilengge. Southern tip of New Britain.

32. Kis. Sepik District.

33. Malangai. Astrolabe Bay area, Madang District.

34. Malol. 3,330. Sepik District.

35. Manam. Ds. also Sepa, Wanami. Manam Island, Madang, New Guinea, and in Sepa and Wanami on the adjacent mainland by emigrants from Manam.

36. Masegi. 565. Talasea Sub-District, New Britain.

37. Matukar. Astrolabe Bay area, Madang District.

38. Megiar. Astrolabe Bay area, Madang District.

39. Mera Mera = Meramera. 920. Talasea Sub-District, New Britain.

40. Mindiri. Astrolabe Bay area, Madang District.

41. Momolili = Momalili. Probably belongs rather to HUON-FINISTERRE.

42. Nakanai = Bileki = Lakalai. 5,834. Willaumez Peninsula, New Britain.

43. Nubami. Morobe District.

44. Peterei. Astrolabe Bay area, Madang District.

45. Sahe = Sake. Southwestern New Britain.

46. Samap. 111. Sepik District.

47. Seleo = Seliu. Seleo Island, close to Aitape, Sepik District.

48. Sisano. Sepik District.

49. Suain = Ulau-Suein. 909. Sepik District.

50. Suam. Morobe District.

51. Swit. Astrolabe Bay area, Madang District.

52. Tami = Taémi. Tami Island off the coast of the Morobe District.

53. Terebu = Turupu. 4,000. Sepik District.

54. Tuam. Tuam Island, Morobe District.

55. Tumleo. 439. Tumleo Island, close to Aitape, Sepik District.

56. Umboi. Umboi Island.

57. Vitu. Vitu (French) Island, north of western New Britain.

58. Wampur = Laewamba. 2,521 (1937). Morobe District.

59. Wogeo. Sepik District.

60. Yabim = Yabem. 1,606 (1937). Morobe District.

61. Yakamul. 1,318. Sepik District.

62. Yamai. Astrolabe Bay area, Madang District.

63. Yamas. Astrolable Bay area, Madang District.

64. Yoria. Astrolabe Bay area, Madang District.

AFFILIATION. Belongs to OCEANIC subgroup of AUSTRONESIAN. Goodenough (1961) argues for the subgrouping of Nakanai (and, by implication, the whole of WILLAUMEZ) with POLYNESIAN and Fijian within EASTERN OCEANIC.

NORTHWEST = PHILIPPINE AUSTRONESIAN

GROUPING. Lexicostatistical comparisons of one sort or another have been done on limited numbers of the Philippine languages by Fox et al. (1965), Thomas and Healey (1962), Chrétien (1962), Dyen (1965 and earlier). Conklin (1952) groups some of the languages he lists into two groups "indicated by systematic sound correspondences and other linguistic features," but leaves unclassified most of the languages he lists.

Dyen subdivides the NORTHWEST languages into a GORONTALO group, Ilongot, and a PHILIPPINE group. Thomas and Healey also classify the single language, Ilongot, coordinately with other Philippine languages rather than as a member of a group including other Philippine languages. Within the PHILIPPINE group, the classifications mentioned above recognize two large subgroups (e.g., Dyen's SULIC and CORDILLERAN, Thomas and Healey's SOUTHERN PHILIPPINE and NORTHERN PHILIPPINE, Conklin's TAGALOG-TYPE and ILOCANO-TYPE); however, among the classifications there is variation in the composition of these two subgroups, both in terms of the languages included (a language included in one of the two in one classification may belong to a separate, smaller, coordinate subclass in another classification) and in the further subgrouping of the members of these two large subgroups. We do not mention all such differences in subclassification, partly because the classifiers were dealing with different samples — not only with not wholly overlapping languages, but also with different sources of data on the languages.

Constantino (1971) cites an ongoing survey of the languages of the Philippines in which more than 300 dialects have been tentatively identified as belonging to more than 70 languages.

Since Dyen's (1965) classification included more languages than any of the other classifications, languages are listed below under his subgroups. For each of Dyen's subgroups we list first those languages actually classified by Dyen before adding other languages which — had they been classified by him — might have been placed in the same subgroups.

GORONTALIC

1. Gorontalo. 900,000. Northern Celebes.
2. Suwawa = Suwawa-Bunda = Bunda. D. also Bunda. Northern Celebes.

Esser (1938) groups languages numbered 3, 4, 5 with Gorontalo and Suwawa as a GORONTALO subgroup; languages 6, 7, 8, 9, also spoken in the same area of northern Celebes, may belong to the same subgroup.

3. Buol = Bual = Bwo'ol = Bwuolo = Dia. 150,000.
4. Bulanga-Uki = Atinggola = Diu.
5. Kaidipan = Dio.
6. Kwandang.
7. Limboto.
8. Sulamata.
9. Tilamuta.

10. Ilongot = Ilungut = Lingotes. Ds. Abaká = Abaca, Egongot, Ibalao = Ibilao, Italon, Iyongut. 7,640. Luzon, Philippines.

PHILIPPINE

11. Baler = Baler Dumagat. Area of Baler, eastern coastal Luzon. Conklin lists four Dumagat = Dumaget dialect areas: Sierra Madre on Luzon, Polillo Island, Alabat Island and Kalawat Island. Macleod (reported in Voegelin and Voegelin 1965) lists four mutually unintelligible Dumagat groups: Umirey, spoken by 3,300 people on Luzon's east coast from Baler south to 20 kilometers south of Infanta and west to the settled areas of Nueve Ecija, Bulacan and Rizal Provinces, and also on Polillo; Anglats along the Agos River, the mouth of which is near Infanta; and two others for which he gives self-designations and no locations, 'tagi depoinga' and 'tagi ilog', with 100 and 300 speakers, respectively. It is not clear how these are to be identified with the two Dumagat languages of Dyen's sample — Baler and Casiguran (14, below) — which are not closely enough related in his classification to form a subgroup. The majority of Umirey Dumagats are reported to be quite fluent in Tagalog.

BILIC. Thomas and Healey treat these languages as a separate SOUTHERN MINDANAO group coordinate with the group composed of the rest of the PHILIPPINE group plus Ilongot (10, above) and other unsubgrouped languages outside the PHILIPPINE group. McKaughan (1971) adds Tiruray (92, below) to form a SOUTHERN PHILIPPINE group coordinate with a NORTHERN (Ilocano-like) group and a CENTRAL (Tagalog-like) group.

12. Bilaan = Bila-an = Bilanes = Biraan = Baraan = Tagalagad. Ds. also Balud = Sarangani = Tumanao, Buluan = Buluanon = Buluanes. 50,600. Cotabato Province, Mindanao, and Sarangani and Balut Islands.

13. Tagabili = Tagabelies. Ds. Kiamba, Sinolon, Cotabato Province, Mindanao.

14. Casiguran = Casiguran Dumagat. Area of Casiguran, eastern coastal Luzon. See note at Baler (11), above.

CORDILLERAN. Dyen separates Inibaloy (33, below) from all the rest, grouped as NORTH CORDILLERAN.

BANAGIC

15. Atok. Luzon.

GADDANG. Treated by Dyen as a group of the two very closely related languages below; Conklin lists one Gaddang language with dialects Iraya (not the Iraya on Mindoro), Katalangan, Maddukayang, and Yogad (Yogad is a language outside GADDANG, but rather closely related in Dyen's classification). Total 16,700–28,150. Luzon.

16. Christian Gaddang.

17. Pagan Gaddang.

18. Ibanag. Ds. also. Western Agta (1,000), Itawes (2,000 in Cagayan Province). 150,000–300,000. Luzon and Babuyan.

ISNEG. A group of four languages, with Itawi (21) and Malaweg (22) more closely related to each other than to the other two (Dyen). Conklin (1952) treats Isneg = Isnag = Apayao = Apayaw as a single language with dialects Itawi (21), Magapta, Mandaya = Northwest Apayao, Talifugu-Ripang = Southeast Apayao; the first two of these are said by Wolfenden (1963) to represent a single dialect, Kabugao = Central Apayao, which may or may not be the same as the Kabugao dialect of Bayag (20). 8,000–13,500 total speakers. Luzon.

19. Barran. D. also Nabwangan.

20. Bayag. D. also Kabugao.

21. Itawi = Tawit = Tauit.

22. Malaweg.

23. Yogad. Luzon. See note at GADDANG above.

IFUGAO = IFUGAW = IPUGAW. Conklin lists Kiangan (26) and Mayaoyao (27), below, as well as Lagawe = Lagaui, Silipan = Sub-Ifugao = Alímit, Tokukan-Asin = Western Ifugao as dialects of a single Ifugao language. 70,000–80,000 total 'Ifugao.' Luzon.

24. Hanglulu. Forms a subgroup with (25) in Dyen's classification.

25. Kalanguya.

26. Kiangan = Central Ifugao = Pure Ifugao = Quianganes = Gilipanes. Ds. also Banaue, Hapao, Hungduan.

27. Mayaoyao = Mayawyaw = Mayoyao = Pungianes.

IGOROT

28. Bayyu = Bayyo = Bayo. See note with Bontok, below.

29. Bontok = Bontok Igorot = Guianes = Itetapanes. Conklin lists as dialects Bayyu (28), above, Central Bontok, Kadaklan-Barlig, Tinglayan, Bangad = Dananao. Balangao (2,500) may also be a Bontok dialect. 21,000–32,000 total 'Bontok.' Luzon.

30. Kankanay = Kankanai = Lepanto Igorot. Ds. Bakun = Malaya

Bakun(?), Baukok = Amburayan(?), Buguias, Kapangan, Kibungan, Mankayan. 91,460. Luzon.

31. Sagada = Sagada Igorot. Luzon.

32. Ilocano = Iloko. 3,000,000. Luzon, Babuyan, Mindoro, Mindanao.

33. Inibaloy = Inibaloi = Inibiloi = Ibaloi = Nabaloi = Benguet-Igorot. Ds. Bokod, Daklan, Kabayan, Nabaloi, Iwaak. Luzon.

34. Isinay = Isinai = Inmeas. Ds. Aritao, Dupax. 3,970. Luzon.

KALINGA

35. Kalinga = Kinalinga = Calinga = Balbalasang. Ds. Ablig-Saligsig, Balbalasang-Ginaang = Guinanaang = Giná'an, Kalagua = Calauas = Lalaua, Lubuagan, Mallango, Mangali-Lubo, Nabayugan, Sumadel. 41,000. Kalinga Sub-Province, Mountain Province, Luzon.

36. Pinukpuk. D. also Tabuk.

37. Piggattan. Apayao, Luzon.

Other languages which may belong to CORDILLERAN are:

38. Central Agta = Aeta = Eta = Ita = Negrito = Central Cagayan Negrito. 1,500. Cagayan Province, Luzon.

39. Eastern Agta. 1,000. Cugayan Province, Luzon.

40. Atta = Northern Cagayan Negrito. 500. Cagayan Province, Luzon.

41. Pangasinan. 515,160. Luzon.

42. Tinggian = Tinguian = Itneg. 32,820–41,600. Luzon.

43. Dusun. Ds. Banggi Island (divergent), Dali, Kiau, Kimanis, Maradu, Papar, Putatan, Tambunan, Tempasuk including Ida'an, Kahung Saraiyoh, Kedamaian and Tombulion; Tuaran. Along the rivers of the west coast and and in the northern half of Sabah. Possibly closely related to:

44. Bulud-Upi = Buludupi = Orang Sungei. Northeast coast of Sabah between the Sugut River and Tabunak. Montano (reported by Cense and Uhlenbeck 1958) connects it with the Tagalog group of languages; Salzner (1960) groups it with Dusun; possibly immigrants from the Philippines (Cense and Uhlenbeck).

45. Ivatan = Batan. Ds. Batan = Northern Ivatan, Itbayat, Sabtang = Southern Ivatan. 11,000. Batan Islands.

46. Yami. D. also Imurut = Imulud. 1,957. Botel Tobago (Lanyu) Island. Closely related to Ivatan (Dyen 1971).

47. Maranao = Maranaw = Rranao = Lanao = Illanos. D. also Ilanun = Illanun = Lanun = Illanos. 250,000. Largely in Lanao Province, Mindanao; some settlements on coast of North Borneo.

48. Maguindanao = Magindanao = Magindanaw = Magindanau. 150,000–190,000. Cotabato Province, Mindanao. Almost mutually intelligible with Maranao (E. Lee, SIL, personal communication).

49. Taw Sug = Tausug = Sulu = Joloano Sulu. Palawan, Philippines, northeast coast of Borneo. Closely related to Maranao (E. Lee, SIL, personal communication).

MURUTIC. All are spoken on the island of Borneo.

50. Bolongan = Bulungan. Generally grouped with Tarakan (52), below, as dialects of Tidung, which also includes Nonukan, Penchangau, Sedalir, Simbakong = Sembakung. East coast of Borneo between Lahad Datu in Sabah and Bulungan in Indonesian Borneo. Differences from Tarakan perhaps due to stronger Malay influence (Cense and Uhlenbeck).

51. North Borneo Murut = Murut. Ds. Keningau = Dabai, Kuijau, Rundum, Semambu, Tagal, Tengara, Timugan = Temogun; of these Tengara, said to strongly resemble Tarakan (52), and Kuijau, said to be a link between North Borneo Murut and Dusun (43), are probably most divergent. South central Sabah.

52. Tarakan. Some words of Tarakan strongly resemble those of the Tengara dialect of North Borneo Murut (Cense and Uhlenbeck). See Bolongan (50, above).

SULIC
BUKIDNIC

53. Bukidnon = Bukidnon Manobo = Binokid. D. also Banuauon = Banawaw = Banuaon = Banuanon. 40,539. Southern Bukidnon and northeastern Cotabato Provinces, Mindanao.

54. Central Manobo. Mindanao. See note at DIBABAIC, below.

55. Cotabato Manobo. Cotabato Province, Mindanao. See note at DIBABAIC, below.

DIBABAIC. Conklin treats Agusan Manobo, Dibabaon, and Libagnon (= Central Manobo ? or Cotabato Manobo ?) as dialects of a single Manobo language, with over 70,000 speakers. Thomas and Healey treat Dibabaon, Bukidnon, Western Bukidnon Manobo (= Central Manobo ?) and (Southern) Cotabato Manobo as forming a subgroup of their SOUTHERN PHILIPPINE group.

56. Agusan Manobo = Manobo Proper. Mindanao.

57. Dibabaon = Dibabawon = Debabaon. Mindanao Island.

58. Kalamian = Calamiano. D. also Agutaynon = Agutainon. Palawan, Calamian, Agutaya, and Ambulong Islands.

MESOPHILIPPINE

59. Bikol = Bicol = Vicol. At least 10 ds., including Albay-Sorsogon, Baao, Bato, Buhi, Catanduanes, Naga. 2,000,000. Dominant language in Albay, Camarines Sur, Catanduanes, Sorsogon Provinces, the southern half of Camerines Norte and some towns of Masbate (Constantino).

HANUNOIC

60. Buhid = Buíd = Bu'id = Bukid = Buhil = Buquil. Four dialects, including Bangon = Bangot, Baribí = Beribi (Tweddell 1970). 6,000. Mindoro.

61. Hanunóo = Hanono-o = Hampangan = Bulalakao = Minangyan. Ds. Binli, Gubatanon, Kagankan, Waigan, Wawan. 6,000. Mindoro.

62. Batangán = Binatangán = Barangan = Tiron = Bangon = Bangot = Suri. 4,000. Mindoro. Most closely related to Buhid

(Tweddell 1970), so possibly a member of Hanunoic.

IRAYIC. Dyen groups Alangan with Iráya as opposed to a group consisting of Nauhán plus Pula, which Tweddell would subsume under Tadyawán.

63. Alangan. 3,000. Mindoro.
64. Iráya. Ds. include Alag-Bako, Pagbahan, Palauan-Calavite, Pambuhan, Santa Cruz-Kasagi-Calamintao. 6,000–8,000. Mindoro.
65. Nauhan = Taga-kaliwâ. A few hundred. Mindoro. See Tadyawan (67), below.
66. Pula = Pola = Buctulan ? = Durugmun ? 1,000. Mindoro. See Tadyawán (67), below.
67. Tadyawán = Tadianan = Tagáydan = Tagáidan = Balabán. Ds. East Aglubang-Bansód = Bansód, West Aglubang = Baraboy, which may rather be a dialect of Alangan. 1,500–2,000, minus the Nauhan and Pula. Mindoro. Tweddell includes Nauhan and Pula as dialects of Tadyawán.

MANSAKIC
68. Mansaka = Mandaka. Ds. also Karanga, Magosan = Managosan, Pagsupan. 35,403. Southern Mindanao.
69. Tagakaolo = Tagakolu = Tagacola = Kalagan = Calaganes = Calagars = Kagan = Saka. D. also Loac. 21,000 (1942). Cotabato and Davao Provinces.
70. Subanun = Subanu = Subano = Sabanun. Ds. include Buluan-Kipit, Dapitan, Malindang, Sibuguey, Sindangan, Siokun, Tukuran. 72,950. Mindanao.

TAGALIC includes the BISAYAN group, below, which is coordinate with three languages, including Tagalog (79, 80, 81).

BISAYAN. Some of these, at least languages numbered 73 – 78, below, are sometimes treated as a single dialect continuum, labeled 'Bisaya' or 'Binisaya,' although no evidence has been presented to demonstrate such a close relationship (Constantino 1971).

71. Butuanon. Mindanao.
72. Cuyunon = Kuyonon = Kuyunon = Cuyo = Cuyuno = Cuyonon. D. also Ratagnón = Latagnon = Latan = Lactan = Aradigi. 2,000 Ratagnon on Mindoro. Cuyo, Palawan, Mindoro, Sibay, Semirra, Caluya, Ilin Islands.
73. Ilonggo = Ilongo = Binisayang Ilonggo = Hiligaynon = Hiligayna = Hililigaina = Panayan (usually when Aklanon (75) and Kinaraya (76) are added). 2,000,000. Dominant language in Capiz, Iloilo, Negros Occidental and Romblon provinces and some towns in Cotabato, Occidental Mindoro and Oriental Mindoro provinces (Constantino).
74. Sebuano = Cebuano = Cebuan = Binisayang Cebuano = Bisayan = Sebuan = Sugbuhanon = Sugbuanon.

At least seven dialects, including Kantilan, Surigaonon = Surigao; several dialects commonly assigned to Sebuano are not mutually intelligible with the other dialects (Constantino). Perhaps 9,000,000 in 1970. Dominant language in Agusan, Bohol, Bukidnon, Cebu, Davao, Lanao del Norte, the eastern half of Leyte, Misamis Occidental, Misamis, Misamis Oriental, Negros Oriental, Surigao, Zamboanga del Norte, Zamboanga del Sur provinces, and some towns in Cotabato (Constantino).

Other languages which probably belong in the BISAYAN subgroup (Constantino) are:

75. Aklanon = Aklan = Panay.
76. Kinaraya = Hiniraya = Binukidnon. Panay.
77. Romblomanon. Romblon Province.
78. Waray = Waray-Waray = Waraywaray = Samar-Leyte = Leytean = Samaron. Dominant language in Samar and the western half of Leyte.
79. Cagayanon = Jama Mapun. Cagayan Is. in Sulu Archipelago.
80. Manmanua = Mamanua = Mamanwa. 1,000. Agusan and Surigao provinces, Mindanao.
81. Tagalog = Tagal = Tagala = Tagalo. 28,800,000, including second language speakers — projecting that 60% of the population would speak Tagalog by 1967 (Constantino); Tagalog has fewer native speakers than Sebuano. Dominant language in Greater Manila and in Bataan, Batangas, Bulacan, Cavite, Laguna, Marinduque, Nueva Ecija, Occidental Mindoro, Oriental Mindoro, Quezon and Rizal provinces; also in the northern half of Camarines Norte, some towns of Zambales and the cities of Davao and perhaps Cotabato. An official language of the Philippines, beside English and Spanish.

PALAWANIC

82. Babuyan = Babuyan Batak = Batak = Tinitianes. Palawan Is.
83. Palawano = Palawan = Palawanen. Palawan Is.
84. Tagbanua = Tagbanuwá = Tagbanua. Ds. Apurawano = Apurahuano = Central, Silanganen = Bulalacaunos, Tangdulanen. 7,000. Palawan Is.
85. Pampangan = Kapampangan = Pampango = Pampanggan. 641,795. Dominant language in Pampanga Province and in four towns of Tarlac and two towns of Bataan, Luzon Is.

Other languages which probably belong to SULIC, possibly to its MESO-PHILIPPINE subgroup are:

86. Agtaa. Negros Is.
87. Ati = Mundo = Montescos = Kalibugan. Panay.

88. Banton. Banton Is.
89. Bohol = Boholano. Bohol Is.
90. Hantik = Antiqueño = Antique. Panay.
91. Sambali = Sambal. Ds. Iba, Bolinao, Tino = Tina. 81,583. Luzon Is.
92. Tiruray = Teduray = Tirurai = Teguray. 15,919. Mindanao Island.
93. Yakan = Yacanes. 30,348. Basilan Island.

Other unclassified languages of the Philippine Islands which probably belong in the PHILIPPINE subgroup are:

94. Ata. Ds. Dugbatang = Dugbatung, Tugauanum = Tugauanon. 7,900. Mindanao.
95. Bagobo. Ds. also Gianga = Guianga = Guanga = Gulanga, Obo = Tagdapaya, Eto = Atá. 20,890. Mindanao.
96. Isamal. Samal.
97. Ke-néy = Kenne = Queney. Palawan.
98. Kulaman = Culamanes = Sarangani Manobo. 3,600. Mindanao.
99. Mandaya. Mindanao.
100. Mangguangan = Manggulanga = Manguagao. 1,790. Mindanao.
101. Melebuganon. Balabac.
102. Samal = A'a Sama. Ds. Land Samal and Sea Samal = Balangingi. Mindanao and Sulu.

Other languages spoken outside the Philippine Islands which may belong to the NORTHWEST subgroup of AUSTRONESIAN (Cense and Uhlenbeck 1958) are:

103. Bajau = Badjo = Bajao = Badjaw = Luaan = Lutaos = Lutayaos = Orang Laut = Sama (self-designation). Sulu Archipelago and other islands of the Sulu Sea, Celebes Sea, Makassar Straits, Gulf of Tomini (Celebes), including the coast of Celebes and north and east coasts of Borneo. Bajau is probably not one of the WEST INDONESIAN Borneo languages (Cense and Uhlenbeck).
104. Ubian Banadan. Near Kudat, Sabah, and possibly on a Philippine island (Cense and Uhlenbeck).

In addition, two languages spoken in Micronesia, Chamorro and Palau, are often said to have their closest relationships with Philippine languages. Dyen's (1965) lexicostatistical classification did not subgroup either Chamorro or Palau with any other language at a level below his largest subgroup of AUSTRONESIAN, namely, MALAYOPOLYNESIAN. However, Topping (cited by Bender 1971) argues that morphological and syntactic evidence points to the close relationship of Chamorro to Philippine languages. W. K. Matthews (1950) proposed that Palauan shows even closer affinities to Philippine languages than Chamorro does. Hence, these two languages are listed here under NORTHWEST AUSTRONESIAN.

105. Chamorro. 51,000. Guam, 13°24′N 144°48′E (39,000), and north of Guam in the Marianas (12,000 including 2,000 bilingual in Chamorro and Carolinian on Saipan).
106. Palauan. 12,000. Palau Islands, 7°30′N 135°12′E (11,500), Guam 13°24′N 144°48′E (500).

AFFILIATION. Member of the HESPERONESIAN subgroup of AUSTRONESIAN.

PAPUA AUSTRONESIAN (Geographical)

GROUPING. Grace (1955) divides the AUSTRONESIAN languages of the Trust Territory of Papua into two major groups: those of the Central District in contrast to those of the Milne Bay District, the Northern District and the islands between Papua and the Solomons. The latter group is subdivided into five groups: first, the languages of the northern tier of islands (from Kiriwina through Laughlin Island); second, those of the southern tier of islands (from Muguru Island — south of the central part of Milne Bay — to Misima Island in the Luisiade Archipelago); third, those of the north coast of the mainland from Milne Bay to Collingwood Bay; fourth, Dobu (6, below); and fifth, Tagula (45).

Dyen's (1965) sample included only seven of the languages of this area; two of these were not subgrouped with any other AUSTRONESIAN languages; four of them formed a subgroup, MASSIM, also not further subgrouped with any other AUSTRONESIAN languages. However, each of the two ungrouped languages shared more cognates with languages in the MASSIM subgroup than with other languages, and the MASSIM subgroup shared more cognates with Dyen's seventh language than with any other language outside the subgroup. The seventh language, Motu (29, below), is classified by Dyen as belonging to HEONESIAN, the other members of which are otherwise classifiable as EASTERN OCEANIC. The MASSIM = TIP subgroup is further subdivided by Dyen into WEDAUIC (Wedauan, 52, and Keheraran, 20) and DOBIC (Dobu, 6, and Molima, 28). Dyen's ungrouped languages are Panayati (35) and Ubir (49).

Capell (1962a) lists and locates the languages of this area.

1. Anuki. Coastal Milne Bay District.
2. Bohutu. Island south of Milne Bay.
3. Bwaidoga. 8,600. Goodenough Island in D'Entrecasteaux Islands.
4. Daiomoni. Island south of Milne Bay.
5. Daraloia. Coastal Milne Bay District.
6. Dobu. D. also Tewara. Dobu Island, adjacent small islands and the adjacent tip of Normanby Island in the D'Entrecasteaux Islands. The population of the Esa'ala District is 31,182, but it is not known how many of these speak Dobu as a native language rather than as a second language.
7. Doura. Central District, Papua.
8. Duau. Ds. also Bunama, Sawabwala, Urada, Normanby Island.
9. Ewatiaga. Island south of Milne Bay.
10. Galoma. Central District, Papua.
11. Gawa. Marshall Bennett Islands.
12. Gumasi. Fergusson Island and the adjacent Amplett Islands.
13. Guregureu. Normanby Island.
14. Gwabegwabe. Fergusson Island and the adjacent Amplett Islands.
15. Hula. Ds. also Aroma, Keakalo, Keapara, Kerepunu. Central District, Papua.
16. Ikoro. Central District, Papua.
17. Kabadi. Central District, Papua.
18. Kalokalo. Goodenough Island in the D'Entrecasteaux Islands.
19. Karo. Central District, Papua.

20. Keheraran = Kehelala. D. also Basilaki. East Cape and Moresby Island.
21. Kiriwina. 8,600. Kiriwina Island in the Trobriand Islands.
22. Kukuya. Fergusson Island and the adjacent Amplett Islands.
23. Kuni. Central District, Papua.
24. Lala = Pokau = Nala = Nara. Central District, Papua.
25. Maiwara. Island south of Milne Bay.
26. Mekeo. D. also Kovio. Central District, Papua.
27. Miaitopa. Island south of Milne Bay.
28. Molima = Morima. Fergusson Island in the D'Entrecasteaux Islands.
29. Motu. Several thousand. Central District, Papua. Police Motu, a pidgin widely used as a ligua franca in Papua, is based on Motu.
30. Mukawa. Coastal Milne Bay District
31. Murua. Woodlark Island.
32. Nada. Laughlin Island.
33. Nuakata. A small island south of Normanby.
34. Panakrusima. In the Calvados Chain.
35. Panayati. D. also Misima. 10,000. Luisiade Archipelago.
36. Roboda. Normanby Island.
37. Roro. Central District, Papua.
38. Sabari. In the Calvados chain.
39. Salakahadi. Fegusson Island and the adjacent Amplett Islands.
40. Sanaroa. An island between Tewara and Dobu Island. May be a dialect of Dobu or Molima.
41. Sariba. Island south of Milne Bay.
42. Sinaki. Island south of Milne Bay.
43. Sinaugoro. Central District, Papua.
44. Suau. Ds. also Bonarua, Brierley Is., Brumer Is., Daui, Duchateau Is., Heath Is., Igora = Aigora, Mugura = Mugula = Bonabona, Rogea = Logea. Islands south of Milne Bay.
45. Tagula = Sudest = Rewa. 1,900. Sud Est (Tagula) Island.
46. Tavara. Island south of Milne Bay.
47. Tokunu. Alcester Islands.
48. Tubetube. Engineer Island.
49. Ubir. Collingwood Bay in the Northern District.
50. Wagawaga. Island south of Milne Bay.
51. Wari = Ware. Teste Island.
52. Wedauan. Ds. also Awalama, Taupota. Northeast coast of Milne Bay.

AFFILIATION. Belongs in OCEANIC subgroup of AUSTRONESIAN.

SANTA CRUZ AUSTRONESIAN

GROUPING. Grace (1955) treats the languages of the Santa Cruz Islands as forming a subgroup. Davenport (1962) presents lexicostatistical evidence to show that the languages of Utupua Island, 10°20′S 160°30′E (1–3 below), do not form a very closely related group.

1. Aba = Nimbau = Nemboa. 119.
2. Apako = Asimboa. 53.
3. Atago = Tanabili. Only a few sepakers who now also speak Apako.
4. Vanikoro. 125. Vanikoro Island, 11°42′S 166°50′E. Closely related to Atago.

AFFILIATION. Member of OCEANIC subgroup of AUSTRONESIAN.

SOUTH HALMAHERA-WEST NEW GUINEA AUSTRONESIAN (Geographical)

GROUPING. Esser (1938) treats the AUSTRONESIAN languages of southern Halmahera and West New Guinea (West Irian) as forming a single group, subdivided first into a SOUTH HALMAHERA subgroup and a WEST NEW GUINEA group. The WEST NEW GUINEA group is further subdivided into Biak, KUWAI, NUMFOR (in which the Numfor language is opposed to the rest), and WINDESI. Dyen's (1965) lexicostatistical classification included some of the languages from this area; in it, Biak, Numfor, WINDESI and Kuwai (from the KUWAI group) as well as some other WEST NEW GUINEA languages are grouped with languages spoken in the Lesser Sundas and Moluccas as MOLUCCAN; names of these MOLUCCAN languages (as Biak and Numfor) are listed under MOLUCCAN. Those not classified as MOLUCCAN fell into two small groups, HOLLANDIA and BIGIC, and two languages (Arguni and Kasira) which were not subgrouped with any other languages in AUSTRONESIAN.

1. Arguni. Western end of Bomberai Peninsula, West New Guinea = West Irian.

BIGIC
  2. As. Western tip of the Vogelkop, West New Guinea.
  3. Biga. Wakde Island, off Sarmi Coast of northeastern West New Guinea.
  4. Buli. D. also Wajamli = Jawanli? South Halmahera.
  5. Minyafuin = Bahasa Gebi = Gebe. Gebe Island, between Halmahera and
     Waigeo Island.
Other possible members of BIGIC follow.
SOUTH HALMAHERA. Spoken on Halmahera Island, Moluccas (except as indicated).
  6. Gane.
  7. Kajoa. Kajoa Island, west of the center of the southern peninsula of
     Halmahera.
  8. Maba. D. also Bitjoli = Ingli.
  9. East Makian. Makian Islands, west of the neck of the southern peninsula
     of Halmahera.
  10. West Makian Islands.
  11. Patani.
  12. Sawai.
  13. Weda = Were.
NUMFOR. Spoken on islands just west of the Vogelkop of West New Guinea.
  14. Bo'o.
  15. Kofiau.
  16. Miso'ol = Misol.

17. Salawati.
18. Waigeo. Ds. also Amber, Saonek.

HOLLANDIA. 1,000. Hollandia District, West New Guinea.
19. Ormu.
20. Tobati = Yotafa. D. also Kajupulau.
21. Kasira. West New Guinea.

KUWAI. Bomberai Peninsula, West New Guinea.
22. Irahutu. 3,850 (Capell 1962).
23. Nabi. 550 (Capell 1962).
Aiduma (?), Busamma (?) Kajumerah (?), Lakahia (?), Lowai (?) Mangawitu (?). Namatote (?), Terera (?), Tjirerau (?), Triton Bay (?), (Salzner 1960).

AFFILIATION. Members of AUSTRONESIAN, within which KUWAI may be includable in MOLUCCAN, since Dyen classifies the language called Kuwai in MOLUCCAN; but he did not treat the other languages in the group called KUWAI, above.

AWYU = AWJU = MANDOBO

GROUPING. Wurm (1971c) subgroups languages numbered (5) and (7) as AWYU; languages numbered (1), (3), (4), and (6) as AGHU; and languages numbered (2), (8) and (9) as DUMUT. Greenberg (1971) classifies DUMUT as a subgroup of OK. 20,000 total speakers. Southern West Irian.
1. Aghu = Dyair.
2. Kaeti = Nub.
3. Kotogüt.
4. Mitak.
5. Oser = Yenimu = Jenimu.
6. Pisa.
7. Syiagha = Sjiagha.
8. Wambon.
9. Wanggom.

AFFILIATION. Member of CENTRAL AND SOUTH NEW GUINEA.

AZTEC-TANOAN PHYLUM

GROUPING. Sapir (1929) grouped KIOWA-TANOAN and UTO-AZTECAN under AZTEC-TANOAN, as two language families that might be remotely related (and added Zuni to this group, as possibly but doubtfully standing in a remote relationship to UTO-AZTECAN). Whorf and Trager (1937) were the first to attest the relationship between UTO-AZTECAN and TANOAN, but weakly so; the attestation remains problematical.

TANOAN (q. v.)
UTO-AZTECAN (q. v.)

AFFILIATION. Whorf (1935) grouped UTO-AZTECAN and PENUTIAN under

MACRO-PENUTIAN. Bouda (1952) postulates connections between UTO-AZTECAN, CHUCKCHEE, URALIC (FINNO-UGRIC), CAUCASIAN, and Basque.

Baen(n)a = Mbae-una. Less than two dozen. State of Bahia, Brazil (Lorraine Bridgeman, personal communication).

AFFILIATION. Unknown.

BALTIC

GROUPING. Of all major INDO-EUROPEAN branches, BALTIC appears to be the most conservative (Hamp 1959; Senn 1966; Toporov et al. 1966; Zeps 1962). Two of the languages in this group, Jatvian (2) and Old Prussian (5), are classified as WEST BALTIC, and the rest as EAST BALTIC. Though the dialect differentiation which led to the split between WEST and EAST BALTIC occurred long ago (500–300 B.C.), the written literature in the daughter languages appears very late. In particular, the records for languages numbered (1), (6), and (7) are meager; and these languages were replaced by Lettish and Lithuanian.

1. *Curonian.
2. *Jatvian = Suduvian. Traces from as late as nineteenth century.
3. Lettish = Latvian. Ds. Central = Middle Lettish; Eastern = High = Upper Lettish (including Lagalian); Tamian = Western Lettish. 2,000,000. Latvia.
4. Lithuanian. Ds. Aukshtaitish = Aukštaičiai = Aukštaitis = High Lithuanian (the basis of Modern Standard Lithuanian is a subdialect of Aukshtaitsh), Dzūkish, Shamaitish = Samogitian = Žemaitis = Žemaitish = Žemaičiai = Low Lithuanian (the earliest written records in Lithuanian are in this dialect). 3,000,000; primarily in Lithuania, but also: United States (400,000), Brazil (40,000), Argentina (35,000), Great Britain (12,000), Uruguay (10,000), Canada (10,000), Central Western Europe (70,000), and Siberia.
5. *Old Prussian. Formerly in Prussia, or Borussia (in an area later called East Prussia) between the Vistula and the Niemumas = Memel rivers. Extinct since seventeenth century.
6. *Selonian. Spoken in Middle Ages near Dvinsk-Daugavpils (extinct since 1400).
7. *Zemgalian = Semi Gallian. Spoken until the late Middle Ages in the Musalielupe River basin (extinct since 1450).

AFFILIATION. Member of INDO-EUROPEAN. See INDO-EUROEPAN for the debated relationship of BALTIC to SLAVIC; the debate hinges on the issue as to whether the shared traits of BALTIC with SLAVIC are diffusional (as some recent ones indisputably are) or whether they are genetic.

BANDJALANGIC

GROUPING. The BANDJALANGIC languages are spoken on the northeastern coast of New South Wales just over the New South Wales-Queensland boundary, Australia.

1. Kitabal = Kidabal = Kittabool = Kitapul = Gidjoobal = Kuttibul. Ds. also Arakwal = Gundurimba = Tugurimba, Badjelang = Bandjalang = Bunjellung = Bundela = Bundel = Watchee, Kalibal, Widjabal.
2. Yugumbal = Yugambe = Jukamba.

AFFILIATION. Member of PAMA-NYUNGAN.

BANTOID

GROUPING. Greenberg (1966) and Williamson (1971) subsume under BANTOID both those languages formerly known as 'Bantu' ('Bantu Proper', 'Narrow Bantu') and some of those variously known as 'Semi-Bantu' (Johnston 1919, 1922), 'Benue-Cross' (Westermann 1927), and 'Bantoid' (Linguistic Survey of the Northern Bantu Borderland 1956, 1957a, b). The classification and list of languages below include all those classified by Williamson (1971) as BANTOID as well as those considered 'Bantu' by Bryan (1959) and Guthrie (1967–71).

While there is consensus on the relationship of these languages to other BENUE-CONGO languages, consensus is lacking on the validity of BANTOID as a subgroup within BENUE-CONGO and on the subgrouping of BANTOID. The BANTOID languages are divided first into NON-BANTU BANTOID versus BANTU = BROAD BANTU languages. Williamson (1971) lists the NON-BANTU languages in two groups: MAMBILA-WUTE and TIV-BATU. The BROAD BANTU languages are subdivided into six groups, which largely reflect geographical proximity rather than linguistic homogeneity: BANTU = NARROW BANTU, GRASSLANDS BANTU, MAMFE BANTU, MISAJE, NIGERIAN BANTU, and TIKAR. These are further subgrouped as shown in the list below. The list includes BANTU PROPER, but does not include the list of language names which are classified under that group name; these numerous language names appear in a separate article (BANTU PROPER), which is cross-referenced to the BANTOID languages that are listed here.

BANTU = NARROW BANTU = BANTU PROPER (q. v.)
GRASSLANDS BANTU = GRASSFIELD = GRASFIL = GRASFI = PLATEAU BANTOID. The GRASSLANDS group includes six subgroups and six coordinate unsubgrouped languages as listed below. Language names previously listed as members of GRASSLANDS which are not identifiable with those on Williamson's list are given with question marks at the end of the list. The following are surely not all separate languages; apparently varying degrees of mutual intelligibility exist among several of them (Welmers 1971a). The GRASSLANDS languages are spoken mainly in Cameroon.

BAMILEKE
1. Babadjou = Tsaso = Etsaso. Dép. de Bamboutos.
2. Bafang = Fe'fe' = FeFe. Ds. Bakou, Bana, Fa, Kuu = Kun. 67,500. Dép. du Haut-Nkam.
3. Bafou. D. also Dschang-Bangwa = Chang = Atsang = Nwe = Dschangtalk. 41,000. Around Dschang.
4. Bafoussam = Fulsap = Fusap = Fusam. 7,000. Dép. du Mifi.
5. Bagam = Tsogap. Dép. de Bamboutos.

6. Baloum. Dép. de la Menoua.
7. Bamaha. South of Fe'fe'.
8. Bamendiinda ? = Bamdendjina. Dép de Bamboutos.
9. Bamenkombit = Bamenkoumbit. Dép. de Bamboutos.
10. Bamenyam. Dép. de Bamboutos.
11. Bandjoun-Baham = Banjoun = Banjoum = Mandjŭ = Mahŭm = Ngomahŭm. D. also Bayangam. Dép. du Mifi.
12. Banganté = Bangangte = Ndzubuga = Njuboga. 66,700. Dép. du Ndé.
13. Bangwa = Eastern Bangwa = Bangoua-Batoufam ? = Bangou ? Dép. du Nde.
14. Bapi. Dép. du Mifi.
15. Batcham. Dép. de Bamboutos.
16. Batchingou = Bachingou. Dép. du Ndé.
17. Bati. Dép. de Bamboutos.
18. Batié. Dép. du Mifi.
19. Bomougoun-Bamenjou = Bamendjou = Pamunguup = Mundju = (Nega) Bamungup = (Nega) Munju. Ds. also Balessing, Bameka (6,000), Bansoa. 25,000. Dép. du Mifi.
20. Fomopea. Dschang area.
21. Fongondeng = Fongo-Ndeng. Dép. de la Menoua.
22. Foto = Fòtò. Near Dschang.
23. Fotouni. Dép. du Haut-Nkam.
24. Ngwe. Around Fontem, Mamfe Prefecture.
25. Bamoun = Bamun = Shupaman. 75,000. Dép. Bamoun. Used widely as a lingua franca.
26. Bandem. 7,700. Cameroon, Upper Wouri River. Bandem is grouped with NKOM as one of the six subgroups of GRASSLANDS.
27. Biba-Bifang = Beba-Befang. Wum Prefecture.
28. Lamnso = Lamso = Banso = Nso = Nsaw = Bansaw. 22,000. Bamenda Prefecture.
29. Mbem = Kaka. Nkambe Prefecture.
MFUMTE. All are spoken in Nkambe Prefecture.
30. Adere = Arderi.
31. Kọfa. D. also Lus.
32. Kwaja.
33. Ncha.
34. Ndaktup = Bitwi.
35. Ntem = Tschintsche. D. also Wanti = Wante = Wongbo.
NDOP = MELAMBA. All are spoken in Bamenda Prefecture.
36. Bamali.
37. Fanji = Bafa'ndji.
38. Kënsense = Kə́nsə́n'sə́ = Bamessing = Nsei.
39. Muka = Bamunka.
40. Ngo = Babungo.
41. Tshirambọ = Bambalang.

42. Ngaaka = Mungaka = Mungaaka = Munyona = Ba'ni = Bali of Bali Town. Bamenda Prefecture.

NGEMBA = NGOMBA = MAGIMBA = MEGIMBA. Kpati (46) is spoken in Takum, Wukari Division, Nigeria; the others are spoken in Bamenda Prefecture, Cameroon.

43. Awing = Bambulewe. Ds. also Mankon, Pinyin.
44. Bafut = Bafu = Bufë = Fut = Fu.
45. Bamunkum.
46. Kpati.
47. Mandankwe. Ds. also Mbili = Mbele = Bambili, Mbui = Bambui, Nkwen = Bafreng.

NKOM = KOM. Mostly in Bamenda and Wum Prefectures.

48. Bafum. Nigeria ?
49. Bum.
50. Fungom = Western Bafumbum ?
51. Kidzöm = Kidzem = Babanki = Finge.
52. Mme.
53. Nkom = Bikom = Kom = Ikom = Bamekon = Ekom = Etaŋ. D. also Tsam ? 15,000–17,000.
54. Oso = Osso = Ndum.
55. Ukfwọ = Oku.
56. We = Weh.
57. Wum = Yum = Aghem.

58. Nsungli = Nsungali = Nsungni = Ndzungle = Zungle = Limbum = Llimbumi = Wimbun. Ds. Tang = Tan, Wiya = Ndu, Wa(r) = Mbat, Nfumte ? Nkambe Prefecture.

TADKON. Bamenda and Mamfe Prefectures.

59. Menemo = Bameta = Meta = Muta = Uta' = Chubo.
60. Mogamo(wa) = Moghamo = Megamaw.
61. Ngamambo = Eastern Meta.
62. Widekum = Widikum = Burrikem = Tiwirkum = Mbudikem = Iyirikum. 10,000.
63. Apo ?
64. Babouantou = Bapouantou = Papuantu ?
65. Bankwet ?
66. Batongtou ?
67. Mbaw ?

MAMBILA-WUTE

68. Bute = Buti = Vute = Wute = Babute = Babuti = Mfuti = Wetere = Vutere. Ds. also Galim, Suga = Ssuga = Jemjem = Njemnjem. 16,000. East Cameroon.
69. Gandua. West Cameroon.
70. Kamkam = Bungnu = Bunu = Kakaba. 800. Kamkam town, Mambila District, Sardauna Province, Nigeria.

71. Kila. Mambila District, Sardauna Province, Nigeria.
72. Magu. Mambila District, Sardauna Province, Nigeria.
73. Mambila = Mambere = Bamembila = Nor = Omavirre = Katoba = Luen = Torbi = Tagbo = Tongbo = Lagubi. Ds. ? also Atta, Kuma, Mvanip. 15,835. Mambila District, Sardauna Province, Nigeria, and adjacent West Cameroon.
74. Ndoro. 1,200. Ndoro District, Sardauna Province, Nigeria.
75. Tep. Mambila District, Sardauna Province, Nigeria.

MAMFE BANTU. Most of these languages have not been studied and hence they are unclassified within BROAD BANTU. They are spoken in the area around Mamfe, West Cameroon.

76. Age = Esimbi = Simpi. 5,000.
77. Amasi.
78. Anyang.
79. Assumbo = Asumbo = Azumbo = Badzumbo.
80. Kinkwa = Mangen Kinkwa.
81. Menka.
82. Lower Mundani. Ds. also Banteng, Bessali, Betchati, Fonange, Ndzen.
83. Upper Mundani. D. also Bamok.
84. Ngi = Ngie = Angie = Ugie = Mingi = Baminge.
85. Ngonu = Ngunu = Ngwo = Ngwa = Agono.
86. Nyang = Kenyang = Ba(n)yang(i). D. also Kitwii = Manyemen = North Balong.
87. Takamanda = Manta.

MISAJE = METCHO
88. Bunaki. Wum Prefecture.
89. Dzaiven Boka. Wum Prefecture.
90. Kọsin = Kaw. Wum Prefecture.
91. Kumaju = Dumbo. Ds. also Bebedjato, Ngọng = Nzhimamuŋgọŋ, Nọni including Nkọr, Ntshanti. Ngọng is spoken in Wum Prefecture, Nọni in Bamenda Prefecture, and the other dialects in Nkambe Prefecture.

NIGERIAN BANTU. Two unsubgrouped languages Afudu (92) and Mbe (112) are listed with the EKOID and JARAWAN subgroups in NIGERIAN BANTU, which represents a geographical rather than a genetic group.

92. Afudu (a language reported by Koelle 1854, cited by Williamson 1971).

EKOID BANTU. Crabb (1965) treats EKOID as consisting of a number of separate languages, whereas Westermann and Bryan (1952) treat these as dialects of a single language. Crabb subgroups (94) with (97), (95) with (101), and (99) with (100). They are spoken in Ogoja, Abakaliki, and Calabar provinces, Nigeria and Mamfe Division, West Cameroon.

93. Abanyom.
94. Efutop.
95. Ekajuk.

96. Ekoi. Ds. Bendeghe = Bindiga = M̀bùmá, Edjagam = Keaka = Keaqə = Kejaka, Ejagham = Ejagam = Ejaham = Ejam = Ezam = Ekwe = Central Ekoi, Northern Etung = Icuatai, Southern Etung, Kwa = Qua = Aqua = Àbàkpà, Obang = E:afeŋ, Amasi (?), Ndam (?) 90,000.

97. Nde = Atam = Ekamtulu:fu = Mbenkpe = U:dom = Mbofo:n = Befo:n. Ds. also Nselle = Nsele, Nta.

98. Ndoe = Akparabon. Ds. Balep, Ekparabong.

99. Nkim.

100. Nkum = Nkumm.

101. Nmam.

JARAWAN BANTU. Following Thomas (1927), this group of languages is discussed in more detail by Maddieson and Williamson (1973). Languages (109) and (111) are each coordinate with a third subgroup, NIGERIAN, consisting of the other JARAWAN languages.

102. Ḅile = Bille = Billanc(h)i = Kunbille. North-East State, Nigeria, east of Numan along the Benue River.

103. Gubi = Gubawa. D. also Guru. Possibly extinct.

104. Jaku = Jakanci. North-East State, Nigeria, east of Bauchi.

105. Jarawa = Plains Jarawa = Jarawan k̀asa = Jar = Jaranci. Ds. Badawa = Bada = Badanci = (M)bat = Mbada(wa) = Jar, Bankala = Bankal = Bankalawa = Bankalanci, Bobar, Duguri = Duguranci = Jar, Ging-gwak = Gingwak = Gwak = Jaranci, Ligri. North-East State, Nigeria, southeast of Bauchi around Zungur and north of Pankshin, Benue-Plateau State.

106. Kulung = Kuluŋ = Kulũ = Kukuluŋ = Bakulũ = Bakuli = Bambur = Wurkum.

107. Lame. Ds. Bambaro = Bombaro = Bambara = Bomborawa = Bomberawa = Bombarawa = Bambaranci, Gura = Gurawa. Lame District, North-East State, Nigeria.

108. Mama. D. also Kantanawa. Benue-Plateau State, Nigeria, east of Wamba.

109. Mboa. Cameroon, on the river Lom, south of Meiganga. Possibly extinct.

110. Mbul(l)a. D. also Bwazza = Bare = Barawa. North-East State, Nigeria, north of Numan along the Gongola River.

111. Nagumi = (M)bama = (N)gong. Cameroon, north of Gunna. Possibly extinct.

112. Mbe = Western Mbube = Ketuen. Ogoja Division, Ogoja Province, Nigeria.

TIKAR. East Cameroon.

113. Bandobo.

114. Tikar = Tikari = Tikali = Tikare = Tika = Tiker = Tumu. 200,000.

TIV-BATU. Languages numbered (116) and (117) are subgrouped with (120), and

(115) and (119) form a subgroup. All are spoken in Nigeria.

115. Abõ. Abõ town, Tigon District.
116. Balegete. Old Ogoja Province.
117. Batu. Batu town, Tigou District.
118. Becheve. Old Ogoja Province.
119. Bitare = Yukutare = Zuande = Tigong. D. also Njwande. 50,000. Tigon District, Sardauna Province.
120. Tiv = Tivi = Tiwi = Mbitse = Mbitshi = (Munshi = Munchi; pejorative) = Appa. 600,000. Tiv Division, Benue Province.

AFFILIATION. Member of BENUE-CONGO.

BANTU PROPER = NARROW BANTU

GROUPING. The overall areal classification, following, reflects the arrangement espoused by Guthrie (1967-71), i.e., to group languages of BANTU PROPER with respect to a half-dozen major areas. In addition, larger groups can be obtained by combining the WESTERN major areas and opposing them to the EASTERN major areas, and smaller groups can be obtained by dividing each major area into zones.

The numerous languages classified as BANTU PROPER are listed below, either in terms of major areas in which they occur (after Guthrie 1948, 1953, 1967-71), or as a group of closely related but not contiguous languages, KARI (after Bryan 1959). These BANTU PROPER languages are separately numbered and alphabetized for each of the following major areas (as well as for KARI):

(1)–(71) under CENTRAL EASTERN AREA
(1)–(49) under CENTRAL WESTERN AREA
(1)–(6) under KARI
(1)–(102) under NORTH EASTERN AREA
(1)–(146) under NORTH WESTERN AREA
(1)–(34) under SOUTH EASTERN AREA
(1)–(31) under SOUTH WESTERN AREA

CENTRAL EASTERN AREA. The division and subdivision of languages into zones and groups, respectively, is stated here before the languages for the area as a whole are listed. After each of three zones, indicated by the letters G and M and N, and within each zone after named groups, there appear cross-reference numbers in parentheses, which refer to the language list, following, alphabetized for all languages in the CENTRAL EASTERN AREA.

Zone G is subdivided into BENA-KINGA = HEHE (4, 9, 14, 15, 42, 53, 69); GOGO (8, 12); POGOLO (33, 45); SHAMBALA = SHAMBAA (1, 6, 56, 65); SWAHILI (16, 43, 58, 62); (ZIGULA-)ZARAMO (13, 18, 34, 36, 48, 52, 67, 70, 71). Altogether 9,000,000 speakers. Tanzania, Kenya.

Zone M is subdivided into BEMBA (3, 60); BISA-LAMBA (2, 5, 19, 20, 54, 59); FIPA-MAMBWE (7, 25, 44, 49, 50); LENJE-TONGA = ILA (10, 21, 22, 23, 57, 63); Nyakyusa-Konde (38); NYIKA-SAFWA (11, 24, 31, 32, 40, 51, 61, 68). Altogether over 250,000 speakers. Tanzania, Zambia, Zaire.

Zone N is subdivided into MANDA (26, 27, 30, 35, 63); NYANJA (28, 29, 39); SENGA-SENA = NSENGA (17, 37, 41, 46, 47, 55); Tumbuka (66). Altogether 2,000,000 speakers. Tanzania, Zambia, Rhodesia, Mozambique.

1. Asu = (ci-)Athu = Chasu = Pare. 99,000.
2. Aushi = Ushi = usi = Uzhil. 29,000.
3. (ici-)Bemba = Wemba. Ds. also Lembue, Lomotua = Lomotwa, Ngoma, Nwesi. 170,000.
4. (eki-)Bena. 158,000.
5. (ici-)Biisa = Bisa = Wisa. 41,500.
6. (ki-)Bondei = Bonde. 28,000.
7. (ici-)Fiba. 78,000.
8. (ci-)Gogo. 270,000.
9. (eki-)Hehe. 192,000.
10. (ci-)Ila = Sukulumbwe = Shukulumbwe. 130,000.
11. Iwa. 7,000.
12. (ci-)Kagulu = Kaguru = Northern Sagara. D. also (ci-) Megi. 59,500.
13. (ki-)Kami.
14. (eki-)Kinga. 57,000.
15. Kisi(i). 4,000.
16. Komoro = Comoro. Ds. Ngazija = Ngazidja, Njuani = Nzwani = Hinzua = Nzuani = Ngwana = Kingwana.
17. (ci-)Kunda = Chikunda. 73,000.
18. (ki-)Kutu = Khutu. 15,000.
19. (ici-)Lala. Ds. also Ambo = Bambo = Kambonsenga, Luano, Wulima. 64,000.
20. (ici-)Lamba. 70,000–80,000.
21. (ci-)Lenje = Ciina Mukuni. D. also Twa. 33,000.
22. Lundwe.
23. Mala.
24. (ishi-)Malila. 17,500.
25. (ici-)Mambwe = Kimambwe. 15,000.
26. (ci-)Manda = Kimanda = Nyasa. 10,000.
27. (ci-)Matengo = Kimatengo. 58,000.
28. Mazaro.
29. Mbo = Ambo. Ds. also Makanga, Tonga, Tumba.
30. (ci-)Mpoto = Kimpoto = Nyasa. 58,000.
31. Mwanga = (ici-)Namwanga = Nyamwanga = Inamwanga. 32,000.
32. Ndali. 51,000.
33. Ndamba. 19,000.
34. (ki-)Nghwele = Ŋhwele.
35. (ci-)Ngoni = Kingoni = (ki-)Sutu. 103,000.
36. (ki-)Ngulu = Nguru. 65,500.
37. (ci-)Nsenga = Senga. 45,000.
38. (eke-)Nyakyusa = Nyekosa = Niakyusa = Nyikyusa = Sokile = Sokili = Sochile = Mombe Kukwe. Ds. also Kukwe, Mwamba = Lungulu, Ngonde = Konde = Nkonde, Selya = Salya = Seria.

39. (ci-)Nyanja = Chinyanja. Ds. also (ci-)Cewa = Chewa = Cheva = Sheva (653,000), Maŋanja = Manganja = Cimanganja, Peta = Cipeta = Maravi = Marave = Malawi. 965,000.
40. (ishi-)Nyiha = Nyika = Nyixa. 59,000.
41. (ci-)Nyungwe = Teta = Tete.
42. (eki-)Pangwa. 38,000.
43. Pemba = Phemba. Ds. also Hadimu, Tambatu.
44. (ici-)Pimbwe. 8,000.
45. (ci-)Pogolo = Pogoro. 63,000.
46. (ci-)Podzo. 5,000.
47. (ci-)Rue = Cirue.
48. (ki-)Ruguru = Luguru. 179,000.
49. (ici-)Runga = Rungwa. 5,000.
50. (ici-)Rungu = Lungu. 24,000.
51. (ishi-)Safwa. 46,200.
52. (ki-)Sagala = Sagara. 20,000.
53. (eshi-)Sango = Sangu = Rori. 23,000.
54. Seba = Sewa = Shishi. Over 7,000.
55. (ci-)Sena. 200,000.
56. (ki-)Shambaa = Shambala = Sambaa = Sambara = Schambala. 130,000.
57. (ci-)Soli. 13,000.
58. Swahili = Suaheli = Suahili = ki-Swahili. Ds. also Amu = Lamu, (ci-)-Cifundi, Mrima, Mtangata = Mtaŋata, Mvita, Pate = Patta, Siu = Siyu, Unguja, Vumba; also KiGavamenti, KiHindi, KiSerikala, KiSettla = Ki-Settlu, KiShamba, KiVita.
59. (ici-)Swaka = Maswaka. 12,500.
60. (ici-)Taabwa = Tabwa = Rungu. D. also Shila. 13,000.
61. Tambo = Tembo. 3,000.
62. Tikuu = Tikulu = Tukulu = Gunya = Bajuni. D. also (ci-)Mbalazi.
63. (ci-)Tonga = Kitonga =Siska = Sisya = Western Nyasa. 50,000.
64. (ci-)Tonga = Plateau Tonga. Ds. also Leya, Toka = Southern Tonga, We = Valley Tonga. 70,000 to 110,000.
65. (ki-)Tubeta = Taveta.
66. Tumbuka = Tew = Tambuka = Timbuka = Tumboka = Tombucas. Ds. also Fulilwa = Fulirwa, Fungwe, Hewe = Hewa, Kamanga = Henga, Kan-dawire, (ici-)Lambia = Lambya = Lambwa, Nenya, Nthali, (ci-)Poka = Phoka, Senga, Yombe.
67. (ki-)Vidunda. 10,000.
68. (ici-)Wanda = Wandia. 6,300.
69. Wanji. 18,000.
70. (ki-)Zaramo = Dzalamo. D. also Doe = Dohe. 180,000.
71. (ki-)Zigula = Zigua = Zeguha. 112,000.

CENTRAL WESTERN AREA. Languages which are alphabetized below for this area as a whole are divided into two zones, H and L; and each one is subdivided into named groups, followed by cross-reference numbers in parentheses.

Zone H is subdivided into KIKONGO (2, 13, 14, 29, 32, 48); KIMBALA (7, 26); KIMBUNDU (1, 4, 5, 12, 16, 27, 30, 33, 34, 35, 39, 44); KIYAKA (8, 22, 28, 42, 45, 46, 47, 49). Altogether 3,000,000 speakers. Congo (Leopoldville) = Zaire, Congo (Brazzaville), Cabinda, Angola.

Zone L is subdivided into Kaonde (10); LUBA (6, 9, 17, 18, 24, 26, 41); LUNDA (20, 23, 38); NKOYA (21, 25, 31, 36); PENDE (15, 37, 40); SONGE (3, 11, 19, 43). Altogether 3,500,000 speakers. Zaire, Zambia, extending into Angola.

1. Amboim = Mbuiyi.
2. Bembe = (ki-)Beembe.
3. Binji = Bindji. 64,000.
4. (lu-)Bolo = Libolo = Haka.
5. Dembo of Cacuta Caenda.
6. (ki-)Hemba = Luba-Hemba = Eastern Luba.
7. (ki-)Hungana = Huana = Hungaan = Huŋanna.
8. Hungu = (ki-)Holo = Hungo. Ds. also Bunda, Poombo, Puna, Tsotso = Sosso, Yembe. 66,000.
9. (ci-)Kanyoka = Kanioka.
10. (ki-)Kaonde = Cikaonde = Kahonde = Kawonde. 38,000.
11. (lu-)Kete = Kikete.
12. Kibala = Quibala.
13. Kongo = Ikeleve = Kileta = Fiote. Ds. Bwende = (ki-)Bweende = Ngoy = Buende = Fiot, including (ki-)Doondo, (ki-)Gaangala, (ki-)Kaamba (?); Central Kongo = Kikongo = Central Congo, including 'Kongo simplifie' = Ki-Ngoy Luula, (ki-)Mbaamba, (ki-)Mboma, (ki-)Mpaangu, (ki-)Mpese, (ki-)Ndibu, (ki-)Ntaandu, (ki-)Solongo; Eastern Kongo = Fiote; Northeastern Kongo = (ki-)Koongo; Southern Kongo = (Kishi-)Kongo = (Kishi-)Koongo = Xikongo = Southwestern Kongo, including (ki-)Mbaata, (ki-)Nzamba = Nzaamba; Southeastern Kongo, including (ki-)Mbeeko, (ki-)Nkanu, (ki-)P(h)atu, Soso = Sooso; Western (ka-)Kongo = (ka-)Koongo = Fiote, including Cabinda, Luangu; Laadi = Lari = Kilari, including Mbinsa = Mbensa = Kibinsa; (ki-)Yombe, including (ki-)Mbala Mumbala (?), (ki-)Vungunya = 'Yombe classique'; (ki-)Zombo = Nzombo = (ki-)Zoombo. 1,500,000. Kongo is spoken widely as a lingua franca, and as such is known as Fiote = Ikeleve, Ki-Leta = Ki-Tuba = Kongo Commercial = Ki-Kongo Véhiculaire.
14. (ki-)Kunyi.
15. (ki-)Kwese = Ukwese = Pindi.
16. *Lengue = Quilengue.
17. (ki-)Luba-Katanga.
18. Luba-Lulua = Kalebwe = Western Luba = Tshiluba = Ciluba = Luva. Ds. Luba-Kasai = Ciluba = Kasai, (cishi-)lange, Lulua. 3,400,000.
19. Luna = Luna Inkongo = Northern Luba.
20. (ci-)Lunda = Southern Lunda. Ds. also Ndembo = Ndembu. 82,000.
21. Lushange. 9,000.

22. (ki-)Luuwa ?
23. Luwunda = Luunda = (u-)Ruund = Northern Lunda = Lunda Muatia-vua = Lunda Muatiamvua. 20,000.
24. Lwalu. 21,000.
25. Mashasha. 13,000.
26. (ki-)Mbala = Rumbala.
27. (ki-)Mbamba = Bambeiro. Ds. also Mbaka = Ambaquista, Njinga = Ginga = Jinga. Listed by Guthrie (1967-71) in an MBUNDU CLUSTER with Mbundu (30).
28. Mbangala. D. also Yongo.
29. Mboka.
30. Mbundu = (ki-)Ndongo = Dongo = Nbundu = N'Bundo = Kimbundu. 1,000,000. Listed by Guthrie in an MBUNDU CLUSTER with Mbamba (27).
31. (shi-)Mbwera = Mbwela. D. also Lukolwe. 36,000.
32. Ndingi = Ndinzi = Ngingi. D. also (kisi(ma)-)Ngoyo = Woyo.
33. *Ngage.
34. Ngengu = Bondo = Quembo = Mussende.
35. Ngola. 41,000.
36. Nkoya = Shinkoya = Shikalu. 19,000.
37. (ki-)Pende = Pindi = Pinji. 27,000.
38. Salampasu = sala-Mpasu = tshi-sala-Mpasu. D. also Luntu. 60,000.
39. (ki-)Sama = Kissama = Quissama. Tr. Mbundu? 9,000.
40. (u-) Samba = Shankadi = (ki-)Tsaan(ba) ? Ds. also Bazela (?), Holu = Holo.
41. Sanga = Chiluba = Luba-Sang = Southern Luba.
42. (ki-)Shingi = Shinji = Xinji = Nungo = Yungo.
43. (lu-)Songe = Songi = Kisonge = Kalebwe = Northeastern Luba = Yembe. Ds. also Bakwa-Luntu, Lwalu, Mbala. 200,000. Used as a lingua franca, known as 'kisonge universel'.
44. Songo = Sungu. 15,000.
45. (ki-)Soonde ?
46. (ki-)Suku. 74,000.
47. Tembo.
48. (ki-)Vili = Fiot.
49. (ki-)Yaka. D. also Ngoongo.

KARI. Altogether 7,000 speakers.
1. Bodo. Sudan, Central African Republic.
2. Boguru. Ds. = Trs. 'Babukur, Boguru (75), Kogoro. Sudan, Congo (Leo-poldville) = Zaire.
3. Homa. Sudan.
4. Kari = Likarili = Kare. 4,000–5,000. Zaire (1,000); Central African Republic (3,000–4,000).
5. (li-)Ngbee = Mangbele. 30. Zaire.
6. Ngbinda = Bungbinda = 'Bangbinda. Sudan, Zaire.

NORTH EASTERN AREA. The 102 languages listed below are consecutively numbered and alphabetized. Both their division and subdivision into zones and groups are given here, with parenthetic cross-reference numbers matching the numbered language in the list following.

Zone D is subdivided into BEMBE-KABWARI (5, 13, 29, 33, 36, 67); BIRA-HUKU = BIRA plus NYALI (4, 7, 8, 9, 10, 11, 32, 38, 55, 58, 76); KONJO = NANDE (44, 63, 62, 71); LEGA KALANGA (1, 2, 3, 31, 35, 47, 49, 51, 87, 101, 102); MBOLE-ENA (21, 50, 56, 60); RUANDA-RUNDI (22, 27, 28, 79, 80, 89, 97). Altogether over 1,000,000 speakers. Zaire extending into Uganda, Rwanda, Burundi, Tanzania.

Zone E is subdivided into CHAGA = SHAKA (15, 25, 37, 81, 82); HAYA-JITA (14, 19, 30, 34, 41, 45, 69, 100); KIKIYU-KAMBA (17, 20, 39, 42, 59, 94); MASABA-LUHYA (53, 54, 73, 75, 83); NYIKA-TAITA (18, 65, 77, 93); NYORO-GANDA (16, 24, 26, 40, 68, 72, 74, 84, 85, 86, 92, 96); RAGOLI-KURIA = GUSII (24, 46, 52, 61, 64, 88, 98, 99). Altogether 7,000,000 speakers. Uganda, Kenya, Tanzania extending into Zaire.

Zone F is subdivided into ILAMBA-IRANGI = NILYAMBA (48, 57, 66, 78); SUKUMA-NYAMWEZI (12, 43, 70, 90, 91); TONGWE (6, 95). Altogether 2,000,000 speakers. Tanzania.

1. Amba = Rwamba = Ku-amba = Kwamba = Hamba = Bulebule = Ruwenzori Bira = Kibira. Ds. also (ki-)Hyanzi, (ku-)Suwa. 48,000.
2. Bali = (li-)Baali = South Eastern Bua = Bango. Ds. Bafwa Ndaka, Bakundumu, Bekeni, Bemili. 38,000.
3. Bangobango = (ki-)Bangubangu. Ds. also (ki-)Buyu = Bujwe, (ki-)Sanzi (?).
4. Beeke = Ibeeke. Zaire.
5. (e-)Beembe = (i-)Bembe.
6. Bende. 7,000.
7. (ki-)Bila = Ku-bira = Forest Bila. 5,700.
8. Bira = Sese = Sumburu. D. also Plains Bira = Kibira (31,700) (?).
9. Western Bira = Babira = Babeda = Babera = Babila. 4,000.
10. Budu. Ds. also Bafwagada, Balika, Malamba, Matta, Mokoda. 83,000. Zaire.
11. Bugombe = Ebugombe. 12,000.
12. (iki-) Bungu.
13. Buyi.
14. Bwisi-Talinga = Mawisi. 6,000. Zaire, Beni Territory.
15. Caga = Shaka = Kishaka = Chaga = Chagga = Dschagga. Ds. (ki-) Hai = Meru, (ki-) Mashami = Macame = Machame = Madschame, (ki-) Moci = Moshi, Shira, (ki-) Rhombo = Rombo, Vunjo = (ki-) Wunjo = Marangu. 237,000.
16. (olu-) Ciga = (oru-) Chiga = Kiga. 272,000.
17. (ke-) Daiso = Kidhaiso = Sageju = Segeju = Sengeju.
18. (ki-) Digo. 32,000.
19. (eci-) Dzindza = Jinja = Zinza = Zinja = Ziba. 67,000.
20. (ke-) Embo = (ki-) Embu. 203,500.
21. Ena = (ba-) Enya = (wa-) Genia = Genya = Zimba.

22. Fuliro = (iki-) Fuliiru = Fuliiro = Furiiro. 56,000.
23. (olu-) Ganda = Luganda. 1,500,000.
24. (eke-) Gusii = Guzii = Kisii = Kosova. 255,000.
25. (ki-) Gweno.
26. (lu-) Gwere = Olugwere = Lugwere. 162,000.
27. (iki-) Ha. 286,000.
28. Hangaza. 54,000.
29. Havu = (eki-) Haava. Ds. also Hwindja = Lwindja, Lindja, Longe-longe, Shi, Ziba. 50,000. May be same language as 43, below.
30. (oru-) Hima = Hema = Huma. Over 3,800. Congo (Leopoldville) = Zaire, Rwanda, Burundi.
31. Holoholo = (ki-) Horohoro = Guha = Kalanga. 2,000.
32. Huku = Hoko = Nyali = Nyari. Ds. also (li-) Bombi, (li-) Bvanuma = Vanuma = South Nyali = Bambutuku, (li-) Nyali = North Nyali. 13,000.
33. (ki-) Hunde = (ru-) Kobi. 33,500.
34. (eci-) Jita = Kwaya. 97,000.
35. (ki-) Kaanu. 3,510.
36. Kabwari.
37. Kahe. 1,800.
38. Kaiku = Ikaiku.
39. (ke-) Kamba = Kikamba. 612,000.
40. (lu-) Kenyi.
41. (eki-) Kerebe = Ecikerebe = Kerewe. D. also Kara. 31,000.
42. Kikuyu = Gikuyu = Gekoyo. 1,000,000.
43. (ki-) Kimbu. 9,000. May be same language as 29, above.
44. (olu-) Konzo = Rukonjo = Konjo = Kondjo. 162,000.
45. (olu-) Kooki.
46. (eke-) Koria = (eki-) Kuria = Kurya = Tende. Ds. also Kiroba, Simbiti, Sweta. 94,000.
47. (ki-) Kuumu = Kọmọ = Kumu. Tr. Badoombi = Bakuumu = Barumbi.
48. (ki-) Langi = Kelangi = Irangi. 95,000.
49. (ke-) Lega = Rega. Ds. also (ki-) Leega, (i-) Leega imuzimu, Tumbwe (7,997). Over 33,000.
50. (ki-) Lengola.
51. (li-) Liko = Toriko. Trs. Mabiti, Maliko. 26,000.
52. (l-) Logooli = Llogole = Ragoli = Maragoli.
53. Luhya = Luyia = Luluhya = Luluyia. Ds. also (lu-) Gwe (?), (lu-) Hanga = Oluhanga = Kawanga = Oluwanga, (lw-) Isuxa = Isukha = (lw-) Idaxo = Idakho = Itakho = Kakamega = Kakumega, (lu-) Kakelewa = Lewi, Kisa = Lushisa, (lu-) Maraci, (lu-) Marama, (lu-) Nyala, Taconi = Tatsoni = Tadjoni, (lu-) Tiriki, (lu-) Tsootso = Tsotso, (lu-) Xaayo = Khayo = Tindi. 654,000.
54. Masaba = Lumasaba. Ds. also (ulu-) Bukusu, Central = (ulu-) Dadiri, (lu-) Gisu = (ulu-) Gishu, (ulu-) Kisu, Northern, Southern = (ulu-) Buya. 487,000.

55. Mbo = Imbo = Kimbo. 2,000. Congo (Leopoldville).
56. (lo-) Mbole. Ds. = Trs. also Inja; Keembo (of Opale), including Botunga, Yaamba, Yaikole, Yaisu, Yangonda; Nkembe. 90,000 to 100,000.
57. Mbugwe. 7,500.
58. (i-) Mbuti = Kumbuti = Kimbuti. Tr. Bambuti Pigmies.
59. (ke-) Mero = (ki-) Meru. 350,000.
60. Mituku = Kinya-Mituku = Mętǫkǫ.
61. (iki-) Nata = Ikoma. 9,500.
62. Ndaaka = Indaaka. 4,750. Zaire, Epulu Territory.
63. (oru-) Ndandi = Nandi = Ndande = N. Nande. Ds. also (eki-) Lega = (eki-) Hambo; Nande, including (eki-) Kumbule, (eki-) Mate, (eki-) Tangi; (eki-) Sanza; (eki-) Shu = (eki-) Shukaali (?); (eki-) Songoora; (eki-) Swaga = (eki-) Kira; (eki-) Yira. 225,000.
64. (iki-) Ngurimi = Ngoreme = Ngruimi = Nguruimi. 11,800.
65. Nika = Nyika. Ds. Conyi, Durama, Giryama, Kauma, Rabai. 39,000.
66. (eke-) Nilamba = (ki-) Niramba = Iramba = Ilamba. 170,000.
67. Nyabungu = (ki-) Tembo. 15,000. Ds. also (ki-) Nyindu, (eki-) Rhinyirhinyi.
68. (olu-) Nyala = Nyara.
69. (eki-) Nyambo = Runyambo. D. also (ru-) Karagwe = Ururagwe. 4,000.
70. (ki-) Nyamwesi = Namwezi, Ds. also Konongo (15,000), Mweri = Ki-na-mweri = Sumbwa (60,000), (ki-)Nyanyembe, Takama = Garaganza. 365,000.
71. Nyanga. 25,000.
72. (alu-) Nyankole = Runyankore = Nyankore = Oru-nyankore = Lunyankole = Nkole. Ds. Hima = Huma, (etshi-) Hororo = Ruhororo, (oru-) Tagwenda = Takwenda. 773,000.
73. (olu-) Nyole = lunyole = lunyore = Nyoole = Nyore. 134,000.
74. (oru-) Nyoro = Runyoro = Rutooro = Gungu = Kyopi. 592,000.
75. (olu-) Nyule. 57,000.
76. Peri = Pere = Pili = Pakombe. Ds. Baidumba, Beka, Bili, Hokohoko, (e-) Leedji, (e-) Tike.
77. (ki-) Pokomo = Pfokomo. 16,500.
78. (ki-) Remi = Keremi = Limi = Rimi = Nyaturu = Wanyaturu = Turu. 180,000.
79. Ruanda = Urunyarwanda = Runyarwanda = Nyaruanda = Runyaruanda. Ds. Bafumbwa; Hutu, including Lera = Urulera = (iki-) Hera, Ndara, (iki-) Shobyo, (igi-) Tshiga = (uru-, i-) Kiga, (i-) Tshogo = (ki-) Ndogo; Tutsi = Tus(s)i; (igi-) Kiga; Ruanda Proper, including Ganza = S. Buganza, (i-) Ndara, (i-) Ndorwa = Rukiga = Ruciga (678,000), (iki-nya-) Ndugu; Twa = Rutwa. 2,283,000 (563,000 in Uganda).
80. (iki-) Rundi = Urundi. 2,185,000 (191,000 in Uganda).
81. Rusha = Arusha = Kuma.
82. (ki-) Rwo.
83. (olu-) Saamia = Lusa(a)mia = Samia = Samya. D. also (lu-) Gwe ? 124,000.

84. (olu-) Sese. Ds. also (olu-) Gaya, (olu-) Vuma.
85. (lu-) Singa ?
86. (olu-) Soga = lusoga. Ds. Northern, Southern. 745,000.
87. (ke-) Songola = Binja. D. also (ke-) Gengele.
88. Sonjo = Sonyo.
89. (uru-) Subi = Shubi = Sinja. 74,000.
90. (ki-) Sukuma = Gwe. D. also Kiya. 890,000.
91. (ki-) Sumbwa.
92. (oru-) Syan = Lusyan = Bantu Sabei. 10,000.
93. Taita = Teita. Ds. also (ki-) Dabida, (ki-) Sagala = Sagalla = Teri. 6,330.
94. (ki-) Tharaka = Saraka. D. also Chuka.
95. (ki-) Tongwe. 8,000.
96. (oru-) Toro = (oru-) Tooro. 163,000.
97. Vinza. 3,000.
98. Ware ?
99. (iki-) Zanaki. Ds. also Girango (?), Ikizu (?), (iki-) Isenyi (?), Ndali, Siora. 23,000.
100. (olu-) Ziba = Ekiziba = (olu-) Haya = Ekihaya. Ds. also Bumbira, Edangabo, Hamba, Hangiro, Mwani, Nyakisasa, Yoza. 264,000.
101. Zimba = S. Binja ? 50,000.
102. Zyoba. Ds. Vira, Masanze.

NORTH WESTERN AREA. The 146 languages of this area are divided by zones and subdivided by groups within zones, except that languages numbered 31, 96, and 102 are not grouped in the zones which follow.

Zone A is subdivided into BAFIA (42, 45, 55, 99); BASA (7, 8, 10, 65, 73, 107); BUBE (-BENGA) (11, 15, 27, 144); DUALA (3, 18, 19, 23, 37, 90, 109, 114, 125); KAKA (46, 59, 113); LUNDU-BALONG = MBO plus LUNDU (6, 9, 26, 70, 81); MAKA-NJEM = MAKAA (24, 52, 72, 80, 91, 104, 122); SANAGA (4, 12, 74, 101, 142); YAUNDE-FANG (14, 29, 39, 40, 41, 43). Altogether over 1,300,000 speakers. Cameroon, Rio Muni, Gabon, extending into Congo (Brazzaville) and Central African Republic.

Zone B is subdivided into KELE = KOTA (50, 53, 76, 119, 140); MBETE (75, 79, 87); Myene (92); NJABI (38, 108, 135, 137, 138); SHIRA-PUNU (69, 115, 117, 121); TEKE (5, 126, 127, 128, 129, 130, 131, 141); TENDE-YANZI (22, 33, 85, 86, 89, 134, 143); TSOGO (47, 136). Altogether over 350,000 speakers. Gabon, Congo (Brazzaville) extending into Zaire.

Zone C is subdivided into BANGI-NTUMBA = NGALA (17, 20, 21, 28, 63, 67, 68, 71, 94, 98, 106, 116, 118, 120); KUBA (30, 32, 62, 124, 139); MBOSHI (1, 54, 56, 60, 82, 84, 97); MONGO-NKUNDO (61, 88, 95); NGOMBE (2, 13, 16, 34, 35, 36, 48, 57, 100, 132, 146); NGUNDI = PANDE (25, 64, 77, 83, 93, 103, 111); (SOKO-) KELE (44, 51, 66, 78, 112, 123); TETELA (49, 58, 105, 110, 133, 145). Altogether over 1,000,000 speakers. Zaire, Congo (Brazzaville), Central African Republic.

1. Akwa.
2. (le-) Angba = Aŋgba = Aŋba = Ngelima = Beo = Tungu = (le-) Boro = Buru = Pseudo-Bangelima.

3. Baakpe = Mokpe = Bakwiri = Kweli = Kwili = Kwiri. Over 15,500.
4. Bacenga = Betsinga = Betzinga. 10,000.
5. Bali = Ambali = Tio = Teo = Tyo.
6. Balong = South Balong = Balung. 2,000.
7. Banen = Banend = Penin = Penyin. Ds. = Trs. Banen proper (24,500), including: Eling, Itundu, Logananga, Ndogbang, Ndogband, Ndokbiakat, Ndoktuna, Bonek = Ponek = (Otang) atomb; Mandi = Lemande; Yambeta. 26,500.
8. Bankon = Abo. 10,000.
9. Barue = West Kundu = Lue. 5,000.
10. Bas(s)a = Koko = Mvele. Ds. = Trs. North (Ba) Koko'; South (Ba) Koko'; Mbene, including Bakem, Dibeng, Dibum, Mbang, Ndokama, Ndokbele, Ndokpenda, Nyamtam, Yabasi (150,000). 170,000.
11. Batanga = Tanga. Ds. Banaka = Banoh = Noho = Nohu = Noko, Banoo = Noo, Bapoko = Poko = Naka = Puku. Over 2,000.
12. Bati.
13. (li-) Bati = Baati = (li-) Benge. D. also Napagisene, including Apagibeti = Gezon.
14. Bëbële (= Bamvele)-Gbïgbïl (= Bobili(s)). 24,000.
15. Benga.
16. (li-) Boa = Bali = Bango = Bua = Napagibetini.
17. Bobangi = Bangi = Rebu = Dzamba.
18. Bobea = Bobe = Bota = Wovea. 600.
19. Bodiman. 2,000.
20. Boko = Iboko.
21. Bolondo. 1,000.
22. (ki-) Boma = Buma. 8,000.
23. Bomboko = Bamboko = Bambuku = Bumbuko = Mboko. 2,500.
24. Bomwali. Tr. also Lino.
25. Bongili = Bongiri = Bungiri.
26. Bonkeng = Bonken = Pendia. 1,500.
27. Bube = Bobe = Bubi = Ediya = Fernandian. Ds. Northern Bobe, South-Eastern Bobe, South-Western Bobe.
28. (i-)Buja = Budja. Ds. Baonga, Basoa-Basoko, Yamongiri. 100,000.
29. Bulu (= Boulou)-Bënë (= Bane). Trs. Yelinda, Yembama, Yengono, Zaman. 170,000.
30. Busooŋ = Kuba = Mbale = Bushong(o) = Shongo = Bamongo = Mongo = Ganga. Ds. = Trs. Djembe, Ngende, Ngombe = Ngombia, Ngongo, Pianga = Panga = Tshobwa = Shobwa = Shoba. 29,000.
31. Cinga = Bundum = Kombe. 12,600.
32. Dengese = Nkutu = Ndengese = Ileo. 4,000.
33. Dï = Diŋ = Dinga = Dziŋ = Dzing = Idzing.
34. Dianga.
35. 'Doko. Ds. also Bwela = Buela = Lingi.
36. Doko of Ngiri.

37. Duala = Douala. D. also Kole = Bakolle. 23,000. Used as a lingua franca over a wide area of western part of Cameroon.
38. (li-)Duma = Adouma = Aduma = Douma. 10,000.
39. Eki = Badjia = Mvang = Omvang. 3,000.
40. Eton. 112,000.
41. Ewondo = Jaunde = Yaunde. Ds. Avak = Bafök = Bafuk = Bavek, including Lapak, Meŋgaŋ (?), Yasem; Bakja = Badjia (14,000); Mvëlë = Yezum = Yesoum = Yezum (140,000); Yangafëk = Yangafuk' (5,500). 93,000. 'Ewondo populaire' used as a lingua franca in central part of Cameroon.
42. (la-)Fa' = Fak = Balom. 4,000.
43. Faŋ = Fang = Fãn = Fañwe. Ds. Northern Faŋ = Ntum = Pamue = Pangwe, Southern Faŋ = Make; Fang of Gabon, Fang of Ogowe = Pahouin. 200,000.
44. Fuma = Foma = 'pseudo-Bambole.'
45. (la-)Kaaloŋ = (la-) Mboŋ. 50.
46. Kako = Kaka = Yaka. 37,000.
47. Kande = Okande.
48. (li-)Kango.
49. (o-)Kela = Lemba. 80,000–100,000.
50. Kele. Ds. also Bubi (4,000), Ngom = Bangomo (11,000), West Kele. 15,000.
51. (e-)Kele = Lokele. Ds. = Trs. LiLeko, Mbooso, Yalikoka (7,000), Yaokandja, Yawembe. 26,000.
52. Konabem(b(e))-Bekwil (= Bakwele). 8,000.
53. Kota = Mahongwe = Shake. 28,000.
54. Koyo.
55. (ra-)Kpa = Bafia. 15,000.
56. (li-)Kuba.
57. Kunda.
58. Kusu = (lo-)Kutsu = Kongola = Fuluka. 26,000.
59. Kwakum = Akpwakum = Bakum = Pakum. D. also Azom ? 3,000.
60. Kwala = Likwala = Likouala.
61. Lalia. 30,000.
62. Lele = Usilele. 26,000.
63. Likila = Bangela = Baloba.
64. Lobala. D. also Bomboli = Bombongo.
65. Lombi = Rombi = Barombi. 1,000.
66. Lombo = Olombo = Turumbu. 10,500.
67. Loi-Ngiri. Ds. Jamba-Makutu, Libinja, Loi = Boloi = Baato Baloi = Rebu, Mampoko, Manganji, Ngiri, Nunu.
68. Losengo = Lusengo. Ds. Boloki = Bologi = Buluki; Kangana; Leko = Eleko = (lo-)Leku; Mangala = Bangala = Lingala = Mangala; (li-)Mbudza; (li-)Mpesa; Ndolo; (li-)Poto = Lifoto, including Bumwangi, Busu Djanga, Empesa Poko, Esumbu, Kunda, Kumba, Lusengo Poto, Mongala Poto, Mongo, Ngundi. 1,000,000.

69. (i-)Lumbu. 12,000.
70. Lundu = Londo = Balundu. Ds. also Bakundu = Lokundu = Kundu, Batanga-Bima = Baima = Bauma, Ekumbe-Mbonge, Ngoro = Ngolo. 24,000.
71. (lo-)Mabaale = Mabale. Ds. also Banza, Bembe, Lipanja, Lobo = Balobo = Bodjinga = Bokula = Bonkembe, Mbinga.
72. Maka(a) = Mäkaa. 51,500.
73. Mandi = Lemande. D. also Yambeta. 2,000 to 2,550.
74. Mangisa. 14,000.
75. (gi-)Mbaama = Mbamba = Bakota = ba-Mbaama. 12,000.
76. Mbaŋwe. 2,000.
77. Mbati = Isongo = Lissongo. 15,000.
78. Mbesa = Mobesa.
79. Mbete = Mbede = Obamba. 20,000 to 35,000.
80. Mbimu. Ds. also Medjime = Medzime = Baagato = North Bangatu (4,500), Mpõmpõ = Bombo = Boumboum = Mbumbum = Mpompo = Kaka of Sala (4,000), Mpiemo = Bidjuki (7,500). Trs. Biakumbo, Bikum, Kpabili. 16,500.
81. Mbo = Ngen = Bareko = Baneka (?) Ds. also Bafo = Bafaw = Balondo (?) = Babong (?), Kaa = Bakaka, (a-)koose = Muamenam = Bakosi = Bakossi = Nkosi, Loŋ = Elong, Mwahet = Manehas = Bakaka, Nenũ = Ninong, Swase = Basosi = (N-)sw ?so. 22,500.
82. Mboko.
83. Mbomotaba = Bamitaba.
84. Mbosi = Mboshi.
85. Mbuun = Mbunu = Mbunda.
86. (e-)Mfinu = Funika = Mfununga. Ds. also Ntsiam, Ntswar.
87. Minduumo = Mindumbu = Ndumu = Nduumo = Ndumbo = Doumbou = Dumbu = Ondoumbo = Ondumbo. Ds. Epigi, Kanandjoho, Kuya, Nyani. 4,000.
88. Mongo-Nkunbo = Mongo-Nkundu. Ds. Bakutu, Bukala = Kala, Ekonda Mongo = Lomongo (80,000), (Bo)Longo, Mpama (6,000), Nkundo = Lonkundu = Lonkundo = Lolo, South Nkundo = Panga = Titu = Buli = Oli, Wangata, Yalima = Yajima. Over 200,000.
89. Mpuono. Ds. also Mpuun.
90. Mulimba = Malimba = Limba. 3,500.
91. Mvumbo = Ngumba = Mabi = Mabea = Bisiwo. 10,000.
92. Myene. Ds. also Dyumba = Adjumba = Adyumba, Enenga (5,000), Galwa = Galoa = (Union) Omyene (2,000), Mpongwe = Mpongoué = Npongué = Pongoué (1,000), Nkomi, Rongo = Orungu. Over 10,000.
93. Ndaanda = Kpala.
94. Ndobo = Ndoobo.
95. Ngando. 121,000.
96. Ngando-Kota = Bodzanga = Bangandou = Bagandou. Close to Ngundi.
97. Ngare.

98. (la-)Ngayaba = Djanti. 1,000.

99. Ngele of Irebu.

100. Ngombe. Ds. also (li-)Binza = Bindja, (di-)Gendja = Genja, Gendza-Baali, Wiinza-Baali. 150,000.

101. Ngoro.

102. (i-)Ngul. Not grouped, close to Teke-Yans (Zone C).

103. Ngundi = Ngondi.

104. Njëm-Bajue. Ds. = Trs. Bajue = Badjue, Esel, Kozime, Njëm = Ndjëm = Djem = Dzimu = Kozime = Zimu. 20,000.

105. Nkutu = Nkutshu = Nkucu = Bankutu. Ds. Elembe, Hamba, (lo-)Kalo, Kongola-Meno, Ngongo, (lo-)Saka.

106. (lo-)Ntombo-Bolia. Ds. = Trs. Bolia = Bokoki of Ruki River, Ntomba = Lontomba, Sakan(yi), Soko. Over 45,000.

107. Nyõ'õ = Nyokon. D. also Fuŋ. 3,000–4,000.

108. (yi-)Nzebi = Njabi = Bandzabi = Ndjabi = Ndjevi. 20,000–40,000.

109. Oli = Ewodi = Wouri = Wuri. 3,500.

110. Ombo = Loombo = hombo = Songola. Ds. also Jonga (?), Langa (?), Mbuli.

111. (i-)Pande = Ndjeli = Linyeli = Linzeli. D. also Bogongo = Bogoŋgo = Bukongo = Bongili = Bongiri.

112. Poke = Topoke = Tofoke. Ds. = Trs. also Baluombila, Liutwa, Likolo, (A)lomboki = 'pseudo-Lokele.' 46,000.

113. Pol-Pomo. Ds. Pɔl = Pul = Poli, Pomo. Over 2,200.

114. Pongo-Mungo = Pongo-Mongo. 7,500.

115. (yi-)Punu. 46,000.

116. (ki-)Sakata. D. also (ki-)Djia.

117. (yi-)Sangu = Shango. 18,000.

118. Saw.

119. Sekiyani = Bulu = Sheke.

120. (ke-)Senegele.

121. (i-)Sira = Shira. 17,000.

122. So. 6,000. Cameroon.

123. So = Soko = Eso = Heso. 6,000 Zaire.

124. Songomeno. 30,000–40,000.

125. Su = Isu(wa) = Isubu = Subu = Bimba. Less than 500.

126. Central Teke. Ds. Boõ = Boma = (e-)Boõ (6,000), Ndzindzihu = Ndzindziu = Njinju = Nziku = Nzinzihu = Ndzikou (9,000).

127. East Teke. Ds. also Mosieno, (esi-)Ngee = Ɲee.

128. North Teke = Teke. Ds. (ka-)Njiniɲi = Ndjinini = Njikini = Nzikini = Djikini (9,000), Tege-kali = (ka-)Tege = Tégué (15,000). 24,000.

129. North East Teke. Ds. = Trs. Mpũ = Mpũmpũ, Ngangoulou = Ngungwel = Ngungulu.

130. South Teke. Ds. Fumu = Ifumu = Mfumu (200), Kukẅa = Chikuya = Kukuya = Koukouya (11,000).

131. West Teke = South West Teke. Ds. Kwe = Wuõ, (i-)Laali = Lali,

Tsaayi = Tsayi = Ntsaayi = Tsaye (30,000); (i-)Yaa = Yaka (2,000).
132. (li-)Tembo.
113. (o-)Tetela = Sungu. 30,000.
134. (ki-)Tiini = Tende = Tiene. 15,000.
135. (i-)Tsaangi = Tsangi = Tcengui = Tchangui. 10,000.
136. Tsogo = Mitsogo = Apindji.
137. Vili.
138. Wandji. 6,000.
139. Wongo = Gongo = Tuk(k)ongo = Tukungo = Ndjembe = Bakong. 2,000–8,000.
140. Wumbvu. 4,000.
141. (i-)Wuumu = Wumbu.
142. Yambasa. 27,000.
143. Yanzi = (i-)Yans = Yansi. Ds. Mbiem, Mpur, Ntsuo, Eastern Yans, Yeei = Yey.
144. Yasa. D. also Kombe = Ngumbi.
145. Yela = Kutu = Boyela. 33,000.
146. Yewa = Napagibetini.

SOUTH EASTERN AREA. Languages of this area are subdivided into two zones, P and S, which are in turn subdivided into named groups; but one ungrouped language, Venda (33), is coordinate with the named groups in Zone S.

Zone P is subdivided into MAKUA (3, 7, 10, 20); MATUMBI = NGINDO (6, 11, 12, 16, 19, 25); YAO (8, 9, 14, 17, 34). Altogether 2,000,000 speakers. Tanzania, Mozambique, Malawi.

Zone S languages are subdivided into CHOPI (2, 29); NGUNI (13,15, 18, 21, 22, 23); SHONA (1, 5, 26), SOTHO-TSWANA (27, 28, 32; sometimes considered dialects of a single language); TSWA-RONGA = TSONGA (4, 24, 30, 31); Venda (33). Altogether 13,000,000. Rhodesia, Botswana, South Africa, Swaziland, Lesotho.

1. Birwa.
2. (shi-)Chopi = Tschopi = (shi-)Copi = (ki-)Lenge.
3. (ci-)Cuabo = Chuabo = Chuambo = Cuambo = Lolo.
4. Gwamba = Gwapa.
5. Karanga = Karaŋa. Ds. also Duma, Govera = Gobera, Jena, Mhari = Mari, Ngova = Ngoba, Nyubi = Nyu'bi.
6. Kuchi.
7. (i-)Lomwe = Lomue = Lolo = Cilowe = Nguru = Western Makua.
8. (ci-)Mabiha = Mavia = Maviha = Mawia = Mawiha. 70,000.
9. (ci-)Makonde = Chininakonde. 281,000.
10. (i-)Makua = Makoa = Makoane = Makwa = Mato. D. also Medo = Northern Makua. 1,000,000.
11. (ki-)Matumbi. 41,000.
12. Mbunga. 10,000.
13. *Old Mfengu = Fingo.
14. (ci-)Mwera = Mwela. 126,000.

15. (isi-)Ndebele = Tabele = Tebele = Nde'bele. 158,000.
16. (ki-)Ndengereko. 53,000.
17. (ci-)Ndonde = Kimawanda. 12,000.
18. Ndzundza.
19. (ki-)Ngindo. 85,000.
20. (i-)Ngulu = Nguru = Mihavane = Mihavani = Mihawani.
21. Nguni. Ds. (isi-)Swati = Swazi = Tekela = Tekeza, including 'Baca = isi-bala, Hlubi = isi-lubi (250,000); (isi-)Xhosa = Xosa = Kaffer = Kaffir, including Bomvana, Gaika = Ncqika, Gcaleka = isi-g/aleka, Mpondo, Mpondomse = isi-mpondomisi = Mpondomisi, Ndlambe, isi-ŋg!ika, Xesibe = isi-//esibe (over 2,500,000); Zulu = Zunda, including Ngoni = Nguni, (isi-)Zulu (with Lala, Qwabe, Zulu of Natal, Zulu of Zululand). 3,000,000. Ngoni may be more closely allied to the Swati dialect.
22. Nrebele.
23. (isi-)Piki = (isi-)Lololo = Fanakala = Fanekalo = Kitchen Kaffir.
24. (shi-)Ronga. Ds. also Konde. 1,000,000.
25. (ki-)Ruihi = Rufiji. 71,000.
26. Shona. Ds. Kalanga = Kalaŋa = Kalaŋga = Kalana = Western Shona, including Kalaka = Kalanga; Korekore = Chishona = Northern Shona, including Budya, Gova = Goba, Nyongwe, Pfunde, Shangwe = Shaŋwe, Sipolilo, Tabara = Tavara, Tande, Urungwe; Lilima = Humbe (with Peri, Talahundra); Manyika (including Hungwe, Boka, Bunji, Bvumba, Domba, Guta, Here, Jindwi, Karombe, Nyamuka, Nyatwe, Unyama); Ndau = Sofala = Southeastern Shona, including Danda, Garwe, Shanga, Tonga; Rozwi = Rozvi = Rozi (with Nambzya, Nyai); Teve = Tebe; Zezeru = Zezuru = Central Shona = Chiswina = Chishona including Harava = Haraba, (va-)Kwachikwakwa = Cikwakwa, (va-)Kwazwimba =Zimba, Mbire, Njanja, Nobvu, Nohwe, Shawasha, Tsunga = Tsuŋga.
27. Northern Sotho = Transvaal Sotho = (se-)Pedi. Ds. Khutswe = Khutswi = Kutswe; Lobedu = (khi-)Lubedu = Lovedu, including Phalaburwa, Tlokwa = Tokwa = Tlokoa = Dogwa; Pai = Mbai = Mbayi; Pedi, including Koni = Tsweni = Tswene, Kwena, Kxaxa = Kgaga, Masemola = Masemula; Xananwa = Gananwa, including (thi-)Phalaburwa = Phala-borwa, Pulana. 800,000.
28. Southern Sotho = Suthu = (se-)Sotho = Suto. Ds. also Phuthi, Taung.
29. (gi-)Tonga = Shengwe.
30. (shi-)Tsonga = Gwamba = Thonga = Tonga = Shangaan. Ds. also Bila = Vila, Hlanganu = Shi-laŋganu = Shangaan, Jonga = Djonga, Ngwalungu =shi-ŋwaluŋgu. 1,000,000.
31. (shi-)Tswa = Sheetswa = Xitswa = Dzibi = Dzonga. D. also Hlengwe = shi-leŋgwe, including Khambana, Makwakwe. 500,000.
32. (se-)Tswana = Chuana = Cauna = Coana = Tšwana. Ds. also Kgalagadi = Kxalaxari = Khalahadi = Kxhalaxdi; Kgatla = Kxhatla = Khatla, includ-ing Kwena = Koena, Ngwaketse = Ŋwaketsi; Lete; Nwato = ŋwatu = Mangwato = Tawana; Rolong = Roloŋ, including Hurutshe = Hurutsi,

Thlaping = Thlapiŋ = Tlapi, Thlaro = Thlaru. 852,000.

33. (ce-)Venda = (tshi-)Venda. Ds. also Phani, Tavhatsindi.
34. (ci-)Yao = Ayo = Djao = Adsawa = Adsoa = Ayawa = Achawa = Hiao = Hyao = Haiao = Veiao = Wajao. Over 408,000.

SOUTH WESTERN AREA. The languages of this area are divided into Zones K and R, with named grouped subdivisions in each zone. The ungrouped language, Lozi (8), is coordinate with the grouped languages in Zone K; two ungrouped languages, Herero (2) and Yeye (31), are coordinate with named groups in Zone R.

The subdivisions in Zone K are CHOKWE-LUCHAZI (1, 9, 10, 12, 16, 18, 24, 26); Lozi (8); LUYANA (5, 6, 11, 13, 14, 15, 19, 20, 27, 28); SUBIYA (29, 30). Altogether 1,000,000 speakers. Botswana, Zambia, Angola, Zaire.

The subdivisions in Zone R are Herero (2); NDONGA = KUANYAMA (4, 7, 22, 23); UMBUNDU (3, 17, 21, 25); Yeye = Yei (31). Altogether 1,500,000 speakers. Angola, South-West Africa, Botswana.

1. Ciokwe = Cokwe = Chokwe = Tschokwe = Cioko = Shioko = Tshiok = Djok = Tschiboko. D. also (mi-)Nungo. Over 600,000.
2. Herero = Otjiherero = Otyiherero. Ds. also Cimba = Himba = Tjimba = Simba, Mbandieru. 25,000.
3. Khumbi.
4. Kwambi.
5. Kwangwa. D. also Mwenyi = Mweni = Muenyi. 26,500.
6. Kwangari = Kwangali. Ds. also Mbogedo = Diriku = Diriko = Gciriku, Mbukushu = Mbukuhu = Mambukush = Mampukush = Goba, Sambyu = Sambio.
7. (oci-)Kwanyama = Humba = Cuanyama = Kuanyama = Oshikuanjama = Osikuanjama.
8. (si-)Lozi = Rozi = Rotse = Rozvi = Kololo. 70,000.
9. (ci-)Lucazi = Luchazi = Lujazi = Ponda. 60,000.
10. (ci-)Luimbi = Luimbe = Lwimbi. Ds. also Ambwela, Ngangela = Ganguella. 500.
11. Luyana = Luana = Luano = Luyi = Louyi = Lui = Rouyi. D. also Kwandi. 3,500.
12. Lwena = Luena = Lovale = Luvale = Lubale. 90,000.
13. Makoma. 8,000.
14. Mashi = Maṣi. 4,500.
15. (esi-)Mbowe. 5,500.
16. (ci-)Mbunda = Mbuunda = Gimbunda = Kimbunda. 25,000.
17. (u-)Mbundu = M'Bundo = Quimbundo = Kimbunda = Nano = Mbali = Mbari. 1,300,000.
18. Mbwela = Mbwera = Ambuella.
19. Mdundulu = Imilangu. 22,000.
20. Mishulundu.
21. Ndombe.
22. (oci-)Ndonga = Ambo = Oshindonga = Osidonga.

23. Ngandyera.
24. Nkangala.
25. (lu-)Nyaneka. Ds. also Humbe, Mwila. 40,000.
26. Nyengo. 5,000.
27. Shanjo = Ṣanjo = Ṣango. 8,000.
28. Simaa. Over 9,000.
29. (eci-)subia = subiya = Subya = Soubiya = (ci-)Ikuhane = Ikwahani.
30. (eci-)Totela. 14,000.
31. Yeye = Yeei = Yei = Ciyei = Yeyi = Kuba = Koba.

AFFILIATION. BANTU PROPER is a member of BANTOID of BENUE-CONGO.

BARBACOAN

GROUPING. The BARBACOAN family has two branches, CAYAPA-COLORADO (those numbered 1–4) and PASTO (number 5 plus the other possible members of BARBACOAN, the names of which follow but are unnumbered below).

CAYAPA-COLORADO
1. *Caranki = Caranqui = Cara. Ecuador.
2. Cayapa. 4,000. Cayapas river and its tributaries in northwestern Ecuador.
3. Colorado. 600. Between Quito and coast in Ecuador.
4. *Nigua. Possibly not extinct. Ecuador.

PASTO
5. Cuaquer = Coaiquer = Coaiker. Colombia.
(?) *Colima. Possibly not extinct. Colombia.
(?) *Muellamues. Colombia.
(?) *Patia. Possibly not extinct. Colombia.
(?) *Pasto. Colombia, Ecuador.
(?) *Sindagua = Malba. Colombia.

AFFILIATION. Member of MACRO-CHIBCHAN phylum.

Basque = Euskara = Eskuara = Úskara = Euskera = Heuskara. Ds. Guipúzcoan, Labourdin, Eastern Lower Navarrese, Northern Upper Navarrese, Southern Upper Navarrese, Western Lower Navarrese, Souletin, Viscayan (the most divergent as well as the most widely spoken). 600,000–700,000. France (90,000), Spain (the Guipúzcoan, Northern Upper Navarrese, Southern Upper Navarrese, and Viscayan dialects are spoken only in Spain; the other dialects are represented in France), and North America.

AFFILIATION. Basque has been variously compared to Berber (Gèze 1883), 'NUBIAN' and 'HAMITIC' (Schuchardt 1912, 1913), and to ALGONQUIAN (de Charency 1867, de Yrizar 1950). Some scholars have also compared Basque with extinct European languages as Iberian (Baehr 1948, Tovar 1950). Lafon (1944, 1947, 1951) and Uhlenbeck (1946, 1947) have supported the older view (Luchaire 1877) that Basque is the direct descendant of the language of the Aquitanians (who occupied the region between the Garonne River, the Pyrenees, and the Atlantic in the time of Julius Caesar) and the Vascones (who once occupied the greater part of the Spanish Navarre and adjacent areas). Bouda (1949), after Trombetti (1926), Lafon (1933), and Uhlenbeck (1946, 1947), holds that the only remote relationship of substance is with CAUCASIAN.

BENUE-CONGO PHYLUM

GROUPING. The term BENUE-CONGO was introduced by Greenberg (1966) for the group composed, for the most part, of the Nigerian and Cameroonian members of the earlier 'Semi-Bantu' grouping discussed by Johnston (1919, 1922) and others, with the addition of the BANTU languages, which Greenberg subsumed under the BANTOID subgroup of 'Semi-Bantu'. See also reports by Jacquot and Richardson (1954), Westermann and Bryan (1952), Williamson and Shimizu (1968), and Williamson (1971, 1973). The four major groups of BENUE-CONGO are:

BANTOID (q.v.).
CROSS-RIVER BENUE-CONGO (q.v.).
JUKUNOID BENUE-CONGO (q.v.).
PLATEAU BENUE-CONGO (q.v.).

AFFILIATION. Member of NIGER-CONGO.

CROSS RIVER BENUE-CONGO

GROUPING. Greenberg (1966) recognized three subgroups of CROSS RIVER. On the basis of further published and unpublished evidence Williamson (1971, 1973) expands Greenberg's classification, dividing Greenberg's subgroup 2 into four subgroups coordinate with Greenberg's subgroup 3 within a DELTA-CROSS division of CROSS RIVER. Maddieson (1974) supplied additional names and subclassification. The DELTA-CROSS division may be more closely related to KWA languages than to other languages within BENUE-CONGO (Williamson; Welmers 1971b).

CROSS-RIVER 1 = BENDI = BOKI-EBEKWARA. Mainly spoken in the northern part of South-Eastern State, Nigeria, by some 150,000 people altogether. Boki (4) is divergent from the other languages in this group.
1. Afrike. Ds. Afrike = Ochagbe = Okpeche, Ibafal, Oboso, Okorogung, Okorotung.
2. Bekwarra = Bekworra(h) = Ebekwara. D. also Yakoro.
3. Bete = Mbete = Bette = Dama. D. also Bendi.
4. Boki = Bokyi = Okii = Nki. Ds. Basua = Bashua, Boje = Bojie, Irruan, Kwakwagom, Nsadop, Osokom. Trs. Ndir, Ukwese, Utang, Yon.
5. Bumaji.
6. Gayi = Alegi = Alege = Uge.
7. Mbeafal = Eastern Mbube.
8. Obanliku. Ds. Basang, Bebi, Bishiri, Bisu = Gayi, Busi = Beve.
9. Ubang.
10. Ukpe. D. also Bayobiri.

DELTA-CROSS

CROSS-RIVER 3 = UPPER CROSS. Languages (11), (17), (18), (19), (20), (21) and (24) form an EASTERN subgroup, to which (11) has been added by Maddieson, and languages (12), (13), (14), (15), (16), (22), (23) form a WESTERN subgroup. Except for Tita (25) and some dialects of Oring (22), these languages are spoken in the upper part of the Cross River drainage, South-Eastern State, and adjoining areas of East-Central State, Nigeria.

11. Agoi = Robambami.
12. Agwagwune. Ds. Abayong, Agwagwune = Akunakuna = Akurakura = Gwune, Erei, Obini = (A)bini = Abine, Odim = (A)dim.
13. Akpet.
14. Biakpan. D. also Ikun.
15. Kohumono = Bahumono = Bahumunu = Humono. Ds. include Ebom = Uzokpo, Ediba = Hotaba, Nile, Usumutong = Hozumutong.
16. Kukele = Ukel(l)e. 20,300.
17. Legbo = Agbo = Gbo. Ds. include Ekureku, Igbo Imaban, Lebama = Higidi.
18. Leyig(h)a = Yigha = Asiga.
19. Mbembe. Ds. include Adun = Edun, E(g)hum = Ohana, Enyen, Epiapum = Ephyapum = Iyamoyong = Iyamitet, Eshuapum = Appiapum = Apiapun, Ofatura, Ofumbongha, Osopong.
20. Nkukoli = Nkokolle = Ekuri.
21. Olulumo = Lulumo. Ds. include Ikom, Okuni.
22. Oring = Kɔring = Orri. Ds. Okpoto(-Mtezi), Ufia, Ufiom = Effiium, Utonkon. Ufia and Utonkon are spoken in Utonkon District, Idoma Division, Benue-Plateau State; Okpoto and Ufiom in Abakiliki Division, East-Central State.
23. Umon.
24. Yakurr = (Lo)kö = Lomömo = Luko = Lukə = Yako = Yakə. 20,000.
25. Tita = Hoai Petel. At Hoai Petel, Jalingo District, North-Eastern State.

LOWER CROSS = EFIK-ANDONI. Andoni (26), is divergent from the other members of this Nigerian group.

26. Andoni = Obolo. 50,000. Obolo District, Opobo Division.
27. Efik. Ds. An(n)ang (Annang Division), Efik = Calabar (along the east bank of the Cross River from Akpap to just over the Cameroon border), Ibibio (Uyo and Ikot-Ekpene divisions and southern Enyong Division). 1,000,000–2,000,000. As the language of Calabar town, Efik became a literary language in the nineteenth century and a local lingua franca.
28. Eket = Ekit.
29. Ibino = Ibeno = Ibuno.
30. Okobo. Okobo-Oron District, Eket Division.
31. Oron. Okobo-Oron District, Eket Division.

CENTRAL DELTA = ABUA-OGBỊA. Rivers State, Nigeria.

32. Abua(n).
33. Afakani.
34. Abulome = Abuloma = Obulom.
35. Ḅukuma = Ogbonuagum.
36. Kugbo.
37. Mini.
38. Oḍual.
39. Ọgbịa. Ds. Anyama, Kolo, Oloiḅiri.
40. Ogbogolo.

CALABAR RIVER = SOUTHEASTERN DELTA CROSS. There may be other languages in this group, as Odut.

41. Bakpinka = Uwet. Around Uwet.
42. Kiong = Okonyong = Akoiyang.
43. Ododop = Korop = Erorup. Northeast of Calabar along the Nigerian-Cameroon border.
44. Uyanga = Basanga ?

OGONI = OKUNI. 76,300. Ogoni Division, Rivers State, Nigeria.

45. Eleme.
46. Gokana.
47. Khana = Kana.

AFFILIATION. Member of BENUE-CONGO.

PLATEAU BENUE-CONGO

GROUPING. Languages included in PLATEAU BENUE-CONGO are subgrouped I through VII, after Greenberg (1966). A few changes in the subgrouping of particular languages are made after Williamson (1971) and additional names are added after Williamson and Shimizu (1968) and Westermann and Bryan (1952). The PLATEAU languages are spoken in the northern states of Nigeria.

I. Greenberg divides PLATEAU I into two groups: (a) and (b).

(a) Williamson [after Rowlands (1962)] divides I(a) into Reshe (15) and a NIGER PROVINCE group within which languages (4), (5), (6), (10), (11), (14), (17) form one subgroup, and languages (1), (2), (3), (7), (9), (12), (13), (16) form another. Niger and Kabba Provinces.

1. Basa = Basa-Kaduna = Basawa.
2. Basa-Komo = Bassa-Komo = Bassa-Kwomu.
3. Bushi = Baushi = Bauchi = Kushi.
4. Dakakari = Dakkakarri = Dakarkari = Dakarchi = Dakarawa = Dabai ? = Clela = Chilila. Tr. also Lilawa = lila = lilana ?
5. Dukawa = Duka = Dukanchi = Hune. 18,778.
6. Gelewa = Geer-ni.
7. Gurmana.
8. Kambari = Kambali = Kamberchi = Kamberawa = Kamber(r)i = Cumbri = Evadi = Yauri = Cishingyini = Shingini = Ashingi. Ds.

Central, South-Western; also Kukawa ? 67,000.

9. Kamuku = Kenji = Jinda = Majinda. Ds. include Achifawa = Achipawa, Ucinda.

10. Kelawa = Keri-ni = Kellini = Adoma = Domawa.

11. Lyase-ne = Bangawa = Bangi.

12. Ngwoi = Ngwe.

13. Pongo = Pongu = Arringeu.

14. Puku-nu = Fakawa.

15. Reshe = Bareshe = Tsureshe = Gunganoi = Gungawa = Gunganchi. Trs. Bararawa, Lapawa = Lupawa, Larawa = Laro = Larauwa, Reshe. 10,000.

16. Ura.

17. Wipsi-ni = Zusu.

(b) Languages (19), (20), (24), (26), (27), (28), (29), (30), (31), (32), (34), (35), (38), (39), (40), (41), (42) and (43) form a CENTRAL group; (21), (22), (33) and (36) form a NORTHERN group, and (23) and (37) form another subgroup.

18. Amap = Ama = Amawa = Amo = Amon(g). 3,547.

19. Anaguta.

20. Buji = Bujawa = Buze = Buje = Ano. 2,256.

21. Butawa = Buta = Mbutawa = Mbotuwa = Ba-Buche = Ba-Mbutu (9,218). D. also Ningawa ? (3,700).

22. Chamo.

23. Chawai = Chawe = Chawi = Atsam = Atsama. 8,584.

24. Gure = Igbiri = Pugbiri. D. also Dungi = Dwingi ? 3,000–5,000.

25. Gyema(wa).

26. Janji = Jenji = Anafejazi = Anajanzi. 360.

27. Jerawa proper = Anazele = Jere. 4,520.

28. Kahugu = Kagu = Kapugu = Anirago = Agari. 1,000.

29. Kaivi = Kaibi.

30. Kiballo.

31. Kinuku.

32. Kitimi.

33. Kuda = Kudawa. 2,000–4,000.

34. Kurama = Akurmi = Azumu = Bukurmi.

35. Kuzamani = Rishuwa.

36. Ningi.

37. Piti = Epit = Pitti = Abisi = Bisi. 1,589.

38. Rebina = Rebinawa = Rebini-wa = Gurum = Bunu = Ì-búnú = Gurrun = Narabuna. 4,106.

39. Rumaya = Rumaiya.

40. Ruruma.

41. Sanga(wa). 1,700.

42. Sheni.

43. Surubu = Srubu.

44. Taura(wa). 810.

Chokobo = Chokobawa = Azure ? 424.
Gezewa = Geji ? 1,305.
Gussum = Gusum = Gusawa = Anibau = Ibau ? 996.
Guzawa = Gusuwa ? 1,360.

II. Williamson, who modifies Greenberg's classification by adding Yeskwa (63) to PLATEAU II, questions the inclusion of Eloyi (47) in this group. If they belong in PLATEAU II, Eloyi and Migili (60) constitute separate subgroups, each co-ordinate with a subgroup consisting of the rest of the PLATEAU II languages. This remaining large subgroup is further divided into five subgroups: (a) languages numbered (57), (59) and (63); (b) = JABA includes (51), (53) and (55); (c) includes (61), (62); (d) = CENTRAL includes (45), (50), (54) and (56); (e) includes (46), (48), (49), (53) and (58). Most are spoken in Zaria Province.

   45. Afusare = Fizere = Jarawan Dutse = Hill Jarawa = Jari. D. also Forum. 30,000.
   46. Doka.
   47. Eloyi = Afo = Epe.
   48. Idon(g).
   49. Ikulu = Ikolu = Ankulu = (Ba)nkulu. 5,594.
   50. Irigwe = Iregwe = Irregwe = Rigwe = Aregwe = Aregwa = Idafan = Kwoll. 13,493. Plateau Province, Jos Division, Birom Tribal Area.
   51. Jaba = Ham = Ada = Doma. Ds. also Chori, Kenyi, Samban.
   52. Kadara = Adara = Peda. 17,700.
   53. Kagoma = Gwong = Gyong. 6,125.
   54. Kaje = Kajji = Kache = Ajio = Baju. 24,500.
   55. Kamantan = Kamanton = Zamangan = Angan. 6,970.
   56. Katab = Tyap = Atyap. Ds. also Ataka = Attaka (5,000), Kachichere = Aticheraak = Titchaat = Dororo (700), Kafauchau = Kabbau-chau (970), Kagoro = Agwolok = Agwot = Aguro (10,566), Morwa = Moroa = Asolio = Aholio = Asulio (5,726).
   57. Koro.
   58. Kuturmi = Ada.
   59. Lungu = Adong.
   60. Migili = Koro.
   61. Nandu.
   62. Tari.
   63. Yeskwa = Yasgua.
   Kajuru = Adjure ? 5,560.

III

   64. Aten = Etien = Ganawuri = Jal. 4,000.
   65. Birom = Biroom = Berom = Burum = Burumawa = Worom = Shosho = Akuut = Kibo = Kibbo = Kibyen.
   66. Chara = Chera = Tera = Terea = Teria = Terria = Nfa = Fachara = Fakara = Pakara. 735.

IV. Languages numbered (68), (71), and (76) form one subgroup; (69), (70), (72), and (73) form another.

    67. Ayu. 3,000.

    68. Boyawa = Boi.

    69. Gwanto.

    70. Kaninkwom = Kaninkon = Kaningkon = Kanikwum = Tum. Ds. also Kanufi, Nidem = I-Nidem = Inidem.

    71. Kwanka = Kadum.

    72. Mada = Nunku = Yidda. 23,500.

    73. Ninzam. 4,500.

    74. Pai = Dalong.

    75. Rukuba.

    76. Shal.

V

    77. Eggon = Egon = Megon. Ds. also Hill Mada = Madda, Matatarwa (?), Matengala ?

    78. Rindre = Rindri = Lindri = Nungu.

    79. Yashi.

VI

    80. Horom = Kaleri.

    81. Mabo = Kaleri.

    82. Pyem = Pyam = Paiem = Pein = Fem = Fyam = Fyeum. 3,000–5,000.

VII

    83. Basherawa = Bashar = Borrom = Burrum = Burumawa = Burmawa = Bogh. 20,000.

    84. Yergham = Yergam = Yergum = Apa = Appa = Torah. 30,000. Plateau Province, Shendam Division.

    AFFILIATION. Member of BENUE-CONGO.

*Beothuk = Beothuc = Bethuck = Bethuk = Newfoundland = Red Indians. Newfoundland.

    AFFILIATION. The proposal that Beothuk be classified as an ALGONQUIAN language, most recently urged by Hewson (1968), is not accepted by all Algonquianists.

BERBER

    GROUPING. Languages in the BERBER family numbered (1) through (5) and (7), below, but not (6), are spoken (for the most part) west of those included in the ZENATI group (8–24). Some of these languages, as Siwa (18), are spoken in isolated desert communities; some, as Mzab (14), are spoken in BERBER villages interspersed among villages in which Arabic is the primary language; and a couple of BERBER languages, Guanche (1) and Jerba (13), are spoken on Atlantic and Mediterranean islands, respectively, although the latter is also spoken on the mainland of Tunisia. Basset (1952) notes that Arabic, as a trade language, is often a second language for men who speak primarily one of the BERBER languages.

Applegate (1964) regards the subgrouping of BERBER languages to be a reflection of structural (especially phonological) similarities among those grouped together under TAMAZIGHT-RIFF-KABYLE (3–5), and under ZENATI (8–24). Altogether, more than 11,000,000 speakers, most of whom are concentrated in Algeria (5,000,000) and Morocco (4,800,000), with some 60,000 in Tunisia; 36,000 in Libya; 35,000 in Mauritania and Senegal; and fewer speakers elsewhere, except for the 50,000 widely scattered speakers of Tuareg (6).

1. Guanche. Canary Islands.
2. Shilha. Morocco, from the Grand Atlas south to the River Dra; east to Algeria, at Tabelbala (Applegate 1958).

TAMAZIGHT-RIFF-KABYLE GROUP
3. Kabyle. Algeria.
4. Riff. Ds. Arzeu, Igzennaian, Iznacen, Senhaja de Srair. Algeria, Morocco.
5. Tamazight. Ds. Central Atlas (Morocco), South Oran (Algeria).

6. Tuareg. Ds. Ahaggar (Algeria), Air (Niger), Ajjer (Algeria, Libya), Ghadames (Libya), Ioullemmeden (Niger, Mali, Nigeria).
7. Zenaga. Mauritania, Senegal.

ZENATI GROUP
8. Awjilah. Libya.
9. Chaouia. Algeria.
10. Ghardaia. Algeria.
11. Gourara. Algeria.
12. Jabal Nafusah. Ds. Jemmari, Zuwarah. Libya.
13. Jerba. Tunisia.
14. Mzab. Algeria.
15. Ouargla. Ds. Oued Righ, Temacin, Touggourt. Algeria.
16. Sawknah. Libya.
17. Sened. Tunisia.
18. Siwa. United Arab Republic (Western Desert).
19. Tamezret. Tunisia.
20. Taoujjout. Tunisia.
21. Tidikelt. Algeria.
22. Tmagourt. Tunisia.
23. Touat. Algeria.
24. Zaoua. Tunisia.

AFFILIATION. Member of AFROASIATIC.

BINANDERE

GROUPING. As reported by Wurm (1971c) the percentage of cognates (on limited lexicostatistical lists) shared between Zia (17, below) and Suena (13) and

Yekora (16) — 67% and 68%, respectively — is close to that sometimes taken to be correlated with being dialects of a single language. Maiheari (10), included by Greenberg (1971b), is treated as unclassified by Wurm. Hooley and McElhanon (1970) add Guhu Samane (6). The BINANDERE languages are spoken on the coast and hinterland from the southeastern corner of Morbobe District, New Guinea at least to Cape Nelson near the eastern border of Northern District, with some extension into the Gulf District, Papua.

1. Aeka = Aiga. 1,500.
2. Ambasi = Tain-daware. 500.
3. Bareji.
4. Baruga. D. also Agaiambo ? 1,300.
5. Binandere = Binandele. 3,000.
6. Guhu Samane = Mid-Waria. D. also Paiwa = Paiawa = Payawa. 4,000. Southeastern Morobe District, New Guinea.
7. Gaina.
8. Hunjara = Koko.
9. Korape = Korafi = Kwarafe = Okeine. 3,500.
10. Maiheari = Mai-hea-ri. Gulf District.
11. Notu = Ewage. 10,000.
12. Orokaiva. 25,000.
13. Suena = Yema = Yema-Yarawe. 1,400.
14. Yega = Okeina.
15. Yega of Gona. 900.
16. Yekora. 300.
17. Zia = Tsia. D. also Mawai. 3,300.

Greenberg also includes in BINANDERE: Adaua, Amara, Berepo, Giumu, Jauwa = Dobudura, Jegasa-Sarau, Mambare, Musa River, Upper Musa, Tahari including Aru and Duvera, Totore, Yoda. These names are mostly from earlier sources, especially Ray, and some of them probably represent alterate names for, or dialects of, the languages listed above.

AFFILIATION. Member of SOUTH-EAST NEW GUINEA.

BISMARCK ARCHIPELAGO

GROUPING. Grace (1955) classifies as one subgroup of his OCEANIC subgroup the languages of the Islands of New Ireland (3°20′S 152°00′E), New Hanover (2°30′S 150°15′E), Duke of York (4°10′S 152°28′E), the eastern half of New Britain (5°40′S 151°00′E), and adjacent small islands. The three languages of the New Hanover-New Ireland area and four of the languages of eastern New Britain included in Dyen's (1965) classification did not share sufficient basic vocabulary with each other or with any other language of the family to be subgrouped. The other three languages of eastern New Britain in Dyen's sample constitute UVOLIC, in which Mamusi (16) and Mengen (18) are more closely related to each other than either is to Uvol (33). The UVOLIC group is also not subgrouped with other AUSTRONESIAN languages in Dyen's classification.

1. Anir Island. 4°5′S 153°42′E.
2. Dang = Iavongai. New Hanover Island.
3. Dyaul. Dyaul Island.
4. Fesoa = Fissoa = Butam. Northern New Ireland.
5. Gelik. D. also Kinsal = Hinsal. South central New Ireland.
6. Gunantuna = Blanche Bay = Tinata Tuna = Tuna = New Britain = Kuanua. D. also Malu (Duke of York Island). Used as a lingua franca throughout New Britain and New Ireland and spoken as a native language on the Gazelle Peninsula of New Britain.
7. Kanapit. South central New Ireland.
8. King. Southern New Ireland.
9. Komalu = Kanalu = Barok. South central New Ireland.
10. Kulube = Kolube. D. also Ugana. South central New Ireland.
11. Lamasa. Southern New Ireland.
12. Lambon. Southern New Ireland.
13. Lemusmus. Northern New Ireland.
14. Lihir = Lir. Lihir Island, 3°05′S 152°35′E.
15. Lote. Eastern New Britain.
16. Mamusi = Kakuna. 920 in Cape Hoskins Patrol Post Division, plus others outside. Eastern New Britain.
17. Maututu. Eastern New Britain.
18. Mengen. Eastern New Britain.
19. Muliama. D. also Konomola. Southern New Ireland.
20. Mussau = Musau. D. also Emirau. Mussau Island (St. Matthias Group), 1°30′S 149°48′E, Emirau Island, 1°40′S 150°00′E.
21. Nalik = Ligagun. North central New Ireland.
22. Nisan = Nissan. Nisan Island, 4°30′S 154°14′E.
23. Nokon. Southern New Ireland.
24. Omo = Tigak. Northern New Ireland.
25. Pala = Patpatar. Southern New Ireland.
26. Peleata. Eastern New Britain.
27. Pililo. Pililo Island, 6°11′S 149°02′E.
28. Rogo. Eastern New Britain.
29. Siar. Southern New Ireland.
30. Tabar. Tabar Islands, 2°56′S 152°00′E.
31. Tanga. Tanga Islands, 3°30′S 153°15′E.
32. Tomoip = Tomoyp = Tumuip. Eastern New Britain.
33. Uvol. Eastern New Britain.
34. Vele Uasi. Eastern New Britain.

AFFILIATION. Member of OCEANIC subgroup of AUSTRONESIAN.

*Bithynian. A non-INDO-EUROPEAN language of ancient Asia Minor known chiefly from Greek traditions (Meyer 1897, Holl 1908).

AFFILIATION. None known.

BODO-NAGA-KACHIN

GROUPING. Languages listed below are separately alphabetized under BODO and NAGA and KACHIN, but are numbered consecutively, (1) through (21). These three groups of languages are taken to be subgroups of one major group, BODO-NAGA-KACHIN, after Morse (1965). Other classifications differ. Thus, Burling (1967), Shafer (1955), and Grierson (1903–1927) list languages numbered 5, 7, 12, 13, and 21, below, as a group coordinate with Burmese in the 'Burma Branch' of BURMESE-LOLO. The BODO and NAGA languages are spoken mainly in India (Assam); KACHIN in northern Burma.

BODO. Burling (1959) groups languages numbered 3 and 4 in a KOCH group coordinate with languages numbered 1 and 2. Shafer (1955) classifies BODO in a 'Barish Section' of his 'Baric Division' of SINO-TIBETAN. India: Assam and neighboring states.

1. Bodo = Boro. Ds. also Dimasa (15,000), Kachari, Mech. 20,000. Brahmaputra Valley.
2. Garo. 250,000–300,000. Standard in northeastern part of the Garo Hills in westernmost Assam.

KOCH. This subgroup is said to include several separate languages, two of which are named — (3) and (4), following. 10,000.

3. Atong. Southeastern part of the Garo Hills District.
4. Wanang = Garo of Jalpaiguri. A few hundred. Along Western border of Garo Hills near the marketplace of Garabadha.

NAGA = NORTHERN NAGA = TANGSA. These languages should not be confused with the NAGA of NAGA-KUKI-CHIN. The estimate given for the number of NAGA speakers is ambiguous; it may include the 75,000 NAGA of NAGA-KUKI-CHIN. Shafer (1955) classifies the NAGA-TANGSA languages in a 'Nagish Section' of his 'Baric Division' of SINO-TIBETAN, but excludes Lepcha (5), which he classifies as a member of NAGA-KUKI-CHIN (q. v.).

5. Lepcha = Leptśa = Róng = Rongpa = Lepoha = Nünpa. 34,894 (1909). Doar, Sikkim, Western Bhutan, Eastern Nepal.
6. Tangsa. Ds. Angwanku = Tableng, Mulung; Banpara, Mutonia; Chang = Tśang (6,000); Have = Hewa; Khemsing; Longphi; Lungchang; Lungri; Moklum; Mośang = Mosang, Śangge = Sanke; Namsangia; Paipi; Ponthai; Rong-Rang, Tikhak; Tśingmegnu = Tamlu; Yogli. 400,000. Lists from Shafer (1955) and Morse (1965) overlap only for Mosang = Mośang and Sangge = Sanke. Morse, on the basis of fieldwork with several of these, indicates they might be considered 'widely divergent dialects' of a single language.

KACHIN = JINGPAW = CHINGHPAW = CHINGPA'O = SHANTOU YEH-JEN = P'U?MAN = P'OK = AP'U = HKANG. Shafer (1955) treats these languages under a 'Katśinish Section' of his 'Burmic' (languages numbered 8, 9, 10, 11 following), and under a 'Northern Unit' in his 'Burmic' (languages numbered 7, 12, 13, 21, following); and under a 'Nungish Section' in his 'Burmic' (languages numbered 16, 17, 18, 19, following). Possibly because the Rawang (18) are sometimes referred to as 'Nung', Shafer neglected the subgroup NUNG (14, 15). This NUNG group might be, alternatively, classified in the GYARUNG-MISHMI family. K'ung Chang (1967) classifies Ach'ang (7) with languages of the BURMESE-LOLO family. Little is known about language boundaries and subgroups within KACHIN; thus, RAWANG, NUNG, and possibly Chingpaw (8), may be a single subgroup under KACHIN. Similar or even occasionally identical dialect names are also assigned to different languages; e.g., in (12), (13), and (21) below. 500,000. North Burma in the Kachin Hills and extending from the Hukwang valley eastward along the Tibetan frontier, down the Chinese frontier as far south as Kentung State, and extending into Assam on the west and Yunnan on the east.

    7. Ach'ang = Atśang. Ds. also Maingtha, Ngatśang.
    8. Chingpaw = Chingp'o = Chinghpaw = Jinghpaw = Singhpo = Theinbaw = Kachin = Ye Jein = Ye Yeh = Khang. 20,000 in China, over 150,000 in Burma. Naga Hills in Burma to western Yunnan. 'Chingpaw' is sometimes used as the name for a larger group including, e.g., the Lashi and Maru, below.
    9. Dźili.
  10. Hkaku.
  11. Kauri = Khauri = Gauri. Burma (Sinlum).
  12. Lashi = Lasi = Letsi = Lets'i = Lechi = Chashan = Ac'ye = Ngac'ang. Burma, largely in the Htawgaw subdivision.
  13. Maru = Lawng = Laungwaw = Lawngvaw = Lansu = Lang = Mulu = Malu = Diso. Burma, largely in the Htawgaw subdivision.

NUNG. Around middle reaches of the Salween River, north Burma and Yunnan.
  14. Nora = Nózà = Norra. Ds. also Byabe, Kizolo, Lama (3,000).
  15. Nung = Anung = Anoong = Nu = Lu = Lutze = Kwinp'ang = Kuhpang = Kwingsang = Fuch'ye. Ds. also Cholo, Gwaza, Miko. 10,000.

RAWANG
  16. Krangku.
  17. Lòngmì = Lùngmì.
  18. Rawang = Ganung-Rawang = Hkanung = Kanung = Nung = Taron = Kiutze = Ch'opa. Ds. also Agu, Hpungsi, Htiselwang, Matwanly, Melam, Metu, Mutwang, Serhta, Serwang, Tamalu = Dămalo, Tukiumu, Wadamkong, Wahke. 60,000. 75 to 100 different dialects, some of which are mutually unintelligible to others.
  19. Zithúng = Zitung.
20. Tangsarr.
21. Tsaiwa = Atši = Atzi = Szi. Ds. also Langwa, Lech'i, Polo. 50,000 in China. Lu-hsi, Jui-li, Lung-ch'uan and Ying-chiang districts in the Te-hung Autonomous Chou (Chang 1967), and the Sadon subdivision of Burma.

AFFILIATION. Member of TIBETO-BURMAN.

BOGIA = MONUMBO.

GROUPING. Wurm (1971c) reports that Capell's (1951) classification has been expanded on the basis of Z'graggen (1968). With more recent fieldwork Z'graggen (1970) has reclassified Wurm's BOGIA into three groups: ADELBERT RANGE, MADANG, and RAMU. Greenberg's (1971b) MONUMBO (all of which is included in Wurm's BOGIA) is most closely identifiable with Z'graggen's RAMU except that Greenberg includes Monumbo (55) and Lilau (54) (as does Wurm, who subgroups the two as MONUMBO), but Z'graggen excludes both from RAMU, classifying them rather as belonging to TORRICELLI.

Z'graggen postulates a distant relationship between his ADELBERT RANGE and MADANG, but none between either and RAMU. Wurm includes a few languages as being unsubclassifiable in BOGIA; those which are not subclassified by Z'graggen are given at the end of the list below. The BOGIA languages are spoken almost entirely in the Madang District, with a few in the adjacent areas of the Sepik District, New Guinea.

ADELBERT RANGE. Bunabun (1, below) and Banara (14) are classified in NORTH-EAST NEW GUINEA by Greenberg.

ISUMRUD
    1. Bunabun = Bunubun. 430.
    2. Dimir = Boskien ? 1,270.
    3. Korak. 170.
    4. Malas. 190.
    5. Waskia. 6,650.

JOSEPHSTAAL
    6. Ikudun. 880.
    7. Katiati. 2,300.
    8. Moresada. 150.
    9. Osum. 570.
    10. Pondoma. 330.
    11. Wadaginam. 460.
    12. Mugil = Saker = Bunu. 1,700.

PIHOM. The single language of Wurm's CENTRAL subgroup of BOGIA which appears in Z'graggen's classification is placed in PIHOM; the other languages in Wurm's CENTRAL are added below.
    13. Amaimon. 370.
    14. Banara = Moando ? (Capell 1962a).
    15. Bepour. 95.
    16. Malala. 600.
    17. Mawak. 1,010.
    18. Musar. 500.
    19. Parawen = Bilakura ? 500.
    20. Pay. 600.
    21. Pila. 530.
    22. Saki. 2,240.
    23. Suaru. 580.
    24. Tani. 2,270.
    25. Ulingan. 1,210.

26. Wagimuda. 2,260.
27. Wanambere. 440.
28. Wanuma. 1,210.
29. Yaben. D. also Mosimo ? 657.
30. Yakiba. 2,240.

WANANG
31. Angaua = Anaberg ? 1,990.
32. Atemple. 700.
33. Emerum. 460.
34. Musak. 240.

MADANG (of Z'graggen). Includes all the languages of Wurm's EASTERN subgroup of BOGIA, which are the only languages in Wurm's classification which belong to this MADANG subgroup. Halopa (41) and Rempi (46) are classified in NORTHEAST NEW GUINEA by Greenberg.

35. Amele. 4,110.
36. Bau. 1,690.
37. Foran. 800.
38. Gal.
39. Garuh. 1,730.
40. Garus. 1,900.
41. Halopa = Nobanob = Nupanob = Botelkude. 1,720.
42. Isebe. 770.
43. Kare. 340.
44. Mawan. 220.
45. Nake.
46. Rempi = Rempin = A'e. 450.
47. Saruga. 90.
48. Sumau. 770.
49. Urigina. 1,560.
50. Usino. 1,050.
51. Utu. 580.
52. Wamas.
53. Yoidik. 200.

MONUMBO. Classified in TORRICELLI by Z'graggen.
54. Lilau = Ngaimbom. 410.
55. Monumbo. 450.

RAMU. Z'graggen's classification agrees with Wurm's in treating Awar (60), Bosngun (64), Gamei (66), Kayan (72), Murisapa (75, not mentioned by Z'graggen), and Watam (81) as a single OTTILIEN-WESTERN subgroup. Z'graggen adds to Wurm's TANGGUM [Igom (69) and Tanggum (79)] two languages not mentioned by Wurm: Andarum (58) and Tanguat (80).

56. Adjora = Adjoria ? 370. Sepik District.
57. Akrukay. 150.

58. Andarum. 1,020.
59. Anor. 390.
60. Awar = Nubia. 500.
61. Ayom = Aiome.
62. Ayon = Aion = Aione. 560. Sepik District.
63. Banaro. 1,000. Upper Keram River, Sepik District.
64. Bosngun = Bosman ? 2,000.
65. Breri. 720.
66. Gamei = Gamai. 930.
67. Giri. 1,540.
68. Gorovu. 46. Sepik District.
69. Igom. 730.
70. Itutang. 370.
71. Kambot. 500. Lower Keram River, Sepik District.
72. Kayan = Kaian. 230.
73. Makarub = Mikarew. 5,660.
74. Midsivindi. 910.
75. Murisapa = Murusapa. 152.
76. Rao. 3,340.
77. Romkuin = Romkun.
78. Sepen. 870.
79. Tanggum = Tanggu = Tangu. 2,430.
80. Tanguat. 570.
81. Watam = Kopar. 600.

82. Aregerek ? 500.
83. Gapun ? 60. Sepik District.
84. Kowaki ? 60.
85. Kuanga ?
86. Moira ?
87. Poroporo = Porapora ? 400. Sepik District.
88. Ufien ? 50.

AFFILIATION. Member of CENTRAL NEW GUINEA macro-phylum (Wurm); of NORTH NEW GUINEA (Greenberg).

BORORO = OTUQUE = OTUKE = BOROTUKE = BOROTUQUE

GROUPING. The BORORO and OTUQUE language groups were formerly considered as separate, but all more recent authorities join them as two branches of one family (Mason 1950). The BORORO branch is composed of six languages (numbered 1–6), spoken in the lowlands of Mato Grosso, Brazil, or possibly of eight if Coroa and Coxipo are included. The OTUQUE languages are probably all extinct; they were spoken in the extensions of the Mato Grosso lowlands into eastern Bolivia.

BORORO = COROADO
1. Acioné.

2. Aravira.
3. Biriuné.
4. Eastern Bororo = Orarimugodoge. 500–1,000.
5. Western Bororo. Ds. Cabasal, Campanya.
6. Umotinā = Barbado.
? Coroa.
? Coxipo.

OTUQUE = OTUQUI = OTUKE
7. *Covareca.
8. *Curuminaca.
9. *Otuque = Otuké = Louxiru. Possibly not extinct.
? *Coraveca. D. also Curavé.
? *Curucaneca.
? *Tapii.

AFFILIATION. Member of MACRO-GE-BORORO group within GE-PANO-CARIB.

Borrado = Quinigua = Guinigua = Quinicuane. Mexico (formerly between the Sierra Madre Oriental and the Sierra Tamaulipa la Nueva, and between the Rio Grande and the Rio del Pilón Grande).

AFFILIATION. Suggested by Gursky (1964) to be HOKAN on the basis of del Hoyo's (1960) vocabularies.

BOTOCUDO = AIMBORE = BORUN

GROUPING. The BOTOCUDO family of languages is to be distinguished from other groups by the same name. The source of the confusion is that 'Botocudo' refers to wearers of large lip plugs. The BOTOCUDO languages are, or were, spoken in the states of Minas Gerais and Espirito Santo in Brazil. Of the nine languages listed, three (numbers 1, 7, 9) are considered independent of BOTOCUDO by many authors (Mason 1950).
1. *Anquet = Anket.
2. *Araná = Aranya. Possibly not extinct.
3. Chonvugn = Crenak. Possibly not extinct.
4. *Crecmun. Possibly not extinct.
5. *Gueren.
6. *Gutucrac. D. (?) also Minya-yirugn = Minhagirun. Possibly not extinct.
7. Nacnhanuc = Nacnyanuk.
8. Nacrehe = Nakrehe = Nachehe.
9. *Yiporok = Giporok = Giporoc. D. (?) also Poicá = Poyishá = Požitxá.

AFFILIATION. Member of MACRO-GE within GE-PANO-CARIB.

BOUGAINVILLE

GROUPING. Allen and Hurd (1965) present a classification on the basis of glottochronology in which the BOUGAINVILLE languages are subgrouped as below. Greenberg's (1971b) classification agrees with that of Allen and Hurd on those languages for which data were available to him. Wurm (1971c) differs from Allen and Hurd in the level at which language boundaries should be assigned, and hence lists more 'languages' than they. All are spoken in the southeastern three-quarters of Bougainville Island in the Solomons.

EASTERN = NASIOI-NAGOVISI-SIWAI-BUIN
    BUIN
        1. Baitsi = Sigisigero. 534. May be a dialect of Siwai.
        2. Buin = Telei = Rugara. 7,553.
        3. Siwai = Motuna. 5,580.
        4. Uitai. 1,060. May be a dialect of Buin.
    NASIOI
        5. Koromira. May be a dialect of Nasioi ?
        6. Nagovisi = Sibbe. 4,619.
        7. Nasioi. D. also Koianu. 9,643.
        8. Simeku. 1,011. May be a dialect of Nasioi.

WESTERN = KUNUA-KERIAKA-ROTOKAS-EIVO. Atsilima (9), Eivo (10), and Rotokas (13) form a ROTOKAS subgroup.
    9. Atsilima. 112. May be a dialect of Rotokas.
  10. Eivo. 1,118.
  11. Keriaka. 991.
  12. Kunua = Konua. 1,337.
  13. Rotokas. 3,408.

AFFILIATION. Member of INDO-PACIFIC (Greenberg).

BUNABAN

GROUPING. Spoken in the Fitzroy River basin southeast of Derby, Western Australia, Australia.

1. Bunaba = Bunapa = Punaba.
2. Gunian = Koneyandi = Konejandi = Kunian = Kunan.
    AFFILIATION. Member of AUSTRALIAN macro-phylum.

BURERAN

GROUPING. These languages are spoken in north central Australia.

1. Barera = Burera = Bawera = Jikai = Tchikai. Ds. also Gunaidbe, Gudjalavia. 350. Blyth River, area north of the Tomkinson River, Cape Stewart and coast east to Wallamungo.
2. Gorogone = Gungorogone. South of the Tomkinson River.

AFFILIATION. Member of AUSTRALIAN macro-phylum.

BURMESE-LOLO = LOLO-BURMESE

GROUPING. Except for the classification of Tsaiwa and Maru, the grouping of languages under BURMESE-LOLO is based on successive revisions after Grierson (1903–1927). The list below reflects — but for the exception noted — the revision of Grierson by Shafer (1955) as well as that of Shafer by Morse (1965), and includes language names supplied by Burling (1967). Tsaiwa and Maru (as well as their dialects and/or closely related languages), are here included in the BODO-NAGA-KACHIN group, after Morse (1965), while the other classifiers include them in the BURMESE subgroup of BURMESE-LOLO.

In the list which follows, Burmese appears as a single language (1), followed by various LOLO-MOSO subgroups among which MINCHIA languages are separately grouped in an uncertain but possible subgroup of LOLO; finally, LOLO-MOSO languages numbered (34) through (51) are listed alphabetically without specific subgrouping.

1. Burmese = Bāmā(-čaka) = Myen. Ds. also Arakanese = Rakhaing = Maghī (221,950), Chaungtha (34,600), Danu = Tāruw (60,950), Inle, Intha (56,850), Mergui = Merguese, Taungyo = Tāru Tavoya(n) = Dawé (159,200), Yabein, Yanbye (326,650), Yaw (900). Burma, Bangladesh. 15,000,000. There are in addition 3,000,000 speakers for whom Burmese is a second language.

LOLO-MOSO = LOLO. 3,000,000.

    EAST LOLO = TONKIN (Shafer). Vietnam.

        2. Black Khoany.

        3. White Khoany.

        4. Mung.

    LOLO PROPER. Shafer's NYI in the 'Central Unit' of his 'Lolo Branch.'

        5. Ahi.

        6. Lolopho.

        7. Nyi.

        8. Tśökö = Tcholo.

        9. Weining.

    NORTH(ERN) LOLO

        10. Kangsiangying.

        11. Kiaokio.

        12. Laichau.

        13. Nee.

        14. Nuoku.

        15. Pakishan.

        16. Thongho.

        17. Tudza.

        18. Ulu.

    SOUTH(ERN) LOLO. Shafer (1955) includes two subgroups in his 'Southern Unit': PHUNOI (languages numbered 22, 23, 27, 28 and 2, 3, 4, above), and AKHA (languages numbered 19, 20, 21, 24, 25, 26, 29). He also includes Lahu (41) in this group. These languages are spoken in adjacent countries: Laos, eastern Burma, Thailand.

19. Akha = Aka = Kaw. 33,000.
20. Ako = Akö. 800.
21. Asong.
22. Hwethom.
23. Khaskhong.
24. Kui = Kwi. 3,700.
25. Menghwa.
26. Phana.
27. Phunoi = Punoi.
28. Pyen. 1,300.
29. Won.

MINCHIA. Possibly a LOLO group: the classification of MINCHIA is obscured by massive borrowing from Chinese.

30. Eryuan.
31. Hoking.
32. Minchia = Minkia.
33. Tali.

LOLO-MOSO ungrouped languages. Shafer (1955) says Mro (47) may be a MON-KHMER language. Shafer includes 34, 40, 44, 49 in a 'Luish section' and 51 as a 'Taman section' of his 'Burmish.' K'un Chang (1967) treats 38, 39, 41, 42, 46 as an 'I' subgroup of TIBETO-BURMAN. Sihia (50) is classified by Shafer as an independent branch of his 'Burmish.'

34. *Andro.
35. *Chairel. Probably the Tshairel of NAGA-KUKI-CHIN.
36. Daingnet.
37. Duampu.
38. Hani.
39. I.
40. Kadu = Asak. D. also Ganan.
41. Lahu = Moso. Ds. also Lahuna = Black Lahu, Luhusi = Luhushi = Red Lahu, Mossu (Laos). 139,000. China, Burma, Thailand, Laos.
42. Lis(s)u = Lis(s)haw = Lesuo = Leisu = Lëshuoop'a = Lëjengoup'a = Loisu = Chung = Cheli = Chedi. Ds. also Kesopo, Kosopho, Lipha, Lipho, Nu-chiang. 245,800. China, Yün-nan and Sze-ch'uan provinces.
43. Manyak = Menia = Menya.
44. Nameji.
45. Phupha.
46. Moso = Mosso = Nahsi = Noshi = Nakhi = Lomi. D. also Dion. China, Yün-nan province.
47. Mro = Mro-Mru. 20,000.
48. Sak = Thet = That. 35,250.
49. *Sengmai.
50. *Sihia = Hsishsia.
51. Taman.

AFFILIATION. Member of TIBETO-BURMAN.

Burushaski = Biltum = Yeshkun = Khajuna = Kunjuti. Ds. Hunza, Nagir, Werchik-war = Jasin (7,500 speakers). 27,500 (1931). States of Hunza and Nagir and also the Jasin District to the west in Pakistan.

AFFILIATION. None known.

CADDOAN

GROUPING. Caddo (1) is classified by Chafe (1971) as equally divergent from two other CADDOAN languages, Pawnee, Wichita (3, 4). The remaining language, Kitsai, (2), now extinct, was once spoken in the southern Plains; so also were representative dialects of languages (1) and (4).

1. Caddo = Caddoe = Kadohadacho. Trs. Cahinnio, Hasinai, Kadohadacho, Nanatsoho, Upper Nasoni, Upper Natchitoches, Upper Yatasi. 300 to 400. Oklahoma. Formerly in northeastern Texas extending into southwestern Arkansas.
2. *Kitsai = Kitchai = Kitsei = Quichais = Quidehais. Formerly Texas, but prehistorically Oklahoma.
3. Pawnee. Ds. Arikara = Arikare = Arickaree = Arickara = Ric(c)ara = Riccaree = Riccari(e) = Rikara = Ris = Ree, including Awahu, Hachepiriinu, Hia, Hoksukhaunu, Hosukhaunukarerihu, Hukawirat, Kaka, Lohoocat, Okos, Paushuk, Sukhutix, Tukatuk, Tukstanu. 200 to 300. On the Missouri River in North Dakota (formerly also South Dakota). The Arikara dialect is geographically separated from Pawnee = Pahni = Pani = Pany = Pawne = Pawnee Picts = Pawni = Picts = Toweahge = Kitka, including Chaui = Grand Pawnee, Kitkehahki = Republican Pawnee, Pitahauerat = Tapage Pawnee, Skidi = Skiri Pawnee. 400 to 600. Oklahoma, Wyoming, Nebraska, Kansas (formerly on the Platte River, Nebraska). Chafe (1973) says non-Arikara Pawnee bands — except the divergent Skidi Pawnee — were dialectically homogeneous.
4. Wichita = Black Pawnee = Panis = Quivira = Witshita. 100 to 200. Oklahoma (formerly in territory from middle Arkansas River in Kansas to Brazos River in Texas).

*Adai = Adahi = Adage = Adaihe = Adaize = Addaise = Watao ? Haina ?

AFFILIATION. Member of MACRO-SIOUAN phylum.

Callahuaya = Callawaya. Zone Callawaya, Bautista Saavedra Province, Bolivia.

AFFILIATION. Regarded as an unclassified language by Key and Key (1967)—i.e., with unknown affiliations.

*Calusa = Caloosa = Coloosa = Calos = Carlos. Southern half of Florida and the keys extending to Key West. In 1763 a remnant of some 80 families was removed to Havana, but Calusa continued to be encountered Florida until the end of the second Seminole war (1842).

AFFILIATION. Calusa is classified as a language isolate (a single language without known sister languages) on the authority of Gatschet (1884); the Calusa are linguistically unaffiliated with—i.e., not in the same family as—their neighbors, the Timucua, or with languages of the MUSKOGEAN family, as Seminole.

CAMACÁN

GROUPING. Five extinct languages formerly spoken in Eastern Brazil comprise the CAMACÁN family. There is general agreement that the five languages form a group, but subgrouping is less clear. Mason (1950) groups only numbers (4) and (5) as forming a CAMACÁN = KAMAKÁN subgroup.

1. *Catethoy = Katathoy = Catethoi = Cutashó = Kotoxó.
2. *Masacará.
3. *Menián = Manyá.
4. *Mongoyó = Mongoio.
5. *Monshocó = Ezeshio.

AFFILIATION. Member of MACRO-GE within GE-PANO-CARIB.

*Cappadocian. A non-INDO-EUROPEAN language of ancient Asia Minor known chiefly from Greek traditions (Kretschmer 1896, Holl 1908, Goetze 1957).

AFFILIATION. None known.

CARAJÁ = CARAYÁ = KARAYÁ = KARADŽÁ

GROUPING. Three languages are listed as composing the CARAJÁ family, although Lipkind (1948) says the linguistic differences are 'on a dialectic level.'

1. Carajá = Carayá = Karayá = Karadžá. 500–1,000. Border regions of the states of Mato Grasso, Pará, and Goiás, Brazil. D. also *Carajahi = Karayaki (possibly not extinct). Northeast of the Carajá.
2. Chamboa = Schambioá = Šambioá = Chimbioá = Ximbioá. Northern tip of Goiás, Brazil.
3. Javahé = Javahai = Javae = Yavahé = Yavahai = Zavažé = Shavayé = Jawagé. 250–500. South of the Carajá.

AFFILIATION. Member of MACRO-GE within GE-PANO-CARIB (Davis 1968).

*Carian. A little known language of Asia Minor attested by a few inscriptions (Friedrich 1931, 1932, 1952, Brandenstein 1935, Mentz 1940, Robert 1950, Masson 1954, Goetze 1957, Vryonis 1971, Masson 1973).

AFFILIATION. None known.

CARIB

GROUPING. The CARIB languages constitute one of the largest families in South

America, both in number of languages and geographical spread, but the internal relationships of the languages have not been worked out on a comparative linguistic basis. It is possible that we are concerned with a CARIB phylum rather than a family. It is also possible that some non-CARIB languages may have been included in lists of CARIB languages.

The languages are grouped and subgrouped on a primarily geographic basis, with little variation by most authors; the three major groups, NORTHERN, NORTH-WESTERN, and SOUTHERN are given here after Mason (1950) without further sub-grouping. The languages are, or were, spoken in Trinidad, Venezuela, Surinam, French Guiana, Guyana, Brazil, and Colombia. Island Carib, which is often assigned to the NORTHERN branch, is actually an ARAWAKAN language.

The NORTHERN branch extends from Trinidad and Venezuela eastward through Guyana, Surinam, and French Guiana, southward into Brazil as far as the Amazon and westward into Colombia. The NORTHWESTERN branch is confined to Venezuela, Colombia, and a small extension into Peru. The SOUTHERN branch is entirely south of the Amazon in Brazil.

Palmela (language number 78) was formerly treated as independent, and Pimenteira (79) was earlier classified in the BOTOCUDA family of MACRO-GE by some, and as independent by others. Carare (52) is often classified as ARAWAKAN. All languages of the CHOCO group formerly classified as CARIBAN have been reclassified, following Greenberg (1960a), as a family within MACRO-CHIBCHAN.

NORTHERN

1. Acawai. D. also Patamona. Guyana.
2. Apalai. D. also *Aracuaju. 250. Brazil.
3. Arecuna = Jaricuna = Pemon. Ds. also Camaracoto, Taulipang = Taurepan = Ipurucoto (500). Possibly the 500 figure includes speakers of other languages, Venezuela.
4. *Arinagoto. Possibly not extinct. Venezuela.
5. Azumara. Possibly extinct. Brazil.
6. *Bonarí. Brazil.
7. Carib. Ds. Calinya (Surinam), Caribice (Guyana), Galibi (500 in Brazil, French Guiana, Guyana, Surinam). 5,000.
8. Carijona = Omagua = Umawa. Ds. Caicuchana = Caicushana, Guagua, Guake = Guaque, Hianacoto, Mahotoyana, Riama, Tsahatsaha = Saha, Yacaoyana. Colombia.
9. *Carinapagoto = Carinepagoto. Trinidad.
10. *Chacopata. Venezuela.
11. *Chayma = Chaima = Sayma = Warapiche. Ds. also Guaga, Tagare.
12. *Core. Possibly not extinct. Venezuela.
13. *Cumanagoto. Venezuela.
14. Cumayena = Ocomayana. Surinam.
15. *Cunewara = Cuneguara. Venezuela.
16. Diau. Guyana.
17. Ingaricó. 500. Guyana and Brazil.

18. *Jauaperi = Yauaperi = Crishana. Possibly not extinct. D. also Atroahy.
19. Macushi = Macusi = Macussi = Teweya = Teueia. 2,500 in Guyana; others in Brazil.
20. Mapoyo = Mapoye. Venezuela.
21. Maquiritare = Maquiritai = Makiritare. Ds. also Cunuana, Decuana = Wainungomo, Ihuruana, Maitsi, Mayongong = Yecuana (1,000). Venezuela.
22. Monoico. Guyana.
23. Mutuan. Brazil.
24. Oyana = Oiana = Uaiana = Wayana = Alukuyana = Upurui. Ds. also Rucuyen, Urucuiana = Urucena. 350 in Surinam; 100 in Brazil; others in French Guiana.
25. *Palank = Palenque = Guarine. Venezuela.
26. Panari. 1,000. West central Venezuela.
27. *Paraviyana = Paravilhana. Brazil.
28. Pariagoto = Paria = Guayuno. Venezuela.
29. Pauchiana = Paushiana. Brazil.
30. *Pauxi = Pauchi. Possibly not extinct. Brazil.
31. Pianocotó = Parucutu = Parukutu = Catauian = Catawian. 500. Guyana and Brazil.
32. *Piritu. Venezuela.
33. *Purucoto = Porocoto = Puricoto = Urucoto. Possibly not extinct. Brazil.
34. Quenoloco = Keneloco. Guyana and Brazil.
35. Sapara. Brazil and Colombia.
36. *Shikiana = Chikena = Chiquena. Brazil.
37. *Taparito. Possibly not extinct. Venezuela.
38. *Tivericoto. Possibly not extinct. Brazil.
39. Trio. 780. Surinam.
40. Uaica = Waica. Said not to be the same as Waica of the WAICA family. Venezuela.
41. Uaimiri = Waimiry. Brazil.
42. Urucuena (listed by McQuown (1955) as an alternate name for Urucuiana, which is a dialect of Oyana).
43. Waiwai = Uaiuai = Uaieue = Ouayeone. 150. Guyana and Brazil.
44. Wayumara = Uaiumare = Guimara. Possibly extinct. Brazil.
45. *Xiparicot = Shiparicot = Chipa. Venezuela.
46. Yabarana. Ds. also Curasicana, Wokiare = Uaiquiare.

NORTHWESTERN
47. *Arvi. Colombia.
48. *Bubure = Coronado. May not be extinct. Venezuela.
49. *Buga. Colombia.
50. Burede. Venezuela.
51. Camaniba. Colombia.
52. Carare. Ds. *Colima = Tapas (trs. Curipa, Marpapi, *Murca), Naura, Nauracoto. Venezuela.

53. *Carate. Venezuela.
54. *Cauca. Ds. (?) Ancerma (trs. also Caramanta, Cartama, Guaca, Nori), Antioquia (trs. also Buritica, Corome, Evéjico), Arma (tr. also Pozo), Quimbaya (trs. also Paucura, Picara, Carrapa). Colombia.
55. *Cenu = Zenu. Ds. (?) Cenufanu, Nutabare = Nutabé, Tahami. Colombia.
56. Chaké. Ds. also Macoa, Pariri, Tucuco. Venezuela.
57. *Chanco. Peru.
58. *Gorrón. Colombia.
59. *Guanao. Colombia (?), Venezuela.
60. Mape. Ds. Aguas Blancas, Aricuaisa, Catatumbo, Chapara, Cunaguasata, Irapeno, Macoa, Macoita, Manastara, Maraca, Sicacao. Tucuco, Yasa. Venezuela.
61. *Muso = Muzo. Colombia.
62. Opón. Colombia.
63. *Panche. Ds. Guali, Guazquia, Marqueton. Colombia.
64. *Patagón. Peru.
65. *Patangoro = Palenque. Ds. Doyma, Guagua, Guaríno, Tamana, Zamana. Colombia.
66. Pemeno. Venezuela.
67. *Pijao. Ds. Cacataima, Cutiba, Irico, Quindio, Toche. Colombia.
68. Yarigui = Quiriquire = Kirikire. Ds. Araya, Chiarcota, Guamaca, Tholomeo, Topocoro, Topoyo. Venezuela.
69. *Zapara. Venezuela.

SOUTHERN
70. Akuku = Acucu. Brazil.
71. Apalakiri = Apalaquiri = Calapalo. 250. Brazil.
72. *Apiaca. Possibly not extinct. Brazil.
73. *Arara = Ajujure. Possibly not extinct. Brazil.
74. Bacaïri. 250. Brazil.
75. Guicurú = Kurkuro = Cuicutl. 250. Brazil.
76. Mariape-Nahuqua. Brazil.
77. Naravute. Brazil.
78. Palmela = Palmella. Sa do Norte tributary of the Amazon; southwestern-most Carib language. Brazil.
79. *Pimenteira. Parraiba River of Brazil far east of any other Carib language. Brazil.
80. *Timirem = Pariri. Possibly not extinct. Brazil.
81. Yamarikuma = Jamarikuma = Jamaricuma. Brazil.
82. Yarumá = Jarumá. Brazil.

AFFILIATION. Member of MACRO-CARIB within GE-PANO-CARIB.

MACRO-CARIB PHYLUM

GROUPING. Greenberg (1960a) includes three language families and one isolated language (Cucura) in MACRO-CARIB. This phylum is represented in every country of the northern half of South America except Ecuador. The CARIB family (q.v.) is the most extensive and by far the largest, whereas the PEBA-YAGUAN (q.v.) and WITOTOAN (q.v.) families are quite small and restricted almost entirely to Peru and Colombia as western representatives of MACRO-CARIB.

Greenberg is the first to accord both PEBA-YAGUAN and WITOTOAN a position parallel to CARIB in a larger MACRO-CARIB grouping. The PEBA-YAGUAN family was first considered independent, then of probable CARIBAN affiliation, but later, again, as independent. Whereas WITOTOAN was originally thought to be CARIBAN, it was later classified by some as a member of MACRO-TUPI-GUARANI.

*1. *Cucura. Formerly spoken near the Verde River of Mato Grosso, Brazil.

   AFFILIATION. Member of GE-PANO-CARIB.

*Cataonian. A non-INDO-EUROPEAN language of ancient Asia Minor known chiefly from Greek traditions (Ruge 1919).
   AFFILIATION. None known.

CAUCASIAN

   GROUPING. Three groups of CAUCASIAN are listed below:
      NORTHEAST CAUCASIAN (languages numbered 1 through 27);
      NORTHWEST CAUCASIAN (languages numbered 28 through 30);
      SOUTH CAUCASIAN (languages numbered 31 through 33).
The relationship between these groups is not altogether certain. They appear to be quite remotely related, e.g., more so than languages in different branches of INDO-EUROPEAN; it is even possible that SOUTH CAUCASIAN may not be genetically related to the northern groups. Kuipers (1963) reports that a genetic relationship between the three groups is taken for granted by Soviet linguists, and that at least the affinity of NORTHEAST and NORTHWEST CAUCASIAN is probable. John Lotz (in Geiger 1959) regards the exact genetic relationship as 'obscure'; see also Meillet and Cohen (1952).

   Eleven members of the Caucasian groups have official status as literary languages:
      Abaza (20,000, the Tapanta dialect of Abkhaz) and Abxazo (65,000, the Abzhui dialect of Abkhaz);
         Avar (270,000);
         Chechen (419,000);
         Dargwa (158,000);
         Georgian (2,700,000);
         Ingush (106,000);
         Kabardian (204,000);
         Lak (64,000);
         Lezghian (223,000);
         Tabasaran (35,000);
         West Circassian (80,000).
Of these, only Georgian has an alphabet of its own; the remainder use the Cyrillic alphabet.

These languages are spoken by five million people in the Caucasus area of the Soviet Union, stretching east and west from the Black Sea to the Caspian Sea, and north and south from the middle reaches of the Kuban River to Iran.

NORTHEAST CAUCASIAN. Languages in this group are divided into four subgroups: AVARO-ANDI-DIDO (languages numbered 1 through 12); LAK-DARGWA (13 and 14); LEZGHIAN = SAMUR (15 to 24); VEJNAX (25 through 27). 1,250,000 speakers, mostly in Daghestan ASSR near the Caspian coast, but also in the Azerbaidzhan SSR, and the Georgian SSR.

AVARO-ANDI-DIDO. These 12 languages are located in an area of the southern Sulak River and its tributaries (Andi Koissu, Avar Koissu, and Kazikumukh Koissu). Avar (2) serves as the literary language of people speaking all the other languages of the AVARO-ANDI-DIDO group. Languages numbered (1), (3), (4), (6), (7), (10) and (11) constitute an ANDI subgroup; languages numbered (5), (8), (9), (12) constitute a DIDO subgroup.

1. Andi. Ds. Gagatl, Kvanxidatl, Munin, Rikvani, Zilo. 8,000.
2. Avar. Ds. Northern, including Salatav, Xunzax = Khunzakh; Southern, including Ancux = Antsukh, Andalal-Gidatl, Batlux, Hid, Karax = Karakh, Zakataly = Char; transitional, including Bacadin, Kaxib, Keleb, Shulanin, Untib. 270,000. Daghestan SSR and to the south in the Azerbaidzhan SSR.
3. Axvax = Akhvakh. Less than 3,000.
4. Bagulal = Kvanada. D. also Tlisi.
5. Bezhita = Kapucha. D. also Gunzib = Xunzal = Khunzal. 1,600.
6. Botlix = Botlikh. D. also Godoberi. 3,500.
7. Chamalal. Ds. Gadyri, including Gachitl, Kvankhi; Gakvari, including Agvali, Richaganik, Tsumada, Tsumada-Urukh; Gigatl.
8. Dido = Tsez = Cez. 7,000.
9. Ginux = Ginukh. 200.
10. Karata. Ds. Anchix, Tokita.
11. Tindi. 5,000.
12. Xvarshi = Khvarshi. D. also Inxokvari. 1,800.

LAK-DARGWA. These two languages are spoken in an area of Daghestan ASSR which extends for 40 miles from the southern Kazikumukh Koissu to the south and east.

13. Dargwa. Ds. Axusha = Ak(k)husha, Cudaxar = Tsudakhar, Dejbuk, Kajtak = Xajdak = Kaitak, Kubachi, Muirin, Sirxin, Uraxa-Urkarax, Xarbuk. 158,000.
14. Lak. Ds. Ashtikulin, Balxar-Calakan = Balkhar-Tsalakan, Kumux = Kumukh, Vicxin = Vitskhin, Vixlin = Vikhlin. 64,000.

LEZGHIAN = SAMUR. The ten languages which follow represent the southernmost of the four subgroups of NORTHEAST CAUCASIAN; spoken in south Daghestan, in adjacent parts of Azerbaidzhan SSR, and in the Georgian SSR.

15. Agul. Ds. also Gekxun, Keren, Koshan. 7,000. Daghestan SSR.
16. Archi. 859. Daghestan SSR.

17. Budux = Budukh. 2,000. Azerbaidzhan SSR.
18. Kryts = Kryc = Kryz. Ds. also Dzhek, Xaput = Khaput. 2,600. Azerbaidzhan SSR.
19. Lezghian. Ds. Axty = Akhty, Garkin (with Anyx, Staly), Gjunej, Kjuri = Kiuri, Kuba. 223,000. Daghestan SSR and Azerbaidzhan SSR.
20. Rutul. Ds. Borch, Ixreko-Muxrek, Shina. 10,000. Daghestan ASSR and Azerbaidzhan SSR.
21. Tabasaran. Ds. Northern = Khanag, Southern. 35,000. Daghestan SSR.
22. Tsaxur = Tsakhur = Caxur. Ds. Kirmitso-Lek, Mikik, Mishlesh. 11,000. Daghestan ASSR and Azerbaidzhan SSR.
23. Udi. Ds. Nidzh = Nizh, Vartashen. 2,000. Azerbaidzhan SSR and Georgian SSR.
24. Xinalug = Khinalug. 100–1,500. Azerbaidzhan SSR.

VEJNAX = VEINAKH = SAMURIAN = KIST

25. Bats = Bac. 2,500. Georgian SSR.
26. Chechen. Ds. Akka = Aux, Cheberloj, Greater Chechen, Galanchog, Itumkala. 419,000. Once located in the now abolished Chechen-Ingush ASSR, a large number of the speakers now live in Kazakh SSR, and a few in the Georgian SSR. Akka is a transitional dialect to Ingush, and the latter is sometimes treated as a dialect of Chechen.
27. Ingush. 106,000. Kazakh SSR, and a few in the Georgian SSR.

NORTHWEST CAUCASIAN. Nearly 500,000 speakers in widely scattered areas on both sides of the main chain of mountains from the Kuban River to Abkhazia to North Osetia.

28. Abxazo = (Abkhaz-)Abaza = Abazin = Abkhaz. Ds. Abzhui, Ashxar = Ashkarwa = Abaza, Bzyb, Samurzakan, Tapanta = Abaza. 85,000. In two locations in the U.S.S.R.: the Abkhaz ASSR south of the mountains along the coast of the Black Sea, and in a group of 15 villages located north of the Cherkes Autonomous Oblast (near the Kuban headwaters); also in Turkey (8,602).
29. Circassian = Adyghe = Adygei = Cherkes. Ds. East Circassian = Upper Circassian = Kabardian, including Baksan, Beslenei, Cherkes, Greater Kabardian, Lesser Kabardian, Kuban, Malka, Mozdok (between the Upper Kuban and Zelenchuk rivers in the Cherkes Autonomous Oblast, and in the eastern part of the Adygei Autonomous Oblast); West Circassian = Lower Circassian = Kiakh = Kjax, including Abadzex = Abadekh, Bzhedux = Bzhedukh, Natuxaj = Natukhaj, Shapsug (including Xukuchi), Temirgoi = Chemgui (located in numerous small enclaves scattered along the Kuban River and its tributaries in the Adygei Autonomous Oblast, and also spoken southeast of Tuapse on the Taman Peninsula). 275,000. Soviet Union, Turkey (66,691), and smaller groups in Syria, Jordan, Israel and Iraq. The two groups, West and East Circassian, may possibly be mutually unintelligible languages; each constitutes the basis of a separate literary language.

30. Ubyx = Ubykh. Nearly extinct. It was spoken north of Abxaz along the Black Sea coast; the last speakers are now near Istanbul, Turkey.

SOUTH CAUCASIAN = KARTVELIAN. 3,000,000. Soviet Union, Turkey, Iran.

31. Georgian. Ds. Eastern, including Ferejdan (in Iran), Ingilo, Kartlian, Kaxetian = Kakhetian, Moxev = Mokhev, Mtiul, Pshav, Tush, Xevsur = Khevsur; Western, including Gurian-Adzhar, Imeretian, Imerxev (in Turkey), Lexchum = Lechkhum, Racha. 2,700,000. Soviet Union (Georgian SSR, Azerbaidzhan SSR), Turkey, Iran. Georgian is the only CAUCASIAN language with over a million speakers, and is the oldest written CAUCASIAN language (dating from about the fifth century when Christian missionaries introduced the Greek alphabet; perhaps influenced by an earlier Aramaic script).

32. Svan. Ds. Lower Bal, Upper Bal, Lashx, Lentex. 13,142–23,000. Northwestern Georgian SSR in the mountainous regions.

33. Zan. Ds. Laz = Chan, including Eastern (with Chxala = Chkhala, and Xopa = Hopa) and Western (with Atina, and Vice-Arxava = Vitse-Arkhava-49,000 total); Mingrelian, including Samurzakan-Zugdidi = Western, and Senaki = Eastern (300,000). 349,000: Soviet Union (302,000); Turkey (47,000). In the Soviet Union Zan is spoken in the Georgian SSR north of the Rion River and in and around the cities of the Abkhaz SSR.

AFFILIATION. Attempts have been made to relate CAUCASIAN genetically with SEMITIC (Trombetti 1902, 1903; Youchmanov 1948), INDO-EUROPEAN (Bopp 1847), Burushaski in India (Morgenstierne 1935), and Sumerian (Bouda 1938). The most promising relationship appears to be that with Basque (Trombetti 1926; Lafon 1933; Bouda 1949); the two together are called 'Ibero-Caucasian' (Holmer 1947), a term sometimes used to refer only to CAUCASIAN.

CENTRAL and SOUTHERN CELEBES (Geographical)

GROUPING. Esser (1938) lists eight apparently coordinate groups of languages on Celebes (Sulawesi) and adjacent small islands.

Dyen's (1965) sample included languages from only four of Esser's groups. Languages from one of these groups ('Gorontalo') were classified with Philippine languages in NORTHWEST AUSTRONESIAN; one language from another one of Esser's groups — his 'Philippine' group — was classified as unsubgrouped in HESPERONESIAN, and another in the more divergent NORTHERN CELEBES was classified as unsubgrouped in MALAYO-POLYNESIAN. From two of Esser's other groups, the four languages compared by Dyen — Bare'e, Buginese Kulawi, Makasarese — formed a CELEBES group. Dyen's classification subgroups Bare'e (29, below) and Kulawi (33) as BAREIC, and Buginese (8) and Makasarese (10) as BUGIC. This division supports the classification of Esser in which Bare'e and Kulawi are included in a TORADJA group while Buginese and Makasarese are included in a SOUTH CELEBES group. Though evidence has not yet been presented to show a special relationship between these and Esser's other three non-Philippine-linked groups — BUNGKU-LAKI, LOINANG-BANGGAI, and MUNA-BUTUNG — these three groups are also listed below.

BUNGKU-LAKI = BUNGKU-MORI

1. Bungku = Nahina. Ds. also Epe plus Routa = Nahina, Marumeme = Maronene = Nahina including Kabaena, Rete = Naida, Tulambatu = Hileo, Watu = Hina, Wowoni = Wawoni = Naida. 180,000. Eastern part of central Celebes and Kabaena Island off southeastern end of Celebes. Subgrouped with (3), Laki (Uhlenbeck 1967).
2. Laiwui = Tambuoki = Kioki. Listed by Salzner (1960) as a dialect of Laki.
3. Laki = Lalaki = Lolaki. Ds. Asera Wanua = Noie, Labea'u = Noihe, Waru = Nehina, Wiwi Rano = Nohina. 125,000. Southeastern Celebes.
4. Landawe.
5. Mapute.
6. Mekongka = Norio. Ds. also Konio, Tamboki.
7. Mori = Aikoa. Ds. Aikoa = West Mori, Padoë = Alalao, Petasia = East Mori = Nahina, Soroako plus Karongsi and Sinongko = Nahina, Tambe'e = South Mori = Ajo. 200,000. Central Celebes.

The following three names and population figures from an Indonesian source are probably alternate names (or places where spoken) for languages listed above rather than additional languages of the group: Bingkokak ? 150,000. Kendari ? 500,000. Kolaka ? 200,000.

SOUTH CELEBES

8. Buginese = De'. D. also Sindjai. 2,500,000. Southern Celebes, western part of central and northern Celebes, with large settlements in coastal southeast Borneo, especially in Kutai, Pasir, and Pegatan.
9. Luwu'. 500,000 may include speakers of the Sindjai dialect of Buginese. Southeastern Celebes. Treated as included in the Sindjai dialect of Buginese by Salzner (1960).
10. Makasarese = Makassar = Macassar = Tawna = Tena. Ds. also Selajar = Salayar = Salayer = Siladja = Silajara, Tonthian = Bonta'eng, Turateya = Turatea. 900,000 in south Celebes, possibly not including 200,000 on Salajar Island just south of Celebes.
11. Mamudju = Udai. D. also Talumpa = Tenteria.
12. Mandarese = Andian. Ds. Balangnipa = Taë', Binuang = Taë', Madjene = Ida = Andiang, Tjampalagian = Tasing, Tjenrana = Andian. 250,000.
13. Masenrempulu. Ds. Batu Lapa, Duri, Enrekang, Kasa, Leta, Maiwa. 250,000.
14. Pitu-ulunna-salu = Pitu Uluna Salu. Ds. Mamasa, Mambië, Mangki = Maki, Rante Bulawan, Tabulahan, Tubi = Ade. 175,000. Mamasa may rather apply to a larger group, possibly the whole language.
15. Sa'dan = Sadang. Ds. Makale, Masamba, Rante Pao, Rongkong plus Kanandede.
16. Seko.
17. Toala.
18. Wotu = La'edo.

Ara ? 75,000.

Bira ? 75,000.
Kadjang ? 50,000.
Tiro ? 75,000.

LOINANG-BANGGAI

19. Balantak = Kosian. 125,000. Eastern part of central Celebes.
20. Banggai. 200,000. Banggai Islands east of central Celebes and western part of Sula in Moluccas.
21. Bobongko = Andio'o = Imbao'o. Possibly extinct.
22. Loinang = Loindang = Madi. D. also Saluan. 100,000 as the number of Saluan may include Loinang. Eastern part of central Celebes.

MUNA-BUTUNG

23. Butung. 200,000 may include speakers of Tukangbesi, below. Butung Island and Tukangbesi Islands off southeastern Celebes.
24. Muna = Mina. Ds. Kapontori = Akido, Northern Muna, Southern Muna. 200,000. Muna Island off southeastern Celebes.
25. Tukangbesi. Ds. also Bonerate including Kalaotoa and Karompa, Wantji = Binongko. Tukangbesi and Bonerate Islands off southeastern Celebes.
26. Wolio. D. also Lajolo = Da'ang. Southern part of Salajer Island off southern Celebes.

TORADJA. All in central Celebes.

27. Bada' = Ti'ara. Ds. also Besoa = Behoa, Hanggira = Da'ara.
28. Banggakoro = Ado.
29. Bare'e. Ds. Lego, Pebato; ds. also Lala'eo = Aunde'e = Nde'e = Unde'e, Po'u mBoto = Are'e, Salu Maoge = A'e'e, Taa consisting of Tare'e including Ampona = Ampana and Wana plus Togia = Tandjo'u = Una-Una. Over 325,000 in central Celebes and Togian Islands.
30. Batui = Baha.
31. Bela = mBelala = Baria.
32. Ganti = Ndepu'u.
33. Kulawi = Moma. D. also Lindu = Tado.
34. Laiwonu = Iba.
35. Leboni = Ha'uwa. Ds. also Rampi = Lambu, Rato.
36. Lore = Lole = Unde. 100,000–140,000.
37. Napu = Bara.
38. Palu = Kaili = Ledo'. Palu d. includes Doï; ds. also Pakuli = Ado, Sidondo = Edo, Sigi = Idja. 200,000–300,000.
39. Pekawa.
40. Pipikoro = Uma Aria. Ds. Benahu = Aria, Uma including Boku, Kantewu, Peana, Tole'e, Winantu-Gimpu.
41. Rapangkaka = Aria.
42. Sausu = Ta'a Dolo. D. also Dolage = Ta'a Doë.
43. Sinohoan = Daido = Ido = Idore'e.
44. Tamungkolowi = Dompa.

45. Tara = Parigi. 125,000. Northern part of central Celebes.
46. Tawaelia = Baria.
47. Tawaili. Ds. Raii = Northern, Torai = Southern.
48. Tobaku = Ompa.
Pamona ? 100,000.
Toradja ? 250,000.

AFFILIATION. Of the languages listed above, four appear in Dyen's classification, forming the CELEBES subgroup of HESPERONESIAN within AUSTRONESIAN; it is
possible that all the others may be classified with these four (see "GROUPING"
above) as also HESPERONESIAN.

NORTHERN CELEBES (Geographical)

GROUPING. Esser (1938) groups the languages listed below into two subgroups.
Within the MINHASA group, (4) is subgrouped with (6), and (2) with (3) and (5). Hardly
any information is available on the languages of the TOMINI subgroup (Uhlenbeck
1967). Additional names are added from Salzner (1960). All are spoken in the northern
part of Celebes Island (Sulawesi).

MINHASA = TON
1. Mongondow = Mongondou = Bolaang-Mongondow = Minhasa ? Ds. also
   Dumoga, Lolajan, Lolak, Pasi, Ponosakan. 400,000.
2. Tombulu.
3. Tondano = Tolou = Tolour. D. also Ka ʔkas-Remboken.
4. Tonsawang.
5. Tonsea'.
6. Tontemboan = Tompakewa. Ds. also Langoan, Tompaso (together
   Makela'i = Maotow), Sonder which, together with Tontemboan d. =
   Matana'i = Maore'.
Ratahan ? 150,000. May be an alternate name of one of the above.

TOMINI
7. Balaesan = Balaisang = Pajo.
8. Bolano = Boano = Djidja.
9. Dampelasa = Dian.
10. Kasimbar = Adjio = Tadjio = Ta'adjio. 100,000.
11. Petapa = Andje = Lole = Tadje.
12. Tinombo = Laudje = Ampibabo. 125,000.
13. Tomini = Tiadje = Tialo = Dondo.
14. Tontoli = Tolitoli = Gage.
15. Umalasa = Nda'u.

AFFILIATION. Esser groups the MINHASA languages with Sangir and the closely
related languages of neighboring islands as a 'Philippine' group of the languages of
Celebes. In Dyen's (1965) lexicostatistical classification, Tontemboan (6, above), the
only one of the languages compared, remains outside the level on which PHILIPPINE

languages are grouped with CELEBES languages within AUSTRONESIAN.

CELTIC = KELTIC

GROUPING. Various groups of Celtic speakers have been found at different times in an east-west distribution from Anatolia to the Atlantic. The CELTIC expansion on the European continent was impeded by Teutonic tribes in the north and by speakers of ITALIC languages in the south; the expansion became a retreat to the west after facing Roman armies.

That Breton is now the only extant variety of CELTIC on the Continent is a consequence of back-tracking: This language was reintroduced from Great Britain to France by refugees who fled from Anglo-Saxon raiders in Britain.

The hypothesis of an 'ITALO-CELTIC' proto-language was supported by Meillet (1908). While concurring with the general consensus that ITALIC and CELTIC are closely related, Watkins (1966) denies that there is any evidence for reconstructability of Proto-Italo-Celtic. But Hamp (personal communication) reports, without regret, that Cowgill has recently come to the defense of the 'ITALO-CELTIC' hypothesis.

Two main groups of CELTIC languages are recognized: BRYTHONIC and GOIDELIC. The distinction between these two groups may be irrelevant for Gaulish (3). Breton, Cornish, Gaulish (?), and Welsh are classified under BRYTHONIC; Irish Gaelic, Manx, and Scottish Gaelic under GOIDELIC; the last three form a dialect continuum (Hamp, personal communication).

BRYTHONIC = BRITTONIC CELTIC = P-CELTIC

1. Breton. Ds. Cornouaillais (southwestern portion of the Peninsula of Brittany around town of Quimper), Leonard (almost northern tip of peninsula), Tregorois (northern part of peninsula around Treguier), Vannetais (southern portion of the peninsula, around town of Vannetais). 900,000. France, Peninsula of Brittany. Probably an early off-shoot of Cornish.
2. *Cornish. Believed extinct since before the 1800s. Formerly Cornwall, England.
3. *Gaulish. Extinct about 500 A.D. From Anatolia (where a Celtic language was spoken by the Galatians) through Italy to France.
4. Welsh = Cymraeg. Ds. Northern Welsh (counties of Anglesey, Carnarvonshire, Merionethshire); Southern (counties of Cardigan, Carmarthen, Merionethshire), Patagonian Welsh (spoken in Chubut Territory, Patagonia, in South America in 1891).100,000 monolingual speakers; 652,750 bilingual. Wales.

GOIDELIC = Q-CELTIC

5. Irish Gaelic. Ds. Connacht in the central area, Leinster in the southeast, Munster in the southwest, Ulster in the north. Standard Irish is based on the Munster dialect. 500,000. Republic of Ireland, and North Ireland. The half-million or more speakers reported by the government may be an exaggeration. The history of Irish is divided into four periods: the Ogham inscriptions period (300 A.D.–600 A.D. ?), Old Irish (600–900 A.D.), Middle Irish (900–1600), Modern Irish (1600–present).

6. *Manx. Formerly spoken on the Isle of Man; extinct in this century.
7. Scottish Gaelic. Concentrated in the north and central counties of Ross, Cromarthy, Sutherland, and Inverness in Scotland, and in the western off-shore islands of Hebrides and the Island of Skye; Nova Scotia (7,000); Cape Breton Island, Canada. Most of the 75,000 Gaelic speakers in Scotland are bilingual; 1,079 monolinguals. Scottish Gaelic originated from a group of Old Irish speakers who migrated to Scotland (beginning in the latter half of the fifth century); it diverged sufficiently in the Modern Irish period to be accorded separate language status.
8. *Pictish. Formerly spoken in Scotland but not necessarily as a CELTIC language.

AFFILIATION. Member of INDO-EUROPEAN.

CHADIC = NIGER-CHAD = BENUE-CHAD

GROUPING. Most languages of the CHADIC family are spoken in an area extending from the area of Lake Chad in Chad to the borderlands of Nigeria, Cameroon, and Central African Republic; Hausa is exceptional in being spoken not only in these borderlands, but also in a much wider area of West Africa, including all of Nigeria, and parts of other nations, as Dahomey, Togo, and Ghana.

The grouping of CHADIC languages given below follows essentially the classification of Newman and Ma (1966) who revised previous classifications. That by Delafosse (1924) was merely geographic; Lukas (1936) proposed a classificatory bifurcation, CHADO-HAMITIC versus MANDARA; later, Lukas (in Westermann and Bryan 1952) added language names to each of his two major groups, but questioned whether these two groups could be combined in a single CHADIC family. Greenberg (1966) abandoned the Lukas bifurcation; instead, he classified his CHAD languages in nine groups, but anticipated that some of these might be subgrouped under fewer major groups. Terry (1971) summarizes classificatory work on CHADIC.

The Newman-Ma classification (with the addition of some language names not included by Newman-Ma but included by Lukas) is reflected in the following list of CHADIC languages, divided into two major groups. One major group of Newman-Ma is BIU-MANDARA; this appears below (with synonyms and near-synonyms) as EAST CHADIC = BIU-MANDARA = CHADIC = MANDARA; Greenberg's groups *3, 4, 5,* and *6* are incorporated in EAST CHADIC in the list below. The other major group in Newman-Ma is PLATEAU-SAHEL; this appears below as WEST CHADIC = PLATEAU-SAHEL = CHADO-HAMITIC; Greenberg's groups *1, 2, 7, 8, 9* are incorporated in WEST CHADIC in the following list. Each major group includes subgroups, as indicated below (after Lukas, for the most part).

Altogether 10,000,000 speakers, of whom 1,000,000 are speakers of CHADIC languages other than Hausa and the other 9,000,000 are speakers of Hausa (of whom 6,000,000 are native speakers); some estimates are as high as 12,000,000, leaving 3,000,000 who speak Hausa as a second language used in trade.

EAST CHADIC = BIU-MANDARA = CHADIC = MANDARA

BATA. Nigeria (Adamawa Province), Cameroon.

1. Bachama = Bacama = Bashamma = Gboare = Abacama = Besema = Bwareba. 11,850. Nigeria, near Numan.
2. Bat(t)a = Demsa Batta = Gboati = Bete = Birsa = Dunu. D. also Bata of Garoua (2,000). 23,000. Cameroon.
3. Cheke = Mapodi = Mubi = Shede = Gujugulu ? Cameroon.
4. Demsa.
5. Gudu = Gudo. D. also Kumbi. Nigeria.
6. Malabu.
7. Njai = Nzangi = Zani = Zany = Njel = Njeny = Nzangyim. Ds. also Holma = Kurndel, Gudi = Gude, Jen, Kobo(ts)chi, Njei. 10,000. Cameroon.
8. Sukur = Sugur = Ssugur. D. also Gudur = Mpsakali = Shakiri ? 1,300. Cameroon.
9. Zumu = Jimo = Zomo = Jirai. Ds. also Muleng, Wadi = Vadi. Nigeria.

BURA

10. Bur(r)a = Bourrah = Huve = Huviya = Toxrica. Ds. = Trs. Ba(r)bur(r) = Babir = Pabir, Burakokra (23,150). 88,700. Nigeria, Cameroon.
11. Chib(b)ak = Chibbuk = Chib(b)ok = Kibaku = Kabak. Nigeria.
12. Kilba = Xibba = Ndirma = Wuding = Pella. 22,800. Nigeria: Adamawa Province, Kilba district.
13. Margi = Marghi = Mirki = Buxidim. Ds. also Duhu, Lassa, Maya, Minthla, Molgoy, Plains Margi. 151,200. Nigeria: Bornu and Adamawa provinces.
14. Podokwo = Paduko = Padoko = Padokwa. Cameroon. Westermann and Bryan (1952) list this language in the MATAKAN-MANDARA group.

HIGI

15. Fali of Kiria. Westermann and Bryan place this language in the BURA group.
16. Fali of Mubi.
17. Fali of Yilbu = Jilbu.
18. Higi = Hiji = Hidj = Kamum = Kapsiki = Hill Margi. Ds. Higi Sinna, Higi Wula, Humsi, Kapsiki, Moda. 15,200. Cameroon.
19. Woga (= Wudir. Ds. also Tur(u), Vemgo, Vizik.

MATAKAM-MANDARA. Greenberg treats the languages here in three subgroups, his groups *4* (languages numbered 20, 21, 23, 26), *5* (Giddar, language numbered 22), and *6* (Mandara, language numbered 25). Newman and Ma group Mandara (25) with other groups in EAST CHADIC (their BIU-MANDARA), but do not include Giddar (22) and Greenberg's group *4* in their BIU-MANDARA.

20. Balda ?
21. Daba. Ds. Fali, Gawar = Gauar = Gaouar = Fali, Hina = Daba Hina = Ina, Musgoi = Musgoy = Musugeu = Musugoi. 13,100. Cameroon, mainly Mokolo subdivision.

22. Gid(d)er = G(u)idar. 37,500. Cameroon (30,000; Guidar subdivision), Chad (7,500; Lere division).
23. Gisiga = Guissiga = Gisohiga = Guissiga Maturua = Muturua = Rum. 18,400. Cameroon, subdivision Kaele.
24. Gwoza = Gwázà.
25. Mandara = Wandala = Ndara = Wandara. D. also Gamergu (9,000). Trs. Gwanje, Jampalam, Kamburwama, Masfeima, Mazagwa, Zlogba. 30,000-40,000. Nigeria, Cameroon.
26. Matakam = Bulahai. D. also Mofu = Muffo = Muf(f)u = Mofou. Over 60,000. Cameroon.
27. Mora. Chad: Mora Massif.
28. Ngaslawe.

TERA
29. Ga'anda = Ganda = Kanda = Gabin = Kabin. 5,400. Nigeria: Adamawa Province.
30. Hin(n)a = Hunna = Pilimdi. 4,350. Nigeria: Tera district and Bornu Province.
31. Jer(r)a = Jara = Jerawa. 2,000. Nigeria: Bornu and Bauchi provinces.
32. Tera = Terawa = Nyimashi = Kemaltu. Ds. also Boga = Poka, Hona = Kilba = Fiteriya = Huene = Bua = Kuturincha = Kuteringa (6,600), Puthlundi (13,154). Nigeria: Adamawa, Gumburku, Bornu, Bauchi provinces.

WEST CHADIC = PLATEAU-SAHEL = CHADO-HAMITIC
AFAWA (after Greenberg)
33. Afawa. 8,000.
34. Barawa of Dass.
35. Diryawa.
36. Gezawa.
37. Miyāwa.
38. Seiyawa. 2,000.
39. Sirawa.
40. Warjawa. 30,000.

BOLEWA
41. Bolewa = Bolenchi = Bolea = Borlawa = Bolawa. Ds. Bara, Fika = Fikankayen = Anpika. 32,000. Nigeria: Bornu and Bauchi provinces.
42. Chongee.
43. Kanakuru = Dera = Bilauum = (Embe)linga = Shellengcha = Tsaba = Gasi. 11,300. Nigeria: Adamawa Province.
44. Kirifawa.
45. Ngamo = Ngamaya = Gamawa. 17,800. Nigeria: Bornu and Bauchi provinces.
46. Pero.
47. Pia = Pai. 2,500.

48. Tangole = Jagjage = Kumba. Ds.   Afudu = Yaffudawa,   Nimalto.
36,000. Nigeria: Bauchi Province.

HAUSA-GWANDARA

49. Hausa = Hausaawaa = Afuno. Ds. Eastern Hausa, Western Hausa.
6,000,000 native speakers. Mainly northern Nigeria and adjoining parts
of Niger.

50. Gwandara. 15,000.

KOTOKO

51. Buduma = Budduma = Bouddouma = Yidena = Yedina. D. also
Kuri = Kakáa. 45,000. Chad: on islands in northeastern and southeastern Lake Chad, some parts of shore.

52. Kotoko = Makari = Mantage = Madaganye = Mida = Labang. Ds.
also   Afade = Avade,   Gulfei = Goulfei = Malbe = Malgwe =
Ngwalkwe, Gwalakwe, Kotoko Daa = Lagwane, Kuseri = Msirr =
'Ũsuri = Mirr,   Logone = Lagwane   (Birni),   Makari = Mpháada,
*Ngala, Shawi = Shoe. 30,000–50,000. Chad: south of Lake Chad
on the Logone River. The people of Ngala and Klesem, on the Shari
River, no longer speak Kotoko, but have adopted Kanuri (NILO-
SAHARAN).

MASA

53. Dari. Ds. Kado, Peve, Tshimiang = čimiaŋ. Chad.

54. Kulung.

55. Lame.

56. Marba. 4,750. Chad, Logone River west of Lai.

57. Masa = Masana = Walai. Ds. Bana(n)a, Yagoua. 52,300. Chad,
Cameroon.

58. Musei = Musey = Mussoi. Ds. Hoho = Banana, (H)ollom, Masa
Gbaya, Ngame. 48,000. Chad-Cameroon borderland.

59. Musgu = Muzgu = Musgum = Mousgou = Musguw = Musgo =
Mulwi = Mamzokoi = Muzugu. Ds. Abi, Beege, Gwai, Pus
(Cameroon), Vulum. 25,000. Chad-Cameroon borderland. This is the
only member of Greenberg's group 7.

60. Sigila. Cameroon, east of Mora.

NGIZIM

61. Auyokawa.

62. Bade = Bede = Bedde. 32,000. Nigeria: Bornu Province.

63. Maha = Magha. Nigeria: Bornu Province, Gujba Division. Placed
in this group by Greenberg (1966) after Newman (1965).

64. Mober = Mobber = Mobeur = Mabar = Matur. 44,800. Nigeria
(Mober and Kanembu districts), Niger.

65. Ngizim = Ngizzem = Ngazam = Kirdiwat = Walu = Gwazum.
39,250. Nigeria: Bornu and Kano Provinces.

66. Shirawa.

PLATEAU

67. Angas(s) = Kerang = Karang = Karang-Ma. Ds. Hill Angas, Plains

Angas = Gurna. 55,250. Nigeria: Plateau Province, Pankshin Division.
68. Ankwe = Kemai = Goemai. 13,500. Nigeria: Plateau Province, Shendam Division.
69. Bwol.
70. Chip.
71. Dimuk.
72. Gerka.
73. Goram.
74. Jorto.
75. Kwolla.
76. Miriam.
77. Montal.
78. Sura = Maghavul. 20,100. Nigeria: Plateau Province, Pankshin Division.
79. Tal.
80. Ron = Baron = Chala = Nafunfia. 11,600. Nigeria: Plateau Province, Pankshin Division.

SOMRAI-SOKORO. This is Greenberg's group 9. Additional language names are from Westermann and Bryan's (1952) SOKORO-MUBI group of their CHADO-HAMITIC, and Tucker and Bryan's (1956) SOMRAI and BUA groups (excluding Bua and Nielim, which are in ADAMAWA of ADAMAWA-EASTERN).

81. Besem(m)e = Unar = Hounar. Central African Republic.
82. 'Bidyo. D. also Waana (3,000). 13,000–14,000. Chad.
83. Buso = Bousso. 40–50. Smiths in Buosso Town.
84. Chiri.
85. Dai = Day = Sara Dai. Ds. Bouna. 600. Chad: Région Moyen-Chari, Districts Moissala and Koumra.
86. Dangaleat. 16,000. Chad: north of Jebel Geira.
87. Dormo. Central African Republic.
88. Fanya = Fana = Fania = Fanian = Mana = Kobe = Nuba? = Nouba(?). 1,500. Chad: between Lake Boli and Lake Iro.
89. Gablai = Kabalai = Lai = Sara Lai. Central African Republic.
90. Gabri = Gaberi = Tshere = Tshiri = Tsiri = Sara Ngabre. Central African Republic.
91. Gam. Central African Republic.
92. Jegu.
93. Jongor = Djongor. Ds. = Trs. Abu Telfan, Jebel Geira. 14,000–16,000. Chad.
94. Karbo.
95. Kim. Ds. Ere = Garap (1,710), Juman = Dzuman = Gerep (720), Kolobo (673), Kosap (1,600). Central African Republic.
96. Miltu = Miltou. District Bousso.
97. Modgel.
98. Mogum. Ds. Koffa (1,000), Mogum of Abu Deia (3,500), Mogum of Melfi (1,750). 6,250. Chad.

99. Mubi = Monjul. Ds. also Kajakse = Kajagise = Kadjagse = Kajaa-kisee (4,000), Masmaje (4,000), Toram (3,650), Wadai-Bergit = Bergit? 22,550. Chad: northeast of Abu Telfan.
100. Nancere = Nantcere. Ds. also Cwa = Chua = Tschwa, Kabalaï, Lele, Nantchoa. 20,000. Central African Republic; Región Logone.
101. Nangire = Nanjeri. Central African Republic.
102. Ndam(m) = Dam = Sara = Ndam. 670. Central African Republic.
103. Sarwa = Sarua = Saroua. Chad: Région Salamat, District Melfi.
104. Sokoro = Bedanga. Ds. also Barein = Baräin = Barain (1,900), Saba (1,700), Tunjur (50). Over 4,000.
105. Somrai = Somray = Somre = Somrei = Sara Soumray. 50,000. Chad-Central African Republic border.
106. Tuburi = Tupuri = Ndore. Ds. Kaele; Yagoua (Cameroon)-Fianga-Pola (Chad). 100,000. Chad, Cameroon. Westermann and Bryan classify this language as a member of 'Mbum'. Tuburi has also been classified as belonging to ADAMAWA.
107. Tumak = Toumak = Tummok = Tumok = Dije = Sara Toumak. Central African Republic.
108. Tunya = Tunia = Tounia = Sara Tounia. 800. Chad, north of Fort Archambault.

AFFILIATION. Member of AFROASIATIC.

CHAPACURA-WANHAMAN

GROUPING. One of the two major groups beside MAIPURAN within the ARAWAKAN family is CHAPACURA-WANHAMAN which is further subgrouped by Mason (1950) as follows: GUAPORE (1–9); MADEIRA (10–13); OCORONO (14–16). Half of the MADEIRA group and all of the OCORONO group are extinct. Northeastern Bolivia and adjacent Brazil.

GUAPORE GROUP. Mason (1950) divides these languages into two subgroups: CHAPACURA (2, 6, 7) and WANHAM = UANHAM = WANYAM = HUANYAM (1, 3, 4, 5, 8, 9).
 1. Cabichi = Cabishi.
 2. Chapacura = Guapore = Guarayo = Tapacura = Huachi.
 3. Cujuna = Cuijana.
 4. Cumana. D. also Cutinaa.
 5. Mataua = Matama.
 6. More = Iten = Guarayo. D. also Itoreauhip. 100.
 7. Quitemoca = Kitemoca. D. also Napeca.
 8. Uanham = Wanyam = Pawumwa. D. also Abitana.
 9. Urunumacan = Urunamacan.

MADEIRA GROUP
 10. *Jaru.
 11. Pacas Novas = Pacahanovo.

12. *Tora(z).
13. Urupa = Txapacura.

OCORONO GROUP. All extinct.
14. *Herisobocono = Herisobocona.
15. *Ororono = Rokorona. D. also Sansimoniano.
16. *San Ignacio. D. also Borija.

AFFILIATION. Member of ARAWAKAN within EQUATORIAL in ANDEAN-EQUATORIAL.

CHARI-NILE = MACRO-SUDANIC

GROUPING. The classification for CHARI-NILE followed by Greenberg (1966) includes two large groups of languages (EASTERN SUDANIC and CENTRAL SUDANIC); it also includes two ungrouped languages, Berta and Kunama, which are accordingly coordinate in classification — each with each of the two large groups of languages mentioned. Marvin Bender (1971) does not have a CHARI-NILE group, and the two ungrouped languages mentioned (Berta and Kunama) are classified as coordinate with KOMAN, directly under NILO-SAHARAN; however, Bender pairs Ingassana with Berta (instead of classifying it in EASTERN SUDANIC, as in the Greenberg classification), thereby obtaining an additional small group of two languages labeled BERTA. This is reflected in the following list, which includes the grouped and ungrouped languages under CHARI-NILE (after Greenberg) but also includes Ingassana (after Bender, if the CHARI-NILE superordinate group were omitted).

BERTA. Ethiopia-Sudan border.
　　1. Berta. Ds. Bararo, Dul, Fadon, Fazoglo = Fazughli, Fecaka = Fecamalga = Nassillok = Hameg, Gamila = Gamili = Quameli = Quamamyl(?), Gobato, Gebelawin, Mabi Tayu, Rikabiyya, Shogale = Shangalla = Hoyalee = Xojalee, Wa-dashi = Fadasi, Wakosho, Watawit = Wetawit = Bats, including Bake ? Shuru ? 28,000.
　　2. Ingassana = Tabi = Metabi = Muntabi = Mamedja = Mamidza = Kamanidi. Trs. also Agadi, Bagis, Buk, Bulmut, Kilgu, Kukuli, Mugum, Sidak. 8,000–20,000.
　3. Kunama = Cunama = Ba(a)da = Ba(a)za = Ba(a)zen = Baden. Ds. Aaimasa = Aymasa, Barka, Bita(a)ma, Ilit = Iilit, Seti(i)t(?), Sogadas, Ti(i)ka. 40,500. Ethiopia, south of the Red Sea and west to Sudan border.

CENTRAL SUDANIC (q.v.)
EASTERN SUDANIC (q.v.)

AFFILIATION. Member of NILO-SAHARAN.

CHIBCHAN

GROUPING. The CHIBCHAN languages may constitute a phylum rather than a family. The EASTERN group (numbered 1–9) clearly belong to one family, but whether the PACIFIC group (numbered 10–12) and WESTERN group (numbered 13–22) are closely enough related to each other and to the EASTERN group to be in the same family is not clear. All of the languages listed here are more closely related to each other than to the languages of other grouping within the MARCO-CHIBCHAN plylum, with the possible exception of the BARBACOAN and INTER-ANDINE family which most scholars, but not Greenberg (1960a) include in the CHIBCHAN family. The EASTERN group is divided into the ARUACO subgroup (those numbered 1, 2, 5, and possibly the three extinct languages Atangue, Guamaca, and Sanha), the CUNDIMARCAN subgroup (numbered 3, 4, 6, 8, 9), and the Rama language (7) coordinate with these two subgroups. The PACIFIC group is divided into the ISTHMIAN subgroup (numbered 10, 11) and the Yolo language (12). The WESTERN group is divided into the TALAMANCA subgroup (located in southern Costa Rica and Northern Panama and numbered 13–15, 18–22) plus Cuna (16) and Guatuso (17) (Mason 1950).

EASTERN

1. Bintucua. Colombia.
2. Cagaba = Kaggaba. Colombia.
3. *Chibcha = Muisca = Mosca. Colombia.
4. *Duit. Colombia.
5. Ica. Colombia.
6. *Morcote. Colombia.
7. Rama. D. also Melchora. Nicaragua.
8. *Sinsiga. Colombia.
9. *Tunebo = Tame. D. also Pedrazá. Colombia.
? *Atangue = Atankez. Possibly not extinct. Colombia.
? *Guamaca. Possibly not extinct. Colombia.
? *Sanha. Possibly not extinct. Colombia.

PACIFIC

10. Burica. Ds. also (may be more than one language) Chaliva, *Changuena = Changina, *Chiriluo = Chiru, Chumula = Chumulu = Chumulue, Day. Panama and Costa Rica. 700 speakers of Burica dialect.
11. Guaymi. Ds. (may be more than one language) Move = Valiente = Nortenyo (15,000), *Muite, *Muoi, Murire = Bukueta = Sabanero (10,000), *Penono-menyo. Escoria and Nata, names of towns, are also sometimes listed as dialects. Northern Panama.
12. Yolo. Colombia.
? *Aburra. Colombia.
? *Jamundi. Colombia.
? *Lile. Colombia.
? *Timba. Colombia.
? *Yameci. Colombia.

WESTERN

13. Boruca = Brunca. Ds. also *Burucaca, *Coto, *Kepo = Quepo, Turucaca. Costa Rica.

14. Bribri = Valiente. 2,000. Ds. Estrella, Pocosi Talamanca, Tariaca, Urinama Valiente. Costa Rica, Panama.
15. Cabecar = Chiripo. D. also Corrhue = Xorrhue. Costa Rica.
16. Cuna. Ds. Chucuna (mainland), *Cueva (mainland), San Blas (island — 20,000). San Blas Islands of Panama and mainland of Panama and Colombia.
17. Guatuso. D. also Corobici and possibly *Cocora and *Gotane, but the former may have been a dialect of (19). 150. Northern Costa Rica.
18. *Guetar. Costa Rica.
19. Suerre = Tucurrique-Orisa. Costa Rica.
20. Terraba = Tirribi = Tiribi = Nortenyo = Quequexque. 700. Ds. (extinct ?) probably Ara, Depso, Lari, Techbi = Teshbi, Tojar, Uren, Zhorquin = Zorquin = Yurquin. Panama.
21. Tucurrike = Tucurrique. D. also Orisa. Costa Rica.
22. *Voto. Costa Rica.

AFFILIATION. Member of MACRO-CHIBCHAN phylum.

MACRO-CHIBCHAN PHYLUM

GROUPING. One of the largest and most widespread of the South American phyla, MACRO-CHIBCHAN centers in Colombia and extends northward through Panama, Costa Rica, Nicaragua, Honduras, El Salvador, and Guatemala, and into Venezuela; southward into Ecuador, Peru, Bolivia, Brazil, and possibly the northern parts of Chile and Argentina. The languages have been subgrouped in a number of crisscrossing ways. The subgrouping here follows, essentially, that of Greenberg (1960a) with some changes based on more recent information and additions of alternate names from earlier sources. The MACRO-CHIBCHAN phylum consists of seven families and nine ungrouped languages.

Greenberg divides the MACRO-CHIBCHAN phylum into two microphyla, CHIBCHA PROPER and PAEZAN. Three subgroups comprise CHIBCHA PROPER: (1) CHIBCHAN (q.v.); (2) MISUMALPAN (q.v.) and the ungrouped languages, Paya, Xinca and Lenca; and (3) WAICAN (q.v.). The PAEZAN group includes the BARBACOAN, CHOCO, INTER-ANDINE, and JIRARAN families (q.v.), plus the remaining ungrouped languages.

The relationship between the BARBACOAN family and the other languages of MACRO-CHIBCHAN has been variously viewed. Formerly, BARBACOAN was listed as separate from MACRO-CHIBCHAN by Brinton (1891) and Chamberlain (1913), but later was considered by Jijón y Caamaño (1941–43) to be a part of the WESTERN group of the CHIBCHAN family. A special relationship has been recognized between the BARBACOAN and INTER-ANDINE languages; Greenberg (1960a) places both within his PAEZAN subdivision.

The CHOCO family was formerly classified as independent or CHIBCHAN, then with CARIBAN by Rivet (1943–44) and Jijón y Caamaño (1941–43), then again with MACRO-CHIBCHAN by Greenberg (1960a). Loewen (1963) preferred the CARIBAN affinity, but allowed for a possible realignment on the basis of similarities between the CHOCO languages and Cuna, a language of the CHIBCHAN family.

Yunca = Yunga, generally classified as part of the YUNCA-PURUHAN phylum of

MACRO-CHIBCHAN has been reclassified as a CHIPAYAN (q.v.) language of the PENUTIAN phylum. Since the YUNCA-PURUHAN phylum was based on scant data (all are extinct except Yunca), the classification of the remaining languages is doubtful. This includes *Cañari = Canyari, *Manteña = Manabita, *Puruha, and the ATALÁN 'family' consisting of *Carake = Caraca = Caraque, *Huancavilca = Wancavilca, *Manta, *Puna, and *Tumbez. These languages were formerly spoken in coastal Ecuador and coastal Northern Peru. The SEC = SECHURA = SEČURA 'family' was also sometimes placed with YUNCA-PURUHAN, but is listed in the ANDEAN division of the ANDEAN-EQUATORIAL phylum by Greenberg.

The MACRO-CHIBCHAN phylum includes the following nine language isolates (without close family affiliations). Atacameño (2) is generally accorded a completely independent position, but Greenberg has classified it in MACRO-CHIBCHAN. Swadesh (1967) places Lenca (4) and Xinca (9) in his 'Macro-Mayan'.

1. *Andakí = Andaquí. Colombia. Possibly a member of the CHIBCHAN family.
2. *Atacameño = Atacama = Cunza = Likananta = Lipe. Northern Chile and northwestern Argentina. Not the same language as Atacame = Esmeralda, which belongs to JIVAROAN.
3. Itonama = Machoto. 2,000 (1967). West of Lake Titicaca in Bolivia.
4. Lenca. Southwestern Honduras and adjacent El Salvador. Ds. also Chilanga, Guaxiquero, *Intibucat, Opatoro, Similaton. Swadesh (1967) regards Chilanga as a separate language.
5. *Matanawi = Matanaui = Matanawü = Mitandu. Possibly not extinct. Brazil.
6. Mura = Muran = Mura-Pirahã = Bohura. 90 plus (1920) and apparently still extant. Brazil.
7. Paya = Taya = Tawka = Seco. Northern Honduras.
8. Warao = Warraw = Uarow = Guarau = Araote = Tivativa. Ds. also Changuane, Mariusa, *Waikeri = Guaiqueri = Guayqueri (may be a separate language and possibly not related). Venezuela.
9. Xinca = Sinca = Shinca = Jinca = Ikomagi = (Guatemalan) Popoloco. Southeastern Guatemala.

AFFILIATION. None known.

CHIMAKUAN

GROUPING. It has been pointed out by Swadesh (1955) that the two languages in the CHIMAKUAN family were mutually unintelligible but so obviously related that there can be no doubt about their belonging to the same family.

1. *Chimakum. Formerly around Port Townsend Bay in Puget Sound.
2. Quileute. Two dozen. La Push — Hoh River, Washington.

AFFILIATION. In the classification by Sapir (1929) every family and language isolate (a single language without closely related sister languages) was classified under one of six phyla, as reflected on the unrevised *Map of North American Indian Languages* by Voegelin and Voegelin (n.d. = 1944), where Quileute (= CHIMAKUAN) appears

under Phylum II, in genetic association with WAKASHAN, Kutenai, SALISH, Yurok
and Wiyot, Beothuk, and ALGONQUIAN, The argument for leaving CHIMAKUAN unaffiliated with respect to phylum classification is given by Voegelin and Voegelin
(1967).

CHINANTECAN

GROUPING. The CHINANTECAN languages and dialects are not clearly delineated.
Robbins (1961) refers to six language complexes, even though CHINANTEC has been
traditionally treated as one language. The seven language names below are those
listed in Wares (1968). Other names of uncertain status are: Huahmi; Hume; Chiltepec.
The CHINANTECAN languages are all spoken in northern Oaxaca, Mexico.

1. Azumacin Chinantec.
2. Lalana Chinantec. 10,000.
3. Ojitlan Chinantec.
4. Palantla Chinantec. 10,000.
5. Quiotepec Chinantec. 3,000.
6. Usila Chinantec. 4,000.
7. Yolox.

AFFILIATION. Member of OTO-MANGUEAN.

CHINESE

GROUPING. The listing of language names to represent either dialects or
separate languages in CHINESE is complicated by two considerations which bear on the
question of which varieties are or are not either mutually intelligible or else ethnolin-
guistically interpretable. First, the same Chinese character writing is used for all
varieties. Second, the descendant of an earlier form of Chinese known as Wen Yen or
Wen Li continues to be used by all educated Chinese, with considerable continuity
of the earlier grammar, for special purposes — for genre in which brevity is a virtue
(e.g., poetry, political slogans, and telegrams). Thus, Chinese can be regarded as an
ethnolinguistic monolith (Voegelin and Voegelin 1964a), while CHINESE is taken to be
an assemblage of several separate languages intertwined in an endless network of
dialects.

The chief early contributors to the problem of classification within this network
were Karlgren (1915–26), Li (1937), Chao (1943) and Shafer (1955). More recently,
Egerod (1967) has summarized generally well-known information, such as the work
of Forrest (1948), as well as the modern treatment of Chinese languages by Yüan
Chia-hua (1960). Within this summary it is pointed out that the boundaries between
Mandarin (5), Wu (8), Hsiang (3), and Kan (4) are the most questionable — with
the latter two least adequately defined. Kan (4) forms a bridge between Hsiang (3) and
Hakka (2). It has been suggested that Hunan (a Hsiang dialect), Kiangsi, Hsiang-kan,
and southern Kiangsi be called 'Hakka-kan.' Hakka (2) stands intermediate between
Mandarin (5) and Cantonese (1). The Min languages (6, 7) can be divided into two
groups, but might be divided into five subgroups (Min Tung = East Min, including

Fuchou; Min Nan = South Min, including Amoy; Min Hsi = West Min, including Ch'angt'ing; Min Pei = North Min, including Chienou; Min Chung = Central Min, including Yungan).

1. Cantonese = Yüeh = Yue. Ds. Canton (including Lungtu, T'oishan, Shekki), Chiangmen, Ch'inchchou, Chiuchiang, Chungshan, Enp'ing, Haoshan, Hop'u, Hsinhui, Junghsien, K'aip'ing, Kaochou, Leichou, Liangyang = Yangchou, Linchou, Nanhai, Popai, Sanshui, Seiyap, Shihch'i, Shunte, T'ashan, Tungkuan, Yangchiang, Yülin, Wuchou. Egerod (1967), unlike Yüan (1960) divides these dialects into five groups: Ch'in Lien (Ch'inchou, Haoshan, Lienchou, Sanshui); Kao Lei (Kaochou, Leichou); Kueinan (southern Kwangsi, Junghsien, Popai, Wuchou, Yülin); Szu-i (Seiyap, including Hsinhui, K'aip'ing, Enp'ing); Yüeh hai (Pearl River Delta and along Western River). 27,000,000. Kwantung and southern part of Kwangsi.

2. Hakka = K'echia = Hokka = K'e. Ds. also Fukien Hakka (including Ch'angt'ing, Chianglo, Shaowu), Hainan Hakka, Jaop'ing Hakka (Taiwan), Kiangsi Hakka (including Lungnan), Kwantung Hakka (including Fengshun, Hsingning, Meihsien, P'ingyüan, T'aoyüan, Tapu, Wahua), Northern Hakka, Sathewkok (Hong Kong New Territories), Taiwan Hakka, Szechwan Hakka (including Huayang). 20,000,000. Hakka is spoken throughout China, side-by-side with other languages; greatest concentration in eastern and northern Kwangtung, Fukien, Kiangsi, Taiwan, Kwangsi, Hunan, Szechwan; in a band from Fukien in the east to Kwangsi in the west.

3. Hsiang = Hunan = Hunanese. Ds. New Hsiang (urban areas), including Ch'angsha = Changsha = Ch'ang Sha = Hengyang, Ch'angte, Hsiangt'an, Iyang, Linhsiang, Shaoyang, Yüehyang, Yungshun; Old Hsiang, including Shuang Feng = Shuangfeng. 26,000,000. Hunan. It is not determined whether Hueichou, in the southern part of Anhwei, is a Hsiang dialect or a divergent member of the otherwise little differentiated Wu dialects.

4. Kan. D. also Nanch'ang = Nan Ch'ang. 13,000,000. Kiangsi and southwestern corner of Hupei, including Tachih, Hsienning, Chiayü, Chu'ungyang.

5. Mandarin = Pei = Northern Chinese. Ds. Northern: Honan (including Chech'eng, Chengchou, Chungho, Hsiangch'ien, Loyang), Hopei (including Changchiak'ou, Ch'angli, Ch'engte, Hantan, Huaian, Kaoch'eng, Linch'eng, Paoting, Peking, Suihsien, T'angshan, Tientsin, Wanhsien, Wanch'üan, Weihsien, Wenan, Yünhsien), Kanyü (northern Kiangsu), Liaoning (including Antung, Ch'anghai, Chuangho, Hsifeng, Hsinmin, Lüta, Shenyang), Shantung (including P'ingtu, Tsinan), also Chi Nan, Hsi Nan; Northwestern = Chin: Kansu (including Chuanglang, K'anglo, Lanchou), Shansi (including Chiachoch'eng, Lich'eng, Pingting, T'aiyüan, Wenshui, Yünch'eng, Yutz'u), Shensi (including Chingpien, Shanghsien, Sian, Wupao, Yench'uan); Southern = Yangtze-Hua = Lower Yan'tze: Anhwei (including Anch'ing = Hwaining, Northern Anhwei), Kiangsu (including Chaohsien, Haian, Hanchou, Hank'ou, Hsinhua, Hsini, Hsüchow, Kanyü [but see Northern Mandarin], Jukao, Jutung, Nanking, Nant'ung, P'eihsien, Tafang, T'aichou, T'aihsien, T'aihsing, T'ungt'ai, Yangchou); Southwestern = Western:

Hupei (including Chiangling, Hank'ou, Hsishui, Huangmei, Huangp'i, Kuangchi, Mach'eng, Tienmen), Szechuwan (including Ch'engtu, Ch'iunglai, Chungking, Fengchieh, Lichuang, Yüch'i), Yünnan (K'unming, Haoch'ing, Hsüanwei, Mengtzu, Pinch'uan, Tali, T'engch'ung, Yungshan), also Loshan, Nan Si Sien. Also Ch'ihshui (Kweichoa); Chün-hua (5,000; Hainan); Nanp'ing (Fukien); Yangyü (Fukien). 387,000,000. Yellow River basin: Hopei, Shantung, Manchuria, part of Inner Mongolia (Northern Mandarin); Shangshi, Shensi, Kansu, Ts'inghai, Ningsia, part of Inner Mongolia (Northwestern Mandarin), Hupei, except southeastern corner, Szechuan, Yünnan, Kweichow, northwestern Kwangsi, northwestern Hunan (Southwestern Mandarin); Anhwei and Kiangsu, south of Yantze except area from Hsüchou to Panfu (Southern Mandarin). Northern Mandarin, in particular Peking speech (Hopei), is the base for the standard, or 'common language' = P'ut'unghua. Forrest (1948) excludes the Northwestern group from his Northern Chinese, setting this group up rather as a coordinate group, which he calls Chin. The above grouping of dialects reflects Chao (1948, 1965), Forrest (1948), and Egerod's (1967) summary of the field, including Yüan (1960).

6. Northern Min = Min Pei = F(o)u Chou = Fuchow = Foochow. Ds. also Fouch'ing, F(o)uchou = Foochow, Fuan, Hsienyu, Kut'ien, P'ut'ien, Shouning; also Kienyang ? Kiening ? 7,000,000. Northwestern part of Fukien, north and south of the Min River.

7. Southern Min = Min Nan. Ds. Ch'ao Shan (Swatow region of Kwangtung), Ch'aochou, southern Chekiang (including Choushan islands, P'ingyang, T'aishun = Szuch'i, Tungt'ou, Yühuan), Southern Fukien (Amoy and Taiwan, the Taiwanese form of which is sometimes referred to as 'Formosan', including Chiehchow, Chinchiang, Lungchi), Hainan Island = Hainanese (Wanning, Wench'ang), Lungtu. 15,000,000.

8. Wu. Southeastern Anhwei: Chich'i, Lingpei; Chekiang: Chingmin, Chinhua, Haiyen, Hsienchü, Ningpo = Ninghsien, T'ungyüan, Wenchou = Wenchow = Wen Chou = Yungkia, Wenling, Yungk'ang; Southern Kiangsu: Chekiang, Chiangyin, Chingchiang, Ch'itung, Ch'uansha, Ch'ungchou, Haimen, Ihsing, Iwu, Liyang, Nant'ung Wu, Nanhui, P'utung, Shanghai, Shaohsing, Suchou = Su Chou, Tanyang, Wuchiang. 46,000,000. Southeastern Anhwei; Kiangsu south of the Yangtze, east of Chenchiang (which is Mandarin), on Ch'ungming Island in the mouth of the Yangtze, and north of the Yangtze in the area of Nant'ung, Haimen, Ch'tung, Chingchiang and Tanyang (the northernmost cities); Chekiang as far south as Ch'üchou, Chinhua and Wenchou.

AFFILIATION. Member of SINO-TIBETAN.

CHINOOK(AN)

GROUPING

1. Chinook Jargon. 10–100 speakers. A pidgin used as a lingua franca from northern California to southern Alaska. Based on Chinook, but with Nootka, French and English as major donor languages.

2. *Lower Chinook = Chenook = Chinuc = Chinuk = Coastal Chinook = Tchi-

noque = Tchinouc = Tshinook = Tshinuk = Tsinuk. D. also Clatsop = Klatsop
= Tlatsop. 26. Oregon (formerly also in Columbia River Delta in Washington).
3. Upper Chinook = Kikct. Ds. Cascades, Clackamas, Kathlamet, Multnomah,
Wasco (10; Oregon and Washington), Wishram (10; Washington). Along Columbia
River in Oregon and Washington.

AFFILIATION. Member of PENUTIAN.

CHIPAYAN = URU-CHIPAYAN = CHIPAYA-URU

GROUPING. Chipaya (1) and Uru (2) have been considered related for some
time (Métraux 1936; Ibarra Grasso 1961; more recently Olson 1964). Stark (1968)
includes Yunca (3, below) as a sister language of CHIPAYAN in a YUNCA-CHIPAYAN
family; though Uhle (1896) had observed the relationship between Yunca and the
CHIPAYAN family, it had long been subgrouped with Puruha, Canari, and other extinct
languages in MACRO-CHIBCHAN (Jijón y Caamaño 1943; Tovar 1961).

1. Chipaya = Puquina = Pukina. 800. Southern end of Bolivian Altiplano.
2. Uru = Uro = Huro = Ochomazo = Uchumi = Kjotsuni = Bukina = Pukina =
Puquina = Urocolla = Uroquilla = Yuracare. Possibly as few as 100. Jancoaqui
and Isla del Sol, small pockets in area of Lake Titicaca and Lake Poopo. Ds. also
on Isla del Sol.
3. *Yunca = Yunga = Yunka = Mochica = Muchik = Chimu = Quingnam. Ds.
also Chanco (?), Eten (?), Mossopé. Formerly spoken on northern coast of Peru.

AFFILIATION. Member of PENUTIAN phylum, with relatively close affinities
to MAYAN (Olson 1964; Stark 1968; Hamp 1967a, 1971), though Lyle Campbell
(1973) presents a negative case for this relationship. The CHIPAYAN family has been
also classified as ARAWAKAN (Créqui-Montfort and Rivet 1925-1927) and MACRO-
CHIBCHAN (Jijón y Camanõ 1943). Yunca has been also classified as MACRO-CHIBCHAN
(Greenberg 1960a), as a sister language of BARBACOAN within MACRO-CHIBCHAN, and as
a language isolate (Chamberlain 1913, Brinton 1901, Swadesh 1959, Tovar 1961).

CHIQUITO

GROUPING. Three languages spoken formerly, according to Key and Key
(1967), in central and eastern Bolivia compose the CHIQUITO family.
1. *Chiquito = Tarapecosi = Yuncarirx.
2. *Churapa = Southern Chiquito.
3. *Penyoqui = Penokikia = Penoki. Ds. also Cuciquia, Pinyoca, Tabiica, Tao.

AFFILIATION. Member of MACRO-GE within GE-PANO-CARIB.

CHOCO = CHOLO

GROUPING. The classification of the dialects of the three extant CHOCO languages
below is that of Loewen (1963). Others distinguish only two languages, treating
Northern and Southern Ẹpẹra as one language, Ẹpẹra = Ẹmpẹra = Ẹmpẹna.

1. Northern Ẹpẹra. Ds. Dabeiba = Dabeibe = Catio = Katio (4,000), Rio Verde (1,000), Sambú = Sambo (5,000), San Jorge = Chimila (1,000). 11,000. Western Colombia and spilling over into Panama.
2. Southern Ẹpẹra. Ds. Bando = Catio (2,000), Chami (2,000), Rio Sucio = Citaró (3,000), Saixa = Saija (1,500), Tado (1,000). 9,500. Colombia, south and west of the Northern Ẹpẹra and along the coast north of the Waunana area.
3. Waunana = Noanamá = Nonama = Chocama = Chanco. 2,500. Western Colombia, in the lower San Juan River basin and along the Pacific coast from the mouth of the San Juan River to the upper reaches of Docordó and Siguirusuá rivers.
? *Cauca. Colombia.
? *Cenu = Zenú. Colombia.

AFFILIATION. Member of MACRO-CHIBCHAN PHYLUM.

CHUKCHEE-KAMCHATKAN = LUORAVETLAN = LUORAWETLAN

GROUPING. Languages numbered (1), (4) and (5) may be dialects of a single language; Kamchadal (3) is quite divergent (Jakobson 1942, Worth 1963, Skorick et al. 1968a). All are spoken in Siberia.

1. Alutor = Al'utor = Aliutor. Ds. Alutorskij, Karaginskij, Palanskij.
2. Chukchee = Chukchi = Luoravetlan. Ds. Enmylinskij, Nunligranskij, Pevekskij, Uellenskij, Xatyrskij. 93.7% of 11,700. Chukchi Peninsula, Chukchi National Okrug, U.S.S.R.
3. Kamchadal = Itel'men. Ds. Napanskij, Sedanskij, Sopočnovskij, Xajrjuzovskij. 36% of 1,100. Eight fishing hamlets in Koryak District.
4. Kerek. Ds. Majna-pil'ginskij, Xatyrskij. Cape Navarin.
5. Koryak = Nymylan. Ds. Apokinskij, Čavčuvenskij, Itkanskij, Kamenskij, Parenskij. 90.5% of 6,300. Koryak National Okrug, U.S.S.R.

AFFILIATION. Swadesh (1959) proposed a relationship between CHUKCHEE-KAMCHATKAN and ESKIMO-ALEUT.

Cilician. A non-INDO-EUROPEAN language of ancient Asia Minor known chiefly from Greek traditions (Kretschmer 1896, Forrer 1937, Erzen 1940).

AFFILIATION. None known.

Cuitlatec(o). Spoken in Guerrero, Mexico, until the middle of the twentieth century (one speaker in 1962) (Escalante Hernández 1962).

AFFILIATION. None known; lexicostatistically it is equally close to Nahuatl (UTO-AZTECAN) and Paya (MACRO-CHIBCHAN) (Arana Osnaya 1959).

CUSHITIC

GROUPING. Languages of the CUSHITIC family are spoken in an area that extends south and west from the Gulf of Aden and the Ethiopian shores of the Red Sea (from Somali Republic to Tanzania and from Ethiopia to adjacent parts of Kenya and Sudan).

The first language listed below, Beja (1), is not subgrouped with any other language; it is coordinate in classification with each of the three language groups or branches of the family (CENTRAL, EASTERN, and SOUTHERN CUSHITIC). This represents the CUSHITIC classification of Bender (1971), after Fleming (1969, 1972), a classification which removes the WESTERN CUSHITIC group in Greenberg (1966) from the CUSHITIC family and places it in another family, OMOTIC (q. v.).

An earlier classification by Huntingford (1956) classified CUSHITIC languages in six geographic 'zones,' after Moreno (1940). Tucker and Bryan (1956, 1966) include languages numbered (24) through (27), below, in a group labeled IRAQW; and they regard languages numbered (24) through (28), below, to be non-CUSHITIC. Though Dolgopoljskij (1966) classified these languages, (24–28), as CUSHITIC, he does not place them in a single SOUTHERN CUSHITIC group.

1. Beja = Bedja = Begia = Bedauye = Bedawiye(t) = Bedawie = Bedya = Bedw. D. also Hadă(a)reb. Trs. Ad Al Bakhit, Ad Ali, (Ad) Elman, Ad Kukal = Kokuduab, Ad Naseh = Ad Nazi, Ad Okud = Ad 'Uqud, Ad Omar (including Ad Al Allam, Al Hamid Awad = Al Hamid Awat, Ad Humbirra, Hassal, Sheneiab), Ad Sheraf = Asheraf, Ad Towas (including Sinkat Keinab = Sinkat Kenab), Amarar, Arteiga, Bedawib = Ibdawi, Beit Awat, Beit Ma(a)la, Beni Amir = Beni Amer = Aamir, Bisharin, Dagga, Diglel, El Hasa, El Gureshab, Handendowa = Hadendoa = Haḑenḑiwa, Hashish Hassanab, Kimmeilab, Labat = Lobat = Labbat = Labet, Morghumab-Kamalab, Shaiab. 150,000 ? (Over 19,000 in Ethiopia.) Sudan, Ethiopia. Greenberg (1966) calls this language NORTHERN CUSHITIC; Bender (1971), NORTH CUSHITIC.

CENTRAL CUSHITIC = AGAU. Called AGAU by Tucker and Bryan (1956), CENTRAL CUSHITIC by Greenberg (1966) and Bender (1971). Bender subgroups into a NORTH group (languages numbered 3, 4, 5) and a SOUTH group (Awiya, 2).

2. Awiya = Awngi = Awi = Damot = Agewmidir = Metekkel = Southern Agew. Ds. also Damot = Damotanya (?), Kunfel = Kumfel, Kwollanyoch.

3. Bilin = Bilen = Belein = Bilayn = Bileno = Bileninya = Bogo(s). Ds. = Trs. Beit Tarke = Bet Tarqe, Beit Tawke = Bet Taqwe. Over 32,000. Ethiopia: Eritrea, Karen Division.

4. Khamir = Kamir = Chamir = Xamir = Khamit = Xamtanga. D. also Khamta = Xamta = Agew of Wag. 5,000. Ethiopia: Avergele District and Lasta and Waag regions.

5. Quara = Qwara = Kwara = Quarina = Quarasa = Koura. Ds. also Kayla = Kaila = Kailinya = Falasha = Falasha Kara = Yihudi (i.e., Jewish) = Qwara (30,000), Qemant = Qimant = Chemant = Kemant = Kimant = Kimantinya = Kəmāntnay (17,000). Ethiopia: Lake Tana region. The Quara dialect is no longer spoken.

EASTERN CUSHITIC. Greenberg (1966) lists the languages and dialects of this group without further subgrouping. Bender (1971) bifurcates EAST CUSHITIC into a HIGHLAND group and a LOWLAND group. Bender has further subgroupings within each of these two major groups: HIGHLAND EAST CUSHITIC is equivalent to Tucker and Bryan's (1956) SIDAMO group; LOWLAND EAST CUSHITIC is equivalent to three groups of Tucker and Bryan (SAHO-AFAR, GALLA, and KONSO-GELERA).

HIGHLAND EAST CUSHITIC = SIDAMO. This group is subdivided by Bender (1971) into NORTH (9), CENTRAL (6, 8, 10), and SOUTH (7) HIGHLAND.

6. Alaba = Halaba. D. also Kembata = Kambatta = Kembatinya, including Kabena = K'abena = Qebena = Adiye = Tambaro = Timbara = Timbaro = T'ambaro = Kambara (250,000). 44,500 (excluding Kembata). Ethiopia.

7. Burji = Bambala = Bembola = Burjina = Amaro. 15,000. Ethiopia: south of Lake Ciamo.

8. Derasa = Darasa = Derasanya = Deresa = Deresinya. 250,000.

9. Hadiyya = Hadya = Hadia = Hadiya = Adiye = Gudella = Gudiela = Marako = Maraquo = Libido. 700,000. Ethiopia, between the Omo and Billate rivers.

10. Sidamo = Sidaminya = Sidama = Sidamonya. 857,000. Ethiopia, between Juba and Webi rivers and Lake Margherita.

LOWLAND EAST CUSHITIC. This group is subdivided by Bender (1971) into NUCLEAR LOWLAND: Afar-Saho (11), BAISO-SOMALOID (13, 20, 21), ARBORE-DASENECH OROMOID with subgroups ARBORE-DASENECH (12, 15), and OROMOID in which (16) is distinguished from KONSOID (14, 18, 19); and WERIZOID: Gawwada (17) and Tsamai (22). Mogogodo (23) is added by Greenberg (1963).

11. Afar-Saho = Saho-Afar. Ds. Afar = Adal = Ṭelṭal = T'elt'al = Dan-(a)kali = Danakil = Denkel = Dangali = Dankali, including Central Afar, Northern Afar, Aussa, Ba'adu (363,000); Saho = Shaho = Sao = Shiho = Shoho, including Assaorta, Hadu = Hazu, Miniferi (121,000). Ethiopia: Eritrea.

12. Arbore = Erbore = Irbore. 1,500. Ethiopia, near Lake Stefanie.

13. Baiso. 500.

14. North Bussa. 1,000.

15. Dasenech = Dasanek = Dathanic = Dathanik = Dathanaik = Dathanaic = Geleb(a) = Gellaba = Gelleb = Gelubba = Marille = Merille = Marle. Tr. Reshaiat = Rechiat = Rachiat = Rusia. 18,000. Ethiopia: north of Lake Rudolf extending into Kenya.

16. Galla = Afan = Oromo. Ds. Arus(s)i = Arsi (1,331,000); Borena = Baran(a) = Booran(a) = Boran Gabbra = Gabra = Gebra = Gare (132,000); Eastern Galla, including Ittu = Kwottu = Qottu = Qwottu (1,077,000), Guji (380,000), Mecha = Mac(c)ha = Wellega = Wollega (1,869,200), Raya (?), Tulema = Tulama = Shewa = Shoa, including Kereyu, Salale (1,946,000); Orma, including Uardai = Wadai = Warday (northern Kenya); Wello = Wollo (75,000). Ethiopia, Kenya.

17. Gawwada = Gauwada = Gawata. Ds. also West Bussa (?) (22,000), Gobeze = Gowase = Gowaze = Goraze = Michile = Orase, Werize

= Innxarsi = Orase = Wazire. 4,000 (Gawwada dialect only). Ethiopia.
18. Gidole = Ghidole = Gardulla = Gidolinya = Cirasha. 5,000. Ethiopia,
    hills near Lake Ciamo.
19. Konso = Komso = Konsinya = Af-Kareti = Gato. 60,000. Ethiopia,
    south of Lake Ciamo in bend of Sagan River.
20. Rendil(l)e = Randile.
21. Somali = Somalinya = Af-Soomaali. Ds. Central, including Digil,
    Digini, MayMay; Common, including Da(a)rod, Dir, Durba, Gada-
    bursi, Hawiy(y)a, Isa = Issa = Issaag, Is'hak, Sab Ogaden; Rahanwein
    = Rahanwen = Rahanwiin, including Jiddu, Tunni. Trs. also Bena(a)-
    dir, Mediban. Over 1,600,000. Somalia, French Somaliland, Kenya,
    Ethiopia.
22. Tsamai = Tsamako = Kulla = Cule = Kuile = Kule = Tamaha ?
    6,500 ?
23. Mogogodo = Mokogodo. Kenya.
Dumé (?); Jamjam = ğamğam ?

SOUTHERN CUSHITIC
24. Alawa = Uwassi = Was(s)i = Asi. 11,000.
25. Burungi = Burunge = Mbulunge = Mbulungu. 11,300. Tanzania: Central
    Province, Kondoa District.
26. Goroa = Gorowa = Fiome = Fiomi. 17,550. Tanzania: Kondoa Central
    Province, and Mbulu District.
27. Iraqw = Iraku = Irakou = Erokh = (Wa-)Mbulu. 111,350. Tanzania:
    Northern Province, Mbule District.
28. Ma'a = Mbugu = Mbougou = Va-Ma'a = Wa Maathi. Tanzania, Eastern
    Province, in Usambara.
29. Sanye = Wa-sanye = Ariangulu = Langulo = Boni = Watta ? Kenya,
    Ethiopia.

AFFILIATION. Member of AFROASIATIC.

DAGA = DIMUGA

GROUPING. Wurm (1971c) points out that doubt is cast upon Ray's (1938)
classification of other languages as closely related to, or dialects of, Daga (2, below)
by the fact that at least one of them on Ray's list — Gwoira — appears not to be
related to Daga or to other members of SOUTH-EAST NEW GUINEA. Greenberg (1971b)
adds other languages to the DAGA group. The DAGA languages are spoken in the
western and northwestern part of the mainland area of Milne Bay District, Papua.

1. Bagoi.
2. Daga = Dimuga = Nawp. 3,500.
3. Galeva.
4. Gwoiden.
5. Jimajima.

6. Kanamara.
7. Maisin.
8. Makiara.
9. Maneao.
10. Moibiri.
11. Onjob.
12. Pue.
13. Tevi.

AFFILIATION. Member of SOUTH-EAST NEW GUINEA.

DALY

GROUPING. Nangumiri (8, below) does not belong to either of the two major subgroups of DALY (Wurm 1971b). The first of these is BRINKEN-WOGAITY, subdivided into BRINKEN, consisting of Brinken (2), Maramanindji (4), and Marengar (6), and WOGAITY consisting of Ame (1), Maranunggu (5), and Wadjiginy (9). The second major subgroup is MULLUK, subdivided into MULLUKMULLUK, consisting of Djeraity (3) and Mullukmulluk (7), and DALY, consisting of Warat (10) and Yunggor (11). The WOGAITY subgroup had formerly been considered to be a single language called Wogait = Wogatj = Wagaitj = Worgite = Worgait = Waggait = Waggite = Waggote = Waggate = Wagatsch = Waogatsch (O'Grady et al. 1966). All these languages are spoken in Northern Territory, Australia.

1. Ame. D. also Manda. Northern side of the Daly River.
2. Brinken = Berringin. Ds. also Maredan, Maretyabin, Marithiel = Marathiel, Nganygit. Between the Daly and Fitzmaurice rivers.
3. Djeraity. Northern shores of Anson Bay, northwards along coast to Port Patterson.
4. Maramanindji = Maramandandji = Marimanindji. Between the Daly and Fitzmaurice rivers.
5. Maranunggu. Vicinity of Hermit Hill and eastward towards the Daly River.
6. Marengar. D. also Tangural.
7. Mullukmulluk = Mullikmullik = Mollakmollak = Mallackmallack. North of the Daly River, south of Darwin.
8. Nangumiri = Nanggumiri = Ngengomeri = Nangimera = Nangimeri = Mariwunini = Nangiomera. D. also Tyemeri = Moil. South of the middle of Daly River.
9. Wadjiginy. D. also Pungupungu. East of the Adelaide River.
10. Warat. Ds. also Kamor, Matngala.
11. Yunggor = Junggor. Between Hermit Hill and Daly River.

AFFILIATION. Member of AUSTRALIAN macro-phylum.

DIERIC

GROUPING. The DIERIC languages are divided into one unsubgrouped language, Karengappa (5); and two subgroups, the KARNA subgroup, consisting of Dieri (2), Pilatapa (6), Jauraworka (3), and Karendala (4), and the NGURA subgroup consisting of Punthamara (7), and Badjiri (1) (O'Grady, Voegelin and Voegelin 1966, Wurm 1971b). O'Grady, Wurm and Hale (1966) and Breen (1971) treat the dialects listed under Punthamara (7, below) as two separate languages: (a) Wongkumera (as known from an earlier wordlist), with the dialects Bitjara and Kalali, and (b) Punthamara with the other dialects, including the spoken form now known as Wongkumara. The DIERIC languages are spoken in an area around the boundaries between Northern Territory, Queensland, South Australia, and New South Wales, Australia.

1. Badjiri = Baddyeri = Byjerri = Baderi = Poidgerry = Badjedi.
2. Dieri = Diari = Diyeri = Dieyerie = Deerie = Dieyrie = Dthee-eri. Ds. also Jandruwanta = Yandruwunta = Yantruwunta = Jendruwonta = Yandrawontha = Yanderawartha = Yanduwulda = Endawarra, Jeljendi = Jeljujendi = Yelya-yendi = Yarleeyandee, Karanguru = Karangura = Kurangooroo, Ngameni = Ngamini = Ngamani = Gnameni = Ngaminni = Ngnaminni = Ahminnie = Uminni = Agaminni = Awmani, Tirari. South Australia.
3. Jauraworka = Jawarawarka = Yauroworka = Yarrawaurka = Yaurorka = Yaurawakka = Jaurorka = Yerawaka = Yowerawoolka = Yowerawarrika. South Australia.
4. Karendala = Kurnandaburi = Kunandaburi. Ds. also Bidia = Birria = Piria, Karuwali = Karawala = Kurrawulla = Karorinje, Kulumali = Ngulangulandji, Kungadutji = Kungaditji = Kungarditchi = Kunatachee, Marulta = Manula. On Cooper Creek at Durham Downs, north to Mount Howitt, east to McGregor Range and to Eromanga, Queensland.
5. Karenggapa = Yalyi = Karrengappa = Kurengappa. Ds. Maljangapa = Malyan-gapa = Maljangaba = Maljangapa = Malyanapa = Mulyanapa = Mulyanappa = Milyauppa = Muliaarpa = Malynapa = Malyapa = Nalyanapa = Multyerra, Wadikali = Wadigali. New South Wales.
6. Pilatapa = Piladapa = Pillatapa = Pulladapa = Berluppa = Pilliapp. South Australia.
7. Punthamara = Bunthomarra = Buntamara = Banthamurra = Bunthaburra. Ds. also Bitjara (?) = Bithara = Pitjara, Kalali = Galali = Kullali = Kullally, Ngandangara = Eromarra = Jarumara = Mambangura (?), Ngurawola (?), Tereila (?) = Diraila = Thiralla, Wongkumara = Wankgumara = Wonkamara = Wonkomarra = Wonkamarra = Wonkamura = Wonkamurra = Wonkubara. Queensland.

AFFILIATION. Member of PAMA-NYUNGAN, which includes not only DIERIC but also PAMA-MARIC. Some languages assigned above to DIERIC may belong rather to PAMA-MARIC (Breen).

DJAMINDJUNGAN

GROUPING. Spoken between the Fitzmaurice and Baine rivers in Northern Territory, Australia.

1. Djamindjung = Jaminjang = Tjaminjun = Djamundon = Murinyuwen.
2. Jilngali.

3. Ngaliwuru.
4. Nungali.

    AFFILIATION. Member of AUSTRALIAN macro-phylum.

DJERAGAN

    GROUPING. O'Grady et al. (1966a, b) divide this family into two groups: the GIDJIC group consisting of Gidja (2), Guluwarin (3) and Lungga (4), and the MIRIWUNIC group consisting of Gadjerong (1) and Miriwun (5). Spoken in the coastal area of the Joseph Bonaparte Gulf on both sides of the Western Australia-Northern Territory boundary line, Australia.

1. Gadjerong = Kadjerong = Kadjeroen.
2. Gidja.
3. Guluwarin.
4. Lungga = Lunga = Loonga.
5. Miriwun = Mirung.

    AFFILIATION. Member of AUSTRALIAN macro-phylum.

DRAVIDIAN

    GROUPING. The DRAVIDIAN family was recognized as a group unrelated to other languages in India as early as 1816, and its status as a language family has never been a matter of controversy. Emeneau (1969) lists 21 and Krishnamurti (1969) lists 22 DRAVIDIAN languages.

    With the exception of Brahui, spoken primarily in Pakistan all DRAVIDIAN languages are concentrated in the south, central, and east portions of the Republic of India. Four of the languages, Tamil, Malayalam, Kannada·and Telugu have independent scripts and literary traditions; Tamil has one of the longest unbroken literary traditions known. The four preceding languages are the only DRAVIDIAN languages "recognized in the relevant schedule of the Constitution of India. These four languages provide the basis for the demarcation of the four linguistic States of South India, which are, respectively, Madras, Kerala, Mysore, and Andhra Pradesh." So states Krishnamurti (1969).

    Less than 10% of the 110,000,000 DRAVIDIAN speakers are bilingual. Two-thirds of the bilinguals have another DRAVIDIAN language as their second language, while the remaining one-third have an INDO-EUROPEAN language as their second language.

    The NORTHERN, CENTRAL, and SOUTHERN branches of DRAVIDIAN are widely accepted, but there has been disagreement as to whether some of the languages are CENTRAL or SOUTHERN. Except as noted, the classification here follows that of Krishnamurti (1969), which, although tentative, is "based on the latest knowledge in the field."

    The small NORTHERN branch is composed of three languages (numbered 1, 11, 14), which are spoken by some 845,000 people, mostly in the states of Bihar, Orissa, and West Bengal of east India and in Pakistan; the CENTRAL branch is composed of 11 or

12 languages (numbered 2, 3, 6, 7, 9, 10, 12, 15, 16, 17, 18, 20, and 22), spoken by 39,000,000 people in the states of Bombay, Madhya Pradesh, Andhra Pradesh, Orissa, and Mysore in central and east India; the SOUTHERN branch is composed of six languages (numbered 4, 5, 8, 13, 19, 21), which are spoken by 70,000,000 people, mostly in the states of Madras, Kerala, and Mysore in south and southwest India and in Ceylon.

Each of the groups above are subclassified in detail by Krishnamurti; only the major divisions of each group are given here. The NORTHERN branch has an eastern division of languages 11 and 14 in east India, separated from Brahui in Pakistan by hundreds of miles. Brahui is itself 800 miles from any other DRAVIDIAN language. The CENTRAL branch is bifurcated into a major group of languages (numbered 3, 7, 9, 10, 12, 15, 18, 20) and a minor group (numbered 2, 6, 16, 17); the minor group is spoken by less than 1 percent of the speakers of the CENTRAL languages. The SOUTHERN branch has a series of subgroupings rather than a single bifurcation such as is found among the CENTRAL languages. However, Kannaḍa (number 4) is more distantly related to the rest (numbered 5, 8, 13, 19, 21) than are any of the latter to each other.

It is possible that there are still DRAVIDIAN languages that have not been discovered; Manḍa (15) was not discovered until 1964 by Burrow and Bhattacharya (1970).

1. Brahui = Brahuidi = Birahui = Kur Galli. Ds. Jharawan (lowland), Kalat Standard = Middle Brahui, Sarawan (upland). 300,000 (1931). Baluchistan (153,000) and Sind (72,000) Provinces of Pakistan, and in the eastern parts of Iran and Afghanistan.

2. Gadba = Gadaba = Ollari = Salur. Ds. Ollari = Hollar Gadbas = Kondkor, Salur = Poya (obsolete). 8,800. Ollari is spoken in villages of Lamtaput and Mundaga Kotri and vicinity; Salur, in the village of the same name and vicinity. The dialects are separated by Gadba of the MUNDA family (q. v.). Krishnamurti (1969) lists Ollari as a separate language.

3. Gondi. Ds. include a 'western' group, which may be distinguished from a Bastar and Chanda or 'eastern', group including Koi = Koya and Maria = Bison-horn Maria. 1,500,000; another million and a half Gonds no longer speak a Dravidian language. Central India with Bastar District of the eastern part of the State of Madhya Pradesh as the primary area of concentration with 365,000 speakers. Other major areas of concentration include 133,000, 87,000, and 60,000 in the neighboring districts of Bhandara and Chanda of Bombay and Balaghat of Madhya Pradesh, respectively; 150,000, 125,000, and 105,000 in the districts of Chhindwara, Bethul, Mandla of western Madhya Pradesh, respectively; 90,000 in the Adilibad district of northern Andhra Pradesh; and a total of 139,000 in the eastern part of the State of Bombay. Smaller numbers are to be found in adjacent areas of these states and also in the states of Orissa (22,000) to the southeast, Bihar (4,000) to the east, and Uttar Pradesh (under 1,000) to the north.

4. Kannaḍa = Kanarese. Ds. include Badaga (67,000), plus various social and regional dialects. 17,000,000. Districts of North and South Santara in Maharashtra, District of Anantapur in Andhra Pradesh, and in the Nilgiri Hills (Badaga dialect) in the mountains of Kotagiri.

5. Kodagu = Coorg. 80,000. Coorg District of Mysore, around Mercara, bordering on the Malayalam language to the south.

6. Kolami = Kolami-Naiki. Ds. include Naikri = Naiki = Naik Pods, but specific information on other dialects is not available. 50,000. Yeotmal District of Bombay and Adilabad District of Andhra Pradesh.

7. Konda = Konda Dora = Kubi. Ds. Northern, Western. 13,000. Koraput District of Orissa. Only one of three tribal sections of the Konda speak Konda; Telugu is spoken by the 'Reddi area' Konda Dora and a dialect of Oriya by the Konda Peroja.

8. Kota. 900 (earlier figures show 4,500). Nilgiri Hills of the mountains of Kotagiri.

9. Koya. Ds. may include Dorli (although Tyler (1968) says it cannot be determined whether Dorli is a dialect of Koya or Gondi). 160,000 to 170,000 (Tyler). Concentrated mainly in Andhra Pradesh, with extensions into Madhya Pradesh and Orissa. Not listed by Emeneau (1969).

10. Kui = Khond = Khondi = Khondo = Kanda = Kodu = Kodulu = Kuinga. Ds. Gumsai = Eastern, Western, plus a great deal of local variation. 510,000. Districts of Puri, Ganjam, Koraput, Dhenkanal, Keonjhar, Phulbani, and Sundargarh in Orissa.

11. Kurukh = Oraon. 1,140,000. Primarily in the northwestern part of the Chota Nagpur Plateau in Bihar State, in the districts of Ranchi (365,000), Palaman (55,000), Purulia, Singbhum, Hazaribagh, Santal Parganas, Gaya, and Shahabad; in the Orissa districts of Sambalpur, Sundargarh, Dhenkanal, and Balasore; and in the West Bengal districts of Jalpaiguri and Darjeeling.

12. Kuwi = Kuvinga = Kond = Southwest Konds. 190,000. Visakhapatnam District of Andhra Pradesh and areas of the cities of Jeypore and Koraput in Orissa.

13. Malayalam = Malayarma = Malabar. Ds. include Pulaya, Yerava. 17,000,000. Primarily in the state of Kerala; also on the Laccadive Islands west of India and in the districts of Nilgiri in Madras and Coorg in Mysore. Considered by some to be a dialect of Tamil, which is separated from Malayalam by a sparsely settled mountainous jungle.

14. Malto = Male = Sauria. 90,000. Rajmahal Hills of northeast Bihar.

15. Manḍa. Kalahandi District of Orissa. Not listed by Krishnamurti (1969).

16. Naiki (of Chanda) = Naik Gonds = Erku. 1,500. Chiefly around the city of Mul in Chanda District of Bombay.

17. Parji = Porojas = Dhurva = Dhruva = Thakara = Tagara = Tugara. Ds. Northeastern, Northwestern, Southern. 20,000. South of Jagdalpur in Bastar District of Madhya Pradesh down through the Kanker Forest Reserve plus a gronp in the Kolab-Sabari Valley in Sukma Zamindari. A few villages extend across the western boundary of Madhya Pradesh into Orissa.

18. Pengo. 1,300. Koraput District of Orissa.

19. Tamil. Ds. Ceylon (including subdialects as Jaffna, Colombo), Northern, Northwestern, Southern, Western, plus caste dialects. 31,000,000. Primarily in southeastern India (28,000,000) in an area composed largely of Madras State plus contiguous districts of Kerala, Andhra, and Mysore: Ceylon (2,000,000); Malaysia, Indonesia, Vietnam (1,000,000); South Africa (250,000); and smaller groups

in Guyana, Fiji, Madagascar, Trinidad, Martinique, Reunion, Mauritius, and Burma. Bugradi, Erukala = Yerukala = Korava = Yenava of Malayalam (?), Irula, Kaikai, and Kasava have been considered as separate languages by Andronov (1960), but they are more generally accepted as minor dialects of Tamil, although apparently more divergent than the geographical dialects listed above. The total number of speakers of these minor dialects is little more than 50,000, located in the forests between the Nilgiri Hills and the Moyar River in the districts of Guntur and Nel, in Andhra, and a few (immigrants) in Madras.

20. Telegu = Gentoo = Andhra. 37,700,000. Andhra Pradesh, Chanda, and Nanded districts of Bombay, adjacent districts of Mysore along the entire length of the Mysore-Andhra border, and in the Coimbatore and Madura districts of Madras (immigrants).

21. Toda. 800. Nilgiri Hills at the junction of the states of Mysore, Kerala, and Madras in the vicinity of Ootacamund.

22. Tuḷu = Tuluva. 940,000. South Kanara District of Mysore state on the west coast of India.

AFFILIATION. Various affiliations outside India have been suggested for DRAVIDIAN. Krishnamurti (1969) dismisses most of them with this comment: "Attempts to trace genetic connections between DRAVIDIAN on the one hand and other languages such as Caucasian, Korean, Egyptian or Sumerian on the other may be passed over in silence, since the methods and materials used in their support have been unimpressive."

Krishnamurti offers scarcely more than silence on Lahovary's four works (1948, 1954, 1957, 1963) 'seeking to establish a relationship between DRAVIDIAN and the languages of the peri-Mediterranean families and Basque.'

More successful attempts have been made to affiliate DRAVIDIAN and URAL-ALTAIC by such men as Caldwell (1913), Burrow (1946), Bouda (1953), Menges (1964), and Andronov (1961). Although far from proved, Krishnamurti believes there are good chances that some remote relationship does connect these two.

DURUBULIC

GROUPING. The DURUBULIC languages are spoken on the southeastern coast of Queensland, Australia.

1. Djendewal = Koenpel. D. also Nununkul = Noonukul = Moondjan.
2. Gowar = Ngugi.
3. Jagara = Jagarabal = Yagara = Turrubul = Yackarabul = Jinibara.

AFFILIATION. Member of PAMA-NYUNGAN.

EASTERN (of ADAMAWA-EASTERN) = UBANGIAN

GROUPING. Greenberg (1966) recognizes a greater number of subgroups for EASTERN than do Bouquiaux and Thomas (in Samarin 1971), who would merge the subgroups numbered I, II, IV, and V into a single subgroup.

I. 300,000. Central African Republic, Cameroons, northwestern Congo.

    1. Gbaya = Baja = Baya = Bwaka = Ngbaka = Gbaka = Gwaka = Gmbu-
aga. D. also Manja = Mandja = Mandjia = Mbaka. Ds. = Trs. Ali = Gbee,
Bagba (5,500), Bangando (2,700), Baya Banou, Bokari, Budigri (5,000),
Gbaya Bianda, Gbaya Bodomo, Gbaya Bokoto, Gbaya Buli, Gbaya Buli
Bukum, Gbaya Kaka, Gbaya Kara = Gbara Kala, Gbaya Lai, Gbofi,
Granu = Banu, Kaka, Manja Baba, Manja Baya, Mbaka = Mandjia
Bakka (17,000), Mombe = Baka Mombe, Ngbaka Gbaya, Ngbaka Manja,
Ngombekaka, Somo, Yangele (2,750).

II

    2. Nabandi = Mongbwandi = Mongwandi = Mbati = Baza. Trs. also Aba-
sango, Bangi, Bwato, Dendi, Mbaati, Nzomboy = Monjomboli. 137,000.
Northwestern Congo.

    3. Sango = Sango Commerical. A lingua franca based on (2) above, with many
French and Bantu words. 1,000,000. Central African Republic, northwestern
Congo, Ubangi-Chari.

    4. Yakoma. Tucker and Bryan (1956) regarded this as a dialect of 3, above.
5,300. Central African Republic ,Yakoma.

Mongoba = Munguba (50) (?); Kazibati = Ganzibati = Hadjibatie =
Kasiboti (365) ?

III. Tucker and Bryan (1956) include the language numbered (6), following, as a
dialect of the language numbered (10), following.

    5. Barambu = Abarambo = Amiangbwa = Balambu = Barambo. 46,000.
Sudan and Congo, in Poko, Ango and Dungu territories.

    6. Nzakara = Ansakara = N'sakara = Sakara = Zakara. 3,000. Congo
(Leopoldville).

    7. Pambia = Apambia. 2,900. Sudan and Central African Republic.

    8. Zande = Asande = Assandeh = Badjande = Nyam-nyam = Niam-niam
= Gnam-gnam = Bazenda = Sande = Sandeh = Zandeh. Ds. Anunga,
Bile, Bomokandi, Dio, Mbomu, Patri Sueh-meridi. 700,000. Sudan, Congo,
Central African Republic.

IV. Tucker and Bryan (1956) include the languages numbered (9) and (13) together
as a dialect cluster. Greenberg does not list the language numbered (12).

    9. Bangba = Abangba. Ds. Alo, Koko, Makudukudu, Merei, Moco, Tibu.
29,000.

    10. Bwaka = Ngbaka Mabo = Ngbaka-Ma'bo = Gbaka = Gwaka = Mbwaka.
Ds. also Gilima, Ngbaka mapi. 17,000. Congo and Central African
Republic.

    11. Gbanziri = Banziri = Gbandere. D. also Buraka. Trs. Bayaka, Ganzi,
Gundi, Mbacca.

    12. Kpala = Gbakpwa = Kpwa(a)la. Northwestern Congo.

    13. Mayogo. Trs. Bakango, Dai = Day = Angai, Maambi, Majugu, Mangbele
= Majogo, Mayko = Maiko, Mayugo. 75,000. Northeastern Congo.

14. Monjombo = Mo(n)djembo = Monzombo. 13,000. Central African Republic, Congo (Brazzaville) and Congo (Leopoldville).
15. Mundu = Mondo = Mondu. 5,000. Sudan and northwestern Congo.

V. Tucker and Bryan (1956) and Welmers (1971) treat languages numbered (16), (17), (22), (23), (24), below, as dialects of a single language, and languages numbered (18), (20), (21), (25) as dialects of another single language. 30,000. Sudan, Congo.

16. Bai = Bari.
17. Bviri = Biri = Gumba = Gamba = Mbegumba = Mvegumba. 16,000.
18. Feroge = Ferohge = Kaligi = Kaliki = Kalige = Kalike.
19. Golo. Tucker and Bryan include this language in (2), above.
20. Indri = Yanderika = Yandirika.
21. Mangaya = Mangaiyat = Mongaiyat.
22. Ndogo.
23. Sere = Basiri = Basili.
24. Tagbu = Tagba = Tagbo.
25. *Togoyo.

VI

26. Dongo. 4,900. Congo, Faradje Territory.
27. Mba = Bamanga = Kimanga = Manga. 16,000. Congo, Banalia Territory.
28. Modunga = Bodunga = Ndunga. 2,500. Congo, Lisala Territory (eight villages).
29. Amadi = Ma = Madi = Madyo. Tucker and Bryan (1956) place Amadi in group **VI**, above. 4,700. Congo, northwest of Niangara.
30. Banda. Ds. Baba = Gbaba, Banda (88,000), Belingo = Bilingo, Bongo, Bria = Mbria, Buru = Borou = Brou = Mbrou = Mbru, Dakpa (6,000), Gbaga = Baga = G'bagga = M'bagga, Gbwende = Bende = Bendi = Gbindi, Gobu = Gabou = Ngobo = Ngobu, Jeto = Djeto = Djioteau, Junguru = Djingburu, Ka = Kha, Langba, Lagba, Linda (27,000), Langwasi = Langbase = Langbwasse, Mbala, Mbanja (70,000–80,000), Mbele = Mbre, Mbi, Mbugu = Bubu = Gbugbu = Mbogu = Mbubu, Mbulu = Mboulou, Mono = Amono (23,000), Mvedere = Vodere = Vidri, Ndi, Ndokpwa = Ndakpwa = Ndokoua = Ndopa, Ngaja = Ngadja, Ngao = Ngawo, Ngapu = Ngapou, Nguru = Ungourra, Nyele = Ndele = Ndere = Ngele, Nyele = Ndri, Sangbanga, Tagbwali, Tambag(g)o = Tombaggo, Togbo = Tagbo (5,500), Vora, Wada = Ouadda, Wasa = Ouassa, Yakpa = Yacoua = Yakpwa = Yakwa (26,000), Yangere (14,000). 350,000. Central African Republic, Congo, and adjacent territories.

Pygmy trs. listed by Welmers as speaking ADAMAWA-EASTERN languages: Babinga, Bamassa, Bayaka, Ganzi, Gundi, Mbacca.

AFFILIATION. Member of ADAMAWA-EASTERN.

ẸDO

GROUPING. Williamson (1968) divides the ẸDO languages (all spoken in

Nigeria) into four groups: CENTRAL (languages numbered 2, 4, 9), DELTA (3, 5, 6), NORTHERN (1, 8, 10, 11, 12, 13, 14, 15, 16), and SOUTHERN (7, 17). Elugbe (1971 and unpublished) and Williamson (1972b) have made revisions in the subclassification of languages in particular groups (see also Williamson and Thomas 1967, Wolff 1959).

1. Aakwọ. Ds. also Ghotuo, Ọkpẹ ? Ọkpẹ is also listed as a dialect of Urhobo (17, below).

2. Bini = Edo. 300,000. Benin City area.

3. Degema = Udekama. Ds. Atala, Usokun = Kala Degema. 5,000. Degema Province, Rivers State.

4. Emai. Ds. also Iuleha, Ora.

5. Engenni = Egene. Ds. Ediro, Inedua, Ogua. 12,200. Ahoada and Yenagoa divisions, Rivers State.

6. Epie. D. also Atisa = Atissa. 26,000. Around Yenagoa, Rivers State. Most speakers are bilingual in one of the ịjọ languages and regard themselves as 'Ịjọ'?

7. Erohwa = Eruhwa = Arokwa. In and around Erohwa and Anibezi in the extreme south of Isoko Division, Mid-Western State. Most Erohwa speakers are bilingual in the Central variety of Isoko (17, below), which is tending to replace Erohwa. Though Erohwa is sometimes classified as one of the Isoko dialects, it is not mutually intelligible with any of them (Mafeni 1972).

8. Ikpeshi. Ds. also Enwan, Sasaru.

9. Ishan = Esan = Isa = Esa. 90,000. Ishan Division, Benin Province.

10. Ivbie. Ds. also Okpela, Atẹ.

11. Iyẹkhee = Etsakọ = Etsakor. Etsako Division, Mid-Western State.

12. Ọkpamheri.

13. Ọsọsọ. Around Ososo.

14. Uhami. D. also Iyayu. Uhami is spoken in the Akoko East District, Akoko Division, Western State; Iyayu is spoken in the Ọwọ Division, Western State.

15. Ukue. D. also Ehuẹun. Akoko East District, Akoko Division, Western State.

16. Uneme.

17. Urhobo. Ds., sometimes treated as separate languages, Isoko = Igabo (derogatory) (135,000), including Northwestern Isoko (Emeror, Illhielogbo, Oghwe), Western Isoko (Enwe), Southwestern Isoko (Igbide, Ume), West-Central Isoko (Olomoro-Emede), Central = Standard Isoko (Uzere, Aviara, Iri), Northern Isoko (Uzoro, Elu, Ofagbe), Niger Isoko (Ase, Ibreda, Unọgbọkọ), Evhro (?), Okpara-Agbado (?); Ọkpẹ; Urhobo, including Abraka, Agbon, Ewu, Olomu, Ughelli, Ughienvwe, Uwherun. Isoko dialects are spoken in the Isoko Division, Mid-Western State except for Niger Isoko spoken in Aboh Division, East-Central State. Sobo is a cover term for the Urhobo and Isoko.

Afenmai = Kukuruku, including Otwa, sometimes listed as an ẸDO language spoken by 125,000 people in Benin and Kabba provinces is apparently a cover term for speakers of some of the languages listed above, since dialects of at least one CENTRAL and one NORTHERN language have been listed as Afenmai dialects.

AFFILIATION. Member of KWA.

*Elamite = Anzanite = Susian = Hozi. Inscriptions dating from 2500 B.C. Spoken in an area corresponding to modern Luristan and Khozistan in Iran. Still spoken in the first century A.D. (Paper 1955, Diakonoff 1967, Reiner 1969).

AFFILIATION. None known.

EQUATORIAL

GROUPING. In contrast to the four major groups (together with relatively numerous single languages) in ANDEAN (q. v.), there are more than twice as many major groups (families) in the EQUATORIAL division of the phylum (but relatively few single languages not classified under one or another family). Of the nine families classified as EQUATORIAL, two are listed here (in alphabetical order), but are treated in separate articles — namely, ARAWAKAN and TUPI. The rest are treated below.

ARAWAKAN (q. v.).

CARIRI. Formerly east central Brazil.
1. Cariri. Ds. also Camuru, *Dzubucua, *Pedra Branca, *Quipea = Kipea. The Camaru dialect may still be spoken.
2. *Pancararú = Pankaru = Pancaru = Pankaravu = Pankaroru. 2,000. On São Francis River in northern Bahia, Brazil.
3. *Sapuya = Sapuia.

4. Cayuvava = Cayawabas = Cayuaba = Kayubaba = Chacobo. Less than 100. Bolivia.

GUAHIBO-PAMIGUA. The family consists of two branches: GUAHIBAN (5–7) and PAMIGUAN (8, 9), both in central and eastern Colombia; GUAHIBAN languages extend into Venezuela.
5. Churoya = Churuya. D. also Bisanigua.
6. Cunimía = Canimia. D. also Guayavero = Guayabero.
7. Guahibo = Guaigua = Guayba = Guajibo = Wahibo = Goahivo = Goahiva. Ds. also Chiricoa (including also Sicuane in Colombia), Cuiba (possibly extinct; including Mella, Ptamo), Yamu. 15,000–45,000. Colombia (10,000–20,000), Venezuela (5,000–20,000).
8. *Pamigua = Bamigua.
9. Tinigua.

MOCOA. Southwestern Colombia.
10. *Otamaco = Otamaca. D. also Taparita = Taparito.
11. *Patoco = Pastoco.
12. *Quillacinga.
13. Sebondoy. Perhaps still spoken.

SALIVAN = SALIBAN = PIAROAN. South central Venezuela.
14. Duniberrenai.
15. Macu.
16. Piaroa. 12,000.

17. *Saliva.

TIMOTE = CUICA-TIMOTE. Highlands of Venezuela. The constituents include a number of tribes or subtribes probably assignable either to Cuica (18) or to Timote (19), namely, Burubusay, Carache, Chejende, Monay, Siquisaye.
18. Cuica. Ds. also Escuquean, Jojoan, Tostoan.
19. Timote. Ds. also Migurian = Chama, Mocochi = Torondoyan, Mocotan = Mukutu = Escaguey, Tapanoan.

20. Trumai = Tramalhys. Less than ten. Until 1962, when a flu epidemic decimated them the Trumai occupied a single village on the right-hand bank of the lower Culuene River.

TUPI (q. v.)

21. Tuyuneri = Tuyoneri = Pucapacuri. Peru.

YURACAREAN. Central Bolivia.
22. Mansinyo = Mansiño = Western Yuracare. D. also *Oromo.
23. Soloto = Eastern Yuracare.

ZAMUCOAN. Spoken in Bolivia and Paraguay in northern Chaco.
24. Northern Zamucoan. Ds. = Trs. Cucarate, Moro, Poturero, Satienyo = Zatieño, Tsiracua.
25. Southern Zamucoan. Ds. = Trs. Caipotorade, Ebidoso, Horio, Imono, Tumereha, Tunacho.

AFFILIATION. As a whole, EQUATORIAL, including ARAWAKAN and TUPI, is classified as a division of ANDEAN-EQUATORIAL.

ESKIMO-ALEUT

GROUPING. Ever since Rasmussen reported his trek *Across Arctic America* (1927), it has been known that all varieties of Greenlandic and Central Eskimo, as well as varieties north of the Yukon in Alaska, are without question dialects of a single Eskimo language — Inuit, (2), below. The language barrier that Rasmussen encountered in Alaska made it impossible for him "without the aid of an interpreter" to communicate with speakers of Yupik, which turns out to have at least four mutually unintelligible dialects — hence separate languages (3, 4, 5, 6), according to Krauss (1973a), who includes an exhaustive bibliography on Eskimo and Aleut linguistic studies from 1945–1970. Aleut is spoken in two or three quite distinct dialects, which are nevertheless mutually intelligible and therefore constitute, according to Krauss, a single language (1).

1. Aleut. Ds. Central Aleut = Atka (Andreanof and Rat Islands and Bering Island in the Komandorskiye group off the Siberian Coast); Eastern Aleut = Unalaska = Umnak (Alaska Peninsula and Fox Islands as far west as Umnak Islands, and also on Pribilof Islands 200 miles north of the Aleutians); Western Aleut = Attu(an) (Near Islands and Copper Island in the Komandorskiye). U.S. (500),

U.S.S.R. (100). Krauss treats Central and Eastern Aleut as a single dialect; hence Western Aleut is a divergent dialect.

2. Inuit = Iñupiat = Inupiaq = Inupik. Ds. Barrow-Inglestatt = Kangianermiut (Alaska, northernmost coast of Norton Sound and parts of northern Alaskan plain, and Kotzebue Sound and Point Barrow). The four Hudson Bay dialects (Canada) are Cumberland Sound Eskimo (Southern Baffin Island, northern coast of Hudson Strait, Frobisher Bay, Cumberland Sound); Iglulik = Iglulingmiut (Fury and Hecla Straits, east coast of Melville Peninsula to Lyon's Inlet) = Aivilik = Aivilingmiut (Repulse Bay and west coast of Roe's Welcome to Chesterfield Inlet) = Tunuermiut (Pond's Inlet); Netsilik = Netsilingmiut = Arviligjuarmiut = Háningajormiut = *Sinimiut = Utkuhigjalingmiut (region around Magnetic Pole from Committee Bay on the east to Simpson Strait to the west); Barren Grounds = Qaernermiut = Kenipitu = Hauneqtôrmiut = Harvaqtôrmiut = Pâdlimiut. Other Canadian ds. are Mackenzie-Coronation, including Copper Eskimos (Canada, Mackenzie River Delta, Coronation Gulf and Bathhurst Inlet); Wales-King, including Kingingmiut, Quavjasâmiut, Ukiuvangmiut = Ukiuvak (Canada, Cape Prince of Wales, westernmost Seward Peninsula on Bering Strait; King Island, Bering Strait). The three dialects of Greenlandic-Labrador are East Greenlandic = Ammassalik = Angmagssalik (Greenland, with N. Kialêq-Pikiutdleq = Kialineq-Pikîteq, N. Umîvik-Ikermiut = Ikermîn, N. Anoritôq = Anoriteq-Aluk = Alik, the southern part of east coast from Blosseville to Cape Farewell, and an extinct group further north on Clavering Island); West Greenlandic (with Julianehaab, Frederikshaab-Hosteinsborg, Egedesminde-Ûmánaq, Upernivik; west coast of Greenland); and Polar = Thule (Greenland, Cape York district at Smith Sound). 43,000 (Greenland), 16,000 (Canada), 6,000 (Alaska), 10 (Siberia).

3. Sirenik (Yupik). 10. Siberia.

4. Central Alaskan Yupik. 14,500. From the north shore of the Alaska Peninsula across Bristol Bay and the Kuskokwim and Yukon deltas to the south shore of Norton Sound, spreading far up the Kuskokwim to Sleetmute and the Yukon to Holy Cross.

5. Pacific Gulf Yupik. 2,000. Prince William Sound (Chugach), Outer Cook Inlet, Kodiak Island, Alaska Peninsula. Popularly called 'Aleut'.

6. St. Lawrence Island Yupik. Ds. also Chaplino and Naukan in Siberia. 1700 (1000 St. Lawrence Island, Alaska, 500 Chaplino, 200 Naukan).

AFFILIATION. The ESKIMO-ALEUT family has been said to be remotely related to one of the Paleosiberian families, CHUCKCHEE-KAMCHATKAN = LUORAWETLAN, by Bouda (1941) and Swadesh (1962, 1964); to URALIC, by Bergsland (1949, 1959); to INDO-EUROPEAN, by Uhlenbeck (1942-45), Thalbitzer (1945, 1948, 1949), and Hammerich (1951); and to the Yahgan language spoken in Tierra del Fuego, by Jenness (1953).

*Eteocretan. An undeciphered script found in Crete (Hrozný 1947).

AFFILIATION. None known.

*Eteocyprian. An undeciphered script found in Cyprus (Pedersen 1938).

AFFILIATION. None known.

*Etruscan. A non-INDO-EUROPEAN language known in Italy from the eighth century B.C. to the fourth century A.D., when it became extinct.

AFFILIATION. Herodotus suggested Lydian affinities, or perhaps Lemnian (Trombetti 1928).

EWE

GROUPING. Speakers of EWE languages total over 1,000,000. Some regard (1) and (2), below, to be dialects of a single language.

1. Ewe. Ds. A(d)ja = Adya (3,000), Awuna = Aŋlo (5,000), Gẽ = Gaingbe = Guingbe = Mina (62,000), Gŭ = Goun = Egun = Alada; Mahi (12,000), Watyi = Ouatchi (124,000); Trs. Glidyi, Ho, Hula = Pea, Peda. Southeastern Ghana, and Togo, Dahomey.
2. Fõ = Fon = Fongbe = Dahomeen = Djedji. Southern Dahomey.

AFFILIATION. Member of KWA phylum.

FREDERIK HENDRIK ISLAND AND SOUTHEAST WEST IRIAN

GROUPING. Wurm (1971c) treats as three separate subgroups of CENTRAL AND SOUTH NEW GUINEA: languages numbered (1), (7), and (14); languages (3), (8), and (10); and languages (5) and (13). Greenberg (1971b) classifies all these as a single subgroup of SOUTHERN.

1. Kanum. 320. Near Australian New Guinea border.
2. Keladdar.
3. Kimaghama. 3,000. Frederik Hendrik Island.
4. Koneraw.
5. Makleu = Maklew. 120. Mainland, just east of Frederik Hendrik Island.
6. Mombum = Komelom. 250. Island adjacent to southeast coast of Frederik Hendrik Island.
7. Moraori. 40. Near Australian border.
8. Ndom. 450. Frederik Hendrik Island.
9. Ngowugar.
10. Riantana. 1,100. Frederik Hendrik Island.
11. Teri-Kawalsch. Frederik Hendrik Island.
12. Toro.
13. Yelmek = Jelmek = Jab. 350. Mainland, just east of Frederik Hendrik Island.
14. Yey = Jei. 1,000. Near Australian border.

AFFILIATION. Member of CENTRAL AND SOUTH NEW GUINEA.

GÃ-ADANGME

GROUPING. Languages (1) and (2), following, are separated by Welmers (1971a) but merged by Westermann and Bryan (1952) as a complex dialect cluster of one language. 250,000.

1. Adangme = Adangbe. Ds. also Ad(d)a, Kpone, Krobo = Klo, Ni(n)go = Nungo, Osuduku, Prampram = Gbugbla, Shai = Se. Spoken in Ada, Ghana, and northeast hinterland of dialects of 2 below.
2. Gã. D. also Gẽ = Gain = Anima. Gã proper: Accra, Ghana, and Anecho area, Togo; Gẽ: along Dahomey coast.

AFFILIATION. Member of KWA phylum.

GARAMAN

GROUPING. Spoken on the northwestern coast of the Northern Territory Australia, north of the Fitzmaurice River.

1. Garama.
2. Murinbata = Marinbata.

AFFILIATION. Member of AUSTRALIAN macro-phylum.

GE = JÊ = ŽE

GROUPING. The GE languages, spoken in Eastern Brazil and extending into Paraguay, are grouped primarily by geographical criteria into three branches, CAINGANG, CENTRAL, and NORTHWEST, with the exception of one ungrouped Brazilian language, *Jeico = Jaico = Jaicuju = Jahycu = Yeico, which became extinct in the 1850s.

The CAINGANG branch is further divided into a TAVEN group (numbered 1–6, of which 1–3 are collectively known as GUALACHO = CORONADO) plus two ungrouped Brazilian languages, *Dorin (possibly not extinct) and Caingang. The latter was formerly considered to be a subgroup of CAINGANG languages, but Weisemann, according to Longacre (1968a), treats Caingang as one language to which she adds Xokreng = Xokleng = Chocren as a dialect; Chocren was formerly considered an independent language of the more inclusive CAINGANG branch of GE. Other Caingang dialects are *Chiqui, Nhacfateitei = Nyacfateitei, and dialects spoken in Paraná, Rio Grande do Sul, and São Paulo.

The CENTRAL GE branch (numbered 7–17) is divided into an ACROA group (7–13) and an ACUA group (14–17). The NORTHWEST GE branch (numbered 18–49) is divided geographically into two groups, CAYAPO (18–29) and EAST TIMBIRA = HOTI (30–49), and two independent languages of Brazil, Apinage = Apinaye (= Mason's West Timbira) and Suya. Probably too many names are listed as representing separate languages in CENTRAL GE.

Wilbert (1962) attempted a lexicostatistical classification of CENTRAL and NORTHWEST GE, which he acknowledged as tentative, but which corresponds largely to the geographical distribution of the languages. He apparently combines the CAYAPO group with Suya in his CAYAPO family; the remainder of NORTHWEST GE he calls the APINAYE family and he calls CENTRAL GE the ACROA family. The classifications, however, are not entirely mutually equivalent since Wilbert's list does not include all the languages, and some of the names are different. So also in the classification of Davis (1968), who groups the GE languages on the basis of comparative studies. The overall grouping given here follows Davis, but his subgroupings, which are not clearly specified to be based on comparative evidence, are not equivalent to previous ones and are not followed here. Location is specified below only if outside of Brazil.

TAVEN GROUP of CAINGANG
1. *Cabelludo. Possibly not extinct.
2. *Chiqui = Chiki.
3. *Guaiana = Guayana.
4. *Gualachi.
5. Ivitorocai = Amho. Paraguay.
6. *Tain = Ingain. Equation of Ingain with Tain rather than Guaiana follows Métraux (1946).

ACROA GROUP of CENTRAL GE
7. North Acroa.
8. South Acroa.
9. Aricobe.
10. *Arua.
11. Guegué = Gogué.
12. *Ponta.
13. *Timbira.

ACUA = AKWA = AKWẼ GROUP of CENTRAL GE
14. *Chacriaba = Shacriaba = Chikriaba.
15. Chavante = Shavante = Crisca = Pusciti = Tapacua.
16. Cherente = Sherenté.
17. *Goya = Goia.

CAYAPÓ = CAIAPO SUBGROUP of NORTHWEST GE
18. Carahó = Karahó.
19. North Cayapo = Cayamo = Caraja = Coroa = Ibiraira. 10,000.
20. *South Cayapo (possibly not extinct).
21. Cruatíre.
22. Curupite.
23. Duludi.
24. Gorotire = Xingu Caiapo. 250.
25. Gradahó = Cradahó = Gradaú.
26. *Ira-Amaire = Purukaru.

27. Pau d'Arco.
28. *Purucarod = Purucaru. D. also Curupite.
29. Uchicrin = Ushicriṅg = Chicri = Byoré.

TIMBIRA GROUP of NORTHWEST GE
30. Apanhecra.
31. Augutge = Gaviose. 2,000.
32. *Caracatage.
33. *Chacamecra.
34. Craho = Kraho = Krao.
35. Creapimcatage = Crepumcateye.
36. *Crenge = Crange = Taže of Cajuapara.
37. Creye = Crenye = Tage of Bacabal.
38. Cricatage = Cricati = Caracaty = Macraia.
39. Gurupy.
40. Macamecran = Pepuchi.
41. *Mehin.
42. *Norocoage.
43. Nucoecamecran = Cucoecamecra.
44. *Paicoge.
45. Piocobge = Pucobge = Bucobu.
46. *Poncatage.
47. *Purecamecran.
48. *Quencatage.
49. Ramcocamecra = Capiecran = Merrime. 500.

AFFILIATION. Member of MACRO-GE within GE-PANO-CARIB.

MACRO-GE = MACRO-JÊ

GROUPING. The MACRO-GE group includes seven or eight language families: BOTOCUDO, CAMACAN, CAINGANG, CARAJÁ, CHIQUITO, GE, MACHACALI, and PURÍ, and seven ungrouped languages (listed below), probably only one or two of which are still spoken. Formerly, the CAMACAN, MACHACALI, and PURÍ families were all taken to be a part of the GE family, rather than MACRO-GE, but later classifiers sometimes separate these and the CAINGANG languages from GE proper. (CAINGANG is treated here under GE; the other families mentioned are treated in separate articles.)

The broad classification given here follows Davis (1968) in part, and follows Greenberg (1960a) elsewhere.

Greenberg treats the CAINGANG languages as coordinate with GE, whereas Davis classifies them as a branch of GE. The CARAJÁ languages and Opaie (included here in MACRO-GE, following Davis) were treated as not related to other languages prior to Greenberg. Greenberg, however, considered the CARAJÁ languages to be coordinate with MACRO-GE in his MACRO-GE-BORORO-CARAJÁ grouping, and classified Opaie with the GUAICURU languages as a constituent of MACRO-PANOAN.

The CHIQUITO family, which was also formerly treated as independent, is classified in MACRO-GE by Greenberg.

Davis classifies CARAJÁ within MACRO-GE rather than coordinate with it. Hamp (1969b), commenting on Davis' conclusions, states that the relation of MACHACALI to CARAJÁ within MACRO-GE is impossible to specify at the present time.

*Patachó, one of the ungrouped languages, was originally classified as a MACHA-CALI language and is so classified by Davis. There is much disagreement on the affinities of Coropo and Malali. Otí is to be distinguished from three other languages, which are also called Chavanté, but which are all of different linguistic affinities.

1. *Coropo. Between the Doce and Parchyba rivers in Brazil.
2. Fulnió = Fornió = Carnijó = Iaté. 1,500 (1946). State of Pernambuco, Brazil.
3. *Guato. Probably extinct. Mato Grosso, Brazil, and adjacent parts of Bolivia.
4. *Malali. Headwaters of the Aracuai River in Brazil.
5. Opaie = Opayé = Ofaye = Opayé Shavanté. Extinct or nearly so. Southern Mato Grosso in Brazil.
6. *Oti = Shavanté = Chavanté = Šavanté = Eochavanté. Brazil.
7. *Patachó = Patashó. May possibly not be extinct. Southeastern Bahia, Brazil from the seaboard inland to the headwaters of the Porto Seguro and the Jucurucu rivers.

AFFILIATION. Member of MACRO-GE-BORORO grouping within GE-PANO-CARIB.

MACRO-GE-BORORO

GROUPING. One family, BORORO (q. v.) and one phylum, MACRO-GE (q. v.), are grouped together by Greenberg (1960a), who also includes the CARAJÁ family (q. v.), as a coordinate member, while Davis (1968) reclassifies CARAJÁ as being within MACRO-GE on the basis of comparative studies. Prior to Greenberg, both BORORO and CARAJÁ were considered to be independent families. Wares (1968b) still lists the Bororo language as unclassified. The languages of these groups are spoken primarily in Brazil, but extend into Bolivia and Paraguay.

AFFILIATION. Member of GE-PANO-CARIB.

GE-PANO-CARIB

GROUPING. Classifications previous to Greenberg (1960a) treated the GE, PANO, and CARIB groups of languages as independent rather than as genetically related. The six members of GE-PANO-CARIB are: three major groupings, MACRO-CARIB, MACRO-GE-BORORO, and MACRO-PANOAN; two families, HUARPE and NAMBI-CUARA; and one language isolate, Taruma. (Each of the groups indicated by capital letters is treated in a separate article.) This classification follows Greenberg.

Both the HUARPE and NAMBICUARA language families were formerly considered independent; i.e., related neither to each other nor to other families.

In general, for the Andean regions of South America, the more widely spread languages are spoken by a million people or even by several million. A paradoxical external feature of GE-PANO-CARIB is its large areal spread (virtually continental) combined with a relatively low number of speakers.

The GE-PANO-CARIB languages are spoken east of the Andean mountain chain from Colombia, Peru, Bolivia, Argentina, Paraguay, and the Brazilian basin of the Amazon to the north-facing coastlines of Brazil, French Guiana, Surinam, Guyana, and Venezuela. These languages are currently spoken by possibly fewer than a million people altogether although estimates run as high as 1.5 million.

*Taruma, the single language isolate, was most often classified as ARAWAKAN or of probable ARAWAKAN affinity prior to Greenberg. It is probably extinct; formerly spoken in Brazil and Paraguay.

AFFILIATION. None known.

*Gergito-Salymean. A non-INDO-EUROPEAN language of ancient Asia Minor known chiefly from Greek traditions.

AFFILIATION. None known (Bürchner 1910, Kretschmer 1896).

GERMANIC

GROUPING. The extinct languages, numbered (1) and (2) following, comprise the EAST GERMANIC group; beside these, the extant GERMANIC languages are traditionally classified either in a NORTH GERMANIC group, including languages (3) and (4), or in a WEST GERMANIC group, including languages (5), (22), and (24), as well as the many ENGLISH-BASED PIDGIN-CREOLES (6–21) and Negerhollands (23).

This traditional tripartite division into EAST, WEST, and NORTH GERMANIC — fully expounded by Streitberg (1896) and Streitberg et al. (1936) and subsequent authorities (Müllenhoff 1890–1920; Hirt 1931–1934; Prokosch 1939) — has recently been challenged. Schwarz (1951, 1956) and Lehmann (1966) offer evidence for a bipartate division into NORTHEASTERN (EAST and NORTH) and WESTERN GERMANIC, a division that was already postulated by Scherer (1868).

Long contact between various groups has led to the diffusion of phonological features which has somewhat obscured the paths of descent from Proto-Germanic. Later changes accounted for by wave theory that swept over NORTH and WEST GERMANIC have led most scholars to reduce the status of WEST GERMANIC languages to a geographical designation. But Voyles (1972) holds that WEST GERMANIC represents the descendants of an actual Germanic proto-language of the same status as NORTH and EAST GERMANIC, thereby controverting Arndt (1959) and Maurer (1952). Voyles postulates the earliest split of Proto-Germanic to have been between EAST GERMANIC and the rest, with a subsequent split between NORTH and WEST GERMANIC.

There are today more than a dozen literary 'languages'; i.e., 'languages' having a particular literary tradition that distinguishes them from other 'languages' having other literary traditions. The literary 'languages' of Insular Scandinavian include Icelandic and Faroese; those of Continental Scandinavian include Danish, Nynorsk, Bokmål, and Swedish; those of Netherlandic-German include Afrikaans, Dutch, Flemish, Low German, Luxemburgian, Standard High German, and Yiddish. But there is, in a coordinate sense, only one literary 'language' for English, and one for Frisian.

Diverse, but not necessarily contradictory, classifications are obtainable from literary 'languages', historical developments, wave theory, and current dialect differentiations which either permit mutual intelligibility or else become barriers to communication. For example, historically, Norwegian would be grouped with Icelandic and Faroese, but while the latter two are mutually intelligible (Insular Scandinavian), Norwegian now shares intelligibility with Danish and Swedish (Continental Scandinavian); and there is a language barrier between Insular and Continental Scandinavian.

EAST GERMANIC

1. *Burgundian. Ds. also spoken by the Gepidae, Rugii, and Vandals. Found in East Germany around 50 A.D.

2. *Gothic. Ds. Crimean Gothic (extant in the sixteenth century when texts were gathered; Bloomfield (1933) indicates that there were some EAST GERMANIC settlements in Crimea which survived until the eighteenth century); Ostrogoth (east side of the Dnieper Diver); Visigoth (west side of the Dnieper River). Gothic speakers inhabited the area of modern Bulgaria, perhaps migrating from Scandinavia prior to 50 A.D. (There are a number of features which Gothic shares with Old Norse as against WEST GERMANIC.) After 100 A.D. the Goths migrated south-eastward from the Vistula; before 250 A.D. they had split into two groups on the east and west plains of the Dnieper.

NORTH GERMANIC = SCANDINAVIAN = NORDIC. All dialects of this group are historically derived from *Old Norse, the language of the Viking Age (700 or 800 to 1050, 1250, or even 1350). Old Norse diverged into Eastern Old Norse (the progenitor of Danish and Swedish) and West Old Norse, the progenitor of Norwegian, Icelandic, and Faroese (Haugen 1968). During the modern period (1525 onward) Insular dialects (Icelandic and Faroese) became isolated from the Continental dialects, which remained in continuous contact.

3. Continental Scandinavian. Ds. Danish (4,700,000 in Denmark, 400,000 in the United States, and 10,000 in Germany; subdialectal division into Northern and Southern on the basis of the so-called 'stφd' feature, usually a 'glottal creak' in Southern corresponding to pitch-stress phenomena in Northern Danish, Norwegian, and Swedish); Norwegian (3,600,000 in Norway, 700,000 in the United States; there are two literary standards: Dano-Norwegian = Bokmål = Riksmål and New Norse = Nynorsk; and within Nynorsk there are urban standards and rural dialects [including Eastern, from Telemark to the Swedish border and north to the Dovre Mountains; Northern, in the three northernmost counties; Trönder, in the trading area of Trondheim; and Western, in the fjord country from Romsdal to Setesdal]); Swedish (7,500,000 in Sweden, 1,000,000 in the United States and Canada, 400,000 in Finland, and a small number in Estonia; grouped into two subdialect groups; the Göta group or South Swedish [including parts of Småland, south Swedish provinces, Värmland, Västergötland], the Svea group or North Swedish [including

Hälsingland, parts of Ostergotland, and Uppland, and the Swedish-speaking parts of Finland and Estonia]).

4. Insular Scandinavian. Ds. Faroese (35,000, on the Dutch-administered Faroe Islands; with practically as many subdialects as there are inhabited islands); Icelandic (180,000 in Iceland, 20,000 in United States; with Northern and Southern subdialects, and some variation between speakers in fishing and in farming communities). Nearly 250,000. Iceland, Faroe Islands, and the United States.

WEST GERMANIC. The languages numbered (5), (22), and (24) following are separated from each other by language barriers of different heights. In the case of English (5), there is neighbor intelligibility between different variants even if distant dialects or a remote dialect and Standard English are not always mutually intelligible; so also for Frisian (22), which is closer to English than either is to Netherlandic-German (24).

In the case of Netherlandic-German, as in the case of English, neighboring dialects are mutually intelligible, even though it is impossible to detect the existence of very much intelligibility, for example, in attempted conversations between speakers of Standard Dutch and Standard German; intelligibility becomes salient only for those speakers who control dialects intervening between the two standards. Though recognizing the dialect diversity in German speaking countries and in The Netherlands, as well as the existence of different literary 'languages', both Bloomfield (1933) and Moulton (1968) regard Netherlandic-German to be a separate, single language because mutual intelligibility obtains between each pair of adjacent dialects in a chain or network that links areas and spans the countries in question.

The paucity of WEST GERMANIC languages (5, 22, 24) is offset by the multitude of ENGLISH-BASED PIDGIN-CREOLES (6–21, below). From the point of view of a true ethnolinguistics — native speaker interpretations of native speaker classifications — there exists a multitude of WEST GERMANIC languages which exceeds the multitude of ENGLISH-BASED PIDGIN-CREOLES. The difference between the ethnolinguistic interpretation and the Bloomfield-Moulton interpretation lies in the point of departure in evaluating intelligibility, from a standard language (or out-of-contact dialect) and from a neighboring dialect, respectively.

5. English. Ds. American (Eastern in New England or northeastern United States, Midland in East-central United States, Southern in southeastern United States and the Caribbean seaboard, Northern-Western in the Great Lakes region and most of the area west of the Mississippi); Australian; British (Eastern [including Cambridge, Rutland, N.E. Northhampton; most of Essex and Hertford, Huntingdon, Bedford, Mid Northhampton; Norfolk and Suffolk; most of Buckingham; Middlesex, S.E. Buckingham, S. Hertford and S.W. Essex], Midland [Lincolnshire; S.E. Lancashire, N.E. Cheshire, N.W. Derby; S.W. Lancashire, south of the Ribble; Mid Lancashire and the Isle of Man; S. Yorkshire; most of Cheshire, N. Staffordshire; most of Derby; Nottingham; Flint and Denbigh; E. Shropshire, S. Staffordshire, most of Warwickshire, S. Derby, Leicestershire], Northern [Northumberland and

N. Durham; S. Durham, most of Cumberland, Westmoreland, N. Lancashire and the hilly parts of W. Yorkshire; N. and E. Yorkshire], Southern [parts of Pembroke and Glamorgan; Wiltshire, Dorset, N. and E. Somerset, most of Gloucester and S.W. Devon; most of Hampshire, Isle of Wight, most of Berkshire, S. Surrey and W. Sussex; N. Gloucester, E. Hereford, Worcester, S. Warwick, N. Oxford, and S.W. Northhampton; most of Oxford; N. Surrey and N.W. Kent; most of Kent and E. Sussex; W. Somerset and N.E. Devon; most of Devon and E. Cornwall; W. Cornwall], Western [W. and S. Shropshire; Hereford, except East Hereford, Radnor, and E. Brecknock]); Canadian (somewhat like the American Northern subdialect, but in some areas British English features are maintained); Irish English (Dublin, in east-central Ireland; Ulster Scots, including Northern Ireland and the northern part of the Republic of Ireland; Wexford, in southeastern Ireland); Scots English (Mid [including W. Angus = W. Forfar, E. and S. Perthshire, Stirling, Fife, Kinross, Klackmannan; Linlithgow = W. Lothian, Edinburg = Mid Lothian, Haddington = E. Lothian, Berwich, and Peebles; E. and W. Dumbarton, S. Argyll, Bute, Renfrew, Glasgow, Lanark, and N. Ayr; S. Ayr, Galloway, and W. Dumfries], Northern [Shetland and Orkney = Insular; Cromarty, Eastern Ross, Black Isle; Caithness and Sutherland; Lower Banff, Aberdeen, Buchan, and Deeside; Inverness, Nairn, Moray, and Upper Banff; Mearns = Kincardine, and E. Angus = E. Forfar], Southern [Roxburg, Selkirk, E. Dumfries and Mid Dumfries]). 300,000,000 (250,000,000 native speakers; 50,000,000 as a second language); United States (more than 180,000,000); British Isles (including Eire, 55,000,000); Canada (13,000,000); Australia (11,000,000); Philippines (11,000,000, mainly as a second language), India (7,000,000, mainly as a second language); New Zealand (2,500,000); Jamaica (1,500,000); Tanganyika (1,500,00, mainly as a second language); Kenya (1,500,000); Nigeria, Ghana, and Uganda (1,000,000 each, as a second language). By world areas: New World (196,000,000), Europe (55,000,000), Pacific (23,000,000), Africa (15,000,000), Asia (8,000,000). There are three recognized historical periods of the English language: *Old English (450–1150), with the dialects Anglian (Northumbrian, Mercian), Kentish, West Saxon; *Old English was substantially influenced by Norse-speaking settlers in the northeast. *Middle English (1150–1500); the Norman Conquest (1066) introduced French influence, which replaced the Scandinavian influence. Modern English (1500 onward) had an extensive influx of foreignisms, particularly from Latin and Greek. The most influential of all dialects of English is that of London, based on the Mercian = East Midland variety (Dieth 1946). Brook (1963) regards all dialects of English as mutually intelligible. American dialects are not so diverse as those of the British Isles (Kurath et al. 1939 onward).

ENGLISH-BASED PIDGIN CREOLES. Two groups are distinguished; a PACIFIC group, which probably shares a common origin with other 'EUROPEAN-BASED PIDGIN-CREOLES' (Whinnom 1965, 1967; Wurm 1971a), and an ATLANTIC group, which shows a divergence from other 'EUROPEAN-BASED PIDGIN-CREOLES' and is probably descended from a Proto-Pidgin English in use along the West African coast in the early sixteenth century (Cassidy 1962; Hall 1966). Pitcairnese, while in the Pacific area, developed independently of any Portuguese influence (DeCamp 1968); it shares features with the ATLANTIC group (Hancock n.d.), suggesting a development from the Proto-Pidgin of the African West Coast. The status of the PACIFIC group of ENGLISH-BASED PIDGIN-CREOLES, however, remains controversial, as it lacks many features of other 'EUROPEAN-BASED PIDGIN-CREOLES' while being at the same time divergent from the ATLANTIC group (DeCamp 1968; Hancock n.d.).

ATLANTIC = CENTRAL ATLANTIC. This group possibly represents the modern descendants of a single English-Pidgin spoken along the West African coast since the early sixteenth century. Cassidy (1962) indicates that English-Pidgin had established itself on the West Coast prior to the mass exportation of slaves. The Gold Coast seaboard would thus be one of the original centers of English-Pidgin, but these varieties were profoundly influenced by the arrival of freed men — the Jamaican Maroons, Nova Scotians, and Black Poor from Britain who arrived in Sierra Leone between 1787 and 1860; from Sierra Leone some went to the Cameroons. This may account for the similarity of Cameroon Pidgin to Krio, grouped in an EAST subgroup, as opposed to the remaining (New World) English-Pidgins, placed in a WEST subgroup.

In the WEST subgroup the varieties of Surinam, e.g., Sranan and Saramaccan and related varieties in the country, are divergent from one another and from other New World varieties. Saramaccan is the most deviant of the ATLANTIC group, with far more Portuguese and African items than are found elsewhere. The close similarity of Pitcairnese and the ATLANTIC group possibly indicates that the mutineers who settled Pitcairn spoke the nautical pidgin of the West African Coast.

The most conservative language is Sranan, which was under the influence of English for only a short time, while the Caribbean varieties — as well as Krio, and Gulla — have been under the constant influence of Standard English varieties for two centuries.

6. Aucaan. Spoken in Surinam.
7. Djuka = Ndjuka = Djoe-Tongo. Along the Marowijne, Cottica, and Commowijne rivers in Surinam. Close affinities with Sranan, such that speakers of Sranan can learn Djuka quite easily.
8. Gulla(h) = Geechee. Formerly widely spoken in Georgia, South Carolina, and nearby Sea Island, but now extinct on the mainland, and even rarely spoken on Sea Island (Turner 1949).
9. Jamaican Creole = Bongo Talk. 1,500,000. Jamaica, Trinidad, Tobago, Guyana, British Honduras, Barbados, St. Lucia, St. Kitts, Anguilla, Nevis, the Netherlands Antilles. Sometimes regarded as a variety of English (Jamaican English) rather than as a separate creole language (William Stewart 1962); there is no clear separation but a continuum, between the Standard English and the Jamaican Creole (Decamp 1971). The extreme varieties of Jamaican Creole and Standard English are mutually unintelligible.
10. Krio = Pidgin Krio = Pidgin English = Talkee Talkee (in first part of nineteenth century). Ds. also Gambian Krio = Aku = Patois

(3,000; Bathhurst, Gambia), Guinea-Senegal (small enclaves where Creole merchants have formed their own Krio-speaking communities), Fernando Po Krio (Creoles originally from Freetown). 20,000–120,000. Sierra Leone: centered in Freetown, Sierra Leone, in various villages in the Sierra Leone Peninsula, on Bonthe, and in the Banana Islands where Creole families have settled; Gambia (Bathhurst); perhaps also in small enclaves in Guinea and Senegal. Employed as a lingua franca throughout Sierra Leone.

11. Pitcairnese. D. also Norfolk Island (a closely related offshoot). Developed from the voluntary settling of Pitcairn Island in 1790 by mutineers from the H.M.S. Bounty. Still spoken on the two islands, Pitcairn and Norfolk, some 4,000 miles away — on the latter by Pitcairn Islanders removed in 1859. Also spoken by second-generation Pitcairn Islanders settled in Australia and New Zealand. It appears that the morphology and lexicon of Pitcairnese are from nautical pidgin rather than Standard English (Hancock n.d.).

12. Saramaccan = Jew Tongo. Ds. Lower Saramaccan, Upper Saramaccan. Spoken along the Surinam and Brownsweg Rivers in Surinam. It appears to be the most deviant of the six English Creoles surveyed by Hancock (n.d.). Saramaccan and Sranan are quite divergent in vocabulary and in phonology. Saramaccan and Djuka are languages of the 'Bush Negroes' (those who escaped plantations during slavery), and Sranan is that of the freed slaves and their descendants (Voorhoeve 1961).

13. Sranan = Sranan Tongo = Taki-Taki = Neng(e)re-Tongo = Kriono = Neger-Engelsch. Ds. also East Sranan, Matuari (spoken on the Saramacca River), West Sranan. 80,000. Coastal belt of Surinam: Paramaribo and surrounding districts. Employed as a lingua franca throughout the country. Cassidy (1962) has suggested that Sranan, which has some Portuguese elements, may be derived from Portuguese sources, but its similarities to Krio weaken this theory (Hancock n.d.).

14. Wescos = Cameroons Pidgin.

PACIFIC. The numerous varieties of ENGLISH-BASED PIDGIN-CREOLES in the PACIFIC group (minus Pitcairnese and Norfolk), both past and present, seem likely to have their origin in Beach-la-Mar. Beach-la-Mar came into use in contacts between Europeans and the native populations in the area from the New Hebrides to the Carolinas (Hall 1966), and is believed derived from Chinese Pidgin-English. Whinnom (1965, 1967) believes these to be relexified Portuguese-based Pidgin-Creole.

15. Australian pidgin. Nearly extinct, but still used in the far north of Australia and in other isolated areas. Its origin antedates Beach-la-Mar, but the two probably have a common origin (Wurm 1971a).

16. Beach-la-Mar = Bislama. 50,000. Used as a lingua franca and contact vernacular in the New Hebrides and Fiji. It was formerly widespread, giving rise to many local varieties which were the ancestors of other PACIFIC AREA ENGLISH-BASED PIDGIN-CREOLES. Its distribution at one

time extended into Polynesia, and it may have played a part in the creation of Hawaiian Pidgin. A number of words of Portuguese origin support the theory that Beach-la-Mar constitutes a relexification of a Portuguese Pidgin, or perhaps of Chinese Pidgin (itself probably a relexified Portuguese Pidgin).

17. Hawaiian Pidgin = Hawaiian English. This Pidgin-Creole probably developed under the influence of the use of Chinese Pidgin by Europeans in Hawaii when speaking to non-Europeans (Wurm 1971a). It undoubtedly existed as a pidgin-creole until the early twentieth century; but continued contact with Standard English has influenced it sufficiently so that it is now mutually intelligible with English, and thus a dialect of English (Voegelin and Voegelin 1964b). DeCamp (1971) has called Jamaican, as well as Hawaiian, a 'post-creole continuum.' Tsuzaki (1966) believes that there are three coexistent systems consisting of an English-based Creole, and a dialect of English (with pidgin associated with immigrants, creole with lower and lower middle classes, and the dialect of English with the upper classes). Tsuzaki (1967) regards the similarities between the ENGLISH-BASED PIDGIN-CREOLES within the Pacific basin, and elsewhere, to be too great to permit an interpretation of chance or parallel development. He thus supports the view of a common origin for all ENGLISH-BASED PIDGINS, and ultimately of all 'EUROPEAN-BASED PIDGIN-CREOLES.'

18. Micronesian Pidgin. Practically extinct. Beach-la-Mar was spoken on the Micronesian Islands as far north as the Carolines; it gave rise to a dialect variant which was widely used until the early part of the twentieth century.

19. Neo-Melanesian = Melanesian Pidgin = New Guinea Pidgin. 500,000, for 10,000 of whom it is their mother-tongue. Predominantly in Rabaul and Port Moresby areas, and on the Admiralty Islands. Little creolization to date, but creolization is now expected to increase (Wurm 1971a). Perhaps the most elaborately developed of the non-creolized pidgins in Oceania. Derived from Beach-la-Mar.

20. Neo-Solomonic = Solomon Island Pidgin. Approximately 50,000. Solomon Islands. Primarily an internative lingua franca. Descended from Beach-la-Mar, which developed locally as the dialect spoken by the indentured laborers returning to the central and eastern Solomon Islands from the sugar-cane areas of North Queensland.

21. *New Zealand = Maori Pidgin. Apparently also a variety of Beach-la-Mar; widely used in New Zealand in the mid-nineteenth century (Hall 1966).

22. Frisian. Ds. East Frisian (1,000; northern part of the Oldenburg region — in strong competition with Ostfriesisch Platt, a Low German dialect); Island Frisian (3,700; in the North Frisian Islands of Sylt, Föhr, and Amrum, and on the Island of Heligoland); North Frisian (12,000; Marsch region of

the Schleswig coast, including the Bökinghard, Darrharde, Gōsharde, and Wredingharde dialects; 30,000 in the United States); West Frisian (350,000; mainly in the province of Friesland in The Netherlands — most speakers are bilingual in Dutch which is replacing West Frisian).

23. Negerhollands is spoken by a few persons in the U.S. Virgin Islands; it is a Dutch-based pidgin-creole that is nearing extinction.

24. Netherlandic-German. Ds. High German — including Middle = Central German (West Central German: Middle Franconian, Moselle Franconian [including Luxemburgian = Letzburgisch], Rhenish Franconian [including Hessisch-Nassauish, Lorraine, Low Hessian, Palatinate]; East Central: *East Prussian, Ostersgebirgisch in Bohemia, Silesian in Prussian and Austrian Silesia and Eastern Bohemia and German Moravia, Thuringian, Upper Saxon in the former Kingdom of Saxony; Yiddish = Judeo-German [*Western Yiddish in Germany, Central Yiddish in Poland, and Eastern Yiddish east of the Vistula — Standard literary Yiddish does not reflect a distinct dialect]); and Upper High) German (Alemannic [High Alemannic, Low Alemannic, Swabian]; Bavarian Austrian [Central Bavarian in the Alps and Lower Austria and Salzburg, North Bavarian spoken north of Regensburg and extending to Nuremburg and Western Bohemia, South Bavarian, spoken in the Bavarian Alps, Tyrol, Styria, and including the Heanzian dialect of Burgenland, Carinthia, the Sette and Tredici Communi south of Trent in northern Italy, and an enclave of Gottschee in Yugoslavia]; High = Upper Franconian [including East Franconian, South Franconian — in the valley of the Neckar and the Murk and the valley of the Main from Würzburg to Bamberg]); Low German — including Afrikaans (the official dialect of the Republic of South Africa, similar to Dutch but with a great deal of morphological leveling); Dutch (a standardized development from Low Franconian, with influence from Low Saxon and Frisian); Flemish (likewise a standardized form of Low Franconian, differing from Dutch primarily in spelling conventions); Plattdeutsch = Modern Low German, including East Low German [of Altmark, Brandenburg, Mecklenburg, Pomerania, Priegnitz, Ukermark]; Low Franconian = Niederfränkish [Bergish, Geldersch, Limburgisch]; Low Saxon [west of the Elbe River: Eastphalian, Engrian, North Low Saxon = Ostfriesisch Platt, Westphalian]) (Keller 1961). Over 115,000,000 (German, 95,000,000; Dutch-Flemish, including Afrikaans, 20,000,000). By political area, East and West Germany (70,000,000), Netherlands (12,000,000), Austria (7,000,000), United States (7,000,000), Belgium (5,000,000), Switzerland (4,000,000), South Africa (4,000,000), France (1,700,000), Poland (1,400,000); and German, Dutch, and Yiddish are spoken by less than 1,000,000 speakers in each of dozens of countries around the world, particularly in Latin America. Standard High German is based on the Central High German dialects, as are Yiddish and Luxemburgian. Afrikaans, Dutch, and Flemish are based on Low Franconian.

AFFILIATION. Member of INDO-EUROPEAN.

GIABALIC

GROUPING. The GIABALIC languages are spoken on the southeastern border of Queensland, Australia.

1. Giabal. Ds. also Kambuwal = Kaombal, Minjangbal = Minyung = Minyowa = Boggangar. Between Allora and about Dalby, east of Gatton; west to Mill-merran.
2. Keinjan. Stanthorpe north to about Hendon, east to Dividing Range; west to beyond Thane.

AFFILIATION. Member of PAMA-NYUNGAN.

Gilyak = Nivkhi. 76.3% of 3,700 Gilya speak the language. Sakhalin Oblast and both sides of Tatar Strait, USSR.

AFFILIATION. Suggested affiliations with YUKAGHIR, ALTAIC, or KOREAN are not generally accepted (Jakobson 1942, 1957; Panfilov 1968, Worth 1963).

GOILALA = KUNIMAIPA

GROUPING. The languages of Wurm's (1971c) GOILALA are listed in three separate subgroups of EASTERN = SOUTH-EAST NEW GUINEA by Greenberg (1971b), who includes in these three groups a number of language names not mentioned by Wurm (those with no population figures below). Greenberg's subgroups are AFORA (languages numbered 1, 2, 5, 8, 16), FUYUGE (languages numbered 6, 9, 14), and KOVIO (languages numbered 4, 7, 10, 11, 12, 13, 15). The GOILALA languages are spoken in the inland northwestern part of the Central District, Papua, extending into the southeastern part of Morobe District, New Guinea.

1. Afoa.
2. Ambo.
3. Biangai. 900. Headwaters of the Bulolo River, Morobe District.
4. Biaru.
5. Debu.
6. Fuyuge = Mafulu. 10,000.
7. Goiefu.
8. Goilala.
9. Kambesi = Tauada.
10. Kovio.
11. Kuepa.
12. Kunimaipa. Ds. include Gajila along the Bubu River, Morobe District. 8,000.
13. Oru Lopiko.
14. Sikube = Kabana.
15. Sini.
16. Tauade = Tauata. 9,000.
17. Were = Wele. 3,500. Headwaters of the Biaru, Waria, and Ono rivers, Morobe District.

AFFILIATION. Member of SOUTH-EAST NEW GUINEA.

GREEK = HELLENIC

GROUPING. Two of the many dialects, of which some are listed below under Ancient Greek (1), are reflected in modern languages: Modern Greek (2) is derived from the classical Attic dialect; Tsakonian (3) is derived from the dialect spoken in Laconia by the Ancient Spartans. At least since the sixteenth century (Bourgnet 1927), a communication barrier between Modern Greek and Tsakonian has kept monolingual speakers of these separate languages out of linguistic contact.

1. *Ancient Greek. Ds. Aeolic, including Asiatic Aeolic, Boeotian, Thessalonian; (Attic-)Ionic; Arcado-Cyprian; Mycenaean; Pamphylian; West Greek (Doric, including Laconian, and Northwest Greek). Ancient mainland Greece (the Peloponnesus, Attica, Boeotia, Thessaly, Locris, Phokis, Aeolia), Crete, Cyprus, Asia Minor. Deciphered by Ventris and Chadwick (1953), Mycenaean Linear B represents the earliest written dialect of Greek — written with a few independent vowel signs beside scores of consonant signs which distinguish phonetically adjacent vowels by graphemic dissimilarity among the signs for the same consonant (Voegelin and Voegelin 1961). This type of writing became extinct with the destruction of Mycenaean cities in Crete (fourteenth century B.C.) and on the Greek mainland (thirteenth and twelfth centuries, B.C.).

2. Modern Greek = Grec = Graecae = Romaic = Neo-Hellenic. Ds. Northeastern, Northwestern, Southeastern, Southwestern. The four dialect groupings are separated by two isogloss lines: one which runs north and south, dividing the dialects into Eastern dialects (local varieties on Chios, the Dodecanese, Cyprus, and Asia Minor) and Western dialects (the remaining geographical area of Greece); and a second isogloss line which divides the dialects into Northern dialects (continental Greece as far south of the Gulf of Corinth and the northern boundary of the Peloponnesos; the two northern Ionian Island groups of Corfu [Kerkira and Paxoi], and Leukas = Levkas, and the Aegean Islands [and including the Andros Island of the Cyclades plus Tinos and Samos, but not Ikaria, of the Dodecanese]), and Southern dialects (the remaining dialects south of those outlined). The dialects may also be broken down into the following varieties: Asia Minor group (including Pontic, Cappadocian), Cretan, Cyclades Island, Cypriot, Dodecanese Islands, Epire-Rumel, Ionian Island, Maniote (including Northern Maniote and Southern Maniote), Northern Aegean Islands (including Lesbian, Samotic, Eubean), Peloponnese (not including Maniote), Saracatsan (a group of Greek nomads in the central mountain regions), Stera Hellas, Southern Italian Greek, Thessalian-Macedonian-Thrace. 7,300,000 in Greece; 95,000 in Turkey; 425,000 in Cyprus; 60,000 in Egypt (Alexandria); 130,000 in Italy; speakers also found in Western Europe, the Balkans (southern Albania, eastern Yugoslavia, Rumania, Bulgaria, and the U.S.S.R. states surrounding the Black Sea: Crimea, Moldavia, Georgia), Africa and parts of North and South America. There is a diglossic relationship between an archaic literary Greek (Katharevousa) and the spoken literary language (Dhimotiki).

3. Tsakonian = Tsaconia. Ds. Kastanitas-Sitena (in the towns of Kastanitas and Sitena), Lenidi-Prastos (in Prastos and Karakovonve, Lenidi, Pramatefti, Sapouna-keida, Tyros). 10,000. Greece, on the eastern coast of the Peloponnesos.

AFFILIATION. Member of INDO-EUROPEAN.

GUAYCURÚ

GROUPING. The four languages of the GUAYCURÚ = GUAICURÚ = WAICURÚ family, now largely extinct, were spoken in the Gran Chaco of northern Argentina and Paraguay and beyond into Bolivia and Brazil. Mason (1950) divides the GUAYCURÚ languages into Mbaya-Guaicuru (number 2) and a FRENTONES group (languages numbered 1, 3, 4). McQuown (1955) lists the names of dialects of numbers (2) and (4), below, as separate languages.

1. *Abipón = Callaga. Ds. (trs. ?) Gulgaissen = Kilvasa, Mapenuss = Yaukanigá, Mpene. Possibly not extinct. Argentina.
2. *Mbaya-Guaicurú. Ds. (trs. ?) Apacachodegodegi = Mbaya Mirim, Caduveo = Cadiguegodi, Eyibogodegi, Gotocogegodegi = Ocoteguebo (?), Guetiadegodi = Guetiadebo, Lichagotegodi = Icachodeguo (?), Payaguá = Lengua (including Sarigué = Cadigue and Magach = Agace = Siacuás = Tacumbu). Paraguay, Brazil, Bolivia.
3. Mocoví = Mbocobi. Argentina.
4. Toba. Ds. (trs. ?) *Aguilot (possibly not extinct), Pilagá; Toba proper includes Chirokina, Cocolot, Guazú, Komlék, Lanyagachek, Michi, Mogosma, Natica. Argentina.

AFFILIATION. Member of MACRO-PANOAN within GE-PANO-CARIB.

GUNWINGGUAN

GROUPING. A GUNWINGGIC group consists of Boun (1), Gundangbon (3), Gunwiggu (4), and Muralidban (6); a YANGMANIC group consists of Wardaman (11), Jungman (5), and possibly Wageman (10) (Wurm 1971b). These languages are spoken from the coastal area of Junction Bay in the north to the Roper River in the south, Northern Territory, Australia.

1. Boun = Buan = Bi. D. also Dalabon. Bulman Gorge and the Wilton River.
2. Djauan = Tjawen = Djauun = Djawanj = Jawin = Chauan = Adowen = Charmong. South of the Alligator Rivers.
3. Gundangbon. D. also Gundei'njekemi. At source of Liverpool River.
4. Gunwiggu = Gunwinggu = Gunwingu = Gunwingo = Gunawitji = Witji = Kulunglutji = Kulunglutchi = Koorungo. Ds. also Gumadir, Gundei'djeme. Has become a lingua franca through adoption as a church language.
5. Jungman = Nolgin = Yangman = Yungman = Yungmun = Yungmunni = Yungmanni = Yungmunee = Yungmunnee = Jongman. Southwest of the source of the Roper River in southern Arnhem Land.
6. Muralidban. D. also Gunbalang = Girdimang (Wurm 1971b).

7. Ngalakan = Ngalagan = Nullakun = Nullikan = Nullikin = Ngalbon = Hongalla = Bigur. North of the Roper River and west of the Wilton River.

8. Ngandi. Upper Wilton River, Mainoru River, east to near source of Rose River.

9. Rembarunga = Rainbarngo. At the western source of the Goider River.

10. Wageman = Wagoman.

11. Wardaman = Wadaman = Wartaman = Warduman = Waderman = Wordaman = Waduman = Yibiwan. South of the Adelaide River.

AFFILIATION. Member of AUSTRALIAN macro-phylum.

GUR = VOLTAIC

GROUPING. The internal relationships of languages in the GUR family, as stated by Greenberg (1966), were considerably revised by Bendor-Samuel (1971). In the latter's large CENTRAL GUR group, MORE-GURMA and GRUSI are brought together as subgroups, and a single language, Tamari (48), is coordinate with them in classification. Beside the CENTRAL GUR group, the remaining coordinate groups are KIRMA-TYURAMA, LOBI, and SENUFO, and these are coordinate with the following single languages: Bargu (1), Bobo (2), Dogon (49), Kulango (52), Seme (61), and Win (76).

1. Bargu = Bariba = Burgu = Batonnun = Batonu. Ds. Kandi, Nikki-Parakou. 240,000. Dahomey, Togo, Nigeria.

2. Bobo = Bwa = Bwamu ? Ds. Bobo(Gbe) = White Bobo = Kyan = Tyan(se), Bobo(Wule) = Red Bobo = Tara(se) = Oulé = Ule = Pwe, Boomu (?), Nyenyege = Bouamou, Sankura = Zara. 389,000. Mali, Upper Volta. Names listed as dialects may be separate languages (Welmers 1971b).

CENTRAL GUR

GRUSI = GURUMSI = GURUNSI. Divided by Bendor-Samuel (1971) into NORTHERN (10, 13, 14, 15), CENTRAL (16, 17), SOUTHERN (4, 6, 19, 21) and EASTERN = TEM (3, 5, 7, 8, 9, 12, 20). Other languages added from Welmers (1971b).

3. Bago.

4. Chakali. 5,000.

5. C(h)ala = Tshala. Togo. Perhaps a dialect of Tem (20).

6. Degha = Buru = Mmfo = Mo. Ivory Coast (800), Ghana (10,000).

7. Delo = (Ntribu). 1,000. Togo. Perhaps a dialect of Tem (20).

8. Dompago = Logba = Legba. 17,000. Perhaps a dialect of Kabre (9), and both are perhaps dialects of Tem (20).

9. Kabre = Cabrai = Kabure = Kabye = Kabiema. 157,000. Togo, Dahomey. Perhaps a dialect of Tem (20).

10. Kasem = Kas(s)ena = Kasene = Kasomse = Kipirse = Awuna = Binyime = Gapershi = Wulisi = Yule. 74,000. Ghana, Upper Volta.

11. Kurumba = Deforo = Fulse = Lilse. 86,000. Upper Volta.

12. Lam(b)a. 29,000. Dahomey. Perhaps a dialect of Tem (20).

13. Lyele = Lele = Lela = Lelese = Lere = L'élé. 61,000. Upper Volta. Possibly a dialect of Kasem (10).

14. Nunuma = Nibulu = Nuna = Nuruma. 43,000. Probably a dialect of Lyele (13), thus of Kasem (10).
15. Pana.
16. Puguli = Pougouli = Buguli = Buguri. 7,500. Upper Volta.
17. Sisala = Hissala = Issala = Sisai. 62,000. Ghana, Upper Volta.
18. Tamprusi = Tampele = Tampole = Tampolem = Tampolense. 100,000. Ghana.
19. Tampulma. 7,000.
20. Tem = Tim(u) = Kotokoli = Cotocoli. 130,000. Dahomey, Togo, Ghana.
21. Vagala = Siti = Sitigo = Kira = Konosara = Paxala. 5,000. Ghana, Ivory Coast.

MORE-GURMA

22. Berba. 44,000. Dahomey.
23. Birifo(r). 90,000. Upper Volta, extending into Ghana. Perhaps a single language with Daagari (25) and Dagara (26) as other dialects.
24. Buli = Buile = Bulea = Bulugu = Kanjago. 63,000. Ghana, Upper Volta.
25. D(a)agari = Dagaba = Daga(r)ti = Dawari. Ds. also Nome, Wali = Wala (47,000). 200,000. Ghana, adjacent Upper Volta. Perhaps a dialect of the same language as Birifor (23) and Dagara (26).
26. Dagara = Dagara-Nura. D. also Nura. 75,000. Perhaps a dialect of the same language as Birifor (23) and Daagari (25).
27. Dagbani = Dagbane = Dagomba = Dagbamba. Ds. Mamprusi = Mampruli (85,000), Nanumba = Nanuni (50,000). 409,000. Ghana, Togo.
28. Dye = Gangam = Ngamgam. 17,000. Togo.
29. Frafra. 138,000. Ghana. Perhaps a dialect of Nankanse (37).
30. Gurma = Gourma(ntche). 127,000–200,000. Upper Volta, Togo.
31. Hanga. 3,000.
32. Konkomba = Kokomba. Tr. Komba (Ghana). Ghana (110,000), Togo (20,000).
33. Kusal(e) = Kusasi. 122,000. Upper Volta, Ghana. Possibly a dialect of Dagbani (27).
34. Moba = B(i)moba = Bema = Moa(b) = Moare. Ghana (32,000), Togo (48,000).
35. Mo(o)re = Mõõre = Mossi = Mole = Moshi. Ds. also Ouagadougou, Saremde, Taolende, Yadre = Yansi, Yanga (7,000). 2,000,000. Upper Volta, Ghana.
36. Namnam = Nabdam = Nabde = Nabdug = Nabrug = Nabt(e). Over 17,000. Ghana.
37. Nankanse = Nankana = Nankani = Fra = Gurenne. 55,000. Ghana, adjacent Upper Volta.
38. Natemba. 17,000. Togo.
39. Nawdam = Naudm = Naoudam = Naoudemba = Losso. 27,000, Welmers (1971b) lists this as a dialect of More (35).

40. Pila(pila) = Kpilakpila = Yom. 40,000. Dahomey.
41. Safalaba. 3,000.
42. Somba = Soma = Some = Tamberma. Ds. also Niende, Yoabu (8,000). 45–72,000. Dahomey, Togo.
43. Soruba-Kuyobe = Biyobe = Meyobe = Solamba. 10,000. Togo, Dahomey (5,000).
44. Takemba = Tankamba. 10,000. Dahomey.
45. Tal(l)ensi = Talansi = Taleni = Talni. 33,000. Ghana.
46. Tayak(o)u. 10,000. Dahomey.
47. Tobote = Busari = Bitshamba = Cemba = Chamba = Tschamina. D. also (A)kas(s)ele = Chamba = Chansi = Che. Ghana (110,000), Togo (20,000).
48. Tamari. 72,000.

49. Dogon = Dogom = Hab(b)e = Kibissi. D. also Tombo. 149,000. Mali, Upper Volta. Bendor-Samuel (1971) questions its inclusion in GUR.

KIRMA-TYURAMA. This group is established as an independent group in GUR by Bendor-Samuel (1971).

50. Kirma = Mbouin = Gwẽ ? = Gouine ? 30,000. Gwẽ is listed by Welmers (1971b) as a dialect of Lobiri (57). This language is placed by Westermann and Bryan (1952) among the SENUFO and LOBIRI languages.
51. Tyurama. 27,000.
52. Kulango = Nabe = Nambai = Ngwala = Zazere. Ds. Kulango (40,000), Loghon = Log(h)oma = Lor(h)on = Loma = Nabe ? (5,000), Tegesye = Tunbe (2,000). 47,000. Ivory Coast. These names listed as dialects may be closely related languages.

LOBI(RI). Bifurcated by Bendor-Samuel (1971) into an EASTERN group (54, 57) and a WESTERN group (53, 55, 59) plus (possibly) Komono (56). 360,000. Moru (58) and Turkana (60) added from Welmers (1971b).

53. Dorhosye = Dorhossie = Doghosie = Dorosie = Dokhobe = Dokhosie. 7,500. Upper Volta. Perhaps a dialect of Lobiri (57).
54. Dya(n) = Dian = Dyane = Dyanu. D. Zanga. 8,000. Upper Volta. Perhaps a dialect of Lobiri (57).
55. Gan(e) = Gan-Lobi = Gã. 51,000. Upper Volta. Perhaps a dialect of Lobiri (57).
56. Komono = Kumwenu. 3,000.
57. Lobi(ri). 211,000. Upper Volta, Ivory Coast.
58. Moru. 10,000. Ivory Coast. Perhaps a dialect of Lobiri (57).
59. Padorho = Padogho = Bodoro. 1,000. Upper Volta. Perhaps a dialect of Gan (55).
60. Turuka = Kpe = Pain = Pin = Turka = Tourouka. 25,000. Upper Volta. Perhaps a dialect of Lobiri (57).

61. Seme. 10,000.

SENUFO. Westermann and Bryan (1952) treat this group as a dialect cluster.
    62. Karaboro = Kama = Karama = Koroma. Ds. Kler, Syer, Tenyer. 25,000.
    Ivory Coast, Upper Volta.
    63. Kulele = Coulailai = Pama. 15,000. Ivory Coast.
    64. Natioro = Natyoro. 1,000. Upper Volta, Ivory Coast, Mali.
    65. Palara = Palaka = Pallakha = Kpa(l)lagha. D. also Wara = Ouala =
    Ouara = Saura (2,000). 7,000–10,000. Ivory Coast.
PANTERA-FANTERA. 3,000. Ghana.
    66. Fantera.
    67. Pantera = Pantara = Nafana = Gambo.
    68. Senari = Senadi = Syenere. Ds. Central Senari (including Kafire, Ksãra,
    Kufuru, Nafãra, Patoro, Pogara, Tãgara, Tagbãri = Mbengui = Niellé,
    Tyebara), Fodõro, Kandere = Tengiela, Nyarafoloro, Papara, Senar.
    Southwest Senari (including Dugubesyẽei, Gara, Nowulo), Takpasyẽeri =
    Messeni, Tenere, Tyebala = Tyebali = Tiébala. 350,000. Ivory Coast.
SUPPIRE-MIANKA. 300,000. Mali.
    69. Mianka = Minianka.
    70. Suppire = Sup'ide = Tagba.
TAGBA(NA)-DYIMINI = DYIMINI-TAGWANA. 85,000. Ivory Coast.
    71. Dyimini = Gimini = Jimini. Ds. Bandogo, Dofama-Dyafolo, Dyamala,
    Folo = Foro, Sĩgala-Tõdala.
    72. Tagbana = Tagwana = Tagbona = Tagouana = Takponin = Kan-
    gable. Ds. Gbõzoro, Niangbo, Niediekaha, Tafire = Tafile = Tafiri.
    73. Tiefo = Tyefo = Tyeforo = Kiefo. 6,500. Mali, Upper Volta.
    74. Tyeliri. Ivory Coast.
    75. Vige = Vigué = Vigye. 3,000.
76. Win = Tusia = Toussia. Ds. Northern Win, Southern Win. 18,000.

AFFILIATION. GUR is a member of NIGER-CONGO.

GYARUNG-MISHMI

GROUPING. Languages grouped together here as GYARUNG-MISHMI are consecutively numbered but separately alphabetized in each of the following subgroups:
EASTERN = EASTERN PRONOMINALIZED HIMALAYAN, including languages numbered (1)
through (21); NON-PRONOMINALIZED, (22) through (33); WESTERN = WESTERN PRONOM-
INALIZED HIMALAYAN, (34) through (47). The sources for classification and revision
of classification are mentioned in prefatory notes to each of these three subgroups.
Roughly speaking, Shafer (1955) tends to accept, with minor revision, Grierson's
(1903–1927) classification; in addition, Shafer proposes alternative classificatory labels,
as noted below.

EASTERN. Three languages included by Grierson (1903–1927) in his EASTERN PRO-
NOMINALIZED HIMALAYAN are listed by Shafer (1955) in his WEST CENTRAL HIMALAYISH
group (languages numbered 3, 12, 19). Shafer bifurcates his EASTERN HIMALAYISH
group into a WESTERN branch (languages numbered 1, 2, 5, 6, 14, 16, 17) and an EASTERN

branch (languages numbered 7, 9, 10, 11, 13, 15, 20, 21). Shafer leaves unclassified (within SINO-TIBETAN) a group that he labels DHIMALISH (languages numbered 4, 18). In Grierson's classification, several of the names listed below as separate languages are considered dialects of Khambu (7); namely, 1, 5, 6, 9, 11, 13, 14, 15, 18. A few of the languages included under EASTERN by Shafer are non-pronominalized (12, 16, 18) and hence are classified by Grierson in his NON-PRONOMINALIZED HIMALAYAN.

1. Bāhing. Nepal, upper valleys. Subgrouped by Shafer with Sunwari (16).
2. Chaurāsya = Tśaurasya. Nepal.
3. Chēpāng = Tśepang. Nepal, central hills.
4. Dhimal = Dhīmāl. 600. Sikkim, India (Darjeeling and Jalpaiguri).
5. Dumi. Nepal, upper valleys. Grouped together by Shafer with Khaling (6) and Rai (14).
6. Khaling. Nepal, upper valleys. Grouped by Shafer with Dumi (5) and Rai (14).
7. Khambū = Khambu = Sangpang = Kirantī = Kulung. Ds. Khambu of Darjeeling district = Nōlōkh Kirant; Khambu of Further Kirant = Pallo Kirant, Khambu of the Hither Kirant = Wallo Kirant, Khambu of the Middle Kirant = Mãjh. Eastern Nepal ('Kirant' country), India (Darjeeling). Grouped together with Nachherēng (13) by Shafer.
8. Kusūndu. Nepal.
9. Lāmbichhōng = Lambitćhong = Chhingtāng = Tśhingtang. Nepal, upper valleys. Grouped by Shafer with Lohōrōng (11), Rōdōng (15), and Waling (20) in a BONTAWA group.
10. Limbu = Tsong = Chang = Monpa = Subah = Suffah = Yakthūngbā. Ds. Fāgūrāī, Fēdopia, Tamarkhōlēā.
11. Lohorong = Lōhōrōng = Balali. Nepal, upper valleys. Grouped by Shafer with Lāmbichhōng (9), Rōdōng (15), and Waling (20) in a BONTAWA group.
12. Magari = Māgari = Magarī. 17,000–19,500. Nepal.
13. Nacherēng = Nāchhēreng = Natśhereng. Nepal. Grouped with Khambū (7) by Shafer.
14. Rai = Jindā. Nepal, between Dud Kosi and Tanbor rivers.
15. Rodong = Rōdōng = Chāmbling. Nepal. Grouped by Shafer with Lambichhōng (9), Lohorong (11), and Waling (20) in a BONTAWA group.
16. Sunwari = Sunwar = Sunuwār.
17. Thulung.
18. Ṭoto = Ṭōṭō. India (Jalpaiguri).
19. Vayu = Vāyu = Hayu. Nepal, both banks of Kosi River in central region of the Himalayas.
20. Waling = Wāling. Ds. also Dungmali = Dūngmālī, Kirante, Rungchhenbung = Rungtśhenbung. Nepal, upper valleys. Grouped by Shafer with Lambichhōng (9), Lohorong (11), and Rodong (15) in a BONTAWA group.
21. Yakha = Yākhā = Yakthomba = Rōi. 1,250–1,700. India (Darjeeling), Nepal, upper valleys.

NON-PRONOMINALIZED. Languages listed below include those from Grierson's

(1903–1927) NON-PRONOMINALIZED HIMALAYAN (those numbered 26, 30, 31), and from his NORTH ASSAM branch (those numbered 22, 23, 24, 25, 28, 29), which are subgroups of his TIBETO-HIMALAYAN branch of TIBETO-BURMAN. Shafer treats most of these languages as unclassified groups (within SINO-TIBETAN), but points out that they are probably members of his BODIC division, or else of his BURMIC division. Shafer proposes group names for MIŚINGISH (22, 24, 33) and GURUNG (26, 30, 32), which he classifies as constituents of his BODIC division, together with Digarish (25), Hruish (28), Midźuish (29), Newarish (31), and Rgyarong (27).

22. Adi = Abor = Miri = Abor-Miri = Miśing. 65,300. India, north hills of the Assam valley, between Bhutan and the Buruli River.
23. Chulikātā Mishmi = Idu. North Assam.
24. Dafla = Daflā = Bangni = Nyising = Nyī-sing. Ds. Apa, Tagen, Tanang.
25. Digāru Mishmi = Taying. D. also Midu = Neda = Methun = Bebejiya. India, northeastern Assam, extending into Tibet.
26. Gurung. 5,211. Nepal. Glover (1971) notes that the latest census data from Nepal (1961) "records 157,778 people claiming Gurung as their mother tongue."
27. Gyarung = Rgyarong. Ds. Pati, Wassu. India (Darjeeling).
28. Hrus(s)o = Aka = Angka(e) = Tenae.
29. Mījū Mishmi = Kaman Mishmi.
30. Murmi = Tāmāng = Ishāng = Sain = Bhōtiā. 38,500. The Valley of Nepal, India (Darjeeling), Sikkim.
31. Nēwārī = Newari. D. also Pahri = Pahrī = Pahī = Paḍhī. 400,000. Central Nepal (in Paton, Bhatgoan, and most of the small towns).
32. Thaksya = Thāksya.
33. Yano.

WESTERN = WESTERN PRONOMINALIZED HIMALAYAN. Shafer includes Thāmī (44) and Bhrāmu (34) as WESTERN GYARUNG-MISHMI, whereas Grierson listed these as EASTERN PRONOMINALIZED. Shafer subdivides his WESTERN as follows: NORTH-NORTHWEST branch (35, 45), NORTHWEST branch (40, 41, 42, 46, 47), ALMORA branch (36, 37, 38, 43), EAST branch (34, 44), and Dźanggali (39). India, north of Almora, in Konowar, Kangra, Lahul, Chamba in the western Himalayas; Nepal; Sikkim.

34. Bhrāmu.
35. Bunan = Bunán. 3,000. Along the Bhaga River northeast 15 miles from its confluence with the Chandra.
36. Byāngsī. 1,600. Almora (Patti Byangs).
37. Chaudāngsī = Tśaudangsi. 1,500. Almora (Patti Chaudangs).
38. Darmiyā. 1,750. Almora (Patti Darma).
39. Jang(g)alī = Dźanggali. 200. Region of Chhipula in Askot Malla. The name Jangali ('of the wilds') is applied to many groups in India; e.g., in Bombay for any Bhīl speaker.
40. Kanāshī = Kanaśi. 1,000. Glen of the Bios Valley; around village of Malāna = Mālāni.
41. Kanāwarī = Kanauri = Kanawi = Kanoreunu Skadd = Kanōrug Skadd

= Tibas Skadd. Ds. also Lower Kanauri = Lower Kănawi, Upper Kanauri, Malhesti = Milchanang = Minchhang = Minchhanäng = Milchang. 13,000–22,000. Kanawar.
42. Manchāti = Monchāti = Mantśati = Patni = Lahul = Chamba Lāhulī. D. also Ranglōī = Gōndlā = Tinan. 4,400. Kahul.
43. Rangkas = Saukiya Khun. 600. Almora.
44. Thāmī. Nepal, Sikkim, Bangladesh.
45. Thebor = Thebör Skadd. Ds. also Kanam, Lippa, Sumtśu, Sungnam, Zangram.
46. Tśikhuli = Chitkhuli.
47. Tukpa.

AFFILIATION. Member of TIBETO-BURMAN.

HALMAHERA = NORTH HALMAHERA

GROUPING. Salzner (1960) lists four subgroups: NORTHWEST (languages numbered 4, 7, 10, below), CENTRAL (3 and 6), WEST (1, 2, 5, 11), and SOUTH (8 and 9). Greenberg's (1971b) classification makes the major division within the group as between SOUTH and the rest. West Makian (12), previously classified as AUSTRONESIAN, is added by Watuseke (1976). The HALMAHERA languages are spoken on the northern part of Halmahera Island in the Moluccas by a total of several thousand people, and on adjacent islands by 12,000 more speakers.

1. Galela.
2. Ibu. Possibly extinct.
3. Ka'u.
4. Loda.
5. Madole = Modole.
6. Pagu = Isam. D. also Tololiku.
7. Tabaru.
8. Ternate.
9. Tidore.
10. Tobelo. Ds. Boëng including Bóbale, Buli, Lollobatta, Mawea, Morotai, Pediwang, Tugutil; Dodinga; Gamsungi including also Gorua, Kokarlamo, Kupa-Kupa, Wohia.
11. Wáioli = Wai. D. also Sahu = Sahu'u = Sau.
12. West Makian = Bahasa Titinéé = Bahasa Desité. 12,000 (1973), of whom 7,000 are on Makian Island and 5,000 on the Kayoa Islands.

AFFILIATION. Member of 'WEST PAPUAN' (Cowan 1957a); of INDO-PACIFIC (Greenberg).

*Hattic=Khattish. Formerly spoken in Asia Minor (Sturtevant and Hahn 1951, Diaknoff 1967, Kammenhuber 1969).

AFFILIATION. None known.

HESPERONESIAN

GROUPING. Though Austronesian languages outside of Polynesia, Melanesia, and Micronesia (except Palau and Chamorro) have been traditionally referred to as 'Indonesian', it has long been recognized that 'Indonesian' is not a homogeneous group and probably "no Proto-Indonesian exclusive of the Oceanic languages ever existed" (Grace 1968, summarizing Milke). The fact that the languages of the eastern islands of Indonesia were divergent from those of the western islands was recognized as early as 1884 by Brandes. This fact is confirmed by Dyen's (1965) lexicostatistical classification, which excludes the languages of eastern Indonesia from HESPERONESIAN, the members of which are listed below:

CELEBES, CENTRAL AND SOUTHERN (q. v.) — at least those languages included in Dyen's comparisons.

NORTHWEST INDONESIAN = PHILIPPINE (q. v.) — except Chamorro and Palauan, which Dyen excludes from both NORTHWEST INDONESIAN and HESPERONESIAN.

WEST INDONESIAN (q. v.) — from which Dyen excludes KALABITIC, MALAGASIC, and Sentah (a Land Dayak dialect), all of which are, however, included in HESPERONESIAN.

Other languages, as Enganno, excluded from WEST INDONESIAN by Dyen are grouped with WEST INDONESIAN only at higher levels of Dyen's classification than HESPERONESIAN.

1. Sangir = Sangihe = Sangil = Sanggil. Ds. Karakitang, Manganitu, Tabukan. 75,000. Sangihe (Sangi) Islands northeast of Celebes, Talaud Islands, and Mindanao, Philippines. Widely used as a mission language from the middle of the nineteenth century; Manganitu d. has "a certain preeminence" (Uhlenbeck 1967).

Esser (1938) groups with Sangir the following three languages, none of which was included in Dyen's sample, so their status as members of HESPERONESIAN has not been attested.

2. Bantik.

3. Bentenan.

4. Talaud. Ds. Kaburuang, Karakelong, Nenusa-Miangas, Salebabu. Talaud Islands, northeast of Sangihe Islands.

AFFILIATION. Member of MALAYO-POLYNESIAN subgroup of AUSTRONESIAN (Dyen).

*Het = Chechehet = Tšetšehet = Čecehet. Only 15 words and some place names are known of this Indian language of Argentina, which became extinct at the end of the eighteenth century.

AFFILIATION. Formerly classified with Puelche (a member of ANDEAN), Het is now treated as a language isolate, the more distant affiliations of which are unknown (Mason 1950).

Hishkaryana. 120. Nhamunda River, northern Brazil (Lorraine Bridgeman, personal communication).

AFFILIATION. Unknown.

HOKAN = HOKAN-COAHUILTECAN = HOKALTECAN PHYLUM

GROUPING. The single languages and language families listed under HOKAN are remotely related to each other, without special subgrouping (other than of languages in attested families). In some instances, tentative groups of languages, as 'COAHUILTECAN', had been suggested to be closely related to each other, but have now come to be regarded as groups of single languages that bear no closer relationship to each other than to other HOKAN languages. But some single languages, as Seri and Cochimi, may be more closely related to languages in a particular family, as YUMAN, than to other HOKAN families.

The early research by Dixon and Kroeber (1913a, b, 1919) brought together under HOKAN the following families and single languages: Chimariko, Esselen, Karok, POMO, the 'SHASTAN' group (now SHASTAN and PALAIHNIHAN), Washo, YANAN, YUMAN.

Subsequently, Sapir (1917, 1920, 1925a) added the following: 'CHONTAL' = TE-QUISTLATECAN, TLAPANECAN, CHUMASH, SALINAN, Seri, and languages of the 'COA-HUILTECAN' group (as noted in the list below).

Occasional additional candidates for inclusion under HOKAN, such as Jicaque, have been proposed by Greenberg and Swadesh (1953).

Jacobsen (1970) criticized the recent tendency of Hokanists to make comparisons of such pairs as PALAIHNIHAN and SHASTAN, SHASTAN and Karok, Karok and Washo, Karok and YANAN, YANAN and Eastern Pomo without assuming that each pair descended from a single proto-language; in fact, cognates from other Hokan languages are often cited as 'additional forms' beside the focus on a paired comparison. Different patterns of correspondence do emerge, but the patterning of a proto-language has not emerged.

1. *Carrizo. Formerly Mexico (near Camargo). Included in Sapir's COAHUILTECAN.
2. *Chimariko. California, formerly on the Canyon of Trinity River.
3. CHUMASH(AN). Barbareño = Santa Inez = Ynezeño, Cuyama, Emigdiano = Ventureño, Interior (?), Island, Obispeño, Purisimeño. Possibly one speaker. Formerly on three northern islands of the Santa Barbara group. There were possibly a number of languages represented (Heizer 1952, 1955).
4. *Coahuilteco = Tejano = Texas = Pajalate. Formerly Mexico (Coahuila, Nuevo Leon, Tamaulipas). Included in Sapir's COAHUILTECAN.
5. *Cochimí = Cochimtee = Cochetimi = Cochima = Cadegomo = Cadegomeño = Didiu = Laimon = Laymon(em) = Laymon-Cochimi = San Javier = San Joaquin = San Xavier = San Francesco Saverio Mission = San Francisco Xavier (de Viggé-Biaundo) Mission. Baja California. Perhaps more than a single language. Troike (1970a) regards it as two distinct groups, labeled Cochimi I and Cochimi II, and makes them coordinate members of a single Hokan subdivision.
6. *Comecrudo. Formerly Mexico (Tamaulipas). Included in Sapir's COAHUILTECAN.

7. *Cotoname. Included in Sapir's COAHUILTECAN.

8. *Esselen = Es(s)ele(neijan) = Eslen = Ecselen = Eskelen = Escelen = Ensen = Ec(c)lema(n)ch = Carmel(o) (Mission) = Huelel = Soledad Mission. Formerly on the upper course of Carmel River, Sur River, and the coast from Point Lopez almost to Point Sur. The HOKAN affinity of Esselen is strongly questioned.

9. Jicaque = Xicaque. Ds. Lean y Mulia, Palmar = Sula, Yora. Perhaps extinct. Northwestern Honduras.

10. Károk = Karuk = Ar(r)ar(r)a = Cahroc = Quoratean = Pehtsék = Pehtsik. D. also Karukawa. 100–1,000. California, northwest coast.

PALAIHNIHAN (q. v.)
POMO (q. v.)

11. *SALINAN. Trs. Playano, San Antonio Salinas, San Miguel Salinas. Formerly California at the headwaters of the Salinas River north to Santa Lucia Peak, and from the sea to the main crest of the Coast Range. Consisted of more than one language, but language boundaries have not been identified.

12. Seri = Ceri = Zeri = Heri = Kukaak = Kmike = Tiburon. Trs. Guayma, Salineros, Serrano, Tepocas, Tiburón, Upanguayma. Few speakers. Mexico, Tiburón Island in Gulf of California; formerly also along the coast of Sonora.

13. SHASTAN = SASTEAN. Trs. Ahotireitsu, Cecilville Indians = Haldokehewuk, Iruaitsu, Kahosadi, Kammatwa. Fewer than ten. California, along the Klamath River and the valleys of Scott and Shasta rivers up to the Oregon border. SHASTAN is believed to have formerly included a number of separate languages.

TEQUISTLATECAN (q. v.)
TLAPANECAN (q. v.)

14. Washo. 100. California-Nevada, on the shores of Lake Tahoe and down the east slope of the Sierra Nevadas.

YANAN (q. v.)
YUMAN (q. v.)

*Pakawa (included in Sapir's COAHUILTECAN) ?

AFFILIATION. The present reduced HOKAN phylum was formerly linked by Sapir (1929) with languages spoken in eastern North America (HOKAN-SIOUAN). Webb (1971) suggests connections with languages of Old World families (DRAVIDIAN and URALIC).

HUARPE = ALLENTIAC

GROUPING. Only two languages (numbered 1, 2) unquestionably belong to this family. McQuown (1955) lists the five here. All were formerly spoken in the upper reaches of the tributaries of the Colorado and Negro rivers in southern Argentina.

1. *Allentiac = Mendoza Huarpe.
2. *Millcayac = Mendocino Huarpe.

3. *Pehuenche.
4. *Puelche (of Cuyo). Probably rather the Puelche of ANDEAN.
5. *Puntano Huarpe.

AFFILIATION. Member of GE-PANO-CARIB.

HUON-FINISTERRE = HUON (PENINSULA)

GROUPING. Hooley and McElhanon (1970) go beyond Wurm (1971c) and Greenberg (1971b) in their identification and classification of languages in this New Guinea group, many of which had not been reported in earlier publications. The two major divisions, HUON = HUON PENINSULA and FINISTERRE, are each further subdivided as shown below. Hooley and McElhanon do not list the WEST group of FINISTERRE languages in detail, since most of them are spoken outside the geographic limit of their paper (the Morobe District, New Guinea); the list below expands their WEST FINIS-TERRE by those languages of Classen's (1970) outline of FINISTERRE not mentioned by Hooley and McElhanon.

FINISTERRE. In and near the Finisterre Mountains.
    EAST FINISTERRE
        ERAP. These languages are labeled Boana=Ne by Capell (1962a). Munkip, Nakama, Nek, Nuk, and Numanggang form a subgroup within ERAP. Watersheds of Busip and Erap Rivers and on the lower Irumu River.
            1. Finungwan. 400.
            2. Gusan. 800.
            3. Mamaa. 200.
            4. Munkip. 100.
            5. Nakama. 900.
            6. Nek. 1,300.
            7. Nimi. 1,400.
            8. Nuk. 1,800.
            9. Numanggang. 2,200.
            10. Sauk. 300.
            11. Uri. 2,000.
        URUWA. Uruwa River basin.
            12. Karangi. 200. Lower Timbe River valley.
            13. Komutu ? 500. Lower Timbe River valley.
            14. Kumdauron. 400.
            15. Mitmit. 100.
            16. Mup. 100.
            17. Sakam. 400. The most divergent URUWA language.
            18. Sindamon. 150.
            19. Som ? 100.
            20. Worin. 400.
        WANTOAT. Southern slopes of Saruwaged Mountains from the Irumu Valley to the Leron Valley.

21. Awara. 900. Possibly a dialect of Wantoat, 26, below.
22. Bam. 600.
23. Irumu = Gumia. 1,800.
24. Leron. 500. Possibly a dialect of Wantoat, 26, below.
25. Saseng. 200.
26. Wantoat. 5,000. Villages in which Wantoat is spoken include Matup = Matap.
27. Yagawak = Kandomin. 400.

YUPNA = JUPNA VALLEY. North of the Finisterre Mountains on both sides of the Madang-Morobe border.

28. Bonkiman. 500.
29. Domung. Madang District.
30. Kewieng. 3,000.
31. Nankina. Madang District.
32. Nokopo. Madang District.

WEST FINISTERRE. Almost entirely in the Madang District.

33. Dahating.

GUSAP-MOT = SURINAM. Surinam River area. All except Ufim are in the Madang District.

34. Gira.
35. Nahu = Naho.
36. Nekgini.
37. Neko. 182.
38. Ngaing = Sor = Mailang. 1850.
39. Rawa = Erawa. 6,000.
40. Ufim. 500.

WARUP. Two or three languages.

HUON. The CENTRAL and NORTHERN divisions are grouped as NORTH-CENTRAL; SOUTHERN and WESTERN are grouped as SOUTH-WEST. Huon Peninsula, Morobe District, except Kovai (60, below).

CENTRAL HUON

41. Burum = Bulum. 3,200. Upper Bulum River valley, south of the Cromwell Range.
42. Kosorong. 1,350. Western slopes of the Mongi River valley, below the junction with the Kua River.
43. Kube = Hube. Ds. Kurungtufu, Yoangen. 4000. Eastern headwaters of the Mongi River, eastern slopes of the lower Kua River valley, Foria River valley.
44. Mindik. 1,500. Western slopes of the lower Kua River valley.
45. Tobo. 3,000. Upper Kua River valley, south of the Cromwell Range.

EASTERN HUON. The status of Dedua is uncertain, since it shows similarities with Kube (43, above) and with Ono in NORTHERN HUON.

46. Dedua ? 4,400. Headwaters of the Masaweng river, south of Mt. Besenona.

47. Kâte. Ds. formerly Mâgobineng, Parec, Wamorâ = Wamolâ, Wanac, Wemo; now only Wemo. 5,600. Used as lingua franca through missionary influence.
48. Mape. Ds. Fuckac, *Naga, Nigâc. 4,600. Along Mape River.
49. Migabac = Migaba'. 1,000.
50. Momare = Momale. 350. North of the Masaweng River.
51. Sene. 12. Near mouth of Masaweng River. Young people speak Kâte only.

NORTHERN HUON
52. Kinalakna. 220.
53. Kumukio. 300.
54. Nomu. 800.
55. Ono. Ds. Amugen, Ziwe. 4,000, plus spoken as a second language by 1,000 Nomu and Sialum speakers. Kalasa census division.
56. Sialum. 600.

SOUTHERN HUON
57. Momolili. 1,500. Hinterland east of Lae.
58. Nabak = Naba = Wain. 9,300. Eastern headwaters of Busa River.

WESTERN HUON
59. Komba. 10,000. North of Cromwell Range, in valleys of Kwama, Andar, and Puleng rivers.
60. Kovai = Umboi. 2,800. Umboi Island, just off Morobe District.
61. Selepet. 5,500. Valleys of Pumune and Kiari rivers.
62. Timbe. 10,000. Timbe River valley and tributaries.

AFFILIATION. Member of CENTRAL NEW GUINEA macro-phylum (Wurm 1971c).

*HURRIAN

GROUPING. Consists of Hurrian (1) and Urartaean (2), below (Speiser 1941).
1. *Hurri(an) = Khurrian. Spoken in ancient Mitanni (with Nuzi as its capital), which extended from northern Mesopotamia into Anatolia. It was written in Akkadian cuneiform.
2. *Urartaean = Vannic Haldean = Kaldic = Khaldean = Chaldean. Formerly spoken in the Mount Ararat region near Lake Van. Information is derived from two inscriptions written in Akkadian cuneiform, dating from the ninth century A.D.

AFFILIATION. None known.

Iberian. Known from a few inscriptions and fragments on coins, Iberian was the language of the people of the Ebro River on the Iberian Peninsula. The Iberian alphabet may represent an older script reshaped under Greek and Punic alphabetic influence. Perhaps once spread all over the Iberian Peninsula, adjacent France, and the neighboring islands of Sardinia, Corsica, and even the British Isles.

AFFILIATION. Linked with Basque by Baehr (1948) and Tovar (1950).

IDOMA = IDOMA-ETULO

GROUPING. Languages numbered (2), (5) and (6), following, are added from Westermann and Bryan (1952) to (1), (3), and (4), which are grouped together in Greenberg (1966).

1. Agatu; rather than a separate language, Agatu is classified as a dialect of (3), Idoma, by Westermann and Bryan (1952).
2. Argo. Nigeria, Lafia Emirate.
3. Idoma. Ds. also Igumale, Okwoga, Otukpa, Otukpo. 118,000. Nigeria, Benue Province.
4. (I)yala. 22,500. Nigeria.
5. Orri. 8,600. Nigeria.
6. Yache (6,600). Nigeria.

AFFILIATION. Member of KWA phylum.

IGBO = IBO

GROUPING. Languages numbered (1) and (3) are geographically discontinuous from (2), below; these are "outlying dialects which are probably better considered as separate languages" (Kay Williamson, personal communication).

1. Ekpeya = Ẹkpẹyẹ. Nigeria, Niger Delta. Mutually unintelligible with Igbo (Clark 1971).
2. Igbo = Ibo. Ds. Cross River = Eastern Igbo, including Abam-Ohaffia, Ada = Edda, Aro; Ika = Western Igbo, including Kwale = Southern Ika, Northern Ika, 'Riverain'; Ogba = Oba = Ogbah; Ogu Uku = Northeastern Igbo; Onitsha = Northern Igbo, including Enugu, Nri-Awka; Owerri = Southern Igbo = Central Igbo including Isu-Ama, Isu-Item, Ohuhu-Ngwa, Oratta-Ikwerri = Ikwere. 6,000,000. Nigeria, southern regions. Ika and Kwale may be two separate languages; perhaps Ogu Uku as well.
3. Izi. Nigeria, northeastern region.

AFFILIATION. Member of KWA phylum.

IJO

GROUPING. The IJO family is a complex of dialects in different degrees of contact rather than a group of separate languages — an impression gained previous to the work of Kay Williamson (1965, 1971, personal communication), who points out that some of the dialects of (1), below, can be said to lack mutual intelligibility, thereby leading to the possible separate language interpretation within IJO. A number of politically 'Ijọ' groups do not speak IJO; e.g., the Apoi, who speak Yoruba, and the Atisa who speak an EDO language.

1. Ijọ = Ijaw = Ijoh. Ds. the major division is between Eastern and Central-Western; (North-) Eastern Ijọ (self-designations are taken from the dialect names following rather than 'Ijọ') including Ibani = Bonny (26,900), Kalabari (292,850), Okrika

(81,000), and Nkọrọ (4,550) which are mutually intelligible and adjacent in a northeast area, just as Akassa = Akaha (4,900) and Nembe = Brass (66,600) are mutually intelligible in a southeast area (and partly so with northeast dialects); Central-Western Ịjọ, whose self-designation is Ịjọ, subdivided areally as South-Central = Lower Ịjọ, including Apoi (3,100), Bassan (8,850), Boma = Bumo (24,600), East Trakiri (3,850), Ikibiri, Ogbom (31,000), Olodiama (13,350), and Oporoma (8,600) which are mutually intelligible with each other and with southeast dialects but not with northeast dialects; North-Central = Upper Ịjọ, including Ekpetiama (9,400), Gbaran (9,400), and Kolokuma (29,500), which are mutually intelligible with each other, with South-Central dialects, partly so with southeast and not at all with northeast dialects; North-East-Central (first reported by Williamson), including the mutually intelligible Amegi-Biseni (4,800) and Okordia (3,600), of which the latter is partly intelligible to North-Central dialects, the former not; North-Western = Western Ịjọ, including Kabo (17,150), Kumbo (11,500), Mein (58,200), West Tarakri (31,700), and Operemar (40,700), which are mutually intelligible with each other, with North-Central and South-Central, but not with North-East-Central nor with Eastern dialects; South-Western (first reported by Williamson), including Arogbo (17,650), Eduwini = Iduwini (9,800), Ọgụlagha (4,200), and Oporoza = Gbaramatu (6,150), which are mutually intelligible with each other, with South-Central and North-West, less so with North-Central, but not with North-East-Central nor with Eastern dialects. 927,750. Ịjọ dialects are spoken in Nigeria, mostly in Degema and Yenagoa Provinces, Rivers State, and in Delta Province, Midwestern State.

AFFILIATION. Member of KWA phylum.

INDIC = INDO-ARYAN

GROUPING. The classifications of Grierson (1903–1927), Chatterji (1945), and Firth (1968) permit listing the INDIC languages in terms of 'zones' (such as CENTRAL INDIC), 'groups' (such as DARDIC), and single languages (such as Romany).

Languages that are included in some of the zones may turn out to constitute INDIC branches, but not enough comparative work has been done to justify equating these zones and groups with established separate branches (Fairbanks 1966). Southworth (1958) and Pattanayak (1966) have now begun studies to establish INDIC branches on a comparative basis.

There are no clear linguistic boundaries between zones; instead, one finds transitional areas of neighboring intelligibility, though there is a genuine boundary between Marathi, on the one hand, and Gujerati, Rajasthani, Western Hindi, and Eastern Hindi, on the other.

The MODERN or NEW INDO-ARYAN languages derive from Old Indo-Aryan and Middle Indo-Aryan (Emeneau 1966). Old Indo-Aryan is represented both by a single dialect, *Classical Sanskrit, and by a set of dialects, *Vedic Sanskrit. The earliest form of Middle Indo-Aryan is found in the *Pali texts. The PRAKRITS, which partially underlie the modern languages, include *Ardhamagadhi, *Avanti, *Maharashtri, *Magadhi, and *Sauraseni.

DARDIC. Morgenstierne (1961) and Emeneau (1966) take the DARDIC languages to be definitely INDIC rather than IRANIAN, even though DARDIC does show divergent features. The languages listed below follow Strand (1973), who follows Morgenstierne. These languages are divided into four groups in addition to two coordinate languages.

CENTRAL = KŌHISTĀNĪ. At least 7,000 speakers. Primarily in the Swat Kohistan in Pakistan.

1. Baškarīk = Gāwrī = Gārwī = Dīrī.
2. Maiyã. Ds. Čilis, Dubērī, Gowro, Kanyawālī. In the Mayo District, Indus Kohistan.
3. Tirāhī.
4. Torwālī.
5. Woṭapūrī-Kaṭārqalāī.

ČITRAL

6. Kalaṣa. Ds. Northern Kalaṣa, Southern Kalaṣa.
7. Khowār = Citrālī = Čitrarī = Arnyiā = Arniyā = Qāšqarī.
8. Kašmīrī = Kēšur. D. also Kaštawāṛi, and transitional dialects to Punjabi. In Jammu and Kashmir (Pakistan and India).

KUNAR

9. Damēlī = Damel. Gid Valley on the east side of the Kunar River in southern Chitral, Pakistan.
10. Gawar-bātī = Narisātī = Narsātī.
11. Šumāštī.
12. Pašaī = Laghmānī = Laurowani = Dēhgānī = Degano. Ds. Northeastern, including Čalās-Kuṛangol and Čugani; Northwestern; Southeastern, including Damenč, Lower Darra-i Nūr, Sum = Ṣale = Ṣāṛī, Upper Darra-i Nūr; Southwestern.

ṢIṆĀ

13. Ḍumākī.
14. Phaluṛa = Palūla = Palola = Ḍangarīk. Ds. Phalūṛa proper = Ašrētī = Ashret = Biyōṛī, in Dir Kohistan, Pakistan; Sāwī = Sau (on the Kunar River, Pakistan). 800–1,000. In a few villages on the eastern side of the lower Chitral Valley.
15. Sina. Ds. Astōrī, Brōkpa, Brōkpa of Drās, Čilāsī, Ḍah, Gilgitī, Gurēzī, Hanū. 100,000. Jammu and Kashmir from the Afghan-Pakistan border to the U.N. cease fire line.

CENTRAL INDIC ZONE. 125,000,000. Western India south of the Himalayas between the Pakistan border and the center of the Indian subcontinent.

16. Banjuri = Labhani. Ds. Bahrupia, Gujarat Banjuri, Kakeri, Labanki, Panjab Banjuri.
17. Bhili. Less than 2,000,000. In mountainous areas where the states of Gujarat, Madhya Pradesh, Maharashtra, Rajasthan converge. Relatively homogeneous but with numerous local variants. Bhili forms a connecting link between Gujarati and Rajasthani.
18. Gujarati = Gujerati. Ds. Gamadia = Gramya (including Ahemedabad [in central and northwest Ahemedabad Province], Anawla = Bhathela [spoken

by the Bathela Brahmans of districts of Surat, Baroda], Eastern Broach, Charotari [in part of Kaira and Baroda districts], Patani [in eastern Mehsana district, Banaskantha district, and Sabarkantha district; Pakistan Gujarati is probably a subdialect of Patani], Patidari [part of Kaira district], Surati [in Surat and Broach districts], Vadorari [part of Kaira and Baroda]); Kakari (spoken by Kekars in the Deccan); Kathiyawadi (on the Kathiawar Peninsula — including Gohilwadi = Bhawnagari, Holadi, Jhalawadi, Sorathi); Kharwa (spoken by Moslem seamen on Piram Island and in part of Ahemedabad Province on the east coast of Kathiawar Peninsula); Parsi (spoken by the Parsis); Standard Gujarati (including Bombay Gujarati, Nagari [spoken by Nagar Brahmans], Patnuli = Saurashtri [spoken by silk weavers of Madras and Deccan], Saurashtra Standard [the speech of educated speakers in state of Gujarat]; Tarimuki = Ghisadi [spoken by wandering blacksmiths in Poona, Satara, Belgaum, Amrasti, Akola, Buldana, and other cities in southern India]). 16,000,000. Mostly in state of Gujarat (15,150,000); also Bombay (840,000), Madhya Pradesh (160,000), Rajasthan (53,000), Mysore (26,000), Andhra Pradesh (16,000), West Bengal (15,000), Madras (15,000), Punjab and Delhi (14,000), Uttar Pradesh (14,000), and less than 10,000 each in Bihar, Orissa, Keerola.

19. Western Hindi = Hindi = Urdu = Hindust(h)ani = Khari-boli. Ds. Bangaru = Hariani = Deswali = Desari = Jatu = Jati = Chamarwa (4,000,000), Braj Bhakha = Braj Bhasha = Antarbedi = Antarvedi (11,500,000), Bundeli = Bundel Khandi (8,000,000), Hindustani (30,000,000), Kanauji (6,000,000). 60,000,000. North central India encompassing central and western portions of Uttar Pradesh, northern Madhya Pradesh, eastern Punjab. There are also colonies of Western Hindi speakers in other parts of the world: Africa (2,000,000), the Guianas (100,000), Surinam (285,000), Fiji (240,176). High Hindi and Urdu serve as literary forms for 30,000,000, and Bazaar Hindi = Chaltu = Chalu = Laghu Hindi serves as a lingua franca for millions more. There are actually four varieties of literary Western Hindi: Hindi = High Hindi = Nagari Hindi = Literary Hindi = Standard Hindi (the Hindi written in Nagari script has been de-Persianized and de-Arabicized, with Sanskrit words introduced); Urdu (written in Arabic script with many Persian and Arabic loans); Dakhini (written in Arabic script, but with little Persianization); Rekhta (a form of Urdu used in poetry). All but the last variety are also represented by spoken subdialects.

20. Khandesi = Ahirani = Dhed Gujari. Ds. also Dangri, Kunbi = Kunbau. 1,000,000. In East and West Khandesi, and in the neighboring districts of Nisik in Maharashtra, and Akola, Nimar and Buldana in Madhya Pradesh.

21. Panjabi = Punjabi = Eastern Panjabi. D. also Dogri-Kongri (in the Kangra district of Panjab State and the southern part of Jammu and Kathua districts of Jammu and Kashmir). 20,000,000. Northwestern India (in the states of Panjab and Rajasthan) and across the border into Pakistan to just west of the city of Lahore. Panjabi and Western Hindi = Urdu are not separated by a language barrier.

22. Rajasthani. Ds. Central-eastern Rajasthani (4,000,000; in the Jaipur, eastern Sikar, northern Tonk, western Sawai Madhopur, Kotah, northern Jhalawar, eastern Bundi districts of Rajasthan Province, and in the Morena and Shivpuri districts of Madhya Bharat [including the Ajmeri, Havauti, Jaipuri, Kishangari, and Sawai Madhopur = Ladi subdialects]); Gujuri (spoken by the Gujurs of the hills north of the Punjab and Pahari areas in Hazara, Swat, and Kashmir); Mal(a)vi (in Chittorgarh and Jhalawar districts of Rajasthan Province, and in the Rajgarh, Shajapur, Mandsaur, Ratlam, Ujjain, western Bhilsa, and western Goona districts of Madhya Bharat Province, in the Raisen and northwest Sehore districts of Bhopal Province, and in the Hoshangabad, Betul, and Nimar districts of Madhya Pradesh Province); Marwari = Me(r)wari (9,000,000; Rajasthan Province in all districts except Jaipur, Kotah, Tonk, Alwar, Bundi Jhalawar, and eastern Ajmer — also in Pakistan and into the Hissar district of the Panjab [including the Eastern, Northern, Southern, Standard, and Western subdialects]); Nimadi (small enclaves in Madhya Pradesh); Northeastern Rajasthans (in the Alwar, Jaipur, Bharatpur, and Sawai Madhopur districts of Rajasthan Province, and in the Gurgaon and Mohindergarh districts of Punjab State [including the Ahirwati and Mewati subdialects]). 22,000,000. Mostly in Rajasthan State; also in Madhya Pradesh State, and along the eastern border of Bahawalpur in Pakistan, and in Punjab State.

EASTERN INDIC ZONE. 140,000,000. India, from the states of Bihar and Orissa to the easternmost part of Assam. The languages of this group developed from the Magadhan Prakrit. The languages listed below are sometimes subdivided as Western Magadhan (the Bhojpuri dialect of Bihari), Central Magadhan (the Maithili and Magahi dialects of Bihari) and Eastern Magadhan (Bengali-Assamese and Oriya). Pattanayak (1966) bifurcates this group, on comparative evidence, into Oriya, on one hand, and Bengali-Assamese, on the other.

23. Bengali = Bangla-Bhasa. Ds. Assamese (including Eastern Assamese, Western Assamese; 6,000,000 in Assam and 10,000,000 in Bangladesh); Bengali (including Central Bengali = Standard Bengali spoken in West Bengal in the districts of Murshidabad, Nadia, Hooghly, Howrah, Calcutta, and the northern part of Midnapore and the eastern half of Burdwan; Eastern Bengali spoken in Bangladesh [including East Central and Haijong]; Northern Bengali, spoken in Bangladesh and West Dinajpur in the state of West Bengal, and the northeastern tip of Purnea in the state of Bihar [including Koch, Siripuria]; Rajbangsi, spoken in Bangladesh in the districts of Jalpaiguri, Cooch Behar, and Darjeeling of West Bengal, and the western borders of the districts of Boalpara and the Garo Hills of Assam [including Bahe, spoken in Darjeeling]; Southeastern Bengali, spoken in Bangladesh [including Chakma]; Southwestern Bengali, spoken in the southern two-thirds of the Bengali-speaking area of Midnapore in West Bengal; Western Bengali, spoken in West Bengal in the districts of Bankura, Birbhum, and the western half of Burdwan, and in Bihar State in Dhanbad, Manbhum, in the northern quarter of Singbum, and in the south and east of Santhal

Parganas [including also Kharia Thar, in Manbhum; Mal Pahoria, in Santhal Parganas and adjoining Birbhum; Saraki]). 76,000,000. Northeastern India in the states of West Bengal, Bihar, and Assam in India; and Bangladesh.

24. Bihari. Ds. Bhojpuri = Bhojpuriya = Hindusthani = Deswali = Khotla = Piscimas (23,500,000 in the Gorakhpur and Banaras divisions of Uttar Pradesh, and in the districts of Champaran, Saran, Shahabad, Palamau, and Ranchi in western Bihar, as well as hundreds of thousands in Calcutta; subdialects include Domra, Madhesi, Nagpuri = Chotar Nagpuri = Sadani = Sadri = Dikkukaji [2,000,000 in the Ranchi and Palamau districts of southwest Bihar], Southern Standard Bhojpuri = Kharwar [7,000,000, Ballia and Ghazipur districts in Uttar Pradesh, Saran, and Shahabad districts in Bihar; considered the standard for Bhojpuri as a whole], Northern Standard Bhojpuri = Gorakhpuri = Sarawaria = Basti [10,000,000 in the districts of Basti, Gorakhpur, and Deoria in Uttar Pradesh, and in Champarahin Bihar], Tharu [Tarai districts of Nepal], Western Standard Bhojpuri = Purbi = Benarsi [6,000,000, in the districts of Azamgarh, Ghazipur, Banaras, Mirzapur, and the extreme tip of Faizabad in Uttar Pradesh]); Magahi (including Central, Northern, Southern; 10,000,000 in south Bihar and in the eastern part of the Patna Division, in most of the north of Chotanagpur Division, and in the Malda District of Bengal); Maithili = Tirahutia (including Central Colloquial, Chikachiki, Eastern Maithili [including Khotta], Johahi, Standard Maithili, Southern Maithili, Western Maithili). 15,000,000 speakers in the whole of the districts of Darbhanga, Musaffarpur, Purnea, Mongyr, and Bhagalpur in Bihar, in the eastern parts of the districts of Champaran and Patna, and the northern part of Santhal Paraganas districts. It is also spoken by the people of the Tarai in Nepal on the borders of Bhagolpur and Tirhut divisions of Bihar.

25. Oriya = Odri = Utkali = Uriya. Ds. Bhatri, spoken in the northeast of the Bastar District of Madhya Pradesh (intermediate between other dialects and Halbi); Halbi = Halabi = Mahari = Mehari, spoken by the Halba (30,000 in Madhya Pradesh, Bastar, Balaghat Chanda, and Bhandara districts, and across the border into the Koraput and other districts of Orissa adjacent to Madhya Pradesh [including Adkuri, Bastari, Chandari, Gachikolo, Mehari, Mari, Sundi, in one group, and the more divergent dialects of Bunjia, Nahari, and Kamari = Kawari]); Mughalbandi = Oriya proper = Standard Oriya, spoken all over Orissa and spilling over into Bihar, Madhya Pradesh, and Andhra Pradesh; Northwest Oriya, spoken in the northernmost part of Raigarh District; Oriya of North Balasore, spoken in the northern Balasore District of Orissa; Oriya of Midnapore, spoken in West Bengal; Oriya of western and northwestern Orissa, spoken on the Orissa-Madhya Pradesh border; Southern Oriya, spoken by some of the lower castes in the district of Visakhapatam in Andhra Pradesh.

26. Eastern Hindi = Kosali (a single language constituting the East-Central Zone).

Ds. Awadhi-Bagheli (20,750,000; Uttar Pradesh, northwestern Madhya Pradesh, and East Madhya Pradesh), Chhattisgarhi = Laria = Khatahi (6,000,000; Madhya Pradesh, Bihar). 30,000,000. India: Uttar Pradesh, Madhya Pradesh, Bihar, Nepal.

27. Marathi (a single language constituting the Southern Zone). Ds. Deccan Marathi = Desi = Dekini (14,500,000; in central Maharashtra), Konkan = Gomataki = Goanese (2,000,000; in the district of Ratnagiri and the area of Goa along the southern Konkan strip of Maharashtra, in the Mysore district of Ramra Shimgoa and the Kamara district of Kerala State); Konkan Standard = Bankoti = Kunabi = North = Central Konkan (3,000,000; in the north and central sections of the Konkan strip of Maharashtra); Varhadi-Nagpuri Marathi (5,000,000; in Eastern Marathi, Madhya Pradesh, Andhra Pradesh). 28,500,000. India: Maharashtra, Madhya Pradesh, Mysore, Andhra Pradesh.

NORTHERN = PAHARI = HIMALAYAN ZONE. 10,000,000. Nepal and most of northwestern India on the slopes of the Himalayas in the states of Punjab and Himachal Pradesh.

28. Garhwali. 1,200,000. In the Garhwal districts of India.
29. Kumauni = Kumaoni. 1,000,000. Northwestern India, primarily in the Almora and Nainital districts.
30. Nepali = Nepalese = Gorkhali = Khas Kura = Parbatiya = Eastern Pahari. 8,000,000. Nepal.
31. Western Pahari. Ds. Baghati, Bradrawah, Chameali, Jaunsari, Kiuthali, Kului, Mandeali, Satlaj, Sirmauri. 2,000.000. India: Himachal Pradesh, Punjab, Uttar Pradesh.

NORTHWEST INDIC ZONE. 20,000,000. Chiefly in Pakistan between the Indo-Pakistani border and the Indus River.

32. Lahnda = Western Panjabi = Hindi. Ds. Northeastern Lahnda in the districts of Jhelum, Rawalpindi, Hazara, Attack, parts of Kashmir, and in Kohat; Northwestern Lahnda in the districts of Jhelum, Peshawar, Hazara, Attack; Standard Lahnda = Southern Lahnda throughout the Panjabi area of Pakistan including Multani, Thali. 15,000,000. Northeast Pakistan.
33. Sindhi. Ds. Kachchi, spoken in the Kutch District of Gujarat State (speakers now largely relocated in Pakistan); Lari, spoken in the northwestern portions of the Kutch District in India, and the southern part of Hyderabad in Pakistan; Lasi, spoken west along the coast from Karachi in Pakistan to the district of Las Bela, Kalat; Macharia, spoken in the Kapurthala district of Panjab State by a migratory tribe of fowlers; Siraiki, spoken from northern Khaipur to the junction of Khaipur, Quetta, and Kalat, to a small section in northeastern Kalat; Thareli, spoken along the western border of Rajasthan State in India, and in the western portions of Hyderabad and Khaipur in Pakistan; Vicholo = Central Hindi, spoken in central and northern Hyderabad and southern Khaipur in Pakistan. 5,000,000. Gujarat and Rajasthan states in India, Hyderabad, Kharpur, Kalat and Quetta in Pakistan. Massive relocations have occurred since the partition of India

and Pakistan; less than a million speakers of Sindhi are now residing in India.

34. Romany = Gypsy. Ds. Armenian, Asiatic, European. The three 'dialects' are probably mutually unintelligible. 450,000–900,000. Asia, Near East, Europe, North America. The major problem in determining the number of speakers of Romany is that of defining the point at which Romany expands itself out of existence; i.e., when it ceases to be a separate language and becomes a dialect of the local language from which it borrows extensively. Instances are the distinction between Romany as a separate language and Rodi = Rotwelsch as a local dialect in Norway and Denmark; and the 'Higher' and 'Lower' Romany in Sweden. Romany speakers are descendants of a group that separated from other INDIC languages of Central India before the middle of the third century B.C. and remained among the NORTHWEST INDIC and DARDIC languages for eight to eleven centuries before migrating across Persia and Armenia and into Europe and eventually to North America.

SINGHALESE-MALDIVIAN. Sri Lanka (Ceylon), and the Maldive and Laccadive Islands. Languages of these islands are separated by clear-cut communication barriers; there are no transitional dialects (Coates 1965).

35. Maldivian = Mahl = Divehi Bas. Nearly 85,000. Maldive Islands and the Island of Minicoy in the Laccadive Islands.

36. Sinhalese = Singhalese = Cingalese. There is a sharp distinction between the literary and the colloquial, e.g., in differences in the number of tenses. There are also three 'secret' dialects; Goyi-basava (used in paddy cultivation to insure the success of crops by having special terms to 'deceive the demons' and to avoid 'unlucky words'); Kall-basava (an analogous hunting variety); Rodiya (spoken by the low-caste Rodiya group). 7,000,000. All parts of Ceylon except the districts of Manner, Vavuiya, Jaffna, and Tringomalee in the north, and Batlicaloa in the east, and the Nuwara Eliya District in the Central Province.

37. Ved(d)a = Vedda(h) = Veddha = Vaedda = Wed(d)a = Weddo = Bed(d)a. 803 (in 1953, but a decade earlier, 2,361; this language is being replaced by Sinhalese). Ceylon, in the remote forests east of the central mountains (370 in the Badulla District, 321 in the Polonnaruwa District). Vedda is sometimes listed as a dialect of Sinhalese; Dharmadasa (1974) offers support for earlier claims that Vedda is a creole developed through contact of Sinhalese speakers and the aboriginal inhabitants of Ceylon. The Veddas have also special 'ritual' and 'jungle' secret languages. There are some Vedda words, shared with the Sinhalese Rodiya dialect, which are not of INDIC or DRAVIDIAN origin.

AFFILIATION. Member of INDO-IRANIAN within INDO-EUROPEAN.

INDO-EUROPEAN

GROUPING. Languages that comprise the main groups or branches of INDO-

EUROPEAN are listed in the following separate articles (q.v.) and discussed in Birnbaum and Puhvel (1966), Cardona et al. (1970), and Lockwood (1972):

Albanian
ANATOLIAN
Armenian
BALTIC
CELTIC
GERMANIC
GREEK
INDO-IRANIAN
   INDIC
   IRANIAN
   NURISTANI
ITALIC
   ROMANCE
SLAVIC
TOCHARIAN

This list yields 15 main groups or branches for INDO-EUROPEAN, not counting the two extinct languages which are listed below (1 and 2).

Fewer branches than this are obtainable by combining some of the main branches and counting only the superordinate branch — as though one counted only INDO-IRANIAN rather than also INDIC, IRANIAN, and NURISTANI. It turns out that the only superordinate branches that are widely accepted in INDO-EUROPEAN are INDO-IRANIAN and ITALIC, though others have been suggested. The two that have been most discussed are 'BALTO-SLAVIC' and 'ITALO-CELTIC'. Neither is wholly accepted.

The 'BALTO-SLAVIC' unity has been criticized by Szemerényi (1957), among others. Senn (1966), however, defended it as a last phase of Proto-Indo-European, but added that the hypothesis of Proto-BALTO-SLAVIC must make reference to the interrelations of BALTIC and SLAVIC with GERMANIC.

An 'ITALO-CELTIC' branch is often less favored than 'BALTO-SLAVIC'; yet Watkins (1966) states that the former is more likely than the latter.

Hamp (1966) surveyed the ancient linguistic situation in the Balkans and Phrygia, and called the relationships of these INDO-EUROPEAN dialects "troublesome and inconclusive." The two languages listed here (1, 2) are sometimes said to be related to Albanian and Armenian, respectively.

1. *Phrygian. Ancient Phrygia.
2. *Thracian. D. also Daco-Mysian. (Ancient Dacia, Dardania, eastern Macedonia). The region bounded by the Black Sea, the Propontis, the Aegean, and the Timachus, Strymon, and Danube rivers.

AFFILIATION. Wider relationships of INDO-EUROPEAN have been most commonly claimed to be with SEMITIC or Egyptian in AFROASIATIC (Möller 1911, Cuny 1943), but various distant relationships with other language families have been suggested, as with URALIC and as with SINO-TIBETAN.

INDO-IRANIAN

GROUPING. The groups of languages classified under INDO-IRANIAN clearly include the following three branches (q.v.):

INDIC
IRANIAN
NURISTANI

The classification of DARDIC languages (by Grierson, 1903–1927) was under IRANIAN; the classification of DARDIC has been revised by Morgenstierne (1961) and Emeneau (1966) to INDIC (q.v.).

AFFILIATION. Member of INDO-EUROPEAN.

EAST INDONESIAN AUSTRONESIAN (Geographic)

GROUPING. Esser (1938) classified the languages of the smaller Indonesian islands (i.e., excluding New Guinea and Halmahera) east of Lombok (in the Sundas) and east of Celebes into the three groups identified below: AMBON-TIMOR, BIMA-SUMBA, SULA-BATJAN. Languages from each of these groups are classified as MOLUCCAN by Dyen (1965). The names of those languages which are classified as MOLUCCAN are given only in MOLUCCAN (q.v.) and not repeated below; additional names are added from Capell (1944), Salzner (1960), and Uhlenbeck (1967) to Esser's classification which follows.

AMBON-TIMOR

1. Ambelau. Ambelau Island off the southeast coast of Buru Island, Moluccas.

ARU = DJUËRI. Aru Islands, east of the Kai Islands and south of the neck of West Irian. Warilau (12) is divergent from the others, which may be dialects of a single language.

2. Kerei = Krei.
3. Koba.
4. Kobro'or.
5. Kola.
6. Komfana = Kongampani.
7. Lola.
8. Mairiri.
9. Trangan.
10. Udjir.
11. Wamar.
12. Warilau.
13. Watulai.
14. Workai.

EAST CERAM. Eastern half of Ceram Island, Moluccas, and the Seram Laut and Watubela islands to the southeast of Ceram, except for the ONIN languages, which are on the Bomberai Peninsula of West Irian.

15. Atiahu.
16. Banda = Eli-Elat. Eastern side of Kai Besar in Kai Islands.

17. Bengoi.
18. Bobot.
19. Boti.
20. Geser = Goram = Gorong. Ds. Goram Laut, Mina mina gorong, Snabi Watubela including Kasiui and Wesi = Esiriun, Tio'or.
21. Hatuë.
22. Hoti.
23. Isal.
24. Kelimuri.
25. Liambata = Lenkaitahe.
26. Ntau.

ONIN

27. Arguni. 200.
28. Bedoanas. 250.
29. Erokwanas. 250.
30. Onin. 600.
31. Uruangnirin. 250.
   Nikuda (?); Ogar (?); Patipi (?); Sepa ?
32. Seran = Ceram.
33. Seti.
34. Silen.
35. Tihoru.
36. Uhei Kachlakin.
37. Wahai = Manusela. Ds. Hatumeten, Hatuolo, Huaulu, Laha, Nusawele = Nusawilih, Saunulu, Waherama.

WEST CERAM. Fieldwork by Indonesian linguists in the early 1960s identified at least six separate languages in the western half of Ceram, languages 38, 45, 47, 48, 50, 52, below. It seems probable that some of the other names added below from earlier lists will turn out to be synonymous names for, or dialects of, these six languages.

38. Amahai.
39. Asilulu. Probably a dialect of Ambonese (in MOLUCCAN).
40. Boana. Boana Island, west of Ceram.
41. Elapaputih.
42. Hoamol. Boana and Kelang islands, west of Ceram.
43. Horuru.
44. Hulung.
45. Iha.
46. Jahalatane.
47. Kaibubu.
48. Kamariang.
49. Lima.
50. Lisabata.
51. Loun.
52. Luhu = Alifuru. Ds. also Batumerah (also spoken on Ambon Island), Piru.

53. Manipa. Manipa Island, west of Ceram.
54. Nuaulu.
55. Nuniali.
56. Sapolewa. Ds. Buria, Huku, Kawa, Lohia, Lumasoal, Manusa, Manuwe, Murinaten, Murikau, Nikulukan, Nuruë, Riring, Wakolo-Patahuë.
57. Seruawan.
58. Soow Huhelia. Manipa Island, west of Ceram.
59. Tala = Wemale. Ds. Ahiolo, Horali, Hunitetu, Kasieh, Kawa = Nutetu Sepa, Lasahata, Mani, Marehunu, Nukuhai, Nutetu Tala, Rumaheler, Sahulau, Saweli, Senahu, Sisiulu, Sumite, Tomuala, Uli = Soahuwe, Wasia.
60. Taluti.
61. Waelulu.

DAMAR. Damar Islands of the same names as the languages, northeast of the eastern tip of Timor, Lesser Sundas.
62. North Damar.
63. South Damar.
64. Nila.
65. Serua.
66. Te'un.

KIMNAVO. Buru Island, west of Ceram. One or more of the names listed below may be synonymous with Buru in MOLUCCAN.
67. Kajeli.
68. Lisela.
69. Masarete.
70. Rana.
71. Waesama.
72. Kupang. Southern tip of Timor.
73. Roma. Roma (Romang) Island, east of Wetar Island, north of Timor.
74. Roti = Rotti. Ds. with *l:* Ba'a, Bilba, Bokai, Dengka, Kolbaffo; with *r:* Renggou = Ringgou, Termanu = Pada, Ti, Unale. Roti Island, southwest of Timor.

EAST TIMOR. Portuguese Timor and border area of Indonesian Timor. Stevens (1967) establishes that Kemak is closely related to languages of this group, and suggests that Waimaha (also previously classified as PAPUAN) may also be.
75. Galoli.
76. Idaté.
77. Kemak.
78. Mambai.
79. Tukudede.
80. Waimaha.
81. Timorese = West Timor. Ds. ? Amabi, Amanubang, East Amarasi, West Amarasi, Belu, Tabenu.
82. Vaikenu = Timol. Ds.? Amakono, Ambenu, Amfuang, Oikusi. Portuguese

enclave in Indonesian Timor.
83. Wetan. Babar Islands northeast of Timor.
WETAR. Wetar Island, north of Timor.
  84. Erai.
  85. Hahutan.
  86. Iliwaki.
  87. Limera.
  88. Tutunohan.
  89. Welemur.

BIMA-SUMBA

90. Bima. Ds. Kolo, Komodo, Sanggar, Toloweri. Eastern end of Sumbawa Island, Lesser Sundas.
91. Manggarai. D. also Ruteng. Western end of Flores Island, Lesser Sundas.

SULA-BATJAN
BATJAN-OBI

92. Batjan. Batjan Island, east of southern Halmahera, Moluccas.
93. Obi = Ombi. Obi Islands, south of Halmahera, Moluccas.
SANANA

94. Mangole. Ds. also Tjapalulu, Ulfola, Waitina. Mangole Island of Sula Islands, Moluccas.
95. Sanana. Ds. also Bega, Falahu, Fatje, Fukuwe'u, Kebau, Molbufa, Pohi Eja, Wajgaj. Sanana Island of the Sula Islands, Moluccas.
TALIABU. Taliabu Island of the Sula Islands, Moluccas.
  96. Biha.
  97. Kadai.
  98. Mange'e.
  99. Mbono = Bono.
 100. Seho.
 101. Talo.

AFFILIATION. All EAST INDONESIAN AUSTRONESIAN subgroups are members of AUSTRONESIAN, within which many or all probably belong in the MOLUCCAN group, since each of these groups of Esser's includes one or more of the MOLUCCAN languages, and for this area Dyen concludes, "Eastern Indonesia is characterized by a large number of relatively diverse languages, many or all of which form a subgroup" (i.e., MOLUCCAN).

WEST INDONESIAN

GROUPING. Esser's (1938) map of the languages of the former Netherlands Indies presented a detailed subgrouping based on all the data then available. Subsequent works by Dutch and Indonesian scholars have largely followed Esser's classification. Salzner (1960) expands Esser's classification with the names of additional languages and numerous dialects. Esser's groups included SUMATRA, JAVA, BALI-SASAK, BORNEO. For further discussion of the languages of Sumatra and Borneo see P.

Voorhoeve (1955) and Cense and Uhlenbeck (1958).

Though Esser's subgrouping was presumably based "mainly ... on genetic considerations" (Uhlenbeck 1967), it is criticized by Dyen (1965) as being "too closely tied to the geography." Dyen's lexicostatistically derived subclasses of the limited number of languages of the area included in his sample cut across island boundaries, with a three-way subdivision of his WEST INDONESIAN: Chru (11, below), the only one of the AUSTRONESIAN languages of Vietnam included in Dyen's sample, BATAK, consisting of three of the languages of Sumatra (20, 56, 60, below) and SUNDIC, which includes languages from all of Esser's groups mentioned above.

Within SUNDIC three languages, Balinese (3) and Sasak (53) — grouped together by Esser — and Gayo (16) of Sumatra are coordinate with each other and with two groups of languages, JAVO-SUMATRA and DAYAK. The JAVO-SUMATRA group is further subdivided into Javanese (19), Sundanese (59), and MALAYIC, in which Malay (34), Minangkabau (38), and Kerintji (24) are more closely related to each other, and Lampung (26) is more closely related to Kroë (25) than any of these is to Achinese (1) or Madurese (32). The DAYAK group consists of three languages: Sampit (52) and Katingan (21), which are more closely related to each other, as a SAMPITIC subgroup, than either is to the third, Ngaju (43); but Dyen's source for Sampit and Katingan is said to be unreliable and full of loanwords; both are usually treated as dialects of Ngaju (Cense and Uhlenbeck 1958).

Dyen excludes Engganno (15, below) from WEST INDONESIAN, and does not subgroup it with any other AUSTRONESIAN language; he also excludes a number of languages of Borneo, namely, those languages of northern Borneo which have long been recognized as being most closely related to Philippine languages, and KALABIT, which consists of Kayan (22), Kenyah (23), and Sarawak Murut (41) as represented by the Kalabit dialect. The KALABIT group may be more closely related to Dyen's PHILIPPINE group than to WEST INDONESIAN. Dyen also excludes from WEST INDONESIAN Maanyan and Land Dayak (as represented in his sample by the Sentah dialect). Maanyan (31) is tentatively grouped with Malagasy (33) as MALAGASIC, a grouping previously suggested by Dahl (1951), but criticized as being premature, since comparisons were not made with a number of other Borneo languages to which Malagasy might equally be expected to be related — a criticism which could also be made of Dyen's classification, since his sample did not include all the languages of the area in which Maanyan is spoken. Sentah (a dialect of 13, below), like MALAGASIC, was subgrouped with WEST INDONESIAN only in the higher-level group, HESPERONESIAN, which includes also the Philippine languages and most languages of Celebes.

Five subgroups of Esser's BORNEO group are represented in the list below:

KLEMANTAN (Embaloh (14), Land Dayak (13)), OT DANUM (Lawangan (27), Maanyan (31), Ngaju (43), Ot Danum (46), Sampit (52)), SEA DAYAK (dialects of Malay (34)), MELANAU (Bintulu (7), Long Pata (29), Melanau (36), Narom (42), possibly Bisaya (8)), KENYAN-BAHAU-KAYAN (Ba Mali (2), Kayan (22), Kenyah (23), Modang (39), Murik (40), Sarawak Murut (41), Punan Ba (47)).

The WEST INDONESIAN languages of Vietnam and Cambodia appear through work by members of the Summer Institute of Linguistics to form a subgroup, CHAMIC, consisting of Bih (6), Cac Gia Roglai (9), Cham (10), Chru (11), Haroy (17), Jarai

(18), Rade (48), Northern Roglai (50), Southern Roglai (51). Bih, Jarai, and Rade form a subgroup within CHAMIC, as opposed to a subgroup consisting of the rest. Cowan (1948) proposed a special relationship between Cham and Achinese, and possibly Selong, listed below as a dialect of Malay.

There are probably fewer separate languages in WEST INDONESIAN than those listed below because "the profusion of languages on Borneo has been overestimated ... even to a certain extent by Ray" (Cense and Uhlenbeck 1958). Where suggestions have appeared on possible alternative grouping of dialects, they are mentioned below.

1. Achinese = Achehnese. Ds. Banda, Baruh, Bueng, Daja, Pase, Pidie = Pedir = Timu, Tunong. 1,000,000. Northern Sumatra.
2. Ba Mali = Bah Malei = Punan. Ds. also Bok, Kajaman, Lahanan = Lanun, Nibong = Nibon, Sekapan = Sekepan, Speng. In Sarawak, on the Baram River around Mt. Dubit, on the Bok River, on a branch of the Labong River, on the Rejang River around Belaga, and on the Baloi River.
3. Balinese. 2,000,000. Bali, northern part of Nusapenida, and western part of Lombok.
4. Basap. Scattered throughout Bulungan, Sangkulirang, and Kutai, Borneo. Sujau Basap, spoken on the Sujau River, may be a separate language. May be most closely related to Punan Ba (47) (Cense and Uhlenbeck 1958).
5. Benkulan = Bengkulu. Western part of southern Sumatra. May be a dialect of Kroë (25, below).
6. Bih. 1,000. Vietnam.
7. Bintulu = Segan. Coastal Sarawak east of Balingian.
8. Bisaya. Ds. also Bekiau = Orang Bukit, Kadayan = Orang Bukit. Coastal Sarawak-Brunei border and Labuan Is. in Brunei Bay.
9. Cac Gia Roglai. 2,000. Vietnam.
10. Cham = Tjam. 150,000. Vietnam (50,000), Cambodia (100,000).
11. Chru = Cru = Churu = Kru. 15,000. Vietnam.
12. Dairi = Dairi Batak = Pakpak. Northern Sumatra. May be a dialect of Karo (20, below).
13. Land Dayak. Ds. Kendayan Dayak and the speech of numerous groups, mostly designated geographically, often by the names of rivers on which they live, e.g., Ambawang Dayak, Balantian, Behe, Berang and Sabungo, Budanoh, Buka, Grogo = Grogoë, Gugu, Gumbang, Ipoh, Karagan, Krokong, Kuap = Quop = Beta = Bikuap, Landu = Lundu, Lara = Luru, Manyukai = Manyuke = Menjuke, Matan, Mentuh Tapuh, Meratei, Punan = Bunan including Murang Punan and Penjabung = Penyabung Punan, Sabutan = Seputan = Saputan, Sadong = Tebakang = Serian = Bukar, Santan and Gurgo, Sarawak Dayak, Sau = Sauh = Biratak, Selakau, Sentah, Serambau = Serambo, Sermah = Bionah, Sering, Setenggau Jagoi, Sidin = Siding, Sinan, Sinding, Singgi = Singhi = Bisingai, Stang, Sumpo, Tringgus, Tubbia. Spoken in southern Sarawak and northwestern Borneo. Dialect divisions have been little investigated, though Aichner (1949) reports five dialects: Lara; Selakau; that of the Upper Sarawak Land

Dayak, including Grogo, Gumbang, Serambau, Setenggau Jagoi and Singgi; that spoken between Penrissen and Sungei Serin; that of the Tebakang (Serian) district. More than one language may be represented; e.g., Cense and Uhlenbeck (1958) "it is not known whether the Seputan or Saputan and the Penyabung ... speak separate languages."

14. Embaloh = Malo = Maloh = Maloh Kalis = Pari = Palin = Sanggau. Tributaries of the upper Kapuas River in western Borneo.

15. Enggano. Probably recently extinct. Enggano Island, west of the southern end of Sumatra.

16. Gayo. Ds. Dorot, Bobasan, Serbodjadi, Tampur. 120,000. Mountain region of northern Sumatra.

17. Haroy = Hroy. 3,000. Vietnam.

18. Jarai. 150,000. Vietnam and Cambodia.

19. Javanese. 45,000,000. Ds. West: Tegal, Tjirebon = Cheribon, Indramaju, Middle Java; East: Banjuwangi, Malang-Pasuruan, Surabaja, Tengger, Tembung Pasisir.

20. Karo = Karo Batak. D. also Alas. Northern Sumatra.

21. Katingan. On Katingan River, south central Borneo. Dialect of Ngadju (Cense and Uhlenbeck 1958).

22. Kayan = Kajan. Ds. also Busang, Uma Baloi, Uma Blubo, Uma Poh, Penihing? Central Indonesian Borneo on upper Kapuas, Mendalem and upper Mahakam rivers; Sarawak on Rejang and Baram rivers. Spoken as a second language by a number of other tribes in the area.

23. Kenyah = Kehja = Kinjin. Ds. ? Lepu Anau, Lepu Pohun, Lepu Pun, Lepu Sawa, Lepu Tau, Long Aki, Long Bangan, Madang, Malang, Sabup = Sambup. Indonesian Borneo in Apo Kayan district at headwaters of Kayan River, on Pujungan River, and possibly on the lower Kayan in the region of the headwaters of the Boh and on the Tawang River in Kutai; in Sarawak on upper Baram and upper Tinjar rivers.

24. Kerintji = Kerinchi = Kinchai. Ds. Akit, Mamaq, Mokomoko, Rawa, Sakei, Talang, Ulu. 170,000. West Sumatra. Kerintji speakers claim intelligibility with Minangkabau, but not vice versa. Treated as a Minangkabau dialect by most sources.

25. Kroë = Kru'i. Southern Sumatra. Kroë plus Komering d. of Lampung are called Njo.

26. Lampung = Api. D. also Komering = Kemering. 200,000. Southern Sumatra. Komering and Kroë together are called Njo.

27. Lawangan = Luwangan. Ds., all names of which are preceded by 'Lawangan' (Salzner 1960): Ajuh, Bakoi = Lampung, Bantian, Banuwang, Bawu, Kali, Karau = Beloh, Lawa (under which are subsumed several groups called Dusun, which may rather be Maanyan), Lolang, Mantararen, Njumit, Paku, Purai, Purung, Tabuyan = Tabojan and Tabojan Tongka, Tuwang. An area from at least Buntok to northwestern Muntai, centering on the Karau River in southwest Borneo.

28. Lonchong = Lontjong = Lawoet ? = Sekah ? Coasts of Banka and Belitung

islands. Possibly extinct. Probably Malay dialect.

29. Long Pata. Ds. also Batu Bla, Berawan. Northern Sarawak.

30. Lubu. 1,000,000. Central region of eastern Sumatra. May be a dialect of Kerintji (24).

31. Maanyan. Ds. include Dusun, Dusun Deyah = Deah (?), Samihim, Sihong. Area in southwest Borneo centering around Tamianglayang between the Barito River and the Karau River on the west and Gunung Meratus in the east.

32. Madurese. Ds. East = Sumenep: Bawean, Pasuruan-Besuki, Sapudi-Kangean; West: Bangkalan, Pamekasan. 5,000,000. Madura and northeastern coast of Java.

33. Malagasy. Ds. eastern = Bara, Betsileo, Betsimisaraka, Bezanozano, Merina = Hova, Sahafatra, Sihanaka, Taifasy, Taimanambondro, Taimoro, Taisaka = Antaisaka, Tambahoaka, Tanala = Antanala including Menabe and Ikongo, Tanosy, Tsimihety; western = Mahafaly, Sakalava, Tanalana, Tandroy, Vezo. 25,000 Bezanozano (1951), 170,000 Tanala (1951). 5,000,000. Malagasy Republic on Madagascar.

34. Malay. Numerous geographic and ethnographic names appear as labels for dialects, the differences between which have been little studied; e.g., Mergui Archipelago: Mergui, Orang Laut including Kappir, Selung = Selong = Moken; Malay Peninsula: Kedah, Kelantan, Perak, Trengganu; Sumatra: Kubu, Palembang, Middle Malay including Besemah = Pasemah, Semendo, Serawaj = Serawai; Bangka Is. : Mentok; Java: Djakarta; Borneo: Bandjarese, Kutai, Labu, Mualang, Ulu = Kapuas = Sintang, Sea Dayak = Iban including Balau, Batang Lupar, Bugau, Milikin, Sekarang = Skarang, Sibuyau = Sabuyau = Sibuian; Celebes: Minhasa Malay = Menado Malay; Ceram: Amboina; and in all areas of Indonesia: the dialect most rapidly changing, Bahasa Indonesia (Teeuw and Emanuels 1961). Literary Malay developed from the standard of the Jahore empire in the seventeenth century, and does not represent the modern spoken dialect of the Johore area of Malaya and the Riau Archipelago, often mistakenly referred to as Standard Malay (Omar 1971). 10,000,000 native speakers may include Kerintji and Minangkabau. Scattered from the Mergui Archipelago to West Irian: Malaysia (over 1,000,000), Riau Islands (1,000,000), coastal area of east Sumatra and Palembang (500,000), southern and southwestern Sumatra (300,000), Borneo (1,500,000), Ceram (100,000), Djakarta, Java (1,000,000).

35. Maporese = Lom = Belom. Still spoken in 1889 in Belinyu district of Bangka Island. Possibly extinct.

36. Melanau = Milano = Belana'u. Ds. Balingian, Bruit, Dalat = Dalad, Daro, Igan, Kanowit, Matu, Mukah = Muka, Oya = Oga, Sibu, Siduan = Seduan = Siduani, Tanjong. Coastal area of the Rejang delta up to the Balingian River, Sarawak.

37. Mentawai. Ds. Simalegi, Sakalagan, Silabu, Taikaku, Saumanganja. 50,000. Mentawai Islands.

38. Minangkabau. Ds. Agam, Batu Sangkar-Pariangan, Pajokumbuh, Si Djundjung, Singkarak, Tanah, Ulu. 2,000,000. West Sumatra. Sometimes treated as a Malay dialect.

39. Modang. Ds. Long Glat, Long Wai = Long Wé = Kelingan (?) = Kelinjau (?), Segai. Northern Indonesian Borneo, on the Gunung Tabur, upper Segah, middle Kelai, Kelinjau, Belayan and upper Mahakam rivers.

40. Murik. Above Claudetown on the Baram River, Sarawak.

41. Sarawak Murut. Ds. Adang, Kelabit = Kalabit including Brung, Lepu Potong and Libbung, Lun Bawang, Lun Daya = Lun Daye, Padas, Treng including Balait and Tabun, Trusan. Across interior Borneo at about 4°N, in an area from Brunei Bay up to the headwaters of the Padas River, down to the headwaters of the Baram and south and southeast into Indonesian Borneo, where most now live in the mountains in which the tributaries of the Sesayap (Sasayap) River arise.

42. Narom. Ds. also Dali, Lelak, Lemiting, Long Kiput, Miri, Tutong. Northern Sarawak.

43. Ngaju = Ngadju = Biadju. Ds. Kahayan = Kahaian, Mangkatip = Mengkatip, Mantangai, Pulopetak; possibly also Katingan and Sampit. On the middle reaches of the Barito River, on all but the upper reaches of the Kapuas and Kahayan rivers, on the Katingan and Mentaya rivers, and as a lingua franca in nearly all of south Borneo.

44. Nias. D. also Batu. 50,000. Nias and Batu islands.

45. Nusa. Southern Nusapenida Is.

46. Ot Danum. Ds. also Ot Murung, Ot Siang; Ot Balawan (?), Ot Banu'u (?), Ot Olang Olang (?), Ot Tuhup ? Upper reaches of rivers of south Borneo, south of the Schwaner Range.

47. Punan Ba = Rejang = Rejang Punan = Punan. Ds. also Beketan = Bakitan = Bukitan = Mangkettan = Mankěta = Pakatan, Punan Batu, Ukit; Punan Gang (?), Punan Lusong ? On the Rejang, Ba (Bah), Kakus, Jelalong and Pandan rivers, Sarawak.

48. Rade = Raday = Rhaday. 80,000. Vietnam and Cambodia.

49. Redjang = Rejang. D. also Lebong. 250,000. Southwestern Sumatra.

50. Roglai, Northern = Radlai = Adlai. 30,000. Vietnam.

51. Roglai, Southern. D. also Rai. 20,000. Vietnam.

52. Sampit. In and around Sampit in southern Borneo. Dialect of Ngaju (Cense and Uhlenbeck 1958).

53. Sasak. D. also Lekong. Eastern Lombok.

54. Sibop. Ds. Lirong, Long Pokun, Tinjar Sibop. On the Tinjar River and elsewhere between the Baram and Rejang rivers, Sarawak.

55. Sichule = Sikule = Wali Banuah. Ds. also Lekon, Simalul, Tapah. Simalur Island.

56. Simalungun = Simelungan = Timur Batak. Northern Sumatra.

57. Simalur = Simulul = Simeuloë = Leng bano. Simalur Island.

58. Sumbawa. Western Sumbawa Island.

59. Sundanese. Ds. Banten, Sundanese = Priangan. 15,000,000. Western Java.

60. Toba = Toba Batak. D. also Angkola = Mandailing. 2,000,000 Toba around Lake Toba, Sumatra.

Samsam ? Sumatra or neighboring island.

AFFILIATION. A member of the Hesperonesian subgroup of Austronesian (Dyen 1965).

INDO-PACIFIC = PAPUAN = NON-AUSTRONESIAN

GROUPING. Greenberg (1958, 1960b, 1971b) proposes a genetic relationship among all the languages that he classifies as INDO-PACIFIC, a relationship previously denied by other scholars in the area (cp. Capell's (1962b) explicit denial in his proposal that they be labeled NON-AUSTRONESIAN rather than PAPUAN, to emphasize their lack of genetic unity). To the languages usually called 'Papuan', Greenberg adds ANDA-MANESE and TASMANIAN.

Besides a 'nuclear' New Guinea group consisting of most of the subgroups of the CENTRAL NEW GUINEA macro-phylum, Greenberg reports there may also be a similarly high level group equivalent to Cowan's (1957a) 'WEST PAPUAN', consisting of HAL-MAHERA, TIMOR-ALOR and WEST PAPUAN, and another consisting of BOUGAINVILLE, NEW BRITAIN, CENTRAL MELANESIAN, and Yele (34, below).

In addition to Greenberg's seven major groups on New Guinea (CENTRAL, EASTERN, NORTHEASTERN, NORTHERN, SOUTHERN, SOUTHWESTERN, and WESTERN) Greenberg (1971b) and Wurm (1971c) list a number of smaller groups (unnumbered below) and single languages (1–35, below), which, largely for lack of data, cannot at present be placed within the larger groups. Besides these unsubgroupable languages, Wurm reports the probable existence of a number of other as-yet-uncontacted and unnamed languages in several areas.

1. Alfendio = Arafundi. 1,000. On the Arafundi River, an eastern tributary of the Karawari, a southern tributary of the Middle Sepik, Sepik District, New Guinea.

ANDAMANESE (q. v.)

2. Asang. Madang District, New Guinea.
3. Baru. Madang District, New Guinea.
4. Bembi. 1,800. Sepik District, New Guinea.
5. Biwat = Munduguma. Lower and Middle Yuat River, Sepik District, New Guinea. May be most closely related to Wapi (30, below), on the Upper Yuat in the Western Highlands District.

BOUGAINVILLE (q. v.)

6. Breenugu. Ds. Ariap, Mamiap. East of the Upper May River, Sepik District, New Guinea.
7. Changriwa. 462. West of the Yuat River and immediately south of the Sepik, Sepik District, New Guinea.
8. Domuna = Dumuna. Madang District, New Guinea.
9. Ganati. 300. Eastern Highlands District, New Guinea.
10. Ganglau. D. ? also Pasa = Siroi. Rai Coast, Madang District, New Guinea.
11. Gumbi. Rai Coast, Madang District, New Guinea.
12. Gwoira. Milne Bay District, New Guinea.

HALMAHERA (q. v.)

13. Kaima. Ds. also Langam, Mongol. 500. Three villages west of the Yuat River and immediately south of the Sepik, Sepik District, New Guinea.

14. Koru Buso. Southeastern Morobe District, New Guinea.

LEFT MAY (q. v.)
LEONARD SCHULTZE (q. v.)
CENTRAL MELANESIAN (q. v.)

15. Mobab. Madang District, New Guinea.

MOMBERAMO RIVER (q. v.)

16. Mumeng. Two languages (Greenberg).
17. Mur. Rai Coast, Madang District, New Guinea.
18. Nagatman. 500. Sepik District, New Guinea.
19. Nakiai. East of the Upper May River, Sepik District, New Guinea.

NEW BRITAIN (q. v.)
CENTRAL NEW GUINEA = HUON-FINISTERRE (q. v.) plus EAST NEW GUINEA HIGHLANDS (q. v.) and WEST NEW GUINEA HIGHLANDS (q. v.)
EASTERN = SOUTH-EAST NEW GUINEA (q. v.)
NORTH NEW GUINEA (q. v.)
NORTHEASTERN NEW GUINEA (q. v.)
SOUTHERN NEW GUINEA, a part of CENTRAL AND SOUTH NEW GUINEA (q. v.)
SOUTHWESTERN NEW GUINEA, a part of CENTRAL AND SOUTH NEW GUINEA (q. v.)
WESTERN NEW GUINEA (q. v.)

20. Ndau. Madang District, New Guinea.
21. Negira. Sepik District, New Guinea.
22. Ondoro.
23. Pagi = Pagei. 500. Sepik District, New Guinea.
24. Sawi. Rai Coast, Madang District, New Guinea.
25. Sunggum. Madang District, New Guinea.

TASMANIAN (q. v.)

26. Tate = Tati. Gulf District, Papua, near Kerema.

TIMOR-ALOR (q. v.)

27. Umana-Kaina. Milne Bay District, New Guinea.
28. Wab. Rai Coast, Madang District, New Guinea.
29. Waisera. 200. Eastern Highlands District, New Guinea.
30. Wapi. 600. Eastern side of the Upper Yuat River, Western Highlands District. May be most closely related to Biwat (5, above) in the Sepik District.
31. Williams River.
32. Yaganon. Rai Coast, Madang District, New Guinea.

33. Yaugang. Madang District, New Guinea.
34. Yele. 1,500. Rossel Island, east of the eastern tip of New Guinea.
35. Yerakai. 326. West of Lake Chambri, Sepik District, New Guinea.

AFFILIATION. None proposed.

INTER-ANDINE = PAEZ-COCONUCO

GROUPING. Three branches, COCONUCAN (languages numbered 1–6), PANA-QUITAN = PAEZ (7–9) and POPAYANENSE (10–11) comprise the INTER-ANDINE family. The BARBACOAN family, sometimes included in INTER-ANDINE, is now considered to be coordinate with INTER-ANDINE in PAEZAN (Greenberg 1960a).

COCONUCAN

1. *Coconuco. Southwestern Colombia.
2. *Guanaco. Southwestern Colombia.
3. Moguez = Guambia. Southwestern Colombia.
4. Polindaro. Southwestern Colombia.
5. *Puben = Pubenaro. Southwestern Colombia.
6. Totoró. Colombia.

PANAQUITAN = PAEZ

7. Paez. 20,000. Southwestern Colombia.
8. Paniquitá = Panikita. Sometimes considered to be a dialect of (7). Southwestern Colombia.
9. *Quilla = Killa. Sometimes listed as member of BARBACOAN or CHIBCHAN. Southwestern Colombia.

POPAYANENSE

10. *Popayán. Southwestern Colombia.
11. *Puracé. May have been a dialect of (10). Southwestern Colombia.

AFFILIATION. Member of MACRO-CHIBCHAN phylum.

IRANIAN

GROUPING. Comparative linguistic evidence reflects an earlier split from Proto-IRANIAN into languages which are now classified as EASTERN and WESTERN IRANIAN. Other additional group classifications merely reflect geographic location rather than paths of descent. Thus, the NORTHERN IRANIAN languages of Russia represent a subgroup of EASTERN IRANIAN; Parachi and Ormuri (included in EASTERN) are sometimes assigned to a 'CENTRAL' group, as is Balochi (even though Balochi is included in WESTERN IRANIAN).

*Avestan is an extinct literary language in which the sacred books of the Zoroastrian religion, *The Avesta*, was written.

EASTERN

NORTHERN = (SAKA-) SCYTHIAN. These languages were formerly spoken in south Russia and as far west as Hungary. Except for Khwarizmian (3) and Khotanese (2), the extinct languages or dialects are known only from Greek inscriptions of south Russia. There are two extant languages of this group: Ossetic, which was probably part of an 'Alanic' complex with Alanic (1); and Yaghnobi (8), which probably is a descendant of the extinct Sogdian (7).

1. *Alanic.
2. *Khotanese = Saka. Known from a Buddhist manuscript in Chinese Turkestan.
3. *Khwarizmian. Known from a few glosses preserved in Arabic books excavated by Soviet archaeologists.
4. Ossetic. Ds. Digoro-Tual = Northwestern = Western, including Digor (in the region of the Urux River) and Tual (Southern Ossetic); Iron = Northeastern = Eastern = Ossetic = Ir = Tagaur = Alagir = Kurtat, along tributaries of the Terek River and along the middle course of the Terek River; *Jassic, formerly spoken in Hungary, became extinct in the sixteenth century. 350,000. North-Ossetian ASSR, Georgian SSR, South-Ossetian AO.
5. *Sarmatian.
6. *Scythian.
7. *Sogdian. The pre-Islamic lingua franca of Central Asia.
8. Yaghnobi. Valley of the Yaghnobi at the headwaters of the Zarafshan River.
9. Ormuri = Bargista. Ds. Kanigurami, in Wazirstan near Kaniguram; Logar, in the Logar Valley.

PAMIR = GHALCHAH GROUP. These languages are spoken in extreme northeastern Afghanistan as well as in adjacent areas in the Soviet Union and Pakistan.

10. Munji = Munjani. Spoken by 200 to 300 familes. Afghanistan in the Munjan region in four dialects, and in Pakistan in one dialect.
11. Sanglechi. Ds. also Ishkashmi, Zebaki. Spoken in the Sanglech Valley and the Ishkashim area, Afghanistan.
12. Parachi. Spoken near Kabul, Afghanistan: in Hindu Kush Valley, in Shutul (400 families), in Ghujulan (100 families), in Nijrau and Tagau (600 families), and in Pachaghan.
13. Pashto = Passtoo = Pakhtoo = Pakhtoo = Pushto = Pashtu = Afghan. Ds. Eastern Afghan = Pakh'to, Kandahari = Pashto, Peshwari = Pakhto. 12,000,000. Pakistan (5,550,000) in the districts of Peshawar, Hazara, Kohat, Bannu, Dera Ismail Khan, and in the Territories of Swat, Buner, Bajaur, as well as in Balochistan and in the Punjab area in the Afghan-Pakistan border areas around Mianwali; Afghanistan (6,500,000) in the southeastern areas of Afghanistan (in the Eastern, Southern, Kandahar, and Farah provinces); over half the people in Kabul speak Pashto, as do one-third of the people in Herat, Qutaghan, and Mazar; also spoken in enclaves in all other areas of Afghanistan (except in Maimana, Badakhashan, and the Daisangi District of Kabul Province).
14. Shughni = Shighni = Khugni. D. also Sarikoli (Soviet Union). Spoken on

both sides of the Afghan-Soviet border, some 30 miles north of Ishkashim.
15. Wakhi. Less than 5,000. Afghanistan east of Ishkashim and still farther east in the upper Yarkhun Valley of Chitral, Pakistan.

WESTERN. Some languages of this group are sometimes subgrouped as 'NORTHWEST' (e.g., Kurdish, Tat, Talysh), or as 'SOUTHERN' (e.g., Persian, Luri, Bakhtiari).

16. Bakhtiari. Southern Iran in two tribal groups: the Hoftlang and the Chaharlang.
17. Balochi = Baluchi. Ds. Eastern, east of Quetta; Western, including Makrani. Pakistan (1,000,000); Afghanistan (200,000); Iran along eastern border adjacent to Pakistan and Afghanistan (600,000); an enclave in the Turkmen SSR in the Merv region (8,000); areas in north Pakistan, India (5,000); and islands of the Persian Gulf and the northern coast of the Arabian Peninsula (15,000).
18. Gabri. Spoken by Persian Zoroastrians in the Yezd and Kerman regions of Iran.
19. Gilaki = Gelaki. Less than 100,000. The Gilan region of Iran.
20. Gurani.
21. Kumzai.

KURDISH. Bacon (1964) lists Zaga Kurdish and Kermanji Kurdish as separate languages. Estimates range from 5,000,000 to 10,000,000. Eastern Turkey (2,000,000), northwestern Iran (1,000,000), northern Syria (250,000), Iraq (900,000), Soviet Armenia (several thousand).

22. Kermanji = Southern Kurdish = Eastern Kurdish. Ds. including Arbil = Irbil, Bingird, Mukri, Pizdar, Riwandiz = Riwanduz, Suleimaniyi (the basis of the Standard used in Baghdad), Surci, Warmawa, Xosnaw.
23. Zaza = Northern Kurdish = Western Kurdish. Ds. including Akre, Amadiye, Barwari, Gulli, Zakho, Sheikhan, Dohuk.
24. Luri. Southwestern Iran.
25. Mazanderani. Northern Iran.
26. Persian. Ds. Afghan Persian, also including Djamchidi = Yemchidi, Firozkodi, Khorasani = Dari, Hazaras, Taimani, Timuri = Taimouri (Afghan Persian is spoken throughout the northcentral portion of Afghanistan from the Iran border on the east to the Pamir Mountains in the northeast along the border of Tadzhik SSR to the north, and Pakistan and Kashmir across the mountains to the south); Tehrani Persian, including Anaraki, Araki, Bandar-Abbasi, Biabanaki, Bihbihani, Birjandi, Hamadani, Jahromi, Judeo-Persian, Kashani, Kazirauni, Kermani, Lari, Mahallati, Na'ini, Qazvini, Seden, Semnani, Shahrudi, Shirazi, Shushtar-Dizfali, Tungistani, Yazdi, Zarandi (central and southcentral Iran); Tajik = Tadjik = Tadzik = Tadzhik, including Galcha in the Pamir Mountains (spoken in northeastern Afghanistan in the areas of Budakhshan, Panjsher, Kabul, and in Tadzhik SSR). 20,000,000. Primarily in Iran, Afghanistan, Tadzhik SSR, Iraq, and the islands of the Persian Gulf. Concentrated most heavily in a belt from the western portion of Iran eastward through northern Afghanistan, and thence north-

eastward into Tadzhik SSR. There are two extinct literary languages of
Persian which represent a historical sequence antedating Modern Persian:
*Old Persian and *Middle Persian (including *Huzvaresh, *Pahlavi, *Parsi,
*Pazend).

27. Talysh. 100,000–150,000. USSR, Talysh region of Iran (50,000). In USSR
along the Caspian coast south of the Viliazh-chai River in the Lenkoran,
Zurand, Astara, and Massala rayons of Azerbaidzhan SSR, and extending
into Iran up to Kepri-chal.

28. Tat. Ds. Jewish Tat, Muslim Tat. 100,000. On both slopes of the eastern
extension of the main Caucasian chain and on the Apsheron Peninsula, in
the coastal zone of the Caspian Sea between Apsheron and Kuba in Azerbaidzhan SSR and Daghestan SSR.

AFFILIATION. Member of INDO-IRANIAN within INDO-EUROPEAN.

IROQUOIS

GROUPING. Chafe (1973) divides IROQUOIS into SOUTHERN (Cherokee, 1 below)
and NORTHERN (the other still-spoken languages plus extinct Laurentian (2) — possibly
also Nottaway (4), since Nottaway appears to have been closely related to Tuscarora
(8). Within the NORTHERN group, the languages of the Five Nations (3, 5, 6) form a
subgroup of such close relationship that "perhaps it is best to regard these languages
as forming a dialect continuum" (Chafe). The dialect continuum nature of the dialects
of (6) was first reported by Wright (anonymous 1842) and further discussed by Voegelin
(1941) and Hickerson et al. (1952). Lounsbury (1961) recognizes, in addition to the
split between Cherokee and NORTHERN, a division between the 'outer' IROQUOIS
languages (1, 2, 8, 9) and the 'inner' or 'Eastern' languages (3, 5, 6). Until the early
period of European colonization a number of other IROQUOIS languages, of which we
have no record, are said by Chafe to have been spoken in Ontario, Quebec, western
New York, Pennsylvania, northern Ohio, Maryland, eastern Virginia, and eastern
North Carolina.

1. Cherokee = Cerochese = Cheerake = Chel-a-ke = Cheleki = Chell-o-kee =
Cherakee = Cheroki = Mountain Cherokee = Alligewi = Alleghany = Talligewi
= Tcálke = Tcerokiéco = Tchálagi = Tscherokese = Tselogi = Southern Iroquoian. 10,000. North Carolina (1,000), Oklahoma (9,000); formerly the southern
end of the Appalachian chain in Tennessee, North Carolina, but including also
parts of South Carolina, Georgia, Alabama, and Virginia.

2. *Laurentian. On the St. Lawrence River in the sixteenth century.

3. Mohawk = Mohaux = Mohaqu = Mohogica (?) = Mohogice (?) = Macquaic
= Mahakuassica = Agnier = Canienga = Caughnawaga = St. Regis. 1,000–
2,000. Ontario, Quebec, New York.

4. *Nottoway. Formerly in southeastern Virginia.

5. Oneida = Oneidah = Oneider = Oneydoe = Onnoiout = St. Xavier = San
Francisco St. Xavier Mission. 1,000–2,000. Ontario, New York, Wisconsin.

6. Seneca. Ds. = Trs. Cayuga = Cayiuker = Quengues = Seneca (more than 1,000;

500–1,000 in Ontario, New York; 200–500 in Oklahoma), Onandaga = Onondago = Onontager = Onnontagué = St. Jean Baptiste = Maqua (?) = Onadagaish (?) = Onandago county ? (100–1,000. Ontario, New York), Seneca = Senecka = Sinicker = Hodenosaunee = Mse Chachtini (2,000–3,000, Ontario, New York). 3,100–5,000. Seneca-Cayuga-Onandaga count as three of the Five (Iroquois) Nations (including also Mohawk and Oneida); later Six Nations (when joined by the Tuscarora).

7. *Susquehannock = Conestoga = Andaste = Minqua. Along the Susquehanna River until about 1763.

8. Tuscarora = Touscarora = Tuskara = Tuskarora = Tuskeruru. 100–300. North Carolina, Pennsylvania, New York and Ontario (formerly in Virginia and North Carolina, on the Tar, Pamlico, and Neuse rivers).

9. *Wyandot = Wanat = Wandot = Weinondot = Wundat = Wyandote = Wyandott(e) = Guyandot = Huron(e). A few speakers survived in Oklahoma until recently (formerly the St. Lawrence Valley and Ontario Province). Group created by merger of the Huron and Tionontati = Petun = Tobacco tribes.

AFFILIATION. Memer of MACRO-SIOUAN phylum.

*Isaurian. A non-INDO-EUROPEAN language of ancient Asia Minor known chiefly from Greek traditions (Holl 1908).

AFFILIATION. None known.

ITALIC

GROUPING. The so-called PRE-ITALIC group of ITALIC languages is a misnomer, since the languages in this group were not necessarily spoken before some of the languages in the remaining two ITALIC groups, which constitute a relatively cohesive pair: LATINO-FALISCAN and UMBRO-SABELLIAN. Information on languages in the controversial PRE-ITALIC group is so meager that the question of their affiliation within ITALIC is in effect unresolved. Sometimes they are classified as intermediate between the two remaining better-attested groups of ITALIC; sometimes the two better-attested groups are taken to be the sole constituents of ITALIC, thereby excluding PRE-ITALIC; sometimes all three groups are taken to be coordinate within ITALIC.

Difficulties encountered in reconstructing Proto-ITALIC from these three groups appear to some to be insolvable; so Beeler (1966).

In the list below, all the languages under the headings LATINO-FALISCAN, UMBRO-SABELLIAN, and PRE-ITALIC are extinct. One language, Old Latin of the fifth century B.C., was ancestral both to literary forms (successively designated 'Classical', 'Post-Classical', and 'Mediaeval' Latin) and to spoken forms (successively designated 'Vulgar' or 'Common Latin', Proto-Romance, and ultimately the modern ROMANCE languages). However, the extant languages are listed in a separate article, ROMANCE (q. v.).

LATIN(O)-FALISCAN = LATINIAN

1. *Camuni. Known from inscriptions of the Val Camonica, the Valley of the

Oglio River north of the Lago d'Iseo. More closely associated with LATIN-FALISCAN than with UMBRO-SABELLIAN.

2. *Faliscan. Centered around its capital, Falerii (modern Civita Castellana) north of Rome and south of Etruria — between Latin and Etruscan speaking areas.

3. *Lanuvian.

4. *Old Latin. Including the dialect of urban Rome beside less known dialects in the area surrounding Rome (Latium). With the Roman conquest and colonialization of all of Italy by the end of the second century B.C., Latin became the language of all Italy over the competing, but unsuccessful, Faliscan and UMBRO-SABELLIAN languages.

5. *Praenestinian.

PRE-ITALIC. This name is a cover term for a number of little-known INDO-EUROPEAN languages spoken in Italy around the fifth century B.C. It is probable that the people of the earlier North Villanovan cultures of Italy (the Palafitticoli, Terramaricoli, and Villanovans) were in part speakers of PRE-ITALIC languages.

6. *Illyrian. D. Messapic (spoken in ancient Apulia and Calabria, now both modern Apulia, on the southeastern 'heel' of the Italian Peninsula in the fifth century B.C.). Known by one inscription of three words from the Balkan Peninsula (now thought to be Greek; Polomé 1966), and from some 200 Messapic inscriptions. Evidently continued to flourish during the first few centuries of the Christian era.

7. *Lepontic. Formerly spoken in the regions around the western lakes and the valleys leading to them in northern Italy in the fifth century B.C. Closely related to *Ligurian (8).

8. *Ligurian. Formerly spoken in Liguria in northwestern Italy around 500 B.C. Known from a small number of glosses and local names. Perhaps intermediate between CELTIC and ITALIC (Whatmough 1937) or predivisional 'Italo-Keltic' (Jullian 1916), or 'Kelto-Ligurian'.

9. *Raetic. Formerly spoken in northeastern Italy, north and south of the Brenner Pass and the Valley of the Adige in the fifth century B.C. Some ancient authors thought Raetic had Etruscan affinities because it used the Etruscan alphabet. Whatmough (1937) and others are convinced that the affinities of *Raetic are with *Illyrian, CELTIC, and GERMANIC; Bonfante (1935) declares that *Raetic is an *Illyrian dialect (6, above).

10. *Old Sabellic = Southern East Italic. Formerly spoken on the Adriatic seaboard on northeastern coast of Italy south of the Po River delta. The 'southern' variety of 'East Italic' is believed to have been INDO-EUROPEAN, while another group, 'Northern East Italic' (known from inscriptions found in Novilaka, Fano, and Pesaro), is believed to have been non-INDO-EUROPEAN (Pulgram 1958).

11. *Sicel. Formerly spoken in Sicily in the fifth century B.C. Closely associated with *Ligurian (8, above).

12. *Venetic. Formerly spoken in northeastern Italy in the region between the

Adige River and the head of the Adriatic Sea (modern Veneto) in the fifth century B.C. Apparently closely related to LATINO-FALISCAN.

UMBRO-SABELLIAN. This name is a cover term for a group of languages more closely related to LATIN-FALISCAN than to PRE-ITALIC. Oscan (13) and Umbrian (14) are grouped together as OSCO-UMBRIAN, in contrast to the lesser known languages, numbered (15) to (21) below, which are known as SABELLIAN.

OSCO-UMBRIAN

    13. *Oscan. Ds. Central Oscan (formerly spoken in the region of modern Campania); Northern Oscan (formerly spoken in the region of modern Abruzzi Molise); Southern Oscan (formerly spoken in a region of modern of modern Calabria, the 'toe' of the Italian Peninsula).

    14. *Umbrian. Formerly spoken north of Rome in the region of modern Umbria, on the headwaters of the Tiber and Arno rivers.

SABELLIAN. Formerly spoken in the hills north and east of Rome. The name SABELLIAN is a cover term for a group of dialects, some of which are closely associated with Oscan, some with Umbrian.

    15. *Aequian.
    16. *Marrucinian.
    17. *Marsian.
    18. *Paelignian.
    19. *Sabine.
    20. *Valscian.
    21. *Vestinian.

AFFILIATION. Member of INDO-EUROPEAN.

IWAIDJAN

GROUPING. Iwaidji (3), and Maung (5) are grouped as IWAIDJIC (O'Grady et al. 1966). Spoken in north central Australia.

1. *?Amarag. East of Van Diemen Gulf.

2. Garik. Doubtfully included by Wurm (1971b).

3. Iwaidji = Wargbi = Jiwaidja = Iwaiji = Eiwaja = Eaewandja = Unalla = Limbakaraja. 55 (1938). Coburg Peninsula.

4. *?Margu. Croker Island.

5. Maung = Arargbi = Maw = Managari. North and South Goulburn Island and neighboring mainland.

AFFILIATION. Member of AUSTRALIAN macro-phylum.

JAKUN

GROUPING. The three JAKUN languages are spoken by an estimated 10,000 people in southern mainland Malaysia west of the SAKAI languages.

1. Beduanda. Northernmost.

2. Jakun = Jaku'd = Jakud'n = Jakoon = Djakun.
3. Kenaboi. Two dialects. Negri Sembilan.

   AFFILIATION. Member of MALACCA group of AUSTRO-ASIATIC phylum.

JAPANESE = JAPANESE-RYUKYUAN

   GROUPING. Elmendorf (1965) finds that three separate languages are spoken
on Okinawa and on adjacent smaller Ryukyu islands. It is, however, generally agreed
that the three languages proposed by Elmendorf are not separate languages but are
dialects of one language. The number of dialects ranges from three to seven, depending on what criterion is used to draw the lines among them (Kanagusuku and Hattori
1955). These dialects — listed as (2), (3), (4) below after Elmendorf — are classified
as the RYUKYUAN group; they, together with Japanese (a single language), constitute
the JAPANESE family (characterized not by many languages but by many diversified
dialects). Even RYUKYUAN can be taken to represent dialects of Japanese (Tōjō 1954).
In every classification, RYUKYUAN represents maximum diversity in the small JAPANESE
family; and the maximum dialectal variation in Japanese itself is in southern Japan,
just north of the Ryukyu islands (Hattori et al. 1955).
   *Old Japanese is known from texts dating from 710–733 A.D. Old Japanese
shows a close correspondence to a 'pre-Japanese' dialect (Roy Miller 1971) called
the 'Koguryŏ' language (named after the Korean state that dominated the peninsula
between 313 and 552). Lee (1963) claims that Japanese descended from this language,
speakers of which "brought the Yayoi culture to northern Kyūshū some 2,300 years
ago."
1. Japanese. Ds. Eastern Japanese, in the Shizuoka, Nagano, Niigata, and areas to
   their east, but excluding the island of Sado and including the following three subdialects: (1) eastern (with five varieties: (a) Tokyo-Yokohama [basis of Standard
   Japanese]; (b) the western Kantō plain area [which encompasses much of suburban
   and metropolitan Tokyo apart from the older downtown region of the city proper,
   most of Kanagawa, central Saitama and westward, most of Gunma, most of the
   Izu Islands, the eastern portion of Shizuoka, the non-Kōfu basin in Yamanashi,
   and the northern part of Nagano]; (c) Central and Western Shizuka, the Kōfu
   basin in Yamanashi, and Central and Southern Nagano; (d) Central and Southern
   portions of the old Echigo area in modern Niigata prefecture; (e) Chiba and
   eastern Saitama area); (2) Northern (with four subdialects: (a) Nan-oo = Ibaragi,
   Tochigi, Miyagi, southern part of Yamagata; northern part of Yamagata and
   southern part of Iwate; (b) Hoku-oo = Aomori, northern part of Iwate, Akita,
   northwestern part of Yamagata; (c) Hoku-etsu = Niigata; (d) Hokkaido); and
   (3) Hachijōjima (on the tiny offshore island of that name). Western Japanese, in
   the Aichi, Gifu, Toyama areas, those parts of Honshū to their west, and Shikoku,
   including Kinki (with three subdialects: (1) Kinki [in Kyoto and Osaka]; (2)
   Hokuriku; (3) Shikoku); as well as non-Kinki (with five subdialects: (1) Gifu-
   Aichi; (2) Totsugawa-Kumano; (3) Chūgoku; (4) Un-paku; (5) Hakata, i.e.,
   southwestern edge of Shikoku). Kyūshū Japanese, on the island of Kyūshū and the

small adjacent islands to the south as far as the Tokara archipelago (including three subdialects: Eastern, Northwestern = Satsuma, and Southwestern). Japan (100,000,000), Taiwan (several thousands), Hawaii (200,000), Continental United States (200,000; mostly in California), Brazil (380,000). Japanese is used as a lingua franca among aboriginal tribes in Taiwan and between some Taiwanese speakers of mutually unintelligible CHINESE languages (as Fukkien and Cantonese). Yamagiwa (1967) uses some of the dialects mentioned in the above summary (from Tōjō 1954; Roy Miller 1967), for purposes of dialect distance testing.

RYUKYUAN = RYUUKYUUAN = LUCHA. 900,000. Ryukyu islands.
2. Central Ryukyuan = Okinawan. Ds. Kikai; Okinawa = Central group (including Northern and Southern subdialects, with the latter including Shuri); Okinoerabu = Okierabu; Sacunan; Tokunosima. 678,000
3. Northern Ryukyuan = Amami-Osima = Oosima. Spoken in the Amami group of islands, which constitute the northernmost inhabited islands of the Ryukyu island chain.
4. Southern Ryukyuan = Sakis(h)ima. Ds. Miyako, Yaeyama = Yayeyama. Spoken in the southern Ryukyus, which run southward toward Formosa (formerly called Sakishima Rettō).

AFFILIATION. Member of ALTAIC (Roy Miller 1971).

JIRARAN

GROUPING. The JIRARAN languages number from three to five, depending on whether languages numbered (2) and (5), below, belong to the family. Number (2) may be a dialect of (5), and (5) may be synonomous with Achaqua, generally considered to be ARAWAKAN. All except (5) are possibly extinct.
1. Ayoman = Ayomano. Venezuela.
2. Cuiba. Venezuela, possibly also Colombia.
3. *Gayón. Possibly not extinct. Venezuela.
4. *Jirajara = Jiraran. Possibly not extinct. Venezuela.
5. Xagua = Ajagua = Achagua ? Venezuela.

AFFILIATION. Member of MACRO-CHIBCHAN phylum.

JIVAROAN

GROUPING. Only five languages are classified under the JIVAROAN division, which is nonetheless coordinate with the large-sized ANDEAN and EQUATORIAL divisions as well as with the moderate sized MACRO-TUCANOAN division within ANDEAN-EQUATORIAL.

1. Candoshi = Kandoshi = Candoxi. Ds. Murato, Shapra. 2,000. Between Morono and Postaza rivers, northern Peru.
2. *Cofan = Kofane. Previously classified as MACRO-CHIBCHAN.
3. *Esmeralda = Atacame. Formerly coast of Ecuador. Previously classified by most sources as MACRO-CHIBCHAN (e.g., Jijón y Camaaño lists Esmeralda and

Yaruro (5) as belonging to a Paleo-Chibchan subdivision of MACRO-CHIBCHAN).

4. Jivaro = Jibaro = Xivaro = Shuara. 20,000. Southeastern Ecuador and north-western Peru. Ds. Achuara = Achuale, Aguaruna (15,000; divergent, possibly a separate language), Ecuadorian Jivaro (including probably *Boloma, *Malacato, *Palta), Huambisa = Huambiza = Wambisa (over 3,000; including Candoa).

5. Yaruro. 3,500–5,000. Southern Venezuela. Sometimes classified as Macro-Chibchan. Jijón y Camaaño (1943) classified Yaruro in a Paleo-Chibchan subdivision of MACRO-CHIBCHAN.

AFFILIATION. Member of ANDEAN-EQUATORIAL.

JUKUNOID

GROUPING. Greenberg (1963b) established JUKUNOID as one of the subgroups of his BENUE-CONGO group, following Westermann (1927). Shimizu (1971a, b) has made the first comparative study of the whole JUKUNOID group and gives the classification outlined below, in which YUKUBEN-KUTEP is coordinate with CENTRAL JUKUNOID, which is further divided into three subgroups. There are altogether 50,000 speakers of JUKUNOID languages in the Nigeria-Cameroon borderland area.

CENTRAL

JUKUN-MBEMBE. The MBEMBE = IZALE = IZARE = NSARE = NƆALE = NDALE = NJARI = AKONTO languages — (1) and (3) below, which are spoken in an area over-lapping the border between North-East State, Nigeria, and Bamenda Province, Cameroon — are also known as TIGON = TIGONG = TIGUM = TUGONG = TUGUN = TUKUM.

1. Ashaku = Ashuku = Atsuku = Akitsikpi = Kusuko = Kaka = Kaka-Banjo = Nfumte.
2. Jukun = Juku = Jukū = Jukum = Jukon = Juku Junkun = Jinkum. Ds. Jibu = Jibawa = Dscuba = Jubu, including Donga and Takum = Dìyī; Kona = Jibi = Jiba (2,000); Wapan = Wapã = Wakari, including Abinsi and Wukan; Wase; Gwana-Pindiga ? 32,000–37,000. The Jibu dialect is spoken by settlements at the easternmost end of the Jukunoid area; a creole has developed from Jibu, and is now spoken in many areas to the west by communities formerly speaking languages numbered (1), (3), (4), (5), (9), and (10) and Chamba (an ADAMAWA language). The Wapan dialect is the dialect of the Jukun capital Wukari and adjoining areas in the central Benue Valley. The name Jukun is sometimes used for some or all of the other JUKUNOID languages.
3. Nama. D. also Kporo.

KPAN-ICEN. Spoken mainly in the southwestern corner of North-East State, Nigeria.

4. Eregba = Regba = Kpan = Kpã = Kpanzon = Kpanzõ = Kpwãtẽ = Hwãye = Appa. Ds. also Apa, Kente, Kentu = Bissaula, Kumbo. Eregba was listed as extinct by Greenberg (1966) but has been redis-covered by Shimizu (1973).

5. Icen = Ichen = Etkywã = Etkyẽ = Kyãtõ = Kyeto = Nyidu.

WURBO. Spoken along the Benue upstream from Jukun in the Muri Division of North-East State, Nigeria.

    6. Bandawa. Ds. also Lau, Minda.

    7. Chomo = Shomo. D. also Karim = Kiyu.

    8. Jiru = Wuyar = Wiyap = Kiru = Kir = Atak.

YUKUBEN-KUTEP

    9. Boritsũ = Yukuben = Oohúm = Balaaben = Difu = Afiteng. Principally in Wukan Division, Benue-Plateau State, Nigeria.

  10. Zumper = Zomper = Zumperi = Zompere = Zumpes = Jompre = Djompra = Djumperi = Kutep = Kuteb = Kutev = Mbarike. 10,000–15,000. Mostly in Wukan Division, Benue-Plateau State, Nigeria.

AFFILIATION. Member of BENUE-CONGO (Greenberg), though recent work by Shimizu (personal communication through Ian Maddieson) tends to confirm the suggestion of Meek (1931) that JUKUNOID is more closely related to some of the languages regarded as KWA than to other BENUE-CONGO languages.

Juma = Yuma = Arara. Still spoken on the tributaries of the Purus River in the state of Amazonas, Brazil (Lorraine Bridgeman, personal communication).

AFFILIATION. Unknown.

KALAPUYA(N) = KALAPOOIAN

GROUPING.

1. Santiam = Kalapuya = Kalapooiah = Calapoo(y)a = Calapooiah = Calapuya = Lúkamiute = Wapatu = Wapatu Lake = Willamot = Mary's River. D. also Mackenzie. 1 or 2 speakers. Oregon.

2. *Tfalati = Tualatin = Tuálati = Tualatims = Tuhwalati = Atfálati = Follaties = Juálati = Wap(p)atu = Wapeto = Wappatoo = Wapto. 44 speakers in 1910 but now extinct. Oregon.

3. *Yonkalla = Yomkallie = Yoncalla. Formerly on the Elk and Calapooya Creeks, Oregon.

AFFILIATION. Member of PENUTIAN, within which it is classified by Shipley (1969) with Takelma in a 'TAKELMAN' group.

KAM-TAI = DAIC

GROUPING. The classification of KAM-TAI which appears below is in terms of the following major groups of constituent languages: KADAI beside KAM-SUI and TAI.

Controversy exists over the status of KADAI. Rather than including KADAI as a major group within KAM-TAI, Benedict (1942, 1966) would place it as a group coordinate with KAM-TAI in an expanded network of relationships that extends into Oceania, where most of the AUSTRONESIAN languages are found; this expansion into a macro-phylum is called 'AUSTRO-TAI'. On the other hand, Gedney (in press) argues that KADAI languages are merely a divergent group of languages within the scope of KAM-TAI languages, which have not been shown to have wider affiliations that extend into Oceania; in particular, Gedney argues that KADAI is to be taken as belonging either in a TAI group (although it is not known which TAI group) or as being closely related to TAI within KAM-TAI.

Beside KADAI, the constituents of the two other branches, and their relationships, are also controverted. Li (1965c) and Gedney (in press) regard TAI and KAM-SUI as two coordinate branches within KAM-TAI. Haudricourt (1966, 1967) has published information on two languages, Ong-Be (8) and Lakkia (6), which are provisionally linked with KAM-SUI. Saek (29) has been usually regarded as a NORTHERN TAI language, but Gedney (1967) believes that it may have diverged from TAI before the establishment of the other TAI branches, and retained some archaic features also found in KAM-SUI.

KADAI. Benedict (1942) divides the KADAI languages into two groups: LI-LAQUA (2, 4) and LATI-KELAO (1, 3).
1. Kelao = Keh-lao = Lao = Thü. Several villages in west-central Kweichow Province, China, ranging into North Vietnam.
2. Laqua = Ka Beo. Upper Rivière Claire Valley of North Vietnam.
3. Lati. 450. Upper Rivière Claire Valley of North Vietnam.
4. Li = Lai = La = Loi = Le = Dli = B'li = B'lai = K'lai = S'lai = Hiai. Ds. Northern Li, Southern Li. Over 1,000,000. Mountainous central and south central parts of the Island of Hainan. Numerous dialects grouped into two dialect groups by Benedict (1942).

KAM-SUI. Lakkia (6) and Ong-Be (8) are possibly independent languages within KAM-TAI, though Haudricourt (1966, 1967) suggests a close connection with KAM-SUI.
5. Kam = Tung = Tong. D. San-chiange. 710,000 (1956). Southeastern Kweichow (Yü-p'ing, T'ien-chu, Chin-p'ing, Li-p'ing, Jung-chiang districts along Hunan border), China.
6. Lak(k)ia. Perhaps an independent language within KAM-TAI (Haudricourt 1967).
7. Mak = Mo. Ds. also Chi, Ching = Cham, Hwa, Lyo, Mo-chia (in Kwangsi Province). A few villages in northwestern Li-po, in Kuei-chou Province, China.
8. (Ong-)Be. Northern coast of Hainan. Perhaps an independent language within KAM-TAI (Haudricourt 1967).
9. Sui = Shui. Ds. San Tung, Sui Ai, Sui Li, Sui-P'o. 133,000. Southeastern Kweichow (San-tu, Jung-chiang, Ts'ung-chiang and Li-po districts along Kwangsi border, and Nan-tan district in Kwangsi), China.
10. T'en = Yanghuang = Yang Huang. A few villages in Hui-shui just south of the provincial capital, Kweiyang, China.

TAI. Li (1959, 1960) and Gedney (in press) group the TAI languages into three sub-groups: SOUTHWESTERN, CENTRAL, and NORTHERN. Haudricourt (1966) would include all of the SOUTHWESTERN group as a single 'WEST' subgroup of a 'SOUTHERN' group, and four languages of the CENTRAL group as an 'EAST' subgroup of his 'SOUTHERN'. The remainder of the CENTRAL group is included in his EASTERN group. He then includes the NORTHERN group as his 'WESTERN', and KAM-SUI as a coordinate 'NORTHERN' group. Gedney (1965a; in press) proposes that SOUTHWESTERN and CENTRAL TAI may be closer to each other as two divisions of one branch, with NORTHERN TAI as a second branch.

CENTRAL TAI = NUNG-THO. Although Li (1959, 1960) places all of these languages in the CENTRAL TAI group, Haudricourt (1966) regards some of them (12, 13, 14) to be constituents of an 'EAST' subgroup of his 'SOUTHERN TAI' (east of the Red River), the 'WEST' subgroup (west of the Red River) being equivalent to Li's SOUTHWESTERN TAI. The remainder of the CENTRAL TAI languages are assigned by Haudricourt to an 'EASTERN' group coordinate with his 'SOUTHERN', but including two languages not mentioned by Li (11, 16). Gedney (in press) admits that boundaries between CENTRAL TAI and SOUTHWESTERN TAI are not clear, but, despite some phonological correspondences in common between some CENTRAL and NORTHERN TAI languages, he believes that this boundary is more definite. Haudricourt included Saek, which is here assigned to NORTHERN TAI after Gedney (1970), in his 'EASTERN'.

11. Man Cao-lan. Vietnam.
12. Nung. Ds. also Lei Ping, Lungchow (China), etc. 170,000 (in Vietnam). North Vietnam, southern China.
13. Tay. Vietnam.
14. Tho = Thu = T'u. 150,000. Vietnam.
15. Tien-pao = T'ien-pao. China.
16. Ts'ün-lao. Vietnam.
17. Yung-chu'un = Yung-shun. China.

NORTHERN TAI = DIOI. Li (1957) bifurcates these languages into Wu-ming (34) and the remaining languages. The languages, exclusive of Wu-ming, are also known as CHUNG(-CHIA) in Kweichow, CHAUNG(-CHIA) in Kwangsi, and JUI= 'JUI = 'JOI = I-CHIA = I-JEN = PU-I = PU(-)YI = DIOI = KUI = KÜEI = GUI. Li proposes JUI as a term for the group opposed to Wu-ming. The JUI languages or dialects are divided into three subgroups, namely: Ch'ien-chiang (18); Po-ai (26); and the remaining languages. Gedney (1965a, b; 1970) has added Yay (35) and Saek (29) to NORTHERN TAI, with the latter as possibly a fourth TAI 'branch' which diverged from PROTO-TAI earlier than the NORTHERN TAI languages; the alternative is that Saek split off in the PRE-TAI period before the PROTO-TAI unity, with close similarities to KAM-SUI. Many of the JUI 'languages' listed below may be dialects of a single language, but Wu-ming (34), Ch'-ien-chiang (18), and Po-ai (26) are not dialects of this language. Li uses district names to designate linguistic materials obtained in a particular area.

18. Ch'ien-chiang.
19. Chaung.
20. Giây. Vietnam.
21. Hsi-lin.
22. Kwei-yang.
23. Ling-yün.

24. Lung-an. Central Kwangsi Province, China.
25. Nhang. Vietnam.
26. Po-ai.
27. Po-se.
28. Qui-châu. Vietnam.
29. Saek = Sek. Speakers numbered in the thousands. East of Tha Khek in Laos, and a few villages across the Mekhong River in northeastern Thailand (Nakhon Phanom Province).
30. Tien-chow. Western Kwangsi, China.
31. T'ien-pa. Shuich'eng district in northeastern Kweichow, China.
32. Ts'e-heng = Dioi. Kweichow Province, China.
33. Tushan = Tu-shan. Southern part of Kweichow Province, China.
34. Wu-ming. Central Kwangsi Province, China.
35. Yay.

SOUTHWESTERN TAI = TAI-SHAN. According to Brown (1965) there are two main groups in SOUTHWESTERN TAI: a single language, Southern Thai (47), and an EAST-CENTRAL group. The latter is subdivided into the CHIANG SAENG languages — including Siamese (45), Phuan (43), Northern Thai (46), and a NORTHWEST subgroup (36, 37, 38, 41, 44, 52) and another group in EAST-CENTRAL which includes Lao (39) and Phu Thai (42).

36. *Ahom. India (Assam).
37. Kham(p)ti = Hkampti = Shan = Khampti Sam. Ds. Assam, N. Burma, Sinkaling Hkamti.
38. Khün = Kuen. Kengtung in Shan States of Burma.
39. Lao = Laotian. Ds. Luang Prabang group (Laos, from Luang Prabang in Laos down the Mekhong River into the Loei Province of Thailand), Vientiene (central and southern Laos and northeastern Thailand in the Provinces of Nong Khai, Udon, Phetchabun, Chaiyaphum, Khon Kaen, Kanlasin, Nakhon Phanom, Mahasarakham, Roi-et, Ubon, Surin Si Saket, Prachinburi, Nakhon Ratchasima, Buriram), Yo (in and around the main towns of the Thai Provinces of Sakhon Nakhon and Nakhon Phanom). 10,000,000. Thailand and Laos.
40. Lü = Lue = Tai Lü. Southern part of Yunnan (Sipsongpanna), China, and adjacent Laos.
41. Maw.
42. Phu Thai. Rural areas of the Thai provinces of Sakon Nakhon and Nakhon Phanom in northeastern Thailand. Little dialect differentiation.
43. Phuan. A few people scattered through central Thailand, mostly around Lopburi. Descendants of a large group moved from Laos by conquering Thai armies 150 years ago.
44. Sha(n) = Thai Yai. Ds. Eastern (centered at Chiang Tung, often spelled Kengtung), Northern (centered at Lashio), Southern (centered at Taunggyi). 2,000,000. Shan States of Burma, Shan States of Yunnan in China, and scattered in northwestern Thailand (particularly the Mae Hong Son area).

45. Siamese = Thai = Central Thai = Standard Thai. 10,000,000. Central Thailand centered on Bangkok. Little geographical variation, but striking social differentiation.
46. Northern Thai = Kammyang. 2,000,000. Mainly in Northern Thailand.
47. Southern Thai. Ds. also Tak Bai and other varieties spoken along the Thai-Malay border (Narathiwat Province). 2,000,000. Thailand (Chumphon, Rahong, Surat, Phangnga, Phuket, Krabi, Nakhon Sithammarat, Trang, Patthalung, Songkhla, Pattani, Satun, Yola, Narathiwat provinces, and Samui Island). The border dialects are quite distinct from the others.
48. Tai Blanc = White Tai. Northwestern Vietnam along the China border.
49. Tai Noir = Black Tai = Dam. 300,000 (Laos). Laos and North Vietnam along the Laotian border.
50. Red Tai. North Vietnam.
51. Tay Nüa. Southern part of Yunnan, China.
52. Ya.
53. Yuan = Yuon = Thai Yuan = Yon. 2,000,000. Lānnā of Phayap region of Thailand.
54. Yunnan Shant'ou = Twelve Districts Shan = Thai Chè = Thai Khè = Tayok = Paiyi.

AFFILIATION. The KAM-TAI languages have traditionally been grouped in a SINITIC branch of SINO-TIBETAN, along with CHINESE and MIAO-YAO, following Maspero (1911). Shafer (1955), however, had serious reservations about the inclusion of KAM-TAI within SINO-TIBETAN at all; and Benedict (1942, 1966; 1967a, b) has postulated an 'AUSTRO-TAI' group linking TAI, KAM-SUI, KADAI, and AUSTRONESIAN, and more recently MIAO-YAO (Benedict 1973).

KANYARA

GROUPING. Thargardi, included in KANYARA by O'Grady et al. (1966) and Wurm (1971b), is reclassified as belonging to MANTHARDA by Klokeid (1968). The KANYARA languages are spoken along the central west coast of Western Australia.

1. Bayungu = Baiong = Baiung = Biong. 20. 23°S 114°E.
2. Talandji = Talaindji = Tallainji = Talanji = Talanjee = Tallainga = Taloinga. D. also Buduna = Burduna = Budina = Budoona = Poordoona. Several score Talandji; fewer than 12 Buduna. 22°S 114°E.
3. *?Wadiwangga.

AFFILIATION. Member of SOUTHWEST PAMA-NYUNGAN.

*Karankawa = Clamcoets = Clamcoche. Trs. also Coapite, Coaque = Coco, Kohani, Kopano. Perhaps also Pataquilla, Quilotes, Tiopane, Tups. Formerly in Texas, between Galveston Bay and Padre Island.

AFFILIATION. Karankawa is now classified as a language isolate (a single language without closely related sister languages), but was classified by Sapir (1929) in genetic association with 'HOKAN-SIOUAN' languages.

KARDU

GROUPING. The KARDU languages are spoken along, and inland from, the coast of west central Western Australia.

1. Inggarda = Jinggarda = Ingara = Ingarrah = Inparra = Kakarakala. Less than 10. 25°S 114°E.
2. Maia = Miah. Cape Cuvier; Salt Lake and Yanrey rivers; from Minilya River south to Gas Coyne River.
3. Malgana = Marlgana = Maldjana = Majanna. Ds. also Buluguda, Takurda, Tamala, Watjandi = Watchandi. 2–3. 26°S 114°E.
4. Muliara = Malleyearra = Meloria. Ds. also Bardimaya (20 speakers), Nugara, Wardal = Wajari, Widi = Cheangwa. 28°S 117°E.
5. Nanda = Nhanda = Yaw = Eau. Ds. also Amangu = Ying = Nyaakurdi, Pulinya. 2. 28°S 115°E.
6. Wadjeri = Wajeri = Waianwonga. Ds. also Kurduwongga, Patimaya. 100. 25°S 118°E.

AFFILIATION. Member of SOUTHWEST PAMA-NYUNGAN.

KAREN

GROUPING. Names of languages or dialects of KAREN from Grierson (1920, 1927) and Shafer (1955) supplement the names of four languages used to reconstruct PROTO-KAREN by Jones (1961). Jones bases his reconstruction on dialects of Pho (numbered 5, below) and of Sgaw (6), and on Palaychi (4) and Taungthu (7), which fall into two branches, (4 and 6) versus (5 and 7).

As a linguistic group name, KAREN is used inclusively for the eight languages following. But as a tribal name Karen is not always used as a name for speakers of all KAREN languages; instead, it may be used exclusively for speakers of Bwe (1), Pho (5), and Sgaw (6), thereby excluding languages that are apparently used by fewer speakers —(2)–(4) and (8) — but excluding also one numerically well represented language, Taungthu (7). Altogether, 1,500,000–2,000,000 speakers of KAREN languages in Lower Burma (in territory shared with other languages from other groups within SINO-TIBETAN), and 60,000–90,000 speakers of KAREN languages in Thailand (along the western border shared with Burma).

1. Bwe = Brè = Bræ = Brec. Ds. also Bre = Brè (6,900), Karenbyu = White Karen = Gebo = Geba (800); Karrennet (3,700); Karrenni = Kaya = Red Karen, including Sinhmaw Mapauk, Yintale (19,000); Mano (1,450); Padaung including Pale, Sawpana (8,500); Sinsin (550); Yinbaw = Yeinbaw (900); Zayein, including Banyang = Banyin, Padeng, Sawtung (5,000).
2. Gheko. 4,000. Yamèthin, Toungoo districts.
3. Mopwa. Ds. also Bilichi, Dermuha.

4. Palaychi.

5. Pho = Pwo = Mutheit = Shu. Ds. Pho of Bassein, Pho of Moulmein. 368,200.

6. Sgaw = Pgha K'nyan = Kayin. Ds. also Mawnepgha, Sgaw of Bassein, Sgaw of Moulmein. 850,750.

7. Taungthu = Pao = Pa-o. 210,550.

8. Wewaw.

AFFILIATION. Member of TIBETO-BURMAN.

KARWAN = KARAWAN

GROUPING. These languages are spoken in the northern border area between the Northwest Territory and Queensland, Australia.

1. Karawa = Karwa = Karrawar = Kurrawar = Korrawa = Leearrawa.

2. Wanji = Wanyi = Wanyee = Wanee.

AFFILIATION. Member of AUSTRALIAN macro-phylum.

Kassite = Cossaean. Formerly spoken in the Zagros Mountain area. Known from a bilingual glossary dated after seventeenth century B.C., but before the conquest of the Kassites by Alexander the Great (Balkan 1954).

AFFILIATION. None known.

Keres = Queres = Keresan. Ds. Acoma (2,000), Cochiti (500), Laguna (3,500), San Felipe (1,000), Santa Ana (350), Santa Domingo (1,500), Zia (300). 7,000. New Mexico (Rio Grande) Pueblos with western outlier pueblo (Acoma). (Wick Miller and Davis 1963).

AFFILIATION. Keres is now classified as a language isolate (a single language without closely related sister languages), but was classified by Sapir (1929) in genetic association with 'HOKAN-SIOUAN' languages.

KHMUIC

GROUPING. The KHMUIC languages are spoken mainly in Laos in numerous enclaves scattered in all directions from Luang Prabang but extending into Thailand. The language names listed here follow Thomas and Headley (1970) and the Summar Institute of Linguistics (1972), but there are a number of other names listed by Pinnow (1959) which may be alternate names, dialect names, or names of different languages (see also Smalley 1973).

1. Khmu' = Khmus = Khmous = Tsa Khmu = Khamûk. D. also Khang = Xá = Xá Câu = Tênh = T'eng = Putênh = Tayhay, including Khang clâu and Khang ai = XáKhao = Khao (22,000, extending into western Nghê An Province, North Vietnam). 100,000. Both sides of Laos-Thailand border and north and south of Luang Prabang in Laos.

2. Lamet = Lemet = Kha Lamet. 6,000.

3. Puôc = Puhooc = Kha Puhoc. 5,000. North Vietnam.
4. Tayhat = Tày Hat. 2,000. Western Nghê An Province, North Vietnam.
5. T'in. Ds. Mal, Pray. 15,000–20,000. Pua and Thung Chang districts of Nan Province, Thailand and adjacent Sayaboury Province of Laos (Filbeck 1971).
6. Yumbri.
? Con. 70.
? Kha Doi-luang = Kha Doy. 60.
? Kha Kon-tu'.
? Kha Kwang-Lim.
? Kven = Khuen.
? Mi.
? Nanhang.
? Pheng = P'eng = Phong = Theng.
? Tong-luang = Kha Tong Luong = Ka Tawng Luang = Phi Taung Luang = Sach = Tac-cui.

AFFILIATION. Member of MON-KHMER (Thomas and Headley 1970).

KHOISAN

GROUPING. The Greenberg (1966) classification of KHOISAN is modified here to reflect the closely similar classification by Bleek (1927, 1929, 1956) and the very different classification by Westphal (1956, 1962a, b, 1963, 1971).

The first two of the classifications mentioned reflect the 'classical' position established by Dorothea Bleek who recognized that HOTTENTOT languages are somehow related to BUSHMAN languages. The preclassical position recognized that BUSHMAN and HOTTENTOT languages shared phonologies characterized by salient click consonants, but held that a genetic relationship between the two groups nevertheless remained unproved. This preclassical position is echoed by Leonard Bloomfield (1933) when he speaks of 'non-Bantu' rather than KHOISAN languages, which fall into "two unrelated speech areas."

In Westphal's divergent classification, BUSHMAN serves as a cover term for five 'unrelated' groups of languages; HOTTENTOT is then a sixth group, unrelated to the others.

The major group below, SOUTH AFRICAN KHOISAN, is subgrouped: CENTRAL, NORTHERN, SOUTHERN. In addition, there are two languages, each coordinate with the major group: Hatsa (1) and Sandawe (2) in Tanzania.

1. Hatsa = Hadza = Hadzapi = Hadzabi = (Wa)kindiga = Kangeju = (Wa)-tindiga. D. also Bali ? 500–600. Tanzania (Kondoa, Merilu districts).
2. Sandawe = Sandawi. 23,366. Tanzania, between the Bubu and Mponde rivers (Kondoa district).

SOUTH AFRICAN KHOISAN

CENTRAL = HOTTENTOT = KHWE-KOVAB. Bleek's CENTRAL BUSHMAN is included in this group. She also include Hatsa in Tanzania (1, above), but reserves her HOTTENTOT as a separate group. Greenberg includes HOTTENTOT in this group but

reserves the Tanzania click languages, Sandawe (2) and Hatsa (1), for separate classification. Westphal (1971) groups these languages into four coordinate HOTTENTOT
subgroups and languages: Kwadi (28), formerly classified by Westphal as an unrelated
language coordinate with HOTTENTOT; NAMA-!ORA (15, 17, 25, 33), TSHU-KHWE =
CENTRAL BUSHMAN, and another single language, San (36). Westphal divides TSHU-
KHWE into seven languages and groups of languages: I (5, 37); II (6); III (12, 10, 20,
22, 27, 29); IV (4, 14, 18, 21, 23, 32); V (34); VI (7, 9, 13, 19, 24); VII (35). Other
languages and dialects listed are not subgrouped in Westphal's classification.

3. Badza.
4. Buka = Bukakhwe = River Bushman = Boga.
5. Danisa = Madenassa = Madanisi = Madinnisane = Danisin = Dansín.
   100. Botswana.
6. Ḍeti = Ḍeṭikhwe = Tete = Tletle. Ds. = Trs. K'erekhwe, Tsh'erekhwe
   (= Tserekhwe of Naron ?).
7. Domkhoe.
8. Dzhika.
9. G//aa(khwe).
10. G//abake = G//abake(n)tshori = Hiechware = Chuware = Masarwa
    = Tati = Tati Bushman.
11. G//am.
12. Ganáde.
13. G//ana(khwe) = Kanakhoe.
14. G//anikwe.
15. Gimsbok Nama = Bushman.
16. G//oro(khwe).
17. *Grikwa = Griqua = Xrikwa = Xirikwa = Gry.
18. Gumahi.
19. G//wi(khwe) = G!wikwe ? = G/wikhwe.
20. Haitshuwau = Haitshuari.
21. Handá(dam) = Handákwe-dam = Ts'ixa = Ts'exa.
22. Hiotshuwau = Tshuwau. 9,587.
23. Hukwe = !Hukwe = Xũ(khwe) = Kxoe = Kwengo = Vakwengo =
    Mbara Kwengo = Glanda-Khwe = Zama = Vazama = Schekere =
    Black Bushman. 5,000–10,000. Angola, S.W.A. (2,000).
24. ≠Khessákhoe.
25. Koran(n)a = !Kora = !Ora = Koraqua = Gorachouqua. 50.
26. Korokwa.
27. Kossee = Kossee-(n)tshori.
28. Kwadi = Cuepe = Cuanhoca = Curoca = Koroca = Bakoroka =
    Makoroko = Mucoroca. Ds. = Trs. Kwise = Bakise = Bacuisso =
    Bakuise = Bakwisso = Moquisse = Kwisso = Vakuise = Moquise,
    Zorotua = Vasorontu. 15,000. Angola.
29. Kwee = Kwe = Kwe-(e)-tshori.
30. Mahura.
31. Masasi.

32. Mohissa.
33. Nama = Namakwa = Namaqwa = Naman = Rooi Nasie. Ds. also
    Dama = Damara = Damakwa = Damaqwa = Berdama = Tama =
    Tamma = Tamakwa = Klipkaffer(n), Kakuya Bushman. By far the
    largest HOTTENTOT ethnic group, perhaps larger than all the others
    combined.
34. Naron = Naro = Nhaurun = Nhauru = //aikwe = /aikwe = //ai-
    //ẽi = //ai// en = //aisan. Ds. ≠amkwe, /anekwe, G!inkwe =
    !giŋkwe, G!okwe, !Kabbakwe, Tsaukwe, Tserekwe, Tsorokwe.
35. n//hai = n/hai-(n)tse'e = Tsaukwe ? D. also Qabékhoe.
36. San = Saan ? Ds. Hain//um = Hei//om = Heikom = Heikom
    Bushman = Hei//om Bushman (3,000–5,000, S.W.A.), Kedi = Keddi
    (500–1,000, Angola, S.W.A.).
37. Shua = Tshumakwe = Shuak(h)we = Mashuakwe. Ds. also //'aiye
    = /Aaye, /hais = /ais, n/oo(khwe) = n//ookhwe, /oree(khwe), tsh'iti
    = Tçaiti = Sili = Shete Tsere.
38. Tshuma.
    Matete (?), G!aŋg!ai (?).
NORTHERN = JU = !XŨ = BUSH-A. Consensus on this group is expressed
by Bleek, Greenberg, and Westphal.
39. Auen = //Au//en = //Au//eĩ = ≠au-//e·n = //Kau-//-e·n =
    Kaukau = //K''au-//en = Koko //Aukwe(?) = //Au-kwe(?) = ≠au-
    kwe ? 4,890. South West Africa, Botswana.
40. Kung = !Kung = !Kũ = !Xũ =! Hũ. Ds. also Dʒu/' oãsi = Ssu Ghassi
    = Zhu/ oase (400), Nogau = Agau(?) = ≠Kungau ? 4,450.
41. Maligo. Angola.
42. !o!uŋ = !O!kung = !O!kuŋ. 1,000–5,000. Angola.
SOUTHERN. Westphal (1971) postulates two groups that constitute Greenberg's
SOUTHERN KHOISAN: TAA and !WI. TAA = ≠HUA = BUSH-B includes languages
numbered 43 and 44, !WI (including Westphal's ŋ/huki = BUSH-C and //xegwe
= BUSH-D) includes languages numbered 45–48.
43. ≠Hua = ≠Hua-⊙wani = Magon(g) = Gxon = !Xon = !Xoŋ =
    !Kõ = !Kɔ = Koon.
44. ŋ/amani. Ds. also Auni = /auni = /auo, Kakia = Masarwa (215), Ki/-
    hazi, ŋ/u//en = nu//e:n = /u//ẽin = ŋ/u/ei(n) = /nu//en = //u-
    //en = Nusan, ŋ/usan = Nusan = Nu-san = Noosan = ŋ/usan, Xatia
    = Katia = Kattea = Khatia = Vaalpens = ≠Kusi = ≠eikusi.
    Union of South Africa, Botswana.
45. ŋ/huki. Ds. also *≠Khomani, //Kxau, *// ŋ!ke = ŋ//-≠e =
    //Ng!ke = //ŋ = /iŋ/ke.
46. Seroa. Ds. also !gã!ŋe = !gã!ne, //ku//e, and a remnant in Lesotho in
    1963.
47. */xam = /kham-ka-!k'e = /kamka!e= /xam-ka-!k'e.
48. *//xegwe = //xegwi = Batwa = Bush-C = Abathwa = Boroa = tloue
    = tloutle = Kloukle = Kxloukxle = amaNkgqwigqwi = amaBusmana

= gi/ /kxi : gwi = Ki/ /kxi : gwi. South-West Africa, Botswana.
*Namib = g/einin = /ganin = /komasan = /huinin = / /obanen ? *Nossob = Hei-g≠uin = g/abe ? *Zimbabwe ? *Natal ? *Bushmanland ?

AFFILIATION. Though represented by the fewest number of languages and language groups among the four major classes of African languages, KHOISAN is nonetheless coordinate with the other three (AFROASIATIC, NIGER-KORDOFANIAN, and NILO-SAHARAN). Greenberg (1966) offers two equally possible interpretations of the few scattered points of morphological resemblance (without vocabulary resemblance) between some KHOISAN languages and some AFROASIATIC languages: either (a) "chance convergences," or (b) reflection of "remote relationship" between KHOISAN and AFROASIATIC "as a whole."

KIKORI RIVER

GROUPING. 5,000 speakers altogether, in all of the Lower and part of the Middle Kikori River area, including the Middle and Upper Omati River area, Gulf District, Papua, Australian New Guinea.
1. Aird Hills.
2. Barika.
3. Dibiasu. Upper Bamu River.
4. Dugene = Dugeme.
5. Dumu = Tumu = Rumu. 300.
6. Kairi.
7. Kasere.
8. Kibene.
9. Kibiri = Kiberi.
10. Kopo-Moniya.
11. Poromi = Porome. 300. Only possibly in KIKORI RIVER (Wurm 1971c). Karima ? Waiiemi ?

AFFILIATION. Member of CENTRAL AND SOUTH NEW GUINEA.

KOIARI = KOITA

GROUPING. Wurm (1971c) divides the six languages of his KOIARI into two subgroups: BARAIC (languages numbered 2, 3, and 21, below) and KOIARIC (languages numbered 15, 16, and 17). Greenberg's (1971b) unsubdivided KOITA includes many additional names, not all of which would be expected to be separate languages, since Greenberg lists any name used by a source in which he found data for comparison; hence, many could be alternate names for, or dialects of, languages in Wurm's list. The KOIARI languages are largely spoken in the Central District of Papua on the coast around Port Moresby and in a wider east-west area up to the dividing range, with some extension into the Northern District.
1. Agi.
2. Aomie. 995.
3. Barai. 2,998.

4. Biagi.
5. Eikiri.
6. Favele.
7. Gosisi = Tobiri.
8. Hagari.
9. Iarumi.
10. Isurara.
11. Itu.
12. Iworo.
13. Kagi.
14. Karukaru.
15. Koiari. 1,776.
16. Mountain Koiari. 3,734.
17. Koita. 2,260.
18. Kokila.
19. Kotoi.
20. Maiari
21. Managalasi. 3,240.
22. Minjori.
23. Mogoni.
24. Neneba.
25. Nigubaiba.
26. Seramina.
27. Suambe.
28. Suku = Amaseba.
29. Uabari.
30. Uberi.
31. Wamai.
32. Wowonga = Wovanga.

AFFILIATION. Member of SOUTH-EAST NEW GUINEA.

KOMAN = COMAN

GROUPING. Though Greenberg (1966) includes Gule (2) under KOMAN, Tucker and Bryan (1956) do not; instead they list Gule separately, outside of the KOMAN family. Marvin Bender (1971) expands KOMAN by the addition of a number of EASTERN SUDANIC languages: BEIER-DIDINGA, Turkana, and NILOTIC.

The chief classificatory difference between Bender and Greenberg can be stated in terms of which languages are taken to be coordinate within KOMAN; they are, according to Bender, languages numbered 2, 3, 4, 5, 6, and 7 in the list following, as well as others not included in the following list. According to Greenberg, they are all the languages following, except Langa (5), which is not excluded from KOMAN but merely omitted.

1. Gule = Hameg = Fecakomodiyo = Fungi. Sudan: Jebel Gule and San and Roro hills. Most Gule speakers are bilingual in Arabic.

2. Gumuz = Gumus = Gumz = Gumis = Guniz = Gunza = Cosa (?) = Shankillinya. Ds. Disoha = Desua, Debatsa, Degoja, Deguba, Dehenda, Dekoka, Dewiya, Dukunza, Dukwaya, Gombo, Jemhwa, Mendeya, Modea, Sai, Sese = Saysay. 53,000. Ethiopia, Sudan.

3. Koma = Kwama = Gwama. Ds. North Koma = Koma of Asosa = Amam = Nokanoka = Gwama = Gwami = Twakwama; South Koma; Koma of Begi (or Beica); Madi(i)n = Modin = Marin = Midin (including Aru). 6,000. Sudan-Ethiopian border.

4. Central Koma = Coma = Ciita = Ansita = Komo = Gokwom = Hayahaya = Koma of Daga. Ds. also Buldit, Kusigilo = Kigille, Kwogo = Kogo. 1,000.

5. Langa. 2,000 ?

6. Northern Mao = Mau = Gwami = Ganza = Ganzo = Koma = Siggoyo = Mayo = Amam = Fadiro. Ds. Dokonu, Kere, Phosko, Shurri = Shirri. 14,000.

7. Uduk = Kwanim Pas = Burun = Kebeirka = Othan = Korara = Kumus. 5,000. Sudan: Upper Nile Province.

AFFILIATION. Member of NILO-SAHARAN.

KORDOFANIAN

GROUPING. Languages of the Sudan in the Nuba Hills west and south of Khartoum in the area that appears on maps as Kordofan are now classified as KORDOFANIAN. The earlier classifications of these languages, as that of Tucker and Bryan (1956), distinguished KOALIB-TAGOI from two supposedly unrelated groups, KATLA and KADUGLI-KRONGO. Languages listed below appear under the group or branch names of Greenberg (1966), namely, KOALIB, TEGALI and TALODI instead of KOALIB-TAGOI; KATLA as in the earlier classification; and TUMTUM instead of KADUGLI-KRONGO (formerly subgrouped as Tulishi (27), Keiga (24), and Kanga (22) in one group, Krongo (25) and Tumtum (29) in another, and the remaining languages under TUMTUM in a third group). Altogether, 200,000 speakers.

KATLA. Sudan, Nuba Hills. Additional names are supplied by Welmers (1961).
1. Katla = Akalak. Ds. Bombori, Kateik, and Kiddu; Kirkpong and Karoka; Koldrong; Julud = Gulud. 8,700.
2. Tima = Lomuriki = Tamanik Lomuriki = Yibwa Lomuriki.

KOALIB = KOALIB-MORO. 80,000–120,000. Heiban (4) may be a dialect of Otoro (8), rather than a separate language.
3. Fungor = Fungur. Ds. = Trs. also Kau = Kao and Nyaro; Werni = Werna. 2,400.
4. Heiban = Dhe-bang. 690.
5. Koalib = Kawalib = Kowalib = Lgalige. Ds. Ngi-nyukwur (3,800), Ngi-rere (4,200), Ngu-nduna (8,976), Ngu-qwurang (8,000). 24,000.
6. Laro = Yillaro = Ŋwullaro. D. also Igwormany.
7. Moro = Dhi-morong. Ds. Abu Leila and Lebu = Dorong (4,100); Acheron (1,216); Umm Dorein = Logorban (460), Umm Gabralla (9,000).

8. Otoro = Dhi-toro = Litoro = Kawama = Kawarma. Ds. Ði-jama, Ðu-gwujur; Ðö-kwara; Do-ŗombe; Dö-göŗindi, Ða-garro; Ðu-guŗila. 10,400.
9. Shwai = Shuway = Ludumör. 2,800.
10. Tira = Thiro = Li-Thiro. Ds. = Trs. Kinderma = Kanderma, Tira el Akhdar = Tira Dagig, Tira Lumum = Luman, Tira Mandi. 10,120.

TALODI = TALODI-MASAKIN. 16,700. Sudan, Talodi, Eliri Range, Masakin Hills, Moro Hills.
11. Eliri. 400. Southern Eliri Range.
12. Lafofa = Kidie. Ds. also Jebel el Amira, (Jebel) Tekeim. 2,000. Sudan, central Eliri Range.
13. Masakin = Mesakin. Ds. = Trs. also Aheima = El Akheimar, Daloka = Taloka; Masakin Gusar = Mesakin Qusar, including Masakin Buram and Masakin Dagig; Masakin Tuwal (= Tiwal = Towal) Hills.
14. Moro Hills. Ds. = Trs. (part of) Acheron, Lumun = Kuku-Lumun, Tacho = Toicho, Torona. 3,800.
15. Talodi = Ga-jomaŋ = A-jomaŋ. 1,200.

TEGALI = TEGALI-TAGOI. 29,000. Sudan, hill region including the Tegali Range, Tumale, Moreb.
16. Tagali = Tegele = Togole. D. also Rashad = Kom = Ŋa-kom = Kome. 5,000.
17. Tagoi = Tagoy. Ds. also Moreb (552), Tumale (1,100).
18. Tingal = Kajakja = Kajaja. May be a dialect of Tagali. 2,100.
19. Tukum = Tukam. 2,000.
20. Turum. 800.

TUMTUM = KADUGLI-KRONGO. 73,000· Sudan, hills south of Nuba Hills area.
21. Kadugli = Kudugli = Dhalla. 18,000 to 19,000.
22. Kanga. Ds. = Trs. also (part of) Abu Sinun; Chiroro and Kursi; Kufa and Lima. 6,340.
23. Katcha = Dholubi. 6,000.
24. Keiga = Aigaŋ. D. also Demik = Rofik. 6,000.
25. Krongo = Korongo = Kurungu = Kadu mo di. D. = Tr. also Fama-Teis-Kua. 11,600.
26. Miri = Kamiri = Muri. 8,000.
27. Tulishi = Tulesh = Thulishi. Ds. also Kamdang, el Kebira = Turuj = Truj = Logoke = Minjimmina. 8,628.
28. Tumma. Ds. = Trs. also Belanya, Krongo Abdullah. 5,200.
29. Tumtum. Ds. = Trs. also Kurondi = Karondi = Korindi, Talassa. 1,300.

AFFILIATION. Member of NIGER-KORDOFANIAN.

KRU

GROUPING. Languages numbered (1)–(5) and (7), below, are those given by

Greenberg (1966); Welmers (1961) extends this list with two additional names (numbered 6 and 8, below), and considers (2), (4), (6), (7) to be a dialect chain in which mutual intelligibility obtains at border-line areas.

1. Bakwe = Bakwo. Ds. also Abi = Abriwi = Abrinyo = Aulo, Hwane = Hwanne = Houne = Hwale = Hwile = Hwine = Bodo, Obwa, Omelokwe, Pya = Pia = Pye = Pie (Westermann and Bryan 1952, who also include Gweabo, 5 below). Trs. Bapo, Bokue = Bokwe = Bakuo, Debue, Digbue, Dioro, Grippuo, Guagui, Haulo, Hena, Inemu, Irapue = Iribue, Irecapo, Kapo = Kopo, Nedio, Nene, Nozo, Plawi = Blapo = Plapo, Prufa, Tabetuo = Tabetouo, Tahu, Toyo = Tuyo, Tuopo, Tuy, Urepo = Orepue, Uroko = Aulopo, Yabue. 16,000. Liberia and Ivory Coast west of Sassandra River.

2. Bassa = Basa = Basso = Gbasa. 150,000. Coast of Liberia and inland.

3. Bete. Ds. Bete = Betegbo with trs. Bobono, Dakuya, Guibono, Loble, Yokogbo, Zelmogbo; Bobwa = Waa = Waya = Wadye = Waga = Wobe = Ouobi; Dida = Wawi with trs. Gobwa, Jivo, Lozwa, Yoko; Godye = Godia = Go with trs. Baleko, Kotroku = Kotrahu, Legre; Kwadya = Kwa = Kwadrewole; Kwaya = Zegbe; Neyo = Newo = Newole = No = Nihiri. Other trs. Gibo, Niabua, Sokwele = Sokya. 150,000–220,000. Between Sassandra and Bandama rivers in Ivory Coast.

4. De = Dewoi = Do. West of Monrovia in Liberia. Now being replaced by WEST ATLANTIC (Gola) and MANDE (Vai) languages.

5. Grebo = Krebo = Gweabo. Ds. Barobo, Jabo = Dyabo, Palipa, Tewi = Tepo. Trs. Bolokwe, Drebo = Tremble, Gbwolo, Nimiah, Nyabo = Pla. 50,000. Between Cess and Cavally rivers, Liberia, and Ivory Coast. Grebo and Jabo may be separate languages.

6. Krahn = Kran = Kra = Kraa = Karan = Pahn. Trs. Neabo, Sapo = Sa, Tchien = Tie = Gien = Kien, Twabo = Te = Tepo. 100,000. Between Cess and Cavally rivers, Liberia, and Ivory Coast, inland from Kru, (7) below.

7. Kru-Krawi = Nana Kru = Kra(wo) = Krao = Klao = Mena Yu. Perhaps over 100,000. Coast of Liberia to Ivory Coast border and inland.

8. Kwaa = Belleh. 25,000. Liberia, south of MANDE speakers (Bandi, Gbunde), separated from other KRU languages by Gola and Kpelle.

AFFILIATION. Member of KWA phylum.

KUKUKUKU = ANGA

GROUPING. Langimar (5, below) is said to be the most divergent language of the group (Wurm 1971c). The KUKUKUKU languages are spoken in the southeastern corner of the Eastern Highlands District, adjacent southwestern Morobe District, and most of the eastern third of the inland part of the Gulf District, Papua, Australian New Guinea.

1. Barua. D.? also Wantakia. 4,000.
2. Kamasa.
3. Kapau. 15,000.

4. Kawacha. 20.

5. Langimar = Langama. 625.

6. Menye. 10,000.

7. Obi. Population combined with (11), below: 1,200.

8. Simbari. 2,000.

9. Wajokeso. D.? also Ampale. 3,000.

10. Yagwoia = Yeghuye. 6,750.

11. Yeripa. 1,200 together with Obi (7).

Ashavi ? Madinava ?

AFFILIATION. Member of CENTRAL and SOUTHERN NEW GUINEA.

KULINIC

GROUPING. Djadjala (1), Taungurong (4), and Wudjawuru (6) comprise a KULIN subgroup, and Marditjali (3) and Tjapwurong (5) a DRUAL subgroup (O'Grady et al. 1966, Wurm 1971b). Spoken in western Victoria, and just over the South Australia and New South Wales boundaries, Australia.

1. Djadjala = Meintangk = Meintank = Worgaia = Painbali. Ds. also Jaara = Yaara = Yaura = Yayauring = Jajaurung = Jajowurrong = Jajowrung = Jajowerong = Jajowrong = Jajoworrong = Jajowerong = Djadjawurung = Jurobaluk = Nirabaluk = Nirababaluk = Panyod = Knenknenwurro, Jardwa = Yardwa-tyalli = Knindowurrong = Djappuminyon, Jarijari = Yariyari = Yarreyarre = Yerriyerri = Yerreyerre = Yairy-yairy = Yarikiluk = Yurra Yurra, Jitajita = Bayangil = Itaita = Ithiithi = Eethaeetha = Yitha = Yitsa, Latjilatji = Laitchi-Laitchi = Litchy-Litchy = Leitchi-Leitchi = Latjoo-Latjoo = Lutchye-Lutchye = Latyoo-Latyoo = Litchoo-Litchoo = Laci-Laci = Laitu-Laitu = Laitu, Muthimuthi = Madimadi = Mathimathi, Ngarkat = Merkani = Merkanie = Mangkarupi = Buripung = Booripung = Boripar = Duwinbarap = Doenbauraket = Tjakulprap = Jakalbarap = Jackalbarap = Jackegilbrab = Jakelbaluk = Ngeruketi = Wragarite, Potaruwutj = Potangola = Woychibirik = Wepulprap = Yaran = Tatiara = Tattayarra = Tyatyalli = Tyeddyuwurru = Wirigirek = Werekatyalli, Warkawarka = Waikywaiky = Wekiweki = Mirdiragoort = Boorong, Waithiwathi = Watthiwatthi = Wattywatty = Wottowotti = Tatitati, Wembawemba = Wambawamba = Womba = Weumba = Waamba = Yambayamba = Yamba, Wotjobaluk. About Werringen and Albacutya lakes.

2. Kurung = Gulyan = Kurungjangbaluk = Werang. Ds. also Kolakngat = Kolacgnat = Coligan = Kolijon, Wathurung = Wathaurung = Wadthaurung = Wudjawurung = Witowurung = Witowurrong = Witawurong = Witowro = Witoura = Wuddyawurru = Wiityahuurong = Wooeewoorong.

3. Marditjali = Keribialbarap. D. also Buandik = Bungandaitj = Bungandaetch = Bungandaetcha = Pungantitj = Pungatitj = Pungandik = Booandik = Boandik = Boandiks = Borandikngolo = Burhwundeirtch = Bungandity.

4. Taungurong = Thagunworong = Dhaguwuru = Thaguwurru = Daguwuru = Daungwurung = Taguniourung = Dhauhurtwurru = Ngooraialum = Ngura-

lungbula = Mouralungbula = Gnurellean = Ooralim = Butherbaluk = Yawan-gillam = Yauungillam = Yowangillam. Ds. also Bunurong = Boonurrong = Boonoorong = Bunwurung = Bunwurru, Djadjuwurung = Djadjuwuru, Wurundjeri = Wurunjeri = Wurrunjeri = Woiwurru = Woiworung = Woewo-rung = Woeewoorong = Wawurong = Wawoorong = Oorongir = Gunung-willam = Ngarukwillam = Kurunjang = Mortnoular = Woiwurung.
5. Tjapwurong = Tyapwurru = Chaapwurru = Pirtkopannoot = Purteetchally = Punoinjon = Kolor. Ds. also Gurnditjmara = Gourndtichmara = Kuurnko-pannoot = Kirurndit, Kirrea = Kirawirung = Kirraewuurong.
6. Wudjawuru.

AFFILIATION. Member of PAMA-NYUNGAN.

KUMBAINGGARIC

GROUPING. The KUMBAINGGARIC languages are spoken along the coast in northeast New South Wales, Australia.

1. Kumbainggar = Kumbainggeri = Kumbaingeri = Kumbainggiri = Kombaing-heri = Koombanggary = Koombangghery = Koombainga = Coombangree = Kombinegherry = Gumbainggar. D. also Banbai = Bahnbi = Ahnbi = Dandai. Headwaters of Mymboida River and across the range towards Urunga, Coffs Harbour, and Bellingen; at Grafton and Glenreagh.
2. Yegir = Jiergera = Yiegera. Lower Clarence River.

AFFILIATION. Member of PAMA-NYUNGAN.

Kutenai = Kutenay = Kutanai = Kootenay = Kootenai = Koetenay = Koetenaice = Cootonais = Kitunahan = Kitunaha = Kutänä = Kootenuha = Kutneha = Cuttonasha = Counarrha = Skalzi = Skalza = Arc-a-plat = Flatbow. Ds. Lower Kutenai, Upper Kutenai. 300–400. Alberta; later Idaho, Washington, Montana, British Columbia.

AFFILIATION. Kutenai is now classified as being without known genetic affiliation, but was classified by Sapir (1929) in genetic association with WAKASHAN, Quileute, SALISH, Yurok and Wiyot, Beothuk, and ALGONQUIAN (cf. also Haas 1965).

KWA

GROUPING. The accepted membership and subgrouping of KWA essentially derives from Westermann (1927). Armstrong (1955) added IDOMA to KWA. Greenberg (1966) adds IJǪ previously classified as an independent group within NIGER-CONGO, and Williamson (1972b) adds Oko-Osanyin and CENTRAL AKOKO, which consist of previously unrecognized languages in Nigeria. Williamson also suggests that Igbirra should form a separate group and not be included in NUPE-GBARI. There have been disputes over the inclusion of the KRU, CENTRAL TOGO, and IJǪ groups within KWA. Westermann and Bryan (1952) exclude IJǪ as well as KRU, CENTRAL TOGO, and IDOMA from KWA. There is some agreement that the languages in the LAGOON, VOLTA-COMOE,

GÃ-ADANGME, and EWE groups, below, belong together in a WESTERN KWA group, which possibly also includes CENTRAL TOGO (Greenberg 1963a, John Stewart 1971); and the YORUBA, Oko-Osanyin, CENTRAL AKOKO, NUPE-GBARI, EDO and IDOMA groups may belong together in a corresponding EASTERN KWA group, probably including IGBO. The validity of KWA as a genetic group has frequently been questioned (e.g., by Greenberg 1963a, Williamson 1971, Welmers 1971a, b) and it is generally agreed that KWA and BENUE-CONGO languages form a single group, the subgroups of which remain to be worked out. The single Oko-Osanyin language is listed below; each of the other subgroups of KWA listed is treated in a separate article:

CENTRAL AKOKO
EDO
EWE
GÃ-ADANGME
IDOMA
IGBO
ỊJỌ
KRU
LAGOON
NUPE-GBARI
1. Oko-Osanyin. Ogori and Magongo towns, Igbirra Division, Kwara State, Nigeria.
CENTRAL TOGO
YORUBA
VOLTA-COMOE

AFFILIATION. Member of NIGER-CONGO.

LAGOON

GROUPING. The LAGOON language names are suggested by Welmers (1961) from various sources; he notes that their separate language status remains to be established. Their combined number of speakers is 120,000–160,000. They are spoken between Grand Bassam and Grand Lahou in the lagoon area of Ivory Coast. Many speakers of languages numbered 1, 6, 7 are bilingual or at least 'understand' one of the AKAN languages, as Anyi. Adyukru (2) is included in WEST ATLANTIC by Westermann and Bryan (1952) (and 2 may alternatively remain outside any family grouping within NIGER-CONGO); Ahizi (3) may alternatively belong in the KRU or LAGOON family.

1. Abe = Abbe(y) = Abi = Aby. 20,000–25,000. Bandama River area.
2. Adyukru = Adioukrou = Adjukru = Agyuku = Ajukru = Burburi = Ogyukru. 20,000–30,000. Cercle Lagunes north of Ebrié Lagoon.
3. Ahizi=Aizi. 10,000 or less. Between Dabu and Krafi on Ebrié Lagoon.
4. Akye = Attié = Atchi = Atshe = Kurobu. Trs. Atobu, Bode = Akye-Kotoko, Kete, Nedi = Memmi, Ngadye. 50,000–60,000. Hinterland of Comoe River.
5. Aladian = Al(l)adyan = Alagian = Alagya = Aragya = Jackjack. 7,000–8,000. Between the sea and Ebrié Lagoon in Cercle Abijan.

6. Ari = Abi(d)ji = Adidji. 6,000 to 11,000. Bandama River.
7. Avikam = Avekom = Brinya = Gbandu = Kwakwa = Lahu. 7,000–9,000. Grand Lahou.
8. Gwa = Agwa = Gwabyo = Mbato = Mgbato = Potu. 4,000–6,000. Potou Lagoon.
9. Kyama = Kiama = Gyuman = Tyaman = Ebrie. 11,500. Between Comoe and Agnéby rivers above Ebrié Lagoon, and east of Petit Bassam.

AFFILIATION. Member of KWA phylum.

LARAKIAN

GROUPING. These languages are spoken near Darwin in western Arnhem Land, Australia.

1. Larakia = Larrakia = Larrakeah = Larrakeeyah = Larrakiha = Laragia = Larragea = Larrekiya = Larreekeeyah = Larikia = Larrikia = Larrikiya = Larriquia.
2. Wuna.

AFFILIATION. Member of AUSTRALIAN macro-phylum.

LEFT MAY

GROUPING. Samo (6, below) is divergent from the rest (Healey, as reported by Wurm 1971c). These languages are spoken in the area of the Left May River, a western tributary of the May River, which is a southern tributary of the Upper Sepik River in the Sepik District, New Guinea. There are about 2,000 speakers of LEFT MAY languages altogether.

1. Apaka. Ds also Abi, Aboa.
2. Asowi.
3. Laro.
4. Nakwi. Ds. also Aukot, Mumupra.
5. Nimo. D. also Wasuai.
6. Samo.

AFFILIATION. Member of INDO-PACIFIC, within which it may be most closely related to BUSA of NORTH NEW GUINEA (Wurm).

LEONARD SCHULTZE

GROUPING. Pai (1) and Walio (3) are more closely related to each other than either is to the others or than the other two are to each other (Wurm 1971c). These languages are spoken along the Leonard Schultze River, a southern tributary of the Upper Sepik River in the Sepik District, New Guinea.

1. Pai. 100.
2. Tuwari = Aliapmin. 122.

3. Walio. 110.
4. Yabio. 100.

    AFFILIATION. Member of INDO-PACIFIC.

*Linear A. Cretan predecessor of Mycenean Linear B type of writing. Linear A is still undeciphered (Middle Minoan after 2,000 B.C.); found only in Crete.

    AFFILIATION. Unknown.

LOYALTY ISLANDS = LIFIC

    GROUPING. All the languages spoken in the Loyalty Islands, except the Polynesian Outlier Uvea, form a subgroup (Dyen 1965).

1. Iai = Wen Yai. 1,000 (1939). Uvea, 20°25′S 166°39′E.
2. Lifu = Dehu = De'u. 6,000 (1939). Lifu Island, 21°15′S 167°32′E.
3. Nengone. 3,000 (1939). Maré Island, 21°53′S 163°30′E.

    AFFILIATION. Subgroup of OCEANIC within AUSTRONESIAN.

LULE-VILELA-CHARRUA

    GROUPING. Inadequate data on the languages of this extinct South American family make it impossible to assign any grouping or to determine whether there was more than one language. Jose Pedro Rona (1965), University of Uruguay, has been able to determine that there were four dialect groups in Uruguay (numbers 1–3, 5). Guenoa (3) was formerly listed as an alternate name for Charrua (2).

1. *Chana = Tšaná = Tschaná = Čaná = Yaro. Uruguay.
2. *Charrua = Čarrua = Tšarrua. Uruguay.
3. *Güenoa. Uruguay.
4. *Lule. Ds. (trs. ?) Great Lule, Small Lule with subgroups Isistiné, Oristiné, Tokistiné. Argentina.
5. *Minuane. Argentina, Uruguay.
6. *Vilela. Ds. (trs. ?) also Atalalá, Chunupí = Sinipé = Chulupí (with subgroups Ocolé, Yecoanita, Yooc = Yoo = Wamalca), Ipa, Omoampa = Umuapa, Pasain = Pazaine, Takete, Vacaa, Wamalca, Yoconoampa = Yecunampa. Argentina.

    AFFILIATION. Member of MACRO-PANOAN within GE-PANO-CARIB.

*Lyconian. A non-INDO-EUROPEAN language of ancient Asia Minor known chiefly from Greek traditions.

    AFFILIATION. None known.

MABAN

    GROUPING. Tucker and Bryan (1956) classify Mimi (4), below, as an ungrouped language rather than as a member of their MABA group, and question whether their

MABA languages may not instead represent a dialect cluster of a single language. Greenberg (1966) includes the following languages and/or dialects under MABAN. Central African Republic, Chad (mainly Wadai), Sudan (Dar Fur).

1. Karanga = Kurunga. Ds. also Baxa, Fa(a)la = Bakka, Konyare, Mo(o)yo.
2. Maba(a) = Mabak = Mabang = Bura Maban = Ouaddaien. Ds. also Abkar, Kajanga(n), Kelingan, Malanga, Ma(n)daba = Ma Dala, Ma(n)dala = Ma Ndaba, Nyabadan. Trs. Abu Sharin = Absharin, Kashmere = Kachmere = Kaschemere = Kashmeree, Kodoi = Kodoï, Kondongo, Kujina, Runga = Runa, Uled Djemma = Aulad Djema = Uled Jemaa. 9,000. Sudan (Wadai).
3. Mas(s)alit = (Kaana) Masala. D. also Marba = Marfa. Chad (73,500), Sudan (27,000).
4. Mimi = Andan(ti) = Mututu = Mime. 15,000. Sudan.
Màkú(?); Mànyan(?); Mige = Míkí(?); Rataning ?

AFFILIATION. Member of NILO-SAHARAN.

MABUIAGIC

GROUPING. The MABUIAGIC languages are spoken on the Torres Strait Islands north of Queensland, Australia.
1. Dauan. D. also Saibai.
2. Kaurareg = Kowrarega = Karualaig. Ds. also Jam = Yam, Mabuiag, Masig, Muralag, Tutu.

AFFILIATION. Member of PAMA-NYUNGAN.

MACHACALI = MASHACALI

GROUPING. According to Mason (1950), six 'languages' with equal rank belong to this South American family. McQuown (1955) adds a seventh (number 7). Only two of the languages are still extant. Davis (1968) apparently considers these to be dialects of a single language and lists the members of the family as Machacali, Malali, and Patachó; the latter two are otherwise classified as ungrouped languages of MACRO-GE (q.v.).

1. *Capocho = Caposhó = Koposo.
2. *Cumanacho = Kumanaxó.
3. Machacali = Maxakali = Maxakari. State of Minas Gerais, Brazil.
4. *Macuni = Maconi.
5. Monocho = Monoxó. 250. State of Minas Gerais, Brazil.
6. *Panhame = Panyame = Pañame.
7. *Paraxim.

AFFILIATION. Member of MACRO-GE within GE-PANO-CARIB.

MAIDU(AN) = PUJUNAN

GROUPING. A number of alternate names refer to Maidu: Meidoo = Michopo

= Digger = Hololupai = Konkau = Konkow = Nakum = Pujuni = Secumne = Sekumne = Tsmak = Yuba = Yupu.

1. Mountain Maidu = Northeast Maidu. Fewer than ten. California.
2. Northwest Maidu = Konkow = Concow. 10–100 speakers. Central California, lower foothills of the Sierra Nevada.
3. Southern Maidu = Nisenan = Neeshenam = Nishinam = Punji = Wapumni. Fewer than ten. Central California, foothills of the Sierra Nevada.
4. *Valley Maidu. California, formerly spoken between Sacramento and the Sierra foothills.

AFFILIATION. Member of PENUTIAN.

MAILU

GROUPING. Wurm (1971c) treats Mailu (12, below) as only distantly related to the five languages listed by him as members of the YAREBA family (languages numbered 1, 2, 3, 11, 14). Of the many other names listed by Greenberg (1971b) as members of MAILU, two (Keveri and Nemea) are said by Wurm to be alternant names for, or dialects of, YAREBA languages. Others can probably be identified with languages in the YAREBA family on the basis of Loukotka's (1962) grouping of them with languages in the family. Comparison of Loukotka's classification with others makes it seem likely that other names — some of those he placed in the same subgroups — may represent dialects of single languages. The list below represents a reduction of Greenberg's MAILU list by grouping of some names after Loukotka, plus Wurm. Because different criteria were used in preparing their lists, the number of actual languages involved and the boundaries between them may be shown to be quite different on further fieldwork. Languages of the YAREBA family are spoken inland in the eastern corner of the Central District extending into the southeastern corner of the Northern District, Papua. Other MAILU languages are spoken in adjacent parts of the same districts, with Mailu (12) extending into the Milne Bay District from the eastern coast of the Central District.

1. Baridzi. 300.
2. Bauwaki = Bawaki. Ds. ? also Avini, Saroa, Yabura, Keveri (?), Nemea ? The total number of speakers of Bauwaki and Binahari (3, below) is 2,000.
3. Binahari. Ds. ? also Dom = Domu, Merani, Monomor, Morawa, O'oku, Keveri (?), Nemea ? Combined population with Bauwaki: 2,000.
4. Boli = Bori.
5. Buari. Ds. ? also Doriaidi, Moikoidi, Neme, Okandi.
6. Domara.
7. Gebi.
8. Kororo.
9. Lauuna.
10. Lauwa = Lawa.
11. Magori. Few speakers.
12. Mailu = Magi. A few thousand ?

13. Orai-iu.

14. Yareba. 2,200.

> *AFFILIATION.* Member of SOUTHEAST NEW GUINEA.

MAIPURAN

> *GROUPING.* Of the two major groups (the other is CHAPACURA-WANHAMAN) within the ARAWAKAN family, MAIPURAN is further subgrouped by Noble (1965) so as to reflect comparative method evidence. This subgrouping now replaces the four coordinate geographical groups within ARAWAKAN formulated by Mason (1950). In this subgrouping a single language, Shebayo (31), is taken to be coordinate in classification with each of the six subgroups below, and NORTHERN MAIPURAN (q. v.).

BANIVA-YAVITERO

1. Baniva = Avani = Ayane = Abane. D. also Quirruba. Colombia, Venezuela.
2. Yavietero = Paraene. Colombia, Venezuela.

EASTERN MAIPURAN.
This subgroup consists of the 'XINGÚ' languages (3, 4, 6, 8), formerly classified by Mason (1950) in SOUTHERN, and Palicur (7) and Marawan (5), formerly classified in NORTHERN.

3. Custenau.
4. Jaulapiti = Yaulapiti.
5. *Marawa(n) = Maraon.
6. Mehinacú = Minaco. 100. Brazil.
7. Palicur = Palijur. 500. Brazil, possibly Guyana.
8. Uaura = Waura = Aura. 250.

PRE-ANDINE MAIPURAN.
Schmidt (1926), Rivet (1924) and Loukotka (1935) included *Apolista, which Noble (1965) regards as a separate subgroup in the ARAWAKAN family (coordinate with MAIPURAN), and Rivet (1924) included Palicur and Marawan (now classified in EASTERN MAIPURAN). Mason (1950) divides the languages listed below into four subgroups: AMAZONIAN (21, 28), CUTINANA (13, 14, 15), JURUÁ-PURÚS (9, 11, 12, 16, 17, 18, 20, 27), and MONTAÑA (10, 19, 22, 23, 24, 25, 26).

9. Cacharari = Casharari.
10. Campa = Atìri. Ds. also Autaniri = Unconino, Anti, Camatica, Catongo, Chicheren, Pangoa, Quimbiri, Quirinairi, Tampa, Ugunichiri, Unini. 33,000. Eastern Peru.
11. Canamari = Kanamari. 500. Brazil.
12. Catiana.
13. Cujisenajeri = Cujigeneri = Cuchitineri. Brazil.
14. Cuniba.
15. Cutinana. Brazil.
16. Cutuquina = Catukina.
17. Inapari.
18. Ipurina = Kangite. D. also Cangutu. 1,000. Brazil.
19. Machiguenga = Macheyenga = Amachengue. 10,000.

20. Maniteneri. Brazil.
21. Maraua = Marawa. Brazil.
22. Masco = Moeno. D. also Huachipairi = Wachipairi = Amarakaire =
    Greachipari. 200.
23. Piro. Ds. also Chontaquiro, Simirinch. 10,000. Peru.
24. Pucpacuri.
25. Puncuri.
26. Sirimeri.
27. Uainamari = Wainamari. Brazil.
28. Uaraicu = Uraicu = Araicu. Brazil.

PARESSI-SARAVECA
29. Paressi = Pareche = Ariti. 500. Brazil.
30. Saraveca. Brazil, Bolivia.

31. *Shebayo. Formerly Trinidad.

SOUTHERN MAIPURAN. This subgroup is the traditional SOUTHERN ARAWA-
KAN, plus the 'PARANA' group (34, 37, 40 below), which Rivet (1924) classified as
ARAUAN, and minus the 'XINGUAN' group (now included in EASTERN MAIPURAN), and
minus Paressi and Saraveca (now classified as an independent group in MAIPURAN —
(29) and (30) above). This leaves two groups, PARANA (34, 37, 40) and BOLIVIAN (32, 33,
35, 36, 38, 39) in SOUTHERN MAIPURAN.
32. Bauré = Chiquimiti. Ds. also Carmelita (in Carmen), Ignacionao (2,500),
    Joaquiniano (in San Joaquín), Trinitario, San Javierano (50). 3,000–4,000.
    Bolivia.
33. Cachiniti = Cashiniti. D. also Uaimare = Waimare.
34. Chané = West Parana. D. also Izocenyo. Paraguay, Bolivia.
35. Chiquito. Ds. also Paiconeca, Paunaca.
36. Cozarini. Ds. Paressi Cabishi, Wild Cabishi, Mahibarez.
37. Guana = Chuala = Chana = East Parana. Ds. also Echoaldi = Chararana
    = Echonoana, Equinao = Kinihínao, Layana = Niguecactemigi. Paraguay,
    Brazil.
38. Iranche = Irantxe. Ds. also Sacuriu-ina, Tahuru-ina, Timalatia. 250. Brazil.
39. Moxo = Mojo = Morocosi. D. also Trinitarios. 1,500. Brazil, Bolivia,
    Paraguay.
40. Tereno = Terena = Etelena. 5,000. Brazil.

WAPISHANAN = RIO BRANCO
41. Atorai = Dauri. D. also Maiopitian = Maopityan = Mapidian. Brazil,
    Guyana.
42. Uapichana = Wapishana = Wapitxano = Vapidiana. D. also *Amariba.
    Brazil (1,500), Guyana (2,500).

AFFILIATION. Member of ARAWAKAN within EQUATORIAL in ANDEAN-EQUATO-
RIAL.

NORTHERN MAIPURAN

GROUPING. Three single languages (numbered 1, 9, 10, below) are coordinate in classification with the half-dozen subgroups that include more than one language. This is essentially the classification of Mason (1950), who summarizes previous classifications.

1. *Araua = Aruan = Arua. Brazil. Possibly extant.

CAQUETION

2. Achagua. Ds. also Amarizana, Caouri, Chapan, Chucuna, Masivaribeni, Tayaga, Tayagua, Yaguai. Venezuela.
3. Caquetio. Ds. also Axagua, Guaicari. Venezuela.
4. Motilon = Motilone. 3,000.
5. *Tecua. Formerly in Colombia.

GUAYUPEAN

6. *Esperigua = Operigua.
7. *Guayupe.
8. Sae.

9. *Jaoi. Formerly in Trinidad.
10. Island Carib = Black Carib = Cabre = Caberne = Calino = Calinya = Callinago = Calinyaku = Kariphuna. Ds. Barranco, Hopkins, Livingstone, Punta Gorda, Roatán Island, Seine Bight, Stann Creek, Truxillo. 30,000. British Honduras, Guatemala, Honduras; formerly also in Lesser Antilles (excluding Trinidad). Surviving in Dominica and St. Vincent until about 1920.

ORINOCO. Languages numbered 11 and 12 below were listed as independent in EASTERN by Mason (1950), but classified as ORINOCO by Schmidt (1926).
11. Arequena = Arekena = Warekena = Uariquena. Brazil, Colombia, Venezuela.
12. Baré (so-called in Venezuela) = Barauna = Barauana = Barawana (so-called in Brazil).
13. Guinao = Temomoyamo = Temomeyeme = Quinhao = Inao. D. also Guaniare (Venezuela). Closely related to Piapoco (16) and Catapolitani (21).
14. *Maipure = Mejepure. Venezuela.
15. Mauacua = Mawacua. Colombia, Venezuela.

PIAPOCOAN

16. Piapoco = Dzaze. Colombia.
17. Mitua. Colombia.

RIO NEGRO. Mason (1950) divides these languages into an independent language, Uirina (43), and six 'divisions': IZANENI = BANIVA (20, 21, 22, 25, 31, 33, 38, 40); MARITIPARANA (24, 36, 37, 40, 44); MAWACA = MAUACA (18, 27, 30, 34, 35); TARIANAN (26, 41); YAPURA 'A' (32, 42); YAPURA 'B' (23, 28, 29, 39). An additional language, Cariaia (19), is grouped in RIO NEGRO by Schmidt (1926).
18. Adzaneni = Adiana = Tatu. Colombia, Brazil.

19. Cariaia = Cariaya. Brazil.
20. Carútana. Ds. Adaru, Arara, Baniva do Icana = Issana, Dzaui = Dzawi, Jauarete = Yawarete Tapuya, Jurupari = Yurupari Tapuya, Mapache, Uadzoli = Wadzoli, Urubu. 250 (may not include all dialects). Brazil.
21. Catapolitani. Brazil.
22. Caua. D. also Hohodene = Hohodeni = Huhuteni. Brazil.
23. Cauichana = Cayuishana = Cawishana. Brazil.
24. Cauyarí = Caryari. Colombia.
25. Cuati = Costi = Capite. Brazil, Colombia.
26. Itayaine = Iyaine. Brazil.
27. Jabaana = Yabaana. Brazil.
28. Jumana = Yumana = Chimana. Brazil.
29. *Manao. Formerly Brazil.
30. Mandauaca = Mandawaca. Brazil.
31. Mapanai = Ira. Brazil.
32. Mariate.
33. Moriuene = Moriwene = Moriwene Máuline = Sucuriyu. Brazil.
34. Masaca. Brazil.
35. Masaca. Venezuela. May be a different language than 34, above.
36. Matapi. Colombia.
37. Menimehe. Colombia.
38. Paioariene = Payualiene = Pacu.
39. Passe = Pasé. Colombia, Brazil.
40. Siuci = Siusí. Ds. also Ipeca = Cumata, Waliperi = Veliperi. Brazil.
41. Tariana. 1,000. Brazil.
42. Uainuma = Wainuma. Colombia, Brazil.
43. Uirina = Wiriná. Brazil.
44. Yucuna. Colombia.

TA-ARAWAKAN. Taino, included in this subgroup by Mason, is classified by Taylor (1958) as a single language within the ARAWAKAN family coordinate with MAIPURAN.

45. Goajiro = Guajiro. 40,000. The Goajiro Peninsula of Colombia (30,000); and Venezuela (10,000). The largest Indian group in Colombia.
46. Guanebucan. Perhaps a subgroup of Goajiro.
47. Lokono = (Continental) Arawak. Guyana (British Guiana) and French Guiana; formerly also in adjacent areas (including Trinidad).
48. Paraujano = Parauhano. Ds. Alile, Toa. Venezuela.

AFFILIATION. Member of the MAIPURAN group of ARAWAKAN within EQUA-TORIAL in ANDEAN-EQUATORIAL.

MALACCA = MALAKKA = ASLIAN

GROUPING. On the basis of Skeat and Blagden (1906), who detailed all the linguistic material then available, Pinnow (1959) groups SEMANG, SAKAI, and JAKUN as forming the MALACCA group, which he also refers to as a SOUTH group of the eastern

AUSTRO-ASIATIC languages. The affiliation of these groups as a division of AUSTRO-ASIATIC is not firmly established. Diffloth (1973) apparently excludes JAKUN from the group, renamed ASLIAN. The MALACCA languages are located entirely in mainland Malaysia, with the exception of a few Semang speakers in southern Thailand, and are thus geographically isolated from the remaining AUSTRO-ASIATIC languages.

JAKUN (q. v.)
SAKAI (q. v.)
SEMANG (q. v.)

AFFILIATION. Member of AUSTRO-ASIATIC phylum.

MALAYO-POLYNESIAN

GROUPING. Dyen (1965) introduces a new sense for 'Malayo-Polynesian'; Dyen's MALAYO-POLYNESIAN is the largest single subgroup of AUSTRONESIAN, including most (but not nearly all) AUSTRONESIAN languages. He includes the following as subgroups of MALAYO-POLYNESIAN.

CELEBES, NORTHERN (q. v.) — at least Tontemboan
Chamorro — excluded from WEST INDONESIAN (q. v.)
FORMOSAN (q. v.) — at least the EAST FORMOSAN subgroup
'HEONESIAN' = EASTERN OCEANIC (q. v.) plus Motu of PAPUAN AUSTRONESIAN (q. v.)
HESPERONESIAN (q. v.)
EAST INDONESIAN (GEOGRAPHIC) (q. v.) — to the extent that the languages may belong to MOLUCCAN
MOLUCCAN (q. v.)
Palau — excluded from WEST INDONESIAN (q. v.)

AFFILIATION. Member of AUSTRONESIAN.

MANDE = MALI = MALE = MELE = MANDINGO

GROUPING. The MANDE languages numbered (1)–(15) are grouped under the (NORTHERN-) WESTERN branch, and further subgrouped; those numbered (16)–(23) are grouped under the (SOUTHERN-) EASTERN branch, and further subgrouped. This follows the classification of Welmers (1958), followed by Greenberg (1966) and of Westermann and Bryan (1952), of bifurcating languages in the MANDE family — but in different ways. Welmers' classification includes the old MANDE-TAN plus Susu in a NORTHERN group (languages numbered 1–10), but does not place the major cleavage in MANDE here; rather, Welmers adds SOUTHWESTERN (languages numbered 11–14, the old MANDE FU minus Busa, reclassified in EASTERN, and Susu) to NORTHERN as one branch of the bifurcation. Welmers' other branch, SOUTHERN-EASTERN, includes SOUTHERN (languages numbered 19–23) and EASTERN (languages numbered 16–18). Languages numbered (10), (11), (13) have syllabaries (Dalby 1967), though those for (10) and (11) are not widely used.

Bambara (1), Dyula (2), and Malinke (7) may well be divergent dialects of a single

language (referred to as Manda-Kã = Mandekan) having 3 million speakers who are
segregated into various tribes; likewise, Vai (10) and Kono (5) may be dialects of
another single language; two of the languages listed below, Mwa (22) and Nwa (23),
may instead be additional dialects of Kweni (20).

NORTHERN-WESTERN
  NORTHERN = NORTHWESTERN
    1. Bambara = Bamana (Koma). Ds. also Dyangirte, Kagoro = Kogoro
       (17,000–27,000), Kalongo = Kalunka, Masasi = Bambara Masasi,
       Nyamosa, Somono, Toro = Toro ga = Toro ke. 900,000–1,200,000.
       Senegal, Mali, Upper Volta.
    2. Dyula = Dyula ka. Ds. also Ble (200 to 500, Upper Volta), Dafing =
       Dafe (Upper Volta, Ghana), Dyankanka = Dyaka = Diakanke =
       Dyaŋe (Mali, Upper Volta). Trs. Dyula = Jula = Dyoula = Dioula =
       Dyula ke = Wankara (Ghana) = Wa = Febe = Ndyura = Kaga =
       Sogha = Dyokereu. 1,140,000. East-central Ivory Coast, Upper Volta,
       Ghana. Dyula is also a term used to refer to the speech of traders and
       minority enclaves in the Bambara-Malinke complex of the northern
       Ivory Coast and Mali.
    3. Huela = Hwela = Vuela = Vwela. D. also Numu = Noumou (11,000–
       50,000). 50,000. Ivory Coast.
    4. Khasonke = Kasso = Kassonke = Xasouke. 53,000–71,000. Mali.
    5. Kono = Kondo. 112,000. Liberia, Mali, Sierra Leone. Probably a
       dialect of Vai (11; Welmers 1971).
    6. Ligbi = Bondo = Ligone = Ligony = Ligoui = Ligwi = Nighi =
       Nigone = Nigoni = Nigui = Taba. 50,000. Ivory Coast.
    7. Malinka = Malinke = Manding(o) = Mandingue = Mandinka =
       Manenka = Mandinka = Meninka = Maninka = Mande. Ds. also
       Konya = Dyomande (Liberia), Koranko = Kouranke = Kuranke =
       Kuranko (a form of Guinean Malinka; 36,600, Guinea; 73,500, Sierra
       Leone), Lele, North, South, and West Malinke, Manya = Commendi
       = Komendi = Manimo (Liberia), Mau = Mahu = Mauka (Ivory
       Coast), Minya = Folo, Sidya = Sidianka = Sidyanka (Guinea, Portu-
       guese Guinea), Wasulu. 1,200,000. Senegal, Guinea, Portuguese Guinea,
       Liberia, Ivory Coast, Mali, Gambia, Sierra Leone. 'Malinke' normally
       refers to West Malinke (Senegal, Portuguese Guinea, Gambia), while
       Mandinka = Maninka is used to refer to Guinea-Ivory Coast Mali
       forms. In Liberia and Sierra Leone the term Mandingo is a cover term
       for any of the dialects in question.
    8. Soninke. Ds. also Azer = Azjer = Ajer = Masiin = Taghdansh (50,000,
       Mali), Bozo = Sorko = Sorogo (30,000–87,000, Mali and neighboring
       nations). Trs. Aser = Adjer = Azer, Aswanik, Dyakamke, Gadyaga,
       Marka, Markanka, Nono, Saracole, Sarakol(l)e, Serahuli, Sarawule,
       Tonbakai, Wakove. 457,000. Senegal (30,000), Mauritania (22,000),
       Mali (283,000), Upper Volta (100,000), scattered colonies across West

Africa (e.g., Niger, Gambia (10,000), Portuguese Guinea (2,000).

9. Sus(s)u = Soussou = Soso. D. also Yalunka = Dyalonke = Djallonke = Jalonco = Jolonke = Yalunke. Sierra Leone.

10. Vai = Gallinas = Karo = Kondo = Kono = Terebendyuke = Vei = Vy. 96,000. Liberia, Sierra Leone.

SOUTHWESTERN. Kpelle is divergent from the other languages.

11. Kpelle = Akpese = Gbeize = Gberese = Gbese = Gerze = Guerzé = Gerse = Kpelese = Kpelesetina = Kpese = Kperese = Kpwes(s)i Pessa = Pessi = Pessy. 250,000–500,000. Liberia, Guinea.

12. Loko = Landogo. 76,000. Sierra Leone, Guinea.

13. Loma = Balu = Buzi = Busi = Bouze = Domor = Jokoi = Loghoma = Looma = Loonago = Toa = Toale = Toali = To(o)ma. Ds. also Gbunde = Boo = Gboo de = Kimbuzi = Briama = Bulyarma, Gisima = Gizima, Siama = Weima, Wuboma, Weima = Koimaka = Weima Buzi = Wymar Bouzie. 260,000. Liberia, Guinea.

14. Mende = Boumpé = Hulo = Huro = Kossa = Kos(s)o = Mendi. Ds. also Gbandi = Bandi = Gbande = Mamboŋa = Mamboma = Yawa Ziru (?) (35,000, Liberia), Ko = Comende = Kolomende = Ko-Mende, Kpa = Gbamende = Kpa-Mende, Sewa = Komboyo Mende = Sewa-Mende. 586,000–1,000,000. Sierra Leone, Liberia.

15. Sya = Sia = Sã. Ds. also Bobo Fing = Black Bobo = Bobo Fĩ = Bulse = Finng. 4,000. Upper Volta, Mali.

SOUTHERN-EASTERN BRANCH
EASTERN

16. Bisa = Bisan = Bisapele = Boussan = Boussanse = Bouzantchi = Busang = Busani = Busanse = Busansi. 127,000. Upper Volta, Ghana.

17. Busa = Bisagwe = Boko = Bɔkɔ = Bokoberu = Boko Bussawa = Bokolawa = Busagwe = Boussa = Busanchi = Kamberi Beri-beri = Kenga = Kyenga = Kyenga-wa = Shanga = Shangawa = Tyenga = Zugweya. 30,000. Dahomey, Nigeria. The similarity of alternate names with (16), above, is probably due to the fact that some have considered (16) and (17) to be a single language (including Westermann and Bryan 1952).

18. Samo = Nangerge Sembla = Ninisi = Samogo = Samogho = Samojo = Samorho = Samoxo = Sano = Sanu = Semou = Semu. Ds. Northeastern and Southwestern, also Sembla = Sambila. 128,000. Upper Volta, Mali. This may include two or more languages (Welmers 1971).

SOUTHERN

19. Dan = Da = Dã = Ge = Gema = Gio = Gyo = Mebe = Ngere = Samia = Yakuba. 100,000. Liberia and adjoining Ivory Coast.

20. Kweni = Gagu = Gouro = Gurnmbo = Guro = Lo. Ds. also Gan = Birifgbẽ = Ganne = Gbeinngn (50,000), Gagu = Gban (50,000), Kanga Bono, Suamle = Menne, Tura (20,000). 210,000. Ivory Coast.

21. Mano = Maa = Ma = Manon = Mawi = Mia. 45,000–150,000. Liberia, Guinea.
22. Mwa = Mona = Moni = Monu = Mouin = Mwẽ. Ivory Coast.
23. Nwa = Nwã = Narã = Nona. Ivory Coast.

AFFILIATION. Member of NIGER-CONGO phylum.

MANGERIAN

GROUPING. Spoken in north central Australia, near Oenpelli, east of the East Alligator River in northern Arnhem Land.
1. Mangeri.
2. Uningangk.

AFFILIATION. Member of AUSTRALIAN macro-phylum.

MANGUEAN = CHOROTEGAN = CHIAPANEC-MANGUEAN

GROUPING. Though one MANGUEAN language, (2), was spoken far to the south of the other language, (1), these two extinct languages are reported to have been quite similar.

1. *Chiapaneco. State of Chiapas, Mexico.
2. *Mangue = Chorotega = Diria = Orotina. Ds. also Diria and Nagrandan in Nicaragua, Nicoya, Orisi and Orotinya = Orotina in Costa Rica; Choluteca = Chorotega in Honduras and El Salvador.

AFFILIATION. Member of OTO-MANGUEAN phylum; this has been questioned by Fernandez de Miranda et al. (1959, 1961).

MANTHARDA

GROUPING. Klokeid (1968) adds Thargari (3, below) to the languages grouped by O'Grady et al. (1966a, b) and Wurm (1971b). The MANTHARDA languages are spoken in west central Western Australia.

1. Djiwali = Jiwali = Jivali. Capricorn Range, Ashburton River south and east of the junction with Hardey River.
2. Tenma. Head of Henry River; Kenneth Range; Frederick River.
3. Thargari = Targari = Dargari = Tarkarri. 12–20. 24°S 115°E.
4. *?Warienga = Warianga = Woorienga = Woorenga = Wariwonga = Warriwonga. 24°S 116°E.

AFFILIATION. Member of SOUTHWEST PAMA-NYUNGAN.

MARAN

GROUPING. Mara (2) and Wandaran (3) are subgrouped as MARIC (O'Grady et al. 1966). All three languages are spoken in north central Australia.

1. Alawa = Allawa = Allua = Allowa = Alowa = Leealowa = Kallana = Allowiri = Allaura. On both sides of the Hodgson River in Arnhem Land.
2. Mara = Gariyimar = Marra = Leelawarra. On both sides of the Roper River in southeastern Arnhem Land.
3. Wandaran = Wandarang = Nawariyi. North of the Mara language in Arnhem Land.

AFFILIATION. Member of the AUSTRALIAN macro-phylum.

MARIND = YAQAY-MARIND-BOAZI

GROUPING. Wurm (1971c) subgroups languages numbered (1), (4), and (6) as opposed to a subgroup consisting of the rest. Southeastern West Irian, extending into the Lake Murray area of Western District, Papua, Australian New Guinea.
1. Bian = Northwest Marind = Boven Mbian ? 900.
2. Boazi = Boadji = Kuni. Ds. ? also Babwa, Biak, Gabgab, Jabga, Konmak, Lake Murray. 1,600.
3. Dea. Total population with (7), below, 1,200.
4. Marind = Southeast Marind = Tugeri. Ds. include Gawir. 6,000.
5. Suki = Wiram. 1,000. Included in MARIND only tentatively by Wurm.
6. Yaqay = Jaqai = Sohur = Mapi. 8,000.
7. Zimakani. D. also Baegwa. Total population with Dea (3, above), 1,200.

AFFILIATION. Member of CENTRAL AND SOUTH NEW GUINEA.

MARNGU

GROUPING. The MARNGU languages are spoken along the Western Australian coast in the area of Eighty Mile Beach.
1. Karadjeri = Garadjeri = Karadhari. From south point of Roebuck Bay southwest to a place 10 miles north of Anna Plains Station, inland about 70 miles.
2. Mangala = Manala = Minala. Jurgurra Creek, Edgar Range.
3. Nyangumarda = Njangamada = Nyangamada = Nangamada = Njangumarda = Nangamurda. D. also Bedengo = Pedong = Peedong = Pidunga = Peedona = Pardoo = Paṭaṭoŋ. Eighty Mile Beach north of Cape Kerandren to Anna Plains; inland about 80 miles.

AFFILIATION. Member of SOUTHWEST PAMA-NYUNGAN.

MATACO

GROUPING. The seven languages in this family belong to two branches: MATACO (numbered 4–7) and MACA (numbered 1–3). The MATACO branch is further subdivided into (4) and (5), and (6) and (7). The languages of the MATACO family extend like a chain from the Andean foothills almost to the Paraguay River across the Gran Chaco of northern Argentina and Paraguay, extending into Bolivia. There were about 20,000 speakers at the end of the nineteenth century, many of whom worked as lumberjacks or on sugar plantations and were thereby being assimilated into the Spanish-speaking linguistic community.

MACA
1. *Guentuse. Possibly still extant. Argentina, Paraguay.
2. *Lengua = Cochaboth. Paraguay.
3. Maca = Enimaga. Extinct in Argentina, but not in Paraguay.

MATACO
4. Ashushlay = Axluslay = Chulupi = Chonopi = Sotiagay = Tapiete. Paraguay.
5. Choroti = Xolota = Yofuaha. Argentina, Paraguay.
6. Mataco. Ds. (trs. ?) Guisnay, Nocten = Octenai. 600 in Bolivia, 10,000 in Argentina, Paraguay.
7. Mataguayo. Ds. (trs. ?) Abucheta, Huexuo = Hueshuo, Pesatupe, Vejoz. Argentina.

AFFILIATION. Member of MACRO-PANOAN within GE-PANO-CARIB.

MAYAN

GROUPING. The internal relationship of languages in the MAYAN family has attracted many classifiers and reclassifiers from the time of Orozco y Berra (1864) to the present; the leading modern classifiers are McQuown (1956), Kaufman (1964, 1969), Grimes (1969). A typical contemporary difference in classification appears when McQuown (who is followed in the grouping below) is compared with Kaufman. The latter obtains fewer groups — namely, seven — by the expediency of merging three pairs of McQuown's groups: CHOLAN with TZELTALAN (languages numbered 1–3, and 23–25); Chujean (4) with KANJOBALAN (7, 8); QUICHÉAN (16–22) with Kekchi (9).

CHOLAN. Some investigators regard (1)–(3), below, to be dialects of one language.
1. Chol = Cholti = Choloid. Ds. *Acala (?), Chol Lacandon, *Choltí (extinct Chol ?), *Chorti, *Manche (?), Toquequa. 32,800. Tabasco and east Chiapas, Mexico.
2. Chontal of Tabasco. 15,500. East Tabasco, Mexico.
3. Chortí = Cholti = Chorte. 33,000. East Guatemala (east Chiquimula Department), and neighboring Honduras.
Moianec (?) = Choroti ?

4. Chujean = Chuh = Chuj = Chuje = Chuhe. 14,000. Western Guatemala.

HUASTECAN
5. Chicomuceltec = Coxoh.
6. Huastec = Huasteca = Huastecan = Huasteco = Houastéque = Huastek(a) = Huastéque = Huaxteca = Huaxteco = Huaxtèque = Guasteca = Guasteco = Guexteca. Ds. Potosino, Veracruzano. 40,000 ? (6,500 monolinguals). Veracruz, San Luis Potosi, and Oaxaca, Mexico.

KANJOBALAN = KANHOBALAN
7. Jacaltec(a). 12,000. Northwest Guatemala (Jacaltenango and Concepción, Huehuetenango Department).

8. Kanjobal = Kanhobal = Conob. Ds. also Subinha-Solomec. 40,000. Western Guatemala.

9. Kekchí = Cacchi = Caché = Cachi = Caichi = Cakchi = Cakgi = Cechi = Kachice = Kahchi = Kakchi = K'ekchi' = Quecchi = Quekchi. 250,000. Guatemala (mostly Alta Verapaz Department), enclave in south British Honduras (650). Formerly grouped with Pokonchi (18) and Pokomam (17), which have been reassigned to QUICHÉAN (Grimes 1969).

MAMEAN = MAMEAN-IXILIAN

10. Aguacatec(an) = Coyotin = Chalchitec. Ds. Aguacatan, Chajul, Chalchitan, Cotzal, Nebaj. 8,000. Guatemala (Huehuetenango Department).
11. Ixil. 25,000. Northwest highlands of Guatemala (northern Quiché Department).
12. Mam(e) = Mem = Zaklapahkap = Zaklohpakap = Zaklopahkap = Zaklopacap. Ds. Tacana = Tacaneco, Taquial, Tlatman, Tupancal, Tutuapa. 285,000. Western Guatemala (270,000), Mexico (southern Chiapas; 16,500).
13. Teco. 5,000. Southern Mexico and Western Guatemala (Kaufman 1969).

14. Maya = Mayo = Mopan = Peten = Punctunc = Patunc = Itza = Ttzae = Yucatan = Yucatana = Yucatanice = Yucatano = Yucatec(a) = Yucateco = Yucatèque = Yucatese. Ds. Icaiche (Yucatan, Mexico), Itza (northern Guatemala, Lake Péten), Lacandon = Yucatec Lacandon (Yucatan, Chiapas, Tabasco in Mexico), Mopan = Moapan (south British Honduras; Guatemala), Santa Cruz (northeast Yacatan), Yucatec = Maya proper (Yucatan, Tabasco in Mexico). 300,000. The Peninsula of Yucatán in British Honduras, northern Guatemala (Peten Department), and in Mexico (Yucatan, Campeche, Quintana Roo, Chiapas, Oaxaca, Tamaulipas, Zacatecas; 81,000). McQuown (1956) lists four dialects: Itza, Lacandone, Mopan, Yucatec. Kaufman (1964) lists Yucatecan-Lacadón and Mopan-Itza as two languages.
15. Motozintlec(o) = Mochó = Motochintlec = Mototzintlec = Motozintleca. 4,000 ? Southeast Chiapas, Mexico.

QUICHÉAN. Previously, Pokonchi (18) and Pokomam (17) were listed with Kekchí (9) in a 'KEKCHIAN' group. This grouping was revised by Grimes (1969).
16. Cakchiquel = Cachiquel. 225,000. Guatemala (Chimaltenango, Sololá, Esquintla, Quiche and Sacatepéquez departments).
17. Pokomam = Pocomom = Pocomanice = Pokoman = Pokomane. 25,000. Guatemala, El Salvador, Honduras. Listed by Mason (1940) as a dialect of 'Pokom', coordinate with Pokonchi (18, below).
18. Pokonchi = Pocomchi = Poncham = Poconchice = Pokonchine = Pokonchini. More than 37,500. North central Guatemala (Alta Verapaz, Baja Verapaz, Quiche). Listed by Mason (1940) as a dialect of 'Pokom', coordinate with Pokomam (17, above).
19. Q(u)iché = Queche = Qviche = Kechi = Kichai = Kiché = San Miguel Chicah (= Quiche de Rabinal) = Tiche = Guatemala = Guatemalec(a) = Ultateca(t) = Ultateco. Over 300,000. Guatemala, Mexico (Chipayas).

20. *Rabinal = Achi.
21. Tzutuhil = Tzutujil = Tzutohile = Tzutuchil(e) = Atiteca = Zacapula = Zacatula = Zutugil = Zutuhil. 25,000. South and west of Lake Atitlan, Guatemala.
22. Uspantec(a) = Uspanteco. 3,000. Central Guatemala, about 35 miles west of Cobán.

TZELTALAN = TZOTZILAN = QUELEM = QUÉLÈNE = TZELTALOID. Mexico (Chiapas).

23. Tojolabal = Toholabal = Chañabal = Chaneabal = Zapaluta. 3,780.
24. Tzeltal = Tzendal = Tzental = Zendal = Sendal = Cendal = Celtala = Celdala = Celdale. Ds. Bachahom, Highland Tzeltal, Lowland Tzeltal. 56,000.
25. Tzotzil = Zotzil = Zozil = Zotzlem(?) = Tzinanteco = Quélène = Quelem = Cinanteco = Chamula. Ds. Chamula, Huixteco, San Andres, Zincanteco. 65,000.

Api = Apay = Apayac ? Chiapas, Mexico.

AFFILIATION. Member of PENUTIAN.

MAYAPIC = WANAMARIC

GROUPING. The MAYAPIC languages are spoken in Queensland, Australia.

1. Mayapi = Maiabi = Myabi = Miappe = Myappe = Miubbi.
2. Maykulan = Maikulung = Mygoolan = Mykoolan = Micoolan = Mikkoolan = Maikulan.
3. Wanamara = Wunamara = Wunumara = Woonamurra = Unamara = Oonoo-murra.

AFFILIATION. Member of PAMA-NYUNGAN.

CENTRAL MELANESIAN

GROUPING. Greenberg (1971b) groups as CENTRAL MELANESIAN the REEF ISLANDS-SANTA CRUZ group recognized by Davenport (1962) and the CENTRAL SOLO-MONS group. Wurm (1971c) suggests affiliation of the CENTRAL SOLOMONS group and BOUGAINVILLE (q.v.).

REEF ISLANDS-SANTA CRUZ = SANTA CRUZ. Languages (1), (2), and (3), spoken on Santa Cruz (Ndeni) Island are subgrouped as NDENI. Though both Davenport and Wurm find three languages in NDENI, they locate their boundaries differently. The locations and first names given below are those of Wurm.

1. Northern Santa Cruz = only part of North-West Santa Cruz. Ds. include Neo on the northern half of Tö Motu Island off the northwestern tip of Santa Cruz. 1,435. Along the north coast and the northern half of the west coast of Santa Cruz.
2. Southeastern Santa Cruz = South Central Santa Cruz and South-East

Santa Cruz. Ds. include Noole. 562. Central to eastern south coast of Santa Cruz.

3. Southwestern Santa Cruz = only part of North-West Santa Cruz. Ds. include Nea. 602. Southern half of the west coast and western half of the south coast of Santa Cruz.

4. Reef Island (Santa Cruz). 3,500. On the main Reef Islands of the Santa Cruz Archipelago.

CENTRAL SOLOMONS

5. Baniata = Banata. 800. Rendova Island, the southernmost island of the New Georgia group.

6. Bilua. 2,000. Vela Lavella Island, the westernmost island of the New Georgia group.

7. *? Kazukuru. Ds.? also Dororo, Gulili = Guliguli. Formerly in the north-western part of New Georgia Island.

8. Laumbe = Lavukaleve. Several thousand. Russell Islands, between New Georgia group and Guadalcanal.

9. Savo = Savosavo. Several hundred. Savo Island, north of the western end of Guadalcanal.

AFFILIATION. Member of INDO-PACIFIC.

MIAO-YAO

GROUPING. Chang (1967) postulates the following bifurcation of languages: Miao (2) versus the YAO group (languages numbered 1, 3, 4). Laka, (1) below, is generally classified as MIAO-YAO, but is regarded as one of the KAM-TAI languages by Mao and Chou (1962) on the basis of vocabulary similarities. Black Miao may be a separate language instead of a dialect of (2) (Fang-Kuei Li 1967), and Punu (4) may be a dialect of Miao (2). 3,000,000. Primarily in Kuei-chou (1,800,000); also Szechuan, Hu-nan, Kuang-hsi, Hainan, extending into northern Vietnam, Laos, and Thailand; a few in the mountainous area of the Shan states of Burma.

1. Laka. 6,000. Ta-yao-shan Autonomous District of the Kuang-hsi Autonomous Region for the Chuang people.

2. Miao = Hmong = Hmung = Hmo = Hsiung = Hunan Miao. Ds. Black Miao = Hei = Heh Miao; Flowery Miao, including Yi = Thai Miao; Green = Blue Miao, Red Miao, White Miao. 250,000,000 in China, North Vietnam, Laos, and Thailand. Located in three dialect groups in China: (a) Szu-ch'uan, western and central Kuei-chou, eastern Yün-nan, western part of the Autonomous Region for the Chuang people in Kuang-hsi (1,150,000; Puna perhaps identified with this group); (b) Hua-yüan, Feng-huang, Chi-shou, Ku-chang, Lu-hsi, Pao-ching districts in Hunan, and the Sung-t'ao Autonomous District for the Miao people in Kuei-chou (440,000); (c) K'ai-li, Lei-shan, Ma-chiang, Huang-p'ing, Chin-p'ing, Li'ping, Ts'ung-chiang, Jung-chiang districts in Kuei-chou, the Ta-miao-shan Autonomous District for the Miao people and the San-chiang Autonomous District for the Kam people in Kuang-hsi, and in the T'ung-tao Autonomous

District for the Kam people in Hunan (900,000).

3. Mien = Yao = Man. Ds. Pia-min (districts of Ch'üan-chou, Kuan-yang, Kung-
ch'eng in Kuang-hsi (21,000); Tsao-min (Lien-nan in Kuang-tung and I-chang
District in Hunan (29,000)); and a group in the Kuang-hsi Autonomous Region
for the Chuang people, and in Hu-nan, Kuang-tung, Yün-nan, and Kuei-chou
provinces (260,000). 300,000 in China, 200,000 in North Vietnam and Laos (60,000),
and in Thailand; perhaps Burma.

4. Punu. Ds. Chiung-nai (Ta-yao-shan Autonomous District for the Yao people in
Kuang-hsi); Pa-heng = Pa-wu (San-chiang and Lung-sheng districts in Kuang-hsi;
Li-p'ing and Jung-chiang districts in Kuei-chou); Wu-nai (Lung-hui, T'ung-tao,
Hsü-p'u districts in Hu-nan); Yu-no (Hsing-an and Lung-sheng districts in Kuang-
hsi); and a group in 20 districts of Kuang-hsi (including Tu-an, Pa-ma, Ma-shan,
Shang-lin, Nan-tan, Ho-ch'ih), Yün-nan (Chiung-nai district), and Tu-shan
(Kuei-chou).

AFFILIATION. Member of SINO-TIBETAN; Shafer (1955) questioned this classification, regarding the relationship to be at best remote. Schmidt (1926) suggested
genetic affinities with KAM-TAI languages; this is now supported by Benedict
1973a). Forrest (1948) postulates a relationship to MON-KHMER. On the other hand,
Chinese scholars, as Li (1965a), have maintained the affinity of MIAO-YAO, KAM-TAI,
and CHINESE in a 'SINITIC' branch of SINO-TIBETAN. Downer (1971) has recently
supported the SINO-TIBETAN relationship of MIAO-YAO, as a separate branch from
CHINESE and TIBETO-BURMAN.

MICRONESIAN = NUCLEAR MICRONESIAN

GROUPING. The languages spoken in the Caroline Islands from Truk west
to Tobi (with the exception of Palau and Yap) form a chain of mutually intelligible
dialects with cognate percentages on basic lexicostatistical lists close to or above
Dyen's 'language-limit' of 70%, but both cognate percentages and intelligibility
decrease between dialects separated by intervening dialects, most noticeably at the
extremes of the chain (Byron Bender 1971). Dyen's (1965) comparisons classified
the dialects from this area in his sample as two languages (labeled 'Trukese' and
'Wolean'), grouped together as TRUKIC. On the basis of comparisons of a larger
number of TRUKIC dialects, Bender aligns them differently into three languages,
Carolinian, Trukese and Ulithian, below. Ponapean (6) and TRUKIC are closer to
each other than either is to other languages of the group.

Dyen excludes Nauruan (5) and Yapese (9) from any possible subgrouping with
NUCLEAR MICRONESIAN = his CAROLINIAN. Bender classifies both as 'questionably'
NUCLEAR languages; Grace (1955) treats all the languages of Micronesian (except
Chamorro, Palau, and the Polynesian Outlier languages) as a single subgroup.

1. Carolinian. Ds. Namonuito (500 speakers), Pulap (400), Pulusuk (300), Puluwat
(400), Satawal (350), possibly also Elato and Lamotrek, listed with Ulithi (8,
below); the dialects on Saipan (2,000 speakers, many of whom are bilingual in
Chamorro) appear to be identical with those of the islands from which the popula-

tion is derived. 4,000. Saipan, 15°10′N 145°45′E; the atolls in the Carolines from 9°00′–6°40′N 146°30′–150°12′E.

2. Gilbertese. 44,000. Gilbert Islands, 3°21′N 4°00′S 169°00′–177°00′E (38,000), Nui in the Ellice Islands, 7°15′S 177°10′E (600), Nauru 0°31′S 166°56′E (1000), Ocean Island (2,500), other Pacific islands where Gilbertese have been resettled (2,000).

3. Kusaiean. 3,600. Kusai, 5°15′N 163°00′E.

4. Marshallese. Ds. Ralik, Ratak. 19,000. Marshall Islands, 6°00′–12°00′N 163°00′–172°00′E.

5. Nauruan. Less than 3,000. 0°31′S 166°56′E.

6. Ponapean. 15,300. Ds., on Ponape that of Kiti municipality contrasts with the rest; also Mokiol (800), Ngatik (500), Pingelap (1,000). 6°00′–7°03′N 157°35′–160°48′E. Some dialects are so divergent (e.g., Ponape proper as compared to Mokil) that Ponapean might be considered more than one language.

7. Trukese. Ds. in Truk Lagoon: Eastern, Western = Faichuk, both with subdivisions; also Hall Islands, Mortlocks, with lower (southernmost) Mortlocks more divergent than upper. 26,000. Truk Islands 7°20′N 151°45′E (18,500), Hall Islands 8°50′N 152°00′E (950), Mortlock Islands 5°45′N 153°50′E (18,500), Ponape (migrants from the Mortlocks).

8. Ulithian. Ds. Fais, Ngulu, Sorol are included in Ulithi proper (with three slightly differentiated dialects, including Mogmog, on Ulithi (total 850)); Sonsoral including also Merir, Pulo Anna, Tobi (total 300); Woleai including other atolls in the area, of which Elato and Lamotrek may be linguistically closer to Satawal of Carolinian (1, above) (total 1,360). 2,510. Ulithi, 10°00′N 139°35′E; Sonsoral, 5°20′N 132°13′E; Tobi 3°01′N 131°10′E; Woleai, 7°24′N 143°52′E.

9. Yapese. 4,000 plus 50 on Ngulu who are bilingual in Ulithian. Yap, 9°30′N 138°09′E.

AFFILIATION. A member of OCEANIC (Grace 1955); often listed as a branch of AUSTRONESIAN not closely affiliated with any other languages, as by W. K. Matthews (1950). Also treated as a subgroup of the languages of Melanesia, as by Dempwolff (1937). Izui (1965) takes particular Micronesian languages and classifies them as Indonesian, Melanesian, or Polynesian.

MIRNINY

GROUPING. The MIRNINY languages are spoken in southern Western Australia.

1. Kalamai = Takalako = Njindango = Natingero. 30°S 119°E.

2. Mirning = Mirniny = Miriñ = Mining = Meening = Wanbiri = Warnabirrie = Warnabinnie = Wanmaraing = Yirkla = Ikala = Ikula. Ds. also Kalarko = Malba, Ngadjunma = Bardojunga. 32°S 122–129°E.

AFFILIATION. Member of SOUTHWEST PAMA-NYUNGAN.

MISUMALPAN

GROUPING. Although commonly assumed to be a phylum, MISUMALPAN is listed here as a small family in Nicaragua and Honduras. Miskito and Sumo appear to be languages closely related to each other; Swadesh (1959) on the basis of glottochronology finds that Matagalpa is as closely related to Miskito and Sumo as the latter are to each other.

Other names probably represent geographically restricted groups which belonged to one of the three languages listed. Thus, Bambana may have been a name for speakers of Sumo who lived on the Bambana River.

1. Matagalpa. Central highlands of Nicaragua and extending into Honduras.
2. Miskito = Misquito = Mosquito = Mosco. Ds. Honduran Miskito = Mam. Tawira = Tauira (Pearl Lagoon to Bemuna and may thus include the group called Baymuna = Baymunana = Baldam), Wanki = Wangki. Cabo = Kabo is also listed as the dialect used by missionaries, but probably represents a geographically restricted group included in the above dialects. Lowlands of Nicaragua and Honduras, from Pearl Lagoon to Black River.
3. Sumo = Sumu. Ds. Northern, Southern. Trs. Northern: remnants of Bawihka = Bawahca = Bauihca, *(?)Ku, Panamaka = Panamaca (subgroups: Carawala = Carahuala, Tunki = Tungui), *(?)Prinsu = Prinzo, *(?)Silam, Twahka = Twahca = Tauahca = Taguaca (subgroups: Coco, Lacu, Pispi, Wasabane = Huasabane); Southern: the nearly extinct (1950) Boa, Kukra = Cucra, Ulva = Ulua = Ulwa = Wulwa, Yusku; unclassified: Musutepes and Yasica. Honduras, Nicaragua.

AFFILIATION. Member of MACRO-CHIBCHAN.

MIWOK-COSTANOAN

GROUPING. The MIWOK and COSTANOAN languages form two coordinate groups in the MIWOK-COSTANOAN family. MIWOK = MEWAN = MOQUELUMNAN is subdivided into five EASTERN MIWOK languages (4, 7–10) and two WESTERN MIWOK languages (5, 6), after Broadbent and Callaghan (1960), and EASTERN is further subdivided into SIERRA MIWOK (including Central (4), Northern (7) and Southern (10)), and Plains Miwok (8) and Saclan (9). Callaghan (1971), in a review of the position of Saclan (9), places it in EASTERN MIWOK with close ties to both Plains (8) and Northern Sierra (7) Miwok. These seven MIWOK languages are listed below after the COSTANOAN languages.

COSTANOAN. The COSTANOAN languages were spoken on the coast and in the coastal valleys of north central California, from the head of the San Pablo Bay branch of San Francisco Bay to about 30 miles south of Salinas. They all became extinct before much more than wordlists had been recorded in most of them. Though language boundaries cannot be determined on the basis of the existing data, the following dialects have been established (Beeler 1961).

1. Northern Costanoan. Ds. East Bay (including Huchiun = Juichun, Niles = Chocheño, San Jose, San Lorenzo), San Francisco, Santa Clara, Santa Cruz.
2. Southern Costanoan. Ds. Monterey, Mutsun = San Juan Bautista, Rumsen = Runsien = San Carlos = Carmel, Soledad. Mutsun and Soledad are more closely related to each other than either is to Rumsen.

3. Karkin.

MIWOK
4. Central Sierra Miwok. Five speakers. California (formerly upper valleys of the Stanislause and Tuolumne).
5. Coast Miwok. Ds. also Bodega, Huimen (Beeler 1961), Marin Miwok. One speaker. California (formerly coast from San Francisco Bay to Bodega Bay). Bodega and Marin Miwok are possibly separate languages (Callaghan 1970).
6. Lake Miwok. Fewer than ten. California (Clear Lake basin).
7. Northern Sierra Miwok. 20–30. California (formerly upper valleys of Mokelumne and Calaveras rivers).
8. Plains = Valley Miwok. One speaker. California (formerly deltas of the San Joaquin and Cosumnes rivers).
9. *Saclan = Saklan = Bay Miwok.
10. Southern Sierra Miwok. 20 speakers. California (formerly along headwaters of the Merced and Chowchilla rivers and on Mariposa Creek).

AFFILIATION. Member of PENUTIAN.

MIXE-ZOQUE(AN) = ZOQUEAN

GROUPING

1. *Aguacatec(a) = Aguacatecan. Formerly Guatemala.
2. Mixe = Mije = Ayuc = Ayook = Guichiovian = Tapijualapane-Mixe. Ds. Northern, Southern. 34,687 (1960). Mexico (Oaxaca and Veracruz States).
3. Oluta. Southern Vera Cruz, Mexico.
4. Sayula. 4,000. North side of Isthmus of Tehuantepec; Veracruz, Mexico.
5. Sierra Popoluca = Populuca = Popoluca of (Southern) Veracruz = Popoluco of Pueblo. 10,000–12,000. Mexico (Veracruz, Puebla, Oaxaca).
6. *Tapachultec = Tapachulteca = Tapachula = Soconusca. Near border of Mexico and Guatemala. Perhaps a dialect of Mixe (2).
7. *Tapixulapan = Tapijulapa = Tapijulapa(n). Perhaps a dialect of Mixe.
8. Texixtepec = Texistepec. Mexico (Veracruz).
9. Zoque = Zoke = Zoc = Çoque = Loque = Sok(u)e = Troc = Tzoc = Chimalapa. Ds. Copainala, Ocotopec, Ostuacan. 20,000. Northern Chiapas and adjacent Oaxaca and Tabasco, Mexico.

AFFILIATION. Member of PENUTIAN.

MIXTECAN = MACRO-MIXTECAN = AMUZGO-MIXTECAN

GROUPING. Formerly the MIXTECAN family was thought to include Amuzgo, and the family was also referred to by the names MACRO-MIXTECAN and AMUZGO-MIXTECAN, but Longacre (1966) has shown that Amuzgo is a single language coordinate with the half-dozen families in the OTO-MANGUEAN phylum. Longacre (1957) demonstrated the position of Trique in MIXTECAN. Holland (1959) suggests that there are 11 distinct Mixtec languages and 3 Cuicatec languages in Oaxaca, Mexico; but he identifies them by zone numbers rather than language names.

1. Cuicatec (Cuicateco). 10,000 (1946). Northeastern Oaxaca, Mexico.
2. Mixtec = Mixteco. Ds. Cuilapa, Cuixtlahuac, Mictlantongo, Montanyes; Nochiztlan, Tamazulaxa, Tepuzculano, Tlaxiaco, Xaltepec, Yanhuitlan. Geographical dialects are also listed in Wares (1968a), but the correlation of these names with the other dialects listed is not clear: Ayutla Mixtec, Eastern Mixtec, Guerrero Mixtec, Huajuapan Mixtec, Jicaltepec Mixtec, San Esteban Mixtec, San Miguel Mixtec, San Pedros Molinos Mixtec, Santo Thomas Mixtec. 170,000 (1930). Mexico: states of Oaxaca, Guerrero, Puebla.
3. Trique = Trike. 3,000 (1930).

> *AFFILIATION.* Member of OTO-MANGUEAN phylum; see Swadesh (1960).

*Mohenjo-Daro. An ancient, undeciphered script from Harrappa and Mohenjo-Daro along the Indus River in Pakistan (Hunter 1934).
> *AFFILIATION.* The script has been compared with those of Asia and Crete (Hrozny 1947) and with that of the Easter Island tablets (Métraux 1938).

MOLUCCAN AUSTRONESIAN

> *GROUPING.* Dyen (1965) grouped most of the eastern Indonesian languages which were included in his sample as MOLUCCAN, or most closely related to languages which definitely belonged to the MOLUCCAN group. We list below all those languages which Dyen classified as unquestionably MOLUCCAN, or possibly MOLUCCAN, except SARMIC, which Grace (1970) classifies as OCEANIC. Dialect names and other information are added from Salzner (1960) and Capell (1962a). Many, or all, of the languages of the EAST INDONESIAN (geographic) group (q.v.) probably belong to an as-yet-undefined larger group which includes the languages listed below.

AMBIC
1. Ambonese. Ds. Alang, Asilulu, Haruku, Hatu, Hila, Kaitetu, Liang = Bahasa Eti on Ceram, Liliboi, Nusulaut, Saparua, Wakasihu. Amboina (Ambon) Island, adjacent small islands to the east and adjacent coastal Ceram, Moluccas.
2. Paulohi. Amboina Island.
3. Bonfia. Ceram Island.
4. Buru. Buru Island, west of Ceram, Moluccas.
5. Endeh. Ds. Aku, including Tanah Kunu, and Djau, including Ngao, are subgroups of Endeh; Ngada ? Flores Island, Lesser Sundas. Ngada may be, rather, a dialect of Sikka (14) or a separate language closely related to Sikka (Uhlenbeck 1967).

FORDATIC
6. Fordat = Fordate. Ds. also Maktian, Molu, Selaru, Selvasan, Sera. Tanimbar Islands, Moluccas.
7. Jamden = Jamdena. Tanimbar Islands.

8. Kei = Kai. Ds. Ewab, Kei Tanimbar = Atnebar, Kur, Ta'am. Kei (Kai) Islands and Tanimbar Islands, Moluccas.

9. Havunese = Hawu = Sawu = Savu = Sabu. Ds. Liae, Mesara, Raidjua, Seba, Timu. 40,000. Sawu and Raidjua Islands, south of Flores and west of Timor, Lesser Sundas.

10. Kuiwai = Kowiai = Kaiwai. 600. Bomberai Peninsula, West Irian.

LETIC. Small islands east of Timor, Lesser Sundas.

11. Kisar. Oirata, sometimes listed as a dialect of Kisar, is classified by Greenberg (1971b) as belonging to INDO-PACIFIC. Therefore, Loikera, said to be closely related to Oirata (Uhlenbeck) may also be INDO-PACIFIC rather than AUSTRONESIAN.

12. Leti. Ds. Lire Leti: Lakor, Leti, Moa; Literi Lagona: Anlutur, Babar, Iliara, Imroin, Kokowari, Letwurung, Luang, Manowui, Sermata, Tela'a, Tepa, Wetoki.

13. Sekar = Seka. 450. Bomberai Peninsula, West Irian.

SIKKIC

14. Sikka. D. also Lio ? Central Flores Island, Lesser Sundas. Lio may be a separate, closely related language (Uhlenbeck).

15. Solor. Ds. Eastern: Belang, Kluang, Lamatukan, Lerek, Lodobelolon; Central: Takä; Western: Bari, Eon, Laän. Solor Island, off eastern tip of Flores, Lesser Sundas.

16. Sobojo. Taliabo Island of the Sula Islands, Moluccas.

17. Sumba. Ds. Kambera, Wewewa (Uhlenbeck 1967); Eastern: Lendi = Rendi, Massokarera, Melolo, Waidjelu; Western: Anakalang, Kodi = Kudi, Laboja = Lamboja, Lauli, Larua = Loura, Lolina, Mamboru = Memboro, Wajewa, Wanukaka (Salzner 1960). Sumba Island, south of Flores, Lesser Sundas.

18. Tettum = Tetum. Timor Island, Lesser Sundas.

An additional subgroup and an 'ungrouped' language were excluded from MOLUCCAN in Dyen's main classification, though their highest percentages of cognates with languages belonging to larger groups were with MOLUCCAN languages. A later refiguring of the percentages (Dyen 1965, Appendix) revealed 'a closer relationship' of these to MOLUCCAN:

GEELVINK. Coast of, and islands in, Geelvink Bay, northern West Irian.

BIAKIC. 40,000 speakers, of whom half are literate in Numfor and Bahasa Indonesia (Capell 1962a).

19. Biak. Ds. Ariom, Bosnik, Dwar, Fairi, Jenures, Korim, Mandusir, Mofu, Opiaref, Padoa, Penasifu, Samberi, Sampori (Mokmer), Sor, Sorendidori, Sorrido, Sundei, Wadibu, Wardo, Wari, Warsa; Supiori (?) including Korrido, Sowek, Wabudori, Wafordori; Padaido (?) including Bromsi, Jeri. Biak Island and adjacent Supiori and Padaido (Padeaido, Padaidori) Islands.

20. Numfor = Nufoor = Numfoor = Noemfoor = Mafoor. Ds. Kamer, Mapia,

Mios Num, Mios Wa'ar, Monoarfu, Rumberpon, Vogelkop. Numfoor Island, surrounding small islands and adjacent Vogelkop coast.

WANDAMIC

21. Japen. Ds.? Ansus, Jobi, Pom, Serui, Wo'oi. Japen Island.
22. Kurudu. Kurudu (Koeroedoe) Island.
23. Wandamen = Wondama = Windesi = Windessi. Ds. Ambumi = Waropen of Wandamen Bay, Bentuni-Wamesa, Dasener, Umar. 14,000, of whom one-quarter are literate in Wandamen, one-half in Bahasa Indonesia (Capell 1962a).

24. Waropen. Ds. Napan, Mo'or (Mo'or Islands)?, Waropen Kai. 6,000, of whom one-quarter are literate in Bahasa Indonesia (Capell 1962a). East side of Geelvink Bay, West Irian.

AFFILIATION. Member of MALAYO-POLYNESIAN group of AUSTRONESIAN (Dyen 1965).

MOMBERAMO RIVER (Geographic ?)

GROUPING. Greenberg (1971b) reports two possibly related groups in the area of the Momberamo River system of West Irian (Indonesian New Guinea). One of these consists of the languages numbered (2) and (3) below, the other of the languages numbered (1), (5), (6), (7), (9), and (10). Wurm (1971c) lists three other languages in the area (4, 8, 11).

1. Borumessu. Lower Momberamo River.
2. Kauwerawet. Lower Momberamo River.
3. Koassa = Kamboi Ramboi. Lower Momberamo River.
4. Manaü.
5. Pauwi. Lower Momberamo River. May be more than one language.
6. Sidjuai. Lower Momberamo River.
7. South River = Sudflüss.
8. Tarunggare. West of the Momberamo River.
9. Tori.
10. Tori Aikwawakai = Tori Aikwakai. Near junction of the Idenburg and Momberamo rivers.
11. Warembori. East of the mouth of the Momberamo River.

AFFILIATION. A member of INDO-PACIFIC, possibly in the WESTERN NEW GUINEA subgroup (Greenberg).

MONGOL(IAN)

GROUPING. According to Poppe (1955), the traditional classification of MONGOLIAN into an 'EASTERN' and a 'WESTERN' group of languages is linguistically irrelevant and does not take into account the position of Mongul (6). In the following list, Dagur, Mongour, and Mongul (languages numbered 2, 5, and 6) are separate languages, and the remainder (those numbered 1, 3, 4, 7, 8, and 9) enjoy various degrees of partial intelligibility with each other — at least with languages in neighboring groups, but they are not counted as dialects of a fourth Mongol language (beside languages 2, 5, 6). The dialect-language boundaries are especially difficult to discern because Khalkha (3) is used as a lingua franca in places where languages numbered (1), (4), (7), (8) and (9) are spoken. 2,500,000–5,000,000. Central Asia from Afghanistan to Manchuria.

1. Buryat. Ds. Alat, Bargu-Buryat (4,500), Barguzin, Bokhan, Bulagat, Ekhirit, Khori = Eastern Buryat (including Agat), Ninžne-Udinsk, Oka, Sartul, Tsongol, Tunka, Ungin. 290,000. Soviet Union, in Buryat ASSR in the area of Lake Baikal to the north of Outer Mongolia. Ekhirit, Ungin, Nižne-Udinsk and Alat, Bokhan, and Tunka are spoken of collectively as 'Western Buryat.'

2. Dagur. Ds. Bataxan, Hailar, Tsitsikhar. 10,000–100,000. China, in three Manchurian communities, of which that in the Nonni Valley is the largest.

3. Khalkha. Ds. Dariganga, Hotoguitu, Kamnigan, Eastern Khalkha, Khalkha of Ulan Bator, Western Khalkha. Over 700,000. Mongolian People's Republic, and small enclaves outside of Mongolia. Used as a lingua franca beyond Mongolia.

4. Khorčin. Ds. also Arkhorčin, Barin, Darkhan, Gorlos, Jaliat, Jarut, Jastu, Kharbin, Kharčin (350,000), Ogirut. 900,000. Chinese People's Republic.

5. Mongour. Ds. also Aragwa, Fulannara, Hu-tsu, Khalči-guor, Lin-hsia, Ming-ho, Narin-guor, San-ch'uan, Ta-T'ung, T'ien-yu, Wu-yang-pu, Yung-ching. Chinese People's Republic, West Kansu. 50,000–60,000.

6. Mongul. Ds. Baghtan, Herat, Maimana, Mangut, Marda of Kundar, Šawit. Afghanistan, on western perimeter of the MONGOL family.

7. Oirat = Western Mongul. Ds. Bait, Buzawa = Derbet of the Don, Dambi-elet, Derbet of Kobdo, Dzakhačin, Kalmyk = Oirat of the Volga, Mingat, Oirat of Kobdo, Olut of the Ili Valley, Torgut of the Altai, Torgut of the Koko-nor, Torgut of Orenburg, Uriangkhai of the Altai. 253,000. Scattered throughout the Sino-Russian borderlands in the region of Issyk-kul and the T'ien Shan Mountains, and further east to the borders of Outer Mongolia; in the United States (700), in New Jersey and a community near Philadelphia.

8. Ordos. Ds. also Abagai, Abaganar, Abaza, Čakhar, Dalat, Durben-Khukhet, Jasak, Jugan, Kešikten, Khangin, Khučit, Otok, Sunit, Tumet, Ujumčin, Urat, Ušing, Wang. 375,000. The Ordos dialect is spoken in the Chinese province of Sui Yang, and the Čakhar dialect is spoken in the Čakhar Territory of Inner Mongolia.

9. Pao-an (5,000). Ds. also Dakheczja, K'ang-lo, Ning-ting, Santa, Šera-Yögur, Širingol, Tung-hsiang (160,000), Tung-yên, Yung-ch'êng, Yunnan. 250,000. China, in Kansu Province.

AFFILIATION. Member of ALTAIC.

MON-KHMER

GROUPING. According to the recent classification of Thomas and Headley (1970) based on "lexicostatistic and other supporting evidence," Mon-Khmer comprises seven branches and two ungrouped languages. These include all the groups of languages listed by Pinnow (1959) as MON-KHMER plus Pinnow's NORTHEAST = PALAUNG-WA, including KHMUIC, and NORTH = KHASI subgroups of his EAST group of AUSTRO-ASIATIC. In addition, Thomas and Headley's MON-KHMER includes VIET-MU'Ŏ'NG, which Pinnow excludes from AUSTRO-ASIATIC (q.v.). Although listed here as MON-KHMER, following Thomas and Headley, KHMUIC, PALAUNG-WA, and VIET-MU'Ŏ'NG are treated in separate articles (q.v.). The remaining languages of MON-KHMER as listed below are those grouped as BAHNARIC (with subdivisions NORTH BAHNARIC, SOUTH BAHNARIC and WEST BAHNARIC), KATUIC, MONIC, and PEARIC plus the two ungrouped languages, Khasi and Khmer.

Thomas and Headley subdivide BAHNARIC into NORTH (= Pinnow's BAHNAR plus Sedang), SOUTH (= Pinnow's CHƏMA plus MNONG) and WEST (= Pinnow's JƏRU plus BRAO). Smith and Gregerson (1973) suggest that Bahnar (1, below) does not belong to NORTH BAHNARIC, but, rather, constitutes a separate subgroup, CENTRAL BAHNARIC, to which Alak (listed as 33, below, in the KATUIC subgroup) may also belong. So also, Cua (2, under NORTH BAHNARIC below) constitutes a separate subgroup, EAST BAHNARIC. The KATUIC subgroup includes Pinnow's KUOY and SUOY. Pinnow's CAMBODIAN includes both KHMER and PEARIC, whereas Thomas and Headley believe there is sufficient evidence for giving PEARIC the status of a distinct branch within MON-KHMER, with a high number of loans from KHMER. The ungrouped languages are Khasi (57) and Khmer (58).

BAHNARIC
NORTH BAHNARIC. Smith and Gregerson suggest that within NORTH BAHNARIC, (3) is subgrouped with (6), and (5) with (10). They list Takua (11, below) as either a dialect of, or closely related to, Cua (2, below), which they treat as EAST BAHNARIC.

1. Bahnar. Ds. Alakong, Bahnar Bŏnŏm, Bahnar Rengao, Gŏlar, Jŏlong, Kontum, Krem, Tŏlo. 85,000. Ankhe, Kontum, and Pleiku provinces, Vietnam.
2. Cua = Kor = Traw = Bong Miêu. 10,000–15,000. Northern Quảng Ngãi Province extending into southern Quảng Tín Province, Vietnam.
3. Duan.
4. Halăng = Haleng = Alang = Selong = Kŏyong. 10,000. Western Kontum Province, Vietnam.
5. Hrê = Davak = Dá Vách. Ds. also Crêg = Kare, Rabah = Tava, Taliang. 80,000. Western and southern Quảng Ngãi Province, Vietnam.
6. Jeh = Dié = Yeh. Ds. Dràm, Jeh Brilar, Jeh Perak, Langya. 10,000. Northwestern Kontum Province and possibly spilling over into southwestern Quảng Tín Province, Vietnam, and into Laos.
7. Kayŏng = Cagiủŏng = Cà Giòng = Katang. Northwestern Quảng Ngãi Province and at Mangbak, northeastern Kontum Province, Vietnam.
8. Mŏnŏm = Bŏnàm = Menam. 5,000. Eastern Kontum Province, Vietnam.
9. Rengao = Rŏngao = Rangao. 10,000–15,000. Northwest of Bahnar (1)

and southwest of Sedang (10) and partially between both in Kontum Province, Vietnam.

10. Sedang = Hadang = Hŏteang = Hŏteă = Rŏteă. 40,000. Northern Kontum Province, Vietnam.

11. Takua = Kotua = Duan (?) = Quảng Tín Katu = Langya(?). Small group. Trà My area of Quảng Tín Province and extending into Kontum and Quảng Ngãi provinces, Vietnam.

12. Tŏdrah = Didrah. D. also Modra. Possibly a dialect of Sedang. 5,000. Southeastern Kontum Province, Vietnam.

Banum (?), Galar (?), Hagu (?), Hajung (?), Halong (?), Jalung (?), Kamrang (?), Triêng = Strieng ? (possibly a dialect of Hrê or Jeh, spoken in western Quảng Tín Province and in Laos).

SOUTH BAHNARIC

13. Chrau = Jro = Ro = Tamun. Ds. Bajiêng, Butwa, Chalah, Jro, Mrả, etc. 15,000. Lòng Khánh, Bình Tuy, Phảơc Tuy and Biên Hoả provinces of Vietnam.

14. Kŏho. Ds. Chil, Kalŏp, Lat, Maa = Chau-Ma, Nop, Riơn, Sre, Tala, Tring. 100,000. Centered in Tuyên Đức and Lâm Đông provinces of Vietnam and extending into Quảng Đức, Long Khánh, Bình Tuy, Nính Tuận and Khánh Hoà provinces.

15. Central Mnong = Pnong. Ds. Biat, Bu Dâng, Bu Nâr = Bunơr, Bu Rung, Dih Bri, Preh, Rŏhong (?). 23,000. Spread over a large area in western Vietnam highlands southwest of the AUSTRONESIAN Rade.

16. Eastern Mnong. Ds. Chil, Gar = Pnom Gar (10,000 in southern Darlạc and northwestern Tuyên Đức provinces, South Vietnam), Kuanh = Khwanh (small group in mountains west of Lạc Thiện, Vietnam), Rŏlŏm = Rlam = Lŏm (5,000–10,000 around Lạc Thiện).

17. Southern Mnong. Ds. Nong, Prâng. 12,000. Mostly in Quảng Đức Province.

18. Stieng. Ds. Budip, Bulach, Bulŏ. 48,000. Phươc Long and Binh Long provinces, Vietnam, and eastern Khmer Republic.

Badung (?), Preng (?), Tipri ?

WEST BAHNARIC

19. Brao = Braou = Proue (?) (see Nyaheun, 27, below) = Lue. Northeastern Khmer Republic. Brao and Laveh (25) may be dialects of the same language.

20. Campuơn = Tampuen = Kha Tampuon = Proon(s) = Lamam.

21. Cheng = Jeng.

22. Hun = Hin = Niahon.

23. Kravet = Kowet = Khvek. Northeastern Khmer Republic.

24. Krủng. Northeastern Khmer Republic.

25. Laveh. Attopeu-Boloven area of southern Laos.

26. Loven = Boloven = Jru = Jaru. Attopen-Boloven area of southern Laos.

27. Nyaheun = Prou. Attopen-Boloven area of southern Laos.

28. Oi = Huei. Southern Laos.
29. Pragar.
30. Sapuan.
31. Sok = Souk = Suk = Su.
32. Suq = Sou = Sue ?

KATUIC
33. Alak.
34. Antor.
35. Brũ = Baroo = Brôu = Leu = Leung = Muong Leong = Tri = Quảngtrị
    Vân Kiêu. 40,000. Ds. also Galler and Makong = Mangkoong in North
    Vietnam and Laos, and probably also Khua and Tri. Quảng Trị Province
    and more recently Thùa Thiên Province of South Vietnam since the 1968
    Tet offensive. Extends also into Laos and North Vietnam.
36. Ca-lơ = Moi-Cu-lơ.
37. Ir. Near Saravane in Laos.
38. Kaleung =Kha Lung.
39. Kantu = Kontu = High Katu. Ds. Pilủ, Taluy, Tangpril.
40. Kasseng = Koseng = Talieng.
41. Kataang.
42. Katu = Phường Katu = Teu = Attouat = Kao = Khat = Thap = Nguôn
    Tà = Tả River Vân Kiêu. 20,000–30,000. Quảng Nam and Thửa Thiên
    provinces of Vietnam and extending into Laos.
43. Kuy = Kui = Kuoy = Cuoi = Khamenboran = Old Khmer.
44. Leun. Near Saravane in Laos.
45. Lor = Klor. Near Saravane in Laos.
46. Mahai.
47. Malo.
48. Ngeq. D. also Nkriang. Ngeq and Ta'oih (below) may be dialects of the same
    language.
49. Nialuok = Chhao-bon. Thailand.
50. Pacỏh = Pokoh = Bô = River Vân Kiêu. D. also Pahi. 15,000. Thửa Thiên
    and Quảng Trị Provinces of South Vietnam and extending into Laos.
51. Phuảng = Phường = Hửu River Vân Kiêu. Small group. Around Asau in
    western Thửa Thiên Province, South Vietnam, between the Katu and Pacỏh.
52. So = Kah So.
53. Soui = Souei.
54. Tảoih = Ta-ôih = Kantua = (Kha)Tahoi ? Small group. West of Asau in
    Thửa Thiên Province of South Vietnam and extending into Laos.
55. Tong.
56. Veh = Lave = Love. Laveh of WEST BAHNARIC ?
    Chari (?) = Shari, Duon (?), Khoi ?

57. Khasi = Khasia = Khassee = Cossyah = Kyi. Ds. Standard Khasi including
    Cherrapunji; Lyngngam = Lngngam, Synteng = Pnar, War, and possibly Cachar
    and Sylhet. 193,000. South-central section of the Khasi and Jaintia Hills District

of central Assam, India.

58. Khmer = Cambodian. Between 6,500,000 and 7,000,000 speakers spread over most of the Khmer Republic (Cambodia) including 185,000 in eastern Thailand and more than 500,000 in areas of southwestern Vietnam.

MONIC

59. Mon = Peguan = Talaing. Ds. Mon Nya = Ye, Mon Tang = Pegu, Mon Te = Mataban-Moulmein. 415,000. Burma (350,000) in eastern delta region from east of Rangoon as far as Ye and Thailand (65,000) in Rat Buri and Kanchanaburi provinces along the Khwae Noi River up to the Burmese border.

60. Niakuol.

PEARIC

61. Angrak = Anskrak = Ansrak. Kampot Province, Khmer Republic. Headley (1973b) doubts the existence of the Angrak.

62. Chong = Shong = Xong. Along the Thai-Khmer Republic border in Pursat Province, Khmer Republic, and Trat Province, Thailand, northwest of the Păr.

63. Pear = Por. Western Khmer Republic, in the Cardamon Mountains of Pursat Province.

64. Samre. Siem Reap Province, Khmer Republic.

65. Sauch = Saoch = Saotch. Kampot Province, Khmer Republic. May have been the same people as the Chong, (62), above (Headley, 1973b).

AFFILIATION. Member of AUSTRO-ASIATIC.

MULAHA

GROUPING. Greenberg (1971b) groups the languages listed below as MULAHA. Wurm (1971c) reports that Mulaha (4) does not appear to belong to SOUTHEAST NEW GUINEA, but he includes Kwale (2), as a 'family-type language isolate' — i.e., a language with no close relatives, which consists of a dialect continuum in which nonadjacent dialects, especially at the extremes of the continuum, are very divergent; hence, his Kwale (2) might possibly include Garia (1) and Manukolu (3), not mentioned by him.

1. Garia.
2. Kwale. 1,183. Central District, Papua, east of Port Moresby, from the coast halfway to the dividing range.
3. Manukolu = Lakume.
4. *Mulaha. D. also Iaibu. Formerly on coast of Central District, Papua, east of Port Moresby.

AFFILIATION. Member of SOUTH-EAST NEW GUINEA.

MUNDA

GROUPING. The MUNDA languages, after INDIC and DRAVIDIAN, constitute the next largest language grouping in India. More than 5 million people speak these languages, with Santali (10) alone spoken by over half this number. Ten languages account for the remaining MUNDA speakers, although Zide (1969) says there are possibly more MUNDA languages not yet discovered. The languages are spoken in three separate geographical areas of India with, in addition, some speakers of Kharia (6) in the Andaman and Nicobar Islands.

Genetically, the SOUTH = SORA-GADABA = KORAPUT (languages numbered 1–3, 9, 11) and CENTRAL = KHARIA-JUANG (languages numbered 4, 6) groups form one branch of MUNDA (GREATER SOUTH MUNDA = SOUTH) and the EASTERN = KHERWARI group (languages numbered 8 and 10) plus Kurku (7) (= Pinnow's WEST) form the other branch (NORTH), although it is the more distantly related CENTRAL and EAST groups that are geographically contiguous and even overlapping. The classification here follows Pinnow (1966) and Zide (1969). De Armond (1973) divides SOUTH MUNDA into three subgroups: (1, 2, 9); (5, 11); (4, 6).

The EAST and CENTRAL groups are located in the Chota Nagpur plateaus of Bihar State (primarily in the districts of Santal Parganas, Ranchi, and Singhbhum) and in Orissa to the south and Bengal to the north plus the insular outliers of Kharia. The SOUTH group is spoken in the Andhra Pradesh and Orissa border area, inland from the city of Visakhapatnam on the coast, between the Mahanadi River in the north and the Godavari River in the south.

Kurku (7) is considerably removed to the west from the other MUNDA languages.

The population figures for the MUNDA languages come from the 1951 Census of India or from Pinnow (1959) unless indicated otherwise. Where there are differing figures, both are given; usually the higher figure is from Pinnow.

It seems likely but not certain that Mundari (8) is no more than one language. Pinnow (1966) considers Mundari to be only one language with several dialects; Stampe (1965–66) says of the dialects "Their degree of mutual intelligibility . . . is so high as to qualify many of them as dialects, rather than distinct languages."

1. Gata? = Gataq = Getaq = Didei = Didey = Didayi = Dire. Less than 2,000 (Stampe 1965–66). Koraput District of Orissa.
2. Gorum = Pareng = Parenga = Parengi = Gadaba (erroneously according to Stampe) of Vizigapatam. Figures range from less than 100 to 10,000, the latter being the more widely accepted. Koraput District of Orissa.
3. Gutob = Gadaba. Ds. include Gadba, Gudwa = Bodo = Bodo-Gadaba = Sodia. Estimates vary from 32,500–54,000. Koraput District of Orissa and Srikakulam and Visakhapatnam districts of Andhra Pradesh. For reconstructions based on (3), (1), and (9), see De Armond (1973).
4. Juang = Patua = Patra-Saara. 13,000–16,000. Mainly in Keonjhar District of Orissa.
5. Juray.
6. Kharia. Ds. include Dudh. 111,000–160,000. Primarily Ranchi District of Bihar; also Raigarh District of Madhya Pradesh, Sundargarh District of Orissa, and some in West Bengal, Assam, and the Andaman and Nicobar Islands.
7. Kurku = Korku = Muwasi = Muasi = Kuri. 175,000 (Stampe 1965–66) to

189,000. Mainly in northwest Madhya Pradesh; also in Amravati District of Maharashtra.

8. Mundari = Mundari-Ho. Ds. Asuri including also Brijia = Koranti, Manjhi (5,000 in Raigarh in East Madhya Pradesh, Sambalpur and Oriya in Orissa, and other scattered areas); Bhumij (estimates vary from 102,000–360,000, located primarily in Mayurbhanj District of Orissa); Birhor = Birhar [600 (Stampe 1966) to 1,500 in Hazaribagh, Singbhum, and Ranchi districts of Bihar; approaching extinction]; Ho = Lankakol [400,000 (Stampe 1966) to 600,000 mainly in Singbhum District of Bihar and Mayurbhanj District of Orissa]; Koda = Kora including also Bankara, Birbhum, and Dhangon [(7,000–25,000 mainly in Sambalpur District of Orissa and in East Madhya Pradesh (Dhangon)]; Korwa including also Ernga = Singli [(16,000 in 1961 census, but Stampe (1966) says K. C. Bahl estimates there are one-third that many, all of whom are probably bilingual]; Mundari including also Hasada?, Kera?, Latar, and Naguri (600,000, mainly in southern and western portions of the Ranchi District of Bihar and also in other districts of Bihar, areas of Orissa, West Bengal, and beyond Bengal); Turi (2,000–4,000 in Raigarh in East Madhya Pradesh, Sambalpur and Oriya in Orissa and other scattered areas). Total population 1.3–1.7 million.

9. Remo = Bondo = Bonda = Bonda Poroja = Nanqa Poroja. 2,500; very few are monolingual. Koraput District of Orissa.

10. Santali. Ds. Karmali = Kohle (7,000), Mahle (4,000), Santali (2,812,000). In a strip of territory about 300 miles long from the Ganges in the north to the Baitarani in the south. This includes Santal Parganas, Purulia, Hazaribagh, Singbhum, Purnea, Dhanbad, and other districts of Bihar; Mayurbhanj and others in Orissa; Midnapur, Bankura, Burdwan, Birbhum, West Dinajpur, and others in West Bengal; Assam Plains in Assam; and other scattered settlements.

11. Sora = Saora = Savara = Sabara. 200,000–360,000. Mainly in the Ganjam District of Orissa; also in the Koraput and Phulbani districts of Orissa, the Plains Division of Assam, and other areas.

AFFILIATION. Member of AUSTRO-ASIATIC.

MURNGIC

GROUPING. Djinba (2), Jarnango (5), and Jandjinung (4) are each coordinate with the remaining languages which form a YULNGU subgroup (O'Grady et al. 1966). The MURNGIC languages are spoken in the northeast tip of Arnhem Land, Northern Territory, Australia.

1. Dalwongo = Dalwangu.
2. Djinba = Jinba = Djimba = Outjanbah = Yulngi. Upper Goyder River, west of the Ridorngu.
3. Gobabingo = Kupapuyngu = Gubabuyngu = Gobabwingu. Ds. also Djabu, Djambarbwingu, Gumaidji = Gomaidj = Gumadj, Manggalili, Mararba = Maroura = Marowera = Jakajako = Yaakoyaako = Waimbo. Used as a lingua franca through adoption as a church language (Wurm 1971b).

4. Jandjinung = Yandijinang = Yandjinung = Djariwidji = Djinang = Wulaki. Western bank of Goyder River and upper part of Blyth River, coast east of Crocodile Islands.
5. Jarnango = Yarnango = Yulngo. Ds. also Garmalangga, Gurjindi.
6. Riraidjango = Riraidjangu. Ds. also Galbu, Warameri = Waramiri. West side of Melville Bay.
7. Ritarungo = Ridarngo = Rittarungo = Ritaringo = Ritarngo = Ridarngu. Headwaters of the Goyder and Walker rivers.
8. Ubulgara.
9. Wagilag. D. also Manggura.
10. Wan?guri = Wan'guri.

AFFILIATION. Member of PAMA-NYUNGAN.

MUSKOGEAN = MUSKHOGEAN

GROUPING. Haas (1941, 1949) distinguishes an Eastern division, represented by Choctaw (3, below), from a Western division, represented by the rest of MUSKOGEAN — namely, Alabama (1), *Apalachee (2), Hitchiti (4), Koasiti (5), and Muskogee = Creek, including Seminole (6, below).

1. Alabama. Ds. also Powokti, Tawas, possibly including Muklasa and Tuskegee. 200–400. Texas (formerly on upper course of Alabama River, Alabama).
2. *Apalachee. Formerly in Florida.
3. Choctaw = Chacta(w) = Chactawice = Chactawisch = Chahta = Chahta-Muskokee = Chocktaw = Choktah = Choktaw. Ds. Northeastern Choctaw, Southern = Sixtown Choctaw, Western Choctaw; d. also Chickasaw = Chic(k)-asa = Chi(c)kasah = Chikasha = Chikkasah = Chakchiuma = Napochi. 10,000 Choctaw, 2,000–3,000 Chickasaw. Oklahoma; formerly Mississippi and adjacent parts of Alabama.
4. Hitchiti = Hitchitathi = Hichita = Hitciteco = Hitchitee = Apalachicola = Ocute(?). Ds. Hitchiti, perhaps including Chiaba (possibly extinct, Alabama, Florida; aboriginally Chattahoochee County, Georgia); d. also Mikasuki = Mekusuky = Miccosukee = Mikasuke (700, now divided into the Oklahoma Mikasuki, and the Florida Mikasuki, misleadingly known as the 'Big Cypress band of Seminole').
5. Koasati = Koassati = Koosatis = Shati = Texas Koasati = Louisiana Koosati = Coassatte = Coosada = Coosauda = Coosawda = Coushatta = (A)Coste(?) = Costehe(?). Possibly including the Kaskimpo = (I)Casqui. 100–200, Louisiana and Texas (formerly lower Pine Island in the Tennessee River).
6. Muskogee = Maskogi = Maskoke = Maskoki = Mukkogee = Muscogee = Muscoghe = Muscogulge = Muscoki = Muskhogee = Muskogh = Muskohge = Muskohgee = Muskoke = Muskokee = Muskoki = Creek = Crick = Crickice (10,000, Oklahoma, Alabama; formerly Georgia, South Carolina, Alabama). D. also Seminole (300, Florida).

AFFILIATION. Member of MACRO-ALGONQUIAN.

*Myriandynian. A non-INDO-EUROPEAN language of ancient Asia Minor known chiefly from Greek traditions (Ruge 1930).

AFFILIATION. None known.

*Mysian. An unknown language of Asia minor attested by a fifth century B.C. inscription (Kretschmer 1934).

AFFILIATION. Said by the ancients to be a mixture of Lydian and Phrygian.

NA-DENE PHYLUM

GROUPING. The Sapir (1915) - Hymes (1956) - Pinnow (1966) classification of two languages — Haida, (1) below, and Tlingit (2) — with ATHAPASCAN-EYAK, is based on typological resemblances and on the assumption that all these can be shown to be descended from an apex node representing the phylum proto-language. Krauss (1973b) finds that this family-tree classification cannot be supported by regular sound correspondences between Haida, Tlingit, and the daughter languages of ATHAPASCAN-EYAK, but admits that, despite the paucity of NA-DENE lexica, there is "obvious and intimate relationship exhibited in the general morphological structure," especially between Tlingit and ATHAPASCAN-EYAK. Much the same question was raised by Goddard (1920).

ATHAPASCAN-EYAK (q.v.).

1. Haida = Skittagetan. Ds. Masset Haida, including Kaigani in Alaska (northern end of Queen Charlotte Islands and in Howkan, Klinkwan, and Kassan, southern part of Prince Wales Island, Alaska); Skidegate Haida (central Queen Charlotte Isl and). 200. Queen Charlotte Islands off coast of British Columbia (100) and adjoining coast of Alaska (100).
2. Tlingit = Koluschan. Ds. Wrangell; Yakutat; and the speech at Auk, Chilkat, Huna, Killisnoo, Sitka, Taku. 1,000–2,000 (Alaska), 100–200 (British Columbia, Yukon). Throughout southeastern Alaska from Dixon entrance and Portland Canal to Copper River, except south end of Prince Wales Island; British Columbia, Yukon.

AFFILIATION. Shafer (1952, 1957) and Swadesh (1962) revived Sapir's (1925b) and Morice's (1914) SINO-TIBETAN-NA-DENE hypothesis. Haas (1964a) has proposed wider affiliations of NA-DENE to Yuchi and SIOUAN; a relationship has also been suggested with TUNGUS (John Campbell 1898; Morice 1914).

NAGA-KUKI-CHIN = KUKI-CHIN = KUKISH

GROUPING. Grierson (1903–1927) groups some SINO-TIBETAN languages under NAGA, others under KUKI, and still others under CHIN; Shafer (1955) classifies most of these languages under his 'KUKISH' section of his 'BURMIC' division, with various subdivisions, as noted below. One language (Lepcha) that is listed by Shafter under his KUKISH section is listed instead under our BODO-NAGA-KACHIN (q.v.); and two languages from Grierson's list are included below (numbered 39 and 84) as coordinate members of our NAGA-KUKI-CHIN group, rather than as members of one of the subgroups.

The classification that follows reflects both Grierson and Shafer, as revised by Morse (1965). This yields a list of NAGA-KUKI-CHIN languages that are consecutively numbered (1–88), but separately alphabetized for each subgroup under five major groups (CHIN, KUKI, LAKHER, NAGA, and WESTERN groups), and for four ungrouped single languages (those numbered 39, 58, 59, 84) which are classificatory coordinates of the five major groups.

CHIN. Burma (Chin Hills) and India (Assam).

CENTRAL CHIN. Shafer's CENTRAL branch of his KUKISH is subdivided into three coordinate units: (a) LASHAI, languages numbered (1), (4), (16), (17), (25); (b) HAKA, languages numbered (3), (19), (21), (28); and (c) Kapwi, a single language numbered (7), following. Kwangli (11), Laizo (12), and Zahao (25) are also known as SHIMRIN, with a total population of 20,000. Other names are added from Grierson.

1. Bom. Burma, Falam area, Chin Hills.
2. Bwel. Haka subdivision.
3. Haka = Lai = Baungshè. 85,000. Falam area, Chin Hills.
4. Hmar. 2,000–5,500. Falam area, Chin Hills.
5. Hsemtung. Haka subdivision.
6. Haulngo = Haulngo. 5,000. Falam area, Chin Hills.
7. Kapwi = Kabui ?
8. Khualringklang = Kwahring Klang. Haka subdivision.
9. Klang-Klang = Tlantlang. 5,000. Haka subdivision.
10. Kwals(h)im = Kwelshin = Kweshin = Mi Err. 4,000. Falam area, Chin Hills.
11. Kwangli. Falam area, Chin Hills.
12. Laizo. Falam area, Chin Hills.
13. Lawthve = Matupi.
14. Lente = Lyente. Falam area, Chin Hills.
15. Lomban. Falam area, Chin Hills.
16. Lushai = Lushēi. Ds. also Dulien, Ngente. 70,000. Falam area, Chin Hills.
17. Pankhu. Falam area, Chin Hills.
18. Senthang. Haka subdivision.
19. Sonśe = Shonshe.
20. Tashōn = Tashon = Shunkla. 85,000. Falam area, Chin Hills.
21. Taungtha = Rongtuw. 26,000. Pakokku district.
22. Tawr. Falam area, Chin Hills.
23. Vamtu. Haka subdivision.
24. Yokwa. 2,700. Haka subdivision.
25. Zahao = Yahow = Lyen-lyem.
26. Zanniat. 7,000. Falam area, Chin Hills.

27. Zokhaoh. Haka subdivision.
28. Zotung = Bandžogi. Haka subdivision.

NORTHERN CHIN. Burma, Tiddim area, Chin Hills, and India (Assam).
29. Kamhau = Kamhow = Kanhow. 65 ?
30. Ralte. 17,000. Also in Assam.
31. Siyin = Siyang = Sizang = Shi-zang. 3,000.
32. Sokte. 21,500.
33. Thado = Thādo-pao. 31,600–36,500. Ds. also Shingsol, Shīk-Shinshum. Also in Assam.
34. Vuite = Paite = Paithe. 15,500. Also in Assam, Lushai Hills.
35. Yos = Yo(?) = Zo ? 4,500 ?

SOUTHERN CHIN. Burma, Kanpetlet subdivision and Arakan Hill Tracts.
36. Ašo = A-shö = Šo = Shö = Shoa = Khyang. Ds. = Trs. Chinbon (11,000), Chittagong, Lemyo, Minbu, Sandoway, Thayetmyo. 95,500 ?
37. Chinbok = Chinbe = Tšinbok. D. also Yawdwin. 21,000.
38. Khami = Khweymi = Khimi = Khumi. Including Matu, Yindi = Yindu. 20,000. Also in Bengal, Chittagong Hill Tracts.

39. Hor = Horpa. Eastern Tibet.

KUKI = OLD KUKI. These languages are divided into two groups by Grierson (1903–1927); a smaller group including languages numbered (40), (44), (50), and a larger group of languages numbered (41), (43), (45), (48), and (52). Shafer also includes languages numbered (42), (46), (49), (51), and (53). and has five subdivisions: CENTRAL, languages numbered (40), (43), (50), (52); CENTRAL PERIPHERAL = KOLRENG, languages numbered (47), (48), (53); SOUTHERN = LAMGANG, languages numbered (41), (45); WESTERN, (42), (44), (46), (51); and a single language, Kyau, numbered (49).
40. Aimal. 750.
41. Anal. 2,650.
42. Biate.
43. Chiru = Tširu.
44. Fallam = Hallam. 11,000.
45. Hiroi-Lamgang. 750.
46. Hrangkhol = Rāngkhōl = Hrangchol. 8,500.
47. Kolhreng. 1,000.
48. Kom. 2,000.
49. Kyau = Chaw = Kyaw. 250.
50. Langrong = Lengreng. 6,250.
51. Southern Luhupa.
52. Purum = Púram. 300.
53. Tarao.

LAKHER. India, Lushai Hills in Assam.
54. Mara = Lakher = Zao. Ds. also Hawthai, Tlongsai. 1,100.
55. Sabeu.
56. Shandu = Šandu = Shendu.

57. Zeuhnang.

58. Langet.

59. Meithei = Meithlei = Mēklē = Mēkhalī = Mailhai = Manipuri = Kat̲he = Pōṇṇā. 240,000–315,000.

NAGA. Burma.

> EASTERN NAGA. Shafer's EASTERN branch, Grierson's WESTERN NAGA.
>> 60. Angami. D. also Tengima = Chākromá. 35,400–39,000.
>> 61. Dayang.
>> 62. Rengma = Unza. Ds. also Anyo = Eastern Rengma, Iseni-Kotsenu, Ntenyi, Nzonyu = Nzong. 5,000.
>> 63. Simi = Sema. Ds. also Kezhama = Keźama, Sopvoma = Māo Naga (10,000). 28,000–40,000.
>> 64. Tśakrima = Chakrimā. Ds. also Dzunu, Kehena, Mima = Nāli. 8,500.
>> 65. Zumoni = Zhimomi.
> 66. Naga-Mikir = Mikir. 89,500–110,000. A single language coordinate with the other NAGA groups (EASTERN, NORTHERN, and SOUTHERN).

NORTHERN NAGA. Shafer's NORTHERN NAGA branch, Grierson's CENTRAL NAGA.
>> 67. Ao = Hatiggorīa = Dupdoria. Ds. Chungli = Tśungli, Changki = Tśanki, Tungsen, Tunli. 15,500–30,000.
>> 68. Hlota = Lhota = Kyŏ = Kyon = Kyontsü = Tsŏntsü = Kantsii = Miklai. 18,500–22,000.
>> 69. Khari.
>> 70. Longla.
>> 71. Mongsen.
>> 72. Tensa.
>> 73. Thukumi.
>> 74. Yachumi = Yatśumi = Yimtśurr.
>> 75. Yatśam.

> SOUTHERN NAGA. Shafer's LUHUPA branch. Shafer subdivides this group into three units: (a) MARING, languages numbered (76), (81), (1,500–2,350 speakers); (b) KUPOME, languages numbered (77), (78), (79), (80), (26,000); (c) TANGKUL, languages numbered (82), (83), (30,000). India, Assam.
>> 76. Khoibu.
>> 77. Khunggoi = Khangoi.
>> 78. Kupome.
>> 79. Central Luhupa.
>> 80. Northern Luhupa.
>> 81. Maring.
>> 82. Tangkul. Ds. also Phadang, Ukrul.
>> 83. Tśamphung.

84. Tshairel = Chairel. India, Southeastern Assam.

WESTERN. Assam and Burma.

85. Empeo = Kachcha Nagas. 8,100–10,300.
86. Kabiu. Ds. also Khoirao. 1,000–15,000.
87. Kwoireng = Liyāng. D. also Miyāng Khāng (5,000) ? 400–5,000.
88. Maram. 5,000. Burma, Southern Haka subdivision.

AFFILIATION. Member of TIBETO-BURMAN.

Nahali = Nihali = Kalṭo. 750–1,200; Bhattacharya (1957) says these estimates are too high. India, mainly around the village of Temi = Tembi, 25 miles east of Burhanpur, in Nimar District of Madhya Pradesh.

AFFILIATION. None known. Pinnow (1959, 1963) would make Nahali coordinate with MUNDA in his WESTERN branch of AUSTRO-ASIATIC, but others, as Kuiper (1966) and Shafer (1940), view it as an independent language. Zide (1969) is doubtful of any affinity with MUNDA. According to Kuiper (1966), 36% of the vocabulary (in a test list of 503 words) is from Kurku, a MUNDA language, and 4% from an older Munda stratum; 9% is of Dravidian origin and 24% has no correspondences in India. Presumably, the remaining 27% are Indic.

NAMBICUARA = NHAMBICUARA

GROUPING. Only relatively recently discovered, the three languages of the NAMBICUARA family are spoken in the Mato Grosso region of Brazil. Lévi-Strauss (as reported by Mason 1950) groups the languages numbered (1) and (2) as NAMBICUARA PROPER; he labels (3), which is so different it may not belong to the same family, Pseudo-Nambicuara.

1. Northeast Nambicuara. Ds. Anunze, Cocuzu = Kokuzu, Congore, Nene.
2. Southwest Nambicuara. Ds. Cabichi = Kabishi, Tagnani, Tamainde, Tarute, Tashuite, Tauite, Uaintazu.
3. Sabane.

AFFILIATION. Member of GE-PANO-CARIB.

NARRINYERIC

GROUPING. The NARRINYERIC languages are spoken on the southeast coast of South Australia and inland on the boundary line between South Australia, Victoria, and New South Wales.

1. Maraura = Ngult = Maroura = Marowera = Jakajako = Yaakoyaako = Waimbo. Ds. also Kureinji = Karin = Kerinma = Karinma = Karingma = Orangema = Keramin = Kemendok = Pintwa, Ngintait = Inteck.
2. Nganguruku = Mirili. Ds. also Erawirung = Eraweerung = Erawirrangu = Erawiruck = Yerraruck = Yirau = Yiran, Ngaiawang = Ngaiwung = Ngaiyau = Aiawung = Aiawong = Iawung = Nggauaiyowangko = Birta = Pitta = Pieta = Peeita = Meru, Ngawait = Nauait = Nanait = Niawoo = Ngawaijung = Narwejung = Eritark = Njawatjurk. On Murray River from Mannum to

South Rhine River junction.

3. Tanganekald = Dadungalung = Korni = Tenggi = Tangane = Tanganalum = Tunga = Thunga = Thungah = Milmenrura. Ds. also Jarildekald = Jaralde = Yarilde = Yaralde = Yarrildie = Narrinyeri, Ngaralta = Wanaulum = Wanjakalde = Wanyakalde = Wunyakalde = Wanakald = Ngaralt = Ngaraltu, Peramangk = Paramangk = Peramarma = Mereldi = Merildakald = Marimejuna = Wangarainbula, Portaulun = Bordawulung = Portalaun = Warawalde, Ramindjeri = Ramong = Raminyeri = Ramindjerar = Ramingara = Danganararumindjeri = Tarbanawalun, Warki = Koraulun = Warkend. Coast along Ninety Mile Beach and about lakes Victoria and Wellington from Lakes Entrance west to mouth of Merriman Creek.

AFFILIATION. Member of PAMA-NYUNGAN.

Natu. A few speakers in Pacatuba, Sergipe, Brazil (Lorraine Bridgeman, personal communication).

AFFILIATION. None known.

NEW BRITAIN

GROUPING. Greenberg (1971b) hesitantly includes Uasi (7, below) in this group, since it seems to be at least as close to BOUGAINVILLE languages as to NEW BRITAIN languages. Sufficient data were also not available for the definite classification of Panaras (4). All are spoken on New Britain, except Panaras, which is spoken on New Ireland. Populations and additional names are given by Wurm (1971c).

1. Anem = Karaiai. Western end of north coast.
2. Baining. Ds. include Gaktai. 4,000–5,000. Gazelle Peninsula.
3. Kol = Kole. D. also Sui. Interior north of Jacquinot Bay on southeast coast.
4. Panaras. Ds. ? Letatan ant Limalua. Northwest coast of New Ireland.
5. Sulka. 1,000. Along the south side of Wide Bay on the southeast coast.
6. Taulil. D. also Butam. Both are almost extinct. Formerly in the northern part of the Gazelle Peninsula.

7. Uasi = Wasi = Ata = Peleata. Inland in the eastern central area.
On New Britain: Idne (?); on New Ireland: Leket ?

AFFILIATION. Member of INDO-PACIFIC (Greenberg).

NEW CALEDONIA

Grace (1955) treats the languages of New Caledonia, 21°28′S 164°15′E, as one group with possible subdivisions. Leenhardt (1946) regards all the languages of northern New Caledonia as forming one subgroup of closely related languages and the languages of the southern part of the island as forming another. Dyen's (1965) lexicostatistical classification confirms a north-south division for those languages in his sample, but groups the NORTHERN and SOUTHERN languages together only on his highest level, AUSTRONESIAN. The total population of New Caledonia in

1960 was 78,000. Capell (1954) laments the fact that many New Caledonians have abandoned their AUSTRONESIAN languages in favor of French.

NORTHERN. Dyen's NORTHERN NEW CALEDONIAN is subdivided into two groups — CAMUHIC (in which 3 and 11 are more closely related to each other than either is to 2), and THUANGIC (8, 12) — and a single language, Paici (9).

1. 'Avekè. 100.
2. Camuhi = Camuki = Tyamuhi = Wagap. 1,200. Wagap, 20°53'S 165°17'E.
3. Haeke = 'Aeke = Kone. 600. Koné 21°04'S 164°52'E.
4. 'Moaekè. 50.
5. 'Moavèkè. 400.
6. Moenebeng = Pwebo. 500.
7. Nemi. Ds. also Jawe = Ubach (400), Pinje (80), Poai = Yengen = Yehen (1,000). 2,180.
8. Nenema. Ds. Fwagumwak = Koumac, Yalasu, Belep. 1,100. Nénéma, 20°01'S 163°56'E.
9. Paici = Pati = Poneriwen = Poneriven. 2,000. Poneriven, 21°05'S 165°24'E.
10. Poapoa. 150.
11. Pwamei = Poamei. 500.
12. Thuanga = θuanga = Yuanga = Nyua-Bonde. 1,050.
13. *Wamoang. Three speakers in 1939.

SOUTHERN. Dyen's SOUTHERN NEW CALEDONIAN is subdivided into WAILIC (18, 19), NUMEIC (20, 21), and Hameha (17).

14. Aro. 300.
15. Boewe. 400.
16. Ciri. 600.
17. Hameha = Anesu = Kanala. 1,500.
18. Haragurè = 'Aragùrè = Thio. 500.
19. Houailou = Wailu = Wai = Ajie. D. also Arha. 4,000, plus 150 Arha. Houailou, 21°17'S 165°38'E.
20. Kwenyi = Kunie. Ds. also Kapone = Duauru, Uen = Ouen. 1,100.
21. Nadubea = Dubea = Dumbea = Wameni. 700. Dumbea, 22°10'S 166°27'E.
22. Neku. 150.
23. *Sirhe. 18 speakers in 1939.

AFFILIATION. A subgroup of the OCEANIC subgroup of AUSTRONESIAN.

CENTRAL NEW GUINEA MACRO-PHYLUM

GROUPING. Wurm (1971c) expands his earlier CENTRAL NEW GUINEA macro-phylum by the tentative inclusion of BOGIA, MURIK, NORTH PAPUAN, and SEPIK, all of which are included in NORTH NEW GUINEA by Greenberg (1971b), and by the inclusion of GOLIATH, which Wurm places in CENTRAL AND SOUTH, and of KUKUKUKU, which Greenberg places in CENTRAL AND SOUTH, by virtue of its inclusion in his SOUTH-WESTERN. Greenberg groups as CENTRAL NEW GUINEA Wurm's HUON, EAST NEW GUINEA HIGHLANDS, and WEST NEW GUINEA HIGHLANDS. Greenberg reports that there "appears to be a nuclear New Guinea" group, but he includes only his CENTRAL NEW GUINEA, NORTH NEW GUINEA, and SOUTHERN and SOUTHWESTERN (= CENTRAL AND SOUTH), and excludes NORTHEAST NEW GUINEA (which overlaps with Wurm's BOGIA), and SOUTHEAST = EAST NEW GUINEA.

BOGIA, MURIK, NORTH PAPUAN, SEPIK (tentatively, Wurm), or all of
    NORTH NEW GUINEA (q.v.) (Greenberg)
HUON-FINISTERRE (q.v.)
CENTRAL AND SOUTH NEW GUINEA (q.v.)
SOUTHEAST NEW GUINEA (q.v.)
EAST NEW GUINEA HIGHLANDS (q.v.)
WEST NEW GUINEA HIGHLANDS (q.v.)

AFFILIATION. Wider affiliations presently not determinable (Wurm); member of INDOPACIFIC (Greenberg).

CENTRAL AND SOUTH NEW GUINEA = SOUTHERN NEW GUINEA and SOUTHWESTERN NEW GUINEA

GROUPING. Wurm's (1971c) CENTRAL AND SOUTHERN NEW GUINEA includes most of the languages of both Greenberg's (1971b) SOUTH and SOUTHWESTERN groups. Greenberg's SOUTHERN = KIWAIIC includes the following subgroups discussed below: AGÖB, FREDERIK HENDRIK ISLAND AND SOUTHEAST WEST IRIAN, GOGODALA, KIKORI RIVER, KIWAI (subgrouped with BAMU AND TURAMA RIVERS and Ipikoi), MOREHEAD RIVER, and ORIOMO RIVER. Greenberg's SOUTHWESTERN = MARIND-OK includes AWYU, KUKUKUKU, MARIND, OK, and TIRIO. Greenberg's and Wurm's classifications also differ in the inclusion or exclusion of particular subgroups and occasionally in the subgrouping of particular languages. Wurm includes the ASMAT subgroup and, tentatively, the GOLIATH subgroup, both of which Greenberg leaves ungrouped but reports that they will probably be shown to be most closely related to WESTERN NEW GUINEA. Wurm also includes Fasu, which Greenberg places in EAST NEW GUINEA HIGHLANDS. Wurm treats KUKUKUKU as probably most closely related to EAST NEW GUINEA HIGHLANDS or HUON PENINSULA, and reports that connections have not yet been found between BAMU AND TURAMA RIVERS and Ipikoi and any other language in the area; hence, he includes neither in CENTRAL AND SOUTH NEW GUINEA. Wurm sets up one large subgroup of CENTRAL AND SOUTH NEW GUINEA within which ASMAT, AWYU, OK, and Mombum (a language placed in FREDERIK HENDRIK ISLAND AND SOUTHEAST WEST IRIAN by Greenberg) are said to be more closely related to each other than they are to GOGODALA, KIKORI RIVER, SIWAI, MARIND, ORIOMO RIVER, PARE-SAMO-BEAMI-BOSAVI, TIRIO, Fasu, or Miriam (a language placed in ORIOMO RIVER by Greenberg). This large subgroup is coordinate with each of the three subgroups of FREDERIK HENDRIK ISLAND AND SOUTHEAST WEST IRIAN, with Oksapmin (19, below), and with each of the other subgroups listed below except the excluded KUKUKUKU and BAMU AND TURAMA RIVERS. In a supplementary section written later than the body of the paper, Wurm reports that NORTH PAPUAN (q.v.) also belongs to CENTRAL AND SOUTH NEW GUINEA, and that Voorhoeve has suggested revision of the internal classification of CENTRAL AND SOUTH NEW GUINEA. Wurm also suggests that Foi and Duna, previously classified as belonging to EAST NEW GUINEA HIGHLANDS, belong rather to CENTRAL AND SOUTH NEW GUINEA.

AGÖB (q.v.)

ASMAT (q.v.)

AWYU (q.v.)

BAMU AND TURAMA RIVERS. Gulf District, Papua.
1. Karami. Middle Turama River.
2. Mahigi. Middle Bamu River.
3. Pepeha = Eme-eme. Coast between the Turama and Omati river deltas. Tapapi = Tapari ?

FREDERIK HENDRIK ISLAND AND SOUTHEAST WEST IRIAN (q.v.)

GOGODALA = GOGODARA. 7,500. Just north of the Fly Estuary, Western District, Papua. The GOGODALA languages may also include Suki, a language Wurm tentatively classified as belonging to MARIND.
4. Gogodala.
5. Waruna.

GOLIATH. A few thousand speakers altogether. Northeastern West Irian.
6. Goliath.
7. Korappun = Erok.
8. Naltje = T-Valley.
9. Wanam.

10. Ipikoi. Gulf District, Papua.

KIKORI RIVER (q.v.)

KIWAI. From south of the Fly Delta, Western District, Papua, across the islands of the Delta and along the coast into the western quarter of the Gulf District.
11. Bamu Kiwai. Ds. Buniki, Damerakaram, Dibiri, Maipani, Oropai, Pirupiru, Sisiaini. 5,000. Bamu River, Western District.
12. Northern Kiwai. Ds. Era River plus Iwainu and Urama; Goaribari, including Goari, Kerewa and Turama rivers. 5,500.
13. Southern Kiwai. Ds. Doropodai, Doumori = Domouri = Domori, Hibaradai, Hiwi, Kiwai Proper, Kubira, Mawata, Pagona, Peran, Sui, Turituri = Tureture.
14. Wabuda. 1,500. Ds. also Gesoa, Sogero.

KUKUKUKU (q.v.)

MARIND (q.v.)

MOREHEAD RIVER. Southwestern half of the area between the Fly River and the south coast, Western District, Papua. The MOREHEAD RIVER group consists of two subgroups: BENSBACH in the west and MOREHEAD in the east.
15. Dorro. 400, together with the Keraki.
16. Keraki.
17. Parb. 100.

18. Peremka. Ds. Gambadi, Semariji. 900.
Bangu (?), Dapo (?), Dungerwab (?), Jimina-kana (?), Karigari (?), Keba-nagara (?), Mani (?), Moi-e (?), Nausaku (?), Nenium = Wakamara (?), Nombuio (?), Noraia (?), Potaia (?), Sanana (?), Tunjuamu (?), Wandatokwe ? Greenberg includes these with three of the MOREHEAD RIVER languages in two separate subgroups of his SOUTHERN.

OK (q.v.)

19. Oksapmin. Ds.? Eriku = Eribu, Gaugutianap, Tarangap, Tekin, Wengbit. 4,000. Small area of southern Sepik District, with some overlap into the Western Highlands District, Australian New Guinea.

ORIOMO RIVER = EASTERN TRANS-FLY (q.v.)
PARE-SAMO-BEAMI-BOSAVI (q.v.)
TIRIO = MUTUM. Southern bank and hinterland of the Fly Estuary, Western District, Papua.
    20. Mutum. 357.
    21. Tagota. 100.
    22. Tirio. 350.
    Anima (?), Arama (?), Pisirami ?

AFFILIATION. Member of CENTRAL NEW GUINEA macro-phylum (Wurm).

NORTH NEW GUINEA

GROUPING. Greenberg (1971b) includes in a single NORTH NEW GUINEA group six subgroups and a number of unsubgrouped languages. Two of the subgroups, SENTANI and TAMI, are subsumed under Wurm's (1971c) NORTH PAPUAN (q.v.); the languages of a third subgroup are included in Wurm's SEPIK (q.v.). Two of Greenberg's remaining subgroups, BOGIA = MONUMBO and MURIK, are said by Wurm to be possibly related to each other (and ultimately to CENTRAL NEW GUINEA), but the third, TORRI-CELLI = ARAPESHAN, is not grouped with the other two at any level by Wurm. Wurm reports that BUNA, not treated by Greenberg, may prove to be related to BOGIA; hence it is listed below.

A few of Greenberg's unsubgrouped NORTH NEW GUINEA languages form three small groups in Wurm's classification: BUSA, SENAGI, and KWOMTARI. Wurm reports that Laycock's preliminary comparisons between KWOMTARI and TORRICELLI showed no relationship between the two.

Greenberg distinguishes a NORTHEASTERN NEW GUINEA = MADANG group from his NORTH NEW GUINEA group. The five languages of Greenberg's NORTHEASTERN which are included in Wurm's classification are included in BOGIA, as the others would presumably have been had they been treated.

1. Apris.

BOGIA (q.v.).
BUNA. About 3,000 speakers altogether. Eastern Sepik District.

2. Buna. 935.
3. Bungain.
4. Komasanu.
5. Muniwara.
6. Tumaru = Tumara. D. also Mandi, of which there are 80 speakers.
7. Urimo.
8. Yauaǧepa.

BUSA
    9. Amto. More than the 189 encountered. South of the Upper Sepik River, extending toward the headwaters of the Left May River. May be related to LEFT MAY (Wurm).
  10. Busa. 226. North of the Upper Sepik River.

KWOMTARI. Kwomtari (14) and Biaka (11) are more closely related to each other than either is to Fas (13) or Baibai (12). Amanab Subdistrict extending into the Aitape and Lumi Subdistricts of the West Sepik District.
  11. Baibai. 314.
  12. Biaka. 400.
  13. Fas. 866.
  14. Kwomtari. 780.

MURIK = NOR-PONDO. Kambot, included in this group by Greenberg, is classified as BOGIA by Z'Graggen (cited by Wurm). Coast and hinterland west of the mouth of the Sepik River, with one language on Lake Chambri in the central Sepik District.
  15. Angoram = Pondo = Tjimundo. 4,000. Lower Sepik River.
  16. Chambri = Tshamberi. 1,000. Southeastern shore of Lake Chambri.
  17. Murik = Nor. 1,000. On the coast west of the mouth of the Sepik River.
  18. Tabriak. 1,000. Lower Korowori River.
  19. Yimas. 1,000. Middle Korowori River.

NORTHEAST NEW GUINEA ? (q. v.)

20. Nori. Sepik District.

NORTH PAPUAN ? (q. v.)

SENAGI. This group may include other undescribed or unencountered languages in West Irian (Wurm). The two languages listed below are spoken largely in the Sepik District in the area in which the Sepik extends along and over the border of West Irian, but the languages extend into West Irian.
  21. Kamberataro = Komberatoro. 687 in Australian New Guinea, 1,000 in West Irian.
  22. Senagi. 1,256.

SEPIK ? (q. v.)

23. Siaute.

TORRICELLI (q. v.)
24. Yuri. 1,000. Sepik District, near West Irian border.

AFFILIATION. The BOGIA, MURIK, and possibly BUNA subgroups belong to CENTRAL NEW GUINEA, but the other subgroups have not been shown to belong to larger groups (Wurm); member of INDO-PACIFIC (Greenberg).

NORTHEASTERN NEW GUINEA = MADANG

GROUPING. Greenberg (1971b) distinguishes NORTHEASTERN from his NORTH NEW GUINEA group of languages. Wurm's (1971c) classification does not make such a distinction. Only five languages of Greenberg's NORTHEASTERN appear in Wurm's classification or Z'graggen's (1970) classification; they are included in the BOGIA group of NORTH NEW GUINEA, two of them in Z'graggen's ADELBERT RANGE subgroup, one in RAMU, and two in his MADANG. These five languages which are listed under BOGIA, are not included below. All the languages listed below are spoken in the Madang District.

1. Ate.
2. Bawaipa.
3. Bogadjim.
4. Bonaputa-Mapu.
5. Bongu.
6. Burumana.
7. Dagoi.
8. Damun.
9. Em.
10. Englam.
11. Gorendu.
12. Jimjam.
13. Kaliko.
14. Kemba.
15. Koliku.
16. Langtup.
17. Male.
18. Maragum.
19. Matepi.
20. Mis.
21. Misdao.
22. Panim.
23. Shongu.
24. Sungumana = Sungum.
25. Tombenam.
26. Uom.
27. Wenke.
28. Wuong.

AFFILIATION. Members of NORTH NEW GUINEA (Wurm 1971c, by implication); member of INDO-PACIFIC (Greenberg, 1971b).

SOUTH-EAST NEW GUINEA = EASTERN

GROUPING. Wurm (1971c) and Greenberg (1971b) are in essential agreement on the languages they group as 'SOUTH-EAST NEW GUINEA' and 'EASTERN', respectively. However, Wurm reports of the TOARIPI group that it "cannot at this stage of our knowledge be connected with" the other groups; he also treats one of the unsubgrouped languages (Koriki 1, below) as unclassified, and only raises the possibility that evidence may ultimately be adduced for the inclusion of DAGA. Subgrouping differences between the two classifications include the fact that Wurm's single GOILALA group is divided into three groups by Greenberg. Wurm treats KOIARI, MULAHA, the YAREBA subgroup of the MAILU group, but not the rest of the MAILU, and the unsubgrouped language Manubara (not treated by Greenberg) as being more closely related to each other than to other members of SOUTH-EAST NEW GUINEA. Membership in subgroups of particular groups and numbers of speakers are based on sources cited in Wurm.

BINANDERE (q. v.)
DAGA (q. v.).
GOILALA (q. v.).
KOIARI (q. v.).

1. Koriki = Namau = Maipua. 5,000. Eastern side of Purari Delta in the Gulf District, Papua.

MAILU (q. v.).

2. Manubara. D. also Koriko. 2,255 (1,414 Manubara, 841 Koriko). Wurm (1971c) treats Manubara and Koriko as a single language on the basis of their high level of mutual intelligibility. Inland, east of Port Moresby, Central District, extending into Northern District, Papua.

MULAHA (q. v.).
TOARIPI (q. v.).

AFFILIATION. Member of CENTRAL NEW GUINEA macro-phylum (Wurm 1971c).

WESTERN NEW GUINEA = WEST PAPUAN

GROUPING. Greenberg (1971b) excludes from his WESTERN NEW GUINEA group the languages of northern Halmahera, Timor, and Alor, which Cowan (1957a) includes in his 'WEST PAPUAN', but otherwise his classification closely agrees with that of Cowan. The first of Greenberg's four subgroups below combines several of Cowan's subgroups ('Northern Vogelkop', 'Eastern Vogelkop', 'Southern Vogelkop') and two of Anceaux's (1958) Bomberai Peninsula subgroups. Greenberg also reports that ASMAT, classified by Wurm (1971c) as belonging to CENTRAL AND SOUTH NEW GUINEA, bears a special relationship to WESTERN NEW GUINEA, if it is not actually a member of it, as does possibly MOMBERAMO RIVER. In addition to the four definite subgroups below, Greenberg leaves Arare and Tanamerah as unsubgrouped, and Yava as only tentatively placed in WESTERN NEW GUINEA, probably as a separate subgroup. Other sources, especially Capell (1962a), mention additional languages in the same area, which have not yet been classified but might be expected to belong to WESTERN NEW GUINEA; these names are given at the end of the list below. The WESTERN NEW GUINEA languages are spoken on the Vogelkop, Bomberai Peninsula, and on islands in Geelvink Bay, West Irian.

I

1. Amberbaken.
2. Barau. 150.
3. Bira.
4. Etna Bay. Probably several languages in Etna Bay area (Wurm).
5. Faranyao = Faranjao.
6. Itigo.
7. Kampong Baru = Yaban ? Ds. also Arandai (?), Weriagar (?)
8. Konda.
9. Mairasi. 1,000.
10. Mansibaber.
11. Mantion. D. also Manikion.
12. Meninggo = Meax.
13. Mogetemin.
14 Mor. 60.
15. Najarago.
16. Puragi.
17. Solowat.
18. Tarof.
19. Yahadian = Jahadian. D. also Nerigo.

II. Languages (20) and (24) are grouped as KALABRA; languages (21), (22) and (23) as MOI-KARON.

20. Kalabra.
21. Karon.
22. Madik.
23. Moi = Waipu.
24. Moraid.
25. Seget.
26. Tehit.
27. Waliem.

III

28. Aitinjo.
29. Asli-Sidi.
30. Ayamaru = Ajamaru.
31. Maibrat.

IV = IHA
> 32. Baham = Patimuni. 450.
> 33. Iha = Kapaur. 5,500.
> 34. Karas 170.

Arare On the Juliana River.

Tanahmerah. 400.

Yava. Ds. include Mantembu, Saweroe. Central Japen Island, Geelvink Bay.

On the Vogelkop: Arfak (?), Hattam (?), Kaibus (?), Mansim (?), Meyach (?), Mogao (?), Samalek (?); on the Bomberai Peninsula: Faur (?), Kaitero (?), Modan (?)

> *AFFILIATION.* Member of INDO-PACIFIC (Greenberg, 1971b).

EAST NEW GUINEA HIGHLANDS

> *GROUPING.* Foi, MIKARU, and PAWAIA each constitute a separate subgroup as opposed to a subgroup consisting of all the rest (Wurm 1971c and earlier). Greenberg (1971b) subgroups Fasu (12, below), classified by Wurm as a member of CENTRAL AND SOUTH NEW GUINEA, with Foi (13). Wurm includes PAWAIA only tentatively; Greenberg leaves PAWAIA as not subclassified within INDO-PACIFIC.

1. Duna. 14,000. Western end of Western and Southern Highlands districts.

ENGA-HULE-WIRU = WEST CENTRAL = (formerly) ENGA-HULE-POLE-WIRU. Western half of Western Highlands and all across Southern Highlands districts.

> ENGA

> > 2. Enga = Caga = Tsaga = Tchaga. Ds. include Kandep-Aruni-Karintsu, Laiap, Mae = Wabag, Maramuni, Paloko, Sirunki, Syaka = Tchak, Waka, Wale-Tarua, Wape, Wapi, Yandapu = Jandapu-Taro-Muritaka; also Kyaka = Baiyer Enga. 119,000.

> > 3. Ipili. D. also Paiela. 4,500.

> 4. Huli. D. also Huliduna. 54,000.

> 5. Lemben = Iniai. 650.

MENDI. Some of the Pole, formerly listed as speaking a dialect or language in this group, speak Kewa (7); others, Sau (10).

> > 6. Augu. 3,100.
> > 7. Kewa = Kewapi = Kewa Pi. 47,000.
> > 8. Magi. 2,000.
> > 9. Mendi = Angal Heneng. 25,000.
> > 10. Sau. 2,611.

> 11. Wiru. 11,540.

12. Fasu. 750. Between Lake Kutubu and Mt. Bosavi in southwestern Southern Highlands District.

13. Foi. Ds. also Fimaga, Ifigi, Kafa, Kutubu, Mubi. 2,600. South-central Southern Highlands District.

GADSUP-AUYANA-AWA-TAIRORA = KAINANTU = EASTERN. Centered in Kainantu Subdistrict of Eastern Highlands District.

GAUWA

14. Auyana. Ds. include Kawaina, Kosena including Arora and Asempa; also Usurufa = Uturupa. 5,265. Bee (1965) treats Usurufa as a separate language from Auyana, though Wurm (1971c) found 76% cognates on a restricted list.

15. Awa. 1,200–1,500. Ds. Ilakia, Northeastern (villages of Tawaina, Yona), Southern (villages of Agamusi, Amoraba, Mobuta), Tauna. On Lamari River in southeast corner of Eastern Highlands District (Loving 1968).

16. Gadsup. Ds. also Agarabe, Oyana. 7,000–15,000.

TAIRORA. May be one language, or three, with (17) and (18) forming a single language (McKaughan 1968).

17. Binumarien. 125.

18. Kambaira. 135.

19. Tairora. Ds. also Obura, Suwaira, Northern, Southern, and possibly (17) and (18) above. 8,180–11,000. Southern Tairora may possibly be a separate language.

20. Waffa. 940. Headwaters of Waffa River in Kaiapit Subdistrict of Morobe District.

Erima (?), Tsinyaji (?) (Greenberg 1971b).

GENDE–SIANE–GAHUKU–KAMANO–FORE = EAST-CENTRAL. Central half of Eastern Highlands District and small adjacent area of Madang District.

FORE

21. Fore. 12,020.

22. Gimi. 16,735.

GAHUKU

23. Benabena. 11,765.

24. Gahuku = Gafuku. D. also Asaro, including Gama (11,600). 22,990.

GENDE. Madang District.

25. Biyom 400.

26. Gende = Iwam = Bundi. 8,000.

KAMANO

27. Kamano. D. also Kanite = Kemiju Jate (2,585). 33,925.

28. Keigana = Keijagana Jate. Ds. also Yagaria (14,295), Yate = Jate (3,990). 26,725.

SIANE

29. Siane. Ds. Komunku = Komonggu, including Emenyo tribe; Koreipa = Korefa; Ono = Ono-Keto; Ramfau = Lambau. 15,335.

30. Yabiyufa = Yaviyufa = Jafijufa. 4,465.

HAGEN–WAHGI–JIMI–CHIMBU = CENTRAL. Eastern half of the Western Highlands District, with a small overlap into Southern Highlands and western quarter of the Eastern Highlands districts.

CHIMBU. (32) and (33) are treated by Salisbury (1962) as a single language, Dene, with three dialects: Gai, Mami-Duma, Siati.

31. Chimbu = Kuman. Ds. include Dom = Tabare-Dom, Golin, Gumine,

Marigl, Nondiri, Salt = Iui; also Nagane = Genagane, Sinasina = Sinesine. 119,255.
32. Chuave = Tjuave. D. also Elimbari, including Sua. 20,965.
33. Nomane. D. also Kiari. 3,680.

JIMI

34. Maring = Yoadabe-Watoare = Karamba-Kambegl. 4,500.
35. Narak. D. also Kandawo = Gandja. 10,000.
36. Medlpa = Moglei = Hagen. Ds. also Aua, Gawigl = Kauil, Tembagla. 90,775.
37. Wahgi = Middle Wahgi. Ds. Gimi, Kambia, Kunjip, Kuno, Kup-Minj, Nangamp (village)-Banz-Nondugl, Pukamigl-Andegabu. Speakers south of the Wahagi River are collectively called Kuma; those north of the river, Ndanga; both together, Nangamp.

KARAM. Westernmost central Madanh District and a small adjacent area in Western Highlands.
38. Gants = Gaj. Several thousand, as combined number of speakers of Gants and Kobon (40).
39. Karam = Aförö. 10,000–14,000.
40. Kobon. Several thousand, combined with Gants (38).

MIKARU. Extreme southern Chimbu District and central inland area of Gulf District. Wurm (1971c, after Franklin) subgroups (44) and (45), below, as NORTHERN, (42) and (45) as WESTERN, (41) and (47) as SOUTHERN, (43) and (48) as EASTERN; in addition, there are unnamed languages in a CENTRAL subgroup, with a few hundred speakers altogether. Greenberg classifies Foraba (42), Ro (47), and Sesa (48) as members of same subgroup of his SOUTHERN NEW GUINEA as the languages which Wurm groups as KIKORI (after Franklin), a subgroup of CENTRAL AND SOUTHERN NEW GUINEA (q. v.).
41. Bara. 50.
42. Foraba. 1,500 total speakers of Foraba and Polopa (46).
43. Ibukairu. 500 total speakers of Ibukairu and Sesa (48).
44. Kewah. 300.
45. Mikaru. D. also Elu. 4,000.
46. Polopa. 1,500 combined with Foraba (42).
47. Ro = Keai = Worugi. 200.
48. Sesa. 500 combined with Ibukairu (43).

PAWAIA. Northern part of the Gulf District, with slight overlap into adjacent Eastern Highlands and Chimbu districts. Under 2,000.
49. Aurama.
50. Hauruha. Spoken near the coast, considerably southeast of the main PAWAIA group as represented by Aurama.

AFFILIATION. Member of CENTRAL NEW GUINEA macro-phylum (Wurm).

WEST NEW GUINEA HIGHLANDS = KAPAUKU-BALIEM

GROUPING. Wurm (1971c) treats Uhunduni (8, below) as more closely related to WISSEL LAKES-KEMANDOGA than either is to other members of WEST NEW GUINEA HIGHLANDS. Greenberg's (1971b) subgrouping differs from Wurm's in that Greenberg lists members of Wurm's GREATER DANI in two different subgroups. All the WEST NEW GUINEA HIGHLANDS languages are spoken in the central highlands of West Irian.

GREATER DANI = NDANI = OERINGOEP. 200,000. Baliem River valley system and adjacent areas. Wurm subgroups languages numbered (1) and (2) as opposed to a subgroup composed of (3), (4), (5), with (6) coordinate with both subgroups.

1. Grand Valley Dani. D. also Pesechem = Peseg(h)em ?
2. Western Dani.
3. Nduga.
4. Northern Ngalik.
5. Southern Ngalik
6. Wano.
7. Dem. D. also Dauwa. 500. Eastern side of the Upper Rouffaer River.
8. Uhunduni. D. also Enggipilu. Several thousand. Southeast of the source of the Kemandoga River.

WISSEL LAKES-KEMANDOGA. Wissel Lakes area and Upper Kemandoga River.

9. Kapauku = Ekagi = Ekari. Ds. also Jabi = Yabi, Simori. 10,000.
10. Moni. 15,000–20,000.
11. Wolani = Wodani = Woda. 5,000.

AFFILIATION. Member of CENTRAL NEW GUINEA macro-phylum (Wurm).

NORTHWESTERN NEW HEBRIDES

GROUPING. Capell (1962a) proposed the close affiliation of subgroups consisting of the languages of Malekula Island and those of Santo Island, as distinct from those of NORTHERN NEW HEBRIDES and SOUTHERN NEW HEBRIDES. This distinction is implicit in the difference between Grace (1955) and Grace (1968).

MALEKULA group. 9,900. Malekula and small adjacent islands, 16°44′S 167°45′E.

1. Ahamb.
2 Atchin. 300 (1930). 15°57′S 167°20′E.
3. Aulua (Bay). 16°19′S 167°43′E.
4. Kuliviu. 16°32′S 167°49′E.
5. Lambumbu. 16°12′S 167°23′E.
6. Mewun = Meaun.
7. Nale. Dyen (1965) does not subgroup Nale with any other AUSTRONESIAN language.
8. Nambas. Ds. Big Nambas, Small Nambas.
9. Onua = Unua.

10. Pangkumu (Bay). 16°17'S 167°39'E.
11. Port Sandwich.
12. Sinesip.
13. Uripiv. 100 (1930). 16°04'S 167°27'E.
14. Vao. 400 (1930). 15°54'S 167°18'E.
15. Wala. 300 (1930). 15°58'S 167°22'E.
Fo'oa (?); Lamangkau (?); Laravat (?); Malua (?) (Bay, 15°59'S 167°11'E); Maragaus (?); Nevat (?); Orierh (?); Toman = Taman = Tomman (?) 16°36'S 167°33'E; Winiv (?); Wuli = Wulei (?) 16°33'S 167°147'E.

SANTO group. 6,100. Santo (Espiritu Santo) and adjacent small islands 15°45'S 166°50'E.
16. Cape Cumberland.
17. Eralado.
18. Malo. 15°40'S 167°11'E.
19. Marina = Marino = Big Bay. 15°15'S 166°50'E.
20. Mavia. 15°23'S 167°14'E.
21. Nokuku = Nogugu. 14°55'S 166°35'E.
22. Sakau = Hog Harbour. 15°09'S 167°07'E.
23. Savan.
24. St. Philip's Bay. 15°06'S 166°54'E.
25. Valpay.
26. Wulua.

AFFILIATION. Subgroup of the OCEANIC within AUSTRONESIAN.

SOUTHERN NEW HEBRIDES

GROUPING. Grace (1955) treats the language of the southern New Hebrides as forming a subgroup, but Dyen (1965) does not subgroup either of the languages in his sample (1, 3 below) with any other AUSTRONESIAN language.

1. Aneityum. 310 (1966). Aneityum Island, 20°15'S 169°49'E.
2. Eromanga. Ds. Ifo = Utaha, Potnariven, Sie = Sorung, Yoku = Enyau. 600. Eromanga (Erromango) Island 18°58'S 169°18'E.
3. Tanna. Ds. also Ikyoo, Itonga, Kwamera, Lenakel, Loanatit, Naviliang, Nerauya, Nerokwang, Numerat, Nupuanmen = Wassisi = Waisisi = Weasisi, Rana. 9,500. Tana Island, 19°32'S 169°27'E.
4. Ura. Eromanga Island, 18°58'S 169°18'E. Closely related to Eromanga (2).

AFFILIATION. Subgroup of the OCEANIC subgroup of AUSTRONESIAN.

NGARGA

GROUPING. The NGARGA languages are spoken in the west central part of Northern Territory, Australia.

1. Ngalia = Ngallia = Nambuda. North of Stuart Bluff Range from Central Mount

Wedge west to Mount Cochburn.

2. Ngardi.

3. Walbiri = Walpiri = Walpari = Wailbry = Wailbri = Wolperi = Wolpirra = Waljbiri = Ilpira = Ilpirra = Ilpara = Elpira. Lander Creek below Mount Leichhardt, sand plain north of Mounts Turner, Sexby and Singleton, northwest toward the Granites.

4. Walmanba = Walmala.

5. Wanayaga = Woneiga.

AFFILIATION. Member of SOUTHWEST PAMA-NYUNGAN (Wurm 1971b).

NGAYARDA

GROUPING. The NGAYARDA languages are spoken along the northwestern coast of Western Australia.

1. Bailko = Bailgu = Balgu = Balgoo = Paljgu = Pulgoe = Boolgoo. D. also Pandjima = Panjima. Less than 50. 22°S 120°E.

2. *Binigura = Binnigoora = Biniguru = Binnigora. D. also *Tjuroro = Tjururu = Churoro = Choororo = Chooraroo.

3. Kariera = Karriara = Karriarra = Kyreara = Kaierra. D. also Ngaluma = Ngarluma = Gnalooma = Gnalouma = Gnalluma. Fewer than 40. 21°S 117°E.

4. Kurama = Karama = Korama. D. also Jindjibandi = Jindjibarndi = Indjibandi = Injibandi = Ingibandi = Yingiebandie. More than 200. 21°S 118°E.

5. Mardudunera = Mardudhoonera = Mardatunera = Mardathoni = Mardatuna = Maratunia = Mardadhunira. 10. 21°S 116°E.

6. Ngarla = Wanbarda = Ngurla = Ngirla = Ngala = Gnalla. Fewer than 6. 20°S 119°E.

7. *Noala.

8. Nyamal = Nyamarl = Njamal = Nyamel = Namel = Gnamo. D. also Widugari = Widagari = Widagaree = Weedokarry = Weedookarry. 20. 21°S 119°E.

AFFILIATION. Member of SOUTHWEST PAMA-NYUNGAN (Wurm 1971b).

NGUMBIN

GROUPING. The NGUMBIN languages are spoken in west central Northern Territory, Australia, and across the northeastern Western Australia border.

1. Bunara = Boonarra. Stuart Creek, Western Australia.

2. Djaru = Jaruru = Jaroo. Ds. also Nyiniñ = Njining, Wandjira, Waringari = Waiangara. Halls Creek and southern vicinity, Western Australia.

3. Gurindji. Wave Hill, Northern Territory.

4. Malngin = Malgin. Southwest of the mouth of Victoria River, probably extending to Ord River.

5. Mudbura = Mudbara = Mudburra = Moodburra = Mootburra. Armstrong River and upper Victoria River east of Victoria River Downs; between Stuart Creek and Victoria River.

6. Ngarinman = Airiman = Ngaiman = Ngaimmun = Ngraimun. Victoria River about Jasper Creek.
7. Tjiwarliñ. D. also Wolmeri = Walmadjari = Warmala = Wulumari = Wolmera = Walmaharri = Wolmaharry. Immediately south of the Fitzroy crossing.

AFFILIATION. Member of SOUTHWEST PAMA-NYUNGAN (Wurm 1971b).

NICOBARESE

GROUPING. Formerly listed as one language, NICOBARESE is now listed (following Stampe (1965–1966) and others) as a group of six languages spoken by some 10,000 people in the Nicobar Islands (India) located south of the Andaman Islands and northwest of Sumatra.

1. Car = Pu.
2. Central. Ds. Camorta = Kamorta, Katchal = Kachel = Tehñu, Nancowry = Nancoury, Trinkut = Trinkat.
3. Chowra = Tɔtet.
4. Shom Pen(g) = Inland of Great Nicobar. May be extinct.
5. Southern. Ds. Condul, Great Nicobar, Little Nicobar, Milo.
6. Teressa = Taih-long. Ds. include Bompaka = Paɔhɔt.

AFFILIATION. Member of AUSTRO-ASIATIC phylum (Pinnow 1959).

NIGER-CONGO

GROUPING. Westermann (1927, 1935) attested the relationship of a group of languages he called WEST SUDANIC, and pointed out resemblances between his 'WEST SUDANIC' and BANTU. Greenberg (1966) incorporates BANTU and Ful (Fulani) into 'WEST SUDANIC' and expands the group — newly named NIGER-CONGO — further by the addition of ADAMAWA-EASTERN. Greenberg subclassifies NIGER-CONGO into a half-dozen major coordinate language groups, as indicated in the following list. These groups are discussed here in one or more separate articles. When a major coordinate group is discussed in more than one separate article, the additional articles are included parenthetically in the following list.

Greenberg admits that KWA and BENUE-CONGO "are particularly close to each other and in fact legitimate doubts arise concerning the validity of the division between them." Welmers (cited by Williamson 1971), Williamson (1971, 1973), and Williamson and Shimizu (1968) present evidence for the argument that distinctive criteria for a division between KWA and BENUE-CONGO do not exist, and a new subgrouping of these languages must be worked out.

ADAMAWA-EASTERN (ADAMAWA and EASTERN)
WEST ATLANTIC
BENUE-CONGO (BANTOID, BANTU, CROSS-RIVER, JUKUNOID, and PLATEAU)
GUR = VOLTAIC
KWA (CENTRAL AKOKO, EDO, EWE, GÃ-ADANGME, IDOMA, IGBO, IJO,

KRU, LAGOON, NUPE-GBARI, CENTRAL TOGO, YORUBA and VOL-TA-COMOE)
MANDE

AFFILIATION. Member of NIGER-KORDOFANIAN.

NIGER-KORDOFANIAN = CONGO-KORDOFANIAN

GROUPING. Greenberg bifurcates NIGER-KORDOFANIAN into KORDOFANIAN (q.v.) and NIGER-CONGO (q.v.). The vast majority of NIGER-KORDOFANIAN languages are grouped and subgrouped under NIGER-CONGO.

AFFILIATION. Of the four maximum classes (AFROASIATIC, KHOISAN, NIGER-KORDOFANIAN, and NILO-SAHARAN) postulated for African languages, NIGER-KORDO-FANIAN includes more groups and subgroups and individual languages than those included in any of the other maximum classes mentioned. The languages classified as NIGER-KORDOFANIAN may be said either (a) to be unrelated to languages in the other maximum classes or (b) to show significantly greater resemblances within NIGER-KORDOFANIAN than exist between NIGER-KORDOFANIAN languages and languages in other maximum classes (Greenberg 1966). Some doubts about (a) and (b), especially (b), are discussed by Fodor (1969), and Edgar Gregerson (unpublished ms.) has proposed a macro-phylum including both NIGER-KORDOFANIAN and NILO-SAHARAN.

NILO-SAHARAN PHYLUM

GROUPING. Two ungrouped languages, Fur (1) and Songhai (2), are listed below as coordinate in classification with the grouped languages or families of the NILO-SAHARAN phylum. Differences in classification reflect either (a) the recognition of a CHARI-NILE major group in which the majority of languages of the NILO-SAHARAN phylum are classified or (b) the recognition of a larger KOMAN group of languages and language groups coordinate with KOMAN, which include many of the languages classified under EASTERN SUDANIC by those who recognize a CHARI-NILE major group.

In Greenberg (1966) the grouped languages of the NILO-SAHARAN phylum are subclassified in three small groups (which include up to a half-dozen or so languages in each group), namely KOMAN, MABAN, and SAHARAN, and in a fourth major group, CHARI-NILE, which is bifurcated into CENTRAL SUDANIC and EASTERN SUDANIC.

Bender (1971) does not have a CHARI-NILE group; instead, he reclassifies some of the EASTERN SUDANIC languages and language groups of CHARI-NILE directly under NILO-SAHARAN, thereby obtaining three coordinate lists of languages and language groups for the restricted part of NILO-SAHARAN which he treats — namely, BERTA, Kunama, and his expanded KOMAN (q.v.), which includes Gumuz, Koma, and northern Mao, as well as Turkana, NILOTIC, and BEIER-DIDINGA of EASTERN SUDANIC.

Further details of classificatory differences are noted in the discussion of the grouped languages or families of the NILO-SAHARAN phylum.

CHARI-NILE (q.v., see also CENTRAL SUDANIC and EASTERN SUDANIC)

1. Fur = Fora = Forduŋga = Furawi = Konjara = Kondjara = Kungara. 171,000.

Sudan, Dar Fur, extending into Chad (1,000).

KOMAN (q.v.)
MABAN (q.v.)
SAHARAN (q.v.)

2. Songhai = Sonrai = Soñay. Ds. also Dendi, Zarma = Dyerma. 400,000. Nigeria, Niger, Mali, Upper Volta, Dahomey.

AFFILIATION. Some of the languages classified by Greenberg (1966) and Bender (1971) as NILO-SAHARAN are classified by others either as AFROASIATIC or as NIGER-CONGO (under NIGER-KORDOFANIAN). Greenberg concedes that some of the languages now classified under NIGER-CONGO might be related to languages now classified under NILO-SAHARAN, but these (eastern languages) "if related at all [to NIGER-CONGO languages], display a connection of a more remote nature" (p. 6). Fodor regards Greenberg's NILO-SAHARAN to be the least convincing of the four maximum classes postulated for Africa.

NUPE-GBARI

GROUPING. Williamson (1972b) suggests that Igbirra (3) is sufficiently divergent from the other languages listed below that it should not be included in a subgroup with them, but rather forms a separate, coordinate subgroup of KWA.
1. Gade = Kyedye.
2. Gbari = Gwari = Gwali = Goali. Ds. Gbari Gyenguen = Matai = Gangan, Gbari Kangye = Kwange, Gbari Yamma Gayegi, Gbari Yamma of Paiko. 155,000. Nigeria, north of Niger-Benue confluence in Zaria, Benue, and Niger Provinces.
3. Igbir(r)a = Ebira = Kwotto. Ds. Igbira-Hima = Ihima = Okene Igbira, Igbira-Igu = Bira = Biri = Egu = Ika = Igbira-Rehe, Igbira-Panda = Kwotto = Igbira-Lele = Umaisha Igbira. 150,000. Igbirra Division, Kwara State, and Akoko-Edo Division, Mid-Western State, Nigeria.
4. Nupe. Ds. also Bassa-Nge = Ibara, Dido = Ganagana, Ebe = Abewa = Agalati = Anupe, Kakanda = Akanda, Kupa = Gupa = Kupanchi; Kakanda may be a separate language, rather than a dialect of Nupe. Trs. Batachi, Beni = Bini, Benu, Cakpang, Ebagi, Gbedye, Gwagba, Kusopa, Nupe Zam. 325,000. Nigeria, both banks of the Niger in Ilorin and Niger provinces.

AFFILIATION. Member of KWA phylum.

NŪRISTĀNĪ = KAFIRI

GROUPING. Both the NURISTANI group of languages and the DARDIC group have been reclassified in recent years; both had been classed as IRANIAN by Griersen 1903–1927. The DARDIC languages are now grouped among INDIC languages, while NURISTANI has been given the status of a separate branch within INDO-IRANIAN, coordinate with INDIC and IRANIAN (Morgenstierne 1961; Strand 1973).

1. Aṣkun = Ashkun(d). Ds. Aṣhū̃ṛu-vēri (including Kolatā, Titin Bajaygəl), Gṛamsõ̃ṛa-vīri, Sõ̃ṛu-vīri = Wāmāi. Afghanistan.

2. Kalaṣa-alā = Waigalī = Wai-alā = Waigeli. Ds. Čima-Nišey-alā (including Čima, Nišeygrām in the lower Wāygal Valley)’, Varǰan-alā (including Amešdeš, J̌amač, Vaygal, Veligal, Ẓönčigal, in the upper Wāygal Valley). Afghanistan.

3. Kati = Bašgalī. Ds. Kamvíri (4,000; spoken by the Kom tribe in Kómbrom = Kāmdeš and other villages; by the Kṣto tribe, in Kṣtõ̃rn = Kuštoz [Lamérṭiviri is a dialect variant spoken by Kṣto tribesmen in the settlements of Lameróṭ = Lagorbats and Baḍrə̀γel on the Čitrāl = Kunar River in Pakistan]); Katə́viri (including Eastern Katə́viri in Bɾagə́maṭol and other villages in the upper Landay Sin basin, and a few enclaves in Čitrāl State, Pakistan; Western Katə́viri [including the subdialects of Ktívi = Kantivo, Kulám, Péruk = Papruk, and Ř̃amgə́l]); Mumvíri (in the villages of Mumórm, Maŋgúl, and Saskũ̃; a transitional dialect between Kamvíri and Katə́viri). Afghanistan, Pakistan.

4. Nangalāmi = Nigalāmi. D. also Gṛangal = Gṍgol. Afghanistan.

5. Tregāmī = Gambīrī. Ds. Gambīr, Kaṭār. Afghanistan. Perhaps a dialect of Kalaṣa-alā (2).

6. Wasi-weri = Prasun = Pārūnī = Veron. Ds. Central (in the villages of Sēč, Ücü, Ušüt, and Zumū = Cucum = Satsumgrom); Lower (in the village of Uṣüt); Upper (in the village of Ṣupu). Afghanistan.

AFFILIATION. Member of INDO-IRANIAN within INDO-EUROPEAN.

NYULNYULAN

GROUPING. Spoken in the coastal area surrounding King Sound and as far south as Broome, Australia (Nekes and Worms 1953).

1. Jauor = Yauor = Yauera = Djauor.

2. Nyigina = Njikena = Njigina = Nyigini.

3. Nyulnyul = Nyul-Nyul = Njul-Njul = Niol-Niol = Nyolnyol. Ds. also Bard = Barda = Bardi, Djaberdjaber = Djaberadjaber, Djaui = Towahi = Tohawi = Ewenu = Ewenyoon, Djugun = Djukan = Jukan, Ngormbal, Nimanbur = Nimanboru.

4. Warwa = Warrwa = Warwai = Warrawai.

AFFILIATION. Member of AUSTRALIAN macro-phylum.

OCEANIC = EASTERN AUSTRONESIAN

GROUPING. Though no evidence has been published to show that EASTERN OCEANIC forms a group apart from other members of OCEANIC, it is generally agreed that POLYNESIAN and certain languages of eastern Melanesia are affiliated as an EASTERN OCEANIC division; however, since comparative work has been attempted for only a few of the many possible candidates for affiliation in eastern Melanesia, the exact membership of EASTERN OCEANIC is still uncertain (Grace 1959, Biggs 1965).

Grace's (1955, 1968) NEW HEBRIDES-BANKS subgroup is more inclusive than EASTERN OCEANIC, since it includes the languages of SOUTHERN NEW HEBRIDES and NORTHWESTERN NEW HEBRIDES as well as those of MICRONESIA; in another respect it is less inclusive, since the languages of the southeastern Solomons are excluded.

Milke (1958) excludes from such a group as EASTERN OCEANIC the languages of the Banks and Torres Islands, and those of the southeastern Solomons, but adds to Grace's list of EASTERN OCEANIC languages those of the ADMIRALTIES and WESTERN ISLANDS, NEW CALEDONIA, and the LOYALTY ISLANDS.

Dyen's (1965) HEONESIAN groups Motu of New Guinea with EASTERN OCEANIC languages. Dyen excludes the NUCLEAR MICRONESIAN languages from HEONESIAN in his main classification, but adds that the percentages of lexical items shared by one of the MICRONESIAN languages (Gilbertese) with two members of HEONESIAN (Fijian and POLYNESIAN) would argue for the inclusion of MICRONESIAN in HEONESIAN. Whether or not MICRONESIAN languages are to be included in EASTERN OCEANIC, they are more closely related to EASTERN OCEANIC languages than to those of other OCEANIC subgroups.

Grace (1955) tentatively assigns OCEANIC languages to 19 subgroups in a classification in which each of the groups designated 'Geographic' below forms more than one subgroup, as do LOYALTY ISLANDS and EASTERN OCEANIC. Milke's (1958) subclassification of OCEANIC, based on the reflexes of Proto Oceanic *1, *d, and *R in the daughter languages, yields three subgroups, one of which is equivalent to EASTERN (with the modifications noted above), one of which encompasses the languages of the southeastern Solomons, and the third of which adds the AUSTRONESIAN languages of Geelvink and Humboldt Bays in West Irian (West New Guinea) to the remaining OCEANIC languages. Grace (1970) agrees that some of the languages of West Irian belong to OCEANIC, namely, the SARMIC languages. Dyen classifies SARMIC with or perhaps within MOLUCCAN.

The following groups are treated in separate articles:

ADMIRALTY-WESTERN ISLANDS (GEOGRAPHIC)
BISMARCK ARCHIPELAGO
LOYALTY ISLANDS
MICRONESIAN = NUCLEAR MICRONESIAN
NEW CALEDONIA
NORTHEAST NEW GUINEA (GEOGRAPHIC)
NORTHWESTERN NEW HEBRIDES
SOUTHERN NEW HEBRIDES
EASTERN OCEANIC
PAPUA (GEOGRAPHIC)
SANTA CRUZ
SARMIC
NORTHWESTERN AND CENTRAL SOLOMONS (GEOGRAPHIC)

AFFILIATION. Member of AUSTRONESIAN.

EASTERN OCEANIC

GROUPING. The POLYNESIAN languages are clearly subgrouped with Fijian

(Grace 1959, Pawley 1970); the earlier inclusion of Rotuman in the POLYNESIAN-Fijian subgroup is questioned (Dyen 1965, Biggs 1965, Grace 1967) on the grounds that many of Rotuman's lexical resemblances represent, instead, recent Polynesian borrowings. Goodenough (1961) argues for the inclusion of Nakanai (and, by implication, the rest of the WILLAUMEZ languages of NORTHEAST NEW GUINEA) in the POLYNESIAN-Fijian subgroup. Lau (7, below) and Toqabaita (13) form another subgroup, LAUIC (Dyen 1965).

Dyen's HEONESIAN includes all of those languages listed below which were used in his comparisons (languages numbered 2, 3, 4, 5, 7, 8, 9, 11, 13, below, and POLYNESIAN). All those languages which are definite members of HEONESIAN — except Motu of New Guinea — clearly belong to EASTERN OCEANIC.

The following list begins with those languages for which membership in EASTERN OCEANIC seems certain (1–15); the remainder are organized by geographical groups to include other languages in the area which might be expected to be EASTERN OCEANIC on the basis of their apparent close relationship to languages demonstrably within it.

1. Arosi. D. also Wango. San Cristoval (San Cristobal), southern Solomons, 10°41'S 161°50'E.

2. Bauro. D. also Haununu. San Cristoval, southern Solomons, 10°36'S 161°50'E.

3. Efate. Ds. Eastern = Eton, Havana Harbor; Northern = Lelepa; Southern = Erakor. 3,467. Efate Island, central New Hebrides, 18°02'S 168°29'E.

4. Fijian. Ds. Eastern = eastern Vitu Levu Island, eastern Kadavu, Vanua Levu, Lau, Lomaiviti, Taveumi and Bau Islands; Western = western Vitu Levu, western Kadavu, Waya and Yasawa Islands, with additional variation within and between islands; Bauan is standard and the variety which is written (Schütz 1963, Pawley 1970). 202,176 (1966). Fiji Islands, 16°05'S–19°15'S, 177°00'E–179°40'W.

5. Kerebuto. D. also Baranago. A fraction of the total population of 15,000 (1950). Guadalcanal Island, southern Solomons, 9°30'S 160°00'E.

6. Kwara?ae = Fiu. 7,000. Malaita Island, southern Solomons, 9°00'S 161°00'E.

7. Lau. Ds. also Ngongosila, Saufa. 3,500. Northern Malaita Island, Solomons, 9°00'S 161°00'E.

8. Mahaga. A fraction of the total population of 6,000 (1956). Santa Isabel (Ysabel) Island, central Solomons, 8°00'S 159°00'E.

9. Mota. 350 (1960). Mota (Sugarloaf) Island, Banks Islands, 13°45'S 167°38'E.

10. Nggela = Gela. Nggela Islands, 9°00'S 160°10'E, Florida Island, 9°05'S 160°15'E, and northern Guadalcanal, 9°30'S 160°00'E, southern Solomons.

POLYNESIAN (q. v.)

11. Rotuman. Rotuma, 12°30'S/177°05'E.

12. Sa?a = Apae?aa. 5,000. Malaita Island, southern Solomons, 9°00'S 161°00'E.

13. Toqabaita = To?abaita. Ds. also Baelelea, Baengu. Northern Malaita Island, southern Solomons, 9°00'S 161°00'E.

14. Uluwa. Uluwa (Contrariete) Island, southern Solomons. 9°46'S 161°57'E.

15. Vaturanga. Guadalcanal, southern Solomons. 9°30'S 160°00'E.

EFATE-EPI (geographical). Languages of Efate Island, 18°02'S 168°28'E, Epi Island, 16°59'S 168°29'E, and the small islands in between, including Efate (3, above), are grouped together by Capell (1962a). Languages (16), (17), and (20) are sometimes treated as a single language called Epi. Recent fieldworkers from the University of Hawaii report that Tongoa (21) may be a dialect of 'Epi'; Capell (1962a) considers Tongoa to be "essentially" the same language as Efate (3).

    16. Baki. 200–500. Epi Island.

    17. Bieri = Bieria. 50–125. Epi Island.

    18. Makura. 1150. Makura, Tongoa, Tongariki, Buninga Islands.

    19. Mari. 50–125. Epi Island.

    20. Tasiko = Lemaroro. Ds. also Bierebo, Lamanu, Lewo = Levo = Laëvo = Maluba, Nikaura, Tasiriki. 1100–2500. Epi Island.

    21. Tongoa. Ds. also Buninga, Emua, Metaso, Nguna, Paunangis, Sesake. 2,250. Spoken on small islands of the same names between Efate and Epi, and on Efate.

    Livara (?); Pango (?) Efate Island.

GUADALCANAL (Geographical). Capell (1962a) regards all the languages of Guadalcanal in the southern Solomons (9°30'S 160°00'E), except Marau (44, below), as forming a single group with the following subdivisions. 13,000 total (1960).

    A. (Includes 15, above.)

        22. Gari.

        23. Gua-Hua.

        24. Malango.

        25. Poleo.

    B

        26. Aola.

        27. Datovitu.

        28. Gambata.

        29. Lengo.

    C

        30. Birao.

        31. Longgu.

        32. Moli.

    D

        33. Koo.

        34. Talisi = Tolo.

    35. Inakona.

    Sugu = Suhu ?

MALAITA (Geographical). With (6), (7), (12), (13) and (14) above, Capell subgroups the following languages spoken on or near Malaita Island, 9°00'S 161°00'E.

    A. (Including 7, 13).

        36. Dai. 143.

        37. Malu?u. 4,000.

        38. Takwa.

B

    39. Areare. D. also Doria. 15,000.

    40. I?iaa. 1,000.

    41. Kwaio = Koio. D. also Uru. 4,000.

    42. Kwarekwareo. 1,000.

    43. Langalanga. 2,500.

    44. Marau. Guadalcanal Island.

C (Includes 12, 14).

    45. Oroha.

    46. Ugi. Ugi Island, 10°30′S 161°40′E.

  47. Fataleka. 3,000. Subgrouped with (6), above.

NORTHERN NEW HEBRIDES (Geographical). Grace (1955) groups the languages of the Banks and Torres Islands with those of the northern New Hebrides. These do not form a subgroup in Dyen's (1965) classification, since the two languages of the area which were included in Dyen's comparisons (Mota, 9, above, and Paama, 86, below) were grouped only at his highest level, AUSTRONESIAN. Capell (1962a) places the languages of the Banks and Torres Islands, Aurora, Leper's, and the northern end of Pentecost Island in one subgroup and the rest in another.

    A. Except as noted, all languages in this subgroup are spoken on the Banks Islands, 13°38′S 167°20′E, of which specific islands are noted in brackets.

    48. Alo Teqel.

    49. Bun.

    50. Gog = Gaua. [Gaua.] Total population 370 (1960).

    51. Lakon. [Gaua.]

    52. Lamalanga = North Raga = Katvenua = Qatvenua = Bwatvenua = Vunmarana. 1500 (1959). Northern Pentecost (Raga) Island, 16°05′S 168°28′E, now also southern Aurora Island, 15°17′S 168°16′E.

    53. Leha.

    54. Leon.

    55. Lomrig.

    56. Lusa.

    57. Luwai.

    58. Maewo = Tanoriki. Ds., or closely related dying languages, Arata, Bangoro, Lotora. 838. Aurora (Maewo) Island, 15°17′S 168°16′E.

    59. Malingo.

    60. Merig. 75.

    61. Merlav. 800 (1959). [Mera Lava (Star Peak).]

    62. Mosin. [Vanua Lava.] 500 total population (1960).

    63. Motlav. 800. [Saddle.]

    64. Omba = Walurigi. Ds. also Duindui (most divergent), Lolsiwoi = Lolokara, Lombaha = Lobaha = Lolopwepwe, Longana, Tavalavola. 5,356 (1959). Leper's (Oba, Omba) Island 15°25′S 167°50′E.

    65. Pak. [Vanua Lava.] 500 total population (1960).

    66. Qei.

67. Quatpe.
68. Retan.
69. Rowa.
70. Sasar. [Vanua Lava.] 500 total population (1960).
71. Tasmate.
72. Tekel = Teqel. Over 107. [Ureparapara, 107, and Vanua Lava.]
73. Togla.
74. Tolay.
75. Torres. Ds. Hiw, Lo, Toga, 290. Torres Islands, 13°15'S 166°36'E.
76. Ulrata.
77. East Ureparapara. 110 (1960). [Ureparapara.]
78. Vatrat.
79. Veverau.
80. Volow = Valuva = Valuga. 36. [Saddle.]
81. Vuras = Vureas = Avreas. [Vanua Lava.] 500 total population (1960).

B

82. Central Ambryn. Ds. Fanting, Lonwolwol. 4,200 total for Central, North, and South Ambryn. Ambryn (Ambrin) Island, 16°28'S 158°17'E.
83. North Ambryn. Ds. Magam, Olal. North Ambryn is more closely related to South Raga (88) than to the other languages on Ambryn
84 South Ambryn = Baiap. Ambryn Island.
85. Southeast Ambryn. Ds. Craig Cove, Tavaik. Several hundred Craig Cove speakers in Maat village on Efate Island. May be a dialect of (82) or (84).
86. Paama = Pauma. 3,500. Paama (Pauuma, Lamenu) Island, 16°29'S 168°15'E.
87. Central Raga. Ds. Bwatnapi, Loltong, Melsisi. Pentecost (Raga) Island, 16°05'S 168°28'E. Total population of Pentecost: 5,600.
88. South Raga. Ds. Lolatavola, Ninebulo, Ponorwal. Pentecost Island.

In addition to (1) and (2), above, the remaining language of San Cristoval may also belong to EASTERN OCEANIC:

89. Kahua. Ds. also Anganiwai, Tawarafa, Wanoni = Narihua. San Cristoval, 10°41'S 161°50'E and adjacent Santa Ana (Owa Raha) and Catalina (Owa Riki) Islands.

AFFILIATION. The EASTERN OCEANIC subgroup is a subgroup of the OCEANIC subgroup of AUSTRONESIAN (Grace); to the extent that EASTERN OCEANIC overlaps with 'HEONESIAN,' it belongs to the MALAYO-POLYNESIAN group of AUSTRONESIAN (Dyen).

OK

GROUPING. Wurm (1971c) divides OK into two subgroups: MOUNTAIN, consisting of languages numbered (1), (2), (6), (8), (9), (11), (12), (14), (15), (16), and LOWLAND, consisting of languages numbered (3), (4), (5), (7), (10), (13), (17). Most of Greenberg's (1971b) language names for OK differ from Wurm's, but one of Greenberg's subgroups includes Telefol (14, below) and another includes two of the names in Wurm's LOWLAND, so Greenberg may have essentially the same two subgroups as Wurm. However, Greenberg includes Wurm's DUMUT subgroup of AWYU as a third subgroup. Central New Guinea in the eastern border area of West Irian, Western District of Papua, and Sepik District, Australian New Guinea.

1. Bimin. 1,000.
2. Faiwol = Faiwolmin. 300.
3. Iwur = Iwoer. 1,000.
4. Northern Kati = Niinati. 8,000.
5. Southern Kati = Metomka. 4,000.
6. Kawol. 500.
7. Kowan. 500.
8. Mianmin. 1,500.
9. Ngalum. 15,000.
10. Ninggirum. D. also Kativa. 3,500.
11. Setaman. 'Small'.
12. Sibil. Over 3,000.
13. Upper Tedi. 500.
14. Telefol = Telefool = Teleefool = Telefomin. 4,100.
15. Tifal. Over 3,000.
16. Wagarabai = Suganga. 500.
17. Yonggom = Iongom. 2,000.
Aran (?), Digul (?), Western Donaldson (?), Upper Fly (?), Kandam (?), Marapka (?), Lower Muiu (?), Muju (?), Upper Muju (?), Eastern Tedi (?) (these were grouped with Upper Tedi (13) and Yonggom (17) by Greenberg); Plain Country (?), Unkia (?) (these were grouped with Telefol (14) by Greenberg).

AFFILIATION. Member of CENTRAL AND SOUTH NEW GUINEA.

OMOTIC

GROUPING. The OMOTIC family has been recently identified as being separate from, rather than a part of CUSHITIC (q. v.). Tucker and Bryan (1966) revised their earlier classification (1956) of CUSHITIC by distinguishing CUSHITIC from PARTIALLY CUSHITIC; under the latter they included languages which are grouped below under WEST OMOTIC. So also, Moreno (1940) pointed out a classificatory cleavage within his CUSHITIC; he grouped separately some of those languages which are classified below in a separate OMOTIC family, following Bender (1971) and Fleming (1969, 1972).

EAST OMOTIC = AROID = BAKO. Ethiopia, east of Omo river.
1. Ari = Aro = Are = Ara = Bak(k)o = Bak(k)a = Bio = Shankillinya. Ds. = Trs. also Gozza, Ubamer. 32,000.
2. Banna = Beshada = Hamer = Amar = Hamar = (H)amar Kok(k)e = Hamerkoke = Nkamar. 22,500.
3. Biya = Biye ?
4. Dime. 2,000.

5. Karo = Kerre. 600. Perhaps mutually intelligible with Banna (2, above). Gayi ?

WEST OMOTIC

JANJERO-KEFOID-OMETA-GIMIRA. Bender (1971) classifies these in three coordinate subgroups: (a) Janjero (9); (b) KEFOID: NORTH (14, 18) and SOUTH (11, 15); (c) OMETO-GIMIRA: GIMERA (7, 17) and OMETO — OMETO = OMATE = WAMATE, which is subgrouped further into Kachama (10); ORTHODOX OMETO: Male (13), Basketo (6), NUCLEAR (16, 19), and LACUSTRINE (12, 20). Chara (8) probably belongs to OMETO, but its position is not yet clear.

6. Basketo = Mesketo. 9,000.
7. Bencho = Bienescio = Bienesho = Benesho = Gimir(r)a = Ghimir(r)a. D. also Mieru.
8. Chara = C'ara. 1,000 ?
9. Janjero = Jenjero = Giangero = Janjerinya = Janjor = Jangor = Yangaro = Yemma = Yamna = Yemna = Yämma = Yemsa = Zingero. 1,000 ?
10. Kachama = K'ac'ama = Kacama = Haruro = Gatzamba. 500 ?
11. Kefa = Ka(f)fa = Kafficho = Kefinya = Caffa = Caffina = Coffino = Kafico = Kafice = Gomaro. D. also Bosha = Garo.
12. Koyra = Bad(d)itu = Kwera = Nuna = Amarro. D. Gidicho = Harro. 5,000.
13. Male. 12,000.
14. Southern Mao = Busashi = Busasi = Anfillo. 1,000.
15. Mocho = Mochinya = Shekka.
16. Oyda. 3,000 ?
17. She = Sce = Kaba.
18. Shinasha = Scinascia = Shat = Zet = Bworo. 4,000.
19. Walamo = Wolamo = Vollamo = Wolataita = Wolaitsa = Walait(t)a = Wollaminya. Ds. also Dache = Gerese; Dorze = Dorzinya (3,000); Gemu; Gofa; Kullo = Dauro = Dawro = Dawaro = Ometay, including Konta, Kucha = Cucia = Kosha = Kusha = Kasha = Koysha (82,000); Zala. Trs. Balta, Borodda, Chencha Ganta, Otschollo, Ub(b)a. 908,000.
20. Zayse = Zaysse = Zaysinya. Ds. Zergulla, Zergullinya. 21,000.

MAJOID

21. Maji = Magi = Majinya = Twoyu = Diz(z)u = Dizi. 18,000 ?
22. Nao = Na'o. 5,000 ?
23. Sheko = Sciacco = Tschako = Dizu = Shak(k)o. 23,000 ?
Doko (?); Dollo (?); Gamo (?); Kaba (?)

AFFILIATION. Member of AFROASIATIC.

Ördek-Burnu. Known from inscriptions in Syria dating from the ninth century B.C.

AFFILIATION. None known positively; comparisons with SEMITIC are unconvincing (Meillet and Cohen 1952).

ORIOMO RIVER = EASTERN TRANS-FLY

GROUPING. Miriam (5, below), included in this group by Greenberg (1971b), is treated as a separate, coordinate subgroup of CENTRAL AND SOUTHERN by Wurm (1971c). Eastern third of the area between the Fly Delta and Estuary and the south coast, Western District, Papua, and Torres Strait islands.
1. Bine = Kunini = Masingle = Masingara. 1,365.
2. Gidra = Oriomo. 1,565.
3. Gizra = Gijara ? 547.
4. Jibu.
5. Miriam = Mer. 500. Several islands in Torres Strait.

AFFILIATION. Member of CENTRAL AND SOUTH NEW GUINEA.

OTO-MANGUEAN = MACRO-OTOMANGUEAN = OLMECA-OTOMANGUE

GROUPING. Six families (each treated in separate articles): CHINANTECAN, MANGUEAN, MIXTECAN, OTOMIAN, POPOLOCAN, ZAPOTECAN; and one ungrouped language, Amuzgo, comprise OTO-MANGUEAN.

Amuzgo was classified as MIXTECAN until Longacre (1966) demonstrated that it was no closer to the MIXTECAN languages than to some of the other OTO-MANGUEAN families. He concluded that it should be classified separately within OTO-MANGUEAN.

Gudschinsky (1959) grouped POPOLOCAN and MIXTECAN in her reconstruction of Proto-Popotecan = OLMECAN, but Longacre (1961) argues that these two are not necessarily more closely related to each other than to any of the other families. Swadesh (1960) would add Huave to OTO-MANGUEAN while excluding CHINANTECAN and MANGUEAN and changing the name to 'OTO-HUAVE'; Longacre (1961) argues against this reshuffling; see also Bartholomew (1965).

With the exception of the MANGUEAN languages, which Longacre suggests were spoken by a group who emigrated southward and became separated, the OTO-MAN-GUEAN languages are all spoken in a concentrated area centering in the state of Oaxaca, Mexico, and extending into the states of Guerrero, Puebla, and Veracruz.

1. Amuzgo. 8,000 (1930). States of Guerrero and Oaxaca, Mexico.

AFFILIATION. Among the phyla represented by families of languages spoken in Middle America, OTO-MANGUEAN is unique by virtue of being the only phylum that is represented exclusively in Middle America. The other phyla represented in Middle America are in part — often for the most part — also represented by languages spoken north of Mexico or south of Panama Canal — or both, in the case of PENUTIAN.

OTOMIAN = OTOMI-PAME

GROUPING. The OTOMIAN languages are classified into three branches of two languages each: a NORTHERN BRANCH comprising the languages numbered (1) and (6);

a CENTRAL BRANCH comprising (3) and (5); and a SOUTHERN BRANCH comprising (2) and (4).

1. Chichimeca-Jonaz = Chichimeco = Chichimeca = Meco = Jonaz. 800 (1956). State of Guanajuato, Mexico.
2. Matlatzinca = Pirinda. Less than 2,000 (1940). State of Mexico, Mexico.
3. Mazahua. 80,000 (1940). States of Mexico and Michoacán, Mexico.
4. Ocuiltec = Ocuilteca = Ocuilteco = Atzinca. Few speakers. San Juan Acingo area of State of Mexico, Mexico.
5. Otomi = Othomi. Ds. Ixtenco (State of Tlaxcala, Mexico), Northeastern = Sierra (States of Hidalgo, Veracruz, and Puebla, Mexico), Northwestern (90,000, State of Hidalgo and adjacent areas of Mexico and Queretaro, Mexico), Southwestern (State of Mexico, Mexico). 215,000 (1930).
6. Pame = (Pame-)chichimeca. Ds. North, South. About 2,500 (1947). States of San Luis Potosi and Hidalgo.

AFFILIATION. Member of OTO-MANGUEAN phylum.

PALAIHNIHAN = ACHUMAWI-ATSUGEWI

GROUPING. The fact that Atsugewi speakers are bilingual in Achumawi (but not conversely) may have influenced the early California classification (Achumai-Atsugewi as a closely related branch within a 'SHASTA-ACHOMAWI' family). More recent work by Olmstead (1959) has shown that the PALAIHNIHAN family has only two members — (1) and (2), below — and that Shasta of the SHASTAN family bears no special relationship within HOKAN to PALAIHNIHAN. Haas (1963) does not accept Olmstead's thesis in quite such strong terms; Shasta may still be somewhat closer to PALAIHNIHAN than to other groups in HOKAN (cf. Olmstead (1965) for a reply to Haas' remarks).

1. Achumawi = Achomawi = Pit(t) River. 10 to 100. California, northeast.
2. Atsugewi. Fewer than 10. California, northeast.

AFFILIATION. Member of HOKAN phylum.

PALAUNG-WA = SALWEEN

GROUPING. The PALAUNG-WA affiliation as listed here excludes the KHMUIC (q. v.) languages classified as an eastern branch of PALAUNG-WA by Pinnow (1959). The languages now classified as PALAUNG-WA are spoken primarily in Burma and Thailand. There were 176,000 speakers of these languages in Burma in 1931. Some groups labelled Lawa (5, below) in Thailand are PALAUNG-WA; some are not, and not even MON-KHMER, according to Thomas and Headley (1970).

1. Angku. Ds. also Amok = Hsen-Hsum, Monglwe = Loi = Tailoi of Mong-Lwe.
2. Danaw.
3. Kawa-Yunnan.
4. Khamed.

5. Lawa. Ds. Bo Luang, Mape, Pa Pao = Chaobon, Umpai. 4,000. Thailand.
6. Mang = Mang U'. 700. Lai Châu Province, North Vietnam.
7. Palaung = Rumai. Ds. Darang, Manton, Nam Hsan, Shan states. 139,000. Burma.
8. Riang-lang = Riang = Yang Sek = Yang Wan Kun. Burma.
9. Wa. Ds. En, Praok, Son, Tailoi = Wa-kut, Vu = Wa-Vu, Wa = Kentung. Burma.

AFFILIATION. Member of MON-KHMER.

PALEOSIBERIAN = HYPERBOREAN

This name is a cover term for three language families and a language isolate found in the Paleosiberian culture area in Siberia, namely: CHUKCHEE-KAMCHATKAN, Gilyak, YENISEIAN, YUKAGHIR (q. v.). An additional family, ESKIMO-ALEUT, is included by Soviet scholars but not by American scholars. Jakobson (1942) and Worth (1963) doubt that the Asiatic families are related even in a phylum linguistic sense; scholars cited by Jakobson claim genetic connections for each of the four families to various families outside the Paleosiberian area, as ESKIMO-ALEUT, ALTAIC, SINO-TIBETAN, and the Ainu language.

PAMA-MARIC

GROUPING. Wurm (1971b) makes a number of revisions in the sudgrouping of O'Grady, Wurm and Hale (1966) and O'Grady, Voegelin and Voegelin (1966); e.g., realigning the dialect constituents of a number of languages and expanding the YARA subgroup to include the languages of the earlier ATHERTON-PAMA subgroup and what was earlier thought to be one language of the MARI subgroup. Breen (1971) proposes further realignment of dialects and sets up a new subgroup, KAPU, which consists of the MARI subgroup, some languages from DIERIC (a subgroup of PAMA-NYUNGAN), and Janda, which Wurm treats as unsubgrouped in PAMA-NYUNGAN. In addition to the subgroups listed below, Wurm lists four unsubgrouped languages (numbered 1, 2, 3, and 6, below).

The PAMA-MARIC languages are spoken in the northeast tip of Arnhem Land, the Torres Strait Islands, the Cape York Peninsula, central and southern Queensland, and the north central boundary of New South Wales, Australia.

1. Koko-Ya'o. Eastern portion of the Cape York Peninsula. Wurm (1971b) questions whether this is a separate subgroup by itself.
2. Kunggara = Koonkurri = Ungorri = Gulf Pama. From Karumba north to Delta Downs; inland to Midlothian and Lotus Vale.
3. Lamalama = Bay Pama. Port Stewart.

MARI. Central Queensland and along the coast between Repulse Bay and Broad Sound.
4. Koa = Goa = Guwa = Goamulgo.
5. Mandandanji. Ds. also Barada, Barna, Biria = Birigaba = Breeaba, Gia = Kia = Bumbarra = Bumburra, Iningai = Muttaburra = Moothaburra = Mootaburra = Tateburra = Thararrabura, Jagalingu = Wakelbara, Jam-

bina = Yambeena, Jangga, Jimun, Jirandali = Yerrunthully = Irendely = Dalebura = Pooroga, Juipera = Juwibara, Kabelbara = Kabalbara = Kaiabara = Yettiṃaralla, Kairi = Khararya, Kangulu = Kanoloo, Karing-bal = Kaingbul = Karranbal, Koamu = Guamu = Kuam = Kaombal, Kongabula = Ongabula = Khungabula, Kunggari = Gungar = Kungeri = Kungri = Ungorri, Kunja, Kuungkari = Koonkerri = Kungeri = Koon-gerri = Yangeberra = Yankibura, Marnganji = Murngain = Murgoin = Murgoan, Mian = Munkibura = Munkieburra, Nguro, Pitjara = Bidjera = Peechera, Wadjabangai = Kun-Gait, Wadjelang = Wadjalang, Wangan, Wiri = Wierdi = Widi.

6. Mbarabam. Previously considered unrelated to other Australian languages, now shown to be closely related to adjacent PAMA-MARIC languages (Wurm 1971b, Dixon 1966a, b).

EASTERN PAMA. Queensland.

7. Koko Bujundji. Annan River; south to Rossville; west to Annan-Normanby Divide.

8. Koko Imudji = Koko Yimidir = Kuku Yimidyi = Kokojimoji = Koko-yimidir. From the Annan and Endeavor rivers to the northern side of Cape Flattery.

9. Koko Jelandji = Kuku Yalanji = Kuku Yalandji = Kokoyellanji = Koko Yerlandji = Kokoyerlantji = Kokolerlantchi. Ds. also China Camp, Koko Bididji, Koko Walandja = Koko Katji (head of the East Normandby River; west to Dividing Range), Wulpura (headwaters of Daintree River). Head-waters of East Normandby River; at Kings Plains; south to headwaters of Daintree River.

10. Koko Yawa. Upper Hann and Kennedy rivers.

MIDDLE PAMA. Southern portion of Cape York Peninsula.

11. Kandju = Ka·ntyu = Kanju = Kandyu = Kantju = Kanyu = Karnju = Karntju = Karnyu = Karnu = Kamdhue.

12. Ombila = ʔumpila = Umpila = Ompeila = Ompela = Umpilo. Cape Sidmouth and north nearly to Night Island.

13. Taior = Ku·k Thayori = Kokkotaijari.

14. Wik Muminh. Inland from Aurukun.

15. Wikepa = Wikʔep = Wik Epa. Near Cape Keerweer.

16. Wikmean = Wik Meʔnh = Wik Mean.

17. Wikmunkan = Wik Mungkan = Wik Munkan. Inland from Edward River to Aurukon.

18. Wikngatara = Wik Ngathara = Wik Ngatara = Wik Alkan. D. also Wik Ngandjara. Between Archer and Holroyd rivers.

NORTHERN PAMA. From the northern side of the Watson River to the tip of the Cape York Peninsula.

19. Alngith = Laynngith. D. also Linngithig.

20. Aritinngithig. Head of the Hey River.

21. Awngthim. Ds. Mamngayt = Mamngayth, Nra?angith = Ntra'ngith = Ntrawa'ngayth, Tjanngayth, as opposed to Nrwa?a. The mouth of the Emblay and Mission rivers.
22. Jinwun = Yinwum. South of Moreton on the Batavia River and west to Cox Creek.
23. Mbeiwum = Mbiywom = Kok Mbewam. Middle and upper Watson River and on Myall Creek.
24. Mpalitjan. D. also Lotiga = Luthig = Okara. Middle and upper Ducie area and west to Cox Creek.
25. Nggoth = Ŋkoṯ = Ngkoth. Between the Embley and Hey rivers south of their junction.
26. Otati = Oradhi = Uradhi = Wotati = Wutati = Wotadi. D. also Jathai-kana = Yaraikana. From the tip of Cape York Peninsula south to the Dalhunty River.

SOUTHERN PAMA. Southwestern position of the Cape York Peninsula.
27. Aghu Tharnggala.
28. Ogondyan.

WESTERN PAMA. Southern west coast of Cape York Peninsula.
29. Koko Mindjan = Kokominjen = Kokomindjin = Kokomandjoen. Ds. Jir Joront = Yir? Yoront, Koko Yak, Yir Thangedl, Yir Tjutjam.
30. Koko Pera = Kokobera.
31. Kundjen. Ds. Uwayan, Uwinkan, Uwolkol = Ulkulu, as opposed to Oykangant.

YARA. Inland and along the coast of east central Queensland, opposite the Great Barrier Reef.
32. Bandjin = Bijai.
33. Ilba = Yukkaburra = Mungerra = Eneby = Pegulloburra. Ds. also Bindal, Jangaa, Juru, Koko Patun, Kutjala, Mitjamba = Kumbulmara, Tagalag = Targalag = Takalak = Dagalang, Wulgurukaba. On Cape River west to Dividing Range; north probably to Goldsborough.
34. Nawagi = Ngawigi. Southwest of Herbert River; principally on high ranges.
35. Wakaman = Warkaman = Warkeeman = Warkamin = Warkeemon. Ds. also Agwamin = Ak-Waumin = Wamin = Wommin = Waumin = Wawmin = Walamin, Bulaway, Djabugay = Tjapukai = Tjapukandi = Tjapukanja = Tjabogaitjandji = Tjabogaitjanji = Kokonjunkulu = Koko-nyungalo = Koko-Tjumbundji = Hileman = Njakali = Nyakali, Djangun, Djirbal = Djirubal = Tjirbal = Chirpalji, Djiru, Giramay = Keramai = Kiramay = Kiramai = Wombelbara, Gulngay = Gulngui, Mamu, Muluridji = Mulurutji = Mulu Rutʸi = Molloroiji = Mularitchee = Kokomoloroitji = Kakomoloroij, Ngadjan = Ngatjan = Ngadja = Ngachanji = Ngaitjandji, Wargamy = Warkamai, Warungu, Yidin = Idinji = Yiti·ntyi = Yukkaburra = Mungera = Eneby = Pegullobura = Ịdin, including Wudjar.

36. Yirgay. Ds. also **Gunggay, Madjay, Wanjur.**

AFFILIATION. Member of PAMA-NYUNGAN.

PAMA-NYUNGAN

GROUPING. Wurm (1971b) makes some revision in the subclasses of PAMA-NYUNGAN as given by O'Grady et al. (1966), and adds several previously unlisted languages. On the basis of recent survey work on Queensland languages, Breen (1971) proposes some revisions of the O'Grady-Wurm classifications. A major proposal is the introduction of KARNIC as a subgroup consisting of Arabana (2, below), Mitakudi (14), some of the DIERIC languages, and PITTAPITTIC. A second major proposal involves the PAMA-MARIC subgroup (q.v.). But Wurm's classification is reflected in the list of 20 (unnumbered) subgroups and 17 (numbered) languages given below.

PAMA-NYUNGAN languages are spoken across most of Western Australia, the central and southern parts of Northern Territory, Queensland (except for the northwest), South Australia, New South Wales, and Victoria.

1. *Aniwan. Previously considered unrelated to the other Australian languages, now classified as belonging in PAMA-NYUNGAN (Wurm 1971b). New South Wales.

2. Arabana = Arabuna = Arrabunna = Arrabonna = Arapani = Urapuna = Urabuna = Urabunna = Ngarabana = Rabuna = Wangarabana = Wong-kurapuna = Wangarabunna. Ds. also Wanggadjaga, Wongkamala = Wonka-mundla = Wangkamala, Wongkanguru = Wangkanguru = Wongkongaru = Wonkanguru = Wonkonguru = Ongkonguru = Wonkaooroo = Wonggongaru = Wonkongaru = Wonkaoora = Wongonooroo = Wonkongnuru = Wonkag-nurra = Wychinga. West side of Lake Eyre to Stuart Range, Macumba Creek to Coward Springs, South Australia.

ARANDIC (q.v.)
BANDJALANGIC (q.v.)

3. Bandjerang = Pangerang = Dadarawa = Bandjalang = Banjgaranj. New South Wales.

4. Bratauolung = Kurnic = Bradawulung = Bradowoolong = Brataualung = Bratanolung = Tarrawarracka = Tarrawarrachal. Ds. also Bidawal = Bidwill = Bidwelli = Biduelli = Beddiwell = Birdhawal = Birdawal = Bidhawal = Bidwell = Birtowall, Brabralung = Brabrawurung = Brabrolung = Brabrolong = Brabirawilung = Brabriwoolong = Tirthung = Tirtalowakani, Braiakaulung = Brajagawulung = Brayakaulung = Braiakolung = Brayakau, Krauatungu-lang = Kroatungolung = Grawadungalung = Krowithunkoolo, Tatungalung =Tatungolung = Tatoongolong = Tatunga = Bouliboul. Victoria.

DIERIC (q.v.)
DURUBULIC (q.v.)
GIABALIC (q.v.)

5. Jaitmathang = Jaithmathang = Jadjmadang = Yaitmathang = Balangamida

= Theddoramittung = Tharamirttong.= Theddora = Jandangara = Gunda-nora. D. also Duduruwa = Dhudhuroa Victoria.

6. Jalanga = Yalarnnga = Yellanga = Yelina. On Wills River from south of Duchess to Fort William; on Burke River north to Chatsworth; at Noranside and Buckingham Downs, Queensland.

7. Janda = Yanda. Head of the Hamilton River, north of Warenda, Queensland.

8. Kalibamu. Between Leichhardt River and Morning Inlet; inland to Floraville and Punchbowl.

9. Kalkutung = Kalkadung = Kalkatungu.

10. Karanti = Garundi. D. also Gudanda ? On the coast facing the Gulf of Carpen-taria immediately west of the Cape York Peninsula. Wurm (1971b) questions whether this and Kukaty (11, below) each represent a separate subgroup.

11. Kukaty. From Donor Hills north to Gulf of Carpentaria; at Inverleigh and Tempe Downs.

12. Kula = Darling = Kurnu = Guerno = Kornu = Cornu = Koono = Kuno. Ds. also Bagundji = Barkindji = Barkinji = Barkungee = Bahkunji = Bah-kunjy = Parkungi = Parkengee = Bakanji = Bakandi = Bargunji, Bandjigali, Barindji = Barrengee = Berriait, Danggali = Dangali = Danggadi = Tun-garlee = Tongaranka, Naualko = Ngunnhalgri = Unelgo = Bungyarlee = Milpulko = Mailpurlgu, Parundji = Paruindi = Paruinji = Parooinge = Barungi = Barinji = Bahroonjee = Barongee = Barrengee = Barunga, Wandji-walku = Wanyuwalgu = Wanjiwalku = Weyneubulkoo = Wonipalku = Wanyabalku = Wonjimalku = Pono, Wiljakali = Wilyakali = Wiljagali = Wilya = Willo. New South Wales.

KULINIC (q.v.)
KUMBAINGGARIC (q.v.)
MABUIAGIC (q.v.)
MAYAPIC = WANAMARIC (q.v.)

13. Mitaka = Mittaka. D. also ? Marrula = Marula = Marulta = Marunada = Marunuda. Southwestern corner of Queensland.

14. Mitakudi = Maithakari = Maidakadi = Maitakudi = Midhaga = Maytagoori = Mythugadi = Mythuggadi = Mythaguddi = Mittagurdi = Mitagurdi = Mitakoodi = Mitroogoordi. Cloncurry north to Canobie on Cloncurry River, Queensland.

15. Murawari = Morowari = Marawari = Murrawarri = Muruwurri = Moora-warree = Moorawarrie = Marraawarree = Murri. On border between New South Wales and Queensland.

MURNGIC (q.v.)
NARRINYERIC (q.v.)
PAMA-MARIC (q.v.)
SOUTHWEST PAMA-NYUNGAN (q.v.)
PITTAPITTIC (q.v.)
TANGKIC (q.v.)

WAKA-KABIC (q.v.)
WAKAYA-WARLUWARIC (q.v.)

16. Walangama. On Carron River and Walker Creek; west to Normanton; east to Croydon; south to Belmore Creek; north to Stirling. Queensland. Wurm (1971b) questions the status of this as a separate subgroup.

17. Warumungu = Waramanga = Waramungu. Northern Territory.

WIRADJURIC (q.v.)
YOTAYOTIC (q.v.)
YUIN-KURIC (q.v.)

AFFILIATION. Member of AUSTRALIAN macro-phylum.

SOUTHWEST PAMA-NYUNGAN = NYUNGIC

GROUPING. The ten subgroups listed below are treated in separate articles (q.v.). The two remaining languages, which are not subgrouped with each other or any others, are listed below. The SOUTHWEST PAMA-NYUNGAN languages are spoken in the greater part of Western Australia, in the western half of Northern Territory, and in South Australia extending west and south of Lake Eyre.

1. Juat = Nyunga. Ds. also Badimara, Balardong = Ballardong = Ballerdokking = Waljuk = Toode-nunjer, Kaneang, Koreng = Kuriny = Corine = Qualup, Minang = Minung = Meenung = Mearn-anger, Nanakati, Nyakinyaki = Njakinjaki = Kokar = Karkar = Kikkar, Pibelmen = Peoplemen = Bibulman = Bebleman = Meeraman = Nurram = Bibbulmun, Pinjarup = Pinjarra, Wadjuk = Whadjuk = Whajook = Yooard = Yooadda = Minalnjunga = Minnal-Yungar = Yungur, Wardandi = Wadarandee = Wardandie = Kardagur, Wiilman = Wheelman = Weel = Weal = Weil = Will = Jaburu, Wudjari = Wadjari = Widjara = Warangoo = Warranger = Warrangle = Ngokwurring = Ngokgurring = Nonga = Nunga = Yunga = Daran. South of 30°S and west of 122°E.

KANYARA
KARDU
NGARGA
NGAYARDA
NGUMBIN
MANTHARDA
MARNGU
MIRNINY
WATI

2. Wirangu = Wirrung = Wirrunga = Warrangoo = Nyaŋga = Njaŋga = Nangga.

YURA

AFFILIATION. Member of PAMA-NYUNGAN of the AUSTRALIAN macro-phylum.

PANO

GROUPING. Numbering perhaps 15,000 speakers, the PANOAN languages are divided into three geographic groups: CENTRAL (numbered 1–15 below), spoken around the Amazon headwaters in Peru and in adjacent Brazil; SOUTHEAST (numbered 16–20), spoken in the Madeira-Madre de Dios tributaries area of northeast Bolivia and adjacent Brazil; and SOUTHWEST (numbered 21–23), spoken in the Onambari River basin in Peru (Mason 1950). The SOUTHEAST languages are collectively called PACAWARA. Jurua-Purus (8) includes a number of tribes whose linguistic affiliations with each other or other Panoan groups have not been ascertained; they probably represent dialects of a single language, although some may be different languages.

Shell, in an unpublished reconstruction of Panoan languages cited by Longacre (1968a), classifies seven of the languages on the basis of shared phonological innovations and with some attention to shared lexical innovations. Though a limited number of languages were treated in detail, Shell's work is sufficient to show that the geographical grouping does not represent the historical grouping. For example, her classification showed Capanahua (2) and Conibo (6) of CENTRAL to be most closely related to Chacobo (18) of SOUTHEAST and only much more distantly related to Cashibo (3), another CENTRAL language.

CENTRAL

1. Amahuaca = Amawaca = Amenguaca(?) = Sayaco. Ds. Inuvaken, Viwivakeu. 3,000–4,000. Peru and Brazil.
2. Capanahua = Kapanawa. Ds. also Busquipani. Peru.
3. Cashibo = Caxibo = Comabo. Ds. Buninahua = Buninawa, Cacataibo, Caxinyo = Cashiño, Puchanahua = Puchanawa, Runyo, Xirino = Shirino. Peru.
4. Cashinawa. D. also Sheminawa. Brazil.
5. Catuquina = Catukina = Caripuna = Juanauo. Ds. Arara (including Shawanawa), Ararapina, Ararawa, Saninawa (including Saninawacana). Brazil. To be distinguished from other languages of the same name.
6. Conibo = Chama = Tschama = Čama. Ds. also Setebo = Setibo (subdialects Panobo, Sensi), Shipibo (subdialects *Manamabo (probably extinct), Manaua, Sinabo). Peru.
7. *Culino = Curina. Brazil.
8. Jurua-Purus. Ds. (trs. ?) Aranaua, Canamari, Chipinaua, Contanaua, Espino, Jaminaua = Yaminawa, Jauanaua = Yawanawa, Jauavo = Yauavo, Jumbanaua, Jura, Manaua = Manamabobo, Pacanaua, Poianaua, Runanaua = Rununawa, Tuchinaua. Juruá-Perús river basin in Brazil; Peru.
9. Marinaua. Brazil.
10. *?Maspo. D. also(?) Epetineri = Impenitari. Peru.
11. Niarawa = Niaragua. Peru.
12. Nucuini. D. also Cuyanawa. Brazil.
13. Pichobo = Pisobo = Pitsubo = Pichaba = Pisabo. Ds. also Mochobo = Mochovo = Univitza (including Comobo), Sobiobo = Saboibo = Saboyo

= Soyboibo = Bolbo (including Ruanawa). Peru.
14. *Puyamanawa. Peru.
15. Remo. D. also Sacuya. Peru.

SOUTHEAST
16. Capuibo. Bolivia. 30 (if Capuibo = Pacawara in Key and Key 1967).
17. Caripuná = Jau-navo. Ds. Jacariá, Pamá = Pamaná. Brazil.
18. Chacobo. 135 (1962). Bolivia.
19. Sinabo = Gritones. Brazil.
20. Zurina. Brazil.

SOUTHWEST
21. *Arasa = Arasaire = Arazaire = Aratsaira.
22. Arauá. Peru.
23. *Atsahuaca = Atsawaca. Ds. *Chaspa = Atsahuaca, Yamiaca = Hasuñeri
    = Haauñeiri. Possibly not extinct. Peru.

AFFILIATION. Branch of PANO-TACANA family in MACRO-PANOAN within GE-
PANO-CARIB.

MACRO-PANOAN PHYLUM

GROUPING. The four families and two language isolates which constitute the
MACRO-PANOAN phylum are spread over a wide area from Peru eastward to Brazil and
Bolivia and southward to Paraguay and Argentina.

The classification followed here is that of Greenberg (1960a) except that (a) Lule
and Vilela are combined with Charrua and three other languages of Uruguay into one
family and (b) Opaié of his GUAYCURU-OPAJE has been reclassified under MACRO-GE
following Davis (1968).

Since Brinton (1891), Lule and Vilela have been treated as members of the same
family by all scholars except Loukotka (1935) and Greenberg (1960a). Because of the
paucity of Lule data it may never be possible to demonstrate that these are members
of the same family. Nor is it certain that the names represent single languages; the
assignments of some tribal names to one or the other conflict. Nimuendajú (1931–32)
listed Güenoa, an extinct language of Uruguay, as a Vilela-speaking tribe and Mason
(1950) suggested the unclassified Charrua as a possible distant relative. Rona (1965)
of the University of Uruguay has been able through intensive work with all the
available linguistic information, including three newly discovered vocabularies, to
identify all of the various tribal names of Uruguay, including Güenoa and Charrua,
as synonyms for — or subgroups of — only four groups and to show that these
dialects or languages are closely related to Vilela. Longacre (1968a) cites an unpublished manuscript of Benigno Ferrario, which he feels presents convincing argu-
ments for the genetic relationship of these languages to Mataco.

The four families GUAYCURÚ, LULE-VILELA-CHARRUA, MATACO, PANO-TACANA, and
two ungrouped languages, Mascoy and Moseten, are coordinate members of MACRO-
PANOAN. (The two branches of PANO-TACANA are treated in separate articles, as are
each of the other families.)

Formerly, GUAYCURÚ and MATACO were considered members of a 'MACRO-GUAICURU' phylum, but this is no longer regarded as a separate linguistic unit. Prior to Greenberg, PANO, TACANA, and Moseten were each generally accepted as independent families, although as Suárez (1969) points out, there was early evidence for their relationship. Suarez would combine PANO-TACANA and Moseten as being more closely related to each other than to the other families and languages grouped under MACRO-PANOAN and even questions whether they are related to the other families.

1. *Mascoy. One of the two ungrouped languages of the phylum and sometimes erroneously called Enimaga = Maca, Mascoy was formerly spoken by 19 bands (1809) on both sides of the Pilcomayo and Paraguay rivers and above the confluence of these rivers in the Gran Chaco of Paraguay. Ds. also Angaite (including Enerslet), Caiotugui, Cashquiha = Guana, Lengua = Gecoinlahaac; Mascoy proper includes Machicui = Tujetge, Sanapana, Sapaqui = Sapuki = Conamesma.

2. Moseten = Mesetene = Mosetano. Another ungrouped language, Moseten, has traditionally been called a family, although Mason (1950) says of the names listed for Moseten, ". . . it is not certain how these are related, which ones are synonyms, or whether the linguistic divergences are on a dialectic level or greater." More recent authors, Key and Key (1967) and Suárez (1969) speak of it as a single language. Ds. Chimane (subdialects (or synonyms ?) Chamano, Chimaniza, Chumano, Nawazi-Montji), Moseten (subdialects (or synonyms ?) Amo, Aparono, Chumpa, Cunana, Magdaleno, Muchanes, Punnucana, Rache, Tucupi). 500 ? (1967). Formerly spoken along the Wopi and Quiquire rivers in Bolivia by people who were relocated to the missions of Covendo, Santa Ana, and Muchanes in the late nineteenth century.

AFFILIATION. Member of GE-PANO-CARIB.

*Paphlagonian. A non-INDO-EUROPEAN language of ancient Asia Minor known chiefly from Greek traditions.

AFFILIATION. None known (Swanson 1948).

NORTH PAPUAN

GROUPING. Wurm (1971c) divides NORTH PAPUAN into one large subgroup, TAMI (consisting of ARSO, SKO, SKOFRO, WARIS, and several unsubgrouped languages), coordinate with several smaller subgroups: NIMBORAN, SENTANI, UPPER TOR, Demta, and Uria. However, Wurm questions Cowan's (1957b, c) inclusion of SKO in the TAMI subgroup on the basis that SKO seems to be no more closely related to the other TAMI languages than to other subgroups of NORTH PAPUAN, and reports that it may actually be more closely related to the TORRICELLI languages than to NORTH PAPUAN languages. Greenberg (1971b) treats the NORTH PAPUAN languages as two independent subgroups of his NORTH NEW GUINEA. One of these is TAMI (not further subgrouped, but including the SKO languages), and the other, 'SENTANI', combines Wurm's other NORTH PAPUAN subgroups. The NORTH PAPUAN languages are spoken in northeastern West Irian, with some overlap across the border into Australian New Guinea.

1. Demta.

NIMBORAN. Total speakers 10,000.
  2. Gresi = Gresik.
  3. Kamtuk.
  4. Mekwei = Mekei = Menggwei = Waibron Bano-Demenggong.
  5. Nimboran. 3,000.
  6. Kwansu = Kuangsu. D. also Bonggrang.

SENTANI
  7. Sentani. D. also Nafri. 6,000.
  8. Tanahmerah = Tenah-Merah. 4,000 ?

TAMI. Tami River area on the north coast, just west of the West Irian-Australian New Guinea border, with some extension across the border.
  ARSO
      9. Arso. 600.
      10. Nyao = Njao = Awye = Awje. 400.
      11. Tabu. 400. Only tentatively included in ARSO.
  12. Dera.
  13. Djanggu.
  14. Kiamerop.
  15. Kilmeri. D.(?) also Krisa. 1,800 plus 468 Krisa.
  16. Molof. 400.
  SKO. May be a single language (Capell 1962a). Subgrouped with Upper Tami (23), below.
      17. Sangke. 1,200.
      18. Sko = Seko = Sekou. 350.
      19. Vanimo. The total number of speakers of Vanimo and Wutong (20, below) is 2,000.
      20. Wutong. See (19), above.
  SKOFRO
      21. Skofro. 50.
      22. Wembi = Yeti. 350.
  23. Upper Tami. Wurm lists as 'families' of unspecified membership, subgrouped with SKO, above.
  24. Wagarindem.
  WARIS
      25. Amanab. 2,700.
      26. Ampas. 500.
      27. Daonda. 100.
      28. Simog. 140.
      29. Sowanda. 850.
      30. Wanya = Wanja = Wina ?
      31. Waris. 3,000.
UPPER TOR

32. Berrik = Berik. 1,000.
33. Bonerif.
34. Dabe.
35. Foja.
36. Ittik.
37. Kwerba.
38. Kwesten.
39. Manter.
40. Saberi.
Boven Tor ?

41. Uria.
Kaure ? Mawes ?

AFFILIATION. Possibly member of CENTRAL NEW GUINEA macro-phylum (Wurm); NORTH NEW GUINEA (Greenberg).

PARE-SAMO-BEAMI-BOSAVI

GROUPING. Wurm (1971c) divides this group into four subgroups: AWIN-PARE (languages numbered 3, 4, 9); Beami (5); Bosavi (7); SAMO-KUBO-BIBO (languages numbered 1, 2, 6, 8, 10). Greenberg classifies Awin (4?), the only language of this group which he treats, as belonging to OK. Northern and northwestern Western District, Papua.

1. Aibe.
2. Alibu = Waribu. 600.
3. East Awin = Akium-Pare. 900.
4. West Awin = Akium-Awim = Aekyom. 6,500.
5. Beami. 3,000.
6. Bibo = Gebusi. 500.
7. Bosavi. 1,200.
8. Kubo-Daba. 500.
9. Pare = Pari. D. also Ba. 1,400.
10. Samo = Supe. 550.

AFFILIATION. Member of CENTRAL AND SOUTH NEW GUINEA.

PEBA-YAGUAN = PEBAN = YAGUAN

GROUPING. Only two of the three PEBA-YAGUAN languages are still extant. They are spoken in Peru west of Iquito on the Marañon and Amazon rivers and in the Peru-Brazil-Colombia border area.

1. *Peba. Ds. also Caumari, Cauwachi, Pacaya. Peru. Possibly to be equated with the Pebas dialect of Yagua below.
2. Yameo. Ds. Alabono, Amaona, Masamai, Mikeano, Nahuapo, Napeano, Parrano, Yarrapo, and possibly Camuchivo, Mazan, and San Regino. San Regis area of Peru.

3. Yagua = Yegua = Yahua. Ds. Atacuari, Colombia, Gochaquinas, Pebas. Peru in the Peru-Brazil-Colombia border area and possibly in enclaves in Brazil and Colombia.

AFFILIATION. Member of MACRO-CARIB within GE-PANO-CARIB.

PENUTIAN PHYLUM

GROUPING. The first grouping of related families into a PENUTIAN phylum was done by Dixon and Kroeber (1919); their grouping did not extend PENUTIAN beyond the so-called California PENUTIAN, and included only four families (MAIDU, MIWOK-COSTANOAN, WINTU, YOKUTS). In the half-century following 1919, several language families and isolates have been successively added to the PENUTIAN phylum by Sapir (1929), by McQuown (1955), by Stanley Newman (1964), recently also by Olson (1964), Stark (1968, 1970), and Hamp (1971). It is the more recent contributors to the hypothesis who have found evidence for and argued for, the PENUTIAN connection of languages spoken in western South America. In sum, a dozen separate language families beside nine different language isolates (single languages without closely related sister languages) are said to be remotely related to each other within the PENUTIAN phylum.

According to the PENUTIAN hypothesis, Araucanian and the CHIPAYAN family of languages are members of the phylum, which extends from southwestern South America northward through Central America and Mexico and the western states of the United States up into northwestern Canada. However, in the classification by Greenberg (1960a), Araucanian and CHIPAYAN are placed in the ANDEAN EQUATORIAL phylum among other languages which are spoken in South America, without particular North American relationships.

1. Araucanian = Araukan = Aucanian = Aucan = Mapuche. 200,000. Chile (chiefly in provinces of Bío-Bío, Malleco and Cautin); also Argentina (an additional 8,000; Neuguén province). Ds. Huiliche = Huilliche = Huilli = Guiliche = Wiliche = Veliche = Chilote (including perhaps Cunco = Cuncho = Junco = Guinche = Cunches = Cunchi = Kuncho = Chikiyami, Pichi Huilliche = Huillipehuenche), Pehuenche = Pewenche = Pegüenche (including also Moluche = Mapuche = Vilimuluche), Picunche = Picones. Other dialect names, mostly Argentinean Araucanian, include: Manzanero, Ranquel(che) = Ranquele = Ranquelines, Serano Huilche, Sanguelche. Perhaps also Calillehet, Chulilaukünnu, Diuihet = Divihet = Diviche, Leuvuche, Taluhet = Taluche; these may, however, bear a closer affinity to Het (q.v.).

2. *Cayuse = Cayus = Kayouse = Kayux = Wailetpu. Formerly about the head-waters of Wallawalla, Umatilla and Grande Ronde rivers, Washington and Oregon. Formerly Cayuse and Molale were thought to be closely related sister languages; Rigsby (1966) has shown that the two are but remotely related to each other (within PENUTIAN) rather than being members of what was once called the "WAIILAT-PUAN" family.

CHINOOK (q.v.)

CHIPAYAN (q.v.)

3. Coos. Fewer than 10. Coos Bay, Oregon.

4. Huave = Huavean = Guave = Guavi = Huavi = Huazonteco = Wabi. 7,000. Mexico (Juchitlan and Tehuantepec departments, Oaxaca). Classified by Mason (1940) as coordinate with the MIXE-ZOQUEAN family in his MIZOCUAVEAN stock. Freeland and Sapir (1930) proposed PENUTIAN affiliation instead, as did Greenberg (1960a); Swadesh (1959) proposed OTO-MANGUEAN affiliation.

KALAPUYA (q.v.)

5. Klamath = Moáklaks = Lutuami = Lutuamian. D. also Modoc. 100 (Klamath; Oregon), 10–100 Modoc; California).

MAIDU (q.v.)
MAYAN (q.v.)
MIWOK-COSTANOAN (q.v.)

6. *Mólale = Molele = Molal(l)a. Trs. Chakankni, Chimbuiha, Mukanti. Formerly Washington and Oregon in the valley of the Deschutes River; later west into Molala and Santiam River valleys, and to headwaters of the Umpqua and Rogue rivers.

SAHAPTIN-NEZ PERCE (q.v.)

7. *Takelma = Takilma = Lowland Takelma. Formerly middle course of the Rogue River, Oregon. Classified by Shipley (1969) in a TAKELMAN group with KALAPUYAN.

TOTONACAN (q.v.)

8. Ts(h)ims(h)ian = Tshimshean = Tchim'-chæ-an' = Chim(m)(e)syan = Skeena Indians = Spuch'-æ-lotz = Kilgat. Ds. also Gitksan Tsimshian, Niska Tsimshian. 3,000. British Columbia and Alaska; traditional provenience interior rather than coastal.

WINTUN (q.v.)
YAKONAN (q.v.)
YOKUTS (q.v.)

9. Zuni. 3,500. New Mexico. Affiliated with PENUTIAN by Stanley Newman (1964).

AFFILIATION. Whorf (1935) grouped PENUTIAN and UTO-AZTECAN into MACRO-PENUTIAN. Shipley (1957) indicated some lexical resemblances between Yuki and PENUTIAN.

Pisidian. A non-INDO-EUROPEAN languages of ancient Asia Minor, known chiefly from Greek traditions.

AFFILIATION. None known (Johannes Friedrich 1932; Kretschmer 1896; Swanson 1948).

PITTAPITTIC = PALKU

GROUPING. Breen (1971) treats PITTAPITTIC as a PALKU subgroup of a larger KARNIC subgroup of PAMA-NYUNGAN. He realigns the dialects of the two languages given below (after Wurm 1971b and O'Grady et al. 1966), placing Wangkadjera as a dialect of the same language as Ulaolinya, with the second PALKU language consisting of the remaining dialects of Wurm's Wangkadjera. These languages are spoken in west central Queensland near the border of Northern Territory, Australia.

1. Ulaolinya = Yoolanlanya = Lanima. At Carlo Springs on Upper Mulligan River.
2. Wangkadjera. Ds. also Karanya = Karanja = Kurrana = Mooraboola = Moorloobullo = Ooloopooloo = Ngulubulu, Kungkalenya = Kungkalenja = Kungkulenje = Koonkodenya = Kiomkoolenya = Koonkalinya, Lanima, Mayuli = Majuli = Miorli, Pittapitta = Pitapita = Bitta Bitta, Rakkaia = Rukkia, Ringuringu = Ringoringo = Ringa Ringa = Ringaringa = Ringa Oringaroo.

AFFILIATION. Member of PAMA-NYUNGAN.

POLYNESIAN

GROUPING. Biggs (1971) groups 54 linguistically differentiated "communalects" into the 27 languages listed below. On the basis of mutually exclusive features, two major subdivisions are distinguished (Pawley 1966, 1967): TONGIC (26 and 27, in the list below) and NUCLEAR (1–25). The larger of these two, NUCLEAR, is subgrouped into EASTERN (1–11) and SAMOIC-OUTLIER (12–25, listed in alphabetical order, including a few inside the Polynesian triangle—Ellicean, Futunan, Pukapukan, and Samoan—and the rest outside this triangle; hence, Polynesian 'Outliers').

This major grouping is essentially the same as an earlier classification by Elbert (1953), whose TONGIC (26 and 27, as below; but also Futunan) is grouped with SAMOIC-OUTLIER as WESTERN POLYNESIAN.

Dyen's (1965) lexicostatistics permit an alternative classification into two large groups and three separate languages. The two large groups are EASTERN (excluding Maori) and WESTERN (including TONGIC, but excluding two Outliers); the three separate languages are Maori and the two Outliers that are excluded from WESTERN, Kapingamarangi and Nukuoro.

NUCLEAR

EASTERN. The first subgrouping distinguishes Easter Island (1) from the rest of EASTERN (2–11), known as CENTRAL or CENTRAL EASTERN. The CENTRAL group is further subdivided into MARQUESIC (3 and 6) and TAHITIC (4, 5, 7, 8, 9, 10, 11); within TAHITIC, Biggs distinguishes a few languages (4, 5, and by implication 7 and 8) as a subgroup. This leaves Hawaiian (2) as CENTRAL, but beyond that it is classifiable in one of two ways: Hawaiian is included in TAHITIC by Elbert but placed in MARQUESIC by Green (1966), who treats Marquesan as two languages, with Southeastern Marquesan and Hawaiian having a common development apart from Northwestern Marquesan. Rapa (9) and some dialects of Tuamotuan (11) are also assigned to MARQUESIC by Green.

1. Easter Island = Rapanui = Pascuenese. Fewer speakers than the island's population of 1200 (1967). 27°S 190°W.

2. Hawaiian. Home language of 250 people on Ni'ihau and a few scattered individuals on other Hawaiian islands. 19°–22°N 155°–160°W.

3. Mangareva. 600–700 (1963). Mangarevan cluster in Gambier Islands, 23°S 135°W.

4. Maori = New Zealand Maori. Ds. North Island, divided into Western, with three sub-areas (North Auckland peninsula, Waikato-King Country area, and Taranaki-Wanganui River area); and Eastern (including part of the Bay of Plenty and Urewera hinterland); and *South Island. 100,000, all bilingual in English. 33°–53°S 167°–179°E.

5. Cook Islands Maori = Rarotongan = Kuki Airani. Ds. also Aitutaki, Atiu, Mangaia, Manihiki-Rakahanga, Mauke, Mitiaro; Rarotongan is Standard. 19,250 in 13 inhabited Cook Islands and an additional 2,500 in New Zealand. 18°–23°S 156°–163°W.

6. Marquesan. Ds. Northern = islands of Nukuhiva, 'Uapou, 'Uahuka; Southern = islands of Hiva'oa, Fatuhiva, and Tahuata, with minor dialect differences between or within islands. 5,000 plus a few hundred in Tahiti. 8°–10°N 138°–142°W.

7. *Moriori. Chatham Islands, 44°S 177°W. Probably developed from South Island or eastern North Island Maori (Biggs).

8. Penrhyn = Tongareva. 591 (1966). 9°S 158°W. Almost mutually intelligible with Cook Islands Maori (Biggs; treated as a divergent dialect of Cook Islands by other sources, e.g., Dyen).

9. Rapa. 250 (1962); Tahitian also spoken. 27°S 144°W. Possibly a dialect of Tahitian (Biggs).

10. Tahitian = Neo-Tahitian. Ds. also Rurutu in the Australs (22°S 151°W), Tubuai (23°S 149°W), possibly also Rapa, 9, above. Less than 66,000 total population (1959), but also lingua franca for the Tuamotus, Marquesas, Gambiers, and Australs. Tahiti and Society Islands, 16°–17°S 148°–155°W.

11. Tuamotuan = Pa'umotuan. Less than 7,000 on about 50 atolls of the Low or Dangerous Archipelago plus about 2,000 in Tahiti. 14°–23°S 135°–149°W.

SAMOIC-OUTLIER. This group includes "probably" all of the Outliers (Biggs). Ellicean (12), Luangiua (16), Mele-Fila (18), and Tikopia (24) are subgrouped as ELLICEAN by Dyen. Biggs recognizes three "well-marked" Outlier subgroups: the Northwest Outliers (15 and 19), the Central Outliers (16) and the New Hebrides Outliers (14 and 18).

12. Ellicean. D. also Tokeluan; Ellicean ds.: northern = Nanumanga, Nanumea, Niutao islands; southern = Nukufetau, Vaitupu, Funafuti, Nukulailai = Nukulaelae; most northerners also know southern, which is official. Most Ellicean speakers understand Samoan through church use. Fewer speakers than inhabitants of Ellice group (6,124) in 1966; (Gilbertese, another language, is spoken on Nui), plus over 200 Elliceans

on Nauru, about 2,000 in Tokelaus (Union Group), plus 500 Toke-
lauans in New Zealand, 100 on Swain's Island (Olosega), plus some in
Hawaii. Ellicean is spoken on seven of the nine inhabited Ellice Islands,
6°S–10°S 176°E–180°E; and on Tokelau Islands, 8°–9°S 172°W; and on
Swain's Island, 11°S 171°W.

13. Futuna = East Futuna. 2,629 (1967). Futuna (Hoorn) Islands, 14°S
178°W.

14. West Futuna = Erronan. D. also Aniwa. 500 (1967). Futuna, 20°S
170°W; Aniwa, 19°S 170°W.

15. Kapingamarangi. 1,000 (700 on Kapingamarangi, plus several hundred
on Ponape (Byron Bender 1971). 1°N 154°E.

16. Luangiua = Leuangiua = Ontong Java = Northern Outlier Polynesian.
Ds. also Nukumanu = Tasman, Nukuria = Nuguria, Sikaiana =
Sikayana = Sikiana, Takuu = Taku = Tauu = Tau ? = Mortlocks.
Fewer speakers than 1750 total population of the islands. Ontong Java
(Lord Howe), 6°S 160°E; Tasman Islands, 5°S 159°E; Nukuria (Fead)
3°S 155°E; Sikaiana (Stewart), 8°S 163°E; Mortlock (Takuu) Islands,
5°S 157°E. May be more than one language (Biggs 1969).

17. Mae = Mwae = Emae = Emwae = Emai = Mai. 200–300; also
speak Tongoan. Two villages on Emae (Three Hills, Sesake) Island,
17°S 168°E.

18. Mele. D. also Fila. Over 1000 in Mele village on Efate, plus 500 on Fila;
Mele Island is more or less deserted. Islands in Vila Harbor and on
adjacent Efate Island, 18°S 168°E.

19. Nukuoro. 260, plus 125 on Ponape; many older speakers are bilingual
in Ponopean. 4°N 155°E.

20. Pileni = Pilheni = Reef Island. D. also Taumako = Duff. Less than
500 (1962). Taumako, Matema, Nupani, Nukapu, Pileni, Nifiloli
(Nufiloli) in the Duff (Wilson) Islands and Reef (Swallow) Islands,
10°S 166°–168°E. (The Polynesian-inhabited islands are known collectively as Te Vaiakau; Nalogo is uninhabited; Aua is inhabited only
seasonally; now two small settlements on Santa Cruz.)

21. Pukapukan. 684 (1966) plus some speakers in Rarotonga and
New Zealand. Pukapuka Island in northern Cook Islands,
11°S 166°W.

22. Rennellese = Munggava = Mugaba. D. also Bellona = Munggiki.
1,760 (1963). Rennell, 12°S 161°E, and Bellona, 11°S 160°E.

23. Samoan. Only minor geographic dialect differences, but great phono-
logical and lexical differences distinguish Formal from Colloquial
Samoan. Fewer speakers than the total population of 155,550 (1966–7),
plus 4,000 Western Samoans in New Zealand and a few hundred
American Samoans in the United States. Savai'i and 'Upolu islands in
Western Samoa, 14°S 172°W; Tutuila and Manu'a group in American
(Eastern) Samoa, 14°S 170°W.

24. Tikopia. D. also Anuta. 1,500 Tikopia including those on Russell Island

and in Honiara, Guadalcanal; 200 on Anuta. Tikopia, 12°S 169°E; Anuta (Cherry), 12°S 170°E.

25. West Uvea. Less than 2,500 population (1963). Uvea in the Loyalty Islands, 21°S 167°E.

TONGIC. The classification of East Uvean and Niuafo'ou is complicated by the fact that they share innovations with NUCLEAR languages and hence might be classified with them; but they are listed as dialects of Tongan (26) because they are mutually intelligible with Tongan, perhaps only through intensive contact.

26. Tongan. Ds. also Niuafo'ou, Niuatoputapu, Uvean = East Uvean. 74,000 Tongan d. speakers (1966); 1,300 Niuafo'ou (1946); 1,400 Niuatoputapu; 5,705 Uvean (1967). Tonga (Friendly) Islands, 15°–24°S and 173°–177°W, including Niuafo'ou (Tin Can) Island, 16°S 176°W, and Niuatoputapu (Keppel) Island, 16°S 174°W; Uvea (Wallis) Island, 13°S 176°W.

27. Niuean = Niuefekai. 5,000 (1966), plus several hundred now in New Zealand. 19°S 170°W.

AFFILIATION. The POLYNESIAN group is a subgroup of the EASTERN OCEANIC subgroup of AUSTRONESIAN (Grace 1959; Biggs 1965).

POMO

GROUPING. Halpern (1964) summarized previous work on the internal classification of the seven POMO languages for which Barrett (1908) was the first to supply vocabulary lists. In the past decade, Oswalt (1964) classified three of the languages (2, 3, and 5, below) as coordinate with each other and distinguished from the remaining four languages, which are more closely related to each other. In the classification by Halpern (1964) the family tree shows a bifurcation, with Southeastern Pomo (5) below appearing on one side and the other languages on the other. Subsequently, Oswalt (1971) adopts a bifurcation classification, setting off Southeastern Pomo from the others and specifying in detail the degree of closeness of the others. Thus, after the bifurcation, the separation of Eastern Pomo (2) and Northeastern Pomo (3) preceded the separation of the remaining group of languages comprising Northern Pomo (4) and languages to the south of it (Central Pomo (1), Southwestern Pomo (7), Southern Pomo (6)). Webb (1971) groups Southeastern Pomo and Eastern Pomo as descendants of Proto-Lake Pomo. She follows Halpern in treating Northeastern Pomo as a descendant of Proto-Russian River Pomo, along with all the other languages, but suggests that Northeastern separated from the rest of the Proto-Russian River dialects before Proto-Lake Pomo had separated from them.

The following alternate names appear either for POMO or for one of the languages, groups, or subgroups in this family: Ballo-Kai-Pomo = Cabanapo = Habenapo = H'hana = Kábinapok = Khabenapo = Khana = Kalanapan = Kulanapan = Kulanapo = Ungieskie(?) = Venaambakaia = Venambakaiia = Yokaia.

1. Central Pomo. Ds. Point Arena, Hopland, Ukiah. Fewer than 40. California.

2. Eastern Pomo = Clear Lake Pomo. Around Clear Lake in the Sacramento River valley. Aboriginally three dialects; only traces remaining.

3. Northeastern Pomo = Salt Pomo. One speaker. California, formerly Coast Range Valley of Story Creek (a tributary of the Sacramento River).
4. Northern Pomo. Ds. Guidiville, Sherwood Valley. Fewer than 40. California.
5. Southeastern (Clear Lake) Pomo = Lower Lake Pomo. Fewer than 10. California, along eastern shores of Clear Lake.
6. Southern Pomo = Gallinoméro. Fewer than 40. California.
7. Southwestern Pomo = Kashaya. 50. California.

AFFILIATION. Member of HOKAN.

*Pontic. A non-INDO-EUROPEAN language of ancient Asia Minor, known chiefly through Greek traditions (Danoff, 1962).

AFFILIATION. None known.

POPOLOCAN = OLMECAN = MAZATECAN

GROUPING. The POPOLOCAN languages numbered (1), (2), (4) form a POPOLOC branch, and Mazatec (3) constitutes another branch.
1. Chocho = Chuchon = Chucholtec = Chuchotec. 600 (1930). State of Oaxaca, Mexico.
2. Ixatec = Ixateco. Santa Maria Ixcatlán area of the state of Oaxaca, Mexico.
3. Mazatec = Mazateco. Ds. Anawtla, Huautla de Jiménez, Mazatlán de Flores, San Jerónimo Tecoatl, San Miguel Huautla, San Miguel Soyaltepec, San Pedro Ixcatlán, Santa María Jiotes. Gudschinsky (1959) also classifies the dialects as Eastern High, Northern Valley Low, Southern Valley Low, Western High. 85,000. States of Oaxaca and Puebla, Mexico.
4. Popoloc = Popoloca. 10,000 (1930). States of Oaxaca and Puebla, Mexico.

AFFILIATION. Member of OTO-MANGUEAN phylum.

PURÍ = COROADO

GROUPING. The PURÍ are not to be confused with CAINGANG and BORORO groups which are also called COROADO. Both of the PURÍ languages are probably extinct.

1. *Coroado. Ds. Cobanipake, Maritong, Sasaricon, Tamprun. Eastern part of state of Minas Gerais, Brazil.
2. *Purí. Ds. Sabonan, Shamishuna, Wambori. Eastern part of state of Minas Gerais, Brazil.

AFFILIATION. Member of MACRO-GE within GE-PANO-CARIB.

ROMANCE = ROMANIC

GROUPING. There is complete agreement that ROMANCE languages descended from Old Latin, but some disagreement on the possible paths of descent.
For Pei (1945) and for Politzer (1949) a sharp distinction is possible between

the descendant literary and nonliterary or spoken languages: (1) 'Classical', 'Post-Classical', 'Medieval', Latin, and (2) 'Vulgar' or 'common' Latin. Thus, on the path of descent to Romanic dialects ancestral to modern ROMANCE languages there may have been a development around 800 A.D. from a unified 'Vulgar Latin' (sometimes regarded as a 'corrupted' form of Classical Latin). However, this interpretation is regarded by Hall (1950) as reflecting a confusion between the known history of written Latin and the reconstructed history of vernacular Latin.

Pulgram (1950) traces the path of descent as follows: Old Latin > Classical Latin (late Republic and early Empire) > Post-classical (second century to about the seventh century) > Mediaeval Latin (eighth century onward). The eighth century also marks the break between written Latin and written Romance dialects; it was not until after the stigma of inferiority was removed from the vernaculars that the first texts began to appear.

Spoken Latin had long been differentiated into dialects, about which little is known; Hall (1950) places PROTO-ROMANCE in the late Republican and early Empire period, i.e., during the period when classical Latin was the written style. Cicero noted that dialect variation in spoken Latin reflected the distinction between *urbanitas* of the Roman aristocracy and the countrified *rusticitas* pronunciation.

Pulgram noted a traditional bifurcation of ROMANCE: the La Spezia-Rimini line, which roughly divides continental Italy from peninsular Italy. Both the Italian dialects south of the La Spezia-Rimini line, and the BALKAN ROMANCE languages are grouped in an 'EASTERN' group, while those Italian dialects north of the La Spezia-Rimini line and the remainder of the ROMANCE languages are grouped in a 'WESTERN' group.

Hall (1950), however, places Italian unambiguously with 'WESTERN' in an 'ITALO-WESTERN' subgroup, as opposed to his EASTERN subgroup (i.e., BALKAN). But Hall (after Wagner 1938, and others) subgroups both 'ITALO-WESTERN' and EASTERN in a larger 'CONTINENTAL' group, which is coordinate with a 'SOUTHERN' group that has divergent dialects of Italian as constituents (namely, Calabrian, Lucanian, Sardinian, and Sicilian).

The bifurcation into 'EASTERN' and 'WESTERN' is based on the isoglosses which are found along the La Spezia-Rimini line, while the more complex classification of Hall is based on sound correspondences. The constituents of ROMANCE are possibly:

BALKAN = EASTERN ROMANCE
GALLO-ROMANCE
IBERO-ROMANCE
Italian (ITALO-ROMANCE)
RHAETO-ROMANCE.

This, in general, reflects Hall's earlier subgroups (except for the inclusion of his 'SOUTHERN' dialects as divergent dialects of Italian); both in 1950 and in his recent (1974) family-tree figure, Hall places Proto-Rhaeto-Romance under Proto-Gallo-Romance.

BALKAN ROMANCE = EASTERN. This sometimes includes Italian dialects south of the La Spezia-Rimini line of isoglosses which separates continental from peninsular Italian in the 'EASTERN' group of ROMANCE languages.

1. *Dalmato-Romanic = Dalmatian. D. also Vegliotic = Vegliot. The last speaker died in the late nineteenth century on the island of Krk (Veglia). Formerly, coast and interior of Balkans (Macedonia, Albania, and parts of Greece).

2. Rumanian = Balkan Romance = Roumanian = Romanian. Ds. Daco-Rumanian, including Moldavian = Eastern Daco-Rumanian (with the Bessarabian, Bukovina, and perhaps the Dobrugea subdialects), Transylvanian = Western Daco-Rumanian (with Banat), Walachian = Southern Daco-Rumanian = Standard Rumanian (with Mutenia and Oltenia subdialects); Istro-Rumanian (Istrian Peninsula of Yugoslavia by 1,500 speakers); Macedo-Rumanian = Arumanian = Aromanian (Pindus Mountains of southern Yugoslavia, northern Greece and eastern Albania); Meglenitic = Megleno-Rumanian = Meglenite (Meglen region of northwest Salonika in Greece by 12,000 speakers). Rumania (16,000,000); Soviet Union (2,500,000); and Yugoslavia, Bulgaria, Greece, and Albania (875,000); the United States and Canada (7,500,000).

GALLO-ROMANCE

3. French. Ds. Standard French (Île de France, or Paris); Franco-Provençal (including Dauphinois, Lyonnais, Neuchâtelais, Savoyard, Valaisien, Vandois, along the Franco-Italian frontier, and a small speech island in southern Italy in the localities of Faeto and Celle S. Vito in the province of Foggia in Apulia); Gascon; Northern French (including Norman, Picard, and Wallon, on the one hand, and Angevin, Berrichon, Bourbonnais, Bourguignon, Franc-comtois, Gallot, Lorraine, Poitevin, and Saintongeais, on the other). 52,000,000 (as a first language; at least 12,000,000 as a second language). France and Corsica (43,000,000), Canada (5,000,000), Belgium (4,000,000), Africa (5,000,000), Vietnam (4,000,000 as a second language), Switzerland (five cantons east of French border: Fribourg, Genève, Neuchâtel, Valais, Vaud; 1,000,000), Italy (in the Val d'Aossa), Haiti (400,000 as a second language), French Polynesia (25,000 as a second language), Monaco, The Lesser Antilles (particularly Guadeloupe, Martinique, and St. Lucia).

4. French Creole. Ds. Agalega (Agalega Islands), Chagos, Guyana French (French Guiana); Haitian Creole (4,500,000–4,750,000); Indian Ocean Creole (about 300,000, Mauritius, Seychelles, Réunion); Lesser Antilles (800,000, on Guadeloupe, Les Saintes, Marie-Galante, Martinique, Dominica, Trinidad, Grenada, St. Lucia); Louisiana Creole = Negro French (400,000, Louisiana in the United States); Madagascar, New Caledonia Pidgin = Bichelemar (virtually extinct; relexification of English-based Beach-la-Mar); New Hebrides French Pidgin (use not widespread; also a relexification of Beach-la-Mar); Rodriguez (17,000); South Vietnam = Annamito French. Perhaps as many as 5,500,000 speakers. The Caribbean, French Guiana, the United States, Madagascar, the Indian Ocean, South Vietnam, New Caledonia, New Hebrides. Of all the European-based Pidgin-Creoles, French Creole is the most homogenous. All dialects of the Caribbean and the Indian Ocean are mutually

intelligible, and probably the Southeast Asian and Oceanic varieties as well (De Camp 1968; William Stewart 1962, Valdman 1968). Whinnom (1956, 1965) proposes the monogenesis of all European-based Pidgin-Creoles from an ancestor such as Sabir, the Mediterranean lingua franca of the Middle Ages.

5. Provençal = Occitan = South French. Ds. also Alpine Provençal, Auvergnat (within which Haut is distinguished from Bas), Caussenard, Languedocien (also distinguishing Haut from Bas), Limousin, and Provençal of southern Provence. 9,500,000. Southern France, along the Franco-Italian border in Italy from Ventimiglia in the south to Turin in the north, and in the valleys leading down to the Po River in Italy. In France, Provençal and Standard French were once separate languages, according to the criterion of lack of intelligibility, but because of dialect leveling over generations of army service and increased school attendance (in which Standard French is taught) the barrier between the two languages in France has been transformed from a language barrier to a dialect barrier.

IBERO-ROMANCE

6. Catalan. Ds. Catalonian, Insular Catalan (Balearic Islands), Valencian. 5,000,000. Spain (4,800,000; Catalonia, Valencia Provinces, and the Balearic Islands), France (200,000; Roussillon region), and in Alghero on Sardinia.

7. Mozarabic.

8. Portuguese. Ds. Central (in Beira); Galician = Northern Portuguese (Galicia in Spain, northern Portugal provinces of Entre-Minho-e-Douro and Traz-oz-Montes); Insular (Madeira and Azores; Brazilian Portuguese most similar to this dialect); Southern (Estremenho, including Lisbon; Aleutejo, Algarve). 76,000,000. Portugal (9,100,000), Brazil (64,000,000), Spain (2,000,000), United States (200,000), Portuguese possessions in Africa (Guinea, Angola, Mozambique; 1,400,000), Goa (250,000), Macao (4,000), Portuguese Timor in the Lesser Sundas, east of Java. The Southern dialect, as spoken in Lisbon, is the basis for Standard Portuguese.

PORTUGUESE-BASED PIDGIN-CREOLES. Less diverse than ENGLISH-BASED PIDGIN-CREOLES, PORTUGUESE-BASED PIDGIN-CREOLES do not exhibit the uniformity characteristic of French Creole, and they are not all mutually intelligible. It is believed that all PORTUGUESE-BASED PIDGIN-CREOLES diffused from an Afro-Portuguese Pidgin-Creole along with Portuguese colonial and imperial expansion. Most oceanic varieties are extinct except for the variety spoken in Portuguese Timor and those which have been relexified into SPANISH-BASED PIDGIN-CREOLES (Ternateño, and associated languages or dialects). The classification of Papiamento (12), with both Portuguese and Spanish as donors, is disputed, and the Dutch and English inclusions give it the appearance of a 'creolized Esperanto' (DeCamp 1968; Navarro Tomás 1953). Spoken or formerly spoken on the Cape Verde Islands of the coast of Africa, the African mainland, the Indian Ocean and the Indian subcontinent; in southeast Asia, Macao, the China coast (Hongkong, Shanghai), the Philippines, Indonesia, perhaps formerly as far east as Hawaii in Polynesia.

9. Indo-Portuguese. India (in the former Portuguese colonies, as Goa).

10. Macanese. Macao. 4,000 in Hongkong.
11. *Moluccas Pidgin.
12. Papiamento. 200,000. Dutch West Indies (the islands of Curacao, Aruba, Bonaire). Considered Portuguese-based by Valdman (1968), and Navarro Tomás (1953).
13. Portuguese Guinea. 50,000.
14. São Tomé. 8,000.
15. Senegal.
16. Timor Pidgin. Portuguese Timor.
17. *Tugu. Java.
18. Spanish = Castilian. Ds. Andalusian, Argonese, Asturan, Castilian, Ladino = Judeo-Spanish, Leonese. 150,000,000. Spain (27,000,000), Central America (40,000,000), Caribbean (9,500,000), South America (54,000,000), United States (2,500,000), Philippines (500,000), Africa (100,000). Latin American dialects are derived from the European dialects listed above (other than Ladino). Pachuco is a kind of bilingual slang spoken across the American Southwest from El Paso to Los Angeles; it serves partly as a language of concealment from older Mexican-American speakers who are not fully bilingual and who cannot interpret the Spanish archaisms or the English idioms introduced into Pachuco by younger speakers.

SPANISH-BASED PIDGIN-CREOLES. These are largely in the Philippines. All but one, Bamboo Spanish (19), are directly or indirectly descended from Ternateño, which developed out of a Portuguese-based pidgin with strong Spanish relexification.

19. Bamboo Spanish. Perhaps still spoken by a few older generation Chinese shopkeepers. Davao Province, Philippines. Used by Japanese when they occupied the area; died out after they left.
20. *Caviteño. 18,000 (1942; became rapidly extinct). Ternateño evacuees to the municipal district of Ermita in the Philippines were re-evacuated to the province of Cavite and housed in the Tanza, San Roque, and New Ternate settlements.
21. Davaueño = Abakay Spanish. 3,500 (1942; slowly dying out). In modern Davao Province in southeastern Mindanao.
22. Ermitaño. From speech of Ternate newcomers after Caviteño deportation. 12,000. (1942; near extinction).
23. Ternateño. Ternate, a small island on the western side of Halmahera Island in the Moluccas. Developed out of a Portuguese-based pidgin established prior to Spanish occupancy with strong Spanish relexification.
24. Zamboangueño = Chabacano. From elements of Ermitaño or Caviteño spoken by Tagalog troops in the present province of Zamboango in western Mindanao. 1,300 (1942; still common in Zamboanga City and surrounding villages).
25. Italian = Italo-Romance. Ds. Central (including Marchigiano, Modern Roman, Northern Latian, Umbrian); Northern (including Gallo-Italian [Emilian, Ligurian, Genovan, Lombard = Milanese, Piedmontese]; Ticanese

in the Swiss Canton Ticino; Venetian [Istrian, Tretine, Venetian proper]);
Southern (Abruzzese, Apulian, Calabrian, Campanian, Lucanian, Sardinian
[Campidanian, Gallurese, Logodurese], Sicilian); Tuscan-Corsican (includ-
ing Corsican, Florentine, Southern Tuscan [Siena, Arezzo], Western Tuscan
[Lucca, Pisa]). About 56,000,000. Italy (43,000,000), Sicily (4,700,000),
Sardinia (1,400,000), Switzerland (200,000), France (including Corsica,
1,000,000), Yugoslavia (300,000), Republic of San Marino (20,000), the
United States (3,500,000), Argentina (1,200,000), Brazil (500,000), Canada
(100,000), and Somalia, Ethiopia, Libya. The Italian dialects are very divergent; although there is neighbor intelligibility between adjacent dialects,
dialect speakers from noncontiguous regions often need to communicate
in Standard Italian (the dialect of Modern Rome). There is an isogloss
line — important not only to Italian, but to all ROMANCE — which runs from
La Spezia on the Tyrrhenian Sea to Rimini on the Adriatic Sea, roughly
separating continental from peninsular Italy (Pulgram 1958). This line of
isoglosses is the basis for a classification of ROMANCE languages into an
'EASTERN' subgroup (Rumanian, Dalmatian, Vegliotic, and the Italian
dialects south of the La Spezia-Rimini line; i.e., Central, Southern, and
Sardinian), and a 'WESTERN' subgroup (the Northern dialects of Italian
and all other ROMANCE languages). Hall (1950) separates out Calabrian,
Lucanian, Sardinian, and Sicilian as constituents of an independent
'SOUTHERN ROMANCE' group, which is opposed to a 'PROTO-CONTINENTAL'
group which has 'ITALO-WESTERN' and 'EASTERN' as coordinate constituents.

RHAETO-ROMANCE = RAETO-ROMANCE = RHETO-ROMANCE =
LADIN = RHAETIAN. The RHAETO-ROMANCE languages are often treated as a
single group, sometimes in the GALLO-ROMANCE group (Hall 1950), though it is generally agreed that RHAETO-ROMANCE languages do not share a common history (see,
e.g., Pulgram 1958). 450,000. Alpine regions of southeastern Switzerland and northern
Italy. Friulian (26) and the Ladin east of the Adige River (27) are possibly closely
associated with the Venetian dialect of Italian; the Ladin west of the Adige River is
perhaps associated with the Lombard dialect of Italian.

26. Friulian. 400,000. Italy (Friuli, in the region between the Alps and the head
   of the Adriatic Sea, with the center at Udine; the area is noted for its trilingual-
   ism; Friulian, Italian and German are used by the same speakers in different
   culture spaces).
27. Ladin. 12,000. Southern Tyrol in Italy (in the Alto Adige and the Dolomites).
28. Romansch = Grishun = Rumauntsch. Ds. Engadine (Upper and Lower;
   the Inn Valley as far as the Austrian border, Switzerland), Oberland Grishun
   (Upper Rhine Valley, Germany).
29. *Sabir. The lingua franca of Mediterranean ports (particularly Algiers and North
   Africa) during the Middle Ages. The grammar and lexicon was largely ROMANCE,
   particularly Portuguese, French, and Italian.

AFFILIATION. Member of INDO-EUROPEAN.

SAHAPTIN-NEZ PERCE

GROUPING

1. Nez Perce = Nez Percé(s) = Chopunnish = Nùmípotitókĕn = Numipu = Numípu = Saaptins = Sahapotins = Sahaptin. Ds. Lower Nez Perce, Upper Nez Perce. 500–1,000. Idaho, Washington (Colville Reservation), Oregon (Umatilla Reservation).

2. Sahaptin = Sahaptian = Northern Sahaptin = Shahaptin. Ds. Columbia River = Umatilla = Rock Creek = John Day = Celilo = Tygh Valley = Tenino, Northeast = Wanapam = Walla Walla = Wawyukma = Palouse, Northwest = Yakima = Kittitas = Upper Cowlitz = Upper Nisqually = Klikitat. 2,750.

AFFILIATION. Member of PENUTIAN.

SAHARAN = EAST SAHARAN

GROUPING. Greenberg (1966) subgroups languages numbered (1) with (2) and (3) with (4), following. Chad, and adjoining areas of Nigeria, Niger, Libya, Sudan.

1. Kanembu = Kanambukanambu. Trs. Bad(d)e, Baribu, Chiroa, Diabu, Galabu, Kadjidi, Kankena, Kanku = Konku, Maguemi. Over 2,250. Chad, Niger.

2. Kanuri = Aga = Baribari = Zan. Trs. Badawai = Kanuri, Dogara = Dagara (19,300), Fadawu, Jetko = Dietko (1,120), Kagama = Kanuri, Kanembu, Karda, Koyam = Kwayam (9,000), Kuburi (550), Lare = Larewa = Lerewa (24,000), Mabar = Mober = Mobber = Mobeur = Mavar = Mafar (28,000), Manga (150,000), Ngumatiwu, Tsugurti (1,150). Nigeria: mainly Bornu Province also in Sokoto, Kano, Zaria, Bauchi provinces; Niger, 1,000,000–2,000,000.

3. Tebu = Tubu = Tibbu = Toubau = Daza. Ds. also Dazza, Dazaga = Dazzaga. Trs. Alaliwa; Amma Borkua; Anka(z)a = Anakatza = Nakaza; Atemata; Bulgeida, including Bultu = Bultoa, Dalea = Dalia = Nas Maramma, Iria = Irie = Yiri, Jagada = Diagada = Dschagada = Musu, Sangada = Koroa = Dobus Hillal; Dirkawa; Dogorda = Dugorda; Dongosa = Donza = Dosa, including Bidea, Tiwa, Yarda, Yenoa = Yinoa = ulad Amian; Gadiwa = Gudua = Gaduwa = Qudawa; Gaida = Gaeda; Gor'an = Goranes; Joarda; Kashirda = Kasherda = Kecherda = Kesherda = Sakerda = Sakarda; Kreda = Karda = Karra, including Bogarea = Aulad Bugar, Iria, Jura, Karda, Norea, Yorda, Yorda, Ngalamiya; Murdia; Norea = Nawarma; Sher(a) Fada = Churafada; Taura; Tebia; Yelmana; Yuruwa = Yuroa; Wannala = Wandal(l)a; Worabba = Warabba = Orabba. Mainly in Chad, extending into Niger.

4. Teda = Tuda = Toda = Tudaga. Ds. = Trs. Brawia, Chigaa, Gunda, Tomagera, Tua. Over 16,000. Chad, extending into Libya.

5. Zaghawa = Zagaoua = Berri = Beri-aa = Merida = Kebadi. Ds. Berti (Sudan), Bideyat = Baele = Anna = Awe = Terawia (3,000). 60,000. Chad, Sudan: Dar Fur. The Berti are bilingual in Arabic (Tucker and Bryan 1956).

AFFILIATION. Member of NILO-SAHARAN.

SAKAI = SENOIC = CENTRAL ASLIAN

GROUPING. Pinnow (1959) follows Skeat and Blagden (1906) in listing groups of SAKAI dialects bearing geographical labels as given below. Diffloth (1973) lists three 'SENOIC' languages, Semai, Temiar, Jah Hut. Diffloth excludes the Southern Sakai (4, below) from SAKAI, treating (4) as a separate SEMELAIC = SOUTHERN ASLIAN group. The SAKAI languages are confined to inland areas of Malaya except south of Kuala Lumpur where they extend to the coast. The total number of speakers is estimated at 10,000.

1. Central = Semai. Ds. Blanya = Lengkuas, Chendariang, Jelai, Mt. Berumban, Orang Tanjong (of Ulu Langat), Serau, Slim, Sungai Raya, Sungkai, Sənoi (of Ulu Pahong), Tapah, Ulu Gedang, Ulu Kampar.
2. Eastern = Jah Hut. Ds. Inner, including Kerdau, Krau, Krau of Ketiar = Tengganu, Kuala Tembeling, Pulau Guai; Outer, including Ulu Ceres = Cheres, Ulu Tembeling.
3. Northern = Temiar. Ds. Grik, Kenderong, Kenering, Po-Klo = Sakai Bukit of Temongoh, Sakai of Plus Korbu, Sungai Piah, Tanjong Rambutan, Tembe? = Tembi, Ulu Kinta = Kinta Sakai.
4. Southern. Ds. Southeastern, including Bera, Serting, Ulu Indau, Ulu Palong; Southwestern, including Besisi = Mah Meri = Besisi of Kuala Langot, Besisi of Malakka, Besisi of Negre Sembilan, Orang Bukit of Ulu Langat, Selangor Sakai.

AFFILIATION. Member of MALACCA group of AUSTRO-ASIATIC phylum.

SALISH

GROUPING. Thompson and Kinkade (1974) regard the lexicostatistic classification of Swadesh (1950) as a point of departure for further work on subclassification yielding the following three major groups: COAST (languages numbered 4, 7, 9, 12, 14, 15, 17, 19, 20, 23), INTERIOR (languages numbered 5, 6, 10, 11, 13, 18, 21), OLYMPIC (2, 3, 8, 16), and two single languages, Bella Coola (1) and Tillamook (22), which are coordinate with the grouped languages. Further details of subclassification are given by Kinkade (1972) and Thompson (1973).

1. Bella Coola = Belacoola = Belhoola = Bellacoola = Bellechoolo = Bilechula = Bilkula = Billechoola = Billechoula = Billechula = Bilqula = Friendly Village = Salmon River = Tallion Nation. 100–400. British Columbia.
2. Lower Chehalis. Fewer than 10. Washington.
3. Upper Chehalis = Chehalis = Kwaiailk = Nusulph = Noosoluph = Noosolup'h = Noosolupsh. D. also Satsop. Fewer than 10. Washington.
4. Clallam = Klallam = Noosdalum = Nusdalum = Sklallam. Fewer than 10. Washington, British Columbia.
5. Coeur d'Alene = Skitsamish = Skitsuish = Skitswish = Schitsui. 10–100. Idaho.
6. Columbian = Wenatchi-Columbia = Middle Columbia = Sinkiuse = Sinkiuse-Columbia = Moses-Columbia = Peshkwaus = Piskwaus. Ds. also Chelan, Wenatchee. 75–100. Washington.

7. Comox = Comux = Komuk = Komookhs = Çatloltq = Çatloltx. D. also Sliammon (500–600; Malaspina Inlet). 100–1,000. British Columbia.

8. Cowlitz = Cowlitch = Kaultits = Kawelitsk = Kowelitz = Kuwalitsk. Nearly extinct. Washington.

9. Halkomelem = Halcomelem = Nanaimo-(Lower) Fraser. Ds. Chemainus, Chehalis, Cowichan, Chilliwack, Katzie, Kwantlen, Lower Fraser River, Nanaimo, Musqueam, Sumas, Tait. 100–1,000. British Columbia.

10. Kalispel = Kalispelm = Kulleespelm = Kullespelm = Salish = Selish = Lingua Selica (including Upper Kalispel = Upper Pend(s) d'Oreilles, Flathead, in Montana; Lower Kalispel = Lower Pend(s) d'Oreilles = Kalispel proper, in Idaho and Washington), Ds. also Chewelah, Spokane = Spokan = Tsakaitsitlin (100–200), Washington. 600–1,200. Washington, Idaho, Montana.

11. Lillooet = Liloeet = Lilowat = Loquilt = Chin. 1,000–2,000. British Columbia.

12. Nooksack = Nooksak = Nuksahk = Nuksak = Nooksahk = Nootsack = Mooksahk. Nearly extinct. Washington.

13. Okanogan = Okanagan = Okanagon = Okinakan = Okinagan = Okinaken = Wakyanakane. Ds. also Colville = Schwoyelpi = Shwoyelpi = Skoyelpi = Kettle Falls = Basket People = Whe-el-po (322, Washington), Lakes, Methow = Chilowhist, Nespelim, Sanpoil (202). 1,000–2,000. Washington, British Columbia.

14. *Pentlatch = Pentlash = Pentlatc = Puntlatch = Puntlatsh = Puntledge. South Vancouver Island in British Columbia.

15. Puget Sound Salish = Puget = Toughnowawmish. Ds. Northern Puget Sound (Skagit, Snohomish), Southern Puget Sound (Duwamish, Muckleshoot, Nisqualli, Puyallup, Snoqualmie, Suquamish). 10–20. Washington.

16. Quinault = Quinaietl. Fewer than 10. Washington.

17. Seshelt = Sechelt = Seechelt = Seshalt = Sicatl = Shishiatl. Fewer than 10. British Columbia.

18. Shuswap = Shooswaap = Shooswap = Shushwapumsh = Atna = Ahtena. 1,000–2,000. British Columbia.

19. Squamish = Squawmish = Skay-wa-mish. 10–100. British Columbia.

20. Northern Straits Salish. Ds. Lummi = Há-lum-mi = Hookluhmic = Nooh-lummi = Nookluolamic = Nūh-lum-mi = Nūkh'-lum-mi = Qtlumi (fewer than 10), Saanich = Sanetch (10–50), Songish = Songhees = Lkungen (nearly extinct), Sooke = Sock = Tsohke = Sâ'ok = Achiganes (nearly extinct). Washington, British Columbia, S. Vancouver Island.

21. Thompson = Thompson River Indians = Nikutamuk = Nikutemuk = Nitklakapamuk = Ntlakyapmuk = Neetlakapamuch = Neklakapamuk = Netlakapamuk = Nicoutemuch. 1,000–2,000. British Columbia.

22. Tillamook = Tilamuk = Talamoh = Kilamook = Ntsietshaw = Ntsietshawus. D. also Siletz. Nearly extinct. Oregon.

23. Twana = Toanhuch = Toanhooch = Tuadhu = Skokomish. Fewer than 10. Washington.

AFFILIATION. In the classification by Sapir (1929), SALISH is a member of a phylum which includes also WAKASHAN, Kutenai, Quileute, Yurok and Wiyot, Beothuk, and ALGONQUIAN. The argument for leaving SALISH unaffiliated with respect to phylum classification is given by Voegelin and Voegelin (1967) and Thompson (1973).

SARMIC

GROUPING. Dyen (1965) groups languages (4) and (5) below, as SOBEIC and (1), (2) and (6) as TARPIC. This division is supported by Grace's (1970) comparisons, which would add (3) to SOBEIC.

1. Anus. Anus Island and a settlement on the adjacent northwest coast of New Guinea.
2. Bonggo = Armopa. Armopa region on coast, 139°36'E.
3. Masimasi. Masimasi Island.
4. Moar = Wakde ? Wakde Island.
5. Sobei. Sarmi region on coast, 138°45'E.
6. Tarpia = Tarfia.
Arimoa ?

AFFILIATION. The SARMIC languages were not grouped with any other AUSTRO-NESIAN language in Dyen's main lexicostatistic classification. A later refiguring of the percentages (Dyen 1965, Appendix) revealed a closer relationship of SARMIC to MOLUC-CAN, in which SARMIC was probably to be included. However, Grace (1970) classifies SARMIC as belonging to the OCEANIC subgroup of AUSTRONESIAN on the basis of comparison of forms from all the SARMIC languages with Proto-Oceanic forms.

SEMANG = JAHAIC = NORTHERN ASLIAN

GROUPING. The three or more SEMANG languages are spoken by some 2,000 people, mainly in the inland area of northern mainland Malaysia, but extending across the border into Thailand.

1. Pangan = Jahai. Ds. Belimbing, Galas, Hiu-Semang, Jalor, Kerbat, Kwala Aring, Lebir, Pǝtani, Sai, Sam, Teliang, Ulu, Ulu Aring, Ulu Kǝlantan.
2. Lowland Semang. Ds. Begbie's Semang, Juru, Orang Benua = Newbold's Semang, Swamp Semang (of Ulu Krian).
3. Semang Proper. Ds. Ijoh = Ijok, Jarum, Jeher = Sakai Tanjong of Temongoh, Kedah = Quedah, Plus, Ulu Sǝlama.

AFFILIATION. Member of MALACCA group of AUSTRO-ASIATIC phylum.

SEMITIC

GROUPING. The languages of the SEMITIC family listed below are grouped under NORTH SEMITIC, with subgrouping into *Akkadian (1), NORTHWEST SEMITIC (languages numbered 2–9, below); and under SOUTH SEMITIC, with subgrouping into SOUTHWEST SEMITIC (languages numbered 23 and 24, below) and SOUTHEAST SEMITIC. The latter subgroup is then subclassified: languages numbered (10) and (11), below, are each coordinate with the 16 languages classified as ETHIOPIC, making a total of three classificatory coordinates for SOUTHEAST SEMITIC.

The SEMITIC languages are distributed in three contiguous areas: in (a), non-African parts of Southwest Asia from the confluence of the Tigris and Euphrates to the Mediterranean, extending also into Transcaucasian regions of the Soviet Union; and in (b), the peninsula of Saudi Arabia, which is solidly SEMITIC in speech; and in (c), a vast area in North Africa, extending roughly from the Atlantic to the Red Sea, in which SEMITIC and non-SEMITIC languages are often interspersed.

Languages of Ethiopia grouped under ETHIOPIC (numbered 12–22, below) are spoken neither in (a) Southwest Asia nor in (b) the peninsula of Saudi Arabia. But the languages of Ethiopia are not entirely ETHIOPIC because Arabic and some CUSHITIC and OMOTIC languages are spoken in Ethiopia, beside or among ETHIOPIC languages. On the basis of Hellenistic sources, Leslau (1945) observes that Ethiopia was occupied by CUSHITIC speakers before the southward SEMITIC migrations in the first millennium B.C. — but the first SEMITIC inscriptions in Ethiopia are dated between 300 and 400 A.D.

NORTH SEMITIC

1. *Akkadian = Assyro-Babylonian = Northeast Semitic. Ds. Assyrian, Babylonian, Neo-Babylonian, Chaldean. Formerly Ancient Babylonia, Assyria, Chaldea.

NORTHWEST SEMITIC

2. *Amorite. Formerly northern Syria.
3. East Aramaic. Ds. Aisor (over 20,000; USSR, Iran, Iraq); *Babylonian Aramaic; *Mandaic = Mandaean (Sabaeans of lower Mesopotamia); Modern Aramaic; Syriac, including Eastern = Nestorian, Western = Jacobite (Syria); *Talmudic Tarqum. 10,000–100,000; Kurdistan, Israel.
4. West Aramaic. Ds. also *Biblical, *Judeo-Aramaic, *Palestinian (Christian), *Palmyrene, *Nabataean, *Samaritan. Lebanon, Syria (villages of Ma'lūla, Baḥ'a, Ǧuba'dīn); Ancient Palestine, Palmyra, Sinai.
5. *Hamat.
6. Hebrew. Ds. *Ancient; *Biblical; Classical = Liturgical; Mishnaic, Modern, including Standard = Israeli = Europeanized (Sephardic = Hispano-Portuguese and Ashkenazic = East European), and Oriental = Arabized = Yemenite; Rabbinic. 2,500,000. Israel, United States, Europe, elsewhere.
7. *Moabite.
8. *Phoenician. Ds., in historical order, may be *Old Byblos = Byblian, *Byblos = Byblian, before *Old Phoenician, *Phoenician, *Punic, *Neo-Punic = Colloquial Punic (Friedrich and Röllig 1970, Naveh 1973); *Yaudi has also been listed as a Phoenician dialect. Byblos as known from second-millennium inscriptions, which are a mixture of hieroglyphic and alphabetic writing, is sometimes identified as belonging to INDO-EUROPEAN (Hrozny 1945) rather than being identified with Phoenician, as by Dhorme (1946-48).

9. *Ugaritic.

SOUTH SEMITIC
SOUTHEAST SEMITIC

10. *Old South Arabic. Ds. Hadramaut, Himyarite, Lihyanite, Minaean, Qataban-Aswan, Sabean = Sabaean.

11. Modern South Arabic = Mahri-Sokotri. Ds. Botahari-Harsusi, Kuria Muria, Mahri (near Mahra), Shahari = Qarawi = Ehkili, Sokotri = Soqotri (on island of Sokotra in the Gulf of Aden). Certain regions of southern Arabia between Hadramaut and Oman; also on five islands off coast of Saudi Arabia.

ETHIOPIC = ETHIOSEMITIC = AFRICAN SEMITIC. These languages are subclassified by Marvin Bender (1971) into three groups: NORTH (languages numbered 14, 21, 28; CENTRAL (languages numbered 12, 13 as coordinate members); SOUTH (languages numbered 15, 16, 17, 18, 19, 20 — with languages 15, 19, 20 subgrouped into a NORTH GURAGE = SIMEN GURAGINYA, 16 and 18 in a WEST GURAGE, and 17 as an ungrouped language).

12. Amharic = Amarin(n)ya = Amharinya = Kuchumba. D. also Argobba = Argobbinya = Islam, including Ankober = North-(ern) Argobba, Harer = South(ern) Argobba (1,000 ?). 7,800,400 (excluding Argobba).

13. *Gafat = Gafatinya. Spoken south of the Blue Nile until about the middle of the nineteenth century.

14. Geez = Ge'ez = Ethiopic. While no longer spoken as a daily vernacular, it remains a liturgical language with a large body of religious and historical literature.

15. Gogot = Dobi.

16. Central West Gurage = Guragie = Gouraghie = Gurague = Gwemara = Chaha Cluster. Ds. Chaha = Cheha, Ezha = Eza = Izha, Gumer = Gwemara, Gura. 542,400 (total for all Gurage languages (16), (17), (18).

17. East Gurage = Guragie = Gouraghie = Gurague. Ds. also Harari = Adare = Gesinan (13,000), Inneqor = Enneqor = Innek'or = Mesqan = Selti = Silti, Urbareg = Ulbarag = Urbarag = Wurbereq, Walani = Wolane = Wulane, Zway = Laqi.

18. Peripheral West Gurage. Ds. Enor = Ener, Geto = Gieta = Gyeto = Gyeta, Indegegn = Indegagne = Endegen = Indagen = Endagany, Ennemor = Ennamor = Innemor = Inor, Mesmes, Mesqan = Masqan = Maskan.

19. Muher = Muxer. Tr. Ane-bet.

20. Soddo. Ds. Aymelle, Galiya, Kistane. Tr. Edi-bet.

21. Tigre = Khassa = Xassa. Ds. Bogos, Habaab, Mensa = Mansa9. Trs. also eastern Beni Amir. 117,000.

22. Tigrinya = Tigriña = Tigrigna = Tigrai = Tigray = Habesha. 3,559,300.

SOUTHWEST SEMITIC

23. Classical Arabic. Spoken by the educated as a lingua franca in all parts of the Arabic speaking world.

24. Modern (Colloquial) Arabic. Ds. Algerian, including Bedouin dialects, Algiers, Constantine, Oran, Arabian, including Bedouin dialects, Datina, Hadramaut, Hijaz, Mecca, Muscat, Najd, Oman, Yemen; Egyptian-Tunisian, including Cairo, dialects of lower Egypt, Sfax (east coast of Tunisia, Takruna, Tripolis-Bedouin, Tripolis-City, Tunis); Iraqian, including Bagdad, Bedouin dialects, Mosul, Mardin; Maltese; Moroccan, including city dialects, Houwara, Sus, Taza, Warga; Southwest Saharan = Hassani; Sudan; Syro-Palestinian Aleppo, including Beirut, Damascus, Jerusalem, Habab, Lebanon, Nomadic dialects, Saida, Semi-Nomadic dialects. 50–80 million. Arabian Peninsula, the Fertile Crescent, North Africa. Dialects spoken across North Africa, excluding Egypt, are often called Maghribi = Maghrebi, and distinguished from Zanzibari (dialect of Zanzibar).

AFFILIATION. Member of AFROASIATIC (Greenberg 1966). Fischel (1964) has reviewed the argument, especially as proposed by Sapir, for including SEMITIC as a member of the INDO-EUROPEAN family.

SEPIK

GROUPING. Wurm (1971c) tentatively unites three subgroups — SEPIK HILL, MIDDLE SEPIK, and UPPER SEPIK — into a single SEPIK group. Greenberg (1971b) groups two of the UPPER SEPIK languages, Mayo (36) and Wogamusin (38), with the languages of MIDDLE SEPIK, leaves two other UPPER SEPIK languages, Abau (28) and Iwam (32), as unclassified and does not mention any of the other UPPER SEPIK languages or any of the SEPIK HILL languages. The SEPIK HILL languages are much more closely related to each other than are the subgroups of MIDDLE SEPIK and UPPER SEPIK (Wurm). The SEPIK languages are spoken in the Sepik District, Australian New Guinea.

SEPIK HILL. South of the Middle Sepik River.
1. Alamblak. 1,066.
2. Bahinemo = Wogu = Gahom. 309.
3. Bisis. 355.
4. Bitara. 100.
5. Gabiano. 98.
6. Hewa. 2,000.
7. Kaningra. 327.
8. Kapriman = Wasare. 1,164.
9. Mari. 147.
10. Piame.
11. Sanio. 500–550.
12. Setiali. 200.
13. Sumariup. 79.

14. Umairof. 100.
15. Watakataui. 159.

MIDDLE SEPIK = NDU-KWOMA. In this group, KWOMA and NDU are more closely related to each other than either is to Namie (19) (Wurm).
    KWOMA. North of the Middle Sepik River.
        16. Gawanga = Kwanga. 7,520.
        17. Kwoma = Washkuk. 2,240.
        18. Seim = Nihamber = Mende = Sambu = Womsak. 3,180.
    19. Namie = Nemia = Watalu. 3,090.
    NDU. From the Middle Sepik River to the north coast, with a slight extension south of the river; locations of individual languages are mapped by Laycock (1965).
        20. Abelam. Ds. include Maprik and Wosera. 29,188.
        21. Boiken. Ds. Kwusaun, Yengoru = Yangoru. 17,332.
        22. Buiamanambu. 60.
        23. Iatmul = Big Sepik. Ds. include Nyaura. 7,887.
        24. Manambu. 1,448.
        25. Ngala. 52.
    26. Sawos = Tshwosh. 1,850. May be a dialect of Iatmul (23).
        27. Yelogu. 63.

UPPER SEPIK. Wurm, after Laycock (1968), divides UPPER SEPIK into three subgroups: RAM, TAMA, and a subgroup consisting of languages numbered 28, 29, 31, 32, and 39, below, within which Chenapian (31) and Iwam (32) are probably much more closely related to each other than to any of the others. Three almost unknown languages, Auwan (30) and two as yet unnamed languages — one with 100 speakers, the other with 1,040 — are treated as probably belonging to UPPER SEPIK, but are left unsubgrouped within it.
    28. Abau. 3,390. May extend into West Irian.
    29. Amal = Magaleri. 330.
    30. Auwan.
    31. Chenapian. 150.
    32. Iwam. 1,160.
    RAM
        33. Autu = Kamnum. 400.
        34. Bouye = Buiye. 560.
        35. Karawa. 40.
    TAMA
        36. Mayo = Yesan-Mayo. D. also Warasai. 800.
        37. Mehek = Me'ek = Driafleisuma = Indinogosima. 3,450.
        38. Pahi = Lugitama = Wansum. 520.
    39. Wogamusin = Wongamusin. 340.

AFFILIATION. Member of CENTRAL NEW GUINEA macro-phylum (Wurm); of NORTH NEW GUINEA (Greenberg).

*Sidetic = Sidetic Cappadocian. A little known language of Asia Minor attested by two Sidetic-Greek bilingual inscriptions of the third to second century B.C.

AFFILIATION. None known (Mansel 1965, Goetze 1957).

SINO-TIBETAN

GROUPING. It is the older, more liberal, classifications of SINO-TIBETAN that have now come under critical scrutiny. Shafer (1955) rejected the bifurcation within SINO-TIBETAN of 'SINITIC' versus TIBETO-BURMAN. Traditionally, 'SINITIC' was supposed to have three major constituents (CHINESE, KAM-TAI, and MIAO-YAO), while TIBETO-BURMAN was supposed to include a number of major constituents; specifically, BODO-NAGA-KACHIN, BURMESE-LOLO, GYARUNG-MISHMI, KAREN, NAGA-KUKI-CHIN and TIBETAN are the six major constituents adopted here from the somewhat more complex classifications of the sources.

Bodman (1971) grants that TIBETO-BURMAN constitutes a natural assemblage of major constituents within SINO-TIBETAN, but is uncertain how CHINESE may be related to which constituent in TIBETO-BURMAN; past comparisons have been largely focused on comparing CHINESE with Classical Tibetan, without broader exploration in TIBETO-BURMAN.

Any special relationship of KAM-TAI and MIAO-YAO, respectively, to CHINESE within 'SINITIC' has been rejected or questioned by (among others) Greenberg (1957a), Schutz (1971), and Benedict (1972 and earlier). As for KAM-TAI (q. v.), this constituent has been claimed to have special relationships with AUSTRONESIAN (q. v.) rather than with CHINESE.

The wider relationship of MIAO-YAO is expected by some to be found in Asia rather than in Oceania. Thus, Downer (1971) offers tentative support either for the possible inclusion of MIAO-YAO in SINO-TIBETAN, or else for some more remote relationship of MIAO-YAO to SINO-TIBETAN.

Note that no further reference is made to 'SINITIC', while the other major constituents and the assemblage of constituents in TIBETO-BURMAN are treated in separate articles (q. v.):

CHINESE
KAM-TAI
MIAO-YAO
TIBETO-BURMAN
    BODO-NAGA-KACHIN
    BURMESE-LOLO
    GYARUNG-MISHMI
    KAREN
    NAGA-KUKI-CHIN
    TIBETAN

DZORGAISH = DZORGAIC = CH'IANG. The half-dozen DZORGAISH languages, following, remain unclassified within SINO-TIBETAN: some would classify these with GYARUNG-MISHMI or TIBETAN (Shafer 1955).

1. Ch'iang.
2. Dzorgai.
3. Kortse.
4. Outer Mantse.
5. Pingfang.
6. Thotśu = Thochu ?

AFFILIATION. Schmidt (1926) postulated a relationship of SINO-TIBETAN and AUSTRONESIAN, also including MUNDA and MON-KHMER in his 'AUSTRIC' phylum. Shafer (1952, 1957) proposed a transoceanic link between SINO-TIBETAN in Asia and ATHA-PASCAN in North America.

SIOUAN

GROUPING. The Siouan languages are listed alphabetically below, since their internal relationships, outlined by C. F. Voegelin (1941a), are not known in detail, but have been attested in general by Wolff (1950-51); details are in Chafe (1973).

In the northern Plains two languages (3 and 6) constitute one linguistic sub-group (Crow-Hidatsa) which does not include Mandan (7) — despite the proximity of (6) and (7) — although Chafe (1971) places (7) closer to (3, 6) than to any other Siouan branch.

Several different tribes are dialectically distinguished, but speak one language, Dhegiha (5); as a single language, (5) is grouped with Dakota (4) and with the sub-group Chiwere-Winnebago (2, 10) — and possibly with the hard to classify Mandan (7) — in a MISSISSIPPI VALLEY branch.

This largest Siouan branch is flanked by the branch (3, 6), already mentioned and by another branch consisting of the subgroup Biloxi-Ofo (1, 9) in the south, and Tutelo (8) in the east.

1. *Biloxi. Formerly lower course of Pascagoula River in Mississippi, and from there through Mississippi to Louisiana, Texas, and Oklahoma.
2. Chiwere = Čiwere. Ds. Iowa = Ioway = Nadouessioux Maskoutens = Nez Percés = Pahodja (100–200; formerly primarily in Iowa, also Minnesota and Missouri); *Missouri = Missouria = Missourie; Oto = Otta = Otto(e) (100–500; formerly on lower course of Platte River or neighboring banks of the Missouri). Iowa, Minnesota, Missouri, Oklahoma, Kansas, Nebraska.
3. Crow = Absaraka = Absároke = Aubsároke = Belantsea = Corbeaux = Earchetinue = Upsároka = Upsaropa. 3,000. Montana, Wyoming.
4. Dakota = Sioux = Nadowa(y). Ds. Assiniboin(e) = Ston(e)y (1,000–2,000, Montana, Alberta, Saskatchewan); Santee = Dakota proper (3,000–5,000, Minnesota, North and South Dakota, Nebraska, Montana, Manitoba); Teton = Lakota, including the Og(a)l(l)ala = Ogallah, Brulé and (H)unkpapa bands (10,000–15,000, South Dakota, Montana, Manitoba); Yankton (together with Assiniboine = Nakota), including the Yantonai (1,000–2,000, North and South Dakota, Montana).
5. Dhegiha = ₵egiha = θegiha. Ds. = Trs. Kansa = Kaw (10–100; Oklahoma;

formerly along Kansas River in Kansas); Omaha = Maha (over 1,000; Nebraska, aboriginally along Missouri River in eastern Nebraska); Osage, including Great Osages, Little Osages (100–400; Oklahoma, formerly on Osage River, Missouri, later also on Missouri River); Ponca (100–1,000; Oklahoma and Nebraska, aboriginally on Missouri River in Nebraska), Quapaw = Akansa = Arkansas (less than 10; Oklahoma, formerly near the mouth of the Arkansas River in Arkansas). Traditional provenience SW Indiana.

6. Hidatsa = Hiratsa = Gros Ventre (of the Missouri) = Minatar(r)e(e) = Minitaree = Minitari = Minnataree = Minnetahse = Minetaree = Minitaree = Mönnitarri. 1,000–2,000. North Dakota in Fort Berthold area (formerly on the Missouri River in North Dakota).

7. Mandan = Mawatani = Numakaki = Numangkake = Sepohskanumakahkee = Wahtani. Fewer than 10. North Dakota.

8. *Tutelo = Katera = Shateras. Formerly Virginia, near Salem; other SIOUAN languages were also spoken in Virginia and the Carolinas.

9. *Ofo = Ofogoula = Mosopelea = Mosoperea = Chongue = Ossipe = Ouesperie = Ouispe = Ushpee. Formerly Mississippi and then Louisiana.

10. Win(n)ebago = Hochangara = Puant = Nipegon. 1,000–2,000. Nebraska, Wisconsin (formerly on south side of Green Bay extending to Lake Winnebago, Wisconsin).

AFFILIATION. Member of MACRO-SIOUAN, with closest affinity to Catawba in that phylum.

MACRO-SIOUAN PHYLUM

GROUPING. The remote genetic relationship between three language families and the three language isolates (1, 2, 3), listed below, is reflected in the MACRO-SIOUAN classification arrived at in 1964 (see *AFFILIATION* below).

The relationship of the SIOUAN family to the language isolate Catawba (1) is so close as to have tempted Wolff (1950–51) to reconstruct Catawba (with the non-controversial Siouan languages) in Proto-SIOUAN. Siebert (1945) was the first to give detailed evidence of the special relationship of Catawba to SIOUAN.

CADDOAN (q.v.); Chafe (1973) gives evidence for relating this family to IROQUOIAN and SIOUAN.

1. Catawba = Katába = Katahba = Ushery = Isa = Ysa = Issa = Iswa. Fewer than 10. South Carolina (formerly York and Lancaster counties, extending into North Carolina and Tennessee).

IROQUOIAN (q.v.); Chafe (1973) summarizes evidence for the relationship of this family to SIOUAN.
SIOUAN (q.v.)

2. Yuchi = Euchee = Uche = Uchee = Uchi = Utchee = Youchee = Yuchian = Chisca = Rickohockans ? 10–100. Oklahoma (formerly in eastern Tennessee, Kentucky, west Florida; also reported in South Carolina, Georgia, Alabama, Illinois).

3. *Woccon. In eastern North Carolina until the war of 1711–1713, after which the survivors may have joined the Tuscarora or the Catawba. Most closely related to Catawba, of which it may have been a dialect. Of the small vocabulary preserved, some words show resemblances to Yuchi (Crawford 1974).

AFFILIATION. In effect, Sapir (1929) included MACRO-SIOUAN in his HOKAN-SIOUAN. This earlier, more inclusive phylum was revised in subsequent classifications by Pinnow (1964) and at the FIRST CONFERENCE ON AMERICAN INDIAN LANGUAGES (1964); motivation for rejection of the former and for consensus reached at the latter is reported in detail by Voegelin and Voegelin (1967).

The HOKAN (q.v.) languages are now treated as a phylum, unrelated to the MACRO-SIOUAN phylum. Haas (1964b) recalls that Sapir used to speak of HOKAN-SIOUAN as his "wastepaper basket" group.

SLAVIC = SLAVONIC

GROUPING. Birnbaum (1966) defends the tripartite division of SLAVIC into an EAST, WEST, and SOUTH branch in the light of synchronic dialectology, but warns that it does not reflect a "consistent, rectilinear evolution;" what it does reflect is "many-layered" diachronic phenomena. The underlying dialects of the earlier 'common Slavic' are East Slavic (an independent development traceable to a pre-literate Proto-Russian, or the literate 'Old Russian'); 'Lekhitic' (Polish, Pomeranian, Polabian dialects); Sorbian = Lusatian; Czechoslovak; Sloveno-Serbocroatian; Macedo-Bulgarian.

There are 13 literary standard SLAVIC 'languages', but these literary 'languages' are not necessarily separated by spoken-language barriers. Between the nuclei formed by the literary 'languages' there are scarcely any linguistic frontiers, since transitional dialects connect each area. Even across the non-SLAVIC belt of language between Czechoslovakian and Serbocroatian there is a fair degree of intelligibility. Further, Lunt (1968) reports that "Almost any two intelligent Slavs can manage fairly quickly to establish elementary communication on a simple conversational level. . . ." Fodor (1961) finds the cognate density in SLAVIC to be above 80% for all SLAVIC 'languages', with most above 90%. In terms of structural features, there are two important isogloss lines: one in the north, which separates Ukrainian-Bielorussian from Polish, and another which separates Polish-Ukrainian from Slovak; and one in the south, which separates Bulgarian and Serbocroatian. These isogloss lines do not seriously impair intelligibility.

In terms of immediate intelligibility, SLAVIC can be grouped into three 'zones': EAST SLAVIC (Bielorussian, Russian, Ukrainian), SOUTH SLAVIC (Bulgarian, Macedonian, Serbocroatian, Slovene), and WEST SLAVIC (Czech, Kashubian, Lower Lusatian, Upper Lusatian, Polish, Slovak). Fourteen languages are listed below under these three 'zones', with the two Lusatian dialects listed as a single language, and with the inclusion of separate entries for the extinct Polabian and Old Church Slavonic.

The earliest attested SLAVIC language was Old Church Slavonic (SOUTH SLAVIC). Cyril and Methodius devised a script (Glagolitic), generally superseded by Cyrillic a century later. Though this script was devised in the ninth century, extant manuscripts date from the eleventh century. The Cyrillic alphabet is used by Orthodox Slavs (Bulgarians, Macedonians, Serbians, Russians, Bielorussians, Ukrainians); the Latin alphabet is used by Catholic Slavs (Poles, Czechs, Slovaks, Lusatians, Slovenes, and Croatians); and the Glagolitic alphabet was used at least until the nineteenth century by Dalmatian and Montenegrian Catholics.

Over 250,000,000 speakers for all SLAVIC. Except for a few border minorities in Europe, and North Americans with SLAVIC mother tongues, nearly all SLAVIC languages are spoken in countries with SLAVIC majorities: Poland, Czechoslovakia, Yugoslavia, Bulgaria, and the Union of Soviet Socialist Republics; the border minority exceptions include Upper and Lower Lusatian spoken in the German Democratic Republic (East Germany). At their first historical appearance, before the SLAVIC expansion, the Slavic homeland was north of the Carpathian mountains, in present-day Eastern Poland and Western Ukraine. The expansion was to the northeast into present-day Russia; west as far as East Germany; south over the Carpathians into Bohemia and Slovakia; and across the Danube into the Balkan Peninsula.

EAST(ERN) SLAVIC. This group comprises a series of transitional dialects between Russian and Bielourissian, and Bielorussian and Ukrainian (but not between Russian and Ukrainian). Bielorussian-Russian split from Ukrainian only in the thirteenth century; Bielorussian and Russian split in the sixteenth and seventeenth centuries. In terms of immediate mutual intelligibility, the EAST SAVIC zone is a single language.

1. Bielorussian = Byelorussian = Belorussian = White Russian = White Ruthenian. Ds. Northwestern (transitional from Russian to the Southwestern dialects), Southwestern (transitional into Northern Ukrainian). 10,000,000. Bielorussian SSR, minorities in Poland and Soviet Lithuania. The Russian Cyrillic alphabet was introduced for Bielorussian in 1908 and modified in 1917–18.

2. Russian = Great Russian. Ds. Central (a narrow belt from northwest to southwest across European Russian extending from Pskov to the Kalinin and Moscow area, and from a little north of Ryazan to Penza, and almost from Saratov on the Volga); Northern (including Leningrad-Novgorod (west), Olonets, Pomorsk, Vladimir-Volga, Vologda-Kirov (east)); Southern (stretching southwest from the central region to the boundaries of Bielorussian and Ukrainian-speaking areas, and starting just south of Rzhev in the north). 150,000,000. U.S.S.R. The primary cleavage is between the Northern and Southern dialects, with the Central dialect sharing features of both. The literary standard is based on Moscow speech (Central). Russonorsk can be said to be a Russian-based pidgin-creole, but might just as well be said to be Norwegian-based, since about half the lexicon of this pidgin-creole represents a relexification of one or the other of the languages mentioned; early in the twentieth century Russonorsk was spoken by Russians and Scandinavians (and probably by Lapps) in the overlapping area of northwest Russian and northeast Scandinavia.

3. Ukrainian = Little Russian. Ds. Eastern (in the Great or Dnieper Ukraine), Western (in Galicia, Podolia, Polesia, and Volhynia — formerly in Poland;

and a strip in Bukovina, which was formerly Rumanian; and in Subcar-
pathian Russia, which was formerly in Czechoslovakia). 40–45 million.
Ukrainian SSR and Soviet republics adjacent to Ukraine; also in Siberia,
Poland, and Slovakia. Shevelov (1965) divides Ukrainian into four dialects;
Northwestern, Southwestern, Eastern, and Carpathian; others divide
Ukrainian into three, rather than four, dialects: Southeastern, Northern,
and Western.

SOUTH(ERN) SLAVIC. This group split into 'Eastern' (Bulgarian) and 'Western'
(Serbocroatian, Slovenian) divisions, with Macedonian being placed either as 'Eastern'
(Lunt 1955) or as transitional (Ivić 1953, 1958). In terms of intelligibility, SOUTH
SLAVIC (like EAST SLAVIC) is a single language. 28,000,000. Primarily Yugoslavia and
Bulgaria. The split between Bulgarian-Macedonian and Slovenian-Serbocroatian is
much deeper than that of Russian-Ukrainian.

4. Bulgarian. Ds. Northeastern (spoken in an area or corridor extending south
   of Pazardžik); Western (spoken in an oblique line or corridor from NNE to
   SSW extending west of Nikopol on the Danube to the Greek frontier, with
   an eastern bulge around Cepino). 8,000,000. Bulgaria and adjacent U.S.S.R.
   (Bessarabia), Yugoslavia (Dimitrovgrad and Bosiljgrad districts), Greece
   (Moslem Pomaks in Thrace); and Catholic Bulgarians in Yugoslav and
   Rumanian Banat. The dialects are variously divided according to phono-
   logical developments (De Bray 1951). Another common division is into
   Central, Eastern, and Western dialects.

5. Macedonian. Ds. Eastern (in the Štip and Pirin region of southwestern
   Bulgaria); Northern (in the Kumanovo-Kratovo region of southeastern
   Yugoslavia); Southern (in the Kukus and Voden region of northern Greece);
   Southeastern (in the region of Gevgelija, Strumica, and Lake Dojran in
   southern Yugoslavia); Southwestern (in the Kostur and Lerin regions of
   northern Greece); Western (a central subdialect of Western in the Veles,
   Prilep, Kičevo, and Bitola regions in southeastern Yugoslavia; another
   subdialect spoken in the Debar-Galčnik region of southeastern Yugoslavia).
   1,000,000. Yugoslavia (Macedonia Republic). Bulgaria, Greece (Kastoria-
   Florina-Edessa region), and a few villages in Albania. In recent years Macedonian became a literary language based on the central subdialect of the
   Western dialect; this literary language is now (since 1943) recognized in
   Yugoslavia as a national language.

6. *Old Church Slav(on)ic. Used as the liturgical language of the various
   Orthodox and Byzantine Catholic churches of the Slavic nation.

7. Serbocroatian. Ds. Čakavian = 'the Ča dialect' (northern Dalmatian area
   of western Yugoslavia and on some Adriatic Islands); Kajkavian = 'the
   Kaj dialect' (northwestern Croatia in northern Yugoslavia; transitional to
   Slovenian); Štokavian = 'the Što dialect' (including East Hercegovina,
   Istrian Ikavian, Kosova-Resava, Late Ikavian, Rumanian Serbocroatian
   dialects, Slavonian, Šumadija-Vojvodina, Zeta-Lovćen); Torlakian (extreme
   southeastern Yugoslavia on the border of Macedonia, Bulgaria, and Albania).

17,000,000. Yugoslavia, Serbia, Bosnia-Hercegovina, Montenegro; minorities in Hungary, Rumania, Austrian Burgenland, Czechoslovakia (one or two villages), southern Italy (Campobasso Province). It is an important second language in Slovenia and Macedonia. The standard literary language is based on the Štokavian dialect for both Serbs and Croats. Differences in orthographies partly reflect political differences and partly dialect differences, with Cyrillic for an eastern variant and Latin for a western variant. The Catholic Dalmatians to some extent use their Glagolitic script (in the Slavonic liturgy).

8. Slovene = Slovenian. Ds. include Lower Carniola, Upper Carniola. 2,000,000. Yugoslavia (Peoples Republic of Slovenia); in Carniola, and southern parts of Styria and Carinthia; minorities in Italy (Udine Province and the Vale of Resia), Austria, Hungary, and the United States (180,000). The literary language is a compromise between the Lower Carniola and the Upper Carniola dialects, based primarily on the local dialect of Dolenjsko. The dialects of Slovene are extremely diverse; they developed during a thousand-year period characterized by lack of political and cultural unity (the two dialects mentioned being two fairly large dialect groups). Most Slovenes are bilingual in Serbocroatian, which they learn in school, but there are transitional dialects between Slovene and Serbocroatian which are closer than the literary languages.

WEST(ERN) SLAVIC. Birnbaum (1966) divides the traditional WEST SLAVIC branch, in terms of isoglosses, as descending from three common Slavic dialects (making this the most diverse of the three 'zones'). The descendants of these can be considered as a 'Northern language' (Polish, Kashubian, and the extinct Polabian), a 'West Central language' (Upper and Lower Lusatian), and a 'Southern language' (Czech and Slovak). As a consequence of diffusion and leveling due to contact since proto-times (if, indeed, it is possible to reconstruct a Proto-WEST-SLAVIC language), Czech and Slovak are now classified with the unquestionable WEST SLAVIC languages, Polish and Lusatian.

9. Czech. Ds. Central (the basis of the Czech literary language; centered in Prague in central Bohemia); Czecho-Moravian; Hanák (Moravia, centered in Brno and Prosětjov); Lach = Yalach (in Silesia; forms a transition to Polish, on the one hand, and to Eastern Slovak, on the other); Northeastern (northeast Bohemia); Southwestern (southwestern Bohemia). 10,000,000. Western Czechoslovakia, and the historic Czech lands of Bohemia, Moravia and Silesia; small Czech communities are also found in Poland. All Czech and Slovak dialects are mutually intelligible.

10. Kashubian = Cassubian. D. also Slovincian. 200,000. Poland (left bank of the Lower Vistula in north central Poland on the seaboard west of Gdansk = Danzig running inland in a narrow strip toward the southwest from Gdynia). Heavily Germanicized. There are transitional dialects between Kashubian proper, Slovenian, and Polish.

11. Lusatian = Sorbian = Wendish. Ds. Eastern Sorbian, around Muskau,

or Mužakow; Lower Lusatian = Low Sorbian = Lower Wendish = Dolna Lužica = Southern Lusatian = Saxon Lusatian (around Baudzen, or Budyšin; with a literary standard). 150,000. East Germany bordering north-west Czechoslovakia and southwest Poland extending east in a line from Berlin to Dresden but centered on the upper reaches of the Spree or Sprjewa River. Both literary standards in Lusatian used the Roman form of Latin script until the seventeenth century, when the Gothic form of writing was introduced in Lower Lusatian; the oldest written documents date from the late fifteenth century. Nearly all Lusatians are bilingual in German. Upper Lusatian resembles Polish, and Lower Lusatian resembles Slovak and Old Czech. In the Middle Ages when the Lusatian territory was more extensive than it is now, it was flanked by Polabian (to the north), Polish (to the east), and Czech (to the south), thereby functioning as an intermediate zone.

12. *Polabian. North of Lusatian.

13. Polish. Ds. Mazovian (centered on Warsaw); Małopolska = Little Polish (centered around Cracow); Silesian (centered at Katowice); Wielkopolska-Kujawy (centered around Poznań in Wielkopolska and Inowroław in Kujawy). 33,000,000. Poland; minorities in U.S.S.R. (500,000); the Těšin district of Czechoslovakia (100,000); Germany (100,000); Rumania (10,000); as well as Canada (130,000) and the United States (3,000,000).

14. Slovak. Ds. Central (basis of literary language); Eastern (affinities with Polish); Western (closer to Eastern than to Central). 4,000,000. Eastern Czechoslovakia in the Tatra Mountains, and in the surrounding foothills north of Hungary; minorities in Hungary and Yugoslav Vojvodina. All Czech and Slovak dialects are mutually intelligible, but Eastern Slovak and Bohemian Czech are probably the least intelligible to the other Czech-Slovak dialects. Slovak might well serve as a SLAVIC lingua franca, since it shares features with EAST, WEST, and SOUTH SLAVIC.

AFFILIATION. Member of INDO-EUROPEAN.

NORTHWESTERN AND CENTRAL SOLOMONS AUSTRONESIAN (Geographical)

GROUPING. Grace (1955) treats the languages of Bougainville Island, Buka Island, and the Bougainville Straits as forming a single subgroup of OCEANIC. Dyen (1965) subgroups seven of these languages as BUKA, but classifies the other two languages of the area in his sample, Banoni (1, below) and Mono (5), as grouped either with each other or with BUKA only at his highest level, AUSTRONESIAN.

The languages of Choiseul Island constitute another subgroup, as do those of the New Georgia Archipelago (Grace 1955, Capell 1962a, Dyen 1965).

Grace treats the languages of the southeastern Solomons (at least as far as the center of Santa Isabel) as forming another subgroup of OCEANIC. Most of these languages probably belong to the EASTERN subgroup of OCEANIC (q.v.); however, some of the languages of Santa Isabel appear not to belong to EASTERN OCEANIC. It is those which appear to be non-EASTERN OCEANIC languages that are listed below (25, 26).

BUKA. Dyen's BUKA languages are subdivided into NORTHWEST (languages 2, 4, 6, 11; further subdivided into 2, 4 as opposed to 6, 11), TEOPIC (8, 12), and Saposa (10).

1. Banoni. 12,500. Southwestern Bougainville.
2. Hanahan = Halia. 3,000–4,000. Northeastern Buka, 5°15'S 154°35'E.
3. Kilinailau. Kilianilau Islands 4°45'S 155°20'E.
4. Lontes = Lontis. Northern Buka, Lontas ? 4°51'S 152°53'E.
5. Mono. 1,300 (1931). In the Bougainville Straits. 6°55'S 156°10'E., on Treasury (Mono) Island, 7°25'S 155°30'E, Fauro Island, 6°55'S 156°05'E, and Shortland Island 7°05'S 155°45'E (where it is spoken by the Alu = Alo).
6. Petats. 10,000, including second-language speakers. Native on Petats (5°20'S 154°33'E), Pororan (5°12'S 154°32'E) and Hitau Islands (5°10'S 154°30'E) off the west coast of Buka; as a lingua franca throughout Buka Passage area.
7. Piva. 300. Piva River, 6°16'S 155°04'E, Bougainville. Grouped by Capell (1962a) with Banoni (1).
8. Raosiara. Northeastern Bougainville, 6°00'S 155°00'E. May be a dialect of Teop (12).
9. Sailo. 1,450 (1959). Buka.
10. Saposa. 200. Saposa Island 5°35'S 154°43'E.
11. Sumoun. Western Buka. May be a dialect of Petats (6).
12. Teop. 1,600 (1959). Northeastern Bougainville, Teop (Tiop) 5°35'S 155°05'E.
13. Timputs. 1,150.
14. Torau. 800.
      Halisa (?), Hanon (?), Matsungan (5°24'S 154°34'E)(?), Rorovana (6°10'S 155°32'E)(?), Taiof (5°31'S 154°39'E)(?), Uruava ?

CHOISEUL. The total population of Choiseul Island, 7°30'S 157°30'E, was 5,000 in 1950. Languages (15) and (16) form a subgroup as opposed to a subgroup consisting of (17) and (18) (Dyen 1965).

15. Sengan = Sengga = Sisingga. Ds. also Babatana = Bambatana, Kuboro = Kumboro.
16. Sirio.
17. Vagua = Tavola = Tavula.
18. Varisi.
Gongoroi(?), Gubinengo = Tuga(?), Katazi(?), Katoratele(?), Kirungella(?), Kiposaka = Tipasaka(?), Kunambena = Kurubena = Mbota(?), Liuliu(?), Lömaumbi(?), Maran(?), Moli = Mole(?), Ruruvai = Ruravai(?), Subi(?), Tasobi(?), Taura = Raura = Laura(?), Vasengasenga = Singasinga(?), Virulata(?), and on small islands off Choiseul: Tamatamba = Tabataba = Tarikukuri(?), Vagena(?), Velaviuru(?).

NEW GEORGIA. Dyen's NEW GEORGIA is subdivided into ROVIANIC (21, 24), LUNGGIC (19, 22), and Marovo (23). The total population of New Georgia was given as 2,294 in 1959; Capell (1962a) estimates numbers of speakers at more than twice that number.

19. Duke = Nduke. 732. Nduke (Kolombangara) Island 8°00'S 157°10'E.

20. Kia. 1,250. Northern end of Santa Isabel. Grouped with Roviana (24) by Capell (1962a).

21. Kusage. D. also Hoava. New Georgia, 8°14′S 157°15′E.

22. Lungga = Luqu. Ds. also Kubokota, Madegugusu. 1,500–2,000. Ganongga (Luqa, Ranonga, Vesu Gogota) Island, 8°00′S 156°34′E and Simbo (Eddystone) Island, 8°18′S 156°34′E.

23. Marovo. Ds. also Bareke, Vangunu. 3,000(?), plus 2,000(?), second-language speakers. New Georgia Island and Vangunu Island, 8°40′S 158°00′E.

24. Roviana = Rubiana. Over 3,000? New Georgia Island.
Batuna(?), Burongo(?), Eongo(?), Gatukai = Ngatokae(?), Podokana(?), Ramata = Ngerasi(?), Tetepari(?), Ugele (400 speakers, northern Rendova Island, 8°33′S 157°17′E)(?), Viru = Kuvilana(?), Wanawana ?

SANTA ISABEL (Geographic). Total population 6,000 (1956).

25. Bogotu = Bogota. Ds. also Hageule, Vulava. 1500. Southern Santa Isabel (Ysabel) Island 8°00′S 159°00′E.

26. Zabana. Not subgrouped with any other AUSTRONESIAN language by Dyen (1965).

Central Santa Isabel small tribes are only doubtfully classified as AUSTRONESIAN speaking: Aara-Maringe(?), Gao = Nggao(?), Hogirano(?), Jajao(?), Kakatio(?), Kilokaka(?), Longgahaja = Logahaja(?), Maga(?), Susulu ?

AFFILIATION. Member of OCEANIC subgroup of AUSTRONESIAN.

CENTRAL SUDANIC

GROUPING. The classification of CENTRAL SUDANIC, following, incorporates information from Tucker and Bryan (1956) and from Greenberg (1966). Though Greenberg does not support Tucker and Bryan's bifurcation of the various groups into two 'larger units', BONGO-BAGIRMI and MORU-MANGBETU, he does otherwise reflect, with some modification, Tucker and Bryan's subgrouping of CENTRAL SUDANIC. Altogether 1,250,000 speakers. Chad, Central African Republic, and adjacent Sudan Uganda, Congo (Leopoldville)=Zaire.

BAGIRMI

1. Babalia ?
2. Bagirmi = Baghirmi = Baguirme = (Tar) Barma = Tar Bagrimma = Lis(i). 30,000–40,000. Chad.
3. Dis(s)a ?
4. Gele ?
5. Gula ?
6. Kenga = Kenge = Kenya = Cenge = Bokiyo. 20,000–25,000. Chad.
7. Kuka = Kouka. Ds. also *Abu Simmin, Bilala = Bulala = Boulala = Ma-(-ge), Mudogo = Medogo = Midogo = Modogo = Kodoi.

BONGO

8. Baka = (Tara) Baaka. 2,600. Congo (Leopoldville).

9. 'Beli = Beili. Ds. also Gberi = Gbara = Muda (600); Lori (1,000); Modo, including Modo Kirim and Modo Lali (1,700); Sopi = Supi (1,600), *Wetu. 9,900. Sudan.

10. Bongo = Bungu = Dor. Over 2,400. Sudan.

11. Morokodo = Ma'di. Ds. also Biti (280), Madu, Nyamusa (1,200), Wira. Over 4,600. Sudan.

KARA

12. Furu = Gbaya. Ds. = Trs. Gbaya, Mbanja, Ngbaka. 5,000. Congo(Kinshasa), Territoire Bosobolo.

13. Kara = Yamegi. Ds. also Gula = Goula, Ŋguru = Bubu = Koyo. Sudan, eastern Equatoria Province.

14. Yulu-Binga. Ds. Aja, Binga = Biŋa, Yulu, 2,800. Sudan.

15. Kresh = Kreish = Kredj = Kreich = Kpala = Kpara. Ds. Dongo (100), Gbaya(-ndogo), Kresh-dogo (1,800), Naka = Kpara = Hofra = Kresh-Hofra = Kpala-Hofra (3,600), Woro = Oro = Ori (400).

16. Lendu = Bale(ndru) = Balega = Walega. Ds. Northern Lendu = Bale-da = Ba(a)-da, including 'Bahema = Wahema = Ziida = Joda, Bale-da of Fataki, Mambisa = Bambisa = Go = Go-da, Oke'bu(ke) = Ke-da, Pi-da of Kwanduma and Rethi (Zaire: Territoires Djugu, and Mahagi); Southern Lendu = Dru = Ndru = Dru-na, including Kabona, Monobi, Zadu (Uganda: Toro District, West Nile District). 110,000–250,000.

MANGBETU

17. Asua(ti) = Aka = Asua-e.

18. Mangbetu = Mangbettu = Amangbetu = Namangbetu. Ds. also Abulu = Naaburi-ti = Naaberu-ti = Aberu = Babeyru = Aaberu = Naaberu (1,500), Lombi = Lumbi = Odyalombi-to = Barumbi = BaLumbi (8,100), Mabisanga = Namabisanga = Amabisanga (4,000), Maele = Malele = Emalele = Nemalele (13,000), Makere = Namakere-ti = Amakere = Namakere (17,500), Majuu = Maidjuwu = Namajuu = Amajuu (8,200), Mangbele, Meje = Nameje-ti = Medje = Medye = Megye = Emeeje = Nemeeje (13,200), Popol = Namapopoi(-ti) = Amapopoi. 100,000–500,000. Some of the dialects listed here may instead be separate languges.

MANGBUTU-EFE

19. Mamvu-Efe. Ds. Amengi; Efe = Efe-e (10,000); Lese = (W)alese =(B)alese, including Andali, Lese Karo = Upstream Lese, Mabeni, Ndese = Lese Dese, Vonkutu = Obi (20,100); Mamvu = Momvu = Momfu = Mudo (29,355); Mvu'ba = Mvuba = Bambuba = Bamvuba = Mvuba-a = Obi-ye. 60,000. Zaire, Uganda.

20. Mangbutu(li) = Mombutu = Wambutu. Ds. also Awimeri = A'imeri, Bambodo, Mangbutu Karo = Upstream Mangbutu, Mangbutu Lobo = Downstream Mangbutu. 8,700. Zaire.

21. Ndo. Ds. Membi = Membi(?), Ndo Avari = Avari-tu = Avere (4,000), Ndo Oke'bu = Kebu-tu = Kebu (9,000). Zaire-Uganda border.

MORU-MA'DI. The languages listed separately as High Lugbara (25) and Low Lugbara (26) may be dialects of a single language.

22. Avukaya = Avokaya = Abukeia. Ds. = Trs. Äjigä = Ädjígä (-ti) = Ojigä = Agamoru, Ogambi, OjiLä = Odzila = Odziliwa. 5,200. Sudan, Zaire.

23. Käliko = Keliko = Madi(-ti). 18,000. Zaire, Sudan.

24. Logo(-ti) = Logo Kuli. Ds. = Trs. also Akori, Bäri-Logo = Bäri(-ti), Obileba, Ogamaru = Northern Logo, Tabulago = TabuLoba. Over 54,000. Zaire, Sudan.

25. High Lugbara = Uruleba(-ti) = Logbware, Lugware = Lugori = Lubari. Ds. Alur(u), Aiva, Lui = Zaki, Maratsa, Nyo = Nyio, Oka, Padzulu. 144,000. Uganda, Zaire. The total Lugbara population is about 350,000 in Uganda (see also 26).

26. Low Lugbara = Andreleba(-ti). Ds. Kulu'ba, Uludri. 78,000. Uganda. (See also 25 for population.)

27. Ma'di(-ti) = Madi. Ds. also 'Burulo, Lokai, Madi Subdistrict dialect (Sudan), Olu'bo = Luluba = Olubo-go = Olubo-ti, Pandikeri, West Nile district dialect (Sudan). About 114,000 in Uganda. Mainly Uganda, Sudan (Madi Subdistrict, Opari district, West Nile district).

28. Moru = Kala Moru. Ds. Ägi = Kala Agi = Moru Agi, Ändri = Moru Ändri, 'Bäli'bä = Boliba = Balimba, Kädiro = Kala Kädiro si = Moru Kädiro = Kediru = Kadiru = Kedero, Lamama'di, Miza = Moru Miza, Wa'di = Moru Wa'di = Wa'di(-ti). 23,000. Sudan.

SARA. All the languages following, excepting Vale, may be dialects of a single Sara language. Central African Republic, Chad.

29. Gambai = Gamba = Sara Gambai = Ngambai = Gambay. Ds. also Daba of Gore, Laka = Lak = Lag = Kabba Laka (40,000), Sara Mbai of Doba = Mbai Gor ? (85,000), Sara Murũn. Over 235,000.

30. Kaba = Sara Kaba = Kabba. Ds. Kaba Boho, Kaba Bumaŋga, Gula of Moufa, Kaba Jaha, Kaba Ndim = Ndemi = Sara Ndemi = Démi, Kaba Ndoko of Ndele, Kaba Sime. 11,500.

31. Kaba Dunjo = Sara. Ds. also Kaba Jiŋge = Dendje = Dindje, Kaba Joko = Ndioko, Kaba Mbaŋga, Kaba Na, Kaba Tie = Tye. 17,000.

32. Mbai = Sara Mbai = Bai = Mbay = Mbaye = Pa Mbai Moisala = Pa Mbai Daŋbo. Ds. Daba of Batangafo, Kaba of Batangafo. 73,000.

33. Sara proper. Ds. (Sara) Gulai = Goulaye = Gulei, (Sara) Majingai = Midjinngay = Modjingaye = Moggingain = Maji-ngai, Nar = Peni, Sara Ngama = Ngama. Over 45,000.

34. Vale. Ds. also Nduka, Tana = Tele = Tane.

Horo(?); Kusuvulu(?); Sara Hii(?); Butu ?

AFFILIATION. Member of NILO-SAHARAN phylum.

EASTERN SUDANIC

GROUPING. Group I languages are known simply as languages belonging to the EASTERN SUDANIC family, while the EASTERN SUDANIC languages under II and III are also known by distinguishing labels: NILOTIC and NILO-HAMITIC, respectively.

The classificatory question revolves on the interpretation given to generally acknowledged similarities between Group III languages and CUSHITIC in AFROASIATIC as well as between Group III and Group I and II languages — subgroups of EASTERN SUDANIC classified in CHARI-NILE of NILO-SAHARAN. The balance of weighing similarities may be indeterminate for the wider classification of Group III languages, or at least insufficient for classifying Group III with Group I and Group II languages, as argued, among others, by Tucker and Bryan (1956); or the balance may permit the classification of Group III languages on a coordinate basis with groups I and II, under EASTERN SUDANIC, as argued by Greenberg (1955, 1957b and 1971a).

Group III languages are labeled NILO-HAMITIC = PARANILOTIC = GREAT LAKES = EASTERN NILOTIC, and by variants of these names to imply different classifications, as noted in the summary of the controversy following, which centers on Group III. Group III is classified as EASTERN SUDANIC by Greenberg (1966), but by both Hohenberger (1958) and Huntingford (1956) as constituting a hybrid link between CUSHITIC (hence, AFROASIATIC) and Groups I and II of EASTERN SUDANIC (hence, NILO-SAHARAN). Struck (1911) and others follow Meinhof's earlier (1910) classification of Group III as HAMITIC (hence, AFROASIATIC) languages spoken in the Nilotic area. Westermann (1921) distinguishes between the NILOTIC or northern division of languages (termed by him NILOTO-SUDANIC) and a southern division (termed SOUTHERN GREAT LAKES). Murray (1920) classified Group III languages (termed by him NILO-HAMITIC) with some Group I languages, in particular with NUBIAN. Tucker and Bryan (1966) classify Group III — GREAT LAKES languages — with Group II, NILOTIC languages, and take the similarities between Group III languages and CUSHITIC to be evidence of borrowing, thereby not supporting the hybrid status of Group III languages with AFROASIATIC, which Hohenberger (1956) espoused.

I. Marvin Bender (1971), concerned primarily with languages of Ethiopia, groups BEIER-DIDINGA = SURMA (Tucker and Bryan 1956) with Nara = Barya = Barea (17) as a singe 'NARA-SURMA' subgroup.

BEIER-DIDINGA = SURMA. Marvin Bender (1971) classifies languages numbered 2, 4, 5, 6, 7, 8, 9 as a SURMA group, with all but Masongo (4) in a CENTRAL SURMA group, with 6 and 9 forming one subgroup, and languages numbered 2, 5, 7, 8 forming another subgroup; the latter are further subdivided into Kwegu (2), Mekan (5), and Mursi-Tirma (7, 8). 60,000. Ethiopia, Sudan.

1. Didinga = 'Di'diŋa = Xaroxa = Toi = Lango. Ds. = Trs. Chukudum = Nagichot, Lowudo. 3,000–11,500. Sudan.
2. Kwegu = Kwegi = Bacha = Menja = Nyidi(ni) = Yidi(nich). 600. Ethiopia.
3. Longarim = Larim(init) = Boya. 1,000–4,000. Sudan.
4. Masongo = Mesengo = Masengo = Mushango = Mojang(o) = Ujang = Mogeno = Majangir = Magianghir = Manjanjiro = Tama = Tdama = Ttama = Dama. Over 28,000.
5. Mekan = Me'en = Mieken = Meqan = Daim = Suro = Shuro =

Surbm = Surma = Durma = Tishana = Teshina = Tishena = Bachuma = Golda = Goldea = Goldiya = Sogore. D. also Bodi. 38,000.

6. Murle = Murleny = Murule = Marille = Marle = Merille = Beir = Ajiba = Adjibba = Agiba = Ajibba = Bangalam = Kapeta = Epeita = Kapeita = Lotilla = Olam. Ds. = Trs. Boma Murle = Ngalam, Omo Murle = Mandarec = Ṇandarec, Ol ci Lotilla = Pibor Murle. 40,000. Ethiopia.

7. Murzu = Mursi = Murzi = Dama = Mun(i) = Ngalibong(?) = Ngaliabong(?) = Kalibong ? 8,500.

8. Tirma = Tirima = Suri-Tirma-Tid = Nikorama = Nyikorama. Ds. Suri = Surma = Korma = Corma = Churma = Shuri = Dhuri = Kichepo = Kachipa = Kachepo = Kachipo = Dhuäk = Thuak = Zuak = Dzuak, Tid(i) = Cach = Chaich = Cac = Caci = Cai = Guredirma = Kamartani = Karabachich = Nkoraṃa = Murutuin = Dolot. 8,500.

9. Zelmamu = Zelmamo = Zulmamu = Zilmamo = Tsilmano = Balethi = Baletha. 2,000.

DAJU = DAGU. Altogether 100,000 speakers. Sudan (Dar Fur, Kordofan, and Equatoria provinces), Chad.

10. Daju = Dagu of Dar Dadjo = Saaroŋge. 27,000. Chad: Wadai Province.

11. Daju = Dagu of Dar Fur = Finiŋga = Daju Ferne. Ds. also Baygo = Baigo = Bego = Beko (200). 2,800. Sudan.

12. Daju = Dagu of Dar Sila = Bokoruge = Bokorike. 32,000. Chad.

13. Daju of West Kordoton = Beke. 6,000. Sudan.

14. Liguri. Ds. also Saburi, Tallau = Talau = Talo. 2,000. Sudan: Nuba Hills.

15. Njalgulgule = Nyoolne = Ngulgule = Begi = Bege = Beko = Njangulgule. 900. Sudan.

16. Shatt. 9,000.

17. Nara = Barya = Barea. 25,000. Ethiopia: Eritrea.

NUBIAN. Altogether 1,000,000 speakers. Sudan, extending into Egypt.

18. Birked = Birqed = Birged = Birkit = Murgi = Kajjara.

19. Dongola-Kenuz. Ds. Dongola = Dongolawi = Dangagla, Kenuz = Kenuzi = Kunuzi. Northern Sudan, along the Nile.

20. Kordofanian Nubian = Hill Nubian. Ds. = Trs. Dair = Daier = Thaminyi (ni be) (225), Dilling = Delen = Warki (m be), El Hugeirat (202), Ghulfan = Gulfan = Wunci (m be) (3,260), Kadaru = Kadaro = Kadero = Kaderu = Kodoro = Kodhin (ni ai) (1,668), Western Kadaru, Karko = Garko = Kithoniri (she) (2,122), Kundugr, Wali = Walari (she) (487).

21. Mahas-Fiyadikka. Ds. Mahas = Mahasi = Mahass, Fiyadikka = Fedicca = Fadicha = Fadija = Fiadidja.

22. Midob = Meidob = Tidda. Ds. = Trs. Shelkota, Torti, Urrti. 1,800.

NYIMANG. 26,000–37,000. Sudan, Nuba Hills.

23. Afitti = Ditti = Unietti. 2,900.
24. Nyimang = Nyiman = Ama. 26,000–37,000.

TAMA. Altogether 150,000 speakers. Sudan (Dar Fur Province) extending into Chad.

25. Kibet. Ds. also Dagel (5,000 to 6,000), Mur(r)u = Murro (1,000). 16,000–22,000.
26. Mararit = Merarit = Mararet = Abiyi = Abiri = Ebiri. Ds. also Abu Sharib. 42,000.
27. Sungor = Asongori. Ds. = Trs. Girga, Walad Dulla. 39,000.
28. Tama = Tamongobo = Tamok = Tamot. Ds. also Erenga, including Asungore, Madungore, Sha(a)le (7,500); Jabaal = Mileere (6,000); Orra = Gimr = Qimr = Haura (1,500). Over 45,000.

TEMEIN. Sudan: Nuba Hills.

29. Keiga Jirru = Keiga Girru. 1,400.
30. Temein = Rone. 2,300.

TEUSO. Uganda.

31. Dorobo.
32. Nuangeya = Nyuangia = Nyangiya = Upale.
33. Tepes = Tepeth.
34. Teuso = Teuth = Ngulak. 1,500.

II. NILOTIC = WESTERN NILOTIC. Greenberg (1966) subclassifies the languages below into three groups: (a) Burun (40); (b) Shilluk (54), Anuak (38), Akoli (36), Lango (47), Alur (37), Luo (48), Lwo = Jur (50), Bor (39); and (c) DINKA (41–44), NUER (52, 53). Marvin Bender (1971) distinguishes between EAST NILOTIC: (a) Burun (40); (b) Maban (51); and WEST NILOTIC: (a) Anuak (38), Shilluk (54), DINKA (41–44) and (b) NUER (52, 53). Tucker and Bryan (1956) set up four subgroups: (a) DINKA (41–44); (b) NUER (52, 53); (c) NORTHERN LWO: Shilluk (54), Anuak (38), Burun (40), Maban (51), Lwo = Jur (50), Thuri (55), Bor (39); (d) SOUTHERN LWO: Akoli (36), Lango (47), Kumam (45), Labwor (46), Lwo = Chopi (49), Alur (37), Adhola (35), Luo = Nyife (48). Altogether, 4,000,000 speakers. Sudan and Uganda, extending into Zaire, Kenya, and Ethiopia.

35. Adhola = Dhopadhola = Budama. 153,000 (Uganda). Uganda (Mbale District) extending into Kenya.
36. Akoli = Acholi = Acooli = Shuli = Log Acoli = Dok Acoli = Gang = Lango. Tr. Payira. 420,000 (Uganda). Uganda, extending into Sudan (Opari District).
37. Alur = Dho Alur = Aluru = Alulu = Lur = Jo Alur. Ds. = Trs. Jokot, Jo Nam, Mambisa, Wanyoro. Over 200,000 (181,000, Uganda).
38. Anuak = Anywak = Anywaq = Anwak = (Dho) Anywaa = Nuro = Yambo. Trs. also Acoli = Madi, Päri = Fari = Berri = Lokoro = Lopol. Over 56,000. Sudan.
39. Bor = Dhe Bor = Jo Bor = Rodi. 6,000.
40. Burun = Barun = Hill Barun = Burun Proper = Northern Burun = Lange = Cai. Ds. = Trs. also Abuldugu = Bogon = Mugo-Mborkoina,

Kurmuk = Tarat = Boit = Mekormuk, Mufwa = Mopo, Mughaja =
Mumughadja, Ragreig. 18,000. Sudan.

DINKA = DINQA = JIENG = JIANG. 500,000–2,000,000. Sudan, Ethiopia.
  41. Agar. Ds. Aliab = Thany, Ciec = Cic = Chich = Kwac = Ajak =
      Ador, Gok. 16,000.
  42. Bor. Ds. Bor Gok (5,800), Boathoi = (Bor) Athoic = Atoc (5,200), Ghol
      (2,000), Nyarueng = Nyarweng = Narreweng (2,000), Twi (8,800).
  43. Padang. Ds. Abialang = Dinka = Ibrahim, including Akoon, Bawom
      = Bowom, Giel (7,200); Don(g)jol (9,000); Luac = Luaic (700);
      Ngok = Ngork = Jok (21,000); Paloc = Poloic, including Age(e)r =
      Ageir, Abuya, Beer, Niel = Nyel (13,500); Rut (515); Ruweng; Thoi
      (400).
  44. Rek = Raik. Ds. Abiem, including Ajong Dit = Ajuong Dit, Ajong
      Thi = Ajuong Thi, Akany Kok = Akern Jok, Apuoth = Apwot,
      Anei = Wun Anei (13,800); Agwok; Apuk; Awan; Lau; Malual =
      Malwal, including Atoktou = Atokto, Duli(i)t, Korok, (M)akem,
      Peth (9,400); Paliet = Baliet, including Ajak, Buoncuai = Bon Shwai
      = Bwoncwai, Kongder = Kondair = Kongdeer, Thany Bur =
      Tainbour (4,400); Palioupiny = Palioping = Palyoupiny, including
      Akjuet = Ajwet, Akuang Ayat = Akwat Ayat, Cimel = Cemel =
      Chimiel, Gomjuer = Gomjier (8,300); Tuic = Twic = Twich = Twij,
      including Adhiang, Amiol, Nyang, Thon (12,600). Over 40,000.
  45. Kumam = Kuman = Kumum = Ikumama = Akum = Akokolemu
      = Ikokolemu. 96,000. Uganda.
  46. Labwor = Tobur. 5,000. Uganda.
  47. Lango = Leb Laŋo = Laŋo Miro. 534,000. Uganda (Lango and Acholi
      districts).
  48. Luo = Dho Luo = Nyife = Nife = Jo Luo = (Wa-)Gaya. 800,000. Kenya,
      Tanzania.
  49. Lwo = Chopi = Dhopaluo = Dho Pa Lwo = Jafalu = Shepalu = Shifalu.
      5,000–6,000. Uganda.
  50. Lwo = Jur = Giur = Luo = Dhe Lwo = Jur Lwo = Jo Lwo. 20,000.
  51. Maban = Maaban = Meban = Southern Burun = Gura = Tungan =
      Barga = Tonko. Ds. also Jumjum = Berin = Olga = Wadega. Over 20,000.

NUER. 250,000–500,000. Sudan, extending into Ethiopia.
  52. Atuot = Atwot. Ds. also Apak = Afak, Aril. 8,000.
  53. Nuer = (Thog)Naath = A(b)bigar. Ds. Do(o)r (1,600), Eastern Jikany
      (17,600); Western Jikany = Jikain = Jekaing = Jikain (2,935); Lou =
      Lau (12,500), Nyuong (1,100); Thiang (2,500), including Bul (5,900),
      Gawaar = Gaweir, Jagai (2,400), La(a)k (6,700), Leek = Leik (4,900).
      40,000.
  54. Shilluk = (Dho)Colo. 110,000. Sudan.
  55. Thuri = Dhe Thuri = Jo Thuri = Wada Thuri. Ds. = Trs. also Bodho =
      Dhe Bood(h)o = Dembo = Demen = Dombo, Colo = Dhe Colo = Jur
      Shol = Jo Colo, Manangeer = Jur Manangeer. 8,000–13,500.

III. NILO-HAMITIC = EASTERN NILOTIC = PARANILOTIC = GREAT
LAKES. The NILO-HAMITIC group includes two subgroups, NANDI (languages
numbered 59–61) and TESO (languages numbered 63–66), and four individual languages;
Bari (56), Lotuho (57), Maasai (58), and Ngasa (62). Altogether, 1,780,000. Sudan
and Uganda, extending into Kenya, Tanzania and Ethiopia.

56. Bari. Ds. Kakwa = Kakua = Kwakwak (84,000. Sudan; 573,000, Uganda);
Kuku (24,000; Uganda), Mondari = Mandari = Mundari = Shir = Chir
= Kir (36,000; Sudan), Nyangbara = Nyangwara = Nyambara (18,000;
Sudan-Zaire border), Nyepu = Nyefu = Nyepo = Nypho (2,800–3,500;
Sudan), Pöjulu = Päjulu = Fadjulu = Fajelu, including Madi (26,000;
Sudan). Trs. 'Dupi, Kulu'ba, Liggi, Lui, Tomonok. 226,000, including
35,000 Bari proper.

57. Lotuho = Otuxo = Lotuxo = Lotuko = Latuko = Lattuka = Olotorit.
Ds. Dongotono = Dongotolo, Koriok = Koriuk (2,500), Lango = Laŋo
(3,900 with Dongotono and Logir), Logir, Logiri, Lokoya = Lokoiya =
Lokoja = (L)owoi = (L)oirya (12,400), Lomya (1,000), Lopi = Loprit =
Lolopit, Lorwama = Lowama, including Lokathan = Ketebo (sometimes
classified as belonging to Teso), Lowudo. Over 66,000. Sudan.

58. (Il-)Maasai = Masai = (Ol-)Maa = Kwavi = Wakwavi = Wakwafi =
(L)oikop = Oigob = Lumbwa. Ds. (I-)Sampur = Sambur = Samburu =
Burkeneji, Tiamus = Njamusi = Njemps = Il-tyamus = Ol-tyamusi. Trs.
(Il-)Arusa = Arusha (Tanzania), Baraguyu (Tanzania), (Il-)Dalalekutuk
(Kenya), (Il-)Damat (Kenya), Kaputiei (Kenya, Tanzania), (Il-)Keekonyokie
(Kenya), (Il-) Kisongo (Kenya, Tanzania), (Il-)Loodokilani (Kenya), (Il-)
Matapato (Kenya), Oitai = Iloytai (Kenya), (Il-)Purko (Kenya), (I-)Sikirari
(Kenya), ·(I-)Siria (Kenya), Wuasinkishu = Wasin Gishu = Guas Ngishu
(Kenya). 190,000. Tanzania, Kenya.

NANDI = SOUTHERN

59. Nandi = Ngalekap Nandi = Nandiek = Cemuel = Il-tiengwali. Ds.
Akiek = Okiek, Dorobo = Ndorobo = Nderobo = Torobo (1,500),
Keyo = Elgeyo = Keyu = Keyyo = Keyyek (40,500), Kipsikis =
Kipsigis = Kipsiki = Lumbwa (160,000), Kipsorai = Sore, Kony =
Elonyi = Elgon (Masai), Konjek, Mbai, Pok = Lako = Lago =
Bagwet, Sabaot = Sabaut (25,500), Sapiny = Sabei = Savei = Sebei
= Saviny = Kamecak (572,000; Uganda), Terik = Nyangori =
Nyangnori, Tuken = Tugen = Tugin = Tukin = Kamasia = Kama-
saya (66,000). Over 450,000. Kenya, Uganda, Tanzania.

60. Pokot = Päkot = Suk = Pokwot = Kimunkon = Upe. Ds. also
Endo(To) = Cepleng (7,200), Kadam = Ngikadama, Markwet =
Marakwet = Maragwetl = Merkwet (22,300). 90,000. Kenya, Uganda.

61. Tatog(a) = Tataru. Trs. Bajut = Bayuta = Barabaik = Barabaig =
Baraban, Bianjit, Buradik, Daragwajek, Dororajek, Ghumbiek, Gisamajenk, Iseimajek = Simajek = Simityek, Mangat'k, Reimojik, Rutageink = Rotageink. 64,000. Tanzania.

62. Ngasa = Ongamo. 1,000. Tanzania.

TESO
63. Karamojong = A-karimojong = Ŋikaramojong = Lango Dyang. Ds. also
    Dodos = Dodoth = Dodotho = Dodosi = Ng-Dudutho = I-Dudutho
    (20,200), Jie = Ngi-jiye = E-jiot (18,200), Jiye, Ngiakwai = Nginyakwai
    (1,000), Ngi-gatio. 100,000, including 55,600 Karamojong proper.
64. Teso = Ateso = Iteso = Ikumama = Bakedi = Bakidi = Itesyo =
    Itesio = Etossio = Elgumi = Wamia. Ds. also Lokathan = Biri =
    Ketebo (actually a dialect of Lotuho?), Nyangeya = Nyangia = Nipori
    = Poren = Ngapore = Ngiaŋgeya, Orom = Rom. Uganda (Teso and
    Mbole districts), Kenya (Northern Nyanza district).
65. Toposo = (Akeroa) Toposa = Topotha = Taposa = Dabossa =
    Akara = Kare = Khumi = Huma = Kum(i), Abo. Ds. also Donyiro
    Dongiro = Idongiro, Nyangatom = Nyamatom. 34,000. Sudan.
66. Turkana = Inyangatom = Bume = Buma = Bumi = Donyiro =
    Donyoro. 85,000–95,000. Kenya, Sudan, Ethiopia.

67. *Meroitic. Language of the ancient Meroitic Kingdom of Egypt and the Sudan.
Unclassified within EASTERN SUDANIC (Greenberg, 1971a).

AFFILIATION. Member of CHARI-NILE in NILO-SAHARAN.

*Sumerian. Ds. eme-KU (the official dialect), eme-SAL (the dialect most often used
in hymns and incantations). Sumerian has the oldest known alphabetic writing system
in the world, with inscriptions dating from 3,100 B.C. This language was spoken in
southern Mesopotamia during the third millennium B.C., and replaced in the next
millennium by Akkadian. It continued in written form until near the beginning of
the Christian era.

AFFILIATION. None known.

TACANA = TAKANA = TECANÁ

GROUPING. The TACANA branch of the PANO-TACANA family, numbering some
30 languages, is divided on an apparently geographical basis by Mason (1950) into
four groups of languages plus three ungrouped languages, all of which are (or were)
spoken in northwest Bolivia and adjacent southeast Peru (Mary Key 1968). The
ARAONA languages (numbered 1–4) are all spoken in Bolivia along the Beni and
Madre de Dios rivers; the CHIRIGUA subgroup (numbered (5–7) is located northeast
of the upper reaches of the Beni River in Bolivia; the TACANA subgroup (numbered
8–21) is spoken by 3,000–4,000 people down-river from the Chirigua group; and the
TIATINAGUA subgroup (numbered 22–29) is spoken west of and adjacent to the TACANA
language area along the upper Beni, Madidi, and Undumo rivers of Bolivia and Peru.
Ungrouped are: *Arasa (possibly not extinct, Peru), *Guariza = Guaziza (Bolivia),
and Yamaluba (Peru and Bolivia). Key and Key (1967) list 50 speakers of 'Araona'
and 1,000 speakers of Reyesano, but it is not clear with which, if any, of the languages
listed here they are to be equated. Presumably many of the languages not marked
as extinct are in fact extinct, since Key and Key do not list them.

ARAONA = ARAUNA = ARAHUNA
    1. Capachene = Kapaheni. Bolivia.
    2. Cavineña = Cavinenyo = Cavineño = Cavinya = Caviña = Kavina. 500.
    Bolivia. Possibly two languages; Mason (1950) lists Caviña and Cavineño
    separately, but Key and Key (1967) list only Cavineña.
    3. Mabenaro. Bolivia.
    4. Machui = Machuvi. Bolivia.

CHIRIGUA = CHIRIBA = TŠIRIGUA = TŠIRIBA
    5. *Chumana. Possibly not extinct. Bolivia.
    6. Maropa. Bolivia.
    7. *Sapibocona. Bolivia.

TACANA = TUCANA = TAKANÁ
    8. Ayaychuna. Bolivia.
    9. Babayana. Bolivia.
  10. Chiliuvo. Bolivia.
  11. Chivamona. Bolivia.
  12. Idiama. D. also Isiama. Bolivia.
  13. Pamaino. Bolivia.
  14. Pasaramona. Bolivia.
  15. Saparuna. Bolivia.
  16. Siliama. Bolivia.
  17. Tumapasa = Maracani. Bolivia.
  18. Turamona = Toromona. Bolivia.
  19. Uchupiamona. Bolivia.
  20. Yabaypura. Bolivia.
  21. Yubamona. Bolivia.

TIATINAGUA
  22. Baguaja = Baguajairi. Bolivia.
  23. Chama = Eseejja. 300. Bolivia.
  24. Chuncho = Chunchu. Peru and Bolivia.
  25. Echoja. Peru and Bolivia.
  26. Guacanahua = Guanacanahua = Guarayo. Bolivia.
  27. Huanayo. Peru and Bolivia.
  28. Kinaki = Quinaqui. Peru and Bolivia.
  29. Mohino. Peru and Bolivia.
Reyesano ?

AFFILIATION. Branch of PANO-TACANA family in MACRO-PANOAN within GE-PANO-CARIB.

TANGKIC = TANGIC

GROUPING. The TANGIC languages are spoken on the north coast between Queensland and Northern Territory, Australia.

1. Gayardilt = Malununda. Ds. also Ganggalida, Jakula = Jugula, Njangga = Yanggal = Nyangga. Bentinck Island, Gulf of Carpentaria.

2. Lardil = Kunana = Laierdila. 270. Mornington Island and Forsyth Islands.

AFFILIATION. Member of PAMA-NYUNGAN.

TANOAN = KIOWA-TANOAN

GROUPING. Since other TANOAN languages are spoken in Pueblo societies, and Kiowa is not, it once seemed natural to assume that the cultural distance between Kiowa and the rest would be matched by a parallel linguistic distance — that Kiowa would turn out to be a divergent member of the TANOAN family, or perhaps not wholly within the family but a connecting link between the TANOAN and UTO-AZTECAN families (Trager 1951). However, ever since the connections between Kiowa and TANOAN were sketched by Harrington (1910, 1928), it has become clear that Kiowa is a full-fledged sister language within TANOAN, which is — reflecting the earlier expectation — still often labeled the KIOWA-TANOAN family.

The extinct Piro was regarded by Harrington (1909) as TANOAN, with its closest affinities to Tiwa. Leap (1971) attributes the special relationship of Piro to Tiwa as due to borrowing, and questions the inclusion of Piro in TANOAN. The question is whether languages spoken in Pueblo societies belong to three families (TANOAN, UTO-AZTECAN, and KERESAN) or to four language families (the three just mentioned and the family of which Piro was the last survivor).

1. Kiowa = Káyowē = Kiaway = Tepda = Tepkínägo = Tideing Indians = Manrhoat(?) = Quichuan ? 2,000. Oklahoma (formerly in Montana, Wyoming, South Dakota, Colorado, Oklahoma; also Mexico (Coahuila, Chihuahua, Durango).

2. *Piro.

3. Tewa = Taowa = Tegua = Tehua = Telma = Tigua. Ds. or villages: Hano = Hopi-Tewa = Arizona Tewa (200); Nambé (200); Pojoaque = Pojuaque = Pojuate (fewer than 10(?), New Mexico); San Ildefonso (250?); San Juan (1,000); Santa Clara (500–600); Tesuque = Tezuque (200, New Mexico). 2,500. New Mexico, north of Albuquerque; Hopi First Mesa (Hano), Arizona.

4. Tiwa. Ds. or villages: Isleta = Ysletta (2,000), Sandia (100–200), Taos (1,200) = Picuris = Picoris (100). 3,600. New Mexico.

5. Towa = Jemez. Ds. Jemez, Pecos. 1,250. New Mexico.

AFFILIATION. Member of AZTEC-TANOAN.

Tarasca(n) = Tarasken = Tarasco = Tala = P'orepeča = Porepecha = Purepeča = Mechoacan = Mechuacā = Michoacano = Michuacan. 50,000 (1968). Mexico (Michoacan, Guerrero, Guanajuato, Jalisco). Dialectal variation has been charted by Paul Friedrich (1971).

AFFILIATION. Long regarded as a language without known genetic affiliation, McQuown (1955) pointed out a possible genetic association of Tarascan with TOTO-NACAN, MAYAN, and MIXE-ZOQUE, thereby claiming that Tarascan is a member of PENUTIAN.

TASMANIAN

GROUPING. Schmidt (1952) on the basis of the limited available materials on the TASMANIAN languages, which became extinct at the end of the nineteenth century, recognized five possible languages, divided into two groups. G. N. O'Grady's reassessment of the material (cited by Wurm 1971b) yielded two languages: Northern Tasmanian, corresponding to Schmidt's Northern; and Southern Tasmanian, corresponding to Schmidt's Northeastern, Mideastern, Southeastern, and Western.

AFFILIATION. Member of INDO-PACIFIC (Greenberg 1971b).

TEQUISTLATECAN = CHONTAL

GROUPING. There are two groups of TEQUISTLATECAN speakers: a coastal group and a mountain group (Paul Turner 1967, 1969; Waterhouse 1969). 8,000–9,000.
1. Tlamelula.
2. Mountain Tequistlateco.

AFFILIATION. Member of HOKAN.

TIBETAN

GROUPING. Difficulties in accounting for dialect versus separate language varieties make it unclear whether TIBETAN represents two languages, as listed below, or as many as four separate languages, or as few as one language with all reported varieties being dialects of such a possible single language.

Grierson (1903–1927) used a single language name, Bhōṭiā, as a cover term under which he listed 14 dialects, bifurcated into a pair of groups that correspond to languages numbered (1) and (2) below.

Shafer (1955) divides his branch called 'Bodish' (equivalent to Bhōṭiā) into four groups of dialects, namely, West, East, Central, and South: the last named group includes only two dialects, Groma and Sikkimese. The 'West Bodish' group is included under language numbered (1), below; the other 'Bodish' groups are included under (2).

The basis for the two-language division of TIBETAN is given by Roy Miller (1955).

Both Bhōṭiā and Bodish are derived from 'bod' of Classical Tibetan, which in practice is taken as the proto-language from which the modern dialects have descended. Hoffman (1967) has now discovered Žaṅ-žuṅ, another classical language of Tibet, now extinct, which he counts as a sister language of Classical Tibetan.

1. Central Tibetan = Bhōṭiā of Tibet = Bhotanta = Huniyā = Kazi = Lama = Shalgno. Ds. also Ãba = Batang, Choni = Chona, Dä-njong-kä = Dandźongka = Sikkamese = Bhōṭiā of Sikkim (10,000–20,000), Dartsemdo = Tatsienlu, Dru, Garhwal = Bhōṭiā of Garhwal (4,300), Groma = Tromawa (including Upper and Lower Groma), Gtsang, Hanniu, Jad = Dźad = Bhōṭiā of Tehri Garhwal (100), Kāgatē (11,500), Kumaun, Lhasa = Dbus = Ü, Lhoke = Bhōṭiā of Dukpa = Bhōṭiā of Bhutan (5,100–8,500), Lhoskad = Hloka, Mnyamskad = Nyamkat = Bud-kat = Bod-skad = Sangyas = Sangs-Rgyas = Bhōṭiā of Upper Kanawar (1,550), Ngambo = Amdo, Nganshuenkuan = Anshuenkuan Nyarong, Panakha-

Panags, Paurong, Sharpā = Bhōṭiā of northwestern Nepal (900–5,200), Sotati-po, Sikkim, Spiti (3,550), Tseku, Takpa = Dwags.
2. West Tibetan = West Bodish. Ds. also Balti = Baltī = Sbalt = Bhōṭiā of Baltistan, including Purik = Burig = Bhōṭiā of Purik (135,500–148,000); Kham = Khams = Khams-yal = Bhōṭiā of Khams (11,400; eastern Tibet, between Ü Province and China); Ladakhi = Ladakhī = Ladwags = Budhī = Bod Buṭun = Mar-yul, including Hanu, Leh, Rong, Sham (29,800–33,300); Lahul = Lāhulī = Bhōṭiā of Lahul (450–1,600). India (Kashmir), eastern Tibet.

AFFILIATION. Member of TIBETO-BURMAN.

TIBETO-BURMAN

GROUPING. In general, TIBETO-BURMAN includes all SINO-TIBETAN languages except those classified as CHINESE, KAM-TAI, and MIAO-YAO; in particular, TIBETO-BURMAN is a cover term for the following groups treated in separate articles (q.v.):

BODO-NAGA-KACHIN
BURMESE-LOLO
GYARUNG-MISHMI
KAREN
NAGA-KUKI-CHIN
TIBETAN.

Of these groups, TIBETAN is the northernmost; all the rest are found south of Tibet and eastward through Burma into adjacent states of Southeast Asia.

The validity of some aspects of this TIBETO-BURMAN classification is open to critical question, as appears in the summary by Benedict (1972) of SINO-TIBETAN comparative work. The TIBETAN group is the only TIBETO-BURMAN group that has been extensively compared with CHINESE (Bodman 1971).

AFFILIATION. Member of SINO-TIBETAN.

TIMOR-ALOR

GROUPING. Abui and Oirata, sometimes listed as AUSTRONESIAN, are placed in this group by Greenberg (1971b).

1. Abui = Baruë = Barawahing = Namatalaki. Ds. also Kaluiwa, Laral, Makadai, and possibly Kabola(?) including Hamap(?), Kamáng(?), Kawél(?) = Limbur(?), Kelong(?) including Makunabein(?), Kolana-Wersin(?), Kui-Kramang(?) including Malua(?), Lumu(?), Maneta(?), Pandai(?), Seboda(?), Wululi(?). Alor.
TIMOR. Languages (3) and (4) are more closely related to each other than either is to (2) (Greenberg). All are spoken on Timor, except Oirata on nearby Kisar. Kemak, previously listed in this group, has been shown to be AUSTRONESIAN by Stevens (1967).
2. Bunak = Buna'. 50,000.
3. Makasai = Makassai.
4. Oirata.
Dagodá(?); Kairui(?), Midik(?), Naumik(?).

AFFILIATION. Member of 'WEST PAPUAN' (Cowan 1957a); member of INDO-PACIFIC (Greenberg).

*Timucua(na) = Timuquan(a) = Florida = Floridiana. Ds., after Granberry (1956): Eastern (including Mocama, Tucururu, Yafera), Southern (including Acuera, Tocobaga), Western (including Potano, Tawasa, Utina = Timucua proper). From the Aucilla River in northwest Florida to the Tampa Bay region on the Gulf coast and the Indian River region on the Atlantic coast; from north Cumberland Island in a line north of the Okeefenokee Swamp west to the Aucilla River.

AFFILIATION. In the classification by Sapir (1929), Timacua is listed (with a query) as a member of the 'HOKAN-SIOUAN' phylum. The argument for leaving Timacua unaffiliated with respect to phylum classification is given by Voegelin and Voegelin (1967).

TJINGILI-WAMBAYAN

GROUPING. Wambaya (3, below) and Ngarndji (1) are grouped as WAMBAYIC (Wurm 1971b). These languages are spoken in the eastern part of the Northern Territory, Australia.

1. Ngarndji.
2. Tjingilu = Tjingili. Mount Grayling (Rennes Springs) in the south to Newcastle Waters in the north, Ashburton Range in the east.
3. Wambaya = Wambaia = Wombya = Wom-by-a = Yumpia = Umbaia. D. also Kutandji. West of the northern part of the Barkly Tableland.

AFFILIATION. Member of the AUSTRALIAN macro-phylum.

TLAPANECAN = SUBTIABA-TLAPANEC = SUPANEC(AN) = SUBTIABA-TLAPANEC-YOPI

GROUPING. Mason (1940), after Radin (1932–33), argues that these languages, widely separated geographically, represent recent dispersions.

1. *Maribichicoa = Maribo = Guatajigiola. Northeastern part of El Salvador, on the Guatajiguala River. Possibly a member of this group.
2. *Subtiaba. Plains of Léon, Republic of Nicaragua on the Pacific slope.
3. Tlapanec = Tlapaneco = Tlappanec = Tiapaneco = Chocho. 14,000–16,000. East central and southwest Guerrero extending to the coast, Mexico.
Yopi = Jope = Yope = Yoppi ?

AFFILIATION. Member of HOKAN (Sapir 1925).

TOARIPI = ELEMA

GROUPING. These four languages were first recognized as a family by Ray (1907). The percentages of cognates on a limited word list shared between the four (68–76%), as shown by Wurm (1971c), make it seem possible that they may be dialects of a single language. The TOARIPI languages are spoken on the east of the Gulf District, Papua, between the Vailala River and the eastern border of the district.

1. Kerema. 3,100.
2. Orokolo. 6,200.
3. Toaripi = Motumotu. Ds. also Elema = Haira, Kairi-Kaura(?), Milareipi, Uaripi ? 16,800.
4. Vailala. 4,200.

   AFFILIATION. Member of SOUTH-EAST NEW GUINEA.

TOCHARIAN

   GROUPING. Winter (1961) and Lane (1966) are recent authorities for the view that at least two separate TOCHARIAN languages had been spoken in Central Asia. These languages are known from sixth century manuscripts found in Chinese Turkestan. A third manuscript may represent a third language, but the evidence is too meager to permit interpretation (Burrow 1937; Lane 1966). Lane suggests that Tocharian A represents a petrified liturgical language, while Tocharian B remained a spoken language during the same period.

1. *Tocharian A. Chinese Turkestan. Tocharian A may have been originally restricted to the Turfan region, and later brought to Karashar by monks as a written language for use in monasteries (Lane 1966).
2. *Tocharian B. Ds. Central (especially represented by the Šorčuq texts near Karashar); Eastern (to which belong the Sängim, Murtuq, Xočo, and Toyoq texts, in the Turfan area); and Western (exemplified by the Ming-Öy Qizil texts, near Kucha). The spoken language of the region of Kucha in the early part of the second half of the first millennium A.D. Tocharian B was also spoken in Turfan and Karashar beside Tocharian A (1, above).

   AFFILIATION. Member of INDO-EUROPEAN; more closely affiliated with Armenian and 'THRACO-PHRYGIAN' than with other languages of the family.

CENTRAL TOGO = TOGO REMNANT= TOGORESTSPRACHEN

   GROUPING. Struck (1912) was the first to recognize the CENTRAL TOGO languages as a group. Anyimere (9) was added by Westermann (1927) and Basila (3) by Bertho (1952). Heine (1968) groups languages (1)–(7) together as the NA branch, versus languages (8)–(14), the KA branch. Within the NA branch languages, (1), (2), (5), and (7) are closely related. Within the KA branch, Kebu (12) and Anyimere (9) are divergent from the rest; Avatime (10) and Nyangbo-Tafi (14) are close enough to raise the question of dialectal status; and (8), (11) and (13) form a group.

NA

1. Adele = Sedere. Trs. also Delo, Lolo. 8,000. Togo (Circonscription d' Atakpame) and Ghana (Volta Region) borderland.

2. Akpafu = Siwu. Ds. also Lolobi. 8,230. Ghana, Volta Region, around Mpeasem and Todji.
3. Basila = Gisida. Ds. Gikolodjya, Gilempla, Giseda. 4,750. Dahomey, around Bassila, Cercle de Djougou and immediately adjoining parts of Togo.
4. Lefana = Lelemi = Buem. Ds. Lefana, Lelemi. 14,900.
5. Likpe = Likpele = Sekpele = Dikpele = Mu. 7,140. Ghana, Kukurantumi and southward, Volta Region.
6. Logba = Ekpana. 2,090. Ghana, north of Amedzote, Volta Region.
7. Santrokofi = Sele. 3,230. Ghana, 3 villages north of Hohoe, Volta Region.

KA

8. Ahlõ = Ahlon = Axlõ = Ago. 2,900. Togo, Canton Bogo-Ahlon of Circonscription de Klouto.
9. Anyimere = Animere. 250. Ghana, Volta Region, two villages, Kecheibi and Kunda.
10. Avatime = Siyase = Siya. 6,920. Ghana, Volta Region around Amedzofe.
11. Bowili = Liwuli = Siwuri. 3,280. Ghana, Volta Region, from the Volta Lake eastward to Amanfro on the Hohoe-Jasikan road.
12. Kebu = Kabu = Kagbarika = Kəgbərikə = Akébou = Akebu = Ekbebe. 17,252. Togo, Canton Akébou of Circonscription d'Akposso and immediately adjoining areas of Ghana.
13. Kposo = Ikposo = Akposo. Ds. Amou Oblou, Ikponu, Iwi = Uwi, Litime = Badou, Logbo, Uma. 80,000. Togo, Circonscription d'Akposso and immediately adjoining areas of Ghana.
14. Nyangbo = Bagbo = Batrugbu. D. also Tafi. 3,290. Ghana, Volta Region, between Amedzofe and the River Dayi.

AFFILIATION. Member of KWA. Christaller (1889) grouped CENTRAL TOGO among the KWA languages, a position supported by Greenberg (1966). Struck (1912), however, grouped them with the 'Semi-Bantu' languages, essentially the same position as De Wolf (1971) has proposed (see NIGER-CONGO), and Köhler (1953) has suggested that they belong with the GUR languages. Heine (1968) accepts the affiliation with KWA, noting especial similarity with the GAUNG group of the VOLTA-COMOE family (cf. Westermann 1922).

TORRICELLI = ARAPESHAN = WAPEI-PALEI

GROUPING. Wurm (1971c) tentatively subgroups the languages as shown below on the basis of Laycock (1968) and on further work by Laycock, as yet unpublished. In addition to the languages listed below, Laycock also tentatively includes SKO, which Wurm classifies as NORTH PAPUAN, and the two languages of Wurm's MONUMBO subgroup of BOGIA in NORTH NEW GUINEA. The TORRICELLI languages are spoken in the Torricelli Mountains in the northwestern part of the West Sepik District, New Guinea, and to the northeast in the adjoining coastal and hinterland area. In addition to the languages listed below, TORRECELLI includes on its central southwestern border an unnamed language spoken by 460 people.

ARAPESH. Coastal central Sepik District.
  1. Bumbita Arapesh = Bambita = Muhiang. 1,990.
  2. Mountain Arapesh. 8,000.
  3. Southern Arapesh. 8,070.
4. Bragat. 360.
5. Eiteip. 380.
6. Kalp = Urim. 1,970.
7. Kavu.

MAIMAI. Wurm subgroups Heyo (9), Siliput (10), and Yahang (13).
  8. Beli = Akuwagel = Mukili. 1,200.
  9. Heyo = Arinwa = Lolopani = Ruruhip. 1,710.
  10. Siliput = Mai. 210.
  11. Urat = Urakin = Wasepnau. 3,560.
  12. Wiaki = Wiakei = Menandon = Minendon. 530.
  13. Yahang = Ya'unk = Rurihi'ip = Ruruhip.

PALEI
  14. Agi = Ori. 650.
  15. Kayik = Menandon = Minendon = Wanap.
  16. Kombio? 2,150.
  17. Lou = Torricelli. 740.

  PALEI
    18. Aiku = Umbrak-Aiku = Menandon = Minendon = Monanda = Monandu. 790.
    19. Aru = Alatil Eru. 120.
    20. Aruop = Alatil = Lau'u = Lauisaranga. 470.
    21. Nambi = Menandon = Minandon = Mitang. 470.
  WAPEI
    22. Alu = Dia = Metru. 1,850.
    23. Au. 3,900.
    24. Elkei = Olkoi. 1,400.
    25. Galu = Metru = Sinagen. 200.
    26. Gnau ? 940.
    27. Ningil = Ral. 500.
    28. Olo = Orlei = Wape = Wapi. 8,800.
    29. Yau. 120.
    30. Yil. 2,100.
    31. Yis. 460.
  32. Yambes? 670.

33. Valman = Koroko. 600.

WEST WAPEI
  34. Oni = Aunalei = Onele. 1,200.
  35. Seta = Aunalei. 140.

36. Seti = Aunalei. 110.

37. Wam = Wom. 1,890.
38. Yapunda = Reiwo. 70.

AFFILIATION. Member of NORTH NEW GUINEA (Greenberg 1971b).

TOTONACAN
GROUPING

1. Totonac(a) = Totonacca = Totonaco = Totonak(a) = Totonaken = Totonaquæ = Totonaque = Totonicapan = Totonoco = Tonaca = Totolaca = Naolingo = Natimolo. Ds. Chacahuaxtli (in Xalpan and Pentepec), Coast, Ipapana (in Augustine missions), Papantla, Sierra, Tatimolo (in Noalingo), TatiquiJhati (in high Sierras). Coast, Papantla and Sierra are listed after Mason (1940), the others after Zambrano (1752). 63,800. Mexico (northern part of State of Puebla and part of Veracruz, with a few in Hidalgo and Distrito Federal).
2. Tepehua = Tepewa. 4,000. Mexico, in small territory where states of Veracruz, Hidalgo, and Pueblo converge.

AFFILIATION. Member of PENUTIAN.

MACRO-TUCANOAN

GROUPING. There is a clear-cut bifurcation in the grouping of MACRO-TUCANOAN languages: those belonging to the PUINAVE family (23, 24) in contrast to all other constituents. The latter comprise two language families — CATUQUINA and TUCANOAN — as well as eight single languages. One of these single languages is called Macu (20); this Macu should not be confused with a language known by the same name in the PUINAVE family(23). As a nonlinguistic term, 'Macu' means *forest tribes.*

1. Auaque = Auake = Arutani. Possibly extinct. Venezuela.
2. Caliana. Possibly extinct. Venezuela.
3. Caninchana. 25. Northeastern Bolivia on Brazilian border.

CATUQUINA = CATUKINA FAMILY. The dialect and language boundaries are uncertain. The following represents Nimuendajú's 1931–32 presentation followed by Mason (1950) and McQuown (1955). Altogether 2,000 speakers. Eastern Brazil.

    4. Amenadiapa = Amena Dyapa.
    5. Bendiapa.
    6. Burue.
    7. Cadiudiapa.
    8. Canadiapa = Cana Dyapa.
    9. Canamari. 250–500.
    10. Catawishi = Catauichi.
    11. Catuquina = Catukina. Ds. also Cutiadapa = Kutia-Dyapa. 500–1,000.
    12. Catuquino = Catukino.
    13. Hondiapa = Mondiapo = Hon-Dyapá.
    14. Marodiapa = Marö Dyapa.

15. Paraua = Parawa.
16. Tauare = Taware. Ds. also the Caduquilidiapa = Cadekili-Dyapa, Uadio-paranindiapa = Wadyo-Paraniñ-Dyapa.
17. Tucundiapa = Mangeroma = Tucano Dyapa = Tucun Dyapá.
18. Uiridiapa = Wiri-Dyapa.
19. Ururudiapa = Ururu-Dyapa.

20. Macu. Probably still spoken. Guiana area of Brazil, in general region of Auaque and Caliana.
21. Movima = Mobima. 2,000. Venezuela.
22. Muniche = Munichi = Otonabe = Paranapura. Ds. Churitura = Churitana, Muchimo. 200 (1925). On the Paranapura River.

PUINAVE = MACU = GUAIPUNAVO FAMILY. Macu and Puinave are placed as a separate subdivision of MACRO-TUCANOAN by Greenberg (1960a). Macu may represent several languages, some of which may not even belong to the PUINAVE family.

23. Macu. Ds. include Kerari, Nadobo, Papuri, Tikie, Yapooa.
24. Puinave. Ds. Eastern (Bravos, Guaripa), Western = Mansos.

TUCANOAN = BETOYAN FAMILY. Classified on a geographical basis into an EASTERN group (languages numbered 25, 26, 29, 30, 31, 32, 34, 35) and a WESTERN group (languages numbered 27, 28, 33). 10,000. Colombia, Ecuador, Peru, Brazil. Reconstructions of PROTO-TUCANOAN are discussed by Watlz and Wheeler (1972).

25. Boloa.
26. Buhagana. Trs. Buhagana proper, including Doa, Omoa, Sara, Tsaina, Tsoloa, Yaba; Hobacana; Macuna.
27. Correguaje. D. also Tama (including the Ayrico).
28. Coto = Payagua. 500.
29. Cubeo. Ds. Bahuna, Coroa = Coroua = Corowa (also Colombia); Baniua, Julaimaua (Brazil); Hahanana (1,000, Colombia), Holona.
30. Cueretu. Possibly including the Cashiita = Caxiita.
31. Des(s)ana. 800–1,100 (in 1900; possibly including the then few Yapua).
32. Erulia.
33. Piojé-Sioni. Ds. = Trs. Encabellado (including Amaguaje, Campaya, Cieguaje, Guaciguaje, Macaguaje, Piojé = Pioche, Santa Maria, Secoya-Gai, Sioni).
34. Tucano = Takuna = Tukana (including the Araspaso, Neenoa, Yohoraa = Curaua, Uina Tupuyo). Ds. = Trs. also Carapana, Pamoa, Tuyuca (including Bara, Tsola), Wanana = Uanana = Anana (including Waina = Uaiana, Uaicana, Uainana, Piratapuyo), Wasona = Uasona.
35. Yahuna. Ds. also Opaina, Datuana.

36. Tucuna. 15,000. Northwestern Brazil.
37. *Yuri = Juri. Middle Amazon.

AFFILIATION. Member of ANDEAN-EQUATORIAL.

TUNGUS

GROUPING. The TUNGUS languages are bifurcated into two groups: NORTHERN (languages numbered 1–6) and SOUTHERN (languages numbered 7–17). Designations such as 'MANCHU,' 'MANCHU-TUNGUS,' and 'MANCHU-TUNGUSIC' wrongly imply 'MANCHU' as opposed to 'TUNGUS.' 180,000. Eastern Siberia.

NORTHERN TUNGUS = NORTHWESTERN TUNGUS = EVENKI.

1. Even = Lamut. Ds. also Arman; Eastern, including Indigirka, Kamčatka, Kolyma-Omolon, Okhotsk, Ola (basis for the literary language), Tompon, Verkhne-Kolymsk; Northern = Western dialects, including Lamunkhin, Sarkyryr; Yukagir. 6,700.

2. Evenki. Ds. Eastern, including Aldan (with subdialects Jeltulak Timpton, Tommot), Ayano-Maj, Barguzin, Kur-Urmi, Olekminsk (with subdialects Kalar, Tokko, Tungir), Sakhalin, Tuguro-Čumikan, Učur, Zeysko-Burelin; Northern, including Erbogočen, Ilimpeya Nakanna, Tutončana; Southern, including North Baikal, Baunt, Cis-Baikelia, Nepa, Nižne-Nepsk, Podkamennaya Tunguska (basis of the literary language, with subdialects Baykit, Čemdalsk, Poligus, Učama, Vanavara), Sym, Tokma-Verkholensk, Tokminsko-Tutur. 12,750.

3. Manegir.
4. Negidal. Ds. Nizovsk, Verkhovsk.
5. Oročon.
6. Solon.

SOUTHERN TUNGUS. Bifurcated into two subgroups: SOUTHEASTERN TUNGUS = NANAJ, 6,900 speakers (subdivided into a NANAJ group, languages numbered 7, 8, 9, 11, 13, 15, 16 and a UDIHE group, languages numbered 14, 17); and a SOUTHWESTERN = MANCHU group (languages numbered 10, 12).

7. Akani.
8. Birar.
9. Gold. Ds. Kuro-Urmi, Sunggari, Torgon (the basis of the literary language), Ussuri.
10. Ju-chen.
11. Kile = Kire.
12. Manchu. D. also Sibo = Colloquial Manchu.
13. Olča.
14. Oroč. Ds. Kjakela = Kjakar = Kekar, Namunka (1,450), Oričen, Tez (500).
15. Orok.
16. Samagir. Ds. Amur, Baikal, Gorin.
17. Udihe. Ds. Anjuski, Bikin, Iman, Khor (the basis of the literary language), Khungari, Samargin, Sikhota alin (800).

AFFILIATION. Member of ALTAIC.

TUPI

GROUPING. After ARAWAKAN (q.v.), TUPI is the 'largest' family classified under EQUATORIAL (q.v.). A single language in TUPI — Puruborá (7) — is coordinate in classification with the half-dozen groups of languages listed below. This appraisal represents the lexicostatistic classification of Rodrigues (1958) supplemented by information from earlier classifications by Trager (1948), Mason (1950), and McQuown (1955). All languages in the TUPI family are spoken south of the Amazon River, with the exception of Oyampí (29); the forebears of present-day speakers of Oyampí migrated to French Guiana two centuries ago.

ARIKEM. This group consists of three languages, all extinct.
1. *Arikem = Ariqueme. Formerly spoken in Amazonas, Brazil.
2. *Kabišiana = Cabichiana = Kabixiâna = Cabichinana = Capichana. Formerly spoken in the Territory of Rondônia, Brazil.
3. *Karitiana. Formerly spoken in Amazonas, Brazil.

MONDE. Spoken in the Rondônia Territory, Brazil.
4. *Aruá. D. also Aruáši = Aruachi.
5. *Digüt.
6. *Mondé. D. also Sanamaikã = Sanamaica = Salamãi.

7. Puruborá = Burubora. 50–100. Territory of Rondônia, Brazil (headwaters of the São Miguel River, a tributary of the Guaporé River).

RAMARAMA = ROMARAMAN. Formerly spoken in the general area of southern Amazonas and Rondônia Territory in Brazil; now extinct.
8. *Arara.
9. *Ramarama = Itanga. D. also Ntogapid = Itogapuc.
10. *Urukú.
11. *Urumí.

TUPARI
12. Guaratégaya = Koaratira = Guaratira = Amniapé = Mequéns = Kanoé = Guarategaja. Rondônia Territory, Brazil.
13. Kepkiriwat = Quepiquiriquat. Rondônia Territory, Brazil.
14. Makurap = Macurap. Spoken along the Branco River, a tributary of the Guaporé River, Rondônia, Brazil.
15. Tuparí. 50. Right bank of the Branco River, a tributary of the Guaporé River, Rondônia Territory, Brazil.
16. Wayoró = Uaiora = Wajaru = Ayurú. D. also Apičum. Rondônia Territory, Brazil.

TUPI-GUARANI. This group is divided into three subgroups and a single language (Guayakí, 20): I (17, 18, 19, 21, 22, 23, 29, 30, 31, 33, 34, 35, 36); II (24, 28); III (25, 26, 27, 32).
17. *Apiaka = Apiaca. Ds. also *Arino, *Pari-bitete, Tapiitin, *Tepanhuna = Tapanhuna. Near confluence of São Manoel River, Mato Grosso State, Brazil.
18. Awetí = Aueto = Auití = Arauite = Arauine. Less than 50, left side of the

Curisevu River, a headwater of the Xingu River, Mato Grosso State, Brazil.

19. Canoeiro = Ava = Abá = Canoe = Canoa. A few groups in Goiás State, Brazil (high ground between the Formosa River and the eastern branch of the Araguaia River).

20. Guayakí = Guoyagui.

21. Kamayurá = Camaiura = Kamayirá. 100–250, on Lake Ipavu close to Curisevu River, a headwater of Xingu River, Mato Grosso State, Brazil.

22. Kawaíb = Cawahib = Cauaiua = Cauhib = Cabahyba = Jauareta-Tapiia. Ds. Mialát (16 in 1938, upper Leitão River, Brazil), Parintintin (100–250, Ipixuna River in Amazonas State), Pawaté = Paranauat = Paranawat (100 in Rondônia Territory on tributaries of the Jiparaná = Machado River and on the Sono River), Wirafed = Uirafed (50, Rondônia Territory). Other local names associated with Kawaíb: Apairande, *Catuquinaru, Odiahuibe, Tapechiche = Taipechiche. Under 500. Brazil (Amazonas State and Rondônia Territory).

23. Kayabí = Caiabi = Parua = Maquiri. About 500. Formerly in the southeastern section of Amazonas State, Brazil — now moving to the Manitsáu-aassu River, a tributary of the Xingu River, Mato Grosso State, Brazil.

24. Kokama = Cocama. Ds. also *Kokamilla = Cocamilla = Pambadeque (formerly in Peru), *Xibitaona (formerly in Peru). 10,000. Peru, Colombia, Brazil border area.

25. *Kuruáya = Caravare = Curuaia. Formerly in Pará State, Brazil.

26. Maué = Mabue = Mawé = Maragua = Andirá = Arapium = Sataré. Region of the Lower Madeira River (on the Andirá, Urupadi, and Mamura riveıs), Amazonas, Brazil.

27. Munduruku = Mundurucu = Weidyenye = Paiquize = Pari = Caras = Pretas. 1,000–1,500. Middle and upper Tapajós River, and canal system of lower Madeira, Maué-Assu, Abacaxis, and Canumã rivers, Pará State, Brazil.

28. Omagua = Compeva. Ds. also *Aizuare = Aissuari, *Curacirari = Curazicari, Curucicuri = Curuzicari, *Paguana = Paguara.

29. Oyampí = Oiumpian = Api. Ds. also Emérillon, including *Araguaju = Ur(u)aguassu = Uruaguacu, *Cussari, *Guaiapi, *Paiquipiranga = Parichy; Calina, *Gamacom. French Guiana and Brazil (Amapá Territory).

30. Pauserna = Guarayu-Ta. About 25. Eastern Bolivia.

31. Šeta = Sheta = Cheta = Xeta = Aré. Ds. also Botocudo, Chocleng, Ivapare, Notobotocudo, Pihtadyovoc, Shocleng.

32. Sirionó = Chori. Ds. Curungua, Jande, Nyeoze-Nee, Tirinie. 5,000. Eastern Bolivia.

33. Takuñapé.

34. Tapirapé. 100–250. On the Tapirapé River, an eastern tributary of the Araguáia River in Mato Grosso State, Brazil.

35. Tenetehara. Ds. Anambé, Asurini (250–500, Pará State, Brazil), Gwažažara = Guajajara (4,000, Maranhão State, Brazil — possibly including Guajá = Ayaya = Wazaizara = Guaxare (100–250), Manaže = Amanage = Manaxo = Manajo = Manazo = Amanyé (less than 300–550 — including Parakana

= Parocana, between the upper Jacondá and Tocantins rivers — Pará State, Brazil on the Garratão and Ararandeuára tributaries of the Capim River, and the Cairaré and Moju rivers), Tembé (1,000–2,500 along Gurupi and Guamí rivers), Turiwara = Turiuara, Urubú(s) (500–1,000, Pará and Maraanhão states, Brazil). Local groups also listed under Tenetehara: Araquaia, *Ararandeura, Cuperob(an) = Cubenepre = Cupelobo, He, *Jacunda = Amiranha, *Jandiahi, *Miranho, *Nhengahiba, *Pacajan = Pucaja, *Tapiraua = Anta. 2,000–3,000, Pará and Maranhão States, Brazil.

36. Tupi. Ds. Čiriguano = Chiriguano = Aba = Camba = Tembeta (20,000, Bolivia and Argentina); Guarani (1,000,000 in Paraguay, 3,000–4,000 in Brazil), including Old Guarani and Avañeẽ = Modern Guarani — names of local groups possibly represent separate subdialects (*Arechane, Carijo, Chandule, *Guaracaio, *Guarambaré, *Itatin, *Taiobe, *Taruma, *Tobatin); Guarayú (5,000 in Bolivia; possibly including Araibaya, Carabere, Cario, Moterecoa = Moperacoa, Pirataguari = Pitaquari, Quiriticoci, Varai); Kaiwa = Kaingua = Caingua = Cayua, including Apapokuva = Apapocuva, Mbia = Mbya — other local names have also been listed under Kaiwa (Avachiripa, Avahuguai, Apitere, Baobera, Baticola, Carima, Catanduva, Cheiru, Chiripa, *Guayana, Jatahy, *Montese, Oguiva = Oguaiva = Oguana, Paiguassu, *Tanygua, Terenoke, Yvytigua); *Palmer (Bolivia and Paraguay); *Poroquicoa (Bolivia); Tapiete = Tirumbae = Yanaigua (Bolivia and Paraguay); Tupi, including Old Tupi = Tupinamba (the lingua geral) and Modern Tupi = Ñeegatú = Nheengatu = Coastal Tupian, and possibly Potiguara = Pitonara (500–1,000) — other names listed as Tupi dialects or languages may represent local groups of Tupinamba speakers in the sixteenth and seventeenth centuries in eastern Brazil (Amoipira, Apigapigtana, Arabojara, Aricobe, Cæte, Muriapigtanga, Potiguara, Rariguara, Tamoia, Tamoio, Timimino, Tobajara, Tupina, Tupiniquin, Viatin); *Ubegua (Bolivia and Paraguay). Over 1,000,000. Brazil, Paraguay, Argentina, Bolivia.

YURUNA. This group is divided into two subgroups, with Manitsawá (37) as one and Sipaya (38) and Yuruna (39) as the other.

37. *Manitsawá = Mantizula = Manitsaua. D. also *Arupai = Urupaya. Formerly spoken on the Manitsaua-missu tributary of the upper Xingu River, Mato Grosso State, Brazil.

38. *Šipaya = Chipaia = Achipaie = Chipaya = Xipáya. Formerly spoken along the Irirí and Curuá tributaries of the Middle Xingu River in Pará State, Brazil.

39. Yuruna = Jaruna = Iuruna. 500–1,000. Pará State, Brazil.

AFFILIATION. Member of EQUATORIAL within ANDEAN-EQUATORIAL.

TURKIC

GROUPING. The TURKIC languages are remarkably homogeneous; Raun (1956) points out that the divergence of the daughter languages from Proto-Turkic can be measured in centuries rather than millennia. Chuvash (1, below) is the most divergent language, and the only extant representative of a BULGAR group, in contrast to the rest (COMMON TURKIC). The latter is subdivided into groups by Baskakov (1962) and in the collective work *Philologiae Turcicae Fundamenta* (Deny et al. 1959-64), yielding the following subgroups of TURKIC:

Chuvash (language numbered 1)
CENTRAL TURKIC
EASTERN TURKIC = KARLUK
NORTHERN TURKIC = EASTERN HUNNIC
SOUTHERN TURKIC = OGHUZ
WESTERN TURKIC.

See also Loewenthal (1957). The earliest extant form of TURKIC is *Old Turkic, known from monumental inscriptions dated from 680–740 A.D. There are some 50,000,000 speakers of TURKIC languages; wherever possible, Soviet statistical data from *Izvestija*, No. 90 (1971) are given below.

1. Chuvash. Ds. Anatri = Lower Chuvash = Southern Chuvash, Viryal = Upper Chuvash = Northern Chuvash. 1,472,000. Russia, in the Chuvash ASSR.

CENTRAL TURKIC

2. Karakalpak. Ds. Northeastern, in the Karauzyak, Takhtakupyr, and Muinak rayons; Southwestern, in the rest of Karakalpakia. 228,000. Soviet Union, in Karakalpak ASSR, the Khorezm oblast of Uzbekistan, and in Ferghana and in the Astrakhan oblast. Also spoken in Afghanistan (2,000).
3. Kazakh. Ds. Northeastern, Southern, Western. 5, 193,000. Soviet Union.
4. 'Kypchak dialects of Uzbek'.
5. Nogai. Ds. also Ak-Nogai, in the Cherkes Oblast; Kara-Nogai, in the rayon of the Stavropol' Krai. 47,000. Soviet Union, in the Stravropol' Krai and Cherkes autonomous oblast in Northern Caucasus.

EASTERN TURKIC = KARLUK

6. Khoton = Choton. Northwestern Mongolia.
7. Uighur. Ds. Southern, including Aqsu, Kashgar-Yarkend (with Yengi Hissar subdialect), Khotan-Kerya (with Cherchen subdialect); Northern, including Ili = Kulja = Taranchi, Kucha-Turfan (in the Kucha, Qarašahr, Qomul, Turfan oasis), Lobnor. 3,640,000 in Sinkiang Province, China; 153,000 in the Soviet Union.
8. Uzbek. Ds. Karluko-Chigile-Uighur, Kypchak, Lokhay, Oghuz, Qurama, Sart. Soviet Union (9,066,000), Afghanistan (1,200,000).

WESTERN TURKIC. This group includes the PONTO-CASPIAN subgroup (10, 11, 12), and the URALIAN subgroup (9, 13). In Baskakov's classification these represent two subgroups of his 'KYPCHAK' group: KYPCHAK-POLOVETSIAN = KYPCHAK-COMANIAN, and KYPCHAK-BULGAR, respectively.

9. Bashkir. Ds. Burzhan = Western Bashkir, Kuvakan = Mountain Bashkir, Yurmaty = Steppe Bashkir. 821,000. Mainly in Bashkir ASSR.
10. Karachay = Qaračay (58,000). D. also Balkar (58,300). Soviet Union,

in the Caucasus and Kirghiz SSR.

11. Karaim. Ds. Eastern, Northwestern. Less than 1,000. Soviet Union, in Lithuanian SSR and the southern Ukraine.

12. Kumyk. Ds. Buinak = Middle Kumyk, Khaidak = Southern Kumyk, Khasav-Yurt = Northern Kumyk. 186,000. Soviet Union, in Daghestan ASSR. Used as a lingua franca.

13. Tatar. Ds. Kazan Tatar = Central Tatar (1,500,000, mostly in Tatar ASSR); Mishar Tatar = Western Tatar (300,000, mostly outside of Tatar ASSR in adjoining oblasts and republics); 'Mixed dialects,' including Astrakhan Tatar (43,000), Kasimov-Tatar (5,000), Teptyar (300,000), Uralian Tatar (110,000, with Kriashon = Nogais); Siberian Tatar (100,000, including Baraba, Irtysh, Ishim, Tara, Tobol', Tom, Tura, Tuymeń, Yalutorov). 5,289,000. Soviet Union, in Tatar ASSR, Siberia, and adjacent areas.

NORTHERN TURKIC = EASTERN HUNNIC

14. Altai. Ds. Altai-Kizhi, including Maima-Kizhi (spoken along the rivers Katuń, Sema, Peschanaya, Charysh, Ursul, and Maima); Tälägit, including Chuy and Tälägit-Tölös; Teleut = Telengut (along the rivers Bolshoi and Malyi Bachat). 49,000.

15. Northern Altai. Ds. Chalkandu = Shalkandu = Lebe d Tatar (2,000), Kumandy (7,000), Tuba (7,000).

16. Chulym = Melet Tatar. Ds. Lower Chulym, Middle Chulym; also spoken by the Käcik = Käzik and the Küärik. Soviet Union, spoken in the basin of the Chulym River (a tributary of the Ob River).

17. Khakas = Abakan Turks = Abakan Tatars = Yenisei Turks = Yenisei Tatars. Ds. Beltir, Kacha, Kamassian (200), Kyzyl, Sagai, Shor. 56,000. Soviet Union.

18. Kirghiz. Ds. Northern Kirghiz, Southern Kirghiz. 1,435,000. Soviet Union in the Kirghiz SSR, the Sinkiang-Uighur Autonomous Region of the CPR, the Kazakh SSR, the Uzbek SSR, the Tajik SSR; and in Afghanistan.

19. Shor = Aba = Kondoma Tatar = Mras Tatar = Kuznets Tatar = Tom - Kuznets Tatar. Ds. Kondoma, Mrassa. 12,000, Soviet Union. This language is not to be confused with the Shor dialect of Khakas.

20. Tofa = Karagas. Less than 600. Soviet Union.

21. Tuva = Tuba = Soyon [sg.] = Soyod [pl.] = Uriangkhai = Tannu-Tuva. 137,000.

22. Yellow Uighur = Sarygh Uygur. D. also Salar. Soviet Union.

23. Yakut = Sakha. D. including Dolgan (3,500 in Taimyr National Okrug). 285,000. Soviet Union.

SOUTHERN = SOUTHWESTERN = OGHUZ TURKIC

24. Azerbaijani. Ds. Eastern (Soviet Union, including Baku, Derbent, Kuba, Lenkoran, Sal'iany, Šemakha); Central (Soviet Union, including Kirovabad, Šuša = Karabakh); Eastern Anatolian = Karapapakh; Northern (Soviet Union, including Kutkašen, Nukha, Zakataly = Mugoly); Northern Iranian (including Täbris); Southern (Soviet Union, including Erevan, Nakhičevań,

Ordubad); Southern Iranian (including Äynallu, Qašqay); Western (Soviet Union, including Airym, Borčala, Kazakh, Kyzylbaš, Terekeme). Azerbaijanian Soviet Republic (4,301,000), Iranian Azerbaijania (2,500,000).

25. Gagauz. Ds. Eastern = Bulgar, Western = Maritime. 147,000. Soviet Union (Ukrainian and Moldavian Republics), eastern Bulgaria, Romania.

26. Balkan Gagauz Turkish. Ds. Gajol, Gerlovo Turks, Karamanli, Kyzylbaš, Macedonian Gagauz (4,000), Surguch (7,000), Tozluk Turks, Yuruk = Konyar (Macedonia).

27. Khalaj. Central Iran. Previously believed to be a dialect of Azerbaijani, Khalaj is, rather, a separate, very archaic TURKIC language (Doerfer et al., 1971).

28. Turkish = Osmanli. Ds. Eastern, Western = Danubian. 24,000,000. Turkey. Also in Bulgaria, Cyprus, Soviet Union (73,000).

29. Crimean Turkish = Crimean Tatar. Removed from the southern shore of the Crimea Peninsula to Uzbek SSR after World War II.

30. Turkmen. Ds. 'marginal dialects' (including Anauli, Khasarli, Nerezim, Nokhurli = Nohur; in the valleys of Kopet-Dag and along the shores of the Amu-Darya River); 'nonmarginal dialects' (including Čavdur, Esarï = Esary, Göklen, Salyr, Saryq, Teke, Yomud); Trukhmen (Stavropol region). Turkmen Soviet Republic (1,508,000), and Iran and Afghanistan (an additional 500,000).

AFFILIATION. Member of ALTAIC.

*Tyrrhenian = Lemnian. Island of Lemnos, known from a sixth century B.C. inscription of ten lines (Johannes Friedrich 1932; Kretschmer 1941; Swanson 1948).

AFFILIATION. Possibly related to Etruscan.

URAL-ALTAIC

GROUPING. For well over a century, it has been noted that URALIC and ALTAIC languages are either typologically or (also) genetically related. When the relationship is counted as typological rather than genetic, well-attested similarities are taken to be a consequence of borrowing between URALIC (q.v.)—an unquestioned language family —and the problematic constituents in ALTAIC (q.v.). When the relationship is counted as genetic, the constituents in ALTAIC are taken to be descended from Proto-Altaic, which, together with Proto-Uralic, are supposed to be descended from a still earlier proto-language.

AFFILIATION. None known.

URALIC

GROUPING. The URALIC languages listed below are constituents of the following two main branches:

FINNO-UGRIC (languages numbered 1–23);

SAMOYEDIC (languages numbered 24–28).

In general, the cognate density among languages in the FINNO-UGRIC branch is relatively high; in particular, it is twice as high as that between any FINNO-UGRIC language and any SAMOYEDIC language measured by Raun (1956) (and SAMOYEDIC languages appear to be as homogeneous among themselves as are FINNO-UGRIC languages). Most, but not all, FINNO-UGRIC languages are now found in Europe, in contrast to the SAMOYEDIC languages, most of which have their present residence and probably their provenience in Asia. Where applicable, Soviet statistical data from *Izvestija*, No. 90 (1971) are given below; see also *Jazyki narodov SSSR* (1966).

The FINNO-UGRIC languages are subgrouped under FINNIC (1–8), and under LAPPIC (9–16), which together constitute the FINNO-LAPPIC group. They are also subgrouped under PERMIC (17, 18). There are three languages subgrouped under UGRIC (19–21), of which the two (20–21) spoken along the Ob River are known as OB-UGRIC. They are also subgrouped under VOLGAIC (22–23), and this group together with the FINNO-LAPPIC group constitutes a FINNO-VOLGAIC major group which is coordinate with PERMIC, as a second major group of FINNO-PERMIC, which in turn is coordinate with UGRIC. Finally, as already mentioned, FINNO-UGRIC as a main branch of URALIC is coordinate with SAMOYEDIC (24–28), as a second main branch.

FINNIC = BALTO-FINNIC

1. (North) Estonian. Estonia. 962,000 (including speakers of 2, below).
2. South Estonian. Southeastern Estonia.
3. Finnish. Ds. Eastern including Savo; Western, including Häme. 4,000,000 (Finland), 43,000 (Soviet Union), 200,000 (elsewhere). The Eastern dialects merge gradually into Karelian (5 below).
4. Ingrian. 350 native speakers. Soviet Union.
5. Karelian. Ds. Karelian proper, including Northern, Novgorod, Southern, and Tver = Kalinin; Ludic; Olonetsian. 92,000 (Soviet Union). Ludic is transitional between Olonetsian and Vepsian (7, below).
6. Livonian. Less than 500. Mostly in Latvia in a few villages westward from the northernmost point of Domesnes in Curonia.
7. Vepsian. About 8,000 in 1959. Soviet Union.
8. Votic. A few old people in Ingria adjacent to northeastern Estonia.

LAPPIC. 30,000: Norway (19,000), Sweden (8,000), Finland (2,000), and the Kola Peninsula of the Soviet Union (1,000). The following languages are often grouped areally as NORTHWESTERN (11–13), SOUTHERN (15, 16), and EASTERN (9, 10, 14); or politically as Norwegian Lapp (13), SWEDISH LAPP (11, 12, 15, 16), Finnish Lapp (9), and RUSSIAN LAPP (10, 14).

9. Inari Lapp. Finland, around Lake Inari.
10. Kola Lapp. Soviet Russia.
11. Lule Lapp. Sweden, along the Lule River in Gellivare and Jokkmokk; Norway, in Tysfjord, Hamarøy, and Folden.
12. Pite Lapp. Sweden, along the Pite River in Arjeplog and Arvidsjaur; Norway, between Saltenfjord and Ranenfjord.
13. Ruija Lapp. Norway, in Finnmark, Troms, and Ofoten; Sweden, in Kare-

suando and Jukkasjärvi; Finland, in Utsjoki, Enontekiö, and the reindeer breeders of Sodankylä. About two-thirds of all Lapp speakers speak Ruija Lapp.

14. Skolt Lapp. Soviet Russia around Petsamo in the west of Kola Peninsula.
15. Southern Lapp. Sweden, in Jemtland and Herjedalen; Norway, in Hatfjell-dalen and Wefsen, southward to Røros.
16. Ume Lapp. Sweden along the Ume River southward, Lycksele, Mala, Sorsele.

PERMIC. The two PERMIC languages listed below are very close; their date of separation linguistically was in the eighth century A.D.
17. Votyak = Udmurt. D. also Besserman. 582,000. Soviet Union. Dialect differentiation is slight even in Besserman, which has an apparent TURKIC structure.
18. Zyrian = Komi. Ds. Komi-Permyak, Komi-Zyrian, Yaźva (4,000). Together 402,000. Soviet Union.

UGRIC
19. Hungarian. Ds. Alföld (the Hungarian lowland), 'Beyond Danube' (west of the Danube), Danube-Tisza (between the Danube and the Tisza), 'King's Pass,' Northeastern, Northwestern, Székely (in Transylvania), Western. 13,500,000. Hungary, and neighbouring countries, plus 160,000 in the Soviet Union. Hungarian is closer to Vogul than to Ostyak.
20. Ostyak = Xanty. Ds. Eastern, Northern, Southern including Konda. About 14,500. Soviet Union.
21. Vogul = Mansi. Ds. East Vogul including Konda, North Vogul, South Vogul, West Vogul, Konda. 4,100. Soviet Union.

VOLGAIC
22. Cheremis = Mari. Ds. Eastern, Displaced Eastern, Western. 546,000, Soviet Union.
23. Mordvin. Ds. Erzja, Mokša = Moksha. About 983,000. Soviet Union.

SAMOYEDIC. Spoken over an immense area in the Soviet Union.
24. Ostyak Samoyed = Selkup. Ds. Ket = Tym = Southern, Taz = Northwestern = Northern. A couple of thousand. Along the Taz River and in the Narym District.
25. Sayan Samoyed. One speaker of the Kamas dialect in 1970; other dialects as Karagas, Koibal, Motor, Soyot, and Taigi are no longer spoken.
26. Tavgy = Tawgi Samoyed = Nganasan = Ŋanasan. Taymyr Peninsula in Siberia. About 750.
27. Yenisei Somoyed = Enec = Enets = Yenets. Perhaps 300 speakers of two dialects. The Lower Yenisei River around Dudinka. Appears to be transitional between Yurak and Tavgy Samoyed.
28. Yurak Samoyed = Nenec = Nenets. D. Forest, Tundra. About 24,000. Spread in an immense tundra area from the mouth of the Northern Dvina in Europe to the delta of the Yenisei in Asia.

AFFILIATION. Member of URAL-ALTAIC.

UTO-AZTECAN

GROUPING. The internal relationships of UTO-AZTECAN languages are not well understood. Multiple groupings — with a couple or at most a few constituent languages in each branch — are, of course, attestable, but they leave open the question as to whether two or more smaller divisions represent a larger branch. Thus, NUMIC, SOUTHERN CALIFORNIA SHOSHONEAN, Tübatulabal, and Hopi might be representatives of a larger SHOSHONEAN group, although evidence for this, marshaled by Voegelin, Voegelin, and Hale (1962), is less strong than that marshaled for the SONORAN group and for the AZTECAN group. The traditional trichotomy, as stated by Sapir (1930) among others, was first challenged by Whorf (1935), who argued that the SHOSHONEAN languages in the north do not form a homogeneous group in contrast to the AZTECAN languages in the south, and that the geographically intermediate SONORAN languages do not constitute a single group coordinate with the other two. Lamb (1964), after Whorf, would replace SONORAN with multiple groupings which distinguish Pima (15), Pima Bajo (16), and Tepehuan (18), as PIMIC, from Cahita (11), Opata (14), Tarahumara (17), and Yaqui (19), as TARACAHITIC, from Cora (12), and Huichol (13), as CORIC. On the basis of lexicostatistic evidence, Hale (1964) distinguishes most SONORAN languages in his sample (those numbered 12, 15, 16, 18, 19) from Tarahumara (17, below). Wick Miller (1964 and 1967) does not confirm this entirely.

A number of extinct languages in northeastern Mexico, as Guachichil and Pelones, have sometimes been classified as UTO-AZTECAN (Swanton 1940); these languages are probably no longer classifiable (Gursky 1963).

AZTEC(AN) = NAHUATLAN

1. *Mecayapan. Mexico.
2. Nahua = Nahoa = Mexicano = Aztec(a). Ds. also Acasaquastlan, Culhua, Nahuat(e) (including Zacapoaxtla), Nahual(t), Nahuatl = Naguatl(e) (including Matlapa, Milpa Atla, Tetelcinco), Niguira(n). 1,000,000. Mexico: Puebla, Hidalgo, Veracruz, Guerrero, San Luis Potosi, Tlaxcala, Oaxaca, Mexico, Morelos, Durango, Distrito Federal, Zacatecas, Baja California.
3. Pipil. Ds. also *Alagüilac, *Bagaces, *Chuchures, *Nahuatlato, *Nicarao, *Toltec = (Toltec-)Chichimec. El Salvador, Southern Guatemala, Northern Honduras.
4. Pochutla. Mexico, Pacific coast of Oaxaca State.
5. *Tamaulipeco ?

6. Hopi = Hopitu = Moqui = Shinumo. 4,800. Northeastern Arizona.

NUMIC = PLATEAU SHOSHONEAN. The term Paiute (= Pah-utah = Pah-yutah = Pah-Ute = Paiuli = Paiulee = Pai-ute = Paiyute = Pa-uta = Payusita = Piede = Piute = Pi Ute) is used ambiguously in reference to Southern and Northern Paiute.

7. Mono = Monachi. 100–500. Eastern California.

8. Northern Paiute = Paviotso. Ds. also Bannock = Bannack = Diggers (fewer than 20, Idaho; formerly southeast Idaho, northwest Colorado, north Utah, west Wyoming, southwest Montana, Oregon), Snake (east Oregon). 2,000. California, Idaho, Nevada.

9. Southern Paiute (less than 500). Ds. also Chemehuevi = Chemuevi = Chemegue = Chimehuevi = Tantawaits = Tä'n-ta'wats (100–200, California, Arizona), Kawaiisu (fewer than 10, California). Ute = Uta(h) = Yuta(h) (2,000–4,000, Utah and Colorado; previously also in New Mexico).

10. Shoshoni = Schoschone = Schoshone = Shoshone = Shoshonee = Shoshonie = Snake = Tosauwihi = Wihínasht. Ds. also Comanche = Camanche = Ca-mán-chee = Comanch = Komanche = Komantsche = Allebome = Hietan = Jetan = Llanero = Meco = Näuni = Nüma = Paduca (1,300, Oklahoma; Wyoming, Nebraska, Kansas, Oklahoma, Texas), Gosiute = Gossi Ute = Kusiuta, Panamint = Ke-at = Koso (10–100; California), Wind River (Wyoming). 5,000. California, Nevada, Idaho, Oregon, Wyoming, Utah.

SONORAN

11. *Cáhita = Caita. Ds. Bamoa, Sinaloa = Cinaloa = Sinalua, Zuaque; also Guasave (including Achire, Ahome, Comopori, Vacoreque), Ocoroni, Tahue = Tahueco = Thehuoco = Zuaque, Tapahue, Taracahitan = Acaxee = Topia (including Sabaibo, Papudo, Tebaca, Tecaya, Xixime?), Vorohio ? Some classifiers regard the dialects of a language still spoken (19, below: Yaqui and Mayo) to be among the major dialects of Cahita.

12. Cora = Nayit(i) = Chora = Chota = Coraice = Teacuacitzia = Teacuaeitzica = Ateanaca = Muutzicat. Ds. = Trs. also *Coano, *Huaynamoto, *Zayahueco. 3,731. Mexico, middle course of the Rio Grande de Santiago, state of Jalisco, central coastal region of Sinaloa; Nayarit. Perhaps related to another language, *Totorame = Pinome.

13. Huichol(a) = Cuachichil. D. also *Guachicil(e) ? 4,000–5,000. Mexico: Jalisco, Nayarit, Durango, Puebla, Coahuila, Nuevo Leon, Zacatecas, San Luis Potosi. Perhaps related to another language, *Tecual.

14. *Opata = Ópataice = Ore = Ure = Sorora = Tegüima = Tequima. Ds. also *Concha(?), *Java.

15. Pima = Pime(ria) = Pimo. Ds. Papago = Papabicotan, including Ahngam, Ge Aji, Gigimai, Huhhu'ula, Huhuwash, Kokololodi, Totoguani; Pima, including Kohadk. 18,000 (5,000 Pima; 13,000 Papago). Arizona, Mexico (Sonora).

16. Pima Bajo = Nebome = Nevoma = Nevome = Cora = Lower Pima. Mexico (Sonora, Chihuahua).

17. Tarahumar(a) = Tarahumare = Tarauhmarice = Taraumara = Tarrahumara = Corohio = Raramuri. 50,000–60,000. Mexico: Chihuahua, Sinoloa, Durango, Sonora.

18. Tepehuan = Tepegua = Tepeguan(a) = Tepehua(na) = Tepehuane = Tepehuano. Ds. also Tepecano, Northern Tepehuane, Southern Tepehuane.

1,766. Mexico: Chihuahua, Durango, Nayarit; also Sonora, Jalisco. May be more than one language or divergent dialects of Pima-Papago.

19. Yaqui. Ds. Mayo (1,837, Sonora and Sinaloa, Mexico), Yaqui = Hiaki = Hiaque (545, Sonora and Chihuahua; 3,000, Arizona). 10,000 Yaqui and Mayo, Mexico.

TAKIC = SOUTHERN CALIFORNIA SHOSHONEAN
  CUPAN = LUISISH = LUISEÑO-CAHUILLA

20. Cahuilla = Cahuillo = Kahweya = Kawia = Kauvuya. 12. California, around Palm Springs.

21. Cupeño = Kupa (Bright and Hill 1967; Hill and Hill 1968). Fewer than 10. California.

22. Luiseño = San Luis Mission = San Luis Rey (Mission) = San Luis Rey de Francia = Saint Louis Mission = Reyano. D. perhaps *Juañeno(?) = San Juan Capestrano = San Juan Capistrano (Mission) = Netēla = Gaitchim. 100–200. California, around Pala.

23. *Gabrieleño = Gabrielino = San Gabriel Mission = Kīj = Kizh = Tobikhar. Ds.? also *Fernandeño, Nicoleño (formerly San Nicolas Island, California).

24. Serrano = Meco = Takhatn. 2 or 3. California. Ds.? *Alliklik, *Kitanemuk = Kikitamar = Kikitanum, *Vanyume.

25. Tübatulabal. Fewer than 10. California, south fork of Kern River (formerly also on the north fork).

*Giamina ?

AFFILIATION. Member of AZTEC-TANOAN phylum.

VIỆT-MU'ỜNG = VIETNAMUONG = ANNAM-MUONG

GROUPING. Prior to Thomas and Headley (1970), Vietnamese and Mu'ờng were listed as the only members of the group. On the basis of materials by Tuyên (1963), Thomas and Headley include three other languages which presumably are spoken entirely in North Vietnam — Arem, Mày = Rục and Tày poọng. Thompson (1973) clarifies that Tuyên (1963: 68 and fn. to end plate VIII) himself considers Mày, Rục, Arem and Tày poọng to be all dialects of Mu'ờng, and that the forms cited largely agree with words given for the same localities by H. Maspero (1912), who also considered them Mu'ờng dialects. Tuyên's vocabularies are in any case severely limited (c. 100 words and phrases) and would not seem to warrant setting up three new languages.

1. Mu'ờng. 390,000. In a long line of sometimes widely separated mountain valley enclaves extending from the Black River of northern Vietnam (west of Hanoi) southward to Quảng-bình province (not far north of Hue). Some groups now relocated south of the 1954 partition line.

2. Vietnamese. Ds. Northern = Tonkinese, Central = High Annamese, Southern = Cochinchinese. The centers of these dialects are Hanoi, Hue, and Saigon, respectively. Maspero (1912) considered the north-central (Haut-Annam) dialects

very divergent from the balance of the dialect continuum; he classified them as a separate dialect branch coordinate with Tonkinese-Cochinchinese (the latter including south-central [Bas-Annam] forms of speech). Essential descriptive materials are still lacking for further study of Vietnamese dialectology; see Thompson (1965). 28,000,000. Vietnam extending into Cambodia (many have been repatriated since the 1970 invasion of Cambodia) and with enclaves in Laos and Thailand. The total outside Vietnam may not exceed 500,000.

AFFILIATION. Member of MON-KHMER.

VOLTA-COMOE = AKAN

GROUPING. Westermann and Bryan (1952) include three languages in this group; Greenberg (1966) added Abure (12) and Metyibo (13), which Westermann and Bryan placed in LAGOON. John Stewart (1971) has reported that the number of languages in this family is much greater than had been supposed; the language and dialect divisions listed below follow Stewart and Welmers (1971b).

CENTRAL VOLTA-COMOE = TANO. This group is divided into a WEST CENTRAL = BIA subgroup (consisting of languages numbered 1, 3, 4 and 5), on the one hand, and Akan (2), on the other. Languages (1) and (5) versus (3) and (4) form further subdivisions of the WEST CENTRAL subgroup.
1. Ahanta = Anta.
2. Akan = Twi-Fante. Ds. Akan, Ak(y)em, Asante = Ashanti, Fante = Fanti = Mfantse, Twi = Tshi = Chwee = Akwapem = Akuapem. 2,000,000. Ghana. Akem plus Asante is also designated as 'Ashanti'. Twi and Fante are sometimes considered as separate languages because of separate writing traditions, though they are largely mutually intelligible.
3. Anyi = Agni. Ds. also Afema = Samwi = Sãwi, Anufo = Brus(s)a = Brissa = Buressa (Ivory Coast, Ghana), Baule = Bauolé = Bowli (373,000, Ivory Coast), Ndyenye, Safwi = Assaye. 450,000. Ivory Coast, Ghana.
4. Chakosi = Tiokossi = Anufo. Northern Togo, Ghana, Dahomey.
5. Nzema = Nzima = Zimba = Amanya = Asoko = Awa = Gura.

EASTERN VOLTA-COMOE = GUAN(G)
6. Achode. Ghana.
7. Awutu = Afutu = Efutu(?) Ghana.
8. Chiripon-Lete-Anum = Cherepong-Larteh-Anum. Ghana.
9. Guan(g) = Gbanya(ng) = Gomoa = Gonja = Gwanja = Nkogna = Ngbanyito. Ds. Anyanga, Atyoti, Brong = Abron(g), Nawuri = Chumuru = Nchum(m)ur(r)u, Nkami, Nkunya = Nkonya. 53,000. Ghana.
10. Krachi. Ghana.
11. Yeji. Ghana.

WESTERN VOLTA-COMOE = ONA
12. Abure = Abouré = Abonwa = Akapless. 7,000–8,000. Ivory Coast, Grand Bassam to Abi Lagoon.

13. Metyibo = Mekibo = Betibe = Byetri = Agua = Ewutere = Ewuture = Papaire = Vet(e)re = Vitré. 3,000–4,000. Ivory Coast, Grand Bassam and Assinie lagoons.

AFFILIATION. Member of KWA.

WAICAN = WAIKAN = UAICAN = GUAICAN = CHIRINAN = SHIRINAN = GUAHARIBAN = YANOMAMA

GROUPING. The WAICAN family may consist of only two languages or may even be a single language; Borgman et al. (1965) say that Shirishana is mutually unintelligible with all the other dialects which appear to form a language complex (even though many of the other dialects appear to be not mutually intelligible). Thus Samatari is said to be 'mutually unintelligible with many if not most' dialects of Central Waica. Carime = Xauari and Pusaracau are listed as separate units by McQuown (1955) and others, but because of their central location they are probably alternate dialect or tribal names. Migliazza (1972) distinguishes four languages: Yanoman, Yanomamɨ, and Yanam, and Sanɨma.

1. Waica. Ds. Central, Samatari, Shamatari, Shiriana, Southern (all dialects of Shamatari and Central are mutually intelligible). Trs. Central: Aykamteri, Maita = Maracana (?), Marashiteri, Parahuri, Parimiteri, Waica, Samatari: Gauharibo, Koatãteri, Mitiwari; unclassified: Kadimani, Shidishana (= Shirishana language?), Tocoshina, Yanomani = Yanoama, Zirizan. 25,000. Brazil and Venezuelan border area in the neighborhood of the divide between the Amazon and Orinoco watersheds.
2. Shirishana = Shirishiana = Kirishiana = Xirixana. Few. Mucajaí River in Brazil east of the Central dialect of Waica.

AFFILIATION. Member of MACRO-CHIBCHAN.

*WAICURIAN = GUAYCURAN

GROUPING. Mason (1940) reported reasons for considering Pericú to be a language related to Waicuri.
1. *Pericú. Tip of Baja California.
2. *Waicuru = Waikur(i) = Waikurio = Vaicura = Waikuru = Guaicuro = Guaycuro = Guaicura = Guajiquiro = Guajiquiro = Guaicuri = Guaikuri = Guaikuru = Guaricuri = Vaicura. Ds. = Trs. Aripa. Cora, Didú, Edú, Guaycura, Ika, Monqui, Uchita = Utciti = Utchitie. Formerly in Baja California between 24° and 25°N.

AFFILIATION. Briton (1891) first proposed YUMAN connections for WAICURIAN; this was disputed by Kroeber (1915). The HOKAN affinities other than YUMAN — are most recently postulated on scanty data by Gursky (1966).

WAKA-KABIC

GROUPING. The WAKA-KABIC group is divided into three subgroups: MIYAN, consisting of Djakunda (3) and Dungidjau (4); THAN, consisting of Dalla (1) and Taribeleng (5); and KINGKEL, consisting of Darambal (2) and Wadja (6) (O'Grady et al. 1966, Wurm 1971b). These languages are spoken in the area between Broad Sound and Brisbane on the coast of Queensland, Australia.

1. Dalla = Mooloola = Dalleburra. Ds. also Batjala = Badjela = Patyala, Kabikabi = Kabi = Karbi = Dippil. Along extreme southern coast.
2. Darambal = Tharumbal = Darawal = Tarumbal = Tarumbul = Charumbul. D. also Koinjmal = Koinjimal = Gonjmal = Guñmal = Kooinmerburra = Kungmal = Kunglaburra = Mamburra. Coast inland to Boomer Range at Marlborough, Yeppoon, Yambe, Rockhampton, and Gracemere.
3. Djakunda. D. also Korenggoreng = Curanggurang = Guranggurang = Gurenggureng = Gooranggorang = Korrengkorreng. Between Upper Boyne and Auburn rivers, north of Hawkwood, south to Dividing Range.
4. Dungidjau. Ds. also Ngoera = Njalbo = Kaiabara, Wakawaka = Wakkawakka = Waka = Woga = Wokka = Wogga = Wokkari = Nukunukubara = Wa. Stradbrake Island.
5. Taribeleng = Taribelang = Tarribelung = Yawaim = Ginginburra = Wokka. Ds. also Goeng = Goonine = Meeroni = Maroonee, Tulua. Vicinity of Bundaberg; inland to about Walla; north to Avondale, along Kolan River.
6. Wadja = Wadjainggo = Waindjago = Wainggo = Maudalgo. Ds. also Bayali, Kangulu = Kaangooloo = Khang = Kongulu = Kongalu = Konguli. Streams on the side of Expedition Range, south to Bigge Range east nearly to Dawson River.

AFFILIATION. Member of PAMA-NYUNGAN.

WAKASHAN

GROUPING. Recent classifications support the traditional grouping of WAKASHAN into two branches: KWAKIUTLAN and NOOTKAN (with three languages in each).

KWAKIUTLAN

1. Bella Bella. D. also Heilsuk. 100–1,000 speakers. Milbank Sound, British Columbia.
2. Haisla. D. also Kitamat. 100–1,000 speakers. Douglas Channel, British Columbia.
3. Kwakiutl. Some 1,000 speakers. Coast of British Columbia and adjacent end of Vancouver Island.

NOOTKAN. Languages numbered (4) and (5), below, are more closely related to each other than either is to Nootka (6) (Haas 1969).

4. Makah. Fewer than 10. Washington.
5. Nitinat. 10–100 speakers. Vancouver Island, British Columbia.
6. Nootka. Ds. also Kyoquot, Tsishaath, and Ucuelet. Possibly as many as 1,800 speakers. Vancouver Island, British Columbia.

AFFILIATION. In the classification by Sapir (1929) every family was classified under one of six phyla, as reflected on the unrevised *Map of North American Indian Languages* by Voegelin and Voegelin (n.d. = 1944), where WAKASHAN appears under Phylum II in genetic association with Kutenai, Quileute, SALISH, Yurok and Wiyot, Beothuk, and ALGONQUIAN. The argument for leaving WAKASHAN unaffiliated with respect to phylum classification is given by Voegelin and Voegelin (1967).

WAKAYA-WARLUWARIC

GROUPING. The WAKAYA-WARLUWARIC languages are spoken in an area around the east central Northern Territory-Queensland boundary line, Australia.

1. Wakaya = Wakaja = Waggaia = Wagai = Waagai = Waagi = Warkya = Worgaia = Worgai = Workia = Leewakya = Ukkia.
2. Warluwara = Maula = Walookera = Wolga = Wollegara = Wlookera = Yunnalinka.

AFFILIATION. Member of PAMA-NYUNGAN.

WATI = WESTERN DESERT

GROUPING. There are some 4,000 speakers of WATI languages scattered across central Western Australia, southwestern Northern Territory and northwestern South Australia (Wurm 1971*b*; Douglas 1964).

1. Kardutjara. 24°S/123°E. Ds. also Antakirinya = Andagirinja = Antakerrinya = Andekarinja = Antekarinja = Andrgrinji = Andigarina = Andingiri = Antigerinya = Andjiringna = Unterrgerrie = Tangara = Yandairunga = Mbenderinga = Madutara = Aldolinga = Andekerinja (27°S 134°E), Godoga, Ibarga = Ibarrga = Ibargo, Inawonga, Jangkundjara = Jangundjara = Jankunzazzara = Wirtjapokandja, Jumu (23°S 129°E), Kiyadjara, Koara, Kokata = Gugada = = Kukatha = Kukata = Kokatha = Koogatho = Kugurda = Koogurda = Koocatho = Kokit-ta = Maduwonga = Madutara (30°S 134°E), Konin, Kukatja = Kukacha = Luritja = Luritcha = Loritja = Loritcha = Lurritji = Aluridja Loorudgie = Loorudgee = Juluridja = Maduntara = Maiulatara = Ooldea, Madoitja = Wainawonga, Maduwonga, Mandijildjara, Mandjindja = Mandjindjara = Manjinjiwonga, Mardo = Mardudjara, Mount Margaret (28°S 122°E), Murunitja = Mooroon, Nana = Nganadjara, Nangatajara = Nangatadjara, Ngadawongga = Ngadhawonga = Ngarawonga, Ngadatjara = Ngadadjara, Ngalawonga, Ngalea = Ooldean = Ngalia (32°S 132°E), Ngurlu, Nyanyamara, Pawututjara, Pindiini = Wonggai, Pini = Pirniritjara, Pintubi = Bindibu = Pintupi = Bindabu, Pitjantjatjara = Pitjandjara = Pitjandjadjara = Pitjindjatjara = Pitkindjara = Pitjindjiara = Pitjanzazara = Wongapitjira = Wongapitcha, Targudi = Targoodi, Tarpuntjari, Tjalkadjara = Barduwonga, Tjeraridjal, Tjitiyamba = Tjitijamba, Walyen = Waljwan = Waljen, Warburton Ranges (26°S 128°E), Waula = Nagiuwonga, Wirdinya = Wirdinja = Woordinya, Yulbaridja = Julbre = YuḷapaRitᵞa (coast between Wallal and Broome). Pitjantjatjara is widely known through adoption as a church language.

2. Wanman = Warnman. Western Desert area between Walmadjari and Ibarga areas.

AFFILIATION. Member of SOUTHWEST PAMA-NYUNGAN.

WINTUN = WINTOON = COPEHAN

GROUPING

1. Nomlaki = Nomlackee = Tehama = Tehema. Fewer than 5.
2. Patwin = Copeh = Suisun = Colouse = Kopé = Korusi = Numsu = Mag Readings. 10–100. California (north of San Francisco Bay).
3. Winiu(n) = Trinity (County). Ds. Central = Wintu, Northern = Wintun. 20–30; California (west side of Sacramento Valley from the river to the Coast Range).

AFFILIATION. Member of PENUTIAN.

WIRADJURIC

GROUPING. Bigumbil (2) is set off from a 'MAIN' subgroup consisting of the languages numbered 1 and 3–8, below (O'Grady et al. 1966). The WIRADJURIC languages are spoken in central New South Wales and the south central portion of Queensland, Australia.

1. Barunggam = Murrungama = Murrumningama. Queensland.
2. Bigumbil = Miyal = Bigambul = Pikambul = Bigambal = Beegumbul = Pikambal = Pikumbul = Pickumbil. Ds. also Gujambal, Kwaimbal, Weraeria = Warairai = Wallaroi = Wolroi = Walaro = Wolaroi = Wullaroi. On the New South Wales and Queensland border.
3. Kamilaroi = Gamilaroi = Kamilarai = Kamilroi = Kamalarai = Koomilroi = Gunilroi = Guminilroi = Gumilray = Camleroy = Euhahlayi. D. also Koinberi = Koinberri = Gunjbarai. In northern New South Wales around Walgett.
4. Nguri = Gnoree. New South Wales.
5. Wiradjuri = Wiradhuri = Wiraduri = Wiradjeri = Wiradhari = Wirraidyuri = Wiratheri = Wirashuri = Werogery = Woradjera = Wordjerg = Wira-Athorree = Wirajeree = Wirraiyarrai = Wirracharee. D. also Geawegal = Gwegal. The entire area west of the Dividing Range from a little north of the Murray River to about the Macquarie River, New South Wales.
6. Wiriwiri. Gwydir River from Moree to Bingara, north to Warialda and Gilgil Creek. New South Wales.
7. Wongaibon = Wongagibun = Wonghibon = Wonghi = Wombungee. Ds. also Baranbinja = Burranbinya = Burrunbinya = Barrumbinya, Ngemba = Ngiamba = Ngeumba = Ngiumba = Gaiamba, Weilwan = Walywan. East central New South Wales.
8. Yualyai = Ualari = Yualai. D. also Juwalarai = Yualarai = Yerraleroi = Uollaroi. Northeastward from Narran Lake to Angledool; east to Walgett; on Narran and Bokhara rivers.

AFFILIATION. Member of PAMA-NYUNGAN.

WITOTOAN = HUITOTOAN

GROUPING. The internal classification of the WITOTOAN languages is, according to Mason (1950), "exceedingly and unusually controversial and uncertain." Other than noting that languages numbered 4–9 constitute a 'BORA-MIRANYA' group, no attempt at classification is given here. It is questionable whether numbers 1–3 and 10–11 are WITOTOAN at all. The WITOTOAN languages are spoken mainly in southeastern Colombia between the Caqueta and Putumayo Rivers, with some extending into Brazil and with speakers of some languages transported as laborers into Peru.

1. *Northern Andoque. Colombia.
2. *Southern Andoque. Colombia.
3. *Araracuara. Colombia.
4. Bora. Colombia.
5. Fitita. Colombia.
6. Ocaina = Ducaiya. Colombia plus about 200 transported to northeastern Peru in the 1930s.
7. Miranya = Andoquero = Carapana. Colombia.
8. Muenane = Muinani = Muinane. 100. Colombia.
9. Nonuya = Achiote = Anyonola. Colombia.
10. *Oregon. Colombia.
11. *Resigero. Possibly not extinct. Colombia.
12. Witoto = Huitoto. Ds. Minica, Muinánï, Murui. 4,000–5,000 in Colombia, 80 or more families transported to Peru in the 1930s. About 100 in Brazil.

AFFILIATION. Member of MACRO-CARIB within GE-PANO-CARIB.

WORORAN

GROUPING. Three subgroups: UNGARINYNIC = NGARINYINIC, consisting of Munumburu (5), Ungarinyin (7), Wolyamidi (10); WORORIC, consisting of Jaudjibara (3), Mailnga (4), Umida (6), Unggarangi (8), Unggumi (9), Worora (11); and WUNAMBALIC, consisting of Bagu (1), Gambre (2), Wunambal (12) (Wurm 1971*b*). Spoken from Derby to Wyndham and from the coast to about 200 miles inland in northern Western Australia, Australia.

1. Bagu = Ba:gu. Ds. also Gwini = Gwi:ni = Cuini, Miwa.
2. Gambre.
3. Jaudjibara.
4. Mailnga.
5. Munumburu. Ds. also Guidj.
6. Umida.
7. Ungarinyin = Ungarinjin = Ngarinyin = Narrinyind. D. also Wilawila.
8. Unggarangi.
9. Unggumi = Ungami = Wongkami.
10. Wolyamidi = Woljamidi = Wolyamini = Molyamidi = Yamandil. Ds. also Manungu, Waladjangari, Walar.

11. Worora = Wororra = Wurara.

12. Wunambal = Unambal = Wummabal = Wunambullu.

AFFILIATION. Member of AUSTRALIAN macro-phylum.

YAKONAN

GROUPING

1. *Alsea = Alséya. D. also Yaquina = Yakwina = Yakon(a). Fewer than 10 (1930). Oregon (formerly on Alsea River and Bay).

2. Siuslaw. D. also Lower Umpqua = Kuitish. Fewer than 10. Oregon (on or near Siuslaw River; Kuitish formerly on Upper Rogue River).

AFFILIATION. Member of PENUTIAN.

YANAN

GROUPING. It appears that the family consisted of only two languages, formerly spoken in California, from Pit River to Rock Creek, and from the edge of Sacramento Valley to the headwaters of the eastern tributaries of the Sacramento River.

1. *Yahi.

2. *Yana proper. Ds. Central, Northern, Southern.

AFFILIATION. Member of HOKAN.

YENISEIAN = YENISEI-OSTYAK

GROUPING. Only one of this group of 'Paleosiberian' languages is still spoken in Russia.

1. *Arin.

2. *Asan.

3. *Cottian = Kotu = Kott. Ds. also Mana.

4. Ket = Yenisei-Ostyak. 77.1 % of 1,100 Ket are speakers of Ket. East of the Khanty-Mansi National Okrug, Krasnoyarsk Kray, along the upper and middle Yenisei.

AFFILIATION. None generally accepted (Dul'zon 1968; Jakobson 1942; Krejnovic 1968; Worth 1963).

YOKUTS = MARIPOSAN

GROUPING

1. Foothill North Yokuts. Ds. Kings River, including Aiticha, Choinimni, Chukaimina, Entimbich, Gashowu = Goshowi, Kocheyali(?); Northern Foothill, including Chu(c)kchansi, Dalinchi, Dumna, Kechayi, Toltichi(?); Poso Creek = Paleuyami, including possibly Kumachisi(?); Tule-Kaweah, including Bokninuwad, Kawia, Wükchamni, Yawdanchi, Yokod. 10-20. California, San Joaquin River and the slopes of the Sierra Nevada.

2. *Foothill South Yokuts = Buena Vista. Ds. Hometwoli, Tuholi, Tulamni.

3. *Valley Yokuts. Ds. Northern, including Chauchila, Chulamni; Southern, including Tachi = Tatché = Telame = Telami, Yauelmani = Yawelmani. Formerly central California, southern San Joaquin Valley.

AFFILIATION. Member of PENUTIAN (Golla 1964; Kroeber 1963; Stanley Newman 1944 and 1946).

YORUBA

GROUPING. In internal relationship, the language numbered (1), following, is quite close to (2), but Itsekiri, listed below as a dialect of (2), is "normally regarded by speakers as a separate language" (Kay Williamson, p.c.). Southwestern Nigeria, extending into Dahomey and with an enclave in Togo.

1. Igala = Igara. 100,000.
2. Yoruba. Ds. Akoko, Anago (the 'Yoruba' of Togo), Aworo = Akanda, Bunu = Eki, Egba, Ekiti, Gbedde, Ife, Igbona, Ijebu, Ijesha, Ila, Ilorin, Itsekiri = Ishekiri =Shekiri = Jek(i)ri, Iworo, Jumu, Ondo, Owe, Oyo-Ibadan-Efe = Yoruba proper =Standard Yoruba, Yagba. About 6,000,000.

AFFILIATION. Member of KWA phylum.

YOTAYOTIC

GROUPING. The YOTAYOTIC languages are spoken in New South Wales and just across the Murray River in Victoria, Australia.

1. Baraparapa = Burraburburaba = Barababaraba = Barrababarraba = Boorabirraba = Burappa = Burabura = Booraboora = Burapper = Karraba = Boort.
2. Jabulajabula = Narinari.
3. Jotijota = Yotayota = Jotajota.

AFFILIATION. Member of PAMA-NYUNGAN.

YUIN-KURIC

GROUPING. The YUIN-KURIC family comprises two subgroups: YUIN, consisting of Gandangara (2), Ngarigo (5), Ngunawal (6), Thaua (7), and Thurawal (8); and KURI consisting of Darkinung (1), Jukambal (3), Ngamba (4), Wanarua (9), and Worimi (10) (O'Grady et al. 1966). These languages are spoken along the coast of New South Wales, Australia.

1. Darkinung = Darginyung = Darkinjung = Karkinung. Counties of Hunter, Northumberland, and Cook to Hawkesbury rivers.
2. Gandangara = Gundungurra = Gundaahmyro. Ds. also Daruk = Dharruk = Dharrok = Dharuk, Iora, Kameraigal = Cameragal = Cammerraygal. At Goveburn and Berrima; down Hawkesbury River to about Camden.
3. Jukambal = Yugumbil = Yukambal = Yukambil = Yookambul = Yookumbil = Ukumbil = Yookumble = Yurimbil = Ucumble = Ngarabal = Ngarrabul = Pregalgh.

4. Ngamba. D. also Dainggati = Dangadi = Danggetti = Dhangatty = Thangatti = Thangatty = Dangati = Tangetti = Burgadi = Boorkutti, Ngaku. From Nanning River north to Rolland Plains.
5. Ngarigo = Ngarigu = Ngaruku = Ngaragu = Ngundura = Ngarego = Ngarago = Garego = Ngarruga = Bemeringal. D. also Wolgal = Walgalu.
6. Ngunawal = Ngaonawal = Nungawal = Yarr = Ngennigenwurro = Yiilima.
7. Thaua = Thawa = Thauaira = Thoorga = Thurga = Tadermanji = Djiringanj = Tauaira = Guyangalyuin. Ds. also Walbanga = Bugellimangi = Thoorga = Thurga, Wandanian = Tharumba = Kurialyuin. Northern half of county of Auckland.
8. Thurawal = Dharawa = Thurrawal = Turuwul = Turrubul = Tharawal = Turuwull. D. also Wodiwodi = Wadiwadi.
9. Wanarua = Wonarua = Wonnarua = Wannerawa. D. also Awabakal = Awabagal = Lake Macquarie.
10. Worimi = Warrimee = Warimai = Warrimi. Ds. also Birpai = Bilpai = Biribi = Birripai = Bripi = Birrapee = Birippi, Kattang = Kutthung = Gadang = Gutthan. Hunter River to near Tuncurry, along coast; inland to about Glendon Brook and head of Myall Creek.

AFFILIATION. Member of PAMA-NYUNGAN.

YUKAGHIR

GROUPING. Spoken in Siberia.
1. *Chuvantzy.
2. Yukaghir = Jukagir = Odul. Ds. Kolyma, Tundra.
AFFILIATION. Krejnovič rejects Collinder's proposal of affiliation with ALTAIC (Krejnovič 1958, 1968; Jakobson 1942; Worth 1963).

YUKI(AN)

GROUPING
1. Wappo = Ashochimi = Soteomellos = Sotomieyos. Ds. Central Wappo, Lile'ek Wappo, Northern Wappo, Southern Wappo, Western Wappo; dialects surviving in 1964: Geyserville and Napa (River). One speaker (1970). California (formerly between Clear Lake and San Franscisco Bay).
2. (Northwest) Yuk(a)i = Yuke(h). Ds. also Coast Yuki, Huchnom. One speaker (1970). California (formerly north of San Francisco Bay, in the Coast Range, and west of it).

AFFILIATION. In the classification by Sapir (1929), Yuki (= YUKIAN) is a member of 'HOKAN-SIOUAN.' Elmendorf (1968) summarizes and argues in partial agreement with Voegelin and Voegelin (1967) that YUKIAN be regarded as un-affiliated with respect to phylum classification, but anticipates that future research will turn up some genetic association of YUKIAN with SIOUAN (Elmendorf 1964), or with PENUTIAN (Shipley 1957), or with HOKAN (Gursky 1965).

YUMAN

GROUPING. Two pairs of YUMAN languages constitute the DELTA-CALIFORNIA group (1, 2, below) and the PAI group (4, 5, below), which are coordinate with two single languages (Kiliwa (3) and (Up)River Yuman (6)), yielding altogether a four-way classification of YUMAN languages. Some variations of this four-way classification have appeared ever since the 1943 classification by Kroeber. Both Wares (1968a) and Walker (1970) classify Paipai (4) with Upland Yuman (5), and Diegueño (2) with Delta Yuman (1), which accounts for all the languages except two (3, 6, below).

DELTA-CALIFORNIAN

1. Delta River Yuman = Delta. Ds. Cocopa = Cucapá, *Kohuana, *Halyik-wamai = Kikima = Quícama. 200. Yuma and Laveen (with the Maricopa), Arizona; 110, Sonora (city of San Luis Rio Colorado). There may be a couple of Kohuana who retain some knowledge of the language among the Maricopa in Laveen, Arizona.

2. Diegueño. Ds. Ipai = Northern Diegueño = Western Diegueño, Tipai = Southern Diegueño = Eastern Diegueño, including Kuʔahl = Kuʔał = Koʹał (Robles, 1964); (Langdon 1968, 1970). 10–100. Southern California, Baja California. The Tipai of La Huerta also refer to themselves as 'Cochimi' (Robles 1964; Troike 1970a).

3. Kiliwa = Kiliwi = Kiliwee = Yukaliwa. 60 (34 people in 9 families; Robles 1964). Northern Baja California (Trinidad Valley). Joel (1964) indicates linguistic relationships to be sought to the south (Cochimi), Mauricio Mixco (1970) indicates possible affinities with the PAI branch.

PAI

4. Paipai = Akwa'ala = Akwaʔala = Awaʔala. 152 (Robles 1964). Baja California (Santa Catarina Valley).

5. Upland Yuman = Arizona Yuman =Highlands Yuman = Northern Yuman = Northwest Arizona Yuman. Ds. Havasupai = Coconino = Tonto (350), Walapai = Hualapai = Jaguallapai = Matáveke-paya (800), Yavapai = Apache-Mojave = Apache-Yuma = Mohave-Apache = Tonto = Tulkepa = Tulkepaia = Yampai = Yampio = Yavapai-Apache = Yavape = Yavepe Kutcan = Yavipai = Yuma Apache (800). Northern and central Arizona. Division of Walapai-Havasupai into two dialects was a result of United States military and Bureau of Indian Affairs artificial division of the two groups.

6. (Up)River = Central Yuman. Ds. Maricopa = Cocomaricopa = Opa (500; Phoenix area, Laveen and Lehi communities), Mohave = Mojave = Mohao = Amojave = Jamajabs = Hummock'havi = Iat = Soyopas (1,300; Colorado River at Parker, Arizona, and Needles, California), Yuma = Yumaya = Kutchan = Cuchan = Kwitcyan = Kertchan = Chirumas = Cetguanes = Tonto (1,000; Colorado River, Yuma area). The Maricopa have absorbed the *Halyikwamai = Kikima = Quícama and *Kohuana (of the DELTA YUMAN group), and the *Hal-

chidom = Halchidhom(a) (traces of which remain in the leveled Maricopa) and
*Kavelchadom = Kaveltcadom = Kavelchadhom = Opa.

AFFILIATION. Member of HOKAN phylum. An especially close relationship
between each of two single HOKAN languages (Cochimi, Seri) with languages of the
YUMAN family has been occasionally noted, as by Troike (1970*a*).

YURA

GROUPING. The YURA languages are spoken along the coast and in the east
central portion of South Australia, south of Lake Eyre.

1. Jadliaura = Jadlijawara = Yadliura = Arabatura = Wonoka. Ds. also Kaurna
= Kaura = Coorna = Koornawarra = Nganawara = Kurumidlanta = Mili-
pitingara = Widninga = Winnaynie = Meyu, Narangga = Naranga = Nanunga
= Narranga = Narranggu = Narrangu = Adjahdurah = Turra, Ngadjuri =
Wirameyu = Manuri = Ngadhuri = Ngarluri = Aluri = Alury = Eeeleeree =
Wirameju = Wirrameyu = Wirramayo = Wirramaya = Wiramaya = Wirra =
Weera = Eura = Manu = Monnoo = Manuley, Nukuna = Nukunu = Nuguna
= Nukunnu = Nookoona = Noocoona = Nokunna = Pukunna = Wongaidya
= Tyura = Doora = Warra.
2. Kuyani = Gujani = Kujani = Kuyanni = Kwiana = Kooyiannie = Cooyiannie
= Kooyeeunna = Kooteeuna = Koonarie.
3. Nawu = Nauo = Nawo = Naua = Nowo = Growoo = Battara.
4. Pangkala = Pankarla = Parnkala = Bangala = Banggala = Bahanga-la =
Pankalla = Punkalla = Bungela = Bungeha = Kortabina.
5. Wailpi = Wipie. D. also Adnyamathana = Adnyamatana = Nuralda = Binbarnja = Kanjimata = Anjimatana = Benbakanjamata = Anjiwatana = Anjamutina = Anyamatana = Unyamootha = Kudnamietha = Kutchnamoota =
Keydnjamarda = Mardala = Mardula = Umbertana = Nimbalda = Nimbaldi =
Nimalda.

AFFILIATION. Member of SOUTHWEST PAMA-NYUNGAN.

ZAPOTECAN

GROUPING. The number of separate languages in the ZAPOTECAN family has
not yet been agreed upon. Longacre (1964) would not include the language numbered
(1), below, in the family; for (2) he lists seven different languages, among some of
which (according to de Angulo and Freeland (1933)) there exists mutual intelligibility,
and hence different dialects rather than different languages. Swadesh (1947) says
that the main divisions within ZAPOTECAN are apparently two separate sets
of divergent dialects, numbered (1) and (2), following, but that some of the
dialects in set (2) especially may be divergent enough to be listed as separate
languages.

1. Chatino. Ds. Taltaltepec, Yaitepec, Zenzontepec. 20,000 (1961). State of Oaxaca,
Mexico.

2. Zapotec = Zapateco. Ds. Southern Mountain = Miahuatlan = Miahuateco, Valleys = Valley-Isthmus = Central (75,000 (1953)), Northern Mountain with distinct subdialects: Northwest = Sierra de Juraez = Ixtlan = Serrano and Northeast = Sierra de Villa Alta = Yalálag = Rincón. 200,000. Mostly in state of Oaxaca, Mexico.

AFFILIATION. Member of OTO-MANGUEAN phylum.

REFERENCES

Aichner, P. (1949). "Some Notes on Land-Dayaks. Their language." *Sarawak Museum Journal* 5 (new series = 16 old):1.95–7.

Allen, Jerry, and Conrad Hurd (1963). *Languages of the Cape Hoskins Patrol Post Division of the Talasea Sub-District, New Britain.* (Port Moresby.)

———— (1965). *Languages of the Bougainville District.* (Port Moresby.)

Anceaux, J. C. (1958). "Languages of the Bomberai Peninsula." *Nieuw-Guinea Studiën* 2.109–21.

Andronov, M. S. (1960). *Tamil'skij jazyk.* (Moscow.)

———— (1961). "New Evidence of Possible Linguistic Ties Between the Deccan and the Urals." In *Dr. R. P. Sethu Pillai Silver Jubilee Commemoration Volume.* (Madras.)

———— (1964). "Materials for a Bibliography of Dravidian Linguistics." *Tamil Culture* 11.3–50.

Anonymous [Wright, Ashur] (1842). *Spelling-Book in Seneca Language: with English Definitions.* (Buffalo Creek Reservation, N.Y.)

Applegate, J. R. (1958). "An Outline of the Structure of Shilha." *American Council of Learned Societies Publication Series B*, Aids No. 11.

———— (1964). Consultant data incorporated in C. F. and F. M. Voegelin, "Languages of the World: African Fascicle One." *Anthropological Linguistics* 6: 5.295–307.

Arana Osnaya, Evangelina (1959). "Afinidades lingüisticas del Cuitlateco." *Actas del XXXII Congreso Internacional de Americanistas* 2.560–72. (San José, Costa Rica.)

Armstrong, Robert G. (1955). "The Idoma-Speaking Peoples." In Darryl Forde et al. (eds.), *Peoples of the Niger-Benue Confluence, Ethnographic Survey of Africa Part X.* (London.)

Arndt, W. W. (1959). "The Performance of Glottochronology in Germanic." *Language* 35.180–92.

Baehr, G. (1948). "Baskisch und Iberisch." *Eusko-Jakintza*, Vol. II.

Balkan, Kemal (1954). *Kassitenstudien: 1. Die Sprache der Kassiten.* Translated by Fr. R. Kraus. *American Oriental Series* 37. (New Haven.)

Barrett, S. A. (1908). "The Ethno-geography of the Pomo and Neighboring Indians." *University of California Publications in American Archaeology and Ethnology* 6.1–332.

Bartholomew, Doris A. (1965). *The Reconstruction of Otopamean.* Ph. D. dissertation, University of Chicago.

Baskakov, N. A. (1962). *Introduction to the Study of Turkic Languages* (in Russian); second edition 1969. (Moscow.)

Basset, André (1952). *La Langue Berbère.* International African Institute, *Handbook of African Languages*, Part I. (London.)

Basu, Dwijendra Nath (1955). "A General Note on the Andamese Languages." *Indian Linguistics* 16. 214–25, Chatterji Jubilee Volume.

Bee, Darlene L. (1965). *Usarufa: A Descriptive Grammar.* Ph.D. thesis, Indiana University.

Beeler, Madison S. (1955). "Saclan." *International Journal of American Linguistics* 21.201–209.

———— (1959). "Saclan Once More." *International Journal of American Linguistics* 25.67–8.

———— (1961). "Northern Costanoan." *International Journal of American Linguistics* 27.191–7.

———— (1966). "The Interrelations within Italic." In Henrik Birnbaum and Jaan Puhvel (eds.) *Ancient Indo-European Dialects.* (Berkeley and Los Angeles.)

Bender, Byron W. (1971). "Micronesian Languages." In Thomas A. Sebeok (ed.), *Current Trends in Linguistics, Vol. 8.* (The Hague.)

Bender, Marvin (1971). "The Languages of Ethiopia." *Anthropological Linguistics* 13: 5.

Bendor-Samuel, John T. (1971). "Niger-Congo, Gur." In Thomas A. Sebeok, ed., *Linguistics in Sub-Saharan Africa, Current Trends in Linguistics*, Vol. 7. (The Hague.)

Benedict, Paul K. (1941). *Sino-Tibetan Philology.* Vol. I. (Berkeley.)

———— (1942). "Thai, Kadai, and Indonesian: A New Alignment in Southeastern Asia." *American Anthropologist* 44.576–601.

———— (1966). "Austro-Thai." *Behavior Science Notes* 1: 4.227–261.

—— (1967a). "Austro-Thai Studies: Material Culture and Kinship Terms." *Behavior Science Notes* 2: 3.203–204.

—— (1967b). "Austro-Thai Studies: 3. Austro-Thai and Chinese." *Behavior Science Notes* 2: 4.275–336.

—— (1972). *Sino-Tibetan Conspectus.* (Cambridge.)

—— (1973a). "Austro-Thai and Austroasiatic, The 'Austro Linkage'." Paper presented at the First International Conference on Austroasiatic Linguistics, Honolulu, January 2–6, 1973.

—— (1973b). *Austro-Thai Studies.* (New Haven.)

Bergsland, Knut. (1949). "Litt om setningsbygningen i samojedisk og eskimoisk," *Det norske videns-kaps-akademie i Oslo,* 15–17. (Oslo.)

—— (1959). "The Eskimo-Uralic Hypothesis." *Journal de la Société Finno-Ougrienne* 61.1–29.

Bertho, J. (1952). "Les dialects du Moyen-Togo." *Bulletin d'IFAN* Serie B 14.1046–1107.

Bhattacharya, S. (1957). "Field Notes on Nahali." *Indian Linguistics* 17.245ff.

Bianchi, E. (1943). *La Lingua Italiana.* (Florence.)

Bidwell, Charles E. (1970). *The Slavic Languages: Their External History.* (Pittsburgh.)

Biggs, Bruce (1965). "Direct and Indirect Inheritance in Rotuman." *Lingua* 14.383–415.

—— (1971). "The Languages of Polynesia." In Thomas A. Sebeok (ed.), *Current Trends in Linguistics,* Vol. 8. (The Hague.)

Birnbaum, H. (1966). "The Dialects of Common Slavic." In H. Birnbaum and J. Puhvel (eds.), *Ancient Indo-European Dialects.* (Berkeley and Los Angeles.)

—— (1975). "Typological, Genetic, and Areal Linguistics—An Assessment of the State of the Art in the 1970s." *Foundations of Language* 13.267-91.

Birnbaum, H., and J. Puhvel (eds.) (1966). *Ancient Indo-European Dialects.*(Berkeley and Los Angeles.)

Bleek, Dorothea F. (1927). "The Distribution of the Bushman Languages in South-Africa." In *Festschrift Meinhof.* (Glückstadt and Hamburg.)

—— (1929). *Comparative Vocabularies of Bushman Languages.* (Cambridge.)

—— (1956). *A Bushman Dictionary.* American Oriental Society. (New Haven.)

Bloomfield, Leonard (1933). *Language.* (New York.)

—— (1946). "Algonquian." In Harry Hoijer et al., *Linguistic Structures of Native America.* Viking Fund Publications in Anthropology 6.

Bodman, N. C. (1971). "Some Phonological Correspondences Between Chinese and Tibetan." Paper presented at the 4th International Sino-Tibetan Conference, October 8–10, Bloomington, Indiana. To appear as "Chinese and Tibetan Correspondences: A Summary and Overview" in *Current Trends in Sino-Tibetan Linguistics* (forthcoming).

Boller, Anton (1857). "Nachweis, dass das Japanische zum Ural-Altaischen Stamme Gehört." *Sitzungsberichte der philos.-histor. Classe der Kais. Akademie der Widdenschaften, Wien* 33.393–481.

Bonfante, Guiliano (1935). "Quelques Aspects du Problème de la Langue Rétique." *Bulletin de la Société Linguistique de Paris* 26.141–54.

Bopp, F. (1847). *Die Kaukasischen Glieder des Indoeuropäischen Sprachstamms.* (Berlin.)

Borgman, Donald, Sandra Cue, Sue Albright, Marril Seeley, and Joseph E. Grimes (1965). "The Waican Language." *Anthropological Linguistics* 7: 7.1–4.

Bouda, Karl (1938). *Die Beziehungen des Sumerischen zum Baskischen, Westkaukasischen und Tibeti-schen.* (Leipzig.)

—— (1941). "Beitrage zur kaukasischen und siberischen Sprachwissenschaft, 4, Das Tschuk-tschische." *Abhandlung für die Kunde des Morgenlandes* 26: 1. (Leipzig.)

—— (1949). *Baskisch-Kaukasische Etymologien.* (Heidelberg.)

—— (1952). "Die Verwandtschaftsverhältnisse der Tschuktschischen Sprachgruppe (Tschuk-tschisch, Korjakisch, Kamtschadalisch)." *Acta Salmanticensia, Filosofia y Letras* 5: 6.

—— (1953). "Dravidisch und Uralaltaisch." In *Ural-Altaische Jahrbücher.* (Wiesbaden.)

Bourguet, E. (1927). *Le Dialect Laconien.* (Paris.)

Brandenstein, W. (1935). "Karische Sprache." *Pauly-Wissowa Realencyclopädie, Suppl.* 6.140–46.

Brandes, J. L. A. (1884). *Bijdrage tot de vergelijkende klankeer der Westeresche afdeeling van de Maleisch-Polynesische Taalfamilie.* Diss. Leiden. (Utrecht.)

Breen, J. G. (1971). "Aboriginal Languages of Western Queensland (Preliminary Version)." *Linguistic Communications* 5.1–88. (Monash University.)

Bright, William, and Jane Hill (1967). "Linguistic History of Cupeño." In Dell Hymes and William Bittle (eds.), *Studies in Southwestern Ethnolinguistics*. (The Hague.)

Brinton, Daniel Garrison (1891). *The American Race: A Linguistic Classification and Ethnographic Description of the Native Tribes of North and South America*. (New York; 1901, Philadelphia.)

Broadbent, S., and C. A. Callaghan (1960). "Comparative Miwok: A Preliminary Study." *International Journal of American Linguistics* 26: 301–16.

Brook, G. L. (1963). *English Dialects*. (Oxford.)

Brown, J. M. (1965). *From Ancient Thai to Modern Dialects*. (Bangkok.)

Bruens, A. (1942–5). "The Structure of Nkom and Its Relations to Bantu and Sudanic." *Anthropos* 37.40.827–66.

Bryan, M. A. (1948). *Distribution of the Nilotic and Nilo-Hamitic Languages of Africa*. (London.)

—— (1959). *The Bantu Languages of Africa*. International African Institute, *Handbook of African Languages*. (London.)

Bürchner, L. (1910). "Gergis." *Pauly-Wissowa Realencyclopädie* 13.1248–49.

Burling, Robbins (1959). "Proto-Bodo." *Language* 35.433–453.

—— (1967). *Proto Lolo-Burmese*. Indiana University Research Center Publications in Anthropology, Folklore, and Linguistics 43. (Bloomington.)

Burrow, T. (1937). *The Language of the Kharoṣṭhi Documents from Chinese Turkestan*. (Cambridge.)

—— (1946). "Dravidian Studies IV." *Bulletin of the School of Oriental and African Studies* 11.328–356.

Burrow, T., and S. Bhattacharya (1970). *The Pengo Language*. (Oxford.)

Calder, W. M. (1911). "Corpus Inscriptionum Neo-Phrygiarum." *Journal of Hellenic Studies* 31.161–215.

Caldwell, R. (1913). *A Comparative Grammar of the Dravidian or South-Indian Family of Languages*. (London.)

Callaghan, Catherine A. (1970). *Bodega Miwok Dictionary*. University of California Publications in Linguistics 60. (Berkeley.)

—— (1971). "Saclan: A Reexamination." *Anthropological Linguistics* 13.448–56.

Campbell, Rev. John (1898). "The Dénés of America Identified with the Tungus of Asia." *Transactions of the Canadian Institute* 5.167–223.

Campbell, Lyle (1973). "Distant Genetic Relationship and the Maya-Chipaya Hypothesis." *Anthropological Linguistics* 15.115–35.

Capell, A. (1937). "The Structure of Australian Languages." *Oceania* 8.1.27–61.

—— (1943). *The Linguistic Position of South-eastern Papua*. (Sydney.)

—— (1944). "Peoples and Languages of Timor." *Oceania* 14.330–7, 15.19–48.

—— (1951). "Languages of Bogia District, New Guinea." *Oceania* 22.130–47, 178–207.

—— (1954). *A Linguistic Survey of the South-Western Pacific*. South Pacific Commission Technical Paper No. 70. (Nouméa.)

—— (1962a). *A Linguistic Survey of the South-Western Pacific*. (New and revised edition.) South Pacific Commission Technical Paper No. 136. (Nouméa.)

—— (1962b). "Oceanic Linguistics Today." *Current Anthropology* 3.371–429.

—— (1963). *Linguistic Survey of Australia*. Australian Institute of Aboriginal Studies. (Canberra.)

—— (1971). "History of Research in Australian and Tasmanian Languages." In Thomas A. Sebeok (ed.), *Current Trends in Linguistics* 8. (The Hague.)

Caratzas, S. C. (1958). *L'Origindes Dialectes Néo-Grecs de L'Italie Meridionale. Institut d' études byzantines et néo-hellénique*. (Paris.)

Cardona, G., H. M. Hoenigswald, and A. Senn, eds. (1970). *Indo-European and Indo-Europeans*. (Philadelphia.)

Cassidy, F. G. (1962). "Toward the Recovery of Early English-African Pidgin." In *Symposium on Multilingualism* (*Brazzaville*), Commission de Cooperation Technique en Afrique, Publication

No. 87. (London.)

Cense, A. A., and E. M. Uhlenbeck (1958). *Critical Survey of Studies on the Language of Borneo.* Koninklijk Instituut voor Taal-, Land- en Volkenkunde, Bibliographical Series 2. (The Hague.)

Chafe, Wallace L. (1962). "Estimates Regarding the Present Speakers of North American Indian Languages." *International Journal of American Linguistics* 28.162–71.

———— (1971). Consultant data supplementing C. F. and F. M. Voegelin, "Languages of the World: Native America Fascicle One." *Anthropological Linguistics* 6: 6.1–149.

———— (1973). "Siouan, Iroquoian, and Caddoan." In Thomas A. Sebeok (ed.), *Current Trends in Linguistics*, Vol. 10. (The Hague.)

Chamberlain, A. F. (1913). "Linguistic Stocks of South American Indians." *American Anthropologist* 15.236–247.

Chang K'un (1967). "National Languages." In Thomas A. Sebeok (ed.), *Current Trends in Linguistics: Linguistics in East Asia and South East Asia*, Vol. II. (The Hague.)

Chao, Y. R. (1943). "Languages and Dialects in China." *Geographical Journal* 102.63–6.

———— (1948). *Mandarin Primer. An Intensive Course in Spoken Chinese.* (Cambridge, Mass.)

———— (1965). *Grammar of Spoken Chinese.* (Berkeley.)

Chatterji, Suniti Juman (1945). *Languages and the Linguistic Problem.* Oxford Pamphlets on Indian Affairs No. 11. (Oxford.)

Chrétien, C. Douglas (1962). "A Classification of Twenty-one Philippine Languages." *Philippine Journal of Science* 91.485–506.

Christaller, J. G. (1889). "Sprachproben aus dem Sudan von 40-60 Sprachen und Mundarten hinter der Gold- und Sklavenküste." *Zeitschrift für afrikanische Sprachen* 3.133–154.

Claasen, Oren (1970). Summary of O. R. Claasen and K. A. McElhanon, "Languages of the Finisterre Range, New Guinea." *Pacific Linguistics*. In press. Paper presented at Indiana University.

Clark, David J. (1971). "Three 'Kwa' Languages of Eastern Nigeria." *The Journal of West African Languages* 8: 1.27–36.

Cohen, Marcel (1947). *Essai comparatif sur le vocabulaire et la phonétique du chamito-sémitique.* (Paris.)

Collinder, Björn (1940). *Jukagirisch und Uralisch.* Uppsala Universitets Årsskrift 1940.8.

Collinder, Björn (ed.) (1957). *Survey of the Uralic Languages.* (Stockholm.)

Conklin, Harold C. (1952). "Outline Gazetteer of Native Philippine Ethnic and Linguistic Groups." Mimeograph.

Constantino, Ernesto (1971). "Tagalog and Other Major Languages of the Philippines." In Thomas A. Sebeok (ed.), *Current Trends in Linguistics*, Vol. 8. (The Hague.)

Cowan, H. K. J. (1948). "Aanteekeningen betreffende de verhouding van het Atjehsch tot de Mon-Khmer-talen." *Bijdragen tot de Taal-, Land- en Volkenkunde, uitgegeven door het Koninklijk Instituut voor Taal-, Land- en Volkenkunde* 104.429–514.

Cowan, H. K. J. (1957a). "A Large Papuan Language Phylum in West New Guinea." *Oceania* 28.159–67.

———— (1957b). "Prospect of a 'Papuan' Comparative Linguistics." *Bijdragen tot de Taal-, Land- en Volkenkunde, uitgegeven door het Koninklijk Instituut voor Taal-, Land- en Volkenkunde* 113.70–91.

———— (1957c). "Een Tweede groote Papoea-taalgroepering in Nederlands Nieuw-Guinea." *Nieuw-Guinea Studiën* 1.107–18.

Crabb, D. W. (1965). *Ekoid Bantu Languages of Ogoja*, Part I. West African Language Monograph Series, 4. Cambridge. (London.)

Cramer, Maria (1962). "Ein Koptischer Brief aus dem Jahre 1848". *Zeitschrift der Deutschen Morganlandischen Gesellschaft* (NF 36). 86–93.

Crawford, James M. (1974). "Some Possible Relationships for Yuchi." Paper presented at the 1974 meetings of the American Anthropological Association.

Créqui-Montfort, G. de, and Paul Rivet (1925–27). "Linguistique bolivienne. La langue uro ou pukina." *Journal de la Société des Américanistes de Paris* 17.211–44; 18.111–99; 19.57–116.

Cuny, A. (1943). *Recherches sur le vocalisme, le consonantisme et la formation des racines en 'nostratique'.* (Paris.)

Curr, E. M. (1886-7). *The Australian Race.* Four vols. (London.)

Dahl, Otto Chr. (1951). *Malgache et Maanjan. Une comparaison linguistique. Studies of the Egede Institute* 3. (Oslo.)

Dalby, David (1965). "The Mel Languages: A Reclassification of Southern 'West Atlantic'." *African Languages* 7.171–179.

———— (1967). "A Survey of the Indigenous Scripts of Liberia and Sierra Leone: Vai, Mende, Loma, Kpelle and Bassa." *African Language Studies* 8 1–51.

Danoff, Chr. M. (1962). "Pontos Euxeinos." *Pauly-Wissowa Realencyclopädie*, Suppl. 9.865–1175.

Dauzat, A. (1940). *L'Europe Linguistique*. (Paris.)

Davenport, William (1962). "Comment on A. Capell, Oceanic Linguistics Today." *Current Anthropology 3,400–2.*

Davis, Irvine (1968). "Some Macro-Jê Relationships." *International Journal of American Linguistics* 34.42–47.

de Angulo, Jaime, and L. S. Freeland (1933). "Zapotekan Linguistic Group. A Comparative Study of Chinanteco, Chocho, Mazateco, Cuicateco, Mixteco, Chatino, and Especially of Zapoteco Proper and Its Dialects." *International Journal of American Linguistics* 8.1–38; 111–30.

DeArmond, Richard A. (1973). "Reconstruction of Proto-Gutob-Remo-Geta ?." Paper presented at the First International Conference on Austroasiatic Linguistics, Honolulu, January 2–6, 1973.

De Bray, R. G. A. (1951). *The Slavonic Languages*. (London.)

DeCamp, D. (1968). "The Field of Creole Language Studies." Paper for *Conference on Pidginization and Creolization*, April 9–12, University of the West Indies, Mona, Jamaica.

———— (1971). "Toward a Generative Analysis of a Post-creole Speech Continuum." In D. Hymes (ed.), *Pidginization and Creolization of Languages*. (London.)

de Charencey, H. (1867). *Des Affinités de la Langue Basque avec les Idiomes du Nouveau-Monde*. (Caen.)

Delafosse, Maurice (1924). "Les langues du Soudan et de la Guinée." In A. Meillet and M. Cohen, *Les langues du Monde*. (Paris.)

———— (1929). *La language mandingue et ses dialects (Malinké, Bambara, Dioula)*. (Paris.)

del Hoyo, E. (1960). "Vocablos de la Lengua Quinigua de los Indios Borrados del Noreste de México." *Anuario del Centro de Estudios Humanístics*, Universidade de Nuevo León 1: 1.489–515.

Dempwolff, Otto (1937). "Deduktive Anwendung des Urindonesischen auf Austronesische Einzelsprachen." *Zeitschrift für Eingeborenen-Sprachen*, Beiheft 17.

Deny, Jean, et al. (eds.) (1959, 1964). *Philologiae Turcicae Fundamenta*. (Wiesbaden.)

De Wolf, P. P. (1971). *The Noun Class System of Proto-Benue-Congo*. (The Hague.)

de Yrizar, P. (1950). *Sobre el carácter pasivo del verbo transitivo, o del verbo de acción, en el vascuence y en algunas lenguas del Norte de América*. (San Sebastián, Real Sociedad Vascongada de Amigos del País.)

Dharmadasa, K. N. O. (1974). "The Creolization of an Aboriginal Language: The Case of Vedda in Sri Lanka (Ceylon)." *Anthropological Linguistics* 16.

Dhorme, M. Ed. (1946–48). "Déchiffrement des Inscriptions Pseudo-Hiéroglyphiques de Byblos." *Syria. Revue d'art Oriental et d'Archéologie* 25.1–35. (Paris.)

Diakonoff, I. M. (1967). *Jazyki Drevnej Perednej Azii*. (Moscow.)

Dieth, Eugene (1946). "A New Survey of English Dialects." *Transactions of the Philological Society* 32.

Diffloth, Gérard (1973a). "Minor-Syllable Vocalism in Senoic Languages." Paper presented at the First International Conference on Austroasiatic Linguistics, Honolulu, January 2–6, 1973.

———— (1973b). "The Position of Senoic in the Mon-Khmer Sub-family." Paper presented at the First International Conference on Austroasiatic Linguistics, Honolulu, January 2–6, 1973.

Dixon, R. B., and A. L. Kroeber (1913a). "New Linguistic Families in California." *American Anthropologist*, n.s., 15.647–755.

———— (1913b). "Relationship of the Indian languages of California." *Science*, n.s., 37.225.

———— (1919). *Linguistic Families of California. University of California Publications in American Archaeology and Ethnology* 16.47–118.

Dixon, R. M. W. (1966a). "Mbabaram: A Dying Australian Language." *Bulletin of the School of Oriental Studies* 29: 1.97–122.

———— (1966b). *Mbabaram Phonology*. (Hertford.)

Doerfer, Gerhard, et al. (1971). *Khalaj Materials. Uralic and Altaic Series* 115. (Bloomington.)

Dolgopoljskij, A. B. (1966). "Materialy pro sravnitelno-istoriceskoj fonetike kusitskix jazykov: gubnye i dentaljnye smyčnye v načalijnom položenii." In B. A. Upsenskij (ed.), *Jazyki Afriki* 35–38. (Moscow.)

Douglas, W. H. (1964). *An Introduction to the Western Desert Language of Australia*. Revised ed., *Oceanic Linguistics Monographs* 4.

Downer, G. B. (1971). "The Further Relationships of the Miao-Yao languages." Paper presented at the 4th International Sino-Tibetan Conference, October 8–10, Bloomington, Indiana. To appear in the *Shafer Memorial Volume*.

DuBois, Cora Alice (1944). *The People of Alor*. (Minneapolis.)

Dul'zon, A. P. (1968). *Ketskij jazyk*. (Tomsk.)

Dyen, Isidore (1963). "The Position of the Malayopolynesian Languages of Formosa." *Asian Perspectives* 7.261–71.

———— (1964). "Comment on Movement of the Malayo-Polynesians: 1500 B.C. to A.D. 500." *Current Anthropology* 5.387–8.

———— (1965). *A Lexicostatistical Classification of the Austronesian Languages. Indiana University Publications in Anthropology and Linguistics* 19.

———— (1966). "The Position of Favorlang among the Austronesian Languages of Formosa." Paper presented at XIth Pacific Science Congress in Tokyo. (Mimeographed.)

———— (1971). "The Austronesian Languages of Formosa." In Thomas A. Sebeok (ed.), *Current Trends in Linguistics* Vol. 8. (The Hague.)

Egerod, Søren (1967). "Dialectology." In Thomas A. Sebeok (ed.), *Linguistics in East Asia and South East Asia, Current Trends in Linguistics* 2. (The Hague.)

Elbert, Samuel H. (1953). "Internal Relationships of Polynesian Languages and Dialects." *Southwestern Journal of Anthropology* 9.147–73.

Elcock, W. D. (1960). *The Romance Languages*. (London.)

Elmendorf, W. W. (1963). "Yukian-Siouan Lexical Similarities." *International Journal of American Linguistics* 29.300–9.

———— (1964). "Item and Set Comparison in Yuchi, Siouan, and Yukian." *International Journal of American Linguistics* 30.328–40.

———— (1965). "Impressions of Ryukyuan-Japanese Diversity." *Anthropological Linguistics* 7:3.1–3.

———— (1968). "Lexical and Cultural Change in Yukian." *Anthropological Linguistics* 10:7.1–41.

Elugbe, Benjamin E. (1971). "The Edo Languages of Akoko Division." *Research Notes* 4: 1.35–8. University of Ibadan, Nigeria.

———— (1972). *Comparative Edo Phonology*. Ph.D. thesis, University of Ibadan, Nigeria.

Emeneau, Murray B. (1966). "The Dialects of Old Indo-Aryan." In H. Birnbaum and J. Puhvel (eds.), *Ancient Indo-European Dialects*. (Berkeley and Los Angeles.)

———— (1969). "The Non-literary Dravidian Languages." In Thomas A. Sebeok (ed.), *Current Trends in Linguistics* Vol. 5. (The Hague.)

Erzen, A. (1940). *Kilikien bis zum Ende der Perserherrschaft*. (Borna, Leipzig.)

Escalante Hernández, Roberto (1962). *El Cuitlateco. Instituto Nacional de Antropologia e Historia, Departamento de Investigaciones Antropológicas, Publ.* 9. (Mexico.)

Esser, S. J. (1938). "Languages." In *Atlas van Tropish Nederland*, sheet 9, 9b. (Amsterdam.)

Fairbanks, G. H. (1966). "Preface" in Pattanayak (1966), q.v.

Farfán, J. M. B. (1954). "Cronología Quechua-Aymara Según el Cálculo Estadístico." *Revista del Museo Nacional* (Lima) 23.50–55.

Fernandez de Miranda, Maria Teresa, Morris Swadesh, and Robert Weitlaner (1959). "Some Findings on Oaxaca Language Classification and Culture Terms." *International Journal of American Linguistics* 25.54–58.

Fernandez de Miranda, Maria Teresa and Robert Weitlaner (1961). "Sobre Algunas Relaciones de la Familia Mangue." *Anthropological Linguistics* 3: 7.1–99.

Ferrario, Benigno (1956). "La Dialettologia della Runa-Simi." *Orbis* 5.131–40.

Ferrell, Raleigh. (1968). "The Pazeh-Kahabu Language." *Bulletin of the Department of Archaeology and Anthropology* Nos. 31–32.73–97. National Taiwan University.

Filbeck, David (1971). *T'in, A Historical Study*. Indiana University Ph.D. dissertation.

Firth, J. R. (1968). "Indian Languages." *Encyclopaedia Britannica*, Vol. 12.103–4.

Fischel, Henry A. (1964). Consultant data incorporated in C. F. and F. M. Voegelin, "Languages of the World: African Fascicle One." *Anthropological Linguistics* 6: 5.281–83.

Fleming, H. C. (1969). "The Classification of West Cushitic within Hamito-Semitic." In D. F. McCall (ed.), *Eastern African History*. (New York.)

—— (1972). "Classification of Cushitic and Omotic Languages." In Bender, Cooper, Ferguson, et al. *Language in Ethiopia*, Chap. 3. (London and Addis Abbaba.)

Fodor, István (1961). "The Validity of Glottochronology on the Basis of the Slavonic Languages." *Studia Slavica* 7: 4.295–346.

—— (1969). *The Problems in the Classification of the African Languages*. Center for Afro-Asiatic Research of the Hungarian Academy of Sciences. (Budapest.)

Forrer, E. (1937). "Kilikien zur Zeit des Hatti-Reiches." *Klio* 30 (NF 12). 135–86.

Forrest, R. A. D. (1948). *The Chinese Language*. (London.)

Fox, Robert B., Willis E. Sibley, and Fred Eggan (1953; published 1965). "A Preliminary Glotto-chronology for Northern Luzon." *Asian Studies* 3.103–13. Paper presented at Eighth Pacific Science Congress, Manila, 1953.

Franklin, K. J. (1968). "Languages of the Gulf District." *Pacific Linguistics*, A, 16.

Freeland, L. S., and E. Sapir (1930). "The Relationship of Mixe to the Punutian Family." *International Journal of American Linguistics* 6.28–33.

Friedrich, Johannes (1931). *Hethitisch und "Kleinasiatische" Sprachen. Geschichte der indo-germanischen Sprachwissenschaft*, II, 5, 1. (Berlin, Leipzig.)

—— (1932). *Kleinasiatische Sprachdenkmäler (Kleine Texte für Vorlesungen und Übungen)*. (Berlin.)

—— (1952). "Karer in Numidien ?" *Orientalia* (NS) 21.231–33.

Friedrich, Johannes, and Wolfgang Röllig (1970). *Phönizisch-punische Grammatik*, 2d ed. Analecta Orientalia, 46. (Rome.)

Friedrich, Paul (1971). "Dialectal Variation in Tarascan Phonology." *International Journal of American Linguistics* 37.164–87.

Gatschet, Albert (1884). *Creek Migration Legends* I. 13. (Philadelphia.)

Gedney, William J. (1965a). "Saek, A Displaced Northern Tai Language." Paper read at the Annual Meeting of the Linguistic Society of America, Chicago.

—— (1965b). "Yay, A Northern Tai Language." *Lingua* 14.180–193.

—— (1967). "Thailand and Laos." In Thomas A. Sebeok (ed.), *Linguistics in East Asia and South East Asia, Current Trends in Linguistics* Vol. 2. (The Hague.)

—— (1970). "The Saek Language of Nakhon Phanom Province." *The Journal of the Siam Society* 58: 1.67–87.

—— (In press). *Future Directions in Comparative Tai Linguistics. Language Science Monographs*.

Geiger, B. et al. (1959). *Peoples and Languages of the Caucasus*. (The Hague.)

Gelb, I. J. (1964). "Sumerian." *Encyclopaedia Britannica* 21.

Gèze, L. (1883). *De Quelques Rapports entre les Languages Berbères et le Basque*. (Toulouse.)

Glover, Warren W. (1971). "Three Gurung Equivalents of English *Be*." *Journal of The Tribhuvan University. Special Linguistic Number*. Tribhuvan University (Kirtipur, Nepal.)

Goddard, Ives (1967). "Notes on the Genetic Classification of the Algonquian Languages." *Contributions to Anthropology: Linguistics I, National Museum of Canada Bulletin* 214.

Goddard, P. E. (1920). "Has Tlingit a Genetic Relation to Athapascan ?" *International Journal of American Linguistics* 1.266–79.

Goetze, Albrecht (1957). *Kulturgeschichte des alten Orients: Kleinasien*. (Munich.)

Golla, Victor K. (1964). "Comparative Yokuts Phonology." In William Bright (ed.), *Studies in Californian Linguistics. University of California Publications in Linguistics* 34.54–66.

Goodenough, Ward (1961). "Migrations Implied by Relationships of New Britain Dialects to Central Pacific Languages." *Journal of the Polynesian Society* 70.112–36.

Gordon, Cyrus H. (1966). *Evidence for the Minoan Language.* (Ventnor, N.J.)

Grace, George W. (1955). "Subgrouping of Malayo-Polynesian: A Report of Tentative Findings." *American Anthropologist* 57.337–9.

——— (1959). *The Position of the Polynesian Languages within the Austronesian Language Family. Indiana University Publications in Anthropology and Linguistics* 16.

——— (1967). "Effect of Heterogeneity in the Lexicostatistical Test List: The Case of Rotuman." In G. A. Highland et al. (eds.), *Polynesian Culture History Essays in Honour of Kenneth P. Emory.* Bishop Museum Special Publication 56 (Honolulu.)

——— (1968). "Classification of the Languages of the Pacific." In Andrew P. Vayda (ed.), *People and Cultures of the Pacific: An Anthropological Reader.*

——— (1970). "Notes on the Phonological History of the Austronesian Languages of the Sarmi Coast." *Working Papers in Linguistics* 2: 9.55–104. (University of Hawaii.)

Granberry, Julian (1956). "Timucua I: Prosodics and Phonemics of the Mocama Dialect." *International Journal of American Linguistics* 22.97–105.

Gray, Louis H. (1934). *Introduction to Semitic Comparative Linguistics.* (New York.)

Green, Roger (1966). "Linguistic Subgrouping within Polynesia: The Implications for Prehistoric Settlement." *Journal of the Polynesian Society* 75.6–38.

Greenberg, Joseph H. (1955). *Studies in African Linguistic Classification.* (New Haven.)

——— (1957). *Essays in Linguistics.* (Chicago.)

——— (1957b). "Nilotic, 'Nilo-Hamitic', and Hamito-Semitic: A Reply." *Africa* 27.364–377.

——— (1958). "Report on the Classification of the Non-Austronesian Languages of the Pacific." Ms.

——— (1960a). "The General Classification of Central and South American Languages." In Anthony F. C. Wallace (ed.), *Selected Papers of the Fifth International Congress of Anthropological and Ethnological Sciences.* (Philadelphia.)

——— (1960b). "Indo-Pacific Etymologies." Ms.

——— (1963a). "History and Status of the Kwa-Problem." *Actes du second colloque international de linguistique Négro-Africaine.* (Dakar.)

——— (1963b). *The Languages of Africa. International Journal of American Linguistics* 29(1), Part 2.

——— (1963c). "The Mogogodo, a Forgotten Cushitic People." *Journal of African Languages* 2, Part 1.29–43.

——— (1966). *The Languages of Africa.* (Bloomington and The Hague.)

——— (1971a). "Nilo-Saharan and Meroitic." In Thomas A. Sebeok (ed.), *Linguistics in Sub-Saharan Africa, Current Trends in Linguistics,* Vol. 7. (The Hague.)

——— (1971b). "The Indo-Pacific Hypothesis." In Thomas A. Sebeok (ed.), *Current Trends in Linguistics,* Vol. 8. (The Hague.)

Greenberg, Joseph H., and Morris Swadesh (1953). "Jicaque as a Hokan-Language." *International Journal of American Linguistics* 19.216–222.

Grierson, Sir George A. (1903–1927). *Linguistic Survey of India,* 11 vols. (Calcutta.)

Grimes, J. L. (1969). "A Reclassification of the Quichean and Kekchian (MAYAN) Languages." Paper presented at the 68th Annual meeting of the American Anthropological Association, New Orleans.

Gudschinsky, Sarah C. (1959). *Proto-Popotecan. Indian University Publications in Anthropology and Linguistics* 15.

Gursky, Karl-Heinz (1963). "Die Stellung der Sprachen von Nordost-Mexiko und Süd-Texas." *Abhandlungen der Völkerkundlichen Arbeitsgemeinschaft,* Bd 4, Nortorf. (Germany.)

——— (1964). "The Linguistic Position of the Quinigua Indians." *International Journal of American Linguistics* 30.325–7.

——— (1965). "Zur Frag der Historischer Stellung der Yuki-Sprachfamilie." *Abhandlungen der*

Völkerkundlichen Arbeitsgemeinschaft 8.1–25.

——— (1966). "On the Historical Position of Waikuri." *International Journal of American Linguistics* 32.41–5.

Guthrie, Malcolm (1948). "Classification of the Bantu Languages," *Handbook of African Languages*. International African Institute. (London.)

——— (1953). "The Bantu Languages of Western Equatorial Africa," *Handbook of African Languages*. International African Institute. (London.)

——— (1967–71). *Comparative Bantu*. 4 vols. (Farnborough, Hants, England.)

Haas, Mary R. (1941). "The Classification of the Muskogean Languages." In Spier, Hallowell, and Newman (eds.), *Language, Culture, and Personality*. (Menasha, Wisconsin.)

——— (1949). "The Position of Apalachee in the Muskogean Family." *International Journal of American Linguistics* 15.121–27.

——— (1958a). "Algonkian-Ritwan: The End of a Controversy." *International Journal of American Linguistics* 24.159–173.

——— (1958b). "A New Linguistic Relationship in North America: Algonkian and the Gulf Languages." *Southwestern Journal of Anthropology* 14.231–264.

——— (1959). "Tonkawa and Algonkian." *Anthropological Linguistics* 1: 2.1–6.

——— (1960). "Some Genetic Affiliations of Algonkian." In *Culture in History, Essays in Honor of Paul Radin*, S. Diamond, ed. (New York.)

——— (1963). "Shasta and Proto-Hokan." *Language* 39.40–59.

——— (1964a). "Athabascan, Tlingit, Yuchi and Siouan." *International Congress of Americanists, Proceedings* 25: 2.495–500.

——— (1964b). "California Hokan." In William Bright (ed.), *Studies in California Linguistics., University of California Publications in Linguistics* 34.73–87.

——— (1965). "Is Kutenai Related to Algonkian ?" *Canadian Journal of Linguistics* 10.77ff.

——— (1966). "Wiyot-Yurok-Algonkian and Problems of Comparative Algonkian." *International Journal of American Linguistics* 32.101–107.

——— (1969). "Swanton and the Biloxi and Ofo Dictionaries." *International Journal of American Linguistics* 35.286–290.

Hale, Kenneth (1964). "The Sub-grouping of Uto-Aztecan Languages: Lexical Evidence for Sonoran." *International Congress of Americanists, Proceedings* 25: 2.511–18.

Hall, Robert A. Jr. (1950). "The Reconstruction of Proto-Romance." *Language* 26.6–27.

——— (1966). *Pidgin and Creole Languages*. (Ithaca.)

——— (1974). *External History of the Romance Languages*. (New York, London, Amsterdam.)

Halpern, A. L. (1964). "A Report on a Survey of Pomo Languages." In W. Bright (ed.), *Studies in California Linguistics. University of California Publications in Linguistics* 34.88–93.

Hammerich, Louis L. (1951). "Can Eskimo Be Related to Indo-European ?" *International Journal of American Linguistics* 17.217–223.

Hamp, Eric P. (1959). "Buividze Lithuanian Phonemes." *International Journal of Slavic Linguistics and Poetics I*.

——— (1965). Consultant information included in C. F. and F. M. Voegelin, "Languages of the World: Indo-European Fascicle One." *Anthropological Linguistics* 7: 8.90–99.

——— (1966). "The Position of Albanian." In Birnbaum and Puhvel (eds.), *Ancient Indo-European Dialects*. (Berkeley and Los Angeles.)

——— (1967a). "On Maya-Chipayan." *International Journal of American Linguistics* 33.74–6.

——— (1967b). "Two Armenian Etymologies." *Revue des Etudes Arméniennes* (N.S.) 4.15–7.

——— (1969a). "Armenian *harb, hars, harc'*." *Reveue des Etudes Arméniennes* (N.S.) 6.15–7.

——— (1969b). "On Maxacali, Karaja, and Macro-Jê." *International Journal of American Linguistics* 35.269–70.

——— (1969c). "On the Problem of Ainu and Indo-European." *Eighth Congress of Anthropological and Ethnological Sciences*, pp. 100–102. (Tokyo, 1968; pub. Tokyo, 1969.)

——— (1971). "On Mayan-Araucanian Comparative Phonology." *International Journal of American*

Linguistics 37.156–9.

———— (1972). "Albanian." In Thomas A. Sebeok (ed.), *Current Trends in Linguistics* Vol. 9. (The Hague.)

Hancock, I. F. (n.d.). "A Provisional Comparison of the English-Based Atlantic Creoles, with Comparative Word-Lists." Ms.

Harrington, J. P. (1909). "Notes on the Piro Language." *American Anthropologist* 11.563–94.

———— (1910). "On Phonetic and Lexical Resemblances between Kiowan and Tanoan." *American Anthropologist* 12.119–123.

———— (1928). "Vocabulary of the Kiowa Language." *Bureau of American Ethnology, Bulletin* 84. (Washington.)

———— (1943). "Hokan Discovered in South America." *Journal of the Washington Academy of Science* 33.334–44.

Hattori Shirō, Haruhiko Kindaichi, Ooki Hayashi, and Susumu Ohno (1955). "Nihon-go (Japanese)." In Ichikawa, Sanki, and Shiro Hattori (eds.), *Sekai Gengo Gaisetsu* (An Introduction to the Languages of the World). II. (Tokyo.)

Hattori Shirō and Mashibo Chiri (1955–56). "Lexicostatistic Study of the Ainu Dialects." *Minzokugaku-Kenkyu* (The Japanese Journal of Ethnology) 24.21–66. [Abstract by Hauro Aoki in IJAL 27.358–60, 1961.]

Haudricourt, André G. (1948). "Les Phonèmes et le vocabulaire du Thai Commun." *Journal Asiatique* 263.197–238.

———— (1956). "De La Restitution des Initials dans les Languages Monosyllabiques: Le Problème du Thai Commun." *Bulletin de la Société Linguistique de Paris* 52.310–313.

———— (1966). "The Limits and Connections of Austroasiatic in the Northeast." In N. H. Zide (ed.), *Studies in Comparative Austroasiatic Linguistics*. (The Hague.)

———— (1967). "La Langue Lakkia." *Bulletin de la Société de Linguistique de Paris* 62.165–182.

Haugen, Einar I. (1968). "Scandinavian Languages." *Encyclopaedia Britannica*, Vol. 19: 1138–9.

Headley, Robert K., Jr. (1973a). "Some Sources of Chamic Vocabulary." Paper presented at the First International Conference on Austroasiatic Linguistics. Honolulu, January 2–6, 1973.

———— (1973b). "The Position of Khmer in the Mon-Khmer Family." Paper presented at the First International Conference on Austroasiatic Linguistics. Honolulu, January, 2–6, 1973. Also, consultant information supplied by personal communication, April 1973.

Heine, Bernd (1968). *Die Verbreitung und Gliederung der Togorestsprachen*. (Berlin.)

———— (1973). "Zur genetischen Gliederung der Bantu-Sprachen." *Afrika und Übersee* 56.164–85.

Heizer, Robert F. (1952). "California Indian Linguistic Records: The Mission Indian Vocabularies of Alphonse Pinart." *University of California Anthropological Records* 15.1–84.

———— (1955). "California Indian Linguistic Records: The Mission Indian Vocabularies of H. W. Henshaw." *University of California Anthropological Records* 15.85–202.

Hewson, John (1968). "Beothuk and Algonkian: Evidence Old and New." *International Journal of American Linguistics* 34.85–93.

Hickerson, Harold, Glen D. Turner, and Nancy P. Hickerson (1952). "Testing Procedures for Estimating Transfer of Information among Iroquois Dialects." *International Journal of American Linguistics* 18.1–8.

Hill, Jane H., and Kenneth C. Hill (1968). "Stress in the Cupan (Uto-Aztecan) Languages." *International Journal of American Linguistics* 34.232–41.

Hirt, H. (1931–34). *Handbuch des Urgermanischen*, Vol. I–III. (Heidelberg.)

Hockett, Charles F. (1948). "Implications of Bloomfield's Algonquian Studies." *Language* 24.117–131.

Hodge, Carleton T. (1968). "Afroasiatic '67." *Language Sciences* 1.13–21.

Hoernle, A. F. R. (1880). *A Comparative Grammar of the Goudian Languages*. (London.)

Hoffman, Helmut (1967). 'Žaṅ-žuṅ: The Holy Language of Bon-po." *Zeitschrift der Deutschen Morgenländischen Gesellschaft* 117: 2.375–381.

Hohenberger, J. (1956). "Comparative Masai Word List." *Africa* 26.281–9.

———— (1958). "Some Notes on Nilotic, 'Nilo-Hamitic', and Hamito-Semitic by Joseph H. Greenberg." *Africa* 28.37–41.

Hoijer, Harry (1938). "The Southern Athapascan Languages." *American Anthropologist* 40.75–87.

—— (1945–49). "The Apachean Verb." *International Journal of American Linguistics* 11.193–203; 12.1–13, 51–9; 14.247–259; 15.12–22.

—— (1960). "Athapascan Languages of the Pacific Coast." In Stanley Diamond (ed.), *Culture in History, Essays in Honor of Paul Radin*. (New York.)

Holl, C. (1908). "Das Fortleben der Volkssprachen in Kleinasien im nachchristlicher Zeit." *Hermes* 43.240–54.

Holland, William R. (1959). "Dialect Variations of the Mixtec and Cuicatec Areas of Oaxaca, Mexico." *Anthropological Linguistics* 1: 8.25–31.

Holmer, Nils M. (1947). "Ibero-Caucasian as a Linguistic Type." *Studia Linguistica* 1.

—— (1963). "On the History and Structure of the Australian Languages." *Australian Essays and Studies III*.

Homburger, L. (1955). "L'Inde et l'Afrique." *Journal de la Société des Africanistes* 25.13–18. (Paris.)

Hooley, B. A., and K. A. McElhanon (1970). "Languages of the Morobe District-New Guinea." In Wurm and Laycock (eds.), *Pacific Linguistic Studies in Honour of Arthur Capell. Pacific Linguistics*, C, 13.

Hrozný, B. (1945). "La Stèle Hiéroglyphique de Byblos." *Académie des Inscriptions et Belles Lettres. Comptes rendus des Séances de L'Anée* 1945, pp. 382–385 (Paris.)

—— (1947). *Histoire de l'Asie anterieure, de l'Inde et de la Crète*. (Paris.)

—— (1949). *Les Inscriptions Crètoises*. (Prague.)

Hunter, G. R. (1934). *The Script of Harappa and Mohenjo-Daro and Its Connection with Other Scripts*. (London.)

Huntingford, G. W. B. (1956). "The 'Nilo-Hamitic' Languages." *Southwest Journal of Anthropology* 12.200–222.

Hymes, Dell H. (1956). "Na-Déné and Positional Analysis of Categories." *American Anthropologist* 58.624–638.

Ibarra Grasso, Dick Edgar (1961). "La Lingüistica Indigena de Bolivia y las Lenguas Andinas." In *A William Cameron Townsend*. (Mexico.)

Ivić, P. (1953). "On the Present State of the Study of Standard Macedonian." *Word* 9.325–38.

——(1958). *Die Serbokroatischen Dialekte; ihre Structur und Entwicklung*, Vol I. (S-Gravenhage).

Izui, Hisanosuke (1965). "The Languages of Micronesia: Their Unity and Diversity." *Lingua* 14.349–59.

Jackson, Frances L. (1972). "Proto Mayan." In Esther Matteson (ed.), *Comparative Studies in Amerindian Languages*. (The Hague.)

Jacobsen, William H., Jr. (1970). "Observations on the Yana Stop Series in Relationship to Problems of Comparative Hokan Phonology." Paper presented at the Hokan Conference, University of California, San Diego.

Jacquot, A., and I. Richardson (1954). "Report of the Western Team." *Linguistic Survey of the Northern Bantu Borderland Vol. 1, Part I*. International African Institute. (London.)

Jakobson, Roman (1942). "The Paleosiberian Languages." *American Anthropologist* 44.602–20.

—— (1955). *Slavic Languages*. (Oxford.)

—— (1957). "Notes on Giljak." *Academia Sinica, Bulletin of the Institute of History and Philology*. I.

Jazyki narodov SSSR (1966). *Tom tretij. Finno-ugorskie i samodijskie jazyki* (Moscow.)

—— (1974). *Main Trends in the Science of Language*. (New York, Evanston, San Francisco, London.)

Jenness, Diamond (1953). "Did the Yahgan Indians of Tierra del Fuego speak an Eskimo Tongue ?" *International Journal of American Linguistics* 19.128–131.

Jensen, Hans (1959). *Altarmenische Grammatik*.

—— (1969). *Sign, Symbol and Script*. (New York.)

Jijón y Caamaño, Jacinto (1941–3). *El Ecuador interandino y occidental*. 3 vols. (Quito.)

—— (1943). "Las Lenguas del Sur de Centro America y el Norte y Centro del Oeste de Sud-America." *El Ecuador Interandino y Occidental* 3.605.

Joel, Judith (1964). "Classification of the Yuman Languages." In W. Bright (ed.), *Studies in California Linguistics. University of California Publications in Linguistics* 34.99–105.

Johnson, Sir H. H. (1919). *A Comparative Study of the Bantu and Semi-Bantu Languages.* (Oxford.)

Johnston, H. H. (1919 and 1922). *A Comparative Study of Bantu and Semi-Bantu.* 2 vols. (Oxford.)

Jokl, Norbert (1911). *Studien zur albanesischen Etymologie und Wortbildung.* (Vienna.)

———— (1927). "Kelten und Albaner." *Symbolae Grammaticae in Honorem Ioannis Rozwadowski* 1.235–250. (Cracoviae.)

Jones, Robert B., Jr. (1961). "Karen Linguistic Studies." *University of California Publications in Linguistics* 25.

Jullian, Camille (1916). "L'époque Italo-Celtic. De Son Existence." *Revue des Etudes Anciennes* 18.263–76.

Kammenhuber, Annelies (1969). "Hattisch." *Altkleinasiatische Sprachen*, pp. 428–546, *Handbuch der Orientalistik*, Erste Abteilung, II Band, 1 und 2 Abschnitt, Lieferung 2. (Leiden, Cologne.)

Kanagusuku, Chōei and Shiro Hattori (1955). Ryukyu-go (Ryukyuan). In Ichikawa, Sanki, and Shiro Hattori (eds.), *Sekai Gengo Gaisetsu* (An Introduction to the Languages of the World). II. (Tokyo.)

Karlgren, Bernard (1915–26). "Études sur la Phonologie Chinoise." *Archives d'Études Orientales.* (Upsala.)

Kaufman, Terrence (1964). "Materiales Lingüísticos para el estudio de la Relaciones Internas y Externas de la Familia de Idiomes Mayanos." In *Desarrollo Cultural de los Mayas*, a special publication of Seminario de Cultura Maya.

———— (1969). "Teco — A New Mayan Language." *International Journal of American Linguistics* 35.154–174.

Keller, R. E. (1961). *German Dialects.* (Manchester.)

Key, Harold, and Mary Key (1967). "Bolivian Indian Tribes: Classification, Bibliography and Map of Present Language Distribution." *Summer Institute of Linguistics Publications in Linguistics and Related Fields.* (Norman.)

Key, Mary Ritchie de (1968). *Comparative Tacanan Phonology.* (The Hague.)

Kinkade, M. Dale (1972). "Proto-Eastern Interior Salish Vowels." *International Journal of American Linguistics* 38.26–48.

Klaproth, H. J. (1823). *Asia Polyglotta;* cited by Miller (1971).

Klokeid, Terry J. (1968). Supplementary information to Geoffrey N. O'Grady, C. F. and F. M. Voegelin (1966).

Köhler, Oswin (1953). "Review of Westermann, D., and M. A. Bryan *The Languages of West Africa.*" *Afrika und Übersee* 37.187–190.

Krauss, Michael E. (1970). Consultant data supplementing C. F. and F. M. Voegelin." Languages of the World: Native America Fascicle One," *Anthropological Linguistics* 6: 6.80–83.

———— (1973a). "Eskimo-Aleut." In Thomas A. Sebeok (ed.), *Current Trends in Linguistics*, Vol. 10. (The Hague.)

———— 1973b). "Na-Dene." In Thomas A. Sebeok (ed.), *Current Trends in Linguistics*, Vol. 10: *Native Languages of the Americas.* (The Hague.)

Krejnovič, E. A. (1958). *Jukagirskij jazyk.* (Moscow-Leningrad.)

———— (1968). "Jukagirskij jazyk." *Jazyki narodov SSSR*, V. (Leningrad.)

Kretschmer, P. (1896). *Einleitung in die Geschichte der griechischen Sprache.* (Göttingen.)

———— (1934). "Literaturberichte für die Jahre 1931 und 1932: Griechisch." *Glotta; Zeitschrift für Griechische und Lateinische Sprache* 22.193–270 (cf. 201ff).

———— (1941). "Die tyrrhenischen Inschriften der Stele von Lemnos." *Glotta* 29.89–98.

Krishnamurti, Bh. (1961). *Telugu verbal bases: A Comparative and Descriptive Study. University of California Publications in Linguistics.* 24.

———— (1969). "Comparative Dravidian Studies." In Thomas A. Sebeok (ed.), *Current Trends in Linguistics.* Vol. 5. (The Hague.)

Kroeber, A. L. (1915). "Serian, Tequistlatecan, and Hokan." *University of California Publications.*

————(1943). "Classification of the Yuman Languages." *University of California Publications in Linguistics* 1.21–40.

————(1963). "Yokuts Dialect Survey." *Anthropological Records* 11(3). (Berkeley.)

Krueger, John R. (1961). "Review of Poppe 1960." *Journal of the American Oriental Society* 81.70–74.

Kuiper, F. B. J. (1962). "Nahali, A Comparative Study." *Mededelingen der Koninklijke Nederlandse Akademie van Wetenschappen* 25.239–352.

————(1966). "The Sources of Nahali Vocabulary." In Norman H. Zide (ed.), *Studies in Comparative Austroasiatic Linguistics*. (The Hague.)

————(1963). "Caucasian." In Thomas A. Sebeok (ed.), *Current Trends in Linguistics*. Vol. 1. (The Hague.)

Kurath, Hans, and others (1939). *The Handbook of Linguistic Geography of New England*. (Providence.)

Lafon, R. (1933). "Basque et Langues Kartvèles." *Revue Internationale des Études Basques* 24: 2.

————(1944). "Appendix" to Volume One of *Le Système du Verbe Basque au XVIe Siècle*. Publications de l'Université de Bordeaux. (Bordeaux.)

————(1947). "L'état Actuel du Problème des Origines de la Langue Basque." *Eusko-Jakintza* fasc. I, II, V–VI.

————(1951). "Les Origines de la Langue Basque, État Actuel de la Question." In *Conférénces de l'Institute de Linguistique de l'Université de Paris*.

Lahovary, N. (1948). "Aperçus nouveau sur de rapports insoupçonnes du basque et des langues dravidiennes." *Boletin de la Real Academia de Buenas Letras de Barcelona* 21.

————(1954). "Substrat linguistic méditerranéen, basque et dravidien." *Substrat en langues classiques*. (Firenze.)

————(1957). *La diffusion des langues anciennes du Proche-Orient: Leurs relations avec le basque, le dravidien et les parlers indo-européens primitifs*. (Berne.)

————(1963). *Dravidian Origins and the West*. (Madras.)

Lamb, Sydney M. (1964). "The Classification of the Uto-Aztecan Languages: A Historical Survey." *University of California Publications in Linguistics* 34.106–25.

Landar, Herbert (1973). "The Tribes and Languages of North America: A Check List." In Thomas A. Sebeok (ed.), *Current Trends in Linguistics, Linguistics in North America* Vol. 10. (The Hague.)

Lane, George S. (1966). "On the Interrelationships of the Tocharian Dialects." In Birnbaum and Puhvel (eds.), *Ancient Indo-European Dialects*. (Berkeley and Los Angeles.)

Langdon, Margaret (1968). "The Proto-Yuman Demonstrative System." *Folia Linguistica* 2: 1.61–81.

————(1970). *A Grammar of Diegueño*. *University of California Publications in Linguistics* 66.

Lanyon-Orgill, Peter A. (1961). Introductory note to "Comparative Vocabulary of Formosan Languages," Naoyoshi Ogawa and Erin Asai. *Journal of Austronesian Studies* 2: 2.5–32.

Laycock, D. C. (1965). *The Ndu Language Family (Sepik District, New Guinea)*. Linguistic Circle of Canberra Publications, Series, C, No. 1.

————(1968). "Languages of the Lumi Sub-District (West Sepik District, New Guinea)." *Oceanic Linguistics* 7.36–66.

Leap, William L. (1971). "Who Were the Piro ?" *Anthropological Linguistics* 13: 7.321–30.

Lee Ki-moon (1963). "A Genetic View on Japanese." *Chōsen gakuhō* 27.94–105.

Leenhardt, Maurice (1946). *Langues et dialectes de l'Austro-Mélanésie*. Travaux et Mémoires de l'Institut d'Ethnologie XLVI.

Lehmann, W. P. (1966). "The Grouping of the Germanic Languages." In Birnbaum and Puhvel (eds.), *Ancient Indo-European Dialects*. (Berkeley and Los Angeles.)

Leslau, W. (1945). "The Influence of Cushitic on the Semitic Languages of Ethiopia: A Problem of Substratum." *Word* 1.59–82.

Li Fang-Kuei (1930). *Mattole: An Athapaskan Language*. (Chicago.)

————(1937). "Language and Dialects." *Chinese Year Book*. (Shanghai.)

————(1954). "Consonant Clusters in Tai." *Language* 30.368–79.

————(1957). "The Jui Dialect of Po-ai and Northern Tai." *Bulletin of the Institute of History and Philology Academia Sinica* 29.315–322.

———— (1959). "Classification by Vocabulary: Tai Dialects." *Anthropological Linguistics* 1: 2.15–21.

———— (1960). "A Tentative Classification of Tai Dialects." In S. Diamond (ed.), *Culture in History, Essays in Honor of Paul Radin*. (New York.)

———— (1965a). Consultant information incorporated in C. F. and F. M. Voegelin "Languages of the World: Sino-Tibetan Fascicle ONE." *Anthropological Linguistics* 6: 3.

———— (1965b). "Some Problems in Comparative Athabascan." *Canadian Journal of Linguistics* 10.129–34.

———— (1965c). "The Tai and Kam-Sui Languages." *Lingua* 14.148–79.

———— (1967). "Linguistics in Taiwan." In Thomas A. Sebeok (ed.), *Current Trends in Linguistics 2: Linguistics in East Asia and Southeast Asia*. (Mouton.)

Lipkind, William (1948). "The Caraja." In Julian H. Steward (ed.), *Handbook of South American Indians*. Vol. 3. 179–91. (Washington.)

Lockwood, W. B. (1972). *A Panorama of Indo-European Languages*. (London.)

Loewen, Jacob A. (1963). "Chocó I: Introduction and Bibliography." *International Journal of American Linguistics* 29.239–263.

Loewenthal, Rudolf (1957). *The Turkic Languages and Literatures of Central Asia, a Bibliography*. (The Hague.)

Longacre, Robert E. (1957). *Proto Mixtecan. Indiana University Research Center in Anthropology, Folklore, and Linguistics* 5.

———— (1961). "Swadesh's Macro-Mixtecan Hypothesis." *International Journal of American Linguistics* 27.9–29.

———— (1964). "Progress in Otomanguean Reconstruction." In Horace G. Lunt (ed.), *Proceedings of the Ninth International Congress of Linguists*. (The Hague.)

———— (1966). "On Linguistic Affinities of Amuzgo." *International Journal of American Linguistics* 32.46–49.

———— (1968a). "Comparative Reconstruction of Indigenous Languages." In Thomas A. Sebeok (ed.), *Current Trends in Linguistics*. Vol. 4. (The Hague.)

———— (1968b). "Proto-Quechumaran: An Ethnolinguistic Note." *Ethnohistory* 15: 4.403–13.

Loukotka, Čestmír (1935). *Clasificacíon de las lenguas sudamericanas. Edición "Linguística sudamericana,"* No. 1. (Prague.)

———— (1962). "Comment on 'Oceanic Linguistics Today' by Arthur Capell." *Current Anthropology* 3.415.

Loukotka, Čestmír, and Peter A. Lanyon-Orgill (1958). "A Revised Classification of the Formosan Languages." *Journal of Austronesian Studies* 1: 3.56–63.

Lounsbury, Floyd G. (1961). "Iroquois-Cherokee Linguistic Relations." *Symposium on Cherokee-Iroquois Culture*. Bureau of American Ethnology Bulletin 180. (Washington, D.C.)

Loving, Richard. (1968). "The Dialects of Awa." In McKaughan (1968), q. v.

Lowie, R. H. (1965). *Letters from Edward Sapir to Robert H. Lowie, with an Introduction and Notes by Robert H. Lowie*. (Berkeley.)

Luchaire, A. (1877). *Les Origines Linguistiques de l'Aquitaine*. (Paris.)

Lukas, J. (1936). "The Linguistic Situation in the Lake Chad area in Central Africa." *Africa* 9.322–49.

Lunt, Horace (1955). *Grammar of the Macedonian Literary Language*. (Skopje.)

———— (1968). "Slavic Languages." *Encyclopaedia Britannica* Vol. 20.644–46.

Mackenzie, D. N. (1961). *Kurdish Dialect Studies*, Vols. 1, 2. (London.)

Maddieson, Ian (1974). Consultant information to supplement articles on BENUE-CONGO and KWA languages in C. F. and F. M. Voegelin, *Index of the World's Languages*. Final Report on HEW Contract OEC-0-9-097717-1252 (014).

Maddieson, Ian and Kay Williamson (1973). "Jarawan Bantu." *African Language Review* 10.

Mafeni, Bernard O. W. (1972). "The Language of the Isoko People." In Obaro Ikime (ed.), *The Isoko People: A Historical Survey*. (Ibadan.)

Mansel, Aüf Mufid (1965). "Side." *Pauly-Wissowa Realencyclopädie*, Suppl. 10.879–918.

Mao Tsung-wu and Chou Tsu-yao (1962). "A Brief Description of the Languages of the Yao People."

Chung-kuo yü-wen (Chinese Language and Writing) 113.141–8.

Martin, Samuel (1966). "Lexical Evidence Relating Korean to Japanese." *Language* 42.185–251.

Martinet, André (1962). *A Functional View of Language*. (Oxford.)

Mason, J. Alden (1940). "The Native Languages of Middle America." In C. L. Hay et al. (eds.), *The Maya and Their Neighbors*. (New York.)

—— (1950). "The Languages of South American Indians." *Handbook of South American Indians* 6.157–317, Bureau of American Ethnology Bulletin 143. (Washington, D. C.)

Maspero, Henri (1911). "Contribution à l'étude du Système Phonétique des Langues Thai." *Bulletin de l'École Française d'Extrême-Orient* 11.153–69.

—— (1912). "Etudes sur la phonétique historique de la langue annamite: les initiales." *Bulletin de l'École Française d'Extrême-Orient* 12: 1.1–127.

Masson, Olivier (1954). "Épigraphie asianique: bibliographie relative aux inscriptions lyciennes, cariennes, lydiennes et phrygiennes." *Orientalia* (NS) 23.439–42.

—— (1973). "Que savons-nous de l'écriture et de la langue des Cariens ?" *Bulletin de la Société de Linguistique de Paris* 68: 1.187–213.

Matteson, Esther (1972). "Proto Arawakan." In Esther Matteson (ed.), *Comparative Studies in Amerindian Languages*. (The Hague.)

Matthews, G. Hubert (1958). *Handbook of Siouan Languages*. University of Pennsylvania dissertation. Dissertation Abstracts 18: 2.135 (1958).

Matthews, W. K. (1950). "Characteristics of Micronesian." *Lingua* 3.419–37.

Maurer, Friedrich (1952). *Nordgermanen und Alemannen*. (Bern, München.)

McElhanon, K. A. (1967). "Preliminary Observations on Huon Peninsula Languages." *Oceanic Linguistics* 6.1–45.

McKaughan, Howard (1964). "A Study of Divergence in Four New Guinea Languages." *American Anthropologist* 66, No. 4, Part II, pp. 98–120.

—— (ed.) (1968). *Anthropological Studies in the Eastern Highlands of New Guinea*, Vol. I. (Seattle.)

—— (1971). "Minor Languages of the Philippines." In Thomas A. Sebeok (ed.), *Current Trends in Linguistics*. Vol. 8. (The Hague.)

McLenden, Sally (1972). "Proto Pomo." *University of California Publications in Linguistics*.

McQuown, Norman A. (1955). "The Indigenous Languages of Latin America." *American Anthropologist* 57.501–570.

—— (1956). "The Classification of the Mayan Languages." *International Journal of American Linguistics* 22.193–195.

Meek, C. K. (1931). *A Sudanese Kingdom: An Ethnographical Study of the Jukun-speaking Peoples of Nigeria*. (London.)

Meillet, A. (1908). *Les Dialectes Indo-Européens*. (Paris.)

Meillet, A., and M. Cohen (1952). *Les Langues du Monde*. (Paris.)

Meinhof, C. (1910). *Die moderne Sprachforschung in Afrika*. (Berlin.)

Menges, Karl H. (1964). "Altajisch und Drāviḍsch." *Orbis* 13.66–103.

Mentz, A. (1940). "Schrift und Sprache der Karer." *Indogermanische Forschungen* 57.265–81.

Métraux, Alfred (1936). "Contribution à l'ethnographie et à la lingistique des Indiens Uro d'Ancoaqui (Bolivie)." *Journal de la Société des Américanistes de Paris* 28.75–110.

—— (1938). "The Proto-Indian Script and the Easter Island Tablets." *Anthropos* 33.218–239.

—— (1946). "The Caingang." In Julian H. Steward (ed.), *Handbook of South American Indians*. Vol. 1, Bureau of American Ethnology Bulletin 143. (Washington, D. C.)

Meyer, Eduard (1897). "Bithynia: Bevölkerung, Geschichte." *Pauly-Wissowa Realencyclopädie* 5.510–22.

Michelson, Truman (1912). "Preliminary Report on the Linguistic Classification of Algonquian Tribes." *28th Annual Report of the Bureau of American Ethnology* 221–290. (Washington, D. C.)

Migliazza, Ernest C. (1972). *Yanomama Grammar and Intelligibility*. Ph. D. dissertation, Indiana University.

Milke, Wilhelm (1958). "Zur inneren Gliederung und geschichtlichen Stellung der ozeanisch-austronesischen Sprachen." *Zeitschrift für Ethnologie* 83.58–62.

Miller, Roy Andrew (1955). "The Independent Status of the Lhasa Dialect within Central Tibetan." ORBIS 4.49–55.

—— (1967). *The Japanese Language*. (Chicago and London.)

—— (1971). *Japanese and the Other Altaic Languages*. (Chicago and London.)

Miller, Wick R. (1964). "The Shoshonean languages of Uto-Aztecan." *University of California Publications in Linguistics* 34.145–48.

—— (1967). *Uto-Aztecan Cognate Sets*. University of California Publications in Linguistics 48.

Miller, Wick R., and Irvine Davis (1963). "Proto-Keresan Phonology." *International Journal of American Linguistics* 29.310–330.

Mixco, Mauricio (1970). "Kiliwa and Proto-Yuman." Paper read at the Conference on Hokan Languages, University of California at San Diego, April 1970.

Möller, Hermann (1911). *Vergleichendes indogermanisch-semitisches Wörterbuch*. (Güttingen.)

Moreno, M. M. (1940). *Manuale di Sidamo*. (Milano.)

Morgenstierne, Georg (1926). *Report on a Linguistic Mission to Afghanistan*. Institut for Sammenlignende Kulturforskning serie 1–2. (Oslo.)

—— (1935). Preface to Lorimer's *The Burushaski Language*, Vol. 1. (Oslo.)

—— (1961). "Dardic and Kafir Languages." *The Encyclopaedia of Islam, New Edition*, Vol. 2, Fasc. 25. (Leiden.)

Morice, A. G. (1914). "Northwestern Dénés and Northeastern Asiatics." *Transactions of the Canadian Institute* 10.131–193.

Morse, Robert (1965). Consultant information incorporated in C. F. and F. M. Voegelin, "Languages of the World: Sino-Tibetan Fascicle Five." *Anthropological Linguistics* 7: 6.

Moulton, W. G. (1968). "Germanic Languages." *Encyclopaedia Britannica*, Vol. 10: 237–9.

Müllenhoff, K. (1890–1920). *Deutsche Altertumskunde* 1–5. (Berlin.)

Murdock, George P. (n. d.). Information incorporated in the Human Relations Area File. (New Haven.)

Murray, G. W. (1920). "The Nilotic Languages, a Comparative Essay." *Journal Royal Anthropological Institute* 50.327–368.

Navarro Tomás, Tomás (1953). "Observaciones sobre el papiamento." *Nueva Revista de Filologia Hispanica* 7.183–9 (Mexico.)

Naveh, Joseph (1973). "Review of Phönizisch-punische Grammatik by Johannes Friedrich and Wolfgang Röllig." *Journal of the American Oriental Society* 93.588–9.

Nekes, H., and E. A. Worms (1953). "Nyulnyul Grammar." In *Australian Languages, Micro-Bibliothece Anthropos*, Vol. 10.

Newman, Paul (1965). "A Brief Note on the Maha Language." *Journal of African Languages* 2: 1.57–8.

Newman, Paul, and Roxana Ma (1966). "Comparative Chadic: Phonology and Lexicon." *Journal of African Languages* 5.218–251.

Newman, Stanley S. (1944). *Yokuts Language of California*. Viking Fund Publication in Anthropology 2. (New York).

—— (1946). "The Yawelmani Dialect of Yokuts." In H. Hoijer (ed.), *Linguistic Structures of Native America*. Viking Fund Publication in Anthropology 6. (New York.)

—— (1964). "Comparison of Zuni and California Penutian." *International Journal of American Linguistics* 30.1–13.

Nikigawa, A. (1953). "A Classification of the Formosan Languages." *Journal of Austronesian Studies* 1: 1.145–51.

Nimuendajú, Curt (1931–32). "Idiomas indígenas del Brasil." *Revista del Instituto de Etnología de la Universidad de Tucumán* 2.543–618.

Noble, G. Kingsley (1965). *Proto-Arawakan and Its Descendants*. International Journal of American Linguistics 31: 3, Part II, Publication 38 of the Indiana University Research Center in Anthropology, Folklore, and Linguistics.

O'Grady, G. N., S. A. Wurm, and K. L. Hale (1966a). *Map of Aboriginal Languages of Australia (A Preliminary Classification).* Department of Linguistics, University of Victoria, B. C.
O'Grady, G. N., C. F. Voegelin, and F. M. Voegelin (1966b). *Languages of the World: Indo-Pacific Fascicle Six. Anthropological Linguistics* 8: 2.
Olmstead, David L. (1959). "Palaihnihan and Shasta III. Dorsal Stops." *Language* 35.637–644.
——— (1964). *History of Palaihnihan Phonology. University of California Publications in Linguistics* 35.
——— (1965). "Phonemic Change and Subgrouping." *Language* 41.303–307.
Olson, R. D. (1964). "Mayan Affinities with Chipaya of Bolivia I: Correspondences." *International Journal of American Linguistics* 30.313–324.
Omar, Asmah Haji (1971). "Standard Language and the Standardization of Malay." *Anthropological Linguistics* 13.75–89.
Orozco y Berra, Manuel (1864). *Géografía de las lenguas y carta etnográfica de México.* (Mexico.)
Orr, Carolyn, and R. E. Longacre (1968). "Proto-Quechumaran." *Language* 44.528–55.
Oswalt, R. L. (1964). "The Internal Relationships of the Pomo Family of Languages." *The 35th International Congress of Americanists, Actas y Memorias,* 413–421. (Mexico.)
——— (1971). Supplementary consultant information to C. F. and F. M. Voegelin, "Native America Fascicle One." *Anthropological Linguistics* 6: 6 (1964).

Panfilov, V. Z. (1968). "Nivxskij jazyk." *Jazyki naradov SSSR,* V, pp. 408–434. (Leningrad.)
Paper, Herbert H. (1955). *The Phonology and Morphology of Royal Achaemenid Elamite.* (Ann Arbor.)
Parker, Gary J. (1963). "La Clasificacíon genética de los Dialectos Quechuas." *Revista del Museo Nacional* (Lima) 32.241–52.
——— (1969a). "Comparative Quechua Phonology and Grammar I: Classification." *Working Papers in Linguistics* (Hawaii) 1.65–87.
——— (1969b). "Comparative Quechua Phonology and Grammar IV: The Evolution of Quechua A." *Working Papers in Linguistics* (Hawaii) 1.149–203.
Pattanayak, Debi Prasanna (1966). *A Controlled Historical Reconstruction of Oriya, Assamese, Bengali and Hindi.* (The Hague.)
Pawley, Andrew (1966). "Polynesian Languages: A Subgrouping Based on Shared Innovations in Morphology." *Journal of the Polynesian Society* 75.39–64.
——— (1967). "The Relationships of Polynesian Outlier Languages." *Journal of the Polynesian Society* 76.259–296.
——— (1970). "Grammatical Reconstruction and Change in Polynesia and Fiji." In S. A. Wurm and D. C. Laycock (eds.), *Pacific Linguistic Studies in Honour of Arthur Capell. Pacific Linguistics,* C, 13.
Pedersen, Holger (1900). "Albanesisch und Armenisch." *Kuhn's Zeitschrift* 36.340–341.
——— (1903). "Türkische Lautgesetze." *Zeitschrift der Duetschen Morgenlandischen Gesellschaft* 75.560–561.
——— (1938). *Mélanges E. Boisacq* II, pp. 161–165. (Bruxelles.)
Pei, Mario A. (1945). "Reflections on the Origin of the Romance Languages." *Romanic Review* 36.
Pinnow, Heinz-Jürgen (1959). *Versuch Einer Historischen Lautlehre der Kharia-Sprache.* (Wiesbaden.)
——— (1963). "The Position of the Munda Languages within the Austroasiatic family." In H. L. Shorto (ed.), *Linguistic Comparison in South East Asia and the Pacific.* (London.)
——— (1964). *Die nordamerikanischen Indianersprachen: ein Überblick über ihren Bau und ihre Besonderheiten.* (Wiesbaden.) [Reviewed by Voegelin and Voegelin (1967).]
——— (1966). *Grundzüge einer historischen Lautlehre des Tlingit: Ein Versuch.* (Wiesbaden.)
——— (1966). "The Verb in the Munda Languages." In Norman H. Zide (ed.), *Studies in Comparative Austroasiatic Linguistics.* (The Hague.)
Pitkin, Harvey, and William Shipley (1958). "Comparative Survey of California Penutian." *International Journal of American Linguistics* 24.174–188.
Politzer, Robert L. (1949). "On the Emergence of Romance from Latin." *Word* 5.131–4.
Polomé, Edgar G. (1966). "The Position of Illyrian and Venetic." In Henrik Birnbaum and Jaan Puhvel, eds., *Ancient Indo-European Dialects.* (Berkeley and Los Angeles.)

Poppe, Nicholas (1955). "Introduction to Mongolian Comparative Studies." *Mémoires de la Société Finno-Ougrienne* 110. (Helsinki.)
—— (1960). *Vergleichende Grammatik der Altaischen Sprachen, Teil 1, Vergleichende Lautlehre.* Porta Linguarum Orientalium, neue Serie, 4. (Wiesbaden.) [Reviewed by Krueger (1961), Street (1962).]
Prokosch, E. (1939). *A Comparative Germanic Grammar.* (Philadelphia.)
Puhvel, J. (1966). "Dialectal Aspects of the Anatolian Branch of Indo-European." In Birnbaum and Puhvel (eds.), *Ancient Indo-European Dialects.* (Berkeley and Los Angeles.)
Pulgram, E. (1950). "Spoken and Written Latin." *Language* 26.458–66.
—— (1958). *The Tongues of Italy.* (Cambridge, Mass.)

Radin, P. (1932–33). "Notes on the Tlappanecan Language of Guerrero." *International Journal of American Linguistics* 8.45–72.
Rasmussen, K. (1927). *Across Arctic America.* (New York.)
Raun, Alo (1956). "Über die sogenannte lexikostatistische Methode oder Glottochronologie und ihre Anwendung auf das Finnisch-Ugrische und Turkische." *Ural-Altaische Jahrbücher* Band XXVIII, pp. 151–154. (Wiesbaden.)
Raun, Alo, David Francis, C. F. Voegelin, and F. M. Voegelin (1965). "Languages of the World: Boreo-Oriental Fascicle One." *Anthropological Linguistics* 7: 1.
Ray, S. H. (1907). *Reports of the Cambridge Anthropological Expedition to the Torres Staits, Vol. III, Linguistics.* (Cambridge.)
—— (1926). *A Comparative Study of the Melanesian Island Languages.* (Cambridge.)
—— (1938). "The Languages of the Eastern and South-Eastern Divisions of Papua." *Journal of the Royal Anthropological Society of Great Britain and Ireland* 68.153–208.
Reiner, Erica (1969). "The Elamite Language." *Altkleinasiatischen Sprachen,* pp. 54–118, *Handbuch der Orientalistik,* Erste Abteilung, II Band, 1 und 2 Abschnitt, Lieferung 2. (Leiden, Cologne.)
Rensch, Calvin R. (In press). *Comparative Otomanguean Phonology.* Language Science Monographs.
Richardson, I. (1957). *Linguistic Survey of the Northern Bantu Borderland.* Volume Two. International African Institute. (London.)
Rigsby, Bruce (1966). "On Cayuse-Molala Relatability." *International Journal of American Linguistics* 32.369–378.
Rivet, Paul (1924). "Langues de l'Amérique des Sud et des Antilles." In A. Meillet and Marcel Cohen (eds.), *Les Langues du Monde.* (Paris.)
—— (1943–44). "La Lengua Chocó." *Revista del Instituto Etnologico Nacional Bogotá* 1.131–196; 2.297–349.
Robbins, Frank E. (1961). "Quiotepec Chinantec Syllable Patterning." *International Journal of American Linguistics* 27.237–250.
Robert, L. (1950). "Inscriptions inédites en langue carienne." *Hellenica* 8.1–38.
Robles, Carlos (1964). "Investigacion lingüistica sobre las grupos indigenas de estado de Baja California." *Anales del Instituto Nacional de Antropología e Historia* 17.275–301.
Rodrigues, Arion D. (1958). "Classification of Tupí-Guaraní." *International Journal of American Linguistics* 24.231–4.
Rona, Jose Pedro (1965). Paper presented at Indiana University.
Rowlands, E. C. (1962). "Notes on Some Class Languages of Northern Nigeria." *African Language Studies* 3.71–83.
Ruge, W. (1919). "Kataonia." *Pauly-Wissowa Realencyclopädie* 20.2478–79.
—— (1927). "Lykaonia." *Pauly-Wissowa Realencyclopädie* 13.2253–55.
—— (1930). "Verwandtschaft mit den Thrakern." *Pauly-Wissowa Realencyclopädie* 28.1747–49.

Salisbury, R. F. (1962). "Notes on Bilingualism and Linguistic Change in New Guinea." *Anthropological Linguistics* 4: 7.1–13.
Salzner, R. (1960). *Sprachenatlas des Indopazifischen Raumes.* 2 vols. (Wiesbaden.)

Samarin, William J. (1971). "Adamawa-Eastern." In Thomas A. Sebeok (ed.), *Linguistics in Sub-Saharan Africa, Current Trends in Linguistics*, Vol. 7. (The Hague.)

Sapir, Edward (1913). "Wiyot and Yurok, Algonkin Languages of California." *American Anthropologist* 15.617–646.

—— (1915). "The Na-Dene Languages, a Preliminary Report." *American Anthropologist* 17.534–558.

—— (1917). "The Position of Yana in the Hokan Stock." *University of California Publications in American Archeology and Ethnology* 13.1–34.

—— (1920). "The Hokan and Coahuiltecan Languages." *International Journal of American Linguistics* 1.280–290.

—— (1925a). "The Hokan Affinity of Subtiaba in Nicaragua." *American Anthropologist* 27.402–35, 491–521.

—— (1925b). "The Similarity of Chinese and Indian Languages." *Science* 62, No. 1607, p. xii.

—— (1929). "Central and North American Indian Languages." *Encyclopaedia Britannica*, 14th ed. 5.138–141.

—— (1930). "Southern Paiute, a Shoshonean Language." *American Academy of Arts and Sciences, Proceedings* 65: 1.

Sapir, J. David (1971). "West Atlantic: An Inventory of the Languages, Their Noun Class Systems, and Consonant Alternation." In Thomas A. Sebeok (ed.), *Current Trends in Linguistics*, Vol. 7. (The Hague.)

Scherer, W. (1868). *Zur Geschichte der Deutschen Sprache*. (Berlin.)

Schmalstieg, William R., and Benjaminš Jēgers (translators) (1971). *Jānis Endzelīns' Comparative Phonology and Morphology of the Baltic Languages*. (The Hague.)

Schmidt, Wilhelm (1906). "Die Mon-Khmer-Völker, Ein Bindeglied zwischen Völkern Zentralasiens und Austronesiens." *Archiv für Anthropologie* 33, N.F. 5.

—— (1919a). *Die Gliederung der Australischen Sprachen*. (Vienna.)

—— (1919b). *Der Personalpronomina in den Australischen Sprachen*. (Vienna.)

—— (1926). *Die Sprachfamilien und Sprachenkreise der Erde*. (Heidelberg.)

—— (1952). *Die Tasmanischen Sprachen. Publications de la Commission d'Enquête linguistique*. 5. (Utrecht.)

Schuchardt, H. (1912). "Nubisch und Baskisch." *Revue Internationale des Études Basques*, p. 282.

—— (1913). "Baskisch und Hamitisch." *Revue Internationale des Études Basques*, p. 289.

Schütz, Albert J. (1963). "Phonemic Typology of Fijian Dialects." *Oceanic Linguistics* 2.62–79.

Schutz, Noel W., Jr. (1971). "Tai and Austronesian: A Study in Remote Linguistic Classification." Paper presented at the 4th International Sino-Tibetan Conference, October 8–10, Bloomington, Indiana. To appear in the *Shafer Memorial Volume*.

Schwarz, E. (1951). *Goten, Nordgermanen, Angelsachsen. Studien zur Ausgliederung der germanischen Sprachen*. (Bern.)

—— (1956). *Germanische Stammeskunde*. (Heidelberg.)

Senn, A. (1966). "The Relationships of Baltic and Slavic." In Birnbaum and Puhvel (eds.), *Ancient Indo-European Dialects*. (Berkeley and Los Angeles.)

Shafer, Robert (1940). "Nahali, a Linguistic Study in Paleoethnography." *Harvard Journal of Asian Studies* 5.346–371.

—— (1952). "Athabascan and Sino-Tibetan." *International Journal of American Linguistics* 18.12–19. [Reviewed by M. Swadesh, *International Journal of American Linguistics* 18.178–181 (1952).]

—— (1955). "Classification of the Sino-Tibetan Languages." *Word* 11: 1.94–111.

—— (1957). "Note on Athabascan and Sino-Tibetan." *International Journal of American Linguistics* 23.116–117.

Shevelov, G. (1965). *Prehistory of Slavic*. (New York.)

Shimizu Kiyoshi (1971a). "Preliminary Report on the Comparative Study of Jukun, Togong and Mbembe." *Actes du 8eme Congres International de Linguistique Africaine*, Universite d'Abidjan. (Abidjan.)

—— (1971b). *Comparative Jukunoid: An Introductory Survey*. Ph.D. thesis, University of Ibadan.

—— (1973). "The Jukunoid Languages in the Polyglotta Africana, Part I, Eregba." *African Language Review* 9.

378

Shipley, William (1957). "Some Yukian-Penutian Lexical Resemblances." *International Journal of American Linguistics* 23.269–74.
—— (1969). "Proto Takelman." *International Journal of American Linguistics* 35.226–230.
Siebert, F. T., Jr. (1945). "Linguistic Classification of Catawba." *International Journal of American Linguistics* 11.100–104, 221–218.
Sinor, Denis (1972). Personal communication.
Skeat, Walter William, and Charles Otto Blagden (1906). *Pagan Races of the Malay Peninsula.* Vol. 2. (London.)
Skorik, P. Ja., et al. (1968a). "Čukotsko-Kamčatskie jazyki." *Jazyki narodov SSSR,* V, pp. 235–351. (Leningrad.)
—— (1968b). "Paleoaziatskie jazyki." *Jazyki narodov SSSR,* V. (Mongol'skie, Tunguso-man' čžurskie i paleoaziatskie jazyki), pp. 233–473.
Smalley, William (1973). "Bibliography of Khmu ?" In *Mon-Khmer Studies IV.* (Carbondale.)
Smith, Kenneth, and Kenneth J. Gregerson (1973). "The Placement of Bahnar among North or South Bahnaric." Paper presented at the First International Conference on Austroastic Linguistics. Honolulu, January 2–6, 1973.
Southworth, F. (1958). *A Test of the Comparative Method (A Historically Controlled Reconstruction Based on Four Modern Indic Languages).* Ph.D. dissertation, Yale.
Speiser, E. A. (1941). *Introduction to Hurrian.* Annual of the American Schools of Oriental Research. (New Haven.)
Stampe, David (1965–66). "Recent Work in Munda Linguistics. I, II, III, IV." *International Journal of American Linguistics* 31.332–341, 32.74–80, 164–168, 390–397.
Stang, Christian S. (1966). *Vergleichende Grammatik der baltischen Sprachen.* (Oslo.)
Stankiewicz, Edward, and Dean Worth (1966, 1970). *A Selected Bibliography of Slavic Linguistics,* Vols. 1, 2. (The Hague.)
Stark, Louisa R. (1968). "Mayan Affinities with Yunga of Peru." Paper presented at the annual meeting of the American Anthropological Association.
—— (1970). "Mayan Affinities with Araucanian." *Papers from the Sixth Regional Meeting of the Chicago Linguistic Society.* (Chicago.)
Steinthal, Heymann (1890). "Der Verhaltniss, das Zwischen dem Ketschua und Aymara besteht." *Proceedings of the Seventh International Congress of Americanists,* pp. 462–64. (Berlin.)
Stevens, Alan M. (1967). "Kemak: An Austronesian Language." *Anthropological Linguistics* 9:1.26–32.
Stewart, John M. (1971). "Niger-Congo, Kwa." In Thomas A. Sebeok (ed.), *Current Trends in Linguistics, Linguistics in Sub-Saharan Africa,* Vol. 7. (The Hague.)
Stewart, William A. (1962). "Creole Languages in the Caribbean." In Frank A. Rice (ed.), *Study of the Role of Second Languages in Asia, Africa, and Latin America.* (Washington, D.C.)
Strand, Richard F. (1973). "Notes on the Nūristānī and Dardic Languages." *Journal of the American Oriental Society* 93.297–305.
Street, J. C. (1962). "Review of Poppe 1960." *Language* 38.92–98.
Streitberg, W. (1896). *Urgermanische Grammatik.* (Heidelberg.)
Streitberg, W., V. Michels, and M. H. Jellinek (1936). *Germanisch. Die Erforschung der Indogermanischen Sprachen.* (Berlin, Leipzig.)
Struck, Bernhard (1911). "Die Sprach de Tatoga und Irakuleute." In F. R. Jaeger, *Der Hochland der Riesenkrater.* (Berlin.)
—— (1912). "Einige Sudan-Wortstämme." *Zeitschrift für Kolonialsprachen* 2.233–253, 309–323.
Sturtevant, Edgar H. (1933). *A Comparative Grammar of the Hittite Language.* (Philadelphia.)
Sturtevant, Edgar H., and E. Adelaide Hahn (1951). *A Comparative Grammar of the Hittite Language,* Vol. 1. Revised ed. (New Haven.)
Suárez, Jorge A. (1969). "Moseten and Pano-Tacanan." *Anthropological Linguistics* 11.255–266.
Suárez, Yolanda Lastra de (1970). "Categorías Posicionales en Quechua y Aymara." *Anales de Antropología* 7.263–84. (Mexico.)
Summer Institute of Linguistics (1972). "Vietnam Minority Languages." Mimeograph. (Saigon.)
Swadesh, Morris (1947). "Phonemic Structure of Proto-Zapotec." *International Journal of American Linguistics* 13.220–230.

—— (1950). "Salish Internal Relationships." *International Journal of American Linguistics* 16.157–167.

—— (1955). "Chemakum Lexicon Compared with Quileute." *International Journal of American Linguistics* 21.60–72.

—— (1959). *Mapas de Clasificación Lingüística de México y las Américas*. Cauadernos del Instituto de Historia, Serie Anthropológia No. 8. Universidad Nacional Autonoma de Mexico. (Mexico.)

—— (1960). "The Oto-Manguean Hypothesis and Macro-Mixtecan." *International Journal of American Linguistics* 26.79–111.

—— (1962). "Linguistic Relations Across Bering Strait." *American Anthropologist* 64.1262–91.

—— (1963). Comment in *Current Anthropology* 4.318.

—— (1964). "Linguistic Overview." In Norbeck and Jennings (eds.), *Prehistoric Man in the New World*. (Chicago.)

—— (1967). "Lexicostatistic Classification." In Norman A. McQuown (ed.), *Handbook of Middle American Indians, Linguistics* Vol. 5. (Austin.)

Swanson, Donald C. (1948). "A Select Bibliography of the Anatolian Languages." *Bulletin of the New York Public Library* 52.234–43, 300–313.

Swanton, J. R. (1940). *Linguistic Material from the Tribes of Southern Texas and Northeastern Mexico*. Bureau of American Ethnology Bulletin 127. (Washington, D.C.)

Szemerényi, Oswald (1957). "The Problem of Balto-Slav Unity — A Critical Survey." *Kratylos* 2.97–123.

Talbot, P. Amaury (1926). *The Peoples of Southern Nigeria*. Vol. IV. (Oxford.)

Tamura Suzuko (1967). "Studies of the Ainu Language." In Thomas A. Sebeok (ed.), *Current Trends in Linguistics*, Vol. 2. (The Hague.)

Taylor, Douglas (1958). "The Place of Island Carib within the Arawakan Family." *International Journal of American Linguistics* 24.153–6.

Teeter, Karl (1967). "Genetic Classification in Algonquian." In *Contributions to Anthropology: Linguistics I (Algonquian)*. National Museum of Canada Bulletin 214, *Anthropological Series* 78.

Teeuw, A., and H. W. Emanuels (1961). *A Critical Survey of Studies on Malay and Bahasa Indonesia*. Koninklijk Instituut voor Taal-, Land- en Volkenkunde, Bibliographical Series 5. (The Hague.)

Terry, R. R. (1971). "Chadic." In Thomas A. Sebeok (ed.), *Current Trends in Linguistics, Linguistics in Sub-Saharan Africa*, Vol. 7 (The Hague.)

Thalbitzer, W. (1945). "Uhlenbeck's Eskimo-Indoeuropean Hypothesis: A Critical Revision." *Travaux du Cercle Linguistique de Copenhague* 1.66–96.

—— (1948). "On the Eskimo Language." *Proceedings of the International Congress of Americanists* 26: 2.403–406.

—— (1949). "Possible Contacts between Eskimos and Old World Languages." In *Indian Tribes of Aboriginal America. Proceedings of the International Congress of Americanists* 29: 3.50–54.

Thomas, David, and Alan Healey (1962). "Some Philippine Language Subgroupings." *Anthropological Linguistics* 4: 9.22–33.

Thomas, David, and Robert K. Headley (1970). "More on Mon-Khmer Subgroupings." *Lingua* 25.398–418.

Thomas, Northcote W. (1927). "The Bantu Languages of Nigeria." *Festschrift Meinhof*, pp. 65–72. (Hamburg.)

—— (1931). In Meek, *The Northern Tribes of Nigeria*, Vol. 2. (London.)

Thompson, Laurence C. (1965). *A Vietnamese Grammar*. (Seattle.)

—— (1973). "Proto-Viet-Muong Phonology." In Philip N. Jenner, Laurence C. Thompson, and Stanley Starosta (eds.), *Austroasiatic Studies*. (Honolulu.)

—— (1973). "The Northwest." In T. A. Sebeok (ed.), *Current Trends in Linguistics, Linguistics in North America*, Vol. 10. (The Hague.)

—— (1974). Consultant information to supplement "Viet-Muong" in C. F. and F. M. Voegelin, *Index of the World's Languages*. Final Report on HEW Contract OEC-0-9-097717-1252(014).

Thompson, Laurence C., and M. Dale Kinkade (1974). Consultant information to supplement C. F.

380

and F. M. Voegelin, "Languages of the World: Native America Fascicle One." *Anthropological Linguistics* 6: 6.1–149.

Tōjō, Misao (1954). *Nihon Hōgengaku* [The Dialectology of Japan]. (Tokyo.)

Toporov, V. N., et al. (1966). "Baltijskie Jazyki." In *Jazyki Narodov SSSR, I. Indoeuropejskie Jazyki*, pp. 455–527. (Moskow.)

Torero, A. (1964). "Los Dialectos Quechuas." *Anales Cieutificos* 2.446–78.

Tovar, Antonio (1950). "Léxico de las Inscripciones Ibéricas (Celtibérico e Ibérico)." In *Est.dios Dedicados a D. Ramon Menéndez Pidal*. (Madrid.)

—————— (1961). *Catálogo de las lenguas de América del Sur*. (Buenos Aires.)

Trager, George L. (1948). "The Indian Languages of Brazil." *International Journal of American Linguistics* 14.43–48.

—————— (1951). "Linguistic History and Ethnographic History in the Southwest." *Journal of the Washington Academy of Sciences* 41.341–3.

Troike, Rudolph C. (1970a). "The Linguistic Classification of Cochimi." Paper presented at the Hokan Conference, University of California, San Diego.

—————— (1970b). Consultant information to supplement C. F. and F. M. Voegelin, "Native America Fascicle One." *Anthropological Linguistics* 6: 6 (1964).

Trombetti, A. (1902–03). "Della Relazioni della lingue Caucasische con le Lingue Camito-Semitiche e con altri gruppi linguistici." *Giornale della Societa Asiatica Italiana* 15 and 16. (Florence.)

—————— (1926). *Le Origini della Lingua Basca*. (Bologne.)

—————— (1928). *La Lingua Etrusca*. (Firenze.)

Tsuzaki, S. M. (1966). "Hawaiian English: Pidgin, Creole, or Dialect ?" *Pacific Speech* 1: 2.25–8.

—————— (1967). "General Characteristics of Hawaiian English." Paper read at the 57th Annual Convention, National Council of Teachers of English, Nov. 24. Mimeographed. (Honolulu.)

Tucker, A. N., and M. A. Bryan (1956). "The Non-Bantu Languages of North Eastern Africa." *Handbook of African Languages* Part III. International African Institute. (London.)

—————— (1957). *Linguistic Survey of the Northern Bantu Borderland*. Vol. Four. International African Institute. (London.)

—————— (1966). "Linguistic Analyses: The Non-Bantu Languages of North-Eastern Africa." *Handbook of African Languages*. International African Institute. (London.)

Turner, L. D. (1949). *Africanisms in the Gullah Dialect*. (Chicago.)

Turner, Paul R. (1967). "Seri and Chontal (Tequistlateco)." *International Journal of American Linguistics* 33.235–239.

—————— (1969). "Proto-Chontal Phonemes." *International Journal of American Linguistics* 35.34–37.

Tuyên, Vương Hoàng (1963). *Các Dân Tộc Nguồn Gốc Nam-Á ở Miền Bắc Việt Nam*. (Hanoi.)

Tweddell, Colin E. (1970). "The Identity and Distribution of the Mangyan Tribes of Mindoro, Philippines." *Anthropological Linguistics* 12.189–207.

Tyler, Stephen A. (1968). *Koya: An Outline Grammar*. *University of California Publications in Linguistics*. 54.

Uhle, Max (1896). "Über die Sprache der Uros in Bolivia." *Globus* 69.19.

—————— (1912). "Los Origenes de Los Incas." *Proceedings of the International Congress of Americanists* 17.318–23.

Uhlenbeck, C. C. (1942–45). "Ur- und altindogermanische Anklänge im Wortschatz des Eskimo." *Anthropos* 27–40.133–148.

—————— (1946). "Gestaaf de en Vermeende Affiniteiten van het Baskisch." In *Mededeelingen der Koninklijke Nederlandsche van Wetenschappen*.

—————— (1948). "La Langue Basque et la Linguistique Général." *Lingua* 1.57–76.

Uhlenbeck, E. M. (1967). "Indonesia and Malaysia." In Thomas A. Sebeok (ed.), *Current Trends in Linguistics, Linguistics in East Asia and South East Asia*. Vol. 2. (The Hague.)

Valdman, A. (1968). "Créole et Français aux Antilles." In *Le Français I: Créoles et Contacts Africains, Annales de La Faculté des Lettres et Sciences Humaines de Nice. No. 7*.

Vaillant, A. (1950–66). *Grammaire Comparée des Langues Slaves.* (Paris.)

Ventris, Michael, and John Chadwick (1953). "Evidence for Greek Dialect in the Mycenaean Archives." *Journal of Hellenic Studies* 73.84–103.

Voegelin, C. F. (1941a). "Internal Relationships of Siouan Languages." *American Anthropologist* 43.246–249.

——— (1941b). "North American Indian Languages Still Spoken and Their Genetic Relationships." In Leslie Spier, A. Irving Hallowell, and Stanley S. Newman (eds.), *Language, Culture, and Personality.* (Menasha, Wisconsin.)

——— (1969). "Review of *Contributions to Anthropology: Linguistics I (Algonquian)*." *American Anthropologist* 71.366–7.

Voegelin, C. F., and E. W. Voegelin (n.d. = 1944). "Map of North American Indian Languages." *American Ethnological Society, Publication No. 20.*

Voegelin, C. F., and F. M. Voegelin (1961). "Typological Classification of Systems with Included, Excluded and Self-sufficient Alphabets." *Anthropological Linguistics* 3: 1.55–96.

——— (1964a). "Languages of the World: Sino-Tibetan Fascicle One." *Anthropological Linguistics* 6: 3.

——— (1964b). "Languages of the World: Indo-Pacific Fascicle Two." *Anthropological Linguistics* 6: 7.

——— (1965). "Languages of the World: Indo-Pacific Fascicle Four." *Anthropological Linguistics* 7: 2.

——— (1966). "Map of North American Indian Languages." *American Ethnological Society*, Revised Publication 20.

——— (1967). "Review of *Die nordamerikanischen Indianersprachen: ein Überblick über ihren Bau und ihre Besonderheiten* by Heinz-Jürgen Pinnow." *Language* 43.573–83.

Voegelin, C. F., F. M. Voegelin, and Kenneth Hale (1962). *Typological and Comparative Grammar of Uto-Aztecan: I (Phonology).* Indiana University Publications in Anthropology and Linguistics 17.

Von der Gabelentz, H. C. (1861–73). *Die melanesischen Sprachen.* 2 vols. (Leipzig.)

Voorhoeve, P. (1955). *Critical Survey of Studies on the Languages of Sumatra.* Koninklijk Instituut voor Taal-, Land- en Volkenkunde, Bibliographical Series 1. (The Hague.)

Voorhoeve, J. (1961). "A Project for the Study of Creole Language History in Surinam." In R. B. Le Page (ed.), *Proceedings.*

Voyles, J. B. (1972). "The Problem of West Germanic." *Folia Linguistica* 5: 1, 2. 117–150.

Vryonis, Speros, Jr. (1971). *The Decline of Medieval Hellenism in Asia Minor and the Process of Islamization from the Eleventh through the Fifteenth Century.* (Berkeley, Los Angeles, London.)

Wagner, M. L. (1938). "Flessione Nominale Verbale del Sardo Antico e Moderno." *Italia Dialettale* 14.93–170.

Walker, Willard (1970). "Diegueno Plural Formation." *Linguistic Notes from La Jolla* 4.1–16.

Waltz, Nathan E., and Alva Wheeler (1972). "Proto Tucanoan." In *Comparative Studies in Amerindian Languages.* (The Hague.)

Wares, Alan C. (1968a). "A Comparative Study of Yuman Consonantism." (The Hague.)

——— (1968b). *"Bibliography of the Summer Institute of Linguistics 1935–1968.* Summer Institute of Linguistics. (Santa Ana, Calif.)

Watkins, Calvert (1965). Consultant information included in C. F. and F. M. Voegelin, "Languages of the World: Indo-European Fascicle One," *Anthropological Linguistics* 7: 3.90–99.

——— (1966). "Italo-Celtic Revisited." In H. Birnbaum and J. Puhvel (eds.), *Ancient Indo-European Dialects.* (Berkeley and Los Angeles.)

Waterhouse, Viola (1969). "Oaxaca Chontal in Reference to Proto-Chontal." *International Journal of American Linguistics* 35.231–233.

Watuseke, F. S. (1976). "West Makian, a Language of the North Halmahera Group of the West Irian Phylum." *Anthropological Linguistics* 18.

Webb, Nancy (1971). *A Statement of Some Phonological Correspondences among the Pomo Languages.* Indiana University Publications in Anthropology and Linguistics 26.

382

Wei, Jacqueline (1962). "Dialectal Differences between Three Standard Varieties of Persian." Ms.

Welmers, William E. (1958). "The Mande Languages." *Georgetown University Monograph Series* 11.9–24. (Washington, D.C.)

—— (1961). Ms. "The Languages of the World Files." Indiana University.

—— (1971a). Consultant information for C. F. and F. M. Voegelin, *Index of the World's Languages*. Final Report on HEW Contract OEC-0-9-097717-1252(014).

—— (1971b). "Checklist of African Language and Dialect Names." In Thomas A. Sebeok (ed.), *Current Trends in Linguistics, Linguistics in Sub-Saharan Africa*, Vol. 7. (The Hague.)

—— (1971c). "Niger-Congo, Mande." In Thomas A. Sebeok (ed.), *Current Trends in Linguistics, Linguistics in Sub-Saharan Africa*, Vol. 7. (The Hague.)

Westermann, D. (1911). *Die Sudansprachen, eine sprachvergleichende Studie*. (Hamburg.)

—— (1921). *The Shilluk People*. (Berlin.)

—— (1922). *Die Sprache der Guang in Togo und auf der Goldküste und fünf andere Togosprachen*. (Berlin.)

—— (1927). "Die westlichen Sudansprachen und ihre Beziehungen zum Bantu." *Mitteilungen des Seminars für orientalische Sprachen*, Vol. 30. (Berlin.)

—— (1928). "Die Westatlantische Gruppe der Sudansprachen." *Mitteilungen des Seminars für Orientalische Sprachen*. (Berlin.)

—— (1935). "Nominalklassen in westafrikanischen Klassensprachen und in Bantusprachen." *Mitteilungen des Seminars für orientalische Sprachen* 38: 3.1-55.

—— (1953). "African Languages." *Encyclopaedia Britannica*.

Westermann, D., and M. A. Bryan (1952). "The Languages of West Africa." *Handbook of African Languages*, Part II. International African Institute. (London.)

Westphal, E. O. J. (1956). "The Non-Bantu Languages of Southern Africa," supplement to *The Non-Bantu Languages of North-Eastern Africa*, International African Institute, *Handbook of African Languages*. Part III. pp. 158–173.

—— (1962a). "A Reclassification of Southern African Non-Bantu Languages." *Journal of African Languages* 1: 1.1–8.

—— (1962b). "On Classifying Bushman and Hottentot Languages." *African Language Studies* 3.30–48.

—— (1963). "The Linguistic Prehistory of Southern Africa: Bush, Kwadi, Hottentot, and Bantu Linguistic Relationships." *Africa* 33: 3.237–65.

—— (1971). "The Click Languages of Southern and Eastern Africa." In Thomas A. Sebeok (ed.), *Current Trends in Linguistics, Linguistics in Sub-Saharan Africa*, Vol. 7. (The Hague.)

Whatmough, Joshua (1937). *The Foundations of Roman Italy*. (London.)

Wheeler, Alva (1972). "Proto Chibchan." In Esther Matteson (ed.), *Comparative Studies in Amerindian Languages*. (The Hague.)

Whinnom, K. (1956). *Spanish Contact Vernaculars in the Philippine Islands*. (Hong Kong.)

—— (1965). "The Origin of European-Based Pidgins and Creoles." *Orbis* 14.509–27.

—— (1967). "Linguistic Hybridization and the 'Special Case' of Pidgins and Creoles." Mimeographed.

Whorf, Benjamin L. (1935). "The Comparative Linguistics of Uto-Aztecan." *American Anthropologist* 37.600–8.

Whorf, B. L., and G. L. Trager (1937). "The Relationship of Uto-Aztecan and Tanoan." *American Anthropologist* 39.609–24.

Wilbert, Johannes (1962). "A Preliminary Glottochronology of Ge." *Anthropological Linguistics* 4: 2.17–25.

Williamson, Kay (1965). *Grammar of Kolokuma Dialect of Ịjọ*. West African Language Monograph Series, 2. (Cambridge.)

—— (1968). "Introduction to 'Comparative Edo Wordlists'." *Research Notes* 1: 4.1–4. University of Ibadan, Nigeria.

—— (1971). "The Benue-Congo Languages and Ịjọ." In Thomas A. Sebeok (ed.), *Current Trends in Linguistics*, Vol. 7. (The Hague.)

—— (1972a). "The Nigerian Rivers Readers Project." *The Linguistic Reporter* 14: 6.1,2.

—— (1972b). "Kwa Languages of Nigeria." Ms.

—— (1973). *Benue-Congo Comparative Wordlist*. Vol. II. (West African Linguistic Society, Ibadan.)

Williamson, Kay, and Elaine Thomas (1967). *Wordlists of Delta Edo: Epie, Engenni, Degema*. Institute of African Studies, University of Ibadan, Nigeria.

Williamson, Kay, and Shimizu Kiyoshi (1968). *Benue-Congo Comparative Wordlist* (West African Linguistic Society. Ibadan)

Winter, Werner (1961). "Lexical Interchange between 'Tocharian' A and B." *Journal of the American Oriental Society* 81.271–280.

—— (1966). "Traces of Early Dialectal Diversity in Old Armenian." In Birnbaum and Puhvel (eds.), *Ancient Indo-European Dialects*. (Berkeley and Los Angeles.)

Wolfenden, Elmer (1963). "Isnes Phonemes." Ms.

Wolff, Hans (1950–51). "Comparative Siouan I–IV." *International Journal of American Linguistics* 16.61–6, 113–21, 168–78, 17.197–204.

—— (1959). "Niger Delta Languages I: Classification." *Anthropological Linguistics* 1: 8.32–53.

—— (1963). "Noun Classes and Concord in Birom." In M. Houis et al. (eds.), *Actes du Second Colloque International de Linguistique Négro Africaine*. West African Languages Survey. (Dakar.)

Worrell, William H., and Werner Vycichl (1942). "Popular Traditions of the Coptic Language." In William H. Horrell (ed.), *Coptic Texts*. University of Michigan Studies, Humanistic Series, Vol. 46. (Ann Arbor.)

Worth, Dean S. (1963). "Paleosiberian." In Thomas A. Sebeok (ed.), *Current Trends in Linguistics, Soviet and East European Linguistics*, Vol. 1. (The Hague.)

Wurm, Stephen A. (1962). "Eastern, Western and Southern Highlands, Territory of Papua and New Guinea." In A. Capell, *A Linguistic Survey of the South-Western Pacific*. South Pacific Commission. (Nouméa, New Caledonia.)

—— (1971a). "Pidgins, Creoles and Lingue Franche." In Thomas A. Sebeok (ed.), *Current Trends in Linguistics*, Vol. 8. (The Hague.)

—— (1971b). "Classifications of Australian Languages." In Thomas A. Sebeok (ed.), *Current Trends in Linguistics*, Vol. 8. (The Hague.)

—— (1971c). "The Papuan Linguistic Situation." In Thomas A. Sebeok (ed.), *Current Trends in Linguistics*, Vol. 8. (The Hague.)

—— (1972). *Languages of Australia and Tasmania. Janua Linguarum, Series Critica*, 1.

Yamagiwa, Joseph K. (1967). "On Dialect Intelligibility in Japan." *Anthropological Linguistics* 9.1–17.

Youchmanov, N. V. (1948). "Constrictives Laryngeales Sémito-Chamito-Japhétiques." In *Langue et Pensée*, No. 11. (Moscow and Leningrad.)

Yüan Chia-Hua (1960). "Synopsis of Chinese Dialects." *Wén Zi Gǎi Gé Chúbǎnshè*. (Peking.)

Zambrano Bonilla, Jose (1752). *Arte de la lengua Totonaca, conforme a el arte de Antonio Nebrija*. (Puebla.)

Zeps, Valdis J. (1962). *Latvian and Finnic Linguistic Convergences. Indiana University Publications, Uralic and Altaic Series*, Vol. 9.

Z'graggen, John A. (1968). "A Linguistic Survey of the Central North-East Coast of New Guinea." *Gedenkschrift zum 100. Geburstag P. Wilhelm Schmidt. Studia Instituti Anthropos*, Band 21.

—— (1970). "Languages of the Western Madang District." In Wurm and Laycock (eds.), *Pacific Linguistic Studies in Honor of Arthur Capell. Pacific Linguistics*, C, 13.

Zide, Norman H., (ed.), (1966). *Studies in Comparative Austroasiatic Linguistics*. (The Hague.)

—— (1969). "Munda and non-Munda Austroasiatic Languages." In Thomas A. Sebeok (ed.), *Current Trends in Linguistics*, Vol. 5. (The Hague.)

INTRODUCTION TO THE INDEX

Names of groups, subgroups, languages, dialects, tribes and their alternate names which appear in the entry articles are listed below in the Index in alphabetical order with cross-reference to the articles in which they appear.

As in the articles, the names of groups of two or more languages are printed in the Index in capitals (e.g., AZTECAN → UTO-AZTECAN); the names of single languages and dialects are not (e.g., English → GERMANIC).

The names of dialects and tribes are indicated by the abbreviations D. and Tr. after the name of the language to which they belong or speak (e.g., Croatian. Serbocroatian D. → SLAVIC; Pasain. Vilela Tr. → LULE-VILELA-CHARRUA).

Alternate names and spellings are indicated by an equal sign (=) after the name followed by the name given first in the entry listing to enable the reader to more readily find the language in question in the entry (e.g., Latvian = Lettish → BALTIC indicates that in the language list in the BALTIC article, 'Lettish' is the first name listed for that language). The name given first in the entry listing is given below in the Index without its various alternates (e.g., Lettish → BALTIC), but each alternate name appears in the Index in its alphabetical place.

The last name given in an item in the Index is the name of the entry article in which the language or language group is discussed; thus, the AZTECAN group of languages is discussed in the UTO-AZTECAN entry; and so on. (An exception is made in the case of cross-reference to BANTU languages. Since the languages listed in the BANTU article are so numerous, cross-reference in the Index is made to the subgroup within BANTU (e.g., Swahili → CENTRAL EASTERN BANTU) to help the reader in finding the language within the BANTU article.)

For articles which treat groups of languages, as most do, the cross-reference to the article given in the Index below is indicated by an arrow (→) before the name of the entry article. In general, this arrow may also be read as 'belongs to'. But it must be remembered that the classification of some languages is uncertain; i.e., some languages are placed in different groups by different classifiers. On the whole, such controversially classified languages are listed in one entry article only and cross-reference is made only to that entry; e.g., in the entry on NUPE-GBARI it is said that Igbirra probably constitutes a separate subgroup of KWA rather than being a member of NUPE-GBARI, but the cross-reference for Igbirra in the following Index is nonetheless to the NUPE-GBARI entry in which Igbirra is listed. It must also be remembered that the group treated in the entry article in which a language is listed is not necessarily the largest group to which that language belongs. Thus, while English belongs to GERMANIC, and the Index listing refers to the entry on GERMANIC, one learns from the entry on GERMANIC that GERMANIC belongs to INDO-EUROPEAN. So also, Island Carib belongs to, and is listed in the entry on, NORTHERN MAIPURAN, but NORTHERN MAIPURAN belongs to (is a subgroup of) MAIPURAN, which in turn is a subgroup of ARAWAKAN, which is a subgroup of EQUATORIAL, which is a subgroup of ANDEAN-EQUATORIAL.

Some entry articles treat single languages; for dialects of those languages, cross-references are given in the Index as, for example, 'Ezo, Ainu D.', which is to be read as "Ezo is a dialect of Ainu and is listed in the entry on Ainu."

Index references to groups of languages and also to single languages which are the names of entry articles are given as, for example, 'GERMANIC see article', and also as 'Basque see article'. Alternate names of the names of entry articles appear in the Index in the form 'HELLENIC = GREEK', 'Euskara = Basque', for which (again) the final name of the item is the name of the entry.

Occasionally language groupings which have been superseded or are not yet widely accepted are not treated in separate entries, but are mentioned in the article on some relevant language group. Cross-references to such groupings that are open to question are of the form 'HOKAN-SIOUAN see MACRO-SIOUAN'; 'AUSTRIC see AUSTROASIATIC'; as usual in the Index, the final name of the item is the name of the entry article in which the first named group is discussed. So also a few such 'see' items appear in the Index for single ethnographic names which are applied to speakers of more than one language.

Two types of language and dialect names listed in the entries do not appear in the Index. Names of languages which are the same as the name of the entry group to which they belong are not given in the Index; only the name of the group is given (e.g., GREEK, but not Greek → GREEK). In the case of dialects which are referred to only by directional terms or geographical terms or place names (e.g., Southern Highlands or New York City, as dialects of English), cross-references are also omitted from the Index. This is not to say that there are no cross-reference items in the Index which contain directional, geographic, or place-name terms; some languages and groups of languages are known only by such names, as Southern Paiute (as opposed to Northern Paiute, which is a different language), or as the many Oceanic languages and groups of languages which are known by the names of the islands on which they are spoken, as Uvea and LOYALTY ISLANDS. Also, for many parts of the world, detailed maps are not readily enough available to enable the reader to determine that a dialect name is geographical; hence, cross-reference entries appear for dialects with geographical names where these names are not well known.

ALPHABETICAL ORDERING

For hyphenated names we follow what librarians call 'letter-by-letter' alphabetization so that, for example, KAM-SUI appears immediately after Kamrau.

For names without hyphens but with more than one word, we follow 'word-by-word' alphabetization so that, for example, Bo Luang appears between Bo and Boa, rather than after Boloven.

The names of many languages and language groups consist of a linguistic name modified by a directional term, a place name, a geographic name, or other modifier (e.g., an ethnic name). In the Index such names appear with the linguistic name first followed by a comma and then the modifier, where such modifiers are English words (including foreign place names used in English). (Non-English modifiers, as the Austronesian words 'Orang' and 'Ulu', are treated in the word-by-word alphabetization fashion described above.) Thus, both Christian Gaddang and Pagan Gaddang appear under G (as Gaddang, Christian; Gaddang, Pagan); Island Carib appears under C (as Carib, Island); WEST ATLANTIC appears under A (as ATLANTIC, WEST), and so on. When such modifiers are hyphenated with the rest of the name, the name is alphabetized as a single word; thus, INTER-ANDINE appears under I, Mid-Waria appears under M.

The modifier is also not post-posed, but left in its usual initial position when compound names represent single place names as Etna Bay, NEW CALEDONIA, and BISMARCK ARCHIPELAGO; or when two place names are combined to form a linguistic name, as BENUE-CONGO.

Diacritics (as macron, umlaut, tilde, cedilla) are omitted from names in the Index even though such diacritics appear on names within entry articles; thus, Provençal appears in the Index as Provencal, AGÖB as AGOB. This should not cause the reader any particular difficulty in identifying cross-reference names; almost all names which appear in the literature with diacritics also appear in the literature without them. Other phonetic symbols are retained in the Index, as slant lines for clicks, apostrophe for aspiration, glottalization or glottal stop, ʔ for glottal stop, ŋ for velar nasal, and a few others. Those phonetic symbols, which are not similar to ordinary alphabet letters (as /,',ʔ), are ignored in alphabetical ordering; thus //Au//en is alphabetized as though it were spelled Auen, Bare'e as though it were Baree. Those phonetic symbols which are modifications of Roman letters or are Greek letters are alphabetized after the most similar Roman letter; thus, æ appears after a, ə after e, ɨ after i, ɬ after l, ŋ after n, ɔ after o, and θ after t. (In preparing the Index, the distinction between e and ɛ was accidentally ignored; both appear as e.)

INDEX

A

A'a Sama = Samal → NORTHWEST AUS-
TRONESIAN
Aaimasa. Kunama D.→CHARI-NILE
Aakwo→EDO
Aamir=Beni Amir. Beja Tr.→CUSHITIC
Aara-Maringe → NORTHWESTERN AND
CENTRAL SOLOMONS
/Aaye = //'aiye. Shua D.→KHOISAN
Aba→SANTA CRUZ AUSTRONESIAN
Aba. Central Tibetan D.→TIBETAN
Aba = Canoeiro→TUPI
Aba = Ciriguano. Tupi D.→TUPI
Aba = Shor→TURKIC
Abaca = Abaka. Ilongot D.→NORTHWEST
AUSTRONESIAN
Abacama = Bachama→CHADIC
Abadekh → Abadzex. Circassian D.→CAU-
CASIAN
Abadzex. Circassian D.→CAUCASIAN
Abagai. Ordos D.→MONGOLIAN
Abaganar. Ordos D.→MONGOLIAN
Abaka. Ilongot D.→NORTHWEST AUS-
TRONESIAN
Abakan Tatars = Khakas→TURKIC
Abakan Turks = Khakas→TURKIC
Abakay Spanish = Davaueno→ROMANCE
Abakpa = Kwa. Ekoi D.→BANTOID
Abam-Ohaffia. Igbo D.→IGBO
Abanaki = Abnaki. Penobscot D.→ALGON-
QUIAN
Abane = Baniva→MAIPURAN
Abangba = Bangba→EASTERN
Abanyom→BANTOID
Abarambo = Barambu→EASTERN
Abasango. Ngbandi Tr.→EASTERN
Abathwa = //xegwe→KHOISAN
Abau→SEPIK
Abayong. Agwagwune D.→CROSS RIVER
BENUE-CONGO
Abaza. Ordos D.→MONGOLIAN
Abaza = Abxazo→CAUCASIAN
Abaza = Ashxar. Abxazo D.→CAUCASIAN
Abaza = Tapanta. Abxazo D.→CAUCASIAN
Abazin = Abxozo→CAUCASIAN
Abbe = Abe→LAGOON
Abbey = Abe→LAGOON
Abbigar = Nuer→EASTERN SUDANIC
Abe→LAGOON
Abedal = Kakadu→AUSTRALIAN MACRO-
PHYLUM
Abelam→SEPIK
Abenaki = Abnaki. Penobscot D.→ALGON-
QUIAN

Abenakise = Abnaki. Penobscot D.→ALGON-
QUIAN
Abenaqui = Abnaki. Penobscot D.→ALGON-
QUIAN
Aberu = Abulu. Mangbetu D.→CENTRAL
SUDANIC
Abewa=Ebe. Nupe D.→NUPE-GBARI
Abhaz=Abxazo→CAUCASIAN
Abi. Apaka D.→LEFT MAY
Abi. Bakwe D.→KRU
Abi. Musgu D.→CHADIC
Abi = Abe→LAGOON
Abialang. Padang D.→EASTERN SUDANIC
Abidji = Ari→LAGOON
Abiem. Rek D.→EASTERN SUDANIC
Abigar = Nuer→EASTERN SUDANIC
Abiji = Ari→LAGOON
Abine = Obini. Agwagwune D.→CROSS
RIVER BENUE-CONGO
Abinsi. Jukun D.→JUKUNOID
Abipon→GUAYCURU
Abiri = Mararit→EASTERN SUDANIC
Abisi = Piti→PLATEAU BENUE-CONGO
Abitana. Uanham D.→CHAPACURA-
WANHAMAN
Abiyi=Mararit→EASTERN SUDANIC
Abkar. Maba D.→MABAN
Abkhaz = Abxazo→CAUCASIAN
Abkhaz-Abaza = Abxazo→CAUCASIAN
Ablig-Saligsig. Kalinga D.→NORTHWEST
AUSTRONESIAN
Abnake = Abnaki. Penobscot D.→ALGON-
QUIAN
Abnaki. Penobscot D.→ALGONQUIAN
Abnaki = Malecite. Passamaquoddy D.→AL-
GONQUIAN
Abo→BANTOID
Abo = Bankon → NORTH WESTERN
BANTU
Abo = Toposo→EASTERN SUDANIC
Aboa. Apaka D.→LEFT MAY
Abolo = Andoni→CROSS RIVER BENUE-
CONGO
Abonwa = Abure→VOLTA-COMOE
Abor = Adi→GYARUNG-MISHMI
Abor-Miri = Adi→GYARUNG-MISHMI
Aboure = Abure→VOLTA-COMOE
Abraka. Urhobo D.→EDO
Abrinyo = Abi. Bakwe D.→KRU
Abriwi = Abi. Bakwe D.→KRU
Abron = Brong. Guan D.→VOLTA-COMOE
Abrong = Brong. Guan D.→VOLTA-COMOE
Absaraka = Crow→SIOUAN
Absaroke = Crow→SIOUAN

Absharin = Abu Sharin. Maba Tr.→MABAN
Abu Leila. Moro D.→KORDOFANIAN
Abu Sharib. Mararit D.→EASTERN SUDANIC
Abu Sharin. Maba Tr.→MABAN
Abu Simmin. Kuka D.→CENTRAL SUDANIC
Abu Sinun. Kanga Tr.→KORDOFANIAN
Abu Telfan. Jongor Tr.→CHADIC
Abua→CROSS RIVER BENUE-CONGO
ABUA-OGBIA=CENTRAL DELTA→CROSS
    RIVER BENUE-CONGO
Abucheta. Mataguayo Tr.→MATACO
Abui→Timor-Alor
Abukeia = Avukaya→CENTRAL SUDANIC
Abuldugu. Burun Tr.→EASTERN SUDANIC
Abuloma = Abulome → CROSS RIVER
    BENUE-CONGO
Abulome→CROSS RIVER BENUE-CONGO
Abulu. Mangbetu D.→CENTRAL SUDANIC
Abure→VOLTA-COMOE
Aburra→CHIBCHAN
Abuya. Padang D.→EASTERN SUDANIC
Abxazo→CAUCASIAN
Aby = Abe→LAGOON
Abzhui. Abxazo D.→CAUCASIAN
Acala. Chol D.→MAYAN
Acasaquastlan. Nahua D.→UTO-AZTECAN
Acawai→CARIB
Acaxee = Taracahitan. Cahita D.→UTO-
    AZTECAN
Accohanoc. Powhatan Tr.→ALGONQUIAN
Achagua→NORTHERN MAIPURAN
Achagua = Xagua→JIRARAN
Ach'ang→BODO-NAGA-KACHIN
Achawa = Yao→SOUTH EASTERN BANTU
Achehnese = Achinese→WEST INDONESIAN
Acheron. Moro D.→KORDOFANIAN
Acheron. Moro Hills Tr.→KORDOFANIAN
Achi = Rabinal→MAYAN
Achiganes = Sooke. Northern Straits Salish D.
    →SALISH
Achinese→WEST INDONESIAN
Achiote = Nonuya →WITOTOAN
Achipaie = Sipaya→TUPI
Achire. Cahita D.→UTO-AZTECAN
Achode→VOLTA-COMOE
Acholi = Akoli→EASTERN SUDANIC
Achomawi = Achumawi→PALAIHNIHAN
Achuale = Achuara. Jivaro D.→JIVAROAN
Achuara. Jivaro D.→JIVAROAN
Achumawi→PALAIHNIHAN
ACHUMAWI-ATSUGEWI=PALAIHNIHAN
Acione→BORORO
Acira→NORTHEAST NEW GUINEA AUS-
    TRONESIAN

Acoli. Anuak Tr.→EASTERN SUDANIC
Acoma. Keres D.
Acooli = Akoli→EASTERN SUDANIC
Acoste = Koasati→MUSKOGEAN
ACROA→GE
Acroa→GE
ACUA→GE
Acucu = Akuku→CARIB
Acuera. Timucua D.
Ac'ye = Lashi→BODO-NAGA-KACHIN
Ad Al Allam. Beja Tr.→CUSHITIC
Ad Al Bakhit. Beja Tr.→CUSHITIC
Ad Ali. Beja Tr.→CUSHITIC
Ad Elman = Elman. Beja Tr.→CUSHITIC
Ad Humbirra. Beja Tr.→CUSHITIC
Ad Kukal. Beja Tr.→CUSHITIC
Ad Naseh. Beja Tr.→CUSHITIC
Ad Nazi = Ad Naseh. Beja Tr.→CUSHITIC
Ad Okud. Beja Tr.→CUSHITIC
Ad Omar. Beja Tr.→CUSHITIC
Ad Sheraf. Beja Tr.→CUSHITIC
Ad Towas. Beja Tr.→CUSHITIC
Ad 'Uqud = Ad Okud. Beja Tr.→CUSHITIC
Ada. Adangme D.→GA-ADANGME
Ada. Igbo D.→IGBO
Ada = Jaba→PLATEAU BENUE-CONGO
Ada = Kuturmi→PLATEAU BENUE-CONGO
Adage = Adai→CADDOAN
Adahi = Adai→CADDOAN
Adai→CADDOAN
Adaihe = Adai→CADDOAN
Adaize = Adai→CADDOAN
Adal = Afar. Afar-Saho D.→CUSHITIC
ADAMAWA see article
ADAMAWA-EASTERN see article
Adang. Sarawak Murut D.→WEST INDO-
    NESIAN
Adangbe = Adangme→GA-ADANGME
Adangme→GA-ADANGME
Adara = Kadara→PLATEAU BENUE-
    CONGO
Adare = Harari. East Gurage D.→SEMITIC
Adaru. Carutana D.→NORTHERN MAI-
    PURAN
Adaua→BINANDERE
Adda = Ada. Adangme D.→GA-ADANGME
Addaise = Adai→CADDOAN
Ade = Tubi. Pitu-ulunna-salu D.→CENTRAL
    AND SOUTHERN CELEBES
ADELBERT RANGE→BOGIA
Adele→CENTRAL TOGO
Adere→BANTOID
Adhiang. Rek D.→EASTERN SUDANIC
Adhola→EASTERN SUDANIC

Adi→GYARUNG-MISHMI

Adiana = Adzaneni→NORTHERN MAI-
PURAN

Adidji = Ari→LAGOON

Adim = Odim. Agwagwune D.→CROSS
RIVER BENUE-CONGO

Adioukrou = Adyukru→LAGOON

Adiye = Hadiyya→CUSHITIC

Adiye = Kabena. Alaba D.→CUSHITIC

Adja = Aja. Ewe D.→EWE

Adjahdurah = Narangga. Jadliaura D.→YURA

Adjer = Aser. Soninke Tr.→MANDE

Adjibba = Murle→EASTERN SUDANIC

Adjiga = Ajiga. Avukaya Tr.→CENTRAL
SUDANIC

Adjiga-ti = Ajiga. Avukaya Tr.→CENTRAL
SUDANIC

Adjio = Kasimbar→NORTHERN CELEBES

Adjora→BOGIA

Adjoria = Adjora→BOGIA

Adjukru = Adyukru→LAGOON

Adjumba = Dyumba. Myene D.→NORTH
WESTERN BANTU

Adjure = Kajuru→PLATEAU BENUE-
CONGO

Adkuri. Oriya D.→INDIC

Adlia = Northern Roglai→WEST INDONE-
SIAN

ADMIRALTY-WESTERN ISLANDS see
article

Adnyamatana = Adnyamathana. Wailpi D.→
YURA

Adnyamathana. Wailpi D.→YURA

Ado = Banggakoro D.→CENTRAL AND
SOUTHERN CELEBES

Ado = Pakuli. Palu D.→CENTRAL AND
SOUTHERN CELEBES

Adoma = Kelawa → PLATEAU BENUE-
CONGO

Adong = Lungu→PLATEAU BENUE-CONGO

Ador = Ciec. Agar D.→EASTERN SUDANIC

Adouma = Duma → NORTH WESTERN
BANTU

Adowen = Djauan→GUNWINGGUAN

Adsawa = Yao→SOUTH EASTERN BANTU

Adsoa = Yao→SOUTH EASTERN BANTU

Aduipliin. Alacaluf D.→ANDEAN

Aduma = Duma → NORTH WESTERN
BANTU

Adun. Mbembe D.→CROSS RIVER BENUE-
CONGO

Adwipliin = Aduipliin. Alacaluf D.→ANDEAN

Adya = Aja. Ewe D.→EWE

Adygei = Circassian→CAUCASIAN

Adyghe = Circassian→CAUCASIAN

Adyukru→LAGOON

Adyumba = Dyumba. Myene D.→NORTH
WESTERN BANTU

Adzaneni→NORTHERN MAIPURAN

A'e = Rempi→BOGIA

A'e'e = Salu Maoge. Bare'e D.→CENTRAL
AND SOUTHERN CELEBES

Aeka→BINANDERE

'Aeke = Haeke→NEW CALEDONIA

Aekyom = West Awin→PARE-SAMO-BEAMI-
BOSAVI

Aequian→ITALIC

Aeta = Central Agta→NORTHERN AUS-
TRONESIAN

Afade. Kotoko D.→CHADIC

Afak=Apak. Atuot D.→EASTERN SUDANIC

Afakani→CROSS RIVER BENUE-CONGO

Afan = Galla→CUSHITIC

Afao = Afo→PLATEAU BENUE-CONGO

Afar. Afar-Saho D.→CUSHITIC

Afar-Saho→CUSHITIC

Afawa→CHADIC

Afema. Anyi D.→VOLTA-COMOE

Afenmai→EDO

Afghan = Pashto→IRANIAN

Afiteng = Boritsu→JUKUNOID

Afitti→EASTERN SUDANIC

Af-Kareti = Konso→CUSHITIC

Afo→PLATEAU BENUE-CONGO

Afo = Eloyi→PLATEAU BENUE-CONGO

AFOA→GOILALA

Afoa→GOILALA

Aforo = Karam→EAST NEW GUINEA
HIGHLANDS

Afrikaans. Netherlandic-German D.→GER-
MANIC

Afrike→CROSS RIVER BENUE-CONGO

AFROASIATIC see article

Af-Soomaali = Somali→CUSHITIC

Afu = Afo→PLATEAU BENUE-CONGO

Afudu→BANTOID

Afuno = Hausa→CHADIC

Afusare→PLATEAU BENUE-CONGO

Afutu = Awutu→VOLTA-COMOE

Aga = Kanuri→SAHARAN

Agace = Magach. Mbaya-Guaicuru Tr.→
GUAYCURU

Agadi. Ingassana Tr.→CHARI-NILE

Agaiambo. Baruga D.→BINANDERE

Agalati = Ebe. Nupe D.→NUPE-GBARI

Agalega. French Creole D.→ROMANCE

Agam. Minangkabau D.→WEST INDO-
NESIAN

Agaminni = Ngameni. Dieri D.→DIERIC

Agamoru = Ajiga. Avukaya Tr.→CENTRAL SUDANIC

Agar→EASTERN SUDANIC

Agarabe. Gadsup D.→EAST NEW GUINEA HIGHLANDS

Agari = Kahugu→PLATEAU BENUE-CONGO

Agat. Buryat D.→MONGOLIAN

Agatu→IDOMA

AGAU→CUSHITIC

Agau = Nogau. Kung D.→KHOISAN

Agawam. Massachusett Tr.→ALGONQUIAN

Agbo = Legbo→CROSS RIVER BENUE-CONGO

Agbon. Urhobo D.→EDO

Age→BANTOID

Ageer = Ager. Padang D.→EASTERN SUDANIC

Ageir = Ager. Padang D.→EASTERN SUDANIC

Ager. Padang D.→EASTERN SUDANIC

Agew, Southern = Awiya→CUSHITIC

Agew of Wag = Khamta. Khamir D.→CUSHITIC

Agewmidir = Awiya→CUSHITIC

Aghem = Wum→BANTOID

AGHU→AWYU

Aghu→AWYU

Aghu Tharnggala→PAMA-MARIC

Agi→KOIARI

Agi→TORRICELLI

Agi. Moru D.→CENTRAL SUDANIC

Agiba = Murle→EASTERN SUDANIC

Aglubang, West. Tadyawan D.→NORTHWEST AUSTRONESIAN

Aglubang-Bansod, East. Tadyawan D.→ NORTHWEST AUSTRONESIAN

Agni = Anyi→VOLTA-COMOE

Agnier = Mohawk→IROQUOIS

Ago = Ahlo→CENTRAL TOGO

AGOB see article

Agobd = Agob→AGOB

Agoi→CROSS RIVER BENUE-CONGO

Agono = Ngonu→BANTOID

Agta, Central→NORTHWEST AUSTRONESIAN

Agta, Eastern→NORTHWEST AUSTRONESIAN

Agta, Western. Ibanag D.→NORTHWEST AUSTRONESIAN

Agtaa→NORTHWEST AUSTRONESIAN

Agu. Rawang D.→BODO-NAGA-KACHIN

Agua = Metyibo→VOLTA-COMOE

Aguacatec→MIXE-ZOQUE

Aguacatec→MAYAN

Aguacateca = Aguacatec→MIXE-ZOQUE

Aguaruna. Jivaro D.→JIVAROAN

Aguas Blancas. Mape D.→CARIB

Aguilot. Toba Tr.→GUAYCURU

Agul→CAUCASIAN

Aguro = Kagoro. Katab D.→PLATEAU BENUE-CONGO

Agusan Manobo→NORTHWEST AUSTRONESIAN

Agusta = Tolowa. Chasta Costa D.→ATHAPASCAN-EYAK

Agutainon = Agutaynon. Kalamian D.→ NORTHWEST AUSTRONESIAN

Agutaynon. Kalamian D.→NORTHWEST AUSTRONESIAN

Agvali. Chamalal D.→CAUCASIAN

Agwa = Gwa→LAGOON

Agwagwune→CROSS RIVER BENUE-CONGO

Agwamin. Wakaman D.→PAMA-MARIC

Agwok. Rek D.→EASTERN SUDANIC

Agwolok=Kagoro. Katab D.→PLATEAU BENUE-CONGO

Agwot=Kagoro. Katab D.→PLATEAU BENUE-CONGO

Agyuku = Adyukru→LAGOON

Ahaggar. Tuareg D.→BERBER

Ahahnelin = Atsina. Arapaho D.→ALGONQUIAN

Ahamb→NORTHWESTERN NEW HEBRIDES

Ahanta→VOLTA-COMOE

Aheima. Masakin Tr.→KORDOFANIAN

Ahenin = Atsina. Arapaho D.→ALGONQUIAN

Ahi→BURMESE-LOLO

Ahiolo. Tala D.→EAST INDONESIAN

Ahirani = Khandesi→INDIC

Ahirwati. Rajasthani D.→INDIC

Ahizi→LAGOON

Ahlo→CENTRAL TOGO

Ahminnie = Ngameni. Dieri D.→DIERIC

Ahnbi = Banbai. Kumbainggar D.→KUMBAINGGARIC

Ahngam. Pima D.→UTO-AZTECAN

Aholio = Morwa. Katab D.→PLATEAU BENUE-CONGO

Ahom→KAM-TAI

Ahome. Cahita D.→UTO-AZTECAN

Ahotireitsu. SHASTAN Tr.→HOKAN

Ahtena→ATHAPASCAN-EYAK

Ahtena = Shuswap→SALISH

Aiawong = Ngaiawang. Nganguruku D.→ NARRINYERIC

Aiawung = Ngaiawang. Nganguruku D.→ NARRINYERIC

Aibe→PARE-SAMO-BEAMI-BOSAVI

Aiduma→SOUTH HALMAHERA AUSTRO-NESIAN

//ai//ei = Naron→KHOISAN

//ai//en = Naron→KHOISAN

Aiga = Aeka→BINANDERE

Aigaŋ = Keiga→KORDOFANIAN

Aigora = Igora. Suau D.→PAPUA AUSTRO-NESIAN

Aikoa = Mori→CENTRAL AND SOUTHERN CELEBES

Aiku→TORRICELLI

/aikwe = Naron→KHOISAN

//aikwe = Naron→KHOISAN

Aimal→NAGA-KUKI-CHIN

Aimara = Aymara→ANDEAN

AIMBORE = BOTOCUDO

A'imeri = Awimeri. Mangbutu D.→CENTRAL SUDANIC

Ainu see article

Aiome = Ayom→BOGIA

Aion = Ayon→BOGIA

Aione = Ayon→BOGIA

Air. Tuareg D.→BERBER

Aird Hills→KIKORI RIVER

Airiman = Ngarinman→NGUMBIN

/ais = /hais. Shua D.→KHOISAN

//aisan = Naron→KHOISAN

Aisor. East Aramaic D.→SEMITIC

Aissuari = Aizuare. Omagua D.→TUPI

Aiticha. Foothill North Yokuts D.→YOKUTS

Aitinjo→WESTERN NEW GUINEA

Aitutaki. Cook Islands Maori D.→POLY-NESIAN

Aiva. High Lugbara D.→CENTRAL SUDANIC

Aivilik = Iglulik. Inuit D.→ESKIMO-ALEUT

Aivilingmiut = Iglulik. Inuit D.→ESKIMO-ALEUT

//'aiye. Shua D.→KHOISAN

Aizi = Ahizi→LAGOON

Aizuare. Omagua D.→TUPI

Aja. Ewe D.→EWE

Aja. Yulu-Binga D.→CENTRAL SUDANIC

Ajagua = Xagua→JIRARAN

Ajak. Rek D.→EASTERN SUDANIC

Ajak = Ciec. Agar D.→EASTERN SUDANIC

Ajamaru = Ayamaru→WESTERN NEW GUINEA

Ajer = Azer. Soninke D.→MANDE

Ajiba = Murle→EASTERN SUDANIC

Ajibba = Murle→EASTERN SUDANIC

Ajie = Houailou→NEW CALEDONIA

Ajiga. Avukaya Tr.→CENTRAL SUDANIC

Ajio = Kaje→PLATEAU BENUE-CONGO

Ajjer. Tuareg D.→BERBER

Ajmeri. Rajasthani D.→INDIC

Ajo = Tambe'e. Mori D.→CENTRAL AND SOUTHERN CELEBES

A-jomaŋ = Talodi→KORDOFANIAN

Ajong Dit. Rek D.→EASTERN SUDANIC

Ajong Thi. Rek D.→EASTERN SUDANIC

Ajuh. Lawangan D.→WEST INDONESIAN

Ajujure = Arara→CARIB

Ajukru = Adyukru→LAGOON

Ajuong Dit = Ajong Dit. Rek D.→EASTERN SUDANIC

Ajuong Thi = Ajong Thi. Rek D.→EASTERN SUDANIC

Ajwet = Akjuet. Rek D.→EASTERN SUDANIC

Aka = Akha→BURMESE-LOLO

Aka = Asua→CENTRAL SUDANIC

Aka = Hruso→GYARUNG-MISHMI

Aka-beada = Beada. Great Andamanese D. →ANDAMANESE

Akaha = Akassa. Ijo D.→IJO

Akalak = Katla→KORDOFANIAN

AKAN = VOLTA-COMOE

Akan→VOLTA-COMOE

Akanda = Aworo. Yoruba D.→YORUBA

Akanda = Kakanda. Nupe D.→NUPE-GBARI

Akani→TUNGUS

Akansa = Quapaw. Dhegiha D.→SIOUAN

Akany Jok. Rek D.→EASTERN SUDANIC

Akapless = Abure→VOLTA-COMOE

Akara. Iliaura D.→ARANDIC

Akara = Toposo→EASTERN SUDANIC

Akar-Bale = Bale. Great Andamanese D.→ ANDAMANESE

A-karimojong = Karamojong → EASTERN SUDANIC

Akasele. Tobote D.→GUR

Akassa. Ijo D.→IJO

Akassele. Tobote D.→GUR

Akebou = Kebu→CENTRAL TOGO

Akebu = Kebu→CENTRAL TOGO

Akem. Akan D.→VOLTA-COMOE

Akem. Rek D.→EASTERN SUDANIC

Akern Jok = Akany Jok. Rek D.→EASTERN SUDANIC

Akeroa Toposa = Toposo → EASTERN SUDANIC

AKHA→BURMESE-LOLO

Akha→BURMESE-LOLO

Akhmim = Akhmimic. Coptic D.→AFRO-
ASIATIC
Akhmimic. Coptic D.→AFROASIATIC
Akhty = Axty. Lezghian D.→CAUCASIAN
Akhusha = Axusha. Dargwa D.→CAUCASIAN
Akhvakh = Axvax→CAUCASIAN
Akido = Kapontori. Muna D.→CENTRAL
AND SOUTHERN CELEBES
Akiek. Nandi D.→EASTERN SUDANIC
Akit. Kerintji D.→WEST INDONESIAN
Akitsikpi = Ashaku→JUKUNOID
Akium-Awin = West Awin→PARE-SAMO-
BEAMI-BOSAVI
Akium-Pare = East Awin→PARE-SAMO-
BEAMI-BOSAVI
Akjuet. Rek D.→EASTERN SUDANIC
Akka. Chechen D.→CAUCASIAN
Akkadian→SEMITIC
Akkhusha = Axusha. Dargwa D.→CAUCA-
SIAN
Aklan = Aklanon→NORTHWEST AUSTRO-
NESIAN
Aklanon→NORTHWEST AUSTRONESIAN
Ak-Nogai. Nogai D.→TURKIC
Ako→BURMESE-LOLO
Akochakanen = Mahican. Mohegan D.→
ALGONQUIAN
Akoiyang = Kiong→CROSS RIVER BENUE-
CONGO
Akokisa = Atakapa → MACRO-ALGON-
QUIAN
AKOKO, CENTRAL see article
Akoko. Yoruba D.→YORUBA
Akokolemu = Kumam→EASTERN SUDANIC
Akoli→EASTERN SUDANIC
AKONTO = MEMBE→JUKUNOID
Akoon. Padang D.→EASTERN SUDANIC
A-koose. Mbo D. → NORTH WESTERN
BANTU
Akori. Logo Tr.→CENTRAL SUDANIC
Akpafu→CENTRAL TOGO
Akparaboŋ = Ndoe→BANTOID
Akpes = Ibaram-Efifa→CENTRAL AKOKO
Akpese = Kpelle→MANDE
Akpet→CROSS RIVER BENUE-CONGO
Akposo = Kposo→CENTRAL TOGO
Akpwakum = Kwakum→NORTH WESTERN
BANTU
Akre. Zaza D.→IRANIAN
Akrukay→BOGIA
Aku. Endeh D.→MOLUCCAN
Akuang Ayat. Rek D.→EASTERN SUDANIC
Akuapem = Twi. Akan D.→VOLTA-COMOE
Akuku→CARIB

Akum = Kumam→EASTERN SUDANIC
Akunakuna = Agwagwune→CROSS RIVER
BENUE-CONGO
Akurakura = Agwagwune→CROSS RIVER
BENUE-CONGO
Akurmi = Kurama→PLATEAU BENUE-
CONGO
Akuut = Birom→PLATEAU BENUE-CONGO
Akuwagel = Beli→TORRICELLI
Akwa→NORTH WESTERN BANTU
AKWA = ACUA→GE
Akwa ʔala = Paipai→YUMAN
Akwa'ala = Paipai→YUMAN
Akwapem = Twi. Akan D.→VOLTA-COMOE
Akwat Ayat = Akuang Ayat. Rek D.→EAST-
ERN SUDANIC
Ak-Waumin = Agwamin. Wakaman D.→
PAMA-MARIC
AKWE = ACUA→GE
Akye→LAGOON
Akye-Kotoko = Bode. Akye Tr.→LAGOON
Akyem = Akem. Akan D.→VOLTA-COMOE
Al Hamid Awad. Beja Tr.→CUSHITIC
Al Hamid Awat = Al Hamid Awad. Beja Tr.→
CUSHITIC
Alaba→CUSHITIC
Alabama→MUSKOGEAN
Alabono. Yameo D.→PEBA-YAGUAN
Alacaluf→ANDEAN
Alada = Gu. Ewe D.→EWE
Aladian→LAGOON
Aladyan = Aladian→LAGOON
Alag-Bako. Iraya D.→NORTHWEST AUS-
TRONESIAN
Alagian = Aladian→LAGOON
Alagir = Iron. Ossetic D.→IRANIAN
Alaguilac. Pipil D. → UTO-AZTECAN
Alagya = Aladian→LAGOON
Alak→MON-KHMER
Alakaluf = Alacaluf→ANDEAN
Alakong. Bahnar D.→MON-KHMER
Alalao = Padoe. Mori D.→CENTRAL AND
SOUTHERN CELEBES
Alaliwa. Tebu Tr.→SAHARAN
Alamblak→SEPIK
Alang. Ambonese D.→MOLUCCAN
Alang = Halang→MON-KHMER
Alangan→NORTHWEST AUSTRONESIAN
Alanic→IRANIAN
Alante = Balanta→WEST ATLANTIC
Alas. Karo D.→WEST INDONESIAN
Alat. Buryat D.→MONGOLIAN
Alatil = Aruop→TORRICELLI
Alatil Eru = Aru→TORRICELLI

A'latskne-i = Tlatskanai. Kwalhioqua D.→ ATHAPASCAN-EYAK

Alawa→MARAN

Alawa→CUSHITIC

ALBANIAN see article

Albay-Sorsogon. Bikol D. → NORTHWEST AUSTRONESIAN

Albinaquis = Abnaki. Penobscot D.→ALGONQUIAN

Aldolinga = Antakirinya. Kardutjara D.→ WATI

Alege = Gayi → CROSS RIVER BENUE-CONGO

Alegi = Gayi → CROSS RIVER BENUE-CONGO

Aleniano = Leco→ANDEAN

Alese = Lese. Mamvu-Efe D.→CENTRAL SUDANIC

Aleut→ESKIMO-ALEUT

Alfendio→INDO-PACIFIC

ALGIC→MACRO-ALGONQUIAN

Algic = Ojibwa→ALGONQUIAN

ALGONKIAN = ALGONQUIAN

ALGONKIN = ALGONQUIAN

Algonkin = Algonquin. Ojibwa D.→ALGONQUIAN

Algonkin, Old = Algonquin. Ojibwa D.→ ALGONQUIAN

Algonkine = Algonquin. Ojibwa D.→ALGONQUIAN

Algonkinska = Algonquin. Ojibwa D.→ALGONQUIAN

Algonquian = Algonquin. Ojibwa D.→ALGONQUIAN

ALGONQUIAN see article

ALGONQUIAN, MACRO- see article

Algonquin. Ojibwa D.→ALGONQUIAN

Algonquine = Algonquin. Ojibwa D.→ALGONQUIAN

Ali→NORTHEAST NEW GUINEA AUSTRONESIAN

Ali. Gbaya Tr.→EASTERN

Aliab. Agar D.→EASTERN SUDANIC

Aliapmin = Tuwari→LEONARD SCHULTZE

Alibu→PARE-SAMO-BEAMI-BOSAVI

Alifuru = Luhu→EAST INDONESIAN

Alikuluf = Alacaluf→ANDEAN

Alile. Paraujano D. → NORTHERN MAIPURAN

Alimit = Silipan. Ifugao D.→NORTHWEST AUSTRONESIAN

Alisan = Arisan. Tsou D.→FORMOSAN AUSTRONESIAN

Aliutor = Alutor → CHUCKCHEE-KAM-CHATKAN

Alladyan = Aladian→LAGOON

Allaura = Alawa→MARAN

Allawa = Alawa→MARAN

Allebome = Comanche. Shoshoni D.→UTO-AZTECAN

Alleghany = Cherokee→IROQUOIS

Allentiac→HUARPE

ALLENTIAC = HUARPE

Alligewi = Cherokee→IROQUOIS

Alliklik. Serrano D.→UTO-AZTECAN

Allowa = Alawa→MARAN

Allowiri = Alawa→MARAN

Allua = Alawa→MARAN

Alngith→PAMA-MARIC

Alo. Bangba D.→EASTERN

Alo Teqel→EASTERN OCEANIC

Alokuk. Nyada D.→ADMIRALTY-WESTERN ISLANDS

Alomboki. Poke Tr.→NORTH WESTERN BANTU

Alowa = Alawa→MARAN

Alsea→YAKONAN

Alseya = Alsea→YAKONAN

Altai→TURKIC

Altai, Northern→TURKIC

ALTAIC see article

Altai-Kizhi. Altai D.→TURKIC

Al-ta-tin = Sekani. Sekani D.→ATHAPASCAN-EYAK

Alu→TORRICELLI

Alukuyana = Oyana→CARIB

Alulu = Alur→EASTERN SUDANIC

alu-Nyankole=Nyankole→NORTH EASTERN BANTU

Alur→EASTERN SUDANIC

Alur. High Lugbara D.→CENTRAL SUDANIC

Aluri = Ngadjuri. Jadliaura D.→YURA

Aluridja = Kukatja. Kardutjara D.→WATI

Aluru = Alur→EASTERN SUDANIC

Aluru = Alur. High Lugbara D.→CENTRAL SUDANIC

Alury = Ngadjuri. Jadliaura D.→YURA

Alutor→CHUKCHEE-KAMCHATKAN

Al'utor = Alutor→CHUKCHEE-KAMCHATKAN

Alutorskij. Alutor D.→CHUKCHEE-KAMCHATKAN

Alyawarra = Iliaura→ARANDIC

Ama = Amap→PLATEAU BENUE-CONGO

Ama = Nyimang→EASTERN SUDANIC

Amabi. Timorese D.→EAST INDONESIAN

Amabisanga = Mabisanga. Mangbetu D.→ CENTRAL SUDANIC

amaBusmana = / /xegwe→KHOISAN
Amachengue = Machiguenga→MAIPURAN
Amadi→EASTERN
Amadiye. Zaza D.→IRANIAN
Amaguaje. Pioje-Sioni Tr. → MACRO-TUCA-
NOAN
Amahai→EAST INDONESIAN
Amahuaca→PANO
Amaimon→BOGIA
Amajuu = Majuu. Mangbetu D.→CENTRAL
SUDANIC
Amakere = Makere. Mangbetu D.→CENTRAL
SUDANIC
Amakono. Vaikenu D.→EAST INDONESIAN
Amal→SEPIK
Amam = North Koma. Koma D.→KOMAN
Amam = Northern Mao→KOMAN
Amami-Osima = Northern Ryukyuan→JAP-
ANESE
Amampa = Southern Bullom→WEST ATLAN-
TIC
Amanab→NORTH PAPUAN
Amanage = Manaze. Tenetehara D.→TUPI
Amangbetu = Mangbetu→CENTRAL SU-
DANIC
Amangu. Nanda D.→KARDU
amaNkgqwigqwi = / /xegwe→KHOISAN
Amanubang. Timorese D.→EAST INDONE-
SIAN
Amanya = Nzema→VOLTA-COMOE
Amanye = Manaze. Tenetehara D.→TUPI
Amaona. Yameo D.→PEBA-YAGUAN
Amap→PLATEAU BENUE-CONGO
Amapopoi = Popol. Mangbetu D.→CENTRAL
SUDANIC
Amar = Banna→OMOTIC
Amar Koke = Banna→OMOTIC
Amara→BINANDERE
Amarag→IWAIDJAN
Amarakaire = Huachipairi. Masco D.→MAI-
PURAN
Amarar. Beja Tr.→CUSHITIC
Amarasi. Timorese D.→EAST INDONESIAN
Amari. Acira D. → NORTHEAST NEW
GUINEA AUSTRONESIAN
Amariba. Uapichana D.→MAIPURAN
Amarinnya = Amharic→SEMITIC
Amarinya = Amharic→SEMITIC
Amarizana. Achagua D.→NORTHERN MAI-
PURAN
Amaro = Burji→CUSHITIC
Amarro = Koyra→OMOTIC
Amaseba = Suku→KOIARI
Amasi→Bantoid

Amasi. Ekoi D.→BANTOID
Amawa = Amap → PLATEAU BENUE-
CONGO
Amawaca = Amahuaca→PANO
Amba→NORTH EASTERN BANTU
Ambali = Bali→NORTH WESTERN BANTU
Ambaquista = Mbaka. Mbamba D.→CEN-
TRAL WESTERN BANTU
Ambasi→BINANDERE
Ambawang Dayak. Land Dayak D.→WEST
INDONESIAN
Ambelau→EAST INDONESIAN
Ambenu. Vaikenu D.→EAST INDONESIAN
Amber. Waigeo D.→SOUTH HALMAHERA
AUSTRONESIAN
Amberbaken→WESTERN NEW GUINEA
AMBIC→MOLUCCAN
Ambo→GOILALA
Ambo. Lala D. → CENTRAL EASTERN
BANTU
Ambo = Mbo → CENTRAL EASTERN
BANTU
Ambo = Ndonga → SOUTH WESTERN
BANTU
Amboim→CENTRAL WESTERN BANTU
Ambonese→MOLUCCAN
Ambryn, Central→EASTERN OCEANIC
Ambryn, North→EASTERN OCEANIC
Ambryn, South→EASTERN OCEANIC
Ambryn, Southeast→EASTERN OCEANIC
Ambuella = Mbwela→SOUTH WESTERN
BANTU
Ambumi. Wandamen D.→MOLUCCAN
Amburayan = Baukok. Kankanay D. →
NORTHWEST AUSTRONESIAN
Ambwela. Luimbi D.→SOUTH WESTERN
BANTU
Amdo = Ngambo. Central Tibetan D.→TIBET-
AN
Ame→DALY
Amegi-Biseni. Ijo D.→IJO
Amele→BOGIA
Amena Dyapa = Amenadiapa→MACRO-
TUCANOAN
Amenadiapa→MACRO-TUCANOAN
Amengi. Mamvu-Efe D.→CENTRAL SUDAN-
IC
Amenguaca = Amahuaca→PANO
Amesdes. Kalasa-ala D.→NURISTANI
Amfuang. Vaikenu D.→EAST INDONESIAN
Amharic→SEMITIC
Amharinya = Amharıc→SEMITIC
Amho = Ivitorocai→GE
Ami→FORMOSAN AUSTRONESIAN

Ami = Tauran. Ami D.→FORMOSAN AUS-
  TRONESIAN
Amiangbwa = Barambu→EASTERN
Amiol. Rek D.→EASTERN SUDANIC
Amiranha = Jacunda. Tenetehara Tr.→TUPI
Amis = Ami→FORMOSAN AUSTRONE-
  SIAN
Amis = Tauran. Ami D.→FORMOSAN AUS-
  TRONESIAN
≠amkwe. Naron D.→KHOISAN
Amma Borkua. Tebu Tr.→SAHARAN
Ammassalik = East Greenlandic. Inuit D.→
  ESKIMO-ALEUT
Amniape = Guarategaya→TUPI
Amo. Moseten D.→MACRO-PANOAN
Amo = Amap→PLATEAU BENUE-CONGO
Amoipira. Tupi Tr.→TUPI
Amojave = Mohave. River Yuman D.→
  YUMAN
Amok. Angku D.→PALAUNG-WA
Amon = Amap→PLATEAU BENUE-CONGO
Among = Amap→PLATEAU BENUE-
  CONGO
Amono = Mono. Banda D.→EASTERN
Amorite→SEMITIC
Amoskeag. Massachusett Tr.→ALGONQUIAN
Amou Oblou. Kposo D.→CENTRAL TOGO
Amoy. Southern Min D.→CHINESE
Ampale. Wajokeso D.→KUKUKUKU
Ampana = Ampona. Bare'e D.→CENTRAL
  AND SOUTHERN CELEBES
Ampas→NORTH PAPUAN
Ampibabo = Tinombo→NORTHERN CELE-
  BES
Ampona. Bare'e D.→CENTRAL AND SOUTH-
  ERN CELEBES
Amto→NORTH NEW GUINEA
Amu. Swahili D. → CENTRAL EASTERN
  BANTU
Amuesha→ARAWAKAN
Amuexa = Amuesha→ARAWAKAN
Amugen. Ono D.→HUON-FINISTERRE
Amuzgo→OTO-MANGUEAN
Anaberg = Angaua→BOGIA
Anafejazi = Janji → PLATEAU BENUE-
  CONGO
Anago. Yoruba D.→YORUBA
Anaguta→PLATEAU BENUE-CONGO
Anajanzi = Janji → PLATEAU BENUE-
  CONGO
Anakalang. Sumba D.→MOLUCCAN
Anakatza = Ankaa. Tebu Tr.→SAHARAN
Anal→NAGA-KUKI-CHIN
Anambe. Tenetehara D.→TUPI

Anana = Wanana. Tucano Tr.→MACRO-
  TUCANOAN
Anang. Efik D.→CROSS RIVER BENUE-
  CONGO
Anaraki. Persian D.→IRANIAN
ANATOLIAN see article
Anatri. Chuvash D.→TURKIC
Anauli. Turkmen D.→TURKIC
Anawla. Gujarati D.→INDIC
Anazele = Jerawa → PLATEAU BENUE-
  CONGO
Ancerma. Cauca D.→CARIB
Anchix. Karata D.→CAUCASIAN
Ancux. Avar D.→CAUCASIAN
Andagirinja = Antakirinya. Kardutjara D.→
  WATI
Andakerebina. Iliaura D.→ARANDIC
Andaki→MACRO-CHIBCHAN
Andalal-Gidatl. Avar D.→CAUCASIAN
Andali. Mamvu-Efe D.→CENTRAL SUDANIC
ANDAMANESE see article
Andaŋ = Mimi→MABAN
Andaŋti = Mimi→MABAN
Andaqui = Andaki→MACRO-CHIBCHAN
Andarum→BOGIA
Andaste = Susquehannock→IROQUOIS
ANDEAN see article
ANDEAN-EQUATORIAL see article
Andekarinja = Antakirinya. Kardutjara D.→
  WATI
Andekerinja = Antakirinya. Kardutjara D.→
  WATI
Andhra = Telugu→DRAVIDIAN
Andi→CAUCASIAN
Andian = Mandarese → CENTRAL AND
  SOUTHERN CELEBES
Andian = Tjenrana. Mandarese D.→CENTRAL
  AND SOUTHERN CELEBES
Andiang = Madjene. Mandarese D.→CEN-
  TRAL AND SOUTHERN CELEBES
Andigarina = Antakirinya. Kardutjara D.→
  WATI
Andilyaugwa = Groote Eylandt→AUSTRA-
  LIAN MACRO-PHYLUM
Andingiri = Antakirinya. Kardutjara D.→
  WATI
Andio'o = Bobongko → CENTRAL AND
  SOUTHERN CELEBES
Andira = Maue→TUPI
Andje = Petapa→NORTHERN CELEBES
Andjiringna = Antakirinya. Kardutjara D.→
  WATI
Andoa→ANDEAN
Andoni→CROSS RIVER BENUE-CONGO

Andoque, Northern→WITOTOAN
Andoque, Southern→WITOTOAN
Andoquero = Miranya→WITOTOAN
Andra→ADMIRALTY-WESTERN ISLANDS
Andreleba = Low Lugbara→CENTRAL SU-
DANIC
Andreleba-ti = Low Lugbara→CENTRAL SU-
DANIC
Andrginji = Antakirinya. Kardutjara D.→
WATI
Andri. Moru D.→CENTRAL SUDANIC
Andro→BURMESE-LOLO
Ane-Bet. Muher Tr.→SEMITIC
Anei. Rek D.→EASTERN SUDANIC
Aneityum→SOUTHERN NEW HEBRIDES
/ anekwe. Naron D.→KHOISAN
Anem→NEW BRITAIN
Anesu = Hameha→NEW CALEDONIA
Anfillo = Southern Mao→OMOTIC
ANGA = KUKUKUKU
Angadi→ASMAT
Angai = Dai. Mayogo Tr.→EASTERN
Angaite. Mascoy D.→MACRO-PANOAN
Angal Heneng = Mendi→EAST NEW GUIN-
EA HIGHLANDS
Angami→NAGA-KUKI-CHIN
Angan = Kamantan→PLATEAU BENUE-
CONGO
Anganiwai. Kahua D.→EASTERN OCEANIC
Angas→CHADIC
Angass = Angas→CHADIC
Angaua→BOGIA
Angba—NORTH WESTERN BANTU
Angie = Ngi→BANTOID
Angka = Hruso→GYARUNG-MISHMI
Angkae = Hruso→GYARUNG-MISHMI
Angkola. Toba D.→WEST INDONESIAN
Angku→PALAUNG-WA
Angmagssalik = East Greenlandic. Inuit D.→
ESKIMO-ALEUT
Angoram→NORTH NEW GUINEA
Angrak→MON-KHMER
Angwanku. Tangsa D. → BODO-NAGA-
KACHIN
Anhaqui. Bijago D.→WEST ATLANTIC
Anibau = Gussum→PLATEAU BENUE-
CONGO
Anima → CENTRAL AND SOUTH NEW
GUINEA
Anima = Ge. Ga D.→GA-ADANGME
Animere = Anyimere→CENTRAL TOGO
Anir Island→BISMARCK ARCHIPELAGO
Anirago = Kahugu→PLATEAU BENUE-
CONGO

Aniwa. West Futuna D.→POLYNESIAN
Aniwan→PAMA-NYUNGAN
Anjamutina = Adnyamathana. Wailpi D.→
YURA
Anjimatana = Adnyamathana. Wailpi D.→
YURA
Anjiwatana = Adnyamathana. Wailpi D.→
YURA
Ankaa. Tebu Tr.→SAHARAN
Ankaza = Ankaa. Tebu Tr.→SAHARAN
Anket = Anquet→BOTOCUDO
Ankober. Amharic D.→SEMITIC
Ankulu = Ikulu→PLATEAU BENUE-CONGO
Ankwe→CHADIC
Anlutur. Leti D.→MOLUCCAN
Anmatjera. Iliaura D.→ARANDIC
Anna = Bideyat. Zaghawa D.→SAHARAN
Annamese = Vietnamese→VIET-MUONG
Annamito French. French Creole D.→
ROMANCE
ANNAM-MUONG = VIET-MUONG
Annang = Anang. Efik D.→CROSS RIVER
BENUE-CONGO
Ano = Buji→PLATEAU BENUE-CONGO
Anoong = Nung→BODO-NAGA-KACHIN
Anor→BOGIA
Anpika = Fika. Bolewa D.→CHADIC
Anquet→BOTOCUDO
Ansakara = Nzakara→EASTERN
Anshuenkuan = Nganshuenkuan. Central Tibet-
an D.→TIBETAN
Ansita = Central Koma→KOMAN
Anskrak = Angrak→MON-KHMER
Ansrak = Angrak→MON-KHMER
Ansus. Japen D.→MOLUCCAN
Anta = Ahanta→VOLTA-COMOE
Anta = Tapiraua. Tenetehara Tr.→TUPI
Antaisaka = Taisaka. Malagasy D.→WEST
INDONESIAN
Antakerrinya = Antakirinya. Kardutjara D.
→WATI
Antakirinya. Kardutjara D.→WATI
Antanala = Tanala. Malagasy D.→WEST
INDONESIAN
Antarbedi = Braj Bhakha. Western Hindi D.→
INDIC
Antarvedi = Braj Bhakha. Western Hindi D.→
INDIC
Antekarinja = Antakirinya. Kardutjara D.→
WATI
Anti. Campa D.→MAIPURAN
Antigerinya = Antakirinya. Kardutjara D.→
WATI
Antioquia. Cauca D.→CARIB

Antique = Hantik→NORTHWEST AUSTRO-NESIAN

Antiqueno = Hantik→NORTHWEST AUS-TRONESIAN

Antor→MON-KHMER

Antsukh = Ancux. Avar D.→CAUCASIAN

Anuak→EASTERN SUDANIC

Anufo. Anyi D.→VOLTA-COMOE

Anufo = Chakosi→VOLTA-COMOE

Anuki→PAPUA AUSTRONESIAN

Anung = Nung→BODO-NAGA-KACHIN

Anunga. Zande D.→EASTERN

Anunze. Northeast Nambicuara D.→NAMBI-CUARA

Anupe = Ebe. Nupe D.→NUPE-GBARI

Anus→SARMIC

Anuta. Tikopia D.→POLYNESIAN

Anwak = Anuak→EASTERN SUDANIC

Anyama. Ogbia D.→CROSS RIVER BENUE-CONGO

Anyamatana = Adnyamathana. Wailpi D.→YURA

Anyang→BANTOID

Anyanga. Guan D.→VOLTA-COMOE

Anyi→VOLTA-COMOE

Anyimere→CENTRAL TOGO

Anyo. Rengma D.→NAGA-KUKI-CHIN

Anyonola = Nonuya→WITOTOAN

Anywaa = Anuak→EASTERN SUDANIC

Anywak = Anuak→EASTERN SUDANIC

Anywaq = Anuak→EASTERN SUDANIC

Anyx. Lezghian D.→CAUCASIAN

Anzanite = Elamite

Aŋba = Angba→NORTH WESTERN BANTU

Aŋgba = Angba → NORTH WESTERN BANTU

Aŋlo = Awuna. Ewe D.→EWE

Ao→NAGA-KUKI-CHIN

Aola→EASTERN OCEANIC

Aomie→KOIARI

Apa. Dafla D.→GYARUNG-MISHMI

Apa. Eregba D.→JUKUNOID

Apa = Yergham → PLATEAU BENUE-CONGO

Apacachodegodegi. Mbaya-Guaicuru Tr.→GUAYCURU

Apache. Navajo D.→ATHAPASCAN-EYAK

APACHEAN→ATHAPASCAN-EYAK

Apache-Mojave = Yavapai. Upland Yuman D.→YUMAN

Apaches, Prairie = Kiowa Apache→ATHA-PASCAN-EYAK

Apache-Yuma = Yavapai. Upland Yuman D.→YUMAN

Apaeʔaa = Saʔa→EASTERN OCEANIC

Apagibeti. Bati D. → NORTH WESTERN BANTU

Apairande. Kawaib Tr.→TUPI

Apak. Atuot D.→EASTERN SUDANIC

Apaka→LEFT MAY

Apako→SANTA CRUZ AUSTRONESIAN

Apalachee→MUSKOGEAN

Apalachicola = Hitchiti→MUSKOGEAN

Apalai→CARIB

Apalakiri→CARIB

Apalaquiri = Apalakiri→CARIB

Apambia = Pambia→EASTERN

Apanhecra→GE

Apapocuva = Apapokuva. Tupi D.→TUPI

Apapokuva. Tupi D.→TUPI

Aparono. Moseten D.→MACRO-PANOAN

Apay = Api→MAYAN

Apayac = Api→MAYAN

Api→MAYAN

Api = Lampung→WEST INDONESIAN

Api = Oyampi→TUPI

Apiaca→CARIB

Apiaca = Apiaka→TUPI

Apiaka→TUPI

Apiapun = Epiapum. Mbembe D.→CROSS RIVER BENUE-CONGO

Apicum. Wayoro D.→TUPI

Apigapigtana. Tupi Tr.→TUPI

Apinage→GE

Apinaye = Apinage→GE

Apindji = Tsogo → NORTH WESTERN BANTU

Apitere. Tupi Tr.→TUPI

Apo→BANTOID

Apoi. Ijo D.→IJO

Apokinskij. Koryak D.→CHUKCHEE-KAM-CHATKAN

Apolista→ARAWAKAN

Appa = Eregba→JUKUNOID

Appa = Tiv→BANTOID

Appa = Yergham → PLATEAU BENUE-CONGO

Appiapum = Epiapum. Mbembe D.→CROSS RIVER BENUE-CONGO

Appomattoc. Powhatan Tr.→ALGONQUIAN

Apris→NORTH NEW GUINEA

AP'U = KATCHIN→BODO-NAGA-KACHIN

Apuk. Rek D.→EASTERN SUDANIC

Apuoth. Rek. D.→EASTERN SUDANIC

Apurahuano = Apurawano. Tagbanua D.→NORTHWEST AUSTRONESIAN

Apurawano. Tagbanua D. → NORTHWEST AUSTRONESIAN

Apwot = Apuoth. Rek D.→EASTERN SU-
DANIC
Aqsu. Uighur D.→TURKIC
Aqua → Kwa. Ekoi D.→BANTOID
Ara → CENTRAL AND SOUTHERN
CELEBES
Ara. Terraba D.→CHIBCHAN
Ara = Ari→OMOTIC
Arabana→PAMA-NYUNGAN
Arabatura = Jadliaura→YURA
Arabela. Zaparo D.→ANDEAN
Arabic→SEMITIC
Arabic, Modern South→SEMITIC
Arabic, Old South→SEMITIC
Araboiara. Tupi Tr.→TUPI
Arabuna = Arabana→PAMA-NYUNGAN
Aracuaju. Apalai D.→CARIB
Aradigi = Ratagnon. Cuyunon D.→NORTH-
WEST AUSTRONESIAN
Arafundi = Alfendio→INDO-PACIFIC
Araguaju. Oyampi D.→TUPI
Aragure→NEW CALEDONIA
'Aragure = Haragure→NEW CALEDONIA
Aragwa. Mongour D.→MONGOLIAN
Aragya = Aladian→LAGOON
ARAHUNA = ARAONA→TACANA
Araibaya. Tupi Tr.→TUPI
Araicu = Uaraicu→MAIPURAN
Arakanese. Burmese D.→BURMESE-LOLO
Araki. Persian D.→IRANIAN
Arakwal. Kitabal D.→BANDJALANGIC
Arama→CENTRAL AND SOUTH NEW
GUINEA
Aramaic, East→SEMITIC
Aramaic, West→SEMITIC
Aramot→NORTHEAST NEW GUINEA AUS-
TRONESIAN
Aran→OK
Aran. Tulu D.→ADMIRALTY-WESTERN
ISLANDS
Arana→BOTOCUDO
Aranaua. Jurua-Purus Tr.→PANO
Aranda, Eastern. Iliaura D.→ARANDIC
Aranda, Lower→ARANDIC
Aranda, Southern. Iliaura D.→ARANDIC
Aranda, Western. Iliaura D.→ARANDIC
Arandai. Kampong Baru D.→WESTERN NEW
GUINEA
ARANDIC see article
Aranya = Arana→BOTOCUDO
ARAONA→TACANA
Araote = Warao→MACRO-CHIBCHAN
Arapaho→ALGONQUIAN
Arapaho, Southern = Nawathinehena. Arapaho

D.→ALGONQUIAN
Arapahoe = Arapaho→ALGONQUIAN
Arapani = Arabana→PAMA-NYUNGAN
ARAPESH→TORRICELLI
Arapesh, Bumbita→TORRICELLI
Arapesh, Mountain→TORRICELLI
Arapesh, Southern→TORRICELLI
ARAPESHAN = TORRICELLI
Arapium = Maue→TUPI
Arapoho = Arapaho→ALGONQUIAN
Arapohoe = Arapaho→ALGONQUIAN
Araquaia. Tenetehara Tr.→TUPI
Arara→CARIB
Arara→TUPI
Arara. Carutana D.→NORTHERN MAI-
PURAN
Arara. Catuquina D.→PANO
Arara = Juma
Arara = Karok→HOKAN
Araracuara→WITOTOAN
Ararandeura. Tenetehara Tr.→TUPI
Ararapina. Catuquina D.→PANO
Arare→WESTERN NEW GUINEA
Arargbi = Maung→IWAIDJAN
Ararra = Karok→HOKAN
Ararwa. Catuquina D.→PANO
Arasa→TACANA
Arasa→PANO
Arasa. Omurano Tr.→ANDEAN
Arasaire = Arasa→PANO
Araspaso. Tucano D.→MACRO-TUCANOAN
Arata. Maewo D.→EASTERN OCEANIC
Aratsaira = Arasa→PANO
Araua→PANO
Araua→ARAWAKAN
Araua→NORTHERN MAIPURAN
ARAUAN→ARAWAKAN
Araucanian→PENUTIAN
Arauine = Aweti→TUPI
Arauite = Aweti→TUPI
Araukan = Araucanian→PENUTIAN
ARAUNA = ARAONA→TACANA
Aravira→BORORO
Arawak = Lokono → NORTHERN MAI-
PURAN
ARAWAKAN see article
Arawe→NORTHEAST NEW GUINEA AUS-
TRONESIAN
Araya. Yarigui D.→CARIB
Arazaire = Arasa→PANO
Arazo = Arasa. Omurano Tr.→ANDEAN
Arbanasi. Albanian D.
Arber = Albanian
Arbil. Kermanji D.→IRANIAN

Arbore→CUSHITIC
ARBORE-DASENECH OROMOID→CUSHITIC
Arbresh = Albanian
Arc-a-plat = Kutenai
Archi→CAUCASIAN
Arderi = Adere→BANTOID
Ardhamagadhi→INDIC
Are = Ari→OMOTIC
Are = Seta→TUPI
Areare→EASTERN OCEANIC
Arechane. Tupi Tr.→TUPI
Arecuna→CARIB
Are'e = Po'u mBoto. Bare'e D.→CENTRAL AND SOUTHERN CELEBES
Aregerek→BOGIA
Aregwa = Irigwe → PLATEAU BENUE-CONGO
Aregwe = Irigwe → PLATEAU BENUE-CONGO
Arekena = Arequena → NORTHERN MAIPURAN
Arem. Muong D.→VIET-MUONG
Arequena→NORTHERN MAIPURAN
Arfak→WESTERN NEW GUINEA
Argo→IDOMA
Argobba. Amharic D.→SEMITIC
Argobbimya = Argobba. Amharic D.→SEMITIC
Arguni→SOUTH HALMAHERA AUSTRONESIAN
Arguni→EAST INDONESIAN
Arha. Houailou D.→NEW CALEDONIA
Ari→OMOTIC
Ari→LAGOON
Aria = Benahu. Pipikoro D.→CENTRAL AND SOUTHERN CELEBES
Aria = Rapangkaka D.→CENTRAL AND SOUTHERN CELEBES
Ariangulu = Sanye→CUSHITIC
Ariap. Breenugu D.→INDO-PACIFIC
Aricapu see article
Arickara = Arikara. Pawnee D.→CADDOAN
Arickaree = Arikara. Pawnee D.→CADDOAN
Aricobe→GE
Aricobe. Tupi Tr.→TUPI
Aricuaisa. Mape D.→CARIB
Arikapu = Aricapu
Arikara. Pawnee D.→CADDOAN
Arikare = Arikara. Pawnee D.→CADDOAN
ARIKEM→TUPI
Arikem→TUPI
Arikun. Saisiyat D.→FORMOSAN AUSTRONESIAN

Aril. Atuot D.→EASTERN SUDANIC
Arimoa→SARMIC
Arin→YENISEIAN
Arinagoto→CARIB
Arino. Apiaka D.→TUPI
Arinwa = Heyo→TORRICELLI
Ariom. Biak D.→MOLUCCAN
Aripa. Waicuru Tr.→WAICURIAN
Ariqueme = Arikem→TUPI
Arisan. Tsou D.→FORMOSAN AUSTRONESIAN
Aritao. Isinay D.→NORTHWEST AUSTRONESIAN
Ariti = Paressi→MAIPURAN
Aritinngithig→PAMA-MARIC
Arkansas = Quapaw. Dhegiha D.→SIOUAN
Arkhorcin. Khorcin D.→MONGOLIAN
Arma. Cauca D.→CARIB
Arman. Even D.→TUNGUS
Armenian see article
Armopa = Bonggo→SARMIC
Arnaut = Albanian
Arniya = Khowar→INDIC
Arnyia = Khowar→INDIC
Aro→NEW CALEDONIA
Aro. Igbo D.→IGBO
Aro = Ari→OMOTIC
Arogbo. Ijo D.→IJO
AROID = EAST OMOTIC→OMOTIC
Arokwa = Erohwa→EDO
Aromanian = Macedo-Rumanian. Rumanian D.→ROMANCE
Arop→NORTHEAST NEW GUINEA AUSTRONESIAN
Arora. Auyana D.→EAST NEW GUINEA HIGHLANDS
Arosi→EASTERN OCEANIC
Arrabonna = Arabana→PAMA-NYUNGAN
Arrabunna = Arabana→PAMA-NYUNGAN
Arrapaho = Arapaho→ALGONQUIAN
Arrapahoe = Arapaho→ALGONQUIAN
Arrara = Karok→HOKAN
Arrarra = Karok→HOKAN
Arringeu = Pongo → PLATEAU BENUE-CONGO
Arsi = Arusi. Galla D.→CUSHITIC
ARSO→NORTH PAPUAN
Arso→NORTH PAPUAN
Arteiga. Beja Tr.→CUSHITIC
Artuya = Kaititj→ARANDIC
Aru→TORRICELLI
Aru→BINANDERE
Aru. Koma D.→KOMAN
Arua→GE

Arua→TUPI
Arua = Araua→NORTHERN MAIPURAN
Aruachi = Aruasi. Arua D.→TUPI
ARUACO→CHIBCHAN
Aruan = Araua→NORTHERN MAIPURAN
Aruasi. Arua D.→TUPI
Arumanian = Macedo-Rumanian. Rumanian
    D.→ROMANCE
Aruni. Enga D.→EAST NEW GUINEA HIGH-
    LANDS
Aruop→TORRICELLI
Arupai. Manitsawa D.→TUPI
Arusa. Maasai Tr.→EASTERN SUDANIC
Arusha = Arusa. Maasai Tr.→EASTERN
    SUDANIC
Arusha = Rusha → NORTH EASTERN
    BANTU
Arusi. Galla D.→CUSHITIC
Arussi = Arusi. Galla D.→CUSHITIC
Arutani = Auaque→MACRO-TUCANOAN
Arvanitika. Albanian D.
Arvi→CARIB
Arviligjuarmiut = Netsilik. Inuit D.→ESKIMO-
    ALEUT
Arzeu. Riff D.→BERBER
As→SOUTH HALMAHERA AUSTRONE-
    SIAN
Asak = Kadu→BURMESE-LOLO
Asan→YENISEIAN
Asande = Zande→EASTERN
Asang→INDO-PACIFIC
Asante. Akan D.→VOLTA-COMOE
Asaro. Gahuku D.→EAST NEW GUINEA
    HIGHLANDS
Asaruntoa. Andoa Tr.→ANDEAN
Asempa. Auyana D.→EAST NEW GUINEA
    HIGHLANDS
Aser. Soninke Tr.→MANDE
Asera Wanua. Laki D.→CENTRAL AND
    SOUTHERN CELEBES
Ashaku→JUKUNOID
Ashanti = Asante. Akan D.→VOLTA-COMOE
Ashavi→KUKUKUKU
Asheraf = Ad Sheraf. Beja Tr.→CUSHITIC
Ashingi = Kambari→PLATEAU BENUE-
    CONGO
Ashkarwa = Ashxar. Abxazo D.→CAUCA-
    SIAN
Ashkun = Askun→NURISTANI
Ashkund = Askun→NURISTANI
A-sho = Aso→NAGA-KUKI-CHIN
Ashochimi = Wappo→YUKI
Ashret = Phalura Proper. Phalura D.→INDIC
Ashtikulin. Lak D.→CAUCASIAN

Ashuku = Ashaku→JUKUNOID
Ashuru-veri. Askun D.→NURISTANI
Ashushlay→MATACO
Ashxar. Abxazo D.→CAUCASIAN
Asi = Alawa→CUSHITIC
ASIENARA→ASMAT
Asienara→ASMAT
Asiga = Leyigha→CROSS RIVER BENUE-
    CONGO
Asilulu→EAST INDONESIAN
Asilulu. Ambonese D.→MOLUCCAN
Asimboa = Apako→SANTA CRUZ AUSTRO-
    NESIAN
Askun→NURISTANI
ASLIAN = MALACCA
ASLIAN, CENTRAL = SAKAI
ASLIAN, NORTHERN = SEMANG
ASLIAN, SOUTHERN = SEMELAIC →
    SAKAI
Asli-Sidi→WESTERN NEW GUINEA
ASMAT see article
Aso→NAGA-KUKI-CHIN
Asoko = Nzema→VOLTA-COMOE
Asolio = Morwa. Katab D.→PLATEAU
    BENUE-CONGO
Asong→BURMESE-LOLO
Asongori = Sungor→EASTERN SUDANIC
Asowi→LEFT MAY
Asreti = Phalura Proper. Phalura D.→INDIC
Assamese. Bengali D.→INDIC
Assandeh = Zande→EASTERN
Assaorta. Afar-Saho D.→CUSHITIC
Assaye = Safwi. Anyi D.→VOLTA-COMOE
Assiniboin. Dakota D.→SIOUAN
Assiniboine = Assiniboin. Dakota D. →
    SIOUAN
Assiut = Asyutic. Coptic D.→AFROASIATIC
Assumbo→BANTOID
Assunpink = Delaware→ALGONQUIAN
Assyrian. Akkadian D.→SEMITIC
Assyro-Babylonian = Akkadian→SEMITIC
Astori. Sina D.→INDIC
Astrakhan Tatar. Tatar D.→TURKIC
Asu→CENTRAL EASTERN BANTU
Asua→CENTRAL SUDANIC
Asua-e = Asua→CENTRAL SUDANIC
Asuati = Asua→CENTRAL SUDANIC
Asulio = Morwa. Katab D.→PLATEAU
    BENUE-CONGO
Asumbo = Assumbo→BANTOID
Asungore. Tama D.→EASTERN SUDANIC
Asuri. Mundari D.→MUNDA
Asurini. Tenetehara D.→TUPI
Aswanik. Soninke Tr.→MANDE

Asyutic. Coptic D.→AFROASIATIC

Ata→NORTHWEST AUSTRONESIAN

Ata→NORTHEAST NEW GUINEA AUSTRONESIAN

Ata = Eto. Bagobo D.→NORTHWEST AUSTRONESIAN

Ata = Uasi→NEW BRITAIN

Atacama = Atacameno → MACRO-CHIBCHAN

Atacame = Esmeralda→JIVAROAN

Atacameno→MACRO-CHIBCHAN

Atacapa = Atakapa → MACRO-ALGONQUIAN

Atacuari. Yagua D.→PEBA-YAGUAN

Atago→SANTA CRUZ AUSTRONESIAN

Ataguate→ANDEAN

Ataiyal = Atayal→FORMOSAN AUSTRONESIAN

Atak = Jiru→JUKUNOID

Ataka. Katab D.→PLATEAU BENUE-CONGO

Atakapa→MACRO-ALGONQUIAN

Atala. Degema D.→EDO

Atalala. Vilela Tr.→LULE-VILELA-CHARRUA

ATALAN→MACRO-CHIBCHAN

Atam = Nde→BANTOID

Atangue→CHIBCHAN

Atankez = Atangue→CHIBCHAN

Atayal→FORMOSAN AUSTRONESIAN

ATAYALIC → FORMOSAN AUSTRONESIAN

Atchi = Akye→LAGOON

Atchin → NORTHWESTERN NEW HEBRIDES

Ate→NORTHEASTERN NEW GUINEA

Ate. Ivbie D.→EDO

Ateanaca = Cora→UTO-AZTECAN

Atemata. Tebu Tr.→SAHARAN

Atemple→BOGIA

Aten→PLATEAU BENUE-CONGO

Ateso = Teso→EASTERN SUDANIC

Atfalati = Tfalati→KALAPUYA

Athabasca. Chipewyan Tr.→ATHAPASCAN-EYAK

Athabascan, Smith River = Chasta Costa→ATHAPASCAN-EYAK

ATHABASKAN = ATHAPASCAN → ATHAPASCAN-EYAK

ATHAPASCAN→ATHAPASCAN-EYAK

ATHAPASCAN-EYAK see article

ATHERTON PAMA see PAMA-MARIC

Athoic = Borathoi. Bor D.→EASTERN SUDANIC

Athu = Asu→CENTRAL EASTERN BANTU

Ati→NORTHWEST AUSTRONESIAN

Atiahu→EAST INDONESIAN

Aticheraak = Kachichere. Katab D.→PLATEAU BENUE-CONGO

Atina. Zan D.→CAUCASIAN

Atinggola = Bulanga-uki → NORTHWEST AUSTRONESIAN

Atiri = Campa→MAIPURAN

Atisa. Epie D.→EDO

Atissa = Atisa. Epie D.→EDO

Atiteca = Tzutuhil→MAYAN

Atiu. Cook Islands Maori D. → POLYNESIAN

Atka = Central Aleut. Aleut D.→ESKIMO-ALEUT

ATLANTIC, WEST see article

Atna = Shuswap→SALISH

Atnebar = Kei Tanimbar. Kei D.→MOLUCCAN

Atobu. Akye Tr.→LAGOON

Atoc = Borathoi. Bor D.→EASTERN SUDANIC

Atok→NORTHWEST AUSTRONESIAN

Atokto = Atoktou. Rek D.→EASTERN SUDANIC

Atoktou. Rek D.→EASTERN SUDANIC

Atomb = Bonek. Banen Tr.→NORTH WESTERN BANTU

Atong→BODO-NAGA-KACHIN

Atorai→MAIPURAN

Atroahy. Jauaperi D.→CARIB

Atsahuaca→PANO

Atsahuaca = Chaspa. Atsahuaca D.→PANO

Atsam = Chawai → PLATEAU BENUE-CONGO

Atsama = Chawai→PLATEAU BENUE-CONGO

Atsang = Ach'ang→BODO-NAGA-KACHIN

Atsang = Dschang-Bangwa. Bafou D.→BANTOID

Atsawaca = Atsahuaca→PANO

Atsera = Acira→NORTHEAST NEW GUINEA AUSTRONESIAN

Atshe = Akye→LAGOON

Atsi = Tsaiwa→BODO-NAGA-KACHIN

Atsilima→BOUGAINVILLE

Atsina. Arapaho D.→ALGONQUIAN

Atsugewi → PALAIHNIHAN

Atsuku = Ashaku→JUKUNOID

Atta→NORTHWEST AUSTRONESIAN

Atta. Mambila D.→BANTOID

Attacapa = Atakapa → MACRO - ALGONQUIAN

Attaka = Ataka. Katab D.→PLATEAU
BENUE-CONGO
Attakapa = Atakapa → MACRO - ALGON-
QUIAN
Atticmospicayes = Dogrib→ATHAPASCAN-
EYAK
Attie = Akye→LAGOON
Attimospiqaies = Dogrib→ATHAPASCAN-
EYAK
Attouat = Katu→MON-KHMER
Attu = Western Aleut. Aleut D.→ESKIMO-
ALEUT
Attuan = Western Aleut. Aleut D.→ESKIMO-
ALEUT
Atuot → EASTERN SUDANIC
Atwot = Atuot→EASTERN SUDANIC
Atyap = Katab→PLATEAU BENUE-CONGO
Atyoti. Guan D.→VOLTA-COMOE
Atzi = Tsaiwa→BODO-NAGA-KACHIN
Atzinca = Ocuiltec→OTOMIAN
Au→TORRICELLI
Aua→ADMIRALTY-WESTERN ISLANDS
Aua. Medlpa D.→EAST NEW GUINEA
HIGHLANDS
Auake = Auaque→MACRO-TUCANOAN
Auaque→MACRO-TUCANOAN
Aubsaroke = Crow→SIOUAN
Auca = Sabela→ANDEAN
Aucaan→GERMANIC
Aucan = Araucanian→PENUTIAN
Aucanian = Araucanian→PENUTIAN
//Au//ei = Auen→KHOISAN
Auen→KHOISAN
//Au//en = Auen→KHOISAN
≠au-//e n = Auen→KHOISAN
Aueto=Aweti→TUPI
Augu→EAST NEW GUINEA HIGHLANDS
Augutge→GE
Auiti = Aweti→TUPI
Aukot. Nakwi D.→LEFT MAY
Aukshtaitish. Lithuanian D.→BALTIC
Aukstaiciai = Aukshtaitish. Lithuanian D.→
BALTIC
Aukstaitis = Aukshtaitish. Lithuanian D.→
BALTIC
//Au-kwe = Auen→KHOISAN
≠au-kwe = Auen → KHOISAN
Aulad Bugar = Bogarea. Tebu Tr.→SAHARAN
Aulad Djema = Uled Djemma. Maba Tr.→
MABAN
Aulo = Abi. Bakwe D.→KRU
Aulopo = Uroko. Bakwe Tr.→KRU
Aulua→NORTHWESTERN NEW HEBRIDES
Aunalei = Oni→TORRICELLI

Aunalei = Seta→TORRICELLI
Aunalei = Seti→TORRICELLI
Aunde'e = Lala'eo. Bare'e D.→CENTRAL
AND SOUTHERN CELEBES
Auni. ŋ/amani D.→KHOISAN
/auni = Auni. ŋ/amani D.→KHOISAN
/auo = Auni. ŋ/amani D.→KHOISAN
Aura = Uaura→MAIPURAN
Aurama→EAST NEW GUINEA HIGHLANDS
Aushi→CENTRAL EASTERN BANTU
Aussa. Afar-Saho D.→CUSHITIC
AUSTRALIAN MACRO-PHYLUM see article
AUSTRIC see AUSTRO-ASIATIC
AUSTRO-ASIATIC see article
AUSTROASIATIC - VIETNAMESE-MUONG
= AUSTRO-ASIATIC
AUSTRONESIAN see article
AUSTRONESIAN, EASTERN = OCEANIC
AUSTRONESIAN, FORMOSAN see article
AUSTRONESIAN, NORTHEAST NEW
GUINEA see article
AUSTRONESIAN, NORTHWEST see article
AUSTRONESIAN, PAPUA see article
AUSTRONESIAN, SANTA CRUZ see article
AUSTRONESIAN, SOUTH HALMAHERA-
WEST NEW GUINEA see article
AUSTRO-THAI see AUSTRONESIAN
Autaniri. Campa D.→MAIPURAN
Autu→SEPIK
Auve. Andoa Tr.→ANDEAN
Auwan→SEPIK
Aux = Akka. Chechen D.→CAUCASIAN
Auyana→EAST NEW GUINEA HIGHLANDS
Auyokawa→CHADIC
Ava = Canoeiro→TUPI
Avachiripa. Tupi Tr.→TUPI
Avade = Afade. Kotoko D.→CHADIC
Avahuguai. Tupi Tr.→TUPI
Avak. Ewondo D.→NORTH WESTERN
BANTU
Avani = Baniva→MAIPURAN
Avanti→INDIC
Avar→CAUCASIAN
Avari-Tu = Ndo Avari. Ndo D.→CENTRAL
SUDANIC
Avaro-Andi-Dido→CAUCASIAN
Avatime→CENTRAL TOGO
'Aveke→NEW CALEDONIA
Avekom = Avikam→LAGOON
Avere = Ndo Avari. Ndo D.→CENTRAL
SUDANIC
Avestan→IRANIAN
Aviara. Urhobo D.→EDO
Avikam→LAGOON

Avini. Bauwaki D.→MAILU
Avokaya = Avukaya→CENTRAL SUDANIC
Avoyel. Natchez D.→MACRO-ALGONQUIAN
Avreas = Vuras→EASTERN OCEANIC
Avukaya→CENTRAL SUDANIC
Awa→EAST NEW GUINEA HIGHLANDS
Awa = Nzema→VOLTA-COMOE
Awa ?ala = Paipai→YUMAN
Awabagal = Awabakal. Wanarua D.→YUIN-KURIC
Awabakal. Wanarua D.→YUIN-KURIC
Awadhi-Bagheli. Eastern Hindi D.→INDIC
Awahu. Pawnee D.→CADDOAN
Awak→ADAMAWA
Awalama. Wedauan D.→PAPUA AUSTRONESIAN
Awan. Rek D.→EASTERN SUDANIC
Awar→BOGIA
Awara→HUON-FINISTERRE
Awe = Bideyat. Zaghawa D.→SAHARAN
Aweti→TUPI
Awi = Awiya→CUSHITIC
Awimeri. Mangbutu D.→CENTRAL SUDANIC
Awin, East→PARE-SAMO-BEAMI-BOSAVI
Awin, West→PARE-SAMO-BEAMI-BOSAVI
Awing→BANTOID
AWIN-PARE → PARE-SAMO-BEAMI-BOSAVI
Awiya→CUSHITIC
Awje = Nyao→NORTH PAPUAN
Awjilah→BERBER
AWJU = AWYU
Awmani = Ngameni. Dieri D.→DIERIC
Awngi = Awiya→CUSHITIC
Awngthim→PAMA-MARIC
Aworo. Yoruba D.→YORUBA
Awuna. Ewe D.→EWE
Awuna = Kasem→GUR
Awutu→VOLTA-COMOE
Awye = Nyao→NORTH PAPUAN
AWYU see article
Axagua. Caquetio D.→NORTHERN MAIPURAN
Axluslay = Ashushlay→MATACO
Axty. Lezghian D.→CAUCASIAN
Axusha. Dargwa D.→CAUCASIAN
Axvax→CAUCASIAN
Ayamaru→WESTERN NEW GUINEA
Ayan = Basari→WEST ATLANTIC
Ayane = Baniva→MAIPURAN
Ayawa = Yao→SOUTH EASTERN BANTU
Ayaya = Guaja. Tenetehara D.→TUPI
Ayaychuna→TACANA

Aykamteri. Waica Tr.→WAICAN
Aymara→ANDEAN
Aymasa = Aaimasa. Kunama D.→CHARI-NILE
Aymelle. Soddo D.→SEMITIC
Ayo = Yao→SOUTH EASTERN BANTU
Ayom→BOGIA
Ayoman→JIRARAN
Ayomano = Ayoman→JIRARAN
Ayon→BOGIA
Ayook = Mixe→MIXE-ZOQUE
Ayrico. Correguaje D.→MACRO-TUCANOAN
Ayu→PLATEAU BENUE-CONGO
Ayuc = Mixe→MIXE-ZOQUE
Ayuru = Wayoro→TUPI
Aywe'lapc = Kwalhioqua→ATHAPASCAN-EYAK
Azer. Soninke D.→MANDE
Azer = Aser. Soninke Tr.→MANDE
Azerbaijani→TURKIC
Azjer = Azer. Soninke D.→MANDE
Azom. Kwakum D.→NORTH WESTERN BANTU
AZTEC→UTO-AZTECAN
Aztec = Nahua→UTO-AZTECAN
Azteca = Nahua→UTO-AZTECAN
AZTEC-TANOAN see article
Azumara→CARIB
Azumbo = Assumbo→BANTOID
Azumu = Kurama→PLATEAU BENUE-CONGO
Azura = Chokobo→PLATEAU BENUE-CONGO

B

Ba→CENTRAL EASTERN BANTU
Ba. Great Andamanese D.→ANDAMANESE
Ba Mali→WEST INDONESIAN
Ba'a. Roti D.→EAST INDONESIAN
Baa-da = Bale-da. Lendu D.→CENTRAL SUDANIC
Baada = Kunama→CHARI-NILE
Ba'adu. Afar-Saho D.→CUSHITIC
Baagato = Medjime. Mbimu D.→NORTH WESTERN BANTU
Baaka = Baka→CENTRAL SUDANIC
Baakpe→NORTH WESTERN BANTU
Baali = Bali→NORTH EASTERN BANTU
Baao. Bikol D.→NORTHWEST AUSTRONESIAN
Baati = Bati→NORTH WESTERN BANTU
Baato Baloi = Loi. Loi-Ngiri D.→NORTH WESTERN BANTU

Baaza = Kunama→CHARI-NILE
Baazen = Kunama→CHARI-NILE
Baba. Banda D.→EASTERN
Babadjou→BANTOID
Babal. Kari D.→ADAMAWA
Babalia→CENTRAL SUDANIC
Babanki = Kidzom→BANTOID
Babar. Leti D.→MOLUCCAN
Babatana. Sengan D.→NORTHWESTERN
　AND CENTRAL SOLOMONS
Babayana→TACANA
Babeda = Western Bira→NORTH EASTERN
　BANTU
Babera = Western Bira→NORTH EASTERN
　BANTU
Babeyru = Abulu. Mangbetu D.→CENTRAL
　SUDANIC
Babila = Western Bira→NORTH EASTERN
　BANTU
Babines. Carrier Tr.→ATHAPASCAN-EYAK
Babinga→EASTERN
Babir = Babur. Bura Tr.→CHADIC
Babira = Western Bira→NORTH EASTERN
　BANTU
Babok = Bok. Manjaku D.→WEST ATLAN-
　TIC
Babong = Bafo. Mbo D.→NORTH WESTERN
　BANTU
Babouantou→BANTOID
Ba-Buche = Butawa→PLATEAU　BENUE-
　CONGO
'Babukur. Boguru D.→CENTRAL WESTERN
　BANTU
Babun. Lebei D.→ADMIRALTY—WESTERN
　ISLANDS
Babungo = Ngo→BANTOID
Babur. Bura Tr.→CHADIC
Baburr. Bura Tr.→CHADIC
Babusa = Babuza→FORMOSAN　AUSTRO-
　NESIAN
Babute = Bute→BANTOID
Babuti = Bute→BANTOID
Babuyan→NORTHWEST AUSTRONESIAN
Babuyan　Batak = Babuyan→NORTHWEST
　AUSTRONESIAN
Babuza→FORMOSAN AUSTRONESIAN
Babwa. Boazi D.→MARIND
Babylonian. Akkadian D.→SEMITIC
Bac = Bats→CAUCASIAN
'Baca. Nguni D.→SOUTH EASTERN BANTU
Bacadin. Avar D.→CAUCASIAN
Bacairi→CARIB
Bacama=Bachama→CHADIC
Bacenga→NORTH WESTERN BANTU

Bacha = Kwegu→EASTERN SUDANIC
Bachahom. Tzeltal D.→MAYAN
Bachama→CHADIC
Bachingou = Batchingou→BANTOID
Bachuma = Mekan→EASTERN SUDANIC
Bacuisso = Kwise. Kwadi Tr.→KHOISAN
Bada'→CENTRAL　AND　SOUTHERN
　CELEBES
Bada = Badawa. Jarawa D.→BANTOID
Ba-da = Bale-da. Lendu D.→CENTRAL
　SUDANIC
Bada = Kunama→CHARI-NILE
Badaga. Kannada D.→DRAVIDIAN
Badanci = Badawa. Jarawa D.→BANTOID
Badawa. Jarawa D.→BANTOID
Badawai. Kanuri Tr.→SAHARAN
Badde = Bade. Kanembu Tr.→SAHARAN
Badditu = Koyra → OMOTIC
Baddyeri = Badjiri→DIERIC
Bade→CHADIC
Bade. Kanembu Tr.→SAHARAN
Baden = Kunama→CHARI-NILE
Baderi = Badjiri→DIERIC
Badian = Badyara→WEST ATLANTIC
Badimara. Juat D.→SOUTHWEST PAMA-
　NYUNGAN
Baditu = Koyra→OMOTIC
Badjande = Zande→EASTERN
Badjaw = Badjau→NORTHWEST　AUSTRO-
　NESIAN
Badjedi = Badjiri→DIERIC
Badjela = Batjala. Dalla D.→WAKA-KABIC
Badjelang. Kitabal D.→BANDJALANGIC
Badjia = Bakja. Ewondo D.→NORTH WEST-
　ERN BANTU
Badjia = Eki→NORTH WESTERN BANTU
Badjiri→DIERIC
Badjo = Bajau→NORTHWEST　AUSTRO-
　NESIAN
Badjue = Bajue. Njem-Bajue　Tr.→NORTH
　WESTERN BANTU
Badlok.　Waimdra　D.→ADMIRALTY-
　WESTERN ISLANDS
Badoombi. Kuumu Tr.→NORTH EASTERN
　BANTU
Badou = Litime. Kposo D.→CENTRAL TOGO
Badung→MON-KHMER
Badyar = Badyara→WEST ATLANTIC
Badyara→WEST ATLANTIC
Badyaranke = Badyara→WEST ATLANTIC
Badyare = Badyara→WEST ATLANTIC
Badza→KHOISAN
Badzumbo = Assumbo→BANTOID
Baegwa. Zimakani D.→MARIND

Baele = Bideyat. Zaghawa D.→SAHARAN
Baelelea. Toqabaita D.→EASTERN OCEANIC
BAENA see article
Baengu. Toqabaita D.→EASTERN OCEANIC
Baenna = Baena
ba-Enya = Ena→NORTH EASTERN BANTU
Bafa'ndji = Fanji→BANTOID
Bafang→BANTOID
Bafaw = Bafo. Mbo D.→NORTH WESTERN
    BANTU
BAFIA→NORTH WESTERN BANTU
Bafia = Kpa→NORTH WESTERN BANTU
Bafo. Mbo D.→NORTH WESTERN BANTU
Bafok = Avak. Ewondo D.→NORTH WEST-
    ERN BANTU
Bafou→BANTOID
Bafoussam→BANTOID
Bafreng = Nkwen. Mandankwe D.→BANTOID
Bafu = Bafut→BANTOID
Bafuk = Avak.   Ewondo   D.→NORTH
    WESTERN BANTU
Bafum→BANTOID
Bafumbum, Western = Fungom→BANTOID
Bafumbwa. Ruanda D.→NORTH EASTERN
    BANTU
Bafut→BANTOID
Bafwa Ndaka. Bali D.→NORTH EASTERN
    BANTU
Bafwagada.   Western   Bira   D.→NORTH
    EASTERN BANTU
Baga = Gbaga. Banda D.→EASTERN
Baga, Black = Mbulungish→WEST ATLAN-
    TIC
Baga Monson = Mbulungish→WEST ATLAN-
    TIC
Baga Binari→WEST ATLANTIC
Baga Fore = Mbulungish→WEST ATLANTIC
Baga Koga→WEST ATLANTIC
Baga Maduri→WEST ATLANTIC
Baga Mboteni→WEST ATLANTIC
Baga Sitemu→WEST ATLANTIC
Baga Sobane→WEST ATLANTIC
Bagaces. Pipil D.→UTO-AZTECAN
Bagam→BANTOID
Bagandou = Ngando-Kota→NORTH WEST-
    ERN BANTU
Bagba. Gbaya Tr.→EASTERN
Bagbo = Nyangbo→CENTRAL TOGO
Baghati. Western Pahari D.→INDIC
Baghirmi = Bagirmi→CENTRAL SUDANIC
Baghtan. Mongul D.→MONGOLIAN
BAGIRMI→CENTRAL SUDANIC
Bagirmi→CENTRAL SUDANIC
Bagis. Ingassana Tr.→CHARI-NILE

Bagnoun = Banyun→WEST ATLANTIC
Bago→GUR
Bagobo→NORTHWEST AUSTRONESIAN
Bagoi→DAGA
Bagu→WORORAN
Baguaja→TACANA
Baguajairi = Baguaja→TACANA
Baguirme = Bagirmi→CENTRAL SUDANIC
Bagulal→CAUCASIAN
Bagundji. Kula D.→PAMA-NYUNGAN
Bagwet = Pok. Nandi D.→EASTERN SU-
    DANIC
Bah Malei = Ba Mali→WEST INDONESIAN
Baha = Batui→CENTRAL AND SOUTHERN
    CELEBES
Baham→WESTERN NEW GUINEA
Bahanga-la = Pangkala→YURA
Bahasa Eti = Liang. Ambonese D.→MOLUC-
    CAN
Bahasa Gebi = Minyafuin→SOUTH HALMA-
    HERA AUSTRONESIAN
Bahasa Indonesia. Malay D.→WEST INDO-
    NESIAN
Bahe. Bengali D.→INDIC
'Bahema. Lendu D.→CENTRAL SUDANIC
Bahinemo→SEPIK
Bahing→GYARUNG-MISHMI
Bahkunji = Bagundji. Kula D.→PAMA-
    NYUNGAN
Bahkunjy = Bagundji. Kula D.→PAMA-
    NYUNGAN
Bahnar→MON-KHMER
BAHNARIC→MON-KHMER
Bahnbi = Banbai. Kumbainggar D.→KUM-
    BAINGGARIC
Bahroonjee = Parundji. Kula D.→PAMA-
    NYUNGAN
Bahumono = Kohumono→CROSS RIVER
    BENUE-CONGO
Bahumunu = Kohumono→CROSS RIVER
    BENUE-CONGO
Bahun = Banyun→WEST ATLANTIC
Bahuna. Cubeo D.→MACRO-TUCANOAN
Bai→EASTERN
Bai = Mbai→CENTRAL SUDANIC
Baiap = South Ambryn→EASTERN OCEANIC
Baibai→NORTH NEW GUINEA
Baidumba.   Peri   D.→NORTH   EASTERN
    BANTU
Baigo = Baygo.   Daju   D.→EASTERN
    SUDANIC
Bailgu = Bailko→NGAYARDA
Bailko→NGAYARDA
Baima = Batanga-Bima. Lundu D.→NORTH

WESTERN BANTU
Baining→NEW BRITAIN
Bainouk = Banyun→WEST ATLANTIC
Bainuk = Banyun→WEST ATLANTIC
Baiong = Bayungu →KANYARA
Baiso→CUSHITIC
BAISO-SOMALOID→CUSHITIC
Bait. Oirat D.→MONGOLIAN
Baitsi→BOUGAINVILLE
Baiung = Bayungu→KANYARA
Baiyer Enga = Kyaka. Enga D.→EAST NEW
  GUINEA HIGHLANDS
Baja = Gbaya→EASTERN
Bajama. Mumuye D.→ADAMAWA
Bajao = Bajau→NORTHWEST AUSTRO-
  NESIAN
Bajau→NORTHWEST AUSTRONESIAN
Bajaygəl. Askun D.→NURISTANI
Bajieng. Chrau D.→MON-KHMER
Baju = Kaje→PLATEAU BENUE-CONGO
Bajue. Njem-Bajue Tr.→NORTH WESTERN
  BANTU
Bajuni = Tikuu→CENTRAL EASTERN
  BANTU
Bajut. Tatog Tr.→EASTERN SUDANIC
BAK→WEST ATLANTIC
Baka→CENTRAL SUDANIC
Baka = Ari→OMOTIC
Bakaka = Kaa. Mbo D.→NORTH WESTERN
  BANTU
Bakaka = Mwahet. Mbo D.→NORTH
  WESTERN BANTU
Bakandi = Bagundji. Kula D.→PAMA-
  NYUNGAN
Bakango. Mayogo Tr.→EASTERN
Bakanji = Bagundji. Kula D.→PAMA-
  NYUNGAN
Bake = Bats. Berta D.→CHARI-NILE
Bakedi = Teso→EASTERN SUDANIC
Bakem. Basa Tr.→NORTH WESTERN BANTU
Bakhtiari→IRANIAN
Baki→EASTERN OCEANIC
Bakidi = Teso→EASTERN SUDANIC
Bakise = Kwise. Kwadi Tr.→KHOISAN
Bakitan = Beketan. Punan Ba D.→WEST
  INDONESIAN
Bakja. Ewondo D.→NORTH WESTERN
  BANTU
Bakka = Ari→OMOTIC
Bakka = Fala. Karanga D.→MABAN
Bakko = Ari→OMOTIC
BAKO = EAST OMOTIC→OMOTIC
Bako = Ari→OMOTIC
Bakoi. Lawangan D.—WEST INDONESIAN

Bakoko'. Basa Tr.→NORTH WESTERN
  BANTU
Bakolle = Kole. Duala D.→NORTH
  WESTERN BANTU
Bakong = Wongo→NORTH WESTERN
  BANTU
Bakoroka = Kwadi→KHOISAN
Bakosi = Koose. Mbo D.→NORTH WEST-
  ERN BANTU
Bakossi = Koose. Mbo D.→NORTH WEST-
  ERN BANTU
Bakota = Mbaama→NORTH WESTERN
  BANTU
Bakou. Bafang D.→BANTOID
Bakovi→NORTHEAST NEW GUINEA
  AUSTRONESIAN
Bakpinka→CROSS RIVER BENUE-CONGO
Baksa. Hoanya D.→FORMOSAN AUSTRO-
  NESIAN
Baksan. Circassian D.→CAUCASIAN
Bakuise = Kwise. Kwadi Tr.→KHOISAN
Bakuli = Kulung →BANTOID
Bakulu = Kulung→BANTOID
Bakum = Kwakum→NORTH WESTERN
  BANTU
Bakun. Kankanay D.→NORTHWEST AUS-
  TRONESIAN
Bakundu. Lundu D.→NORTH WESTERN
  BANTU
'Bakundumu. Bali D.→NORTH EASTERN
  BANTU
Bakuo = Bokue. Bakwe Tr.→KRU
Bakutu. Mong-Nkundo D.→NORTH WEST-
  ERN BANTU
Bakuumu = Badoombi. Kuumu Tr.→NORTH
  EASTERN BANTU
Bakwa-Luntu. Songe D.→CENTRAL WEST-
  ERN BANTU
Bakwe→KRU
Bakwele = Bekwil. Konabem D.→NORTH
  WESTERN BANTU
Bakwiri = Baakpe → NORTH WESTERN
  BANTU
Bakwisso = Kwise. Kwadi Tr.→KHOISAN
Bakwo = Bakwe→KRU
Balaaben = Boritsu→JUKUNOID
Balaban = Tadyawan→NORTHWEST AUS-
  TRONESIAN
Balaesan→NORTHERN CELEBES
Balaisang = Balaesan → NORTHERN CELE-
  BES
Balait. Sarawak Murut D.→WEST INDO-
  NESIAN
Balali = Lohorong→GYARUNG-MISHMI

Balambu = Barambu→EASTERN

Balangamida = Jaitmathang → PAMA-NYUNG-AN

Balangingi. Samal D.→NORTHWEST AUSTRONESIAN

Balangnipa. Mandarese D.→CENTRAL AND SOUTHERN CELEBES

Balant = Balanta→WEST ATLANTIC

Balanta→WEST ATLANTIC

Balantak→CENTRAL AND SOUTHERN CELEBES

Balante = Balanta→WEST ATLANTIC

Balantian. Land Dayak D.→WEST INDONESIAN

Balardong. Juat D.→SOUTHWEST PAMA-NYUNGAN

Balawa = Bale. Great Andamanese D.→ANDAMANESE

Balbalasang = Kalinga→NORTHWEST AUSTRONESIAN

Balbalasang-Ginaang. Kalinga D.→NORTHWEST AUSTRONESIAN

Balda→CHADIC

Baldam = Baymuna. Miskito D.→MISUMALPAN

Bale. Great Andamanese D.→ANDAMANESE

Bale = Lendu→CENTRAL SUDANIC

Bale-da. Lendu D.→CENTRAL SUDANIC

Balega = Lendu→CENTRAL SUDANIC

Balegete→BANTOID

Baleko. Bete Tr.→KRU

Balendru = Lendu→CENTRAL SUDANIC

Balep. Ndoe D.→BANTOID

Baler→NORTHWEST AUSTRONESIAN

Baler Dumagat = Baler→NORTHWEST AUSTRONESIAN

Balese = Lese. Mamvu-Efe D.→CENTRAL SUDANIC

Balessing. Bomougoun-Bamenjou D.→BANTOID

Baletha = Zelmamu→EASTERN SUDANIC

Balethi = Zelmamu→EASTERN SUDANIC

Balgoo = Bailko→NGAYARDA

Balgu = Bailko→NGAYARDA

Bali→NORTH EASTERN BANTU

Bali→NORTH WESTERN BANTU

Bali. Hatsa D.→KHOISAN

Bali. Yendang D.→ADAMAWA

Bali = Boa→NORTH WESTERN BANTU

Bali of Bali Town = Ngaaka→BANTOID

'Bali'ba. Moru D.→CENTRAL SUDANIC

Baliet = Paliet. Rek D.→EASTERN SUDANIC

Balika. Western Bira D.→NORTH EASTERN BANTU

Balimba = Bali'ba. Moru D.→CENTRAL SUDANIC

Balinese→WEST INDONESIAN

Balingian. Melanau D.→WEST INDONESIAN

Balkar. Karachay D.→TURKIC

Balkhar-Tsalakan = Balxar-Calakan. Lak D.→CAUCASIAN

Ballanta = Balanta→WEST ATLANTIC

Ballante = Balanta→WEST ATLANTIC

Ballardong = Balardong. Juat D.→SOUTHWEST PAMA-NYUNGAN

Ballerdokking = Balardong. Juat D.→SOUTHWEST PAMA-NYUNGAN

Ballo-Kai-Pomo = Pomo→POMO

Baloba = Likila → NORTH WESTERN BANTU

Balobo = Lobo. Mabaale D.→NORTH WESTERN BANTU

Balochi→IRANIAN

Baloi = Loi. Loi-Ngiri D.→NORTH WESTERN BANTU

Balom = Fa'→NORTH WESTERN BANTU

Balondo = Bafo. Mbo D.→NORTH WESTERN BANTU

Balong→NORTH WESTERN BANTU

Balong, North = Kitwii. Nyang D.→BANTOID

Balong, South = Balong→NORTH WESTERN BANTU

Baloum→BANTOID

Balsapuertino = Yamorai. Chayahuita D.→ANDEAN

Balta. Walamo Tr.→OMOTIC

Balti. West Tibetan D.→TIBETAN

Balti = Balti. West Tibetan D.→TIBETAN

BALTIC see article

BALTO-FINNIC = FINNIC→URALIC

Balu = Loma→MANDE

Baluan→ADMIRALTY-WESTERN ISLANDS

Baluchi = Balochi→IRANIAN

Balud. Bilaan D.→NORTHWEST AUSTRONESIAN

BaLumbi = Lombi. Mangbetu D.→CENTRAL SUDANIC

Balundu = Lundu → NORTH WETSERN BANTU

Balung = Balong → NORTH WESTERN BANTU

Baluombila. Poke Tr.→NORTH WESTERN BANTU

Balxar-Calakan. Lak D.→CAUCASIAN

Bam→HUON-FINISTERRE

Bama = Burmese→BURMESE-LOLO

Bama = Nagumi→BANTOID

Bama-caka = Burmese→BURMESE-LOLO

Bamaha→BANTOID
Bamali→BANTOID
Bamana. Batchingou D.→BANTOID
Bamana = Bambara→MANDE
Bamanakoma = Bambara→MANDE
Bamanga = Mba→EASTERN
Bamassa→EASTERN
ba-Mbaama = Mbaama→NORTH WESTERN
    BANTU
Bambala = Burji→CUSHITIC
Bambalang = Tshirambo→BANTOID
Bambana. Sumo D.→MISUMALPAN
Bambara→MANDE
Bambara = Bambaro. Lame D.→BANTOID
Bambara Masasi = Masasi. Bambara D.→
    MANDE
Bambaranci = Bambaro. Lame D.→BANTOID
Bambaro. Lame D.→BANTOID
Bambatana = Babatan. Sengan D.→NORTH-
    WESTERN AND CENTRAL SOLO-
    MONS
Bambeiro = Mbamba→CENTRAL WEST-
    ERN BANTU
Bambili = Mbili. Mandankwe D.→BANTOID
Bambisa = Mambisa. Lendu D.→CENTRAL
    SUDANIC
Bambita = Bumbita Arapesh→TORRICELLI
Bambo = Ambo. Lala D.→CENTRAL EAST-
    ERN BANTU
Bambodo. Mangbutu D.→CENTRAL SU-
    DANIC
Bamboko = Bomboko→NORTH WESTERN
    BANTU
Bambole, Pseudo- = Fuma→NORTH WEST-
    ERN BANTU
Bamboo Spanish→ROMANCE
Bambuba = Mvu'ba. Mamvu-Efe D.→CEN-
    TRAL SUDANIC
Bambui = Mbui. Mandankwe D.→BANTOID
Bambuku = Bomboko→NORTH WESTERN
    BANTU
Bambulewe = Awing→BANTOID
Bambur = Kulung→BANTOID
Bambuti. Mbuti Tr.→NORTH EASTERN
    BANTU
Ba-Mbutu = Butawa→PLATEAU BENUE-
    CONGO
Bambutuku = Bvanuma. Huku D.→NORTH
    EASTERN BANTU
Bameka. Bomougoun-Bamenjou D.→BANTOID
Bamekon = Nkom→BANTOID
Bamembila = Mambila→BANTOID
Bamendiinda→BANTOID
Bamendjina = Bamendiinda→BANTOID

Bamendjou = Bamougoun-Bamenjou→BAN-
    TOID
Bamenkombit→BANTOID
Bamenkoumbit = Bamenkombit→BANTOID
Bamenyam→BANTOID
Bamessing = Kensense→BANTOID
Bameta = Menemo→BANTOID
Bamigua = Pamigua→EQUATORIAL
BAMILEKE→BANTOID
Baminge = Ngi→BANTOID
Bamitaba = Mbomotaba→NORTH WESTERN
    BANTU
Bamoa. Cahita D.→UTO-AZTECAN
Bamok. Upper Mundani D.→BANTOID
Bamongo = Busooŋ→NORTH WESTERN
    BANTU
Bamoun→BANTOID
BAMU AND TURAMA RIVERS→CEN-
    TRAL AND SOUTH NEW GUINEA
Bamun = Bamoun→BANTOID
Bamungup = Bomougoun-Bamenjou→BAN-
    TOID
Bamunka = Muka→BANTOID
Bamunkum→BANTOID
Bamvele = Bebele → NORTH WESTERN
    BANTU
Bamvuba = Mvu'ba. Mamvu-Efe D.→CEN-
    TRAL SUDANIC
Bana. Bafang D.→BANTOID
Banaa. Masa D.→CHADIC
BANAGIC → NORTHWEST AUSTRONE-
    SIAN
Banaka. Batanga D.→NORTH WESTERN
    BANTU
Banana = Banaa. Masa D.→CHADIC
Banana = Hoho. Musei D.→CHADIC
Banara→BOGIA
Banaro→BOGIA
Banata = Baniata→CENTRAL MELANESIAN
Banaue. Kiangan D.→NORTHWEST AUS-
    TRONESIAN
Banawaw = Banuauon. Bukidnon D. →
    NORTHWEST AUSTRONISIAN
Banbai. Kumbainggar D.→KUMBAINGGA-
    RIC
Banda→EASTERN
Banda→EAST INDONESIAN
Banda. Achinese D.→WEST INDONESIAN
Bandar-Abbasi. Persian D.→IRANIAN
Bandawa→JUKUNOID
Bandem→BANTOID
Bandi = Gbandi. Mende D.→MANDE
Bandial. Diola D.→WEST ATLANTIC
Bandjalang = Badjelang. Kitabal D.→BAND-

JALANGIC
Bandjalang = Bandjerang→PAMA NYUNGAN
BANDJALANGIC see article
Bandjerang→PAMA-NYUNGAN
Bandjigali. Kula D.→PAMA-NYUNGAN
Bandjin→PAMA-MARIC
Bandjoun-Baham→BANTOID
Bando. Southern Epera D.→CHOCO
Bandobo→BANTOID
Bandogo. Dyimini D.→GUR
Bandzabi = Nzebi → NORTH WESTERN
    BANTU
Bandzogi = Zotung→NAGA-KUKI-CHIN
Bane = Bene. Bulu D.→NORTH WESTERN
    BANTU
Baneka = Mbo→NORTH WESTERN BANTU
Banen→NORTH WESTERN BANTU
Banen. Banen Tr.→NORTH WESTERN
    BANTU
Banend = Banen → NORTH WESTERN
    BANTU
Banga. Puyuma D.→FORMOSAN AUSTRO-
    NESIAN
Bangad. Bontok D.→NORTHWEST AUSTRO-
    NESIAN
Bangala = Mangala. Losengo D.→NORTH
    WESTERN BANTU
Bangala = Pangkala→YURA
Bangalam = Murle→EASTERN SUDANIC
Bangando. Gbaya Tr.→EASTERN
Bangandou = Ngando-Kota→NORTH WEST-
    ERN BANTU
Bangangte = Bangante→BANTOID
Bangante→BANTOID
Bangaru. Western Hindi D.→INDIC
Bangatu, North = Medjime. Mbimu D.→
    NORTH WESTERN BANTU
Bangawa → Lyase-ne→PLATEAU BENUE-
    CONGO
Bangba→EASTERN
'Bangbinda = Ngbinda→CENTRAL WEST-
    ERN BANTU
Bangela = Likila → NORTH WESTERN
    BANTU
Bangelima, Pseudo- = Angba→NORTH WEST-
    ERN BANTU
Banggai → CENTRAL AND SOUTHERN
    CELEBES
Banggakoro→CENTRAL AND SOUTHERN
    CELEBES
Banggala = Pangkala→YURA
Bangi. Ngbandi Tr.→EASTERN
Bangi = Bobangi → NORTH WESTERN
    BANTU

Bangi = Lyase-ne→PLATEAU BENUE-
    CONGO
BANGI-NTUMBA → NORTH WESTERN
    BANTU
Bangla = Bengali→INDIC
Banglulu→NORTHWEST AUSTRONESIAN
Bangni = Dafla→GYARUNG-MISHMI
Bango = Bali→NORTH EASTERN BANTU
Bango = Boa→NORTH WESTERN BANTU
Bangobango→NORTH EASTERN BANTU
Bangomo = Ngom. Kele D.→NORTH WEST-
    ERN BANTU
Bangon. Buhid D.→NORTHWEST AUSTRO-
    NESIAN
Bangon = Batangan→NORTHWEST AUS-
    TRONESIAN
Bangoro. Maewo D.→EASTERN OCEANIC
Bangot = Bangon. Buhid D.→NORTHWEST
    AUSTRONESIAN
Bangot = Batangan→NORTHWEST AUS-
    TRONESIAN
Bangou = Bangwa→BANTOID
Bangoua→BANTOID
Bangoua-Batoufam = Bangwa→BANTOID
Bangu→CENTRAL AND SOUTH NEW
    GUINEA
Bangubangu = Bangobango→NORTH EAST-
    ERN BANTU
Bangwa→BANTOID
Banhum = Banyun→WEST ATLANTIC
Banhun = Banyun→WEST ATLANTIC
Ba'ni = Ngaaka→BANTOID
Baniata→CENTRAL MELANESIAN
Baniua. Cubeo D.→MACRO-TUCANOAN
Baniva→MAIPURAN
BANIVA = IZANENI→NORTHERN MAI-
    PURAN
Baniva Do Icana. Carutana D.→NORTHERN
    MAIPURAN
BANIVA-YAVITERO→MAIPURAN
Banjgaranj = Bandjerang→PAMA-NYUNGAN
Banjoum = Banjoun-Baham→BANTOID
Banjoun = Bandjoun-Baham→BANTOID
Banjuri→INDIC
Bankal = Bankala. Jarawa D.→BANTOID
Bankala. Jarawa D.→BANTOID
Bankalanci = Bankala. Jarawa D.→BANTOID
Bankalawa = Bankala. Jarawa D.→BANTOID
Bankara. Mundari D.→MUNDA
Bankon→NORTH WESTERN BANTU
Bankoti = Konkan Standard. Marathi D.→
    INDIC
Bankulu = Ikulu→PLATEAU BENUE-
    CONGO

Bankutu = Nkutu → NORTH WESTERN BANTU

Bankwet→BANTOID

Banna→OMOTIC

Bannack = Bannock. Northern Paiute D.→ UTO-AZTECAN

Bannock. Northern Paiute D.→UTO-AZTECAN

Banoh = Banaka. Batanga D.→NORTH WESTERN BANTU

Banoni→NORTHWESTERN AND CENTRAL SOLOMONS

Banoo. Batanga D.→NORTH WESTERN BANTU

Banpara. Tangsa D.→BODO-NAGA-KACHIN

Bansaw = Lamnso→BANTOID

Banso = Lamnso→BANTOID

Bansoa. Bomougoun-Bamenjou D.→BANTOID

Bansod = East Aglubang-Bansod. Tadyawan D.→NORTHWEST AUSTRONESIAN

Banta→WEST ATLANTIC

Bantaurang. Puyuma D.→FORMOSAN AUSTRONESIAN

Banthamurra = Punthamara→DIERIC

Bantian. Lawangan D.→WEST INDONESIAN

Bantik→HESPERONESIAN

BANTOID see article

Banton→NORTHWEST AUSTRONESIAN

BANTU PROPER see article

BANTU, NARROW = BANTU PROPER

Bantu Sabei = Syan→NORTH EASTERN BANTU

Banu = Granu. Gbaya Tr.→EASTERN

Banuanon = Banuauon. Bukidnon D.→ NORTHWEST AUSTRONESIAN

Banuaon = Banuauon. Bukidnon D.→NORTHWEST AUSTRONESIAN

Banuauon. Bukidnon D.→NORTHWEST AUSTRONESIAN

Banum→MON-KHMER

Banuwang. Lawangan D.→WEST INDONESIAN

Banyang. Bwe D.→KAREN

Banyangam. Bandjoun-Baham D.→BANTOID

Banyangi = Nyang→BANTOID

Banyin = Banyang. Bwe D.→KAREN

Banyuk = Banyun→WEST ATLANTIC

Banyun→WEST ATLANTIC

Banyung = Banyun→WEST ATLANTIC

Banza. Mabaale D.→NORTH WESTERN BANTU

Banziri = Gbanziri→EASTERN

Bao→NORTHEAST NEW GUINEA AUSTRONESIAN

Baobera. Tupi Tr.→TUPI

Baol. Serer D.→WEST ATLANTIC

Baol. Wolof D.→WEST ATLANTIC

Baonga. Buja D.→NORTH WESTERN BANTU

Baoule = Baule. Anyi D.→VOLTA-COMOE

Bape = Bapeŋ→WEST ATLANTIC

Bapeŋ→WEST ATLANTIC

Bapi→BANTOID

Bapo. Bakwe Tr.→KRU

Bapoko. Batanga D.→NORTH WESTERN BANTU

Bapouantou = Babouantou→BANTOID

Bara→EAST NEW GUINEA HIGHLANDS

Bara. Bolewa D.→CHADIC

Bara. Malagasy D.→WEST INDONESIAN

Bara. Tucano Tr.→MACRO-TUCANOAN

Bara = Napu→CENTRAL AND SOUTHERN CELEBES

Baraan = Bilaan→NORTHWEST AUSTRONESIAN

Baraan Kalkus = Bok. Manjaku D.→WEST ATLANTIC

Barababaraba = Baraparapa→YOTAYOTIC

Barabaig = Bajut. Tatog Tr.→EASTERN SUDANIC

Barabaik = Bajut. Tatog Tr.→EASTERN SUDANIC

Baraban = Bajut. Tatog Tr.→EASTERN SUDANIC

Baraboy = West Aglubang. Tadyawan D.→ NORTHWEST AUSTRONESIAN

Barada. Mandandanji D.→PAMA-MARIC

Baraguyu. Maasai Tr.→EASTERN SUDANIC

Barai→KOIARI

Barai→NORTHEAST NEW GUINEA AUSTRONESIAN

Barain = Barein. Sokoro D.→CHADIC

Barambo = Barambu→EASTERN

Barambu→EASTERN

Baran. Ami D.→FORMOSAN AUSTRONESIAN

Baran = Borena. Galla D.→CUSHITIC

Barana = Borena. Galla D.→CUSHITIC

Baranago. Kerebuto D.→EASTERN OCEANIC

Baranbinja. Wongaibon D.→WIRADJURIC

Barangan = Batangan→NORTHWEST AUSTRONESIAN

Barao. Berta D.→CHARI-NILE

Baraparapa→YOTAYOTIC

Bararawa. Reshe Tr.→PLATEAU BENUE-CONGO

Barau→WESTERN NEW GUINEA

Barauana = Bare→NORTHERN MAIPURAN

Barauna = Bare→NORTHERN MAIPURAN
Barawa = Bwazza. Mbula D.→BANTOID
Barawa of Dass→CHADIC
Barawahing = Abui→TIMOR-ALOR
Barawana = Bare→NORTHERN MAIPURAN
BARBACOAN see article
Barbado = Umotina→BORORO
Barbareno. CHUMASH Tr.→HOKAN
Barbur. Bura Tr.→CHADIC
Barburr. Bura Tr.→CHADIC
Bard. Nyulnyul D.→NYULNYULAN
Barda = Bard., Nyulnyul D.→NYULNYULAN
Bardi = Bard. Nyulnyul D.→NYULNYULAN
Bardimaya. Muliara D.→KARDU
Bardojunga = Ngadjunma. Mirning D.→ MIRNINY
Barduwonga = Tjalkadjara. Kardutjara D.→ WATI
Bare→NORTHERN MAIPURAN
Bare = Bwazza. Mbula D.→BANTOID
Barea = Nara→EASTERN SUDANIC
Bare'e→CENTRAL AND SOUTHERN CELEBES
BAREIC→CENTRAL AND SOUTHERN CELEBES
Bareji→BINANDERE
Bareko = Mbo→NORTH WESTERN BANTU
Barera→BURERAN
Bareshe = Reshe→PLATEAU BENUE-CONGO
Barga = Maban→EASTERN SUDANIC
Bargista = Ormuri→IRANIAN
Bargu→GUR
Bargu-Buryat. Buryat D.→MONGOLIAN
Bargunji = Bagundji. Kula D.→PAMA-NYUNGAN
Barguzin. Buryat D.→MONGOLIAN
Bari→EASTERN SUDANIC
Bari. Solor D.→MOLUCCAN
Bari = Bai→EASTERN
Bari = Bari-Logo. Logo Tr.→CENTRAL SUDANIC
Baria = Bela→CENTRAL AND SOUTHERN CELEBES
Baria = Tawaelia→CENTRAL AND SOUTHERN CELEBES
Bariai→NORTHEAST NEW GUINEA AUSTRONESIAN
Bariba = Bargu→GUR
Baribari = Kanuri→SAHARAN
Baribi. Buhid D.→NORTHWEST AUSTRONESIAN
Baribu. Kanembu Tr.→SAHARAN
BARIC see BODO-NAGA-KACHIN

Baridzi→MAILU
Barika→KIKORI RIVER
Bari-Logo. Logo Tr.→CENTRAL SUDANIC
Barim→NORTHEAST NEW GUINEA AUSTRONESIAN
Barin. Khorcin D.→MONGOLIAN
Barindji. Kula D.→PAMA-NYUNGAN
Barinji = Parundji. Kula D.→PAMA-NYUNGAN
Bari-ti = Bari-Logo. Logo Tr.→CENTRAL SUDANIC
Barka. Kunama D.→CHARI-NILE
Barkindji = Bagundji. Kula D.→PAMA-NYUNGAN
Barkinji = Bagundji. Kula D.→PAMA-NYUNGAN
Barkungee = Bagundji. Kula D.→PAMA-NYUNGAN
Barma = Bagirmi→CENTRAL SUDANIC
Barna. Mandandanji D.→PAMA-MARIC
Barobo. Grebo Tr.→KRU
Barok = Komalu→BISMARCK ARCHIPELAGO
Barombi = Lombi → NORTH WESTERN BANTU
Baron = Ron→CHADIC
Barongee = Parundji. Kula D. → PAMA-NYUNGAN
Baroo = Bru→MON-KHMER
Barrababarraba = Baraparapa→YOTAYOTIC
Barran→NORTHWEST AUSTRONESIAN
Barrengee = Barindji. Kula D. → PAMA-NYUNGAN
Barrengee = Parundji. Kula D.→PAMA-NYUNGAN
Barrumbinya = Baranbinja. Wongaibon D.→ WIRADJURIC
Baru→INDO-PACIFIC
Barua→KUKUKUKU
Barue→NORTH WESTERN BANTU
Barue = Abui→TIMOR-ALOR
Baruga→BINANDERE
Baruh. Achinese D.→WEST INDONESIAN
Barumbi = Badoombi. Kuumu Tr.→NORTH EASTERN BANTU
Barumbi = Lombi. Mangbetu D.→CENTRAL SUDANIC
Barun = Burun→EASTERN SUDANIC
Barunga = Parundji. Kula D.→PAMA-NYUNGAN
Barunggam→WIRADJURIC
Barungi = Parundji. Kula D.→PAMA-NYUNGAN
Barwari. Zaza D.→IRANIAN

Barya = Nara→EASTERN SUDANIC
BASA→NORTH WESTERN BANTU
Basa→PLATEAU BENUE-CONGO
Basa→NORTH WESTERN BANTU
Basa = Bassa→KRU
Basa-Kaduna = Basa→PLATEAU BENUE-CONGO
Basa-Komo→PLATEAU BENUE-CONGO
Basang. Obanliku D.→CROSS RIVER BENUE-CONGO
Basanga = Uyanga→CROSS RIVER BENUE-CONGO
Basap→WEST INDONESIAN
Basari→WEST ATLANTIC
Basaridu Bandemba = Bedik→WEST ATLANTIC
Basawa = Basa→PLATEAU BENUE-CONGO
Basgali = Kati→NURISTANI
Bashamma = Bachama→CHADIC
Bashar = Basherawa→PLATEAU BENUE-CONGO
Basherawa→PLATEAU BENUE-CONGO
Bashkir→TURKIC
Bashmuric = Fayumic. Coptic D.→AFRO-ASIATIC
Bashua = Basua. Boki D.→CROSS-RIVER BENUE-CONGO
Basila→CENTRAL TOGO
Basilaki. Keheraran D.→PAPUA AUSTRONESIAN
Basili = Sere→EASTERN
Basiri = Sere→EASTERN
Baskarik→INDIC
Basketo→OMOTIC
Basoa-Basoko. Buja D.→NORTH WESTERN BANTU
Basosi = Swase. Mbo D.→NORTH WESTERN BANTU
Basque see article
Bassa→NORTH WESTERN BANTU
Bassa→KRU
Bassa-Komo = Basa-Komc→PLATEAU BENUE-CONGO
Bassa-Kwomu = Basa-Komo→PLATEAU BENUE-CONGO
Bassan. Ijo D.→IJO
Bassa-Nge. Nupe D.→NUPE-GBARI
Basso = Bassa→KRU
Bastari. Oriya D.→INDIC
Basti = Gorkhpuri. Bihari D.→INDIC
Basua. Boki D.→CROSS-RIVER BENUE-CONGO
Bat = Badawa. Jarawa D.→BANTOID
BATA→CHADIC

Bata→CHADIC
Batachi. Nupe Tr.→NUPE-GBARI
BATAK→WEST INDONESIAN
Batak = Babuyan→NORTHWEST AUSTRONESIAN
Batak, Karo = Karo→WEST INDONESIAN
Batak, Timur = Simalungun→WEST INDONESIAN
Batak, Toba = Toba→WEST INDONESIAN
Batan = Ivatan—NORTHWEST AUSTRONESIAN
Batang = Aba. Central Tibetan D.→TIBETAN
Batanga→NORTH WESTERN BANTU
Batanga-Bima. Lundu D.→NORTH WESTERN BANTU
Batangan→NORTHWEST AUSTRONESIAN
Bataxan. Dagur D.→MONGOLIAN
Batcham→BANTOID
Batchingou→BANTOID
Batem-da-kai-ee = Kato→ATHAPASCAN-EYAK
Bateng. Lower Mundani D.→BANTOID
Bati→BANTOID
Bati→NORTH WESTERN BANTU
Baticola. Tupi Tr.→TUPI
Batie→BANTOID
Batjala. Dalla D.→WAKA-KABIC
Batjan→EAST INDONESIAN
Batlux. Avar D.→CAUCASIAN
Bato. Bikol D.→NORTHWEST AUSTRONESIAN
Batongtou→BANTOID
Batonnun = Bargu→GUR
Batonu = Bargu→GUR
Batoufam. Bangoua D.→BANTOID
Batrugbu = Nyangbo→CENTRAL TOGO
Bats→CAUCASIAN
Bats = Watawit. Berta D.→CHARI-NILE
Batta = Bata→CHADIC
Battara = Nawu→YURA
Batu→BANTOID
Batu. Nias D.→WEST INDONESIAN
Batu Bla. Long Pata D.→WEST INDONESIAN
Batu Lapa. Masenrempulu D.→CENTRAL AND SOUTHERN CELEBES
Batu Sangkar-Pariangan. Minangkabau D.→WEST INDONESIAN
Batui→CENTRAL AND SOUTHERN CELEBES
Batumerah. Luhu D.→EAST INDONESIAN
Batuna→NORTHWESTERN AND CENTRAL SOLOMONS
Batwa = / /xegwe→KHOISAN
Batzulnetas = Chistochina. Ahtena D.→ATHA-

PASCAN-EYAK
Bau→BOGIA
Bauan. Fijian D.→EASTERN OCEANIC
Bauchi = Bushi→PLATEAU BENUE-CONGO
Bauihca = Bawihka. Sumo Tr.→MISUMAL-
PAN
Baukok. Kankanay D.→NORTHWEST AUS-
TRONESIAN
Baule. Anyi D.→VOLTA-COMOE
Bauma = Batanga-Bima. Lundu D.→NORTH
WESTERN BANTU
Baungshe = Haka→NAGA-KUKI-CHIN
Baure→MAIPURAN
Bauro→EASTERN OCEANIC
Bauwaki→MAILU
Bavek = Avak. Ewondo D.→NORTH WEST-
ERN BANTU
Bawahca = Bawihka. Sumo Tr.→MISUMAL-
PAN
Bawaipa→NORTHEASTERN NEW GUINEA
Bawaki = Bauwaki→MAILU
Bawera = Barera→BURERAN
Bawichtigoutek = Ojibwa→ALGONQUIAN
Bawihka. Sumo Tr.→MISUMALPAN
Bawom. Padang D.→EASTERN SUDANIC
Bawu. Lawangan D.→WEST INDONESIAN
Baxa. Karanga D.→MABAN
Baya = Gbaya→EASTERN
Baya Banou. Gbaya Tr.→EASTERN
Bayag→NORTHWEST AUSTRONESIAN
Bayaka→EASTERN
Bayaka. Gbanziri Tr.→EASTERN
Bayali. Wadja D.→WAKA-KABIC
Bayang = Nyang→BANTOID
Bayangam→BANTOID
Bayangi = Nyang→BANTOID
Bayangil = Jitajita. Djadjala D.→KULINIC
Baygo. Daju D.→EASTERN SUDANIC
Baymuna. Miskito D.→MISUMALPAN
Baymunana = Baymuna. Miskito D.→MISU-
MALPAN
Bayo = Bayyu→NORTHWEST AUSTRO-
NESIAN
Bayobiri. Ukpe D.→CROSS RIVER BENUE-
CONGO
Bayot→WEST ATLANTIC
Bayungu→KANYARA
Bayuta = Bajut. Tatog Tr.→EASTERN SU-
DANIC
Bayyo = Bayyu→NORTHWEST AUSTRO-
NESIAN
Bayyu→NORTHWEST AUSTRONESIAN
Baza = Kunama→CHARI-NILE
Baza = Ngbandi→EASTERN

Bazela. Samba D.→CENTRAL WESTERN
BANTU
Bazen = Kunama→CHARI-NILE
Bazenda = Zande→EASTERN
Be = Ong-Be→KAM-TAI
Bea = Beada. Great Andamanese D.→ANDA-
MANESE
Beach-la-Mar→GERMANIC
Beada. Great Andamanese D.→ANDA-
MANESE
Beafada = Biafada→WEST ATLANTIC
Beami→PARE-SAMO-BEAMI-BOSAVI
Bear Lake. Dogrib Tr.→ATHAPASCAN-EYAK
Bear River. Mattole D.→ATHAPASCAN-
EYAK
Beaver. Sekani D.→ATHAPASCAN-EYAK
Beba-Befang = Biba-Bifang→BANTOID
Bebedjato. Kumaju D.→BANTOID
Bebejiya = Midu. Digaru Mishmi D.→GYA-
RUNG-MISHMI
Bebele→NORTH WESTERN BANTU
Bebeli→NORTHEAST NEW GUINEA AUS-
TRONESIAN
Bebi. Obanliku D.→CROSS RIVER BENUE-
CONGO
Bebleman = Pibelmen. Juat D.→SOUTHWEST
PAMA-NYUNGAN
Becheve→BANTOID
Beda = Veda→INDIC
Bedanga = Sokoro→CHADIC
Bedauye = Beja→CUSHITIC
Bedawib. Beja Tr.→CUSHITIC
Bedawie = Beja→CUSHITIC
Bedawiye = Beja→CUSHITIC
Bedawiyet = Beja→CUSHITIC
Bedda = Veda→INDIC
Bedde = Bade→CHADIC
Beddiwell = Bidawal. Bratauolung D.→PAMA-
NYUNGAN
Bede = Bade→CHADIC
Bedengo. Nyangumarda D.→MARNGU
Bedfola = Biafada→WEST ATLANTIC
Bedik→WEST ATLANTIC
Bedja = Beja→CUSHITIC
Bedoanas→EAST INDONESIAN
Beduanda→JAKUN
Bedw = Beja→CUSHITIC
Bedya = Beja→CUSHITIC
Beege. Musgu D.→CHADIC
Beegumbul = Bigumbil→WIRADJURIC
Beeke→NORTH EASTERN BANTU
Beembe→NORTH EASTERN BANTU
Beembe = Bembe→CENTRAL WESTERN
BANTU

Beer. Padang D.→EASTERN SUDANIC
Befo:n = Nde→BANTOID
Bega. Sanana D.→EAST INDONESIAN
Bege = Njalgulgule→EASTERN SUDANIC
Begi = Njalgulgule→EASTERN SUDANIC
Begia = Beja→CUSHITIC
Bego = Baygo. Daju D.→EASTERN SUDAN-
    IC
Behe. Land Dayak D.→WEST INDONESIAN
Behoa = Besoa. Bada' D.→CENTRAL AND
    SOUTHERN CELEBES
BEIER-DIDINGA→EASTERN SUDANIC
Beili = 'Beli→CENTRAL SUDANIC
Beir = Murle→EASTERN SUDANIC
Beit Awat. Beja Tr.→CUSHITIC
Beit Maala = Beit Mala. Beja Tr.→CUSHITIC
Beit Mala. Beja Tr.→CUSHITIC
Beit Tarke. Bilin Tr.→CUSHITIC
Beit Tawke. Bilin Tr.→CUSHITIC
Beja→CUSHITIC
Beka. Peri D.→NORTH EASTERN BANTU
Bekeni. Bali D.→NORTH EASTERN BANTU
Beketan. Punan Ba D.→WEST INDONESIAN
Bekiau. Bisaya D.→WEST INDONESIAN
Beko = Baygo. Daju D.→EASTERN SUDAN-
    IC
Beko = Njalgulgule→EASTERN SUDANIC
Bekwarra→CROSS RIVER BENUE-CONGO
Bekwil. Konabem D.→NORTH WESTERN
    BANTU
Bekworra = Bekwarra→CROSS RIVER
    BENUE-CONGO
Bekworrah = Bekwarra→CROSS RIVER BE-
    NUE-CONGO
Bela→CENTRAL AND SOUTHERN CELE-
    BES
Belacoola = Bella Coola→SALISH
Belana'u = Melanau→WEST INDONESIAN
Belang. Solor D.→MOLUCCAN
Belante = Balanta→WEST ATLANTIC
Belantsea = Crow→SIOUAN
Belanya. Tumma Tr.→KORDOFANIAN
Belein = Bilin→CUSHITIC
Belep. Nenema D.→NEW CALEDONIA
Belhoola = Bella Coola→SALISH
'Beli→CENTRAL SUDANIC
Beli→TORRICELLI
Belimbing. Pangan D.→SEMANG
Belingo. Banda D.→EASTERN
Bella Bella→WAKASHAN
Bella Coola→SALISH
Bellacoola = Bella Coola→SALISH
Bellechoolo = Bella Coola→SALISH
Belleh = Kwaa→KRU

Bellona. Rennellese D.→POLYNESIAN
Beloh = Karau. Lawangan D.→WEST INDO-
    NESIAN
Belom = Maporese→WEST INDONESIAN
Belorussian = Bielorussian→SLAVIC
Beltìr. Khakas D.→TURKIC
Belu. Timorese D.→EAST INDONESIAN
Bema = Moba→GUR
BEMBA→CENTRAL EASTERN BANTU
Bemba→CENTRAL EASTERN BANTU
Bembe→CENTRAL WESTERN BANTU
Bembe. Mabaale D.→NORTH WESTERN
    BANTU
Bembe = Beembe→NORTH EASTERN BAN-
    TU
BEMBE-KABWARI → NORTH EASTERN
    BANTU
Bembi→INDO-PACIFIC
Bembola = Burji→CUSHITIC
Bemeringal = Ngarigo→YUIN-KURIC
Bemili. Bali D.→NORTH EASTERN BANTU
Bena→CENTRAL EASTERN BANTU
Benaadir = Benadir. Somali Tr.→CUSHITIC
Benabena→EAST NEW GUINEA HIGH-
    LANDS
Benadir. Somali Tr.→CUSHITIC
Benahu. Pipikoro D.→CENTRAL AND
    SOUTHERN CELEBES
BENA-KINGA→CENTRAL EASTERN BAN-
    TU
Benarsi = Purbi. Bihari D.→INDIC
Benbakanjamata = Adnyamathana. Wailpi D.→
    YURA
Bencho→OMOTIC
Bende→NORTH EASTERN BANTU
Bende = Gbwende. Banda D.→EASTERN
Bendeghe. Ekoi D.→BANTOID
Bendi. Bete D.→CROSS RIVER BENUE-
    CONGO
Bendi = Gbwende. Banda D.→EASTERN
Bendiapa→MACRO-TUCANOAN
Bene. Bulu D.→NORTH WESTERN BANTU
Benesho = Bencho→OMOTIC
Benga→NORTH WESTERN BANTU
Bengali→INDIC
Benge = Bati→NORTH WESTERN BANTU
Bengkulu = Benkulan→WEST INDONESIAN
Bengoi→EAST INDONESIAN
Benguet-Igorot = Inibaloy → NORTHWEST
    AUSTRONESIAN
Beni. Nupe Tr.→NUPE-GBARI
Beni Amer = Beni Amir. Beja Tr.→CUSHITIC
Beni Amir. Beja Tr.→CUSHITIC
Beni Amir. Tigre Tr.→SEMITIC

Benkulan→WEST INDONESIAN
Bentenan→HESPERONESIAN
Bentuni-Wamesa. Wandamen D.→MOLUC-
CAN
Benu. Nupe Tr.→NUPE-GBARI
BENUE-CHAD = CHADIC
BENUE-CONGO PHYLUM see article
BENUE-CONGO, CROSS RIVER see article
BENUE-CONGO, PLATEAU see article
Beo = Angba→NORTH WESTERN BANTU
Beothuc = Beothuk
Beothuk see article
Bepour→BOGIA
Bera. Southeastern Sakai D.→SAKAI
Berang. Land Dayak D.→WEST INDONE-
SIAN
Berawan. Long Pata D.→WEST INDONE-
SIAN
Berba→GUR
BERBER see article
Berdama = Dama. Nama D.→KHOISAN
Berein. Sokoro D.→CHADIC
Berepo→BINANDERE
Bergit = Wadai-Bergit. Mubi D.→CHADIC
Beri-aa = Zaghawa→SAHARAN
Beribi = Baribi. Buhid D.→NORTHWEST
AUSTRONESIAN
Berik = Berrik→NORTH PAPUAN
Berin = Jumjum. Maban D.→EASTERN SU-
DANIC
Berluppa = Pilatapa→DIERIC
'Berom = Birom→PLATEAU BENUE-CON-
GO
Berri = Pari. Anuak Tr.→EASTERN SUDAN-
IC
Berri = Zaghawa→SAHARAN
Berriait = Barindji. Kula D.→PAMA-NYUNG-
AN
Berrik→NORTH PAPUAN
Berringin = Brinken→DALY
BERTA→CHARI-NILE
Berta→CHARI-NILE
Berti. Zaghawa D.→SAHARAN
Besema = Bachama→CHADIC
Beseme→CHADIC
Besemme = Beseme→CHADIC
Beshada = Banna→OMOTIC
Besisi. Southern Sakai D.→SAKAI
Beslenei. Circassian D.→CAUCASIAN
Besoa. Bada'd.→CENTRAL AND SOUTHERN
CELEBES
Bessali. Lower Mundani D.→BANTOID
Besserman. Votyak D.→URALIC
Bet Taqwe = Beit Tawke. Bilin Tr.→CUSHITIC

Bet Tarqe = Beit Tarke. Bilin Tr.→CUSHITIC
Beta = Kuap. Land Dayak D.→WEST INDO-
NESIAN
Betchati. Lower Mundani D.→BANTOID
Bete→CROSS-RIVER BENUE-CONGO
Bete→KRU
Bete = Bata→CHADIC
Betegbo = Bete→KRU
Bethuck = Beothuk
Bethuk = Beothuk
Betibe = Metyibo→VOLTA-COMOE
BETOYAN = TUCANOAN→MACRO-TU-
CANOAN
Betsileo. Malagasy D.→WEST INDONESIAN
Betsimisaraka. Malagasy D.→WEST INDONE-
SIAN
Betsinga = Bacenga→NORTH WESTERN
BANTU
Bette = Bete→CROSS RIVER BENUE-CON-
GO
Betzinga = Bacenga→NORTH WESTERN
BANTU
Beve = Busi. Obanliku D.→CROSS RIVER
BENUE-CONGO
Bezanozano. Malagasy D.→WEST INDO-
NESIAN
Bezhita→CAUCASIAN
Bhathela = Anawla. Gujarati D.→INDIC
Bhatri. Oriya D.→INDIC
Bhawnagari = Gohilwadi. Gujarati D.→INDIC
Bhili→INDIC
Bhojpuri. Bihari D.→INDIC
Bhojpuriya = Bhojpuri. Bihari D.→INDIC
Bhotanta = Central Tibetan→TIBETAN
Bhotia see TIBETAN
Bhotia = Murmi→GYARUNG-MISHMI
Bhramu→GYARUNG-MISHMI
Bhumij. Mundari D.→MUNDA
Bi = Boun→GUNWINGGUAN
BIA = WEST CENTRAL→VOLTA-COMOE
Biabanaki. Persian D.→IRANIAN
Biada = Beada. Great Andamanese D.→
ANDAMANESE
Biadju = Ngaju→WEST INDONESIAN
Biafada→WEST ATLANTIC
Biafar = Biafada→WEST ATLANTIC
Biagi→KOIARI
Biak→MOLUCCAN
Biak. Boazi D.→MARIND
Biaka→NORTH NEW GUINEA
BIAKIC→MOLUCCAN
Biakpan→CROSS RIVER BENUE-CONGO
Biakumbo. Mbimu Tr.→NORTH WESTERN
BANTU

Bian→MARIND
Biangai→GOILALA
Bianjit. Tatog Tr.→EASTERN SUDANIC
Biaru→GOILALA
Biat. Central Mnong D.→MON-KHMER
Biate→NAGA-KUKI-CHIN
Biba-Bifang→BANTOID
Bibbulmun = Pibelmen. Juat D.→SOUTH-
    WEST PAMA-NYUNGAN
Bibo→PARE-SAMO-BEAMI-BOSAVI
Bibulman = Pibelmen. Juat D.→SOUTHWEST
    PAMA-NYUNGAN
Bichelemar = New Caledonia Pidgin. French
    Creole D.→ROMANCE
Bicol = Bikol→NORTHWEST AUSTRONE-
    SIAN
Bidawal. Bratauolung D.→PAMA-NYUNGAN
Bidea. Tebu Tr.→SAHARAN
Bideyat. Zaghawa D.→SAHARAN
Bidhawal = Bidawal. Bratauolung D.→PAMA-
    NYUNGAN
Bidia. Karendala D.→DIERIC
Bidjera = Pitjara. Mandandanji D.→PAMA-
    MARIC
Bidjuki = Mpiembo. Mbimu D.→NORTH
    WESTERN BANTU
Biduelli = Bidawal. Bratauolung D.→PAMA-
    NYUNGAN
Bidwell = Bidawal. Bratauolung D.→PAMA-
    NYUNGAN
Bidwelli = Bidawal. Bratauolung D.→PAMA-
    NYUNGAN
Bidwill = Bidawal. Bratauolung D.→PAMA-
    NYUNGAN
'Bidyo→CHADIC
Bidyogo = Bijago→WEST ATLANTIC
Bi-Dyola = Biafada→WEST ATLANTIC
Bidyola = Biafada→WEST ATLANTIC
Bielorussian→SLAVIC
Bienescio = Bencho→OMOTIC
Bienesho = Bencho→OMOTIC
Bierebo. Tasiko D.→EASTERN OCEANIC
Bieri→EASTERN OCEANIC
Bieria = Bieri→EASTERN OCEANIC
Big Bay = Marina→NORTHWESTERN NEW
    HEBRIDES
Biga→SOUTH HALMAHERA AUSTRONE-
    SIAN
Bigambal = Bigumbil→WIRADJURIC
Bigambul = Bigumbil→WIRADJURIC
BIGIC→SOUTH HALMAHERA AUSTRO-
    NESIAN
Bigola = Badyara→WEST ATLANTIC
Bigumbil→WIRADJURIC

Bigur = Ngalakan→GUNWINGGUAN
Bih→WEST INDONESIAN
Biha→EAST INDONESIAN
Bihari→INDIC
Bihbihani. Persian D.→IRANIAN
Biisa→CENTRAL EASTERN BANTU
Bijago→WEST ATLANTIC
Bijai = Bandjin→PAMA-MARIC
Bijogo = Bijago→WEST ATLANTIC
Bijougot = Biuago→WEST ATLANTIC
Bijuga = Bijago→WEST ATLANTIC
Bikol→NORTHWEST AUSTRONESIAN
Bikom = Nkom→BANTOID
Bikuap = Kuap. Land Dayak D.→WEST
    INDONESIAN
Bikum. Mbimu Tr.→NORTH WESTERN BAN-
    TU
Bila→NORTH EASTERN BANTU
Bila. Tsonga D.→SOUTH EASTERN BANTU
Bila, Forest = Bila→NORTH EASTERN BAN-
    TU
Bilaan→NORTHWEST AUSTRONESIAN
Bila-an = Bilaan→NORTHWEST AUSTRO-
    NESIAN
Bilakura = Parawen→BOGIA
Bilala. Kuka D.→CENTRAL SUDANIC
Bilanes = Bilaan→NORTHWEST AUSTRO-
    NESIAN
Bilauum = Kanakuru→CHADIC
Bilayn = Bilin→CUSHITIC
Bilba. Roti D.→EAST INDONESIAN
Bile→BANTOID
Bile. Zande D.→EASTERN
Bilechula = Bella Coola→SALISH
Bileki = Nakanai → NORTHEAST NEW
    GUINEA AUSTRONESIAN
Bilen = Bilin→CUSHITIC
Bileninya = Bilin→CUSHITIC
Bileno = Bilin→CUSHITIC
Bili. Peri D.→NORTH EASTERN BANTU
Biliau→NORTHEAST NEW GUINEA AUS-
    TRONESIAN
BILIC→NORTHWEST AUSTRONESIAN
Bilin→CUSHITIC
Bilingo = Belingo. Banda D.→EASTERN
Bilkula = Bella Coola→SALISH
Billanchi = Bile→BANTOID
Billanci = Bile→BANTOID
Bille = Bile→BANTOID
Billechoola = Bella Coola→SALISH
Billechoula = Bella Coola→SALISH
Billechula = Bella Coola→SALISH
Biloxi→SIOUAN
Bilpai = Birpai. Worimi D.→YUIN-KURIC

Bilqula = Bella Coola→SALISH
Biltum = BURUSHASKI
Bilua→CENTRAL MELANESIAN
Bima→EAST INDONESIAN
Bimbia = Su→NORTH WESTERN BANTU
Bimin→OK
Bimoba = Moba→GUR
Binahari→MAILU
Binandele = Binandere→BINANDERE
BINANDERE see article
Binatangan = Batangan→NORTHWEST AUS-
TRONESIAN
Binbarnja = Adnyamathana. Wailpi D.→YURA
Bindabu = Pintubi. Kardutjara D.→WATI
Bindal. Ilba D.→PAMA-MARIC
Bindi = Gbwende. Banda D.→EASTERN
Bindibu = Pintubi. Kardutjara D.→WATI
Bindiga = Bendeghe. Ekoi D.→BANTOID
Bindja = Binza. Ngombe D.→NORTH WEST-
ERN BANTU
Bindji = Binji→CENTRAL WESTERN BAN-
TU
Bine→ORIOMO RIVER
Binga. Yulu-Binga D.→CENTRAL SUDANIC
Bingird. Kermanji D.→IRANIAN
Bingkokak→CENTRAL AND SOUTHERN
CELEBES
Bini→EDO
Bini = Beni. Nupe Tr.→NUPE-GBARI
Bini = Obine. Agwagwune D.→CROSS RIVER
BENUE-CONGO
Binigura→NGAYARDA
Biniguru = Binigura→NGAYARDA
Binisayang Cebuano = Sebuano→NORTH-
WEST AUSTRONESIAN
Binisayang Ilonggo = Ilonggo→NORTHWEST
AUSTRONESIAN
Binja = Songola→NORTH EASTERN BANTU
Binja, Southern = Zimba→NORTH EASTERN
BANTU
Binji→CENTRAL WESTERN BANTU
Binli. Hanunoo D.→NORTHWEST AUSTRO-
NESIAN
Binna = Yunger→ADAMAWA
Binnigoora = Binigura→NGAYARDA
Binnigora = Binigura→NGAYARDA
Binokid = Bukidnon→NORTHWEST AUS-
TRONESIAN
Binongko = Wantji. Tukangbesi D.→CEN-
TRAL AND SOUTHERN CELEBES
Bintucua→CHIBCHAN
Bintulu→WEST INDONESIAN
Binuang. Mandarese D.→CENTRAL AND
SOUTHERN CELEBES

Binukidnon = Kinaraya→NORTHWEST AUS-
TRONESIAN
Binumarien→EAST NEW GUINEA HIGH-
LANDS
Binyime = Kasem→GUR
Binza. Ngombe D.→NORTH WESTERN BAN-
TU
Biŋa = Binga. Yulu-Binga D.→CENTRAL SU-
DANIC
Bio = Ari→OMOTIC
Bionah = Sermah. Land Dayak D.→WEST
INDONESIAN
Biong = Bayungu→KANYARA
Bipi→ADMIRALTY-WESTERN ISLANDS
Bira→NORTH EASTERN BANTU
Bira→CENTRAL AND SOUTHERN CELE-
BES
Bira→WESTERN NEW GUINEA
Bira, Plains. Bira D.→NORTH EASTERN
BANTU
Bira, Western→NORTH EASTERN BANTU
BIRA = BIRA-HUKU→NORTH EASTERN
BANTU
Bira = Igbira-Igu. Igbira D.→NUPE-GBARI
Biraan = Bilaan→NORTHWEST AUSTRO-
NESIAN
Birahui = Brahui→DRAVIDIAN
BIRA-HUKU→NORTH EASTERN BANTU
Birao→EASTERN OCEANIC
Birar→TUNGUS
Biratak = Sau. Land Dayak D.→WEST INDO-
NESIAN
Birbhum. Mundari D.→MUNDA
Birdawal = Bidawal. Bratauolung D.→PAMA-
NYUNGAN
Birdhawal = Bidawal. Bratauolung D.→PAMA-
NYUNGAN
Birged = Birked→EASTERN SUDANIC
Birhar = Birhor. Mundari D.→MUNDA
Birhor. Mundari D.→MUNDA
Biri = Bviri→EASTERN
Biri = Igbira-Igu. Igbira D.→NUPE-GBARI
Biri = Lokathan. Teso D.→EASTERN SU-
DANIC
Biria. Mandandanji D.→PAMA-MARIC
Biribi = Birpai. Worimi D.→YUIN-KURIC
Birifgbe = Gan. Kweni D.→MANDE
Birifo = Birifor→GUR
Birifor→GUR
Birigaba = Biria. Mandandanji D.→PAMA-
MARIC
Birippi = Birpai. Worimi D.→YUIN-KURIC
Birinue→BORORO
Biriwa. Limba D.→WEST ATLANTIC

Birjandi. Persian D.→IRANIAN
Birked→EASTERN SUDANIC
Birkit = Birked→EASTERN SUDANIC
Birom→PLATEAU BENUE-CONGO
Biroom = Birom→PLATEAU BENUE-CONGO
Birpai. Worimi D.→YUIN-KURIC
Birqed = Birked→EASTERN SUDANIC
Birrapee = Birpai. Worimi D.→YUIN-KURIC
Birria = Bidia. Karendala D.→DIERIC
Birripai = Birpai. Worimi D.→YUIN-KURIC
Birsa = Bata→CHADIC
Birta = Ngaiawang. Nganguruku D.→NARRI-NYERIC
Birtowall = Bidawal. Bratauolung D.→PAMA-NYUNGAN
Birwa→SOUTH EASTERN BANTU
Bisa→MANDE
Bisa = Biisa→CENTRAL EASTERN BANTU
Bisagwe = Busa→MANDE
BISA-LAMBA→CENTRAL EASTERN BANTU
Bisan = Bisa→MANDE
Bisanigua. Churoya D.→EQUATORIAL
Bisapele = Bisa→MANDE
Bisaya→WEST INDONESIAN
BISAYAN→NORTHWEST AUSTRONESIAN
Bisayan Cebuano = Sebuano→NORTHWEST AUSTRONESIAN
Bisharin. Beja Tr.→CUSHITIC
Bishiri. Obanliku D.→CROSS RIVER BENUE-CONGO
Bisi = Piti→PLATEAU BENUE-CONGO
Bisingai = Singgi, Land Dayak D.→WEST INDONESIAN
Bisis→SEPIK
Bisiwo = Mvumbo→NORTH WESTERN BANTU
Bislama = Beach-la-Mar→GERMANIC
BISMARCK ARCHIPELAGO see article
Bison-horn Maria = Maria. Gondi D.→DRA-VIDIAN
Bissaula = Kentu. Eregba D.→JUKUNOID
Bisu. Obanliku D.→CROSS RIVER BENUE-CONGO
Bitaama = Bitama. Kunama D.→CHARI-NILE
Bitama. Kunama D.→CHARI-NILE
Bitara→SEPIK
Bitare→BANTOID
Bithara = Bitjara. Punthamara D.→DIERIC
Bithynian see article
Biti. Morokodo D.→CENTRAL SUDANIC
Bitjara. Punthamara D.→DIERIC
Bitjoli. Maba D.→SOUTH HALMAHERA

AUSTRONESIAN
Bitshamba = Tobote→GUR
Bitta Bitta = Pittapitta. Wangkadjera D.→PITTAPITTIC
Bitwi = Ndaktup→BANTOID
BIU-MANDARA = EAST CHADIC→CHADIC
Biwat→INDO-PACIFIC
Biya→OMOTIC
Biyan = Basari→WEST ATLANTIC
Biye = Biya→OMOTIC
Biyobe = Soruba-Kuyobe→GUR
Biyom→EAST NEW GUINEA HIGHLANDS
Biyori = Phalura Proper. Phalura D.→INDIC
Black Bushman = Hukwe→KHOISAN
Blackfoot→ALGONQUIAN
B'lai = Li→KAM-TAI
Blanche Bay = Gunantuna → BISMARCK ARCHIPELAGO
Blanya. Central Sakai D.→SAKAI
Blapo = Plawi. Bakwe Tr.→KRU
Ble. Dyula D.→MANDE
B'li = Li→KAM-TAI
Bliss. Diola D.→WEST ATLANTIC
Blood. Blackfoot D.→ALGONQUIAN
Blupblup→NORTHEAST NEW GUINEA AUSTRONESIAN
Blyth River. Barera D.→BURERAN
Bmoba = Moba→GUR
Bo = Pacoh→MON-KHMER
Bo Luang. Lawa D.→PALAUNG-WA
Boa→NORTH WESTERN BANTU
Boa. Sumo Tr.→MISUMALPAN
Boa = Bua→ADAMAWA
Boadji = Boazi→MARIND
Boana→EAST INDONESIAN
Boana = ERAP→HUON-FINISTERRE
Boandik = Buandik. Marditjali D.→KULINIC
Boandiks = Buandik. Marditjali D.→KULINIC
Boano = Bolano→NORTHERN CELEBES
Boazi→MARIND
Bobale. Tobelo D.→NORTH HALMAHERA
Bobangi→NORTH WESTERN BANTU
Bobar. Jarawa D.→BANTOID
Bobasan. Gayo D.→WEST INDONESIAN
Bobe = Bobea→NORTH WESTERN BANTU
Bobe = Bube→NORTH WESTERN BANTU
Bobea→NORTH WESTERN BANTU
Bobili = Gbigbil. Bebele D.→NORTH WESTERN BANTU
Bobilis = Gbigbil. Bebele D.→NORTH WESTERN BANTU
Bobo→GUR
Bobo, Black = Bobo Fing. Sya D.→MANDE

Bobo Fi = Bobo Fing. Sya D.→MANDE

Bobo Fing. Sya D.→MANDE

Bobongko→CENTRAL AND SOUTHERN CELEBES

Bobono. Bete Tr.→KRU

Bobot→EAST INDONESIAN

Bobwa. Bete D.→KRU

Bod Butun = Ladakhi. West Tibetan D.→ TIBETAN

Bode. Akye Tr.→LAGOON

Bodega. Coast Miwok D.→MIWOK-COSTANOAN

Bodho. Thuri Tr.→EASTERN SUDANIC

Bodi. Mekan D.→EASTERN SUDANIC

Bodiman→NORTH WESTERN BANTU

BODISH see TIBETAN

Bodjinga = Lobo. Mabaale D. → NORTH WESTERN BANTU

BODO→BODO-NAGA-KACHIN

Bodo→CENTRAL WESTERN BANTU

Bodo→BODO-NAGA-KACHIN

Bodo = Gudwa. Gutob D.→MUNDA

Bodo = Hwane. Bakwe D.→KRU

Bodo-Gadaba = Gudwa. Gutob D.→MUNDA

BODO-NAGA-KACHIN see article

Bodoro = Padorho→GUR

Bod-skad = Mnyamskad. Central Tibetan D.→ TIBETAN

Bodunga = Modunga→EASTERN

Bodzanga = Ngando-Kota→NORTH WESTERN BANTU

Boeng. Tobelo D.→NORTH HALMAHERA

Boewe→NEW CALEDONIA

Boga. Tera D.→CHADIC

Boga = Buka→KHOISAN

Bogadjim→NORTHEASTERN NEW GUINEA

Bogarea. Tebu Tr.→SAHARAN

Boggangar = Minjangbal. Giabal D.→GIABALIC

BOGIA see article

Bobijiab. Great Andamanese D.→ANDAMANESE

Bogo = Bilin→CUSHITIC

Bogon = Abuldugu. Burun Tr.→EASTERN SUDANIC

Bogongo. Pande D.→NORTH WESTERN BANTU

Bogoŋgo = Bogongo. Pande D.→NORTH WESTERN BANTU

Bogos. Tigre D.→SEMITIC

Bogos = Bilin→CUSHITIC

Bogota = Bogotu→NORTHWESTERN AND CENTRAL SOLOMONS

Bogotu→NORTHWESTERN AND CENTRAL SOLOMONS

Boguru→CENTRAL WESTERN BANTU

Boguru. Boguru D.→CENTRAL WESTERN BANTU

Bohairic = Bohayric. Coptic D.→AFROASIATIC

Bohayric. Coptic D.→AFROASIATIC

Bohol→NORTHWEST AUSTRONESIAN

Boholano = Bohol→NORTHWEST AUSTRONESIAN

Bohura = Mura→MACRO-CHIBCHAN

Bohutu→PAPUA AUSTRONESIAN

Boi = Boyawa→PLATEAU BENUE-CONGO

Boiken→SEPIK

Boit = Kurmuk. Burun Tr. → EASTERN SUDANIC

Bojigniji = Beada. Great Andamanese D.→ ANDAMANESE

Bojigyab = Bogijiab. Great Andamanese D.→ ANDAMANESE

Bok. Ba Mali D.→WEST INDONESIAN

Bok. Manjaku D.→WEST ATLANTIC

Boka. Shona D.→SOUTH EASTERN BANTU

Boka Mombe = Mombe. Gbaya Tr.→EASTERN

Bokai. Roti D.→EAST INDONESIAN

Bokari. Gbaya Tr.→EASTERN

Bokhan. Buryat D.→MONGOLIAN

Boki→CROSS-RIVER BENUE-CONGO

Bokiyo = Kenga→CENTRAL SUDANIC

Bokninuwad. Foothill North Yokuts D.→ YOKUTS

Boko→NORTH WESTERN BANTU

Boko = Busa→MANDE

Boko = Woko→ADAMAWA

Boko Bussawa = Busa→MANDE

Bokoberu = Busa→MANDE

Bokod. Inibaloy D.→NORTHWEST AUSTRONESIAN

Bokoki = Bolia. Ntombo-Bolia Tr.→NORTH WESTERN BANTU

Bokolawa = Busa→MANDE

Bokorike = Daju→EASTERN SUDANIC

Bokoruge = Daju →Eastern Sudanic

Boku. Pipikoro D. → CENTRAL AND SOUTHERN CELEBES

Bokue. Bakwe Tr.→KRU

Bokula = Lobo. Mabaale D.→NORTH WESTERN BANTU

Bokwe = Bokue. Bakwe Tr.→KRU

Bokyi = Boki→CROSS-RIVER BENUE-CONGO

Bola→NORTH EAST NEW GUINEA AUSTRONESIAN

Bola = Mankanya→WEST ATLANTIC

Bolaang-Mongondow = Mongondow → NORTHERN CELEBES

Bolano→NORTHERN CELEBES

Bolawa = Bolewa→CHADIC

Bolbo = Sobiobo. Pichobo D.→PANO

Bolea = Bolewa→CHADIC

Bolenchi = Bolewa→CHADIC

BOLEWA→CHADIC

Bolewa→CHADIC

Bolgo→ADAMAWA

Bolgo Dugag→ADAMAWA

Boli→ADAMAWA

Boli→MAILU

Bolia. Ntombo-Bolia Tr.→NORTH WESTERN BANTU

Boliba = 'Bali'ba. Moru D.→CENTRAL SUDANIC

Bolinao. Sambali D.→NORTHWEST AUS-TRONESIAN

Bolo→CENTRAL WESTERN BANTU

Bolo = Bola→NORTHEAST NEW GUINEA AUSTRONESIAN

Boloa→MACRO-TUCANOAN

Bologi = Boloki. Losengo D. → NORTH WESTERN BANTU

Boloki. Losengo D.→NORTH WESTERN BANTU

Bolom = Northern Bullom→WEST ATLAN-TIC

Bolondo→NORTH WESTERN BANTU

Bolongan→NORTHWEST AUSTRONESIAN

Bolongo. Mongo-Nkundo D.→NORTH WEST-ERN BANTU

Boloven = Loven→MON-KHMER

Bom→WEST ATLANTIC

Bom→NAGA-KUKI-CHIN

Boma→NORTH WESTERN BANTU

Boma. Ijo D.→IJO

Boma = Boo. Central Teke D.→NORTH WESTERN BANTU

Boma Murle. Murle Tr.→EASTERN SUDANIC

Bombali. Temne D.→WEST ATLANTIC

Bombarawa = Bambaro. Lame D.→BANTOID

Bombaro = Bambaro. Lame D.→BANTOID

Bomberawa = Bambaro. Lame D.→BANTOID

Bombi. Huku D.→NORTH EASTERN BANTU

Bombo = Mpompo. Mbimu D.→NORTH WESTERN BANTU

Bomboko→NORTH WESTERN BANTU

Bomboli. Lobala D.→NORTH WESTERN BANTU

Bombongo = Bomboli. Lobala D.→NORTH WESTERN BANTU

Bomborawa = Bambaro. Lame D.→BANTOID

Bombori. Katla Tr.→KORDOFANIAN

Bome = Bom→WEST ATLANTIC

Bomo = Bom→WEST ATLANTIC

Bomokandi. Zande D.→EASTERN

Bomougoun-Bamenjou→BANTOID

Bompaka. Teressa D.→NICOBARESE

Bomsau. Mok D.→ADMIRALTY-WESTERN ISLANDS

Bomvana. Nguni D.→SOUTH EASTERN BANTU

Bomwali→NORTH WESTERN BANTU

Bon. Gula D.→ADAMAWA

Bon Shwai = Buoncuai. Rek D.→EASTERN SUDANIC

Bonabona = Mugura. Suau D.→PAPUA AUSTRONESIAN

Bonam = Monom→MON-KHMER

Bonaputa-Mapu → NORTHEASTERN NEW GUINEA

Bonari→CARIB

Bonarua. Suau D.→PAPUA AUSTRONESIAN

Bonda = Remo→MUNDA

Bonda Poroja = Remo→MUNDA

Bonde = Bondei→CENTRAL EASTERN BANTU

Bondei→CENTRAL EASTERN BANTU

Bondo = Ligbi→MANDE

Bondo = Ngengu→CENTRAL WESTERN BANTU

Bondo = Remo→MUNDA

Bonek. Banen Tr.→NORTH WESTERN BAN-TU

Bonerate. Tukangbesi D.→CENTRAL AND SOUTHERN CELEBES

Bonerif→NORTH PAPUAN

Bonfia→MOLUCCAN

Bong Mieu = Cua→MON-KHMER

Bonggo→SARMIC

Bonggrang. Kwansu D.→NORTH PAPUAN

Bongili→NORTH WESTERN BANTU

Bongili = Bogongo. Pande D. → NORTH WESTERN BANTU

Bongiri = Bogongo. Pande D. → NORTH WESTERN BANTU

Bongiri = Bongili→NORTH WESTERN BAN-TU

BONGO→CENTRAL SUDANIC

Bongo→CENTRAL SUDANIC

Bongo. Banda D.→EASTERN

Bongo Talk = Jamaican Creole→GERMANIC

Bongu→NORTHEASTERN NEW GUINEA

Boni = Sanye→CUSHITIC

Bonkembe = Lobo. Mabaale D.→NORTH

WESTERN BANTU

Bonken = Bonkeng→NORTH WESTERN BANTU

Bonkeng→NORTH WESTERN BANTU

Bonkiman→HUON-FINISTERRE

Bonny = Ibani. Ijo D.→IJO

Bono = Mbono→EAST INDONESIAN

Bonotsek = Taihyo. Atayal D.→FORMOSAN AUSTRONESIAN

Bonta'eng = Tonthain. Makasarese D.→CENTRAL AND SOUTHERN CELEBES

BONTAWA→GYARUNG-MISHMI

Bontok→NORTHWEST AUSTRONESIAN

Bontok Igorot = Bontok → NORTHWEST AUSTRONESIAN

Bonum. Fali D.→ADAMAWA

Bo'o→SOUTH HALMAHERA AUSTRONESIAN

Boo. Central Teke D.→NORTH WESTERN BANTU

Boo = Gbunde. Loma D.→MANDE

Booandik = Buandik. Marditjali D.→KULINIC

Boolgoo = Bailko→NGAYARDA

Boomu. Bobo D.→GUR

Boonarra = Bunara→NGUMBIN

Boonoorong = Bunurong. Taungurong D.→KULINIC

Boonurrong = Bunurong. Taungurong D.→KULINIC

Boorabirraba = Baraparapa→YOTAYOTIC

Booraboora = Baraparapa→YOTAYOTIC

Booran = Borena. Galla D.→CUSHITIC

Boorana = Borena. Galla D.→CUSHITIC

Booripung = Ngarkat. Djadjala D.→KULINIC

Boorkutti = Dainggati. Ngamba D.→YUIN-KURIC

Boorong = Warkawarka. Djadjala D.→KULINIC

Boort = Baraparapa→YOTAYOTIC

Bor→EASTERN SUDANIC

Bor Athoic = Borathoi. Bor. D.→EASTERN SUDANIC

Bor Gok. Bor D.→EASTERN SUDANIC

Bora→WITOTOAN

BORA-MIRANYA→WITOTOAN

Boran Gabbra = Borena. Galla D.→CUSHITIC

Borandikngolo = Buandik. Marditjali D.→KULINIC

Borathoi. Bor D.→EASTERN SUDANIC

Borch. Rutul D.→CAUCASIAN

Bordawulung = Portaulun. Tanganekald D.→NARRINYERIC

Borena. Galla D.→CUSHITIC

Bori = Boli→MAILU

Borija. San Ignacio D.→CHAPACURA-WANHAMAN

Boripar = Ngarkat. Djadjala D.→KULINIC

Boritsu→JUKUNOID

Borlawa = Bolewa→CHADIC

Boro = Angba→NORTH WESTERN BANTU

Boro = Bodo→BODO-NAGA-KACHIN

Boroa = //xegwe→KHOISAN

Borodda. Walamo Tr.→OMOTIC

BORORO see article

BOROTUKE = BORORO

BOROTUQUE = BORORO

Borou = Buru. Banda D.→EASTERN

Borrado see article

Borrom = Basherawa→PLATEAU BENUE-CONGO

Boruca→CHIBCHAN

Borumessu→MOMBERAMO RIVER

BORUN = BOTOCUDO

Bosavi→PARE-SAMO-BEAMI-BOSAVI

Bosha. Kefa D.→OMOTIC

Boskien = Dimir→BOGIA

Bosman = Bosngun→BOGIA

Bosngun→BOGIA

Bosnik. Biak D.→MOLUCCAN

Bota = Bobea→NORTH WESTERN BANTU

Botahari-Harsusi. Modern South Arabic D.→SEMITIC

Botelkude = Halopa→BOGIA

Boti→EAST INDONESIAN

Botlikh = Botlix→CAUCASIAN

Botlix→CAUCASIAN

BOTOCUDO see article

Botocudo. Seta D.→TUPI

Botunga. Mbole D.→NORTH EASTERN BANTU

Boua = Bua→ADAMAWA

Bouamou = Nyenyege. Bobo D.→GUR

Bouddouma = Buduma→CHADIC

BOUGAINVILLE see article

Boulala = Bilala. Kuka D.→CENTRAL SUDANIC

Bouliboul = Tatungalung. Bratauolung D.→PAMA-NYUNGAN

Boulou = Bulu→NORTH WESTERN BANTU

Boumboum = Mpompo. Mbimu D.→NORTH WESTERN BANTU

Boumpe = Mende→MANDE

Boun→GUNWINGGUAN

Bourrah = Bura→CHADIC

Boussa = Busa→MANDE

Boussan = Bisa→MANDE

Boussanse = Bisa→MANDE

Bousso = Buso→CHADIC

Bouye→SEPIK
Bouzantchi = Bisa→MANDE
Bouze = Loma→MANDE
Boven Moian = Bian→MARIND
Boven Tor→NORTH PAPUAN
Bowai. Tulu D.→ADMIRALTY-WESTERN ISLANDS
Bowat. Mokareng D.→ADMIRALTY-WESTERN ISLANDS
Bowili→CENTRAL TOGO
Bowli = Baule. Anyi D.→VOLTA-COMOE
Bowom = Bawom. Padang D.→EASTERN SUDANIC
Boya = Longarim→EASTERN SUDANIC
Boyawa→PLATEAU BENUE-CONGO
Boyela = Yela→NORTH WESTERN BANTU
Bozo. Soninke D.→MANDE
Boko = Busa→MANDE
Brabirawilung = Brabralung. Bratauolung D. →PAMA-NYUNGAN
Brabralung. Bratauolung D.→PAMA-NYUNGAN
Brabrawurung = Brabralung. Bratauolung D. →PAMA-NYUNGAN
Brabriwoolong = Brabralung. Bratauolung D. →PAMA-NYUNGAN
Brabrolong = Brabralung. Bratauolung D. →PAMA-NYUNGAN
Brabrolung = Brabralung. Bratauolung D. →PAMA-NYUNGAN
Bradawulung = Bratauolung → PAMA-NYUNGAN
Bradowoolong = Bratauolung → PAMA-NYUNGAN
Bradrawah. Western Pahari D.→INDIC
Bragat→TORRICELLI
Brahui→DRAVIDIAN
Brahuidi = Brahui→DRAVIDIAN
Braiakaulung. Bratauolung D.→PAMA-NYUNGAN
Braiakolung = Braiakaulung. Bratauolung D. →PAMA-NYUNGAN
Braj Bhakha. Western Hindi D.→INDIC
Braj Bhasha = Braj Bhakha. Western Hindi D. →INDIC
Brajagawulung = Braiakaulung. Bratauolung D.→PAMA-NYUNGAN
Brame = Mankanya→WEST ATLANTIC
Brao→MON-KHMER
Braou = Brao→MON-KHMER
Brass = Nembe. Ijo D.→IJO
Brassa = Balanta→WEST ATLANTIC
Bratanolung = Bratauolung → PAMA-NYUNGAN

Brataualung = Bratauolung→ PAMA-NYUNGAN
Bratauolung→PAMA-NYUNGAN
Bravos. Puinave D.→MACRO-TUCANOAN
Brawia. Teda Tr.→SAHARAN
Brayakau = Braiakaulung. Bratauolung D.→ PAMA-NYUNGAN
Brayakaulung = Braiakaulung. Bratauolung D. →PAMA-NYUNGAN
Bræ = Bwe→KAREN
Bre = Bwe→KAREN
Brec = Bwe→KAREN
Breeaba = Biria. Mandandanji D.→PAMA-MARIC
Breenugu→INDO-PACIFIC
Breri→BOGIA
Breton→CELTIC
Bria. Banda D.→EASTERN
Briama = Gbunde. Loma D.→MANDE
Bribri→CHIBCHAN
Brierley Is. Suau D.→PAPUA AUSTRONESIAN
Brijia. Mundari D.→MUNDA
BRINKEN→DALY
Brinken→DALY
BRINKEN-WOGAITY→DALY
Brinya = Avikam→LAGOON
Bripi = Birpai. Worimi D.→YUIN-KURIC
Brissa = Anufo. Anyi D.→VOLTA-COMOE
Brokpa. Sina D.→INDIC
Bromsi. Biak D.→MOLUCCAN
Brong. Guan D.→VOLTA-COMOE
Brotherton = Mahican. Mohegan D.→ALGONQUIAN
Brou = Bru→MON-KHMER
Brou = Buru. Banda D.→EASTERN
Bru→MON-KHMER
Bruit. Melanau D.→WEST INDONESIAN
Brule. Dakota D.→SIOUAN
Brumer Is. Suau D.→PAPUA AUSTRONESIAN
Brunca = Boruca→CHIBCHAN
Brung. Sarawak Murut D.→WEST INDONESIAN
Brusa = Anufo. Anyi D.→VOLTA-COMOE
Brushwood = Slave. Chipewyan Tr.→ATHAPASCAN-EYAK
Brussa = Anufo. Anyi D.→VOLTA-COMOE
BRYTHONIC→CELTIC
Bu Dang. Central Mnong D.→MON-KHMER
Bu Nar. Central Mnong D.→MON-KHMER
Bu Rung. Central Mnong D.→MON-KHMER
BUA→CHADIC
Bua→ADAMAWA
Bua. Ndrosun D.→ADMIRALTY-WESTERN

ISLANDS
Bua = Boa→NORTH WESTERN BANTU
Bua = Hona. Tera D.→CHADIC
Bua, South Eastern = Bali → NORTH EASTERN BANTU
Bual = Buol→NORTHWEST AUSTRONESIAN
Buan = Boun→GUNWINGGUAN
Buandik. Marditjali D.→KULINIC
Buang→NORTHEAST NEW GUINEA AUSTRONESIAN
BUANIC→GUNWINGGUAN
Buari→MAILU
BUBE→NORTH WESTERN BANTU
Bube→NORTH WESTERN BANTU
BUBE-BENGA→NORTH WESTERN BANTU
Bubi. Kele D.→NORTH WESTERN BANTU
Bubi = Bube→NORTH WESTERN BANTU
Buboi. Nyada D.→ADMIRALTY-WESTERN ISLANDS
Bubu = Mbugu. Banda D.→EASTERN
Bubu = Nguru. Kara D.→CENTRAL SUDANIC
Bubure→CARIB
Bucobu = Piocobge→GE
Buctulan = Pula→NORTHWEST AUSTRONESIAN
Budama = Adhola→EASTERN SUDANIC
Budanoh. Land Dayak D.→WEST INDONESIAN
Budduma = Buduma→CHADIC
Budhi = Ladakhi. West Tibetan D.→TIBETAN
Budigri. Gbaya Tr.→EASTERN
Budina = Buduna. Talandji D.→KANYARA
Budip. Stieng D.→MON-KHMER
Budja = Buja→NORTH WESTERN BANTU
Budjago = Bijago→WEST ATLANTIC
Bud-kat = Mnyamskad. Central Tibetan D.→TIBETAN
Budoona = Buduna. Talandji D.→KANYARA
Budu→NORTH EASTERN BANTU
Budugum. Masa D.→ADAMAWA
Budukh = Budux→CAUCASIAN
Buduma→CHADIC
Buduna. Talandji D.→KANYARA
Budux→CAUCASIAN
Budya. Shona D.→SOUTH EASTERN BANTU
Buela = Bwela. 'Doko D.→NORTH WESTERN BANTU
Buem = Lefana→CENTRAL TOGO
Buena Vista = Foothill South Yokuts→YOKUTS
Buende = Bwende. Kongo D.→CENTRAL WESTERN BANTU

Bueng. Achinese D.→WEST INDONESIAN
Bufe = Bafut→BANTOID
Buga→CARIB
Bugago = Bijago→WEST ATLANTIC
Buganza, Southern = Ganza. Ruanda D.→NORTH EASTERN BANTU
Bugellimangi = Walbanga. Thaua D.→YUIN-KURIC
Bugi→AGOB
BUGIC→CENTRAL AND SOUTHERN CELEBES
Buginese→CENTRAL AND SOUTHERN CELEBES
Bugombe→NORTH EASTERN BANTU
Bugradi. Tamil D.→DRAVIDIAN
Bugudum = Budugum. Masa D.→ADAMAWA
Buguias. Kankanay D.→NORTHWEST AUSTRONESIAN
Buguli = Paguli→GUR
Buguri = Puguli→GUR
Buhagana→MACRO-TUCANOAN
Buhi. Bikol D.→NORTHWEST AUSTRONESIAN
Buhid→NORTHWEST AUSTRONESIAN
Buhil = Buhid→NORTHWEST AUSTRONESIAN
Buhwan. Seediq D.→FORMOSAN AUSTRONESIAN
Buiamanambu→SEPIK
Buid = Buhid→NORTHWEST AUSTRONESIAN
Bu'id = Buhid→NORTHWEST AUSTRONESIAN
Buile = Buli→GUR
BUIN→BOUGAINVILLE
Buin→BOUGAINVILLE
Buinak. Kumyk D.→TURKIC
Buiok. Saisiyat D.→FORMOSAN AUSTRONESIAN
Buiye = Bouye→SEPIK
Buja→NORTH WESTERN BANTU
Bujawa = Buji→PLATEAU BENUE-CONGO
Buje = Buji→PLATEAU BENUE-CONGO
Buji→PLATEAU BENUE-CONGO
Bujwe = Buyu. Bangobango D.→NORTH EASTERN BANTU
Buk. Ingassana Tr.→CHARI-NILE
BUKA→NORTHWESTERN AND CENTRAL SOLOMONS
Buka→KHOISAN
Buka. Land Dayak D.→WEST INDONESIAN
Bukakhwe = Buka→KHOISAN
Bukala. Mongo-Nkundo D.→NORTH WESTERN BANTU

Bukar = Sadong. Land Dayak D.→WEST INDONESIAN

Bukaua→NORTHEAST NEW GUINEA AUSTRONESIAN

Bukawa = Bukaua→NORTHEAST NEW GUINEA AUSTRONESIAN

Bukid = Buhid→NORTHWEST AUSTRONESIAN

BUKIDNIC→NORTHWEST AUSTRONESIAN

Bukidnon→NORTHWEST AUSTRONESIAN

Bukidnon Manobo = Bukidnon → NORTHWEST AUSTRONESIAN

Bukina = Uru→CHIPAYAN

Bukitan = Beketan. Punan Ba D.→WEST INDONESIAN

Bukongo = Bogongo. Pande D.→NORTH WESTERN BANTU

Bukueta = Murire. Guaymi D.→CHIBCHAN

Bukuma→CROSS RIVER BENUE-CONGO

Bukurmi = Kurama → PLATEAU BENUE-CONGO

Bukusu. Masaba D.→NORTH EASTERN BANTU

Bul. Nuer D.→EASTERN SUDANIC

Bulach. Stieng D.→MON-KHMER

Bulagat. Buryat D.→MONGOLIAN

Bulahai = Matakam→CHADIC

Bulala = Bilala. Kuka D.→CENTRAL SUDANIC

Bulalacaunos = Silanganen. Tagbanua D.→ NORTHWEST AUSTRONESIAN

Bulalakao = Hanunoo→NORTHWEST AUSTRONESIAN

Bulama = Mankanya→WEST ATLANTIC

Bulanga-Uki→NORTHWEST AUSTRONESIAN

Bulante = Balanta→WEST ATLANTIC

Bulaway. Wakaman D.→PAMA-MARIC

Buldit. Central Koma D.→KOMAN

Bulea = Buli→GUR

Bulebule = Amba→NORTH EASTERN BANTU

Bulem = Northern Bullom→WEST ATLANTIC

Bulgarian→SLAVIC

Bulgeida. Tebu Tr.→SAHARAN

Buli→GUR

Buli→SOUTH HALMAHERA AUSTRONESIAN

Buli. Tobelo D.→NORTH HALMAHERA

Buli = South Nkundo. Mongo-Nkundo D.→ NORTH WESTERN BANTU

Bulihan. Ndrosun D.→ADMIRALTY-WESTERN ISLANDS

Bulin = Northern Bullom→WEST ATLANTIC

Bullom, Northern→WEST ATLANTIC

Bullom, Southern→WEST ATLANTIC

Bullun = Northern Bullom→WEST ATLANTIC

Bulmut. Ingassana Tr.→CHARI-NILE

Bulo. Stieng D.→MON-KHMER

Bulse = Bobo Fing. Sya D.→MANDE

Bultoa = Bultu. Tebu Tr.→SAHARAN

Bultu. Tebu Tr.→SAHARAN

Bulu→NORTH WESTERN BANTU

Bulu→NORTHEAST NEW GUINEA AUSTRONESIAN

Bulu = Sekiyani → NORTH WESTERN BANTU

Buluan. Bilaan D.→NORTHWEST AUSTRONESIAN

Buluanes = Buluan. Bilaan D.→NORTHWEST AUSTRONESIAN

Buluan-Kipit. Subanun D.→NORTHWEST AUSTRONESIAN

Buluanon = Buluan. Bilaan D.→NORTHWEST AUSTRONESIAN

Bulud-Upi→NORTHWEST AUSTRONESIAN

Buludupi = Bulud-Upi→NORTHWEST AUSTRONESIAN

Buluf. Diola D.→WEST ATLANTIC

Bulugu = Buli→GUR

Buluguda. Malgana D.→KARDU

Buluki = Boloki. Losengo D.→NORTH WESTERN BANTU

Bulum = Burum→HUON-FINISTERRE

Bulungan = Bolongan→NORTHWEST AUSTRONESIAN

Bulyarma = Gbunde. Loma D.→MANDE

Bum→BANTOID

Bum = Bom→WEST ATLANTIC

Buma = Boma→NORTH WESTERN BANTU

Buma = Turkana→EASTERN SUDANIC

Bumaji→CROSS RIVER BENUE-CONGO

Bumbarra = Gia. Mandandanji D.→PAMA-MARIC

Bumbira. Ziba D.→NORTH EASTERN BANTU

Bumbuko = Bomboko→NORTH WESTERN BANTU

Bumburra = Gia. Mandandanji D.→PAMA-MARIC

Bume = Turkana→EASTERN SUDANIC

Bumi = Turkana→EASTERN SUDANIC

Bumwangi. Losengo D.→NORTH WESTERN BANTU

Bun→EASTERN OCEANIC

BUNA→NORTH NEW GUINEA

Buna→NORTH NEW GUINEA

Buna' = Bunak→TIMOR-ALOR

BUNABAN see article

Bunabun→BOGIA

Bunak→TIMOR-ALOR

Bunaki→BANTOID

Bunan→GYARUNG-MISHMI

Bunan = Punan. Land Dayak D.→WEST INDONESIAN

Bunapa = Bunaba→BUNABAN

Bunara→NGUMBIN

Bunda. Hungu D.→CENTRAL WESTERN BANTU

Bunda = Suwawa→NORTHWEST AUSTRONESIAN

Bundel = Badjelang. Kitabal D.→BANDJALANGIC

Bundel Khandi = Bundeli. Western Hindi D.→INDIC

Bundela = Badjelang. Kitabal D.→BANDJALANGIC

Bundeli. Western Hindi D.→INDIC

Bundi = Gende→EAST NEW GUINEA HIGHLANDS

Bundrahai. Bipi D.→ADMIRALTY-WESTERN ISLANDS

Bundum = Cinga → NORTH WESTERN BANTU

Bungain→NORTH NEW GUINEA

Bungandaetch = Buandik. Marditjali D.→KULINIC

Bungandaethca = Buandik. Marditjali D.→KULINIC

Bungandaitj = Buandik. Marditjali D.→KULINIC

Bungandity = Buandik. Marditjali D.→KULINIC

Bungbinda = Ngbinda→CENTRAL WESTERN BANTU

Bungeha = Pangkala→YURA

Bungela = Pangkala→YURA

Bungiri = Bongili → NORTH WESTERN BANTU

Bungku→CENTRAL AND SOUTHERN CELEBES

BUNGKU-LAKI→CENTRAL AND SOUTHERN CELEBES

BUNGKU-MORI = BUNGKU-LAKI→CENTRAL AND SOUTHERN CELEBES

Bungnu = Kamkam→BANTOID

Bungu→NORTH EASTERN BANTU

Bungu = Bongo→CENTRAL SUDANIC

Bungyarlee = Naualko. Kula D.→PAMANYUNGAN

Buniki. Bamu Kiwai D.→CENTRAL AND SOUTH NEW GUINEA

Buninahua. Cashibo D.→PANO

Buninawa = Buninahua. Cashibo D.→PANO

Buninga. Tongoa D.→EASTERN OCEANIC

Bunjellung = Badjelang. Kitabal D.→BANDJALANGIC

Bunji. Shona D.→SOUTH EASTERN BANTU

Bunjia. Oriya D.→INDIC

Bunor = Bu Nar. Central Mnong D.→MON-KHMER

Buntamara = Punthamara→DIERIC

Bunthaburra = Punthamara→DIERIC

Bunthomarra = Punthamara→DIERIC

Bunu. Yoruba D.→YORUBA

Bunu = Mugil→BOGIA

Bunu = Rebina→PLATEAU BENUE-CONGO

Bunubun = Bunabun→BOGIA

Bunum = Bunun→FORMOSAN AUSTRONESIAN

Bunun→FORMOSAN AUSTRONESIAN

Bunurong. Taungurong D.→KULINIC

Bunwurru = Bunurong. Taungurong D.→KULINIC

Bunwurung = Bunurong. Taungurong D.→KULINIC

Buol→NORTHWEST AUSTRONESIAN

Buoncuai. Rek D.→EASTERN SUDANIC

Buquil = Buhid→NORTHWEST AUSTRONESIAN

BURA→CHADIC

Bura→CHADIC

Bura Mabaŋ = Maba→MABAN

Burabura = Baraparapa→YOTAYOTIC

Buradik. Tatog Tr.→EASTERN SUDANIC

Buraka. Gbanziri D.→EASTERN

Burakokra. Bura Tr.→CHADIC

Buram = Mankanya→WEST ATLANTIC

Burama. Mankanya D.→WEST ATLANTIC

Burama = Mankanya→WEST ATLANTIC

Burappa = Baraparapa→YOTAYOTIC

Burapper = Baraparapa→YOTAYOTIC

Burburi = Adyukru→LAGOON

Burduna = Buduna. Talandji D.→KANYARA

Burede→CARIB

BURERAN see article

BURERIC→BURERAN

Buressa = Anufo. Anyi D.→VOLTA-COMOE

Burgadi = Dainggati. Ngamba D.→YUIN-KURIC

Burgu = Bargu→GUR

Burgundian→GERMANIC

Burhwundeirtch = Buandik. Marditjali D.→KULINIC

Buria. Sapolewa D.→EAST INDONESIAN
Burica→CHIBCHAN
Burig = Purik. West Tibetan D.→TIBETAN
Buripung = Ngarkat. Djadjala D.→KULINIC
Buritica. Cauca Tr.→CARIB
Burji→CUSHITIC
Burjina = Burji→CUSHITIC
Burekenji = Sampur. Maasai D.→EASTERN SUDANIC
Burmawa = Basherawa→PLATEAU BENUE-CONGO
Burmese→BURMESE-LOLO
BURMESE-LOLO see article
Burongo→NORTHWESTERN AND CENTRAL SOLOMONS
Burra = Bura→CHADIC
Burraburburaba = Baraparapa→YOTAYOTIC
Burranbinya = Baranbinja. Wongaibon D.→WIRADJURIC
Burrikem = Widekum→BANTOID
Burrum = Basherawa→PLATEAU BENUE-CONGO
Burrunbinya = Baranbinja. Wongaibon D.→WIRADJURIC
Bursu. Mok D.→ADMIRALTY-WESTERN ISLANDS
Buru→MOLUCCAN
Buru. Banda D.→EASTERN
Buru = Angba→NORTH WESTERN BANTU
Buru = Degha→GUR
Burubora = Purubora→TUPI
Burubusay. Cuica D.→EQUATORIAL
Burucaca. Boruca D.→CHIBCHAN
Burue→MACRO-TUCANOAN
'Burulo. Ma'di D.→CENTRAL SUDANIC
Burum→HUON-FINISTERRE
Burum = Birom→PLATEAU BENUE-CONGO
Burumana→NORTHEASTERN NEW GUINEA
Burumawa = Basherawa→PLATEAU BENUE-CONGO
Burumawa = Birom→PLATEAU BENUE-CONGO
Burun→EASTERN SUDANIC
Burun = Uduk→KOMAN
Burun, Hill = Burun→EASTERN SUDANIC
Burun, Northern = Burun→EASTERN SUDANIC
Burun, Southern = Maban→EASTERN SUDANIC
Burunge = Burungi→CUSHITIC
Burungi→CUSHITIC
Burushaski see article
Buryat→MONGOLIAN

Burzhan. Bashkir D.→TURKIC
BUSA→NORTH NEW GUINEA
Busa→MANDE
Busa→NORTH NEW GUINEA
Busagwe = Busa→MANDE
Busamma→SOUTH HALMAHERA AUSTRONESIAN
Busanchi = Busa→MANDE
Busang. Kayan D.→WEST INDONESIAN
Busang = Bisa→MANDE
Busani = Bisa→MANDE
Busanse = Bisa→MANDE
Busansi = Bisa→MANDE
Busari = Tobote→GUR
Busashi = Southern Mao→OMOTIC
Busasi = Southern Mao→OMOTIC
BUSH A = NORTHERN SOUTH AFRICAN KHOISAN→KHOISAN
BUSH B = TAA→KHOISAN
BUSH C = ŋ/huki→KHOISAN
BUSH D = //xegwe→KHOISAN
Bushi→PLATEAU BENUE-CONGO
BUSHMAN→KHOISAN
Bushman = Gimsbok Nama→KHOISAN
Bushman, River = Buka→KHOISAN
BUSHMAN, CENTRAL = TSHU-KHWE→KHOISAN
Bushong = Busooŋ→NORTH WESTERN BANTU
Bushongo = Busooŋ→NORTH WESTERN BANTU
Busi. Obanliku D.→CROSS RIVER BENUE-CONGO
Busi = Loma→MANDE
Buso→CHADIC
Busooŋ→NORTH WESTERN BANTU
Busquipani. Capanahua D.→PANO
Bussa, North→CUSHITIC
Bussa, West = Gobeze. Gawwada D.→CUSHITIC
Busu Djanga. Losengo D.→NORTH WESTERN BANTU
Buta = Butawa→PLATEAU BENUE-CONGO
Butam. Taulil D.→NEW BRITAIN
Butam = Fesoa→BISMARCK ARCHIPELAGO
Butawa→PLATEAU BENUE-CONGO
Bute→BANTOID
Butherbaluk = Taunburong→KULINIC
Buti = Bute→BANTOID
Butu→CENTRAL SUDANIC
Butuanon→NORTHWEST AUSTRONESIAN
Butung→CENTRAL AND SOUTHERN CELEBES

Butwaq. Chrau D.→MON-KHMER

Buxidim = Margi→CHADIC

Buya. Masaba D.→NORTH EASTERN BANTU

BUYANG → ADMIRALITY-WESTERN IS-LANDS

Buyi→NORTH EASTERN BANTU

Buyu. Bangobango D.→NORTH EASTERN BANTU

Buzawa. Oirat D.→MONGOLIAN

Buze = Buji→PLATEAU BENUE-CONGO

Buzi = Loma→MANDE

Bvanuma. Huku D.→NORTH EASTERN BANTU

Bviri→EASTERN

Bvumba. Shona D.→SOUTH EASTERN BAN-TU

Bwa = Bobo→GUR

Bwaidoga→PAPUA AUSTRONESIAN

Bwaka→EASTERN

Bwaka = Gbaya→EASTERN

Bwamu = Bobo→GUR

Bwareba = Bachama→CHADIC

Bwatnapi. Central Raga D.→EASTERN OCE-ANIC

Bwato. Ngbandi Tr.→EASTERN

Bwatvenua = Lamalanga→EASTERN OCE-ANIC

Bwazza. Mbula D.→BANTOID

Bwe→KAREN

Bweende = Bwende. Kongo D.→CENTRAL WESTERN BANTU

Bwel→NAGA-KUKI-CHIN

Bwela. 'Doko D.→NORTH WESTERN BAN-TU

Bwende. Kongo D.→CENTRAL WESTERN BANTU

Bwisi-Talinga→NORTH EASTERN BANTU

Bwol→CHADIC

Bwoncwai = Buoncuai. Rek D.→EASTERN SUDANIC

Bwo'ol = Buol → NORTHWEST AUSTRO-NESIAN

Bworo = Shinasha→OMOTIC

Bwuolo = Buol → NORTHWEST AUSTRO-NESIAN

Byangsi→GYARUNG-MISHMI

Byblian = Byblos. Phoenician D.→SEMITIC

Byblos. Phoenician D.→SEMITIC

Byelorussian = Bielorussian→SLAVIC

Byetri = Metyibo→VOLTA-COMOE

Byjerri = Badjiri→DIERIC

Byore = Uchicrin→GE

Byrre = Kpere. Kari D.→ADAMAWA

Bzhedukh-Temirgoi = Bezhedux. Circassian D. →CAUCASIAN

Bzhedux. Circassian. D.→CAUCASIAN

Bzyb. Abxazo D.→CAUCASIAN

C

Ca Giong = Kayong→MON-KHMER

Cabahyba = Kawaib→TUPI

Cabanapo = Pomo→POMO

Cabasal. Western Bororo D.→BORORO

Cabasal = Western Bororo→BORORO

Cabecar→CHIBCHAN

Cabelludo→GE

Caberne = Island Carib→NORTHERN MAI-PURAN

Cabichi→CHAPACURA-WANHAMAN

Cabichi. Southwest Nambicuara D.→NAMBI-CUARA

Cabichiana = Kabisiana→TUPI

Cabichinana = Kabisiana→TUPI

Cabinda. Kongo D.→CENTRAL WESTERN BANTU

Cabishi, Wild. Cozarini D.→MAIPURAN

Cabishi = Cabichi→CHAPACURA-WANHA-MAN

Cabo. Miskito D.→MISUMALPAN

Cabrai = Kabre→GUR

Cabre = Island Carib→NORTHERN MAI-PURAN

Cac = Tid. Tirma D.→EASTERN SUDANIC

Cac Gia Roglai→WEST INDONESIAN

Cacataibo. Cashibo D.→PANO

Cacataima. Pijao D.→CARIB

Cacchi = Kekchi→MAYAN

Cach = Tid. Tirma D.→EASTERN SUDANIC

Cachar. Khasi D.→MON-KHMER

Cacharari→MAIPURAN

Cache = Kekchi→MAYAN

Cachi = Kekchi→MAYAN

Cachiniti→MAIPURAN

Cachiquel = Cakchiquel→MAYAN

Caci = Tid. Tirma D.→EASTERN SUDANIC

Caddo→CADDOAN

CADDOAN see article

Caddoe = Caddo→CADDOAN

Cadegomeno = Cochimi→HOKAN

Cadegomo = Cochimi→HOKAN

Cadekili-Dyapa = Caduquilidiapa. Tauare D.→ MACRO-TUCANOAN

Cadigue = Sarigue. Mbaya-Guaicuru Tr.→ GUAYCURU

Cadiguegodi = Caduveo. Mbaya-Guaicuru Tr.→ GUAYCURU

Cadiudiapa→MACRO-TUCANOAN
Caduquilidiapa. Tauare D.→MACRO-TUCA-
NOAN
Caduveo. Mbaya-Guaicuru Tr.→GUAYCURU
Caffa = Kefa→OMOTIC
Caffina = Kefa→OMOTIC
Caga→NORTH EASTERN BANTU
Caga = Enga→EAST NEW GUINEA HIGH-
LANDS
Cagaba→CHIBCHAN
Cagayanon→NORTHWEST AUSTRONESIAN
Cagiuong = Kayong→MON-KHMER
Cahinnio. Caddo Tr.→CADDOAN
Cahita→UTO-AZTECAN
Cahokia = Illinois. Miami D.→ALGONQUIAN
Cahroc = Karok→HOKAN
Cahuapana→ANDEAN
CAHUAPANAN→ANDEAN
CAHUAPANAN MAINA = CAHUAPANAN
→ANDEAN
Cahuilla→UTO-AZTECAN
Cahuillo = Cahuilla→UTO-AZTECAN
Cai = Burun→EASTERN SUDANIC
Cai = Tid. Tirma D.→EASTERN SUDANIC
Caiabi = Kayabi→TUPI
CAIAPO = CAYAPO→GE
Caichi = Kekchi→MAYAN
Caicuchana. Carijona D.→CARIB
Caicushana = Caicuchana. Carijona D.→
CARIB
CAINGANG→GE
Caingang→GE
Caingua = Kaiwa. Tupi D.→TUPI
Caiotugui. Mascoy D.→MACRO-PANOAN
Caipotorade. Southern Zamucoan Tr.→EQUA-
TORIAL
Caita = Cahita→UTO-AZTECAN
Cakavian. Serbocroatian D.→SLAVIC
Cakchi = Kekchi→MAYAN
Cakchiquel→MAYAN
Cakgi = Kekchi→MAYAN
Cakhar. Ordos D.→MONGOLIAN
Cakpang. Nupe Tr.→NUPE-GBARI
Cala→GUR
Calabar = Efik→CROSS RIVER BENUE-
CONGO
CALABAR RIVER→CROSS RIVER BENUE-
CONGO
Calaganes = Tagakaolo→NORTHWEST AUS-
TRONESIAN
Calagars = Tagakaolo→NORTHWEST AUS-
TRONESIAN
Calamiano = Kalamian→NORTHWEST AUS-
TRONESIAN

Calapalo = Apalakiri→CARIB
Calapooa = Santiam→KALAPUYA
Calapooiah = Santiam→KALAPUYA
Calapooya = Santiam→KALAPUYA
Calapuya = Santiam→KALAPUYA
Calas-Kurangol. Pasai D.→INDIC
Calauas = Kalagua. Kalinga D.→NORTH-
WEST AUSTRONESIAN
Caliana→MACRO-TUCANOAN
Calillehet. Araucanian D.→PENUTIAN
Calina. Oyampi D.→TUPI
Calinga = Kalinga→NORTHWEST AUSTRO-
NESIAN
Calino = Island Carib→NORTHERN MAI-
PURAN
Calinya. Carib D.→CARIB
Calinya = Island Carib→NORTHERN MAI-
PURAN
Calinyaku = Island Carib→NORTHERN MAI-
PURAN
Callaga = Abipon→GUAYCURU
Callahuaya see article
Callawaya = Callahuaya
Callinago = Island Carib→NORTHERN MAI-
PURAN
Ca-lo→MON-KHMER
Caloosa = Calusa
Calos = Calusa
Calusa see article
Cama = Conibo→PANO
CAMACAN see article
Camaiura = Kamayura→TUPI
Camanche = Comanche. Shoshoni D.→UTO-
AZTECAN
Ca-man-chee = Comanche. Shoshoni D.→
UTO-AZTECAN
Camaniba→CARIB
Camaracoto. Arecuna D.→CARIB
Camatica. Campa D.→MAIPURAN
Camba = Ciriguano. Tupi D.→TUPI
CAMBODIAN see MON-KHMER
Cambodian = Khmer→MON-KHMER
Cameragal = Kameraigal. Gandangara D.→
YUIN-KURIC
Camleroy = Kamilaroi→WIRADJURIC
Cammerraygal = Kameraigal. Gandangara D.→
YUIN-KURIC
Camoria. Central Nicobarese D.→NICOBAR-
ESE
Campa→MAIPURAN
Campanya. Western Bororo D.→BORORO
Campaya. Pioje-Sioni Tr.→MACRO-TUCA-
NOAN
Campuon→MON-KHMER

Camuchivo. Yameo D.→PEBA-YAGUAN
Camuhi→NEW CALEDONIA
CAMUHIC→NEW CALEDONIA
Camuki = Camuhi→NEW CALEDONIA
Camuni→ITALIC
Camuru. Cariri D.→EQUATORIAL
Cana. Aymara Tr.→ANDEAN
Cana = Chana→LULE-VILELA-CHARRUA
Cana Dyapa = Canadiapa→MACRO-TUCA-
    NOAN
Canadiapa→MACRO-TUCANOAN
Canamari→MACRO-TUCANOAN
Canamari→MAIPURAN
Canamari. Jurua-Purus Tr.→PANO
Canari→MACRO-CHIBCHAN
Canchi. Aymara Tr.→ANDEAN
Candoshi→JIVAROAN
Candoxi = Candoshi→JIVAROAN
CANGIN→WEST ATLANTIC
Cangutu. Ipurina D.→MAIPURAN
Caniba = Abnaki. Penobscot D.→ALGON-
    QUIAN
Canienga = Mohawk→IROQUOIS
Canimia = Cunimia→EQUATORIAL
Caninchana→MACRO-TUCANOAN
Canoa = Canoeiro→TUPI
Canoe = Canoeiro→TUPI
Canoeiro→TUPI
Cantonese→CHINESE
Canyari = Canari→MACRO-CHIBCHAN
Caouri. Achagua D.→NORTHERN MAI-
    PURAN
Capachene→TACANA
Capana. Yamamadi D.→ARAWAKAN
Capanahua→PANO
Cape Cumberland→NORTHWESTERN NEW
    HEBRIDES
Capichana = Kabisiana→TUPI
Capiecran = Ramcocamecra→GE
Capinamari. Yamamadi D.→ARAWAKAN
Capite = Cuati→NORTHERN MAIPURAN
Capocho→MACHACALI
Caposho = Capocho→MACHACALI
Cappadocian, Sidetic = Sidetic
Cappadocian see article
Capuibo→PANO
Caquetio→NORTHERN MAIPURAN
CAQUETION→NORTHERN MAIPURAN
Car→NICOBARESE
Cara = Caranki→BARBACOAN
C'ara = Chara→OMOTIC
Carabere. Tupi Tr.→TUPI
Caraca = Carake→MACRO-CHIBCHAN
Caracatage→GE

Caracaty = Cricatage→GE
Carache. Cuica D.→EQUATORIAL
Caraho→GE
Carahuala = Carawala. Sumo Tr.→MISUMAL-
    PAN
CARAJA see article
Caraja = North Cayapo→GE
Carake→MACRO-CHIBCHAN
Caramanta. Cauca Tr.→CARIB
Caranki→BARBACOAN
Caranqui = Caranki→BARBACOAN
Carapana. Tucano Tr.→MACRO-TUCANOAN
Carapana = Miranya→WITOTOAN
Caraque = Carake→MACRO-CHIBCHAN
Carare→CARIB
Caras = Munduruku→TUPI
Carate→CARIB
Caravare = Kuruaya→TUPI
Carawala. Sumo Tr.→MISUMALPAN
CARAYA = CARAJA
Caraya = Caraja→CARAJA
Cari. Great Andamanese D.→ANDAMANESE
Cariaia→NORTHERN MAIPURAN
Carian see article
Cariaya = Cariaia→NORTHERN MAIPURAN
Carib, Island→NORTHERN MAIPURAN
Carib, Black = Island Carib→NORTHERN
    MAIPURAN
CARIB see article
CARIB, MACRO- see article
Caribice. Carib D.→CARIB
Caribou-eaters = Etheneldeli. Chipewyan Tr.→
    ATHAPASCAN-EYAK
Carijo. Tupi Tr.→TUPI
Carijona→CARIB
Carima. Tupi Tr.→TUPI
Carinapagoto→CARIB
Carinepagoto = Carinapagoto→CARIB
Cario. Tupi Tr.→TUPI
Caripuna→PANO
Caripuna = Catuquina→PANO
CARIRI→EQUATORIAL
Cariri→EQUATORIAL
Carlos = Calusa
Carmel = Esselen→HOKAN
Carmel = Rumsen. Southern Costanoan D.→
    MIWOK-COSTANOAN
Carmelo = Esselen→HOKAN
Carnijo = Fulnio→MACRO-GE
Carolinean→MICRONESIAN
CAROLINIAN→MICRONESIAN
Carrapa. Cauca Tr.→CARIB
Carrier→ATHAPASCAN-EYAK
Carrizo→HOKAN

Carrua = Charrua→LULE-VILELA-CHAR-
RUA
Cartama. Cauca Tr.→CARIB
Carutana→NORTHERN MAIPURAN
Caryari = Cauyari→NORTHERN MAI-
PURAN
Cascades. Upper Chinook D.→CHINOOKAN
Cashiita. Cueretu D.→MACRO-TUCANOAN
Cashinawa→PANO
Cashiniti = Cachiniti→MAIPURAN
Cashino = Caxinyo. Cashibo D.→PANO
Cashquiha. Mascoy D.→MACRO-PANOAN
Casiguran→NORTHWEST AUSTRONESIAN
Casiguran Dumagat = Casiguran.→NORTH-
WEST AUSTRONESIAN
Casqui = Kaskimpo. Koasati D.→MUSKO-
GEAN
Cassanga = Kasanga→WEST ATLANTIC
Cassubian = Kashubian→SLAVIC
Castilian = Spanish→ROMANCE
Castors des Prairies = Sarsi→ATHAPASCAN-
EYAK
Cata. Massachusett Tr.→ALGONQUIAN
Catacao→ANDEAN
Catalan→ROMANCE
Catanduanes. Bikol D.→NORTHWEST AUS-
TRONESIAN
Catanduva. Tupi Tr.→TUPI
Cataonian see article
Catapolitani→NORTHERN MAIPURAN
Catatumbo. Mape D.→CARIB
Catauian = Pianocoto→CARIB
Catauichi = Catawishi→MACRO-TUCA-
NOAN
Catawba→MACRO-SIOUAN
Catawian = Pianocoto→CARIB
Catawishi→MACRO-TUCANOAN
Catethoi = Catethoy→CAMACAN
Catethoy→CAMACAN
Catiana→MAIPURAN
Catio = Bando. Southern Epera D.→CHOCO
Catio = Dabeiba. Northern Epera D.→CHOCO
Catloltq = Comox→SALISH
Catloltx = Comox→SALISH
Catongo. Campa D.→MAIPURAN
CATUKINA = CATUQUINA→MACRO-TU-
CANOAN
Catukina = Catuquina→PANO
Catukina = Catuquina→MACRO-TUCA-
NOAN
Catukino = Catuquino→MACRO-TUCA-
NOAN
CATUQUINA→MACRO-TUCANOAN
Catuquina→PANO

Catuquina→MACRO-TUCANOAN
Catuquinaru. Kawaib Tr.→TUPI
Catuquino→MACRO-TUCANOAN
Caua→NORTHERN MAIPURAN
Cauaiua = Kawaib→TUPI
Cauca→CARIB
Cauca→CHOCO
Caucahue. Alacaluf D.→ANDEAN
CAUCASIAN see article
Caucawe = Caucahue. Alacaluf D.→ANDEAN
Caughnawaga = Mohawk→IROQUOIS
Cauhib = Kawaib→TUPI
Cauichana→NORTHERN MAIPURAN
Caumari. Peba D.→PEBA-YAGUAN
Cauwachi. Peba D.→PEBA-YAGUAN
Cauyari→NORTHERN MAIPURAN
Cavcuvenskij. Koryak D.→CHUKCHEE-KAM-
CHATKAN
Cavdur. Turkmen D.→TURKIC
Cavina = Cavinena→TACANA
Cavinena→TACANA
Cavineno = Cavinena→TACANA
Cavinenyo = Cavinena→TACANA
Cavinya = Cavinena→TACANA
Caviteno→ROMANCE
Cawahib = Kawaib→TUPI
Cawishana = Cauichana→NORTHERN MAI-
PURAN
Caxiita = Cashiita. Cheretu D.→MACRO-TU-
CANOAN
Caxinyo. Cashibo D.→PANO
Caxur = Tsaxur→CAUCASIAN
Cayamo = North Cayapo→GE
Cayapa→BARBACOAN
CAYAPA-COLORADO→BARBACOAN
CAYAPO→GE
Cayapo, North→GE
Cayapo, South→GE
Cayawabas = Cayuvava→EQUATORIAL
Cayiuker = Cayuga. Seneca Tr.→IROQUOIS
Cayor. Wolof D.→WEST ATLANTIC
Cayua = Kaiwa. Tupi D.→TUPI
Cayuaba = Cayuvava→EQUATORIAL
Cayuga. Seneca Tr.→IROQUOIS
Cayuishana = Cauichana→NORTHERN MAI-
PURAN
Cayus = Cayuse→PENUTIAN
Cayuse→PENUTIAN
Cayuvava→EQUATORIAL
Cæte. Tupi Tr.→TUPI
Cebuan = Sebuano→NORTHWEST AUSTRO-
NESIAN
Cebuano = Sebuano→NORTHWEST AUS-
TRONESIAN

Cechi = Kekchi→MAYAN
Cecilville. SHASTAN TR.→HOKAN
Cegiha = Dhegiha→SIOUAN
Celdala = Tzeltal→MAYAN
Celdale = Tzeltal→MAYAN
CELEBES, CENTRAL AND SOUTHERN see
  article
CELEBES, NORTHERN see article
Celilo = Columbia River. Sahaptian D.→
  SAHAPTIAN-NEZ PERCE
Celtala = Tzeltal→MAYAN
CELTIC see article
CELTIC, BRITTONIC = BRYTHONIC→
  CELTIC
Cemba = Tobote→GUR
Cemel = Cimel. Rek D.→EASTERN SU-
  DANIC
Cemuel = Nandi→EASTERN SUDANIC
Cendal = Tzeltal→MAYAN
Cenu→CARIB
Cenu→CHOCO
Cenufanu. Cenu D.→CARIB
Cepleng = Endo. Pokot D.→EASTERN SU-
  DANIC
Ceram = Seran→EAST INDONESIAN
Ceri = Seri→HOKAN
Cerochese = Cherokee→IROQUOIS
Cetguanes = Yuma. River Yuman D.→
  YUMAN
ce-Vende = Vende→SOUTH EASTERN
  BANTU
Cewa. Nyanja D.→CENTRAL EASTERN
  BANTU
Cez = Dido→CAUCASIAN
Chaapwurru = Tjapwurong→KULINIC
Chabacano = Zamboangueno→ROMANCE
Chacahuaxtli. Totonac D.→TOTONACAN
Chacamecra→GE
Chacobo→PANO
Chacobo = Cayuvava→EQUATORIAL
Chacopata→CARIB
Chacriaba→GE
Chacta = Choctaw→MUSKOGEAN
Chactaw = Choctaw→MUSKOGEAN
Chactawice = Choctaw→MUSKOGEAN
Chactawisch = Choctaw→MUSKOGEAN
CHADIC see article
CHADO-HAMITIC = WEST CHADIC→
  CHADIC
CHAGA→NORTH EASTERN BANTU
Chaga = Caga→NORTH EASTERN BANTU
Chagga = Caga→NORTH EASTERN BANTU
Chagos. French Creole D.→ROMANCE
Chaha. Central West Gurage D.→SEMITIC

Chaharlang. Bakhtiari Tr.→IRANIAN
Chahta = Choctaw→MUSKOGEAN
Chahta-Muskokee = Choctaw→MUSKOGEAN
Chaich = Tid. Tirma D.→EASTERN SUDAN-
  IC
Chaima = Chayma→CARIB
Chairel→BURMESE-LOLO
Chairel = Tshairel→NAGA-KUKI-CHIN
Chajul. Aguacatec D.→MAYAN
Chakali→GUR
Chakankni. Molale Tr.→PENUTIAN
Chakchiuma = Chickasaw. Choctaw D.→MUS-
  KOGEAN
Chake→CARIB
Chakosi→VOLTA-COMOE
Chakrima = Tsakrima→NAGA-KUKI-CHIN
Chakroma = Tengima. Agami D.→NAGA-
  KUKI-CHIN
Chala→GUR
Chala = Ron→CHADIC
Chalah. Chrau D.→MON-KHMER
Chalchitan. Aguacatec D.→MAYAN
Chalchitec = Aguacatec→MAYAN
Chaldean. Akkadian D.→SEMITIC
Chaldean = Urartaean→HURRIAN
Chaliva. Burica D.→CHIBCHAN
Chalkandu, Northern Altai D.→TURKIC
Chaltu = Bazaar Hindi. Western Hindi D.→
  INDIC
Chalu = Bazaar Hindi. Western Hindi D.→
  INDIC
Cham→ADAMAWA
Cham→WEST INDONESIAN
Cham = Ching. Mak D.→KAM-TAI
Chama→TACANA
Chama = Conibo→PANO
Chama = Migurian. Timote D.→EQUATO-
  RIAL
Chamalal→CAUCASIAN
Chamano. Moseten D.→MACRO-PANOAN
Chamariko→HOKAN
Chamarwa = Bangaru. Western Hindi D.→
  INDIC
Chamba→ADAMAWA
Chamba = Kasele→GUR
Chamba = Tobote→GUR
Chamba Daka = Daka→ADAMAWA
Chamba Lahuli = Manchati → GYARUNG-
  MISHMI
Chamba Lekon = Lekon→ADAMAWA
Chambling = Rodong→GYARUNG-MISHMI
Chamboa→CARAJA
Chambri→NORTH NEW GUINEA
Chameali. Western Pahari D.→INDIC

Chami. Southern Epera D.→CHOCO
CHAMIC→WEST INDONESIAN
Chamicura = Chamicuro→ARAWAKAN
Chamicuro→ARAWAKAN
Chamir = Khamir→CUSHITIC
CHAMITO-SEMITIQUE = AFROASIATIC
Chamo→PLATEAU BENUE-CONGO
Chamorro→NORTHWEST AUSTRONESIAN
Chamula. Tzotzil D.→MAYAN
Chamula = Tzotzil→MAYAN
Chana→LULE-VILELA-CHARRUA
Chana = Guana→MAIPURAN
Chanabal = Tojolabal→MAYAN
Chanawese = Conoy. Mohegan D.→ALGON-
    QUIAN
Chanco→CARIB
Chanco. Yunca D.→CHIPAYAN
Chanco = Waunana→CHOCO
Chandari. Oriya D.→INDIC
Chandule. Tupi Tr.→TUPI
Chane→MAIPURAN
Chaneabal = Tojolabal→MAYAN
Chang. Tangsa D.→BODO-NAGA-KACHIN
Chang = Dschang-Bangwa. Bafou D.→BAN-
    TOID
Chang = Limbu→GYARUNG-MISHMI
Changina = Changuena. Burica D.→CHIB-
    CHAN
Changki. Ao D.→NAGA-KUKI-CHIN
Changriwa→INDO-PACIFIC
Changuane. Warao D.→MACRO-CHIBCHAN
Changuena. Burica D.→CHIBCHAN
Chansi = Kasele→GUR
Chaobon = Pa Pao. Lawa D.→PALAUNG-WA
Chaouia→BERBER
CHAPACURA-WANHAMAN see article
Chapan. Achagua D.→NORTHERN MAI-
    PURAN
Chapara. Mape D.→CARIB
Chaplino. St. Lawrence Island Yupik D.→
    ESKIMO-ALEUT
Char = Zakataly. Avar D.→CAUCASIAN
Chara→OMOTIC
Chara→PLATEAU BENUE-CONGO
Chararana = Echoaldi.   Guana   D.→MAI-
    PURAN
Charca. Aymara Tr.→ANDEAN
Chari→MON-KHMER
Chariar. Great Andamanese D.→ANDAMAN-
    ESE
CHARI-NILE see article
Charmong = Djauan→GUNWINGGUAN
Charotari. Gujarati D.→INDIC
Charrua→LULE-VILELA-CHARRUA

Charumbul=Darambal→WAKA-KABIC
Chashan = Lashi→BODO-NAGA-KACHIN
Chaspa. Atsahuaca D.→PANO
Chasta Costa→ATHAPASCAN-EYAK
Chasu = Asu→CENTRAL EASTERN BANTU
Chatino→ZAPOTECAN
Chauan = Djauan→GUNWINGGUAN
Chauchila. Valley Yokuts D.→YOKUTS
Chaudangsi→GYARUNG-MISHMI
Chaui. Pawnee D.→CADDOAN
Chaui = Chayahuita→ANDEAN
Chau-Ma = Maa. Koho D.→MON-KHMER
Chaungtha. Burmese D.→BURMESE-LOLO
Chaurasya→GYARUNG-MISHMI
Chavante→GE
Chavante = Oti→MACRO-GE
Chaw = Kyau→NAGA-KUKI-CHIN
CHAWAI→PLATEAU BENUE-CONGO
Chawai→PLATEAU BENUE-CONGO
Chawano = Shawnee→ALGONQUIAN
Chawe = Chawai → PLATEAU   BENUE-
    CONGO
Chawi = Chawai → PLATEAU BENUE-
    CONGO
Chawi = Chayahuita→ANDEAN
Chayahuita→ANDEAN
Chayavita = Chayahuita→ANDEAN
Chayenne = Cheyenne→ALGONQUIAN
Chayma→CARIB
Che = Kasele→GUR
Cheangwa = Widi. Muliara D.→KARDU
Cheberloj. Chechen D.→CAUCASIAN
Chebero→ANDEAN
CHEBEROAN→ANDEAN
Chechen→CAUCASIAN
Chedi = Lisu→BURMESE-LOLO
Cheerake = Cherokee→IROQUOIS
Cheha = Chaha. Central West Gurage D.→
    SEMITIC
Chehalis. Halkomelem D.→SALISH
Chehalis, Lower→SALISH
Chehalis, Upper→SALISH
Chehalis = Upper Chehalis→SALISH
Cheiru. Tupi Tr.→TUPI
Chejende. Cuica D.→EQUATORIAL
Cheke→CHADIC
Chel-a-ke = Cherokee→IROQUOIS
Chelan. Columbian D.→SALISH
Cheleki = Cherokee→IROQUOIS
Cheli = Lisu→BURMESE-LOLO
Chell-o-kee = Cherokee→IROQUOIS
Chemainus. Halkomelem D.→SALISH
Chemant = Qemant. Quara D.→CUSHITIC
Chemegue = Chemehuevi. Southern Paiute D.→

UTO-AZTECAN

Chemehuevi. Southern Paiute D.→UTO-AZTECAN

Chemgui = Bezhedux. Circassian D.→CAUCASIAN

Chemuevi = Chemehuevi. Southern Paiute D.→UTO-AZTECAN

Chenapian→SEPIK

Chencha. Walamo Tr.→OMOTIC

Chendariang. Central Sakai D.→SAKAI

Cheng→MON-KHMER

Chenook = Lower Chinook→CHINOOKAN

Chepang→GYARUNG-MISHMI

Chera = Chara→PLATEAU BENUE-CONGO

Cherakee = Cherokee→IROQUOIS

Cherchen. Uighur D.→TURKIC

Cheremis→URALIC

Cherente→GE

Cherepong-Larteh-Anum = Chiripon-Lete-Anum→VOLTA-COMOE

Cheres = Ulu Ceres. Outer Eastern Sakai D.→SAKAI

Cherkes. Circassian D.→CAUCASIAN

Cherkes = Circassian→CAUCASIAN

Cherokee→IROQUOIS

Cheroki = Cherokee→IROQUOIS

Cherrapunji. Khasi D.→MON-KHMER

Chesapeake. Powhatan Tr.→ALGONQUIAN

Cheta = Seta→TUPI

Chetco. Chasta Costa D.→ATHAPASCAN-EYAK

Chetemacha = Chitamacha → MACRO-ALGONQUIAN

Chetimacha = Chitamacha → MACRO-ALGONQUIAN

Cheva = Cewa. Nyanja D.→CENTRAL EASTERN BANTU

Chewa = Cewa. Nyanja D.→CENTRAL EASTERN BANTU

Chewelah. Kalispel D.→SALISH

Cheyenne→ALGONQUIAN

CHƏMA see MON-KHMER

Chhao-bon = Nialuok→MON-KHMER

Chhattisgarhi, Eastern Hindi D.→INDIC

Chhingtang = Lambichhong → GYARUNG-MISHMI

Chi. Mak D.→KAM-TAI

Chiaha. Hitchiti D.→MUSKOGEAN

Ch'iang→SINO-TIBETAN

CHIAPANEC-MANGUEAN→MANGUEAN

Chiapaneco→MANGUEAN

Chiarcota. Yarigui D.→CARIB

Chibak→CHADIC

Chibbak = Chibak→CHADIC

Chibbok = Chibak→CHADIC

Chibbuk = Chibak→CHADIC

Chibcha→CHIBCHAN

CHIBCHAN see article

CHIBCHAN, MACRO see article

Chibok = Chibak→CHADIC

Chibora = Tfuea. Tsou D.→FORMOSAN AUSTRONESIAN

Chibora = Tsuihwan. Bunun D.→FORMOSAN AUSTRONESIAN

Chicasa = Chickasaw. Choctaw D.→MUSKOGEAN

Chich = Ciec. Agar D.→EASTERN SUDANIC

Chicheren. Campa D.→MAIPURAN

Chichimec = Toltec. Pipil D.→UTO-AZTECAN

Chichimeca = Pame→OTOMIAN

Chichimeca-Jonaz→OTOMIAN

Chicimeco = Chichimeca-Jonaz→OTOMIAN

Chickahominy. Powhatan Tr.→ALGONQUIAN

Chickasa = Chickasaw. Choctaw D.→MUSKOGEAN

Chickasah = Chickasaw. Choctaw D.→MUSKOGEAN

Chickasaw. Choctaw D.→MUSKOGEAN

Chickataubut. Massachusett Tr.→ALGONQUIAN

Chicmeca = Chichimeca-Jonaz→OTOMIAN

Chicomuceltec→MAYAN

Chicri = Uchicrin→GE

Ch'ien-chiang→KAM-TAI

Chiga = Ciga→NORTH EASTERN BANTU

Chigaa. Teda Tr.→SAHARAN

Chikachiki. Bihari D.→INDIC

Chikasah = Chickasaw. Choctaw D.→MUSKOGEAN

Chikasha = Chickasaw. Choctaw D.→MUSKOGEAN

Chikena = Shikiana→CARIB

Chiki = Chiqui→GE

Chikiyamt = Cunco. Araucanian D.→PENUTIAN

Chikkasah = Chickasaw. Choctaw D.→MUSKOGEAN

Chikriaba = Chacriaba→GE

Chikunda = Kunda→CENTRAL EASTERN BANTU

Chikuya = Kukwa. South Teke D.→NORTH WESTERN BANTU

Chil. Eastern Mnong D.→MON-KHMER

Chil. Koho D.→MON-KHMER

Chilanga. Lenga D.→MACRO-CHIBCHAN

Chilcotian→ATHAPASCAN-EYAK

Chilila = Dakakari → PLATEAU BENUE-CONGO

Chiliuvo→TACANA
Chilliwack. Halkomelem D.→SALISH
Chilote = Huiliche. Araucanian D.→PENU-
TIAN
Chilowhist = Methow. Okanogan D.→SALISH
Chiltepec→CHINANTECAN
Chiluba = Sanga→CENTRAL WESTERN
BANTU
Chilula. Hupa D.→ATHAPASCAN-EYAK
CHIMAKUAN see article
Chimakum→CHIMAKUAN
Chimalapa = Zoque→MIXE-ZOQUE
Chimana = Jumana → NORTHERN MAI-
PURAN
Chimane. Moseten D.→MACRO-PANOAN
Chimaniza. Moseten D.→MACRO-PANOAN
Chimbioa = Chamboa→CARAJA
CHIMBU→EAST NEW GUINEA HIGH-
LANDS
Chimbu→EAST NEW GUINEA HIGH-
LANDS
Chimbuiha. Molale Tr.→PENUTIAN
Chimehuevi = Chemehuevi. Southern Paiute D.
→UTO-AZTECAN
Chimesyan = Tsimshian→PENUTIAN
Chimiel = Cimel. Rek D.→EASTERN SU-
DANIC
Chimila = San Jorge, Northern Epera D.→
CHOCO
Chimmesyan = Tsimshian→PENUTIAN
Chimmsyan = Tsimshian→PENUTIAN
Chimsyan = Tsimshian→PENUTIAN
Chimu = Yunca→CHIPAYAN
CHIN→NAGA-KUKI-CHIN
Chin = Lillooet→SALISH
Ch'in Lien. Cantonese D.→CHINESE
China Camp. Koko Jelandji D.→PAMA-
MARIC
Chinantec, Azumacin→CHINANTECAN
Chinantec, Lalana→CHINANTECAN
Chinantec, Ojitlan→CHINANTECAN
Chinantec, Quiotepec→CHINANTECAN
Chinantec, Usila→CHINANTECAN
CHINANTECAN see article
Chinbe = Chinbok→NAGA-KUKI-CHIN
Chinbok→NAGA-KUKI-CHIN
Chinbon. Aso Tr.→NAGA-KUKI-CHIN
Chinese, Northern=Mandarin→CHINESE
CHINESE see article
Ching. Mak D.→KAM-TAI
CHINGHPAW = KACHIN→BODO-NAGA-
KACHIN
Chinghpaw = Chingpaw → BODO-NAGA-
KACHIN

CHINGPA'O = KACHIN → BODO-NAGA-
KACHIN
Chingpaw→BODO-NAGA-KACHIN
Chingp'o = Chingpaw → BODO-NAGA-
KACHIN
Chinguil. Gula D.→ADAMAWA
Chininkonde = Makonde → SOUTH EAST-
ERN BANTU
Chinook, Lower→CHINOOKAN
Chinook, Upper→CHINOOKAN
Chinook, Coastal = Lower Chinook→CHI-
NOOKAN
Chinook Jargon→CHINOOKAN
CHINOOKAN see article
Chintagottine. Dogrib Tr.→ATHAPASCAN-
EYAK
Chinuc = Lower Chinook→CHINOOKAN
Chinuk = Lower Chinook→CHINOOKAN
Chinyanja = Nyanja→CENTRAL EASTERN
BANTU
Chip→CHADIC
Chipa = Xiparicot→CARIB
Chipaia = Sipaya→TUPI
Chipaya→CHIPAYAN
Chipaya = Sipaya→TUPI
CHIPAYAN see article
CHIPAYA-URU = CHIPAYAN
Chipewyan→ATHAPASCAN-EYAK
Chipinaua. Jurua-Purus Tr.→PANO
Chipon. Puyuma D.→FORMOSAN AUSTRO-
NESIAN
Chipouais = Ojibwa→ALGONQUIAN
Chippawa = Ojibwa→ALGONQUIAN
Chippaway = Ojibwa→ALGONQUIAN
Chippewa = Ojibwa→ALGONQUIAN
Chipun = Chipon. Puyuma D.→FORMOSAN
AUSTRONESIAN
Chiquena = Shikiana→CARIB
Chiqui→GE
Chiqui. Caingang D.→GE
Chiquimiti = Baure→MAIPURAN
Chiquito→MAIPURAN
Chiquito, Southern = Churapa→CHIQUITO
CHIQUITO see article
Chir = Mondari. Bari D.→EASTERN SUDAN-
IC
Chira. Sec D.→ANDEAN
Chiri→CHADIC
CHIRIBA = CHIRIGUA→TACANA
Chiricahua. Navajo D. → ATHAPASCAN-
EYAK
Chiricoa. Guahibo D.→EQUATORIAL
CHIRIGUA→TACANA
Chiriguano = Ciriguano. Tupi D.→TUPI

Chiriluo. Burica D.→CHIBCHAN
CHIRINAN = WAICAN
Chiripa. Tupi Tr.→TUPI
Chiripo = Cabecar→CHIBCHAN
Chiripon-Lete-Anum→VOLTA-COMOE
Chiroa. Kanembu Tr.→SAHARAN
Chirokina. Toba Tr.→GUAYCURU
Chiroro. Kanga Tr.→KORDOFANIAN
Chirpalji = Djirbal. Wakaman D.→PAMA-
    MARIC
Chiru→NAGA-KUKI-CHIN
Chiru = Chiriluo. Burica D.→CHIBCHAN
Chirumas = Tuma. River Yuman D.→YUMAN
Chisca = Yuchi→MACRO-SIOUAN
Chishona = Korekore. Shona D.→SOUTH
    EASTERN BANTU
Chishona = Zezeru. Shona D.→SOUTH
    EASTERN BANTU
Chistochina. Ahtena D.→ATHAPASCAN-
    EYAK
Chiswina = Zezeru. Shona D.→SOUTH
    EASTERN BANTU
Chitamacha→MACRO-ALGONQUIAN
Chitina. Ahtena D.→ATHAPASCAN-EYAK
Chitkhuli = Tsikhuli→GYARUNG-MISHMI
Chittagong. Aso Tr.→NAGA-KUKI-CHIN
Chiung-nai. Punu D.→MIAO-YAO
Chivamona→TACANA
Chiwere→SIOUAN
Chkhala = Chxala. Zan D.→CAUCASIAN
Chocama = Waunana→CHOCO
Chocheno = Niles. Northern Costanoan D.→
    MIWOK-COSTANOAN
Chocho = Tlapanec→TLAPANECAN
Chocktaw = Choctaw→MUSKOGEAN
Chocleng. Seta D.→TUPI
CHOCO see article
Chocren = Xokreng. Caingang D.→GE
Choctaw→MUSKOGEAN
Choinimni. Foothill North Yokuts D.→
    YOKUTS
Chokobawa = Chokobo→PLATEAU BENUE-
    CONGO
Chokobo→PLATEAU BENUE-CONGO
Choktah = Choctaw→MUSKOGEAN
Choktaw = Choctaw→MUSKOGEAN
Chokwe = Ciokwe → SOUTH WESTERN
    BANTU
CHOKWE-LUCHAZI→SOUTH WESTERN
    BANTU
Chol→MAYAN
Chol Lacandon. Chol D.→MAYAN
CHOLAN→MAYAN
CHOLO = CHOCO

Choloid = Chol→MAYAN
Cholon→ANDEAN
Cholti. Chol. D.→MAYAN
Cholti = Chol→MAYAN
Cholti = Chorti→MAYAN
Choluteca. Mangue D.→MANGUEAN
Chomo→JUKUNOID
CHON→ANDEAN
Chon→ANDEAN
Chona = Choni. Central Tibetan D.→TIBETAN
Chong→MON-KHMER
Chongee→CHADIC
Chongue = Ofo→SIOUAN
Choni. Central Tibetan D.→TIBETAN
Chono. Alacaluf D.→ANDEAN
Chonopi = Ashushlay→MATACO
CHONTAL = TEQUISTLATECAN
Chontal of Tabasco→MAYAN
Chontaquiro. Piro D.→MAIPURAN
Chonvugn→BOTOCUDO
Chonzo = Concho. Cahuapana D.→ANDEAN
Chooraroo = Tjuroro. Binigura D.→NGAY-
    ARDA
Choororo = Tjuroro. Binigura D.→NGAY-
    ARDA
Ch'opa = Rawang→BODO-NAGA-KACHIN
CHOPI→SOUTH EASTERN BANTU
Chopi→SOUTH EASTERN BANTU
Chopi = Lwo→EASTERN SUDANIC
Chopunnish = Nez Perce→SAHAPTIN-NEZ
    PERCE
Chora = Cora→UTO-AZTECAN
Chori. Jaba D.→PLATEAU BENUE-CONGO
Chori = Siriono→TUPI
Chorotega = Choluteca. Mangue D.→MAN-
    GUEAN
Chorotega = Mangue→MANGUEAN
CHOROTEGAN = MANGUEAN
Choroti→MATACO
Choroti = Moianec→MAYAN
Chorte = Chorti→MAYAN
Chorti→MAYAN
Chorti. Chol D.→MAYAN
Chosen = Korean→ALTAIC
Chota = Cora→UTO-AZTECAN
Chotar Nagpuri = Nagpuri. Bihari D.→
    INDIC
Choton = Khoton→TURKIC
Chowra→NICOBARESE
Chrau→MON-KHMER
Christeneaux = Cree→ALGONQUIAN
Chru→WEST INDONESIAN
Chua = Cwa. Nancere D.→CHADIC
Chuabo = Cuabo → SOUTH EASTERN

BANTU
Chuala = Guana→MAIPURAN
Chuambo = Cuabo → SOUTH EASTERN
BANTU
Chuana = Tswana → SOUTH EASTERN
BANTU
Chuang→KAM-TAI
CHUANG = JUI→KAM-TAI
CHUANGCHIA = JUI→KAM-TAI
Chuave→EAST NEW GUINEA HIGHLANDS
Chubo = Menemo→BANTOID
Chucholtec = Chocho→POPOLOCAN
Chuchon = Chocho→POPOLOCAN
Chuchotec = Chocho→POPOLOCAN
Chuchures. Pipil D.→UTO-AZTECAN
Chuckchansi. Foothill North Yokuts D.→
YOKUTS
Chucuna. Achagua D.→NORTHERN MAI-
PURAN
Chucuna. Cuna D.→CHIBCHAN
Chuh = Chujean→MAYAN
Chuhe = Chujean→MAYAN
Chuihwan = Thao→FORMOSAN AUSTRO-
NESIAN
Chuj = Chujean→MAYAN
Chuje = Chujean→MAYAN
Chujean→MAYAN
Chuka. Tharaka D.→NORTH EASTERN
BANTU
Chukaimina. Foothill North Yokuts D.→
YOKUTS
Chukchansi. Foothill North Yokuts D.→YO-
KUTS
Chukchee→CHUKCHEE-KAMCHATKAN
CHUKCHEE-KAMCHATKAN see article
Chukchi = Chukchee → CHUKCHEE-KAM-
CHATKAN
Chukudum. Didinga Tr.→EASTERN SUDAN-
IC
Chulamni. Valley Yokuts D.→YOKUTS
Chulikata Mishmi→GYARUNG-MISHMI
Chulilaukunnu. Araucanian D.→PENUTIAN
Chulupi = Ashushlay→MATACO
Chulupi = Chunupi. Vilela Tr.→LULE-
VILELA-CHARRUA
Chulym→TURKIC
Chumna→TACANA
Chumano. Moseten D.→MACRO-PANOAN
CHUMASH→HOKAN
Chumpa. Moseten D.→MACRO-PANOAN
Chumula. Burica D.→CHIBCHAN
Chumulu = Chumula. Burica D.→CHIBCHAN
Chumulue = Chumula. Burica D.→CHIB-
CHAN

Chumuru = Nawuri. Guan D.→VOLTA-COMOE
Chuncho→TACANA
Chuncho = Leco→ANDEAN
Chunchu = Chuncho→TACANA
CHUNG = JUI→KAM-TAI
Chung = Lisu→BURMESE-LOLO
CHUNGCHIA = JUI→KAM-TAI
Chungli. Ao D.→NAGA-KUKI-CHIN
Chunupi. Vilela Tr.→LULE-VILELA-CHAR-
RUA
Churafada = Sherfada. Tebu Tr.→SAHARAN
Churapa→CHIQUITO
Churitana = Churitura. Muniche D.→MACRO-
TUCANOAN
Churitura. Muniche D.→MACRO-TUCA-
NOAN
Churma = Suri. Tirma D.→EASTERN SU-
DANIC
Churo = Cur. Manjaku D.→WEST ATLANTIC
Churoro = Tjuroro. Binigura D.→NGAY-
ARDA
Churoya→EQUATORIAL
Churu = Chru→WEST INDONESIAN
Churuya = Churoya→EQUATORIAL
Chuvantzy→YUKAGHIR
Chuvash→TURKIC
Chuware = G//abake→KHOISAN
Chuy. Altai D.→TURKIC
Chwee = Twi. Akan D.→VOLTA-COMOE
Chxala. Zan D.→CAUCASIAN
ci-Athu = Asu → CENTRAL EASTERN
BANTU
Cic = Ciec. Agar D.→EASTERN SUDANIC
ci-Cewa = Cewa. Nyanja D.→CENTRAL
EASTERN BANTU
ci-Cifundi = Cifundi. Swahili D.→CENTRAL
EASTERN BANTU
ci-Cuabo = Cuabo → SOUTH EASTERN
BANTU
Ciec. Agar D.→EASTERN SUDANIC
Cieguaje. Pioje-Sioni Tr.→MACRO-TUCA-
NOAN
Cifundi. Swahili D.→CENTRAL EASTERN
BANTU
Ciga→NORTH EASTERN BANTU
ci-Gogo = Gogo → CENTRAL EASTERN
BANTU
ci-Ikuhane = Subia → SOUTH WESTERN
BANTU
ci-Ila = Ila→CENTRAL EASTERN BANTU
Ciina Mukuni = Lenje→CENTRAL EASTERN
BANTU
Ciita = Central Koma→KOMAN
ci-Kagulu = Kagulu→CENTRAL EASTERN

BANTU

ci-Kanyoka = Konyoka→CENTRAL WEST-
ERN BANTU

Cikaonde = Kaonde→CENTRAL WESTERN
BANTU

ci-Kunda = Kunda→CENTRAL EASTERN
BANTU

Cikwakwa = Kwachikwakwa. Shona D.→
SOUTH EASTERN BANTU

Cilasi. Sina D.→INDIC

ci-Lenje = Lenje→CENTRAL EASTERN
BANTU

Cilician see article

Cilis. Maiya D.→INDIC

Cilowe = Lomwe → SOUTH EASTERN
BANTU

Ciluba = Luba-Kasai. Luba-Lulua D.→
CENTRAL WESTERN BANTU

Ciluba = Luba-Lulua → CENTRAL WEST-
ERN BANTU

ci-Lucazi = Lucazi→SOUTH WESTERN
BANTU

ci-Luimbi = Luimbi→SOUTH WESTERN
BANTU

ci-Lunda = Lunda→CENTRAL WESTERN
BANTU

Cima. Kalasa-ala D.→NURISTANI

ci-Mabiha = Mabiha→SOUTH EASTERN
BANTU

ci-Makonde = Mokande→SOUTH EASTERN
BANTU

ci-Manda = Manda→CENTRAL EASTERN
BANTU

Cimanganja = Maŋanja. Nyanja D.→CENTRAL
EASTERN BANTU

Cima-Nisey-ala. Kalasa-ala D.→NURISTANI

ci-Matengo = Matengo→CENTRAL EAST-
ERN BANTU

Cimba. Herero D.→SOUTH WESTERN
BANTU

ci-Mbalazi = Mbalazi. Tikuu D.→CENTRAL
EASTERN BANTU

ci-Mbunda = Mbunda→SOUTH WESTERN
BANTU

ci-Megi = Megi. Kagulu D.→CENTRAL
EASTERN BANTU

Cimel. Rek D.→EASTERN SUDANIC

Cimiaŋ = Tshimiang. Dari D.→CHADIC

ci-Mpoto = Mpoto→CENTRAL EASTERN
BANTU

ci-Mwera = Mwera → SOUTH EASTERN
BANTU

Cinaloa = Sinaloa. Cahita D.→UTO-AZTE-
CAN

Cinanteco = Tzotzil→MAYAN

ci-Ndonde = Ndonde → SOUTH EASTERN
BANTU

Cinga→NORTH WESTERN BANTU

Cingalese = Sinhalese→INDIC

ci-Ngoni = Ngoni → CENTRAL EASTERN
BANTU

ci-Nsenga = Nsenga→CENTRAL EASTERN
BANTU

ci-Nyanja = Nyanja→CENTRAL EASTERN
BANTU

ci-Nyungwe = Nyungwe → CENTRAL EAST
ERN BANTU

Cioko = Ciokwe → SOUTH WESTERN
BANTU

Ciokwe→SOUTH WESTERN BANTU

Cipeta = Peta. Nyanja D.→CENTRAL EAST-
ERN BANTU

Cipo = Sipo→ARAWAKAN

ci-Podzo = Podzo → CENTRAL EASTERN
BANTU

ci-Pogolo = Pogolo → CENTRAL EASTERN
BANTU

Cipoka = Poka. Tumbuka D.→CENTRAL
EASTERN BANTU

Cirasha = Gidole→CUSHITIC

Circassian→CAUCASIAN

Circee = Sarsi→ATHAPASCAN-EYAK

Ciri→NEW CALEDONIA

Ciries = Sarsi→ATHAPASCAN-EYAK

Ciriguano. Tupi D.→TUPI

ci-Rue = Rue→CENTRAL EASTERN BANTU

Cirue = Rue→CENTRAL EASTERN BANTU

ci-Sena = Sena → CENTRAL EASTERN
BANTU

cishi-lange = lange. Luba-Lulua D.→CEN-
TRAL WESTERN BANTU

ci-Soli = Soli→CENTRAL EASTERN BANTU

Citaro = Rio Sucio. Southern Epera D.→
CHOCO

ci-Tonga = Tonga → CENTRAL EASTERN
BANTU

CITRAL→INDIC

Citrali = Khowar→INDIC

Citrari = Khowar→INDIC

Ciwere = Chiwere→SIOUAN

ci-Yao = Yao→SOUTH EASTERN BANTU

Ciyei = Yeye→SOUTH WESTERN BANTU

Clackamas. Upper Chinook D.→CHINOOKAN

Clackstar = Tlatskanai. Kwalhioqua D.→
ATHAPASCAN-EYAK

Clallam→SALISH

Clamcoche = Karankawa

Clamcoets = Karankawa

Clatskanie = Tlatskanai. Kwalhioqua D.→
ATHAPASCAN-EYAK
Clatsop. Lower Chinook D.→CHINOOKAN
Clela = Dakarkari→PLATEAU BENUE-
CONGO
Clistenos = Cree→ALGONQUIAN
COAHUILTECAN see HOKAN
Coahuilteco→HOKAN
Coaiker = Cuaquer→BARBACOAN
Coaiquer = Cuaquer→BARBACOAN
Coana = Tswana→SOUTH EASTERN BANTU
Coano. Cora Tr.→UTO-AZTECAN
Coapite. Karankawa Tr.
Coaque. Karankawa Tr.
Coassatte = Koasati→MUSKOGEAN
Cobanipake. Coroado D.→PURI
Cobiana = Kobiana→WEST ATLANTIC
Cocama = Kokama→TUPI
Cocamilla = Kokamilla. Kokama D.→TUPI
Cochaboth = Lengua→MATACO
Cochetimi = Cochimi→HOKAN
Cochima = Cochimi→HOKAN
Cochimi→HOKAN
Cochimtee = Cochimi→HOKAN
Cochinchinese. Vietnamese D.→VIET-MUONG
Cochiti. Keres D.
Coco. Sumo Tr.→MISUMALPAN
Coco = Coaque. Karankawa Tr.
Cocolot. Toba Tr.→GUAYCURU
Cocomaricopa = Maricopa. River Yuman D.→
YUMAN
Coconino = Havasupai. Upland Yuman D.→
YUMAN
COCONUCAN→INTER-ANDINE
Coconuco→INTER-ANDINE
Cocopa. Delta River Yuman D.→YUMAN
Cocora. Guatuso D.→CHIBCHAN
Cocuzu. Northeast Nambicuara D.→NAMBI-
CUARA
Coeur d'Alene→SALISH
Cofan→JIVAROAN
Coffino = Kefa→OMOTIC
Cogniagui = Konyagi→WEST ATLANTIC
Cokwe = Ciokwe → SOUTH WESTERN
BANTU
Colan→ANDEAN
Coligan = Kolakngat. Kurung D.→KULINIC
Colima→BARBACOAN
Colima. Carare D.→CARIB
Colla. Aymara Tr.→ANDEAN
Collagua. Aymara Tr.→ANDEAN
Collahuaya. Aymara Tr.→ANDEAN
Collao = Colla. Aymara Tr.→ANDEAN
Colo. Thuri Tr.→EASTERN SUDANIC

Colo. Yamamadi D.→ARAWAKAN
Colo = Shilluk→EASTERN SUDANIC
Coloosa = Calusa
Colorado→BARBACOAN
Colouse = Patwin→WINTUN
Columbia River. Sahaptin D.→SAHAPTIN
NEZ PERCE
Columbian→SALISH
Colville. Okanogan D.→SALISH
Coma = Central Koma→KOMAN
Comabo = Cashibo→PANO
COMAN = KOMAN
Comanch = Comanche. Shoshoni D.→UTO-
AZTECAN
Comanche. Shoshoni D.→UTO-AZTECAN
Comecrudo→HOKAN
Comende = Ko. Mende D.→MANDE
Commendi = Manya. Malinka D.→MANDE
Comobo. Pichobo D.→PANO
Comopori. Cahita D.→UTO-AZTECAN
Comoro = Komoro→CENTRAL EASTERN
BANTU
Comox→SALISH
Compeva = Omagua→TUPI
Comux = Comox→SALISH
Con→KHMUIC
Conamesma = Sapaqui. Mascoy D.→MACRO-
PANOAN
Concha. Opata D.→UTO-AZTECAN
Concho. Cahuapana D.→ANDEAN
Condul. Southern Nicobarese D.→NICOBAR-
ESE
Conestoga = Susquehannock→IROQUOIS
CONGO-KORDOFANIAN = NIGER-
KORDOFANIAN
Congore. Northeast Nambicuara D.→NAMBI-
CUARA
Coniagui = Konyagi→WEST ATLANTIC
Conibo→PANO
Conob = Kanjobal→MAYAN
Conoy. Mohegan D.→ALGONQUIAN
Contanaua. Jurua-Purus Tr.→PANO
Conyi. Nika D.→NORTH EASTERN BANTU
Coombangree = Kumbainggar→KUMBAING-
GARIC
Coorg = Kodagu→DRAVIDIAN
Coorna = Kaurna. Jadliaura D.→YURA
Coos→PENUTIAN
Coosada = Koasati→MUSKOGEAN
Coosauda = Koasati→MUSKOGEAN
Coosawda = Koasati→MUSKOGEAN
Cootonais = Kutenai
Cooyiannie = Kuyani→YURA
Copainala. Zoque D.→MIXE-ZOQUE

Copeh = Patwin→WINTUN
COPEHAN = WINTUN
Copi = Chopi→SOUTH EASTERN BANTU
Copper Eskimo. Inuit D.→ESKIMO-ALEUT
Copper Indians = Yellow-knife. Chipewyan Tr.
   →ATHAPASCAN-EYAK
Copper River = Ahtena → ATHAPASCAN-
   EYAK
Coque = Zoque→MIXE-ZOQUE
Coquille. Chasta Costa D.→ATHAPASCAN-
   EYAK
Coquille, Upper = Coquille. Chasta Costa D.→
   ATHAPASCAN-EYAK
Cora = UTO-AZTECAN
Cora. Waicuru Tr.→WAICURIAN
Cora = Pima Bajo→UTO-AZTECAN
Coraice = Cora→UTO-AZTECAN
Coraveca→BORORO
Corbeaux = Crow→SIOUAN
Corchaug. Mohegan Tr.→ALGONQUIAN
CORDILLERAN→NORTHWEST AUSTRO-
   NESIAN
Core→CARIB
Corean = Korean→ALTAIC
CORIC→UTO-AZTECAN
Corine = Koreng. Juat D.→SOUTHWEST
   PAMA-NYUNGAN
Corma = Suri. Tirma D.→EASTERN SUDAN-
   IC
Cornish→CELTIC
Cornu = Kula→PAMA-NYUNGAN
Coroa→BORORO
Coroa. Cubeo D.→MACRO-TUCANOAN
Coroa = North Cayapo→GE
Coroado→PURI
COROADO = BORORO→BORORO
Corobici. Guatuso D.→CHIBCHAN
Corohio = Tarahumara→UTO-AZTECAN
Corome. Cauca Tr.→CARIB
Coronado→ANDEAN
CORONADO = GUALACHO→GE
Coronado = Bubure→CARIB
Coropo→MACRO-GE
Coroua = Coroa. Cubeo D.→MACRO-TUCA-
   NOAN
Corowa = Coroa. Cubeo D. → MACRO-
   TUCANOAN
Correguaje→MACRO-TUCANOAN
Corrhue. Cabecar D.→CHIBCHAN
Cosa = Gumuz→KOMAN
Cossaean = Kassite
Cossyah = Khasi→MON-KHMER
COSTANOAN→MIWOK-COSTANOAN
Costanoan, Northern→MIWOK-COSTANOAN

Costanoan, Southern→MIWOK-COSTANOAN
Coste = Koasati→MUSKOGEAN
Costehe = Koasati→MUSKOGEAN
Costi = Cuati→NORTHERN MAIPURAN
COTO→MACRO-TUCANOAN
Coto. Boruca D.→CHIBCHAN
Cotocoli = Tem→GUR
Cotoname→HOKAN
Cottian→YENISEIAN
Cotzal. Aguacatec D.→MAYAN
Coulailai = Kulele→GUR
Counarrha = Kutenai
Coushatta = Koasati→MUSKOGEAN
Covareca→BORORO
Cowichan. Halkomelem D.→SALISH
Cowlitch = Cowlitz→SALISH
Cowlitz→SALISH
Cowlitz, Upper = Yakima. Sahaptian D.→
   SAHAPTIN-NEZ PERCE
Coxipo→BORORO
Coxoh = Chicomuceltec→MAYAN
Coyotin = Aguacatec→MAYAN
Cozarini→MAIPURAN
Cradaho = Gradaho→GE
Craho→GE
Craig Cove. Southeast Ambryn D.→EASTERN
   OCEANIC
Crange = Crenge→GE
Creapimcatage→GE
Crecmun→BOTOCUDO
Cree→ALGONQUIAN
Creek = Muskogee→MUSKOGEAN
Creg. Hre D.→MON-KHMER
Crenak = Chonvugn→BOTOCUDO
Crenge→GE
Crenye = Creye→GE
Creole. French→ROMANCE
Crepumcateye = Creapimcatage→GE
Creye→GE
Cri = Cree→ALGONQUIAN
Crianæ = Cree→ALGONQUIAN
Cricatage→GE
Cricati = Cricatage→GE
Crick = Muskogee→MUSKOGEAN
Crickice = Muskogee→MUSKOGEAN
Crie = Cree→ALGONQUIAN
Cris = Cree→ALGONQUIAN
Crisca = Chavante→GE
Crise = Cree→ALGONQUIAN
Crishana = Jauaperi→CARIB
CROSS RIVER = BENUE-CONGO, CROSS
   RIVER
Crow→SIOUAN
Cru = Chru→WEST INDONESIAN

Cruatire→GE
Cua→MON-KHMER
Cuabo→SOUTH EASTERN BANTU
Cauchichil = Huichol→UTO-AZTECAN
Cuambo = Cuabo → SOUTH EASTERN BANTU
Cuana = Tswana → SOUTH EASTERN BANTU
Cuanhoca = Kwadi→KHOISAN
Cuanyama = Kwanyama→SOUTH WESTERN BANTU
Cuaquer→BARBACOAN
Cuati→NORTHERN MAIPURAN
Cubenepre = Cuperob. Tenetehara Tr.→TUPI
Cubeo→MACRO-TUCANOAN
Cucapa = Cocopa. Delta River Yuman D.→ YUMAN
Cucarate. Northern Zamucoan Tr.→EQUATORIAL
Cuchan = Yuma. River Yuman D.→YUMAN
Cuchitineri = Cujisenajeri→MAIPURAN
Cucia = Kucha. Walamo D.→OMOTIC
Cuciquia. Penyoqui D.→CHIQUITO
Cucoecamecra = Nucoecamecran→GE
Cucra = Kukra. Sumo Tr.→MISUMALPAN
Cucura→MACRO-CARIB
Cudaxar. Dargwa D.→CAUCASIAN
Cuepe = Kwadi→KHOISAN
Cueretu→MACRO-TUCANOAN
Cueva. Cuna D.→CHIBCHAN
Cugani. Pasai D.→INDIC
Cuiba→JIRARAN
Cuiba. Guahibo D.→EQUATORIAL
Cuica→EQUATORIAL
Cuicatec→MIXTECAN
Cuicateco = Cuicatec→MIXTECAN
CUICA-TIMOTE = TIMOTE→EQUATORIAL
Cuicutl = Guicuru→CARIB
Cuijana = Cujuna→CHAPACURA-WAHNAMAN
Cuilapa. Mixtec D.→MIXTECAN
Cuini = Gwini. Bagu D.→WORORAN
Cuitlatec see article
Cuitlateco = Cuitlatec
Cuixtlahuac. Mixtec D.→MIXTECAN
Cujigeneri = Cujisenajeri→MAIPURAN
Cujisenajeri→MAIPURAN
Cujuna→CHAPACURA-WANHAMAN
Culamanes = Kulaman→NORTHWEST AUSTRONESIAN
Cule = Tsamai→CUSHITIC
Culhua. Nahua D.→UTO-AZTECAN
Culina→ARAWAKAN

Culinha = Culina→ARAWAKAN
Culino→PANO
Culino = Culina→ARAWAKAN
Culle→ANDEAN
Cumana→CHAPACURA-WANHAMAN
Cumanacho→MACHACALI
Cumanagoto→CARIB
Cumata = Ipeca. Siuci D.→NORTHERN MAIPURAN
Cumayena→CARIB
Cumbri = Kambari → PLATEAU BENUE-CONGO
Cuna→CHIBCHAN
Cunaguasata. Mape D.→CARIB
Cunama = Kunama→CHARI-NILE
Cunana. Moseten D.→MACRO-PANOAN
Cunches = Cunco. Araucanian D.→PENUTIAN
Cunchi = Cunco. Araucanian D.→PENUTIAN
Cuncho = Cunco. Araucanian D.→PENUTIAN
Cunco. Araucanian D.→PENUTIAN
CUNDIMARCAN→CHIBCHAN
Cunewara→CARIB
Cuniba→MAIPURAN
Cuniba = Culina→ARAWAKAN
Cunimia→EQUATORIAL
Cunuana. Maquiritare D.→CARIB
Cunza = Atacameno→MACRO-CHIBCHAN
Cuoi = Kuy→MON-KHMER
CUPAN→UTO-AZTECAN
Cupelobo = Cuperob. Tenetehara Tr.→TUPI
Cupeno→UTO-AZTECAN
Cuperob. Tenetehara Tr.→TUPI
Cuperoban = Cuperob. Tenetchara Tr.→TUPI
Cur. Manjaku D.→WEST ATLANTIC
Curacirari. Omagua D.→TUPI
Curanggurang = Korenggoreng. Djakunda D. →WAKA-KABIC
Curasicana. Yabarana D.→CARIB
Curaua = Yohoraa. Tucano D.→MACRO-TUCANOAN
Curave. Coraveca D.→BORORO
Curazicari = Curacirari. Omagua D.→TUPI
Curi = Culina→ARAWAKAN
Curiana = Culina→ARAWAKAN
Curina = Culina→ARAWAKAN
Curina = Culino→PANO
Curipa. Carare Tr.→CARIB
Curoca = Kwadi→KHOISAN
Curonian→BALTIC
Curuaia = Kuruaya→TUPI
Curucaneca→BORORO
Curucicuri. Omagua D.→TUPI
Curucuru = Paumari. Purupuru D.→ARA-

WAKAN
Curuminaca→BORORO
Curungua. Siriono D.→TUPI
Curupite→GE
Curupite. Purucarod D.→GE
Curuzicari = Curucicuri. Omagua D.→TUPI
CUSHITIC see article
Cussari. Oyampi D.→TUPI
Custenau→MAIPURAN
Cutasho = Catethoy→CAMACAN
Cutiadapa. Catuquina D.→MACRO-TUCA-
NOAN
Cutiba. Pijao D.→CARIB
Cutinaa. Cumana D.→CHAPACURA-WAN-
HAMAN
CUTINANA→MAIPURAN
Cutinana→MAIPURAN
Cutshamakin. Massachusett Tr.→ALGON-
QUIAN
Cutshamequin — Cutshamakin. Massachusett
Tr.→ALGONQUIAN
Cuttonasha — Kutenai
Cutuquina→MAIPURAN
Cuur = Cur. Manjaku D.→WEST ATLANTIC
Cuyama. CHUMASH TR.→HOKAN
Cuyanawa. Nucuini D.→PANO
Cuyo = Cuyunon→NORTHWEST AUSTRO-
NESIAN
Cuyonon = Cuyunon→ NORTHWEST AUS-
TRONESIAN
Cuyuno = Cuyunon → NORTHWEST AUS-
TRONESIAN
Cuyunon→NORTHWEST AUSTRONESIAN
Cwa. Nancere D.→CHADIC
Cymraeg = Welsh→CELTIC
Cypawais = Ojibwa→ALGONQUIAN
Czech→SLAVIC
Czecho-Moravian. Czech D.→SLAVIC

D

Da = Dan→MANDE
Da Vach = Hre→MON-KHMER
Daagari = Dagari→GUR
Da'ang = Lajolo. Wolio D.→CENTRAL AND
SOUTHERN CELEBES
Da'ara = Hanggira. Bada' D.→CENTRAL
AND SOUTHERN CELEBES
Daarod = Darod. Somali D.→CUSHITIC
Daba→CHADIC
Daba = Kubo → PARE-SAMO-BEAMI-BO-
SAVI
Daba Hina = Hina. Daba D.→CHADIC

Daba of Batangafo. Mbai D.→CENTRAL
SUDANIC
Daba of Gore. Gambai D.→CENTRAL
SUDANIC
Dabai = Dakakari→PLATEAU BENUE-
CONGO
Dabai = Keningau. Murut D.→NORTHWEST
AUSTRONESIAN
Dabe→NORTH PAPUAN
Dabeiba. Northern Epera D.→CHOCO
Dabeibe = Dabeiba. Northern Epera D.→
CHOCO
Dabida. Taita D.→NORTH EASTERN BANTU
Dabossa = Toposo→EASTERN SUDANIC
Dabu→AGOB
Dabus Hillal = Sangada. Tebu Tr.→SAHARAN
Dache. Walamo D.→OMOTIC
Daco-Mysian. Thracian D.→INDO-EURO-
PEAN
Daco-Rumanian. Rumanian D.→ROMANCE
Dadarawa = Bandjerang→PAMA-NYUNGAN
Dadia→ADAMAWA
Dadiri = Central Masaba. Masaba D.→
NORTH EASTERN BANTU
Dadiya→ADAMAWA
Dadungalung = Tanganekald→NARRINYE-
RIC
Daele. Tuburi D.→CHADIC
Dafe = Dafing. Dyula D.→MANDE
Dafing. Dyula D.→MANDE
Dafla→GYARUNG-MISHMI
Dafpa. Banda D.→EASTERN
DAGA see article
Dagaba = Dagari→GUR
Dagalang = Tagalag. Ilaba D.→PAMA-
MARIC
Dagara→GUR
Dagara = Dogara. Kanuri Tr.→SAHARAN
Dagara-Nura = Dagara→GUR
Dagari→GUR
Da-garro. Otoro D.→KORDOFANIAN
Dagarti = Dagari→GUR
Dagati = Dagari→GUR
Dagbamba = Dagbani→GUR
Dagbane = Dagbani→GUR
Dagbani→GUR
Dagel. Kibet D.→EASTERN SUDANIC
Dagga. Beja Tr.→CUSHITIC
Dagoda→TIMOR-ALOR
Dagoi→NORTHEASTERN NEW GUINEA
Dagomba = Dagbani→GUR
DAGU = DAJU→EASTERN SUDANIC
Dagu of Dar Fur = Daju→EASTERN SUDAN-
IC

Dagu of Dar Sila = Daju→EASTERN SUDAN-IC

Dagu of Dardadjo = Daju→EASTERN SU-DANIC

Dagur→MONGOLIAN

Daguwuru = Taungurong→KULINIC

Dah. Sina D.→INDIC

Dahating→HUON-FINISTERRE

Dahomeen = Fo→EWE

DAI→EASTERN OCEANIC

Dai→CHADIC

Dai. Mayogo Tr.→EASTERN

DAIC = KAM-TAI

Daido = Sinohoan→CENTRAL AND SOUTH-ERN CELEBES

Daier = Dair. Kordofanian Nubian Tr.→EAST-ERN SUDANIC

Daim = Mekan→EASTERN SUDANIC

Dainan. Rukai D.→FORMOSAN AUSTRO-NESIAN

Dainggati. Ngamba D.→YUIN-KURIC

Daingnet→BURMESE-LOLO

Daiomoni→PAPUA AUSTRONESIAN

Dair. Kordofanian Nubian Tr.→EASTERN SU-DANIC

Dairi→WEST INDONESIAN

Dairi Batak = Dairi→WEST INDONESIAN

Daiso→NORTH EASTERN BANTU

Daja. Achinese D.→WEST INDONESIAN

DAJU→EASTERN SUDANIC

Daju→EASTERN SUDANIC

Daju = el Kebira. Tulishi D.→KORDOFA-NIAN

Daju Ferne = Daju→EASTERN SUDANIC

Daka—ADAMAWA

Dakakari→PLATEAU BENUE-CONGO

Dakarawa = Dakakari→PLATEAU BENUE-CONGO

Dakarchi = Dakakari→PLATEAU BENUE-CONGO

Dakarkari = Dakakari→PLATEAU BENUE-CONGO

Dakheczja. Pao-an D.→MONGOLIAN

Dakhini. Western Hindi D.→INDIC

Dakkakarri = Dakakari→PLATEAU BENUE-CONGO

Daklan. Inibaloy D.→NORTHWEST AUS-TRONESIAN

Dako. Chamba D.→ADAMAWA

Dakota→SIOUAN

Dakuya. Bete Tr.→KRU

Dalabon. Bonu D.→GUNWINGGUAN

Dalad = Dalat. Melanau D.→WEST INDO-NESIAN

Dalalekutuk. Maasai Tr.→EASTERN SUDAN-IC

Dalat. Melanau D.→WEST INDONESIAN

Dalat. Ordos D.→MONGOLIAN

Dalea. Tebu Tr.→SAHARAN

Dalebura = Jirandali. Mandandanji D.→PAMA-MARIC

Dali. Dusun D.→NORTHWEST AUSTRO-NESIAN

Dali. Narom D.→WEST INDONESIAN

Dalia = Dalea. Tebu Tr.→SAHARAN

Dalinchi. Foothill North Yukuts D.→YOKUTS

Dalla→WAKA-KABIC

Dalleburra = Dalla→WAKA-KABIC

Dalmatian = Dalmato-Romanic→ROMANCE

Dalmato-Romanic→ROMANCE

Daloka. Masakin Tr.→KORDOFANIAN

Dalong = Pai→PLATEAU BENUE-CONGO

Dalwangu = Dalwongo···MURNGIC

Dalwongo→MURNGIC

DALY see article

Dam = Ndam→CHADIC

Dam = Tai Noir→KAM-TAI

Dama. Mono D.→ADAMAWA

Dama. Nama D.→KHOISAN

Dama = Bete→CROSS RIVER BENUE-CONGO

Dama = Masongo→EASTERN SUDANIC

Dama = Murzu→EASTERN SUDANIC

Damakwa = Dama. Nama D.→KHOISAN

Damalo = Tamalu. Rawang D. → BODO-NAGA-KACHIN

Damaqwa = Dama. Nama D.→KHOISAN

Damar, North→EAST INDONESIAN

Damar, South→EAST INDONESIAN

Damara = Dama. Nama D.→KHOISAN

Damat. Massai Tr.→EASTERN SUDANIC

Dambi-elet. Oirat D.→MONGOLIAN

Damel = Dameli→INDIC

Dameli→INDIC

Damenc. Pasai D.→INDIC

Damerakaram. Bamu Kiwai D.→CENTRAL AND SOUTH NEW GUINEA

Damot. Awiya D.→CUSHITIC

Damot = Awiya→CUSHITIC

Damotanya = Damot. Awiya D.→CUSHITIC

Dampelasa→NORTHERN CELEBES

Damun—NORTHEASTERN NEW GUINEA

Dan→MANDE

Danakali = Afar. Afar-Saho D.→CUSHITIC

Danakil = Afar. Afar-Saho D.→CUSHITIC

Dananao = Bangad. Bontok D.→NORTH-WEST AUSTRONESIAN

Danaw→PALAUNG-WA

Danda. Shona D.→SOUTH EASTERN BANTU
Dandai = Banbai. Kumbainggar D.→KUM-
    BAINGGARIC
Dandzongka = Da-njong-ka. Central Tibetan
    D.→TIBETAN
Dang→BISMARCK ARCHIPELAGO
Dangadi = Dainggati. Ngamba D.→YUIN-KU-
    RIC
Dangagla = Dongola. Dongola-Kenuz D.→
    EASTERN SUDANIC
Dangaleat→CHADIC
Dangali = Afar. Afar-Saho D.→CUSHITIC
Dangali = Danggali. Kula D.→PAMA-NYUN-
    GAN
Danganararumindjeri = Ramindjeri. Tanga-
    nekald D.→NARRINYERIC
Dangarik = Phalura→INDIC
Dangati = Dainggati. Ngamba D.→YUIN-KU-
    RIC
Danggadi = Danggali. Kula D.→PAMA-
    NYUNGAN
Danggali. Kula D.→PAMA-NYUNGAN
Danggetti = Dainggati. Ngamba D.→YUIN-
    KURIC
Dangri. Khandesi D.→INDIC
Dani, Grand Valley→WEST NEW GUINEA
    HIGHLANDS
Dani, Western→WEST NEW GUINEA HIGH-
    LANDS
Dani, Greater→WEST NEW GUINEA HIGH-
    LANDS
Danisa→KHOISAN
Danish. Continental Scandinavian D.→GER-
    MANIC
Danisin = Danisa→KHOISAN
Da-njong-ka. Central Tibetan D.→TIBETAN
Dankali = Afar. Afar-Saho D.→CUSHITIC
Dansin = Danisa→KHOISAN
Danu. Burmese D.→Burmese-Lolo
Daonda→NORTH PAPUAN
Dapitan. Subanun D.→NORTHWEST AUS-
    TRONESIAN
Dapo → CENTRAL AND SOUTH NEW
    GUINEA
Daragwajek. Tatog Tr.→EASTERN SUDANIC
Daraloia→PAPUA AUSTRONESIAN
Darambal→WAKA-KABIC
Daran = Wudjari. Juat D.→SOUTHWEST
    PAMA-NYUNGAN
Darasa = Derasa→CUSHITIC
Darawal = Darambal→WAKA-KABIC
DARDIC→INDIC
Dargari = Thargari→MANTHARDA
Darginyung = Darkinung→YUIN-KURIC

Dargwa→CAUCASIAN
Dari→CHADIC
Dari = Khorasani. Persian D.→IRANIAN
Dariganga. Khalkha D.→MONGOLIAN
Darkhan. Khorcin D.→MONGOLIAN
Darkinjung = Darkinung→YUIN-KURIC
Darkinung→YUIN-KURIC
Darling = Kula→PAMA-NYUNGAN
Darmiya→GYARUNG-MISHMI
Daro. Melanau D.→WEST INDONESIAN
Darod. Somali D.→CUSHITIC
Darra-i Nur. Pasai D.→INDIC
Dartsemdo. Central Tibetan D.→TIBETAN
Daruk. Gandangara D.→YUIN-KURIC
Dasanek = Dasenech→CUSHITIC
Dasenech→CUSHITIC
Dasener. Wandamen D.→MOLUCCAN
Dathanaic = Dasenech→CUSHITIC
Dathanaik = Dasenech→CUSHITIC
Dathanic = Dasenech→CUSHITIC
Dathanik = Dasenech→CUSHITIC
Datovitu→EASTERN OCEANIC
Datuana. Yahuna D.→MACRO-TUCANOAN
Dauan→MABUIAGIC
Daui. Suau D.→PAPUA AUSTRONESIAN
Daungwurung = Taungurong→KULINIC
Dauri = Atorai→MAIPURAN
Dauro = Kullo. Walamo D.→OMOTIC
Dauwa. Dem D.→WEST NEW GUINEA
    HIGHLANDS
Davak = Hre→MON-KHMER
Davaueno→ROMANCE
Dawari = Dagari→GUR
Dawaro = Kullo. Walamo D.→OMOTIC
Dawe = Tavoya. Burmese D.→BURMESE-
    LOLO
Dawro = Kullo. Walamo D.→OMOTIC
Day. Burica D.→CHIBCHAN
Day = Dai→CHADIC
Day = Dai. Mayogo Tr.→EASTERN
DAYAK→WEST INDONESIAN
Dayak, Land→WEST INDONESIAN
Dayak, Sarawak. Land Dayak D.→WEST
    INDONESIAN
Dayak, Sea. Malay D.→WEST INDONESIAN
Dayang→NAGA-KUKI-CHIN
Daza = Tebu→SAHARAN
Dazaga. Tebu D.→SAHARAN
Dazza. Tebu D.→SAHARAN
Dazzaga = Dazaga. Tebu D.→SAHARAN
Dbus = Lhasa. Central Tibetan D.→TIBETAN
De→KRU
De' = Buginese→CENTRAL AND SOUTH-
    ERN CELEBES

De = Gola→WEST ATLANTIC
Dea→MARIND
Deah = Dusun Deyah. Maanyan D.→WEST INDONESIAN
Debabaon = Dibabaon→NORTHWEST AUSTRONESIAN
Debatsa. Gumuz D.→KOMAN
Debu→GOILALA
Debue. Bakwe Tr.→KRU
Decuana. Maquiritare D.→CARIB
Dedua→HUON-FINISTERRE
Deerie = Dieri→DIERIC
Deforo = Kurumba→GUR
Degano = Pasai→INDIC
Degema→EDO
Degha→GUR
Degoja. Gumuz D.→KOMAN
Deguba. Gumuz D.→KOMAN
Dehenda. Gumuz D.→KOMAN
Dehgani = Pasai→INDIC
Dehu = Lifu→LOYALTY ISLANDS
Dejbuk. Dargwa D.→CAUCASIAN
Dek. Kari D.→ADAMAWA
Dekini = Deccan. Marathi D.→INDIC
Dekka = Daka→ADAMAWA
Dekoka. Gumuz D.→KOMAN
Delaware→ALGONQUIAN
Delen = Dilling. Kordofanian Nubian Tr.→ EASTERN SUDANIC
Delewes = Delaware→ALGONQUIAN
Delo→GUR
Delo. Adele Tr.→CENTRAL TOGO
Delta = Delta River Yuman→YUMAN
DELTA-CALIFORNIA→YUMAN
DELTA-CROSS→CROSS RIVER BENUE-CONGO
Dem→WEST NEW GUINEA HIGHLANDS
Dembo→CENTRAL WESTERN BANTU
Dembo = Bodho. Thuri Tr.→EASTERN SUDANIC
Demen = Bodho. Thuri Tr.→EASTERN SUDANIC
Demi = Kaba Ndim. Kaba D.→CENTRAL SUDANIC
Demik. Keiga D.→KORDOFANIAN
Demsa→CHADIC
Demsa Batta = Bata→CHADIC
Demta→NORTH PAPUAN
Denali-Cantwell = Chitina. Ahtena D.→ATHAPASCAN-EYAK
Dendi. Ngbandi Tr.→EASTERN
Dendi. Songhai D.→NILO-SAHARAN
Dendje = Kaba Jiŋge. Kaba Dunjo D.→CENTRAL SUDANIC

Dene see CHIMBU→EAST NEW GUINEA HIGHLANDS
Dengese→NORTH WESTERN BANTU
Dengka. Roti D.→EAST INDONESIAN
Denkel = Afar. Afar-Saho D.→CUSHITIC
Deŋ = Gola→WEST ATLANTIC
Depso. Terraba D.→CHIBCHAN
Dera→NORTH PAPUAN
Dera = Kanakuru→CHADIC
Derambat. Mundrau D. → ADMIRALTY-WESTERN ISLANDS
Derasa→CUSHITIC
Derasanya = Derasa→CUSHITIC
Derbet = Buzawa. Oirat D.→MONGOLIAN
Deresa = Derasa→CUSHITIC
Deresinya = Derasa→CUSHITIC
Desana→MACRO-TUCANOAN
Desari = Bangaru. Western Hindi D.→INDIC
Desi = Deccan. Marathi D.→INDIC
Desnedekenade. Chipewyan Tr.→ATHAPASCAN-EYAK
Desendeyarelottine. Chipewayan Tr.→ATHAPASCAN-EYAK
Dessana = Desana→MACRO-TUCANOAN
Desua = Disoha. Gumuz D.→KOMAN
Deswali = Bangaru. Western Hindi D.→INDIC
Deswali = Bhojpuri. Bihari D.→INDIC
Deti→KHOISAN
Detikhwe = Deti→KHOISAN
De'u = Lifu→LOYALTY ISLANDS
Dewiya. Gumuz D.→KOMAN
Dewoi = De→KRU
Dfola = Biafada→WEST ATLANTIC
Dhaguwuru = Taungurong→KULINIC
Dhalla = Kadugli→KORDOFANIAN
Dhangatty = Dainggati. Ngamba D.→YUIN-KURIC
Dhangon. Mundari D.→MUNDA
Dharawa = Thurawal→YUIN-KURIC
Dharrok = Daruk. Gandangara D.→YUIN-KURIC
Dharruk = Daruk. Gandangara D.→YUIN-KURIC
Dharuk = Daruk. Gandangara D.→YUIN-KURIC
Dhauhurtwurru = Taungurong→KULINIC
Dhe Boodho = Bodho. Thuri Tr.→EASTERN SUDANIC
Dhe Boodo = Bodho. Thuri Tr.→EASTERN SUDANIC
Dhe Bor = Bor→EASTERN SUDANIC
Dhe Colo = Colo. Thuri Tr.→EASTERN SUDANIC
Dhe Lwo = Lwo→EASTERN SUDANIC

Dhe Thuri − Thuri→EASTERN SUDANIC
Dhe-bang = Heiban→KORDOFANIAN
Dhed Gujari = Khandesi→INDIC
Dhegiha→SIOUAN
Dhimal→GYARUNG-MISHMI
Dhimal = Dhimal→GYARUNG-MISHMI
Dhi-morong = Moro→KORDOFANIAN
Dhi-toro = Otoro→KORDOFANIAN
Dho Alur = Alur→EASTERN SUDANIC
Dho Anywaa = Anuak→EASTERN SUDANIC
Dho Colo = Shilluk→EASTERN SUDANIC
Dho Luo = Luo→EASTERN SUDANIC
Dho Pa Lwo = Lwo→EASTERN SUDANIC
Dholubi = Katcha→KORDOFANIAN
Dhopadhola = Adhola→EASTERN SUDANIC
Dhopaluo = Lwo→EASTERN SUDANIC
Dhruva = Parji→DRAVIDIAN
Dhuak = Suri. Tirma D.→EASTERN SUDAN-
IC
Dhudhuroa = Duduruwa. Jaitmathang D.→
PAMA-NYUNGAN
Dhuri = Suri. Tirma D.→EASTERN SUDAN-
IC
Dhurva = Parji→DRAVIDIAN
Di→NORTH WESTERN BANTU
Dia = Alu→TORRICELLI
Dia = Buol→NORTHWEST AUSTRONE-
SIAN
Diabu. Kanembu Tr.→SAHARAN
Diagada = Jagada. Tebu Tr.→SAHARAN
Diakanke = Dyankanka. Dyula D.→MANDE
Dian = Dampelasa→NORTHERN CELEBES
Dian = Dya→GUR
Dianga→NORTH WESTERN BANTU
Diari = Dieri→DIERIC
Diau→CARIB
DIBABAIC→ NORTHWEST AUSTRONE-
SIAN
Dibabaon→NORTHWEST AUSTRONESIAN
Dibabawon = Dibabaon→NORTHWEST AUS-
TRONESIAN
Dibeng. Basa Tr.→NORTH WESTERN BAN-
TU
Dibiasu→KIKORI RIVER
Dibiri. Bamu Kiwai D.→CENTRAL AND
SOUTH NEW GUINEA
Dibolug→AGOB
Dibum. Basa Tr.→NORTH WESTERN BAN-
TU
Dida. Bete D.→KRU
Didayi = Gataʔ→MUNDA
Didei = Gataʔ→MUNDA
Didey = Gataʔ→MUNDA
Didinga→EASTERN SUDANIC

'Di'di a − Didinga→EASTERN SUDANIC
Didiu = Cochimi→HOKAN
Dido→CAUCASIAN
Dido. Nupe D.→NUPE-GBARI
Didrah = Todrah→MON-KHMER
Didu. Waicuru Tr.→WAICURIAN
Die = JEH→Mon-Khmer
Diegueno→YUMAN
Dieri→DIERIC
DIERIC see article
Dietko − Jetko. Kanuri Tr.→SAHARAN
Dieyerie − Dieri→DIERIC
Dieyrie = Dieri→DIERIC
Difu = Boritsu→JUKUNOID
Digaru Mishmi→GYARUNG-MISHMI
Digbue. Bakwe Tr.→KRU
di-Gendja = Gendja. Ngombe D.→NORTH
WESTERN BANTU
Digger = Maidu→MAIDU
Diggers = Bannock. Northern Paiute D.→UTO-
AZTECAN
Digil. Somali D.→CUSHITIC
Digini. Somali D.→CUSHITIC
Diglel. Beja Tr.→CUSHITIC
Digo→NORTH EASTERN BANTU
Digor. Ossetic D.→IRANIAN
Digul→OK
Digut→TUPI
Dih Bri. Central Mnong D.→MON-KHMER
Di-jama. Otoro D.→KORDOFANIAN
Dije = Tumak→CHADIC
Dikkukaji = Nagpuri. Bihari D.→INDIC
Dikpele = Likpe→CENTRAL TOGO
Dilling. Kordofanian Nubian Tr.→EASTERN
SUDANIC
Dim = Odim. Agwagwune D.→CROSS RIVER
BENUE-CONGO
Dimasa. Bodo D.→BODO-NAGA-KACHIN
Dime→OMOTIC
Dimer→BOGIA
DIMUGA = DAGA
Dimuga = Daga→DAGA
Dimuk→CHADIC
Dindje = Kaba Jiŋge. Kaba Dunjo D.→CEN-
TRAL SUDANIC
Dinga = Di→NORTH WESTERN BANTU
Ding-ding. Mumuye D.→ADAMAWA
DINKA→EASTERN SUDANIC
Dinka = Abialang. Padang D.→EASTERN SU-
DANIC
DINQA = DINKA→EASTERN SUDANIC
Diŋ = Di→NORTH WESTERN BANTU
Dio. Zande D.→EASTERN
Dio = Kaidipan→NORTHWEST AUSTRO-

NESIAN

DIOI = NORTHERN TAI→KAM-TAI

DIOI = JUI→KAM-TAI

Dioi = Ts'e-Heng→KAM-TAI

Diola→WEST ATLANTIC

Dion. Moso D.→BURMESE-LOLO

Dioro. Bakwe Tr.→KRU

Dioula = Dyula. Dyula Tr.→MANDE

Dippil = Kabikabi. Dalla D.→WAKA-KABIC

Dir. Somali D.→CUSHITIC

Diraila = Tereila. Punthamara D.→DIERIC

Dire = Gata ?→MUNDA

Diri = Baskarik→INDIC

Diria. Mangue D.→MANGUEAN

Diria = Mangue→MANGUEAN

Diriko = Mbogedo. Kwangari D.→SOUTH
  WESTERN BANTU

Diriku = Mbogedo. Kwangari D.→SOUTH
  WESTERN BANTU

Dirkawa. Tebu Tr.→SAHARAN

Diryawa→CHADIC

Disa→CENTRAL SUDANIC

Diso = Maru→BODO-NAGA-KACHIN

Disoha. Gumuz D.→KOMAN

Dissa = Disa→CENTRAL SUDANIC

Ditti = Afitti→EASTERN SUDANIC

Diu = Bulanga-Uki→NORTHWEST AUS-
  TRONESIAN

Diuihet. Araucanian D.→PENUTIAN

Divehi Bas = Maldivian→INDIC

Diviche = Diuihet. Araucanian D.→PENU-
  TIAN

Divihet = Diuihet. Araucanian D.→PENU-
  TIAN

Diyeri = Dieri→DIERIC

Diyi = Takum. Jukun D.→JUKUNOID

Dizi = Maji→OMOTIC

Dizu = Maji→OMOTIC

Dizu = Sheko→OMOTIC

Dizzu = Maji→OMOTIC

Djaberadjaber = Djaberdjaber. Nyulnyul D.→
  NYULNYULAN

Djaberdjaber. Nyulnyul D.→NYULNYULAN

Djabu. Gobabingo D.→MURNGIC

Djabugay. Wakaman D.→PAMA-MARIC

Djadjala→KULINIC

Djadjawurung = Jaara. Djadjala D.→KULINIC

Djadjuwuru = Djadjuwurung. Taungurong D.
  →KULINIC

Djadjuwurung. Taungurong D.→KULINIC

Djakun = Jakun→JAKUN

Djakunda→WAKA-KABIC

Djallonke = Yalunka. Susu D.→MANDE

Djambarbwingu. Gobabingo D.→MURNGIC

Djamchidi. Persian D.→IRANIAN

Djamindjung→DJAMINDJUNGAN

DJAMINDJUNGAN see article

Djamundon = Djamindjung → DJAMINDJU-
  NGAN

Djanggu→NORTH PAPUAN

Djangun. Wakaman D.→PAMA-MARIC

Djanti = Ngayaba→NORTH WESTERN
  BANTU

Djao = Yao→SOUTH EASTERN BANTU

Djappuminyon = Jardwa. Djadjala D.→KULI-
  NIC

Djariwidji = Jandjinung→MURNGIC

Djaru→NGUMBIN

Djasing = Yasing→ADAMAWA

Djau. Edeh D.→MOLUCCAN

Djauan→GUNWINGGUAN

Djaui. Nyulnyul D.→NYULNYULAN

Djauor = Jauor→NYULNYULAN

Djauun = Djauan→GUNWINGGUAN

Djawanj = Djauan→GUNWINGGUAN

Djedji = Fo→EWE

Djem = Njem. Njem-Bajue Tr.→NORTH
  WESTERN BANTU

Djembe. Busooŋ Tr.→NORTH WESTERN
  BANTU

Djendewal→DURUBULIC

DJERAGAN see article

Djeraity→DALY

Djeto = Jeto. Banda D.→EASTERN

Djia. Sakata D.→NORTH WESTERN BANTU

Djidja = Bolano.→NORTHERN CELEBES

Djikini = Njiniŋi. North Teke D.→NORTH
  WESTERN BANTU

Djimba = Djinba→MURNGIC

Djinang = Jandjinung→MURNGIC

Djinba→MURNGIC

Djingburu = Junguru. Banda D.→EASTERN

Djioteau = Jeto. Banda D.→EASTERN

Djirbal. Wakaman D.→PAMA-MARIC

Djiringanj = Thaua→YUIN-KURIC

Djiru. Wakaman D.→PAMA-MARIC

Djirubal = Djirbal. Wakaman D.→PAMA-
  MARIC

Djiwali→MANTHARDA

Djoe-Tongo = Djuka→GERMANIC

Djok = Ciokwe→SOUTH WESTERN BANTU

Djolof = Dyolof. Wolof D.→WEST ATLAN-
  TIC

Djompra = Zumper→JUKUNOID

Djonga = Jonga. Tsonga D. → SOUTH
  EASTERN BANTU

Djongor = Jongor→CHADIC

Djugun. Nyulnyul D.→NYULNYULAN

Djuka→GERMANIC
Djukan = Djugun. Nyulnyul D.→NYULNY-
ULAN
Djumperi = Zumper→JUKUNOID
Dli = Li→KAM-TAI
Do = De→KRU
Doa. Buhagana Tr.→MACRO-TUCANOAN
Dobi = Gogot→SEMITIC
DOBIC→PAPUA AUSTRONESIAN
Dobu→PAPUA AUSTRONESIAN
Dobudura = Jauwa→BINANDERE
Dodinga. Tobelo D.→NORTH HALMAHERA
Dodos. Karamojong D.→EASTERN SUDANIC
Dodosi = Dodos. Karamojong D.→EASTERN
SUDANIC
Dodoth = Dodos. Karamojong D.→WEST-
ERN SUDANIC
Dodotho = Dodos. Karamojong D.-→EAST-
ERN SUDANIC
Doe. Zaramo D.→CENTRAL EASTERN
BANTU
Doegs = Nanticoke. Mohegan D.→ALGON-
QUIAN
Doenbauraket = Ngarkat. Djadjala D. →
KULINIC
Dofama-Dyafolo. Dyumini D.→GUR
Dogara. Kanuri Tr.→SAHARAN
Doghosie = Dorhosye→GUR
Dogom = Dogon→GUR
Dogon→GUR
Dogorda. Tebu Tr.→SAHARAN
Do-gorindi. Otoro D.→KORDOFANIAN
Dogrib→ATHAPASCAN-EYAK
Dogri-Kongri. Panjabi D.→INDIC
Dogwa = Tlokwa. Northern Sotho D.→SOUTH
EASTERN BANTU
Dohe = Doe. Zaramo D.→CENTRAL EAST-
ERN BANTU
Dohuk. Zaza D.→IRANIAN
Doi. Palu D.→CENTRAL AND SOUTHERN
CELEBES
Dok Acoli = Akoli→EASTERN SUDANIC
Doka→PLATEAU BENUE-CONGO
Dokhobe = Dorhosye→GUR
Dokhosie = Dorhosye→GUR
Doko→OMOTIC
'Doko→NORTH WESTERN BANTU
Doko of Ngiri→NORTH WESTERN BANTU
Dokonu. Northern Mao D.→KOMAN
Do-kwara. Otoro D.→KORDOFANIAN
Dolage. Sausu D.→CENTRAL AND SOUTH-
ERN CELEBES
Dolgan. Yakuts D.→TURKIC
Dollo→OMOTIC

Dolot = Tid. Tirma D.→EASTERN SUDANIC
Dom. Binahari D.→MAILU
Dom. Chimbu D.→EAST NEW GUINEA
HIGHLANDS
Doma = Jaba→PLATEAU BENUE-CONGO
Domara→MAILU
Domawa = Kelawa→PLATEAU BENUE-
CONGO
Domba. Shona D.→SOUTH EASTERN
BANTU
Dombo = Bodho. Thuri Tr.→EASTERN
SUDANIC
Domkhoe→KHOISAN
Domor = Loma→MANDE
Domori = Doumori. Southern Kiwai D.→
CENTRAL AND SOUTH NEW GUINEA
Domouri = Doumori. Southern Kiwai D.→
CENTRAL AND SOUTH NEW GUINEA
Dompa = Tamungkolowi→CENTRAL AND
SOUTHERN CELEBES
Dompago→GUR
Domra. Bihari D.→INDIC
Domu = Dom. Binahari D.→MAILU
Domuna→INDO-PACIFIC
Domung→HUON-FINISTERRE
Donaldson, Western→OK
Dondo = Tomini→NORTHERN CELEBES
Donga→ADAMAWA
Donga. Jukun D.→JUKUNOID
Dongiro = Donyiro. Toposo D.→EASTERN
SUDANIC
Dongo→EASTERN
Dongo. Kresh D.→CENTRAL SUDANIC
Dongo = Donga→ADAMAWA
Dongo = Mbundu→CENTRAL WESTERN
BANTU
Dongol = Donjol. Padang D.→EASTERN
SUDANIC
Dongola. Dongola-Kenuz D.→EASTERN
SUDANIC
Dongola-Kenuz→EASTERN SUDANIC
Dongolawi = Dongola. Dongola-Kenuz D.→
EASTERN SUDANIC
Dongosa. Tebu Tr.→SAHARAN
Dongotolo = Dongotono. Lotuho D.→EAST-
ERN SUDANIC
Dongotono. Lotuho D.→EASTERN SUDANIC
Donjol. Padang D.→EASTERN SUDANIC
Donyanyo = Doyayo→ADAMAWA
Donyayo = Doyayo→ADAMAWA
Donyiro. Toposo D.→EASTERN SUDANIC
Donyiro = Turkana→EASTERN SUDANIC
Donyoro = Turkana→EASTERN SUDANIC
Donza = Dongosa. Tebu Tr.→SAHARAN

Doondo. Kongo D.→CENTRAL WESTERN BANTU

Door = Dor. Nuer D.→EASTERN SUDANIC

Doora = Nukuna. Jadliaura D.→YURA

Dootoodn = Tututni. Chasta Costa D.→ATHA-PASCAN-EYAK

Dor. Nuer D.→EASTERN SUDANIC

Dor = Bongo→CENTRAL SUDANIC

Dorhossie = Dorhosye→GUR

Dorhosye→GUR

Dorhosye→GUR

Doria. Areare D.→EASTERN OCEANIC

Doriaidi. Buari D.→MAILU

Dorin→GE

Dorli. Koya D.→DRAVIDIAN

Dormo→CHADIC

Dorobo→EASTERN SUDANIC

Dorobo. Nandi D.→EASTERN SUDANIC

Do-rombc. Otoro D.→KORDOFANIAN

Doropodai. Southern Kiwai D.→CENTRAL AND SOUTH NEW GUINEA

Dororajek. Tatog Tr.→EASTERN SUDANIC

Dororo. Kazukuru D.→CENTRAL MELANESIA

Dororo = Kachichere. Katab D.→PLATEAU BENUE-CONGO

Dorosie = Dorhosye→GUR

Dorot. Gayo D.→WEST INDONESIAN

Dorro→CENTRAL AND SOUTH NEW GUINEA

Dorze. Walamo D.→OMOTIC

Dorzinya = Dorze. Walamo D.→OMOTIC

Dosa = Dongosa. Tebu Tr.→SAHARAN

Douala = Duala → NORTH WESTERN BANTU

Douma = Duma → NORTH WESTERN BANTU

Doumbou = Minduumo→NORTH WESTERN BANTU

Doumori. Southern Kiwai D. → CENTRAL AND SOUTH NEW GUINEA

Doura→PAPUA AUSTRONESIAN

Doyayo→ADAMAWA

Doyma. Patangoro D.→CARIB

Dram. Jeh D.→MON-KHMER

DRAVIDIAN see article

Driafleisuma = Mehek→SEPIK

Dru. Central Tibetan D.→TIBETAN

Dru. Lendu D.→CENTRAL SUDANIC

DRAUL→KULINIC

Dru-na = Dru. Lendu D.→CENTRAL SUDANIC

Dschagada = Jagada. Tebu Tr.→SAHARAN

Dschagga = Caga → NORTH EASTERN BANTU

Dschamba = Chamba→ADAMAWA

Dschang-Bangwa. Bafou D.→BANTOID

Dschangtalk = Dschang-Bangwa. Bafou D. →BANTOID

Dscuba = Jibu. Jukun D.→JUKUNOID

Dthee-eri = Dieri→DIERIC

DUALA→NORTH WESTERN BANTU

Duala→NORTH WESTERN BANTU

Duampu→BURMESE-LOLO

Duan→MON-KHMER

Duan = Takua→MON-KHMER

Duau→PAPUA AUSTRONESIAN

Duauru = Kapone. Kwenyi D.→NEW CALEDONIA

Dubea = Nadubea→NEW CALEDONIA

Duberi. Maiya D.→INDIC

Ducaiya = Ocaina→WITOTOAN

Duchateau Is. Suau D.→PAPUA AUSTRONESIAN

Dudh. Kharia D.→MUNDA

Duduruwa. Jaitmathang. D.→PAMA-NYUNGAN

Duff = Taumako. Pileni D.→POLYNESIAN

Dufutu = Luhtu. Tsou D.→FORMOSAN AUSTRONESIAN

Dugbatang. Ata D.→NORTHWEST AUSTRONESIAN

Dugbatung = Dugbatang. Ata D.→NORTHWEST AUSTRONESIAN

Dugeme = Dugene→KIKORI RIVER

Dugene → KIKORI RIVER

Dugorda = Dogorda. Tebu Tr.→SAHARAN

Dugubesyeei. Senari D.→GUR

Duguranci = Duguri. Jarawa D.→BANTOID

Duguri. Jarawa D.→BANTOID

Du-gurila. Otoro D.→KORDOFANIAN

Du-gwujur. Otoro D.→KORDOFANIAN

Duhu. Magri D.→CHADIC

Dui = Duru→ADAMAWA

Duindui. Ombo D.→EASTERN OCEANIC

Dutt→CHIBCHAN

Duka = Dukawa→PLATEAU BENUE-CONGO

Dukai = Rukai→FORMOSAN AUSTRONESIAN

Dukanchi = Dukawa→PLATEAU BENUE-CONGO

Dukawa→PLATEAU BENUE-CONGO

Duke→NORTHWESTERN AND CENTRAL SOLOMONS

Dukunza. Gumuz D.→KOMAN

Dukwaya. Gumuz D.→KOMAN

Dul. Berta D.→CHARI-NILE

Duli = Duru→ADAMAWA
Duliit = Dulit. Rek D.→EASTERN SUDANIC
Dulit. Rek D.→EASTERN SUDANIC
Duludi→GE
Duma→NORTH WESTERN BANTU
Duma. Karanga D.→SOUTH EASTERN BANTU
Dumaki→INDIC
Dumbea = Nadubea→NEW CALEDONIA
Dumbo = Kumaju→BANTOID
Dumbu = Minduumo→NORTH WESTERN BANTU
Dume→CUSHITIC
Dumi→GYARUNG-MISHMI
Dumna. Foothill North Yokuts D.→YOKUTS
Dumoga. Mongondow D.→NORTHERN CELEBES
Dumu→KIKORI RIVER
Dumuna = Domuna→INDO-PACIFIC
DUMUT→AWYU
Duna→EAST NEW GUINEA HIGHLANDS
Dungerwalb→CENTRAL AND SOUTH NEW GUINEA
Dungi. Gure D.→PLATEAU BENUE-CONGO
Dungidjau→WAKA-KABIC
Dungmali. Waling D.→GYARUNG-MISHMI
Duniberrenai→EQUATORIAL
Dunu = Bata→CHADIC
Duon→MON-KHMER
Dupa→ADAMAWA
Dupax. Isinay D.→NORTHWEST AUSTRO-NESIAN
Dupdoria = Ao→NAGA-KUKI-CHIN
Dupi. Bari Tr.→EASTERN SUDANIC
Durama. Nika D.→NORTH EASTERN BANTU
Durba. Somali D.→CUSHITIC
Durben-Khukhet. Ordos D.→MONGOLIAN
Duri. Masenrempulu D.→CENTRAL AND SOUTHERN CELEBES
Durma = Mekan→EASTERN SUDANIC
Durru→ADAMAWA
Duru→ADAMAWA
DURUBULIC see article
Durugmun = Pula→NORTHWEST AUSTRO-NESIAN
Dusun→NORTHWEST AUSTRONESIAN
Dusun. Maanyan D.→WEST INDONESIAN
Dusun Deyah. Maanyan D.→WEST INDO-NESIAN
Dutch. Netherlandic-German D.→GERMANIC
Duvera→BINANDERE
Duwamish. Puget Sound Salish D.→SALISH
Duwinbarap = Ngarkat. Djadjala D.→KULI-NIC

Dwags = Takpa, Central Tibetan D.→TIBETAN
Dwar. Biak D.→MOLUCCAN
Dwingi = Dungi. Gure D.→PLATEAU BENUE-CONGO
Dya→GUR
Dyabo = Jabo. Grebo Tr.→KRU
Dyair = Aghu→AWYU
Dyaka = Dyankanka. Dyula D.→MANDE
Dyakamke. Soninke D.→MANDE
Dyalonke = Yalunka. Susu D.→MANDE
Dyamala. Dyimini D.→GUR
Dyamate = Diola→WEST ATLANTIC
Dyan→GUR
Dyane = Dya→GUR
Dyangirte. Bambara D.→MANDE
Dyankanka. Dyula D.→MANDE
Dyanu = Dya→GUR
Dyaŋe = Dyankanka. Dyula D.→MANDE
Dyaul→BISMARCK ARCHIPELAGO
Dye→GUR
Dyegueme = Ndyegem. Serer D. → WEST ATLANTIC
Dyerma = Zarma. Songhai D.→NILO-SAHA-RAN
Dyimini→GUR
Dyoba = Non→WEST ATLANTIC
Dyokereu = Dyula. Dyula Tr.→MANDE
Dyola = Diola→WEST ATLANTIC
Dyolof. Wolof D.→WEST ATLANTIC
Dyomande = Konya. Malinka D.→MANDE
Dyoula = Dyula. Dyula Tr.→MANDE
Dyula→MANDE
Dyula Ka = Dyula→MANDE
Dyula Ke = Dyula. Dyula Tr.→MANDE
Dyumba. Myene D.→NORTH WESTERN BANTU
Dza = Jen→ADAMAWA
Dzad = Jad. Central Tibetan D.→TIBETAN
Dzaiven Boka→BANTOID
Dzakhacin. Oirat D.→MONGOLIAN
Dzalamo = Zaramo→CENTRAL EASTERN BANTU
Dzamba = Bobangi→NORTH WESTERN BANTU
Dzanggali = Jangali→GYARUNG-MISHMI
Dzaui. Carutana D.→NORTHERN MAI-PURAN
Dzawi = Dzaui. Carutana D.→NORTHERN MAIPURAN
Dzaze = Piapoco→NORTHERN MAIPURAN
Dzhek. Kryts D.→CAUCASIAN
Dzhika→KHOISAN

Dzibi = Tswa→SOUTH EASTERN BANTU

Dzili→BODO-NAGA-KACHIN

Dzimu = Njem. Njem-Bajue Tr.→NORTH WESTERN BANTU

Dzindza→NORTH EASTERN BANTU

Dzing = Di→NORTH WESTERN BANTU

Dziŋ = Di→NORTH WESTERN BANTU

Dzonga = Tswa→SOUTH EASTERN BANTU

Dzorgai→SINO-TIBETAN

Dzuak = Suri. Tirma D.→EASTERN SUDAN-IC

Dzubucua. Cariri D.→EQUATORIAL

Dzukish. Lithuanian D.→BALTIC

Dzuman = Juman. Kim. D.→CHADIC

Dzunu. Tsakrima D.→NAGA-KUKI-CHIN

Dzu/'oasi. Kung D.→KHOISAN

E

Eacwandja = Iwaidji→IWAIDJAN

E:afeŋ = Obang. Ekoi D.→BANTOID

Eagle = Katshikotin. Han Tr. → ATHA-PASCAN-EYAK

Earchethinue = Blackfoot→ALGONQUIAN

Earchetinue = Crow→SIOUAN

Easter Island→POLYNESIAN

EASTERN (OF ADAMAWA-EASTERN) see article

Eau = Nanda→KARDU

Ebagi. Nupe Tr.→NUPE-GBARI

Ebe. Nupe D.→NUPE-GBARI

e-Beembe = Beembe → NORTH EASTERN BANTU

Ebekwara = Bekwarra→CROSS RIVER BE-NUE-CONGO

Ebidoso, Southern Zamucoan Tr.→EQUATO-RIAL

Ebira = Igbira→NUPE-GBARI

Ebiri = Mararit→EASTERN SUDANIC

Ebom. Kohumono D.→CROSS RIVER BENUE-CONGO

e-Boo = Boo. Central Teke D.→NORTH WESTERN BANTU

Ebrie = Kyama→LAGOON

Ebugombe = Bubombe→NORTH EASTERN BANTU

Ecclemach = Esselen→HOKAN

Ecclemanch = Esselen→HOKAN

Echemin = Malecite. Passamaquoddy D.→ALGONQUIAN

Echoaldi. Guana D.→MAIPURAN

Echoja→TACANA

Echonoana = Echoaldi. Guana D.→MAI-PURAN

eci-Dzindza = Dzindza→NORTH EASTERN BANTU

eci-Jita = Jita→NORTH EASTERN BANTU

Ecikerebe = Kerebe → NORTH EASTERN BANTU

eci-Subia = Subia → SOUTH WESTERN BANTU

eci-Totela = Totela → SOUTH WESTERN BANTU

Eclemach = Esselen→HOKAN

Eclemanch = Esselen→HOKAN

Ecselen = Esselen→HOKAN

Edangabo. Ziba D.→NORTH EASTERN BANTU

Edda = Ada. Igbo D.→IGBO

Ediba. Kohumono D.→CROSS RIVER BE-NUE-CONGO

Ediba = Kohumono D.→CROSS RIVER BENUE-CONGO

Edi-bet. Soddo Tr.→SEMITIC

Ediro. Engenni D.→EDO

Ediro. Engenni D.→EDO

Ediya = Bube→NORTH WESTERN BANTU

Edjagam. Ekoi D.→BANTOID

Edo = Bini→EDO

Edo = Sidondo. Palu D.→CENTRAL AND SOUTHERN CELEBES

EDO see article

Edu. Waicuru Tr.→WAICURIAN

Edun = Adun. Mbembe D.→CROSS RIVER BENUE-CONGO

Eduwini. Ijo D.→IDO

Eeeleeree = Ngadjuri. Jadliaura D.→YURA

Eethaeetha = Jitajita. Djadjala D.→KULINIC

Efate→EASTERN OCEANIC

Efe. Mamvu-Efe D.→CENTRAL SUDANIC

Efe-e = Efe. Mamvu-Efe D.→CENTRAL SUDANIC

Effium = Ufiom. Oring D.→CROSS RIVER BENUE-CONGO

Efik→CROSS RIVER BENUE-CONGO

EFIK-ANDONI→CROSS RIVER BENUE-CONGO

Efutop→BANTOID

Efutu = Awutu→VOLTA-COMOE

Egba. Yoruba D.→YORUBA

Egene = Engenni→EDO

Eggon→PLATEAU BENUE-CONGO

Eghum. Mbembe D.→CROSS RIVER BENUE-CONGO

Egon = Eggon→PLATEAU BENUE-CONGO

Egongot. Ilongot D.→NORTHWEST AUSTRO-NESIAN

Egu = Igbira-Igu. Igbira D.→NUPE-GBARI

Egun = Gu. Ewe D.→EWE

Egyptian-Coptic→AFROASIATIC

Ehkili = Shahari. Modern South Arabic D.→ SEMITIC

Ehueun. Ekue D.→EDO

Ehum = Eghum. Mbembe D.→CROSS RIVER BENUE-CONGO

Eikiri→KOIARI

≠eikusi = Xatia. ŋ/amani D.→KHOISAN

Eiteip→TORRICELLI

Eivo→BOUGAINVILLE

Eiwaja = Iwaidji→IWAIDJAN

Ejagam = Ejagham. Ekoi D.→BANTOID

Ejagham. Ekoi D.→BANTOID

Ejaham = Ejagham. Ekoi D.→BANTOID

Ejam = Ejagham. Ekoi D.→BANTOID

E-joit = Jie. Karamojong D.→EASTERN SUDANIC

Ekagi = Kapauku→WEST NEW GUINEA HIGHLANDS

Ekajuk→BANTOID

Ekamtulu:fu = Nde→BANTOID

Ekari = Kapauku→WEST NEW GUINEA HIGHLANDS

Ekbebe = Kebu→CENTRAL TODO

eke-Gusii = Gusii→NORTH EASTERN BANTU

eke-Koria = Koria→NORTH EASTERN BANTU

e-Kele = Kele→NORTH WESTERN BANTU

eke-Nilamba = Nilamba→NORTH EASTERN BANTU

eke-Nyakyusa = Nyakyusa→CENTRAL EASTERN BANTU

Eket→CROSS RIVER BENUE-CONGO

Ekhirit. Buryat D.→MONGOLIAN

Eki→NORTH WESTERN BANTU

Eki = Bunu. Yoruba D.→YORUBA

eki-Bena = Bena→CENTRAL EASTERN BANTU

eki-Haavu = Havu→NORTH EASTERN BANTU

eki-Hambo = Lega. Ndandi D.→NORTH EASTERN BANTU

Ekihaya = Ziba→NORTH EASTERN BANTU

eki-Hehe = Hehe→CENTRAL EASTERN BANTU

eki-Kerebe = Kerebe→NORTH EASTERN BANTU

eki-Kinga = Kinga→CENTRAL EASTERN BANTU

eki-Kira = Swaga. Ndandi D.→NORTH EASTERN BANTU

eki-Kumbule = Kumbule Ndandi D.→NORTH EASTERN BANTU

eki-Kuria = Koria→NORTH EASTERN BANTU

eki-Lega = Lega. Ndandi D.→NORTH EASTERN BANTU

eki-Mate = Mate. Ndandi D.→NORTH EASTERN BANTU

eki-Nyambo = Nyambo→NORTH EASTERN BANTU

eki-Pangwa = Pangwa→CENTRAL EASTERN BANTU

eki-Rhinyirhinyi=Rhinyirhinyi. Nyabungu D.→ NORTH EASTERN BANTU

eki-Sanza = Sanza. Ndandi D.→NORTH EASTERN BANTU

eki-Shu = Shu. Ndandi D.→NORTH EASTERN BANTU

eki-Shukaali = Shu. Ndandi D.→NORTH EASTERN BANTU

eki-Songoora = Songoora. Ndandi D.→NORTH EASTERN BANTU

eki-Swaga = Swaga. Ndandi D.→NORTH EASTERN BANTU

Ekii = Eket→CROSS RIVER BENUE-CONGO

eki-Tangi = Tangi. Ndandi D.→NORTH EASTERN BANTU

Ekiti. Yoruba D.→YORUBA

eki-Yira = Yira. Ndandi D.→NORTH EASTERN BANTU

Ekiziba = Ziba→NORTH EASTERN BANTU

Ekoi→BANTOID

EKOID→BANTU

Ekom = Nkom→BANTOID

Ekonda Monŋo. Mongo-Nkundo D.→NORTH WESTERN BANTU

Ekpana = Logba→CENTRAL TODO

Ekaparabong. Ndoe D.→BANTOID

Ekpetiama. Ijo D.→IJO

Ekpeya→IGBO

Ekpeye = Ekpeya→IGBO

Ekumbe-Mbonge. Lundu D.→NORTH WESTERN BANTU

Ekureku. Legbo D.→CROSS RIVER BENUE-CONGO

Ekuri = Nkukoli→CROSS RIVER BENUE-CONGO

Ekwe = Ejagham. Ekoi D.→BANTOID

El Akheimar = Aheima. Masakin Tr.→ KORDOFANIAN

El Gureshab. Beja Tr.→CUSHITIC

El Hasa. Beja Tr.→CUSHITIC

El Hugeirat. Kordofanian Nubian Tr.→EASTERN SUDANIC

El Kebira. Tulishi D.→KORDOFANIAN
Elamite see article
Elapaputih→EAST INDONESIAN
Elato. Ulithian D.→MICRONESIAN
e-Leedji = Leedji. Peri D.→NORTH EASTERN
    BANTU
Eleidlinottine.   Chipewyan   Tr.→ATHAPAS-
    CAN-EYAK
Eleko = Leko. Losengo D.→NORTH WEST-
    ERN BANTU
Elema. Toaripi D.→TOARIPI
ELEMA = TOARIPI
Elembe.   Nkutu   D.→NORTH   WESTERN
    BANTU
Eleme→CROSS RIVER BENUE-CONGO
Elegeyo = Keyo. Nandi D.→EASTERN SU-
    DANIC
Elgon = Kony.   Nandi   D. → EASTERN
    SUDANIC
Elgon Masai = Kony. Nandi D.→EASTERN
    SUDANIC
Elgonyi = Kony.   Nandi   D. → EASTERN
    SUDANIC
Elgumi = Teso→EASTERN SUDANIC
Eli-Elat = Banda→EAST INDONESIAN
Elimbari. Chuave D.→EAST NEW GUINEA
    HIGHLANDS
Eling.   Banen   Tr.→NORTH   WESTERN
    BANTU
Eliri = KORDOFANIAN
Elkei→TORRICELLI
ELLICEAN→POLYNESIAN
Ellicean→POLYNESIAN
Elman. Beja Tr.→CUSHITIC
Elomay = Banyun→WEST ATLANTIC
Elong = Loŋ. Mbo D.→NORTH WESTERN
    BANTU
Eloyi→PLATEAU BENUE-CONGO
Elpira = Walbiri→NGARGA
Elu.   Mikaru   D.→EAST   NEW   GUINEA
    HIGHLANDS
Elunay = Banyun→WEST ATLANTIC
Em→NORTHEASTERN NEW GUINEA
Emae = Mae→POLYNESIAN
Emai→EDO
Emai = Mae→POLYNESIAN
Emalele = Maele. Mangbetu D.→CENTRAL
    SUDANIC
Embaloh→WEST INDONESIAN
Embelinga = Kanakuru→CHADIC
Embo→NORTH EASTERN BANTU
Embu = Embo→NORTH EASTERN BANTU
Emeeje = Meje.   Mangbetu   D.→CENTRAL
    SUDANIC

Eme-eme = Pepeha→CENTRAL AND SOUTH
    NEW GUINEA
eme-KU. Sumerian D.
Emenyo. Siane Tr.→EAST NEW GUINEA
    HIGHLANDS
Emerillon. Oyampi D.→TUPI
Emeror. Urhobo D.→EDO
Emerum→BOGIA
eme-SAL. Sumerian D.
e-Mfinu   =   Mfinu → NORTH   WESTERN
    BANTU
Emigdiano. CHUMASH TR.→HOKAN
Emirau. Mussau D.→BISMARCK ARCHI-
    PELAGO
Empene = Epera→CHOCO
Empeo→NAGA-KUKI-CHIN
EMPERA = EPERA→CHOCO
Empesa Poko. Losengo D.→NORTH WEST-
    ERN BANTU
Emua. Tongoa D.→EASTERN OCEANIC
Emwae = Mae→POLYNESIAN
En. Wa D.→PALAUNG-WA
Ena→NORTH EASTERN BANTU
Encabellado.   Pioji-Sioni   Tr. → MACRO-
    TUCANOAN
Endagany = Indegegn. Peripheral West Gurage
    D.→SEMITIC
Endawarra = Jandruwanta. Dieri D.→DIERIC
Endegen = Indegegn.   Peripheral   West Gurage
    D.→SEMITIC
Endeh→MOLUCCAN
Endo. Pokot D.→EASTERN SUDANIC
Endoto = Endo.   Pokot   D.→EASTERN SU-
    DANIC
Eneadine. Romansch D.→ROMANCE
Eneby = Ilba→PAMA-MARIC
Eneby = Yidin.   Wakaman   D.→PAMA-
    MARIC
Enec = Yenisei Samoyed→URALIC
Enenga.   Myene   D.→NORTH   WESTERN
    BANTU
Ener = Enor.   Peripheral   West   Gurage D.→
    SEMITIC
Enerslet. Mascoy D.→MACRO-PANOAN
Enets = Yenisei Samoyed→URALIC
ENGA→EAST NEW GUINEA HIGHLANDS
Enga→EAST NEW GUINEA HIGHLANDS
Engenni→EDO
Enggano→WEST INDONESIAN
Enggipilu.   Uhunduni   D.→WEST   NEW
    GUINEA HIGHLANDS
Englam→NORTHEASTERN NEW GUINEA
English→GERMANIC
Enimaga see Mascoy→MACRO-PANOAN

Enimaga = Maca→MATACO

Enmylinskij. Chukchee D.→CHUKCHEE-KAMCHATKAN

Ennamor = Ennemor. Peripheral West Gurage D.→SEMITIC

Ennemor. Peripheral West Gurage D.→SEMITIC

Enneqor = Inneqor. East Gurage D.→SEMITIC

Enoo. Alacaluf D.→ANDEAN

Enor. Peripheral West Gurage D.→SEMITIC

Enrekang. Masenrempulu D.→CENTRAL AND SOUTHERN CELEBES

Ensen = Esselen→HOKAN

Entimbich. Foothill North Yokuts D.→YOKUTS

Enugu. Igbo D.→IGBO

Enwan. Ikpeshi D.→EDO

Enwe. Urhobo D.→EDO

Enya = Ena→NORTH EASTERN BANTU

Enyau = Yoku. Eromanga D.→SOUTHERN NEW HEBRIDES

Enyen. Mbembe D.→CROSS RIVER BENUE-CONGO

Eochavante = Oti→MACRO-GE

Eon. Solor D.→MOLUCCAN

Eongo→NORTHWESTERN AND CENTRAL SOLOMONS

Epe. Bungku D.→CENTRAL AND SOUTHERN CELEBES

Epe = Eloyi→PLATEAU BENUE-CONGO

Epeita = Murle→EASTERN SUDANIC

Epera, Northern→CHOCO

Epera, Southern→CHOCO

Epetineri. Maspo D.→PANO

Ephyapum = Epiapum. Mbembe D.→CROSS RIVER BENUE-CONGO

Epiapum. Mbembe D.→CROSS RIVER BE-NUE-CONGO

Epie→EDO

Epigi. Minduumo D.→NORTH WESTERN BANTU

Epii = Piti→PLATEAU BENUE-CONGO

EQUATORIAL see article

Equinao. Guana D.→MAIPURAN

Erai→EAST INDONESIAN

Eralado→NORTHWESTERN NEW HEB-RIDES

ERAP→HUON-FINISTERRE

Erawa = Rawa→HUON-FINISTERRE

Eraweerung = Erawirung. Nganguruku D.→NARRINYERIC

Erawirrangu = Erawirung. Nganguruku D.→NARRINYERIC

Erawiruk = Erawirung. Nganguruku D.→NARRINYERIC

Erawirung. Nganguruku D.→NARRINYERIC

Erbore = Arbore→CUSHITIC

Ere. Kim D.→CHADIC

Eregba→JUKUNOID

Erei. Agwagwune D.→CROSS RIVER BENUE-CONGO

Erenga. Tama D.→EASTERN SUDANIC

Eribu = Eriku. Oksapmin D.→CENTRAL AND SOUTH NEW GUINEA

Eriku. Oksapmin D.→CENTRAL AND SOUTH NEW GUINEA

Erima→EAST NEW GUINEA HIGHLANDS

Eritark = Ngawait. Nganguruku D.→NARRIN-YERIC

Erku = Naiki→DRAVIDIAN

Ermitano→ROMANCE

Erohwa→EDO

Erok = Korappun→CENTRAL AND SOUTH NEW GUINEA

Erokh = Iraqw→CUSHITIC

Erokwanas→EAST INDONESIAN

Eromanga→SOUTHERN NEW HEBRIDES

Eromarra = Ngandangara. Punthamara D.→DIERIC

Erorup = Ododop→CROSS-RIVER BENUE-CONGO

Erronan = West Futuna→POLYNESIAN

Eruhwa = Erohwa→EDO

Erukala. Tamil D.→DRAVIDIAN

Erulia→MACRO-TUCANOAN

ERYTHRAIC = AFROASIATIC

Eryuan→BURMESE-LOLO

Erzja. Morovin D.→URALIC

Esa = Ishan→EDO

Esan = Ishan→EDO

Esari. Turkmen D.→TURKIC

Esary=Esari. Turkmen D.→TURKIC

Escaguey = Mocotan. Timote D.→EQUA-TORIAL

Escelen = Esselen→HOKAN

Escuquean. Cuica D.→EQUATORIAL

Eseejja = Chama→TACANA

Esel. Njem-Bajue Tr.→NORTH WESTERN BANTU

Esele = Esselen→HOKAN

Eseleneijan = Esselen→HOKAN

Esembi = Age→BANTOID

eshi-Sango = Sango→CENTRAL EASTERN BANTU

esi-Mbome = Mbowe→SOUTH WESTERN BANTU

esi-Ngee = Ngee. East Teke D.→NORTH WESTERN BANTU

Esiriun = Wesi. Geser D.→EAST INDONE-
SIAN
Eskelen = Esselen→HOKAN
ESKIMO-ALEUT see article
Eskuara = Basque
Eslen = Esselen→HOKAN
Esmeralda→JIVAROAN
Eso = So→NORTH WESTERN BANTU
Esperigua→NORTHERN MAIPURAN
Espino. Jurua-Purus Tr.→PANO
Essele = Esselen→HOKAN
Esselen→HOKAN
Esseleneijan = Esselen→HOKAN
Estonian = North Estonian→URALIC
Estonian, North→URALIC
Estonian, South→URALIC
Estrella. Bribri D.→CHIBCHAN
Esulau. Diola D.→WEST ATLANTIC
Esumbu. Losengo D.→NORTH WESTERN
BANTU
Etaŋ = Central Agta→NORTHWEST AUS-
TRONESIAN
Eta = Nkom→BANTOID
Etatchogottine. Dogrib Tr.→ATHAPASCAN-
EYAK
Etchaottine = Slave. Chipewyan Tr.→ATHA-
PASCAN-EYAK
Etchemin = Malecite. Passamaquoddy D.→
ALGONQUIAN
Etcheridiegottine. Chipewyan Tr.→ATHA-
PASCAN-EYAK
Etchimi = Malecite. Passamaquoddy D.→
ALGONQUIAN
Etechemin = Malecite. Passamaquoddy D.→
ALGONQUIAN
Etechemine = Malecite. Passamaquoddy D.→
ALGONQUIAN
Etechesottine. Chipewyan Tr.→ATHAPAS-
CAN-EYAK
Etelena = Tereno→MAIPURAN
Eten. Yunca D.→CHIPAYAN
Eteocretan see article
Eteocyprian see article
Etheneldeli. Chipewyan Tr.→ATHAPASCAN-
EYAK
ETHIOPIC→SEMITIC
Ethiopic = Geez→SEMITIC
ETHIOSEMITIC = ETHIOPIC→SEMITIC
Etten = Aten→PLATEAU BENUE-CONGO
e-Tike = Tike. Peri D.→NORTH EASTERN
BANTU
Etkye = Icen→JUKUNOID
Etkywa = Icen→JUKUNOID
Etna Bay→WESTERN NEW GUINEA

Etnemitane = Upper Umpqua→ATHAPAS-
CAN-EYAK
Eto. Bagobo D.→NORTHWEST AUSTRONE-
SIAN
Eton→NORTH WESTERN BANTU
Eton. Efate D.→EASTERN OCEANIC
Etossio = Teso→EASTERN SUDANIC
Etruscan see article
Etsako = Iyekhee→EDO
Etsakor = Iyekhee→EDO
Etsaso = Babadjou→BANTOID
etshi-Hororo = Hororo. Nyankole D.→
NORTH EASTERN BANTU
Etung. Ekoi D.→BANTOID
Euchee = Yuchi→MACRO-SIOUAN
Euhahlayi = Kamilaroi→WIRADJURIC
Euroc = Yurok→MACRO-ALGONQUIAN
Euskara = Basque
Euskera = Basque
Evadi = Kambari→PLATEAU BENUE-
CONGO
Evejico. Cauca Tr.→CARIB
Even→TUNGUS
Evenki→TUNGUS
EVENKI = NORTHERN TUNGUS→TUN-
GUS
Evhro. Urhobo D.→EDO
Ewab. Kei D.→MOLUCCAN
Ewage = Notu→BINANDERE
Ewatiaga→PAPUA AUSTRONESIAN
EWE see article
Ewenu = Djaui. Nyulnyul D.→NYULNYU-
LAN
Ewenyoon = Djaui. Nyulnyul D.→NYULNYU-
LAN
Ewodi = Oli→NORTH WESTERN BANTU
Ewondo→NORTH WESTERN BANTU
Ewu. Urhobo D.→EDO
Ewutere = Metyibo→VOLTA-COMOE
Ewuture = Metyibo→VOLTA-COMOE
Eyak→ATHAPASCAN-EYAK
Eyibogodegi. Mbya-Guaicuru Tr.→GUAY-
CURU
Eza = Ezha. Central West Gurage D.→SEMIT-
IC
Ezam = Ejagham. Ekoi D.→BANTOID
Ezeshio = Monshoco→CAMACAN
Ezha. Central West Guarage D.→SEMITIC
Ezo. Ainu D.→AINU

F

Fa'→NORTH WESTERN BANTU
Fa, Bafang D.→BANTOID

Faala. Karanga D.→MABAN
Fachara = Chara→PLATEAU BENUE-CONGO
Fada = Biafada→WEST ATLANTIC
Fadasi = Wa-dashi. Berta D.→CHARI-NILE
Fadawu. Kanuri Tr.→SAHARAN
Fadicha = Fiyadikka. Mahas-Fiyadikka D.→EASTERN SUDANIC
Fadija = Fiyadikka. Mahas-Eiyadikka D.→EASTERN SUDANIC
Fadiout = Fadyut. Serer D.→WEST ATLANTIC
Fadiro = Northern Mao→KOMAN
Fadjulu = Pojulu. Bari D.→EASTERN SUDANIC
Fadon. Berta D.→CHARI-NILE
Fadyut. Serer D.→WEST ATLANTIC
Fagnia = Fanya→ADAMAWA
Fagurai. Limbu D.→GYARUNG-MISHMI
Faichuk. Trukese D.→MICRONESIAN
Fairi. Biak D.→MOLUCCAN
Fais. Ulithian D.→MICRONESIAN
Faiwol→OK
Faiwolmin = Faiwol→OK
Fajelu = Polulu. Bari D.→EASTERN SUDANIC
Fajut-Palmerin = Fadyut. Serer D.→WEST ATLANTIC
Fak = Fa'→NORTH WESTERN BANTU
Fakara = Chara→PLATEAU BENUE-CONGO
Fakawa = Puku-nu → PLATEAU BENUE-CONGO
Fala. Karanga D.→MABAN
Falahu. Sanana D.→EAST INDONESIAN
Falanao = Baran. Ami D.→FORMOSAN AUSTRONESIAN
Falasha = Kalya. Quara D.→CUSHITIC
Falasha Kara = Kayla. Quara D.→CUSHITIC
Fali→ADAMAWA
Fali. Daba D.→CHADIC
Fali = Gawar. Daba D.→CHADIC
Fali of Kiria→CHADIC
Fali of Mubi→CHADIC
Fali of Yilbu→CHADIC
Faliscan→ITALIC
Fall Indians = Atsina. Arapaho D.→ALGONQUIAN
Fallam→NAGA-KUKI-CHIN
Falor→WEST ATLANTIC
Fama-Teis-Kua. Krongo Tr.→KORDOFANIAN
Fan = Faŋ→NORTH WESTERN BANTU
Fana = Fanya→CHADIC
Fanakala = Piki→SOUTH EASTERN BANTU
Fanekalo = Piki→SOUTH EASTERN BANTU

Fang = Faŋ→NORTH WESTERN BANTU
Fania = Fanya→CHADIC
Fanian = Fanya→CHADIC
Fanji→BANTOID
Fante. Akan D.→VOLTA-COMOE
Fantera→GUR
Fanti = Fante. Akan D.→VOLTA-COMOE
Fanting. Central Ambryn D.→EASTERN OCEANIC
Fanwe = Faŋ→NORTH WESTERN BANTU
Fanya→ADAMAWA
Fanya→CHADIC
Faŋ→NORTH WESTERN BANTU
Faranjao = Faranyao → WESTERN NEW GUINEA
Faranyao→WESTERN NEW GUINEA
Fari = Pari. Anuak Tr.→EASTERN SUDANIC
Faroese. Insular Scandinavian D.→GERMANIC
Fas-→NORTH NEW GUINEA
Fasu→EAST NEW GUINEA HIGHLANDS
Fataleka→EASTERN OCEANIC
Fatje. Sanana D.→EAST INDONESIAN
Faur→WESTERN NEW GUINEA
Favele→KOIARI
Favorlang = Babuza→FORMOSAN AUSTRONESIAN
Fayumic. Copitic D.→AFROASIATIC
Fazoglo. Berta D.→CHARI-NILE
Fazughli = Fazoglo. Berta D.→CHARI-NILE
Febe = Dyula. Dyula Tr.→MANDE
Fecaka. Berta D.→CHARI-NILE
Fecakomodiyo = Gule→KOMAN
Fecamalga = Fecaka. Berta D.→CHARI-NILE
Fedicca = Fiyadikka. Mahas-Fiyadikka D.→EASTERN SUDANIC
Fedopia. Limbu D.→GYARUNG-MISHMI
Fe ʔfe ʔ = Bafang→BANTOID
Fefe = Bafang→BANTOID
Fellani = Ful→WEST ATLANTIC
Feloup = Flup. Diola D.→WEST ATLANTIC
Felup = Flup. Diola D.→WEST ATLANTIC
Felupe = Fulp. Diola D.→WEST ATLANTIC
Fem = Pyem→PLATEAU BENUE-CONGO
Ferejdan. Geogian D.→CAUCASIAN
Fernandeno. Gabrieleno D.→UTO-AZTECAN
Fernandian = Bube → NORTH WESTERN BANTU
Feroge→EASTERN
Ferohge = Feroge→EASTERN
Fesoa→BISMARCK ARCHIPELAGO
Fetutlin. Han Tr.→ATHAPASCAN-EYAK
Fiadidja = Fiyadikka. Mahas-Fiyadikka D.→EASTERN SUDANIC
Fianga. Tuburi D.→CHADIC

Fianga-Chola. Tupuri D.→ADAMAWA
Fiba→CENTRAL EASTERN BANTU
Fijian→EASTERN OCEANIC
Fika. Bolewa D.→CHADIC
Fikankayen = Fika. Bolewa D.→CHADIC
Fila. Mele D.→POLYNESIAN
Filham = Fogny. Diola D.→WEST ATLANTIC
Fimaga. Foi D.→EAST NEW GUINEA HIGHLANDS
Finge = Kidzom→BANTOID
Fingo = Old Mfengu → SOUTH EASTERN BANTU
Finiŋga = Daju→EASTERN SUDANIC
FINISTERRE→HUON-FINISTERRE
Finng = Bobo Fing. Sya D.→MANDE
FINNIC→URALIC
Finnish→URALIC
FINNO-LAPPIC→URALIC
FINNO-UGRIC→URALIC
FINNO-VOLGAIC→URALIC
Finungwan→HUON-FINISTERRE
Fiome = Goroa→CUSHITIC
Fiomi = Goroa→CUSHITIC
Fiot = Bwende. Kongo D.→CENTRAL WESTERN BANTU
Fiot = Vili→CENTRAL WESTERN BANTU
Fiote = Eastern Kongo. Kongo D.→CENTRAL WESTERN BANTU
Fiote = Kongo→CENTRAL WESTERN BANTU
Fiote = Western Kongo. Kongo D.→CENTRAL WESTERN BANTU
FIPA-MAMBWE→CENTRAL EASTERN BANTU
Fire Nation = Potawatomi→ALGONQUIAN
Firozkodi. Persian D.→IRANIAN
Fissoa = Fesoa→BISMARCK ARCHIPELA-GO
Fiteriya = Hona. Tera D.→CHADIC
Fitita→WITOTOAN
Fiu = Kwara ʔae→EASTERN OCEANIC
Fiyadikka. Mahas-Fiyadikka D.→EASTERN SUDANIC
Fizere = Afusare→PLATEAU BENUE-CONGO
Flancs-de-Chien = Dogrib→ATHAPASCAN-EYAK
Flatbow = Kutenai
Flathead. Kalispel D.→SALISH
Flemish. Netherlandic-German D.→GERMANIC
Florida = Timucua
Floridiana = Timucua
Flup. Diola D.→WEST ATLANTIC

Fly, Upper→OK
Fo→EWE
Fogny. Diola D.→WEST ATLANTIC
Foi→EAST NEW GUINEA HIGHLANDS
Foja→NORTH PAPUAN
Follaties = Tfalati→KALAPUYA
Folle Avoine = Menomini→ALGONQUIAN
Folo. Dyimini D.→GUR
Folo = Minya. Malinka D.→MANDE
Foma = Fuma→NORTH WESTERN BANTU
Fomopea→BANTOID
Fon = Fo→EWE
Fonange. Lower Mundani D.→BANTOID
Fongbe = Fo→EWE
Fongondeng→BANTOID
Fongo-Ndeng = Fongondeng→BANTOID
Fony = Fogny. Diola D.→WEST ATLANTIC
Fo'oa→NORTHWESTERN NEW HEBRIDES
Foochow = Northern Min→CHINESE
Fora. Balanta D.→WEST ATLANTIC
Fora = Fur→NILO-SAHARAN
Foraba→EAST NEW GUINEA HIGHLANDS
Foran→BOGIA
Fordat→MOLUCCAN
Fordate = Fordat→MOLUCCAN
FORDATIC→MOLUCCAN
Forduŋga = Fur→NILO-SAHARAN
FORE→EAST NEW GUINEA HIGHLANDS
Fore→EAST NEW GUINEA HIGHLANDS
Formosan. Southern Min D.→CHINESE
Fornio = Fulnio→MACRO-GE
Foro = Folo. Dyimini D.→GUR
Forum. Afusare D.→PLATEAU BENUE-CONGO
Foto→BANTOID
Fotouni→BANTOID
Fox→ALGONQUIAN
Fra = Nankanse→GUR
Frafra→GUR
Franconian. Netherlandic-German D.→GERMANIC
Franco-Provencal. French D.→ROMANCE
FREDERIK HENDRIK ISLAND AND SOUTHEAST WEST IRIAN see article
French→ROMANCE
French, South = Provencal→ROMANCE
FRENTONES→GUAYCURU
Frisian→GERMANIC
Friulian→ROMANCE
Fu = Bafut→BANTOID
Fuchow = Northern Min→CHINESE
Fuch'ye = Nung→BODO-NAGA-KACHIN
Fuckac. Mape D.→HUON-FINISTERRE
Fukuwe'u. Sanana D.→EAST INDONESIAN

Ful→WEST ATLANTIC
Fula = Ful→WEST ATLANTIC
Fulah = Ful→WEST ATLANTIC
Fulani = Ful→WEST ATLANTIC
Fulannara. Mongour D.→MONGOLIAN
Fulbe = Ful→WEST ATLANTIC
Fulfede = Ful→WEST ATLANTIC
Fulfulde = Ful→WEST ATLANTIC
Fuliro = Fuliro→NORTH EASTERN BANTU
Fuliiru = Fuliro→NORTH EASTERN BANTU
Fulilwa. Tumbuka D.→CENTRAL EASTERN
    BANTU
Fuliro→NORTH EASTERN BANTU
Fulirwa = Fulilwa. Tumbuka D.→CENTRAL
    EASTERN BANTU
Fulnio→MACRO-GE
Fulsap = Bafoussam→BANTOID
Fulse = Kurumba→GUR
Fuluka = Kusu→NORTH WESTERN BANTU
Fulup = Flup. Diola D.→WEST ATLANTIC
Fuma→NORTH WESTERN BANTU
Fumu. South Teke D.→NORTH WESTERN
    BANTU
Fungi = Gule→KOMAN
Fungom→BANTOID
Fungor→KORDOFANIAN
Fungur = Fungor→KORDOFANIAN
Fungwe. Tumbuka D.→CENTRAL EASTERN
    BANTU
Funika = Mfinu → NORTH WESTERN
    BANTU
Fuŋ. Nyo'o D.→NORTH WESTERN BANTU
Fur→NILO-SAHARAN
Furawi = Fur→NILO-SAHARAN
Furiiro = Fuliro→NORTH EASTERN BANTU
Furu→CENTRAL SUDANIC
Fusam = Bafoussam→BANTOID
Fusap = Bafoussam→BANTOID
Fut = Bafut→BANTOID
Futa = Ful→WEST ATLANTIC
Futuna→POLYNESIAN
Futuna, West→POLYNESIAN
Futuna, East = Futuna→POLYNESIAN
FUYUGE→GOILALA
Fuyuge→GOILALA
Fwagumwak. Nenema D.→NEW CALEDONIA
Fyam = Pyem→PLATEAU BENUE-CONGO
Fyeum = Pyem→PLATEAU BENUE-CONGO

G

Ga→GA-ADANGME
Ga = Gan→GUR
G//aa→KHOISAN

GA-ADANGME see article
G//aakhwe = G//aa→KHOISAN
Ga'anda→CHADIC
Gaangala. Kongo D.→CENTRAL WESTERN
    BANTU
G//abake→KHOISAN
G//abake ntshori = G//abake→KHOISAN
G//abake tshori = G//abake→KHOISAN
g/abe = Nossob→KHOISAN
Gaberi = Gabri→CHADIC
Gabgab. Boazi D.→MARIND
Gagiano→SEPIK
Gabin = Ga'anda→CHADIC
Gablai→CHADIC
Gabou = Gobu. Banda D.→EASTERN
Gabra = Borena. Galla D.→CUSHITIC
Gabri→CHADIC
Gabri→IRANIAN
Gabrieleno→UTO-AZTECAN
Gabrielino = Gabrieleno→UTO-AZTECAN
Gachikolo. Oriya D.→INDIC
Gachitl. Chamalal D.→CAUCASIAN
Gadaba = Gorum→MUNDA
Gadaba = Gutob→MUNDA
Gadabursi. Somali D.→CUSHITIC
Gadang = Kattang. Worimi D.→YUIN-KURIC
Gadba→DRAVIDIAN
Gadba. Gutob D.→MUNDA
GADDANG→NORTHWEST AUSTRONE-
    SIAN
Gaddang, Christian→NORTHWEST AUSTRO-
    NESIAN
Gaddang. Pagan→NORTHWEST AUSTRO-
    NESIAN
Gade→NUPE-GBARI
Gadiwa. Tebu Tr.→SAHARAN
Gadjerong→DJERAGAN
Gadsup→EAST NEW GUINEA HIGH-
    LANDS
GADSUP-AUYANA-AWA-TAIRORA→EAST
    NEW GUINEA HIGHLANDS
Gaduwa = Gadiwa. Tebu Tr.→SAHARAN
Gadyaga. Soninke Tr.→MANDE
Gadyri. Chamalal D.→CAUCASIAN
Gae. Andoa Tr.→ANDEAN
Gaeda = Gaida. Tebu Tr.→SAHARAN
Gaelic, Irish→CELTIC
Gaelic, Scottish→CELTIC
Gafat→SEMITIC
Gafatinya = Gafat→SEMITIC
Gafuku = Gahuku→EAST NEW GUINEA
    HIGHLANDS
Gagadu = Kakadu→AUSTRALIAN MACRO-
    PHYLUM

Gagatl. Andi D.→CAUCASIAN
Gagauz→TURKIC
Gagauz Turkish, Balkan→TURKIC
Gage = Tontoli→NORTHERN CELEBES
Gagu. Kweni D.→MANDE
Gagu = Kweni→MANDE
Gahom = Bahinemo→SEPIK
GAHUKU→EAST NEW GUINEA HIGH-LANDS
Gahuku→EAST NEW GUINEA HIGH-LANDS
Gai see CHIMBU→EAST NEW GUINEA HIGHLANDS
Gaiamba = Ngemba. Wongaibon D.→WIRAD-JURIC
Gaida. Tebu Tr.→SAHARAN
Gaika. Nguni D.→SOUTH EASTERN BANTU
Gain = Fe. Ga D.→GA-ADANGME
Gaina→BINANDERE
Gaingre = Ge. Ewe D.→EWE
Gaitchim = Juaneno. Luiseno D.→UTO-AZTECAN
Gaj = Gants→EAST NEW GUINEA HIGH-LANDS
Gajila. Kunimaipa D.→GOILALA
Gajol. Balkan Gagauz Turkish D.→TURKIC
Ga-joماŋ = Talodi→KORDOFANIAN
Gaktai. Baining D.→NEW BRITAIN
Gakvari. Chamalal D.→CAUCASIAN
Gal→BOGIA
Galabu. Kanembu Tr.→SAHARAN
Galali = Kalali. Punthamara D.→DIERIC
Galanchog. Chechen D.→CAUCASIAN
Galar→MON-KHMER
Galas. Pangan D.→SEMANG
Galbu. Riraidjango D.→MURNGIC
Galcha. Persian D.→IRANIAN
Galek→NORTHEAST NEW GUINEA AUS-TRONESIAN
Galela→NORTH HALMAHERA
Galeva→DAGA
Galibi. Carib D.→CARIB
Galice→ATHAPASCAN-EYAK
Galician. Portuguese D.→ROMANCE
Galim. Bute D.→BANTOID
Galiya. Soddo D.→SEMITIC
GALLA→CUSHITIC
Galla→CUSHITIC
Galler. Bru D.→MON-KHMER
Gallinas = Vai→MANDE
Gallinomero = Southern Pomo→POMO
GALLO-ROMANCE→ROMANCE
Galoa = Galwa. Myene D.→NORTH WEST-ERN BANTU

Galoli→EAST INDONESIAN
Galoma→PAPUA AUSTRONESIAN
Galu→TORRICELLI
Galwa. Myene D.→NORTH WESTERN BANTU
G//am→KHOISAN
Gam→CHADIC
Gama. Gahuku D.→EAST NEW GUINEA HIGHLANDS
Gamacom. Oyampi D.→TUPI
Gamadia. Gujarati D.→INDIC
Gamai = Gamei→BOGIA
Gamawa = Ngamo→CHADIC
Gamba = Bviri→EASTERN
Gamba = Gambai→CENTRAL SUDANIC
Gambadi. Peremka D.→CENTRAL AND SOUTH NEW GUINEA
Gambai→CENTRAL SUDANIC
Gambata→EASTERN OCEANIC
Gambay = Gambai→CENTRAL SUDANIC
Gamba = Dyolof. Wolof D.→WEST ATLAN-TIC
Gambir. Tregami D.→NURISTANI
Gambiri = Tregami→NURISTANI
Gambo = Pantera→GUR
Gambre→WORORAN
Gamei→BOGIA
Gamergu. Mandara D.→CHADIC
Gamgam = Jamjam→CUSHITIC
Gamila. Berta D.→CHARI-NILE
Gamilaroi = Kamilaroi→WIRADJURIC
Gamili = Gamila. Berta D.→CHARI-NILE
Gamo→OMOTIC
Gamsungi. Tobelo D.→NORTH HALMA-HERA
Gan→GUR
Gan. Kweni D.→MANDE
G//ana→KHOISAN
Ganade→KHOISAN
Ganagana = Dido. Nupe D.→NUPE-GBARI
G//anakhwe = G//ana→KHOISAN
Ganan. Kadu D.→BURMESE-LOLO
Gananwa = Xananwa. Northern Sotho D.→SOUTH EASTERN BANTU
Ganati→INDO-PACIFIC
Ganawuri = Aten→PLATEAU BENUE-CONGO
Ganda→NORTH EASTERN BANTU
Ganda = Ga'anda→CHADIC
Gandangara→YUIN-KURIC
Gandja = Kandawo. Narak D.→EAST NEW GUINEA HIGHLANDS
Gandua→BANTOID
Gane→GUR

Gane = SOUTH HALMAHERA AUSTRO-NESIAN
!ga!ne = !ga!ŋe. Seroa D.→KHOISAN
Gang = Akoli→EASTERN SUDANIC
Ganga = Busooŋ→NORTH WESTERN BANTU
Gangam = Dye→GUR
Gangan = Gbari Gyenguen. Gbari D.→NUPE-GBARI
Ganggalida. Gayardilt D.→TANGKIC
Ganglau→NORTHEAST NEW GUINEA AUSTRONESIAN
Ganglau→INDO-PACIFIC
Ganguella = Ngangela. Luimbi D.→SOUTH WESTERN BANTU
G//anikwe→KHOISAN
/ganin = Namib→KHOISAN
Ganja→WEST ATLANTIC
Gan-Lobi = Gan→GUR
Ganne = Gan. Kweni D.→MANDE
Ganta. Walamo Tr.→OMOTIC
Ganti→CENTRAL AND SOUTHERN CELEBES
Gants→EAST NEW GUINEA HIGHLANDS
Ganung-Rawang = Rawang→BODO-NAGA-KACHIN
Ganza. Ruanda D.→NORTH EASTERN BANTU
Ganza = Northern Mao→KOMAN
Ganzi→EASTERN
Ganzi. Bganziri Tr.→EASTERN
Ganzibati = Kazibati→EASTERN
Ganzo = Northern Mao→KOMAN
!ga!ŋe. Seroa D.→KHOISAN
G!aŋg!ai→KHOISAN
Gao→NORTHWESTERN AND CENTRAL SOLOMONS
Gaouar = Gawar. Daba D.→CHADIC
Gapershi = Kasem→GUR
Gapun→BOGIA
Gar. Eastern Mnong D.→MON-KHMER
Gara. Senari D.→GUR
Garadjeri = Karadjeri→MARNGU
Garaganza = Takama. Nyamwesi D.→NORTH EASTERN BANTU
Garama→GARAMAN
GARAMAN see article
Garap = Ere. Kim D.→CHADIC
Gardulla = Gidole→CUSHITIC
Gare = Borena. Galla D.→CUSHITIC
Garego = Ngarigo→YUIN-KURIC
Garhwal. Central Tibetan D.→TIBETAN
Garhwali→INDIC
Gari→EASTERN OCEANIC

Garia→MULAHA
Gariyimar = Mara→MARAN
Garkin. Lezghian D.→CAUCASIAN
Garko = Karko. Kordofanian Nubian Tr.→EASTERN SUDANIC
Garmalangga. Jarnango D.→MURNGIC
Garo→BODO-NAGA-KACHIN
Garo = Bosha. Kefa D.→OMOTIC
Garo of Jalpaiguri = Wanang→BODO-NAGA KACHIN
Garua = Karua→NORTHEAST NEW GUINEA AUSTRONESIAN
Garuh→BOGIA
Garundi = Karanti→PAMA-NYUNGAN
Garus→BOGIA
Garwe. Shona D.→SOUTH EASTERN BANTU
Garwi = Baskarik→INDIC
Gashowu. Foothill North Yokuts D.→YOKUTS
Gasi = Kanakuru→CHADIC
Gaspesien = Micmac→ALGONQUIAN
Gataʔ→MUNDA
Gataq = Gataʔ→MUNDA
Gato = Konso→CUSHITIC
Gatukai→NORTHWESTERN AND CENTRAL SOLOMONS
Gatzamba = Kachama→OMOTIC
Gaua = Gog→EASTERN OCEANIC
Gauar = Gawar. Daba D.→CHADIC
Gaugutianap. Oksapmin D.→CENTRAL AND SOUTH NEW GUINEA
Gaulish→CELTIC
Gauri = Kauri→BODO-NAGA-KACHIN
GAUWA→EAST NEW GUINEA HIGH LANDS
Gauwada = Gawwada→CUSHITIC
Gaviose = Augutge→GE
Gawa→PAPUA AUSTRONESIAN
Gawaar. Nuer D.→EASTERN SUDANIC
Gawanga→SEPIK
Gawar. Daba D.→CHADIC
Gawar-bati→INDIC
Gawata = Gawwada→CUSHITIC
Gaweir = Gawaar. Nuer D.→EASTERN SUDANIC
Gawigl. Medlpa D.→EAST NEW GUINEA HIGHLANDS
Gawir. Marind D.→MARIND
Gawri = Baskarik→INDIC
Gawwada→CUSHITIC
Gaya. Sese D.→NORTH EASTERN BANTU
Gaya = Luo→EASTERN SUDANIC
Gayardilt→TANGKIC
Gayi→CROSS-RIVER BENUE-CONGO
Gayi→OMOTIC

Gayi = Bisu. Obanliku D.→CROSS RIVER BENUE-CONGO

Gayo→WEST INDONESIAN

Gayon→JIRARAN

Gbaba = Baba. Banda D.→EASTERN

Gbaga. Banda D.→EASTERN

G'bagga = Gbaga. Banda D.→EASTERN

Gbaka = Gbaya→EASTERN

Gbakpwa = Kpala→EASTERN

Gbamende = Kpa. Mende D.→MANDE

Gban = Gagu. Kweni D.→MANDE

Gbande = Gbandi. Mende D.→MANDE

Gbandere = Gbanziri→EASTERN

Gbandi. Mende D.→MANDE

Gbandu = Avikam→LAGOON

Gbanya = Guan→VOLTA-COMOE

Gbanyang = Guan→VOLTA-COMOE

Gbanziri→EASTERN

Gbara = Gberi. 'Beli D. → CENTRAL SUDANIC

Gbara Kala = Gbaya Kara. Gbaya Tr.→EASTERN

Gbaramatu = Oporoza. Ijo D.→IJO

Gbaran. Ijo D.→IJO

Gbari→NUPE-GBARI

Gbari Gyenguen. Gbari D.→NUPE-GBARI

Gbari Kangye. Gbari D.→NUPE-GBARI

Gbari Yamma. Gbari D.→NUPE-GBARI

Gbasa = Bassa→KRU

Gbaya→EASTERN

Gbaya. Furu Tr.→CENTRAL SUDANIC

Gbaya. Kresh D.→CENTRAL SUDANIC

Gbaya = Furu→CENTRAL SUDANIC

Gbaya Bianda. Gbaya Tr.→EASTERN

Gbaya Bodomo. Gbaya Tr.→EASTERN

Gbaya Bokoto. Gbaya Tr.→EASTERN

Gbaya Buli. Gbaya Tr.→EASTERN

Gbaya Buli Bukum. Gbaya Tr.→EASTERN

Gbaya Kaka. Gbaya Tr.→EASTERN

Gbaya Kara. Gbaya Tr.→EASTERN

Gbaya Lai. Gbaya Tr.→EASTERN

Gbaya-ndogo = Gbaya. Kresh D.→CENTRAL SUDANIC

Gbedde. Yoruba D.→YORUBA

Gbedye. Nupe Tr.→NUPE-GBARI

Gbee = Ali. Gbaya Tr.→EASTERN

Gbeinngn = Gan. Kweni D.→MANDE

Gbeize = Kpelle→MANDE

Gberese = Kpelle→MANDE

Gberi. 'Beli D.→CENTRAL SUDANIC

Gbese = Kpelle→MANDE

Gbigbil. Bebele D.→NORTH WESTERN BANTU

Gbindi = Gbewende. Banda D.→EASTERN

Gbo = Legbo→CROSS RIVER BENUE-CONGO

Gboare = Bachama→CHADIC

Gboati = Bata→CHADIC

Gbofi. Gbaya Tr.→EASTERN

Gboo De = Gbunde. Loma D.→MANDE

Gbugbla = Prampram. Adangme D.→GA-ADANGME

Gbugbu = Mbugu. Banda D.→EASTERN

Gbunde. Loma D.→MANDE

Gbwende. Banda D.→EASTERN

Gcaleka. Nguni D.→SOUTH EASTERN BANTU

Gciriku = Mbogedo. Kwangari D.→SOUTH WESTERN BANTU

GE see article

GE, MACRO- see article

Ge. Ewe D.→EWE

Ge. Ga D.→GA-ADANGME

Ge = Dan→MANDE

Ge Aji. Pima D.→UTO-AZTECAN

Geawegal. Wiradjuri D.→WIRADJURIC

Geba = Karenbyu. Bwe D.→KAREN

Gebe = Minyafuin→SOUTH HALMAHERA AUSTRONESIAN

Gebelawin. Berta D.→CHARI-NILE

Gebi→MAILU

Gebo = Karenbyu. Bwe D.→KAREN

GE-BORORO, MACRO- see article

Gebra = Borena. Galla D.→CUSHITIC

Gebusi = Bibo→PARE-SAMO-BEAMI-BOSAVI

Gecoinlahaac = Lengua. Mascoy D.→MACRO-PANOAN

Geechee = Gullah→GERMANIC

GEELVINK→MOLUCCAN

Geer-ni = Gelewa→PLATEAU BENUE-CONGO

Geez→SEMITIC

Ge'ez = Geez→SEMITIC

Geg. Albanian D.

g/einin = Namib→KHOISAN

Geji = Gezewa→PLATEAU BENUE-CONGO

Gekoyo = Kikuyu→NORTH EASTERN BANTU

Gekxun. Agul D.→CAUCASIAN

Gela = Nggela→EASTERN OCEANIC

Gelaki = Gilaki→IRANIAN

Gelama. Mundang D.→ADAMAWA

Gele→CENTRAL SUDANIC

Geleb = Dasenech→CUSHITIC

Geleba = Dasenech→CUSHITIC

Gelewa→PLATEAU BENUE-CONGO

Gelik→BISMARCK ARCHIPELAGO

Gellaba = Dasenech→CUSHITIC
Gelleb = Dasenech→CUSHITIC
Gelubba = Dasenech→CUSHITIC
Gema = Dan→MANDE
Gemu. Walamo D.→OMOTIC
Genagane = Nagane. Chimbu D.→EAST NEW GUINEA HIGHLANDS
GENDE→EAST NEW GUINEA HIGHLANDS
Gende→EAST NEW GUINEA HIGHLANDS
GENDE-SIANE-GAHUKU-KAMANO-FORE →EAST NEW GUINEA HIGHLANDS
Gendja. Ngombe D.→NORTH WESTERN BANTU
Gendza-Baali. Ngombe D.→NORTH WESTERN BANTU
Genge = Kenga→CENTRAL SUDANIC
Gengele. Songola D.→NORTH EASTERN BANTU
Gengle→ADAMAWA
Genia = Ena→NORTH EASTERN BANTU
Genja = Gendja. Ngombe D.→NORTH WESTERN BANTU
Gentoo = Telugu→DRAVIDIAN
Genya = Ena→NORTH EASTERN BANTU
Georgian→CAUCASIAN
GE-PANO-CARIB see article
Gepidae. Burgundian D.→GERMANIC
Gerep = Juman. Kim D.→CHADIC
Gerese = Dache. Walamo D.→OMOTIC
GERGITO-SALYMEAN see article
Gerka→CHADIC
Gerlovo Turks. Balkan Gagauz Turkish D.→ TURKIC
German. Netherlandic-German D.→GERMANIC
GERMANIC see article
Gerse = Kpelle→MANDE
Gerze = Kpelle→MANDE
Geser→EAST INDONESIAN
Gesinan = Harari. East Gurage D.→SEMITIC
Gesoa. Wabuda D.→CENTRAL AND SOUTH NEW GUINEA
Getag = Gata ?→MUNDA
Geto. Peripheral West Gurage D.→SEMITIC
Gezawa→CHADIC
Gezewa→PLATEAU BENUE-CONGO
Gezon = Apagibeti. Bati D.→NORTH WESTERN BANTU
Ghadames. Tuareg D.→BERBER
GHALCHAH = PAMIR→IRANIAN
Ghardaia→BERBER
Gheg = Geg. Albanian D.
Gheko→KAREN

Ghidole = Gidole→CUSHITIC
Ghimira = Bencho→OMOTIC
Ghimirra = Bencho→OMOTIC
Ghisadi = Tarimuki. Gujarati D.→INDIC
Ghizi = Kisi→WEST ATLANTIC
Ghol. Bor D.→EASTERN SUDANIC
Ghotuo. Aakwo D.→EDO
Ghulfan. Kordofanian Nubian Tr.→EASTERN SUDANIC
Ghumbiek. Tatog Tr.→EASTERN SUDANIC
Gia. Mandandanji D.→PAMA-MARIC
Giabal→GIABALIC
GIABALIC see article
Giamina→UTO-AZTECAN
Gianga. Bagobo D.→NORTHWEST AUSTRONESIAN
Giangero = Janjero→OMOTIC
Giay→KAM-TAI
Gibo. Bete Tr.→KRU
Gidar = Gider→CHADIC
Gidder = Gider→CHADIC
Gidempla. Basila D.→CENTRAL TOGO
Gider→CHADIC
Gidicho. Koyra D.→OMOTIC
Gidja→DJERAGAN
GIDJIC→DJERAGAN
Gidjiya = Gunavidji→AUSTRALIAN MACRO-PHYLUM
Gidjoobal = Kitabal→BANDJALANGIC
Gidole→CUSHITIC
Gidolinya = Gidole→CUSHITIC
Gidra→ORIOMO RIVER
Giel. Padang D.→EASTERN SUDANIC
Gien = Tchien. Krahn Tr.→KRU
Gieta = Geto. Peripheral West Gurage D.→ SEMITIC
Gigimai. Pima D.→UTO-AZTECAN
Gijara = Gizra→ORIOMO RIVER
Gikolodjya. Basila D.→CENTRAL TOGO
Gikuyu = Kikuyu→NORTH EASTERN BANTU
gi/ /kxi:gwi = / /xegwe→KHOISAN
Gilaki→IRANIAN
Gilbertese→MICRONESIAN
Gilgiti. Sina D.→INDIC
Gilima. Bwaka D.→EASTERN
Gilipanes = Kiangan→NORTHWEST AUSTRONESIAN
Gili'q!ulawas = Kwalhioqua→ATHAPASCAN-EYAK
Gilyak see article
gi-Mbaama = Mbaama→NORTH WESTERN BANTU

Gimbunda = Mbunda→SOUTH WESTERN BANTU
GIMERA→OMOTIC
Gimi→EAST NEW GUINEA HIGHLANDS
Gimi. Wahgi D.→EAST NEW GUINEA HIGHLANDS
Gimini = Dyimini→GUR
Gimira = Bencho→OMOTIC
Gimirra = Bencho→OMOTIC
Gimr = Orra. Tama D.→EASTERN SUDANIC
Gimsbok Nama→KHOISAN
Gina'an = Balbalasang-Ginaang. Kalinga D.→ NORTHWEST AUSTRONESIAN
Ginga = Njinga. Mbamba D.→CENTRAL WESTERN BANTU
Ging-Gwak. Jarawa D.→BANTOID
Ginginburra = Taribeleng→WAKA-KABIC
Gingwak = Ging-Gwak. Jarawa D.→BANTOID
G!inkwe. Naron D.→KHOISAN
Ginukh = Ginux→CAUCASIAN
Ginux→CAUCASIAN
!giŋkwe = G!inkwe. Naron D.→KHOISAN
Gio = Dan→MANDE
Giporoc = Yiporok→BOTOCUDO
Giporok = Yiporok→BOTOCUDO
Gira→HUON-FINISTERRE
Giramay. Wakaman D.→PAMA-MARIC
Girango. Zanaki D.→NORTH EASTERN BANTU
Girdimang = Gunbalang. Muralidban D.→ GUNWINGGUAN
Girga. Sungor Tr.→EASTERN SUDANIC
Giri→BOGIA
Giryama. Nika D.→NORTH EASTERN BANTU
Gisamajenk. Tatog Tr.→EASTERN SUDANIC
Giseda. Basila D.→CENTRAL TOGO
Gishu = Masaba→NORTH EASTERN BANTU
Gisida = Basila→CENTRAL TOGO
Gisiga→CHADIC
Gisima. Loma D.→MANDE
Gisohiga = Gisiga→CHADIC
Gissi = Kisi→WEST ATLANTIC
Gisu = Masaba→NORTH EASTERN BANTU
Gitksan. Tsimshian D.→PENUTIAN
gi-Tonga = Tonga→SOUTH EASTERN BANTU
Giumu→BINANDERE
Giur = Lwo→EASTERN SUDANIC
Gizi = Kisi→WEST ATLANTIC
Gizima = Gisima. Loma D.→MANDE
Gizra→ORIOMO RIVER

Gjunej. Lezghian D.→CAUCASIAN
Glanda-Khwe = Hukwe→KHOISAN
Glidyi. Ewe Tr.→EWE
Gmbuaga = Gbaya→EASTERN
Gnalla = Ngarla→NGAYARDA
Gnalluma = Ngaluma. Kariera D.→NGAYARDA
Gnalooma = Ngaluma. Kariera D.→NGAYARDA
Gnalouma = Ngaluma. Kariera D.→NGAYARDA
Gnameni = Ngameni. Dieri D.→DIERIC
Gnam-gnam = Zande→EASTERN
Gnamo = Nyamal→NGAYARDA
Gnau→TORRICELLI
Gnoree = Nguri→WIRADJURIC
Gnurellean = Taungurong→KULINIC
Go = Godye. Bete D.→KRU
Go = Mambisa. Lendu D.→CENTRAL SUDANIC
Goa = Koa→PAMA-MARIC
Goahiva = Guahibo→EQUATORIAL
Goahivo = Guahibo→EQUATORIAL
Goajiro→NORTHERN MAIPURAN
Goali = Gbari→NUPE-GBARI
Goamulgo = Koa→PAMA-MARIC
Goanese = Konkan. Marathi D.→INDIC
Goari. Northern Kiwai D.→CENTRAL AND SOUTH NEW GUINEA
Goaribari. Northern Kiwai D.→CENTRAL AND SOUTH NEW GUINEA
Goba = Gova. Shona D.→SOUTH EASTERN BANTU
Goba = Mbukushu. Kwangari D.→SOUTH WESTERN BANTU
Gobabingo→MURNGIC
Gobabwingu = Gobabingo→MURNGIC
Gobato. Berta D.→CHARI-NILE
Gobera = Govera. Karanga D.→SOUTH EASTERN BANTU
Gobeze. Gawwada D.→CUSHITIC
Gobla = Gola→WEST ATLANTIC
Gobu. Banda D.→EASTERN
Gobwa. Bete Tr.→KRU
Gochaquinas. Yagua D.→PEBA-YAGUAN
Go-da = Mambisa. Lendu D.→CENTRAL SUDANIC
Godia = Godye. Bete D.→KRU
Godye. Bete D.→KRU
Goemai = Ankwe→CHADIC
Goeng. Taribeleng D.→WAKA-KABIC
Gofa. Walamo D.→OMOTIC
Gog→EASTERN OCEANIC
GOGO→CENTRAL EASTERN BANTU

Gogo→CENTRAL EASTERN BANTU

Gogo. Bipi D.→ADMIRALTY-WESTERN ISLANDS

Gogoda. Kardutjara D.→WATI

GOGODALA→CENTRAL AND SOUTH NEW GUINEA

Gogodala→CENTRAL AND SOUTH NEW GUINEA

GOGODARA = GOGODALA→CENTRAL AND SOUTH NEW GUINEA

Gogol = Grangal. Nangalami D.→NURISTANI

Gogot→SEMITIC

Gogue = Guegue→GE

Gohilwadi. Gujarati D.→INDIC

Goia = Goya→GE

GOIDELIC→CELTIC

Goiefu→GOILALA

GOILALA see article

Gok. Agar D.→EASTERN SUDANIC

Gokana→CROSS RIVER BENUE-CONGO

Goklen. Turkmen D.→TURKIC

G!okwe. Naron D.→KHOISAN

Gokwom = Central Koma→KOMAN

Gola→WEST ATLANTIC

Gola. Mumuye D.→ADAMAWA

Gola = Badyara→WEST ATLANTIC

Golar. Bahnar D.→MON-KHMER

Gold→TUNGUS

Golda = Mekan→EASTERN SUDANIC

Goldea = Mekan→EASTERN SUDANIC

Goldiya = Mekan→EASTERN SUDANIC

GOLIATH→CENTRAL AND SOUTH NEW GUINEA

Goliath→CENTRAL AND SOUTH NEW GUINEA

Golin. Chimbu D.→EAST NEW GUINEA HIGHLANDS

Golo→EASTERN

Gomaidj = Gumaidji. Gobabingo D.→MURNGIC

Gomaro = Kefa→OMOTIC

Gomataki = Konkan. Marathi D.→INDIC

Gombo. Gumuz D.→KOMAN

Gomjier = Gomjuer. Rek D.→EASTERN SUDANIC

Gomjuer. Rek D.→EASTERN SUDANIC

Gomoa = Guan→VOLTA-COMOE

Gondi→DRAVIDIAN

Gondla = Rangloi. Manchati D.→GYARUNG-MISHMI

Gong = Nagumi→BANTOID

Gonge. Kari D.→ADAMAWA

Gongo = Wongo→NORTH WESTERN BANTU

Gongoroi→NORTHWESTERN AND CENTRAL SOLOMONS

Gonja = Guan→VOLTA-COMOE

Gonjmal = Koinjmal. Darambal D.→WAKA-KABIC

Goom. Duru D.→ADAMAWA

Goonine = Goeng. Taribeleng D.→WAKA-KABIC

Gooranggorang = Korenggoreng. Djakunda D.→WAKA-KABIC

Gorachouqua = Korana→KHOISAN

Goram→CHADIC

Goram = Geser→EAST INDONESIAN

Goram Laut. Geser D.→EAST INDONESIAN

Gor'an. Tebu Tr.→SAHARAN

Goranes = Gor'an. Tebu Tr.→SAHARAN

Gorendu→NORTHEASTERN NEW GUINEA

Gorkhali = Nepali→INDIC

Gorkhpuri. Bihari D.→INDIC

Gorlos. Khorcin D.→MONGOLIAN

G//oro→KHOISAN

Goroa→CUSHITIC

Gorogone→BURERAN

G//orokhwe = G//oro→KHOISAN

Gorong = Geser→EAST INDONESIAN

GORONTALIC→NORTHWEST AUSTRONESIAN

Gorontalo→NORTHWEST AUSTRONESIAN

Gorotire→GE

Gorovu→BOGIA

Gorowa = Goroa→CUSHITIC

Gorron→CARIB

Gorua. Tobelo D.→NORTH HALMAHERA

Gorum→MUNDA

Gorzae = Gobeze. Gawwada D.→CUSHITIC

Goshowi = Gashowu. Foothill North Yokuts D.→YOKUTS

Gosisi→KOIARI

Gosiute. Shoshoni D.→UTO-AZTECAN

Gossi Ute = Gosiute. Shoshoni D.→UTO-AZTECAN

Gotane. Guatuso D.→CHIBCHAN

Gothic→GERMANIC

Gotocogegodegi. Mbaya-Guaicuru Tr.→GUAYCURU

Gouine = Kirma→GUR

Goula = Gula. Kara D.→CENTRAL SUDANIC

Goulaye = Gulai. Sara D.→CENTRAL SUDANIC

Goulfei = Gulfei. Kotoko D.→CHADIC

Goun = Gu. Ewe D.→EWE

Gouraghie = Central West Gurage→SEMITIC

Gouraghie = East Gurage→SEMITIC
Gourara→BERBER
Gourma = Gurma→Gur
Gourmantche = Gurma→GUR
Gournditchmara = Gurnditjamara. Tjapwu-
    rong D.→KULINIC
Gouro = Kweni→MANDE
Gova. Shona D.→SOUTH EASTERN BANTU
Govera. Karanga D.→SOUTH EASTERN
    BANTU
Gowar→DURUBULIC
Gowase = Gobeze. Gawwada D.→CUSHITIC
Gowaze = Gobeze. Gawwada D.→CUSHITIC
Gowro. Maiya D.→INDIC
Goya→GE
Goyi-basava. Sinhalese D.→INDIC
Gozza. Ari Tr.→OMOTIC
Gradaho→GE
Gradau = Gradaho→GE
Graecae = Greek→GREEK
Graged→NORTHEAST NEW GUINEA AUS-
    TRONESIAN
Gramsəra-Viri. Askun D.→NURISTANI
Gramya = Gamadia. Gujarati D.→INDIC
Grangal. Nangalami D.→NURISTANI
Granu. Gbaya Tr.→EASTERN
GRASFI = GRASSLANDS→BANTOID
GRASFIL = GRASSLANDS→BANTOID
GRASSFIELD = GRASSLANDS→BANTOID
GRASSLANDS→BANTOID
Grawadungalung = Krauatungulang. Bratauo-
    lung D.→PAMA-NYUNGAN
Greachipari = Huachipairi. Masco D.→MAI-
    PURAN
GREAT LAKES = NILO-HAMITIC→EAST-
    ERN SUDANIC
Grebo→KRU
Grec = Greek→GREEK
GREEK see article
Gresi→NORTH PAPUAN
Gresik = Gresi→NORTH PAPUAN
Grik. Northern Sakai D.→SAKAI
Grikwa→KHOISAN
Grippuo. Bakwe Tr.→KRU
Griqua = Grikwa→KHOISAN
Grishun = Romansch→ROMANCE
Gritones = Sinabo→PANO
Grogo. Land Dayak D.→WEST INDONE-
    SIAN
Grogoe = Gorgo. Land Dayak D.→WEST
    INDONESIAN
Groma. Central Tibetan D.→TIBETAN
Groote Eylandt→AUSTRALIAN MACRO-
    PHYLUM

Gros Ventre = Atsina. Arapaho D.→ALGON-
    QUIAN
Gros Ventre = Hidatsa→SIOUAN
Growoo = Nawu→YURA
GRUSI→GUR
Gry = Grikwa→KHOISAN
Gtsang. Central Tibetan D.→TIBETAN
Gu. Ewe D.→EWE
Guaca. Cauca Tr.→CARIB
Guacanahua→TACANA
Guachicil. Huichol D.→UTO-AZTECAN
Guachicile = Guachicil. Huichol D.→UTO-
    AZTECAN
Guaciguaje. Pioje-Sioni Tr.→MACRO-TUCA-
    NOAN
GUADALCANAL→EASTERN OCEANIC
Guaga. Chayma D.→CARIB
Guagua. Carijona D.→CARIB
Guagua. Patangoro D.→CARIB
Guagui. Bakwe Tr.→KRU
GUAHARIBAN = WAICAN
Guaharibo. Waica Tr.→WAICAN
Guahibo→EQUATORIAL
GUAHIBO-PAMIGUA→EQUATORIAL
Gua-Hua→EASTERN OCEANIC
Guaiana→GE
Guaiapi. Oyampi D.→TUPI
GUAICAN = WAICAN
Guaicari. Caquetio D.→NORTHERN MAI-
    PURAN
Guaicura = Waicuru→WAICURIAN
Guaicuri = Waicuru→WAICURIAN
Guaicuro = Waicuru→WAICURIAN
GUAICURU = GUAYCURU
Guaigua = Guahibo→EQUATORIAL
Guaikuri = Waicuru→WAICURIAN
Guaikuru = Waicuru→WAICURIAN
GUAIPUNAVO = PUINAVE→MACRO-
    TUCANOAN
Guaiqueri = Waikeri. Warao D.→MACRO-
    CHIBCHAN
Guaja. Tenetehara D.→TUPI
Guajajara = Gwazazara. Tenetehara D.→TUPI
Guajibo = Guahibo→EQUATORIAL
Guajiquiro = Waicuru→WAICURIAN
Guajiro = Goajiro→NORTHERN MAI-
    PURAN
Guake. Carijona D.→CARIB
Gualachi→GE
GUALACHO→GE
Guali. Panche D.→CARIB
Guallpayo. Andoa Tr.→ANDEAN
Guamaca→CHIBCHAN
Guamaca. Yarigui D.→CARIB

Guambia = Moguez→INTER-ANDINE

Guamu = Koamu. Mandandanji D.→PAMA-
MARIC

GUAN = GUANG→VOLTA-COMOE

Guan→VOLTA-COMOE

Guana→MAIPURAN

Guana = Cashquiha. Mascoy D.→MACRO-
PANOAN

Guanacanahua = Guacanahua→TACANA

Guanaco→INTER-ANDINE

Guanao→CARIB

Guanche→BERBER

Guanebucan→NORTHERN MAIPURAN

GUANG→VOLTA-COMOE

Guang = Guan→VOLTA-COMOE

Guanga = Gianga. Bagobo D.→NORTH-
WEST AUSTRONESIAN

Guaniare. Guinao D.→NORTHERN MAI-
PURAN

GUAPORE→CHAPACURA-WANHAMAN

Guapore = Chapacura → CHAPACURA-
WANHAMAN

Guaque = Guake. Carijona D.→CARIB

Guaracaio. Tupi Tr.→TUPI

Guarambare. Tupi Tr.→TUPI

Guarani. Tupi D.→TUPI

Guarategaja = Guarategaya→TUPI

Guarategaya→TUPI

Guaratira = Guarategya→TUPI

Guarau = Warao→MACRO-CHIBCHAN

Guarayo = Chapacura → CHAPACURA-
WANHAMAN

Guarayo = Guacanahua→TACANA

Guarayo = More→CHAPACURA-WANHA-
MAN

Guarayu. Tupi D.→TUPI

Guarayu-ta = Pauserna→TUPI

Guaricuri = Waicuru→WAICURIAN

Guarine = Palank→CARIB

Guarino. Patangoro D.→CARIB

Guaripa. Puinave D.→MACRO-TUCANOAN

Guariza→TACANA

Guas Ngishu = Wuasinkishu. Maasai Tr.→
EASTERN SUDANIC

Guasaga. Andoa Tr.→ANDEAN

Guasave. Cahita D.→UTO-AZTECAN

Guasteca = Huastec→MAYAN

Guasteco = Huastec→MAYAN

Guatajigiola = Maribichicoa→TLAPANECAN

Guatemala = Quiche→MAYAN

Guatemalec = Quiche→MAYAN

Guatemaleca = Quiche→MAYAN

Guato→MACRO-GE

Guatuso→CHIBCHAN

Guave = Huave→PENUTIAN

Guavi = Huave→PENUTIAN

Guaxare = Guaja. Tenetehara D.→TUPI

Guaxiquero. Lenca D.→MACRO-CHIBCHAN

Guayaki→TUPI

Guayana. Tupi Tr.→TUPI

Guayana = Guaiana→GE

Guayba = Guahibo→EQUATORIAL

Guaycura. Waicuru Tr.→WAICURIAN

GUAYCURAN = WAICURIAN

Guaycuro = Waicuru→WAICURIAN

GUAYCURU see article

Guayma. Seri Tr.→HOKAN

Guaymi→CHIBCHAN

Guayqueri = Waikeri. Warao D.→MACRO-
CHIBCHAN

Guayuno = Pariagoto→CARIB

Guayupe→NORTHERN MAIPURAN

GUAYUPEAN→NORTHERN MAIPURAN

Guaziza = Guariza→TACANA

Guazquia. Panche D.→CARIB

Guazu. Toba Tr.→GUAYCURU

Gubabuyngu = Gobabingo→MURNGIC

Gubatanon. Hanunoo D.→NORTHWEST
AUSTRONESIAN

Gubawa = Gubi→BANTOID

Gubi→BANTOID

Gubinengo→NORTHWESTERN AND CEN-
TRAL SOLOMONS

Gudanda. Karanti D.→PAMA-NYUNGAN

Gude = Gudi. Njai D.→CHADIC

Gudella = Hadiyya→CUSHITIC

Gudi. Njai D.→CHADIC

Gudiela = Hadiyya→CUSHITIC

Gudjalavia. Barera D.→BURERAN

Gudo = Gudu→CHADIC

Gudu→CHADIC

Gudua = Gadiwa. Tebu Tr.→SAHARAN

Gudur. Sukur D.→CHADIC

Gudwa. Gutob D.→MUNDA

Guegue→GE

Guegue = Geg. Albanian D.

Guenoa→LULE-VILELA-CHARRUA

Guentuse→MATACO

Gueren→BOTOCUDO

Guerno = Kula→PAMA-NYUNGAN

Guerze = Kpelle→MANDE

Guetar→CHIBCHAN

Guetiadebo = Guetiadegodi. Mbaya-Guaicuru
Tr.→GUAYCURU

Guetiadegodi. Mbaya-Guaicuru Tr.→GUAY-
CURU

Guexteca = Huastec→MAYAN

Gugada = Kokata. Kardutjara D.→WATI

Gugu. Land Dayak D.→WEST INDONESIAN
Guha = Holoholo → NORTH EASTERN BANTU
Guhu Samane→BINANDERE
GUI = JUI→KAM-TAI
Guianes = Bontok→NORTHWEST AUSTRONESIAN
Guianga = Gianga. Bagobo D.→NORTHWEST AUSTRONESIAN
Guibono. Bete Tr.→KRU
Guichiovian = Mixe→MIXE-ZOQUE
Guicuru→CARIB
Guidar = Gider→CHADIC
Guidj. Munumburu D.→WORORAN
Guilford Indians = Wappinger. Mohegan D.→ALGONQUIAN
Guiliche = Huiliche. Araucanian D.→PENUTIAN
Guimara = Wayumara→CARIB
Guinanaang = Balbalasang-Ginaang. Kalinga D.→NORTHWEST AUSTRONESIAN
Guinao→NORTHERN MAIPURAN
Guinche = Cunco. Araucanian D.→PENUTIAN
Guingbe = Ge. Ewe D.→EWE
Guinigua = Borrado
Guisnay. Mataco Tr.→MATACO
Guissiga = Gisiga→CHADIC
Guissiga Maturua = Gisiga→CHADIC
Gujaaxet. Banyun D.→WEST ATLANTIC
Gujambal. Bigumbil D.→WIRADJURIC
Gujani = Kuyani→YURA
Gujarati→INDIC
Gujerati = Gujarati→INDIC
Guji. Galla D.→CUSHITIC
Gujugulu = Cheke→CHADIC
Gujuri. Rajasthani D.→INDIC
Gula→ADAMAWA
Gula→CENTRAL SUDANIC
Gula. Kara D.→CENTRAL SUDANIC
Gula = Gola→WEST ATLANTIC
Gula Gera = Taataal. Gula D.→ADAMAWA
Gula Iro = Kulaal. Gula D.→ADAMAWA
Gula of Moufa. Kaba D.→CENTRAL SUDANIC
Gulai. Sara D.→CENTRAL SUDANIC
Gulanga = Gianga. Bagobo D.→NORTHWEST AUSTRONESIAN
Gule→KOMAN
Gulei = Gulai. Sara D.→CENTRAL SUDANIC
GULF→MACRO-ALGONQUIAN
Gulfan = Ghulfan. Kordofanian Nubian Tr. →EASTERN SUDANIC

Gulfei. Kotoko D.→CHADIC
Gulgaissen. Abipon Tr.→GUAYCURU
Guliguli = Gulili. Kazukuru D.→CENTRAL MELANESIAN
Gulili. Kazukuru D.→CENTRAL MELANESIAN
Gulkana-Gakona = Chitina Ahtena D.→ATHAPASCAN-EYAK
Gulla = Gullah→GERMANIC
Gullah→GERMANIC
Gulli. Zaza D.→IRANIAN
Gulngay. Wakaman D.→PAMA-MARIC
Gulngui = Gulngay. Wakaman D.→PAMA-MARIC
Gulud = Julud. Katla D.→KORDOFANIAN
Guluwarian→DJERAGAN
Gulyan = Kurung→KULINIC
Gumadir. Gunwiggu D.→GUNWINGGUAN
Gumadj = Gumaidji. Gobabingo D.→MURNGIC
Gumahi→KHOISAN
Gumaidji. Gobabingo D.→MURNGIC
Gumasi→PAPUA AUSTRONESIAN
Gumba = Bviri→EASTERN
Gumbainggar = Kumbainggar→KUMBAINGGARIC
Gumbang. Land Dayak D.→WEST INDONESIAN
Gumbi→INDO-PACIFIC
Gumer. Central West Gurage D.→SEMITIC
Gumia = Irumu→HUON-FINISTERRE
Gumilary = Kamilaroi→WIRADJURIC
Gumine. Chimbu D.→EAST NEW GUINEA HIGHLANDS
Guminilroi = Kamilaroi→WIRADJURIC
Gumis = Gumuz→KOMAN
Gumsai. Kui D.→DRAVIDIAN
Gumus = Gumuz→KOMAN
Gumuz→KOMAN
Gumz = Gumuz→KOMAN
Gunabidji = Gunavidji→AUSTRALIAN MACRO-PHYLUM
Gunaidbe. Barera D.→BURERAN
Gunantuna→BISMARCK ARCHIPELAGO
Gunavidji → AUSTRALIAN MACRO-PHYLUM
Gunawitji → Gunwiggu—GUNWINGGUAN
Gunbalang. Muralidban D.→GUNWINGGUAN
Gunda. Teda Tr.→SAHARAN
Gundaahmyro = Gandangara→YUIN-KURIC
Gundangbon→GUNWINGGUAN
Gundanora = Jaitmathang→PAMA-NYUNGAN

Gundei'djeme. Gunwiggu D.→GUNWING-GUAN

Gundei'njekemi. Gundangbon D.→GUNWING-GUAN

Gundi→EASTERN

Gundi. Gbanziri Tr.→EASTERN

Gundungurra = Gundangara→YUIN-KURIC

Gundurimba = Arakwal. Kitabal D.→BAND-JALANGIC

Gunganchi = Reshe → PLATEAU BENUE-CONGO

Gunganoi = Reshe → PLATEAU BENUE-CONGO

Gungar = Kunggari. Mandandanji D.→PAMA-MARIC

Gungawa = Reshe→PLATEAU BENUE-CONGO

Gunggay. Yirgay D.→PAMA-MARIC

Gungo = Wu. Seediq D.→FORMOSAN AUS-TRONESIAN

Gungorogone = Gorogone→BURERAN

Gungu = Nyoro→NORTH EASTERN BANTU

Gunian→BUNABAN

Gunilroi = Kamilaroi→WIRADJURIC

Guniz = Gumuz→KOMAN

Gunjbarai = Koinberi. Kamilaroi D.→WIRADJURIC

Gunje = Gonge. Kari D.→ADAMAWA

Gunmal = Koinjmal. Darambal D.→WAKA-KABIC

Gunu = Wu. Seediq D.→FORMOSAN AUS-TRONESIAN

Gunungwillam = Wurundjeri. Taungurong D.→KULINIC

Gunwiggu→GUNWINGGUAN

GUNWINGGIC→GUNWINGGUAN

Gunwinggu = Gunwiggu→GUNWINGGUAN

GUNWINGGUAN see article

Gunwingo = Gunwiggu→GUNWINGGUAN

Gunwingu = Gunwiggu→GUNWINGGUAN

Gunya = Tikuu→CENTRAL EASTERN BAN-TU

Gunyamolo. Banyun D.→WEST ATLANTIC

Gunza = Gumuz→KOMAN

Gunzib. Bezhita D.→CAUCASIAN

Guoyagui = Guayaki→TUPI

Gupa = Kupa, Nupe D.→NUPE-GBARI

GUR see article

Gura. Central West Gurage D.→SEMITIC

Gura. Lame D.→BANTOID

Gura = Maban→EASTERN SUDANIC

Gura = Nzema→VOLTA-COMOE

Gurage, Central West→SEMITIC

Gurage, East→SEMITIC

GURAGE, NORTH→SEMITIC

Gurage, Peripheral West→SEMITIC

Gurage = Central West Gurage→SEMITIC

Guragie = East Gurage→SEMITIC

Gurague = Central West Gurage→SEMITIC

Gurague = East Gurage→SEMITIC

Guraggurang = Korenggoreng. Djakunda D.→WAKA-KABIC

Gurani→IRANIAN

Gurawa = Gura. Lame D.→BANTOID

Gure→PLATEAU BENUE-CONGO

Guredirma = Tid. Tirma D.→EASTERN SU-DANIC

Guregureu→PAPUA AUSTRONESIAN

Gurenggureng = Korenggoreng. Djakunda D.→WAKA-KABIC

Gurenne = Nankanse→GUR

Gurezi. Sina D.→INDIC

Gurgo. Land Dayak D.→WEST INDONESIAN

Gurian-Adzhar. Georgian D.→CAUCASIAN

Gurindji→NGUMBIN

Gurjindi. Jarnango D.→MURNGIC

Gurma→GUR

Gurmana→PLATEAU BENUE-CONGO

Gurna = Plains Angas. Angas D.→CHADIC

Gurnditjmara. Tjapwurong D.→KULINIC

Gurnmbo = Kweni→MANDE

Guro = Kweni→MANDE

Gurrun = Rebina→PLATEAU BENUE-CON-GO

Guru. Gubi D.→BANTOID

Gurum = Rebina→PLATEAU BENUE-CON-GO

GURUMSI = GRUSI→GUR

Gurung→GYARUNG-MISHMI

GURUNSI = GRUSI→GUR

Gurupy→GE

Gusan→HUON-FINISTERRE

GUSAP-MOT→HUON-FINISTERRE

Gusawa = Gussum→PLATEAU BENUE-CON-GO

Gusii→NORTH EASTERN BANTU

GUSII = ROGOLI-KURIA→NORTH EAST-ERN BANTU

Gusilay→WEST ATLANTIC

Gussum→PLATEAU BENUE-CONGO

Gusum = Gussum→PLATEAU BENUE-CONGO

Guta. Shona D.→SOUTH EASTERN BANTU

Gutob→MUNDA

Gutthan = Katang. Worimi D.→YUIN-KURIC

Gutucrac→BOTOCUDO

Guwa = Koa→PAMA-MARIC

Guyana French. French Creole D.→RO-
MANCE
Guyandot = Wyandot→IROQUOIS
Guyangalyuin = Thaua→YUIN-KURIC
Guzawa→PLATEAU BENUE-CONGO
Guzii = Gusii→NORTH EASTERN BANTU
Gwa→LAGOON
Gwabegwabe→PAPUA AUSTRONESIAN
Gwabyo = Gwa→LAGOON
Gwagba. Nupe Tr.→NUPE-GBARI
Gwai. Musgu D.→CHADIC
Gwak = Ging-Gwak. Jarawa D.→BANTOID
Gwaka = Bwaka→EASTERN
Gwaka = Gbaya→EASTERN
Gwalakwe. Kotoko D.→CHADIC
Gwali = Gbari→NUPE-GBARI
Gwama = Koma→KOMAN
Gwama = North Koma. Koma D.→KOMAN
Gwamba→SOUTH EASTERN BANTU
Gwamba = Tsonga→SOUTH EASTERN BAN-
TU
Gwami = North Koma. Koma D.→KOMAN
Gwami = Northern Mao→KOMAN
Gwana-Pindiga. Jukun D.→JUKUNOID
Gwandara→CHADIC
Gwanja = Guan→VOLTA-COMOE
Gwanje. Mandara Tr.→CHADIC
Gwanto→PLATEAU BENUE-CONGO
Gwapa = Gwamba → SOUTH EASTERN
BANTU
Gwari = Gbari→NUPE-GBARI
Gwaza = Gwoza→CHADIC
Gwazazara. Tenetehara D.→TUPI
Gwazum = Ngizim→CHADIC
Gwe. Luhya D.→NORTH EASTERN BANTU
Gwe. Saamia D.→NORTH EASTERN BANTU
Gwe = Kirma→GUR
Gwe = Sukuma→NORTH EASTERN BANTU
Gweabo = Krebo→KRU
Gwegal = Geawegal. Wiradjuri D.→WIRAD-
JURIC
Gwemara = Central West Gurage→SEMITIC
Gwemara = Gumer. Central West Gurage D.→
SEMITIC
Gweno→NORTH EASTERN BANTU
Gwere→NORTH EASTERN BANTU
G//wi→KHOISAN
G//wikhwe = G//wi→KHOISAN
G/wikhwe = G//wi→KHOISAN
G!wikwe = G//wi→KHOISAN
Gwini. Bagu D.→WORORAN
Gwoiden→DAGA
Gwoira→INDO-PACIFIC
Gwomo. Jen D.→ADAMAWA

Gwong. Kagoma D.→PLATEAU BENUE-
CONGO
Gwoza→CHADIC
Gwune = Agwagwune → CROSS RIVER
BENUE-CONGO
Gxon = ≠Hua→KHOISAN
Gyarung→GYARUNG-MISHMI
GYARUNG-MISHMI see article
Gyema = Gyemawa→PLATEAU BENUE-
CONGO
Gyemawa→PLATEAU BENUE-CONGO
Gyeta = Geto. Peripheral West Gurage D.→
SEMITIC
Gyeto = Geto. Peripheral West Gurage D.→
SEMITIC
Gyo = Dan→MANDE
Gyong. Kagoma D.→PLATEAU BENUE-
CONGO
Gypsy = Romany→INDIC
Gyuman = Kyama→LAGOON

H

Ha→NORTH EASTERN BANTU
Haauneiri = Yamiaca. Atsahuaca D.→PANO
Haavu = Havu→NORTH EASTERN BANTU
Habaab. Tigre D.→SEMITIC
Habbe = Dogon→GUR
Habe = Dogon→GUR
Habenapo = Pomo→POMO
Habesha = Tigrinya→SEMITIC
Habitoa. Omurano Tr.→ANDEAN
Hachepiriinu. Pawnee D.→CADDOAN
Hadaareb = Hadareb. Beja D.→CUSHITIC
Hadang = Sedang→MON-KHMER
Hadareb. Beja D.→CUSHITIC
Hadendiwa = Handendowa. Beja Tr.→CUSHI-
TIC
Hadendoa = Handendowa. Beja Tr.→CUSHI-
TIC
Hadia = Hadiyya→CUSHITIC
Hadimu. Pemba D.→CENTRAL EASTERN
BANTU
Hadiya = Hadiyya→CUSHITIC
Hadiyya→CUSHITIC
Hadjibatie = Kazibati→EASTERN
Hadramaut. Old South Arabic D.→SEMITIC
Hadu. Afar-Saho D.→CUSHITIC
Hadya = Hadiyya→CUSHITIC
Hadza = Hatsa→KHOISAN
Hadzabi = Hatsa→KHOISAN
Hadzapi = Hatsa→KHOISAN
Haeke→NEW CALEDONIA
Hagari→KOIARI

Hagen = Medlpa→EAST NEW GUINEA HIGHLANDS

HAGEN - WAHGI- JIMI - CHIMBU → EAST NEW GUINEA HIGHLANDS

Hageule. Bogotu D.→NORTHWESTERN AND CENTRAL SOLOMONS

Hagu→MON-KHMER

Hahanana. Cubeo D.→MACRO-TUCANOAN

Hahutan→EAST INDONESIAN

Hai. Caga D.→NORTH EASTERN BANTU

Haiao = Yao→SOUTH EASTERN BANTU

Haida→NA-DENE

Hailar. Dagur D.→MONGOLIAN

Haina→CADDOAN

Hainanese = Hainan Island. Southern Min D.→ CHINESE

Hain//um. San D.→KHOISAN

Haira = Elema. Toaripi D.→TOARIPI

/ hais. Shua D.→KHOISAN

Haisen. Saaroa D.→FORMOSAN AUSTRO-NESIAN

Haisla→WAKASHAN

Haitian Creole. French Creole D.→ROMANCE

Haitshuari = Haitshuwau→KHOISAN

Haitshuwau→KHOISAN

Hajung→MON-KHMER

HAKA→NAGA-KUKI-CHIN

Haka→NAGA-KUKI-CHIN

Haka = Bolo→CENTRAL WESTERN BAN-TU

Hakka→CHINESE

Halaba = Alaba→CUSHITIC

Halabi = Halbi. Oriya D.→INDIC

Halang→MON-KHMER

Halbi. Oriya D.→INDIC

Halchidhom = Halchidom. River Yuman D.→ YUMAN

Halchidhoma = Halchidom. River Yuman D.→ YUMAN

Halchidom. River Yuman D.→YUMAN

Halcomelem = Halkomelem→SALISH

Haldokehewuk = Cecilville. SHASTAN TR. →HOKAN

Haleng = Halang→MON-KHMER

Halia = Hanahan→NORTHWESTERN AND CENTRAL SOLOMONS

Halikwamai. River Yuman D.→YUMAN

Halisa→NORTHWESTERN AND CENTRAL SOLOMONS

Halkomelem→SALISH

Hallam = Fallam→NAGA-KUKI-CHIN

HALMAHERA see article

Halong→MON-KHMER

Halopa→BOGIA

Ha-lum-mi = Lummi. Northern Straits Salish D.→SALISH

Halyikwamai. Delta River Yuman D.→YUMAN

Ham→NORTHEAST NEW GUINEA AUS-TRONESIAN

Ham = Jaba→PLATEAU BENUE-CONGO

Hamadani. Persian D.→IRANIAN

Hamap. Abui D.→TIMOR-ALOR

Hamar = Banna→OMOTIC

Hamar Koke = Banna→OMOTIC

Hamar Kokke = Banna→OMOTIC

Hamat→SEMITIC

Hamba. Nkutu D.→NORTH WESTERN BANTU

Hamba. Ziba D.→NORTH EASTERN BANTU

Hamba = Amba→NORTH EASTERN BANTU

Hamba = Lega. Ndandi D.→NORTH EAST-ERN BANTU

Hame. Finnish D.→URALIC

Hameg = Fecaka. Berta D.→CHARI-NILE

Hameg = Gule→KOMAN

Hameha→NEW CALEDONIA

Hamer = Banna→OMOTIC

Hamerkoke = Banna→OMOTIC

HAMITIC = AFROASIATIC

HAMITO-SEMITIC = AFROASIATIC

Hammonasset = Wappinger. Mohegan D.→ ALGONQUIAN

Hammonassett = Wappinger. Mohegan D.→ ALGONQUIAN

Hampangan = Hanunoo→NORTHWEST AUS-TRONESIAN

Han→ATHAPASCAN-EYAK

Han = Atakapa→MACRO-ALGONQUIAN

Hanahan→NORTHWESTERN AND CEN-TRAL SOLOMONS

Hanak. Czech D.→SLAVIC

Handa→KHOISAN

Handadam = Handa→KHOISAN

Handakwe-dam = Handa→KHOISAN

Handendowa. Beja Tr.→CUSHITIC

Hanga→GUR

Hanga. Luhya D.→NORTH EASTERN BANTU

Hangaza→NORTH EASTERN BANTU

Hanggira. Bada' D.→CENTRAL AND SOUTHERN CELEBES

Hangiro. Ziba D.→NORTH EASTERN BANTU

Hani→BURMESE-LOLO

Haningajormiut = Netsilik. Inuit D.→ESKIMO-ALEUT

Hankul = Korean→ALTAIC

Hanniu. Central Tibetan D.→TIBETAN

Hano. Tewa D.→TANOAN

Hanon→NORTHWESTERN AND CENTRAL SOLOMONS

Hanono-o = Hanunoo→NORTHWEST AUSTRONESIAN

Hantik→NORTHWEST AUSTRONESIAN

Hanu. Sina D.→INDIC

Hanu. West Tibetan D.→TIBETAN

HANUNOIC→NORTHWEST AUSTRONESIAN

Hanunoo→NORTHWEST AUSTRONESIAN

Hapa→NORTHEAST NEW GUINEA AUSTRONESIAN

Haraba = Harava. Shona D.→SOUTH EASTERN BANTU

Haragure→NEW CALEDONIA

Harari. East Gurage D.→SEMITIC

Harava. Shona D.→SOUTH EASTERN BANTU

Hare. Dogrib Tr.→ATHAPASCAN-EYAK

Harengan. Sori D.→ADMIRALTY-WESTERN ISLANDS

Harer. Amharic D.→SEMITIC

Hariani = Bangaru. Western Hindi D.→INDIC

Haroy→WEST INDONESIAN

Harro = Gidicho. Koyra D.→OMOTIC

Haruku. Ambonese D.→MOLUCCAN

Haruro = Kachama→OMOTIC

Harvaqtormiut = Barren Grounds Eskimo. Inuit D.→ESKIMO-ALEUT

Hasadaʔ. Mundari D.→MUNDA

Hashish Hassanab. Beja Tr.→CUSHITIC

Hassal. Beja Tr.→CUSHITIC

Hasuneiri = Yamiaca. Atsahuaca D.→PANO

Hati = Hittite→ANATOLIAN

Hatiggoria = Ao→NAGA-KUKI-CHIN

Hatsa→KHOISAN

Hattam→WESTERN NEW GUINEA

Hattic see article

Hatu. Ambonese D.→MOLUCCAN

Hatue→EAST INDONESIAN

Hatumeten. Wahai D.→EAST INDONESIAN

Hatuolo. Wahai D.→EAST INDONESIAN

Hatwara. Tari D.→ADMIRALTY-WESTERN ISLANDS

Haulngo = Haulngo→NAGA-KUKI-CHIN

Haulo. Bakwe Tr.→KRU

Hauneqtormiut = Barren Grounds Eskimo. Inuit D.→ESKIMO-ALEUT

Haun\u0075\u006eu. Bauro D.→EASTERN OCEANIC

Haura = Orra. Tama D.→EASTERN SUDANIC

Hauruha→EAST NEW GUINEA HIGHLANDS

Hausa→CHADIC

Hausaawaa = Hausa→CHADIC

HAUSA-GWANDARA→CHADIC

Haʔuwa = Leboni→CENTRAL AND SOUTHERN CELEBES

Havasupai. Upland Yuman D.→YUMAN

Havauti. Rajasthani D.→INDIC

Have. Tangsa D.→BODO-NAGA-KACHIN

Havu→NORTH EASTERN BANTU

Havunese→MOLUCCAN

Hawaiian→POLYNESIAN

Hawiya. Somali D.→CUSHITIC

Hawiyya = Hawiya. Somali D.→CUSHITIC

Hawthai. Mara D.→NAGA-KUKI-CHIN

Hawu = Havunese→MOLUCCAN

Haya = Ziba→NORTH EASTERN BANTU

Hayahaya = Central Koma→KOMAN

HAYA-JITA→NORTH EASTERN BANTU

Hayu = Vayu→GYARUNG-MISHMI

Hazaras. Persian D.→IRANIAN

Hazu = Hadu. Afar-Saho D.→CUSHITIC

He. Tenetehara Tr.→TUPI

Heath Is. Suau D.→PAPUA AUSTRONESIAN

Hebrew→SEMITIC

Heh Miao = Black Miao. Miao D.→MIAO-YAO

HEHE = BENA-KINGA→CENTRAL EASTERN BANTU

Hehe→CENTRAL EASTERN BANTU

Hei = Black Miao. Miao D.→MIAO-YAO

Heiban→KORDOFANIAN

Hei-g≠uin = Nossob→KHOISAN

Heikom = Hain//um. San D.→KHOISAN

Heikom Bushman = Hain//um. San D.→KHOISAN

Heilsuk. Bella Bella D.→WAKASHAN

Hei//om = Hain//um. San D.→KHOISAN

Hei//om Bushman = Hain//um. San D.→KHOISAN

HELLENIC = GREEK

Hema = Hima→NORTH EASTERN BANTU

Hemba→CENTRAL WESTERN BANTU

Hena. Bakwe Tr.→KRU

Henga = Kamanga. Tumbuka D.→CENTRAL EASTERN BANTU

HEONESIAN see OCEANIC

Her. Diola D.→WEST ATLANTIC

Hera = Lera. Ruanda D.→NORTH EASTERN BANTU

Herat. Mongul D.→MONGOLIAN

Here. Shona D.→SOUTH EASTERN BANTU

Herero→SOUTH WESTERN BANTU

Heri = Seri→HOKAN
Herisobocona = Herisobocono → CHAPA-
CURA-WANHAMAN
Herisobocono→CHAPACURA-WANHAMAN
Heso = So→NORTH WESTERN BANTU
HESPERONESIAN see article
Het see article
Heuskara = Basque
Hewa→SEPIK
Hewa = Have. Tangsa D.→BODO-NAGA-
KACHIN
Hewa = Hewe. Tumbuka D.→CENTRAL
EASTERN BANTU
Hewe. Tumbuka D.→CENTRAL EASTERN
BANTU
Heyo→TORRICELLI
H'hana = Pomo→POMO
Hia. Pawnee D.→CADDOAN
Hiai = Li→KAM-TAI
Hianacoto. Carijona D.→CARIB
Hiao = Yao→SOUTH EASTERN BANTU
Hibaradai. Southern Kiwai D.→CENTRAL
AND SOUTH NEW GUINEA
Hibito = Xibito→ANDEAN
Hichita = Hitchiti→MUSKOGEAN
Hid. Avar D.→CAUCASIAN
Hidatsa→SIOUAN
Hidj = Higi→CHADIC
Hiechware = G//abake→KHOISAN
Hietan = Comanche. Shoshoni D.→UTO-
AZTECAN
Higi→CHADIC
Higi Wula. Higi D.→CHADIC
Higidi = Lebama. Legbo D.→CROSS RIVER
BENUE-CONGO
Hiji = Higi→CHADIC
Hikanagi = Mahican. Mohegan D.→ALGON-
QUIAN
Hila. Ambonese D.→MOLUCCAN
Hileman = Djabugay. Wakaman D.→PAMA-
MARIC
Hileo = Tulambatu. Bungku D.→CENTRAL
AND SOUTHERN CELEBES
Hiligayna = Ilonggo→NORTHWEST AUS-
TRONESIAN
Hiligaynon = Ilonggo→NORTHWEST AUS-
TRONESIAN
Hililigaina = Ilonggo→NORTHWEST AUS-
TRONESIAN
Hill Nubian = Kordofanian Nubian→EAST-
ERN SUDANIC
Hima→NORTH EASTERN BANTU
Hima. Nyankole D.→NORTH EASTERN
BANTU

Himba = Cimba. Herero D.→SOUTH WEST-
ERN BANTU
Himyarite. Old South Arabic D.→SEMITIC
Hin = Hun→MON-KHMER
Hina→CHADIC
Hina. Daba D.→CHADIC
Hina = Watu. Bungku D.→CENTRAL AND
SOUTHERN CELEBES
Hinan. Puyuma D.→FORMOSAN AUSTRO-
NESIAN
Hinan = Piana. Puyuma D.→FORMOSAN
AUSTRONESIAN
Hindi, Bazaar. Western Hindi D.→INDIC
Hindi, Eastern→INDIC
Hindi, Western→INDIC
Hindi = Lahnda→INDIC
Hindi = Western Hindi→INDIC
Hindi, Central = Vicholo. Sindhi D.→INDIC
Hindustani. Western Hindi D.→INDIC
Hindustani = Western Hindi→INDIC
Hindusthani = Bhojpuri. Bihari D.→INDIC
Hindusthani = Western Hindi→INDIC
Hiniraya = Kinaraya→NORTHWEST AUS-
TRONESIAN
Hinna = Hina→CHADIC
Hinsal = Kinsal. Gelik D.→BISMARCK AR-
CHIPELAGO
Hinzua = Njuani. Komoro D.→CENTRAL
EASTERN BANTU
Hiotshuwau→KHOISAN
Hiratsa = Hidatsa→SIOUAN
Hiroi = Lamgang→NAGA-KUKI-CHIN
Hishkaryana see article
Hissala = Sisala→GUR
Hitaka. Ainu D.→Ainu
Hitchitathi = Hitchiti→MUSKOGEAN
Hitchitee = Hitchiti→MUSKOGEAN
Hitchiti→MUSKOGEAN
Hitchiteco = Hitchiti→MUSKOGEAN
Hittite→ANATOLIAN
Hittite, Hieroglyphic. Luwian D.→ANA-
TOLIAN
HITTITE-LUWIAN = ANATOLIAN
Hiu-Semang. Pangan D.→SEMANG
Hiw. Torres D.→EASTERN OCEANIC
Hiwi. Southern Kiwai D.→CENTRAL AND
SOUTH NEW GUINEA
Hkaku→BODO-NAGA-KACHIN
Hkampti = Khamti→KAM-TAI
HKANG = KACHIN → BODO-NAGA-KA-
CHIN
Hkanung = Rawang→BODO-NAGA-KACHIN
Hlanganu. Tsonga D.→SOUTH EASTERN
BANTU

Hlengwe. Tswa D.→SOUTH EASTERN BAN-
TU
Hloka = Lhoskad. Central Tibetan D.→TIBE-
TAN
Hlota→NAGA-KUKI-CHIN
Hlubi. Nguni D.→SOUTH EASTERN BANTU
Hmar→NAGA-KUKI-CHIN
Hmo = Miao→MIAO-YAO
Hmong = Miao→MIAO-YAO
Hmung = Miao→MIAO-YAO
Ho. Ewe Tr.→EWE
Ho. Mundari D.→MUNDA
Hoai Petel = Tita→CROSS RIVER BENUE-
CONGO
Hoamol→EAST INDONESIAN
Hoanya→FORMOSAN AUSTRONESIAN
Hobacana. Buhagana Tr.→MACRO-TUCA-
NOAN
Hochangara = Winebago→SIOUAN
Hodenosaunee = Seneca. Seneca Tr.→IRO-
QUOIS
Hofra=Naka. Kresh D.→CENTRAL SUDAN-
IC
Hoftlang. Bakhtiari Tr.→IRANIAN
Hog Harbour = Sakau→NORTHWESTERN
NEW HEBRIDES
Hogirano→NORTHWESTERN AND CEN-
TRAL SOLOMONS
Hoho. Musei D.→CHADIC
Hoho = Wu. Seediq D.→FORMOSAN AUS-
TRONESIAN
Hohodene. Caua D.→NORTHERN MAI-
PURAN
Hohodeni = Hohodene. Caua D.→NORTH-
THERN MAIPURAN
Hoilkut-hoi = Whilkut. Hupa D.→ATHAPAS-
CAN-EYAK
HOKALTECAN = HOKAN
HOKAN see article
Hoking→BURMESE-LOLO
Hokka = Hakka→CHINESE
Hoko = Huku→NORTH EASTERN BANTU
Hokohoko. Peri D.→NORTH EASTERN BAN-
TU
Hoksukhaunu Pawnee D.→CADDOAN
Holadi. Gujarati D→INDIC
HOLLANDIA→SOUTH HALMAHERA AUS-
TRONESIAN
Hollar Gadbas = Ollari. Gadba D.→DRAVI-
DIAN
Hollom = Ollom. Musei D.→CHADIC
Holma. Njai D.→CHADIC
Holo = Holu. Samba D.→CENTRAL WEST-
ERN BANTU

Holo = Hungu→CENTRAL WESTERN BAN-
TU
Holoholo→NORTH EASTERN BANTU
Hololupai = Maidu→MAIDU
Holona. Cubeo D.→MACRO-TUCANOAN
Holu. Samba D.→CENTRAL WESTERN
BANTU
Homa→CENTRAL WESTERN BANTU
Hombo = Ombo→NORTH WESTERN BAN-
TU
Hometwoli. Foothill South Yokuts D.→YO-
KUTS
Hona. Tera D.→CHADIC
Hondiapa→MACRO-TUCANOAN
Hon-Dyapa = Hondiapa → MACRO-TUCA-
NOAN
Hongalla = Ngalakan→GUNWINGGUAN
Hookluhmic = Lummi. Northern Straits Salish
D.→SALISH
Hopa = Xopa. Zan D.→CAUCASIAN
Hopi→UTO-AZTECAN
Hopi Tewa = Hano. Tewa D.→TANOAN
Hopitu = Hopi→UTO-AZTECAN
Hor→NAGA-KUKI-CHIN
Horali. Tala D.→EAST INDONESIAN
Horio. Southern Zamucoan Tr.→EQUATORI-
AL
Horo→CENTRAL SUDANIC
Horohoro = Holoholo→NORTH EASTERN
BANTU
Horom→PLATEAU BENUE-CONGO
Hororo. Nyankole D.→NORTH EASTERN
BANTU
Horpa = Hor→NAGA-KUKI-CHIN
Horuru→EAST INDONESIAN
Hosukhaunukarerihu. Pawnee D.→CADDO
AN
Hotaba=Ediba. Kohumono D.→CROSS RIV-
ER BENUE-CONGO
Hotea = Sedang→MON-KHMER
Hoteang =. Sedang→MON-KHMER
HOTI = EAST TIMBIRA→GE
Hoti→EAST INDONESIAN
Hotoguitu. Khalkha D.→MONGOLIAN
HOTTENTOT = CENTRAL SOUTH AFRI-
CAN KHOISAN→KHOSIAN
Houailou→NEW CALEDONIA
Houasteque = Huastec→MAYAN
Hounar = Beseme→CHADIC
Houne = Hwane. Bakwe D.→KRU
Housatonic = Machican. Mohegan D.→AL-
GONQUIAN
Hova = Merina. Malagasy D.→WEST INDO-
NESIAN

Hoyalee = Shogale. Berta D.→CHARI-NILE
Hozi = Elamite
Hozumutong = Usumutong. Kohumono D.→
    CROSS RIVER BENUE-CONGO
Hpungsi. Rawang D.→BODO-NAGA-KACHIN
Hrangchol = Hrangkhol→ NAGA-KUKI-
    CHIN
Hrangkhol→NAGA-KUKI-CHIN
Hre→MON-KHMER
Hroy = Haroy→WEST INDONESIAN
Hruso→GYARUNG-MISHMI
Hrusso = Hruso→GYARUNG-MISHMI
Hsemtung→NAGA-KUKI-CHIN
Hsen-Hsum = Amok. Angku D.→PALAUNG-
    WA
Hsiang→CHINESE
Hsi-lin→KAM-TAI
Hsishsia = Sihia→BURMESE-LOLO
Hsiung = Miao→MIAO-YAO
Htiselwang. Rawang D.→BODO-NAGA-KA-
    CHIN
!Hu = Kung→KHOISAN
≠HUA = TAA→KHOISAN
≠Hua→KHOISAN
Huachi = Chapacura→CHAPACURA-WAN-
    HAMAN
Huachipairi. Masco D.→MAIPURAN
Huahmi→CHINANTECAN
Hualapai = Walapai. Upland Yuman D.→YU-
    MAN
Hualngo→NAGA-KUKI-CHIN
Huambisa. Jivaro D.→JIVAROAN
Huambiza = Huambisa. Jivaro D.→JIVAROAN
Huana = Hungana→CENTRAL WESTERN
    BANTU
Huanayo→TACANA
Huancavilca→MACRO-CHIBCHAN
HUANYAM = WANHAM→CHAPACURA-
    WANHAMAN
Huanzonteco = Huave→PENUTIAN
≠Hua-Owani = ≠Hua→KHOISAN
Huarani = Sabela→ANDEAN
HUARPE see article
Huasabane = Wasabane. Sumo Tr.→MISU-
    MALPAN
Huash. Ona D.→ANDEAN
Huastec→MAYAN
Huasteca = Huastec→MAYAN
HUASTECAN→MAYAN
Huastecan = Huastec→MAYAN
Huasteco = Huastec→MAYAN
Huastek = Huastec→MAYAN
Hausteka = Huastec→MAYAN
Huasteque = Huastec→MAYAN

Huaulu. Wahai D.→EAST INDONESIAN
Huave→PENUTIAN
Huavi = Huave→PENUTIAN
Huax = Huash. Ona D.→ANDEAN
Huaxteca = Huastec→MAYAN
Huaxteco = Huastec→MAYAN
Huaxteque = Huastec→MAYAN
Huaynamoto. Cora Tr.→UTO-AZTECAN
Hube = Kube→HUON-FINISTERRE
Huchiun. Northern Costanoan D.→MIWOK-
    COSTANOAN
Huchnom. Yuki D.→YUKI
Huei = Oi→MON-KHMER
Huela→MANDE
Huelel = Esselen→HOKAN
Huene = Hona. Tera D.→CHADIC
Hueshuo = Huexuo. Mataguayo Tr.→MATA-
    CO
Huexuo. Mataguayo Tr.→MATACO
Huhhu'ula. Pima D.→UTO-AZTECAN
Huhuteni = Hohodene. Caua D.→NORTHERN
    MAIPURAN
Huhuwash. Pima D.→UTO-AZTECAN
Huichol→UTO-AZTECAN
Huichola = Huichol→UTO-AZTECAN
Huiliche. Araucanian D.→PENUTIAN
Huilli = Huiliche. Araucanian D.→PENUTIAN
Huilliche = Huiliche. Araucanian D.→PENU-
    TIAN
Huillipehuenche = Pichi Huilliche. Araucanian
    D.→PENUTIAN
Huimen. Coast Miwok D.→MIWOK-COSTA-
    NOAN
/huinin = Namib→KHOISAN
Huitoto = Witoto→WITOTOAN
HUITOTOAN = WITOTOAN
Huixteco. Tzotzil D.→MAYAN
Hukawirat. Pawnee D.→CADDOAN
Huku→NORTH EASTERN BANTU
Huku. Sapolewa D.→EAST INDONESIAN
Hukwe→KHOISAN
!Hukwe = Hukwe→KHOISAN
Hula→PAPUA AUSTRONESIAN
Hula. Ewe Tr.→EWE
Huli→EAST NEW GUINEA HIGHLANDS
Huliduna. Huli D.→EAST NEW GUINEA
    HIGHLANDS
Hulo = Mende→MANDE
Hulon. Diola D.→WEST ATLANTIC
Huluf. Diola D.→WEST ATLANTIC
Hulung→EAST INDONESIAN
Huma = Hima→NORTH EASTERN BANTU
Huma = Hima. Nyankole D.→NORTH EAST-
    ERN BANTU

Huma = Toposo→EASTERN SUDANIC

Humba = Kwanyama→SOUTH WESTERN BANTU

Humbe. Nyaneka D.→SOUTH WESTERN BANTU

Humbe = Lilima. Shona D.→SOUTH EASTERN BANTU

Humbolt Bay = Wiyok→MACRO-ALGONQUIAN

Hume→CHINANTECAN

Hummock'havi = Mohave. River Yuman D.→ YUMAN

Humono = Kohumono→CROSS RIVER BENUE-CONGO

Humsi. Higi D.→CHADIC

Hun→MON-KHMER

Hunan = Hsiang→CHINESE

Hunan Miao = Maio→MIAO-YAO

Hunanese = Hsiang→CHINESE

Hunde→NORTH EASTERN BANTU

Hune = Dukawa→PLATEAU BENUE-CONGO

Hungaan = Hungana→CENTRAL WESTERN BANTU

Hungana→CENTRAL WESTERN BANTU

Hungarian→URALIC

Hungduan. Kiangan D.→NORTHWEST AUSTRONESIAN

Hungo = Hungu→ CENTRAL WESTERN BANTU

Hungu→CENTRAL WESTERN BANTU

Hungwe. Shona D.→SOUTH EASTERN BANTU

Hunitetu. Tala D.→EAST INDONESIAN

Huniya = Central Tibetan→TIBETAN

Hunjara→BINANDERE

Hunkpapa = Unkpapa. Dakota D.→SIOUAN

Hunna = Hina→CHADIC

HUNNIC, EASTERN = NORTHERN TURKIC→TURKIC

Hunza. Burushaski D.

Huŋanna = Hungana→CENTRAL WESTERN BANTU

HUON→HUON-FINISTERRE

HUON-FINISTERRE see article

Hupa→ATHAPASCAN-EYAK

Huro = Mende→MANDE

Huro = Uru→CHIPAYAN

Huron = Wyandot→IROQUOIS

Hurone = Wyandot→IROQUOIS

Hurri→HURRIAN

HURRIAN see article

Hurutshe. Tswana D.→SOUTH EASTERN BANTU

Hurutsi = Hurutshe. Tswana D.→SOUTH EASTERN BANTU

Hus→ADMIRALTY-WESTERN ISLANDS

Hu-tsu. Mongour D.→MONGOLIAN

Hutu. Ruanda D.→NORTH EASTERN BANTU

Huve = Bura→CHADIC

Huviya = Bura→CHADIC

Huzvaresh. Persian D.→IRANIAN

Hwa. Mak D.→KAM-TAI

Hwale = Hwane. Bakwe D.→KRU

Hwane. Bakwe D.→KRU

Hwanne = Hwane. Bakwe D.→KRU

Hwaye = Eregba→JUKUNOID

Hwela = Huela→MANDE

Hwethom→BURMESE-LOLO

Hwile = Hwane. Bakwe D.→KRU

Hwindja. Havu D.→NORTH EASTERN BANTU

Hwine = Hwane. Bakwe D.→KRU

Hwotsotenne. Carrier Tr.→ATHAPASCAN-EYAK

Hyanzi. Amba D.→NORTH EASTERN BANTU

Hyao = Yao→SOUTH EASTERN BANTU

HYPERBOREAN = PALEOSIBERIAN

I

I→BURMESE-LOLO

Iai→LOYALTY ISLANDS

Iaibu. Mulaha D.→MULAHA

Iangla→NORTHEAST NEW GUINEA AUSTRONESIAN

Iarumi→KOIARI

Iai = Mohave. Yuman D.→YUMAN

Iate = Fulnio→MACRO-GE

Iatmul→SEPIK

Iavongai = Dang→BISMARCK ARCHIPELAGO

Iawung = Ngaiawang. Nganguruku D.→NARRINYERIC

Iba. Sambali D.→NORTHWEST AUSTRONESIAN

Iba = Laiwonu→CENTRAL AND SOUTHERN CELEBES

Ibafal. Afrike D.→CROSS RIVER BENUE-CONGO

Ibaho. Bunun D.→FORMOSAN AUSTRONESIAN

Ibalao. Ilongot D.→NORTHWEST AUSTRONESIAN

Ibaloi = Inibaloy→NORTHWEST AUSTRO-
NESIAN
Ibanag→NORTHWEST AUSTRONESIAN
Ibani. Ijo D.→IJO
Ibara = Bassa-Nge. Nupe D.→NUPE-GBARI
Ibaram-Efifa→CENTRAL AKOKO
Ibarga. Kardutjara D.→WATI
Ibargo = Ibarga. Kardutjara D.→WATI
Ibarrga = Ibarga. Kardutjara D.→WATI
Ibau = Gussum→PLATEAU BENUE-CONGO
Ibdawi = Bedawib. Beja Tr.→CUSHITIC
Ibeeke = Beeke→NORTH EASTERN BANTU
i-Bembe = Beembe→NORTH EASTERN BAN-
TU
Ibeno = Ibino→CROSS RIVER BENUE-CON-
GO
Iber. Gula D.→ADAMAWA
Iberian see article
IBERO-CAUCASIAN see CAUCASIAN
IBERO-ROMANCE→ROMANCE
Ibibio. Efik D.→CROSS RIVER BENUE-CON-
GO
Ibilao = Ibalao. Ilongot D.→NORTHWEST
AUSTRONESIAN
Ibino→CROSS RIVER BENUE-CONGO
Ibiraira = North Cayapo→GE
IBO = IGBO
Ibo = Igbo→IGBO
Iboho. Seediq D.→FORMOSAN AUSTRO-
NESIAN
Iboko = Boko→NORTH WESTERN BANTU
Ibrahim = Abialang. Padang D.→EASTERN
SUDANIC
Ibu→NORTH HALMAHERA
i-Buja = Buja→NORTH WESTERN BANTU
Ibukairu→EAST NEW GUINEA HIGH-
LANDS
Ibuno = Ibino→CROSS RIVER BENUE-CON-
GO
Ica→CHIBCHAN
Icachodeguo = Lichagotegodi. Mbaya-Guaicuru
Tr.→GUAYCURU
Icaiche. Maya D.→MAYAN
Icasqui = Kaskimpo. Koasati D.→MUSKO-
GEAN
Icelandic. Insular Scandinavian D.→GERMAN-
IC
Icen→JUKUNOID
Ichen = Icen→JUKUNOID
I-CHIA = JUI→KAM-TAI
ici-Bemba = Bemba→CENTRAL EASTERN
BANTU
ici-Biisa = Biisa→CENTRAL EASTERN BAN-
TU

ici-Fiba = Fiba→CENTRAL EASTERN BAN-
TU
ici-Lala = Lala→CENTRAL EASTERN
BANTU
ici-Lamba = Lamba→CENTRAL EASTERN
BANTU
ici-Lambia = Lambia. Tumbuka D.→CEN-
TRAL EASTERN BANTU
ici-Mambwe = Mambwe→CENTRAL EAST-
ERN BANTU
ici-Namwanga = Mwanga→CENTRAL EAST-
ERN BANTU
ici-Pimbwe = Namwanga→CENTRAL EAST-
ERN BANTU
ici-Runga = Runga→CENTRAL EASTERN
BANTU
ici-Rungu = Rungu→CENTRAL EASTERN
BANTU
ici-Swaka = Swaka→CENTRAL EASTERN
BANTU
ici-Taabwa = Taabwa→CENTRAL EASTERN
BANTU
ici-Wanda = Wanda→CENTRAL EASTERN
BANTU
Icuatai = Northern Etung. Ekoi D.→BAN-
TOID
Ida = Madjene. Mandarese D.→CENTRAL
AND SOUTHERN CELEBES
Ida'an. Dusun D.→NORTHWEST AUSTRO-
NESIAN
Idafan = Irigwe→PLATEAU BENUE-CONGO
Idakho = Isuxa. Luhya D.→NORTH EAST-
ERN BANTU
Idate→EAST INDONESIAN
Idaxo = Isuxa. Luhya D.→NORTH EASTERN
BANTU
Idiama→TACANA
Idin = Yidin. Wakaman D.→PAMA-MARIC
Idinji = Yidin. Wakaman D.→PAMA-MARIC
Idja = Sigi. Palu D.→CENTRAL AND
SOUTHERN CELEBES
Idne→NEW BRITAIN
Ido = Sinohoan→CENTRAL AND SOUTH-
ERN CELEBES
IDOMA see article
Idon = Idong→PLATEAU BENUE-CON-
GO
Idong→PLATEAU BENUE-CONGO
Idongiro = Donyiro. Toposo D.→EASTERN
SUDANIC
Idore'e = Sinohoan→CENTRAL AND
SOUTHERN CELEBES
Idu = Chulikata Mishmi→GYARUNG-
MISHMI

I-Dudutho = Dodos. Karamojong D.→EAST-
ERN SUDANIC
Iduwini = Eduwini. Ijo D.→IJO
Idzing = Di→NORTH WESTERN BANTU
Ife. Yoruba D.→YORUBA
Ifigi. Foi D.→EAST NEW GUINEA HIGH-
LANDS
Ifo. Eromanga D.→SOUTHERN NEW HEB-
RIDES
IFUGAO→NORTHWEST AUSTRONESIAN
Ifugao, Central = Kiangan→NORTHWEST
AUSTRONESIAN
Ifugao, Sub- = Silipan. Ifugao D.→NORTH-
WEST AUSTRONESIAN
IFUGAW   =   IFUGAO→NORTHWEST
AUSTRONESIAN
Igabo = Isoko→EDO
Igabo = Isoko. Urhobo D.→EDO
Igala→YORUBA
Igan. Melanau D.→WEST INDONESIAN
Igara = Igala→YORUBA
Igbide. Urhobo D.→EDO
Igbira→NUPE-GBARI
Igbira-Hima. Igbira D.→NUPE-GBARI
Igbira-Igu. Igbira D.→NUPE-GBARI
Igbira-Lele = Igbira-Panda. Igbira D.→NUPE-
GBARI
Igbira-Panda. Igbira D.→NUPE-GBARI
Igbira-Rehe = Igbira-Igu. Igbira D.→NUPE-
GBARI
Igbiri→PLATEAU BENUE-CONGO
Igrirra = Igbira→NUPE-GBARI
IGBO see article
Igbo Imaban. Legbo D.→CROSS RIVER
BENUE-CONGO
Igbona. Yoruba D.→YORUBA
igi-Kiga = Kiga. Ruanda D.→NORTH EAST-
ERN BANTU
igi-Tshiga = Tshiga. Ruanda D.→NORTH
EASTERN BANTU
Iglulik. Inuit D.→ESKIMO-ALEUT
Iglulingmiut = Iglulik. Inuit D.→ESKIMO-
ALEUT
Igom→BOGIA
Igora. Suau D.→PAPUA AUSTRONESIAN
IGOROT→NORTHWEST AUSTRONESIAN
Igumale. Idoma D.→IDOMA
Igwormany. Laro D.→KORDOFANIAN
Igzennaian. Riff D.→BERBER
IHA→WESTERN NEW GUINEA
Iha→WESTERN NEW GUINEA
Iha→EAST INDONESIAN
I-hadja = Kasanga→WEST ATLANTIC
Ihima = Igbira-Hima. Igbira D.→NUPE-
GBARI
Ihuruana. Maquiritare D.→CARIB
Iʔiaa→EASTERN OCEANIC
Iilit = Ilit. Kunamà D.→CHARI-NILE
Iimutsu. Tsou D.→FORMOSAN AUSTRO-
NESIAN
Ijaw = Ijo→IJO
Ijebu. Yoruba D.→YORUBA
I-JEN = JUI→KAM-TAI
Ijesha. Yoruba D.→YORUBA
IJO see article
Ijoh. Semang Proper D.→SEMANG
Ijoh = Ijo→IJO
Ijok = Ijoh. Semang Proper D.→SEMANG
Ika. Igbo D.→IGBO
Ika. Waicuru Tr.→WAICURIAN
Ika = Igbira-Igu. Igbira D.→NUPE-GBARI
Ikaiku = Kaiku→NORTH EASTERN BANTU
Ikala = Mirning→MIRNINY
Ikeleve = Kongo→CENTRAL WESTERN
BANTU
iki-Bungu = Bungu→NORTH EASTERN
BANTU
iki-Fuliiru = Fuliro→NORTH EASTERN
BANTU
i-Kiga = Tshiga. Ruanda D.→NORTH EAST-
ERN BANTU
iki-Ha = Ha→NORTH EASTERN BANTU
iki-Hera = Lera. Ruanda D.→NORTH EAST-
ERN BANTU
iki-Isenyi = Isenyi. Zanaki D.→NORTH
EASTERN BANTU
iki-Nata = Nata→NORTH EASTERN BANTU
iki-Ngurimi = Ngurimi→NORTH EASTERN
BANTU
iki-nya-Ndugu = Ndugu. Ruanda D.→NORTH
EASTERN BANTU
iki-Rundi = Rundi→NORTH EASTERN
BANTU
iki-Shobyo = Shobyo. Ruanda D.→NORTH
EASTERN BANTU
iki-Zanaki = Zanaki→NORTH EASTERN
BANTU
Ikizu. Zanaki D.→NORTH EASTERN BANTU
Ikkillin = Kuchin→ATHAPASCAN-EYAK
Ikokolemu = Kumam→EASTERN SUDANIC
Ikolu = Ikulu→PLATEAU BENUE-CONGO
Ikom. Olulumo D.→CROSS RIVER BENUE-
CONGO
Ikom = Nkom→BANTOID
Ikoma = Nata→NORTH EASTERN BANTU
Ikomagi = Xinca→MACRO-CHIBCHAN
Ikongo. Malagasy D.→WEST INDONESIAN
Ikoro→PAPUA AUSTRONESIAN

Ikpeshi→EDO
Ikponu. Kposo D.→CENTRAL TOGO
Ikposo = Kposo→CENTRAL TOGO
Ikuhane = Subia→SOUTH WESTERN BANTU
Ikula = Mirning→MIRNINY
Ikulu→PLATEAU BENUE-CONGO
Ikumama = Kumam→EASTERN SUDANIC
Ikumama = Teso→EASTERN SUDANIC
Ikum. Biakpan D.→CROSS RIVER BENUE-CONGO
Ikundun→BOGIA
Ikwahani = Subia→SOUTH WESTERN BANTU
Ikwere = Oratta-Ikwerri. Igbo D.→IGBO
Ikyoo. Tanna D.→SOUTHERN NEW HEBRIDES
Ila→CENTRAL EASTERN BANTU
Ila. Yoruba D.→YORUBA
ILA = LENJE-TONGA→CENTRAL EASTERN BANTU
i-Laali = Laali. West Teke D.→NORTH WESTERN BANTU
Ilakia. Awa D.→EAST NEW GUINEA HIGHLANDS
ILAMBA-IRANGI→NORTH EASTERN BANTU
Ilanun. Maranao D.→NORTHWEST AUSTRONESIAN
Il-Arusa = Arusa. Maasai Tr.→EASTERN SUDANIC
Ilba→PAMA-MARIC
Il-Dalalekutuk = Dalalekutuk. Maasai Tr. →EASTERN SUDANIC
Il-Damat = Damat. Maasai Tr.→EASTERN SUDANIC
Ile a la Crosse = Cree→ALGONQUIAN
i-Leega imuzium = Leega imuzimu. Lega D.→ NORTH EASTERN BANTU
Ileo = Dengese→NORTH WESTERN BANTU
Ili. Uighur D.→TURKIC
Iliara. Leti D.→MOLUCCAN
Iliaura→ARANDIC
Ilit. Kunama D.→CHARI-NILE
Iliwaki→EAST INDONESIAN
Iljaura = Iliaura→ARANDIC
Il-Keekonyokie = Keekonyokie. Maasai Tr.→ EASTERN SUDANIC
Il-Kisongo = Kisongo. Maasai Tr.→EASTERN SUDANIC
Illanos = Ilanun. Maranao D.→NORTHWEST AUSTRONESIAN
Illanos = Maranao→NORTHWEST AUSTRONESIAN
Illanun = Ilanun. Maranao D.→NORTH-WEST AUSTRONESIAN
Illhielogbo. Urhobo D.→EDO
Illiaura = Iliaura→ARANDIC
Illinese = Illinois. Miami D.→ALGONQUIAN
Illinice = Illinois. Miami D.→ALGONQUIAN
Illinois. Miami D.→ALGONQUIAN
Illinoise = Illinois. Miami D.→ALGONQUIAN
Il-Loodokilani = Loodokilani, Maasai Tr.→ EASTERN SUDANIC
Illyowra = Iliaura→ARANDIC
Illyrian→ITALIC
Il-Maasai = Maasai→EASTERN SUDANIC
Il-Matapato. Maasai Tr.→EASTERN SUDANIC
Ilocano→NORTHWEST AUSTRONESIAN
Iloko = Ilocano→NORTHWEST AUSTRONESIAN
i-Lomwe = Lomwe→SOUTH EASTERN BANTU
Ilonggo→NORTHWEST AUSTRONESIAN
Ilongo = Ilonggo→NORTHWEST AUSTRONESIAN
Ilongot→NORTHWEST AUSTRONESIAN
Ilorin. Yoruba D.→YORUBA
Iloytai = Oitai. Maasai Tr.→EASTERN SUDANIC
Ilpara = Walbiri→NGARGA
Ilpira = Walbiri→NGARGA
Ilpirra = Walbiri→NGARGA
Il-Purko = Purko. Maasai Tr.→EASTERN SUDANIC
Il-Tiengwali = Nandi→EASTERN SUDANIC
Il-Tyamus = Tiamus. Maasai D.→EASTERN SUDANIC
i-Lumbu = Lumbu→NORTH WESTERN BANTU
Ilungut = Ilongot→NORTHWEST AUSTRONESIAN
Ilutso = Iboho. Seediq D.→FORMOSAN AUSTRONESIAN
Ilyuarra = Iliaura→ARANDIC
i-Makue = Makue→SOUTH EASTERN BANTU
Imatjera = Anmatjera. Iliaura D.→ARANDIC
Imbao'o = Bobongko→CENTRAL AND SOUTHERN CELEBES
Imbo = Mbo→NORTH EASTERN BANTU
i-Mbuti = Mbuti→NORTH EASTERN BANTU
Imeretian. Georgian D.→CAUCASIAN
Imerxev. Georgian D.→CAUCASIAN
Imilangu = Mdundulu→SOUTH WESTERN BANTU

Imono. Southern Zamucoan Tr.→EQUATO-
RIAL
Impenitari = Epetineri. Maspo D.→PANO
Imroin. Leti D.—MOLUCCAN
Imulud = Imurut. Yami D.→NORTHWEST
AUSTRONESIAN
Imurut. Yami D.→NORTHWEST AUSTRO-
NESIAN
Ina = Hina. Daba D.→CHADIC
Inaken = Inaquen. Chon D.→ANDEAN
Inakona→EASTERN OCEANIC
Inamwanga = Mwanga→CENTRAL EAST-
ERN BANTU
Inao = Guinao→NORTHERN MAIPURAN
Inapari→MAIPURAN
Inaquen. Chon D.→ANDEAN
Inari Lapp→URALIC
Inawonga. Kardutjara D.→WATI
Inca = Quechua→ANDEAN
Indaaka = Ndaaka→NORTH EASTERN
BANTU
Indagen = Indegegn. Peripheral West Gurage
D.→SEMITIC
i-Ndara = Ndara. Ruanda D.→NORTH
EASTERN BANTU
Indegagne = Indegegn. Peripheral West Gurage
D.→SEMITIC
Indegegn. Peripheral West Gurage D.→
SEMITIC
i-Ndem = Nidem. Kaninkwom D.→PLATEAU
BENUE-CONGO
Indian Ocean Creole. French Creole D.→
ROMANCE
INDIC see article
Indinogosima = Mehek→SEPIK
Indjibandi = Jindjibandi. Kurama D.→NGAY-
ARDA
INDO-ARYAN = INDIC
INDO-EUROPEAN see article
INDO-HITTITE see ANATOLIAN
INDO-IRANIAN see article
INDONESIAN, EAST see article
INDONESIAN, WEST see article
INDO-PACIFIC see article
Indo-Portuguese→ROMANCE
i-Ndorwa = Ndorwa. Ruanda D.→NORTH
EASTERN BANTU
Indri→EASTERN
Inedua. Engenni D.→EDO
Inemu. Bakwe Tr.→KRU
Ingain = Tain→GE
Ingalit→ATHAPASCAN-EYAK
Ingara = Inggarda→KARDU
Ingarico→CARIB

Ingarrah = Inggarda→KARDU
Ingassana→CHARI-NILE
Inggarda→KARDU
Ingibandi = Jindjibandi. Kurama D.→
NGAYARDA
Ingilo. Georgian D.→CAUCASIAN
Ingli = Bitjoli D.→SOUTH HALMAHERA
AUSTRONESIAN
Ingrian→URALIC
i-Ngul = Ngul→NORTH WESTERN BANTU
i-Ngulu = Ngulu→SOUTH EASTERN BANTU
Ingura = Groote Eylandt→AUSTRALIAN
MACRO-PHYLUM
Ingush→CAUCASIAN
Iniai = Lemben→EAST NEW GUINEA
HIGHLANDS
Inibaloi = Inibaloy→NORTHWEST AUSTRO
NESIAN
Inibaloy→NORTHWEST AUSTRONESIAN
Inibiloi = Inibaloy→NORTHWEST AUS-
TRONESIAN
Inidem = Nidem. Kaninkwom D.→PLATEAU
BENUE-CONGO
Iningai. Mandandanji D.→PAMA-MARIC
Inja. Mbole D.→NORTH EASTERN BANTU
Injibandi = Jindjibandi. Kurama D.→NGAY-
ARDA
Inle. Burmese D.→BURMESE-LOLO
Inmeas = Isinay→NORTHWEST AUSTRO-
NESIAN
Innek'or = Inneqor. East Gurage D.→SEMITIC
Innemor = Ennemor. Peripheral West Gurage
D.→SEMITIC
Inneqor. East Gurage D.→SEMITIC
Innxarsi = Werize. Gawwada D.→CUSHITIC
Inor = Ennemor. Peripheral West Gurage D.→
SEMITIC
Inparra = Inggarda→KARDU
Inteck = Ngintait. Maraura D.→NARRIN-
YERIC
INTER-ANDINE see article
Intha. Burmese D.→BURMESE-LOLO
Intibucat. Lenca D.→MACRO-CHIBCHAN
Inuit→ESKIMO-ALEUT
Inupiaq = Inuit→ESKIMO-ALEUT
Inupiat = Inuit→ESKIMO-ALEUT
Inupik = Inuit→ESKIMO-ALEUT
Inuvaken. Amahuaca D.→PANO
Inxokvari. Xvarshi D.→CAUCASIAN
Inyangatom = Turkana→EASTERN SU-
DANIC
/Iŋ/ke = //ŋ!ke. ŋ/huki D.→KHOISAN
Iongom = Yonggom→OK
Iora. Gandangara D.→YUIN-KURIC

Ioullemmeden. Tuareg D.→BERBER

Iowa. Chiwere D.→SIOUAN

Ioway = Iowa. Chiwere D.→SIOUAN

Ipa. Vilela Tr.→LULE-VILELA-CHARRUA

Ipai. Diegueno D.→YUMAN

i-Pande = Pande→NORTH WESTERN BANTU

Ipapana. Totonac D.→TOTONACAN

Ipeca. Siuci D.→NORTHERN MAIPURAN

Ipikoi→CENTRAL AND SOUTH NEW GUINEA

Ipili→EAST NEW GUINEA HIGHLANDS

Ipoh. Land Dayak D.→WEST INDONESIAN

IPUGAW = IFUGAO→NORTHWEST AUS-TRONESIAN

Ipurina→MAIPURAN

Ipurucoto = Taulipang. Arecuna D.→CARIB

Iquito. Andoa Tr.→ANDEAN

Ir→MON-KHMER

Ir = Iron. Ossetic D.→IRANIAN

Ira = Mapanai→NORTHERN MAIPURAN

Ira-Amaire→GE

Irahutu→SOUTH HALMAHERA AUSTRO-NESIAN

Irakou = Iraqw→CUSHITIC

Iraku = Iraqw→CUSHITIC

Iramba = Nilamba→NORTH EASTERN BANTU

Iranche→MAIPURAN

Irangi = Langi→NORTH EASTERN BANTU

IRANIAN see article

Irantxe = Iranche→MAIPURAN

Irapeno. Mape D.→CARIB

Irapue. Bakwe Tr.→KRU

IRAQW→CUSHITIC

Iraqw→CUSHITIC

Iraya→NORTHWEST AUSTRONESIAN

IRAYIC→NORTHWEST AUSTRONESIAN

Irbil = Arbil. Kermanji D.→IRANIAN

Irbore = Arbore→CUSHITIC

Irecapo. Bakwe Tr.→KRU

Iregwe = Irigwe→PLATEAU BENUE-CONGO

Irendely = Jirandali. Mandandanji D.→PAMA-MARIC

Iri. Urhobo D.→EDO

Iria→ASMAT

Iria. Tebu Tr.→SAHARAN

Iribue = Irapue. Bakwe Tr.→KRU

Irico. Pijao D.→CARIB

Irie = Iria. Tebu Tr.→SAHARAN

Irigwe→PLATEAU BENUE-CONGO

Iron. Ossetic D.→IRANIAN

Iroquoian, Southern = Cherokee→IROQUOIS

IROQUOIS see article

Irregwe = Irigwe→PLATEAU BENUE-CONGO

Iruaitsu.→SHASTAN Tr.→HOKAN

Irula. Tamil D.→DRAVIDIAN

Irumu→HUON-FINISTERRE

Isa. Somali D.→CUSHITIC

Isa = Catawba→MACRO-SIOUAN

Isa = Ishan→EDO

Isal→EAST INDONESIAN

Isam = Pagu→NORTH HALMAHERA

Isamal→NORTHWEST AUSTRONESIAN

I-Sampur = Sampur. Maasai D.→EASTERN SUDANIC

Isaurian see article

Isebe→BOGIA

Iseimajek. Tatog Tr.→EASTERN SUDANIC

Iseni-Kotsenu. Rengma D.→NAGA-KUKI-CHIN

Isenyi. Zanaki D.→NORTH EASTERN BANTU

Is'hak. Somali D.→CUSHITIC

Ishan→EDO

Ishang = Murmi→GYARUNG-MISHMI

Ishekiri = Itsekiri. Yoruba D.→YORUBA

ishi-Malila = Malila→CENTRAL EASTERN BANTU

ishi-Nyiha = Nyiha→CENTRAL EASTERN BANTU

ishi-Safwa = Safwa→CENTRAL EASTERN BANTU

isi-bala = 'Baca. Nguni D.→SOUTH EASTERN BANTU

isi-//esiba = Xesibe. Nguni D.→SOUTH EASTERN BANTU

isi-g/aleka = Gcaleka. Nguni D.→SOUTH EASTERN BANTU

I-Sikirari = Sikirari. Maasai Tr.→EASTERN SUDANIC

isi-Lololo = Piki→SOUTH EASTERN BANTU

isi-Lubi = Hlubi. Nguni D.→SOUTH EAST-ERN BANTU

isi-Mpondomisi = Mpondomse. Nguni D.→ SOUTH EASTERN BANTU

Isinai = Isinay→NORTHWEST AUSTRO-NESIAN

Isinay→NORTHWEST AUSTRONESIAN

isi-Ndebele = Ndebele→SOUTH EASTERN BANTU

isi-ŋg!ika. Nguni D.→SOUTH EASTERN BANTU

isi-Piki = Piki→SOUTH EASTERN BANTU

i-Sira = Sira→NORTH WESTERN BANTU

i-Siria = Siria. Maasai Tr.→EASTERN SUDANIC

Isistine. Lule Tr.→LULE-VILELA-CHARRUA

isi-Swati = Swati. Nguni D.→SOUTH EAST-
ERN BANTU

isi-Xhosa = Xhosa. Nguni D.→SOUTH EAST-
ERN BANTU

isi-Zulu = Zulu. Nguni D.→SOUTH EAST-
ERN BANTU

Islam = Argobba. Amharic D.→SEMITIC

Isleta. Tiwa D.→TANOAN

ISNEG→NORTHWEST AUSTRONESIAN

Isoko. Urhobo D.→EDO

Israeli. Hebrew D.→SEMITIC

Issa = Catawba→MACRO-SIOUAN

Issa = Isa. Somali D.→CUSHITIC

Issaag = Isa. Somali D.→CUSHITIC

Issala = Sisala→GUR

Issana = Baniva Do Icana, Carutana D.→
NORTHERN MAIPURAN

Istro-Rumanian. Rumanian D.→ROMANCE

Isu = Su→NORTH WESTERN BANTU

Isu-Ama. Igbo D.→IGBO

Isubu = Su→NORTH WESTERN BANTU

Isu-Item. Igbo D.→IGBO

Isuka = Isuxa. Luhya D.→NORTH EASTERN
BANTU

ISUMRUD→BOGIA

Isurara→KOIARI

Isuwa = Su→NORTH WESTERN BANTU

Isuxa. Luhya D.→NORTH EASTERN BANTU

Iswa = Catawba→MACRO-SIOUAN

Ita = Central Agta→NORTHWEST AUSTRO-
NESIAN

Itaita = Jitajita. Djadjala D.→KULINIC

Itakho = Isuxa. Luhya D.→NORTH EASTERN
BANTU

Italian→ROMANCE

ITALIC see article

Italon. Ilongot D.→NORTHWEST AUSTRO-
NESIAN

Itanga = Ramarama→TUPI

Itatin. Tupi Tr.→TUPI

Itawes. Ibanag D.→NORTHWEST AUSTRO-
NESIAN

Itawi→NORTHWEST AUSTRONESIAN

Itayaine→NORTHERN MAIPURAN

Itbayat. Ivatan D.→NORTHWEST AUSTRO-
NESIAN

Itchali = Kuchin→ATHAPASCAN-EYAK

Itel'men = Kamchadal→CHUKCHEE-KAM-
CHATKAN

Iten = More→CHAPACURA-WANHAMAN

Itesio = Teso→EASTERN SUDANIC

Iteso = Teso→EASTERN SUDANIC

Itesyo = Teso→EASTERN SUDANIC

Itetapanes = Bontok→NORTHWEST AUS-
TRONESIAN

Ithiithi = Jitajita. Djadjala D.→KULINIC

Itigo→WESTERN NEW GUINEA

Itkalyaruin = Kuchin→ATHAPASCAN-EY-
AK

Itkanskij. Koryak D.→CHUKCHEE-KAM-
CHATKAN

Itkasnkij. Koryak D.→CHUKCHEE-KAM-
CHATKAN

Itkpe'lit = Kuchin→ATHAPASCAN-EYAK

Itku'dlin = Kuchin→ATHAPASCAN-EYAK

Itneg = Tinggian→NORTHWEST AUSTRO-
NESIAN

Itogapuc = Nitogapid. Ramarama D.→TUPI

Itonama→MACRO-CHIBCHAN

Itonga. Tanna D.→SOUTHERN NEW HEB-
RIDES

Itoreauhip. More D.→CHAPACURA-WAN-
HAMAN

i-Tsaangi = Tsaangi→NORTH WESTERN
BANTU

Itsekiri. Yoruba D.→YORUBA

i-Tsogo = Tsogo. Ruanda D.→NORTH
EASTERN BANTU

Ittik→NORTH PAPUAN

Ittu. Galla D.→CUSHITIC

Itu→KOIARI

Itucale. Simacu D.→ANDEAN

Itumkala. Chechen D.→CAUCASIAN

Itundu. Banen Tr.→NORTH WESTERN
BANTU

Itutang→BOGIA

Itza. Maya D.→MAYAN

Itza = Maya→MAYAN

Iui = Salt. Chimbú D.→EAST NEW GUINEA
HIGHLANDS

Iuleha. Emai D.→EDO

Iuruna = Yuruna→TUPI

Ivapare. Seta D.→TUPI

Ivatan→NORTHWEST AUSTRONESIAN

Ivaxo = Ibaho. Bunun D.→FORMOSAN AUS-
TRONESIAN

Ivbie→EDO

Ivitorocai→GE

Iwa→CENTRAL EASTERN BANTU

Iwaak. Inibaloy D.→NORTHWEST AUSTRO-
NESIAN

IWAIDJAN see article

Iwaidji→IWAIDJAN

Iwaiji = Iwaidji→IWAIDJAN

Iwainu. Northern Kiwai D.→CENTRAL AND
SOUTH NEW GUINEA

Iwam→SEPIK

Iwam = Gende→EAST NEW GUINEA HIGHLANDS
Iwi. Kposo D.→CENTRAL TOGO
Iwoer = Iwur→OK
Iworo→KOIARI
Iworo. Yoruba D.→YORUBA
Iwur→OK
i-Wuumu = Wuumu→NORTH WESTERN BANTU
Ixatec→POPOLOCAN
Ixateco = Ixatec→POPOLOCAN
Ixil→MAYAN
Ixreko-Muxrek. Rutul D.→CAUCASIAN
Ixtenco. Otomi D.→OTOMIAN
i-Yaa = Yaa. West Teke D.→NORTH WESTERN BANTU
Iyaine = Itayaine→NORTHERN MAIPURAN
Iyala = Yala→IDOMA
i-Yans = Yanzi→NORTH WESTERN BANTU
Iyayu. Uhami D.→EDO
Iyekhee→EDO
Iyiniwok = Cree→ALGONQUIAN
Iyirikum = Widekum→BANTOID
Iyongut. Ilongot D.→NORTHWEST AUSTRONESIAN
IZALE = MBEMBE→JUKUNOID
IZANENI→NORTHERN MAIPURAN
IZARE = MBEMBE→JUKUNOID
Izha = Ezha. Central West Gurage D.→SEMITIC
Izi→IGBO
Iznacen. Riff D.→BERBER
Izocenyo. Chane D.→MAIPURAN

J

Jaara. Djadjala D.→KULINIC
Jab = Yelmek→FREDERIK HENDRIK IS. AND SE WEST IRIAN
JABA→PLATEAU BENUE-CONGO
Jaba→PLATEAU BENUE-CONGO
Jabaal. Tama D.→EASTERN SUDANIC
Jabana→NORTHERN MAIPURAN
Jabal Nafusah→BERBER
Jabga. Boazi D.→MARIND
Jabi. Kapauku D.→WEST NEW GUINEA HIGHLANDS
Jabo. Grebo Tr.→KRU
Jabulajabula→YOTAYOTIC
Jaburu = Wiilman. Juat D.→SOUTHWEST PAMA-NYUNGAN
Jacaltec→MAYAN
Jacalteca = Jacaltec→MAYAN
Jacaria. Caripuna D.→PANO

Jackalbarap = Ngarkat. Djadjala D.→KULINIC
Jackegilbrab = Ngarkat. Djadjala D.→KULINIC
Jackjack = Aladian→LAGOON
Jacobite. East Aramaic D.→SEMITIC
Jacunda. Tenetehara Tr.→TUPI
Jad. Central Tibetan D.→TIBETAN
Jadjmadang = Jaitmathang→PAMA-NYUNGAN
Jadliaura→YURA
Jadlijawara = Jadliaura→YURA
Jafalu = Lwo→EASTERN SUDANIC
Jafijufa = Yabiyufa→EAST NEW GUINEA HIGHLANDS
Jagada. Tebu Tr.→SAHARAN
Jagai. Nuer D.→EASTERN SUDANIC
Jagalingu. Mandandanji D.→PAMA-MARIC
Jagara→DURUBULIC
Jagarabal = Jagara→DURUBULIC
Jagjage = Tangole→CHADIC
Jaguallapai = Walapai. Upland Yuman D.→YUMAN
Jah Hut = Eastern Sakai→SAKAI
Jahadian = Yahadian→WESTERN NEW GUINEA
JAHAIC = SEMANG
Jahai = Pangan→SEMANG
Jahalatane→EAST INDONESIAN
Jahromi. Persian D.→IRANIAN
Jahycu = Jeico→GE
Jaico = Jeico→GE
Jaicuju = Jeico→GE
Jaipuri. Rajasthani D.→INDIC
Jaithmathang = Jaitmathang→PAMA-NYUNGAN
Jaitmathang→PAMA-NYUNGAN
Jajao→NORTHWESTERN AND CENTRAL SOLOMONS
Jajaurung = Jaara. Djadjala D.→KULINIC
Jajowerong = Jaara. Djadjala D.→KULINIC
Jajoworrong = Jaara. Djadjala D.→KULINIC
Jajowrong = Jaara. Djadjala D.→KULINIC
Jajowrung = Jaara. Djadjala D.→KULINIC
Jajowurrong = Jaara. Djadjala D.→KULINIC
Jakajako = Mararba. Gobabingo D.→MURNGIC
Jakajako = Maraura→NARRINYERIC
Jakalbarap = Ngarkat. Djadjala D.→KULINIC
Jakanci = Jaku→BANTOID
Jakelbaluk = Ngarkat. Djadjala D.→KULINIC
Jakoon = Jakun→JAKUN
Jaku→BANTOID
Jaku'd = Jakun→JAKUN

Jakud'n = Jakun→JAKUN
Jakula. Gayardilt D.→TANGKIC
JAKUN see article
Jal = Aten→PLATEAU BENUE-CONGO
Jalanga→PAMA-NYUNGAN
Jaliat. Khorcin D.→MONGOLIAN
Jalonco = Yalunka. Susu D.→MANDE
Jalor. Pangan D.→SEMANG
Jalung→MON-KHMER
Jam. Kaurareg D.→MABUIAGIC
Jama Mapun = Cagayanon→NORTHWEST
    AUSTRONESIAN
Jamac. Kalasa-ala D.→NURISTANI
Jamaican Creole→GERMANIC
Jamajabs = Mohave. River Yuman D.→YU-
    MAN
Jamaricuma = Yamarikuma→CARIB
Jamarikuma = Yamarikuma→CARIB
Jamba = Chamba→ADAMAWA
Jamba-Makutu. Loi-Ngiri D.→NORTH WEST-
    ERN BANTU
Jambina. Mandandanji D.→PAMA-MARIC
Jamden→MOLUCCAN
Jamdena = Jamden→MOLUCCAN
Jaminaua. Jurua-Purus Tr.→PANO
Jaminjang = Djamindjung→DJAMINDJUN-
    GAN
Jamjam→CUSHITIC
Jampalam. Mandara Tr.→CHADIC
Jamundi→CHIBCHAN
Janda→PAMA-NYUNGAN
Jandangara = Jaitmathang→PAMA-NYUN-
    GAN
Jandapu = Yandapu. Enga D.→EAST NEW
    GUINEA HIGHLANDS
Jande. Siriono D.→TUPI
Jandiahi. Tenetehara Tr.→TUPI
Jandjinung→MURNGIC
Jandruwanta. Dieri D.→DIERIC
Jangaa. Ilba D.→PAMA-MARIC
Jangali→GYARUNG-MISHMI
Jangga. Mandandanji D.→PAMA-MARIC
Janggali = Jangali→GYARUNG-MISHMI
Jangkundjara. Kardutjara D.→WATI
Jangor = Janjero→OMOTIC
Jangundjara = Jangkundjara. Kardutjara D.→
    WATI
Janjerinya = Janjero→OMOTIC
Janjero→OMOTIC
Janji→PLATEAU BENUE-CONGO
Janjor = Janjero→OMOTIC
Jankunzazzara = Jangkundjara. Kardutjara
    D.→WATI
Jaoi→NORTHERN MAIPURAN

JAPANESE see article
Japen→MOLUCCAN
Jaqai = Yaqay→MARIND
Jaqaru-Cauqui. Aymara Tr.→ANDEAN
Jar = Jarawa→BANTOID
Jara = Jera→CHADIC
Jarai→WEST INDONESIAN
Jaralde = Jarildekald. Tanganekald D.→NAR-
    RINYERIC
Jaranci = Jarawa→BANTOID
Jarawa→BANTOID
Jarawa→ANDAMANESE
Jarawa, Hill = Afusare→PLATEAU BENUE
    CONGO
Jarawa, Plains = Jarawa→BANTOID
JARAWAN→BANTOID
Jarawan Dutse = Afusare → PLATEAU
    BENUE-CONGO
Jarawan Kasa = Afusare→PLATEAU BENUE-
    CONGO
Jarawan Kasa = Jarawa→BANTOID
Jardwa. Djadjala D.→KULINIC
Jari. Afusare D.→PLATEAU BENUE- CONGO
Jaricuna = Arecuna→CARIB
Jarijari. Djadjala D.→KULINIC
Jarildekald. Tanganekald D.→NARRINYERIC
Jarionga = Jaroinga. Iliaura D.→ARANDIC
Jarnango→MURNGIC
Jarobaluk = Jaara. Djadjala D.→KULINIC
Jaroinga. Iliaura D.→ARANDIC
Jaroo = Djaru→NGUMBIN
Jaru→CHAPACURA-WANHAMAN
Jaru = Loven→MON-KHMER
Jarum. Semang Proper D.→SEMANG
Jaruma = Yaruma→CARIB
Jarumara = Ngandangara. Punthamara D.→
    DIERIC
Jaruna = Yuruna→TUPI
Jaruru = Djaru→NGUMBIN
Jarut. Khorcin D.→MONGOLIAN
Jasak. Ordos D.→MONGOLIAN
Jasin = Werchikwar. Burushaski D.
Jasing = Yasing→ADAMAWA
Jassing = Yasing→ADAMAWA
Jastu. Khorcin D.→MONGOLIAN
Jatahy. Tupi Tr.→TUPI
Jate = Yate. Keigana D.→EAST NEW GUIN
    EA HIGHLANDS
Jathaikana. Otati D.→PAMA-MARIC
Jati = Bangaru. Western Hindi D.→INDIC
Jatu = Bangaru. Western Hindi D.→INDIC
Jatvian→BALTIC
Jauanaua. Jurua-Purus Tr.→PANO
Jauaperi→CARIB

Jauareta-Tapiia = Kawaib→TUPI
Jauarete. Carutana D.→NORTHERN MAI-
PURAN
Jauavo. Jurua-Purus Tr.→PANO
Jaudjibara→WORORAN
Jaulapiti→MAIPURAN
Jau-navo = Caripuna→PANO
Jaunde = Ewondo→NORTH WESTERN BAN-
TU
Jaunsari. Western Pahari D.→INDIC
Jauor→NYULNYULAN
Jauraworka→DIERIC
Jaurorka = Jauraworka→DIERIC
Jauwa→BINANDERE
Java. Opata D.→UTO-AZTECAN
Javae = Javahe→CARAJA
Javahai = Javahe→CARAJA
Javahe→CARAJA
Javanese→WEST INDONESIAN
JAVO-SUMATRA→WEST INDONESIAN
Jawage = Javahe→CARAJA
Jawanli = Wajamli. Buli D.→SOUTH HALMA-
HERA AUSTRONESIAN
Jawarawarka = Jauraworka→DIERIC
Jawe. Nemi D.→NEW CALEDONIA
Jawin = Djauan→GUNWINGGUAN
JE = GE
Jebel El Amira. Lafofa D.→KORDOFANIAN
Jebel Geira. Jongor Tr.→CHADIC
Jebel Tekeim. Lafofa D.→KORDOFANIAN
Jebero = Chebero→ANDEAN
Jegasa-Sarau→BINANDERE
Jegu→CHADIC
Jeh→MON-KHMER
Jeher. Semang Proper D.→SEMANG
Jei = Yey→FREDERIK HENDRIK IS. AND
SE WEST IRIAN
JEICO→GE
Jekaing = Jikany. Nuer D.→EASTERN SUDA-
NIC
Jekiri = Itsekiri. Yoruba D.→YORUBA
Jekri = Itsekiri. Yoruba D.→YORUBA
Jelai. Central Sakai D.→SAKAI
Jeljendi. Dieri D.→DIERIC
Jeljujendi = Jeljendi. Dieri D.→DIERIC
Jelmek = Yelmek→FREDERIK HENDRIK IS.
AND SE WEST IRIAN
Jemez. Towa. D.→TANOAN
Jemez = Towa→TANOAN
Jemhwa. Gumuz D.→KOMAN
Jemjem = Suga. Bute D.→BANTOID
Jemmari. Jabal Nafusah D.→BERBER
Jen→ADAMAWA
Jen. Njai D.→CHADIC

Jena. Karanga D.→SOUTH EASTERN BAN-
TU
Jendruwonta = Jandruwanta. Dieri D.→
DIERIC
Jeng = Cheng→MON-KHMER
Jenimu = Oser→AWYU
Jenjero = Janjero→OMOTIC
Jenji = Janji→PLATEAU BENUE-CONGO
Jenures. Biak D.→MOLUCCAN
Jera→CHADIC
JERAWA→PLATEAU BENUE-CONGO
Jerawa→PLATEAU BENUE-CONGO
Jerawa = Jera→CHADIC
Jerba→BERBER
Jere = Jerawa→PLATEAU BENUE-CONGO
Jeri. Biak D.→MOLUCCAN
Jerra = Jera→CHADIC
Jeru. Great Andamanese D.→ANDAMAN-
ESE
Jetan = Comanche. Shoshoni D.→UTO-AZTE-
CAN
Jetko. Kanuri Tr.→SAHARAN
Jeto. Banda D.→EASTERN
Jew Tongo = Saramaccan→GERMANIC
JƏRU see MON-KHMER
Jhalawadi. Gujarati D.→INDIC
Jharawan. Brahui D.→DRAVIDIAN
JIANG = DINKA→EASTERN SUDANIC
Jiba = Kona. Jukun D.→JUKUNOID
Jibaro = Jivaro→JIVAROAN
Jibawa = Jibu. Jukun D.→JUKUNOID
Jibu→ORIOMO RIVER
Jibu. Jukun D.→JUKUNOID
Jicaque→HOKAN
Jicarilla. Navajo D.→ATHAPASCAN-EYAK
Jiddu. Somali D.→CUSHITIC
Jie. Karamojong D.→EASTERN SUDANIC
Jiegera = Yegir→KUMBAINGGARIC
JIENG = DINKA→EASTERN SUDANIC
Jikai = Barera→BURERAN
Jikain = Jikany. Nuer D.→EASTERN SUDAN-
IC
Jikany. Nuer D.→EASTERN SUDANIC
Jilbu = Fali of Yilbu→CHADIC
Jilngali→DJAMINDJUNGAN
Jimajima→DAGA
Jimina-kana→CENTRAL AND SOUTH NEW
GUINEA
Jimini = Dyimini→GUR
Jimjam→NORTHEASTERN NEW GUINEA
Jimo = Zumu→CHADIC
Jimun. Mandandanji D.→PAMA-MARIC
Jinba = Djinba→MURNGIC
Jinca = Xinca→MACRO-CHIBCHAN

Jinda = Kamuku→PLATEAU BENUE-CON-
GO
Jinda = Rai→GYARUNG-MISHMI
Jindabira = Mbayaka→AGOB
Jindjibandi. Kurama D.→NGAYARDA
Jindjibarndi = Jindjibandi. Kurama D.→NGAY-
ARDA
Jindwi. Shona D.→SOUTH EASTERN BANTU
Jinga = Njinga. Mbamba D.→CENTRAL
WESTERN BANTU
Jinggarda = Inggarda→KARDU
Jinghpaw = Chingpaw→BODO-NAGA-KA-
CHIN
JINGPAW = KACHIN→BODO-NAGA-KA-
CHIN
Jinibara = Jagara→DURUBULIC
Jinja = Dzindza→NORTH EASTERN BANTU
Jinkum = Jukun→JUKUNOID
Jinwun→PAMA-MARIC
Jir Joront. Koko Mindjan D.→PAMA-MARIC
Jirai = Zumu→CHADIC
Jirajara→JIRARAN
Jirandali. Mandandanji D.→PAMA-MARIC
Jiraran = Jirajara→JIRARAN
JIRARAN see article
Jiru→JUKUNOID
Jita→NORTH EASTERN BANTU
Jitajita. Djadjala D.→KULINIC
Jivali = Djiwali→MANTHARDA
Jivaro→JIVAROAN
JIVAROAN see article
Jivo. Bete Tr.→KRU
Jiwaidja = Iwaidji→IWAIDJAN
Jiwali = Djiwali→MANTHARDA
Jiye. Karamojong D.→EASTERN SUDANIC
Jo Alur = Alur→EASTERN SUDANIC
Jo Bor = Bor→EASTERN SUDANIC
Jo Colo = Colo. Thuri Tr.→EASTERN SU-
DANIC
Jo Luo = Luo→EASTERN SUDANIC
Jo Lwo = Lwo→EASTERN SUDANIC
Jo Nam. Alur Tr.→EASTERN SUDANIC
Jo Thuri = Thuri→EASTERN SUDANIC
Joarda. Tebu Tr.→SAHARAN
Jobi. Japen D.→MOLUCCAN
Joda = 'Bahema. Lendu D.→CENTRAL SU-
DANIC
John Day = Columbia River. Sahaptin D.→
SAHAPTIN-NEZ PERCE
JOI = JUI→KAM-TAI
Jojoan. Cuica D.→EQUATORIAL
Jok = Ngok. Padang D.→EASTERN SUDAN-
IC
Jokoi = Loma→MANDE

Jokot. Alur Tr.→EASTERN SUDANIC
Jola = Diola→WEST ATLANTIC
Joloano Sulu = Taw Sug→NORTHWEST AUS-
TRONESIAN
Jolof. Wolof D.→WEST ATLANTIC
Jolof = Wolof→WEST ATLANTIC
Jolong. Bahnar D.→MON-KHMER
Jolonke = Yalunka. Susu D.→MANDE
Jompre = Zumper→JUKUNOID
Jonaz = Chichimeca-Jonaz→OTOMIAN
Jonga. Ombo D.→NORTH WESTERN BANTU
Jonga. Tsonga D.→SOUTH EASTERN BANTU
Jongman = Jungman→GUNWINGGUAN
Jongor→CHADIC
Jope = Yopi→TLAPANECAN
Jorto→CHADIC
JOSEPHSTAAL→BOGIA
Jotajota = Jotijota→YOTAYOTIC
Jotijota→YOTAYOTIC
Jro. Chrau D.→MON-KHMER
Jro = Chrau→MON-KHMER
Jru = Loven→MON-KHMER
JU = NORTHERN SOUTH AFRICAN KHOI-
SAN→KHOISAN
Jualati = Tfalati→KALAPUYA
Juanauo = Catuquina→PANO
Juaneno. Luiseno D.→UTO-AZTECAN
Juang→MUNDA
Juat→SOUTHWEST PAMA-NYUNGAN
Jubu = Jibu. Kukun D.→JUKUNOID
Ju-chen→TUNGUS
Judeo-Aramaic. West Aramaic D.→SEMITIC
Judeo-German = Yiddish. Netherlandic-German
D.→GERMANIC
Judeo-Persian. Persian D.→IRANIAN
Judeo-Spanish = Ladino. Spanish D.→RO-
MANCE
Jugan. Ordos D.→MONGOLIAN
Jugula = Jakula→TANGKIC
JUI→KAM-TAI
Juichun = Huchiun. Northern Costanoan D.→
MIWOK-COSTANOAN
Juipera. Mandandanji D.→PAMA-MARIC
Jukagir = Yukaghir→YUKAGHIR
Jukamba = Yugambe→BANDJALANGIC
Jukambal→YUIN-KURIC
Jukan = Djugun. Nyulnyul D.→NYULNYU-
LAN
Jukon = Jukun→JUKUNOID
Juku. Jar D.→BANTOID
Juku = Jukun→JUKUNOID
Juku Junkun = Jukun→JUKUNOID
Jukum = Jukun→JUKUNOID
Jukun→JUKUNOID

JUKUN-MBEMBE→JUKUNOID
JUKUNOID see article
Jula = Dyula. Dyula Tr.→MANDE
Julaimaua. Cubeo D.→MACRO-TUCANOAN
Julbre = Yulbaridja. Kardutjara D.→WATI
Julud. Katla D.→Kordofanian
Juluridja = Kukatja. Kardutjara D.→WATI
Juma see article
Juman. Kim D.→CHADIC
Jumana→NORTHERN MAIPURAN
Jumbanaua. Jurua-Purus Tr.→PANO
Jumjum. Maban D.→EASTERN SUDANIC
Jumu. Kardutjara D.→WATI
Jumu. Yoruba D.→YORUBA
Junco = Cunco. Araucanian D.→PENUTIAN
Junggor = Yunggor→DALY
Jungman→GUNWINGGUAN
Junguru. Banda D.→EASTERN
Junoi. Great Andamanese D.→ANDAMANESE
JUPNA VALLEY = YUPNA→HUON-FINIS-
　　TERRE
Jur = Lwo→EASTERN SUDANIC
Jur Lwo = Lwo→EASTERN SUDANIC
Jur Manangeer = Manangeer. Thuri Tr.→
　　EASTERN SUDANIC
Jur Shol = Colo. Thuri Tr.→EASTERN SU-
　　DANIC
Jura. Jurua-Purus Tr.→PANO
Jura. Tebu Tr.→SAHARAN
Juray→MUNDA
Juri = Yuri→MACRO-TUCANOAN
Juru. Ilba D.→PAMA-MARIC
Juru. Lowland Semang D.→SEMANG
JURUA-PURUS→MAIPURAN
Jurua-Purus→PANO
Jurupari. Carutana D.→NORTHERN MAI-
　　PURAN
Juwalarai. Yualyai D.→WIRADJURIC
Juwibara = Juipera. Mandandanji D.→PAMA-
　　MARIC

K

KA→CENTRAL TOGO
Ka. Banda D.→EASTERN
Ka Beo = Laqua→KAM-TAI
Ka Tawng Luang = Tong-luang→KHMUIC
Kaa. Mbo D.→NORTH WESTERN BANTU
Kaaloŋ→NORTH WESTERN BANTU
Kaamba. Kongo D.→CENTRAL WESTERN
　　BANTU
Kaana Masala = Masalit→MABAN
Kaangooloo = Kangulu. Wadja D.→WAKA-
　　KABIC

Kaanu→NORTH EASTERN BANTU
Kaba→CENTRAL SUDANIC
Kaba→OMOTIC
Kaba = She→OMOTIC
Kaba Boho. Kaba D.→CENTRAL SUDANIC
Kaba Bumaŋga. Kaba D.→CENTRAL SU-
　　DANIC
Kaba Dunjo→CENTRAL SUDANIC
Kaba Jaha. Kaba D.→CENTRAL SUDANIC
Kaba Jiŋge. Kaba Dunjo D.→CENTRAL
　　SUDANIC
Kaba Joko. Kaba Dunjo D.→CENTRAL
　　SUDANIC
Kaba Mbaŋga. Kaba Dunjo D.→CENTRAL
　　SUDANIC
Kaba Na. Kaba Dunjo D.→CENTRAL
　　SUDANIC
Kaba Ndim. Kaba D.→CENTRAL SUDANIC
Kaba Ndoko. Kaba D.→CENTRAL SUDANIC
Kaba of Batangafo. Mbai D.→CENTRAL
　　SUDANIC
Kaba Tie. Kaba Dunjo D.→CENTRAL SU-
　　DANIC
Kabadi→PAPUA AUSTRONESIAN
Kabaena. Bungku D.→CENTRAL AND
　　SOUTHERN CELEBES
Kabak = Chibak→CHADIC
Kabalai. Nancere D.→CHADIC
Kabalai = Gablai→CHADIC
Kabalbara = Kabelbara. Mandandanji D.→
　　PAMA-MARIC
Kabana = Sikube→GOILALA
Kabanu. Tulu D.→ADMIRALTY-WESTERN
　　ISLANDS
Kabardian. Circassian D.→CAUCASIAN
Kabayan. Inibaloy D.→NORTHWEST AUS-
　　TRONESIAN
Kabba = Kaba→CENTRAL SUDANIC
Kabba Laka = Laka. Gambai D.→CENTRAL
　　SUDANIC
!Kabbakwe. Naron D.→KHOISAN
Kabbau-chau = Kafauchau. Katab D.→PLA-
　　TEAU BENUE-CONGO
Kabelbara. Mandandanji D.→PAMA-MARIC
Kabena. Alaba D.→CUSHITIC
K'abena = Kabena. Alaba D.→CUSHITIC
Kabi = Kabikabi. Dalla D.→WAKA-KABIC
Kabiema = Kabre→GUR
Kabikabi. Dalla D.→WAKA-KABIC
Kabin = Ga'anda→CHADIC
Kabinapok = Pomo→POMO
Kabishi = Cabichi. Southwest Nambicuara D.→
　　NAMBICUARA
Kabisiana→TUPI

Kabiu→NAGA-KUKI-CHIN
Kabixiana = Kabisiana→TUPI
Kabo. Ijo D.→IJO
Kabo = Cabo. Miskito D.→MISUMALPAN
Kabola. Abui D.→TIMOR-ALOR
Kabona. Lendu D.→CENTRAL SUDANIC
Kabre→GUR
Kabu = Kebu→CENTRAL TOGO
Kabugao. Bayag D.→NORTHWEST AUSTRO-
    NESIAN
Kabui = Kapwi→NAGA-KUKI-CHIN
Kabuli. Bipi D.→ADMIRALTY-WESTERN
    ISLANDS
Kabure = Kabre→GUR
Kaburuang. Talaud D.→HESPERONESIAN
Kabwari→NORTH EASTERN BANTU
Kabye = Kabre→GUR
Kabyle→BERBER
Kacama = Kachama→OMOTIC
K'ac'ama = Kachama→OMOTIC
Kacha. Khakas D.→TURKIC
Kachama→OMOTIC
Kachari. Bodo D.→BODO-NAGA-KACHIN
Kachcha Nagas = Empeo→NAGA-KUKI-
    CHIN
Kachchi. Sindhi D.→INDIC
Kache = Kaje→PLATEAU BENUE-CONGO
Kachel = Katchal. Central Nicobarese D.→
    NICOBARESE
Kachepo = Suri. Tirma D.→EASTERN SU-
    DANIC
Kachice = Kekchi→MAYAN
Kachichere. Katab D.→PLATEAU BENUE-
    CONGO
KACHIN→BODO-NAGA-KACHIN
Kachin = Chingpaw→BODO-NAGA-KACHIN
Kachipa = Suri. Tirma D.→EASTERN SU-
    DANIC
Kachipo = Suri. Tirma D.→EASTERN SU-
    DANIC
Kachirai. Paiwan D.→FORMOSAN AUSTRO-
    NESIAN
Kachmere = Kashmere. Maba Tr.→MABAN
Kacik. Chulym D.→TURKIC
KADAI→KAM-TAI
Kadai→EAST INDONESIAN
Kadaklan-Barlig. Bontok D.→NORTHWEST
    AUSTRONESIAN
Kadam. Pokot D.→EASTERN SUDANIC
Kadara→PLATEAU BENUE-CONGO
Kadaro = Kadaru. Kordofanian Nubian Tr.→
    EASTERN SUDANIC
Kadaru. Kordofanian Nubian Tr.→EASTERN
    SUDANIC

Kadayan. Bisaya D.→WEST INDONESIAN
Kaddakie = Kaititj→ARANDIC
Kadero = Kadaru. Kordofanian Nubian Tr.→
    EASTERN SUDANIC
Kaderu = Kadaru. Kordofanian Nubian Tr.→
    EASTERN SUDANIC
Kadiko = Tonkawa → MACRO-ALGON-
    QUIAN
Kadimani. Waica Tr.→WAICAN
Kadiro. Moru D.→CENTRAL SUDANIC
Kadiru = Kadiro. Moru D.→CENTRAL SU-
    DANIC
Kadjagse = Kajakse. Mubi D.→CHADIC
Kadjang→CENTRAL AND SOUTHERN
    CELEBES
Kadjeroen = Gadjerong→DJERAGAN
Kadjerong = Gadjerong→DJERAGAN
Kadjidi. Kanembu Tr.→SAHARAN
Kado. Dari D.→CHADIC
Kadohadacho. Caddo Tr.→CADDOAN
Kadohadacho = Caddo→CADDOAN
Kadu→BURMESE-LOLO
Kadu Mo Di = Krongo→KORDOFANIAN
Kadugli→KORDOFANIAN
KADUGLI-KRONGO = TUTUM→KORDO-
    FANIAN
Kadum = Kwanka → PLATEAU BENUE-
    CONGO
Kaeti→AWYU
Kafa. Foi D.→EAST NEW GUINEA HIGH-
    LANDS
Kafa = Kefa→OMOTIC
Kafauchau. Katab D.→PLATEAU BENUE-
    CONGO
Kaffa = Kefa→OMOTIC
Kaffer = Xhosa. Nguni D.→SOUTH EASTERN
    BANTU
Kafficho = Kefa→OMOTIC
Kaffir = Xhosa. Nguni D.→SOUTH EASTERN
    BANTU
Kafice = Kefa→OMOTIC
Kafico = Kefa→OMOTIC
Kafire. Senari D.→GUR
KAFIRI = NURISTANI
Kaga = Dyula. Dyula Tr.→MANDE
Kagama. Kanuri Tr.→SAHARAN
Kagan = Tagakaolo→NORTHWEST AUS-
    TRONESIAN
Kagankan. Hanunoo D.→NORTHWEST AUS-
    TRONESIAN
Kagate. Central Tibetan D.→TIBETAN
Kagbarika = Kebu→CENTRAL TOGO
Kaggaba = Cagaba→CHIBCHAN
Kagi→KOIARI

Kagi. Bunun D.→FORMOSAN AUSTRONE-
SIAN

Kagoma→PLATEAU BENUE-CONGO

Kagoro. Bambara D.→MANDE

Kagoro. Katab D.→PLATEAU BENUE-
CONGO

Kagu = Kahugu→PLATEAU BENUE-
CONGO

Kagulu→CENTRAL EASTERN BANTU

Kaguru = Kagulu→CENTRAL EASTERN
BANTU

Kah So = So→MON-KHMER

Kahaian = Kahayan. Ngaju D.→WEST INDO-
NESIAN

Kahayan. Ngaju D.→WEST INDONESIAN

Kahchi = Kekchi→MAYAN

Kahe→NORTH EASTERN BANTU

Kahonde = Kaonde→CENTRAL WESTERN
BANTU

Kahosadi. SHASTAN TR.→HOKAN

Kahua→EASTERN OCEANIC

KAHUAPANA = CAHUAPANAN→AN-
DEAN

Kahugu→PLATEAU BENUE-CONGO

Kahung Saraiyoh. Dusun D.→NORTHWEST
AUSTRONESIAN

Kahweya = Cahuilla→UTO-AZTECAN

Kai→NORTHEAST NEW GUINEA AUS-
TRONESIAN

Kai = Kei→MOLUCCAN

Kai Po-mo = Kato→ATHAPASCAN-EYAK

Kaiabara = Kabelbara. Mandandanji D.→
PAMA-MARIC

Kaiabara = Ngoera. Dungidjau D.→WAKA-
KABIC

Kaian = Kayan→BOGIA

Kaibi = Kaivi→PLATEAU BENUE-CONGO

Kaibubu→EAST INDONESIAN

Kaibus→WESTERN NEW GUINEA

Kaidipan→NORTHWEST AUSTRONESIAN

Kaierra = Kariera→NGAYARDA

Kaigani. Haida D.→NA-DENE

Kaikai. Tamil D.→DRAVIDIAN

Kaiku→NORTH EASTERN BANTU

Kaila = Kalya. Quara D.→CUSHITIC

Kaili = Palu→CENTRAL AND SOUTHERN
CELEBES

Kailinya = Kayla. Quara D.→CUSHITIC

Kaima→INDO-PACIFIC

Kainah = Blood. Blackfoot D.→ALGON-
QUIAN

KAINANTU = GADSUP-AUYANA-AWA-
TAIRORA→EAST NEW GUINEA
HIGHLANDS

Kaingbul = Karingbal. Mandandanji D.→
PAMA-MARIC

Kaingua = Kaiwa. Tupi D.→TUPI

Kairi→KIKORI RIVER

Kairi. Mandandanji D.→PAMA-MARIC

Kairi-Kaura. Toaripi D.→TOARIPI

Kairiru→NORTHEAST NEW GUINEA AUS-
TRONESIAN

Kairui→TIMOR-ALOR

Kaitak = Kajtak. Dargwa D.→CAUCASIAN

Kaitero→WESTERN NEW GUINEA

Kaitetu. Ambonese D.→MOLUCCAN

Kaitije = Kaititj→ARANDIC

Kaitish = Kaititj→ARANDIC

Kaititj→ARANDIC

Kaititja = Kaititj→ARANDIC

Kaivi→PLATEAU BENUE-CONGO

Kaiwa→NORTHEAST NEW GUINEA AUS-
TRONESIAN

Kaiwa. Tupi D.→TUPI

Kaiwai = Kuiwai→MOLUCCAN

Kajaakisee = Kajakse. Mubi D.→CHADIC

Kajagise = Kajakse. Mubi D.→CHADIC

Kajaja = Tingal→KORDOFANIAN

Kajakaja→ASMAT

Kajakja = Tingal→KORDOFANIAN

Kajakse. Mubi D.→CHADIC

Kajaman. Ba Mali D.→WEST INDONESIAN

Kajamat = Fogny. Diola D.→WEST AT-
LANTIC

Kajan = Kayan→WEST INDONESIAN

Kajanga. Maba D.→MABAN

Kaje→PLATEAU BENUE-CONGO

Kajeli→EAST INDONESIAN

Kajjara = Birked→EASTERN SUDANIC

Kajji = Kaje→PLATEAU BENUE-CONGO

Kajkavian. Serbocroatian D.→SLAVIC

Kajoa→SOUTH HALMAHERA AUSTRO-
NESIAN

Kajtak. Dargwa D.→CAUCASIAN

Kajumerah→SOUTH HALMAHERA AUS-
TRONESIAN

Kajupulau. Tobati D.→SOUTH HALMAHERA
AUSTRONESIAN

Kajuru→PLATEAU BENUE-CONGO

KAKA→NORTH WESTERN BANTU

Kaka. Gbaya Tr.→EASTERN

Kaka. Pawnee D.→CADDOAN

Kaka = Ashaku→JUKUNOID

Kaka = Kako→NORTH WESTERN BANTU

Kaka = Mbem→BANTOID

Kaka of Sala = Mpompo. Mbimu D.→NORTH
WESTERN BANTU

Kakaa = Kuri. Buduma D.→CHADIC

Kakaba = Kamkam→BANTOID
Kaka-Banjo = Ashaku→JUKUNOID
Kakadju = Kakadu→AUSTRALIAN MACRO-PHYLUM
Kakadu→AUSTRALIAN MACRO-PHYLUM
Kakamega = Isuxa. Luhya D.→NORTH EASTERN BANTU
Kakanda. Nupe D.→NUPE-GBARI
Kakarakala = Inggarda→KARDU
Kakari. Gujarati D.→INDIC
Ka ?kas-Remboken. Tondano D.→NORTH-ERN CELEBES
Kakatio→NORTHWESTERN AND CEN-TRAL SOLOMONS
Kakchi = Kekchi→MAYAN
Kakelewa. Luhya D.→NORTH EASTERN BANTU
Kakhetian = Kaxetian. Georgian D.→CAUCA-SIAN
Kakia. ŋ/amani D.→KHOISAN
Kako→NORTH WESTERN BANTU
Kakomoloroij = Muluridji. Wakaman D.→PAMA-MARIC
ka-Kongo = Western Kongo. Kongo D.→CENTRAL WESTERN BANTU
Kakoongo = Western Kongo. Kongo D.→CENTRAL WESTERN BANTU
Kakua = Kakwa. Bari D.→EASTERN SU-DANIC
Kakumega = Isuxa. Luhya D.→NORTH EASTERN BANTU
Kakumo→CENTRAL AKOKO
Kakuna = Mamusi→BISMARCK ARCHIPEL-AGO
Kakuya Bushman. Nama D.→KHOISAN
Kakwa. Bari D.→EASTERN SUDANIC
Kak-wits = Wailaki→ATHAPASCAN-EYAK
Kala = Bukala. Mongo-Nkundo D.→NORTH WESTERN BANTU
Kala Agi = Agi. Moru D.→CENTRAL SU-DANIC
Kala Degema = Usokun. Degema D.→EDO
Kala Kadiro Si = Kadiro. Moru D.→CENTRAL SUDANIC
Kala Moru = Moru→CENTRAL SUDANIC
Kalabari. Ijo D.→IJO
Kalabit = Kelabit. Sarawak Murut D.→WEST INDONESIAN
KALABRA→WESTERN NEW GUINEA
Kalabra→WESTERN NEW GUINEA
Kalagan = Tagakaolo→NORTHWEST AUS-TRONESIAN
Kalagua. Kalinga D.→NORTHWEST AUS-TRONESIAN

Kalaka. Shona D.→SOUTH EASTERN BANTU
Kalali. Punthamara D.→DIERIC
Kalamai→MIRNINY
Kalamian→NORTHWEST AUSTRONESIAN
Kalana = Kalanga. Shona D.→SOUTH EASTERN BANTU
Kalanapan = Pomo→POMO
Kalanga. Shona D.→SOUTH EASTERN BANTU
Kalanga = Holoholo→NORTH EASTERN BANTU
Kalanga = Kalaka. Shona D.→SOUTH EASTERN BANTU
Kalanguya → NORTHWEST AUSTRONE-SIAN
Kalaŋa = Kalanga. Shona D.→SOUTH EASTERN BANTU
Kalaotoa. Tukangbesi D.→CENTRAL AND SOUTHERN CELEBES
Kalapooiah = Santiam→KALAPUYA
KALAPOOIAN = KALAPUYA
KALAPUYA see article
Kalarko. Mirning D.→MIRNINY
Kalasa→INDIC
Kalasa-ala→NURISTANI
Kalat Standard. Bhahui D.→DRAVIDIAN
Kalatika = Miami→ALGONQUIAN
Kaldic = Urartaean→HURRIAN
Kalebwe = Luba-Lulua→CENTRAL WEST-ERN BANTU
Kalebwe = Songe→CENTRAL WESTERN BANTU
Kaleri = Horom→PLATEAU BENUE-CONGO
Kaleri=Mabo→PLATEAU BENUE-CONGO
Kaleung→MON-KHMER
Kali. Bipi D.→ADMIRALTY-WESTERN ISLANDS
Kali. Lawangan D.→WEST INDONESIAN
Kali = Kari→ADAMAWA
Kaliai→NORTHEAST NEW GUINEA AUS-TRONESIAN
Kalibal. Kitabal D.→BANDJALANGIC
Kalibamu→PAMA-NYUNGAN
Kalibong = Murzu→EASTERN SUDANIC
Kalibugan = Ati→NORTHWEST AUSTRO-NESIAN
Kalige = Feroge→EASTERN
Kaligi = Feroge→EASTERN
Kalike = Feroge→EASTERN
Kaliki = Feroge→EASTERN
Kaliko→CENTRAL SUDANIC
Kaliko→NORTHEASTERN NEW GUINEA

KALINGA→NORTHWEST AUSTRONE-SIAN
Kalinga→NORTHWEST AUSTRONESIAN
Kalinin = Tver. Karelian D.→URALIC
Kalispel→SALISH
Kalispelm = Kalispel→SALISH
Kalisteno = Cree→ALGONQUIAN
Kalkadung = Kalkutung→PAMA-NYUNGAN
Kalkatungu = Kalkutung→PAMA-NYUNGAN
Kalkutung→PAMA-NYUNGAN
Kallana = Alawa→MARAN
Kall-basava. Sinhalese D.→INDIC
Kalmyk. Oirat D.→MONGOLIAN
Kalo. Nkutu D.→NORTH WESTERN BAN-TU
Kalokalo→PAPUA AUSTRONESIAN
Kalongo. Bambara D.→MANDE
Kalop. Koho D.→MON-KHMER
Kalp-→TORRICELLI
Kalto = Nahali
Kaluiwa. Abui D.→TIMOR-ALOR
Kalunka = Kalongo. Bambara D.→MANDE
Kam-→ADAMAWA
Kam→KAM-TAI
Kama = Karaboro→GUR
KAMAKAN = CAMACAN→CAMACAN
Kamalarai = Kamilaroi→WIRADJURIC
Kaman Mishmi = Miju Mishmi→GYARUNG-MISHMI
Kamang. Abui D.→TIMOR-ALOR
Kamanga. Tumbuka D.→CENTRAL EAST-ERN BANTU
Kamanidi = Ingassana→CHARI-NILE
KAMANO→EAST NEW GUINEA HIGH-LANDS
Kamano→EAST NEW GUINEA HIGH-LANDS
Kamantan→PLATEAU BENUE-CONGO
Kamanton = Kamantan→PLATEAU BENUE-CONGO
Kamari. Oriya D.→INDIC
Kamariang→EAST INDONESIAN
Kamartani = Tid. Tirma D.→EASTERN SU-DANIC
Kamas. Sayan Samoyed D.→URALIC
Kamasa→KUKUKUKU
Kamasaya = Tuken. Nandi D.→EASTERN SUDANIC
Kamasia = Tuken. Nandi D.→EASTERN SUDANIC
Kamassian. Khakas D.→TURKIC
Kamayira = Kamayura→TUPI
Kamayura→TUPI
Kamba→NORTH EASTERN BANTU

Kambaira→EAST NEW GUINEA HIGH-LANDS
Kambali = Kambari→PLATEAU BENUE-CONGO
Kambara = Kabena. Alaba D.→CUSHITIC
KAMBARI→PLATEAU BENUE-CONGO
Kambari→PLATEAU BENUE-CONGO
Kambatta = Kembata. Alaba D.→CUSHITIC
Kambera. Sumba D.→MOLUCCAN
Kamberataro→NORTH NEW GUINEA
Kamberawa = Kambari→PLATEAU BENUE-CONGO
Kamberchi = Kambari→PLATEAU BENUE-CONGO
Kamberi = Kambari→PLATEAU BENUE-CONGO
Kamberi Beri-Beri = Busa→MANDE
Kamberri = Kambari→PLATEAU BENUE-CONGO
Kambesi→GOILALA
Kambia. Wahgi D.→EAST NEW GUINEA HIGHLANDS
Kamboi Ramboi = Koassa→MOMBERAMO RIVER
Kambonsenga = Ambo. Lala D.→CENTRAL EASTERN BANTU
Kambot→BOGIA
Kambrau = Iria→ASMAT
Kamburwama. Mandara Tr.→CHADIC
Kambuwal. Giabal D.→GIABALIC
Kamchadal→CHUKCHEE-KAMCHATKAN
Kamdang. Tulishi D.→KORDOFANIAN
Kamdhue = Kandju→PAMA-MARIC
Kamecak = Sapiny. Nandi D.→EASTERN SUDANIC
Kamenskij. Koryak D.→CHUKCHEE-KAM-CHATKAN
Kamer. Numfor D.→MOLUCCAN
Kameraigal. Gandangara D.→YUIN-KURIC
Kamhau→NAGA-KUKI-CHIN
Kamhow = Kamhau→NAGA-KUKI-CHIN
Kami→CENTRAL EASTERN BANTU
Kamilarai = Kamilaroi→WIRADJURIC
Kamilaroi→WIRADJURIC
Kamilroi = Kamilaroi→WIRADJURIC
Kamir = Khamir→CUSHITIC
Kamiri = Miri→KORDOFANIAN
/kamka!e = /xam→KHOISAN
Kamkam→BANTOID
Kammatwa. SHASTAN TR.→HOKAN
Kammyang = Northern Thai→KAM-TAI
Kamnigan. Khalkha D.→MONGOLIAN
Kamnum = Autu→SEPIK
Kamor. Warat D.→DALY

KAMORO = ASMAT
Kamoro→ASMAT
Kamorta = Camorta. Central Nicobarese D.→
  NICOBARESE
Kampong Baru→WESTERN NEW GUINEA
Kamrang→MON-KHMER
Kamrau = Iria→ASMAT
KAM-SUI→KAM-TAI
KAM-TAI see article
Kamtuk→NORTH PAPUAN
Kamu→ADAMAWA
Kamuke. Limba D.→WEST ATLANTIC
Kamuku→PLATEAU BENUE-CONGO
Kamum = Higi→CHADIC
Kamviri. Kati D.→NURISTANI
Kan→CHINESE
Kana = Khana→CROSS RIVER BENUE-
  CONGO
Kanabu = Kanakanabu→FORMOSAN AUS-
  TRONESIAN
Kanagu. Puyuma D.→FORMOSAN AUSTRO-
  NESIAN
Kanakanabu→FORMOSAN AUSTRONE-
  SIAN
Kanakanavu = Kanakanabu→FORMOSAN
  AUSTRONESIAN
Kanakhoe = G//ana→KHOISAN
Kanakuru→CHADIC
Kanala = Hameha→NEW CALEDONIA
Kanalu = Komalu→BISMARCK ARCHIPEL-
  AGO
Kanam. Thebor D.→GYARUNG-MISHMI
Kanamara→DAGA
Kanamari = Canamari→MAIPURAN
Kanambukanambu = Kanembu→SAHARAN
Kanandede. Sa'dan D.→CENTRAL AND
  SOUTHERN CELEBES
Kanandjoho. Minduumo D.→NORTH WEST-
  ERN BANTU
Kanapit→BISMARCK ARCHIPELAGO
Kanarese = Kannada→DRAVIDIAN
Kanashi→GYARUNG-MISHMI
Kanasi = Kanashi→GYARUNG-MISHMI
Kanauji. Western Hindi D.→INDIC
Kanauri = Kanawari→GYARUNG-MISHMI
Kanawari→GYARUNG-MISHMI
Kanawi = Kanawari→GYARUNG-MISHMI
Kanda = Ga'anda→CHADIC
Kanda = Kui→DRAVIDIAN
Kandahari. Pashto D.→IRANIAN
Kandam→OK
Kandawire. Tumbuka D.→CENTRAL EAST-
  ERN BANTU
Kandawo. Narak D.→EAST NEW GUINEA

HIGHLANDS
Kande→NORTH WESTERN BANTU
Kandep. Enga D.→EAST NEW GUINEA
  HIGHLANDS
Kandere. Senari D.→GUR
Kanderma = Kinderma. Tira Tr.→KORDO-
  FANIAN
Kandi. Bargu D.→GUR
Kandju→PAMA-MARIC
Kandomin = Yagawak→HUON-FINISTERRE
Kandoshi = Candoshi→JIVAROAN
Kandyu = Kandju→PAMA-MARIC
Kaneang. Juat D.→SOUTHWEST PAMA-
  NYUNGAN
Kanembu→SAHARAN
Kanembu. Kanuri Tr.→SAHARAN
Kanga→KORDOFANIAN
Kanga Bono. Kweni D.→MANDE
Kangable = Tagbana→GUR
Kangana. Losengo D.→NORTH WESTERN
  BANTU
Kangeju = Hatsa→KHOISAN
Kangianermiut. Inuit D.→ESKIMO-ALEUT
Kangite = Ipurina→MAIPURAN
K'ang-lo. Pao-an D.→MONGOLIAN
Kango→NORTH WESTERN BANTU
Kangsiangying→BURMESE-LOLO
Kangtewu. Pipikoro D.→CENTRAL AND
  SOUTHERN CELEBES
Kangula. Wadja D.→WAKA-KABIC
Kangulu. Mandandanji D.→PAMA-MARIC
Kanhobal = Kanjobal→MAYAN
KANHOBALAN = KANJOBALAN→MA-
  YAN
Kanhow = Kamhau→NAGA-KUKI-CHIN
Kanigurami. Ormuri D.→IRANIAN
Kanikwum = Kaninkwom→PLATEAU BE-
  NUE-CONGO
Kaningkom = Kaninkwom→PLATEAU BE-
  NUE-CONGO
Kaningra→SEPIK
Kaninkon = Kaninkwom→PLATEAU
  BENUE-CONGO
Kaninkwom→PLATEAU BENUE-CONGO
Kanioka = Kanyoka→CENTRAL WESTERN
  BANTU
Kanite. Kamano D.→EAST NEW GUINEA
  HIGHLANDS
Kanjago = Buli→GUR
Kanjimata = Adnyamathana. Wailpi D.→
  YURA
ka-Njiniŋi = Njiniŋi. North Teke D.→NORTH
  WESTERN BANTU
Kanjobal→MAYAN

KANJOBALAN→MAYAN
Kanju = Kandju→PAMA-MARIC
Kankanai = Kankanay→NORTHWEST AUS-
TRONESIAN
Kankanay→NORTHWEST AUSTRONESIAN
Kankena. Kanembu Tr.→SAHARAN
Kanku. Kanembu Tr.→SAHARAN
Kannada→DRAVIDIAN
Kanoe – Guarategaya→TUPI
Kanoloo = Kangulu. Mandandanji D.→PAMA-
MARIC
Kanoreunu Skadd — Kanawari→GYARUNG-
MISHMI
Kanorug Skadd = Kanawari→GYARUNG-
MISHMI
Kanowit. Melanau D.→WEST INDONESIAN
Kansa. Dhegiha D.→SIOUAN
Kantanawa. Mama D.→BANTOID
Kantilan. Sebuano D.→NORTHWEST AUS-
TRONESIAN
Kantju = Kandju→PAMA-MARIC
Kantsii = Hlota→NAGA-KUKI-CHIN
Kantu→MON-KHMER
Kantua = Taoih→MON-KHMER
Ka.ntyu = Kandju→PAMA-MARIC
Kanufi. Kaninkwom D.→PLATEAU BENUE-
CONGO
Kanum→FREDERIK HENDRIK IS. AND SE
WEST IRIAN
Kanung = Rawang→BODO-NAGA-KACHIN
Kanuri→SAHARAN
KANYARA see article
Kanyawali. Maiya D.→INDIC
Kanyoka→CENTRAL WESTERN BANTU
Kanyop = Manjaku→WEST ATLANTIC
Kanyu = Kandju→PAMA-MARIC
Kao = Katu→MON-KHMER
Kao = Kau. Fungor Tr.→KORDOFANIAN
Kao Lei. Cantonese D.→CHINESE
Kaombal = Kambuwal. Giabal D.→GIABALIC
Kaombal = Koamu. Mandandanji D.→PAMA-
MARIC
Kaonde→CENTRAL WEST BANTU
Kapaheni = Capachene→TACANA
Ka-paiwan-an = Shimopaiwan. Paiwan D.→
FORMOSAN AUSTRONESIAN
Kapaiwanan = Shimopaiwan. Paiwan D.→
FORMOSAN AUSTRONESIAN
Kapampangan = Pampangan→NORTHWEST
AUSTRONESIAN
Kapanawa = Capanahua→PANO
Kapangan. Kankanay D.→NORTHWEST
AUSTRONESIAN
Kapau→KUKUKUKU

Kapauku→WEST NEW GUINEA HIGH-
LANDS
KAPAUKU-BALIEM = WEST NEW GUIN-
EA HIGHLANDS
Kapaur = Iha→WESTERN NEW GUINEA
KAPEITA = Murle→EASTERN SUDANIC
Kapeta = Murle→EASTERN SUDANIC
Kapiangan = Kapiyan. Paiwan D.→FORMO-
SAN AUSTRONESIAN
Kapingamarangi→POLYNESIAN
Kapiyan. Paiwan D.→FORMOSAN AUSTRO-
NESIAN
Kapo. Bakwe Tr.→KRU
Kapo. Ndrosun D.→ADMIRALTY-WEST-
ERN ISLANDS
Kapone. Kwenyi D.→NEW CALEDONIA
Kapontori. Muna D.→CENTRAL AND
SOUTHERN CELEBES
Kapore→NORTHEAST NEW GUINEA
AUSTRONESIAN
Kapriman→SEPIK
Kapsiki. Higi D.→CHADIC
Kapsiki = Higi→CHADIC
KAPU→PAMA-MARIC
Kapucha = Bezhita→CAUCASIAN
Kapugu = Kahugu→PLATEAU BENUE
CONGO
Kaputiei. Maasai Tr.→EASTERN SUDANIC
Kapwi→NAGA-KUKI-CHIN
KARA→CENTRAL SUDANIC
Kara→CENTRAL SUDANIC
Kara. Kerebe D.→NORTH EASTERN BANTU
Karabachich = Tid. Tirma D.→EASTERN
SUDANIC
Karaboro→GUR
Karachay→TURKIC
Karadhari = Karadjeri→MARNGU
Karadjeri→MARNGU
KARADZA = CARAJA
Karadza = Caraja→CARAJA
Karagan. Land Dayak D.→WEST INDO-
NESIAN
Karagas. Sayan Samoyed D.→URALIC
Karagas = Tofa→TURKIC
Karaginskij. Alutor D.→CHUKCHEE-
KAMCHATKAN
Karagwe. Nyambo D.→NORTH EASTERN
BANTU
Karaho = Caraho→GE
Karaiai = Anem→NEW BRITAIN
Karaim→TURKIC
Karakalpak→TURKIC
Karakelong. Talaud D.→HESPERONESIAN
Karakh = Karax. Avar D.→CAUCASIAN

Karakitang. Sangir D.→HESPERONESIAN
KARAM→EAST NEW GUINEA HIGH-
    LANDS
Karam→EAST NEW GUINEA HIGHLANDS
Karama = Karaboro→GUR
Karama = Kurama→NGYARDA
Karamanli. Balkan Gagauz Turkish D.→
    TURKIC
Karamba-Kambegl = Maring→EAST NEW
    GUINEA HIGHLANDS
Karami→CENTRAL AND SOUTH NEW
    GUINEA
Karamojong→EASTERN SUDANIC
Karan = Krahn→KRU
Karang = Angas→CHADIC
Karanga→MABAN
Karanga→SOUTH EASTERN BANTU
Karanga. Mansaka D.→NORTHWEST AUS-
    TRONESIAN
Karangi→HUON-FINISTERRE
Karang-Ma = Angas→CHADIC
Karangura = Karanguru. Dieri D.→DIERIC
Karanguru. Dieri D.→DIERIC
Karanja = Karanya. Wangkadjera D.→PITTA-
    PITTIC
Karankawa see article
Kara-Nogai. Nagoi D.→TURKIC
Karanti→PAMA-NYUNGAN
Karanya. Wangkadjera D.→PITTAPITTIC
Karaŋa = Karanga→SOUTH EASTERN
    BANTU
Karas→WESTERN NEW GUINEA
Karata→CAUCASIAN
Karau. Lawangan D.→WEST INDONESIAN
Karawa→KARWAN
Karawa→SEPIK
Karawala = Karuwali. Karendala D.→DIE-
    RIC
KARAWAN = KARWAN
Karax. Avar D.→CAUCASIAN
KARAYA = CARAJA
Karaya = Caraja→CARAJA
Karbi = Kabikabi. Dalla D.→WAKA-KABIC
Karbo→CHADIC
Karda. Kanuri Tr.→SAHARAN
Karda. Tebu Tr.→SAHARAN
Karda = Kreda. Tebu Tr.→SAHARAN
Kardagur = Wardandi. Juat D.→SOUTHWEST
    PAMA-NYUNGAN
KARDU see article
Kardutjara→WATI
Kare→BOGIA
Kare = Creg. Hre D.→MON-KHMER
Kare = Kari→ADAMAWA

Kare = Kari→CENTRAL WESTERN BANTU
Kare = Toposo→EASTERN SUDANIC
Karelian→URALIC
Karen, Red = Karrenni. Bwe D.→KAREN
Karen, White = Karenbyu. Bwe D.→KAREN
KAREN see article
Karenbyu. Bwe D.→KAREN
Karendala→DIERIC
Karenggapa→DIERIC
Kareovan. Kavalan D.→FORMOSAN AUS-
    TRONESIAN
KARI→CENTRAL WESTERN BANTU
Kari→ADAMAWA
Kari→CENTRAL WESTERN BANTU
Kariera→NGAYARDA
Karigari→CENTRAL AND SOUTH NEW
    GUINEA
Kariko = Tonkawa→MACRO-ALGON-
    QUIAN
Karim. Chomo D.→JUKUNOID
Karima→KIKORI RIVER
Karin = Kureinji. Maraura D.→NARRIN-
    YERIC
Karingbal. Mandandanji D.→PAMA-MARIC
Karingma = Kureinji. Maraura D.→NARRIN-
    YERIC
Karinma = Kureinji. Maraura D.→NARRIN-
    YERIC
Karintsu. Enga D.→EAST NEW GUINEA
    HIGHLANDS
Kariphuna = Island Carib→NORTHERN MAI-
    PURAN
Karitiana→TUPI
Karkadoo = Kakadu→AUSTRALIAN MAC-
    RO-PHYLUM
Karkar = Nyakinyaki. Juat D.→SOUTHWEST
    PAMA-NYUNGAN
Karkin→MIWOK-COSTANOAN
Karko. Kordofanian Nubian Tr.→EASTERN
    SUDANIC
KARLUK = EASTERN TURKIC→TURKIC
Karluko-Chigile-Uighur. Uzbek D.→TURKIC
Karmali. Santali D.→MUNDA
KARNA→DIERIC
Karnju = Kandju→PAMA-MARIC
Karntju = Kandju→PAMA-MARIC
Karnu = Kandju→PAMA-MARIC
Karnyu = Kandju→PAMA-MARIC
Karo→OMOTIC
Karo→PAPUA AUSTRONESIAN
Karo→WEST INDONESIAN
Karo = Vai→MANDE
Karok→HOKAN
Karoka. Katla D.→KORDOFANIAN

Karomba. Shona D.→SOUTH EASTERN
BANTU
Karompa. Tukangbesi D.→CENTRAL AND
SOUTHERN CELEBES
Karon→WEST ATLANTIC
Karon→WESTERN NEW GUINEA
Karondi = Kurondi. Tumtum Tr.→KORDO-
FANIAN
Karongsi. Mori D.→CENTRAL AND SOUTH-
ERN CELEBES
Karorinje = Karuwali. Karendala D.→DIERIC
Karra = Kreda. Tebu Tr.→SAHARAN
Karraba = Baraparapa→YOTAYOTIC
Karranbal = Karingbal. Mandandanji   D.→
PAMA-MARIC
Karrawar = Karawa→KARWAN
Karre = Kari→ADAMAWA
Karrengappa = Karenggapa→DIERIC
Karrennet. Bwe D.→KAREN
Karrenni. Bwe D.→KAREN
Karriria = Kariera→NGAYARDA
Karriarra = Kariera→NGAYARDA
Kartlian. Georgian D.→CAUCASIAN
KARTVELIAN→CAUCASIAN
Karua→NORTHEAST NEW GUINEA AUS-
TRONESIAN
Karualaig = Kaurareg→MABUIAGIC
Karuk = Karok→HOKAN
Karukaru→KOIARI
Karukawa. Karok D.→HOKAN
Karuwali. Karendala D.→DIERIC
Karwa = Karawa→KARWAN
KARWAN see article
Kasa. Diola D.→WEST ATLANTIC
Kasa. Masenrempulu D.→CENTRAL AND
SOUTHERN CELEBES
Kasai = Luba-Kasai. Luba-Lulua D.→CEN-
TRAL WESTERN BANTU
Kasanga→WEST ATLANTIC
Kasava. Tamil D.→DRAVIDIAN
Kaschemere = Kashmere. Maba Tr.→MABAN
Kasele. Tobote D.→GUR
Kasem→GUR
Kasena = Kasem→GUR
Kasene = Kasem→GUR
Kasere→KIKORI RIVER
Kasha = Kucha. Walamo D.→OMOTIC
Kashani. Persian D.→IRANIAN
Kashaya = Southwestern Pomo→POMO
Kasherda = Kashirda. Tebu Tr.→SAHARAN
Kashgar-Yarkend. Uighur D.→TURKIC
Kashirda. Tebu Tr.→SAHARAN
Kashmere. Maba Tr.→MABAN
Kashmeree = Kashmere. Maba Tr.→MABAN

Kashubian→SLAVIC
Kasiboti — Kazibati→EASTERN
Kasieh. Tala D.→EAST INDONESIAN
Kasimbar→NORTHERN CELEBES
Kasimov-Tatar. Tatar D.→TURKIC
Kasira→SOUTH HALMAHERA AUSTRO-
NESIAN
Kasiui. Geser D.→EAST INDONESIAN
Kaska. Tahltan D.→ATHAPASCAN-EYAK
Kaskaskia — Illinois. Miami D.→ALGON-
QUIAN
Kaskimpo. Koasati D.→MUSKOGEAN
Kasmiri→INDIC
Kasomse = Kasem→GUR
Kassanga = Kasanga→WEST ATLANTIC
Kassele. Tobote D.→GUR
Kassena = Kasem→GUR
Kasseng→MON-KHMER
KASSITE see article
Kasso = Khasonke→MANDE
Kassonke = Khasonke→MANDE
Kastawari. Kasmiri D.→INDIC
Kataang→MON-KHMER
Katab→PLATEAU BENUE-CONGO
Kataba = Catawba→MACRO-SIOUAN
Katahba = Catawba→MACRO-SIOUAN
Katang = Kayong→MON-KHMER
Katar. Tregami D.→NURISTANI
Katata = Kakadu→AUSTRALIAN MACRO-
PHYLUM
Katathoy = Catethoy→CAMACAN
Kata-tipol = Chipon. Puyuma D.→FORMO-
SAN AUSTRONESIAN
Katazi→NORTHWESTERN AND CENTRAL
SOLOMONS
Katcha→KORDOFANIAN
Katchal. Central Nicobarese D.→NICOBARESE
Kate→HUON-FINISTERRE
ka-Tege = Tege-kali. North Teke D.→NORTH
WESTERN BANTU
Kateik. Katla D.→KORDOFANIAN
Katera = Tutelo→SIOUAN
Katəviri. Kati D.→NURISTANI
Kathe = Meithei→NAGA-KUKI-CHIN
Kathiyawadi. Gujarati D.→INDIC
Kathlamet. Upper Chinook D.→CHINOOKAN
Kati→NURISTANI
Kati, Northern→OK
Kati, Southern→OK
Katia = Xatia. ŋ/amani D.→KHOISAN
Katiati→BOGIA
Katin. Ndrosun D.→ADMIRALTY-WEST-
ERN ISLANDS
Katingan→WEST INDONESIAN

Katio = Dabeiba. Northern Epera D.→CHOCO
Katitcha = Kaititj→ARANDIC
Katitja = Kaititj→ARANDIC
Katitya = Kaititj→ARANDIC
Kativa. Ninggirum D.→OK
KATLA→KORDOFANIAN
Katla→KORDOFANIAN
Kato→ATHAPASCAN-EYAK
Katoba = Mambila→BANTOID
Katoguran. Bunun D.→FORMOSAN AUS-
    TRONESIAN
Katongulan = Katoguran. Bunun D.→FOR-
    MOSAN AUSTRONESIAN
Katoratele→NORTHWESTERN AND CEN-
    TRAL SOLOMONS
Katsausan. Puyuma D.→FORMOSAN AUS-
    TRONESIAN
Katshikotin. Han Tr.→ATHAPASCAN-EYAK
Kattang. Worimi D.→YUIN-KURIC
Kattea = Xatia. ŋ/amani D.→KHOISAN
Kattish = Hattic
Katu→MON-KHMER
Katu, High = Kantu→MON-KHMER
KATUIC→MON-KHMER
Katvenua = Lamalanga→EASTERN OCEAN-
    IC
Katzie. Halkomelem D.→SALISH
Ka'u→NORTH HALMAHERA
Kau. Fungor Tr.→KORDOFANIAN
//Kau-//-en = Auen→KHOISAN
//K"au-//en = Auen→KHOISAN
Kauil = Gawigl. Medlpa D.→EAST NEW
    GUINEA HIGHLANDS
Kaukau = Auen→KHOISAN
Kaultits = Cowlitz→SALISH
Kaura = Kaurna. Jadliaura D.→YURA
Kaurareg→MABUIAGIC
Kaure→NORTH PAPUAN
Kauri→BODO-NAGA-KACHIN
Kaurna. Jadliaura D.→YURA
Kauvuya = Cahuilla→UTO-AZTECAN
Kauwerawet→MOMBERAMO RIVER
Kavalan→FORMOSAN AUSTRONESIAN
Kavelchadhom = Kavelchadom. River Yuman
    D.→YUMAN
Kavelchadom. River Yuman D.→YUMAN
Kaveltcadom = Kavelchadom. River Yuman D.
    →YUMAN
Kaviangan = Kapiyan. Paiwan D.→FORMO-
    SAN AUSTRONESIAN
Kavina = Cavinena→TACANA
Kavu→TORRICELLI
Kaw = Akha→BURMESE-LOLO
Kaw = Kosin→BANTOID

Kawa. Sapolewa D.→EAST INDONESIAN
Kawa. Tala D.→EAST INDONESIAN
Kawa = Bukaua→NORTHEAST NEW GUIN-
    EA AUSTRONESIAN
Kawacha→KUKUKU
Kawaib→TUPI
Kawaiisu. Southern Paiute D.→UTO-AZTE-
    CAN
Kawaina. Auyana D.→EAST NEW GUINEA
    HIGHLANDS
Kawaliap. Buyang D.→ADMIRALTY-WEST-
    ERN ISLANDS
Kawalib = Koalib→KORDOFANIAN
Kawama = Otoro→KORDOFANIAN
Kawanga = Hanga. Luhya D.→NORTH EAST-
    ERN BANTU
Kawari = Kamari. Oriya D.→INDIC
Kawarma = Otoro→KORDOFANIAN
Kawa-Yunnan→PALAUNG-WA
Kawchogottine. Dogrib Tr.→ATHAPASCAN-
    EYAK
Kawchottine = Hare. Dogrib Tr.→ATHAPAS-
    CAN-EYAK
Kawel. Abui D.→TIMOR-ALOR
Kawelitsk = Cowlitz→SALISH
Kawia. Foothill North Yokuts D.→YOKUTS
Kawia = Cahuilla→UTO-AZTECAN
Kawol→OK
Kawonde = Kaonde→CENTRAL WESTERN
    BANTU
Kaxetian. Georgian D.→CAUCASIAN
Kaxib. Avar D.→CAUCASIAN
Kaya = Karrenni. Bwe D.→KAREN
Kayabi→TUPI
Kayan→BOGIA
Kayan→WEST INDONESIAN
Kayik→TORRICELLI
Kayin = Sgaw→KAREN
Kayla. Quara D.→CUSHITIC
Kayong→MON-KHMER
Kayor = Cayor. Wolof D.→WEST ATLANTIC
Kayouse = Cayuse→PENUTIAN
Kayowe = Kiowa→TANOAN
Kayubaba = Cayuvava→EQUATORIAL
Kayux = Cayuse→PENUTIAN
Kazakh→TURKIC
Kazan Tatar. Tatar D.→TURKIC
Kazi = Central Tibetan→TIBETAN
Kazibati→EASTERN
Kazik = Kacik. Chulym D.→TURKIC
Kazirauni. Persian D.→IRANIAN
Kazukuru→CENTRAL MELANESIAN
Kæle. Mundang D.→ADAMAWA
K'e = Hakka→CHINESE

Keai = Ro→EAST NEW GUINEA HIGH-
LANDS
Keaka = Edjagam. Ekoi D.→BANTOID
Keaqə = Edjagam. Ekoi D.→BANTOID
Ke-at = Panamint. Shoshoni D.→UTO-AZTE-
CAN
Kebadi = Zaghawa→SAHARAN
Kebanagara→CENTRAL AND SOUTH NEW
GUINEA
Kebau. Sanana D.→EAST INDONESIAN
Kebeirka = Uduk→KOMAN
Kebu→CENTRAL TOGO
Kebu = Ndo Oke'bu. Ndo D.→CENTRAL
SUDANIC
Kebu-tu = Ndo Oke'bu. Ndo D.→CENTRAL
SUDANIC
Kechayi. Foothill North Yokuts D.→YOKUTS
Kecherda = Kashirda. Tebu Tr.→SAHARAN
Kecchi = Qiche→MAYAN
K'echia = Hakka→CHINESE
Kechua = Quechua→ANDEAN
KECHUMARAN = QUECHUMARAN→AN-
DEAN
Ke-da = Oke'bu. Lendu D.→CENTRAL SU-
DANIC
Kedah. Semang Proper D.→SEMANG
ke-Daiso = Daiso→NORTH EASTERN BAN-
TU
Kedamaian. Dusun D.→NORTHWEST AUS-
TRONESIAN
Keddi = Kedi. San D.→KHOISAN
Kede. Great Andamanese D.→ANDAMANESE
Kedero = Kadiro. Moru D.→CENTRAL SU-
DANIC
Kedi. San D.→KHOISAN
Kediru = Kadiro. Moru D.→CENTRAL SU-
DANIC
Keekonyokie. Maasai Tr.→EASTERN SUDAN-
IC
ke-Embo = Embo→NORTH EASTERN BAN-
TU
Keembo. Mbole D.→NORTH EASTERN BAN-
TU
Kefa→OMOTIC
Kefinya = Kefa→OMOTIC
KEFOID→OMOTIC
ke-Gengele = Gengele. Songola D.→NORTH
EASTERN BANTU
Kehelala = Keheraran→PAPUA AUSTRO-
NESIAN
Kehena. Tsakrima D.→NAGA-KUKI-CHIN
Keheraran→PAPUA AUSTRONESIAN
Keh-lao = Kelao→KAM-TAI
Kei→MOLUCCAN

Kei Tanimbar. Kei D.→MOLUCCAN
Keiga→KORDOFANIAN
Keiga Girru = Keiga Jirru→EASTERN SU-
DANIC
Keiga Jirru→EASTERN SUDANIC
Keigana→EAST NEW GUINEA HIGHLANDS
Keijagana Jate = Keigana→EAST NEW GUIN-
EA HIGHLANDS
Keinjan→GIABALIC
Kejaka = Edjagam. Ekoi D.→BANTOID
ke-Kamba = Kamba→NORTH EASTERN
BANTU
Kekar = Kjakela. Oroc D.→TUNGUS
Kekchi→MAYAN
K'ekchi' = Kekchi→MAYAN
KEKCHIAN see MAYAN
Kela→NORTH WESTERN BANTU
Kela = Kelana→NORTHEAST NEW GUIN-
EA AUSTRONESIAN
Kelabit. Sarawak Murut D.→WEST INDONE-
SIAN
Keladdar→FREDERIK HENDRIK IS. AND
SE WEST IRIAN
Kelana→NORTHEAST NEW GUINEA AUS-
TRONESIAN
Kelangi = Langi→NORTH EASTERN BAN-
TU
Kelao→KAM-TAI
Kelawa→PLATEAU BENUE-CONGO
KELE→NORTH WESTERN BANTU
Kele→NORTH WESTERN BANTU
Keleb. Avar D.→CAUCASIAN
ke-Lega = Lega→NORTH EASTERN BAN-
TU
Keliko = Kaliko→CENTRAL SUDANIC
Kelimuri→EAST INDONESIAN
Kelingan = Long Wai. Modang D.→WEST
INDONESIAN
Kelinjau = Long Wai. Modang D.→WEST
INDONESIAN
Keli ŋgan. Maba D.→MABAN
Kellini = Kelawa→PLATEAU BENUE-CON-
GO
Kelong. Abui D.→TIMOR-ALOR
KELTIC = CELTIC
Kemai = Ankwe→CHADIC
Kemak→EAST INDONESIAN
Kemaltu = Tera→CHADIC
Kemant = Qemant. Quara D.→CUSHITIC
Kemba→NORTHEASTERN NEW GUINEA
Kembata. Alaba D.→CUSHITIC
Kembatinya = Kembata. Alaba D.→CUSHITIC
Kemendok = Kureinji. Maraura D.→NAR-
RINYERIC

Kemering = Komering. Lampung D.→WEST INDONESIAN

ke-Mero = Mero→NORTH EASTERN BANTU

Kemiju Jate = Kanite. Kamano D.→EAST NEW GUINEA HIGHLANDS

Kenaboi→JAKUN

Kendari→CENTRAL AND SOUTHERN CELEBES

Kendayan Dayak. Land Dayak D.→WEST INDONESIAN

Kenderong. Northern Sakai D.→SAKAI

Keneloco = Quenoloco→CARIB

Kenering. Northern Sakai D.→SAKAI

Ke-ney→NORTHWEST AUSTRONESIAN

Kenga→CENTRAL SUDANIC

Kenga = Busa→MANDE

Kenge = Kenga→CENTRAL SUDANIC

Keningau. Murut D.→NORTHWEST AUSTRONESIAN

Kenipitu = Barren Grounds Eskimo. Inuit D.→ESKIMO-ALEUT

Kenistenoag = Cree→ALGONQUIAN

Kenja = Kenyah→WEST INDONESIAN

Kenji = Kamuku→PLATEAU BENUE-CONGO

Kenne = Ke-ney→NORTHWEST AUSTRONESIAN

Kensense→BANTOID

Kente. Eregba D.→JUKUNOID

Kentu. Eregba D.→JUKUNOID

Kenuz. Dongola-Kenuz D.→EASTERN SUDANIC

Kenuzi = Kenuz. Dongola-Kenuz D.→EASTERN SUDANIC

Kenya = Kenga→CENTRAL SUDANIC

Kenyah→WEST INDONESIAN

KENYAN-BAHAU-KAYAN→WEST INDONESIAN

Kenyang = Nyang→BANTOID

Kenyi→NORTH EASTERN BANTU

Kenyi. Jaba D.→PLATEAU BENUE-CONGO

Kepere. Kari D.→ADAMAWA

Kepkiriwat→TUPI

Kepo. Boruca D.→CHIBCHAN

Kera?→ADAMAWA

Kera. Mundari D.→MUNDA

Keraki→CENTRAL AND SOUTH NEW GUINEA

Keramai = Giramay. Wakaman D.→PAMA-MARIC

Keramin = Kureinji. Maraura D.→NARRI-NYERIC

Kerang = Angas→CHADIC

Kerari. Macu D.→MACRO-TUCANOAN

Kerbat. Pangan D.→SEMANG

Kerdau. Inner Eastern Sakai D.→SAKAI

Kere. Northern Mao D.→KOMAN

Kerebe→NORTH EASTERN BANTU

Kerebuto→EASTERN OCEANIC

Kerei→EAST INDONESIAN

Kerek→CHUKCHEE-KAMCHATKAN

K'erekhwe. Deti Tr.→KHOISAN

Kerema→TOARIPI

Keremi = Remi→NORTH EASTERN BANTU

Keren. Agul D.→CAUCASIAN

Keres see article

Kerewa. Northern Kiwai D.→CENTRAL AND SOUTH NEW GUINEA

Kerewe = Kerebe→NORTH EASTERN BANTU

Kereyu. Galla D.→CUSHITIC

Keriaka→BOUGAINVILLE

Keribialbarap = Marditjali→KULINIC

Kerinchi = Kerintji→WEST INDONESIAN

Keri-ni = Kelawa→PLATEAU BENUE-CONGO

Kerinma = Kureinji. Maraura D.→NARRINYERIC

Kerintji→WEST INDONESIAN

Kermani. Persian D.→IRANIAN

Kermanji→IRANIAN

Kerre = Karo→OMOTIC

Kertchan = Yuma. River Yuman D.→YUMAN

ke-Senegele = Senegele→NORTH WESTERN BANTU

Kesherda = Kashirda. Tebu Tr.→SAHARAN

Kesikten. Ordos D.→MONGOLIAN

ke-Songola = Songola→NORTH EASTERN BANTU

Kesopo. Lisu D.→BURMESE-LOLO

Kesur = Kasmiri→INDIC

Ket→YENISEIAN

Ket. Ostyak Samoyed D.→URALIC

Ketagalan→FORMOSAN AUSTRONESIAN

Ketanganau = Katoguran. Bunun D.→FORMOSAN AUSTRONESIAN

Kete→CENTRAL WESTERN BANTU

Kete. Akye Tr.→LAGOON

Ketebo = Lokathan. Lotuho D.→EASTERN SUDANIC

Ketebo = Lokathan. Teso D.→EASTERN SUDANIC

Kettle Falls = Colville. Okanogan D.→SALISH

Ketuen = Mbe→BANTOID

Keveri. Bauwaki or Binahari D.→MAILU

Kewa→EAST NEW GUINEA HIGHLANDS

Kewa Pi = Kewa→EAST NEW GUINEA HIGHLANDS

Kewah→EAST NEW GUINEA HIGHLANDS
Kewapi = Kewa→EAST NEW GUINEA HIGHLANDS
Kewieng→HUON-FINISTERRE
Keydnjamarda = Adnyamathana. Wailpi D.→ YURA
Keyo. Nandi D.→EASTERN SUDANIC
Keyu = Keyo. Nandi D.→EASTERN SUDANIC
Keyyek = Keyo. Nandi D.→EASTERN SUDANIC
Keyyo = Keyo. Nandi D.→EASTERN SUDANIC
Kezama = Kezhama. Simi D.→NAGA-KUKI-CHIN
Kezhama. Simi D.→NAGA-KUKI-CHIN
Kəgbərikə = Kebu→CENTRAL TOGO
Kəmantnay = Qemant. Quara D.→CUSHITIC
Kənsen'se = Kensense→BANTOID
Kentɔhe. Balanta D.→WEST ATLANTIC
Kfwetragottine. Dogrib Tr.→ATHAPASCAN-EYAK
Kgaga = Kxaxa. Northern Sotho D.→SOUTH EASTERN BANTU
Kgalagadi. Iswana D.→SOUTH EASTERN BANTU
Kgatla. Tswana D.→SOUTH EASTERN BANTU
Kha = Ka. Banda D.→EASTERN
Kha Doi-luang→KHMUIC
Kha Doy = Kha Doi-luang→KHMUIC
Kha Kon-tu→KHMUIC
Kha Kwang-Lim→KHMUIC
Kha Lamet = Lamet→KHMUIC
Kha Lung = Kaleung→MON-KHMER
Kha Puhoc = Puoc→KHUMIC
Kha Tampuon = Campuon→MON-KHMER
Kha Tong Luong = Tong-luang→KHMUIC
Khabenapo = Pomo→POMO
Khaidak. Kumyk D.→TURKIC
Khajuna = Burushaski
Khakas→TURKIC
Khalahadi = Kgalagadi. Tswana D.→SOUTH EASTERN BANTU
Khalci-guor. Mongour D.→MONGOLIAN
Khaldean = Urartaean→HURRIAN
Khaling→GYARUNG-MISHMI
Khalkha→MONGOLIAN
Kham. West Tibetan D.→TIBETAN
Khambana. Tswa D.→SOUTH EASTERN BANTU
Khambu→GYARUNG-MISHMI
Khamed→PALAUNG-WA
Khamenboran = Kuy→MON-KHMER

Khami→NAGA-KUKI-CHIN
Khamir→CUSHITIC
Khamit = Khamir→CUSHITIC
/kham-ka- ! k'e = /xam→KHOISAN
Khampti = Khamti→KAM-TAI
Khampti Sam = Khamti→KAM-TAI
Khams = Kham. West Tibetan D.→TIBETAN
Khams-yal = Kham. West Tibetan D.→TIBETAN
Khamta. Khamir D.→CUSHITIC
Khamti→KAM-TAI
Khamuk = Khmu'→KHMUIC
Khana→CROSS RIVER BENUE-CONGO
Khana = Pomo→POMO
Khanag. Tabasaran D.→CAUCASIAN
Khandesi→INDIC
Khang. Khmu' D.→KHMUIC
Khang = Chingpaw→BODO-NAGA-KACHIN
Khang = Kangulu. Wadja D.→WAKA-KABIC
Khang Ai = Khang. Khmu' D.→KHMUIC
Khang Clau = Khang. Khmu' D.→KHMUIC
Khangin. Ordos D.→MONGOLIAN
Khangoi = Khunggoi→NAGA-KUKI-CHIN
Khao = Khang. Khmu' D.→KHMUIC
Khaput = Xaput. Kryts D.→CAUCASIAN
Khararya = Kairi. Mandandanji D.→PAMA-MARIC
Kharbin. Khorcin D.→MONGOLIAN
Kharcin. Khorcin D.→MONGOLIAN
Khari→NAGA-KUKI-CHIN
Kharia→MUNDA
Kharia Thar. Bengali D.→INDIC
Khari-boli = Western Hindi→INDIC
Kharwa. Gujarati D.→INDIC
Kharwar. Bihari D.→INDIC
Khas Kura = Nepali→INDIC
Khasarli. Turkmen D.→TURKIC
Khasav-Yurt. Kumyk D.→TURKIC
Khasi→MON-KHMER
Khasia = Khasi→MON-KHMER
Khaskhong→BURMESE-LOLO
Khasonke→MANDE
Khassa = Tiger→SEMITIC
Khassee = Khasi→MON-KHMER
Khat = Katu→MON-KHMER
Khatahi. Chhattisgarhi. Eastern Hindi D.→ INDIC
Khatahoi = Taoih→MON-KHMER
Khatia = Xatia. ŋ/amani D.→KHOISAN
Khatla = Kgatla. Tswana D.→SOUTH EASTERN BANTU
Khattish = Hattic
Khauri = Kauri→BODO-NAGA-KACHIN

Khayo = Xaayo. Luhya D.→NORTH EAST-
ERN BANTU

Khemsing. Tangsa D.→BODO-NAGA-KA-
CHIN

≠Khessakhoe→KHOISAN

Khevsur = Xevsur. Georgian D.→CAUCA-
SIAN

khi-Lubedu = Lobedu. Northern Sotho D.→
SOUTH EASTERN BANTU

Khimi = Khami→NAGA-KUKI-CHIN

Khinalug = Xinalug→CAUCASIAN

Khmer→MON-KHMER

Khmer, Old = Kuy→MON-KHMER

Khmous = Khmu'→KHMUIC

Khmu'→KHMUIC

KHMUIC see article

Khmus = Khmu'→KHMUIC

Khoany, Black→BURMESE-LOLO

Khoany, White→BURMESE-LOLO

Khoi→MON-KHMER

Khoibu→NAGA-KUKI-CHIN

Khoirao. Kabiu D.→NAGA-KUKI-CHIN

KHOISAN see article

Khoke = Koke→ADAMAWA

≠Khomani. ŋ/huki D.→KHOISAN

Khond = Kui→DRAVIDIAN

Khondi = Kui→DRAVIDIAN

Khorasani. Persian D.→IRANIAN

Khorcin→MONGOLIAN

Khori. Buryat D.→MONGOLIAN

Khotanese→IRANIAN

Khotan-Kerya. Uighur D.→TURKIC

Khotla = Bhojpuri. Bihari D.→INDIC

Khoton→TURKIC

Khotta. Bihari D.→INDIC

Khowar→INDIC

Khua. Bru D.→MON-KHMER

Khualringklang→NAGA-KUKI-CHIN

Khucit. Ordos D.→MONGOLIAN

Khuen = Kven→KHMUIC

Khugni = Shughni→IRANIAN

Khumbi→SOUTH WESTERN BANTU

Khumi = Khami→NAGA-KUKI-CHIN

Khumi = Toposo→EASTERN SUDANIC

Khun→KAM-TAI

Khungabula = Kongabula. Mandandanji D.→
PAMA-MARIC

Khunggoi→NAGA-KUKI-CHIN

Khunzakh = Xunzax. Avar D.→CAUCASIAN

Khurrian = Hurri→HURRIAN

Khutswe. Northern Sotho D.→SOUTH EAST-
ERN BANTU

Khutswi = Khutswe. Northern Sotho D.→
SOUTH EASTERN BANTU

Khutu = Kutu→CENTRAL EASTERN BAN-
TU

Khvarshi = Xvarshi→CAUCASIAN

Khvek = Kravet→MON-KHMER

Khwanh = Kuanh. Eastern Mnong D.→MON-
KHMER

Khwarizmian→IRANIAN

KHWE-KOVAB = CENTRAL S. AFRICAN
KHOISAN→KHOISAN

Khweymi = Khami→NAGA-KUKI-CHIN

Khyang = Aso→NAGA-KUKI-CHIN

Kia→NORTHWESTERN AND CENTRAL
SOLOMONS

Kia = Gia. Mandandanji D.→PAMA-MARIC

Kiakh. Circassian D.→CAUCASIAN

Kiama = Kyama→LAGOON

Kiamba. Tagabili D.→NORTHWEST AUS-
TRONESIAN

Kiamerop→NORTH PAPUAN

Kiangan→NORTHWEST AUSTRONESIAN

Kiaokio→BURMESE-LOLO

Kiapoo = Kikapoo. Fox D.→ALGONQUIAN

Kiari. Nomane D.→EAST NEW GUINEA
HIGHLANDS

Kiau. Dusun D.→NORTHWEST AUSTRO-
NESIAN

Kiaway = Kiowa→TANOAN

Kibaku = Chibak→CHADIC

Kibala→CENTRAL WESTERN BANTU

Kiballo→PLATEAU BENUE-CONGO

ki-Bangubangu = Bangobango→NORTH
EASTERN BANTU

Kibbo = Birom→PLATEAU BENUE-CONGO

ki-Beembe = Bembe→CENTRAL WESTERN
BANTU

Kibene→KIKORI RIVER

Kiberi = Kibiri→KIKORI RIVER

Kibet→EASTERN SUDANIC

Kibi. Ami D.→FORMOSAN AUSTRONE-
SIAN

ki-Bila = Bila→NORTH EASTERN BANTU

Kibinsa = Mbinsa. Kongo D.→CENTRAL
WESTERN BANTU

Kibira = Amba→NORTH EASTERN BANTU

Kibira = Plains Bira. Bira D.→NORTH EAST-
ERN BANTU

Kibiri→KIKORI RIVER

Kibissi = Dogon→GUR

Kibo = Birom→PLATEAU BENUE-CONGO

ki-Boma = Boma→NORTH WESTERN BAN-
TU

ki-Bondei = Bondei→CENTRAL EASTERN
BANTU

Kibuli→AGOB

Kibungan. Kankanay D.→NORTHWEST AUS-
TRONESIAN
ki-Buyu = Buyu. Bangobango D.→NORTH
EASTERN BANTU
ki-Bweende = Bwende. Kongo D.→CENTRAL
WESTERN BANTU
Kibyen = Birom→PLATEAU BENUE-CON-
GO
Kichai = Kitsai→CADDOAN
Kichai = Qiche→MAYAN
Kiche = Qiche→MAYAN
Kichepo = Suri. Tirma D.→EASTERN SU-
DANIC
Kickapoo = Kikapoo. Fox D.→ALGON-
QUIAN
Kidabal = Kitabal→BANDJALANGIC
ki-Dabida = Dabida. Taita D.→NORTH EAST-
ERN BANTU
Kiddu. Katla D.→KORDOFANIAN
Kidhaiso = Daiso→NORTH EASTERN BAN-
TU
Kidie = Lafofa→KORDOFANIAN
ki-Digo = Digo→NORTH EASTERN BANTU
ki-Djia = Djia. Sakata D.→NORTH WEST-
ERN BANTU
ki-Doondo = Doondo. Kongo D.→CENTRAL
WESTERN BANTU
Kidzem = Kidzom→BANTOID
Kidzom→BANTOID
Kiefo = Tiefo→GUR
ki-Embu = Embo→NORTH EASTERN BAN-
TU
Kien = Tchien. Krahn Tr.→KRU
Kiga. Ruanda D.→NORTH EASTERN BANTU
Kiga = Ciga→NORTH EASTERN BANTU
Kiga = Tshiga. Ruanda D.→NORTH EAST-
ERN BANTU
ki-Gaangala = Gaangala. Kongo D.→CEN-
TRAL WESTERN BANTU
Kigavamenti. Swahili D.→CENTRAL EAST-
ERN BANTU
Kigille = Kusigilo. Central Koma D.→KOMAN
ki-Gweno = Gweno→NORTH EASTERN
BANTU
ki-Hai = Hai. Caga D.→NORTH EASTERN
BANTU
Ki/hazi. ŋ/amani D.→KHOISAN
ki-Hemba = Hemba→CENTRAL WESTERN
BANTU
Kihindi. Swahili D.→CENTRAL EASTERN
BANTU
ki-Holo = Hungu→CENTRAL WESTERN
BANTU
ki-Horohoro = Holoholo→NORTH EASTERN
BANTU

ki-Hunde = Hunde→NORTH EASTERN
BANTU
ki-Hungana = Hungana→CENTRAL WEST-
ERN BANTU
ki-Hyanzi = Hyanzi. Amba D.→NORTH EAST-
ERN BANTU
Kij = Gabrieleno→UTO-AZTECAN
ki-Kaamba = Kaamba. Kongo D.→CENTRAL
WESTERN BANTU
ki-Kaanu = Kaanu→NORTH EASTERN
BANTU
Kikamba = Kamba→NORTH EASTERN
BANTU
ki-Kami = Kami→CENTRAL EASTERN
BANTU
ki-Kaonde = Kaonde→CENTRAL WESTERN
BANTU
Kikapoo. Fox D.→ALGONQUIAN
Kikapu = Kikapoo. Fox D.→ALGONQUIAN
Kikct = Upper Chinook→CHINOOKAN
Kikete = Kete → CENTRAL WESTERN
BANTU
Kikima = Halyikwamai. Delta River Yuman
D.→YUMAN
ki-Kimbu = Kimbu→NORTH EASTERN
BANTU
Kikitamar = Kitanemuk. Serrano D.→UTO-
AZTECAN
Kikitanum = Kitanemuk. Serrano D.→UTO-
AZTECAN
KIKIYU-KAMBA→NORTH EASTERN
BANTU
Kikkapoe = Kikapoo. Fox D.→ALGON-
QUIAN
Kikkar = Nyakinyaki. Juat D.→SOUTHWEST
PAMA-NYUNGAN
KIKONGO→CENTRAL WESTERN BANTU
Kikongo = Central Kongo. Kongo D.→CEN-
TRAL WESTERN BANTU
ki-Koongo = Northeastern Kongo. Kongo D.→
CENTRAL WESTERN BANTU
KIKORI RIVER see article
ki-Kunyi = Kunyi→CENTRAL WESTERN
BANTU
ki-Kutu = Kutu→CENTRAL EASTERN BAN-
TU
ki Kuumu = Kuumu→NORTH EASTERN
BANTU
Kikuyu→NORTH EASTERN BANTU
ki-Kwese = Kwese→CENTRAL WESTERN
BANTU
Ki/ /kxi:gwi = / /xegwe→KHOISAN
Kila→BANTOID

Kilamook = Tillamook→SALISH

ki-Langi = Langi→NORTH EASTERN BANTU

Kilari = Laadi. Kongo D.→CENTRAL WESTERN BANTU

Kilba→CHADIC

Kilba = Hona. Tera D.→CHADIC

Kile→TUNGUS

ki-Leega = Leega. Lega D.→NORTH EASTERN BANTU

Kilenge→NORTHEAST NEW GUINEA AUSTRONESIAN

ki-Lenge = Chopi→SOUTH EASTERN BANTU

Kilengge = Kilenge→NORTHEAST NEW GUINEA AUSTRONESIAN

ki-Lengola = Lengola→NORTH EASTERN BANTU

ki-Leta = Kongo→CENTRAL WESTERN BANTU

Kilgat = Tsimshian→PENUTIAN

Kilgu. Ingassana Tr.→CHARI-NILE

Kilinailau→NORTHWESTERN AND CENTRAL SOLOMONS

Kiliwa→YUMAN

Kiliwee = Kiliwa→YUMAN

Kiliwi = Kiliwa→YUMAN

Killa = Quilla→INTER-ANDINE

Killisteno = Cree→ALGONQUIAN

Kilmeri→NORTH PAPUAN

Kilokaka→NORTHWESTERN AND CENTRAL SOLOMONS

ki-Luba-Katanga = Luba-Katanga→CENTRAL WESTERN BANTU

ki-Luuwa = Luuwa→CENTRAL WESTERN BANTU

Kilvasa = Gulgaissen. Abipon Tr.→GUAYCURU

Kim→CHADIC

Kim = Krim→WEST ATLANTIC

Kimaghama→FREDERIK HENDRIK IS. AND SE WEST IRIAN

Kimambwe = Mambwe→CENTRAL EASTERN BANTU

Kimanda = Manda→CENTRAL EASTERN BANTU

Kimanga = Mba→EASTERN

Kimanis. Dusun D.→NORTHWEST AUSTRONESIAN

Kimant = Qemant. Quara D.→CUSHITIC

Kimantinya = Qemant. Quara D.→CUSHITIC

ki-Mashami = Mashami. Caga D.→NORTH EASTERN BANTU

Kimatengo = Matengo→CENTRAL EASTERN BANTU

ki-Matumbi = Matumbi→SOUTH EASTERN BANTU

Kimawanda = Ndonde→SOUTH EASTERN BANTU

ki-Mbaamba = Mbaamba. Kongo D.→CENTRAL WESTERN BANTU

ki-Mbaata = Mbaata. Kongo D.→CENTRAL WESTERN BANTU

KIMBALA→CENTRAL WESTERN BANTU

ki-Mbala = Mbala→CENTRAL WESTERN BANTU

ki-Mbala Mumbala = Mbala Mumbala. Kongo D.→CENTRAL WESTERN BANTU

ki-Mbamba = Mbamba→CENTRAL WESTERN BANTU

ki-Mbeeko = Mbeeko. Kongo D.→CENTRAL WESTERN BANTU

Kimbo = Mbo→NORTH EASTERN BANTU

ki-Mboma = Mboma. Kongo D.→CENTRAL WESTERN BANTU

Kimbu→NORTH EASTERN BANTU

Kimbunda = Mbunda→SOUTH WESTERN BANTU

Kimbunda = Mbundu→SOUTH WESTERN BANTU

KIMBUNDU→CENTRAL WESTERN BANTU

Kimbundu = Mbundu→CENTRAL WESTERN BANTU

Kimbuti = Mbuti→NORTH EASTERN BANTU

Kimbuzi = Gbunde. Loma D.→MANDE

ki-Meru = Mero→NORTH EASTERN BANTU

Kimi = Krim→WEST ATLANTIC

Kimmeilab. Beja Tr.→CUSHITIC

ki-Moci = Moci. Caga D.→NORTH EASTERN BANTU

ki-Mpaangu = Mpaangu. Kongo D.→CENTRAL WESTERN BANTU

ki-Mpese = Mpese. Kongo D.→CENTRAL WESTERN BANTU

Kimpoto = Mpoto→CENTRAL EASTERN BANTU

Kimunkon = Pokot→EASTERN SUDANIC

Kinaki→TACANA

Kinalakna→HUON-FINISTERRE

Kinalinga = Kalinga→NORTHWEST AUSTRONESIAN

Ki-na-mweri = Mweri. Nyamwesi D.→NORTH EASTERN BANTU

Kinaraya→NORTHWEST AUSTRONESIAN

Kinchai = Kerintji→WEST INDONESIAN

ki-Ndengereko = Ndengereko→SOUTH EAST-
ERN BANTU
Kinderma. Tira Tr.→KORDOFANIAN
ki-Ndibu = Ndibu. Kondo D.→CENTRAL
WESTERN BANTU
Kindiga = Hatsa→KHOISAN
ki-Ndogo = Tsogo. Ruanda D.→NORTH
EASTERN BANTU
ki-Ndongo = Mbundu→CENTRAL WESTERN
BANTU
King→BISMARCK ARCHIPELAGO
Kinga→CENTRAL EASTERN BANTU
ki-Nghwele = Nghwele→CENTRAL EAST-
ERN BANTU
ki-Ngindo = Ngindo→SOUTH EASTERN
BANTU
KINGKEL→WAKA-KABIC
Kingoni = Ngoni→CENTRAL EASTERN
BANTU
ki-Ngoy Luula = Kongo Simplifie. Kongo D.→
CENTRAL WESTERN BANTU
ki-Ngulu = Ngulu→CENTRAL EASTERN
BANTU
Kingwana = Njuani. Komoro D.→CENTRAL
EASTERN BANTU
Kinihinao = Equinao. Guana D.→MAIPURAN
Kiningmiut. Inuit D.→ESKIMO-ALEUT
ki-Niramba = Nilamba→NORTH EASTERN
BANTU
Kinjin = Kenyah→WEST INDONESIAN
ki-Nkanu = Nkanu. Kongo D.→CENTRAL
WESTERN BANTU
Kinkwa→BANTOID
Kinsal. Gelik D.→BISMARCK ARCHIPELA-
GO
Kinta Sakai = Ulu Kinta. Northern Sakai D.→
SAKAI
ki-Ntaandu = Ntaandu. Kongo D.→CEN-
TRAL WESTERN BANTU
Kinuku→PLATEAU BENUE-CONGO
Kinya-Mituku = Mituku→NORTH EASTERN
BANTU
ki-Nyamwesi = Nyamwesi→NORTH EAST-
ERN BANTU
ki-Nyanyembe = Nyanyembe. Nyamwesi D.→
NORTH EASTERN BANTU
ki-Nyindu = Nyindu. Nyabungu D.→NORTH
EASTERN BANTU
ki-Nzamba = Nzamba. Kongo D.→CENTRAL
WESTERN BANTU
Kioki = Laiwui→CENTRAL AND SOUTH-
ERN CELEBES
Kiomkoolenya = Kungkalenya. Wangkadjera
D.→PITTAPITTIC

Kiong→CROSS RIVER BENUE-CONGO
Kiowa→TANOAN
Kiowa Apache→ATHAPASCAN-EYAK
KIOWA-TANOAN = TANOAN
Kipatu. Kongo D.→CENTRAL WESTERN
BANTU
Kipea = Quipea. Cariri D.→EQUATORIAL
ki-Pende = Pende→CENTRAL WESTERN
BANTU
Kiphatu. Kongo D.→CENTRAL WESTERN
BANTU
Kipirse = Kasem→GUR
Kipiyan = Kapiyan. Paiwan D.→FORMOSAN
AUSTRONESIAN
ki-Pokomo = Pokomo→NORTH EASTERN
BANTU
Kiposaka→NORTHWESTERN AND CEN-
TRAL SOLOMONS
Kipsigis = Kipsikis. Nandi D.→EASTERN
SUDANIC
Kipsiki = Kipsikis. Nandi D.→EASTERN SU-
DANIC
Kipsikis. Nandi D.→EASTERN SUDANIC
Kipsorai. Nandi D.→EASTERN SUDANIC
Kir = Jiru→JUKUNOID
Kir = Mondari. Bari D.→EASTERN SUDAN-
IC
Kira = Swaga. Ndandi D.→NORTH EAST-
ERN BANTU
Kira = Vagala→GUR
Kiramai = Giramay. Wakaman D.→PAMA-
MARIC
Kiramay = Giramay. Wakaman D.→PAMA-
MARIC
Kirante. Waling D.→GYARUNG-MISHMI
Kiranti = Khambu→GYARUNG-MISHMI
Kirawirung = Kirrea. Tjapwurong D.→KULI-
NIC
Kirdiwat = Ngizim→CHADIC
Kire = Kile→TUNGUS
ki-Remi = Remi→NORTH EASTERN BAN-
TU
Kirghiz→TURKIC
ki-Rhombo = Rhombo. Caga D.→NORTH
EASTERN BANTU
Kirifawa→CHADIC
Kirikire = Yarigui→CARIB
Kirim = Krim→WEST ATLANTIC
Kirishiana = Shirishana→WAICAN
Kiriwina→PAPUA AUSTRONESIAN
Kirkpong. Katla D.→KORDOFANIAN
Kirma→GUR
KIRMA-TYURAMA→GUR
Kirmitso-Lek. Tsaxur D.→CAUCASIAN

Kiroba. Koria D.→NORTH EASTERN BAN-
TU
Kirraewuurong = Kirrea. Tjapwurong D.→
KULINIC
Kirrea. Tjapwurong D.→KULINIC
Kiru = Jiru→JUKUNOID
ki-Ruguru = Ruguru→CENTRAL EASTERN
BANTU
ki-Ruihi = Ruihi→SOUTH EASTERN BANTU
Kirunggela→NORTHWESTERN AND CEN-
TRAL SOLOMONS
Kirurndit = Gurnditjmara. Tjapwurong D.→
KULINIC
ki-Rwo = Rwo→NORTH EASTERN BANTU
Kis→NORTHEAST NEW GUINEA AUS-
TRONESIAN
Kisa. Luhya D.→NORTH EASTERN BANTU
ki-Sagala = Sagala→CENTRAL EASTERN
BANTU
ki-Sagala = Sagala. Taita D.→NORTH EAST-
ERN BANTU
ki-Sakata = Sakata→NORTH WESTERN
BANTU
ki-Sama = Sama→CENTRAL WESTERN
BANTU
ki-Sanzi = Sanzi. Bangobango D.→NORTH
EASTERN BANTU
Kisar→MOLUCCAN
Kiserikala. Swahili D.→CENTRAL EASTERN
BANTU
Kisettla. Swahili D.→CENTRAL EASTERN
BANTU
Kisettlu = Kisettla. Swahili D.→CENTRAL
EASTERN BANTU
Kishaka=Caga→NORTH EASTERN BANTU
Kishamba. Swahili D.→CENTRAL EASTERN
BANTU
ki-Shambaa = Shambaa→CENTRAL EAST-
ERN BANTU
Kishangari. Rajasthani D.→INDIC
Kishi-Kongo = Southern Kongo. Kongo D.→
CENTRAL WESTERN BANTU
Kishi-Koongo = Southern Kongo. Kongo D.→
CENTRAL WESTERN BANTU
ki-Shingi = Shingi→CENTRAL WESTERN
BANTU
Kisi→CENTRAL EASTERN BANTU
Kisi→WEST ATLANTIC
Kisii→CENTRAL EASTERN BANTU
kisima-Ngoyo = Ngoyo. Ndingi D.→CENTRAL
WESTERN BANTU
kisi-Ngoyo = Ngoyo. Ndingi D.→CENTRAL
WESTERN BANTU
ki-Solongo = Solongo. Kongo D.→CENTRAL

WESTERN BANTU
Kisonge = Songe→CENTRAL WESTERN
BANTU
Kisonge Universel =Songe→CENTRAL WEST-
ERN BANTU
Kisongo. Maasai Tr.→EASTERN SUDANIC
ki-Soonde = Soonde→CENTRAL WESTERN
BANTU
Kissama = Sama→CENTRAL WESTERN
BANTU
Kissi = Kisi→WEST ATLANTIC
Kissien = Kisi→WEST ATLANTIC
Kissii = Gusii→NORTH EASTERN BANTU
Kistane. Soddo D.→SEMITIC
Kisu. Masaba D.→NORTH EASTERN BAN-
TU
ki-Suku = Suku→CENTRAL WESTERN
BANTU
ki-Sukuma = Sukuma→NORTH EASTERN
BANTU
ki-Sumbwa = Sumbwa→NORTH EASTERN
BANTU
ki-Sutu = Ngoni→CENTRAL EASTERN
BANTU
ki-Swahili = Swahili→CENTRAL EASTERN
BANTU
Kitabal→BANDJALANGIC
Kitamat. Haisla D.→WAKASHAN
Kitanemuk. Serrano D.→UTO-AZTECAN
Kitapul = Kitabal→BANDJALANGIC
Kitchen Kaffir = Piki→SOUTH EASTERN
BANTU
ki-Tembo = Nyabungu→NORTH EASTERN
BANTU
Kitemoca = Quitemoca→ CHAPACURA-
WANHAMAN
ki-Tharaka = Tharaka→NORTH EASTERN
BANTU
Kithoniri = Karko. Kordofanian Nubian Tr.→
EASTERN SUDANIC
Kithonirishe = Karko. Kordofanian Nubian
Tr.→EASTERN SUDANIC
ki-Tiini = Tiini→NORTH WESTERN BANTU
Kitimi→PLATEAU BENUE-CONGO
Kitka = Pawnee→CADDOAN
Kitehahki. Pawnee D.→CADDOAN
Kitonga = Tonga→CENTRAL EASTERN
BANTU
ki-Tongwe = Tongwe→NORTH EASTERN
BANTU
ki-Tsaan = Samba→CENTRAL WESTERN
BANTU
ki-Tsaanba = Samba→CENTRAL WESTERN
BANTU

Kitsai→CADDOAN
Kitsei = Kitsai→CADDOAN
Kittabool = Kitabal→BANDJALANGIC
Kittim = Krim→WEST ATLANTIC
Kittitas = Yakima. Sahaptin D.→SAHAPTIN-NEZ PERCE
ki-Tuba = Kongo→CENTRAL WESTERN BANTU
ki-Tubeta = Tubeta→CENTRAL EASTERN BANTU
Kitunaha = Kutenai
Kitunahan = Kutenai
Kitwii. Nyang D.→BANTOID
Kiuri = Kjuri. Lezghian D.→CAUCASIAN
Kiuthali. Western Pahari D.→INDIC
Kiutze = Rawang→BODO-NAGA-KACHIN
ki-Vidunda = Vidunda→CENTRAL EASTERN BANTU
ki-Vili = Vili→CENTRAL WESTERN BANTU
Kivita. Swahili D.→CENTRAL EASTERN BANTU
ki-Vungunya = Vungunya. Kongo D.→CENTRAL WESTERN BANTU
KIWAI→CENTRAL AND SOUTH NEW GUINEA
Kiwai, Bamu→CENTRAL AND SOUTH NEW GUINEA
Kiwai, Northern→CENTRAL AND SOUTH NEW GUINEA
Kiwai, Southern→CENTRAL AND SOUTH NEW GUINEA
Kiwai Proper. Southern Kiwai D.→CENTRAL AND SOUTH NEW GUINEA
KIWAIIC→CENTRAL AND SOUTH NEW GUINEA
Kiwarawa = Kavalan→FORMOSAN AUS-TRONESIAN
Kiwit = Kibi. Ami D.→FORMOSAN AUS-TRONESIAN
ki-Wunjo = Vunjo. Caga D.→NORTH EAST-ERN BANTU
Kiya. Sukuma D.→NORTH EASTERN BAN-TU
Kiyadjara. Kardutjara D.→WATI
KIYAKA→CENTRAL WESTERN BANTU
ki-Yaka = Yaka→CENTRAL WESTERN BANTU
ki-Yombe = Yombe. Kongo D.→CENTRAL WESTERN BANTU
Kiyu = Karim. Chomo D.→JUKUNOID
ki-Zaramo = Zaramo→CENTRAL EASTERN BANTU
Kizh = Gabrieleno→UTO-AZTECAN
Kiziere. Mundang D.→ADAMAWA

ki-Zigula = Zigula→CENTRAL EASTERN BANTU
ki-Zombo = Zombo. Kongo D.→CENTRAL WESTER NBANTU
ki-Zoombo = Zombo. Kongo D.→CENTRAL WESTERN BANTU
Kjakar = Kjakela. Oroc D.→TUNGUS
Kjakela. Oroc D.→TUNGUS
Kjax = Kiakh. Circassian D.→CAUCASIAN
Kjotsuni = Uru→CHIPAYAN
Kjuri. Lezghian D.→CAUCASIAN
K'lai = Li→KAM-TAI
Klallam = Clallam→SALISH
Klamath→PENUTIAN
Klang-Klang→NAGA-KUKI-CHIN
Klao = Kru-Krawi→KRU
Klatskanai = Tlatskanai. Kwalhioqua D.→ATHAPASCAN-EYAK
Klatsop = Clatsop. Lower Chinook D.→CHI-NOOKAN
KLEMANTAN→WEST INDONESIAN
Kler. Karaboro D.→GUR
Klikitat = Yakima. Sahaptin D.→SAHAPTIN-NEZ PERCE
Klipkaffer = Dama. Nama D.→KHOISAN
Klipkaffern = Dama. Nama D.→KHOISAN
Klo = Krobo. Adangme D.→GA-ADANGME
Klodesseottine. Chipewyan Tr.→ATHAPAS-CAN-EYAK
Klor = Lor→MON-KHMER
Kloukle = / /xegwe→KHOISAN
Kluang. Solor D.→MOLUCCAN
Kmike = Seri→HOKAN
Knaiakhotana = Tanaina→ATHAPASCAN-EYAK
Knenknenwurro = Jaara. Djadjala D.→KULI-NIC
Knindowurrong = Jardwa. Djadjala D.→KULI-NIC
Knisteneaux = Cree→ALGONQUIAN
Ko. Mende D.→MANDE
Ko = Yakurr→CROSS RIVER BENUE-CON-GO
!Ko = ≠Hua→KHOISAN
Koa→PAMA-MARIC
KOALIB→KORDOFANIAN
Koalib→KORDOFANIAN
KOALIB-MORO = KOLAIB→KORDOFA-NIAN
Ko'aɬ=Kuʔaɬ. Diegueno D.→YUMAN
Koamu. Mandandanji D.→PAMA-MARIC
Koara. Kardutjara D.→WATI
Koaratira = Guarategaya→TUPI
Koasati→MUSKOGEAN

Koassa→MOMBERAMO RIVER

Koassati = Koasati→MUSKOGEAN

Koatateri. Waica Tr.→WAICAN

Koba→EAST INDONESIAN

Koba = Yeye→SOUTH WESTERN BANTU

Kobe = Bakovi→NORTHEAST NEW GUIN-
EA AUSTRONESIAN

Kobe = Fanya→CHADIC

Kobi = Hunde→NORTH EASTERN BANTU

Kobiana→WEST ATLANTIC

Kobilari = Kolbilla→ADAMAWA

Kobon→EAST NEW GUINEA HIGHLANDS

Koboshi. Njai D.→CHADIC

Kobotschi = Kobochi. Njai D.→CHADIC

Kobro'or→EAST INDONESIAN

KOCH→BODO-NAGA-KACHIN

Koch. Bengali D.→INDIC

Kocheyali. Foothill North Yokuts D.→YO-
KUTS

Koda. Mundari D.→MUNDA

Kodagu→DRAVIDIAN

Kodhin = Kadaru. Kordofanian Nubian Tr.→
EASTERN SUDANIC

Kodhinni Ai = Kadaru. Kordofanian Nubian
Tr.→EASTERN SUDANIC

Kodi. Sumba D.→MOLUCCAN

Kodoi. Maba Tr.→MABAN

Kodoi = Mudogo. Kuka D.→CENTRAL SU-
DANIC

Kodoro = Kadaru. Kordofanian Nubian Tr.→
EASTERN SUDANIC

Kodu = Kui→DRAVIDIAN

Kodulu = Kui→DRAVIDIAN

Koena = Kwena. Tswana D.→SOUTH EAST-
ERN BANTU

Koenpel = Djendewal→DURUBULIC

Koetenaice = Kutenai

Koetenay = Kutenai

Kofa→BANTOID

Kofane = Cofan→JIVAROAN

Koffa. Mogum D.→CHADIC

Kofiau→SOUTH HALMAHERA AUSTRO-
NESIAN

Kogo = Kwogo. Central Koma D.→KOMAN

Kogoro. Boguru D.→CENTRAL WESTERN
BANTU

Kogoro = Kagoro. Bambara D.→MANDE

Kohadk. Pima D.→UTO-AZTECAN

Kohani. Karankawa Tr.

KOHISTANI→INDIC

Kohle = Karmali. Santali D.→MUNDA

Koho→MON-KHMER

Kohuana. Delta River Yuman D.→YUMAN

Kohumono→CROSS RIVER BENUE-CONGO

Koi. Gondi D.→DRAVIDIAN

Koianu. Nasioi D.→BOUGAINVILLE

Koiari, Mountain→KOIARI

KOIARI see article

Koibal. Sayan Samoyed D.→URALIC

Koimaka = Weima. Loma D.→MANDE

Koinberi. Kamilaroi D.→WIRADJURIC

Koinberri = Koinberi. Kamilaroi D.→WIRAD-
JURIC

Koinjimal = Koinjmal. Darambal D.→WAKA-
KABIC

Koinjmal. Darambal D.→WAKA-KABIC

Koio = Kwaio→EASTERN OCEANIC

KOITA = KOIARI

Koita→KOIARI

Kok Mbewam = Mbeiwum→PAMA-MARIC

Kokama→TUPI

Kokamilla. Kokama D.→TUPI

Kokar = Nyakinyaki. Juat D.→SOUTHWEST
PAMA-NYUNGAN

Kokarlamo. Tobelo D.→NORTH HALMA-
HERA

Kokata. Kardutjara D.→WATI

Kokatha = Kokata. Kardutjara D.→WATI

Koke→ADAMAWA

Kokila→KOIARI

Kokit-ta = Kokata. Kardutjara D.→WATI

Kokkotaijari = Taior→PAMA-MARIC

Koko. Bangba D.→EASTERN

Koko'. Basa Tr.→NORTH WESTERN BANTU

Koko = Auen→KHOISAN

Koko = Basa→NORTH WESTERN BANTU

Koko = Hunjara→BINANDERE

Koko Bididji. Koko Jelandji D.→PAMA-
MARIC

Koko Bujundji→PAMA-MARIC

Koko Imudji→PAMA-MARIC

Koko Jelandji→PAMA-MARIC

Koko Katji = Koko Walandja. Koko Jelandji
D.→PAMA-MARIC

Koko Mindjan→PAMA-MARIC

Koko Patun. Ilba D.→PAMA-MARIC

Koko Pera→PAMA-MARIC

Koko Walandja. Koko Jelandji D.→PAMA-
MARIC

Koko Yak. Koko Mindjan D.→PAMA-MARIC

Koko Yawa→PAMA-MARIC

Koko Yerlandji = Koko Jelandji→PAMA-MA-
RIC

Koko Yimidir = Koko Imudji→PAMA-MARIC

Kokobera = Koko Pera→PAMA-MARIC

Kokojimoji = Koko Imudji→PAMA-MARIC

Kokolerlantchi = Koko Jelandji→PAMA-
MARIC

Kokololodi. Pima D.→UTO-AZTECAN

Kokomandjoen = Koko Mindjan→PAMA-MARIC

Kokomba = Konkomba→GUR

Kokomindjin = Koko Mindjan→PAMA-MARIC

Kokominjen = Koko Mindjan→PAMA-MARIC

Kokomoloroitji = Muluridji. Wakaman D.→PAMA-MARIC

Kokonjunkulu = Djabugay. Wakaman D.→PAMA-MARIC

Kokonyungalo = Djabugay. Wakaman D.→PAMA-MARIC

Kokori = Nakara→AUSTRALIAN MACRO-PHYLUM

Koko-Tjumbundji = Djabugay. Wakaman D.→PAMA-MARIC

Kokowari. Leti D.→MOLUCCAN

Koko-Ya'o→PAMA-MARIC

Kokoyellanji = Koko Jelandji→PAMA-MARIC

Kokoyerlantji = Koko Jelandji→PAMA-MARIC

Kokoyimidir = Koko Imudji→PAMA-MARIC

Kokuduab = Ad Kukal. Beja Tr.→CUSHITIC

Kokuzu = Cocuzu. Northeast Nambicuara D.→NAMBICUARA

Kol→NEW BRITAIN

Kol. Great Andamanese D.→ANDAMANESE

Kola→EAST INDONESIAN

Kola Lapp→URALIC

Kolacgnat = Kolakngat. Kurung D.→KULINIC

Kolaka→CENTRAL AND SOUTHERN CELEBES

Kolakngat. Kurung D.→KULINIC

Kolami→DRAVIDIAN

Kolana-Wersin. Abui D.→TIMOR-ALOR

Kolata. Askun D.→NURISTANI

Kolbaffo. Roti D.→EAST INDONESIAN

Kolbila = Kolbilla→ADAMAWA

Kolbilla→ADAMAWA

Koldrong. Katla D.→KORDOFANIAN

Kole. Duala D.→NORTH WESTERN BANTU

Kole = Kol→NEW BRITAIN

Kolhreng→NAGA-KUKI-CHIN

Kolijon = Kolakgnat. Kurung D.→KULINIC

Koliku→NORTHEASTERN NEW GUINEA

Kolo. Bima D.→EAST INDONESIAN

Kolo. Ogbia D.→CROSS RIVER BENUE-CONGO

Kolobo. Kim D.→CHADIC

Kolokuma. Ijo D.→IJO

Kololo = Lozi→SOUTH WESTERN BANTU

Kolomende = Ko. Mende D.→MANDE

Kolor = Tjapwurong→KULINIC

KOLRENG→NAGA-KUKI-CHIN

Kolube = Kulube→BISMARCK ARCHIPELAGO

Koluschan = Tlingit→NA-DENE

Kolyma. Yukaghir D.→YUKAGHIR

Kom→NAGA-KUKI-CHIN

Kom. Kati D.→NURISTANI

KOM = NKOM→BANTOID

Kom = Nkom→BANTOID

Kom = Rashad. Tagali D.→KORDOFANIAN

Koma→ADAMAWA

Koma→KOMAN

Koma, Central→KOMAN

Koma = Northern Mao→KOMAN

Koma of Daga = Central Koma→KOMAN

Komalu→BISMARCK ARCHIPELAGO

KOMAN see article

Komanche = Comanche. Shoshoni D.→UTO-AZTECAN

Komantsche = Comanche. Shoshoni D.→UTO-AZTECAN

/komasan = Namib→KHOISAN

Komasau→NORTH NEW GUINEA

Komba→HUON-FINISTERRE

Komba. Konkomba Tr.→GUR

Kombaingheri = Kumbainggar→KUMBAINGGARIC

Kombe. Yasa D.→NORTH WESTERN BANTU

Kombe = Cinga→NORTH WESTERN BANTU

Komberatoro = Kamberataro→NORTH NEW GUINEA

Kombinegherry = Kumbainggar→KUMBAINGGARIC

Kombio→TORRICELLI

Kombo. Diola D.→WEST ATLANTIC

Komboyo Mende = Sewa. Mende D.→MANDE

Kome = Rashad. Tagali D.→KORDOFANIAN

Komelom = Mombum→FREDERIK HENDRIK IS. AND SE WEST IRIAN

Ko-Mende = Ko. Mende D.→MANDE

Komendi = Manya. Malinka D.→MANDE

Komering. Lampung D.→WEST INDONESIAN

Komfana→EAST INDONESIAN

Komi = Zyrian→URALIC

Komi-Permyak. Zyrian D.→URALIC

Komi-Zyrian. Zyrian D.→URALIC

Komkome = Tonkawa→MACRO-ALGONQUIAN

Komlek. Toba Tr.→GUAYCURU

Komo = Central Koma→KOMAN

Komo = Kuumu→NORTH EASTERN BANTU

Komodo. Bima D.→EAST INDONESIAN

Komonggu = Komunku. Siane D.→EAST NEW GUINEA HIGHLANDS

Komono→GUR

Komookhs = Comox→SALISH

Komoro→CENTRAL EASTERN BANTU

Komso = Konso→CUSHITIC

Komuk = Comox→SALISH

Komunku. Siane D.→EAST NEW GUINEA HIGHLANDS

Komutu→HUON-FINISTERRE

Kona. Jukun D.→JUKUNOID

Konabem→NORTH WESTERN BANTU

Konabemb→NORTH WESTERN BANTU

Konabembe→NORTH WESTERN BANTU

Kond = Kuwi→DRAVIDIAN

Konda→DRAVIDIAN

Konda→WESTERN NEW GUINEA

Konda. Ostyak D.→URALIC

Konda. Vogul D.→URALIC

Konda Dora = Konda→DRAVIDIAN

Kondair = Kongder. Rek D.→EASTERN SUDANIC

Konde. Ronga D.→SOUTH EASTERN BANTU

Konde = Ngonde. Nyakyusa D.→CENTRAL EASTERN BANTU

Kondho = Kui→DRAVIDIAN

Kondjara = Fur→NILO-SAHARAN

Kondjo = Konzo→NORTH EASTERN BANTU

Kondkor = Ollari. Gadba D.→DRAVIDIAN

Kondo = Kono→MANDE

Kondo = Vai→MANDE

Kondoma. Shor D.→TURKIC

Kondoma Tatar = Shor→TURKIC

Kondongo. Maba Tr.→MABAN

Konds, Southwest = Kuwi→DRAVIDIAN

Kone = Haeke→NEW CALEDONIA

Konejandi = Gunian→BUNABAN

Koneraw→FREDERIK HENDRIK IS. AND SE WEST IRIAN

Koneyandi = Gunian→BUNABAN

Kongabula. Mandandanji D.→PAMA-MARIC

Kongadavanau = Tona. Rukai D.→FORMOSAN AUSTRONESIAN

Kongalu = Kangulu. Wadja D.→WAKA-KABIC

Kongampani = Komfana→EAST INDONESIAN

Kongana. Hoanya D.→FORMOSAN AUSTRONESIAN

Kongdeer = Kongder. Rek D.→EASTERN SUDANIC

Kongder. Rek D.→EASTERN SUDANIC

Kongo→CENTRAL WESTERN BANTU

Kongo = Southern Kongo. Kongo D.→CENTRAL WESTERN BANTU

Kongo Simplifie. Kongo D.→CENTRAL WESTERN BANTU

Kongola = Kusu→NORTH WESTERN BANTU

Kongola-Meno. Nkutu D.→NORTH WESTERN BANTU

Konguli = Kangulu. Wadja D.→WAKA-KABIC

Kongulu = Kangulu. Wadja D.→WAKA-KABIC

Koni. Northern Sotho D.→SOUTH EASTERN BANTU

Koniagi = Konyagi→WEST ATLANTIC

Konin. Kardutjara D.→WATI

Konio. Mekongka D.→CENTRAL AND SOUTHERN CELEBES

Konjara = Fur→NILO-SAHARAN

Konjek. Nandi D.→EASTERN SUDANIC

KONJO→NORTH EASTERN BANTU

Konjo = Konzo→NORTH EASTERN BANTU

Konkan. Marathi D.→INDIC

Konkan Standard. Marathi D.→INDIC

Konkomba→GUR

Konkone = Tonkawa→MACRO-ALGONQUIAN

Konkow = Maidu→MAIDU

Konkow = Northwest Maidu→MAIDU

Konmak. Boazi D.→MARIND

Kono→MANDE

Kono = Vai→MANDE

Konomola. Muliama D.→BISMARCK ARCHIPELAGO

Konongo. Nyamwesi D.→NORTH EASTERN BANTU

Konosara = Vagala→GUR

Konsinya = Konso→CUSHITIC

Konso→CUSHITIC

KONSO-GELERA→CUSHITIC

KONSOID→CUSHITIC

Konta. Walamo D.→OMOTIC

Kontu = Kantu→MON-KHMER

Kontum. Bahnar D.→MON-KHMER

Konua = Kunua→BOUGAINVILLE

Kony. Nandi D.→EASTERN SUDANIC

Konya. Malinka D.→MANDE

Konyagi→WEST ATLANTIC

Konyar = Yuruk. Balkan Gagauz Turkish D.→
TURKIC
Konyare. Karanga D.→MABAN
Konzo→NORTH EASTERN BANTU
Koŋgbaa = Gola→WEST ATLANTIC
Koo→EASTERN OCEANIC
Koocatho = Kokata. Kardutjara D.→WATI
Koogatho = Kokata. Kardutjara D.→WATI
Koogurda = Kokata. Kardutjara D.→WATI
Kooinmerburra = Koinjmal. Darambal D.→
WAKA-KABIC
Kooki→NORTH EASTERN BANTU
Koombainga = Kumbainggar→KUMBAING-
GARIC
Koombanggary = Kumbainggar→KUM-
BAINGGARIC
Koombangghery = Kumbainggar→KUM-
BAINGGARIC
Koomilroi = Kamilaroi→WIRADJURIC
Koon = ≠Hua→KHOISAN
Koonarie = Kuyani→YURA
Koongerri = Kuungkari. Mandandanji D.→
PAMA-MARIC
Koongo = Northeastern Kongo. Kongo D.→
CENTRAL WESTERN BANTU
Koongo = Southern Kongo. Kongo D.→
CENTRAL WESTERN BANTU
Koongo = Western Kongo. Kongo D.→
CENTRAL WESTERN BANTU
Koonkalinya = Kungkalenya. Wangkadjera
D.→PITTAPITTIC
Koonkerri = Kuungkari. Mandandanji D.→
PAMA-MARIC
Koonkodenya = Kungkalenya. Wangkadjera
D.→PITTAPITTIC
Koonkurri = Kunggara→PAMA-MARIC
Koono = Kula→PAMA-NYUNGAN
Koornawarra = Kaurna. Jadliaura D.→YURA
Koorungo = Gunwiggu→GUNWINGGUAN
Koosati = Koasati→MUSKOGEAN
Koose. Mbo D.→NORTH WESTERN BANTU
Kooteeuna = Kuyani→YURA
Kootenai = Kutenai
Kootenay = Kutenai
Kootenuha = Kutenai
Kooyeeunna = Kuyani→YURA
Kooyiannie = Kuyani→YURA
Kopano. Karankawa Tr.
Kopar = Watam→BOGIA
Kope = Patwin→WINTUN
Kopo = Kapo. Bakwe Tr.→KRU
Kopo-Moniya→KIKORI RIVER
Koposo = Capocho→MACHACALI
Kor = Cua→MON-KHMER

Kora. Great Andamanese D.→ANDAMANESE
Kora = Koda. Mundari D.→MUNDA
!Kora = KORANA→KHOISAN
Korafi = Korape→BINANDERE
Korak→BOGIA
Korama = Kurama→NGAYARDA
Korana→KHOISAN
Koranko. Malinka D.→MANDE
Koranna = Korana→KHOISAN
Koranti = Brijia. Mundari D.→MUNDA
Korape→BINANDERE
Korappun→CENTRAL AND SOUTH NEW
GUINEA
Koraqua = Korana→KHOISAN
Korara = Uduk→KOMAN
Koraulun = Warki. Tanganekald D.→NAR-
RINYERIC
Korava = Erukala. Tamil D.→DRAVIDIAN
Kordofanian Nubian→EASTERN SUDANIC
KORDOFANIAN see article
Korean→ALTAIC
Korefa = Koreipa. Siane D.→EAST NEW
GUINEA HIGHLANDS
Koreipa. Siane D.→EAST NEW GUINEA
HIGHLANDS
Korekore. Shona D.→SOUTH EASTERN
BANTU
Koreng. Juat D.→SOUTHWEST PAMA-
NYUNGAN
Korenggoreng. Djakunda D.→WAKA-KABIC
Koria→NORTH EASTERN BANTU
Koriki→SOUTHEAST NEW GUINEA
Koriko. Manubara D.→SOUTHEAST NEW
GUINEA
Korim. Biak D.→MOLUCCAN
Korindi = Kurondi. Tumtum Tr.→KORDO-
FANIAN
Koriok. Lotuho D.→EASTERN SUDANIC
Koriuk = Koriok. Lotuho D.→EASTERN
SUDANIC
Korku = Kurku→MUNDA
Korma = Suri. Tirma D.→EASTERN
SUDANIC
Korni = Tanganekald→NARRINYERIC
Kornu = Kula→PAMA-NYUNGAN
Koro→PLATEAU BENUE-CONGO
Koro = Migili→PLATEAU BENUE-CONGO
Koroa = Sangada. Tebu Tr.→SAHARAN
Koroca = Kwadi→KHOISAN
Korok. Rek D.→EASTERN SUDANIC
Koroko = Valman→TORRICELLI
Korokwa→KHOISAN
Koroma = Karaboro→GUR
Koromira→BOUGAINVILLE

Korongo = Krongo→KORDOFANIAN
Korop = Ododop→CROSS-RIVER BENUE-
 CONGO
Kororo→MAILU
Korrawa = Karawa→KARWAN
Korrengkorreng = Korenggoreng. Djakunda
 D.→WAKA-KABIC
Korrido. Biak D.→MOLUCCAN
Kortabina = Pangkala→YURA
Korise→SINO-TIBETAN
Koru Buso→INDO-PACIFIC
Korusi = Patwin→WINTUN
Korwa. Mundari D.→MUNDA
Koryak→CHUKCHEE-KAMCHATKAN
Kosali = Eastern Hindi→INDIC
Kosap. Kim D.→CHADIC
Kosena. Auyana D.→EAST NEW GUINEA
 HIGHLANDS
Koseng = Kasseng→MON-KHMER
Kosha = Kucha. Walamo D.→OMOTIC
Koshan. Agul D.→CAUCASIAN
Kosian = Balantak→CENTRAL AND SOUTH-
 ERN CELEBES
Kosin→BANTOID
Koso = Mende→MANDE
Koso = Panamint. Shoshoni D.→UTO-AZTE-
 CAN
Kosopho. Lisu D.→BURMESE-LOLO
Kosorong→HUON-FINISTERRE
Kosova = Gusii→NORTH EASTERN BANTU
Kosove = Ship. Albanian D.
Kossa = Mende→MANDE
Kossee→KHOISAN
Kossee-ntshori = Kossee→KHOISAN
Kossee-tshori = Kossee→KHOISAN
Kosso = Mende→MANDE
Kota→NORTH WESTERN BANTU
Kota→DRAVIDIAN
KOTA = KELE→NORTH WESTERN
 BANTU
Kotofo = Kotopo→ADAMAWA
Kotogut→AWYU
Kotoi→KOIARI
KOTOKO→CHADIC
Kotoko→CHADIC
Kotoko Daa. Kotoko D.→CHADIC
Kotokoli = Tem→GUR
Kotopo→ADAMAWA
Kotoxo = Catethoy→CAMACAN
Kotpojo = Kotopo→ADAMAWA
Kotrahu = Kotroku. Bete Tr.→KRU
Kotroku. Bete Tr.→KRU
Kott = Cottian→YENISEIAN
Kotu = Cottian→YENISEIAN

Kotua = Takua→MON-KHMER
Kotule = Tula→ADAMAWA
Kouka = Kuka→CENTRAL SUDANIC
Koukouya = Kukwa. South Teke D.→NORTH
 WESTERN BANTU
Koumac = Fwagumwak. Nenema D.→NEW
 CALEDONIA
Koura = Quara→CUSHITIC
Kouranke = Koranko. Malinka D.→MANDE
Kovai→HUON-FINISTERRE
Kove = Bakovi→NORTHEAST NEW GUIN-
 EA AUSTRONESIAN
KOVIO→GOILALA
Kovio→GOILALA
Kowaki→BOGIA
Kowalib = Koalib→KORDOFANIAN
Kowan→OK
Kowelitz = Cowlitz→SALISH
Kowet = Kravet→MON-KHMER
Kowiai = Kuiwai→MOLUCCAN
Kowilth = Wiyok→MACRO-ALGONQUIAN
Kowrarega = Kaurareg→MABUIAGIC
Koya→DRAVIDIAN
Koya = Koi. Gondi D.→DRAVIDIAN
Koyam. Kanuri Tr.→SAHARAN
Koyo→NORTH WESTERN BANTU
Koyo = Nguru. Kara D.→CENTRAL SUDAN-
 IC
Koyong = Halang→MON-KHMER
Koyra→OMOTIC
Koysha = Kucha. Walamo D.→OMOTIC
Koyukon→ATHAPASCAN-EYAK
Koyukukhotana = Koyukon→ATHAPASCAN-
 EYAK
Kozime. Njem-Bajue Tr.→NORTH WESTERN
 BANTU
Kozime = Njem. Njem-Bajue Tr.→WESTERN
 BANTU
!Ko = ≠Hua→KHOISAN
Koriŋ = Oring→CROSS RIVER BENUE-
 CONGO
Kpa→NORTH WESTERN BANTU
Kpa. Mende D.→MANDE
Kpa = Eregba→JUKUNOID
Kpabili. Mbimu Tr.→NORTH WESTERN
 BANTU
Kpala→EASTERN
Kpala = Kresh→CENTRAL SUDANIC
Kpala = Ndaanda→NORTH WESTERN
 BANTU
Kpalagha = Palara→GUR
Kpala-Hofra = Naka. Kresh D.→CENTRAL
 SUDANIC
Kpallagha = Palara→GUR

Kpa-Mende = Kpa. Mende D.→MANDE
Kpan = Eregba→JUKUNOID
Kpan = Eregba→JUKUNOID
KPAN-ICEN→JUKUNOID
Kpanzon = Eregba→JUKUNOID
Kpara = Kresh→CENTRAL SUDANIC
Kpara = Naka. Kresh D.→CENTRAL SUDAN-
 IC
Kpati→BANTOID
Kpe = Turuka→GUR
Kpelese = Kpelle→MANDE
Kpelesetina = Kpelle→MANDE
Kpelle→MANDE
Kpere. Kari D.→ADAMAWA
Kperese = Kpelle→MANDE
Kpese = Kpelle→MANDE
Kpilakpila = Pila→GUR
Kpo = Gola→WEST ATLANTIC
Kpone. Adangme D.→GA-ADANGME
Kporo. Nama D.→JUKUNOID
Kposo→CENTRAL TOGO
Kpwaala = Kpala→EASTERN
Kpwala = Kpala→EASTERN
Kpwate = Eregba→JUKUNOID
Kpwesi = Kpelle→MANDE
Kpwessi = Kpelle→MANDE
Kra = Krahn→KRU
Kra = Kru-Krawi→KRU
Kraa = Krahn→KRU
Krachi→VOLTA-COMOE
Krahn→KRU
Kraho = Craho→GE
Kran = Krahn→KRU
Krangku→BODO-NAGA-KACHIN
Krao = Craho→GE
Krao = Kru-Krawi→KRU
Krau. Inner Eastern Sakai D.→SAKAI
Krau of Ketiar. Inner Eastern Sakai D.→
 SAKAI
Krauatungulang. Bratauolung D.→PAMA-
 NYUNGAN
Kravet→MON-KHMER
Krawo = Kru-Krawi→KRU
Krebo = Grebo→KRU
Kreda. Tebu Tr.→SAHARAN
Kredj = Kresh→CENTRAL SUDANIC
Krei = Kerei→EAST INDONESIAN
Kreich = Kresh→CENTRAL SUDANIC
Kreish = Kresh→CENTRAL SUDANIC
Krem. Bahnar D.→MON-KHMER
Kresh→CENTRAL SUDANIC
Kresh-dogo. Kresh D.→CENTRAL SUDANIC
Kresh-Hofra = Naka. Kresh D.→CENTRAL
 SUDANIC

Kri = Cree→ALGONQUIAN
Krih = Cree→ALGONQUIAN
Krim→WEST ATLANTIC
Krio → GERMANIC
Kriono = Sranan→GERMANIC
Krisa. Kilmeri D.→NORTH PAPUAN
Kristinaux = Cree→ALGONQUIAN
Kroatungolung = Krauatungulang. Bratauolung
 D.→PAMA-NYUNGAN
Krobo. Adangme D.→GA-ADANGME
Kroe→WEST INDONESIAN
Krokong. Land Dayak D.→WEST INDONE-
 SIAN
Krongo→KORDOFANIAN
Krongo Abdullah. Tumma Tr.→KORDOFA-
 NIAN
Krowtihunkoolo = Krauatungulang. Bratauo-
 lung D.→PAMA-NYUNGAN
KRU see article
Kru = Chru→WEST INDONESIAN
Kru'i = Kroe→WEST INDONESIAN
Kru-Krawi→KRU
Krung→MON-KHMER
Kryc = Kryts→CAUCASIAN
Kryts→CAUCASIAN
Kryz = Kryts→CAUCASIAN
Ksara. Senari D.→GUR
Ku. Sumo Tr.→MISUMALPAN
!Ku = Kung→KHOISAN
Ku'aḥɬ = Kuˀaɬ. Diegueno D.→YUMAN
Kuala Tembeling. Inner Eastern Sakai D.→
 SAKAI
Kuˀaɬ. Diegueno D.→YUMAN
Kuam = Koamu. Mandandanji D.→PAMA-
 MARIC
Ku-amba = Amba→NORTH   EASTERN
 BANTU
Kuanga→BOGIA
Kuangsu = Kwansu→NORTH PAPUAN
Kuanh. Eastern Mnong D.→MON-KHMER
Kuanua = Gunantuna→BISMARCK ARCHI-
 PELAGO
Kuanyama = Kwanyama→SOUTH WESTERN
 BANTU
Kuap. Land Dayak D.→WEST INDONESIAN
Kuarik. Chulym D.→TURKIC
KUBA→NORTH WESTERN BANTU
Kuba→NORTH WESTERN BANTU
Kuba. Lezghian D.→CAUCASIAN
Kuba = Busooŋ→NORTH WESTERN BANTU
Kuba = Yeye→SOUTH WESTERN BANTU
Kubachi. Dargwa D.→CAUCASIAN
Kuban. Circassian D.→CAUCASIAN
Kube→HUON-FINISTERRE

Kubi = Konda→DRAVIDIAN
Kubira. Southern Kiwai D.→CENTRAL AND
    SOUTH NEW GUINEA
Ku-bira = Bila→NORTH EASTERN BANTU
Kubo→PARE-SAMO-BEAMI-BOSAVI
Kubokota. Lungga D.→NORTHWESTERN
    AND CENTRAL SOLOMONS
Kuboro. Sengan D.→NORTHWESTERN AND
    CENTRAL SOLOMONS
Kuburi. Kanuri Tr.→SAHARAN
Kucha. Walamo D.→OMOTIC
Kuchi→SOUTH EASTERN BANTU
Kuchin→ATHAPASCAN-EYAK
Kuchumba = Amharic→SEMITIC
Kuda→PLATEAU BENUE-CONGO
Kudamuta = Diola→WEST ATLANTIC
Kudawa = Kuda→PLATEAU BENUE-CON-
    GO
Kudi = Kodi. Sumba D.→MOLUCCAN
Kudnamietha = Adnyamathana. Wailpi D.→
    YURA
Kudugli = Kadugli→KORDOFANIAN
//ku//e. Seroa D.→KHOISAN
KUEI = JUI→KAM-TAI
Kueinan. Cantonese D.→CHINESE
Kuen = Khun→KAM-TAI
Kuepa→GOILALA
Kufa. Kanga Tr.→KORDOFANIAN
Kufuru. Senari D.→GUR
Kugama. Yendang D.→ADAMAWA
Kugbo→CROSS RIVER BENUE-CONGO
Kugurda = Kokata. Kardutjara D.→WATI
Kuhpang = Nung→BODO-NAGA-KACHIN
KUI = JUI→KAM-TAI
Kui→DRAVIDIAN
Kui→BURMESE-LOLO
Kui = Kuy→MON-KHMER
Kuijau. Murut D.→NORTHWEST AUSTRO-
    NESIAN
Kui-Kramang. Abui D.→TIMOR-ALOR
Kuile = Tsamai→CUSHITIC
Kuinga = Kui→DRAVIDIAN
Kuitish = Lower Umpqua. Siuslaw D.→YAKO-
    NAN
Kuiwai→MOLUCCAN
Kujani = Kuyani→YURA
Kujiŋ. Maba Tr.→MABAN
Ku·k Thayori = Taior→PAMA-MARIC
Kuka→CENTRAL SUDANIC
Kukaak = Seri→HOKAN
Kukacha = Kukatja. Kardutjara D.→WATI
Kukata = Kokata. Kardutjara D.→WATI
Kukatha = Kokata. Kardutjara D.→WATI
Kukatja. Kardutjara D.→WATI

Kukaty→PAMA-NYUNGAN
Kukele→CROSS RIVER BENUE-CONGO
KUKI→NAGA-KUKI-CHIN
Kuki Airani = Cook Islands Maori→POLYNE-
    SIAN
KUKI-CHIN = NAGA-KUKI-CHIN
KUKISH = NAGA-KUKI-CHIN
Kukra. Sumo Tr.→MISUMALPAN
Kuku. Bari D.→EASTERN SUDANIC
Kuku Yalandji = Koko Jelandji→PAMA-MA-
    RIC
Kuku Yalanji = Koko Jelandji→PAMA-MA-
    RIC
Kuku Yimidyi = Koko Imudji→PAMA-MA-
    RIC
KUKUKUKU see article
Kukuli. Ingassana Tr.→CHARI-NILE
Kuku-Lumun = Lumun. Moro Hills Tr.→KOR-
    DOFANIAN
Kukuluŋ = Kulung→BANTOID
Kukuruku = Afenmai→EDO
Kukuya→PAPUA AUSTRONESIAN
Kukuya = Kukwa. South Teke D.→NORTH
    WESTERN BANTU
Kukwa. South Teke D.→NORTH WESTERN
    BANTU
Kukwe. Nyakyusa D.→CENTRAL EASTERN
    BANTU
Kula→PAMA-NYUNGAN
Kulaal. Gula D.→ADAMAWA
Kulalau = Kunanau. Paiwan D.→FORMOSAN
    AUSTRONESIAN
Kulaman→NORTHWEST AUSTRONESIAN
Kulanapan = Pomo→POMO
Kulanapo = Pomo→POMO
Kulango→GUR
Kulawi→CENTRAL AND SOUTHERN CELE-
    BES
Kule = Tsamai→CUSHITIC
Kulele→GUR
KULIN→KULINIC
Kulina = Culina→ARAWAKAN
KULINIC see article
Kulino = Culina→ARAWAKAN
Kuliviu→NORTHWESTERN NEW HEB-
    RIDES
Kulja = Ili. Uighur D.→TURKIC
Kulla = Tsamai→CUSHITIC
Kullali = Kalali. Punthamara D.→DIERIC
Kullally = Kalali. Punthamara D.→DIERIC
Kulleespelm = Kalispel→SALISH
Kullespelm = Kalispel→SALISH
Kullo. Walamo D.→OMOTIC
Kulu = Kulung→BANTOID

Kulu'ba. Bari Tr.→EASTERN SUDANIC

Kulu'ba. Low Lugbara D.→CENTRAL SUDAN-
IC

Kulube→BISMARCK ARCHIPELAGO

Kului. Western Pahari D.→INDIC

Kulumali. Karendala D.→DIERIC

Kulung→BANTOID

Kulung→CHADIC

Kulung = Khambu→GYARUNG-MISHMI

Kulunglutchi = Gunwiggu→GUNWINGGU-
AN

Kulunglutji = Gunwiggu→GUNWINGGUAN

Kuluŋ = Kulung→BANTOID

Kum = Toposo→EASTERN SUDANIC

Kuma. Mambila D.→BANTOID

Kuma. Wahgi D.→EAST NEW GUINEA
HIGHLANDS

Kuma = Rusha→NORTH EASTERN BANTU

Kumachisi. Foothill North Yokuts D.→YO-
KUTS

Kumaju→BANTOID

Kumam→EASTERN SUDANIC

Kuman = Chimbu→EAST NEW GUINEA
HIGHLANDS

Kuman = Kumam→EASTERN SUDANIC

Kumanaxo = Cumanacho→MACHACALI

Kumandy. Northern Altai D.→TURKIC

Kumaoni = Kumauni→INDIC

Kumaun. Central Tibetan D.→TIBETAN

Kumauni→INDIC

Kumba→ADAMAWA

Kumba. Losengo D.→NORTH WESTERN
BANTU

Kumba = Tangole→CHADIC

Kumbaingeri = Kumbainggar→KUMBAING-
GARIC

KUMBAINGGARIC see article

Kumbainggeri = Kumbainggar→KUMBAING-
GARIC

Kumbainggiri = Kumbainggar→KUMBAING-
GARIC

Kumbi. Gudu D.→CHADIC

Kumbo. Eregba D.→JUKUNOID

Kumbo. Ijo D.→IJO

Kumboro = Kuboro. Sengan D.→NORTH-
WESTERN AND CENTRAL SOLO-
MONS

Kumbule. Ndandi D.→NORTH EASTERN
BANTU

Kumbulmara = Mitjamba. Ilba D.→PAMA-
MARIC

Kumbuti = Mbuti→NORTH EASTERN BAN-
TU

Kumdauron→HUON-FINISTERRE

Kumfel = Kunfel. Awiya D.→CUSHITIC

Kumi = Toposo→EASTERN SUDANIC

Kumu = Kuumu→NORTH EASTERN BAN-
TU

Kumukh = Kumux. Lak D.→CAUCASIAN

Kumukio→HUON-FINISTERRE

Kumum = Kumam→EASTERN SUDANIC

Kumus = Uduk→KOMAN

Kumux. Lak D.→CAUCASIAN

Kumwenu = Komono→GUR

Kumyk→TURKIC

Kumzai→IRANIAN

Kun = Kuu. Bafang D.→BANTOID

Kunabi = Konkan Standard. Marathi D.→
INDIC

Kunama→CHARI-NILE

Kunambena→NORTHWESTERN AND CEN-
TRAL SOLOMONS

Kunan = Gunian→BUNABAN

Kunana = Lardil→TANGKIC

Kunanau. Paiwan D.→FORMOSAN AUSTRO-
NESIAN

Kunandaburi = Karendala→DIERIC

Kunant = Mansoanka→WEST ATLANTIC

Kunante = Mansoanka→WEST ATLANTIC

KUNAR→INDIC

Kunatachee = Kungadutji. Karendala D.→DIE-
RIC

Kunbau = Kunbi. Khandesi D.→INDIC

Kunbi. Khandesi D.→INDIC

Kunbille = Bile→BANTOID

Kuncho = Cunco. Araucanian D.→PENUTIAN

Kunda→NORTH WESTERN BANTU

Kunda→CENTRAL EASTERN BANTU

Kunda. Losengo D.→NORTH WESTERN
BANTU

Kundjen→PAMA-MARIC

Kundu = Bakundu. Lundu D.→NORTH WEST-
ERN BANTU

Kundu, West = Barue→NORTH WESTERN
BANTU

Kundugr. Kordofanian Nubian Tr.→EASTERN
SUDANIC

Kunfel. Awiya D.→CUSHITIC

Kung→KHOISAN

!Kung = Kung→KHOISAN

Kungaditji = Kungadutji. Karendala D.→
DIERIC

Kungadutji. Karendala D.→DIERIC

Kun-Gait = Wadjabangai. Mandandanji D.→
PAMA-MARIC

Kungara = Fur→NILO-SAHARAN

Kungarakany→AUSTRALIAN MACRO-PHY-
LUM

Kungarditchi = Kungadutji.   Karendala   D.→
    DIERIC
≠Kungau = Nogau.   Kung D.→KHOISAN
Kungeri = Kunggari.   Mandandanji D.→PAMA-
    MARIC
Kungeri = Kuungkari.   Mandandanji   D.→
    PAMA-MARIC
Kunggara→PAMA-MARIC
Kunggari. Mandandanji D.→PAMA-MARIC
Kungkalenja = Kungkalenya. Wangkadjera D.→
    PITTAPITTIC
Kungkalenya. Wangkadjera D.→PITTAPITTIC
Kungkulenje = Kungkalenya.   Wangkadjera
    D.→PITTAPITTIC
Kunglaburra = Koinjmal.   Darambal   D.→
    WAKA-KABIC
Kungmal = Koinjmal. Darambal D.→WAKA-
    KABIC
Kungri = Kunggari.   Mandandanji D.→PAMA-
    MARIC
Kuni→PAPUA AUSTRONESIAN
Kuni = Boazi→MARIND
Kunian = Gunian→BUNABAN
Kunie = Kwenyi→NEW CALEDONIA
Kunike, Deep. Temne D.→WEST ATLANTIC
Kunimaipa→GOILALA
KUNIMAIPA = GOILALA
Kunini = Bine→ORIOMO RIVER
Kunja. Mandandanji D.→PAMA-MARIC
Kunjip. Wahgi D.→EAST NEW GUINEA
    HIGHLANDS
Kunjuti = Burushaski
Kuno. Wahgi D.→EAST NEW GUINEA
    HIGHLANDS
Kuno = Kula→PAMA-NYUNGAN
Kunua→BOUGAINVILLE
Kunuzi = Kenuz. Dongola-Kenuz D.→EAST-
    ERN SUDANIC
Kunyi→CENTRAL WESTERN BANTU
KUOY see MON-KHMER
Kuoy = Kuy→MON-KHMER
Kup. Mundrau D.→ADMIRALTY-WEST-
    ERN ISLANDS
Kupa. Nupe D.→NUPE-GBARI
Kupa = Cupeno→UTO-AZTECAN
Kupa-Kupa. Tobelo D.→NORTH HALMA-
    HERA
Kupanchi = Kupa. Nupe D.→NUPE-GBARI
Kupang→EAST INDONESIAN
Kupapuyngu = Gobabingo→MURNGIC
Kup-Minj. Wahgi D.→EAST NEW GUINEA
    HIGHLANDS
Kupome→NAGA-KUKI-CHIN
Kur. Kei D.→MOLUCCAN

Kur Galli = Brahui→DRAVIDIAN
Kurama→PLATEAU BENUE-CONGO
Kurama→NGAYARDA
Kurangooroo = Karanguru. Dieri D.→DIERIC
Kuranke = Koranko. Malinka D.→MANDE
Kuranko = Koranko. Malinka D.→MANDE
Kurdish, Eastern = Kermanji→IRANIAN
Kurdish, Northern = Zaza→IRANIAN
Kurdish, Southern = Kermanji→IRANIAN
Kurdish, Western = Zaza→IRANIAN
Kurduwongga. Wadjeri D.→KARDU
Kureinji. Maraura D.→NARRINYERIC
Kurengappa = Karenggapa→DIERIC
KURI→YUIN-KURIC
Kuri. BUDUMA D.→CHADIC
Kuri = Kurku→MUNDA
Kuria = Koria→NORTH EASTERN BANTU
Kuria Muria. Modern South Arabic D.→
    SEMITIC
Kurialyuin = Walbanga.   Thaua   D.→YUIN-
    KURIC
Kuriny = Koreng.   Juat   D.→SOUTHWEST
    PAMA-NYUNGAN
Kurku→MUNDA
Kurkuro = Guicuru→CARIB
Kurmuk. Burun Tr.→EASTERN SUDANIC
Kurnandaburi = Karendala→DIERIC
Kurndel = Holma. Njai D.→CHADIC
Kurnic = Bratauolung→PAMA-NYUNGAN
Kurnu = Kula→PAMA-NYUNGAN
Kurobu = Akye→LAGOON
Kurondi. Tumtum Tr.→KORDOFANIAN
Kuro-Urmi. Gold D.→TUNGUS
Kurrana = Karanya. Wangkadjera D.→PITTA-
    PITTIC
Kurrawar = Karawa→KARWAN
Kurrawulla = Karuwali.   Karendala D.→
    DIERIC
Kursi. Kanga Tr.→KORDOFANIAN
Kurtat = Iron. Ossetic D.→IRANIAN
Kuruaya→TUPI
Kurubena = Kunambena→NORTHWESTERN
    AND CENTRAL SOLOMONS
Kurudu→MOLUCCAN
Kurukh→DRAVIDIAN
Kurumba→GUR
Kurumidlanta = Kaurna. Jadliaura D.→YURA
Kurung→KULINIC
Kurunga = Karanga→MABAN
Kurungjangbaluk = Kurung→KULINIC
Kurungtufu. Kube D.→HUON-FINISTERRE
Kurungu = Krongo→KORDOFANIAN
Kurunjang = Wurundjeri. Taungurong D.→
    KULINIC

Kurya = Koria→NORTH EASTERN BANTU
Kusage→NORTHWESTERN AND CENTRAL
  SOLOMONS
Kusaiean→MICRONESIAN
Kusal→GUR
Kusale→GUR
Kusasi = Kusal→GUR
Kuseki = Kumba→ADAMAWA
Kuseri. Kotoko D.→CHADIC
Kusha = Kucha. Walamo D.→OMOTIC
Kushi = Bushi→PLATEAU BENUE-CONGO
≠Kusi = Xatia. ŋ/amani D.→KHOISAN
Kusigilo. Central Koma D.→KOMAN
Kusiuta = Gosiute. Shoshoni D.→UTO-AZ-
  TECAN
Kuskokwim. Ingalit D.→ATHAPASCAN-
  EYAK
Kuskokwim, Upper→ATHAPASCAN-EYAK
Kusopa. Nupe Tr.→NUPE-GBARI
Kusu→NORTH WESTERN BANTU
Kusuko = Ashaku→JUKUNOID
Kusundu→GYARUNG-MISHMI
Kusuvulu→CENTRAL SUDANIC
Kusuwa. Amba D.→NORTH EASTERN BAN-
  TU
Kutana = Kutenai
Kutanai = Kutenai
Kutandji. Wambaya D.→TJINGILI-WAMBA-
  YAN
Kutcha-Kutchin = Kuchin→ATHAPASCAN-
  EYAK
Kutchamakin = Cutshamakin. Massachusett
  Tr.→ALGONQUIAN
Kutchan = Yuma. River Yuman D.→YUMAN
Kutchin = Kuchin→ATHAPASCAN-EYAK
Kutchnamoota = Adnyamathana. Wailpi D.→
  YURA
Kuteb = Zumper→JUKUNOID
Kutenai see article
Kutenay = Kutenai
Kutep = Zumper→JUKUNOID
Kuteringa = Hona. Tera D.→CHADIC
Kutev = Zumper→JUKUNOID
Kutia-Dyapa = Cutiadapa. Catuquina D.→
  MACRO-TUCANOAN
Kutin→ADAMAWA
Kutine = Kutin→ADAMAWA
Kutinn→ADAMAWA
Kutjala. Ilba D.→PAMA-MARIC
Kutneha = Kutenai
Kutsu = Kusu→NORTH WESTERN BANTU
Kutswe = Khutswe. Northern Sotho D.→
  SOUTH EASTERN BANTU
Kutthung = Kattang. Worimi D.→YUIN-KU-

RIC
Kuttibul = Kitabal→BANDJALANGIC
Kutu→CENTRAL EASTERN BANTU
Kutu = Yela→NORTH WESTERN BANTU
Kutubu. Foi D.→EAST NEW GUINEA HIGH-
  LANDS
Kuturincha = Hona. Tera D.→CHADIC
Kuturmi→PLATEAU BENUE-CONGO
Kuu. Bafang D.→BANTOID
Kuumu→NORTH EASTERN BANTU
Kuungkari. Mandandanji D.→PAMA-MARIC
Kuurnkopannoot = Gurnditjmara. Tjapwurong
  D.→KULINIC
Kuvakan. Bashkir D.→TURKIC
Kuvarawan = Kavalan→FORMOSAN AUS-
  TRONESIAN
Kuvilana = Viru→NORTHWESTERN AND
  CENTRAL SOLOMONS
Kuvinga = Kuwi→DRAVIDIAN
KUWAI→SOUTH HALMAHERA AUSTRO-
  NESIAN
Kuwalitsk = Cowlitz→SALISH
Kuwarawan = Kavalan→FORMOSAN AUS-
  TRONESIAN
Kuwi→DRAVIDIAN
Kuy→MON-KHMER
Kuya. Minduumo D.→NORTH WESTERN
  BANTU
Kuyani→YURA
Kuyanni = Kuyani→YURA
Kuyonon = Cuyunon→NORTHWEST AUS-
  TRONESIAN
Kuyunon = Cuyunon→NORTHWEST AUS-
  TRONESIAN
Kuzamani→PLATEAU BENUE-CONGO
Kuznets Tatar = Shor→TURKIC
Kvanada = Bagulal→CAUCASIAN
Kvankhi. Chamalal D.→CAUCASIAN
Kvanxidatl. Andi D.→CAUCASIAN
Kven→KHMUIC
KWA see article
Kwa. Ekoi D.→BANTOID
Kwa = Kwadya. Bete D.→KRU
Kwaa→KRU
Kwaatay→WEST ATLANTIC
Kwac = Ciec. Agar D.→EASTERN SUDANIC
Kwachikwakwa. Shona D.→SOUTH EASTERN
  BANTU
Kwadi→KHOISAN
Kwadrewole = Kwadya. Bete D.→KRU
Kwadya. Bete D.→KRU
Kwahring Klang = Khualringklang→NAGA-
  KUKI-CHIN
Kwaiailk = Upper Chehalis→SALISH

Kwaimbal. Bigumbil D.→WIRADJURIC
Kwaio→EASTERN OCEANIC
Kwaja→BANTOID
Kwakiutl→WAKASHAN
KWAKIUTLAN→WAKASHAN
Kwakum→NORTH WESTERN BANTU
Kwakwa = Avikam→LAGOON
Kwakwak = Kakwa. Bari D.→EASTERN SU-
DANIC
Kwala→NORTH WESTERN BANTU
Kwala Aring. Pangan D.→SEMANG
Kwale→MULAHA
Kwale. Igbo D.→IGBO
Kwalhioqua→ATHAPASCAN-EYAK
Kwalshim = Kwalsim→NAGA-KUKI-CHIN
Kwalsim→NAGA-KUKI-CHIN
Kwama = Koma→KOMAN
Kwamba = Amba→NORTH EASTERN BAN-
TU
Kwambi→SOUTH WESTERN BANTU
Kwamera. Tanna D.→SOUTHERN NEW HEB-
RIDES
Kwandang→NORTHWEST AUSTRONESIAN
Kwandi. Luyana D.→SOUTH WESTERN
BANTU
Kwanga = Gawanga→SEPIK
Kwangali = Kwangari→SOUTH WESTERN
BANTU
Kwangari→SOUTH WESTERN BANTU
Kwange = Gbari Kangye. Gbari D.→NUPE-
GBARI
Kwangli→NAGA-KUKI-CHIN
Kwangwa→SOUTH WESTERN BANTU
Kwanim Pas = Uduk→KOMAN
Kwanka→PLATEAU BENUE-CONGO
Kwansu→NORTH PAPUAN
Kwantlen. Halkomelem D.→SALISH
Kwanyama→SOUTH WESTERN BANTU
Kwara = Quara→CUSHITIC
Kwaraʔae→EASTERN OCEANIC
Kwarafe = Korape→BINANDERE
Kwarekwareo→EASTERN OCEANIC
Kwavi = Maasai→EASTERN SUDANIC
Kwaya. Bete D.→KRU
Kwaya = Jita→NORTH EASTERN BANTU
Kwayam = Koyam. Kanuri Tr.→SAHARAN
Kwazwimba. Shona D.→SOUTH EASTERN
BANTU
Kwe. West Teke D.→NORTH WESTERN
BANTU
Kwe = Kwee→KHOISAN
Kwee→KHOISAN
Kwe-e-tshori = Kwee→KHOISAN
Kwegi = Kwegu→EASTERN SUDANIC

Kwegu→EASTERN SUDANIC
Kwei-yang→KAM-TAI
Kweli = Baakpe→NORTH WESTERN BAN-
TU
Kwelshin = Kwalsim→NAGA-KUKI-CHIN
Kwena. Northern Sotho D.→SOUTH EAST-
ERN BANTU
Kwena. Tswana D.→SOUTH EASTERN BAN-
TU
Kwengo = Hukwe→KHOISAN
Kweni→MANDE
Kwenyi→NEW CALEDONIA
Kwera = Koyra→OMOTIC
Kwerba→NORTH PAPUAN
Kwese→CENTRAL WESTERN BANTU
Kweshin = Kwalsim→NAGA-KUKI-CHIN
Kwesten→NORTH PAPUAN
Kwe-tshori = Kwee→KHOISAN
Kwi = Kui→BURMESE-LOLO
Kwiana = Kayani→YURA
Kwili = Baakpe→NORTH WESTERN BAN-
TU
Kwingsang = Nung→BODO-NAGA-KACHIN
Kwinp'ang = Nung→BODO-NAGA-KACHIN
Kwiri = Baakpe→NORTH WESTERN BAN-
TU
Kwise. Kwadi Tr.→KHOISAN
Kwisso = Kwise. Kwadi Tr.→KHOISAN
Kwitcyan = Yuma. River Yuman D.→YUMAN
Kwogo. Central Koma D.→KOMAN
Kwoireng→NAGA-KUKI-CHIN
Kwoll = Irigwe→PLATEAU BENUE-CONGO
Kwolla→CHADIC
Kwollanyoch. Awiya D.→CUSHITIC
KWOMA→SEPIK
Kwoma→SEPIK
KWOMTARI→NORTH NEW GUINEA
Kwomtari→NORTH NEW GUINEA
Kwotto = Igbira→NUPE-GBARI
Kwotto = Igbira-Panda. Igbira D.→NUPE-
GBARI
Kwottu = Ittu. Galla D.→CUSHITIC
Kwusaun. Boiken D.→SEPIK
Kxalaxari = Kgalagadi. Tswana D.→SOUTH
EASTERN BANTU
//Kxau. ŋ/huki D.→KHOISAN
Kxaxa. Northern Sotho D.→SOUTH EASTERN
BANTU
Kxhalaxdi = Kgalagadi. Tswana D.→SOUTH
EASTERN BANTU
Kxhatla = Kgatla. Tswana D.→SOUTH EAST-
ERN BANTU
Kxloukxle = //xegwe→KHOISAN
Kxoe = Hukwe→KHOISAN

Kyaka. Enga D.→EAST NEW GUINEA HIGH-
LANDS
Kyama→LAGOON
Kyan = Bobo Gbe. Bobo D.→GUR
Kyato = Icen→JUKUNOID
Kyau→NAGA-KUKI-CHIN
Kyaw = Kyau→NAGA-KUKI-CHIN
Kyedye = Gade→NUPE-GBARI
Kyenga = Busa→MANDE
Kyenga-wa = Busa→MANDE
Kyeto = Icen→JUKUNOID
Kyi = Khasi→MON-KHMER
Kyo = Hlota→NAGA-KUKI-CHIN
Kyon = Hlota→NAGA-KUKI-CHIN
Kyontsu = Hlota→NAGA-KUKI-CHIN
Kyopi = Nyoro→NORTH EASTERN BANTU
Kyoquot. Nootka D.→WAKASHAN
Kypchak→TURKIC
Kypchak. Uzbek D.→TURKIC
KYPCHAK-BULGAR→TURKIC
KYPCHAK-COMANIAN = KYPCHAK-PO-
LOVETSIAN→TURKIC
KYPCHAK-POLOVETSIAN→TURKIC
Kyreara = Kariera→NGAYARDA
Kyzyl. Khakas D.→TURKIC
Kyzylbas. Balkan Gagauz Turkish D.→TURKIC

L

La = Li→KAM-TAI
Laadi. Kongo D.→CENTRAL WESTERN
BANTU
Laak = Lak. Nuer D.→EASTERN SUDANIC
Laali. West Teke D.→NORTH WESTERN
BANTU
La'alua = Saaroa→FORMOSAN AUSTRO-
NESIAN
La'aluwa = Haisen. Saaroa D.→FORMOSAN
AUSTRONESIAN
Laan. Solor D.→MOLUCCAN
La'aroa = Saaroa→FORMOSAN AUSTRO-
NESIAN
Labahan. Mokareng D.→ADMIRALTY-WEST-
ERN ISLANDS
Labang = Kotoko→CHADIC
Labat. Beja Tr.→CUSHITIC
Labbat = Labat. Beja Tr.→CUSHITIC
Labea'u. Laki D.→CENTRAL AND SOUTH-
ERN CELEBES
Labet = Labat. Beja Tr.→CUSHITIC
Labhani = Banjuri→INDIC
Laboja. Sumba D.→MOLUCCAN
Labu' = Hapa→NORTHEAST NEW GUINEA
AUSTRONESIAN

Labwor→EASTERN SUDANIC
Lacandon. Maya D.→MAYAN
Lach. Czech D.→SLAVIC
Lachira = Chira. Sec D.→ANDEAN
Laci-Laci = Latijilatji. Djadjala D.→KULINIC
Lactan = Ratagnon. Cuyunon D.→NORTH-
WEST AUSTRONESIAN
Lacu. Sumo Tr.→MISUMALPAN
Ladakhi. West Tibetan D.→TIBETAN
Ladi = Sawai Madhopur. Rajasthani D.→IN-
DIC
LADIN = RHAETO-ROMANCE→ RO-
MANCE
Ladin→ROMANCE
Ladino. Spanish D.→ROMANCE
Ladwags = Ladakhi. West Tibetan D.→TIBET-
AN
La'edo = Wotu→CENTRAL AND SOUTH-
ERN CELEBES
Laevo = Lewo. Tasiko D.→EASTERN OCEAN-
IC
Laewamba = Wampur→NORTHEAST NEW
GUINEA AUSTRONESIAN
la-Fa' = Fa'→NORTH WESTERN BANTU
Lafofa→KORDOFANIAN
Lag = Laka. Gambai D.→CENTRAL SUDAN-
IC
Lagalian. Lettish D.→BALTIC
Lagaui = Lagawe. Ifugao D.→NORTHWEST
AUSTRONESIAN
Lagawe. Ifugao D.→NORTHWEST AUSTRO-
NESIAN
Lagba. Banda D.→EASTERN
Laghmani = Pasai→INDIC
Laghu Hindi = Bazaar Hindi. Western Hindi
D.→INDIC
Lago = Pok. Nandi D.→EASTERN SUDANIC
LAGOONS see article
Lagoons = Tolowa. Chasta Costa D.→ATHA-
PASCAN-EYAK
Lagubi = Mambila→BANTOID
Laguna. Keres D.
Lagwane = Kotoko Daa. Kotoko D.→CHADIC
Lagwane = Logone. Kotoko D.→CHADIC
Lagwane Birni = Logone. Kotoko D.→CHAD-
IC
Laha. Wahai D.→EAST INDONESIAN
Lahanan. Ba Mali D.→WEST INDONESIAN
Lahnda→INDIC
Lahu→BURMESE-LOLO
Lahu = Avikam→LAGOON
Lahul. West Tibetan D.→TIBETAN
Lahul = Manchati→GYARUNG-MISHMI
Lahuli = Lahul. West Tibetan D.→TIBETAN

Lahuna. Lahu D.→BURMESE-LOLO
Lai = Gablai→CHADIC
Lai = Haka→NAGA-KUKI-CHIN
Lai = Li→KAM-TAI
Laiap. Enga D.→EAST NEW GUINEA HIGH-
    LANDS
Laichau→BURMESE-LOLO
Laierdila = Lardil→TANGKIC
Laimon = Cochimi→HOKAN
Laitchi-Laitchi = Latjilatji. Djadjala D.→KU-
    LINIC
Laitu = Latjilatji. Djadjala D.→KULINIC
Laitu-Laitu = Latjilatji. Djadjala D.→KULIN-
    IC
Laiwonu→CENTRAL   AND   SOUTHERN
    CELEBES
Laiwui→CENTRAL   AND   SOUTHERN
    CELEBES
Laizo→NAGA-KUKI-CHIN
Lajolo. Wolio D.→CENTRAL AND SOUTH-
    ERN CELEBES
Lak→CAUCASIAN
Lak. Nuer D.→EASTERN SUDANIC
Lak = Laka.   Gambai   D.→CENTRAL
    SUDANIC
Laka→MIAO-YAO
Laka. Gambai D.→CENTRAL SUDANIC
Laka Mbere. Kari D.→ADAMAWA
la-Kaaloŋ = Kaaloŋ→NORTH   WESTERN
    BANTU
Lakahia→SOUTH HALMAHERA AUSTRO-
    NESIAN
Lakalai = Nakanai→NORTHEAST   NEW
    GUINEA AUSTRONESIAN
LAK-DARGWA→CAUCASIAN
Lake Macquarie = Awabakal. Wanarua D.→
    YUIN-KURIC
LAKHER→NAGA-KUKI-CHIN
Lakher = Mara→NAGA-KUKI-CHIN
Laki→CENTRAL   AND   SOUTHERN
    CELEBES
Lakia→KAM-TAI
Lakka. Kari D.→ADAMAWA
Lakkia = Lakia→KAM-TAI
Lako = Pok. Nandi D.→EASTERN SUDANIC
Lakon→EASTERN OCEANIC
Lakor. Leti D.→MOLUCCAN
Lakota = Teton. Dakota D.→SIOUAN
Lakume = Manukolu→MULAHA
Lala→CENTRAL EASTERN BANTU
Lala→PAPUA AUSTRONESIAN
Lala. Nguni D.→SOUTH EASTERN BANTU
Lala.   Talu   D.→ADMIRALTY-WESTERN
    ISLANDS

Lala = Yunger→ADAMAWA
Lala'eo. Bare'e D.→CENTRAL AND SOUTH-
    ERN CELEBES
Lalaki = Laki→CENTRAL AND SOUTHERN
    CELEBES
Lalaua = Kalagua. Kalinga D.→NORTHWEST
    AUSTRONESIAN
Lali = Laali. West Teke D.→NORTH WEST-
    ERN BANTU
Lalia→NORTH WESTERN BANTU
Laliklik = Rikiriki. Paiwan D.→FORMOSAN
    AUSTRONESIAN
Lama→GUR
Lama = Central Tibetan→TIBETAN
Lamalama→PAMA-MARIC
Lamalanga→EASTERN OCEANIC
Lamam = Campuon→MON-KHMER
Lamama'di. Moru D.→CENTRAL SUDANIC
Lamangkau → NORTHWESTERN   NEW
    HEBRIDES
Lamanu. Tasiko D.→EASTERN OCEANIC
Lamasa→BISMARCK ARCHIPELAGO
Lamatukan. Solor D.→MOLUCCAN
Lamba→CENTRAL EASTERN BANTU
Lamba→GUR
Lambau = Ramfau. Siane D.→EAST NEW
    GUINEA HIGHLANDS
Lambia. Tumbuka D.→CENTRAL EASTERN
    BANTU
Lambichhong→GYARUNG-MISHMI
Lambitchong = Lambichhong→GYARUNG-
    MISHMI
Lamboja = Laboja. Sumba D.→MOLUCCAN
Lambon→BISMARCK ARCHIPELAGO
la-Mboŋ = Kaaloŋ→NORTH   WESTERN
    BANTU
Lambu = Rampi. Leboni D.→CENTRAL AND
    SOUTHERN CELEBES
Lambumbu→NORTHWESTERN NEW HE-
    BRIDES
Lambwa = Lambia. Tumbuka D.→CENTRAL
    EASTERN BANTU
Lambya = Lambia. Tumbuka D.→CENTRAL
    EASTERN BANTU
Lame→BANTOID
Lame→CHADIC
Lamertiviri. Kati D.→NURISTANI
Lamet→KHMUIC
LAMGANG→NAGA-KUKI-CHIN
Lamnso→BANTOID
Lamotrek. Ulithian D.→MICRONESIAN
Lampung→WEST INDONESIAN
Lampung = Bakoi.   Lawangan   D.→WEST
    INDONESIAN

Lamso = Lamnso→BANTOID

Lamu = Amu. Swahili D.→CENTRAL EAST-
ERN BANTU

Lamut = Even→TUNGUS

Lanao = Maranao→NORTHWEST AUSTRO-
NESIAN

Landawe→CENTRAL AND SOUTHERN
CELEBES

Landogo = Loko→MANDE

Landoma = Landuma→WEST ATLANTIC

Landouman = Landuma→WEST ATLANTIC

Landu. Land Dayak D.→WEST INDONESIAN

Landuma→WEST ATLANTIC

Lang = Maru→BODO-NAGA-KACHIN

Langa→KOMAN

Langa. Ombo D.→NORTH WESTERN
BANTU

Langalanga→EASTERN OCEANIC

Langam. Kaima D.→INDO-PACIFIC

Langama = Langimar→KUKUKUKU

la-Ngayaba = Ngayaba→NORTH WESTERN
BANTU

Langba. Banda D.→EASTERN

Langbase = Langwasi. Banda D.→EASTERN

Langbwasse = Langwasi. Banda D.→EASTERN

Lange. Luba-Lulua D.→CENTRAL WESTERN
BANTU

Lange = Burun→EASTERN SUDANIC

Langet→NAGA-KUKI-CHIN

Langi→NORTH EASTERN BANTU

Langimar→KUKUKUKU

Lango→EASTERN SUDANIC

Lango. Lotuho D.→EASTERN SUDANIC

Lango = Akoli→EASTERN SUDANIC

Lango = Didinga→EASTERN SUDANIC

Lango Dyang = Karamojong→EASTERN
SUDANIC

Langoan. Tontemboan D.→NORTHERN CEL-
EBES

Langrong→NAGA-KUKI-CHIN

Langtup→NORTHEASTERN NEW GUINEA

Langulo = Sanye→CUSHITIC

Langwa. Tsaiwa D.→BODO-NAGA-KACHIN

Langwasi. Banda D.→EASTERN

Langya. Jeh D.→MON-KHMER

Langya = Takua→MON-KHMER

Lanima. Wangkadjera D.→PITTAPITTIC

Lanima = Ulaolinya→PITTAPITTIC

Lankakol = Ho. Mundari D.→MUNDA

Lansu = Maru→BODO-NAGA-KACHIN

Lanun = Ilanun. Maranao D.→NORTHWEST
AUSTRONESIAN

Lanun = Lahanan. Ba Mali D.→WEST INDO-
NESIAN

Lanuvian→ITALIC

Lanyagachek. Toba Tr.→GUAYCURU

Laŋo = Lango. Lotuho D.→EASTERN SU-
DANIC

Lado Miro = Lango→EASTERN SUDANIC

Lao→KAM-TAI

Lao = Kelao→KAM-TAI

Laotian = Lao→KAM-TAI

Lapacho = Apolista→ARAWAKAN

Lapak. Ewondo D.→NORTH WESTERN
BANTU

Lapalapa = Leco→ANDEAN

Lapawa. Reshe Tr.→PLATEAU BENUE-
CONGO

Lapp, Southern→URALIC

LAPPIC→URALIC

Lapuchu = Apolista→ARAWAKAN

Laqi = Zway. East Gurage D.→SEMITIC

Laqua→KAM-TAI

Lara. Land Dayak D.→WEST INDONESIAN

Laragia = Larakia→LARAKIAN

LARAKIAN see article

Laral. Abui D.→TIMOR-ALOR

Larauwa = Larawa. Reshe Tr.→PLATEAU
BENUE-CONGO

Laravat→NORTHWESTERN NEW HEB-
RIDES

Larawa. Reshe Tr.→PLATEAU BENUE-
CONGO

Lardil→TANGKIC

Lare. Kanuri Tr.→SAHARAN

Larewa = Lare. Kanuri Tr.→SAHARAN

Lari. Persian D.→IRANIAN

Lari. Sindhi D.→INDIC

Lari. Terraba D.→CHIBCHAN

Lari = Laadi. Kongo D.→CENTRAL WEST-
ERN BANTU

Laria = Chhattisgarhi. Eastern Hindi D.→
INDIC

Larikia = Larakia→LARAKIAN

Larim = Longarim→EASTERN SUDANIC

Lariminit = Longarim→EASTERN SUDANIC

Laro→KORDOFANIAN

Laro→LEFT MAY

Laro = Larawa. Reshe Tr.→PLATEAU BE-
NUE-CONGO

Larragea = Larakia→LARAKIAN

Larrakeah = Larakia→LARAKIAN

Larrakeeyah = Larakia→LARAKIAN

Larrakia = Larakia→LARAKIAN

Larrakiha = Larakia→LARAKIAN

Larreekeeyah = Larakia→LARAKIAN

Larrekiya = Larakia→LARAKIAN

Larrikia = Larakia→LARAKIAN

Larrikiya = Larakia→LARAKIAN
Larriquia = Larakia→LARAKIAN
Larua. Sumba D.→MOLUCCAN
Lasa. Margi D.→CHADIC
Lasahata. Tala D.→EAST INDONESIAN
LASHAI→NAGA-KUKI-CHIN
Lashi→BODO-NAGA-KACHIN
Lasi. Sindhi D.→INDIC
Lasi = Lashi→BODO-NAGA-KACHIN
Lassik. Nongatl D.→ATHAPASCAN-EYAK
Lat. Koho D.→MON-KHMER
Latagnon = Ratagnon. Cuyunon D.→NORTH-
    WEST AUSTRONESIAN
Latan = Ratagnon. Cuyunon D.→NORTH-
    WEST AUSTRONESIAN
Latar. Mundari D.→MUNDA
Lati→KAM-TAI
LATI-KELAO→KAM-TAI
Latin → ITALIC
LATIN-FALISCAN = LATINO-FALISCAN
    →ITALIC
LATINIAN = LATINO-FALISCAN→ITALIC
LATINO-FALISCAN→ITALIC
Latjilatji. Djadjala D.→KULINIC
Latjoo-Latjoo = Latjilatji. Djadjala D.→
    KULINIC
Lattuka = Lotuho→EASTERN SUDANIC
Latuko = Lotuho→EASTERN SUDANIC
Latvian = Lettish→BALTIC
Latyoo-Latyoo = Latjilatji. Djadjala D.→
    KULINIC
Lau→EASTERN OCEANIC
Lau. Bandawa D.→JUKUNOID
Lau. Rek D.→EASTERN SUDANIC
Lau = Lou. Nuer D.→EASTERN SUDANIC
Laudje = Tinombo→NORTHERN CELEBES
Laues. Ndrosun D.→ADMIRALTY-WEST-
    ERN ISLANDS
LAUIC→EASTERN OCEANIC
Lauisaranga = Aruop→TORRICELLI
Laukanu = Kelana→NORTHEAST NEW
    GUINEA AUSTRONESIAN
Lauli. Sumba D.→MOLUCCAN
Laumbe→CENTRAL MELANESIAN
Laungwaw = Maru→BODO-NAGA-KACHIN
Laura = Taura→NORTHWESTERN AND
    CENTRAL SOLOMONS
Laurentian→IROQUOIS
Laurowani = Pasai→INDIC
Lau'u = Aruop→TORRICELLI
Lauuna→MAILU
Lauwa→MAILU
Lave = Veh→MON-KHMER
Laveh→MON-KHMER

Lavukaleve = Laumbe→CENTRAL MELANE-
    SIAN
Lawa→PALAUNG-WA
Lawa. Lawangan D.→WEST INDONESIAN
Lawa = Lauwa→MAILU
Lawangan→WEST INDONESIAN
Lawng = Maru→BODO-NAGA-KACHIN
Lawngvaw = Maru→BODO-NAGA-KACHIN
Lawoet = Lonchong→WEST INDONESIAN
Lawthve→NAGA-KUKI-CHIN
Layana. Guana D.→MAIPURAN
Laymon = Cochimi→HOKAN
Laymon-Cochimi = Cochimi→HOKAN
Laymonem = Cochimi→HOKAN
Laynngith = Alngith→PAMA-MARIC
Laz. Zan D.→CAUCASIAN
Le = Li→KAM-TAI
Lean y Mulia. Jicaque D.→HOKAN
le-Angba = Angba→NORTH WESTERN
    BANTU
Leb Laŋo = Lango→EASTERN SUDANIC
Lebama. Legbo D.→CROSS RIVER BENUE-
    CONGO
Lebed Tatar = Chalkandu. Northern Altai
    D.→TURKIC
Lebei→ADMIRALTY-WESTERN ISLANDS
Lebir. Pangan D.→SEMANG
Lebong. Redjang D.→WEST INDONESIAN
Leboni→CENTRAL AND SOUTHERN
    CELEBES
le-Boro = Angba→NORTH WESTERN
    BANTU
Lebou. Wolof D.→WEST ATLANTIC
Lebu. Moro D.→KORDOFANIAN
Leca = Leco→ANDEAN
Lecan = Leco→ANDEAN
Lecheyal. Alacaluf D.→ANDEAN
Lech'i. Tsaiwa D.→BODO-NAGA-KACHIN
Lechi = Lashi→BODO-NAGA-KACHIN
Lechkum = Lexchxum. Georgian D.→CAUCA-
    SIAN
Leco→ANDEAN
Ledo' = Palu→CENTRAL AND SOUTHERN
    CELEBES
Leealowa = Alawa→MARAN
Leearrawa = Karawa→KARWAN
Leedji. Peri D.→NORTH EASTERN BANTU
Leega. Lega D.→NORTH EASTERN BANTU
Leega Imuzimu. Lega D.→NORTH EASTERN
    BANTU
Leek. Nuer D.→EASTERN SUDANIC
Leelawarra = Mara→MARAN
Leewakya = Wakaya→WAKAYA-WARLU-
    WARIC

Lefana→CENTRAL TOGO
LEFT MAY see article
Lega→NORTH EASTERN BANTU
Lega. Ndandi D.→NORTH EASTERN BANTU
LEGA-KALANGA → NORTH EASTERN BANTU
Legba = Dompago→GUR
Legbo→CROSS RIVER BENUE-CONGO
Lego. Bare'e D.→CENTRAL AND SOUTHERN CELEBES
Lego = Lekon→ADAMAWA
Legre. Bete Tr.→KRU
Leh. West Tibetan D.→TIBETAN
Leha→EASTERN OCEANIC
Lehar→WEST ATLANTIC
Lei Ping. Nung D.→KAM-TAI
Leik = Leek. Nuer D.→EASTERN SUDANIC
Leisu = Lisu→BURMESE-LOLO
Leitchi-Leitchi = Latjilatji. Djadjala D.→KULINIC
Leiwa. Tulu D.→ADMIRALTY-WESTERN ISLANDS
Lejengoup'a = Lisu→BURMESE-LOLO
Leket→NEW BRITAIN
Lekhitic→SLAVIC
Leko. Losengo D.→NORTH WESTERN BANTU
Leko = Lekon→ADAMAWA
Lekon→ADAMAWA
Lekon. Sichule D.→WEST INDONESIAN
Lekong. Sasak D.→WEST INDONESIAN
Leku = Leko. Losengo D.→NORTH WESTERN BANTU
Lela = Lyele→GUR
Lelak. Narom D.→WEST INDONESIAN
Lele→NORTH WESTERN BANTU
Lele. Malinka D.→MANDE
Lele. Nancere D.→CHADIC
Lele = Lyele→GUR
L'ele = Lyele→GUR
Lelemi = Lefana→CENTRAL TOGO
Lelepa. Efate D.→EASTERN OCEANIC
Lelese = Lyele→GUR
Lemande = Mandi→NORTH WESTERN BANTU
Lemande = Mandi. Banen Tr.→NORTH WESTERN BANTU
Lemaroro = Tasiko→EASTERN OCEANIC
Lemba = Kela→NORTH WESTERN BANTU
Lemben→EAST NEW GUINEA HIGHLANDS
Lembue. Bemba D.→CENTRAL EASTERN BANTU
Lemet = Lamet→KHMUIC
Lemiting. Narom D.→WEST INDONESIAN

Lemnian = Tyrrhenian
Lemusmus→BISMARCK ARCHIPELAGO
Lemyo. Aso Tr.→NAGA-KUKI-CHIN
Lenakel. Tanna D.→SOUTHERN NEW HEBRIDES
Lenape. Delaware D.→ALGONQUIAN
Lenapee = Lenape. Delaware D.→ALGONQUIAN
Lenapi = Lenape. Delaware D.→ALGONQUIAN
Lenca→MACRO-CHIBCHAN
Lendi. Sumba D.→MOLUCCAN
Lendu→CENTRAL SUDANIC
Leng Bano = Simalur→WEST INDONESIAN
Lenge = Chopi→SOUTH EASTERN BANTU
Lengo→EASTERN OCEANIC
Lengola→NORTH EASTERN BANTU
Lengreng = Langrong→NAGA-KUKI-CHIN
Lengua→MATACO
Lengua. Mascoy D.→MACRO-PANOAN
Lengua = Payagua. Mbaya-Guaicuru Tr.→GUAYCURU
Lengue→CENTRAL WESTERN BANTU
Lenje→CENTRAL EASTERN BANTU
LENJE-TONGA → CENTRAL EASTERN BANTU
Lenkaitahe = Liambata→EAST INDONESIAN
Lennape = Lenape. Delaware D.→ALGONQUIAN
Lennappe = Lenape. Delaware D.→ALGONQUIAN
Lenni = Lenape. Delaware D.→ALGONQUIAN
Lenni-Lenape = Lenape. Delaware D.→ALGONQUIAN
Lente→NAGA-KUKI-CHIN
Leon→EASTERN OCEANIC
LEONARD SCHULTZE see article
Lepanto Igorot = Kankanay→NORTHWEST AUSTRONESIAN
Lepcha→BODO-NAGA-KACHIN
Lepoha = Lepcha→BODO-NAGA-KACHIN
Lepontic→ITALIC
Leptsa = Lepcha→BODO-NAGA-KACHIN
Lepu Anau. Kenyah D.→WEST INDONESIAN
Lepu Pohun. Kenyah D.→WEST INDONESIAN
Lepu Potong. Sarawak Murut D.→WEST INDONESIAN
Lepu Pun. Kenyah D.→WEST INDONESIAN
Lepu Sawa. Kenyah D.→WEST INDONESIAN
Lepu Tau. Kenyah D.→WEST INDONESIAN
Lera. Ruanda D.→NORTH EASTERN BANTU

Lere. Mundang D.→ADAMAWA
Lere = Lyele→GUR
Lerek. Solor D.→MOLUCCAN
Lerewa = Lare. Kanuri Tr.→SAHARAN
Leron→HUON-FINISTERRE
Lesau. Nyada D.→ADMIRALTY - WESTERN
   ISLANDS
Lese. Mamvu-Efe D.→CENTRAL SUDANIC
Lese Dese = Ndese. Mamvu-Efe D.→CEN-
   TRAL SUDANIC
Leshuoop'a = Lisu→BURMESE-LOLO
Lesuo = Lisu→BURMESE-LOLO
Leta. Masenrempulu D.→CENTRAL AND
   SOUTHERN CELEBES
Letatan. Panaras D.→NEW BRITAIN
Lete. Tswana D.→SOUTH EASTERN BANTU
Leti→MOLUCCAN
Letsi = Lashi→BODO-NAGA-KACHIN
Lets'i = Lashi→BODO-NAGA-KACHIN
Lettish→BALTIC
Letwurung. Leti D.→MOLUCCAN
Letzburgisch = Luxemburgian. Netherlandic-
   German D.→GERMANIC
Leu = Bru→MON-KHMER
Leuangiua = Luangiua→POLYNESIAN
Leun→MON-KHMER
Leung = Bru→MON-KHMER
Leuvuche. Araucanian D.→PENUTIAN
Levo = Lewo. Tasiko D.→EASTERN OCEAN-
   IC
Lewi = Kakelewa. Luhya D.→NORTH EAST-
   ERN BANTU
Lewo. Tasiko D.→EASTERN OCEANIC
Lexchxum. Georgian D.→CAUCASIAN
Leya. Tomga D.→CENTRAL EASTERN
   BANTU
Leyiga = Leyigha→CROSS RIVER BENUE-
   CONGO
Leyigha→CROSS RIVER BENUE-CONGO
Leytean = Waray→NORTHWEST AUSTRO-
   NESIAN
LEZGHIAN→CAUCASIAN
Lezghian→CAUCASIAN
Lgalige = Koalib→KORDOFANIAN
Lhasa. Central Tibetan D.→TIBETAN
Lhaten = Sekani. Sekani D.→ATHAPASCAN-
   EYAK
Lhoke. Central Tibetan D.→TIBETAN
Lhoskad. Central Tibetan D.→TIBETAN
Lhota = Hlota→NAGA-KUKI-CHIN
Li→KAM-TAI
Liae. Havunese D.→MOLUCCAN
Liambata→EAST INDONESIAN
Liang. Ambonese D.→MOLUCCAN

Liap. Buyang D.→ADMIRALTY-WESTERN
   ISLANDS
Liaro. Kisi D.→WEST ATLANTIC
li-Baali = Bali→NORTH EASTERN BANTU
li-Bati = Bati→NORTH WESTERN BANTU
Libbung. Sarawak Murut D.→WEST INDO-
   NESIAN
li-Benge = Bati→NORTH WESTERN BANTU
Libido = Hadiyya→CUSHITIC
Libinja. Loi-Ngiri D.→NORTH WESTERN
   BANTU
li-Binza = Binza. Ngombe D.→NORTH
   WESTERN BANTU
Libo→ADAMAWA
li-Boa = Boa→NORTH WESTERN BANTU
Libolo = Bolo→CENTRAL WESTERN BAN-
   TU
li-Bombi = Bombi. Huku D.→NORTH EAST-
   ERN BANTU
li-Bvanuma = Bvanuma. Huku D.→NORTH
   EASTERN BANTU
Lichagotegodi. Mbaya-Guaicuru Tr.→GUAY-
   CURU
li-Duma = Duma→NORTH WESTERN BAN-
   TU
LIFIC = LOYALTY ISLANDS
Lifoto = Poto. Losengo D.→NORTH WEST-
   ERN BANTU
Lifu→LOYALTY ISLANDS
Ligbi→MANDE
Liggi. Bari Tr.→EASTERN SUDANIC
Ligone = Ligbi→MANDE
Ligony = Ligbi→MANDE
Ligoui = Ligbi→MANDE
Ligri. Jarawa D.→BANTOID
Liguri→EASTERN SUDANIC
Ligurian→ITALIC
Ligwi = Ligbi→MANDE
Lihir→BISMARCK ARCHIPELAGO
Lihyanite. Old South Arabic D.→SEMITIC
Likananta = Atacameno→MACRO-CHIB-
   CHAN
li-Kango = Kango→NORTH WESTERN
   BANTU
Likango = Kango→NORTH WESTERN BAN-
   TU
Likarili = Kari→CENTRAL WESTERN
   BANTU
Likəs-utsia= Bok. Majaku D.→WEST ATLAN-
   TIC
Likila→NORTH WESTERN BANTU
Liko→NORTH EASTERN BANTU
Likolo. Poke Tr.→NORTH WESTERN
   BANTU

Likouala = Kwala→NORTH WESTERN BANTU

Likpe→CENTRAL TOGO

Likpele = Likpe→CENTRAL TOGO

li-Kuba = Kuba→NORTH WESTERN BANTU

Likwala = Kwala→NORTH WESTERN BANTU

Lila = Lilawa. Dakakari Tr.→PLATEAU BENUE-CONGO

Lilana = Lilawa. Dakakari Tr.→PLATEAU BENUE-CONGO

LI-LAQUA→KAM-TAI

Lilau→BOGIA

Lilawa. Dakakari Tr.→PLATEAU BENUE-CONGO

Lile→CHIBCHAN

Lileko. Kele Tr.→NORTH WESTERN BANTU

Liliboi. Ambonese D.→MOLUCCAN

li-Liko = Liko→NORTH EASTERN BANTU

Lilima. Shona D.→SOUTH EASTERN BANTU

Lilisha = Rikiriki. Paiwan D.→FORMOSAN AUSTRONESIAN

Lillooet→SALISH

Liloeet = Lillooet→SALISH

Lilowat = Lilooet→SALISH

Lilse = Kurumba→GUR

Lima→EAST INDONESIAN

Lima. Kanga Tr.→KORDOFANIAN

Limalua. Panaras D.→NEW BRITAIN

Limba→WEST ATLANTIC

Limba = Mulimba→NORTH WESTERN BANTU

Limbakaraja = Iwaidji→IWAIDJAN

Limboto→NORTHWEST AUSTRONESIAN

Limbu→GYARUNG-MISHMI

li-Mbudza = Mbudza. Losengo D.→NORTH WESTERN BANTU

Limbum = Nsungli→BANTOID

Limbur = Kawel. Abui D.→TIMOR-ALOR

Limera→EAST INDONESIAN

Limi = Remi→NORTH EASTERN BANTU

li-Mpesa. = Mpesa. Losengo D.→NORTH WESTERN BANTU

Linapi = Lenape. Delaware D.→ALGONQUIAN

Linda. Banda D.→EASTERN

Lindja. Havu D.→NORTH EASTERN BANTU

Lindri = Rindre→PLATEAU BENUE-CONGO

Lindrou. Lebei D.→ADMIRALTY-WESTERN ISLANDS

Lindu. Kulawi D.→CENTRAL AND SOUTHERN CELEBES

Linear A see article

Linear B. Ancient Greek D.→GREEK

Linga = Kanakuru→CHADIC

Lingala = Mangala. Losengo D.→NORTH WESTERN BANTU

li-Ngbee = Ngbee→CENTRAL WESTERN BANTU

Lingi = Bwela. 'Doko D.→NORTH WESTERN BANTU

Lingotes = Ilongot→NORTHWEST AUSTRONESIAN

Lingua Selica = Kalispel→SALISH

Ling-yun→KAM-TAI

Lin-hsia. Mongour D.→MONGOLIAN

Linngithig. Alngith D.→PAMA-MARIC

Lino. Bomwali Tr.→NORTH WESTERN BANTU

Lintchanre. Dogrib Tr.→ATHAPASCAN-EYAK

li-Nyali = Nyali. Huku D.→NORTH EASTERN BANTU

Linyeli = Pande→NORTH WESTERN BANTU

Linzeli = Pande→NORTH WESTERN BANTU

Lio. Sikka D.→MOLUCCAN

Lipan. Navajo D.→ATHAPASCAN-EYAK

Lipanja. Mabaale D.→NORTH WESTERN BANTU

Lipe = Atacameno→MACRO-CHIBCHAN

Lipha. Lisu D.→BURMESE-LOLO

Lipho. Lisu D.→BURMESE-LOLO

li-Poto = Poto. Losengo D.→NORTH WESTERN BANTU

Lippa. Thebor D.→GYARUNG-MISHMI

Lir = Lihir→BISMARCK ARCHIPELAGO

Lirong. Sibop D.→WEST INDONESIAN

Lis = Bagirmi→CENTRAL SUDANIC

Lisabata→EAST INDONESIAN

Lisela→EAST INDONESIAN

Lishaw = Lisu→BURMESE-LOLO

Lisi = Bagirmi→CENTRAL SUDANIC

LISRAMIC = AFROASIATIC

Lisshaw = Lisu→BURMESE-LOLO

Lissongo = Mbati→NORTH WESTERN BANTU

Lissu = Lisu→BURMESE-LOLO

Lisu→BURMESE-LOLO

Litchoo-Litchoo = Litjilatji. Djadjala D.→KULINIC

Litchy-Litchy = Latjilatji. Djadjala D.→KULINIC

li-Tembo = Tembo→NORTH WESTERN BANTU

Litembo = Tembo→NORTH WESTERN BANTU

li-Thiro = Tira→KORDOFANIAN
Lithuanian→BALTIC
Litime. Kposo D.→CENTRAL TOGO
Litoro = Otoro→KORDOFANIAN
Liuliu→NORTHWESTERN AND CENTRAL
    SOLOMONS
Liutwa. Poke Tr.→NORTH WESTERN BAN-
    TU
Livara→EASTERN OCEANIC
Livonian→URALIC
Liwuli = Bowili→CENTRAL TOGO
Liyang = Kwoireng→NAGA-KUKI-CHIN
Lkungen = Songish. Northern Straits Salish
    D.→SALISH
Llamba = Nilamba→NORTH EASTERN
    BANTU
Llanero = Comanche. Shoshoni D.→UTO-
    AZTECAN
Llimbumi = Nsungli→BANTOID
Llogole = Logooli→NORTH EASTERN BAN-
    TU
l-Logooli = Logooli→NORTH EASTERN
    BANTU
Lngngam = Lyngngam. Khasi D.→MON-
    KHMER
Lo. Torres D.→EASTERN OCEANIC
Lo = Kweni→MANDE
Loac. Tagakaolo D.→NORTHWEST AUSTRO-
    NESIAN
Loanatit. Tanna D.→SOUTHERN NEW HEB-
    RIDES
Lobaha = Lombaha. Omba D.→EASTERN
    OCEANIC
Lobala→NORTH WESTERN BANTU
Lobat = Labat. Beja Tr.→CUSHITIC
Lobedu. Northern Sotho D.→SOUTH EAST-
    ERN BANTU
LOBI→GUR
Lobi→GUR
LOBIRI→GUR
Lobiri→GUR
Loble. Bete Tr.→KRU
Lobnor. Uighur D.→TURKIC
Lobo. Mabaale D.→NORTH WESTERN BAN-
    TU
Loda→NORTH HALMAHERA
Lodobelolon. Solor D.→MOLUCCAN
Log Acoli = Akoli→EASTERN SUDANIC
Logahaja = Longgahaja→NORTHWESTERN
    AND CENTRAL SOLOMONS
Logananga. Banen Tr.→NORTH WESTERN
    BANTU
Logar. Ormuri D.→IRANIAN
Logba→CENTRAL TOGO

Logba = Dompago→GUR
Logbo. Kposo D.→CENTRAL TOGO
Logea = Rogea. Suau D.→PAPUA AUSTRO-
    NESIAN
Loghoma = Loghon. Kulango D.→GUR
Loghoma = Loma→MANDE
Loghon. Kulango D.→GUR
Logir. Lotuho D.→EASTERN SUDANIC
Logiri. Lotuho D.→EASTERN SUDANIC
Logo→CENTRAL SUDANIC
Logo Kuli = Logo→CENTRAL SUDANIC
Logoke = El Kebira. Tulishi D.→KORDOFA-
    NIAN
Logoma = Loghon. Kulango D.→GUR
Logone. Kotoko D.→CHADIC
Logooli→NORTH EASTERN BANTU
Logorban = Umm Durein. Moro D.→KORDO-
    FANIAN
Logo-ti = Logo→CENTRAL SUDANIC
Lohia. Sapolewa D.→EAST INDONESIAN
Lohoocat. Pawnee D.→CADDOAN
Lohorong→GYARUNG-MISHMI
Loi. Loi-Ngiri D.→NORTH WESTERN BAN-
    TU
Loi. Tulu D.→ADMIRALTY-WESTERN IS-
    LANDS
Loi = Li→KAM-TAI
Loi = Monglwe. Angku D.→PALAUNG-WA
Loikera see Kisar→MOLUCCAN
Loikop = Maasai→EASTERN SUDANIC
Loinang→CENTRAL AND SOUTHERN
    CELEBES
LOINANG-BANGGAI→CENTRAL   AND
    SOUTHERN CELEBES
Loindang = Loinang→CENTRAL AND
    SOUTHERN CELEBES
Loi-Ngiri→NORTH WESTERN BANTU
Loirya = Lokoya. Lotuho D.→EASTERN SU-
    DANIC
Loisu = Lisu→BURMESE-LOLO
Loitja. Tawi D.→ADMIRALTY→WESTERN
    ISLANDS
Lokai. Ma'di D.→CENTRAL SUDANIC
lo-Kalo = Kalo. Nkutu D.→NORTH WEST-
    ERN BANTU
Lokathan. Lotuho D.→EASTERN SUDANIC
Lokathan. Teso D.→EASTERN SUDANIC
Lokele = Kele→NORTH WESTERN BANTU
Lokele, Pseudo- = Lomboki. Poke Tr.→NORTH
    WESTERN BANTU
Lokhay. Uzbek D.→TURKIC
Loko→MANDE
Loko = Yakurr→CROSS RIVER BENUE-
    CONGO

Lokoiya = Lokoya. Lotuho D.→EASTERN SUDANIC

Lokoja = Lokoya. Lotuho D.→EASTERN SUDANIC

Lokono→NORTHERN MAIPURAN

Lokoro = Pari. Anuak Tr.→EASTERN SUDANIC

Lokoya. Lotuho D.→EASTERN SUDANIC

Lokundu = Bakundu. Lundu D.→NORTH WESTERN BANTU

lo-Kutsu = Kusu→NORTH WESTERN BANTU

Lola→EAST INDONESIAN

Lolajan. Mongondow D.→NORTHERN CELEBES

Lolak. Mongondow D.→NORTHERN CELEBES

Lolaki = Laki→CENTRAL AND SOUTHERN CELEBES

Lolang. Lawangan D.→WEST INDONESIAN

Lole = Lore→CENTRAL AND SOUTHERN CELEBES

Lole = Petapa→NORTHERN CELEBES

lo-Leku = Leko. Losengo D.→NORTH WESTERN BANTU

Lolina. Sumba D.→MOLUCCAN

Lollobatta. Tobelo D.→NORTH HALMAHERA

Lolo. Adele Tr.→CENTRAL TÓGO

LOLO = LOLO-MOSO→BURMESE-LOLO

Lolo = Cuabo→SOUTH EASTERN BANTU

Lolo = Lomwe→SOUTH EASTERN BANTU

Lolo = Nkundo. Mongo-Nkundo D.→NORTH WESTERN BANTU

Lolobi. Akpafu D.→CENTRAL TOGO

LOLO-BURMESE = BURMESE-LOLO

Lolokara = Lolsiwoi. Omba D.→EASTERN OCEANIC

Lololo = Piki→SOUTH EASTERN BANTU

LOLO-MOSO→BURMESE-LOLO

Lolopani = Heyo→TORRICELLI

Lolopho→BURMESE-LOLO

Lolopit = Lopit. Lotuho D.→EASTERN SUDANIC

Lolopwepwe = Lombaha. Omba D.→EASTERN OCEANIC

Lolsiwoi. Omba D.→EASTERN OCEANIC

Loltavola. South Raga D.→EASTERN OCEANIC

Loltong. Central Raga D.→EASTERN OCEANIC

Lom = Maporese→WEST INDONESIAN

Lom = Rolom. Eastern Mnong D.→MON-KHMER

Loma→MANDE

Loma = Loghon. Kulango D.→GUR

lo-Mabaale = Mabaale→NORTH WESTERN BANTU

Lomaumbi→NORTHWESTERN AND CENTRAL SOLOMONS

Lombaha. Omba D.→EASTERN OCEANIC

Lomban→NAGA-KUKI-CHIN

Lombi→NORTH WESTERN BANTU

Lombi. Mangbetu D.→CENTRAL SUDANIC

Lombo→NORTH WESTERN BANTU

Lomboki. Poke Tr.→NORTH WESTERN BANTU

lo-Mbole = Mbole→NORTH EASTERN BANTU

Lomi = Moso→BURMESE-LOLO

Lomomo = Yakurr→CROSS RIVER BENUE-CONGO

Lomongo = Ekonda Mongo. Mongo-Nkundo D.→NORTH WESTERN BANTU

Lomotua. Bemba D.→CENTRAL EASTERN BANTU

Lomotwa = Lomotua. Bemba D.→CENTRAL EASTERN BANTU

Lomrig→EASTERN OCEANIC

Lomue = Lomwe→SOUTH EASTERN BANTU

Lomuriki = Tima→KORDOFANIAN

Lomwe→SOUTH EASTERN BANTU

Lomya. Lotuho D.→EASTERN SUDANIC

Lonchong→WEST INDONESIAN

Londo = Lundu→NORTH WESTERN BANTU

Long Aki. Kenyah D.→WEST INDONESIAN

Long Bangan. Kenyah D.→WEST INDONESIAN

Long Glat. Modang D.→WEST INDONESIAN

Long Kiput. Narom D.→WEST INDONESIAN

Long Pata→WEST INDONESIAN

Long Pokun. Sibop D.→WEST INDONESIAN

Long Wai. Modang D.→WEST INDONESIAN

Long We = Long Wai. Modang D.→WEST INDONESIAN

Longana Omba D.→EASTERN OCEANIC

Longarim→EASTERN SUDANIC

Longe-longe. Havu D.→NORTH EASTERN BANTU

Longgahaja→NORTHWESTERN AND CENTRAL SOLOMONS

Longgu→EASTERN OCEANIC

Longla→NAGA-KUKI-CHIN

Longmi→BODO-NAGA-KACHIN

Longo. Mongo-Nkundo D.→NORTH WESTERN BANTU

Longphi. Tangsa D.→BODO-NAGA-KACHIN
Longuda→ADAMAWA
Loniu. Mokareng D.→ADMIRALTY-WEST-
ERN ISLANDS
Lonkundo = Nkundo. Mongo-Nkundo D.→
NORTH WESTERN BANTU
Lonkundu = Nkundo. Mongo-Nkundo D.→
NORTH WESTERN BANTU
Lontes→NORTHWESTERN AND CENTRAL
SOLOMONS
Lontis = Lontes→NORTHWESTERN AND
CENTRAL SOLOMONS
Lontjong = Lonchong→WEST INDONESIAN
Lontomba = Ntomba. Ntombo-Bolia Tr.→
NORTH WESTERN BANTU
lo-Ntombo-Bolia = Ntombo-Bolia→NORTH
WESTERN BANTU
Lonwolwol. Central Ambryn D.→EASTERN
OCEANIC
Loŋ. Mbo D.→NORTH WESTERN BANTU
Loodokilani. Maasai Tr.→EASTERN SUDAN-
IC
Looma = Loma→MANDE
Loombo = Ombo→NORTH WESTERN BAN-
TU
Loonago = Loma→MANDE
Loonga = Lungga→DJERAGAN
Loorudgee = Kukatja. Kardutjara D.→WATI
Loorudgie = Kukatja. Kardutjara D.→WATI
Lopas = Tolowa. Chasta Costa D.→ATHAPAS-
CAN-EYAK
Lopit. Lotuho D.→EASTERN SUDANIC
Lopol = Pari. Anuak Tr.→EASTERN SUDAN-
IC
Loprit = Lopit. Lotuho D.→EASTERN SU-
DANIC
Loque = Zoque→MIXE-ZOQUE
Loquilt = Lillooet→SALISH
Lor→MON-KHMER
Lore→CENTRAL AND SOUTHERN CELE-
BES
Lorengau. Tulu D.→ADMIRALTY-WEST-
ERN ISLANDS
Lorhon = Loghon. Kulango D.→GUR
Lori. 'Beli D.→CENTRAL SUDANIC
Loritcha = Kukatja. Kardutjara D.→WATI
Loritja = Kukatja. Kardutjara D.→WATI
Loron = Loghon. Kulango D.→GUR
Lorwama. Lotuho D.→EASTERN SUDANIC
lo-Saka = Saka. Nkutu D.→NORTH WEST-
ERN BANTU
Losengo→NORTH WESTERN BANTU
Losso = Nawdam→GUR
Lote→BISMARCK ARCHIPELAGO

Lotiga. Mpalitjan D.→PAMA-MARIC
Lotilla = Murle→EASTERN SUDANIC
Lotora. Maewo D.→EASTERN OCEANIC
Lotuho→EASTERN SUDANIC
Lotuko = Lotuho→EASTERN SUDANIC
Lotuxo = Lotuho→EASTERN SUDANIC
Lotuxo = Lotuho→EASTERN SUDANIC
Lou→TORRICELLI
Lou. Baluan D.→ADMIRALTY-WESTERN
ISLANDS
Lou. Nuer D.→EASTERN SUDANIC
Louise-Tyone = Chitina. Ahtena D.→ATHA-
PASCAN-EYAK
Louisiana Creole. French Creole D.→RO-
MANCE
Loun→EAST INDONESIAN
Loup = Mahican. Mohegan D.→ALGON-
QUIAN
Loura = Larua. Sumba D.→MOLUCCAN
Louxiru = Otuque→BORORO
Louyi = Luyana→SOUTH WESTERN BAN-
TU
Lovale = Lwena→SOUTH WESTERN BAN-
TU
Love = Veh→MON-KHMER
Lovedu = Lobedu. Northern Sotho D.→SOUTH
EASTERN BANTU
Loven→MON-KHMER
Lowa. Buyang D.→ADMIRALTY-WESTERN
ISLANDS
Lowai→SOUTH HALMAHERA AUSTRO-
NESIAN
Lowakai. Tulu D.→ADMIRALTY-WEST-
ERN ISLANDS
Lowama = Lorwama. Lotuho D.→EASTERN
SUDANIC
Lowoi = Lokoya. Lotuho D.→EASTERN SU-
DANIC
Lowudo. Didinga Tr.→EASTERN SUDANIC
Lowudo. Lotuho D.→EASTERN SUDANIC
LOYALTY ISLANDS see article
Lozi→SOUTH WESTERN BANTU
Lozwa. Bete Tr.→KRU
Lu→KAM-TAI
Lu = Nung→BODO-NAGA-KACHIN
Luaan = Bajau→NORTHWEST AUSTRO-
NESIAN
Luac. Padang D.→EASTERN SUDANIC
Luaic = Luac. Padang D.→EASTERN SU-
DANIC
Luana = Luyana→SOUTH WESTERN BAN-
TU
Luang. Leti D.→MOLUCCAN
Luangiua→POLYNESIAN

Luangu. Kongo D.→CENTRAL WESTERN BANTU

Luano. Lala D.→CENTRAL EASTERN BANTU

Luano = Luyana→SOUTH WESTERN BANTU

LUBA→CENTRAL WESTERN BANTU

Luba, Eastern = Hemba→CENTRAL WESTERN BANTU

Luba, Northeastern = Songe→CENTRAL WESTERN BANTU

Luba, Northern = Luna→CENTRAL WESTERN BANTU

Luba, Southern = Sanga→CENTRAL WESTERN BANTU

Luba, Western = Luba-Lulua→CENTRAL WESTERN BANTU

Luba-Hemba = Hemba→CENTRAL WESTERN BANTU

Luba-Kasia. Luba-Lulua D.→CENTRAL WESTERN BANTU

Luba-Katanga→CENTRAL WESTERN BANTU

Lubale = Lwena→SOUTH WESTERN BANTU

Luba-Lulua→CENTRAL WESTERN BANTU

Luba-Sanga = Sanga→CENTRAL WESTERN BANTU

Lubedu = Lobedu. Northern Sotho D.→ SOUTH EASTERN BANTU

lu-Bolo = Bolo→CENTRAL WESTERN BANTU

Lubu→WEST INDONESIAN

Lubuagan. Kalinga D.→NORTHWEST AUSTRONESIAN

Lucazi→SOUTH WESTERN BANTU

LUCHA = RYUKYUAN→JAPANESE

Luchazi = Lucazi→SOUTH WESTERN BANTU

Ludic. Karelian D.→URALIC

Ludumor = Shwai→KORDOFANIAN

Lue = Barue→NORTH WESTERN BANTU

Lue = Brao→MON-KHMER

Lue = Lu→KAM-TAI

Luen = Mambila→BANTOID

Luena = Lwena→SOUTH WESTERN BANTU

Luf→ADMIRALTY-WESTERN ISLANDS

Lugagun = Nalik→BISMARCK ARCHIPELAGO

Luganda = Ganda→NORTH EASTERN BANTU

Lugbara, High→CENTRAL SUDANIC

Lugbara, Low→CENTRAL SUDANIC

lu-Gisu = Masaba→NORTH EASTERN BANTU

Lugitama = Pahi→SEPIK

Luguru = Ruguru→CENTRAL EASTERN BANTU

lu-Gwe = Gwe. Luhya D.→NORTH EASTERN BANTU

lu-Gwe = Gwe. Saamia D.→NORTH EASTERN BANTU

lu-Gwere = Gwere→NORTH EASTERN BANTU

Lugwere = Gwere→NORTH EASTERN BANTU

lu-Hanga = Hanga. Luhya D.→NORTH EASTERN BANTU

Luhtu. Tsou D.→FORMOSAN AUSTRONESIAN

Luhu→EAST INDONESIAN

Luhupa, Central→NAGA-KUKI-CHIN

Luhupa, Northern→NAGA-KUKI-CHIN

Luhupa, Southern→NAGA-KUKI-CHIN

Luhushi = Luhusi. Lahu D.→BURMESE-LOLO

Luhusi. Lahu D.→BURMESE-LOLO

Luhya→NORTH EASTERN BANTU

Lui. Bari Tr.→EASTERN SUDANIC

Lui. High Lugbara D.→CENTRAL SUDANIC

Lui = Luyana→SOUTH WESTERN BANTU

Luimbe = Luimbi→SOUTH WESTERN BANTU

Luimbi→SOUTH WESTERN BANTU

Luiseno→UTO-AZTECAN

LUISISH = CUPAN→UTO-AZTECAN

Lujazi = Lucazi→SOUTH WESTERN BANTU

lu-Kakelewa = Kakelewa. Luhya D.→NORTH EASTERN BANTU

Lukamiute = Santiam→KALAPUYA

lu-Kenyi = Kenyi→NORTH EASTERN BANTU

lu-Kete = Kete→CENTRAL WESTERN BANTU

Lukə = Yakurr→CROSS RIVER BENUE-CONGO

Luko = Yakurr→CROSS RIVER BENUE-CONGO

Lukolwe. Mbwera D.→CENTRAL WESTERN BANTU

Lule→LULE-VILELA-CHARRUA

Lule Lapp→URALIC

LULE-VILELA-CHARRUA see article

Lulua. Luba-Lulua D.→CENTRAL WESTERN BANTU

Luluba = Olu'bo. Ma'di D.→CENTRAL SUDANIC

Luluhya = Luhya→NORTH EASTERN BAN-
TU

Lulumo = Olulumo→CROSS RIVER BENUE-
CONGO

Luluyia = Luhya→NORTH EASTERN BAN-
TU

Luman = Tira Lumun. Tira Tr.→KORDO-
FANIAN

lu-Maraci = Maraci. Luhya D.→NORTH EAST-
ERN BANTU

lu-Marama = Marama. Luhya D.→NORTH
EASTERN BANTU

Lumasaba = Masaba→NORTH EASTERN
BANTU

Lumasoal. Sapolewa D.→EAST INDONESIAN

Lumbi = Lombi. Mangbetu D.→CENTRAL
SUDANIC

Lumbu→NORTH WESTERN BANTU

Lumbwa = Kipsikis. Nandi D.→EASTERN
SUDANIC

Lumbwa = Maasai→EASTERN SUDANIC

Lummi. Northern Straits Salish D.→SALISH

Lumu. Abui D.→TIMOR-ALOR

Lumun. Moro Hills Tr.→KORDOFANIAN

Lun Bawang. Sarawak Murut D.→WEST INDO-
NESIAN

Lun Daya. Sarawak Murut D.→WEST INDO-
NESIAN

Lun Daye = Lun Daya. Sarawak Murut D.→
WEST INDONESIAN

Luna→CENTRAL WESTERN BANTU

Luna Inkongo = Luna→CENTRAL WEST-
ERN BANTU

Lund. Manjaku D.→WEST ATLANTIC

LUNDA—CENTRAL WESTERN BANTU

Lunda→CENTRAL WESTERN BANTU

Lunda, Northern = Luwunda→CENTRAL
WESTERN BANTU

Lunda, Southern = Lunda→CENTRAL WEST-
ERN BANTU

Lunda Muatiamvua = Luwunda→CENTRAL
WESTERN BANTU

Lunda Muatiavua = Luwunda→CENTRAL
WESTERN BANTU

Lundret. Tongo D.→ADMIRALTY-WEST-
ERN ISLANDS

LUNDU→NORTH WESTERN BANTU

Lundu→NORTH WESTERN BANTU

Lundu = Landu. Land Dayak D.→WEST
INDONESIAN

LUNDU-BALONG→NORTH   WESTERN
BANTU

Lundwe→CENTRAL EASTERN BANTU

Lunga = Lungga→DJERAGAN

Lung-an→KAM-TAI

Lungchang. Tangsa D.→BODO-NAGA-KA-
CHIN

Lungchow. Nung D.→KAM-TAI

Lungga→DJERAGAN

Lungga→NORTHWESTERN AND CENTRAL
SOLOMONS

LUNGGIC→NORTHWESTERN AND CEN-
TRAL SOLOMONS

Lungmi = Longmi→BODO-NAGA-KACHIN

Lungri. Tangsa D.→BODO-NAGA-KACHIN

Lungu→PLATEAU BENUE-CONGO

Lungu = Rungu→CENTRAL EASTERN BAN-
TU

Lungulu = Mwamba. Nyakyusa D.→CEN-
TRAL EASTERN BANTU

Luntu. Salampasu D.→CENTRAL WESTERN
BANTU

lu-Nyala = Nyala. Luhya D.→NORTH EAST-
ERN BANTU

lu-Nyaneka = Nyaneka→SOUTH WESTERN
BANTU

Lunyankole = Nyankole→NORTH EASTERN
BANTU

Lunyole = Nyole→NORTH EASTERN BAN-
TU

Lunyore = Nyole→NORTH EASTERN BAN-
TU

Luo→EASTERN SUDANIC

Luo = Lwo→EASTERN SUDANIC

LUORAVETLAN = CHUKCHEE-KAM-
CHATKAN

Luoravetlan = Chukchee→CHUKCHEE-KAM-
CHATKAN

LUORAWETLAN = CHUKCHEE-KAM-
CHATKAN

Lupaca. Aymara Tr.→ANDEAN

Lupacca = Lupaca. Aymara Tr.→ANDEAN

Lupawa = Lapawa. Reshe Tr.→PLATEAU
BENUE-CONGO

Luqu = Lungga→NORTHWESTERN AND
CENTRAL SOLOMONS

Lur = Alur→EASTERN SUDANIC

Luri→IRANIAN

Luritcha = Kukatja. Kardutjara D.→WATI

Luritja = Kukatja. Kardutjara D.→WATI

Lurritji = Kukatja. Kardutjara D.→WATI

Luru = Lara. Land Dayak D.→WEST INDO-
NESIAN

Lus. Kofa D.→BANTOID

Lusa→EASTERN OCEANIC

Lusaamia = Saamia→NORTH EASTERN
BANTU

Lusamia = Saamia→NORTH EASTERN BANTU

Lusatian→SLAVIC

Lusengo = Losengo→NORTH WESTERN BANTU

Lusengo Poto. Losengo D.→NORTH WESTERN BANTU

Lushai→NAGA-KUKI-CHIN

Lushange→CENTRAL WESTERN BANTU

Lushei = Lushai→NAGA-KUKI-CHIN

Lushisa = Kisa. Luhya D.→NORTH EASTERN BANTU

lu-Singa = Singa→NORTH EASTERN BANTU

Lusoga = Soga→NORTH EASTERN BANTU

lu-Songe = Songe→CENTRAL WESTERN BANTU

Lusyan = Syan→NORTH EASTERN BANTU

Lutaos = Bajau→NORTHWEST AUSTRONESIAN

Lutayaos = Bajau→NORTHWEST AUSTRONESIAN

Lutchye-Lutchye = Latjilatji. Djadjala D.→KULINIC

Luthig = Lotiga. Mpalitjan D.→PAMA-MARIC

lu-Tiriki = Tiriki. Luhya D.→NORTH EASTERN BANTU

lu-Tsootso = Tsootso. Luhya D.→NORTH EASTERN BANTU

Lutuami = Klamath→PENUTIAN

Lutze = Nung→BODO-NAGA-KACHIN

Luunda = Luwunda→CENTRAL WESTERN BANTU

Luuwa→CENTRAL WESTERN BANTU

Luva = Luba-Lulua→CENTRAL WESTERN BANTU

Luvale = Lwena→SOUTH WESTERN BANTU

Luwai→EASTERN OCEANIC

Luwangan = Lawangan→WEST INDONESIAN

Luwian→ANATOLIAN

Luwu'→CENTRAL AND SOUTHERN CELEBES

Luwunda→CENTRAL WESTERN BANTU

lu-Xaayo = Xaayo. Luhya D.→NORTH EASTERN BANTU

Luxemburgian. Netherlandic-German D.→GERMANIC

LUYANA→SOUTH WESTERN BANTU

Luyana→SOUTH WESTERN BANTU

Luyi = Luana→SOUTH WESTERN BANTU

Luyia = Luhya→NORTH EASTERN BANTU

Lwalu→CENTRAL WESTERN BANTU

Lwalu. Songe D.→CENTRAL WESTERN BANTU

Lwena→SOUTH WESTERN BANTU

lw-Idaxo = Isuxa. Luhya D.→NORTH EASTERN BANTU

Lwimbi = Luimbi→SOUTH WESTERN BANTU

Lwindja = Hwindja. Havu D.→NORTH EASTERN BANTU

lw-Isuxa = Isuxa. Luhya D.→NORTH EASTERN BANTU

LWO→EASTERN SUDANIC

Lwo→EASTERN SUDANIC

Lyase-ne→PLATEAU BENUE-CONGO

Lycian. Luwian D.→ANATOLIAN

Lyconian see article

Lydian→ANATOLIAN

Lyele→GUR

Lyen-lyem = Zahao→NAGA-KUKI-CHIN

Lyente = Lente→NAGA-KUKI-CHIN

Lyngngam. Khasi D.→MON-KHMER

Lyo. Mak D.→KAM-TAI

M

Ma = Amadi→EASTERN

Ma = Bilala. Kuka D.→CENTRAL SUDANIC

Ma = Mano→MANDE

Ma Dala = Madaba. Maba D.→MABAN

Ma Ndaba = Madala. Maba D.→MABAN

Maa. Koho D.→MON-KHMER

Maa = Maasai→EASTERN SUDANIC

Maa = Mano→MANDE

Ma'a = Mbugu→CUSHITIC

Maaban = Maban→EASTERN SUDANIC

Maambi. Mayogo Tr.→EASTERN

Maanyan→WEST INDONESIAN

Maasai→EASTERN SUDANIC

Maba→MABAN

Maba→SOUTH HALMAHERA AUSTRONESIAN

Mabaa = Maba→MABAN

Mabaale→NORTH WESTERN BANTU

Mabak = Maba→MABAN

Mabale = Mabaale→NORTH WESTERN BANTU

Maban→EASTERN SUDANIC

MABAN see article

Mabang = Maba→MABAN

Mabar. Kanuri Tr.→SAHARAN

Mabar = Mober→CHADIC

Mabea = Mvumbo→NORTH WESTERN BANTU

Mabenaro→TACANA

Mabeni. Mamvu-Efe D.→CENTRAL SUDAN-
IC
Mabi = Mvumbo→NORTH WESTERN
BANTU
Mabi Tayu. Berta D.→CHARI-NILE
Mabiha→SOUTH EASTERN BANTU
Mabisanga. Mangbetu D.→CENTRAL SU-
DANIC
Mabiti. Liko Tr.→NORTH EASTERN BANTU
Mabo→PLATEAU BENUE-CONGO
Mabue = Maue→TUPI
Mabuiag. Kaurareg D.→MABUIAGIC
MABUIAGIC see article
MACA→MATACO
Maca→MATACO
Maca see Mascoy→MACRO-PANOAN
Macaguaje. Pioje-Sioni Tr.→MACRO-TUCA-
NOAN
Macame = Mashami. Caga D.→NORTH
EASTERN BANTU
Macamecran→GE
Macanese→ROMANCE
Macassar = Makasarese→CENTRAL AND
SOUTHERN CELEBES
Maccha = Mecha. Galla D.→CUSHITIC
Macedonian→SLAVIC
Macedo-Rumanian. Rumanian D.→ROMANCE
Macha = Mecha. Galla D.→CUSHITIC
MACHACALI see Article
Machame = Mashami. Caga D.→NORTH
EASTERN BANTU
Macheyenga = Machiguenga→MAIPURAN
Machias = Passamaquoddy→ALGONQUIAN
Machicui. Mascoy D.→MACRO-PANOAN
Machiguenga→MAIPURAN
Machoto = Itonama→MACRO-CHIBCHAN
Machui→TACANA
Machuvi = Machui→TACANA
Macicani = Mahican. Mohegan D.→ALGON-
QUIAN
Mackenzie. Santiam D.→KALAPUYA
Macoa. Chake D.→CARIB
Macoa. Mape D.→CARIB
Macoita. Mape D.→CARIB
Maconi = Macuni→MACHACALI
Macquaic = Mohawk→IROQUOIS
Macraia = Cricatage→GE
MACU = PUINAVE→MACRO-TUCANOAN
Macu→MACRO-TUCANOAN
Macu→EQUATORIAL
Macuna. Buhagana Tr.→MACRO-TUCA-
NOAN
Macuni→MACHACALI
Macurap = Makurap→TUPI

Macushi→CARIB
Macusi = Macushi→CARIB
Macussi = Macushi→CARIB
Mada→PLATEAU BENUE-CONGO
Mada, Hill. Eggon D.→PLATEAU BENUE-
CONGO
Madaba. Maba D.→MABAN
Madaganye = Kotoko→CHADIC
Madala. Maba D.→MABAN
MADANG→BOGIA
Madang. Kenyah D.→WEST INDONESIAN
MADANG = NORTHEASTERN NEW
GUINEA
Madanisi = Danisa→KHOISAN
Madda = Hill Mada. Eggon D.→PLATEAU
BENUE-CONGO
Madegugusu. Lungga D.→NORTHWESTERN
AND CENTRAL SOLOMONS
MADEIRA→CHAPUCURA-WANHAMAN
Madenassa = Danisa→KHOISAN
Madhesi. Bihari D.→INDIC
Ma'di→CENTRAL SUDANIC
Madi. Bari D.→EASTERN SUDANIC
Madi = Acoli. Anuak Tr.→EASTERN SU-
DANIC
Madi = Amadi→EASTERN
Madi = Kaliko→CENTRAL SUDANIC
Madi = Loinang→CENTRAL AND SOUTH-
ERN CELEBES
Madi = Ma'di→CENTRAL SUDANIC
Ma'di = Morokodo→CENTRAL SUDANIC
Madiha→ARAWAKAN
Madiin = Madin. Koma D.→KOMAN
Madik→WESTERN NEW GUINEA
Madimadi = Muthimuthi. Djadjala D.→
KULINIC
Madin. Koma D.→KOMAN
Madinava→KUKUKUKU
Madinnisane = Danisa→KHOISAN
Madi-ti = Kaliko→CENTRAL SUDANIC
Ma'di-ti = Ma'di→CENTRAL SUDANIC
Madjay. Yirgay D.→PAMA-MARIC
Madjene. Mandarese D.→CENTRAL AND
SOUTHERN CELEBES
Madoitja. Kardutjara D.→WATI
Madole→NORTH HALMAHERA
Madschame = Mashami. Caga D.→NORTH
EASTERN BANTU
Madu. Morokodo D.→CENTRAL SUDANIC
Madungore. Tama D.—EASTERN SUDANIC
Maduntara = Kukatja. Kardutjara D.→WATI
Madurese→WEST INDONESIAN
Madutara = Antakirinya. Kardutjara D.→
WATI

Madutara = Kokata. Kardutjara D.→WATI
Maduwonga. Kardutjara D.→WATI
Maduwonga = Kokata. Kardutjara D.→WATI
Madyak = Manjaku→WEST ATLANTIC
Madyo = Amadi→EASTERN
Mae→POLYNESIAN
Mae. Enga D.→EAST NEW GUINEA HIGH-
    LANDS
Maele. Mangbetu D.→CENTRAL SUDANIC
Maewo→EASTERN OCEANIC
Mafar = Mabar. Kanuri Tr.→SAHARAN
Mafoor = Numfor→MOLUCCAN
Mafulu = Fuyuge→GOILALA
Mag Readings = Patwin→WINTUN
Maga→NORTHWESTERN AND CENTRAL
    SOLOMONS
Maga. Rukai D.→FORMOSAN AUSTRO-
    NESIAN
Magach. Mbaya-Guaicuru Tr.→GUAYCURU
Magadhi→INDIC
Magahi. Bihari D.→INDIC
Magaleri = Amal→SEPIK
Magam. North Ambryn D.→EASTERN
    OCEANIC
Magari→GYARUNG-MISHMI
Magdaleno. Moseten D.→MACRO-PANOAN
Ma-ge = Bilala. Kuka D.→CENTRAL SU-
    DANIC
Magha = Maha→CHADIC
Maghavul = Sura→CHADIC
Maghi = Arakanese. Burmese D.→BURMESE-
    LOLO
Maghrebi = Maghribi. Arabic D.→SEMITIC
Maghribi. Arabic D.→SEMITIC
Magi→EAST NEW GUINEA HIGHLANDS
Magi = Mailu→MAILU
Magi = Maji→OMOTIC
Magianghir = Masongo→EASTERN SUDAN-
    IC
MAGIMBA = NGEMBA→BANTOID
Magindanao = Maguindanao→NORTHWEST
    AUSTRONESIAN
Magindanau = Maguindanao→NORTHWEST
    AUSTRONESIAN
Magindanaw = Maguindanao→NORTHWEST
    AUSTRONESIAN
Magobineng. Kate D.→HUON-FINISTERRE
Magon = ≠Hua→KHOISAN
Magong = ≠Hua→KHOISAN
Magori→MAILU
Magosan. Mansaka D.→NORTHWEST AUS-
    TRONESIAN
Magu→BANTOID
Maguemi. Kanembu Tr.→SAHARAN

Maguindanao→NORTHWEST   AUSTRO-
    NESIAN
Mah Meri = Besisi. Southern Sakai D.→SAKAI
Maha→CHADIC
Maha = Omaha. Dhegiha D.→SIOUAN
Mahafaly. Malagasy D.→WEST INDONESIAN
Mahaga→EASTERN OCEANIC
Mahai→MON-KHMER
Mahakuassica = Mohawk→IROQUOIS
Mahallati. Persian D.→IRANIAN
Maharashtri→INDIC
Mahari = Halbi. Oriya D.→INDIC
Mahas. Mahas-Fiyadikka D.→EASTERN
    SUDANIC
Mahas-Fiyadikka→EASTERN SUDANIC
Mahasi = Mahas. Mahas-Fiyadikka D.→
    EASTERN SUDANIC
Mahass = Mahas. Mahas-Fiyadikka D.→
    EASTERN SUDANIC
Mahi. Ewe D.→EWE
Mahibarez. Cozarini D.→MAIPURAN
Mahican. Mohegan D.→ALGONQUIAN
Mahican = Mohegan→ALGONQUIAN
Mahicann = Mahican. Mohegan D.→ALGON-
    QUIAN
Mahigi→CENTRAL AND SOUTH NEW
    GUINEA
Mahikan = Mahican. Mohegan D.→ALGON-
    QUIAN
Mahl = Maldivian→INDIC
Mahle. Santali D.→MUNDA
Mahongwe = Kota→NORTH WESTERN
    BANTU
Mahotoyana. Carijona D.→CARIB
Mahri. Modern South Arabic D.→SEMITIC
Mahri-Sokotri = Modern South Arabic→
    SEMITIC
Mahu = Mau. Malinka D.→MANDE
Mahum = Bandjoun-Baham→BANTOID
Mahura→KHOISAN
Mai = Mae→POLYNESIAN
Mai = Siliput→TORRICELLI
Maia→KARDU
Maiabi = Mayapi→MAYAPIC
Maiari→KOIARI
Maibrat→WESTERN NEW GUINEA
Maidakadi = Mitakudi→PAMA-NYUNGAN
Maidjuwu = Majuu. Mangbetu D.→CENTRAL
    SUDANIC
MAIDU see article
Maiheari→BINANDERE
Mai-hea-ri = Maiheari→BINANDERE
Maiko = Mayko. Mayogo Tr.→EASTERN
Maikulan = Maykulan→MAYAPIC

Maikulung = Maykulan→MAYAPIC
Mailang = Ngaing→HUON-FINISTERRE
Mailhai = Meithei→NAGA-KUKI-CHIN
Mailnga→WORORAN
Mailpurlgu = Naualko. Kula D.→PAMA-
NYUNGAN
MAILU see article
MAIMAI→TORRICELLI
Maima-Kizhi. Altai D.→TURKIC
Maimana. Mongul D.→MONGOLIAN
Maingtha. Ach'ang D.→BODO-NAGA-
KACHIN
Maiopitian. Atorai D.→MAIPURAN
Maipani. Bamu Kiwai D.→CENTRAL AND
SOUTH NEW GUINEA
Maipua = Koriki→SOUTHEAST NEW
GUINEA
Maipua — Koriki→SOUTHEAST NEW
GUINEA
MAIPURAN see article
MAIPURAN, NORTHERN see article
Maipure—NORTHERN MAIPURAN
Mairasi→WESTERN NEW GUINEA
Mairiri→EAST INDONESIAN
Maisin→DAGA
Maita. Waica Tr.→WAICAN
Maitakudi = Mitakudi→PAMA-NYUNGAN
Maithakari = Mitakudi→PAMA-NYUNGAN
Maithili. Bihari D.→INDIC
Maitsi. Maquiritare D.→CARIB
Maiulatara = Kukatja. Kardutjara D.→WATI
Maiwa. Masenrempulu D.→CENTRAL AND
SOUTHERN CELEBES
Maiwara→PAPUA AUSTRONESIAN
Maiya→INDIC
Majangir = Masongo→EASTERN SUDANIC
Majanna = Malgana→KARDU
Maji→OMOTIC
Majinda = Kamuku→PLATEAU BENUE-
CONGO
Majingai. Sara D.→CENTRAL SUDANIC
Maji-ngai = Majingai. Sara D.→CENTRAL
SUDANIC
Majinya = Maji→OMOTIC
Majna-pil'ginskij. Kerek D.→CHUKCHEE-
KAMCHATKAN
Majogo = Mangbele. Mayogo Tr.→EASTERN
MAJOID→OMOTIC
Majugu. Mayogo Tr.→EASTERN
Majuli = Mayuli. Wangkadjeri D.→PITTA-
PITTIC
Majuu. Mangbetu D.→CENTRAL SUDANIC
Mak→KAM-TAI
Maka→NORTH WESTERN BANTU

MAKAA = MAKA-NJEM→NORTH WEST-
ERN BANTU
Makaa = Maka→NORTH WESTERN BANTU
Makadai. Abui D.→TIMOR-ALOR
Makah→WAKASHAN
Makale. Sa'dan D.→CENTRAL AND
SOUTHERN CELEBES
Makanga. Mbo D.→CENTRAL EASTERN
BANTU
MAKA-NJEM→NORTH WESTERN BANTU
Makari. Kotoko D.→CHADIC
Makari = Kotoko→CHADIC
Makarub→BOGIA
Makasarese→CENTRAL AND SOUTHERN
CELEBES
Makassai = Məkasai→TIMOR-ALOR
Makassar — Makasarese→CENTRAL AND
SOUTHERN CELEBES
Makatao. Siraya D.—FORMOSAN AUSTRO-
NESIAN
Make — Southern Faŋ. Faŋ D.→NORTH
WESTERN BANTU
Makedonnija. Albanian D.
Makela'i. Tontemboan D.→NORTHERN
CELEBES
Maken Rek D.→EASTERN SUDANIC
Makere. Mangbetu D.→CENTRAL SUDANIC
Maki = Mangki. Pitu-ulunna-salu D.→
CENTRAL AND SOUTHERN CELEBES
Makian, East→SOUTH HALMAHERA AUS-
TRONESIAN
Makian, West→HALMAHERA
Makiara→DAGA
Makiritare = Maquiritare→CARIB
Makleu→FREDERIK HENDRIK IS AND
SE WEST IRIAN
Maklew = Makleu→FREDERIK HENDRIK
IS AND SE WEST IRIAN
Makoa = Makua→SOUTH EASTERN
BANTU
Makoane = Makua→SOUTH EASTERN
BANTU
Makoma→SOUTH WESTERN BANTU
Makonde→SOUTH EASTERN BANTU
Makong. Bru D.→MON-KHMER
Makoroko = Kwadi→KHOISAN
Maktian. Fordat D.→MOLUCCAN
Maku→MABAN
MAKUA→SOUTH EASTERN BANTU
Makua→SOUTH EASTERN BANTU
Makua, Northern = Medo. Makua D.→SOUTH
EASTERN BANTU
Makua, Western = Lomwe→SOUTH EAST-
ERN BANTU

Makudukudu. Banga D.→EASTERN
Makunabein. Abui D.→TIMOR-ALOR
Makura→EASTERN OCEANIC
Makurap→TUPI
Makwa = Makua→SOUTH EASTERN BAN-
TU
Makwakwe. Tswa D.→SOUTH EASTERN
BANTU
Mal. T'in D.→KHMUIC
Mal Pahoria. Bengali D.→INDIC
Mala→CENTRAL EASTERN BANTU
Malabar = Malayalam→DRAVIDIAN
Malabu→CHADIC
MALACCA see article
MALAGASIC see WEST INDONESIAN
Malagasy→WEST INDONESIAN
Malai. Lebei D.→ADMIRALTY-WESTERN
ISLANDS
Malai. Ndrosun D.→ADMIRALTY-WEST-
ERN ISLANDS
MALAITA→EASTERN OCEANIC
MALAKKA = MALACCA
Malala→BOGIA
Malali→MACRO-GE
Malamba. Western Bira D.→NORTH EAST-
ERN BANTU
Malang. Kenyah D.→WEST INDONESIAN
Malanga. Maba D.→MABAN
Malangai→NORTHEAST NEW GUINEA
AUSTRONESIAN
Malango→EASTERN OCEANIC
Malas→BOGIA
Malavi. Rajasthani D.→INDIC
Malaweg→NORTHWEST AUSTRONESIAN
Malawi = Peta. Nyanja D.→CENTRAL EAST-
ERN BANTU
Malay→WEST INDONESIAN
Malayalam→DRAVIDIAN
Malayarma = Malayalam→DRAVIDIAN
MALAYIC→WEST INDONESIAN
MALAYO-POLYNESIAN see article
Malba = Kalarko. Mirning D.→MIRNINY
Malba = Sindagua→BARBACOAN
Malbe = Gulfei. Kotoko D.→CHADIC
Maldivian→INDIC
Maldjana = Malgana→KARDU
Male→OMOTIC
Male→NORTHEASTERN NEW GUINEA
MALE = MANDE
Male = Malto→DRAVIDIAN
Malechite = Malecite. Passamaquoddy D.→
ALGONQUIAN
Malecite. Passamaquoddy D.→ALGONQUIAN
MALEKULA→NORTHWESTERN NEW

HEBRIDES
Malele = Maele. Mangbetu D.→CENTRAL
SUDANIC
Malgana→KARDU
Malgin = Malngin→NGUMBIN
Malgwe = Gulfei. Kotoko D.→CHADIC
Malhesti. Kanawari D.→GYARUNG-MISHMI
Malhommes = Menomini→ALGONQUIAN
MALI→MANDE
Maliko. Liko Tr.→NORTH EASTERN
BANTU
Malila→CENTRAL EASTERN BANTU
Malimba = Mulimba ·NORTH WESTERN
BANTU
Malindang. Subanun D.→NORTHWEST
AUSTRONESIAN
Malingo→EASTERN OCEANIC
Malinka→MANDE
Malinke = Malinka→MANDE
Maliseet = Malecite. Passamaquoddy D.→
ALGONQUIAN
Malisete = Malecite. Passamaquoddy D.→
ALGONQUIAN
Malisit = Malecite. Passamaquoddy D.→
ALGONQUIAN
Maljangaba = Maljangapa. Karenggapa D.→
DIERIC
Maljangapa. Karenggapa D.→DIERIC
Malka. Circassian D.→CAUCASIAN
Mallackmallack = Mullukmulluk→DALY
Mallango. Kalinga D.→NORTHWEST AUS-
TRONESIAN
Malleyearra = Muliara→KARDU
Malngin→NGUMBIN
Malo→MON-KHMER
Malo→NORTHWESTERN NEW HEBRIDES
Malo = Embaloh→WEST INDONESIAN
Maloh = Embaloh→WEST INDONESIAN
Maloh Kalis = Embaloh→WEST INDONE-
SIAN
Malol→NORTHEAST NEW GUINEA
AUSTRONESIAN
Malto→DRAVIDIAN
Malu. Gunantuna D.→BISMARCK ARCHI-
PELAGO
Malu = Maru→BODO-NAGA-KACHIN
Malua→NORTHWESTERN NEW HEBRIDES
Malua. Abui D.→TIMOR-ALOR
Malual. Rek D.→EASTERN SUDANIC
Maluba = Lewo. Tasiko D.→EASTERN
OCEANIC
Malununda = Gayardilt→TANGKIC
Malu ʔu→EASTERN OCEANIC
Malvi. Rajasthani D.→INDIC

Malwal = Malual. Rek D.→EASTERN SU-
DANIC
Malyanapa = Maljangapa. Karenggapa D.→
DIERIC
Malyangapa = Maljangapa. Karenggapa D.→
DIERIC
Malyapa = Maljangapa. Karenggapa D.→
DIERIC
Malynapa = Maljangapa. Karenggapa D.→
DIERIC
Mam→MAYAN
Mam. Miskito D.→MISUMALPAN
Mama→BANTOID
Mamaa→HUON-FINISTERRE
Mamanua = Manmanua→NORTHWEST AUS-
TRONESIAN
Mamanwa = Manmanua→NORTHWEST
AUSTRONESIAN
Mamaq. Kerintji D.→WEST INDONESIAN
Mamasa. Pitu-ulunna-salu D.→CENTRAL
AND SOUTHERN CELEBES
Mambai→EAST INDONESIAN
Mambai = Manbai→ADAMAWA
Mambangura = Ngandangara. Punthamara
D.→DIERIC
Mambare→BINANDERE
Mambere = Mambila→BANTOID
Mambie. Pitu-ulunna-salu D.→CENTRAL AND
SOUTHERN CELEBES
Mambila→BANTOID
Mambisa. Alur Tr.→EASTERN SUDANIC
Mambisa. Lendu D.→CENTRAL SUDANIC
Mamboma = Gbandi. Mende D.→MANDE
Mamboŋa = Gbandi. Mende D.→MANDE
Mamboru. Sumba D.→MOLUCCAN
Mambukush = Mbukushu. Kwangari D.→
SOUTH WESTERN BANTU
Mamburra = Koinjmal. Darambal D.→WAKA-
KABIC
Mambwe→CENTRAL EASTERN BANTU
Mame = Mam→MAYAN
MAMEAN→MAYAN
MAMEAN-IXILIAN = MAMEAN→MAYAN
Mamedja = Ingassana→CHARI-NILE
Mamiap. Breenugu D.→INDO-PACIFIC
Mami-Duma see CHIMBU→EAST NEW
GUINEA HIGHLANDS
Mamidza = Ingassana→CHARI-NILE
Mamngayt. Awngthim D.→PAMA-MARIC
Mamngayth = Mamngayt. Awngthim D.→
PAMA-MARIC
Mampa = Southern Bullom→WEST ATLAN-
TIC
Mampoko. Loi-Ngiri D.→NORTH WESTERN

BANTU
Mampruli = Mamprusi. Dagbani D.→GUR
Mamprusi. Dagbani D.→GUR
Mampukush = Mbukushu. Kwangari D.→
SOUTH WESTERN BANTU
Mampwa = Southern Bullom→WEST ATLAN-
TIC
Mamu. Wakaman D.→PAMA-MARIC
Mamudju→CENTRAL AND SOUTHERN
CELEBES
Mamusi→BISMARCK ARCHIPELAGO
Mamvu. Mamvu-Efe D.→CENTRAL SUDAN-
IC
Mamvu-Efe→CENTRAL SUDANIC
Mamzokoi = Musgu→CHADIC
Man = Mien→MIAO-YAO
Man Cao-lan→KAM-TAI
Mana→ADAMAWA
Mana. Cottian D.→YENISEIAN
Mana = Fanya→CHADIC
Manabita = Mantena→MACRO-CHIBCHAN
Managalasi→KOIARI
Managari = Maung→IWAIDJAN
Managobla = Gola→WEST ATLANTIC
Managosan = Magosan. Mansaka D.→
NORTHWEST AUSTRONESIAN
Manajo = Manaze. Tenetehara D.→TUPI
Manala = Mangala→MARNGU
Manam→NORTHEAST NEW GUINEA
AUSTRONESIAN
Manamabo. Conibo D.→PANO
Manamabobo = Manaua. Jurua-Purus Tr.→
PANO
Manambu→SEPIK
Manangeer. Thuri Tr.→EASTERN SUDANIC
Manao→NORTHERN MAIPURAN
Manastara. Mape D.→CARIB
Manatahqua = Cutshamakin. Massachusett
Tr.→ALGONQUIAN
Manau→MOMBERAMO RIVER
Manaua. Conibo D.→PANO
Manaua. Jurua-Purus Tr.→PANO
Manaxo = Manaze. Tenetehara D.→TUPI
Manaze. Tenetehara D.→TUPI
Manbai→ADAMAWA
Mancagne = Mankanya→WEST ATLANTIC
Mancanka = Mankanya→WEST ATLANTIC
Manchati→GYARUNG-MISHMI
Manche. Chol D.→MAYAN
Manchu→TUNGUS
MANCHU = SOUTHWESTERN→TUNGUS
MANDA→CENTRAL EASTERN BANTU
Manda→CENTRAL EASTERN BANTU
Manda→DRAVIDIAN

Manda. Ame D.→DALY
Mandaba = Madaba. Maba D.→MABAN
Mandaean = Mandaic. East Aramaic D.→
SEMITIC
Mandaic. East Aramaic D.→SEMITIC
Mandailing = Angkola. Toba D.→WEST
INDONESIAN
Mandaka = Mansaka→NORTHWEST AUS-
TRONESIAN
Manda-Ka see MANDE
Mandala = Madala. Maba D.→MABAN
Mandan→SIOUAN
Mandandanji→PAMA-MARIC
Mandankwe→BANTOID
Mandara→CHADIC
MANDARA = EAST CHADIC→CHADIC
Mandarec = Omo Murle. Murle Tr.→EAST-
ERN SUDANIC
Mandarese→CENTRAL AND SOUTHERN
CELEBES
Mandari = Baga Maduri→WEST ATLANTIC
Mandari = Mondari. Bari D.→EASTERN
SUDANIC
Mandarin→CHINESE
Mandauaca→NORTHERN MAIPURAN
Mandawaca = Mandauaca→NORTHERN
MAIPURAN
Mandaya→NORTHWEST AUSTRONESIAN
Mande = Malinka→MANDE
MANDE see article
Mandeali. Western Pahari D.→INDIC
Mandekan see MANDE
Mandfaque = Manjaku→WEST ATLANTIC
Mandi→NORTH WESTERN BANTU
Mandi. Banen Tr.→NORTH WESTERN
BANTU
Mandi. Tumaru D.→NORTH NEW GUINEA
Mandijildjara. Kardutjara D.→WATI
Manding = Malinka→MANDE
Mandingi = Northern Bullom→WEST AT-
LANTIC
MANDINGO = MANDE
Mandingo = Malinka→MANDE
Mandingue = Malinka→MANDE
Mandinka = Malinka→MANDE
Mandjia = Manja. Gbaya D.→EASTERN
Mandjia Bakka = Mbaka. Gbaya Tr.→EAST-
ERN
Mandjindja. Kardutjara D.→WATI
Mandjindjara = Mandjindja. Kardutjara D.→
WATI
Mandju = Bandjoun-Baham→BANTOID
MANDOBO = AWYU
Mandrica. Albanian D.

Mandusir. Biak D.→MOLUCCAN
Mandyak = Manjaku→WEST ATLANTIC
Mandyako = Manjaku→WEST ATLANTIC
Mane. Balanta D.→WEST ATLANTIC
Maneao→DAGA
Maneaters = Tonkawa→MACRO-ALGON-
QUIAN
Manegir→TUNGUS
Manehas = Mwahet. Mbo D.→NORTH
WESTERN BANTU
Manenka = Malinka→MANDE
Maneta. Abui D.→TIMOR-ALOR
Manfaco = Manjaku→WEST ATLANTIC
Mang→PALAUNG-WA
Mang U' = Mang→PALAUNG-WA
Manga. Kanuri Tr.→SAHARAN
Manga = Mba→EASTERN
Mangaia. Cook Islands Maori D.→POLY-
NESIAN
Mangaiyat = Mangaya→EASTERN
Mangakonkia = Miami→ALGONQUIAN
Mangala→MARNGU
Mangala. Losengo D.→NORTH WESTERN
BANTU
Mangali-Lubo. Kalinga D.→NORTHWEST
AUSTRONESIAN
Manganitu. Sangir D.→HESPERONESIAN
Manganja = Maɲanja. Nyanja D.→CENTRAL
EASTERN BANTU
Manganji. Loi-Ngiri D.→NORTH WESTERN
BANTU
Mangarai→AUSTRALIAN MACRO-PHYLUM
Mangareva→POLYNESIAN
Mangat'k. Tatog Tr.→EASTERN SUDANIC
Mangawitu→SOUTH HALMAHERA AUS-
TRONESIAN
Mangaya→EASTERN
Mangbei = Manbai→ADAMAWA
Mangbele. Mangbetu D.→CENTRAL SU-
DANIC
Mangbele. Mayogo Tr.→EASTERN
Mangbele = Ngbee→CENTRAL WESTERN
BANTU
Mangbettu = Mangbetu→CENTRAL SUDAN-
IC
MANGBETU→CENTRAL SUDANIC
Mangbetu→CENTRAL SUDANIC
Mangbutu→CENTRAL SUDANIC
Mangbutu Karo. Mangbutu D.→CENTRAL
SUDANIC
MANGBUTU-EFE→CENTRAL SUDANIC
Mangbutuli = Mangbutu→CENTRAL SU-
DANIC
Mange'e→EAST INDONESIAN

Mangen Kinkwa = Kinkwa→BANTOID
Mangeri→MANGERIAN
MANGERIAN see article
Mangeroma = Tucundiapa→MACRO-TU-CANOAN
Manggalili. Gobabingo D.→MURNGIC
Manggarai→EAST INDONESIAN
Mangguangan→NORTHWEST AUSTRO-NESIAN
Manggulanga = Mangguangan→NORTHWEST AUSTRONESIAN
Manggura. Wagilag D.→MURNGIC
Mangisa→NORTH WESTERN BANTU
Mangkarupi = Ngarkat. Djadjala D.→KULI-NIC
Mangkatip. Ngaju D.→WEST INDONESIAN
Mangkettan = Beketan. Punan Ba D.→WEST INDONESIAN
Mangki. Pitu-ulunna-salu D.→CENTRAL AND SOUTHERN CELEBES
Mangkoong = Makong. Bru D.→MON-KHMER
Mangole→EAST INDONESIAN
Manguagao = Mangguangan→NORTHWEST AUSTRONESIAN
Mangue→MANGUEAN
MANGUEAN see article
Mangut. Mongul D.→MONGOLIAN
Mangwato = Nwato. Tswana D.→SOUTH EASTERN BANTU
Manhasset. Mohegan D.→ALGONQUIAN
Mani→CENTRAL AND SOUTH NEW GUINEA
Mani. Tala D.→EAST INDONESIAN
Manihiki-Rakahanga. Cook Islands Maori D.→POLYNESIAN
Manikion. Mantion D.→WESTERN NEW GUINEA
Manimo = Manya. Malinka D.→MANDE
Maninka = Malinka→MANDE
Manipa→EAST INDONESIAN
Manipuri = Meithei→NAGA-KUKI-CHIN
Maniteneri→MAIPURAN
Manitsaua = Manitsawa→TUPI
Manitsawa→TUPI
Manja. Gbaya D.→EASTERN
Manja Baba. Gbaya Tr.→EASTERN
Manjaco = Manjaku→WEST ATLANTIC
Manjaku→WEST ATLANTIC
Manjanjiro = Masongo→EASTERN SU-DANIC
Manjhi. Mundari D.→MUNDA
Manjiak = Manjaku→WEST ATLANTIC
Manjinjiwonga = Mandjindja. Kardutjara D.→

WATI
Mankanha = Mankanya→WEST ATLANTIC
Mankanya→WEST ATLANTIC
Mankayan. Kankanay D.→NORTHWEST AUSTRONESIAN
Manketa = Beketan. Punan Ba D.→WEST INDONESIAN
Mankon. Awing D.→BANTOID
Manmanua→NORTHWEST AUSTRONE-SIAN
Mano→MANDE
Mano. Bwe D.→KAREN
Manobo, Central→NORTHWEST AUSTRO-NESIAN
Manobo, Cotabato→NORTHWEST AUS-TRONESIAN
Manobo, Sarangani = Kulaman→NORTH-WEST AUSTRONESIAN
Manobo Proper = Agusan Manobo→NORTH-WEST AUSTRONESIAN
Manon = Mano→MANDE
Manowui. Leti D.→MOLUCCAN
Manrhoat = Kiowa→TANOAN
Mansa9 = Mensa. Tigre D.→SEMITIC
Mansaka→NORTHWEST AUSTRONESIAN
MANSAKIC→NORTHWEST AUSTRONE-SIAN
Mansi = Vogul→URALIC
Mansibaber→WESTERN NEW GUINEA
Mansim→WESTERN NEW GUINEA
Mansino = Mansinyo→EQUATORIAL
Mansinyo→EQUATORIAL
Mansoanka→WEST ATLANTIC
Mansos. Puinave D.→MACRO-TUCANOAN
Manta→MACRO-CHIBCHAN
Manta = Takamanda→BANTOID
Mantage = Kotoko→CHADIC
Mantangai. Ngaju D.→WEST INDONESIAN
Mantararen. Lawangan D.→WEST INDONE-SIAN
Mantauran. Rukai D.→FORMOSAN AUS-TRONESIAN
Mantembu. Yava D.→WESTERN NEW GUINEA
Mantena→MACRO-CHIBCHAN
Manter→NORTH PAPUAN
MANTHARDA see article
Mantion→WESTERN NEW GUINEA
Mantizula = Manitsawa→TUPI
Mantsati = Manchati→GYARUNG-MISHMI
Mantse, Outer→SINO-TIBETAN
Manu = Ngadjuri. Jadliaura D.→YURA
Manubara→SOUTHEAST NEW GUINEA
Manukolu→MULAHA

Manula = Marulta. Karendala D.→DIERIC
Manuley = Ngadjuri. Jadliaura D.→YURA
Manungu. Wolyamidi D.→WORORAN
Manuri = Ngadjuri. Jadliaura D.→YURA
Manusa. Sapolewa D.→EAST INDONESIAN
Manusela = Wahai→EAST INDONESIAN
Manuwe. Sapolewa D.→EAST INDONESIAN
Manx→CELTIC
Manya. Malinka D.→MANDE
Manya = Menian→CAMACAN
Manyak→BURMESE-LOLO
Manyaŋ→MABAN
Manyemen = Kitwii. Nyang D.→BANTOID
Manyika. Shona D.→SOUTH EASTERN
    BANTU
Manyukai. Land Dayak D.→WEST INDO-
    NESIAN
Manyuke—Manyukai. Land Dayak D.→WEST
    INDONESIAN
Manzancro. Araucanian D.--·PENUTIAN
Maŋanja. Nyanja D.--CENTRAL EASTERN
    BANTU
Mao, Northern--·KOMAN
Mao, Southern--·OMOTIC
Mao Naga = Sopvoma. Simi D.→NAGA-
    KUKI-CHIN
Maopityan = Maiopitian. Atorai D.→MAI-
    PURAN
Maore' = Sonder. Tontemboan D.→NORTH-
    ERN CELEBES
Maori→POLYNESIAN
Maori, Cook Islands→POLYNESIAN
Maotow = Makela'i. Tontemboan D.→
    NORTHERN CELEBES
Mapache. Carutana D.→NORTHERN MAI-
    PURAN
Mapanai→NORTHERN MAIPURAN
Mapauk. Bwe D.→KAREN
Mape→CARIB
Mape→HUON-FINISTERRE
Mape. Lawa D.→PALAUNG-WA
Mapenuss. Abipon Tr.→GUAYCURU
Mapi = Yaqay→MARIND
Mapidian = Maiopitian. Atorai D.→MAI-
    PURAN
Mapodi = Cheke→CHADIC
Maporese→WEST INDONESIAN
Mapoye = Mapoyo→CARIB
Mapoyo→CARIB
Maprik. Abelam D.→SEPIK
Mapuche = Araucanian→PENUTIAN
Mapuche = Moluche. Araucanian D.→PENU-
    TIAN
Mapute→CENTRAL   AND   SOUTHERN
    CELEBES
Maqua = Onandaga. Seneca Tr.→IROQUOIS
Maquiri = Kayabi→TUPI
Maquiritai = Maquiritare→CARIB
Maquiritare→CARIB
Mara→MARAN
Mara→NAGA-KUKI-CHIN
Maraca. Mape D.→CARIB
Maracana. Andoa Tr.→ANDEAN
Maracana = Maita. Waica Tr.→WAICAN
Maracani = Tumapasa→TACANA
Maraci. Luhya D.→NORTH EASTERN
    BANTU
Maradu. Dusun D.→NORTHWEST AUSTRO-
    NESIAN
Maragaus→NORTHWESTERN NEW HEB-
    RIDES
Maragoli — Logooli--NORTH EASTERN
    BANTU
Maragua - Mauc→TUPI
Maragum--·NORTHEASTERN NEW GUINEA
Maragwet — Markwet. Pokot D.--·EASTERN
    SUDANIC
Marako = Hadiyya→CUSHITIC
Marakwet = Markwet. Pokot D.→EASTERN
    SUDANIC
Maram→NAGA-KUKI-CHIN
Marama. Luhya D.→NORTH EASTERN
    BANTU
Maramandandji = Maramanindji→DALY
Maramanindji→DALY
Maramuni. Enga D.→EAST NEW GUINEA
    HIGHLANDS
Maran→NORTHWESTERN AND CENTRAL
    SOLOMONS
Maran = Baran. Ami D.→FORMOSAN
    AUSTRONESIAN
MARAN see article
Maranao→NORTHWEST AUSTRONESIAN
Maranaw = Maranao→NORTHWEST AUS-
    TRONESIAN
Marangu = Vunjo. Caga D.→NORTH EAST-
    ERN BANTU
Maranunggu→DALY
Maraon = Marawa→MAIPURAN
Marapka→OK
Maraquo = Hadiyya→CUSHITIC
Mararba. Gobabingo D.→MURNGIC
Mararet = Mararit→EASTERN SUDANIC
Mararit→EASTERN SUDANIC
Marashiteri. Waica Tr.→WAICAN
Marathi→INDIC
Marathiel = Marithiel. Brinken D.→DALY
Maratsa. High Lugbara D.→CENTRAL

SUDANIC
Maratunia = Mardudunera→NGAYARDA
Marau→EASTERN OCEANIC
Maraua→MAIPURAN
Maraura→NARRINYERIC
Marave = Peta. Nyanja D.→CENTRAL EASTERN BANTU
Maravi = Peta. Nyanja D.→CENTRAL EASTERN BANTU
Marawa→MAIPURAN
Marawa = Maraua→MAIPURAN
Marawari = Murawari→PAMA-NYUNGAN
Marawurei. Tawi D.→ADMIRALTY-WESTERN ISLANDS
Marba→CHADIC
Marba. Masalit D.→MABAN
Marda. Mongul D.→MONGOLIAN
Mardadhunira = Mardudunera→NGAYARDA
Mardala = Adnyamathana. Wailpi D.→YURA
Mardathoni = Mardudunera→NGAYARDA
Mardatuna = Mardudunera→NGAYARDA
Mardatunera = Mardudunera→NGAYARDA
Marditjali→KULINIC
Mardo. Kardutjara D.→WATI
Mardudhoonera = Mardudunera→NGAYRDA
Mardudjara = Mardo. Kardutjara D.→WATI
Mardudunera→NGAYARDA
Mardula = Adnyamathana. Wailpi D.→YURA
Maredan. Brinken D.→DALY
Marehunu. Tala D.→EAST INDONESIAN
Marengar→DALY
Mareschet = Malecite. Passamaquoddy D.→ ALGONQUIAN
Mareschit = Malecite. Passamaquoddy D.→ ALGONQUIAN
Mareschite = Malecite. Passamaquoddy D.→ ALGONQUIAN
Maretyabin. Brinken D.→DALY
Mafra = Marba. Masalit D.→MABAN
Marghi = Margi→CHADIC
Margi→CHADIC
Margi, Hill. Higi D.→CHADIC
Margu→IWAIDJAN
MARI→PAMA-MARIC
Mari→EASTERN OCEANIC
Mari→SEPIK
Mari. Oriya D.→INDIC
Mari = Cheremis→URALIC
Mari = Mhari. Karanga D.→SOUTH EASTERN BANTU
Maria. Gondi D.→DRAVIDIAN
Mariape-Nahuqua→CARIB
Mariate→NORTHERN MAIPURAN
Maribichicoa→TLAPANECAN

Maribo = Maribichicoa→TLAPANECAN
MARIC→MARAN
Maricopa. River Yuman D.→YUMAN
Marigl. Chimbu D.→EAST NEW GUINEA HIGHLANDS
Marille = Dasenech→CUSHITIC
Marille = Murle→EASTERN SUDANIC
Marimanindji = Maramanindji→DALY
Marimejuna = Peramangk. Tanganekald D.→ NARRINYERIC
Marin = Madin. Koma D.→KOMAN
Marin Miwok. Coast Miwok D.→MIWOK-COSTANOAN
Marina→NORTHWESTERN NEW HEBRIDES
Marinaua→PANO
MARIND see article
MARIND-OK→CENTRAL AND SOUTH NEW GUINEA
Maring→EAST NEW GUINEA HIGHLANDS
Maring→NAGA-KUKI-CHIN
Marino = Marina→NORTHWESTERN NEW HEBRIDES
MARIPOSAN = YOKUTS
Marithiel. Brinken D.→DALY
MARITIPARANA→NORTHERN MAIPURAN
Maritong. Coroado D.→PURI
Mariusa. Warao D.→MACRO-CHIBCHAN
Marivunini = Nangumiri→DALY
Marka. Soninke Tr.→MANDE
Markanka. Soninke Tr.→MANDE
Markwet. Pokot D.→EASTERN SUDANIC
Marle = Dasenech→CUSHITIC
Marle = Murle→EASTERN SUDANIC
Marlgana = Malgana→KARDU
Marnganji. Mandandanji D.→PAMA-MARIC
MARNGU see article
Maro Dyapa = Marodiapa→MACRO-TUCANOAN
Marodiapa→MACRO-TUCANOAN
Maronene = Marumeme. Bungku D.→CENTRAL AND SOUTHERN CELEBES
Maroonee = Goeng. Taribeleng D.→WAKAKABIC
Maropa→TACANA
Maroura = Mararba. Gobabingo D.→MURNGIC
Maroura = Maraura→NARRINYERIC
Marovo→NORTHWESTERN AND CENTRAL SOLOMONS
Marowera = Mararba. Gobabingo D.→MURNGIC
Marowera = Maraura→NARRINYERIC

Marpapi. Carare Tr.→CARIB
Marquesan→POLYNESIAN
MARQUESIC→POLYNESIAN
Marqueton. Panche D.→CARIB
Marra = Mara→MARAN
Marraawarree = Murawari→PAMA-NYUN-
GAN
Marrucinian→ITALIC
Marrula. Mitaka D.→PAMA-NYUNGAN
Marshallese→MICRONESIAN
Marsian→ITALIC
Maru→BODO-NAGA-KACHIN
Marula = Marrula. Mitaka D.→PAMA-NYUN-
GAN
Marulta. Karendala D.→DIERIC
Marulta = Marrula. Mitaka D.→PAMA-NYUN-
GAN
Marumeme. Bungku D.→CENTRAL AND
SOUTHERN CELEBES
Marun. Luf D.→ADMIRALTY-WESTERN
ISLANDS
Marunada = Marrula. Mitaka D.→PAMA-
NYUNGAN
Marunuda = Marrula. Mitaka D.→PAMA-
NYUNGAN
Marwari. Rajasthani D.→INDIC
Mary's River = Santiam→KALAPUYA
Mar-yul = Ladakhi. West Tibetan D.→
TIBETAN
MASA→CHADIC
Masa→ADAMAWA
Masa→CHADIC
Masa Gbaya. Musei D.→CHADIC
Masaba→NORTH EASTERN BANTU
MASABA-LUHYA→NORTH EASTERN
BANTU
Masaca→NORTHERN MAIPURAN
Masacara→CAMACAN
Masai = Maasai→EASTERN SUDANIC
Masakin→KORDOFANIAN
Masakin Buram. Masakin Tr.→KORDOFA-
NIAN
Masakin Dagig. Masakin Tr.→KORDOFA-
NIAN
Masakin Gusar. Masakin Tr.→KORDOFA-
NIAN
Masakin Tuwal. Masakin Tr.→KORDOFA-
NIAN
Masala = Masalit→MABAN
Masalit→MABAN
Masamai. Yameo D.→PEBA-YAGUAN
Masamba. Sa'dan D.→CENTRAL AND
SOUTHERN CELEBES
Masana = Masa→CHADIC

Masanze. Zyoba D.→NORTH EASTERN
BANTU
Masarete→EAST INDONESIAN
Masarwa = G / / abake→KHOISAN
Masarwa = Kakia. ŋ/amani D.→KHOISAN
Masasi→KHOISAN
Masasi. Bambara D.→MANDE
Masco→MAIPURAN
Mascouten = Illinois. Miami D.→ALGON-
QUIAN
Mascouten = Potawatomi→ALGONQUIAN
Mascoy→MACRO-PANOAN
Masegi→NORTHEAST NEW GUINEA AUS-
TRONESIAN
Masemola. Northern Sotho D.→SOUTH EAST-
ERN BANTU
Masemula = Masemola. Northern Sotho D.→
SOUTH EASTERN BANTU
Masengo = Masongo→EASTERN SUDANIC
Masenrempulu→CENTRAL AND SOUTH-
ERN CELEBES
Masfeima. Mandara Tr.→CHADIC
MASHACALI = MACHACALI
Mashami. Caga D.→NORTH EASTERN
BANTU
Mashasha→CENTRAL WESTERN BANTU
Mashi→SOUTH WESTERN BANTU
Mashuakwe = Shua→KHOISAN
Masi = Mashi→SOUTH WESTERN BANTU
Masig. Kaurareg D.→MABUIAGIC
Masiin = Azer. Soninke D.→MANDE
Masimasi→SARMIC
Masingara = Bine→ORIOMO RIVER
Masingle = Bine→ORIOMO RIVER
Masivaribeni. Achagua D.→NORTHERN MAI-
PURAN
Maskan = Mesqan. Peripheral West Gurage
D.→SEMITIC
Maskogi = Muskogee→MUSKOGEAN
Maskoke = Muskogee→MUSKOGEAN
Maskoki = Muskogee→MUSKOGEAN
Masmaje. Mubi D.→CHADIC
Masongo→EASTERN SUDANIC
Maspo→PANO
Masqan = Mesqan. Peripheral West Gurage
D.→SEMITIC
Massachusett→ALGONQUIAN
Massaco = Wappinger. Mohegan D.→ALGON-
QUIAN
Massacoe = Wappinger. Mohegan D.→
ALGONQUIAN
Massalit = Masalit→MABAN
Massapeque. Mohegan Tr.→ALGONQUIAN
Massasoits = Wampanoag. Massachusett D.→

ALGONQUIAN

Masset. Haida D.→NA-DENE

MASSIM→PAPUA AUSTRONESIAN

Massokarera. Sumba D.→MOLUCCAN

Maswaka = Swaka→CENTRAL EASTERN BANTU

Mata. Tupuri D.→ADAMAWA

Mataban-Moulmein = Mon Te. Mon D.→ MON-KHMER

MATACO see article

Matagalpa→MISUMALPAN

Mataguyo→MATACO

Matai = Gbari Gyenguen. Gbari D.→NUPE-GBARI

Matakam→CHADIC

MATAKAM-MANDARA→CHADIC

Matama = Mataua→CHAPACURA-WAN-HAMAN

Matan. Land Dayak D.→WEST INDONESIAN

Matana'i = Sonder. Tontemboan D.→NORTHERN CELEBES

Matanaui = Matanawi→MACRO-CHIBCHAN

Matanawi→MACRO-CHIBCHAN

Matanawu = Matanawi→MACRO-CHIBCHAN

Matap = Matup. Wantoat D.→HUON-FINISTERRE

Matapato. Maasai Tr.→EASTERN SUDANIC

Matapi→NORTHERN MAIPURAN

Matatarwa. Eggon D.→PLATEAU BENUE-CONGO

Mataua→CHAPACURA-WANHAMAN

Mataveke-paya = Walapai. Upland Yuman D. →YUMAN

Mate. Ndandi D.→NORTH EASTERN BANTU

Matengala. Eggon D.→PLATEAU BENUE-CONGO

Matengo→CENTRAL EASTERN BANTU

Matepi→NORTHEASTERN NEW GUINEA

Matete→KHOISAN

Mathimathi = Muthimuthi. Djadjala D.→ KULINIC

Matinecock. Mohegan Tr.→ALGONQUIAN

Matla. Western Bira D.→NORTH EASTERN BANTU

Matlapa. Nahua D.→UTO-AZTECAN

Matlatzinca→OTOMIAN

Matngala. Warat D.→DALY

Mato = Makua→SOUTH EASTERN BANTU

Matsungan→NORTHWESTERN AND CENTRAL SOLOMONS

Mattapony. Powhatan Tr.→ALGONQUIAN

Mattole→ATHAPASCAN-EYAK

Matu. Khami D.→NAGA-KUKI-CHIN

Matu. Melanau D.→WEST INDONESIAN

Matuari. Sranan D.→GERMANIC

Matukar→NORTHEAST NEW GUINEA AUSTRONESIAN

MATUMBI→SOUTH EASTERN BANTU

Matumbi→SOUTH EASTERN BANTU

Matup. Wantoat D.→HUON-FINISTERRE

Matupi = Lawthve→NAGA-KUKI-CHIN

Matur = Mober→CHADIC

Matwanly. Rawang D.→BODO-NAGA-KACHIN

Mau. Malinka D.→MANDE

Mau = Northern Mao→KOMAN

MAUACA = MAWACA→NORTHERN MAIPURAN

Mauacua→NORTHERN MAIPURAN

Maudalgo = Wadja→WAKA-KABIC

Maue→TUPI

Mauka = Mau. Malinka D.→MANDE

Mauke. Cook Islands Maori D.→POLYNESIAN

Maula = Warluwara→WAKAYA-WARLU-WARIC

Maung→IWAIDJAN

Maututu→BISMARCK ARCHIPELAGO

Mavar = Mabar. Kanuri Tr.→SAHARAN

Mavia→NORTHWESTERN NEW HEBRIDES

Mavia = Mabiha→SOUTH EASTERN BANTU

Maviha = Mabiha→SOUTH EASTERN BANTU

Maw→KAM-TAI

Maw = Maung→IWAIDJAN

MAWACA→NORTHERN MAIPURAN

Mawacua = Mauacua→NORTHERN MAIPURAN

Mawai. Zia D.→BINANDERE

Mawak→BOGIA

Mawan→BOGIA

Mawata. Southern Kiwai D.→CENTRAL AND SOUTH NEW GUINEA

Mawatani = Mandan→SIOUAN

Mawe = Maue→TUPI

Mawea. Tobelo D.→NORTH HALMAHERA

Mawes→NORTH PAPUAN

Mawi = Mano→MANDE

Mawia = Mabiha→SOUTH EASTERN BANTU

Mawiha = Mabiha→SOUTH EASTERN BANTU

Mawisi = Bwisi-Talinga→NORTH EASTERN BANTU

Mawnepgha. Sgaw D.→KAREN

Maxakali = Machacali→MACHACALI

Maxakari = Machacali→MACHACALI

Maxubi = Aricapu

May. Muong D.→VIET-MUONG

Maya→MAYAN

Maya. Margi D.→CHADIC

MAYAN see article

Mayaoyao→NORTHWEST AUSTRONE-SIAN

Mayapi→MAYAPIC

MAYAPIC see article

Mayawyaw = Mayaoyao→NORTHWEST AUSTRONESIAN

Mayko. Mayogo Tr.→EASTERN

Maykulan→MAYAPIC

Maymay. Somali D.→CUSHITIC

Mayo→SEPIK

Mayo. Yaqui D.→UTO-AZTECAN

Mayo = Maya→MAYAN

Mayo = Northern Mao→KOMAN

Mayogo→EASTERN

Mayongong. Maquiritare D.→CARIB

Mayoyao = Mayaoyao→NORTHWEST AUS-TRONESIAN

Maytagoori = Mitakudi→PAMA-NYUNGAN

Mayugo. Mayogo Tr.→EASTERN

Mayuli. Wangkadjera D.→PITTAPITTIC

Mazagwa. Mandara Tr.→CHADIC

Mazahua→OTOMIAN

Mazan. Yameo D.→PEBA-YAGUAN

Mazanderani→IRANIAN

Mazaro→CENTRAL EASTERN BANTU

Mazatec→POPOLOCAN

MAZATECAN = POPOLOCAN

Mazateco = Mazatec→POPOLOCAN

Mba→EASTERN

Mbaama→NORTH WESTERN BANTU

Mbaata. Kongo D.→CENTRAL WESTERN BANTU

Mbaati. Ngbandi Tr.→EASTERN

Mbacca→EASTERN

Mbacca. Gbanziri Tr.→EASTERN

Mbada = Badawa. Jarawa D.→BANTOID

Mbadawa = Badawa. Jarawa D.→BANTOID

Mbae-una = Baena

M'bagga = Gbaga. Ganda D.→EASTERN

Mbai→CENTRAL SUDANIC

Mbai. Nandi D.→EASTERN SUDANIC

Mbai = Pai. Northern Sotho D.→SOUTH EASTERN BANTU

Mbai Gor = Sara Mbai of Doba. Gambai D.→CENTRAL SUDANIC

Mbaka. Gbaya Tr.→EASTERN

Mbaka. Mbamba D.→CENTRAL WESTERN BANTU

Mbaka = Manja. Gbaya D.→EASTERN

Mbala→CENTRAL WESTERN BANTU

Mbala. Banda D.→EASTERN

Mbala. Songe D.→CENTRAL WESTERN BANTU

Mbala Mumbala. Kongo D.→CENTRAL WESTERN BANTU

Mbalazi. Tikuu D.→CENTRAL EASTERN BANTU

Mbale = Busooŋ→NORTH WESTERN BANTU

Mbali = Mbundu→SOUTH WESTERN BANTU

Mbama = Nagumi→BANTOID

Mbamba→CENTRAL WESTERN BANTU

Mbamba = Mbaama→NORTH WESTERN BANTU

Mbandieru. Herero D.→SOUTH WESTERN BANTU

Mbang. Basa Tr.→NORTH WESTERN BANTU

Mbangala→CENTRAL WESTERN BANTU

Mbanja. Banda D.→EASTERN

Mbanja. Furu Tr.→CENTRAL SUDANIC

Mbaŋwe→NORTH WESTERN BANTU

Mbara Kwengo = Hukwe→KHOISAN

Mbarabam→PAMA-MARIC

Mbari = Mbundu→SOUTH WESTERN BANTU

Mbarike = Zumper→JUKUNOID

Mbat = Badawa. Jarawa D.→BANTOID

Mbat = Wa. Nsungli D.→BANTOID

Mbati→NORTH WESTERN BANTU

Mbati = Ngbandi→EASTERN

Mbato = Gwa→LAGOON

Mbaw→BANTOID

Mbay = Mbai→CENTRAL SUDANIC

Mbaya Mirim = Apacachodegodegi. Mbaya-Guaicuru Tr.→GUAYCURU

Mbaya-Guaicuru→GUAYCURU

Mbayaka→AGOB

Mbaye = Mbai→CENTRAL SUDANIC

Mbayi = Pai. Northern Sotho D.→SOUTH EASTERN BANTU

Mbbamba. Kongo D.→CENTRAL WESTERN BANTU

Mbe→BANTOID

Mbeafal→CROSS RIVER BENUE-CONGO

Mbede = Mbete→NORTH WESTERN BANTU

Mbeeko. Kongo D.→CENTRAL WESTERN BANTU

Mbegumba = Bviri→EASTERN

Mbeiwum→PAMA-MARIC

Mbelala = Bela→CENTRAL AND SOUTH-

ERN CELEBES

Mbele. Banda D.→EASTERN

Mbele = Mbili. Mandankwe D.→BANTOID

Mbem→BANTOID

MBEMBE→JUKUNOID

Mbembe→CROSS RIVER BENUE-CONGO

Mbenderinga = Antakirinya. Kardutjara D.→ WATI

Mbene. Basa Tr.→NORTH WESTERN BANTU

Mbengui = Tagbari. Senari D.→GUR

Mbenkpe = Nde→BANTOID

Mbensa = Nbinsa. Kongo D.→CENTRAL WESTERN BANTU

Mbere. Kari D.→ADAMAWA

Mbesa→NORTH WESTERN BANTU

MBETE→NORTH WESTERN BANTU

Mbete→NORTH WESTERN BANTU

Mbete = Bete→CROSS-RIVER BENUE-CONGO

Mbi. Banda D.→EASTERN

Mbia. Tupi D.→TUPI

Mbiem. Yanzi D.→NORTH WESTERN BANTU

Mbili. Mandankwe D.→BANTOID

Mbimu→NORTH WESTERN BANTU

Mbinga. Mabaale D.→NORTH WESTERN BANTU

Mbinsa. Kongo D.→CENTRAL WESTERN BANTU

Mbire. Shona D.→SOUTH EASTERN BANTU

Mbitse = Tiv→BANTOID

Mbitshi = Tiv→BANTOID

Mbiywom = Mbeiwum→PAMA-MARIC

MBO = LUNDU-BALONG→NORTH WESTERN BANTU

Mbo→NORTH EASTERN BANTU

Mbo→NORTH WESTERN BANTU

Mbo→CENTRAL EASTERN BANTU

Mboa→BANTOID

Mbocobi = Mocovi→GUAYCURU

Mbofo:n = Nde→BANTOID

Mbogedo. Kwangari D.→NORTH WESTERN BANTU

Mbogu = Mbugu. Banda D.→EASTERN

Mboi→ADAMAWA

Mboka→CENTRAL WESTERN BANTU

Mboko→NORTH WESTERN BANTU

Mboko = Bomboko→NORTH WESTERN BANTU

Mbole→NORTH EASTERN BANTU

MBOLE-ENA→NORTH EASTERN BANTU

Mboma. Kongo D.→CENTRAL WESTERN BANTU

Mbomotaba→NORTH WESTERN BANTU

Mbomu. Zande D.→EASTERN

Mbono→EAST INDONESIAN

Mboŋ = Kaaloŋ→NORTH WESTERN BANTU

Mbooso. Kele Tr.→NORTH WESTERN BANTU

Mboshi = Mbosi→NORTH WESTERN BANTU

Mbosi→NORTH WESTERN BANTU

Mbota = Kunambena→NORTHWESTERN AND CENTRAL SOLOMONS

Mbotuwa = Butawa→PLATEAU BENUE-CONGO

Mbougou = Mbugu→CUSHITIC

Mbouin = Kirma→GUR

Mboulou = Mbulu. Banda D.→EASTERN

Mbowe→SOUTH WESTERN BANTU

Mbre = Mbele. Banda D.→EASTERN

Mbria = Bria. Banda D.→EASTERN

Mbrou = Buru. Banda D.→EASTERN

Mbru = Buru. Banda D.→EASTERN

Mbube, Eastern = Mbeafal→CROSS RIVER BENUE-CONGO

Mbube, Western = Mbe→BANTOID

Mbubu = Mbugu. Banda D.→EASTERN

Mbudikem = Widekum→BANTOID

Mbudza. Losengo D.→NORTH WESTERN BANTU

Mbuge. Mok. D.→ADMIRALTY-WESTERN ISLANDS

Mbugu→CUSHITIC

Mbugu. Banda D.→EASTERN

Mbugwe→NORTH EASTERN BANTU

Mbui. Mandankwe D.→BANTOID

Mbuiyi = Amboim→CENTRAL WESTERN BANTU

Mbukuhu = Mbukushu. Kwangari D.→SOUTH WESTERN BANTU

Mbukushu. Kwangari D.→SOUTH WESTERN BANTU

Mbula→BANTOID

Mbuli. Ombo D.→NORTH WESTERN BANTU

Mbulla = Mbula→BANTOID

Mbulu. Banda D.→EASTERN

Mbulu = Iraqw→CUSHITIC

Mbulunge = Burungi→CUSHITIC

Mbulungish→WEST ATLANTIC

Mbulungu = Burungi→CUSHITIC

Mbum. Kari D.→ADAMAWA

Mbuma = Bendeghe. Ekoi D.→BANTOID

Mbumbum = Mpompo. Mbinu D.→NORTH WESTERN BANTU

Mbunai. Mok D.→ADMIRALTY-WESTERN ISLANDS

Mbunda→SOUTH WESTERN BANTU
Mbunda = Mbuun→NORTH WESTERN BANTU
M'bundo = Mbundu→SOUTH WESTERN BANTU
Mbundu→SOUTH WESTERN BANTU
Mbundu. Sama Tr.→CENTRAL WESTERN BANTU
Mbunga→SOUTH EASTERN BANTU
Mbunu = Mbuun→NORTH WESTERN BANTU
Mbutawa = Butawa→PLATEAU BENUE-CONGO
Mbuti→NORTH EASTERN BANTU
Mbuun→NORTH WESTERN BANTU
Mbuunda = Mbunda→SOUTH WESTERN BANTU
Mbwaka = Bwaka→EASTERN
Mbwela→SOUTH WESTERN BANTU
Mbwela = Mbwera→CENTRAL WESTERN BANTU
Mbwera→CENTRAL WESTERN BANTU
Mbwera = Mbwela→SOUTH WESTERN BANTU
Mbya = Mbia. Tupi D.→TUPI
Mdundu→CENTRAL WESTERN BANTU
Mdundulu→SOUTH WESTERN BANTU
Mearn-anger = Minang. Juat D.→SOUTHWEST PAMA-NYUNGAN
Meaun = Mewun→NORTHWESTERN NEW HEBRIDES
Meax = Meninggo→WESTERN NEW GUINEA
Meban = Mban→EASTERN SUDANIC
Mebe = Dan→MANDE
Mecayapan→UTO-AZTECAN
Mech. Bodo D.→BODO-NAGA-KACHIN
Mecha. Galla D.→CUSHITIC
Mechkentowoon. Mohegan Tr.→ALGONQUIAN
Mechoacan = Tarascan
Mechuaca = Tarascan
Meco = Chichimeca-Jonaz→OTOMIAN
Meco = Comanche. Shoshoni D.→UTO-AZTECAN
Meco = Serrano→UTO-AZTECAN
Mediban. Somali Tr.→CUSHITIC
Medje = Meje. Mangbetu D.→CENTRAL SUDANIC
Medjime. Mbimu D.→NORTH WESTERN BANTU
Medlpa→EAST NEW GUINEA HIGHLANDS
Medo. Makua D.→SOUTH EASTERN BANTU
Medogo = Mudogo. Kuka D.→CENTRAL SUDANIC
Medye = Meje. Mangbetu D.→CENTRAL SUDANIC
Medzime = Medjime. Mbimu D.→NORTH WESTERN BANTU
Me'ek→SEPIK
Meeleeceet = Malecite. Passamaquoddy D.→ALGONQUIAN
Me'en = Mekan→EASTERN SUDANIC
Meening = Mirning→MIRNINY
Meenung = Minang. Juat D.→SOUTHWEST PAMA-NYUNGAN
Meeraman = Pibelmen. Juat D.→SOUTHWEST PAMA-NYUNGAN
Meeroni = Goeng. Taribeleng D.→WAKA-KABIC
Megamaw = Mogamo→BANTOID
Megi. Kagulu D.→CENTRAL EASTERN BANTU
Megiar→NORTHEST NEW GUINEA AUSTRONESIAN
MEGIMBA = NGEMBA→BANTOID
Meglenite = Meglenitic. Rumanian D.→ROMANCE
Meglenitic. Rumanian D.→ROMANCE
Megleno-Rumanian = Meglenitic. Rumanian D.→ROMANCE
Megon = Eggon→PLATEAU BENUE-CONGO
Megye = Meje. Mangbetu D.→CENTRAL SUDANIC
Mehari. Oriya D.→INDIC
Mehari = Halbi. Oriya D.→INDIC
Mehek→SEPIK
Mehin→GE
Mehinacu→MAIPURAN
Meidob = Midob→EASTERN SUDANIC
Meidoo = Maidu→MAIDU
Mein. Ijo D.→IJO
Meintangk = Djadjala→KULINIC
Meintank = Djadjala→KULINIC
Meithei→NAGA-KUKI-CHIN
Meithlei = Meithei→NAGA-KUKI-CHIN
Meje. Mangbetu D.→CENTRAL SUDANIC
Mejepure = Maipure→NORTHERN MAIPURAN
Mekan→EASTERN SUDANIC
Mekbengetseq = Taihyo. Atayal D.→FORMOSAN AUSTRONESIAN
Mekei = Mekwei→NORTH PAPUAN
Mekeo→PAPUA AUSTRONESIAN
Mekhali = Meithei→NAGA-KUKI-CHIN
Mekibo = Metyibo→VOLTA-COMOE
Mekle = Meithei→NAGA-KUKI-CHIN

Mekongka→CENTRAL AND SOUTHERN CELEBES

Mekormuk = Kurmuk. Burun Tr.→EASTERN SUDANIC

Mekusuky = Mikasuki. Hitchiti D.→MUSKO-GEAN

Mekwei→NORTH PAPUAN

MEL→WEST ATLANTIC

Melam. Rawang D.→BODO-NAGA-KACHIN

MELAMBA = NDOP→BANTOID

MELANAU→WEST INDONESIAN

Melanau→WEST INDONESIAN

MELANESIAN, CENTRAL see article

Melchora. Rama D.→CHIBCHAN

MELE = MANDE

Mele→POLYNESIAN

Melebuganon→NORTHWEST AUSTRONE-SIAN

Melet Tatar = Chulym→TURKIC

Melicete = Malecite. Passamaquoddy D.→ALGONQUIAN

Melicite = Malecite. Passamaquoddy D.→ALGONQUIAN

Mella. Guahibo D.→EQUATORIAL

Melolo. Sumba D.→MOLUCCAN

Meloria = Muliara→KARDU

Melsisi. Central Raga D.→EASTERN OCEANIC

Mem = Mam→MAYAN

Membi. Ndo D.→CENTRAL SUDANIC

Memboro = Mamboru. Sumba D.→MOLUC-CAN

Memmi = Nedi. Akye Tr.→LAGOON

Mena Yu = Kru-Krawi→KRU

Menabe. Malagasy D.→WEST INDONESIAN

Menam = Monom→MON-KHMER

Menandon = Aiku→TORRICELLI

Menandon = Kayik→TORRICELLI

Menandon = Nambi→TORRICELLI

Menandon = Wiaki→TORRICELLI

Mende→MANDE

Mende = Seim→SEPIK

Mendeya. Gumuz D.→KOMAN

MENDI→EAST NEW GUINEA HIGH-LANDS

Mendi→EAST NEW GUINEA HIGHLANDS

Mendi = Mende→MANDE

Mendocino Huarpe = Millcayac→HUARPE

Mendoza Huarpe = Allentiac→HUARPE

Menemo→BANTOID

Mengen→BISMARCK ARCHIPELAGO

Menggwei = Mekwei→NORTH PAPUAN

Menghwa→BURMESE-LOLO

Mengkatip = Mangkatip. Ngaju D.→WEST INDONESIAN

Menia = Manyak→BURMESE-LOLO

Menian→CAMACAN

Menimehe→NORTHERN MAIPURAN

Meninggo→WESTERN NEW GUINEA

Meninka = Malinka→MANDE

Menja = Kwegu→EASTERN SUDANIC

Menjuke = Manyukai. Land Dayak D.→WEST INDONESIAN

Menka→BANTOID

Menne = Suamle. Kweni D.→MANDE

Mennomonie = Menomini→ALGONQUIAN

Menomene = Menomini→ALGONQUIAN

Menomenee = Menomini→ALGONQUIAN

Menomeni = Menomini→ALGONQUIAN

Menomenie = Menomini→ALGONQUIAN

Menomine = Menomini→ALGONQUIAN

Menominee = Menomini→ALGONQUIAN

Menomini→ALGONQUIAN

Menomonee = Menomini→ALGONQUIAN

Menomoni = Menomini→ALGONQUIAN

Mensa. Tigre D.→SEMITIC

Mentasta. Ahtena D.→ATHAPASCAN-EYAK

Mentawai→WEST INDONESIAN

Mentuh Tapuh. Land Dayak D.→WEST INDONESIAN

Menunkatuk = Wappinger. Mohegan D.→ALGONQUIAN

Menya = Manyak→BURMESE-LOLO

Menye→KUKUKUKU

Meŋgaŋ. Ewondo D.→NORTH WESTERN BANTU

Meqan = Mekan→EASTERN SUDANIC

Mequens = Guarategaya→TUPI

Mer = Miriam→ORIOMO RIVER

Mera Mera→NORTHEAST NEW GUINEA AUSTRONESIAN

Meramera = Mera Mera→NORTHEST NEW GUINEA AUSTRONESIAN

Merani. Binahari D.→MAILU

Merarit = Mararit→EASTERN SUDANIC

Meratei. Land Dayak D.→WEST INDO-NESIAN

Merei. Bangba D.→EASTERN

Mereldi = Peramangk. Tanganekald D.→NAR-RINYERIC

Merguese = Mergui. Burmese D.→BURMESE-LOLO

Mergui. Burmese D.→BURMESE-LOLO

Merida = Zaghawa→SAHARAN

Merig→EASTERN OCEANIC

Merildakald = Peramangk. Tanganekald D.→NARRINYERIC

Merille = Dasenech→CUSHITIC

Merille = Murle→EASTERN SUDANIC
Merina. Malagasy D.→WEST INDONESIAN
Merir. Ulithian D.→MICRONESIAN
Merkani = Ngarkat. Djadjala D.→KULINIC
Merkanie = Ngarkat. Djadjala D.→KULINIC
Merkwet = Markwet. Pokot D.→EASTERN SUDANIC
Merlav→EASTERN OCEANIC
Mero→NORTH EASTERN BANTU
Meroitic→EASTERN SUDANIC
Merric. Mohegan Tr.→ALGONQUIAN
Merrimac = Pennacook. Massachusett D.→ALGONQUIAN
Merrime = Ramcocamecra→GE
Meru = Hai. Caga D.→NORTH EASTERN BANTU
Meru = Mero→NORTH EASTERN BANTU
Meru = Ngaiawang. Nganguruku D.→NARRINYERIC
Merwari = Marwari. Rajasthani D.→INDIC
Mesakin = Masakin→KORDOFANIAN
Mesakin Qusar = Masakin Gusar. Masakin Tr.→KORDOFANIAN
Mesara. Havunese D.→MOLUCCAN
Mescalero. Navajo D.→ATHAPASCAN-EYAK
Mesengo = Masongo→EASTERN SUDANIC
Mesketo = Basketo→OMOTIC
Mesmes = Mesqan. Peripheral West Gurage D.→SEMITIC
MESOPHILIPPINE→NORTHWEST AUSTRONESIAN
Mesqan. Peripheral West Gurage D.→SEMITIC
Mesqan = Inneqor. East Gurage D.→SEMITIC
Messapic. Illyrian D.→ITALIC
Messeni = Takpasyeeri. Senari D.→GUR
Meta = Menemo→BANTOID
Meta, Eastern = Ngamambo→BANTOID
Metabi = Ingassana→CHARI-NILE
Metaso. Tongoa D.→EASTERN OCEANIC
Metekkel = Awiya→CUSHITIC
Methow. Okanogan D.→SALISH
Methun = Midu. Digaru Mishmi D.→GYARUNG-MISHMI
Metoko = Mituku→NORTH EASTERN BANTU
Metomka = Southern Kati→OK
Metru = Alu→TORRICELLI
Metru = Galu→TORRICELLI
Metu. Rawang D.→BODO-NAGA-KACHIN
Metyibo→VOLTA-COMOE
MEWAN = MIWOK→MIWOK-COSTANOAN
Mewari = Marwari. Rajasthani D.→INDIC
Mewati. Rajasthani D.→INDIC

Mewun→NORTHWESTERN NEW HEBRIDES
Mexicano = Nahua→UTO-AZTECAN
Meyobe = Soruba-Kuyobe→GUR
Meyu = Kaurna. Jadliaura D.→YURA
Məkasai→TIMOR-ALOR
Mfantse = Fante. Akan D.→VOLTA-COMOE
Mfinu→NORTH WESTERN BANTU
MFUMTE→BANTOID
Mfumu = Fumu. South Teke D.→NORTH WESTERN BANTU
Mfununga = Mfinu→NORTH WESTERN BANTU
Mfuti = Bute→BANTOID
Mgbato = Gwa→LAGOON
Mhari. Karanga D.→SOUTH EASTERN BANTU
Mi→KHMUIC
Mi Err = Kwalsim→NAGA-KUKI-CHIN
Mia = Mano→MANDE
Miah = Maia→KARDU
Miahuateco = Miahuatlan. Zapotec D.→ZAPOTECAN
Miahuatlan. Zapotec D.→ZAPOTECAN
Miaitopa→PAPUA AUSTRONESIAN
Mialat. Kawaib D.→TUPI
Miami→ALGONQUIAN
Mian. Mandandanji D.→PAMA-MARIC
Mianka→GUR
Mianmin→OK
MIAO-YAO see article
Miappe = Mayapi→MAYAPIC
Miccosukee = Mikasuki. Hitchiti D.→MUSKOGEAN
Michi. Toba Tr.→GUAYCURU
Michigamea = Illinois. Miami D.→ALGONQUIAN
Michile = Gobeze. Gawwada D.→CUSHITIC
Michoacano = Tarascan
Michopo = Maidu→MAIDU
Michuacan = Tarascan
Micmac→ALGONQUIAN
Micmacensi = Micmac→ALGONQUIAN
Micmak = Micmac→ALGONQUIAN
Micoolan = Maykulan→MAYAPIC
MICRONESIAN see article
MICTLANTONGO. Mixtec D.→MIXTECAN
Mid-Waria = Guhu Samane→BINANDERE
Mida = Kotoko→CHADIC
Middle Columbia = Columbian→SALISH
Midhaga = Mitkudi→PAMA NYUNGAN
Midik→TIMOR-ALOR
Midin = Madin. Koma D.→KOMAN
Midjinngay = Majingai. Sara D.→CENTRAL

SUDANIC
Midob→EASTERN SUDANIC
Midogo = Mudogo. Kuka D.→CENTRAL SU-
DANIC
Midsivindi→BOGIA
Midu. Digaru Mishmi D.→GYARUNG-MISH-
MI
Mieken = Mekan→EASTERN SUDANIC
Mien→MIAO-YAO
Mieru. Bencho D.→OMOTIC
Migaba' = Migabac→HUON-FINISTERRE
Migabac→HUON-FINISTERRE
Mige→MABAN
Migili→PLATEAU BENUE-CONGO
Migurian. Timote D.→EQUATORIAL
Mihavane = Ngulu→SOUTH EASTERN BAN-
TU
Mihavani = Ngulu→SOUTH EASTERN BAN-
TU
Mihawani = Ngulu→SOUTH EASTERN BAN-
TU
Mije = Mixe→MIXE-ZOQUE
Miju Mishmi→GYARUNG-MISHMI
Mikarew = Makarub→BOGIA
MIKARU→EAST NEW GUINEA HIGH-
LANDS
Mikaru→EAST NEW GUINEA HIGHLANDS
Mikasuke = Mikasuki. Hitchiti D.→MUSKO-
GEAN
Mikasuki. Hitchiti D.→MUSKOGEAN
Mikeano. Yameo D.→PEBA-YAGUAN
Mikemak = Micmac→ALGONQUIAN
Miki = Mige→MABAN
Mikik. Tsaxur D.→CAUCASIAN
Mikir = Naga-Mikir→NAGA-KUKI-CHIN
Mikkoolan = Maykulan→MAYAPIC
Miklai = Hlota→NAGA-KUKI-CHIN
Mikmak = Micmac→ALGONQUIAN
Mikmaque = Micmac→ALGONQUIAN
Mikud→AGOB
Milano = Melanau→WEST INDONESIAN
Milareipi. Toaripi D.→TOARIPI
Milchanang = Malhesti. Kanawari D.→GYA-
RUNG-MISHMI
Milchang = Malhesti. Kanawari D.→GYA-
RUNG-MISHMI
Mileere = Jabaal. Tama D.→EASTERN SU-
DANIC
Milicete = Malecite. Passamaquoddy D.→AL-
GONQUIAN
Milicite = Malecite. Passamaquoddy D.→AL-
GONQUIAN
Milipitingara = Kaurna. Jadliaura D.→YURA
Millcayac→HUARPE

Millicete = Malecite. Passamaquoddy D.→AL-
GONQUIAN
Milmenrura = Tanganekald→NARRINYERIC
Milo. Southern Nicobarese D.→NICOBARESE
Milpa Alta. Nahua D.→UTO-AZTECAN
Milpulko = Naualko. Kula D.→PAMA-
NYUNGAN
Miltou = Miltu→CHADIC
Miltu→CHADIC
Milyauppa = Maljangapa. Karenggapa D.→
DIERIC
Mima. Tsakrima D.→NAGA-KUKI-CHIN
Mime = Mimi→MABAN
Mimi→CROSS RIVER BENUE-CONGO
Mimi→MABAN
Mimika→ASMAT
Min, Northern→CHINESE
Min, Southern→CHINESE
Min Nan = Southern Min→CHINESE
Min Pei = Northern Min→CHINESE
Mina = Ge. Ewe D.→EWE
Mina = Muna→CENTRAL AND SOUTHERN
CELEBES
Mina Mina Gorong. Geser D.→EAST INDO-
NESIAN
Minaco = Mehinacu→MAIPURAN
Minaean. Old South Arabic D.→SEMITIC
Minala = Mangala→MARNGU
Minalnjunga = Wadjuk. Juat D.→SOUTH-
WEST PAMA-NYUNGAN
Minandon = Nambi→TORRICELLI
Minang. Juat D.→SOUTHWEST PAMA-
NYUNGAN
Minangkabau→WEST INDONESIAN
Minangyan = Hanunoo→NORTHWEST AUS-
TRONESIAN
Minatare = Hidatsa→SIOUAN
Minataree = Hidatsa→SIOUAN
Minatarre = Hidatsa→SIOUAN
Minatarree = Hidatsa→SIOUAN
Minbu. Aso Tr.→NAGA-KUKI-CHIN
Minchhanang = Malhesti. Kanawari D.→GYA-
RUNG-MISHMI
Minchhang = Malhesti. Kanawari D.→GYA-
RUNG-MISHMI
MINCHIA→BURMESE-LOLO
Minchia→BURMESE-LOLO
Minda. Bandawa D.→JUKUNOID
Mindik→HUON-FINISTERRE
Mindiri→NORTHEST NEW GUINEA AUS-
TRONESIAN
Mindumbu = Minduumo→NORTH WEST-
ERN BANTU
Minduumo→NORTH WESTERN BANTU

Minendon = Aiku→TORRICELLI
Minendon = Kayik→TORRICELLI
Minendon = Wiaki→TORRICELLI
Minetaree = Hidatsa→SIOUAN
Mingat. Oirat D.→MONGOLIAN
Ming-ho. Mongour D.→MONGOLIAN
Mingi = Ngi→BANTOID
Mingin→AUSTRALIAN MACRO-PHYLUM
Mingrelian. Zan D.→CAUCASIAN
Minhagirun = Minya-yirugn. Gutucrac D.→
    BOTOCUDO
MINHASA→NORTHERN CELEBES
Minhasa = Mongondow→NORTHERN CELE-
    BES
Minianka = Mianka→GUR
Minica. Witoto D.→WITOTOAN
Miniferi. Afar-Saho D.→CUSHITIC
Minikin = Mingin→AUSTRALIAN MACRO-
    PHYLUM
Mining = Mirning ·MIRNINY
Minitaree = Hidatsa→SIOUAN
Minitari = Hidatsa→SIOUAN
Minjangbal. Giabal D.→GIABALIC
Minjimmina = El Kebira. Tulishi D.→KORDO-
    FANIAN
Minjori→KOIARI
Minkia = Minchia→BURMESE-LOLO
Minkin = Mingin→AUSTRALIAN MACRO-
    PHYLUM
Minnal-Yungar = Wadjuk. Juat D.→SOUTH-
    WEST PAMA-NYUNGAN
Minnataree = Hidatsa→SIOUAN
Minnetahse = Hidatsa→SIOUAN
Minqua = Susquehannock→IROQUOIS
Minthla. Margi D.→CHADIC
Minuane→LULE-VILELA-CHARRUA
Minung = Minang. Juat D.→SOUTHWEST
    PAMA-NYUNGAN
mi-Nungo = Nungo. Ciokwe D.→SOUTH
    WESTERN BANTU
Minya. Malinka D.→MANDE
Minyafuin→SOUTH HALMAHERA AUS-
    TRONESIAN
Minya-yirugn. Gutucrac D.→BOTOCUDO
Minyowa = Minjangbal. Giabal D.→GIABALIC
Minyung = Minjangbal. Giabal D.→GIABALIC
Miorli = Mayuli. Wangkadjera D.→PITTA-
    PITTIC
Mios Num. Numfor D.→MOLUCCAN
Mios Wa'ar. Numfor D.→MOLUCCAN
Miquemaque = Micmac→ALGONQUIAN
Miranho. Tenetehara Tr.→TUPI
Miranya→WITOTOAN
Mirdiragoort = Warkawarka. Djadjala D.→

KULINIC
Miri→KORDOFANIAN
Miri. Narom D.→WEST INDONESIAN
Miri = Adi→GYARUNG-MISHMI
Miriam→CHADIC
Miriam→ORIOMO RIVER
Mirili = Nganguruku→NARRINYERIC
Mirin = Mirning→MIRNINY
Miriwun→DJERAGAN
MIRIWUNIC→DJERAGAN
Mirki = Margi→CHADIC
Mirning→MIRNINY
Mirniny = Mirning→MIRNINY
MIRNINY see article
Mirr = Kuseri. Kotoko D.→CHADIC
Mirung = Miriwun→DJERAGAN
Mis→NORTHEASTERN NEW GUINEA
MISAJE→BANTOID
Misdao→NORTHEASTERN NEW GUINEA
Mishikhwutmetunee = Coquille. Chasta Costa
    D.→ATHAPASCAN-EYAK
Mishlesh. Tsaxur D.→CAUCASIAN
Mishmar Tatar. Tatar D.→TURKIC
Mishulundu→SOUTH WESTERN BANTU
Mising = Adi→GYARUNG-MISHMI
Miskito→MISUMALPAN
Misol = Miso'ol→SOUTH HALMAHERA
    AUSTRONESIAN
Miso'ol→SOUTH HALMAHERA AUSTRO-
    NESIAN
Misquito = Miskito→MISUMALPAN
Missouri. CHIWERE D.→SIOUAN
Missouria = Missouri. CHIWERE D.→SIOU-
    AN
Missourie = Missouri. CHIWERE D.→SIOU-
    AN
MISUMALPAN see article
Mitagurdi = Mitakudi→PAMA-NYUNGAN
Mitak→AWYU
Mitaka→PAMA-NYUNGAN
Mitakoodi = Mitakudi→PAMA-NYUNGAN
Mitakudi→PAMA-NYUNGAN
Mitandu = Matanawi→MACRO-CHIBHCAN
Mitang = Nambi→TORRICELLI
Mitiaro. Cook Islands Maori D.→POLYNE-
    SIAN
Mitiwari. Waica Tr.→WAICAN
Mitjamba. Ilba D.→PAMA-MARIC
Mitmit→HUON-FINISTERRE
Mitroogordi = Mitakudi→PAMA-NYUNGAN
Mitsogo = Tsogo→NORTH WESTERN BAN-
    TU
Mittagurdi = Mitakudi→PAMA-NYUNGAN
Mittaka = Mitaka→PAMA-NYUNGAN

Mitua→NORTHERN MAIPURAN
Mituku→NORTH EASTERN BANTU
Miubbi = Mayapi→MAYAPIC
Miwa. Bagu D.→WORORAN
MIWOK-COSTANOAN see article
MIXE-ZOQUE see article
Mixtec→MIXTECAN
MIXTECAN see article
Mixteco = Mixtec→MIXTECAN
Miyako. Southern Ryukyuan D.→JAPANESE
Miyal = Bigumbil→WIRADJURIC
MIYAN→WAKA-KABIC
Miyang Khang. Kwoireng D.→NAGA-KUKI-
   CHIN
Miyawa→CHADIC
Miza. Moru D.→CENTRAL SUDANIC
Mmani = Northern Bullom→WEST ATLAN-
   TIC
Mme→BANTOID
Mmfo = Degha→GUR
Mnemones = Menomini→ALGONQUIAN
Mnong, Central→MON-KHMER
Mnong, Eastern→MON-KHMER
Mnong, Southern→MON-KHMER
Mnyamskad. Central Tibetan D.→TIBETAN
Mo = Degha→GUR
Mo = Mak→KAM-TAI
Moa. Leti D.→MOLUCCAN
Moa = Moba→GUR
Moab = Moba→GUR
Moabite→SEMITIC
'Moaeke→NEW CALEDONIA
Moaklaks = Klamath→PENUTIAN
Moando = Banara→BOGIA
Moapan = Mopan. Maya D.→MAYAN
Moar→SARMIC
Moare = Moba→GUR
'Moaveke→NEW CALEDONIA
Moba→GUR
Mobab→INDO-PACIFIC
Mobber = Mabar. Kanuri Tr.→SAHARAN
Mobber = Mober→CHADIC
Mober→CHADIC
Mober = Mabar. Kanuri Tr.→SAHARAN
Mobesa = Mbesa→NORTH WESTERN BAN-
   TU
Mobeur = Mabar. Kanuri Tr.→SAHARAN
Mobeur = Mober→CHADIC
Mobima = Movima→MACRO-TUCANOAN
Mocama. Timucua D.
Mo-chia. Mak D.→KAM-TAI
Mochica = Yunca→CHIPAYAN
Mochinya = Mocho→OMOTIC
Mocho→OMOTIC

Mocho = Motozintlec→MAYAN
Mochobo. Pichobo D.→PANO
Mochovo = Mochobo. Pichobo D.→PANO
Moci. Caga D.→NORTH EASTERN BANTU
MOCOA→EQUATORIAL
Mocochi. Timote D.→EQUATORIAL
Mocotan. Timote D.→EQUATORIAL
Mocovi→GUAYCURU
Moda. Higi D.→CHADIC
Modan→WESTERN NEW GUINEA
Modang→WEST INDONESIAN
Modea. Gumuz D.→KOMAN
Modgel→CHADIC
Modin = Madin. Koma D.→KOMAN
Modjembo = Monjombo→EASTERN
Modjingaye = Majingai. Sara D.→CENTRAL
   SUDANIC
Modo. 'Beli D. ·CENTRAL SUDANIC
Modo. Bangba D. ·EASTERN
Modoc. Klamath D.··PENUTIAN
Modogo = Mudogo. Kuka D. ·CENTRAL
   SUDANIC
Modole = Madole→NORTH HALMAHERA
Modra. Todrah D.→MON-KHMER
Modunga→EASTERN
Moenebeng→NEW CALEDONIA
Moeno = Masco→MAIPURAN
Mofou = Mofu. Matakam D.→CHADIC
Mofu. Biak D.→MOLUCCAN
Mofu. Matakam D.→CHADIC
Mogamo→BANTOID
Mogamowa→BANTOID
Mogao→WESTERN NEW GUINEA
Mogeno = Masongo→EASTERN SUDANIC
Mogetemin→WESTERN NEW GUINEA
Moggingain = Majingai. Sara D.→CENTRAL
   SUDANIC
Moghamo = Mogamo→BANTOID
Moglei = Medlpa→EAST NEW GUINEA
   HIGHLANDS
Mogmog. Ulithian D.→MICRONESIAN
Mogogodo→CUSHITIC
Mogoni→KOIARI
Mogosma. Toba Tr.→GUAYCURU
Moguez→INTER-ANDINE
Mogum→CHADIC
Mohao = Mohave. River Yuman D.→YUMAN
Mohaqu = Mohawk→IROQUOIS
Mohaux = Mohawk→IROQUOIS
Mohave. River Yuman D.→YUMAN
Mohave-Apache = Yavapai. Upland Yuman
   D.→YUMAN
Mohawk→IROQUOIS
Moheagan = Mohegan→ALGONQUIAN

Moheakakannsew — Mohegan→ALGON-QUIAN

Moheakannuk = Mohegan→ALGONQUIAN

Mohegan→ALGONQUIAN

Mohenjo-Daro see article

Mohican = Mohegan→ALGONQUIAN

Mohikan = Mohegan→ALGONQUIAN

Mohino→TACANA

Mohissa→KHOISAN

Mohogica — Mohawk→IROQUOIS

Mohogice = Mohawk→IROQUOIS

Moi→WESTERN NEW GUINEA

Moianec→MAYAN

Moibiri→DAGA

Moi-Cu-lo = Ca-lo→MON-KHMER

Moi-e→CENTRAL AND SOUTH NEW GUINEA

MOI-KARON→WESTERN NEW GUINEA

Moikoidi. Buari D.→MAILU

Moil = Tyemeri. Nangumiri D.→DALY

Moingwena = Illinois. Miami D.→ALGON-QUIAN

Moira→BOGIA

Mojang = Masongo→EASTERN SUDANIC

Mojango = Masongo→EASTERN SUDANIC

Mojave — Mohave. River Yuman D.→YUMAN

Mojo — Moxo→MAIPURAN

Mok→ADMIRALTY-WESTERN ISLANDS

Mokareng→ADMIRALTY-WESTERN IS-LANDS

Mokhev = Moxev. Georgian D.→CAUCASIAN

Mokil. Ponapean D.→MICRONESIAN

Moklum. Tangsa D.→BODO-NAGA-KACHIN

Mokmer = Sampori. Biak D.→MOLUCCAN

Mokoda. Western Bira D.→NORTH EASTERN BANTU

Mokogodo = Mogogodo→CUSHITIC

Mokomoko. Kerintji D.→WEST INDONE-SIAN

Mokpe = Baakpe→NORTH WESTERN BAN-TU

Moksa. Mordvin D.→URALIC

Moksha = Moksa. Mordvin D.→URALIC

Molala = Molale→PENUTIAN

Molale→PENUTIAN

Molalla = Molale→PENUTIAN

Molbufa. Sanana D.→EAST INDONESIAN

Moldavian. Rumanian D.→ROMANCE

Mole = Moli→NORTHWESTERN AND CEN-TRAL SOLOMONS

Mole = More→GUR

Molele = Molale→PENUTIAN

Molgoy. Margi D.→CHADIC

Moli→NORTHWESTERN AND CENTRAL SOLOMONS

Moli→EASTERN OCEANIC

Molima→PAPUA AUSTRONESIAN

Mollakmollak = Mullukmulluk→DALY

Molloroiji = Muluridji. Wakaman D.→PAMA-MARIC

Molof→NORTH PAPUAN

Molu. Fordat D.→MOLUCCAN

MOLUCCAN see article

Moluccas Pidgin→ROMANCE

Moluche. Araucanian D.→PENUTIAN

Molyamidi = Wolyamidi→WORORAN

Moma = Kulawi→CENTRAL AND SOUTH-ERN CELEBES

Momale = Momare→HUON-FINISTERRE

Momalili = Momolili→NORTHEST NEW GUINEA AUSTRONESIAN

Momare→HUON-FINISTERRE

Mombe. Gbaya Tr.→EASTERN

Mombe Kukwe = Nyakyusa→CENTRAL EAST-ERN BANTU

MOMBERAMO RIVER see article

Mombum→FREDERIK HENDRIK IS AND SE WEST IRIAN

Mombutu = Mangbutu→CENTRAL SUDAN-IC

Momfu = Mamvu. Mamvu-Efe D.→CENTRAL SUDANIC

Momolili→NORTHEAST NEW GUINEA AUSTRONESIAN

Momolili→HUON-FINISTERRE

Momvu = Mamvu. Mamvu-Efe D.→CEN-TRAL SUDANIC

Mona. Cham D.→ADAMAWA

Mona = Mwa→MANDE

Monachi = Mono→UTO-AZTECAN

Monanda = Aiku→TORRICELLI

Monandu = Aiku→TORRICELLI

Monay. Cuica D.→EQUATORIAL

Monchati = Manchati→GYARUNG-MISHMI

Mondari. Bari D.→EASTERN SUDANIC

MONDE→TUPI

Monde→TUPI

Mondiapo = Hondiapa→MACRO-TUCA-NOAN

Mondjembo = Monjombo→EASTERN

Mondo = Mundu→EASTERN

Mondu = Mundu→EASTERN

Mongaiyat = Mangaya→EASTERN

Mongala Poto. Losengo D.→NORTH WEST-ERN BANTU

Mongbwandi = Ngbandi→EASTERN

Monglwe. Angku D.→PALAUNG-WA

Mongo. Losengo D.→NORTH WESTERN

BANTU

Mongo = Busooŋ→NORTH WESTERN BAN-TU

Mongoba→EASTERN

Mongoio = Mongoyo→CAMACAN

Mongol. Kaima D.→INDO-PACIFIC

MONGOL = MONGOLIAN

MONGOLIAN see article

Mongondou — Mongondow→NORTHERN CELEBES

Mongondow→NORTHERN CELEBES

MONGO-NKUNDO→NORTH WESTERN BANTU

Mongo-Nkundo→NORTH WESTERN BANTU

Mongo-Nkundu = Mongo-Nkundo→NORTH WESTERN BANTU

Mongour→MONGOLIAN

Mongoyo→CAMACAN

Mongsen→NAGA-KUKI-CHIN

Mongul→MONGOLIAN

Mongul, Western = Oirat→MONGOLIAN

Mongwandi = Ngbandi→EASTERN

Moni→WEST NEW GUINEA HIGHLANDS

Moni = Mwa→MANDE

MONIC→MON-KHMER

Monjombo→EASTERN

Monjomboli=Nzomboy. Ngbandi Tr.→EAST-ERN

Monjul = Mubi→CHADIC

MON-KHMER see article

Monnitarri = Hidatsa→SIOUAN

Monno = Ngadjuri. Jaliaura D.→YURA

Mono→ADAMAWA

Mono→UTO-AZTECAN

Mono→NORTHWESTERN AND CENTRAL SOLOMNOS

Mono. Banda D.→EASTERN

Monoarfu. Numfor D.→MOLUCCAN

Monobi. Lendu D.→CENTRAL SUDANIC

Monocho→MACHACALI

Monoico→CARIB

Monom→MON-KHMER

Monomor. Binahari D.→MAILU

Monoxo = Monocho→MACHACALI

Monpa = Limbu→GYARUNG-MISHMI

Monqui. Waicuru Tr.→WAICURIAN

Monshoco→CAMACAN

Montagnais. Cree D.→ALGONQUIAN

Montagnais = Chipewyan. Chipewyan Tr.→ ATHAPASCAN-EYAK

Montagnar = Montagnais. Cree D.→ALGON-QUIAN

Montagnards = Montagnais. Cree D.→AL-GONQUIAN

Montagnie — Montagnais. Cree D.→ALGON-QUIAN

Montal→CHADIC

Montanyes. Mixtec D.→MIXTECAN

Montauckett = Montauk. Mohegan D.→AL-GONQUIAN

Montauk. Mohegan D.→ALGONQUIAN

Monterey. Southern Costanoan D.→MIWOK-COSTANOAN

Montescos — Ati→NORTHWEST AUSTRO-NESIAN

Montese. Tupi Tr.→TUPI

Monu — Mwa→MANDE

MONUMBO→BOGIA

MONUMBO = BOGIA

Monumbo→BOGIA

Monzombo = Monjombo→EASTERN

Moodburra = Mudbura→NGUMBIN

Mooksahk = Nooksack→SALISH

Mooloola = Dalla→WAKA-KABIC

Moondjan = Nununkul. Djendewal D.→DU-RUBULIC

Mo'or. Waropen D.→MOLUCCAN

Mooraboola = Karanya. Wangkadjera D.→ PITTAPITTIC

Moorawarree = Murawari→PAMA-NYUN-GAN

Moorawarrie = Murawari→PAMA-NYUN-GAN

Moore→GUR

Moorloobullo = Karanya. Wangkadjera D.→ PITTAPITTIC

Mooroon = Murunitja. Kardutjara D.→WATI

Mootaburra = Iningai. Mandandanji D.→ PAMA-MARIC

Mootburra = Mudbura→NGUMBIN

Moothaburra = Iningai. Mandandanji D.→ PAMA-MARIC

Mooyo = Moyo. Karanga D.→MABAN

Mopan. Maya D.→MAYAN

Mopan = Maya→MAYAN

Moperacoa = Moterecoa. Tupi Tr.→TUPI

Mopo = Mufwa. Burun Tr.→EASTERN SUDANIC

Mopwa→KAREN

MOQUELUMNAN = MIWOK→MIWOK-COSTANOAN

Moqui = Hopi→UTO-AZTECAN

Moquise = Kwise. Kwadi Tr.→KHOISAN

Moquisse = Kwise. Kwadi Tr.→KHOISAN

Mor→WESTERN NEW GUINEA

Mora→CHADIC

Moraid→WESTERN NEW GUINEA

Moraori→FREDERIK HENDRIK IS AND SE

WEST IRIAN
Morawa. Binahari D.→MAILU
Morcote→CHIBCHAN
Mordvin→URALIC
More→GUR
More→CHAPACURA-WANHAMAN
Moreb. Tagoi D.→KORDOFANIAN
MORE-GURMA→GUR
MOREHEAD RIVER→CENTRAL AND
  SOUTH NEW GUINEA
Moresada→BOGIA
Morghumab-Kamalab. Beja Tr.→CUSHITIC
Mori→CENTRAL AND SOUTHERN CELE-
  BES
Moriil. Gula D.→ADAMAWA
Morima = Molima→PAPUA AUSTRONE-
  SIAN
Moriori→POLYNESIAN
Moriuene→NORTHERN MAIPURAN
Moriwene = Moriuene→NORTHERN MAI-
  PURAN
Moriwene Mauline = Moriuene→NORTHERN
  MAIPURAN
Moro→KORDOFANIAN
Moro. Northern Zamucoan Tr.→EQUATORI-
  AL
Moro Hills→KORDOFANIAN
Moroa = Morwa. Katab D.→PLATEAU BE-
  NUE-CONGO
Morocosi = Moxo→MAIPURAN
Morokodo→CENTRAL SUDANIC
Morong = Lebu. Moro D.→KORDOFANIAN
Morotai. Tobelo D.→NORTH HALMAHERA
Morowari = Murawari→PAMA-NYUNGAN
Mortlocks = Takuu. Luangiua D.→POLYNE-
  SIAN
Mortnoular = Wurundjeri. Taungurong D.→
  KULINIC
Moru→CENTRAL SUDANIC
Moru→GUR
Moru Agi = Agi. Moru D.→CENTRAL
  SUDANIC
Moru Andri = Andri. Moru D.→CENTRAL
  SUDANIC
Moru Kadiro = Kadiro. Moru D.→CENTRAL
  SUDANIC
Moru Miza = Miza. Moru D.→CENTRAL
  SUDANIC
Moru Wa'di = Wa'di. Moru D.→CENTRAL
  SUDANIC
MORU-MA'DI→CENTRAL SUDANIC
Morwa. Katab D.→PLATEAU BENUE-
  CONGO
MOSAN see MACRO-ALGONQUIAN

Mosang. Tangsa D.→BODO-NAGA-KACHIN
Mosang = Mosang. Tangsa D.→BODO-
  NAGA-KACHIN
Mosca = Chibcha→CHIBCHAN
Mosco = Miskito→MISUMALPAN
Moses. Columbian D.→SALISH
Moses-Columbia = Columbian→SALISH
Mosetano = Moseten→MACRO-PANOAN
Moseten→MACRO-PANOAN
Moshi = Moci. Caga D.→NORTH EASTERN
  BANTU
Moshi = More→GUR
Mosieno. East Teke D.→NORTH WESTERN
  BANTU
Mosimo. Yaben D.→BOGIA
Mosin→EASTERN OCEANIC
Moso→BURMESE-LOLO
Moso = Lahu→BURMESE-LOLO
Mosopelea = Ofo→SIOUAN
Mosoperea = Ofo→SIOUAN
Mosquito = Miskito→MISUMALPAN
Mossi = More→GUR
Mosso = Moso→BURMESE-LOLO
Mossope. Yunca D.→CHIPAYAN
Mossu. Lahu D.→BURMESE-LOLO
Mota→EASTERN OCEANIC
Moterecoa. Tupi Tr.→TUPI
Motilon→NORTHERN MAIPURAN
Motilone = Motilon→NORTHERN MAI-
  PURAN
Motlav→EASTERN OCEANIC
Motocintlec = Motozintlec→MAYAN
Motor. Sayan Samoyed D.→URALIC
Mototzintlec = Motozintlec→MAYAN
Motozintlec→MAYAN
Motozintleca = Motozintlec→MAYAN
Motozintleco = Motozintlec→MAYAN
Motu→PAPUA AUSTRONESIAN
Motumotu = Toaripi→TOARIPI
Motuna = Siwai→BOUGAINVILLE
Mouin = Mwa→MANDE
Moundan = Mundang→ADAMAWA
Mount Margaret. Kardutjara D.→WATI
Mountain Indians = Montagnais. Cree D.→
  ALGONQUIAN
Mountainee = Montagnais. Cree D.→ALGON-
  QUIAN
Mountaineers = Chipewyan. Chipewyan Tr.→
  ATHAPASCAN-EYAK
Mountaineers = Montagnais. Cree D.→AL-
  GONQUIAN
Mountainiers = Montagnais. Cree D.→AL-
  GONQUIAN
Mouralungbula = Taungurong→KULINIC

Mousgou = Musgu→CHADIC
Move. Guaymi D.→CHIBCHAN
Movima→MACRO-TUCANOAN
Moxev. Georgian D.→CAUCASIAN
Moxo→MAIPURAN
Moyo. Karanga D.→MABAN
Mozarabic→ROMANCE
Mozdok. Circassian D.→CAUCASIAN
Mpaangu. Kongo D.→CENTRAL WESTERN BANTU
Mpalitjan→PAMA-MARIC
Mpama. Mongo-Nkundo D.→NORTH WESTERN BANTU
Mpene. Abipon Tr.→GUAYCURU
Mpesa. Losengo D.→NORTH WESTERN BANTU
Mpese. Kongo D.→CENTRAL WESTERN BANTU
Mphaada = Makari. Kotoko D.→CHADIC
Mpiemo. Mbimu D.→NORTH WESTERN BANTU
Mpompo. Mbimu D.→NORTH WESTERN BANTU
Mpondo. Nguni D.→SOUTH EASTERN BANTU
Mpondomse. Nguni D.→SOUTH EASTERN BANTU
Mpongoue = Mpongwe. Myene D.→NORTH WESTERN BANTU
Mpongwe. Myene D.→NORTH WESTERN BANTU
Mpoto→CENTRAL EASTERN BANTU
Mpsakali = Gudur. Sukur D.→CHADIC
Mpu. North East Teke Tr.→NORTH WESTERN BANTU
Mpumpu = Mpu. North East Teke Tr.→NORTH WESTERN BANTU
Mpuono→NORTH WESTERN BANTU
Mpur. Yanzi D.→NORTH WESTERN BANTU
Mpuun. Mpuono D.→NORTH WESTERN BANTU
Mras Tatar = Shor→TURKIC
Mrassa. Shor D.→TURKIC
Mrima. Swahili D.→CENTRAL EASTERN BANTU
Mro→BURMESE-LOLO
Mro-Mru = Mro→BURMESE-LOLO
Mru. Chrau D.→MON-KHMER
Mse Chachtini = Seneca. Seneca Tr.→IROQUOIS
Msirr = Kuseri. Kotoko D.→CHADIC
Mtangata. Swahili D.→CENTRAL EASTERN BANTU
Mtiul. Georgian D.→CAUCASIAN

Mu = Likpe→CENTRAL TOGO
Muamenam = Koose. Mbo D.→NORTH WESTERN BANTU
Muasi = Kurku→MUNDA
Mubako = Mumbake→ADAMAWA
Mubi→CHADIC
Mubi. Foi D.→EAST NEW GUINEA HIGHLANDS
Mubi = Cheke→CHADIC
Muchanes. Moseten D.→MACRO-PANOAN
Muchik = Yunca→CHIPAYAN
Muchimo. Muniche D.→MACRO-TUCANOAN
Muckleshoot. Puget Sound Salish D.→SALISH
Mucoroca = Kwadi→KHOISAN
Muda = Gberi. 'Beli D.→CENTRAL SUDANIC
Mudbara = Mudbura→NGUMBIN
Mudbura→NGUMBIN
Mudburra = Mudbura→NGUMBIN
Mudo = Mamvu. Mamvu-Efe D.→CENTRAL SUDANIC
Mudogo. Kuka D.→CENTRAL SUDANIC
Muellamues→BARBACOAN
Muenane→WITOTOAN
Muenyi = Mwenyi. Kwangwa D.→SOUTH WESTERN BANTU
Muffo = Mofu. Matakam D.→CHADIC
Muffu = Mofu. Matakam D.→CHADIC
Mufu = Mofu. Matakam D.→CHADIC
Mufwa. Burun Tr.→EASTERN SUDANIC
Mugaba = Rennellese→POLYNESIAN
Mughaja. Burun Tr.→EASTERN SUDANIC
Mughalbandi. Oriya D.→INDIC
Mugil→BOGIA
Mugo-Mborkoina = Abuldugu. Burun Tr.→EASTERN SUDANIC
Mugula = Mugura. Suau D.→PAPUA AUSTRONESIAN
Mugum. Ingassana Tr.→CHARI-NILE
Mugura. Suau D.→PAPUA AUSTRONESIAN
Muhekaneew = Mohegan→ALGONQUIAN
Muher→SEMITIC
Muhheconnuk = Mohegan→ALGONQUIAN
Muhhekaneew = Mohegan→ALGONQUIAN
Muhhekaneok = Mohegan→ALGONQUIAN
Muhiang = Bumbita Arapesh→TORRICELLI
Muhkekaneew = Mohegan→ALGONQUIAN
Muinane = Muenane→WITOTOAN
Muinani. Witoto D.→WITOTOAN
Muinani = Muenane→WITOTOAN
Muirin. Dargwa D.→CAUCASIAN
Muisca = Chibcha→CHIBCHAN
Muite. Guaymi D.→CHIBCHAN

Muiu, Lower→OK
Muju→OK
Muju, Upper→OK
Muka→BANTOID
Muka = Mukah. Melanau D.→WEST INDO-NESIAN
Mukah. Melanau D.→WEST INDONESIAN
Mukanti. Molale Tr.→PENUTIAN
Mukawa→PAPUA AUSTRONESIAN
Mukili = Beli→TORRICELLI
Mukkogee = Muskogee→MUSKOGEAN
Muklasa. Alabama D.→MUSKOGEAN
Mukri. Kermanji D.→IRANIAN
Mukutu = Mocotan. Timote D.→EQUATO-RIAL
MULAHA see article
Mularitchee = Muluridji. Wakaman D.→PAMA-MARIC
Muleng. Zumu D. →CHADIC
Muliaarpa – Maljangapa. Karenggapa D.→DIERIC
Muliama→BISMARCK ARCHIPELAGO
Muliara→KARDU
Mulimba→NORTH WESTERN BANTU
Mullilmullik = Mullukmulluk→DALY
MULLUK→DALY
MULLUKMULLUK→DALY
Mullukmulluk→DALY
Multani. Lahnda D.→INDIC
Multnomah. Upper Chinook D.→CHINOOK-AN
Multyerra = Maljangapa. Karenggapa D.→DIERIC
Mulu = Maru→BODO-NAGA-KACHIN
Mulu Rutyi = Muluridji. Wakaman D.→PAMA-MARIC
Mulung. Tangsa D.→BODO-NAGA-KACHIN
Muluridji. Wakaman D.→PAMA-MARIC
Mulurutji = Muluridji. Wakaman D.→PAMA-MARIC
Mulwi = Musgu→CHADIC
Mulyanapa = Maljangapa. Karenggapa D.→DIERIC
Mulyanappa = Maljangapa. Karenggapa D.→DIERIC
Mumbake→ADAMAWA
Mumbi = Membi. Ndo D.→CENTRAL SU-DANIC
Mumeng→INDO-PACIFIC
Mumughadja = Mughaja. Burun Tr.→EAST-ERN SUDANIC
Mumupra. Nakwi D.→LEFT MAY
Mumuye→ADAMAWA
Mumuye, Hill = Pugu. Mumuye D.→ADA-MAWA

Mumviri. Kati D.→NURISTANI
Mun = Murzu→EASTERN SUDANIC
Muna→CENTRAL AND SOUTHERN CELEBES
MUNA-BUTUNG→CENTRAL AND SOUTH-ERN CELEBES
Munchi = Tiv→BANTOID
MUNDA see article
Mundang→ADAMAWA
Mundani, Lower→BANTOID
Mundani, Upper→BANTOID
Mundari→MUNDA
Mundari = Mondari. Bari D.→EASTERN SUDANIC
Mundari-Ho = Mundari→MUNDA
Mundju = Bomougoun-Bamenjou→BANTOID
Mundo Ati→NORTHWEST AUSTRONE-SIAN
Mundrau→ADMIRALTY-WESTERN IS-LANDS
Mundu→EASTERN
Munduburew. Waimdra D.→ADMIRALTY-WESTERN ISLANDS
Munduguma = Biwat→INDO-PACIFIC
Mundurucu = Munduruku→TUPI
Munduruku→TUPI
Mung→BURMESE-LOLO
Munga→ADAMAWA
Mungaaka = Ngaaka→BANTOID
Mungaka = Ngaaka→BANTOID
Mungarai = Mangarai→AUSTRALIAN MAC-RO-PHYLUM
Mungera = Yidin. Wakaman D.→PAMA-MARIC
Mungerra = Ilba→PAMA-MARIC
Mungerry = Mangarai→AUSTRALIAN MAC-RO-PHYLUM
Munggava = Rennellese→POLYNESIAN
Munggiki = Bellona. Rennellese D.→POLY-NESIAN
Munguba = Mongoba→EASTERN
Muni = Murzu→EASTERN SUDANIC
Muniche→MACRO-TUCANOAN
Munichi = Muniche→MACRO-TUCANOAN
Munin. Andi D.→CAUCASIAN
Muniwara→NORTH NEW GUINEA
Munjani = Munji→IRANIAN
Munji→IRANIAN
Munju = Bomouboun-Bamenjou→BANTOID
Munkibura = Mian. Mandandanji D.→PAMA-MARIC
Munkieburra = Mian. Mandandanji D.→PAMA-MARIC

Munkip→HUON-FINISTERRE
Munshi = Tiv→BANTOID
Muntabi = Ingassana→CHARI-NILE
Munumburu→WORORAN
Munyona = Ngaaka→BANTOID
Muoi. Guaymi D.→CHIBCHAN
Muong→VIET-MUONG
Muong Leong = Bru→MON-KHMER
Mup→HUON-FINISTERRE
Mur→INDO-PACIFIC
Mura→MACRO-CHIBCHAN
Muralag. Kaurareg D.→MABUIAGIC
Muralidban→GUNWINGGUAN
Muran = Mura→MACRO-CHIBCHAN
Murang Punan. Land Dayak D.→WEST
  INDONESIAN
Mura-Piraha = Mura→MACRO-CHIBCHAN
Murato. Candoshi D.→JIVAROAN
Murawari ·PAMA-NYUNGAN
Murca. Carare Tr. ·CARIB
Murdia. Tebu Tr.·SAHARAN
Murgi = Birked→EASTERN SUDANIC
Murgoan = Marnganji. Mandandanji D. ·
  PAMA-MARIC
Murgoin = Marnganji. Mandandanji D.→
  PAMA-MARIC
Muri = Miri→KORDOFANIAN
Muriapigtanga. Tupi Tr.→TUPI
MURIK→NORTH NEW GUINEA
Murik→NORTH NEW GUINEA
Murik→WEST INDONESIAN
Murikau. Sapolewa D.→EAST INDONESIAN
Murinaten. Sapolewa D.→EAST INDONE-
  SIAN
Murinbata→GARAMAN
Murinbata = Marinbata→GARAMAN
Murinyuwen = Djamindjung→DJAMINDJUN-
  GAN
Murire. Guaymi D.→CHIBCHAN
Murisapa→BOGIA
Muritaka. Enga D.→EAST NEW GUINEA
  HIGHLANDS
Murle→EASTERN SUDANIC
Murleny = Murle→EASTERN SUDANIC
Murmi→GYARUNG-MISHMI
Murngain = Marnganji. Mandandanji D.→
  PAMA-MARIC
MURNGIC see article
Murrawarri = Murawari→PAMA-NYUNGAN
Murri = Murawari→PAMA-NYUNGAN
Murro = Muru. Kibet D.→EASTERN SU-
  DANIC
Murru = Muru. Kibet D.→EASTERN SU-
  DANIC

Murrumningama Barunggam→WIRAD-
  JURIC
Murrungama = Barunggam→WIRADJURIC
Mursi = Murzu→EASTERN SUDANIC
Muru. Kibet D.→EASTERN SUDANIC
Murua→PAPUA AUSTRONESIAN
Murui. Witoto D.→WITOTOAN
Murule = Murle→EASTERN SUDANIC
Murunitja. Kardutjara D.→WATI
Murusapa = Murisapa→BOGIA
Murut→NORTHWEST AUSTRONESIAN
Murut, Sarawak→WEST INDONESIAN
MURUTIC→NORTHWEST AUSTRONE-
  SIAN
Murutuin = Tid. Tirma D.→EASTERN SU-
  DANIC
Muruwurri = Murawari→PAMA-NYUNGAN
Murzi = Murzu→EASTERN SUDANIC
Murzu ·EASTERN SUDANIC
Musa, Upper ·BINANDERE
Musa River ·BINANDERE
Musak→BOGIA
Musar→BOGIA
Musau = Mussau→BISMARCK ARCHIPEL-
  AGO
Muscogee = Muskogee→MUSKOGEAN
Muscoghe = Muskogee→MUSKOGEAN
Muscogulge = Muskogee→MUSKOGEAN
Muscoki = Muskogee→MUSKOGEAN
Musei→CHADIC
Musey = Musei→CHADIC
Musgoi = Musgu→CHADIC
Musgo. Daba D.→CHADIC
Musgoy = Musgoi. Daba D.→CHADIC
Musgu→CHADIC
Musgum = Musgu→CHADIC
Musguw = Musgu→CHADIC
Mushango = Masongo→EASTERN SUDANIC
MUSKHOGEAN = MUSKOGEAN
Muskhogee = Muskogee→MUSKOGEAN
MUSKOGEAN see article
Muskogee→MUSKOGEAN
Muskogh = Muskogee→MUSKOGEAN
Muskohge = Muskogee→MUSKOGEAN
Muskohgee = Muskogee→MUSKOGEAN
Muskoke = Muskogee→MUSKOGEAN
Muskokee = Muskogee→MUSKOGEAN
Muskoki = Muskogee→MUSKOGEAN
Muskotawenewuk = Cree→ALGONQUIAN
Muso→CARIB
Musquakie = Fox→ALGONQUIAN
Musqueam. Halkomelem D.→SALISH
Mussau→BISMARCK ARCHIPELAGO
Mussende = Ngengu→CENTRAL WESTERN

BANTU

Mussoi = Musei→CHADIC
Musu = Jagada. Tebu Tr.→SAHARAN
Musugeu = Musgoi. Daba D.→CHADIC
Musugoi = Musgoi. Daba D.→CHADIC
Musutepes. Sumo Tr.→MISUMALPAN
Muta = Menemo→BANTOID
Mutheit = Pho→KAREN
Muthimuthi. Djadjala D.→KULINIC
Mutonia. Tangsa D.→BODO-NAGA-KACHIN
Mutsun. Southern Costanoan D.→MIWOK-COSTANOAN
Muttaburra = Iningai. Mandandanji D.→PAMA-MARIC
Mutuan→CARIB
MUTUM =TIRIO→CENTRAL AND SOUTH NEW GUINEA
Mutum→CENTRAL AND SOUTH NEW GUINEA
Muturua = Gisiga→CHADIC
Mututu = Mimi→MABAN
Mutwang. Rawang D.→BODO-NAGA-KACHIN
Muutzicat = Cora→UTO-AZTECAN
Muwasi = Kurku→MUNDA
Muxer = Muher→SEMITIC
Muzgu = Musgu→CHADIC
Muzo = Muso→CARIB
Muzugu = Musgu→CHADIC
Mvang = Eki→NORTH WESTERN BANTU
Mvanip. Mambila D.→BANTOID
Mvedere. Banda D.→EASTERN
Mvegumba = Bviri→EASTERN
Mvele. Ewondo D.→NORTH WESTERN BANTU
Mvele = Basa→NORTH WESTERN BANTU
Mvita. Swahili D.→CENTRAL EASTERN BANTU
Mvu'ba.Mamvu-Efe D.→CENTRAL SUDANIC
Mvuba = Mvu'ba. Mamvu-Efe D.→CENTRAL SUDANIC
Mvuba-a = Mvu'ba. Mamvu-Efe D.→CENTRAL SUDANIC
Mvumbo→NORTH WESTERN BANTU
Mwa→MANDE
Mwae = Mae→POLYNESIAN
Mwahet. Mbo D.→NORTH WESTERN BANTU
Mwamba. Nyakyusa D.→CENTRAL EASTERN BANTU
Mwanga→CENTRAL EASTERN BANTU
Mwani. Ziba D.→NORTH EASTERN BANTU
Mwe = Mwa→MANDE
Mwela = Mwera→SOUTH EASTERN BANTU

Mweni = Mwenyi. Kwangwa D.→SOUTH WESTERN BANTU
Mwenyi. Kwangwa D.→SOUTH WESTERN BANTU
Mwera→SOUTH EASTERN BANTU
Mweri. Nyamwesi D.→NORTH EASTERN BANTU
Mwila. Nyaneka D.→SOUTH WESTERN BANTU
Myabi = Mayapi→MAYAPIC
Myappe = Mayapi→MAYAPIC
Myeach→WESTERN NEW GUINEA
Myen = Burmese→BURMESE-LOLO
Myene→NORTH WESTERN BANTU
Mygoolan = Maykulan→MAYAPIC
Mykoolan = Maykulan→MAYAPIC
Myngeen = Mingin→AUSTRALIAN MACRO-PHYLUM
Myriandynian see article
Mysian see article
Mythaguddi = Mitakudi→PAMA-NYUNGAN
Mythugadi = Mitakudi→PAMA-NYUNGAN
Muthuggadi = Mitakudi→PAMA-NYUNGAN
Mzab→BERBER

N

NA→CENTRAL TOGO
Naaberu = Abulu. Mangbetu D.→CENTRAL SUDANIC
Naaberu-ti = Abulu. Mangbetu D.→CENTRAL SUDANIC
Naaburi-ti = Abulu. Mangbetu D.→CENTRAL SUDANIC
Naath = Nuer→EASTERN SUDANIC
Naba = Nabak→HUON-FINISTERRE
Nabak→HUON-FINISTERRE
Nabaloi. Inibaloy D.→NORTHWEST AUSTRONESIAN
Nabaloi = Inibaloy→NORTHWEST AUSTRONESIAN
Nabataean. West Aramaic D.→SEMITIC
Nabayugan. Kalinga D.→NORTHWEST AUSTRONESIAN
Nabdam = Namnam→GUR
Nabde = Namnam→GUR
Nabdug = Namnam→GUR
Nabe = Kulango→GUR
Nabe = Loghon. Kulango D.→GUR
Nabi→SOUTH HALMAHERA AUSTRONESIAN
Nabrug = Namnam→GUR
Nabt = Namnam→GUR

Nabte = Namnam→GUR
Nabwangan. Barran D.→NORTHWEST AUS-
    TRONESIAN
Nachehe = Nacrehe→BOTOCUDO
Nachereng→GYARUNG-MISHMI
Nachhereng = Nachereng→GYARUNG-
    MISHMI
Nacnhanuc→BOTOCUDO
Nacnyanuk = Nacnhanuc→BOTOCUDO
Nacrehe→BOTOCUDO
Nada→PAPUA AUSTRONESIAN
NA-DENE see article
Nadobo. Macu D.→MACRO-TUCANOAN
Nadouessioux Maskoutens = Iowa. Chiwere
    D.→SIOUAN
Nadowa = Dakota→SIOUAN
Nadoway = Dakota→SIOUAN
Nadubea→NEW CALEDONIA
Nafana = Pantera→GUR
Nafara. Senari D.→GUR
Nafri. Sentani D.→NORTH PAPUAN
Nafunfia = Ron→CHADIC
NAGA→BODO-NAGA-KACHIN
NAGA→NAGA-KUKI-CHIN
NAGA, NORTHERN = NAGA→BODO-
    NAGA-KACHIN
Naga. Balanta D.→WEST ATLANTIC
Naga. Bikol D.→NORTHWEST AUSTRONE-
    SIAN
Naga. Mape D.→HUON-FINISTERRE
NAGA-KUKI-CHIN see article
Naga-Mikir→NAGA-KUKI-CHIN
Nagane. Chimbu D.→EAST NEW GUINEA
    HIGHLANDS
Nagara = Nakara→AUSTRALIAN MACRO-
    PHYLUM
Nagari. Gujarati D.→INDIC
Nagatman→INDO-PACIFIC
Nagichot = Chukudum. Didinga Tr.→EAST-
    ERN SUDANIC
Nagir. Burushaski D.
Nagisaran = Nagisaru. Kanakanabu D.→
    FORMOSAN AUSTRONESIAN
Nagisaru. Kanakanabu D.→FORMOSAN
    AUSTRONESIAN
Nagovisi→BOUGAINVILLE
Nagpuri. Bihari D.→INDIC
Nagramadu→ASMAT
Nagrandan. Mangue D.→MANGUEAN
Naguatl = Nahuatl. Nahua D.→UTO-AZTE-
    CAN
Naguatle = Nahuatl. Nahua D.→UTO-AZTE-
    CAN
Nagumi→BANTOID

Naguri. Mundari D.→MUNDA
Nahali see article
Nahankhuotana = Upper Umpqua→ATHA-
    PASCAN-EYAK
Nahari. Oriya D.→INDIC
Nahaton = Cutshamakin. Massachusett Tr.→
    ALGONQUIAN
Nahina = Epe. Bungku D.→CENTRAL AND
    SOUTHERN CELEBES
Nahina = Marumeme. Bungku D.→CENTRAL
    AND SOUTHERN CELEBES
Nahina = Petasia. Mori D.→CENTRAL AND
    SOUTHERN CELEBES
Nahina = Soroako. Mori D.→CENTRAL AND
    SOUTHERN CELEBES
Nahine = Bungku→CENTRAL AND
    SOUTHERN CELEBES
Naho = Nahu→HUON-FINISTERRE
Nahoa = Nahua→UTO-AZTECAN
Nahsi = Moso→BURMESE-LOLO
Na'htchi = Natchez→MACRO-ALGON-
    QUIAN
Nahu→HUON-FINISTERRE
Nahua→UTO-AZTECAN
Nahual. Nahua D.→UTO-AZTECAN
Nahualt = Nahual. Nahua D.→UTO-AZTE-
    CAN
Nahuapo. Yameo D.→PEBA-YAGUAN
Nahuat. Nahua D.→UTO-AZTECAN
Nahuate = Nahuat. Nahua D.→UTO-AZTE-
    CAN
Nahuatl. Nahua D.→UTO-AZTECAN
NAHUATLAN = AZTEC→UTO-AZTECAN
Nahuatlato. Pipil D.→UTO-AZTECAN
Naibun. Paiwan D.→FORMOSAN AUSTRO-
    NESIAN
Naida = Rete. Bungku D.→CENTRAL AND
    SOUTHERN CELEBES
Naida = Wowoni. Bungku D.—CENTRAL
    AND SOUTHERN CELEBES
Naik Gonds = Naiki→DRAVIDIAN
Naik Pods = Naikri. Kolami D.→DRAVIDIAN
Naiki→DRAVIDIAN
Naiki = Naikri. Kolami D.→DRAVIDIAN
Naikri. Kolami D.→DRAVIDIAN
Na'ini. Persian D.→IRANIAN
Najarago→WESTERN NEW GUNEA
Naka. Kresh D.→CENTRAL SUDANIC
Naka = Bapoko. Batanga D.→NORTH WEST-
    ERN BANTU
Nakama→HUON-FINISTERRE
Nakanai→NORTHEST NEW GUINEA AUS-
    TRONESIAN
Nakara→AUSTRALIAN MACRO-PHYLUM

Nakaza = Ankaa. Tebu Tr.→SAHARAN
Nake→BOGIA
Nakeyare. Chamba D.→ADAMAWA
Nakhi = Moso→BURMESE-LOLO
Nakiai→INDO-PACIFIC
Nakota = Yankton. Dakota D.→SIOUAN
Nakrehe = Nacrehe→BOTOCUDO
Nakum = Maidu→MAIDU
Nakwi→LEFT MAY
Nala = Lala→PAPUA AUSTRONESIAN
Nale→NORTHWESTERN NEW HEBRIDES
Nali = Mima. Tsakrima D.→NAGA-KUKI-
   CHIN
Nalik→BISMARCK ARCHIPELAGO
Nalou = Nalu→WEST ATLANTIC
Naltje→CENTRAL AND SOUTH NEW
   GUINEA
Nalu→WEST ATLANTIC
Nalyanapa = Maljangapa. Karenggapa D.→
   DIERIC
Nama→JUKUNOID
Nama→KHOISAN
Namabisanga = Mabisanga. Mangbetu D.→
   CENTRAL SUDANIC
Namahabana = Luhtu. Tsou D.→FORMOSAN
   AUSTRONESIAN
Namajuu = Majuu. Mangbetu D.→CENTRAL
   SUDANIC
Namakaban = Luhtu. Tsou D.→FORMOSAN
   AUSTRONESIAN
Namakabau = Luhtu. Tsou D.→FORMOSAN
   AUSTRONESIAN
Namakere = Makere. Mangbetu D.→CEN-
   TRAL SUDANIC
Namakere-ti = Makere. Mangbetu D.→CEN-
   TRAL SUDANIC
Namakwa = Nama→KHOISAN
Namangbetu = Mangbetu→CENTRAL SU-
   DANIC
Namapopi = Popol. Mangbetu D.→CENTRAL
   SUDANIC
Namapopoi-ti = Popol. Mangbetu D.→CEN-
   TRAL SUDANIC
Namaqwa = Nama→KHOISAN
Namatalaki = Abui→TIMOR-ALOR
Namatote→SOUTH HALMAHERA AUSTRO-
   NESIAN
Namau = Koriki→SOUTHEAST NEW GUIN-
   EA
Nambai = Kulango→GUR
Nambas→NORTHWESTERN NEW HEB-
   RIDES
Nambe. Tewa D.→TANOAN
Nambi→TORRICELLI
NAMBICUARA see article

Nambuda = Ngalia→NGARGA
Nambzya. Shona D.→SOUTH EASTERN
   BANTU
Namchi = Namshi→ADAMAWA
Namci = Namshi→ADAMAWA
Namdji = Namshi→ADAMAWA
Nameje-ti = Meje. Mangbetu D.→CENTRAL
   SUDANIC
Nameji→BURMESE-LOLO
Namel = Nyamal→NGAYARDA
NAME-!ORA→KHOISAN
Namib→KHOISAN
Namie→SEPIK
Namji = Namshi→ADAMAWA
Namnam→GUR
Namonuito. Carolinian D.→MICRONESIAN
Namsangia. Tangsa D.→BODO-NAGA-KA-
   CHIN
Namshi→ADAMAWA
Namtchi = Namshi→ADAMAWA
Namunka. Oroc D.→TUNGUS
Namwanga = Mwanga→CENTRAL EAST-
   ERN BANTU
Namwezi = Nyamwesi→NORTH EASTERN
   BANTU
Nan Ch'ang = Nanch'ang. Kan D.→CHINESE
Nana. Kardutjara D.→WATI
Nana Kru = Kru-Krawi→KRU
Nanaepashemet. Massachusett Tr.→ALGON-
   QUIAN
Nanaimo. Halkomelem D.→SALISH
Nanaimo-Lower Fraser = Halkomelem→SA-
   LISH
NANAJ→TUNGUS
Nanakati. Juat D.→SOUTHWEST PAMA-
   NYUNGAN
Nanatsoho. Caddo Tr.→CADDOAN
Nancere→CHADIC
Nanch'ang. Kan D.→CHINESE
Nancoury = Nancowry. Central Nicobarese
   D.→NICOBARESE
Nancowry. Central Nicobarese D.→NICOBAR-
   ESE
Nanda→KARDU
NANDE = KONJO→NORTH EASTERN
   BANTU
Nande, Northern = Ndandi→NORTH EAST-
   ERN BANTU
NANDI→EASTERN SUDANIC
Nandi→EASTERN SUDANIC
Nandi = Ndandi→NORTH EASTERN BAN-
   TU
Nandiek = Nandi→EASTERN SUDANIC
Nandu→PLATEAU BENUE-CONGO
Nangalami→NURISTANI

Nangamada = Nyangumarda→MARNGU
Nangamp = Wahgi→EAST NEW GUINEA HIGHLANDS
Nangamp-Banz-Nondugl. Wahgi D.→EAST NEW GUINEA HIGHLANDS
Nangamurda = Nyangumarda→MARNGU
Nangatadjara = Nangatajara. Kardutjara D.→ WATI
Nangatajara. Kardutjara D.→WATI
Nangerge Sembla = Samo→MANDE
Nangga = Wirangu→SOUTHWEST PAMA-NYUNGAN
Nanggumiri = Nangumiri→DALY
Nangimera = Nangumiri→DALY
Nangimeri = Nangumiri→DALY
Nangiomera = Nangumiri→DALY
Nangire→CHADIC
Nangumiri→DALY
Nanhang→KHMUIC
Nanjeri = Nangire→CHADIC
Nankana = Nankanse→GUR
Nankani = Nankanse→GUR
Nankanse→GUR
Nankina→HUON-FINISTERRE
Nano = Mbundu→SOUTH WESTERN BANTU
Nanqa Poroja = Remo→MUNDA
Nansemond. Powhatan Tr.→ALGONQUIAN
Nantcere = Nancere→CHADIC
Nantchoa. Nancere D.→CHADIC
Nanticok = Nanticoke. Mohegan D.→ALGONQUIAN
Nanticoke. Mohegan D.→ALGONQUIAN
Nanumba. Dagbani D.→GUR
Nanunga = Narangga. Jadliaura D.→YURA
Nanuni = Nanumba. Dagbani D.→GUR
Nao→OMOTIC
Na'o = Nao→OMOTIC
Naolingo = Totonac→TOTONACAN
Naoudam = Nawdam→GUR
Naoudemba = Nawdam→GUR
Napagibetini = Boa→NORTH WESTERN BANTU
Napagibetini = Yewa→NORTH WESTERN BANTU
Napagisene. Bati D.→NORTH WESTERN BANTU
Napan. Waropen D.→MOLUCCAN
Napanskij. Kamchadal D.→CHUKCHEE-KAMCHATKAN
Napeano. Yameo D.→PEBA-YAGUAN
Napeca. Quitemoca D.→CHAPACURA-WAN-HAMAN
Napochi = Chickasaw. Choctaw D.→MUSKO-GEAN

Napu→CENTRAL AND SOUTHERN CELEBES
Nar. Sara D.→CENTRAL SUDANIC
Nara→EASTERN SUDANIC
Nara = Lala→PAPUA AUSTRONESIAN
Nara = Nwa→MANDE
Narabuna = Rebina→PLATEAU BENUE-CONGO
Narak→EAST NEW GUINEA HIGHLANDS
Naranga = Narangga. Jadliaura D.→YURA
Naranganset. Massachusett D.→ALGONQUIAN
Narangansett = Naranganset. Massachusett D.→ ALGONQUIAN
Narangga. Jadliaura D.→YURA
Naravute→CARIB
Narihua = Wanoni. Kahua D.→EASTERN OCEANIC
Narinari = Jabulajabula→YOTAYOTIC
Narin-guor. Mongour D.→MONGOLIAN
Narisati = Gawar-bati→INDIC
Naro = Naron→KHOISAN
Narom→WEST INDONESIAN
Naron→KHOISAN
Narranga = Narangga. Jadliaura D.→YURA
Narranganset = Naranganset. Massachusett D.→ALGONQUIAN
Narrangansett = Naranganset. Massachusett D.→ ALGONQUIAN
Narranggu = Narangga. Jadliaura D.→YURA
Narrangu = Narangga. Jadliaura D.→YURA
Narreweng = Nyarueng. Bor D.→EASTERN SUDANIC
Narrinyeri = Jarildekald. Tanganekald D.→ NARRINYERIC
NARRINYERIC see article
Narrinyind = Ungarinyin→WORORAN
Narsati = Gawar-bati→INDIC
Narwejung = Ngawait. Nganguruku D.→ NARRINYERIC
Nas Maramma = Dalea. Tebu Tr.→SAHARAN
Nascapee = Naskapi. Cree D.→ALGONQUIAN
Nashua. Massachusett Tr.→ALGONQUIAN
NASIOI→BOUGAINVILLE
Nasioi→BOUGAINVILLE
Naskapee = Naskapi. Cree D.→ALGONQUIAN
Naskapi. Cree D.→ALGONQUIAN
Naskatin. Carrier Tr.→ATHAPASCAN-EYAK
Nasoni, Upper. Caddo Tr.→CADDOAN
Nassillok = Fecaka. Berta D.→CHARI-NILE
Nata→NORTH EASTERN BANTU

Natal→KHOISAN

Nataoran = Tauran. Ami D.→FORMOSAN AUSTRONESIAN

Nataotin. Carrier Tr.→ATHAPASCAN-EYAK

Natches = Natchez→MACRO-ALGONQUIAN

Natchez→MACRO-ALGONQUIAN

Natchitoches, Upper. Caddo Tr.→CADDOAN

Natemba→GUR

Natica. Toba Tr.→GUAYCURU

Natick. Massachusett D.→ALGONQUIAN

Natik = Natick. Massachusett D.→ALGON-QUIAN

Natimolo = Totonac→TOTONACAN

Natingero = Kalamai→MIRNINY

Natinnoh-hoi = Hupa→ ATHAPASCAN-EYAK

Natioro→GUR

Natliatin. Carrier Tr.→ATHAPASCAN-EYAK

Natshereng = Nachereng→GYARUNG-MISH-MI

Natu see article

Natukhaj = Natuxaj. Circassian D.→CAUCA-SIAN

Natuxaj. Circassian D.→CAUCASIAN

Natyoro = Natioro→GUR

Naua = Nawu→YURA

Nauait = Ngawait. Nganguruku D.→NAR-RINYERIC

Naualko. Kula D.→PAMA-NYUNGAN

Naudm = Nawdam→GUR

Naugatuk = Wappinger. Mohegan D.→AL-GONQUIAN

Nauhan→NORTHWEST AUSTRONESIAN

Naukan. St. Lawrence Island Yupik D.→ESKI-MO-ALEUT

Naumik→TIMOR-ALOR

Nauna. Rambutjo D.→ADMIRALTY-WEST-ERN ISLANDS

Nauni = Comanche. Shoshoni D.→UTO-AZTE-CAN

Nauo = Nawu→YURA

Naura. Carare D.→CARIB

Nauracoto. Carare D.→CARIB

Nauruan→MICRONESIAN

Nausaku→CENTRAL AND SOUTH NEW GUINEA

Navaho = Navajo→ATHAPASCAN-EYAK

Navajo→ATHAPASCAN-EYAK

Naviliang. Tanna D.→SOUTHERN NEW HEB-RIDES

Nawagi→PAMA-MARIC

Nawariyi = Wandaran→MARAN

Nawarma = Norea. Tebu Tr.→SAHARAN

Nawathinehena. Arapaho D.→ALGONQUIAN

Nawazi-Montji. Moseten D.→MACRO-PANO-AN

Nawdam→GUR

Nawo = Nauo→YURA

Nawp = Daga→DAGA

Nawu→YURA

Nawunena = Nawathinehena. Arapaho D.→ ALGONQUIAN

Nawuri. Guan D.→VOLTA-COMOE

Nayit = Cora→UTO-AZTECAN

Nayiti = Cora→UTO-AZTECAN

N'bundo = Mbundu→CENTRAL WESTERN BANTU

Nbundu = Mbundu→CENTRAL WESTERN BANTU

Ncha→BANTOID

Nchummurru = Nawuri. Guan D.→VOLTA-COMOE

Nchummuru = Nawuri. Guan D.→VOLTA-COMOE

Nchumurru = Nawuri. Guan D.→VOLTA-COMOE

Nchumuru = Nawuri. Guan D.→VOLTA-COMOE

Ncqika = Gaika. Nguni D.→SOUTH EAST-ERN BANTU

Ndaaka→NORTH EASTERN BANTU

Ndaanda→NORTH WESTERN BANTU

Ndagam = Boli→ADAMAWA

Ndakpwa = Ndokpwa. Banda D.→EASTERN

Ndaktup→BANTOID

NDALE = MBEMBE→JUKUNOID

Ndali→CENTRAL EASTERN BANTU

Ndali. Zanaki D.→NORTH EASTERN BANTU

Ndam→CHADIC

Ndam. Ekoi D.→BANTOID

Ndamba→CENTRAL EASTERN BANTU

Ndamm = Ndam→CHADIC

Ndande = Ndandi→NORTH EASTERN BAN-TU

Ndandi→NORTH EASTERN BANTU

Ndanga. Wahgi D.→EAST NEW GUINEA HIGHLANDS

NDANI = GREATER DANI→WEST NEW GUINEA HIGHLANDS

Ndara. Ruanda D.→NORTH EASTERN BAN-TU

Ndara = Mandara→CHADIC

Ndau→INDO-PACIFIC

Ndau. Shona D.→SOUTH EASTERN BANTU

Nda'u = Umalasa→NORTHERN CELEBES

Nde→BANTOID

Ndebele→SOUTH EASTERN BANTU

Nde'bele = Ndebele→SOUTH EASTERN

BANTU

Nde'e = Lala'eo. Bare'e D.→CENTRAL AND SOUTHERN CELEBES

Ndele = Nyele. Banda D.→EASTERN

Ndembo. Lunda D.→CENTRAL WESTERN BANTU

Ndembu = Ndembo. Lunda D.→CENTRAL WESTERN BANTU

Ndemi = Kaba Ndim. Kaba D.→CENTRAL SUDANIC

Ndengereko→SOUTH EASTERN BANTU

Ndengese = Dengese→NORTH WESTERN BANTU

NDENI→CENTRAL MELANESIAN

Ndepu'u = Ganti→CENTRAL AND SOUTHERN CELEBES

Ndere = Nyele. Banda D.→EASTERN

Nderobo = Dorobo. Nandi D.→EASTERN SUDANIC

Ndese. Mamvu-Efe D.→CENTRAL SUDANIC

Ndi. Banda D.→EASTERN

Ndibu. Kongo D.→CENTRAL WESTERN BANTU

Ndingi→CENTRAL WESTERN BANTU

Ndinzi = Ndingi→CENTRAL WESTERN BANTU

Ndioko = Kaba Joko. Kaba Dunjo D.→CENTRAL SUDANIC

Ndir. Boki Tr.→CROSS-RIVER BENUE-CONGO

Ndirma = Kilba→CHADIC

Ndjabi = Nzebi→NORTH WESTERN BANTU

Ndjeli = Pande→NORTH WESTERN BANTU

Ndjem = Njem. Njem-Bajue Tr.→NORTH WESTERN BANTU

Ndjembe = Wongo→NORTH WESTERN BANTU

Ndjevi = Nzebi→NORTH WESTERN BANTU

Ndjinini = Njiniŋi. North Teke D.→NORTH WESTERN BANTU

Ndjuka = Djuka→GERMANIC

Ndlamba. Nguni D.→SOUTH EASTERN BANTU

Ndo→CENTRAL SUDANIC

Ndo Avari. Ndo D.→CENTRAL SUDANIC

Ndo Oke'bu. Ndo D.→CENTRAL SUDANIC

Ndobo→NORTH WESTERN BANTU

Ndoe→BANTOID

Ndogband. Banen Tr.→NORTH WESTERN BANTU

Ndogbang. Banen Tr.→NORTH WESTERN BANTU

Ndogo→EASTERN

Ndogo = Tsogo. Ruanda D.→NORTH EAST-

ERN BANTU

Ndokama. Basa Tr.→NORTH WESTERN BANTU

Ndokbele. Basa Tr.→NORTH WESTERN BANTU

Ndokbiakat. Banen Tr.→NORTH WESTERN BANTU

Ndokoua = Ndokpwa. Banda D.→EASTERN

Ndokpenda. Basa Tr.→NORTH WESTERN BANTU

Ndokpwa. Banda D.→EASTERN

Ndoktuna. Banen Tr.→NORTH WESTERN BANTU

Ndolo. Losengo D.→NORTH WESTERN BANTU

Ndom→FREDERIK HENDRIK IS AND SE WEST IRIAN

Ndombe→SOUTH WESTERN BANTU

Ndonde→SOUTH EASTERN BANTU

Ndonga→SOUTH WESTERN BANTU

NDONGA-KUANYAMA→SOUTH WESTERN BANTU

Ndongo = Mbundu→CENTRAL WESTERN BANTU

Ndoobo = Ndobo→NORTH WESTERN BANTU

NDOP→BANTOID

Ndopa = Ndokpwa. Banda D.→EASTERN

Ndore = Tuburi→CHADIC

Ndore = Tupuri→ADAMAWA

Ndoro→BANTOID

Ndorobo = Dorobo. Nandi D.→EASTERN SUDANIC

Ndorwa. Ruanda D.→NORTH EASTERN BANTU

Ndoute. Serer D.→WEST ATLANTIC

Ndoute = Ndut→WEST ATLANTIC

Ndrabito. Tawi D.→ADMIRALTY-WESTERN ISLANDS

Ndrabwi. Tulu D.→ ADMIRALTY-WESTERN ISLANDS

Ndramndrau. Tawi D.→ADMIRALTY-WESTERN ISLANDS

Ndranggot. Mokareng D.→ADMIRALTY-WESTERN ISLANDS

Ndranu. Tongo D.→ADMIRALTY-WESTERN ISLANDS

Ndrehet. Lebei D.→ ADMIRALTY-WESTERN ISLANDS

Ndri = Nyele. Banda D.→EASTERN

Ndrihol. Mok D.→ADMIRALTY-WESTERN ISLANDS

Ndroliu. Bipi D.→ADMIRALTY-WESTERN ISLANDS

Ndrosun→ADMIRALTY-WESTERN IS-
LANDS
Ndru = Dru. Lendu D.→CENTRAL SUDAN-
IC
NDU→SEPIK
Ndu = Wiya. Nsungli D.→BANTOID
Nduga→WEST NEW GUINEA HIGHLANDS
Ndugu. Ruanda D.→NORTH EASTERN BAN-
TU
Nduka. Vale D.→CENTRAL SUDANIC
Nduke = Duke→NORTHWESTERN AND
CENTRAL SOLOMONS
NDU-KWOMA = MIDDLE SEPIK→SEPIK
Ndum = Oso→BANTOID
Ndumbo = Minduumo→NORTH WESTERN
BANTU
Ndumu = Minduumo→NORTH WESTERN
BANTU
Ndunga = Modunga→EASTERN
Ndut→WEST ATLANTIC
Nduumo = Minduumo→NORTH WESTERN
BANTU
Nduupa = Dupa→ADAMAWA
Ndyak = Manjaku→WEST ATLANTIC
Ndyander = Ndyanger. Wolof D.→WEST AT-
LANTIC
Ndyanger. Wolof D.→WEST ATLANTIC
Ndyegem. Serer D.→WEST ATLANTIC
Ndyenye. Anyi D.→VOLTA-COMOE
Ndyura = Dyula. Dyula Tr.→MANDE
Ndzen. Lower Mundani D.→BANTOID
Ndzikou = Ndzindzihu. Central Teke D.→
NORTH WESTERN BANTU
Ndzindzihu. Central Teke D.→NORTH WEST-
ERN BANTU
Ndzindziu = Ndzindzihu. Central Teke D.→
NORTH WESTERN BANTU
Ndzubuga = Bangante→BANTOID
Ndzundza→SOUTH EASTERN BANTU
Ndzungle = Nsungli→BANTOID
NE = ERAP→HUON-FINISTERRE
Nea. Southwestern Santa Cruz D.→CENTRAL
MELANESIAN
Neabo. Krahn Tr.→KRU
Nebaj. Aguacatec D.→MAYAN
Nebome = Pima Bajo→UTO-AZTECAN
Nechegansett = Pennacook. Massachusett D.→
ALGONQUIAN
Neda = Midu. Digaru Mishmi D.→GYA-
RUNG-MISHMI
Nedi. Akye Tr.→LAGOON
Nedio. Bakwe Tr.→KRU
Nee→BURMESE-LOLO
Neegatu = Tupi. Tupi D.→TUPI

Neenoa. Tucano D.→MACRO-TUCANOAN
Neeshenam = Southern Maidu→MAIDU
Neetlakapamuch = Thompson→SALISH
Neferipi→ASMAT
Nega Bumungup = Bomougoun-Bamenjou→
BANTOID
Nega Munju = Bomougoun-Bamenjou→BAN-
TOID
Neger-Engelsch = Sranan→GERMANIC
Negerhollands→GERMANIC
Negidal→TUNGUS
Negira→INDO-PACIFIC
Negrito = Central Agta→NORTHWEST AUS-
TRONESIAN
Negrito, Central Cagayan = Central Agta→
NORTHWEST AUSTRONESIAN
Negrito, Northern Cagayan = Atta→NORTH-
WEST AUSTRONESIAN
Nehina = Waru. Laki D.→CENTRAL AND
SOUTHERN CELEBES
Nek→HUON-FINISTERRE
Nekgini→HUON-FINISTERRE
Neklakapamuk = Thompson→SALISH
Neko→HUON-FINISTERRE
Neku→NEW CALEDONIA
Nellagottine. Dogrib Tr.→ATHAPASCAN-
EYAK
Nemalele = Maele. Mangbetu D.→CENTRAL
SUDANIC
Nembe. Ijo D.→IJO
Nemboa = Aba→SANTA CRUZ AUSTRO-
NESIAN
Neme. Buari D.→MAILU
Nemea. Bauwaki or Binahari D.→MAILU
Nemeeje = Meje. Mangbetu D.→CENTRAL
SUDANIC
Nemi→NEW CALEDONIA
Nemia = Namie→SEPIK
Nene. Bakwe Tr.→KRU
Nene. Northeast Nambicuara D.→NAMBI-
CUARA
Neneba→KOIARI
Nenec = Yurak Samoyed→URALIC
Nenema→NEW CALEDONIA
Nenets = Yurak Samoyed→URALIC
Nengere-Tongo = Sranan→GERMANIC
Nengone→LOYALTY ISLANDS
Nengre-Tongo = Sranan→GERMANIC
Nenium→CENTRAL AND SOUTH NEW
GUINEA
Nentego = Nanticoke. Mohegan D.→ALGON-
QUIAN
Nenu. Mbo D.→NORTH WESTERN BANTU
Nenusa-Miangas. Talaud D.→HESPERONE-

SIAN

Nenya. Tumbuka D.→CENTRAL EASTERN BANTU

Neo. Northern Santa Cruz D.→CENTRAL MELANESIAN

Neo-Hellenic = Greek→GREEK

Neo-Melanesian→GERMANIC

Neo-Solomonic→GERMANIC

Neo-Tahitian = Tahitian→POLYNESIAN

Nepalese = Nepali→INDIC

Nepali→INDIC

Nerauya. Tanna D.→SOUTHERN NEW HEBRIDES

Nerezim. Turkmen D.→TURKIC

Nerigo. Yahadian D.→WESTERN NEW GUINEA

Nermonsinnansee = Nawathinehena. Arapaho D.→ALGONQUIAN

Nerokwang. Tanna D.→SOUTHERN NEW HEBRIDES

Nespelim. Okanogan D.→SALISH

Nesquake. Mohegan Tr.→ALGONQUIAN

Nestorian. East Aramaic D.→SEMITIC

Netela = Juaneno. Luiseno D.→UTO-AZTECAN

Netherlandic-German→GERMANIC

Netlakapamuk = Thompson→SALISH

Netsilik. Inuit D.→ESKIMO-ALEUT

Netsilingmiut = Netsilik. Inuit D.→ESKIMO-ALEUT

Nevat→NORTHWESTERN NEW HEBRIDES

Nevoma = Pima Bajo→UTO-AZTECAN

Nevome = Pima Bajo→UTO-AZTECAN

New Britain = Gunantuna→BISMARCK ARCHIPELAGO

NEW BRITAIN see article

New Caledonia Pidgin. French Creole D.→ROMANCE

NEW CALEDONIA see article

NEW GEORGIA→NORTHWESTERN AND CENTRAL SOLOMONS

NEW GUINEA, CENTRAL MACRO-PHYLUM see article

NEW GUINEA, CENTRAL AND SOUTH see article

NEW GUINEA, EASTERN = SOUTHEAST NEW GUINEA

NEW GUINEA HIGHLANDS, EAST see article

NEW GUINEA HIGHLANDS, WEST see article

NEW GUINEA, SOUTHERN see NEW GUINEA, CENTRAL AND SOUTH

NEW GUINEA, SOUTHWESTERN see NEW GUINEA, CENTRAL AND SOUTH

NEW GUINEA, WESTERN see article

NEW HEBRIDES, NORTHERN→EASTERN OCEANIC

NEW HEBRIDES, NORTHWESTERN see article

NEW HEBRIDES, SOUTHERN see article

NEW HEBRIDES-BANKS see OCEANIC

Newari→GYARUNG-MISHMI

Newfoundland = Beothuk

Newo = Neyo. Bete D.→KRU

Newole = Neyo. Bete D.→KRU

Neyo. Bete D.→KRU

Nez Perce→SAHAPTIN-NEZ PERCE

Nez Perces = Iowa. CHIWERE D.→SIOUAN

Nez Perces = Nez Perce→SAHAPTIN-NEZ PERCE

Nfa = Chara→PLATEAU BENUE-CONGO

Nfumte. Nsungli D.→BANTOID

Nfumte = Ashaku→JUKUNOID

Ngaaka→BANTOID

Ngac'ang = Lashi→BODO-NAGA-KACHIN

Ngachanji = Ngadjan. Wakaman D.→PAMA-MARIC

Ngada. Endeh D.→MOLUCCAN

Ngadadjara = Ngadatjara. Kardutjara D.→WATI

Ngadatjara. Kardutjara D.→WATI

Ngadawongga. Kardutjara D.→WATI

Ngadhawonga = Ngadawongga. Kardutjara D.→WATI

Ngadhuri = Ngadjuri. Jadliaura D.→YURA

Ngadja = Ngadjan. Wakaman D.→PAMA-MARIC

Ngadja = Ngaja. Banda D.→EASTERN

Ngadjan. Wakaman D.→PAMA-MARIC

Ngadju = Ngaju→WEST INDONESIAN

Ngadjunma. Mirning D.→MIRNINY

Ngadjuri. Jadliaura D.→YURA

Ngadye. Akye Tr.→LAGOON

Ngage→CENTRAL WESTERN BANTU

Ngaiawang. Nganguruku D.→NARRINYERIC

Ngaiman = Ngarinman→NGUMBIN

Ngaimbom = Lilau→BOGIA

Ngaimmun = Ngarinman→NGUMBIN

Ngaing→HUON-FINISTERRE

Ngaitjandji = Ngadjan. Wakaman D.→PAMA-MARIC

Ngaiuwonga = Waula. Kardutjara D.→WATI

Ngaiwung = Ngaiawang. Nganguruku D.→NARRINYERIC

Ngaiyau = Ngaiawang. Nganguruku D.→NARRINYERIC

Ngaja. Banda D.→EASTERN

Ngaju→WEST INDONESIAN
Ngaku. Ngamba D.→YUIN-KURIC
Ngala→SEPIK
Ngala. Kotoko D.→CHADIC
NGALA = BANGI-NTUMBA→ NORTH WESTERN BANTU
Ngala = Ngarla→NGAYARDA
Ngalagan = Ngalakan→GUNWINGGUAN
Ngalakan→GUNWINGGUAN
Ngalamiya. Tebu Tr.→SAHARAN
Ngalawonga. Kardutjara D.→WATI
Ngalbon = Ngalakan→GUNWINGGUAN
Ngalea. Kardutjara D.→WATI
Ngalek Ap Nandi = Nandi→EASTERN SU-DANIC
Ngalia→NGARGA
Ngalia = Ngalea. Kardutjara D.→WATI
Ngaliabong = Murzu→EASTERN SUDANIC
Ngalibong=Murzu→EASTERN SUDANIC
Ngalik, Northern→WEST NEW GUINEA HIGHLANDS
Ngalik, Southern→WEST NEW GUINEA HIGHLANDS
Ngaliwuru→DJAMINDJUNGAN
Ngallia = Ngalia→NGARGA
Ngalum→OK
Ngaluma. Kariera D.→NGAYARDA
Ngama = Sara Ngama. Sara D.→CENTRAL SUDANIC
Ngamai-iki→AGOB
Ngamambo→BANTOID
Ngamani = Ngameni. Dieri D.→DIERIC
Ngamaya = Ngamo→CHADIC
Ngamba→YUIN-KURIC
Ngambai = Gambai→CENTRAL SUDANIC
Ngambo. Central Tibetan D.→TIBETAN
Ngame. Musei D.→CHADIC
Ngameni. Dieri D.→DIERIC
Ngamgam = Dye→GUR
Ngamini = Ngameni. Dieri D.→DIERIC
Ngaminni = Ngameni. Dieri D.→DIERIC
Ngamo→CHADIC
Nganadjara = Nana. Kardutjara D.→WATI
Nganasan = Tavgy→URALIC
Nganawara = Kaurna. Jadliaura D.→YURA
Ngandangara. Punthamara D.→DIERIC
Ngandi→GUNWINGGUAN
Ngando→NORTH WESTERN BANTU
Ngando-Kota→NORTH WESTERN BANTU
Ngandyera→SOUTH WESTERN BANTU
Ngangela. Luimbi D.→SOUTH WESTERN BANTU
Ngangoulou. North East Teke Tr.→NORTH WESTERN BANTU

Nganguruku→NARRINYERIC
Nganshuenkuan. Central Tibetan D.→TIBETAN
Nganygit. Brinken D.→DALY
Ngao. Banda D.→EASTERN
Ngao. Endeh D.→MOLUCCAN
Ngaonawal = Ngunawal→YUIN-KURIC
Ngapore = Nyangeya. Teso D.→EASTERN SUDANIC
Ngapou = Ngapu. Banda D.→EASTERN
Ngapu. Banda D.→EASTERN
Ngarabal = Jukambal→YUIN-KURIC
Ngarabana = Arabana→PAMA-NYUNGAN
Ngarago = Ngarigo→YUIN-KURIC
Ngaragu = Ngarigo→YUIN-KURIC
Ngaralt = Ngaralta. Tanganekald D.→NARRI-NYERIC
Ngaralta. Tanganekald D.→NARRINYERIC
Ngaraltu = Ngaralta. Tanganekald D.→NAR-RINYERIC
Ngarawonga = Ngadawongga. Kardutjara D.→ WATI
Ngardi→NGARGA
Ngare→NORTH WESTERN BANTU
Ngarego = Ngarigo→YUIN-KURIC
NGARGA see article
Ngarigo→YUIN-KURIC
Ngarigu = Ngarigo→YUIN-KURIC
Ngarinman→NGUMBIN
Ngarinyin = Ungarinyin→WORORAN
NGARINYINIC = UNGARINYINIC→WO-RORAN
Ngarkat. Djadjala D.→KULINIC
Ngarla→NGAYARDA
Ngarluma = Ngaluma. Kariera D.→NGAYAR-DA
Ngarluri = Ndadjuri. Jadliaura D.→YURA
Ngarndji→TJINGILI-WAMBAYAN
Ngarrabul = Jukambal→YUIN-KURIC
Ngarruga = Ngarigo→YUIN-KURIC
Ngaruku = Ngarigo→YUIN-KURIC
Ngarukwillam = Wurundjeri. Taungurong D.→ KULINIC
Ngasa→EASTERN SUDANIC
Ngaslawe→CHADIC
Ngatik. Ponapean D.→MICRONESIAN
Ngatjan = Ngadjan. Wakaman D.→PAMA-MARIC
Ngatokae = Gatukai→NORTHWESTERN AND CENTRAL SOLOMONS
Ngatsang. Ach'ang D.→BODO-NAGA-KA-CHIN
Ngawaijung = Ngawait. Nganguruku D.→ NARRINYERIC
Ngawait. Nganguruku D.→NARRINYERIC

Ngawigi = Nagwagi→PAMA-MARIC
Ngawo = Ngao. Banda D.→EASTERN
Ngayaba→NORTH WESTERN BANTU
NGAYARDA see article
Ngazam = Ngizim→CHADIC
Ngazidja = Ngazija. Komoro D.→CENTRAL
EASTERN BANTU
Ngazija. Komoro D.→CENTRAL EASTERN
BANTU
Ngbaka. Furu Tr.→CENTRAL SUDANIC
Ngabaka = Gbaya→EASTERN
Ngbaka Gbaya. Gbaya Tr.→EASTERN
Ngbaka Mabo = Bwaka→EASTERN
Ngbaka Manja. Gbaya Tr.→EASTERN
Ngbaka Mapi. Bwaka D.→EASTERN
Ngbaka-Ma'bo = Bwaka→EASTERN
Ngbandi→EASTERN
Ngbang. Duru D.→ADAMAWA
Ngbanyito = Guan→VOLTA-COMOE
Ngbee→CENTRAL WESTERN BANTU
Ngbinda→CENTRAL WESTERN BANTU
Ng-Dudutho = Dodos. Karamojong D.→EAST-
ERN SUDANIC
Ngee. East Teke D.→NORTH WESTERN
BANTU
Ngele = Nyele. Banda D.→EASTERN
Ngele of Irebu→NORTH WESTERN BANTU
Ngelima = Angba→NORTH WESTERN BAN-
TU
NGEMBA→BANTOID
Ngemba. Wongaibon D.→WIRADJURIC
Ngen = Mbo→NORTH WESTERN BANTU
Ngende. Busooŋ Tr.→NORTH WESTERN
BANTU
Ngengomeri = Nangumiri→DALY
Ngengu→CENTRAL WESTERN BANTU
Ngennigenwurro = Ngunawal→YUIN-KURIC
Ngeq→MON-KHMER
Nger = Laka Mbere. Kari D.→ADAMAWA
Ngerasi = Ramata→NORTHWESTERN AND
CENTRAL SOLOMONS
Ngere = Dan→MANDE
Ngeruketi = Ngarkat. Djadjala D.→KULINIC
Ngeumba = Ngemba. Wongaibon D.→WIRA-
DJURIC
Ngewin→AUSTRALIAN MACRO-PHYLUM
Nggad = Gao→NORTHWESTERN AND
CENTRAL SOLOMONS
Nggauaiyowangko = Ngaiawang. Nganguruku
D.→NARRINYERIC
Nggela→EASTERN OCEANIC
Nggoth→PAMA-MARIC
Nghwele→CENTRAL EASTERN BANTU
Ngi→BANTOID

Ngiakwai. Karamojong D.→EASTERN
SUDANIC
Ngiamba = Ngemba. Wongaibon D.→WIRA-
DJURIC
Ngi-aŋgeya = Nyangeya. Teso D.→EASTERN
SUDANIC
Ngie = Ngi→BANTOID
Ngi-gatio. Karamojong D.→EASTERN
SUDANIC
Ngi-jiye = Jie. Karamojong D.→EASTERN
SUDANIC
Ngikadama = Kadam. Pokot D.→EASTERN
SUDANIC
Ngindo→SOUTH EASTERN BANTU
NGINDO = MATUMBI→SOUTH EASTERN
BANTU
Ngingi = Ndingi→CENTRAL WESTERN
BANTU
Ngintait. Maraura D.→NARRINYERIC
Nginyakwai — Ngiakwai. Karamojong D.→
EASTERN SUDANIC
Ngi-nyukwur. Kolib D.→KORDOFANIAN
Ngi-rere. Koalib D.→KORDOFANIAN
Ngiri. Loi-Ngiri D.→NORTH WESTERN BAN-
TU
Ngirla = Ngarla→NGAYARDA
Ngiumba = Ngemba. Wongaibon D.→WIRA-
DJURIC
NGIZIM→CHADIC
Ngizim→CHADIC
Ngizzem = Ngizim→CHADIC
//Ng!ke = // ŋ!ke. ŋ /huki D.→KHOISAN
Ngkoth = Nggoth→PAMA-MARIC
Ngnaminni = Ngameni. Dieri D.→DIERIC
Ngo→BANTOID
Ngoba = Ngova. Karanga D.→SOUTH EAST-
ERN BANTU
Ngobo = Gobu. Banda D.→EASTERN
Ngobu = Gobu. Banda D.→EASTERN
Ngoera. Dungidjau D.→WAKA-KABIC
Ngok. Padang D.→EASTERN SUDANIC
Ngokgurring = Wudjari. Juat D.→SOUTH-
WEST PAMA-NYUNGAN
Ngokwurring = Wudjari. Juat D.→SOUTH-
WEST PAMA-NYUNGAN
Ngola→CENTRAL WESTERN BANTU
Ngolo = Ngoro. Lundu D.→NORTH WEST-
ERN BANTU
Ngom. Kele D.→NORTH WESTERN BANTU
Ngoma. Bemba D.→CENTRAL EASTERN
BANTU
Ngomahum = Bandjoun-Baham→BANTOID
NGOMBA = NGEMBA→BANTOID
NGOMBE→NORTH WESTERN BANTU

Ngombe→NORTH WESTERN BANTU

Ngombe. Busooŋ Tr.→NORTH WESTERN BANTU

Ngombekaka. Gbaya Tr.→EASTERN

Ngombia = Ngombe. Busooŋ Tr.→NORTH WESTERN BANTU

Ngonde. Nyakyusa D.→CENTRAL EASTERN BANTU

Ngondi = Ngundi→NORTH WESTERN BANTU

Ngong. Kumaju D.→BANTOID

Ngong = Nagumi→BANTOID

Ngongo. Busooŋ Tr.→NORTH WESTERN BANTU

Ngongo. Nkutu D.→NORTH WESTERN BANTU

Ngongosila. Lau D.→EASTERN OCEANIC

Ngoni→CENTRAL EASTERN BANTU

Ngoni. Nguni D.→SOUTH EASTERN BANTU

Ngonu→BANTOID

Ngoongo. Yaka D.→CENTRAL WESTERN BANTU

Ngooraialum = Taungurong→KULINIC

Ngoreme = Ngurimi→NORTH EASTERN BANTU

Ngork = Ngok. Padang D.→EASTERN SUDANIC

Ngormbal. Nyulnyul D.→NYULNYULAN

Ngoro→NORTH WESTERN BANTU

Ngoro. Lundu D.→NORTH WESTERN BANTU

Ngova. Karanga D.→SOUTH EASTERN BANTU

Ngowugar→FREDERIK HENDRIK IS AND SE WEST IRIAN

Ngoy=Bwende. Kongo D.→CENTRAL WESTERN BANTU

Ngoyo. Ndingi D.→CENTRAL WESTERN BANTU

Ngraimun = Ngarinman→NGUMBIN

Ngruimi = Ngurimi→NORTH EASTERN BANTU

Ngugi = Gowar→DURUBULIC

Ngul→NORTH WESTERN BANTU

Ngulak = Teuso→EASTERN SUDANIC

Ngulangulandji = Kulumali. Karendala D.→DIERIC

Ngulgule = Njalgulgule→EASTERN SUDANIC

Ngult = Maraura→NARRINYERIC

Ngulu→CENTRAL EASTERN BANTU

Ngulu→SOUTH EASTERN BANTU

Ngulu. Ulithian D.→MICRONESIAN

Ngulubulu = Karanya. Wangkadjera D.→PIT-

TAPITTIC

Ngumatiwu. Kanuri Tr.→SAHARAN

Ngumba = Mvumbo→NORTH WESTERN BANTU

Ngumbi = Kombe. Yasa D.→NORTH WESTERN BANTU

NGUMBIN see article

Nguna. Tongoa D.→EASTERN OCEANIC

Ngunawal→YUIN-KURIC

NGUNDI→NORTH WESTERN BANTU

Ngundi→NORTH WESTERN BANTU

Ngundi. Losengo D.→NORTH WESTERN BANTU

Ngu-nduna. Koalib D.→KORDOFANIAN

Ngundura = Ngarigo→YUIN-KURIC

Ngungulu = Ngangoulou. North East Teke Tr.→NORTH WESTERN BANTU

Ngungwel = Ngangoulou. North East Teke Tr.→NORTH WESTERN BANTU

NGUNI→SOUTH EASTERN BANTU

Nguni→SOUTH EASTERN BANTU

Nguni = Ngoni. Nguni D.→SOUTH EASTERN BANTU

Ngunnhalgri = Naualko. Kula D.→PAMA-NYUNGAN

Ngunu = Ngonu→BANTOID

Nguon Ta = Katu→MON-KHMER

Ngu-qwurang. Koalib D.→KORDOFANIAN

NGURA→DIERIC

Nguralungbula = Taungurong→KULINIC

Ngurawola. Punthamara D.→DIERIC

Nguri→WIRADJURIC

Ngurimi→NORTH EASTERN BANTU

Ngurla = Ngarla→NGAYARDA

Ngurlu. Kardutjara D.→WATI

Nguro. Mandandanji D.→PAMA-MARIC

Nguru. Banda D.→EASTERN

Nguru. Kara D.→CENTRAL SUDANIC

Nguru = Lomwe→SOUTH EASTERN BANTU

Nguru = Ngulu→CENTRAL EASTERN BANTU

Nguru = Ngulu→SOUTH EASTERN BANTU

Nguruimi = Ngurimi→NORTH EASTERN BANTU

Ngwa = Ngonu→BANTOID

Ngwaketse. Tswana D.→SOUTH EASTERN BANTU

Ngwala = Kulango→GUR

Ngwalkwe = Gulfei. Kotoko D.→CHADIC

Ngwalungu. Tsonga D.→SOUTH EASTERN BANTU

Ngwana = Njuani. Komoro D.→CENTRAL EASTERN BANTU

Ngwe→BANTOID

Ngwe = Ngwoi→PLATEAU BENUE-CONGO
Ngwo = Ngonu→BANTOID
Ngwoi→PLATEAU BENUE-CONGO
Nhacfateitei. Caingang D.→GE
n//hai→KHOISAN
n/hai-ntse'e = n//hai→KHOISAN
n/hai-tse'e = n//hai→KHOISAN
NHAMBICUARA = NAMBICUARA
Nhanda = Nanda→KARDU
Nhang→KAM-TAI
Nhauru = Naron→KHOISAN
Nhaurun = Naron→KHOISAN
Nheengatu = Tupi. Tupi D.→TUPI
Nhengahiba. Tenetehara Tr.→TUPI
Niabua. Bete Tr.→KRU
Niahon = Hun→MON-KHMER
Niakuol→MON-KHMER
Niakyusa = Nyakyusa→CENTRAL EASTERN
    BANTU
Nialuok→MON-KHMER
Niam-niam = Zande→EASTERN
Niangbo. Tagbana D.→GUR
Niaragua = Niarawa→PANO
Niarawa→PANO
Nias→WEST INDONESIAN
Niawoo = Ngawait. Nganguruku D.→NAR-
    RINYERIC
Nibiltse = Hupa→ATHAPASCAN-EYAK
Nibon = Nibong. Ba Mali D.→WEST INDO-
    NESIAN
Nibong. Ba Mali D.→WEST INDONESIAN
Nibulu = Nunuma→GUR
Nicarao. Pipil D.→UTO-AZTECAN
NICOBARESE see article
Nicola. Chilcotin Tr.→ATHAPASCAN-EYAK
Nicoutemuch = Thompson→SALISH
Nicoya. Mangue D.→MANGUEAN
Nidem. Kaninkwom D.→PLATEAU BENUE-
    CONGO
Nidzh. Udi D.→CAUCASIAN
Niediekaha. Tagbana D.→GUR
Ni'ekeni' = Bear River. Mattole D.→ATHA-
    PASCAN-EYAK
Niel. Padang D.→EASTERN SUDANIC
Nielim→ADAMAWA
Nielle = Tagbari. Senari D.→GUR
Niellim = Nielim→ADAMAWA
Niende. Somba D.→GUR
Nife = Luo→EASTERN SUDANIC
Nigac. Mape D.→HUON-FINISTERRE
NIGER-CHAD = CHADIC
NIGER-CONGO see article
NIGER-KORDOFANIAN see article
Nighi = Ligbi→MANDE

Nigo. Adangme D.→GA-ADANGME
Nigone = Ligbi→MANDE
Nigoni = Ligbi→MANDE
Nigottine. Dogrib Tr.→ATHAPASCAN-EYAK
Nigua→BARBACOAN
Nigubaiba→KOIARI
Niguecactemigi = Layana. Guana D.→MAI-
    PURAN
Nigui = Ligbi→MANDE
Niguira. Nahua D.→UTO-AZTECAN
Niguiran = Niguira. Nahua D.→UTO-AZTEC-
    AN
Nihali = Nahali
Nihamber = Seim→SEPIK
Nihiri = Neyo. Bete D.→KRU
Niinati = Northern Kati→OK
Nika→NORTH EASTERN BANTU
Nikaura. Tasiko D.→EASTERN OCEANIC
Nikki-Parakou. Bargu D.→GUR
Nikorama — Tirma→EASTERN SUDANIC
Nikozliautin. Carrier Tr.→ATHAPASCAN-
    EYAK
Nikuda→EAST INDONESIAN
Nikulukan. Sapolewa D.→EAST INDONE-
    SIAN
Nikutamuk = Thompson→SALISH
Nikutemuk = Thompson→SALISH
Nila→EAST INDONESIAN
Nilamba→NORTH EASTERN BANTU
Nile. Kohumono D.→CROSS RIVER BENUE-
    CONGO
Niles. Northern Costanoan D.→MIWOK-
    COSTANOAN
NILO-HAMITIC→EASTERN SUDANIC
NILO-SAHARAN see article
NILOTIC→EASTERN SUDANIC
NILOTIC, EASTERN = NILO-HAMITIC→
    EASTERN SUDANIC
NILOTIC, WESTERN = NILOTIC→EAST-
    ERN SUDANIC
NILYAMBA = LLAMBA-IRANGI→NORTH
    EASTERN BANTU
Nimadi. Rajasthani D.→INDIC
Nimalda = Adnyamathana. Wailpi D.→YURA
Nimanboru = Nimanbur. Nyulnyul D.→NYUL-
    NYULAN
Nimanbur. Nyulnyul D.→NYULNYULAN
Nimbalda = Adnyamathana. Wailpi D.→YURA
Nimbaldi = Adnyamathana. Wailpi D.→YURA
Nimbari→ADAMAWA
Nimbau = Aba→SANTA CRUZ AUSTRO-
    NESIAN
NIMBORAN→NORTH PAPUAN
Nimboran→NORTH PAPUAN

Nimi→HUON-FINISTERRE

Nimo→LEFT MAY

Ninebulo. South Raga D.→EASTERN OCEAN-IC

Ningalami = Nangalami→NURISTANI

Ningawa. Butawa D.→PLATEAU BENUE-CONGO

Ninggirum→OK

Ningi→PLATEAU BENUE-CONGO

Ningil→TORRICELLI

Ningo = Nigo. Adangme D.→GA-ADANGME

Ning-ting. Pao-an D.→MONGOLIAN

Ninigo→ADMIRALTY-WESTERN ISLANDS

Nining = Nyinin. Djaru D.→NGUMBIN

Ninisi = Samo→MANDE

Ninong = Nenu. Mbo D.→NORTH WESTERN BANTU

Ninzam→PLATEAU BENUE-CONGO

Ninzne-Udinsk. Buryat D.→MONGOLIAN

Niol-Niol = Nyulnyul→NYULNYULAN

Nipegon = Winnebago→SIOUAN

Nipori = Nyangeya. Teso D.→EASTERN SU-DANIC

Nirababaluk = Jaara. Djadjala D.→KULINIC

Nirabaluk = Jaara. Djadjala D.→KULINIC

Niramba = Nilamba→NORTH EASTERN BANTU

Nisan→BISMARCK ARCHIPELAGO

Nisenan = Southern Maidu→MAIDU

Niseygram. Kalasa-ala D.→NURISTANI

Nishinam = Southern Maidu→MAIDU

Niska. Tsimshian D.→PENUTIAN

Nisqualli. Puget Sound Salish D.→SALISH

Nisqually, Upper = Yakima. Sahaptin D.→SAHAPTIN-NEZ PERCE

Nissan = Nisan→BISMARCK ARCHIPELA-GO

Nitinat→WAKASHAN

Nitklakapamuk = Thompson→SALISH

Niuafo'ou. Tongan D.→POLYNESIAN

Niuatoputapu. Tongan D.→POLYNESIAN

Niuean→POLYNESIAN

Niuefekai = Niuean→POLYNESIAN

Nivkhi = Gilyak

Nizh = Nidzh. Udi D.→CAUCASIAN

NJABI→NORTH WESTERN BANTU

Njabi = Nzebi→NORTH WESTERN BANTU

Njai→CHADIC

Njakali = Djabugay. Wakaman D.→PAMA-MARIC

Njakinjaki = Nyakinyaki. Juat D.→SOUTH-WEST PAMA-NYUNGAN

Njal. Kari D.→ADAMAWA

Njalbo = Ngoera. Dungidjau D.→WAKA-KABIC

Njalgulgule→EASTERN SUDANIC

Njamal = Nyamal→NGAYARDA

Njamusi = Tiamus. Maasai D.→EASTERN SU-DANIC

Njangamada = Nyangumarda→MARNGU

Njangga. Gayardilt D.→TANGKIC

Njangumarda = Nyangumarda→MARNGU

Njanja. Shona D.→SOUTH EASTERN BANTU

Njaŋga = Wirangu→SOUTHWEST PAMA-NYUNGAN

Njaŋgulgule = Njalgulgule→EASTERN SU-DANIC

Njao = Nyao→NORTH PAPUAN

NJARI = MBEMBE→JUKUNOID

Njawatjurk = Ngawait. Nganguruku D.→NAR-RINYERIC

Njei. Njai D.→CHADIC

Njel = Njai→CHADIC

Njem. Njem-Bajue Tr.→NORTH WESTERN BANTU

Njem-Bajue→NORTH WESTERN BANTU

Njemnjem. Bute D.→BANTOID

Njemps = Tiamus. Maasai D.→EASTERN SU-DANIC

Njeng = Jen→ADAMAWA

Njeny = Njai→CHADIC

Njigina = Nyigina→NYULNYULAN

Njikena = Nyigina→NYULNYULAN

Njikini = Njiniŋi. North Teke D.→NORTH WESTERN BANTU

Njindango = Kalamai→MIRNINY

Njinga. Mbamba D.→CENTRAL WESTERN BANTU

Njiniŋi. North Teke D.→NORTH WESTERN BANTU

Njinju = Ndzindzihu. Central Teke D.→NORTH WESTERN BANTU

Njo see Kro and Lampung→WEST INDO-NESIAN

Njuani. Komoro D.→CENTRAL EASTERN BANTU

Njuboga = Bangante→BANTOID

Njul-Njul = Nyulnyul→NYULNYULAN

Njumit. Lawangan D.→WEST INDONESIAN

Njwande. Bitare D.→BANTOID

Nkamar = Banna→OMOTIC

Nkami. Guan D.→VOLTA-COMOE

Nkangala→SOUTH WESTERN BANTU

Nkanu. Kongo D.→CENTRAL WESTERN BANTU

Nkembe. Mbole D.→NORTH EASTERN BAN-TU

Nki = Boki→CROSS-RIVER BENUE-CONGO
Nkim→BANTOID
Nkogna = Guan→VOLTA-COMOE
Nkokolle = Nkukoli→CROSS RIVER BENUE-CONGO
Nkokolle = Nkukoli→CROSS RIVER BENUE-CONGO
Nkole = Nyankole→NORTH EASTERN BANTU
NKOM→BANTOID
Nkom→BANTOID
Nkomi. Myene D.→NORTH WESTERN BANTU
Nkonde = Ngonde. Nyakyusa D.→CENTRAL EASTERN BANTU
Nkonya = Nkunya. Guan D.→VOLTA-COMOE
Nkor. Kumaju D.→BANTOID
Nkorama = Tid. Tirma D.→EASTERN SUDANIC
Nkoro. Ijo D.→IJO
Nkosi = Koose. Mbo D.→NORTH WESTERN BANTU
NKOYA→CENTRAL WESTERN BANTU
Nkoya→CENTRAL WESTERN BANTU
Nkriang. Ngeq D.→MON-KHMER
Nkucu = Nkutu→NORTH WESTERN BANTU
Nkukoli→CROSS RIVER BENUE-CONGO
Nkulu = Ikulu→PLATEAU BENUE-CONGO
Nkum→BANTOID
Nkumm = Nkum→BANTOID
Nkundo. Mongo-Nkundo D.→NORTH WESTERN BANTU
Nkunya. Guan D.→VOLTA-COMOE
Nkutshu = Nkutu→NORTH WESTERN BANTU
Nkutu→NORTH WESTERN BANTU
Nkutu = Dengese→NORTH WESTERN BANTU
Nkwen. Mandankwe D.→BANTOID
Nnam→BANTOID
No = Neyo. Bete D.→KRU
Noala→NGAYARDA
Noanama = Waunana→CHOCO
Nobanob = Halopa→BOGIA
Nobvu. Shona D.→SOUTH EASTERN BANTU
Nochiztlan. Mixtec D.→MIXTECAN
Nochpeem = Wappinger. Mohegan D.→ALGONQUIAN
Nocten. Mataco Tr.→MATACO
Noemfoor = Numfor→MOLUCCAN

Nogai→TURKIC
Nogau. Kung D.→KHOISAN
Nogugu = Nokuku → NORTH WESTERN NEW HEBRIDES
Nohina = Wiwi Rano. Laki D.→CENTRAL AND SOUTHERN CELEBES
Noho = Banaka. Batanga D.→NORTH WESTERN BANTU
Nohu = Banaka. Batanga D.→NORTH WESTERN BANTU
Nohur == Nokhurli. Turkmen D.→TURKIC
Nohwe. Shona D.→SOUTH EASTERN BANTU
Noie = Asera Wanua. Laki D.→CENTRAL AND SOUTHERN CELEBES
Noihe = Labea'u. Laki D.→CENTRAL AND SOUTHERN CELEBES
Nokanoka = North Koma. Koma D.→KOMAN
Nokhurli. Turkmen D.→TURKIC
Noko = Banaka. Batanga D.→NORTH WESTERN BANTU
Nokon→BISMARCK ARCHIPELAGO
Nokopo→HUON-FINISTERRE
Nokuku→NORTH WESTERN NEW HEBRIDES
Nokunna = Nukuna. Jadliaura D.→YURA
Nolgin = Jungman→GUNWINGGUAN
Nomane→ EAST NEW GUINEA HIGHLANDS
Nombuio→CENTRAL AND SOUTH NEW GUINEA
Nome. Dagari D.→GUR
Nomlackee = Nomlaki→WINTUN
Nomlaki→WINTUN
Nomu→HUON-FINISTERRE
Non→WEST ATLANTIC
Nona = Nwa→MANDE
Nonama = Waunana→CHOCO
NON-AUSTRONESIAN = INDO-PACIFIC
Nondiri. Chimbu D.→EAST NEW GUINEA HIGHLANDS
None = Non→WEST ATLANTIC
Nong. Southern Mnong D.→MON-KHMER
Nonga = Wudjari. Juat D.→SOUTHWEST PAMA-NYUNGAN
Nongatl→ATHAPASCAN-EYAK
Noni. Kumaju D.→BANTOID
Nono. Soninke Tr.→MANDE
Nonukan. Bolongan D.→NORTHWEST AUSTRONESIAN
Nonuya→WITOTOAN
n/oo. Shua D.→KHOISAN
Noo = Banoo. Batanga D.→NORTH WEST-

ERN BANTU

Noocoona = Nukuna. Jadliaura D.→YURA

Nooh-lum-mi = Lummi. Northern Straits Salish D.→SALISH

n/ookhwe = n/oo. Shua D.→KHOISAN

n//ookhwe = n/oo. Shua D.→KHOISAN

Nookluolamic = Lummi. Northern Straits Salish D.→ SALISH

Nookoona = Nukuna. Jadliaura D.→YURA

Nooksack→SALISH

Nooksahk = Nooksack→SALISH

Nooksak = Nooksack→SALISH

Noole. Southeastern Santa Cruz D.→CENTRAL MELANESIAN

Noonukul = Nununkul. Djendewal D.→DU-RUBULIC

Noosan = ŋ/usan. ŋ/amani D.→KHOISAN

Noosdalum = Clallam→SALISH

Noosoluph = Upper Chehalis→SALISH

Noosolup'h = Upper Chehalis→SALISH

Noosolupsh = Upper Chehalis→SALISH

Nootka→WAKASHAN

NOOTKAN→WAKASHAN

Nootsack = Nooksack→SALISH

Nop. Koho D.→MON-KHMER

Nor = Mambila→BANTOID

Nor = Murik→NORTH NEW GUINEA

Nora→BODO-NAGA-KACHIN

Noraia→CENTRAL AND SOUTH NEW GUINEA

NORDIC = NORTH GERMANIC→GERMANIC

Norea. Tebu Tr.→SAHARAN

Nori→NORTH NEW GUINEA

Nori. Cauca Tr.→CARIB

Norio = Mekongka→CENTRAL AND SOUTHERN CELEBES

Norocoage→GE

NOR-PONDO = MURIK→NORTH NEW GUINEA

Norra = Nora→BODO-NAGA-KACHIN

Nortenyo = Move. Guaymi D.→CHIBCHAN

Nortenyo = Terraba→CHIBCHAN

Norwegian. Continental Scandinavian D.→GERMANIC

Noshi = Moso→BURMESE-LOLO

Nossob→KHOISAN

Notobotocudo. Seta D.→TUPI

Nottoway→IROQUOIS

Notu→BINANDERE

Nouba = Fanya→CHADIC

Noumou = Numu. Huela D.→MANDE

Nousaghauset = Naranganset. Massachusett D. →ALGONQUIAN

Nowo = Nawu→YURA

Nowulo. Senari D.→GUR

Noza = Nora→BODO-NAGA-KACHIN

Nozo. Bakwe Tr.→KRU

Npongue = Mpongwe. Myene D.→NORTH WESTERN BANTU

Nraʔangith. Awngthim D.→PAMA-MARIC

Nrebele→SOUTH EASTERN BANTU

Nri-Awka. Igbo D.→IGBO

Nrwaʔa. Awngthim D.→PAMA-MARIC

N'sakara = Nzakara→EASTERN

NSARE = MBEMBE→JUKUNOID

Nsaw = Lamnso→BANTOID

Nsei = Kensense→BANTOID

Nsele = Nselle. Nde D.→BANTOID

Nselle. Nde D.→BANTOID

NSENGA = SENGA-SENA→CENTRAL EASTERN BANTU

Nsenga→CENTRAL EASTERN BANTU

Nso = Lamnso→BANTOID

Nsungali = Nsungli→BANTOID

Nsungli→BANTOID

Nsungni = Nsungli→BANTOID

N-swɔsə = Swase. Mbo D.→NORTH WESTERN BANTU

Nta. Nde D.→BANTOID

Ntaandu. Kongo D.→CENTRAL WESTERN BANTU

Ntau→EAST INDONESIAN

Ntem→BANTOID

Ntenyi. Rengma D.→NAGA-KUKI-CHIN

Nthali. Tumbuku D.→CENTRAL EASTERN BANTU

Ntlakyapmuk = Thompson→SALISH

Ntogapid. Ramarama D.→TUPI

Ntomba. Ntombo-Bolia Tr.→NORTH WESTERN BANTU

Ntombo-Bolia→NORTH WESTERN BANTU

Ntra'ngith = Nra ʔangith. Awngthim D.→PAMA-MARIC

Ntrawa'ngayth = Nra ʔangith. Awngthim D.—PAMA-MARIC

Ntribu = Delo→GUR

Ntsaayi = Tsaayi. West Teke D.→NORTH WESTERN BANTU

Ntshaautin. Carrier Tr.→ATHAPASCAN-EYAK

Ntshanti. Kumaju D.→BANTOID

Ntsiam. Mfinu D.→NORTH WESTERN BANTU

Ntsietshaw = Tillamook→SALISH

Ntsietshawus = Tillamook→SALISH

Ntsuo. Yanzi D.→NORTH WESTERN BANTU

Ntswar. Mfinu D.→NORTH WESTERN BANTU
Ntum = Northern Faŋ. Faŋ D.→NORTH WEST-ERN BANTU
Nu = Nung→BODO-NAGA-KACHIN
Nuakata→PAPUA AUSTRONESIAN
Nuangeya→EASTERN SUDANIC
Nuaulu→EAST INDONESIAN
Nub = Kaeti→AWYU
Nuba = Fanya→CHADIC
Nubami→NORTHEAST NEW GUINEA AUS-TRONESIAN
Nubia = Awar→BOGIA
NUBIAN→EASTERN SUDANIC
Nu-chiang. Lisu D.→BURMESE-LOLO
Nucoecamecran→GE
Nucuini→PANO
/nu/ /en = ŋ/u/ /en. ŋ/amani D.→KHOISAN
nu/ /e:n = ŋ/u/ /en. ŋ/amani D.→KHOISAN
NUER→EASTERN SUDANIC
Nuer→EASTERN SUDANIC
Nufoor = Numfor→MOLUCCAN
Nugara. Muliara D.→KARDU
Nugubuyu = Nunggubuju→AUSTRALIAN MACRO-PHYLUM
Nuguna = Nukuna. Jadliaura D.→YURA
Nuguria = Nukuria. Luangiua D.→POLYNE-SIAN
Nuh-lum-mi = Lummi. Northern Straits Salish D.→SALISH
Nuk→HUON-FINISTERRE
Nukh-lum-mi = Lummi. Northern Straits Salish D.→SALISH
Nuksahk = Nooksack→SALISH
Nuksak = Nooksack→SALISH
Nukuhai. Tala D.→EAST INDONESIAN
Nukumanu. Luangiua D.→POLYNESIAN
Nukuna. Jadaliaura D.→YURA
Nukunnu = Nukuna. Jadliaura D.→YURA
Nukunu = Nukuna. Jadliaura D.→YURA
Nukunukubara = Wakawaka. Dungidjau D.→WAKA-KABIC
Nukuoro→POLYNESIAN
Nukuria. Luangiua D.→POLYNESIAN
Nullakun = Ngalakan→GUNWINGGUAN
Nullikan = Ngalakan→GUNWINGGUAN
Nullikin = Ngalakan→GUNWINGGUAN
Numa = Comanche. Shoshoni D.→UTO-AZTECAN
Numakaki = Mandan→SIOUAN
Numanggang→HUON-FINISTERRE
Numangkake = Mandan→SIOUAN
NUMEIC→NEW CALEDONIA
Numerat. Tanna D.→SOUTHERN NEW HEB-

RIDES
Numfoor = Numfor→MOLUCCAN
NUMFOR→SOUTH HALMAHERA AUS-TRONESIAN
Numfor→MOLUCCAN
NUMIC→UTO-AZTECAN
Numipotitoken = Nez Perce→SAHAPTIN-NEZ PERCE
Numipu = Nez Perce→SAHAPTIN-NEZ PERCE
Numsu = Patwin→WINTUN
Numu. Huela D.→MANDE
Nuna = Koyra→OMOTIC
Nuna = Nunuma→GUR
NUNG→BODO-NAGA-KACHIN
Nung→KAM-TAI
Nung→BODO-NAGA-KACHIN
Nung = Rawang→BODO-NAGA-KACHIN
Nunga = Wudjari. Juat D.→SOUTHWEST PAMA-NYUNGAN
Nungabuya = Nunggubuju→AUSTRALIAN MACRO-PHYLUM
Nungabuyu = Nunggubuju→AUSTRALIAN MACRO-PHYLUM
Nungali→DJAMINDJUNGAN
Nungawal = Ngunawal→YUIN-KURIC
Nungbuju = Nunggubuju→AUSTRALIAN MACRO-PHYLUM
Nunggubuju→AUSTRALIAN MACRO-PHY-LUM
Nunggubuyu = Nunggubuju→AUSTRALIAN MACRO-PHYLUM
Nungo. Ciokwe D.→SOUTH WESTERN BANTU
Nungo = Nigo. Adangme D.→GA-ADANGME
Nungo = Shingi→CENTRAL WESTERN BANTU
Nungu = Rindre→PLATEAU BENUE-CON-GO
Nungubuju = Nunggubuju→AUSTRALIAN MACRO-PHYLUM
Nunguda = Longuda→ADAMAWA
Nuniali→EAST INDONESIAN
Nunku = Mada→PLATEAU BENUE-CONGO
Nunligranskij. Chukchee D.→CHUCKCHEE-KAMCHATKAN
Nunpa = Lepcha→BODO-NAGA-KACHIN
Nunu. Loi-Ngiri D.→NORTH WESTERN BANTU
Nunuma→GUR
Nununkul. Djendewal D.→DURUBULIC
Nuoku→BURMESE-LOLO
Nupanob = Halopa→BOGIA
Nupe→NUPE-GBARI

Nupe Zam. Nupe Tr.→NUPE-GBARI
NUPE-GBARI see article
Nupuanmen. Tanna D.→SOUTHERN NEW HEBRIDES
Nura. Dagara D.→GUR
Nuralda = Adnyamathana. Wailpi D.→YURA
NURISTANI see article
Nuro = Anuak→EASTERN SUDANIC
Nurram = Pibelmen. Juat D.→SOUTHWEST PAMA-NYUNGAN
Nurue. Sapolewa D.→EAST INDONESIAN
Nuruma = Nunuma→GUR
Nusa→WEST INDONESIAN
Nusan = ŋ/u/ /en. ŋ/amani D.→KHOISAN
Nusan = ŋ/usan. ŋ/amani D.→KHOISAN
Nu-san = ŋ/usan. ŋ/amani D.→KHOISAN
Nusawele. Wahai D.→EAST INDONESIAN
Nusawilih = Nusawele. Wahai D.→EAST INDONESIAN
Nusdalum = Clallam→SALISH
Nusulaut. Ambonese D.→MOLUCCAN
Nusulph = Upper Chehalis→SALISH
Nutabare. Cenu D.→CARIB
Nutabe = Nutabare. Cenu D.→CARIB
Nutetu Sepa = Kawa. Tala D.→EAST INDO-NESIAN
Nutetu Tala. Tala D.→EAST INDONESIAN
Nwa→MANDE
Nwato. Tswana D.→SOUTH EASTERN BANTU
Nwe = Dschang-Bangwa. Bafou D.→BAN-TOID
Nwesi. Bemba D.→CENTRAL EASTERN BANTU
Nyaakurdi = Amangu. Nanda D.→KARDU
Nyabadan. Maba D.→MABAN
Nyabungu→NORTH EASTERN BANTU
Nyacfateitei. Caingang D.→GE
Nyada→ADMIRALTY-WESTERN ISLANDS
Nyaheun→MON-KHMER
Nyai. Shona D.→SOUTH EASTERN BANTU
Nyakali = Djabugay. Wakaman D.→PAMA-MARIC
Nyakinyaki. Juat D.→SOUTHWEST PAMA-NYUNGAN
Nyakisasa. Ziba D.→NORTH EASTERN BANTU
Nyakyusa→CENTRAL EASTERN BANTU
Nyala→NORTH EASTERN BANTU
Nyala. Luhya D.→NORTH EASTERN BANTU
NYALI→NORTH EASTERN BANTU
Nyali. Huku D.→NORTH EASTERN BANTU
Nyali = Huku→NORTH EASTERN BANTU
Nyali. South = Bvanuma. Huku D.→NORTH

EASTERN BANTU
Nyamal→NGAYARDA
Nyamarl = Nyamal→NGAYARDA
Nyamatom = Nyangatom. Toposo D.→EAST-ERN SUDANIC
Nyambara = Nyangbara. Bari D.→EASTERN SUDANIC
Nyambo→NORTH EASTERN BANTU
Nyamel = Nyamal→NGAYARDA
Nyamkat = Mnyamskad. Central Tibetan D.→TIBETAN
Nyam-nyam = Zande→EASTERN
Nyamosa. Bambara D.→MANDE
Nyamtam. Basa Tr.→NORTH WESTERN BANTU
Nyamuka. Shona D.→SOUTH EASTERN BANTU
Nyamusa. Moro Kodo D.→CENTRAL SU-DANIC
Nyamwanga = Mwanga→CENTRAL EAST-ERN BANTU
Nyamwesi→NORTH EASTERN BANTU
Nyaneka→SOUTH WESTERN BANTU
Nyang→BANTOID
Nyang. Rek D.→EASTERN SUDANIC
Nyanga→NORTH EASTERN BANTU
Nyangamada = Nyangumarda→MARNGU
Nyangatom. Toposo D.→EASTERN SUDAN-IC
Nyangbara. Bari D.→EASTERN SUDANIC
Nyangbo→CENTRAL TOGO
Nyangeya. Teso D.→EASTERN SUDANIC
Nyangga = Njangga. Gayardilt D.→TANGKIC
Nyangia = Nyangeya. Teso D.→EASTERN SUDANIC
Nyangiya = Nuangeya→EASTERN SUDANIC
Nyangnori = Terik. Nandi D.→EASTERN SUDANIC
Nyangori = Terik. Nandi D.→EASTERN SUDANIC
Nyangumarda→MARNGU
Nyangwara = Nyangbara. Bari D.→EASTERN SUDANIC
Nyani. Minduuno D.→NORTH WESTERN BANTU
NYANJA→CENTRAL EASTERN BANTU
Nyanja→CENTRAL EASTERN BANTU
Nyankole→NORTH EASTERN BANTU
Nyankore = Nyankole→NORTH EASTERN BANTU
Nyanra. Iatmul D.→SEPIK
Nyanyamara. Kardutjara D.→WATI
Nyanyembe. Nyamwesi D.→NORTH EAST-ERN BANTU

Nyaŋga = Wirangu→SOUTHWEST PAMA-NYUNGAN

Nyao→NORTH PAPUAN

Nyara = Nyala→NORTH EASTERN BANTU

Nyarafoloro. Senari D.→GUR

Nyari = Huku→NORTH EASTERN BANTU

Nyaro. Fungor Tr.→KORDOFANIAN

Nyarong. Central Tibetan D.→TIBETAN

Nyaruanda = Ruanda—NORTH EASTERN BANTU

Nyarueng. Bor D.→EASTERN SUDANIC

Nyarweng = Nyarueng. Bor D.→EASTERN SUDANIC

Nyasa = Manda→CENTRAL EASTERN BANTU

Nyasa = Mpoto→CENTRAL EASTERN BANTU

Nyasa, Western = Tonga→CENTRAL EASTERN BANTU

Nyaturu = Remi→NORTH EASTERN BANTU

Nyatwe. Shona D.→SOUTH EASTERN BANTU

Nyefu = Nyepu. Bari D.→EASTERN SUDANIC

Nyekosa = Nyakyusa→CENTRAL EASTERN BANTU

Nyel = Niel. Padang D.→EASTERN SUDANIC

Nyele. Banda D.→EASTERN

Nyengo→SOUTH WESTERN BANTU

Nyenyege. Bobo D.→GUR

Nyeoze-Nee. Siriono D.→TUPI

Nyepo = Nyepu. Bari D.→EASTERN SUDANIC

Nyepu. Bari D.→EASTERN SUDANIC

Nyi→BURMESE-LOLO

NYI = LOLO PROPER→BURMESE-LOLO

Nyidi = Kwegu→EASTERN SUDANIC

Nyidini = Kwegu→EASTERN SUDANIC

Nyidu = Icen→JUKUNOID

Nyife = Luo→EASTERN SUDANIC

Nyigina→NYULNYULAN

Nyigini = Nyigina→NYULNYULAN

Nyiha→CENTRAL EASTERN BANTU

Nyika = Nika→NORTH EASTERN BANTU

Nyika = Nyiha→CENTRAL EASTERN BANTU

NYIKA-SAFWA→CENTRAL EASTERN BANTU

NYIKA-TAITA→NORTH EASTERN BANTU

Nyikorama = Tirma→EASTERN SUDANIC

Nyikyusa = Nyakyusa→CENTRAL EASTERN BANTU

Nyilem = Nielim→ADAMAWA

NYIMANG→EASTERN SUDANIC

Nyimang→EASTERN SUDANIC

Nyimaŋ = Nyimang→EASTERN SUDANIC

Nyimashi = Tera→CHADIC

Nyindu. Nyabungu D.→NORTH EASTERN BANTU

Nyinin. Djaru D.→NGUMBIN

Nyio = Nyo. High Lugbara D.→CENTRAL SUDANIC

Nyi-sing = Dafla→GYARUNG-MISHMI

Nyising = Dafla→GYARUNG-MISHMI

Nyixa = Nyiha→CENTRAL EASTERN BANTU

Nymylan = Koryak→CHUKCHEE-KAMCH-ATKAN

Nyo. High Lugbara D.→CENTRAL SUDANIC

Nyokon = Nyo'o→NORTH WESTERN BANTU

Nyole→NORTH EASTERN BANTU

Nyoli, North = Nyali. Huku D.→NORTH EASTERN BANTU

Nyolnyol = Nyulnyul→NYULNYULAN

Nyomi = Nyominka. Serer D.→WEST ATLANTIC

Nyominka. Serer D.→WEST ATLANTIC

Nyongnepa = Mumbake→ADAMAWA

Nyongwe. Shona D.→SOUTH EASTERN BANTU

Nyo'o→NORTH WESTERN BANTU

Nyoole = Nyole→NORTH EASTERN BANTU

Nyoolne = Njalgulgule→EASTERN SUDANIC

Nyore = Nyole→NORTH EASTERN BANTU

Nyoro→NORTH EASTERN BANTU

NYORO-GANDA→NORTH EASTERN BANTU

Nypho = Nyepu. Bari D.→EASTERN SUDANIC

Nyua-Bonde = Thuanga→NEW CALEDONIA

Nyuangia = Nuangeya→EASTERN SUDANIC

Nyubi. Karanga D.→SOUTH EASTERN BANTU

Nyu'bi = Nyubi. Karanga D.→SOUTH EASTERN BANTU

Nyule→NORTH EASTERN BANTU

Nyulnyul→NYULNYULAN

Nyul-Nyul = Nyulnyul→NYULNYULAN

NYULNYULAN see article

Nyunga = Juat→SOUTHWEST PAMA-NYUNGAN

NYUNGIC = SOUTHWEST PAMA-NYUNGAN

Nyungwe→CENTRAL EASTERN BANTU

Nyuong. Nuer D.→EASTERN SUDANIC

Nzaamba = Nzamba. Kongo D.→CENTRAL WESTERN BANTU

Nzakara→EASTERN

Nzamba. Kongo D.→CENTRAL WESTERN BANTU

Nzangi = Njai→CHADIC

Nzangyim = Njai→CHADIC

Nzebi→NORTH WESTERN BANTU

Nzema→VOLTA-COMOE

Nzhimamuŋgoŋ = Ngong. Kumaju D.→BANTOID

Nzikini = Njiniŋi, North Teke D.→NORTH WESTERN BANTU

Nziku = Ndzindzihu. Central Teke D.→ NORTH WESTERN BANTU

Nzima = Nzema→VOLTA-COMOE

Nzinzihu = Ndzindzihu. Central Teke D.→ NORTH WESTERN BANTU

Nzombo = Zombo. Kongo D.→CENTRAL WESTERN BANTU

Nzomboy. Ngbandi Tr.→EASTERN

Nzong = Nzonyu. Rengma D.→NAGA-KUKI-CHIN

Nzonyu. Rengma D.→NAGA-KUKI-CHIN

Nzuani = Njuani. Komoro D.→CENTRAL EASTERN BANTU

Nzwani = Njuani. Komoro D.→CENTRAL EASTERN BANTU

Ŋ

ŋ/ / = / /ŋ!ke. ŋ/huki D.→KHOISAN

ŋ/amani→KHOISAN

Ŋanasan = Tavgy→URALIC

Ŋandarec = Omo Murle. Murle Tr.→EASTERN SUDANIC

ŋ/ /-≠e = / /ŋ!ke. ŋ/huki D.→KHOISAN

Ŋee = Ngee. East Teke D.→NORTH WESTERN BANTU

ŋgalam = Boma Murle. Murle Tr.→EASTERN SUDANIC

Ŋguru. Kara D.→CENTRAL SUDANIC

ŋ/huki→KHOISAN

Ŋhwele = Nghwele→CENTRAL EASTERN BANTU

Ŋikaramojong = Karamojong→EASTERN SUDANIC

/ /ŋ!ke. ŋhuki D.→KHOISAN

Ŋkot = Nggoth→PAMA-MARIC

ŋ/u/ei = ŋ/u/ /en. ŋ/amani D.→KHOISAN

ŋ/u/ein = ŋ/u/ /en. ŋ/amani D.→KHOISAN

ŋ/u/ /en. ŋ/amani D.→KHOISAN

ŋ/usan. ŋ/amani D.→KHOISAN

Ŋwaketsi = Ngwaketse. Tswana D.→SOUTH EASTERN BANTU

ŋwatu = Nwato. Tswana D.→SOUTH EASTERN BANTU

ŋwullaro = Laro→KORDOFANIAN

O

Oa. Coronado Tr.→ANDEAN

Oba = Ogba. Igbo D.→IGBO

Obamba = Mbete→NORTH WESTERN BANTU

/ /obanen = Namib→KHOISAN

Obang. Ekoi D.→BANTOID

Obanliku→CROSS RIVER BENUE-CONGO

Obi→KUKUKUKU

Obi→EAST INDONESIAN

Obi = Vonkutu. Mamvu-Efe D.→CENTRAL SUDANIC

Obileba. Logo Tr.→CENTRAL SUDANIC

Obini. Agwagwune D.→CROSS RIVER BENUE-CONGO

Obispeno. CHUMASH Tr.→HOKAN

Obi-ye = Mvu'ba. Mamvu-Efe D.→CENTRAL SUDANIC

Objeboa = Ojibwa→ALGONQUIAN

Objibwa = Ojibwa→ALGONQUIAN

Objibwe = Ojibwa→ALGONQUIAN

Obo. Bagobo D.→NORTHWEST AUSTRONESIAN

Obose. Afrike D.→CROSS RIVER BENUE-CONGO

OB-UGRIC→URALIC

Obulom = Abulome→CROSS RIVER BENUE-CONGO

Obura. Tairora D.→EAST NEW GUINEA HIGHLANDS

Obwa. Bakwe D.→KRU

Ocaina→WITOTOAN

Occitan = Provencal→ROMANCE

OCEANIC see article

OCEANIC, EASTERN see article

Ochagbe = Afrike→CROSS RIVER BENUE-CONGO

Ochepwa = Ojibwa→ALGONQUIAN

Ochippeway = Ojibwa→ALGONQUIAN

Ochomazo = Uru→CHIPAYAN

oci-Kwanyama = Kwanyama→SOUTH WESTERN BANTU

oci-Ndonga = Ndonga→SOUTH WESTERN BANTU

Ocole. Vilela Tr.→LULE-VILELA-CHARRUA

Ocoroni. Cahita D.→UTO-AZTECAN

OCORONO→CHAPACURA-WANHAMAN

Ocoteguebo = Gotocogegodegi. Mbaya-Guaicuru Tr.→GUAYCURU

Ocotopec. Zoque D.→MIXE-ZOQUE

Octenai = Nocten. Mataco Tr.→MATACO
Ocuiltec→OTOMIAN
Ocuilteca = Ocuiltec→OTOMIAN
Ocuilteco = Ocuiltec→OTOMIAN
Ocute = Hitchiti→MUSKOGEAN
Odahwah = Ottawa. Ojibwa D.→ALGON-
QUIAN
Odiahuibe. Kawaib Tr.→TUPI
Odim. Agwagwune D.→CROSS RIVER BE-
NUE-CONGO
Odjibway = Ojibwa→ALGONQUIAN
Ododop→CROSS-RIVER BENUE-CONGO
Odri = Oriya→INDIC
Odschibwa = Ojibwa→ALGONQUIAN
Odual→CROSS RIVER BENUE-CONGO
Odul = Yukaghir→YUKAGHIR
Odut→CROSS RIVER BENUE-CONGO
Odyalombi-to = Lombi. Mangbetu D.→CEN-
TRAL SUDANIC
Odzila = Ojila. Avukaya Tr.→CENTRAL
SUDANIC
Odziliwa = Ojila. Avukaya Tr.→CENTRAL
SUDANIC
OERINGOEP = GREATER DANI→WEST
NEW GUINEA HIGHLANDS
Ofatura. Mbembe D.→CROSS RIVER BENUE-
CONGO
Ofaye = Opaie→MACRO-GE
Ofo→SIOUAN
Ofogoula = Ofo→SIOUAN
Ofumbongha. Mbembe D.→CROSS RIVER
BENUE-CONGO
Oga = Oya. Melanau D.→WEST INDONE-
SIAN
Ogalala = Oglala. Dakota D.→SIOUAN
Ogallah = Oglala. Dakota D.→SIOUAN
Ogallala = Oglala. Dakota D.→SIOUAN
Ogamaru. Logo Tr.→CENTRAL SUDANIC
Ogambi. Avukaya D.→CENTRAL SUDANIC
Ogar→EAST INDONESIAN
Ogba. Igbo D.→IGBO
Ogbah = Ogba. Igbo D.→IGBO
Ogbia→CROSS RIVER BENUE-CONGO
Ogbogolo→CROSS RIVER BENUE-CONGO
Ogbom. Ijo D.→IJO
Ogbonuagum = Bukuma→CROSS RIVER
BENUE-CONGO
Oghuz. Uzbek D.→TURKIC
OGHUZ = SOUTHERN TURKIC→TURKIC
Oghwe. Urhobo D.→EDO
Ogirut. .Khorcin D.→MONGOLIAN
Oglala. Dakota D.→SIOUAN
Ogllala = Oglala. Dakota D.→SIOUAN
Ogondyan→PAMA-MARIC

OGONI→CROSS RIVER BENUE-CONGO
Ogu Uku. Igbo D.→IGBO
Ogua. Engenni D.→EDO
Oguaiva = Oguiva. Tupi Tr.→TUPI
Oguana = Oguiva. Tupi Tr.→TUPI
Oguiva. Tupi Tr.→TUPI
Ogulagha. Ijo D.→IJO
Ogyukru = Adyukru→LAGOON
Ohana = Eghum. Mbembe D.→CROSS RIVER
BENUE-CONGO
Ohuhu-Ngwa. Igbo D.→IGBO
Oi→MON-KHMER
Oiana = Oyana→CARIB
Oigob = Maasai→EASTERN SUDANIC
Oikop = Maasai→EASTERN SUDANIC
Oikusi. Vaikenu D.→EAST INDONESIAN
Oirat→MONGOLIAN
Oirata→TIMOR-ALOR
Oirata see Kisar→MOLUCCAN
Oirya = Lokoya. Lotuho D.→EASTERN
SUDANIC
Oitai. Maasai Tr.→EASTERN SUDANIC
Oiumpian = Oyampi→TUPI
Ojebwa = Ojibwa→ALGONQUIAN
Ojibbewa = Ojibwa→ALGONQUIAN
Ojibbeway = Ojibwa→ALGONQUIAN
Ojibbwa = Ojibwa→ALGONQUIAN
Ojibua = Ojibwa→ALGONQUIAN
Ojibue = Ojibwa→ALGONQUIAN
Ojibwa→ALGONQUIAN
Ojibwauk = Ojibwa→ALGONQUIAN
Ojibway = Ojibwa→ALGONQUIAN
Ojibwemowin = Ojibwa→ALGONQUIAN
Ojiga = Ajiga. Avukaya Tr.→CENTRAL
SUDANIC
Ojila. Avukaya Tr.→CENTRAL SUDANIC
Ojipue = Ojibwa→ALGONQUIAN
OK see article
Oka. Buryat D.→MONGOLIAN
Oka. High Lugbara D.→CENTRAL SUDANIC
Okanagan = Okanogan→SALISH
Okanagon = Okanogan→SALISH
Okande = Kande→NORTH WESTERN
BANTU
Okandi. Buari D.→MAILU
Okanogan→SALISH
Okara = Lotiga. Mpalitjan D.→PAMA-MARIC
Oke'bu. Lendu D.→CENTRAL SUDANIC
Oke'buke = Oke'bu. Lendu D.→CENTRAL
SUDANIC
Okeina = Korape→BINANDERE
Okeina = Yega→BINANDERE
o-Kela = Kela→NORTH WESTERN BANTU
Okene Igbira = Igbira-Hima. Igbira D.→

NUPE-GBARI

Okiek = Akiek. Nandi D.→EASTERN SU-
DANIC

Okii = Boki→CROSS-RIVER BENUE-
CONGO

Okinagan = Okanogan→SALISH

Okinakan = Okanogan→SALISH

Okinaken = Okanogan→SALISH

Okinawan = Central Ryukyuan→JAPANESE

Okobo→CROSS RIVER BENUE-CONGO

Okonyong = Kiong→CROSS RIVER BENUE-
CONGO

Oko-Osanyin→KWA

Okordia. Ijo D.→IJO

Okorogung. Afrike D.→CROSS RIVER BE-
NUE-CONGO

Okorotung. Afrike D.→CROSS RIVER BE-
NUE-CONGO

Okos. Pawnee D.→CADDOAN

Okpamheri→EDO

Okpara-Agbado. Urhobo D.→EDO

Okpe. Aakwo or Urhobo D.→EDO

Okpeche = Afrike→CROSS RIVER BENUE-
CONGO

Okpela. Ivbie D.→EDO

Okpoto-Mteze. Oring D.→CROSS RIVER
BENUE-CONGO

Okrika. Ijo D.→IJO

Oksapmin→CENTRAL AND SOUTH NEW
GUINEA

Oku = Ukfwo→BANTOID

!O! kung = !o! uŋ→KHOISHAN

Okuni. Olulumo D.→CROSS RIVER BENUE-
CONGO

OKUNI = OGONI→CROSS RIVER BENUE-
CONGO

!O!kuŋ = !o!uŋ→KHOISAN

Okwoga. Idoma D.→IDOMA

Ol Ci Lotilla. Murle Tr.→EASTERN SUDANIC

Ola. Even D.→TUNGUS

Olal. North Ambryn D.→EASTERN OCEANIC

Olam = Murle→EASTERN SUDANIC

Olca→TUNGUS

Old Mfengu→SOUTH EASTERN BANTU

Olga = Jumjum. Mban D.→EASTERN SU-
DANIC

Oli→NORTH WESTERN BANTU

Oli = South Nkundo. Mongo-Nkundo D.→
NORTH WESTERN BANTU

Olkoi = Elkei→TORRICELLI

Ollari. Gadba D.→DRAVIDIAN

Ollom. Musei D.→CHADIC

Ol-Maa = Maasai→EASTERN SUDANIC

OLMECAN = POPOLOCAN

OLMECA-OTOMANGUE =OTO-MANGUE-
AN

Olo→TORRICELLI

Olodiama. Ijo D.→IJO

Oloibiri. Ogbia D.→CROSS RIVER BENUE-
CONGO

Olombo = Lombo→NORTH WESTERN
BANTU

Olomoro-Emede. Urhobo D.→EDO

Olomu. Urhobo D.→EDO

Olonetsian. Karelian D.→URALIC

Olotorit = Lotuho→EASTERN SUDANIC

Ol-tyamusi = Tiamus. Maasai D.→EASTERN
SUDANIC

Olu'bo. Ma'di D.→CENTRAL SUDANIC

Olubo-go = Olu'bo. Ma'di D.→CENTRAL
SUDANIC

Olubo-ti = Olu'bo. Ma'di D.→CENTRAL
SUDANIC

olu-Ciga = Ciga→NORTH EASTERN BANTU

Olue = Bobo Wule. Bobo D.→GUR

olu-Ganda = Ganda→NORTH EASTERN
BANTU

olu-Gaya = Gaya. Sese D.→NORTH EASTERN
BANTU

Olugwere = Gwere→NORTH EASTERN
BANTU

Oluhanga = Hanga. Luhya D.→NORTH
EASTERN BANTU

olu-Haya = Ziba→NORTH EASTERN
BANTU

olu-Konzo = Konzo→NORTH EASTERN
BANTU

olu-Kooki = Kooki→NORTH EASTERN
BANTU

Olulumo→CROSS-RIVER BENUE-CONGO

olu-Nyala = Nyala→NORTH EASTERN
BANTU

olu-Nyole = Nyole→NORTH EASTERN
BANTU

olu-Nyule = Nyule→NORTH EASTERN
BANTU

olu-Saamia = Saamia→NORTH EASTERN
BANTU

olu-Sese = Sese→NORTH EASTERN BANTU

olu-Soga = Soga→NORTH EASTERN
BANTU

Olut. Oirat D.→MONGOLIAN

Oluta→MIXE-ZOQUE

olu-Vuma = Vuma. Sese D.→NORTH EAST-
ERN BANTU

Oluwanga = Hanga. Luhya D.→NORTH
EASTERN BANTU

olu-Ziba = Ziba→NORTH EASTERN BANTU

OLYMPIC→SALISH
Omagua→TUPI
Omagua = Carijona→CARIB
Omaha. Dhegiha D.→SIOUAN
OMATE = OMETO→OMOTIC
Omavirre = Mambila→BANTOID
Omba→EASTERN OCEANIC
Ombi = Obi→EAST INDONESIAN
Ombila→PAMA-MARIC
Ombo→NORTH WESTERN BANTU
Omelokwe. Bakwe D.→KRU
Ometay = Kullo. Walamo D.→OMOTIC
OMETO→OMOTIC
Omo→BISMARCK ARCHIPELAGO
Omo Murle. Murle Tr.→EASTERN SUDANIC
Omoa. Buhagana Tr.→MACRO-TUCANOAN
Omoampa. Vilela Tr.→LULE-VILELA-CHAR-
    RUA
OMOTIC see article
Ompa = Tobaku→CENTRAL AND SOUTH-
    ERN CELEBES
Ompeila = Ombila→PAMA-MARIC
Ompela = Ombila→PAMA-MARIC
Omurano→ANDEAN
Omvang = Eki→NORTH WESTERN BANTU
Omyene = Galwa. Myene D.→NORTH WEST-
    ERN BANTU
ONA→VOLTA-COMOE
Ona→ANDEAN
ONA-CHON = CHON→ANDEAN
Onadagaish = Onandaga. Seneca Tr.→IRO-
    QUOIS
Onandaga. Seneca Tr.→IROQUOIS
Ondo. Yoruba D.→YORUBA
Ondoro→INDO-PACIFIC
Ondoumbo = Minduumo→NORTH WEST-
    ERN BANTU
Ondumbo = Minduumo→NORTH WESTERN
    BANTU
Oneida→IROQUOIS
Oneidah = Oneida→IROQUOIS
Oneider = Oneida→IROQUOIS
Onele = Oni→TORRICELLI
Oneydoe = Oneida→IROQUOIS
Ongabula = Kongabula. Mandandanji D.→
    PAMA-MARIC
Ongamo = Ngasa→EASTERN SUDANIC
Ong-Be→KAM-TAI
Onge. Jarawa D.→ANDAMANESE
Ongkonguru = Wongkanguru. Arabana D.→
    PAMA-NYUNGAN
Oni→TORRICELLI
Onian = Basari→WEST ATLANTIC
Onin→EAST INDONESIAN

Onitsha. Igbo D.→IGBO
Onjob→DAGA
Onnoiout = Oneida→IROQUOIS
Onnontague = Onandaga. Seneca Tr.→IRO-
    QUOIS
Ono→HUON-FINISTERRE
Ono. Siane D.→EAST NEW GUINEA HIGH-
    LANDS
Ono-Keto = Ono. Siane D.→EAST NEW
    GUINEA HIGHLANDS
Onondago = Onandaga. Seneca Tr.→IRO-
    QUOIS
Onontager = Onandaga. Seneca Tr.→IRO-
    QUOIS
Ontong Java = Luangiua→POLYNESIAN
Onua→NORTHWESTERN NEW HEBRIDES
Oohum = Boritsu→JUKUNOID
O'oku. Binahari D.→MAILU
Ooldea = Kukatja. Kardutjara D.→WATI
Ooldean = Ngalea. Kardutjara D.→WATI
Ooloopooloo = Karanya. Wangkadjera D.→
    PITTAPITTIC
Oonoomurra = Wanamara→MAYAPIC
Ooralim = Tangurong→KULINIC
Oorongir = Wurundjeri. Taungurong D.→
    KULINIC
Oosima = Northern Ryukyuan→JAPANESE
Opa = Kavelchadom. River Yuman D.→
    YUMAN
Opa = Maricopa. River Yuman D.→YUMAN
Opaie→MACRO-GE
Opaina. Yahuna D.→MACRO-TUCANOAN
Opata→UTO-AZTECAN
Opataice = Opata→UTO-AZTECAN
Opatoro. Lenca D.→MACRO-CHIBCHAN
Opaye = Opaie→MACRO-GE
Opaye Shavante = Opaie→MACRO-GE
Openango = Passamaquoddy→ALGONQUIAN
Operemar. Ijo D.→IJO
Operigua = Esperigua→NORTHERN MAI-
    PURAN
Opiaref. Biak D.→MOLUCCAN
Opon→CARIB
Oporoma. Ijo D.→IJO
Oporoza. Ijo D.→IJO
Opuhnarke = Delaware→ALGONQUIAN
Opunoho = Mantauran. Rukai D.→FORMO-
    SAN AUSTRONESIAN
Ora. Emai D.→EDO
!Ora = Korana→KHOISAN
Orabba = Worabba. Tebu Tr.→SAHARAN
Oradhi = Otati→PAMA-MARIC
Orai-iu→MAILU
Orang Benua. Lowland Semang D.→SEMANG

Orang Bukit. Southwestern Sakai D.→SAKAI
Orang Bukit = Bekiau. Bisaya D.→WEST INDONESIAN
Orang Bukit = Kadayan. Bisaya D.→WEST INDONESIAN
Orang Laut = Bajau→NORTHWEST AUSTRONESIAN
Orang Sungei = Bulud-Upi→NORTHWEST AUSTRONESIAN
Orang Tanjong. Central Sakai D.→SAKAI
Orangema = Kureinji. Maraura D.→NARRINYERIC
Orango. Bijago D.→WEST ATLANTIC
Oraon = Kurukh→DRAVIDIAN
Orarimugodoge = Eastern Bororo→BORORO
Orase = Gobeze. Gawwada D.→CUSHITIC
Orase = Werize. Gawwada. D.→CUSHITIC
Oratta-Ikwerri. Igbo D.→IGBO
Ordek-Burnu see article
Ordos→MONGOLIAN
Ore = Opata→UTO-AZTECAN
/oree. Shua D.→KHOISAN
/oreekhwe = /oree. Shua D.→KHOISAN
Oregon→WITOTOAN
Orepue = Urepo. Bakwe Tr.→KRU
Ori = Agi→TORRICELLI
Ori = Woro. Kresh D→CENTRAL SUDANIC
Oricen. Oroc D.→TUNGUS
Orierh→NORTHWESTERN NEW HEBRIDES
Oring→CROSS RIVER BENUE-CONGO
ORINOCO   ARAWAKAN→NORTHERN MAIPURAN
Oriomo = Gidra→ORIOMO RIVER
ORIOMO RIVER see article
Orisa. Tucurrike D.→CHIBCHAN
Orisi. Mangue D.→MANGUEAN
Oristine. Lule Tr.→LULE-VILELA-CHARRUA
Oriya→INDIC
Orlei = Olo→TORRICELLI
Orma. Galla D.→CUSHITIC
Ormu→SOUTH HALMAHERA AUSTRONESIAN
Ormuri→IRANIAN
Oro = Woro. Kresh D.→CENTRAL SUDANIC
Oroc→TUNGUS
Orocon→TUNGUS
Oroha→EASTERN OCEANIC
Orok→TUNGUS
Orokaiva→BINANDERE
Orokolo→TOARIPI
Orom. Teso D.→EASTERN SUDANIC
Oromo. Mansinyo D.→EQUATORIAL
Oromo = Galla→CUSHITIC

OROMOID→CUSHITIC
Oron→CROSS RIVER BENUE-CONGO
Oropai. Bamu Kiwai D.→CENTRAL AND SOUTH NEW GUINEA
Ororono→CHAPACURA-WANHAMAN
Orotina = Mangue→MANGUEAN
Orotina = Orotinya. Mangue D.→MANGUEAN
Orotinya. Mangue D.→MANGUEAN
Orra. Tama D.→EASTERN SUDANIC
Orri→IDOMA
Orri = Oring→CROSS RIVER BENUE-CONGO
Oru Lopiko→GOILALA
oru-Chiga = Ciga→NORTH EASTERN BANTU
oru-Hima = Hima→NORTH EASTERN BANTU
oru-Ndandi = Ndandi→NORTH EASTERN BANTU
Orungu = Rongo. Myene D.→NORTH WESTERN BANTU
oru-Nyankore = Nyankole→NORTH EASTERN BANTU
oru-Nyoro = Nyoro→NORTH EASTERN BANTU
Oruro = Aymara→ANDEAN
oru-Syan = Syan→NORTH EASTERN BANTU
oru-Tagwenda = Tagwenda. Nyankole D.→NORTH EASTERN BANTU
oru-Tooro = Toro→NORTH EASTERN BANTU
oru-Toro = Toro→NORTH EASTERN BANTU
Osage. Dhegiha D.→SIOUAN
Oscan→ITALIC
OSCO-UMBRIAN→ITALIC
Oser→AWYU
Oshikuanjama = Kwanyama→SOUTH WESTERN BANTU
Oshindonga = Ndonga→SOUTH WESTERN BANTU
Osidonga = Ndonga→SOUTH WESTERN BANTU
Osikuanjama = Kwanyama→SOUTH WESTERN BANTU
Osmanli = Turkish→TURKIC
Oso→BANTOID
Osopong. Mbembe D.→CROSS RIVER BENUE-CONGO
Ososo→EDO
Ossetic→IRANIAN
Ossipe = Ofo→SIOUAN

Osso = Oso→BANTOID
Ostrogoth. Gothic D.→GERMANIC
Ostuacan. Zoque D.→MIXE-ZOQUE
Ostyak→URALIC
Ostyak Samoyed→URALIC
Osuduku. Adangme D.→GA-ADANGME
Osum→BOGIA
Ot Balawan. Ot Danum D.→WEST INDO-
  NESIAN
Ot Banu'u. Ot Danum D.→WEST INDO-
  NESIAN
OT DANUM→WEST INDONESIAN
Ot Danum→WEST INDONESIAN
Ot Murung. Ot Danum D.→WEST INDO-
  NESIAN
Ot Olang Olang. Ot Danum D.→WEST
  INDONESIAN
Ot Siang. Ot Danum D.→WEST INDONESIAN
Ot Tuhup. Ot Danum D.→WEST INDO-
  NESIAN
Otamaca = Otamaco→EQUATORIAL
Otamaco→EQUATORIAL
Otangatomb = Bonek. Banen Tr.→NORTH
  WESTERN BANTU
Otati→PAMA-MARIC
Otchilpwe = Ojibwa→ALGONQUIAN
o-Tetela = Tetela→NORTH   WESTERN
  BANTU
Othan = Uduk→KOMAN
Othomi = Otomi→OTOMIAN
Oti→MACRO-GE
O-til'-tin = Kuchin→ATHAPASCAN-EYAK
Otjiherero = Herero→SOUTH WESTERN
  BANTU
Oto. CHIWERE D.→SIOUAN
OTO-HUAVE   see   OTO-MANGUEAN
Otok. Ordos D.→MONGOLIAN
OTO-MANGUEAN see article
OTOMANGUEAN, MACRO = OTO-MAN-
  GUEAN
Otomi→OTOMIAN
OTOMIAN see article
OTOMI-PAME = OTOMIAN
Otonabe = Muniche→MACRO-TUCANOAN
Otoro→KORDOFANIAN
Otschollo. Walamo Tr.→OMOTIC
Otta = Oto. CHIWERE D.→SIOUAN
Ottawa. Ojibwa D.→ALGONQUIAN
Ottawwaw = Ottawa. Ojibwa D.→ALGON-
  QUIAN
OTTILIEN→BOGIA
Otto = Oto. CHIWERE D.→SIOUAN
Ottoe = Oto. CHIWERE D.→SIOUAN
Ottowa = Ottawa. Ojibwa D.→ALGONQUIAN

OTUKE = BORORO
OTUKE = OTUQUE→BORORO
Otuke = Otuque→BORORO
Otukpa. Idoma D.→IDOMA
Otukpo. Idoma D.→IDOMA
OTUQUE→BORORO
OTUQUE = BORORO
Otuque→BORORO
OTUQUI = OTUQUE→BORORO
Otuxo = Lotuho→EASTERN SUDANIC
Otwa. Afenmai D.→EDO
Otyiherero = Herero→SOUTH WESTERN
  BANTU
Ouadda = Wada. Banda D.→EASTERN
Ouaddaien = Maba→MABAN
Ouagadougou. More D.→GUR
Ouala = Wara. Palara D.→GUR
Ouara = Wara. Palara D.→GUR
Ouargla→BERBER
Ouassa = Wasa. Banda D.→EASTERN
Ouatchi Watyi. Ewe D.→EWE
Ouaycone   Waiwai→CARIB
Oued Righ. Ouargla D.→BERBER
Ouen = Uen. Kwenyi D.→NEW CALEDONIA
Ouesperie = Ofo→SIOUAN
Ouispe = Ofo→SIOUAN
Oulof = Wolof→WEST ATLANTIC
!o!uŋ→KHOISAN
Ouobi = Bobwa. Bete D.→KRU
Outaouk = Ottawa. Ojibwa D.→ALGON-
  QUIAN
Outjanbah = Djinba→MURNGIC
Owaragees = Pennacook. Massachusett D.→
  ALGONQUIAN
Owe. Yoruba D.→YORUBA
Owerri. Igbo D.→IGBO
Owoi = Lokoya. Lotuho D.→WESTERN SU-
  DANIC
Oya. Melanau D.→WEST INDONESIAN
Oyampi→TUPI
Oyana→CARIB
Oyana. Gadsup D.→EAST NEW GUINEA
  HIGHLANDS
Oyda→OMOTIC
Oykangant. Kundjen D.→PAMA-MARIC
Oyo-Ibadan-Efe. Yoruba D.→YORUBA

                              P

Pa Mbai Daŋbo = Mbai→CENTRAL SU-
  DANIC
Pa Mbai Moisala = Mbai→CENTRAL SU-
  DANIC
Pa Pao. Lawa D.→PALAUNG-WA

Paama→EASTERN OCEANIC
Paani. Duru D.→ADAMAWA
Pabir = Babur. Bura Tr.→CHADIC
Pacahanova = Pacas Novas→CHAPACURA-WANHAMAN
Pacajan. Tenetehara Tr.→TUPI
Pacanaua. Jurua-Purus Tr.→PANO
Pacas Novas→CHAPACURA-WANHAMAN
PACAWARA→PANO
Pacaya. Peba D.→PEBA-YAGUAN
Pacer Band = Kiowa Apache→ATHAPASCAN-EYAK
Pachien. Puyuma D.→FORMOSAN AUSTRONESIAN
Pachuco. Spanish D.→ROMANCE
Pacoh→MON-KHMER
Pacu = Paioariene→NORTHERN MAIPURAN
Pada = Termanu. Roti D.→EAST INDONESIAN
Padaido. Biak D.→MOLUCCAN
Padang→EASTERN SUDANIC
Padas. Sarawak Murut D.→WEST INDONESIAN
Padaung. Bwe D.→KAREN
Padeng. Bwe D.→KAREN
Padhi = Pahri. Newari D.→GYARUNG-MISHMI
Padi→INDO-PACIFIC
Padlimiut = Barren Grounds Eskimo. Inuit D.→ESKIMO-ALEUT
Padoa. Biak D.→MOLUCCAN
Padoe. Mori D.→CENTRAL AND SOUTHERN CELEBES
Padogho = Padorho→GUR
Padoko = Podokwo→CHADIC
Padokwa = Podokwo→CHADIC
Padorho→GUR
Paduca = Comanche. Shoshoni D.→UTO-AZTECAN
Paduko = Podokwo→CHADIC
Padzulu. High Lugbara D.→CENTRAL SUDANIC
Paegan = Piegan. Blackfoot D.→ALGONQUIAN
Paelignian→ITALIC
Paez→INTER-ANDINE
PAEZ = PANAGUITAN→INTER-ANDINE
PAEZ-COCONUCO = INTER-ANDINE
Paəhət = Bompaka. Teressa D.→NICOBARESE
Pagbahan. Iraya D.→NORTHWEST AUSTRONESIAN
Pagei = Pagi→INDO-PACIFIC

Pagona. Southern Kiwai D.→CENTRAL AND SOUTH NEW GUINEA
Pagsupan. Mansaka D.→NORTHWEST AUSTRONESIAN
Pagu→NORTH HALMAHERA
Paguana. Omagua D.→TUPI
Paguara = Paguana. Omagua D.→TUPI
PAHARI→INDIC
Pahari, Western→INDIC
Pahari, Eastern = Nepali→INDIC
Pa-heng. Punu D.→MIAO-YAO
Pahi→SEPIK
Pahi. Pacoh D.→MON-KHMER
Pahi = Pahri. Newari D.→GYARUNG-MISHMI
Pahlavi. Persian D.→IRANIAN
Pahn = Krahn→KRU
Pahni = Pawnee→CADDOAN
Pahodja = Iowa. CHIWERE D.→SIOUAN
Pahouin. Faŋ D.→NORTH WESTERN BANTU
Pahri. Newari D.→GYARUNG-MISHMI
PAI→YUMAN
Pai→PLATEAU BENUE-CONGO
Pai→LEONARD SCHULTZE
Pai. Northern Sotho D.→SOUTH EASTERN BANTU
Pai = Pia→CHADIC
Paiawa = Paiwa. Guhu Samane D.→BINANDERE
Paichien = Pachien. Puyuma D.→FORMOSAN AUSTRONESIAN
Paici→NEW CALEDONIA
Paicoge→GE
Paiconeca. Chiquito D.→MAIPURAN
Paiela. Ipili D.→EAST NEW GUINEA HIGHLANDS
Paiem = Pyem→PLATEAU BENUE-CONGO
Paiguassu. Tupi Tr.→TUPI
Pain = Turuka→GUR
Painbali = Djadjala→KULINIC
Paioariene→NORTHERN MAIPURAN
Paipai→YUMAN
Paipi. Tangsa D.→BODO-NAGA-KACHIN
Paiquipiranga. Oyampi D.→TUPI
Paiquize = Munduruku→TUPI
Paite = Vuite→NAGA-KUKI-CHIN
Paithe = Vuite→NAGA-KUKI-CHIN
Paitsiana = Haisen. Saaroa D.→FORMOSAN AUSTRONESIAN
Paiute, Northern→UTO-AZTECAN
Paiute, Southern→UTO-AZTECAN
Paiwa. Guhu Samane D.→BINANDERE
Paiwan→FORMOSAN AUSTRONESIAN
PAIWANIC→FORMOSAN AUSTRONESIAN

Paiyi = Yunnan Shant'ou→KAM-TAI
Pajade = Badyara→WEST ATLANTIC
Pajadinca = Badyara→WEST ATLANTIC
Pajadinka = Badyara→WEST ATLANTIC
Pajalate = Coahuilteco→HOKAN
Pajo = Balaesan→NORTHERN CELEBES
Pajokumbuh. Minangkabau D.→WEST INDO-
    NESIAN
Pajulu = Pojulu. Bari D.→EASTERN SUDAN-
    IC
Pak→EASTERN OCEANIC
Pak→ADMIRALTY-WESTERN ISLANDS
Pakara = Chara→PLATEAU BENUE-CONGO
Pakatan = Beketan. Punan Ba D.→WEST
    INDONESIAN
Pakawa→HOKAN
Pakh'to. Pashto D.→IRANIAN
Pakhto = Peshwari. Pashto D.→IRANIAN
Pakhtoo = Pashto→IRANIAN
Pakishan→BURMESE-LOLO
Pakombe = Peri→NORTH EASTERN BANTU
Pakot = Pokot→EASTERN SUDANIC
Pakpak = Dairi→WEST INDONESIAN
Paku. Lawangan D.→WEST INDONESIAN
Pakuli. Palu D.→CENTRAL AND SOUTH-
    ERN CELEBES
Pakum = Kwakum→NORTH WESTERN
    BANTU
Pala→BISMARCK ARCHIPELAGO
Palaic→ANATOLIAN
PALAIHNIHAN see article
Palaka = Palara→GUR
Palank→CARIB
Palanskij. Alutor D.→CHUKCHEE-KAM-
    CHATKAN
Palara→GUR
Palatoŋ = Bedengo. Nyangumarda D.→
    MARNGU
Palauan→NORTHWEST AUSTRONESIAN
Palauan-Calavite. Iraya D.→NORTHWEST
    AUSTRONESIAN
PALAUNG-WA see article
Palawan = Palawano→NORTHWEST AUS-
    TRONESIAN
Palawanen = Palawano→NORTHWEST AUS-
    TRONESIAN
PALAWANIC→NORTHWEST AUSTRONE-
    SIAN
Palawano→NORTHWEST AUSTRONESIAN
Palaychi→KAREN
Pale. Bwe D.→KAREN
PALEI→TORRICELLI
Palenque = Palank→CARIB
Palenque = Patangoro→CARIB

PALEOSIBERIAN see article
Paleuyami = Poso Creek. Foothill North Yokuts
    D.→YOKUTS
Pali→INDIC
Palicur→MAIPURAN
Paliet. Rek D.→EASTERN SUDANIC
Palijur = Palicur→MAIPURAN
Palin = Embaloh→WEST INDONESIAN
Palioping = Palioupiny. Rek D.→EASTERN
    SUDANIC
Palioupiny. Rek D.→EASTERN SUDANIC
Palipa. Grebo Tr.→KRU
Paljgu = Bailko→NGAYARDA
PALKU = PITTAPITTIC
Pallakha = Palara→GUR
Palmar. Jicaque D.→HOKAN
Palmela→CARIB
Palmella = Palmela→CARIB
Palmer. Tupi D.→TUPI
Palmyrene. West Aramaic D.→SEMITIC
Paloc. Padang D.→EASTERN SUDANIC
Paloko. Enga D.→EAST NEW GUINEA
    HIGHLANDS
Palola = Phalura→INDIC
Palouse = Wanapam. Sahaptin D.→SAHAP-
    TIN-NEZ PERCE
Palu→CENTRAL AND SOUTHERN CELE-
    BES
Palula = Phalura→INDIC
Palyoupiny = Palioupiny. Rek D.→EASTERN
    SUDANIC
Pam. Baluan D.→ADMIRALTY-WESTERN
    ISLANDS
Pama→ARAWAKAN
Pama. Caripuna D.→PANO
Pama = Kulele→GUR
Pama, Bay = Lamalama→PAMA-MARIC
Pama, Gulf = Kunggara→PAMA-MARIC
PAMA, EASTERN→PAMA-MARIC
PAMA, MIDDLE→PAMA-MARIC
PAMA, NORTHERN→PAMA-MARIC
PAMA, SOUTHERN→PAMA-MARIC
PAMA, WESTERN→PAMA-MARIC
Pamaino→TACANA
PAMA-MARIC see article
Pamana = Pama→ARAWAKAN
Pamana = Pama. Caripuna D.→PANO
PAMA-NYUNGAN see article
PAMA-NYUNGAN, SOUTHWEST see article
Pamari = Paumari. Purupuru D.→ARAWA-
    KAN
Pambadeque = Kokamilla. Kokama D.→TUPI
Pambia→EASTERN
Pambuhan. Iraya D.→NORTHWEST AUS-

TRONESIAN

Pame→OTOMIAN

Pame-Chichimeca = Pame→OTOMIAN

Pamigua→EQUATORIAL

PAMIR→IRANIAN

Pammari = Paumari. Purupuru D.→ARAWA-KAN

Pamoa. Tucano Tr.→MACRO-TUCANOAN

Pamona→CENTRAL AND SOUTHERN CELEBES

Pampa = Puelche→ANDEAN

Pampangan→NORTHWEST AUSTRONE-SIAN

Pampanggan = Pampangan→NORTHWEST AUSTRONESIAN

Pampango = Pampangan→NORTHWEST AUSTRONESIAN

Pamue = Northern Faŋ. Faŋ D.→NORTH WESTERN BANTU

Pamunguup = Bomougoun-Bamenjou→BAN-TOID

Pamunkey. Powhatan Tr.→ALGONQUIAN

Pana→GUR

Pana. Kari D.→ADAMAWA

PANAGUITAN→INTER-ANDINE

Panakha-Panags. Central Tibetan D.→TIBE-TAN

Panakrusima→PAPUA AUSTRONESIAN

Panamaca = Panamaka. Sumo Tr.→MISU-MALPAN

Panamaka. Sumo Tr.→MISUMALPAN

Paname = Panhame→MACHACALI

Panamint. Shoshoni D.→UTO-AZTECAN

Panaras→NEW BRITAIN

Panari→CARIB

Panay = Aklanon→NORTHWEST AUS-TRONESIAN

Panayan = Ilonggo→NORTHWEST AUS-TRONESIAN

Panayati→PAPUA AUSTRONESIAN

Pancararu→EQUATORIAL

Pancaru = Pancararu→EQUATORIAL

Panche→CARIB

Pandai. Abui D.→TIMOR-ALOR

Pande→NORTH WESTERN BANTU

PANDE = NGUNDI→NORTH WESTERN BANTU

Pandikeri. Ma'di D.→CENTRAL SUDANIC

Pandjima. Bailko D.→NGAYARDA

Panga = Pianga. Busooŋ Tr.→NORTH WEST-ERN BANTU

Panga = South Nkundo. Mongo-Nkundo D.→ NORTH WESTERN BANTU

Pangan→SEMANG

Pangasinan→NORTHWEST AUSTRONESIAN

Pangerang = Bandjerang→PAMA-NYUNGAN

Pangkala→YURA

Pangkumu→NORTHWESTERN NEW HEB-RIDES

Pango→EASTERN OCEANIC

Pangtsah = Ami→FORMOSAN AUSTRO-NESIAN

Pangwa→CENTRAL EASTERN BANTU

Pangwe = Northern Faŋ. Faŋ D.→NORTH WESTERN BANTU

Panhame→MACHACALI

Pani. Kari D.→ADAMAWA

Pani = Pawnee→CADDOAN

Panikita = Paniquita→INTER-ANDINE

Panim→NORTHEASTERN NEW GUINEA

Paniquita→INTER-ANDINE

Panis = Wichita→CADDOAN

Panjabi→INDIC

Panjabi, Eastern = Panjabi→INDIC

Panjabi, Western = Lahnda→INDIC

Panjima = Pandjima. Bailko D.→NGAYARDA

Pankalla = Pangkala→YURA

Pankaravu = Pancararu→EQUATORIAL

Pankarla = Pangkala→YURA

Pankaroru = Pancararu→EQUATORIAL

Pankaru = Pancararu→EQUATORIAL

Pankhu→NAGA-KUKI-CHIN

PANOAN see article

PANOAN, MACRO see article

Panobo. Conibo D.→PANO

Panon. Duru D.→ADAMAWA

Pantara = Pantera→GUR

Pantera→GUR

Pany = Pawnee→CADDOAN

Panyame = Panhame→MACHACALI

Panyod = Jaara. Djadjala D.→KULINIC

Pa-o = Taungthu→KAREN

Pao = Taungthu→KAREN

Pao-an→MONGOLIAN

Papabieotan = Papago. Pima D.→UTO-AZTECAN

Papago. Pima D.→UTO-AZTECAN

Papaire = Metyibo→VOLTA-COMOE

Papantla. Totonac D.→TOTONACAN

Papar. Dusun D.→NORTHWEST AUSTRO-NESIAN

Papara. Senari D.→GUR

Pape→ADAMAWA

Papei = Papel→WEST ATLANTIC

Papel→WEST ATLANTIC

Paphlagonian see article

Papiamento→ROMANCE

Papitalai. Mokareng D.→ADMIRALTY-

WESTERN ISLANDS
Papora→FORMOSAN AUSTRONESIAN
PAPUAN = INDO-PACIFIC
PAPUAN, NORTH see article
PAPUAN, WEST = WESTERN NEW GUINEA
Papuantu = Babouartou→BANTOID
Papudo. Cahita D.→UTO-AZTECAN
Papuri. Macu D.→MACRO-TUCANOAN
Parachi→IRANIAN
Paraene = Yavitero→MAIPURAN
Parahuri. Waica Tr.→WAICAN
Parakana. Tenetehara D.→TUPI
Paramangk = Peramangk. Tanganekald D.→ NARRINYERIC
Paran. Seediq D.→FORMOSAN AUSTRO-NESIAN
PARANA→MAIPURAN
Parana, East = Guana→MAIPURAN
Parana, West = Chane→MAIPURAN
Paranapura = Muniche→MACRO-TUCA-NOAN
Paranauat = Pawate. Kawaib D.→TUPI
Paranawat = Pawate. Kawaib D.→TUPI
PARANILOTIC = NILO-HAMITIC→EAST-ERN SUDANIC
Paraua→MACRO-TUCANOAN
Parauhano = Paraujano→NORTHERN MAI-PURAN
Paraujano→NORTHERN MAIPURAN
Paravilhana = Paraviyana→CARIB
Paraviyana→CARIB
Parawa = Paraua→MACRO-TUCANOAN
Parawen→BOGIA
Paraxim→MACHACALI
Parb→CENTRAL AND SOUTH NEW GUINEA
Parbatiya = Nepali→INDIC
Pardoo = Bedengo. Nyangumarda D.→ MARNGU
Pare→PARE-SAMO-BEAMI-BOSAVI
Pare = Asu→CENTRAL EASTERN BANTU
Parec. Kate D.→HUON-FINISTERRE
Pareche = Paressi→MAIPURAN
Pareng = Gorum→MUNDA
Parenga = Gorum→MUNDA
Parengi = Gorum→MUNDA
Parenskij. Koryak D.→CHUKCHEE-KAM-CHATKAN
PARE-SAMO-BEAMI-BOSAVI see article
Paressi→MAIPURAN
Paressi Cabishi. Cozarini D.→MAIPURAN
PARESSI-SARAVECA→MAIPURAN
Pari. Anuak Tr.→EASTERN SUDANIC

Pari = Embaloh→WEST INDONESIAN
Pari = Munduruku→TUPI
Pari = Pare→PARE-SAMO-BEAMI-BOSAVI
Paria = Pariagoto→CARIB
Pariagoto→CARIB
Pari-bitete. Apiaka D.→TUPI
Parichy = Paiquipiranga. Oyampi D.→TUPI
Parigi = Tara→CENTRAL AND SOUTHERN CELEBES
Parimiteri. Waica Tr.→WAICAN
Parintintin. Kawaib D.→TUPI
Pariri. Chake D.→CARIB
Pariri =Timirem→CARIB
Parji→DRAVIDIAN
Parkengee = Bagundji. Kula D.→PAMA-NYUNGAN
Parkungi = Bagundji. Kula D.→PAMA-NYUNGAN
Parnkala = Pangkala→YURA
Parocana = Parakana. Tenetehara D.→TUPI
Parooinge = Parundji. Kula D.→PAMA-NYUNGAN
Parrano. Yameo D.→PEBA-YAGUAN
Parsi. Gujarati D.→INDIC
Parsi. Persian D.→IRANIAN
Parua = Kayabi→TUPI
Parucutu = Pianocoto→CARIB
Paruindi = Parundji. Kula D.→PAMA-NYUNGAN
Paruinji = Parundji. Kula D.→PAMA-NYUNGAN
Parukutu = Pianocoto→CARIB
Parundji. Kula D.→PAMA-NYUNGAN
Paruni = Wasi-weri→NURISTANI
Pasa. Ganglau D.→INDO-PACIFIC
Pasai→INDIC
Pasain. Vilela Tr.→LULE-VILELA-CHARRUA
Pasamaquoddice = Passamaquoddy→ALGON-QUIAN
Pasaramona→TACANA
Pascuenese = Easter Island→POLYNESIAN
Pase. Achinese D.→WEST INDONESIAN
Pase = Passe→NORTHERN MAIPURAN
Pashtoo→IRANIAN
Pashtu = Pashto→IRANIAN
Pasi. Mongondow D.→NORTHERN CELEBES
Passam. Yendang D.→ADAMAWA
Passamaquoddy→ALGONQUIAN
Passe→NORTHERN MAIPURAN
Passto = Pashto→IRANIAN
PASTO→BARBACOAN
Pasto→BARBACOAN
Pastoco = Patoco→EQUATORIAL
Paswam = Agob→AGOB

Patacho→MACRO-GE
Patagon→CARIB
Patamona. Acawai D.→CARIB
Patangoro→CARIB
Patani. Gujarati D.→INDIC
Patano→SOUTH HALMAHERA AUSTRO-
 NESIAN
Pataquilla. Karankawa Tr.
Patasho = Patacho→MACRO-GE
Patchəag = Montauk. Mohegan D.→ALGON-
 QUIAN
Patchogue. Mohegan Tr.→ALGONQUIAN
Patchogue = Montauk. Mohegan D.→ALGON-
 QUIAN
Pate. Swahili D.→CENTRAL EASTERN
 BANTU
Pati. Gyarung D.→GYARUNG-MISHMI
Pati = Paici→NEW CALEDONIA
Patia→BARBACOAN
Patidari. Gujarati D.→INDIC
Patimaya. Wadjeri D.→KARDU
Patimuni = Baham→WESTERN NEW GUI-
 NEA
Patipi→EAST INDONESIAN
Patni = Manchati→GYARUNG-MISHMI
Patnuli. Gujarati D.→INDIC
Patoco→EQUATORIAL
Patool. Gula D.→ADAMAWA
Patoro. Senari D.→GUR
Patpatar = Pala→BISMARCK ARCHIPEL-
 AGO
Patra-Saara = Juang→MUNDA
Patri Sueh-meridi. Zande D.→EASTERN
Patsaval = Tachaban. Paiwan D.→FORMO-
 SAN AUSTRONESIAN
Patsavan = Tachaban. Paiwan D.→FORMO-
 SAN AUSTRONESIAN
Patta = Pate. Swahili D.→CENTRAL EAST-
 ERN BANTU
Patu. Kongo D.→CENTRAL WESTERN
 BANTU
Patua = Juang→MUNDA
Patunc = Maya→MAYAN
Patusi. Mok D.→ADMIRALTY-WESTERN
 ISLANDS
Patwin→WINTUN
Patyala = Batjala. Dalla D.→WAKA-KABIC
Pau D'arco→GE
Pauchi = Pauxi→CARIB
Pauchiana→CARIB
Paucura. Caura Tr.→CARIB
Paulohi→MOLUCCAN
Pauma = Paama→EASTERN OCEANIC
Paumari. Purupuru D.→ARAWAKAN

Pa'umotuan = Tuamotuan→POLYNESIAN
Paunaca. Chiquito D.→MAIPURAN
Paunangis. Tongoa D.→EASTERN OCEANIC
Paurong. Central Tibetan D.→TIBETAN
Pauserna→TUPI
Paushiana = Paushiana→CARIB
Paushuk. Pawnee D.→CADDOAN
Pauwi→MOMBERAMO RIVER
Pauxi→CARIB
Pava. Omurano Tr.→ANDEAN
Paviotso = Northern Paiute→UTO-AZTECAN
PAWAIA→EAST NEW GUINEA HIGH-
 LANDS
Pawate. Kawaib D.→TUPI
Pawne = Pawnee→CADDOAN
Pawnee→CADDOAN
Pawnee, Black = Wichita→CADDOAN
Pawnee Picts = Pawnee→CADDOAN
Pawni = Pawnee→CADDOAN
Pa-wu = Pa-heng. Punu D.→MIAO-YAO
Pawumwa = Uanham→CHAPACURA-WAN-
 HAMAN
Pawututjara. Kardutjara D.→WATI
Paxala = Vagala→GUR
Pay→BOGIA
Paya→MACRO-CHIBCHAN
Payagua. Mbaya-Guaicuru Tr.→GUAYCURU
Payagua = Coto→MACRO-TUCANOAN
Payawa = Paiwa. Guhu Samane D.→BINAN-
 DERE
Payira. Akoli Tr.→EASTERN SUDANIC
Payniken. Chon D.→ANDEAN
Payualiene = Paioariene→NORTHERN MAI-
 PURAN
Pazaine = Pasain. Vilela Tr.→LULE-VILELA-
 CHARRUA
Pazeh→FORMOSAN AUSTRONESIAN
Pazehe = Pazeh→FORMOSAN AUSTRO-
 NESIAN
Pazeh-Kahabu = Pazeh→FORMOSAN AUS-
 TRONESIAN
Pazend. Persian D.→IRANIAN
Pazzehe = Pazeh→FORMOSAN AUSTRONE-
 SIAN
Pea = Hula. Ewe Tr.→EWE
Peana. Pipikoro D.→CENTRAL AND
 SOUTHERN CELEBES
Pear→MON-KHMER
PEARIC→MON-KHMER
Peaux-de-Lievres = Hare. Dogrib Tr.→ATHA-
 PASCAN-EYAK
Peba→PEBA-YAGUAN
PEBAN = PEBA-YAGUAN
Pebas. Yagua D.→PEBA-YAGUAN

Pebato. Bare'e D.→CENTRAL AND SOUTH-
ERN CELEBES
PEBA-YAGUAN see article
Pecixe = Yu. Manjaku D.→WEST ATLANTIC
Pecos. Towa D.→TANOAN
Peda. Ewe Tr.→EWE
Peda = Kadara→PLATEAU BENUE-CONGO
Pedi. Northern Sotho D.→SOUTH EASTERN
BANTU
Pedi = Northern Sotho→SOUTH EASTERN
BANTU
Pedir = Pidie. Achinese D.→WEST INDONE-
SIAN
Pediwang. Tobelo D.→NORTH HALMAHERA
Pedong = Bedengo. Nyangumarda D.→
MARNGU
Pedra Branca. Cariri D.→EQUATORIAL
Pedraza. Tunebo D.→CHIBCHAN
Peechera = Pitjara. Mandandanji D.→PAMA-
MARIC
Peedona = Bedengo. Nyangumarda D.→
MARNGU
Peedong = Bedengo. Nyangumarda D.→
MARNGU
Peeita = Ngaiawang. Nganguruku D.→NAR-
RINYERIC
Pegu = Mon Tang. Mon D.→MON-KHMER
Peguan = Mon→MON-KHMER
Peguenche = Pehuenche. Araucanian D.→
PENUTIAN
Pegullobura = Yidin. Wakaman D.→PAMA-
MARIC
Pegulloburra = Ilba→PAMA-MARIC
Pehtsek = Karok→HOKAN
Pehtsik = Karok→HOKAN
Pehuenche→HUARPE
Pehuenche. Araucanian D.→PENUTIAN
Pei = Mandarin→CHINESE
Pein = Pyem→PLATEAU BENUE-CONGO
Pekawa→CENTRAL AND SOUTHERN
CELEBES
Pelam = Puyuma→FORMOSAN AUSTRO-
NESIAN
Peleata→BISMARCK ARCHIPELAGO
Peleata = Uasi→NEW BRITAIN
Peli. Mok D.→ADMIRALTY-WESTERN IS-
LANDS
Pella = Kilba→CHADIC
Pelones see UTO-AZTECAN
Pemba→CENTRAL EASTERN BANTU
Pemeno→CARIB
Pemon = Arecuna→CARIB
Penasifu. Biak D.→MOLUCCAN
Penchangau. Bolongan D.→NORTHWEST
AUSTRONESIAN
Pend d'Oreilles. Kalispel D.→SALISH
PENDE→CENTRAL WESTERN BANTU
Pende→CENTRAL WESTERN BANTU
Pendia = Bonkeng→NORTH WESTERN
BANTU
Pends d'Oreilles = Pend d'Oreilles. Kalispel
D.→SALISH
P'eng = Pheng→KHMUIC
Pengo→DRAVIDIAN
Peni = Nar. Sara D.→CENTRAL SUDANIC
Penihing. Kayan D.→WEST INDONESIAN
Penin = Banen→NORTH WESTERN BANTU
Penjabung. Land Dayak D.→WEST INDO-
NESIAN
Pennacook. Massachusett D.→ALGONQUIAN
Penobscot→ALGONQUIAN
Penobscotice = Penobscot→ALGONQUIAN
Penoki = Penyoqui→CHIQUITO
Penokikia = Penyoqui→CHIQUITO
Penonomenyo. Guaymi D.→CHIBCHAN
Penrhyn→POLYNESIAN
Pentaguot = Penobscot→ALGONQUIAN
Pentlash = Pentlatch→SALISH
Pentlatc = Pentlatch→SALISH
Pentlatch→SALISH
PENUTIAN see article
Penyabung Punan = Penjabung. Land Dayak
D.→WEST INDONESIAN
Penyin = Banen→NORTH WESTERN BAN-
TU
Penyoqui→CHIQUITO
Peoplemen = Pibelmen. Juat D.→SOUTH-
WEST PAMA-NYUNGAN
Peoria = Illinois. Miami D.→ALGONQUIAN
Pepeha→CENTRAL AND SOUTH NEW
GUINEA
Pepel = Papel→WEST ATLANTIC
Pepicokia = Miami→ALGONQUIAN
Pepohwan. Hoanya D.→FORMOSAN AUS-
TRONESIAN
Pepuchi = Macamecran→GE
Pequot. Mohegan D.→ALGONQUIAN
Peramangk. Tanganekald D.→NARRINYERIC
Peramarma = Peramangk. Tanganekald D.→
NARRINYERIC
Peran. Southern Kiwai D.→CENTRAL AND
SOUTH NEW GUINEA
Pere = Kpere. Kari D.→ADAMAWA
Pere = Peri→NORTH EASTERN BANTU
Pereba = Wom→ADAMAWA
Peremka→CENTRAL AND SOUTH NEW
GUINEA
Peri→NORTH EASTERN BANTU

Peri. Shona D.→SOUTH EASTERN BANTU
Pericu→WAICURIAN
PERMIC→URALIC
Pero→CHADIC
Persian→IRANIAN
Pesatupe. Mataguayo Tr.→MATACO
Pesechem. Grand Valley Dani D.→WEST
NEW GUINEA HIGHLANDS
Pesegem = Pesechem. Grand Valley Dani D.→
WEST NEW GUINEA HIGHLANDS
Peseghem = Pesechem. Grand Valley Dani D.→
WEST NEW GUINEA HIGHLANDS
Peshera = Enoo. Alacaluf D.→ANDEAN
Peshkwaus = Columbian→SALISH
Peshwari. Pashto D.→IRANIAN
Pessa = Kpelle→MANDE
Pessi = Kpelle→MANDE
Pessy = Kpelle→MANDE
Peta. Nyanja D.→CENTRAL EASTERN
BANTU
Petapa→NORTHERN CELEBES
Petasia. Mori D.→CENTRAL AND SOUTH-
ERN CELEBES
Petats→NORTHWESTERN AND CENTRAL
SOLOMONS
Peten = Maya→MAYAN
Peterei→NORTHEAST NEW GUINEA AUS-
TRONESIAN
Peth. Rek. D.→EASTERN SUDANIC
Petun = Tionontati. Wyandot D.→IROQUOIS
Peul = Ful→WEST ATLANTIC
Peve. Dari D.→CHADIC
Pevekskij. Chukchee D.→CHUKCHEE-KAM-
CHATKAN
Pewenche = Pehuenche. Araucanian D.→
PENUTIAN
Pǝlhilh = Yu. Manjaku D.→WEST ATLANTIC
Pǝtani. Pangan D.→SEMANG
Pfokomo = Pokomo→NORTH EASTERN
BANTU
Pfunde. Shona D.→SOUTH EASTERN
BANTU
Pgha K'nyan = Sgaw→KAREN
Phadang. Tangkul D.→NAGA-KUKI-CHIN
Phalaborwa = Phalaburwa. Northern Sotho
D.→SOUTH EASTERN BANTU
Phalaburwa. Northern Sotho D.→SOUTH
EASTERN BANTU
Phalura→INDIC
Phana→BURMESE-LOLO
Phani. Vende D.→SOUTH EASTERN BANTU
Phatu. Kongo D.→CENTRAL WESTERN
BANTU
Phemba = Pemba→CENTRAL EASTERN

BANTU
Pheng→KHMUIC
Phi Taung Luang = Tong-luang→KHMUIC
PHILIPPINE→NORTHWEST AUSTRONE-
SIAN
Philip's Indians = Wampanoag. Massachusett
D.→ALGONQUIAN
Pho→KAREN
Phoenician→SEMITIC
Phoka = Poka. Tumbuka D.→CENTRAL
EASTERN BANTU
Phong = Pheng→KHMUIC
Phosko. Northern Mao D.→KOMAN
Phrygian→INDO-EUROPEAN
Phu Thai→KAM-TAI
Phuan→KAM-TAI
Phuang→MON-KHMER
PHUNOI→BURMESE-LOLO
Phunoi→BURMESE-LOLO
Phuong = Phuang.→MON-KHMER
Phuong Katu = Katu→MON-KHMER
Phupha→BURMESE-LOLO
Phuthi. Southern Sotho D.→SOUTH EASTERN
BANTU
Pia→CHADIC
Pia = Pya. Bakwe D.→KRU
Piame→SEPIK
Pia-min. Mien D.→MIAO-YAO
Pianga. Busooŋ Tr.→NORTH WESTERN
BANTU
Piankashaw = Miami→ALGONQUIAN
Pianocoto→CARIB
Piapoco→NORTHERN MAIPURAN
PIAPOCOAN→NORTHERN MAIPURAN
Piaroa→EQUATORIAL
PIAROAN = SALIVAN→EQUATORIAL
Pibelmen. Juat D.→SOUTHWEST PAMA-
NYUNGAN
Pibor Murle = Ol Ci Lotilla. Murle Tr.→
EASTERN SUDANIC
Picara. Cauca Tr.→CARIB
Pichaba = Pichobo→PANO
Pichi Huilliche. Araucanian D.→PENUTIAN
Pichobo→PANO
Pickumbil = Bigumbil→WIRADJURIC
Picones = Picunche. Araucanian D.→PENU-
TIAN
Picoris = Picuris. Tiwa D.→TANOAN
Pictish see CELTIC
Picts = Pawnee→CADDOAN
Picunche. Araucanian D.→PENUTIAN
Picuris. Tiwa D.→TANOAN
Pi-da. Lendu D.→CENTRAL SUDANIC
Pidgin, Cameroons = Wescos→GERMANIC

Pidgin English = Krio→GERMANIC
Pidgin Krio = Krio→GERMANIC
Pidie. Achinese D.→WEST INDONESIAN
Pidunga = Bedengo. Nyangumarda D.→MAR-
    NGU
Pie = Pya. Bakwe D.→KRU
Piegan. Blackfoot D.→ALGONQUIAN
Pieta = Ngaiawang.   Nganguruku   D.→
    NARRINYERIC
Piggatan→NORTHWEST AUSTRONESIAN
PIHOM→BOGIA
Pihtadyovoc. Seta D.→TUPI
Pijao→CARIB
Pikambal = Bigumbil→WIRADJURIC
Pikambul = Bigumbil→WIRADJURIC
Piki→SOUTH EASTERN BANTU
Pikumbul = Bigumbil→WIRADJURIC
Pila→GUR
Pila→BOGIA
Piladapa = Pilatapa→DIERIC
Pilaga. Toba Tr.→GUAYCURU
Pilam = Pinan.   Puyuma   D.→FORMOSAN
    AUSTRONESIAN
Pilam = Puyuma→FORMOSAN AUSTRO-
    NESIAN
Pilapila→GUR
Pilatapa→DIERIC
Pileni→POLYNESIAN
Pilheni = Pileni→POLYNESIAN
Pili = Peri→NORTH EASTERN BANTU
Pililo→BISMARCK ARCHIPELAGO
Pilimdi = Hina→CHADIC
Pillager = Ojibwa→ALGONQUIAN
Pillatapa = Pilatapa→DIERIC
Pilliapp = Pilatapa→DIERIC
Pilu. Kantu D.→MON-KHMER
Pima→UTO-AZTECAN
Pima, Lower = Pima Bajo→UTO-AZTECAN
Pima Bajo→UTO-AZTECAN
Pimbwe→CENTRAL EASTERN BANTU
Pime = Pima→UTO-AZTECAN
Pimenteira→CARIB
Pimeria = Pima→UTO-AZTECAN
PIMIC→UTO-AZTECAN
Pimo = Pima→UTO-AZTECAN
Pin = Turuka→GUR
Pinan. Puyuma D.→FORMOSAN AUSTRO-
    NESIAN
Pinche. Omurano Tr.→ANDEAN
Pindi = Kwese→CENTRAL WESTERN BAN-
    TU
Pindi = Pende→CENTRAL WESTERN BAN-
    TU
Pindiini. Kardutjara D.→WATI

Pingelap. Ponapean D.→MICRONESIAN
Pingfang→SINO-TIBETAN
Pini. Kardutjara D.→WATI
Pinjarra = Pinjarup. Juat D.→SOUTHWEST
    PAMA-NYUNGAN
Pinjarup. Juat D.→SOUTHWEST PAMA-
    NYUNGAN
Pinje. Nemi D.→NEW CALEDONIA
Pinji = Pende→CENTRAL   WESTERN
    BANTU
Pintubi. Kardutjara D.→WATI
Pintupi = Pintubi. Kardutjara D.→WATI
Pintwa = Kureinji. Maraura D.→NARRIN-
    YERIC
Pinukpuk→NORTHWEST AUSTRONESIAN
Pinyin. Awing D.→BANTOID
Pinyoca. Penyoqui D.→CHIQUITO
Pioche = Pioje. Pioje-Sioni Tr.→MACRO-
    TUCANOAN
Piocobge→GE
Pioje. Pioje-Sioni Tr.→MACRO-TUCANOAN
Pioje-Sioni→MACRO-TUCANOAN
Pipikoro→CENTRAL   AND   SOUTHERN
    CELEBES
Pipil→UTO-AZTECAN
Pirataguari. Tupi Tr.→TUPI
Piratapuyo.   Tucano   Tr.→MACRO-TUCA-
    NOAN
Pirdima = Southern Aranda. Iliaura D.→
    ARANDIC
Piria = Bidia. Karendala D.→DIERIC
Piritu→CARIB
Pirniritjara = Pini. Kardutjara D.→WATI
Piro→TANOAN
Piro→MAIPURAN
Piro see TANOAN
Pirtkopannoot = Tjapwurong→KULINIC
Piru. Luhu D.→EAST INDONESIAN
Pirupiru. Bamu Kiwai D.→CENTRAL AND
    SOUTH NEW GUINEA
Pisa→AWYU
Pisabo = Pichobo→PANO
Piscataway = Conoy. Mohegan D.→ALGON-
    QUIAN
Piscimas = Bhojpuri. Bihari D.→INDIC
Pisidian see article
Pisirami→CENTRAL AND SOUTH NEW
    GUINEA
Piskwaus = Columbian→SALISH
Pisobo = Pichobo→PANO
Pispi. Sumo Tr.→MISUMALPAN
Pit River = Achumawi→PALAIHNIHAN
Pitahauerat. Pawnee D.→CADDOAN
Pitapita = Pittapitta. Wangkadjera D.→PIT-

TAPITTIC
Pitaquari = Pirataguari. Tupi Tr.→TUPI
Pitcairnese→GERMANIC
Pite Lapp→URALIC
Piti→PLATEAU BENUE-CONGO
Pitjandjadjara = Pitjantjatjara. Kardutjara D.→ WATI
Pitjandjara = Pitjantjatjara. Kardutjara D.→ WATI
Pitjantjatjara. Kardutjara D.→WATI
Pitjanzazara = Pitjantjatjara. Kardutjara D.→ WATI
Pitjara. Mandandanji D.→PAMA-MARIC
Pitjara = Bitjara. Punthamara D.→DIERIC
Pitjindjatjara = Pitjantjatjara. Kardutjara D.→ WATI
Pitjindjiara = Pitjantjatjara. Kardutjara D.→ WATI
Pitkindjara = Pitjantjatjara. Kardutjara D.→ WATI
Pitonara = Potiguara. Tupi D.→TUPI
Pitsubo = Pichobo→PANO
Pitt River = Achumawi→PALAIHNIHAN
Pitta = Ngaiawang. Nganguruku D.→NAR-RINYERIC
Pittapitta. Wangkadjera D.→PITTAPITTIC
PITTAPITTIC see article
Pitti = Piti→PLATEAU BENUE-CONGO
Pitu Uluna Salu = Pitu-ulunna-salu→CEN-TRAL AND SOUTHERN CELEBES
Pitu-ulunna-salu→CENTRAL AND SOUTH-ERN CELEBES
Pityilu→ADMIRALTY-WESTERN ISLANDS
Piura. Sec D.→ANDEAN
Piva→NORTHWESTERN AND CENTRAL SOLOMONS
Pizdar. Kermanji D.→IRANIAN
Plain Country→OK
Plapo = Plawi. Bakwe Tr.→KRU
PLATEAU = PLATEAU BENUE-CONGO
PLATEAU-SAHEL = WEST CHADIC→ CHADIC
Plats-Cotes-de-Chien = Dogrib→ATHAPAS-CAN-EYAK
Plattdeutsch. Netherlandic-German D.→GER-MANIC
Plawi. Bakwe Tr.→KRU
Playano. Salinan Tr.→HOKAN
Plus. Semang Proper D.→SEMANG
Pnar = Synteng. Khasi D.→MON-KHMER
Pnom Gar = Gar. Eastern Mnong D.→MON-KHMER
Pnong = Central Mnong→MON-KHMER
Po-ai→KAM-TAI

Poai. Nemi D.→NEW CALEDONIA
Poamei = Pwamei→NEW CALEDONIA
Poapoa→NEW CALEDONIA
Poavosa = Babuza D.→FORMOSAN AUS-TRONESIAN
Pochutla→UTO-AZTECAN
Pocomchi = Pokonchi→MAYAN
Poconcham = Pokonchi→MAYAN
Poconchice = Pokonchi→MAYAN
Pocosi Talamanca. Bribri D.→CHIBCHAN
Podawahdmih = Potawatomi→ALGONQUIAN
Podokana→NORTHWESTERN AND CEN-TRAL SOLOMONS
Podokwo→CHADIC
Podunk = Wappinger. Mohegan D.→ALGON-QUIAN
Podzo→CENTRAL EASTERN BANTU
Pogara. Senari D.→GUR
POGOLO→CENTRAL EASTERN BANTU
Pogolo→CENTRAL EASTERN BANTU
Pogoro = Pogolo→CENTRAL EASTERN BANTU
Pohi Eja. Sanana D.→EAST INDONESIAN
Poianaua. Jurua-Purus Tr.→PANO
Poica. Yiporok D.→BOTOCUDO
Poidgerry = Badjiri→DIERIC
Pojoaque. Tewa D.→TANOAN
Pojuaque = Pojoaque. Tewa D.→TANOAN
Pojuate = Pojoaque. Tewa D.→TANOAN
Pojulu. Bari D.→EASTERN SUDANIC
Pok. Nandi D.→EASTERN SUDANIC
P'OK = KACHIN→BODO-NAGA-KACHIN
Poka. Tumbuka D.→CENTRAL EASTERN BANTU
Poka = Boga. Tera D.→CHADIC
Pokau = Lala→PAPUA AUSTRONESIAN
Poke→NORTH WESTERN BANTU
Po-Klo. Northern Sakai D.→SAKAI
Poko = Bapoko. Batanga D.→NORTH WEST-ERN BANTU
Pokoh = Pacoh→MON-KHMER
Pokom see MAYAN
Pokomo→NORTH EASTERN BANTU
Pokonchi→MAYAN
Pokonchine = Pokonchi→MAYAN
Pokonchini = Pokonchi→MAYAN
Pokot→EASTERN SUDANIC
Pokwot = Pokot→EASTERN SUDANIC
Pol. Pol-Pomo D.→NORTH WESTERN BANTU
Pola. Tuburi D.→CHADIC
Pola = Pula→NORTHWEST AUSTRONE-SIAN
Polabian→SLAVIC

Pole see MENDI
Poleo→EASTERN OCEANIC
Poli = Pol. Pol-Pomo D.→NORTH WESTERN
  BANTU
Polindaro→INTER-ANDINE
Polish→SLAVIC
Polo. Tsaiwa D.→BODO-NAGA-KACHIN
Poloic = Paloc. Padang D.→EASTERN SU-
  DANIC
Polopa→EAST NEW GUINEA HIGHLANDS
Pol-Pomo→NORTH WESTERN BANTU
POLYNESIAN see article
Pom. Japen D.→MOLUCCAN
POMO see article
Ponam→ADMIRALTY-WESTERN ISLANDS
Ponapean→MICRONESIAN
Ponca. Dhegiha D.→SIOUAN
Poncatage→GE
Ponda = Lucazi→SOUTH WESTERN BANTU
Pondo. Kari D.→ADAMAWA
Pondo — Angoram→NORTH NEW GUINEA
Pondoma→BOGIA
Ponek = Bonek. Banen Tr.→NORTH WEST-
  ERN BANTU
Poneriven = Paici→NEW CALEDONIA
Poneriwen = Paici→NEW CALEDONIA
Pongo→PLATEAU BENUE-CONGO
Pongo-Mongo = Pongo-Mungo→NORTH
  WESTERN BANTU
Pongo-Mungo→NORTH WESTERN BANTU
Pongoue = Mpongwe. Myene D.→NORTH
  WESTERN BANTU
Pongu = Pongo→PLATEAU BENUE-CONGO
Ponna = Meithei→NAGA-KUKI-CHIN
Pono = Wandjiwalku. Kula D.→PAMA-
  NYUNGAN
Ponorwal. South Raga D.→EASTERN OCEAN-
  IC
Ponosakan. Mongondow D.→NORTHERN
  CELEBES
Ponta→GE
Ponthai. Tangsa D.→BODO-NAGA-KACHIN
Pontic see article
PONTO-CASPIAN→TURKIC
Poŋaal. Gula D.→ADAMAWA
Poodawahduhme = Potawatomi→ALGON-
  QUIAN
Poombo. Hungu D.→CENTRAL WESTERN
  BANTU
Poordoona = Buduna. Talandji D.→
  KANYARA
Pooroga = Jirandali. Mandandanji D.→PAMA-
  MARIC
Popayan→INTER-ANDINE

POPAYANENSE→INTER-ANDINE
Popol. Mangbetu D.→CENTRAL SUDANIC
Popoloc→POPOLOCAN
Popoloca = Popoloc→POPOLOCAN
POPOLOCAN see article
Popoloco, Guatemalan = Xinca→MACRO-
  CHIBCHAN
Popoluca of Vera Cruz = Sierra Popoluca→
  MIXE-ZOQUE
Popoluco of Pueblo = Sierra Popoluca→
  MIXE-ZOQUE
POPOTECAN see OTO-MANGUEAN
Populuca = Sierra Popoluca→MIXE-ZOQUE
Por = Pear→MON-KHMER
Porapora = Poroporo→BOGIA
Poren = Nyangeya. Teso D.→EASTERN
  SUDANIC
P'orepeca = Tarascan
Porepecha — Tarascan
Porocoto = Purucoto→CARIB
Porojas — Parji→DRAVIDIAN
Porome = Poromi→KIKORI RIVER
Poromi→KIKORI RIVER
Poroporo→BOGIA
Poroquicoa. Tupi D.→TUPI
Port Sandwich→NORTHWESTERN NEW
  HEBRIDES
Portalaun = Portaulun. Tanganekald D.→
  NARRINYERIC
Portaulun. Tanganekald D.→NARRINYERIC
Portuguese→ROMANCE
Po-se→KAM-TAI
Potaia→CENTRAL AND SOUTH NEW
  GUINEA
Potangola = Potaruwutj. Djadjala D.→KULI-
  NIC
Potano. Timucua D.
Potaruwutj. Djadjala D.→KULINIC
Potatuck. Mohegan Tr.→ALGONQUIAN
Potawatomi→ALGONQUIAN
Potawatomie = Potawatomi→ALGONQUIAN
Potawatomy = Potawatomi→ALGONQUIAN
Potawotami = Potawatomi→ALGONQUIAN
Potawotamic = Potawatomi→ALGONQUIAN
Potawotamie = Potawatomi→ALGONQUIAN
Potawottami = Potawatomi→ALGONQUIAN
Potawottamie = Potawatomi→ALGONQUIAN
Potewateme = Potawatomi→ALGONQUIAN
Potewatemi = Potawatomi→ALGONQUIAN
Potewatimi = Potawatomi→ALGONQUIAN
Potewattomie = Potawatomi→ALGONQUIAN
Potewotomi = Potawatomi→ALGONQUIAN
Potiguara. Tupi D.→TUPI
Potiguara. Tupi Tr.→TUPI

Potiwattomie = Potawatomi→ALGONQUIAN
Potnariven. Eromanga D.→SOUTHERN NEW HEBRIDES
Poto. Losengo D.→NORTH WESTERN BANTU
Potomac. Powhatan Tr.→ALGONQUIAN
Potosino. Huastec D.→MAYAN
Potowatome = Potawatomi→ALGONQUIAN
Potowatomie = Potawatomi→ALGONQUIAN
Potowotomi = Potawatomi→ALGONQUIAN
Potowotomie = Potawatomi→ALGONQUIAN
Potrwatame = Potawatomi→ALGONQUIAN
Potrwatome = Potawatomi→ALGONQUIAN
Pottawatameh = Potawatomi→ALGONQUIAN
Pottawatomi = Potawatomi→ALGONQUIAN
Pottawatomie = Potawatomi→ALGONQUIAN
Pottawotami = Potawatomi→ALGONQUIAN
Pottawotamie = Potawatomi→ALGONQUIAN
Pottawotomi = Potawatomi→ALGONQUIAN
Pottawotomie = Potawatomi→ALGONQUIAN
Pottawottami = Potawatomi→ALGONQUIAN
Pottawottamie = Potawatomi→ALGONQUIAN
Potu = Gwa→LAGOON
Poturero. Northern Zamucoan Tr.→EQUA-TORIAL
Po'u mBoto. Bare'e D.→CENTRAL AND SOUTHERN CELEBES
Pougouli = Puguli→GUR
Poutouatomi = Potawatomi→ALGONQUIAN
Powhatan→ALGONQUIAN
Powhattan = Powhatan→ALGONQUIAN
Powokti. Alabama D.→MUSKOGEAN
Poya = Salur. Gadba D.→DRAVIDIAN
Poyisha = Poica. Yiporok D.→BOTOCUDO
Pozitxa = Poica. Yiporok D.→BOTOCUDO
Pozo. Cauca Tr.→CARIB
Praenestinian→ITALIC
Pragar→MON-KHMER
PRAKRIT→INDIC
Prampram. Adangme D.→GA-ADANGME
Prang. Southern Mnong D.→MON-KHMER
Praok. Wa D.→PALAUNG-WA
Prasun = Wasi-weri→NURISTANI
Pray. T'in D.→KHMUIC
Pregalgh = Jukambal→YUIN-KURIC
Preh. Central Mnong D.→MON-KHMER
PRE-ITALIC→ITALIC
Preng→MON-KHMER
Pretas = Munduruku→TUPI
Priinda = Matlatzinca→OTOMIAN
Prinsu. Sumo Tr.→MISUMALPAN
Prinzo = Prinsu. Sumo Tr.→MISUMALPAN
Proon = Campuon→MON-KHMER
Proons = Campuon→MON-KHMER

Prou = Nyaheun→MON-KHMER
Proue = Brao→MON-KHMER
Provencal→ROMANCE
Prufa. Bakwe Tr.→KRU
Prussian, Old→BALTIC
Pshav. Georgian D.→CAUCASIAN
Ptamo. Guahibo D.→EQUATORIAL
Pu = Car→NICOBARESE
Puant = Winnebago→SIOUAN
Puben→INTER-ANDINE
Pubenaro = Puben→INTER-ANDINE
Pucaja = Pacajan. Tenetehara Tr.→TUPI
Pucapacuri = Tuyuneri→EQUATORIAL
Puchanahua. Cashibo D.→PANO
Puchanawa = Puchanahua. Cashibo D.→PANO
Puchikwar. Great Andamanese D.→ANDA-MANESE
Pucobge = Piocobge→GE
Pucpacuri→MAIPURAN
Pue→DAGA
Puelche→ANDEAN
Pugbiri→PLATEAU BENUE-CONGO
Puget = Puget Sound Salish→SALISH
Pugu. Mumuye D.→ADAMAWA
Puguli→GUR
Puhooc = Puoc→KHMUIC
PU-I = JUI→KAM-TAI
PUINAVE→MACRO-TUCANOAN
Puinave→MACRO-TUCANOAN
PUJUNAN = MAIDU
Pujuni = Maidu→MAIDU
Pukamigl-Andegabu. Wahgi D.→EAST NEW GUINEA HIGHLANDS
Pukapukan→POLYNESIAN
Pukina = Chipaya→CHIPAYAN
Pukina = Uru→CHIPAYAN
Puku = Bapoko. Batanga D.→NORTH WESTERN BANTU
Pukunna = Nukuna. Jadliaura D.→YURA
Puku-nu→PLATEAU BENUE-CONGO
Pul = Pol. Pol-Pomo D.→NORTH WESTERN BANTU
Pula→NORTHWEST AUSTRONESIAN
Pulana. Northern Sotho D.→SOUTH EAST-ERN BANTU
Pulap. Carolinian D.→MICRONESIAN
Pulau Guai. Inner Eastern Sakai D.→SAKAI
Pulaya. Malayalam D.→DRAVIDIAN
Pulgoe = Bailko→NGAYARDA
Pulinya. Nanda D.→KARDU
Pulladapa = Pilatapa→DIERIC
Pulo Anna. Ulithian D.→MICRONESIAN
Pulopetak. Ngaju D.→WEST INDONESIAN
Pulusuk. Carolinian D,→MICRONESIAN

Puluwat. Carolinian D.→MICRONESIAN
P'U?MAN = KACHIN→BODO-NAGA-KA-CHIN
Puna→MACRO-CHIBCHAN
Puna. Hungu D.→CENTRAL WESTERN BANTU
Punaba = Bunaba→BUNABAN
Punan. Land Dayak D.→WEST INDONESIAN
Punan = Ba Mali→WEST INDONESIAN
Punan = Punan Ba→WEST INDONESIAN
Punan Ba→WEST INDONESIAN
Punan Batu. Punan Ba D.→WEST INDONE-SIAN
Punan Gang. Punan Ba D.→WEST INDO-NESIAN
Punan Lusong. Punan Ba D.→WEST INDO-NESIAN
Punctunc = Maya→MAYAN
Puncuri→MAIPURAN
Pundru. Waimdra D.→ADMIRALTY-WESTERN ISLANDS
Pungandik = Buandik. Marditjali D.→KULINIC
Pungantitj = Buandik. Marditjali D.→KULINIC
Pungatitj = Buandik. Marditjali D.→KULINIC
Pungianes = Mayaoyao→NORTHWEST AUS-TRONESIAN
Pungupungu. Wadjiginy D.→DALY
Punic. Phoenician D.→SEMITIC
Punjabi = Panjabi→INDIC
Punji = Southern Maidu→MAIDU
Punkalla = Pangkala→YURA
Punnucana. Moseten D.→MACRO-PANOAN
Punoi = Phunoi→BURMESE-LOLO
Punoinjon = Tjapwurong→KULINIC
Puntano Huarpe→HUARPE
Punthamara→DIERIC
Puntlatch = Pentlatch→SALISH
Puntlatsh = Pentlatch→SALISH
Puntledge = Pentlatch→SALISH
Punu→NORTH WESTERN BANTU
Punu→MIAO-YAO
Puoc→KHMUIC
Puquina = Chipaya→CHIPAYAN
Puquina = Uru→CHIPAYAN
Purace→INTER-ANDINE
Puragi→WESTERN NEW GUINEA
Purai. Lawangan D.→WEST INDONESIAN
Puram = Purum→NAGA-KUKI-CHIN
Purbi. Bihari D.→INDIC
Purecamecran→GE
Purepeca = Tarascan

PURI see article
Puricoto = Purucoto→CARIB
Purik. West Tibetan D.→TIBETAN
Purisimeno. CHUMASH Tr.→HOKAN
Purko. Maasai Tr.→EASTERN SUDANIC
Purteetchally = Tjapwurong→KULINIC
Purubora→TUPI
Purucarod→GE
Purucaru = Purucarod→GE
Purucoto→CARIB
Puruha→MACRO-CHIBCHAN
Purukaru = Ira-Amaire→GE
Purum→NAGA-KUKI-CHIN
Purung. Lawangan D.→WEST INDONESIAN
Purupuru→ARAWAKAN
Pus. Musgu D.→CHADIC
Pusciti = Chavante→GE
Pushto = Pashto→IRANIAN
Putatan. Dusun D.→NORTHWEST AUSTRO-NESIAN
Putawatomi = Potawatomi→ALGONQUIAN
Putenh = Khang. Khmu' D.→KHMUIC
Puthlundi. Tera D.→CHADIC
Puyallup. Puget Sound Salish D.→SALISH
Puyamanawa→PANO
PUYI = JUI→KAM-TAI
Puyuma→FORMOSAN AUSTRONESIAN
Pwamei→NEW CALEDONIA
Pwe = Bobo Wule. Bobo D.→GUR
Pwebo = Moenebeng→NEW CALEDONIA
Pwo = Pho→KAREN
Pya. Bakwe D.→KRU
Pyam = Pyem→PLATEAU BENUE-CONGO
Pye = Pya. Bakwe D.→KRU
Pyem→PLATEAU BENUE-CONGO
Pyen→BURMESE-LOLO
Pyuma = Chipon. Puyuma D.→FORMOSAN AUSTRONESIAN
Pyuma = Puyuma→FORMOSAN AUSTRO-NESIAN

Q

Qabekhoe. n//hai D.→KHOISAN
Qaernermiut = Barren Grounds Eskimo. Inuit D.→ESKIMO-ALEUT
Qaracay = Karachay→TURKIC
Qarawi = Shahari. Modern South Arabic D.→SEMITIC
Qasqari = Khowar→INDIC
Qataban-Aswan. Old South Arabic D.→SEMITIC
Qatvenua = Lamalanga→EASTERN OCEAN-IC

Qazvini. Persian D.→IRANIAN
Qebena = Kabena. Alaba D.→CUSHITIC
Qei→EASTERN OCEANIC
Qemant. Quara D.→CUSHITIC
Qiche→MAYAN
Qimant = Qemant. Quara D.→CUSHITIC
Qimr = Orra. Tama D.→EASTERN SUDANIC
Qottu = Ittu. Galla D.→CUSHITIC
Qtlumi = Lummi. Northern Straits Salish D.→
    SALISH
Qua = Kwa. Ekoi D.→BANTOID
Quaddie = Passamaquoddy→ALGONQUIAN
Qualup = Koreng. Juat D.→SOUTHWEST
    PAMA-NYUNGAN
Quamamyl = Gamila. Berta D.→CHARI-NILE
Quameli = Gamila. Berta D.→CHARI-NILE
Quang Tin Katu= Takua→MON-KHMER
Quapaw. Dhegiha D.→SIOUAN
Quara→CUSHITIC
Quarasa = Quara→CUSHITIC
Quarina = Quara→CUSHITIC
Quatpe→EASTERN OCEANIC
Quavjasamiut. Inuit D.→ESKIMO-ALEUT
Qudawa = Gadiwa. Tebu Tr.→SAHARAN
Quecchi = Kekchi→MAYAN
Queche = Qiche→MAYAN
Quechua→ANDEAN
QUECHUMARAN→ANDEAN
Quedah = Kedah. Semang Proper D.→
    SEMANG
Quekchi = Kekchi→MAYAN
QUELEM = TZELTALAN→MAYAN
Quelem = Tzotzil→MAYAN
QUELENE = TZELTALAN→MAYAN
Quelene = Tzotzil→MAYAN
Quembo = Ngengu→CENTRAL WESTERN
    BANTU
Quencatage→GE
Queney = Ke-ney→NORTHWEST AUSTRO-
    NESIAN
Quengues = Cayuga. Seneca Tr.→IROQUOIS
Quenoloco→CARIB
Quepiquiriquat = Kepkiriwat→TUPI
Quepo = Kepo. Boruca D.→CHIBCHAN
Quequexque = Terraba→CHIBCHAN
Queres = Keres
Quianganes = Kiangan→NORTHWEST AUS-
    TRONESIAN
Quibala = Kibala→CENTRAL WESTERN
    BANTU
Quicama = Halyikwamai. Delta River Yuman
    D.→YUMAN
Quichais = Kitsai→CADDOAN
Qui-chau→KAM-TAI

Quiche = Qiche→MAYAN
QUICHEAN→MAYAN
Quichua = Quechua→ANDEAN
Quichuan = Kiowa→TANOAN
Quidehais = Kitsai→CADDOAN
Quilengue = Lengue→CENTRAL WESTERN
    BANTU
Quileute→CHIMAKUAN
Quilla→INTER-ANDINE
Quillacinga→EQUATORIAL
Quilotes. Karankawa Tr.
Quimbaya. Cauca D.→CARIB
Quimbiri. Campa D.→MAIPURAN
Quimbundo = Mbundu→SOUTH WESTERN
    BANTU
Quinaietl = Quinault→SALISH
Quinaqui = Kinaki→TACANA
Quinault→SALISH
Quindio. Pijao D.→CARIB
Quingnam = Yunca→CHIPAYAN
Quinhao = Guinao→NORTHERN MAI-
    PURAN
Quinicuane = Borrado
Quinigua = Borrado
Quinnipiac = Wappinger. Mohegan D.→
    ALGONQUIAN
Quinnipiak = Wappinger. Mohegan D.→
    ALGONQUIAN
Quipea. Cariri D.→EQUATORIAL
Quirinairi. Campa D.→MAIPURAN
Quiripi = Wappinger. Mohegan D.→ALGON-
    QUIAN
Quiriquire = Yarigui→CARIB
Quiriticoci. Tupi Tr.→TUPI
Quirruba. Baniva D.→MAIPURAN
Quissama = Sama→CENTRAL WESTERN
    BANTU
Quitemoca→CHAPACURA-WANHAMAN
Quivira = Wichita→CADDOAN
Quoddy = Passamaquoddy→ALGONQUIAN
Quop = Kuap. Land Dayak D.→WEST
    INDONESIAN
Quoratean = Karok→HOKAN
Qurama. Uzbek D.→TURKIC
Qviche = Qiche→MAYAN
Qwabe. Nguni D.→SOUTH EASTERN
    BANTU
Qwara = Kayla. Quara D.→CUSHITIC
Qwara = Quara→CUSHITIC
Qwottu = Ittu. Galla D.→CUSHITIC

R

Rabah. Hre D.→MON-KHMER

Rabai. Nika D.→NORTH EASTERN BANTU

Rabbit Skins = Hare. Dogrib Tr.→ATHAPAS-CAN-EYAK

Rabinal→MAYAN

Rabuna = Arabana→PAMA-NYUNGAN

Racha. Georgian D.→CAUCASIAN

Rache. Moseten D.→MACRO-PANOAN

Rachiat = Reshaiat. Dasenech Tr.→CUSHITIC

Raday = Rade→WEST INDONESIAN

Rade→WEST INDONESIAN

Radlai = Northern Roglai→WEST INDONE-SIAN

Raetic→ITALIC

RAETO-ROMANCE = RHAETO-ROMANCE →ROMANCE

Raga, Central→EASTERN OCEANIC

Raga, North = Lamalanga→EASTERN OCEANIC

Raga, South→EASTERN OCEANIC

Ragoli = Logooli→NORTH EASTERN BANTU

RAGOLI-KURIA→NORTH EASTERN BAN-TU

Ragreig. Burun Tr.→EASTERN SUDANIC

Rahanwein. Somali D.→CUSHITIC

Rahanwen = Rahanwein. Somali D.→CUSH-ITIC

Rahanwiin = Rahanwein. Somali D.→CUSH-ITIC

Rai→GYARUNG-MISHMI

Rai. Southern Roglai D.→WEST INDO-NESIAN

Raidjua. Havunese D.→MOLUCCAN

Raii. Tawaili D.→CENTRAL AND SOUTH-ERN CELEBES

Raik = Rek→EASTERN SUDANIC

Rainbarngo = Rembarunga→GUNWING-GUAN

Raisha. Paiwan D.→FORMOSAN AUSTRO-NESIAN

Rajasthani→INDIC

Rajbangsi. Bengali D.→INDIC

Rakhaing = Arakanese. Burmese D.→BUR-MESE-LOLO

Rakkaia. Wangkadjera D.→PITTAPITTIC

ra-Kpa = Kpa→NORTH WESTERN BANTU

Ral = Ningil→TORRICELLI

Ralik. Marshallese D.→MICRONESIAN

Ralte→NAGA-KUKI-CHIN

RAM→SEPIK

Rama→CHIBCHAN

RAMARAMA→TUPI

Ramarama→TUPI

Ramata→NORTHWESTERN AND CEN-TRAL SOLOMONS

Rambutjo→ADMIRALTY-WESTERN IS-LANDS

Ramcocamecra→GE

Ramfau. Siane D.→EAST NEW GUINEA HIGHLANDS

Ramindjerar = Ramindjeri. Tanganekald D.→ NARRINYERIC

Ramindjeri. Tanganekald D.→NARRINYERIC

Ramingara = Ramindjeri. Tanganekald D.→ NARRINYERIC

Raminyeri = Ramindjeri. Tanganekald D.→ NARRINYERIC

Ramong = Ramindjeri. Tanganekald D.→ NARRINYERIC

Rampi. Leboni D.→CENTRAL AND SOUTH-ERN CELEBES

RAMU→BOGIA

Rana→EAST INDONESIAN

Rana. Tanna D.→SOUTHERN NEW HEB-RIDES

Randile = Rendile→CUSHITIC

Rangao = Rengao→MON-KHMER

Rangkas→GYARUNG-MISHMI

Rangkhol = Hrangkhol→NAGA-KUKI-CHIN

Rangloi. Manchati D.→GYARUNG-MISHMI

Ranquel. Araucanian D.→PENUTIAN

Ranquelche = Ranquel. Araucanian D.→ PENUTIAN

Ranquele = Ranquel. Araucanian D.→PENU-TIAN

Ranquelines = Ranquel. Araucanian D.→ PENUTIAN

Rante Bulawan. Pitu-ulunna-salu D.→CEN-TRAL AND SOUTHERN CELEBES

Rante Pao. Sa'dan D.→CENTRAL AND SOUTHERN CELEBES

Rao→BOGIA

Raokrik = Rikiriki. Paiwan D.→FORMOSAN AUSTRONESIAN

Raosiara→NORTHWESTERN AND CEN-TRAL SOLOMONS

Rapa→POLYNESIAN

Rapangkaka→CENTRAL AND SOUTHERN CELEBES

Rapanui = Easter Island→POLYNESIAN

Rappahannock. Powhatan Tr.→ALGON-QUIAN

Raramuri=Tarahumara→UTO-AZTECAN

Rariguara. Tupi Tr.→TUPI

Rarotongan = Cook Islands Maori→POLY-NESIAN

Rashad. Tagali D.→KORDOFANIAN

Ratagnon. Cuyunon D.→NORTHWEST AUS-

TRONESIAN
Ratahan→NORTHERN CELEBES
Ratak. Marshallese D.→MICRONESIAN
Rataning→MABAN
Rato. Leboni D.→CENTRAL AND SOUTH-
ERN CELEBES
Raura = Taura→NORTHWESTERN AND
CENTRAL SOLOMONS
Rawa→HUON-FINISTERRE
Rawa. Kerintji D.→WEST INDONESIAN
RAWANG→BODO-NAGA-KACHIN
Rawang→BODO-NAGA-KACHIN
Raya. Galla D.→CUSHITIC
Rebina→PLATEAU BENUE-CONGO
Rebinawa = Rebina→PLATEAU BENUE-
CONGO
Rebini-wa = Rebina→PLATEAU BENUE-
CONGO
Rebu = Bobangi→NORTH WESTERN BAN-
TU
Rebu = Loi. Loi-Ngiri D.→NORTH WEST-
ERN BANTU
Rechiat = Reshaiat. Dasenech Tr.→CUSHITIC
Redjang→WEST INDONESIAN
Red-knife = Yellow-knife. Chipewyan Tr.→
ATHAPASCAN-EYAK
Redwood Indians = Whilkut. Hupa D.→ATHA-
PASCAN-EYAK
Ree = Arikara. Pawnee D.→CADDOAN
Reef Island→CENTRAL MELANESIAN
Reef Island = Pileni→POLYNESIAN
REEF ISLANDS-SANTA CRUZ→CENTRAL
MELANESIAN
Rega = Lega→NORTH EASTERN BANTU
Regba = Eregba→JUKUNOID
Reimojik. Tatog Tr.→EASTERN SUDANIC
Reiwo = Yapunda→TORRICELLI
Rejang = Punan Ba→WEST INDONESIAN
Rejang = Redjang→WEST INDONESIAN
Rejang Punan = Punan Ba→WEST INDO-
NESIAN
Rek→EASTERN SUDANIC
Rekhta. Western Hindi D.→INDIC
Rembarunga→GUNWINGGUAN
Remi→NORTH EASTERN BANTU
Remo→PANO
Remo→MUNDA
Rempi→BOGIA
Rempin = Rempi→BOGIA
Rendi = Lendi. Sumba D.→MOLUCCAN
Rendile→CUSHITIC
Rendille = Rendile→CUSHITIC
Rengao→MON-KHMER
Renggou. Roti D.→EAST INDONESIAN

Rengma→NAGA-KUKI-CHIN
Rennellese→POLYNESIAN
Reshaiat. Dasenech Tr.→CUSHITIC
Reshe→PLATEAU BENUE-CONGO
Resigero→WITOTOAN
Retan→EASTERN OCEANIC
Rete. Bungku D.→CENTRAL AND SOUTH-
ERN CELEBES
Rethi. Lendu D.→CENTRAL SUDANIC
Rewa = Tagula→PAPUA AUSTRONESIAN
Reyano = Luiseno→UTO-AZTECAN
Reyesano→TACANA
Rgyarong = Gyarung→GYARUNG-MISHMI
Rhaday = Rade→WEST INDONESIAN
RHAETIAN = RHAETO-ROMANCE→
ROMANCE
RHAETO-ROMANCE→ROMANCE
RHETO-ROMANCE = RHAETO-RO-
MANCE→ROMANCE
Rhinyirhinyi. Nyabungu D.→NORTH EAST-
ERN BANTU
Rhombo. Caga D.→NORTH EASTERN
BANTU
Riama. Carijona D.→CARIB
Riang = Riang-lang→PALAUNG-WA
Riang-lang→PALAUNG-WA
Riantana→FREDERIK HENDRIK IS AND
SE WEST IRIAN
Ricara = Arikara. Pawnee D.→CADDOAN
Riccara = Arikara. Pawnee D.→CADDOAN
Riccaree = Arikara. Pawnee D.→CADDOAN
Riccari = Arikara. Pawnee D.→CADDOAN
Riccarie = Arikara. Pawnee D.→CADDOAN
Richaganik. Chamalal D.→CAUCASIAN
Rickohockans = Yuchi→MACRO-SIOUAN
Ridarngo = Ritarungo→MURNGIC
Ridarngu = Ritarungo→MURNGIC
Riff→BERBER
Rigwe = Irigwe→PLATEAU BENUE-CONGO
Rikabiyya. Berta D.→CHARI-NILE
Rikara = Arikara. Pawnee D.→CADDOAN
Rikiriki. Paiwan D.→FORMOSAN AUSTRO-
NESIAN
Rikvani. Andi D.→CAUCASIAN
Rimi = Remi→NORTH EASTERN BANTU
Rindre→PLATEAU BENUE-CONGO
Rindri = Rindre→PLATEAU BENUE-CON-
GO
Ringa Oringaroo = Ringuringu. Wangkadjera
D.→PITTAPITTIC
Ringa Ringa = Ringuringu. Wangkadjera D.→
PITTAPITTIC
Ringaringa = Ringuringu. Wangkadjera D.→
PITTAPITTIC

Ringgou = Renggou. Roti D.→EAST INDO-
NESIAN
Ringoringo = Ringuringu. Wangkadjera D.→
PITTAPITTIC
Ringuringu. Wangkadjera D.→PITTAPITTIC
RIO BRANCO = WAPISHANAN→MAI-
PURAN
RIO NEGRO ARAWAKAN→NORTHERN
MAIPURAN
Rio Sucio. Southern Epera D.→CHOCO
Rion. Koho D.→MON-KHMER
Ripere = Kpere. Kari D.→ADAMAWA
Riraidjango→MURNGIC
Riraidjangu = Riraidjango→MURNGIC
Riring. Sapolewa D.→EAST INDONESIAN
Ririo→NORTHWESTERN AND CENTRAL
SOLOMONS
Ris = Arikara. Pawnee D.→CADDOAN
Rishuwa = Kuzamani→PLATEAU BENUE-
CONGO
Ritaringo = Ritarungo→MURNGIC
Ritarngo = Ritarungo→MURNGIC
Ritarungo→MURNGIC
Rittarungo = Ritarungo→MURNGIC
RITWAN see MACRO-ALGONQUIAN
Riwandiz. Kermanji D.→IRANIAN
Riwanduz = Riwandiz. Kermanji D.→IRA-
NIAN
Rlam = Rolom. Eastern Mnong D.→MON-
KHMER
Ro→EAST NEW GUINEA HIGHLANDS
Ro = Chrau→MON-KHMER
Roamaina = Omurano→ANDEAN
Roba. Yunger D.→ADAMAWA
Robambami = Agoi→CROSS RIVER BENUE-
CONGO
Roboda→PAPUA AUSTRONESIAN
Rock Creek = Columbia River. Sahaptin D.→
SAHAPTIN-NEZ PERCE
Rockaway. Mohegan Tr.→ALGONQUIAN
Rocky Mountain Indians = Sekani. Sekani D.→
ATHAPASCAN-EYAK
Rodi = Bor→EASTERN SUDANIC
Rodiya. Sinhalese D.→INDIC
Rodong→GYARUNG-MISHMI
Rofik = Demik. Keiga D.→KORDOFANIAN
Rogea. Suau D.→PAPUA AUSTRONESIAN
Roglai, Cac Gia→WEST INDONESIAN
Roglai, Northern→WEST INDONESIAN
Roglai, Southern→WEST INDONESIAN
Rogo→BISMARCK ARCHIPELAGO
Rohong. Central Mnong D.→MON-KHMER
Roi = Yakha→GYARUNG-MISHMI
Rokorona = Ororono→CHAPACURA-WAN-
HAMAN
Rolom. Eastern Mnong D.→MON-KHMER
Rolong. Tswana D.→SOUTH EASTERN
BANTU
Roloŋ = Rolong. Tswana D.→SOUTH EAST-
ERN BANTU
Rom = Orom. Teso D.→EASTERN SUDANIC
Roma→EAST INDONESIAN
Romaic = Greek→GREEK
Romance, Balkan = Rumanian→ROMANCE
ROMANCE see article
Romanian = Rumanian→ROMANCE
ROMANIC = ROMANCE
Romansch→ROMANCE
Romany→INDIC
ROMARAMAN = RAMARAMA→TUPI
Rombi = Lombi→NORTH WESTERN
BANTU
Romblomanon→NORTHWEST AUSTRONE-
SIAN
Rombo = Rhombo. Caga D.→NORTH EAST-
ERN BANTU
Romkuin→BOGIA
Romkun = Romkuin→BOGIA
Ron→CHADIC
Rone = Temein→EASTERN SUDANIC
Rong. West Tibetan D.→TIBETAN
Rong = Lepcha→BODO-NAGA-KACHIN
Ronga→SOUTH EASTERN BANTU
Rongao = Rengao→MON-KHMER
Rongkong. Sa'dan D.→CENTRAL AND
SOUTHERN CELEBES
Rongo. Myene D.→NORTH WESTERN
BANTU
Rongpa = Lepcha→BODO-NAGA-KACHIN
Rong-Rang. Tangsa D.→BODO-NAGA-KA-
CHIN
Rongtuw = Taungtha→NAGA-KUKI-CHIN
Rooi Nasie = Nama→KHOISAN
Rori = Sango→CENTRAL EASTERN BANTU
Roro→PAPUA AUSTRONESIAN
Rorovana→NORTHWESTERN AND CEN-
TRAL SOLOMONS
Rotageink = Rutageink. Tatog Tr.→EASTERN
SUDANIC
Rotea = Sedang→MON-KHMER
Roti→EAST INDONESIAN
Rotokas→BOUGAINVILLE
Rotse = Lozi→SOUTH WESTERN BANTU
Rotti = Roti→EAST INDONESIAN
Rotuman→EASTERN OCEANIC
Roumanian = Rumanian→ROMANCE
Roundhead = Cree→ALGONQUIAN
Routa. Bungku D.→CENTRAL AND SOUTH-

ERN CELEBES
Rouyi = Luyana→SOUTH WESTERN BANTU
Roviana→NORTHWESTERN AND CENTRAL SOLOMONS
ROVIANIC→NORTHWESTERN AND CENTRAL SOLOMONS
Rowa→EASTERN OCEANIC
Rozi = Lozi→SOUTH WESTERN BANTU
Rozi = Rozwi. Shona D.→SOUTH EASTERN BANTU
Rozvi = Lozi→SOUTH WESTERN BANTU
Rozvi = Rozwi. Shona D.→SOUTH EASTERN BANTU
Rozwi. Shona D.→SOUTH EASTERN BANTU
Rranao = Maranao→NORTHWEST AUSTRONESIAN
Ruanawa. Pichobo D.→PANO
Ruanda→NORTH EASTERN BANTU
RUANDA-RUNDI→NORTH EASTERN BANTU
Rubiana = Roviana→NORTHWESTERN AND CENTRAL SOLOMONS
Ruc = May. Muong D.→VIET-MUONG
Ruciga = Rukiga. Ruanda D.→NORTH EASTERN BANTU
Rucuyen. Oyana D.→CARIB
Rue→CENTRAL EASTERN BANTU
Rufiji = Ruihi→SOUTH EASTERN BANTU
Ruftu = Luhtu. Tsou D.→FORMOSAN AUSTRONESIAN
Rugara = Buin→BOUGAINVILLE
Rugii. Burgundian D.→GERMANIC
Ruguru→CENTRAL EASTERN BANTU
Ruhororo = Hororo. Nyankole D.→NORTH EASTERN BANTU
Ruihi→SOUTH EASTERN BANTU
Ruija Lapp→URALIC
Rukai→FORMOSAN AUSTRONESIAN
ru-Karagwe = Karagwe. Nyambo D.→NORTH EASTERN BANTU
Rukiga. Ruanda D.→NORTH EASTERN BANTU
Rukkia = Rakkaia. Wangkadjera D.→PITTA-PITTIC
ru-Kobi = Hunde→NORTH EASTERN BANTU
Rukonjo = Konzo→NORTH EASTERN BANTU
Rukuba→PLATEAU BENUE-CONGO
Rum = Gisiga→CHADIC
Rumaheler. Tala D.→EAST INDONESIAN
Rumai = Palaung→PALAUNG-WA
Rumaiya = Rumaya→PLATEAU BENUE-CONGO

Rumanian→ROMANCE
Rumauntsch = Romansch→ROMANCE
Rumaya→PLATEAU BENUE-CONGO
Rumbala = Mbala→CENTRAL WESTERN BANTU
Rumberpon. Numfor D.→MOLUCCAN
Rumsen. Southern Costanoan D.→MIWOK-COSTANOAN
Rumu = Dumu→KIKORI RIVER
Runanaua. Jurua-Purus Tr.→PANO
Rundi→NORTH EASTERN BANTU
Rundum. Murut D.→NORTHWEST AUSTRONESIAN
Runga→CENTRAL EASTERN BANTU
Runga. Maba Tr.→MABAN
Rungchhenbung. Waling D.→GYARUNG-MISHMI
Rungtshenbung = Rungchhenbung. Waling D.→GYARUNG-MISHMI
Rungu→CENTRAL EASTERN BANTU
Rungu = Taabwa→CENTRAL EASTERN BANTU
Rungwa = Runga→CENTRAL EASTERN BANTU
Runsien = Rumsen. Southern Costanoan D.→MIWOK-COSTANOAN
Rununawa = Runanaua. Jurua-Purus Tr.→PANO
Runyambo = Nyambo→NORTH EASTERN BANTU
Runyankore = Nyankole→NORTH EASTERN BANTU
Runyaruanda = Ruanda→NORTH EASTERN BANTU
Runyarwanda = Ruanda→NORTH EASTERN BANTU
Runyo. Cashibo D.→PANO
Runyoro = Nyoro→NORTH EASTERN BANTU
Ruŋa = Runga. Maba Tr.→MABAN
Ruravai = Ruruvai→NORTHWESTERN AND CENTRAL SOLOMONS
Rurihi'ip = Yahang→TORRICELLI
Ruruhip = Heyo→TORRICELLI
Ruruhip = Yahang→TORRICELLI
Ruruma→PLATEAU BENUE-CONGO
Rurutu. Tahitian D.→POLYNESIAN
Ruruvai→NORTHWESTERN AND CENTRAL SOLOMONS
Rusha→NORTH EASTERN BANTU
Rusia = Reshaiat. Dasenech Tr.→CUSHITIC
Russian→SLAVIC
Russian, Great = Russian→SLAVIC
Russian, Little = Ukrainian→SLAVIC

Russian, White = Bielorussian→SLAVIC
Russonorsk see Russian→SLAVIC
Rut. Padang D.→EASTERN SUDANIC
Rutageink. Tatog Tr.→EASTERN SUDANIC
Ruteng. Manggarai D.→EAST INDONESIAN
Ruthenian, White = Bielorussian→SLAVIC
Rutooro = Nyoro→NORTH EASTERN BANTU
Rutul→CAUCASIAN
Rutwa = Twa. Ruanda D.→NORTH EASTERN BANTU
Ruund = Luwunda→CENTRAL WESTERN BANTU
Ruweng. Padang D.→EASTERN SUDANIC
Ruwenzori Bira = Amba→NORTH EASTERN BANTU
Rwamba = Amba→NORTH EASTERN BANTU
Rwo→NORTH EASTERN BANTU
RYUKYUAN→JAPANESE
Ryukyuan, Central→JAPANESE
Ryukyuan, Northern→JAPANESE
Ryukyuan, Southern→JAPANESE

S

Sa = Sapo. Krahn Tr.→KRU
Sa = Sya→MANDE
Sa?a→EASTERN OCEANIC
Saamia→NORTH EASTERN BANTU
Saan = San→KHOISAN
Saanich. Northern Straits Salish D.→SALISH
Saaptins = Nez Perce→SAHAPTIN-NEZ PERCE
Saaroa→FORMOSAN AUSTRONESIAN
Saaroŋge = Daju→EASTERN SUDANIC
Saarua = Saaroa→FORMOSAN AUSTRONESIAN
Sab Ogaden. Somali D.→CUSHITIC
Saba. Sokoro D.→CHADIC
Sabaean = Sabean. Old South Arabic D.→SEMITIC
Sabaibo. Cahita D.→UTO-AZTECAN
Sabane→NAMBICUARA
Sabanero = Murire. Guaymi D.→CHIBCHAN
Sabanun = Subanun→NORTHWEST AUSTRONESIAN
Sabaot. Nandi D.→EASTERN SUDANIC
Sabara = Sora→MUNDA
Sabari→PAPUA AUSTRONESIAN
Sabari. Ami D.→FORMOSAN AUSTRONESIAN
Sabaut = Sabaot. Nandi D.→EASTERN SU-DANIC

Sabean. Old South Arabic D.→SEMITIC
Sabei = Sapiny. Nandi D.→EASTERN SUDANIC
Sabela→ANDEAN
SABELLIAN→ITALIC
Sabellic, Old→ITALIC
Saberi→NORTH PAPUAN
Sabeu→NAGA-KUKI-CHIN
Sabine→ITALIC
Sabir→ROMANCE
Saboibo = Sobiobo. Pichobo D.→PANO
Sabon. Tongo D.→ADMIRALTY-WESTERN ISLANDS
Sabonan. Puri D.→PURI
Saboyo = Sobiobo. Pichobo D.→PANO
Sabtang. Ivatan D.→NORTHWEST AUSTRONESIAN
Sabu = Havunese→MOLUCCAN
Sabungo. Land Dayak D.→WEST INDONESIAN
Sabup. Kenyah D.→WEST INDONESIAN
Saburi. Liguri D.→EASTERN SUDANIC
Sabutan. Land Dayak D.→WEST INDONESIAN
Sac = Sauk. Fox D.→ALGONQUIAN
Sach→VIET-MUONG
Sach = Tong-luang→KHMUIC
Sack = Sauk. Fox D.→ALGONQUIAN
Saclan→MIWOK-COSTANOAN
Saconnet. Massachusett D.→ALGONQUIAN
Sacuriu-ina. Iranche D.→MAIPURAN
Sacuya. Remo D.→PANO
Sa'dan→CENTRAL AND SOUTHERN CELEBES
Sadang = Sa'dan→CENTRAL AND SOUTHERN CELEBES
Sadani = Nagpuri. Bihari D.→INDIC
Sadar = Shadal. Mankanya D.→WEST ATLANTIC
Sadong. Land Dayak D.→WEST INDONESIAN
Sadri = Nagpuri. Bihari D.→INDIC
Sae→NORTHERN MAIPURAN
Saek→KAM-TAI
Safalaba→GUR
Safen→WEST ATLANTIC
Safroko. Limba D.→WEST ATLANTIC
Safwa→CENTRAL EASTERN BANTU
Safwi. Anyi D.→VOLTA-COMOE
Sagada→NORTHWEST AUSTRONESIAN
Sagai. Khakas D.→TURKIC
Sagala→CENTRAL EASTERN BANTU
Sagala. Taita D.→NORTH EASTERN BANTU

Sagalla = Sagala. Taita D.→NORTH EASTERN BANTU

Sagar, Northern = Kagulu→CENTRAL EASTERN BANTU

Sagara = Sagala→CENTRAL EASTERN BANTU

Sagara, Northern = Kagulu→CENTRAL EASTERN BANTU

Sageju = Daiso→NORTH EASTERN BANTU

Saha = Tsahatsaha. Carijona D.→CARIB

Sahafatra. Malagasy D.→WEST INDONESIAN

Sahapotins = Nez Perce→SAHAPTIN-NEZ PERCE

Sahaptian = Sahaptin→SAHAPTIN-NEZ PERCE

Sahaptin→SAHAPIN—NEZ PERCE

SAHAPTIN-NEZ PERCE see article

SAHARAN see article

Sahe→NORTHEAST NEW GUINEA AUSTRONESIAN

Sahidic. Coptic D.→AFROASIATIC

Sahkey = Sauk. Fox D.→ALGONQUIAN

Saho. Afar-Saho D.→CUSHITIC

SAHO-AFAR→CUSHITIC

Saho-Afar = Afar-Saho→CUSHITIC

Sahu. Waioli D.→NORTH HALMAHERA

Sahulau. Tala D.→EAST INDONESIAN

Sahu'u = Sahu. Waioli D.→NORTH HALMAHERA

Sai. Gumuz D.→KOMAN

Sai. Pangan D.→SEMANG

Saibai. Dauan D.→MABUIAGIC

Saija = Saixa. Southern Epera D.→CHOCO

Sailo→NORTHWESTERN AND CENTRAL SOLOMONS

Sain = Murmi→GYARUNG-MISHMI

Saint Croix = Passamaquoddy→ALGONQUIAN

Sairakis = Taiai. Saisiyat D.→FORMOSAN AUSTRONESIAN

Saisat = Saisiyat→FORMOSAN AUSTRONESIAN

Saiset = Saisiyat→FORMOSAN AUSTRONESIAN

Saisett = Saisiyat→FORMOSAN AUSTRONESIAN

Saisiat = Saisiyat→FORMOSAN AUSTRONESIAN

Saisiet = Saisiyat→FORMOSAN AUSTRONESIAN

Saisirat = Saisiyat→FORMOSAN AUSTRONESIAN

Saisiyat→FORMOSAN AUSTRONESIAN

Saixa. Southern Epera D.→CHOCO

Sak→BURMESE-LOLO

Saka. Nkutu D.→NORTH WESTERN BANTU

Saka = Khotanese→IRANIAN

Saka = Tagakaolo→NORTHWEST AUSTRONESIAN

SAKAI see article

Sakai Tanjong = Jeher. Semang Proper D.→SEMANG

Sakalagan. Mentawai D.→WEST INDONESIAN

Sakalava. Malagasy D.→WEST INDONESIAN

Sakam→HUON-FINISTERRE

Sakan. Ntombo-Bolia Tr.→NORTH WESTERN BANTU

Sakanyi. Ntombo-Bolia Tr.→NORTH WESTERN BANTU

Sakara = Nzakara→EASTERN

Sakarda = Kashirda. Tebu Tr.→SAHARAN

SAKA-SCYTHIAN→IRANIAN

Sakata→NORTH WESTERN BANTU

Sakau→NORTHWESTERN NEW HEBRIDES

Sake = Sahe→NORTHEAST NEW GUINEA AUSTRONESIAN

Sakei. Kerintji D.→WEST INDONESIAN

Saker = Mugil→BOGIA

Sakerda = Kashirda. Tebu Tr.→SAHARAN

Sakewi = Sauk. Fox D.→ALGONQUIAN

Sakha = Yakuts→TURKIC

Saki→BOGIA

Sakis = Sauk. Fox D.→ALGONQUIAN

Sakishima = Southern Ryukyuan→JAPANESE

Sakisima = Southern Ryukyuan→JAPANESE

Saklan = Saclan→MIWOK-COSTANOAN

Salakahadi→PAPUA AUSTRONESIAN

Salale. Galla D.→CUSHITIC

Salamai = Sanamaika. Monde D.→TUPI

Salampasu→CENTRAL WESTERN BANTU

sala-Mpasu = Salampasu→CENTRAL WESTERN BANTU

Salar. Yellow Uighur D.→TURKIC

Salatav. Avar D.→CAUCASIAN

Salawati→SOUTH HALMAHERA AUSTRONESIAN

Salayar = Selajar. Makasarese D.→CENTRAL AND SOUTHERN CELEBES

Salayer = Salajar. Makasarese D.→CENTRAL AND SOUTHERN CELEBES

Sale = Sum. Pasai D.→INDIC

Salebabu. Talaud D.→HESPERONESIAN

SALIBAN = SALIVAN→EQUATORIAL

Salien. Bipi D.→ADMIRALTY-WESTERN ISLANDS

SALINAN→HOKAN

Salineros. Seri Tr.→HOKAN
SALISH see article
Salish = Kalispel→SALISH
Saliva→EQUATORIAL
SALIVAN→EQUATORIAL
Saloum. Wolof D.→WEST ATLANTIC
Salt. Chimbu D.→EAST NEW GUINEA HIGHLANDS
Salt Pomo = Northeastern Pomo→POMO
Salteaux. Ojibwa D.→ALGONQUIAN
Salu Maoge. Bare'e D.→CENTRAL AND SOUTHERN CELEBES
Saluan. Loinang D.→CENTRAL AND SOUTHERN CELEBES
Salur. Gadba D.→DRAVIDIAN
SALWEEN = PALAUNG-WA
Salya = Selya. Nyakyusa D.→CENTRAL EASTERN BANTU
Salyr. Turkmen D.→TURKIC
Sam. Pangan D.→SEMANG
Sama→CENTRAL WESTERN BANTU
Sama = Bajau→NORTHWEST AUSTRONE-SIAN
Samagir→TUNGUS
Samal→NORTHWEST AUSTRONESIAN
Samalek→WESTERN NEW GUINEA
Samap→NORTHEAST NEW GUINEA AUS-TRONESIAN
Samaritan. West Aramaic D.→SEMITIC
Samar-Leyte = Waray→NORTHWEST AUS-TRONESIAN
Samaron = Waray→NORTHWEST AUSTRO-NESIAN
Samatari. Waica Tr.→WAICAN
Samba→CENTRAL WESTERN BANTU
Samba = Chamba→ADAMAWA
Sambaa = Shambaa→CENTRAL EASTERN BANTU
Sambal = Sambali→NORTHWEST AUSTRO-NESIAN
Sambali→NORTHWEST AUSTRONESIAN
Samban. Jaba D.→PLATEAU BENUE-CONGO
Sambara = Shambaa→CENTRAL EASTERN BANTU
Samberi. Biak D.→MOLUCCAN
Sambila = Sembla. Samo D.→MANDE
Sambio = Sambyu. Kwangari D.→SOUTH WESTERN BANTU
Sambioa = Chamboa→CARAJA
Sambo = Sambu. Northern Epera D.→CHOCO
Sambu. Northern Epera D.→CHOCO
Sambu = Seim→SEPIK
Sambup = Sabup. Kenyah D.→WEST INDO-NESIAN
Sambur = Sampur. Maasai D.→EASTERN SUDANIC
Samburu = Sampur. Maasai D.→EASTERN SUDANIC
Sambyu. Kwangari D.→SOUTH WESTERN BANTU
Samia = Dan→MANDE
Samia = Saamia→NORTH EASTERN BANTU
Samihim. Maanyan D.→WEST INDONESIAN
Samo→MANDE
Samo→LEFT MAY
Samo→PARE-SAMO-BEAMI-BOSAVI
Samoan→POLYNESIAN
Samogho = Samo→MANDE
Samogitian = Shamaitish. Lithuanian D.→BALTIC
Samogo = Samo→MANDE
SAMOIC-OUTLIER→POLYNESIAN
Samojo = Samo→MANDE
SAMO-KUBO-BIBO→PARE-SAMO-BEAMI-BOSAVI
Samorho = Samo→MANDE
Samoxo = Samo→MANDE
SAMOYEDIC→URALIC
Sampit→WEST INDONESIAN
SAMPITIC→WEST INDONESIAN
Sampori. Biak D.→MOLUCCAN
Sampur. Maasai D.→EASTERN SUDANIC
Samre→MON-KHMER
Samsam→WEST INDONESIAN
SAMUR = LEZGHIAN→CAUCASIAN
Samurzakan. Abxazo D.→CAUCASIAN
Samurzakan-Zugdidi. Zan D.→CAUCASIAN
Samwi = Afema. Anyi D.→VOLTA-COMOE
Samya = Saamia→NORTH EASTERN BANTU
San→KHOISAN
San Andres. Tzotzil D.→MAYAN
San Antonio Salinas. Salinan Tr.→HOKAN
San Carlos. Navajo D.→ATHAPASCAN-EYAK
San Carlos = Rumsen. Southern Costanoan D.→MIWOK-COSTANOAN
San Felipe. Keres D.
San Francesco Saverio Mission = Cochimi→HOKAN
San Francisco. Northern Costanoan D.→MIWOK-COSTANOAN
San Francisco St. Xavier = Oneida→IROQUOIS
San Francisco Xavier Mission = Cochimi→HOKAN
San Gabriel Mission = Gabrieleno→UTO-AZTECAN

San Ignacio→CHAPACURA-WANHAMAN
San Ildefonso. Tewa D.→TANOAN
San Javier = Cochimi→HOKAN
San Joaquin = Cochimi→HOKAN
San Jorge. Northern Epera D.→CHOCO
San Jose. Northern Costanoan D.→MIWOK-COSTANOAN
San Juan. Tewa D.→TANOAN
San Juan Bautista = Mutsun. Southern Costanoan D.→MIWOK-COSTANOAN
San Juan Capistrano = Juaneno. Luiseno D.→UTO-AZTECAN
San Lorenzo. Northern Costanoan D.→MIWOK-COSTANOAN
San Luis Mission = Luiseno→UTO-AZTECAN
San Miguel Chicah = Qiche→MAYAN
San Miguel Salinas. Salinan Tr.→HOKAN
San Regino. Yameo D.→PEBA-YAGUAN
San Tung. Sui D.→KAM-TAI
San Xavier = Cochimi→HOKAN
SANAGA→NORTH WESTERN BANTU
Sanamaica = Sanamaika. Monde D.→TUPI
Sanamaika. Monde D.→TUPI
Sanana→CENTRAL AND SOUTH NEW GUINEA
Sanana→EAST INDONESIAN
Sanapana. Mascoy D.→MACRO-PANOAN
Sanaroa→PAPUA AUSTRONESIAN
San-chiange. Kam D.→KAM-TAI
San-ch'uan. Mongour D.→MONGOLIAN
Sandawe→KHOISAN
Sandawi = Sandawe→KHOISAN
Sande→EASTERN
Sandeh→EASTERN
Sandia. Tiwa D.→TANOAN
Sandoway. Aso Tr.→NAGA-KUKI-CHIN
Sandu = Shandu→NAGA-KUKI-CHIN
Sanetch = Saanich. Northern Straits Salish D.→SALISH
Sanga→CENTRAL WESTERN BANTU
Sanga = Sangawa→PLATEAU BENUE-CONGO
Sangada. Tebu Tr.→SAHARAN
Sangawa→PLATEAU BENUE-CONGO
Sangbanga. Banda D.→EASTERN
Sanggar. Bima D.→EAST INDONESIAN
Sanggau = Embaloh→WEST INDONESIAN
Sangge. Tangsa D.→BODO-NAGA-KACHIN
Sanggil = Sangir→HESPERONESIAN
Sangihe = Sangir→HESPERONESIAN
Sangil = Sangir→HESPERONESIAN
Sangir→HESPERONESIAN
Sangke→NORTH PAPUAN
Sanglechi→IRANIAN

Sango→EASTERN
Sango→CENTRAL EASTERN BANTU
Sango = Shanjo→SOUTH WESTERN BANTU
Sangpang = Khambu→GYARUNG-MISHMI
Sangs-Rgyas = Mnyamskad. Central Tibetan D.→TIBETAN
Sangu→NORTH WESTERN BANTU
Sangu = Sango→CENTRAL EASTERN BANTU
Sanguelche. Araucanian D.→PENUTIAN
Sangyas = Mnyamskad. Central Tibetan D.→TIBETAN
Sanha→CHIBCHAN
Sanima→WAICAN
Saninawa. Catuquina D.→PANO
Saninawacana. Catuquina D.→PANO
Sanio→SEPIK
Sanjo = Shango→SOUTH WESTERN BANTU
Sanke = Sangge. Tangsa D.→BODO-NAGA-KACHIN
Sankhican = Delaware→ALGONQUIAN
Sankihani = Delaware→ALGONQUIAN
Sankikani = Delaware→ALGONQUIAN
Sankitani = Delaware→ALGONQUIAN
Sankura. Bobo D.→GUR
Sano = Samo→MANDE
Sanpoil. Okanogan D.→SALISH
Sansimoniano. Ororono D.→CHAPACURA-WANHAMAN
Sanskrit→INDIC
Santa. Pao-an D.→MONGOLIAN
Santa Ana. Keres D.
Santa Clara. Northern Costanoan D.→MIWOK-COSTANOAN
Santa Clara. Tewa D.→TANOAN
Santa Cruz. Northern Costanoan D.→MIWOK-COSTANOAN
Santa Cruz. Maya D.→MAYAN
SANTA CRUZ = REEF ISLANDS-SANTA CRUZ→CENTRAL MELANESIAN
Santa Cruz, Northern→CENTRAL MELANESIAN
Santa Cruz, Southeastern→CENTRAL MELANESIAN
Santa Cruz, Southwestern→CENTRAL MELANESIAN
Santa Cruz, Reef Island = Reef Island→CENTRAL MELANESIAN
Santa Domingo. Keres D.
Santa Inez = Barbareno. CHUMASH Tr.→HOKAN
Santa Maria. Pioje-Sioni Tr.→MACRO-TUCANOAN
Santali→MUNDA

Santan. Land Dayak D.→WEST INDONESIAN
Santee. Dakota D.→SIOUAN
Santiam→KALAPUYA
SANTO→NORTHWESTERN NEW HEBRIDES
Santrokofi→CENTRAL TOGO
Sanu = Samo→MANDE
Sanye→CUSHITIC
Sanza. Ndandi D.→NORTH EASTERN BANTU
Sanzi. Bangobango D.→NORTH EASTERN BANTU
Sao = Saho. Afar-Saho D.→CUSHITIC
Sao = Thao→FORMOSAN AUSTRONESIAN
Sao Tome→ROMANCE
Saoch = Sauch→MON-KHMER
Saok = Sooke. Northern Straits Salish D.→SALISH
Saonek. Waigeo D.→SOUTH HALMAHERA AUSTRONESIAN
Saora = Sora→MUNDA
Saotch = Sauch→MON-KHMER
Sapaqui. Mascoy D.→MACRO-PANOAN
Sapara→CARIB
Saparua. Ambonese D.→MOLUCCAN
Saparuna→TACANA
Sapibocona→TACANA
Sapiny. Nandi D.→EASTERN SUDANIC
Sapo. Krahn Tr.→KRU
Sapolewa→EAST INDONESIAN
Sapondralis. Bipi D.→ADMIRALTY-WESTERN ISLANDS
Saposa→NORTHWESTERN AND CENTRAL SOLOMONS
Saprek. Puyuma D.→FORMOSAN AUSTRONESIAN
Sapuan→MON-KHMER
Sapuia = Sapuya→EQUATORIAL
Sapuki = Sapaqui. Mascoy D.→MACRO-PANOAN
Saputan = Sabutan. Land Dayak D.→WEST INDONESIAN
Sapuya→EQUATORIAL
SARA→CENTRAL SUDANIC
Sara→CENTRAL SUDANIC
Sara. Buhagana Tr.→MACRO-TUCANOAN
Sara = Kaba Dunjo→CENTRAL SUDANIC
Sara Dai=Dai→CHADIC
Sara Gambai = Gambai→CENTRAL SUDANIC
Sara Gulai = Gulai. Sara D.→CENTRAL SUDANIC
Sara Hii→CENTRAL SUDANIC
Sara Kaba = Kaba→CENTRAL SUDANIC

Sara Lai = Gablai→CHADIC
Sara Majingai = Majingai. Sara D.→CENTRAL SUDANIC
Sara Mbai = Mbai→CENTRAL SUDANIC
Sara Mbai of Doba. Gambai D.→CENTRAL SUDANIC
Sara Murun. Gambai D.→CENTRAL SUDANIC
Sara Ndam = Ndam→CHADIC
Sara Ndemi = Kaba Ndim. Kaba D.→CENTRAL SUDANIC
Sara Ngabre = Gabri→CHADIC
Sara Ngama. Sara D.→CENTRAL SUDANIC
Sara Soumray = Somrai→CHADIC
Sara Toumak = Tumak→CHADIC
Sara Tounia = Tunya→CHADIC
Saracole. Soninke Tr.→MANDE
Saraka = Tharaka→NORTH EASTERN BANTU
Saraki. Bengali D.→INDIC
Sarakole. Soninke Tr.→MANDE
Sarakolle. Soninke Tr.→MANDE
Saramaccan→GERMANIC
Sarangani = Balud. Bilaan D.→NORTHWEST AUSTRONESIAN
Sarar = Bok. Manjaku D.→WEST ATLANTIC
Saraveca→MAIPURAN
Sarawan. Brahui D.→DRAVIDIAN
Sarawaria = Gorkhpuri. Bihari D.→INDIC
Sarawule. Soninke Tr.→MANDE
Sarcee = Sarsi→ATHAPASCAN-EYAK
Saremde. More D.→GUR
Sari→ADAMAWA
Sari = Sum. Pasai D.→INDIC
Sariba→PAPUA AUSTRONESIAN
Sarigue. Mbaya-Guaicuru Tr.→GUAYCURU
Sarikoli. Shughni D.→IRANIAN
Sarmatian→IRANIAN
SARMIC see article
Saroa. Bauwaki D.→MAILU
Saroua = Sarwa→CHADIC
Sarsi→ATHAPASCAN-EYAK
Sart. Uzbek D.→TURKIC
Sartul. Buryat D.→MONGOLIAN
Sarua = Sarwa→CHADIC
Saruga→BOGIA
Sarwa→CHADIC
Saryh Uygur = Yellow Uighur→TURKIC
Saryq. Turkmen D.→TURKIC
Sasak→WEST INDONESIAN
Sasar→EASTERN OCEANIC
Sasaricon. Coroado D.→PURI
Sasaru. Ikpeshi D.→EDO
Saseng→HUON-FINISTERRE

Saskathewan = Cree→ALGONQUIAN
SASTEAN = SHASTAN→HOKAN
Sastica = Blackfoot→ALGONQUIAN
Sastika = Blackfoot→ALGONQUIAN
Sastikaa = Blackfoot→ALGONQUIAN
Sastotene = Sekani. Sekani D.→ATHAPAS-CAN-EYAK
Sasuchan. Sekani D.→ATHAPASCAN-EYAK
Sasuten = Sasuchan. Sekani D.→ATHAPAS-CAN-EYAK
Satare = Maue→TUPI
Satawal. Carolinian D.→MICRONESIAN
Satchotugottine. Dogrib Tr.→ATHAPASCAN-EYAK
Sate = Kumba→ADAMAWA
Satienyo. Northern Zamucoan Tr.→EQUATO-RIAL
Satlaj. Western Pahari D.→INDIC
Satsop. Upper Chehalis D.→SALISH
Sau→EAST NEW GUINEA HIGHLANDS
Sau. Land Dayak D.→WEST INDONESIAN
Sau. Mundrau D.→ADMIRALTY-WESTERN ISLANDS
Sau = Sahu. Waioli D.→NORTH HALMA-HERA
Sau = Sawi. Phalura D.→INDIC
Sau = Thao→FORMOSAN AUSTRONESIAN
Sauch→MON-KHMER
Saufa. Lau D.→EASTERN OCEANIC
Sauh = Sau. Land Dayak D.→WEST INDO-NESIAN
Sauk→HUON-FINISTERRE
Sauk. Fox D.→ALGONQUIAN
Sauki = Sauk. Fox D.→ALGONQUIAN
Saukie = Sauk. Fox D.→ALGONQUIAN
Saukiya Khun = Rangkas→GYARUNG-MISHMI
Saulteurs = Salteaux. Ojibwa D.→ALGON-QUIAN
Saumanganja. Mentawai D.→WEST INDO-NESIAN
Saunulu. Wahai D.→EAST INDONESIAN
Saura = Wara. Palara D.→GUR
Sauraseni→INDIC
Saurashtri = Patnuli. Gujarati D.→INDIC
Sauria = Malto→DRAVIDIAN
Sausu→CENTRAL AND SOUTHERN CELE-BES
Savan→NORTHWESTERN NEW HEBRIDES
Savana = Shawnee→ALGONQUIAN
Savanahica = Shawnee→ALGONQUIAN
Savanahice = Shawnee→ALGONQUIAN
Savanna = Shawnee→ALGONQUIAN
Savante = Oti→MACRO-GE

Savara = Sora→MUNDA
Savei = Sapiny. Nandi D.→EASTERN SUDAN-IC
Saviny = Sapiny. Nandi D.→EASTERN SU-DANIC
Savo→CENTRAL MELANESIAN
Savo. Finnish D.→URALIC
Savosavo = Savo→CENTRAL MELANESIAN
Savu = Havunese→MOLUCCAN
Saw→NORTH WESTERN BANTU
Sawai→SOUTH HALMAHERA AUSTRO-NESIAN
Sawai Madhopur. Rajasthani D.→INDIC
Sawano = Shawnee→ALGONQUIAN
Sawanou = Shawnee→ALGONQUIAN
Sawanwan = Shawnee→ALGONQUIAN
Saweli. Tala D.→EAST INDONESIAN
Saweroe. Yava D.→WESTERN NEW GUINEA
Sawi→INDO-PACIFIC
Sawi. Phalura D.→INDIC
Sawi = Afema. Anyi D.→VOLTA-COMOE
Sawit. Mongul D.→MONGOLIAN
Sawk = Sauk. Fox D.→ALGONQUIAN
Sawkee = Sauk. Fox D.→ALGONQUIAN
Sawknah→BERBER
Sawos→SEPIK
Sawpana. Bwe D.→KAREN
Sawtung. Bwe D.→KAREN
Sawu = Havunese→MOLUCCAN
Sayaco = Amahuaca→PANO
Sayan Samoyed→URALIC
Sayma = Chayma→CARIB
Saysay = Sese. Gumuz D.→KOMAN
Sayula→MIXE-ZOQUE
Sazek = Seediq→FORMOSAN AUSTRONE-SIAN
Sbalt = Balti. West Tibetan D.→TIBETAN
SCANDINAVIAN = NORTH GERMANIC→GERMANIC
Scandinavian, Continental→GERMANIC
Scandinavian, Insular→GERMANIC
Sce = She→OMOTIC
Schambala = Shambaa→CENTRAL EAST-ERN BANTU
Schambioa = Chamboa→CARAJA
Schawanese = Shawnee→ALGONQUIAN
Schekere = Hukwe→KHOISAN
Scheyenne = Cheyenne→ALGONQUIAN
Schitsui = Coeur d'Alene→SALISH
Schoschone = Shoshoni→UTO-AZTECAN
Schoshone = Shoshoni→UTO-AZTECAN
Schwoyelpi = Colville. Okanogan D.→SALISH
Sciacco = Sheko→OMOTIC
Scinascia = Shinasha→OMOTIC

Scoffie = Naskapi. Cree D.→ALGONQUIAN

Scotuks = Passamaquoddy→ALGONQUIAN

Scythian→IRANIAN

Se = Shai. Adangme D.→GA-ADANGME

Seba→CENTRAL EASTERN BANTU

Seba. Havunese D.→MOLUCCAN

Sebei = Sapiny. Nandi D.→EASTERN SU-
DANIC

Seboda. Abui D.→TIMOR-ALOR

Sebondoy→EQUATORIAL

Sebuan = Sebuano→NORTHWEST AUSTRO-
NESIAN

Sebuano→NORTHWEST AUSTRONESIAN

Sec→ANDEAN

Secatogue. Mohegan Tr.→ALGONQUIAN

Sechelt = Seshelt→SALISH

Sechura = Sec→ANDEAN

Seco = Paya→MACRO-CHIBCHAN

Secoya-Gai. Pioje-Sioni Tr.→MACRO-TUCA-
NOAN

Secumne = Maidu→MAIDU

Secura = Sec→ANDEAN

Sedalir. Bolongan D.→NORTHWEST AUS-
TRONESIAN

Sedang→MON-KHMER

Sedanskij. Kamchadal D.→CHUKCHEE-KAM-
CHATKAN

Seden. Persian D.→IRANIAN

Sedere = Adele→CENTRAL TOGO

Sedik = Seediq→FORMOSAN AUSTRONE-
SIAN

Sediq = Seediq→FORMOSAN AUSTRONE-
NESIAN

Seduan = Siduan. Melanau D.→WEST INDO-
NESIAN

Seechelt = Seshelt→SALISH

Seedik = Seediq→FORMOSAN AUSTRONE-
SIAN

Seediq→FORMOSAN AUSTRONESIAN

Segai. Modang D.→WEST INDONESIAN

Segan = Bintulu→WEST INDONESIAN

Segeju = Daiso→NORTH EASTERN BANTU

Seget→WESTERN NEW GUINEA

Segum. Serer D.→WEST ATLANTIC

Seho→EAST INDONESIAN

Seim→SEPIK

Seiyawa→CHADIC

Sek = Saek→KAM-TAI

Seka = Sekar→MOLUCCAN

Sekah = Lonchong→WEST INDONESIAN

Sekani→ATHAPASCAN-EYAK

Sekapan. Ba Mali D.→WEST INDONESIAN

Sekar→MOLUCCAN

Sekepan = Sekapan. Ba Mali D.→WEST IN-

DONESIAN

Sekhwan. Kanakanabu D.→FORMOSAN AUS-
TRONESIAN

Sekiyani→NORTH WESTERN BANTU

Seko→CENTRAL AND SOUTHERN CELE-
BES

Seko = Sko→NORTH PAPUAN

Sekou = Sko→NORTH PAPUAN

Sekpele = Likpe→CENTRAL TOGO

Sekumne = Maidu→MAIDU

Sela. Limba D.→WEST ATLANTIC

Selajar. Makasarese D.→CENTRAL AND
SOUTHERN CELEBES

Selakau. Land Dayak D.→WEST INDONE-
SIAN

Selangor. Southwestern Sakai D.→SAKAI

Selaru. Fordat D.→MOLUCCAN

Selcnam = Shelknam. Ona D.→ANDEAN

Sele = Santrokofi→CENTRAL TOGO

Seleo→NORTHEAST NEW GUINEA AUS-
TRONESIAN

Selepet→HUON-FINISTERRE

Selish = Kalispel→SALISH

Seliu = Seleo→NORTHEAST NEW GUINEA
AUSTRONESIAN

Selkup = Ostyak Samoyed→URALIC

Selong = Halang→MON-KHMER

Selonian→BALTIC

Selti = Inneqor. East Gurage D.→SEMITIC

Selvasan. Fordat D.→MOLUCCAN

Selya. Nyakyusa D.→CENTRAL EASTERN
BANTU

Sema = Simi→NAGA-KUKI-CHIN

Semai = Central Sakai→SAKAI

Semambu. Murut D.→NORTHWEST AUS-
TRONESIAN

SEMANG see article

Semariji. Peremka D.→CENTRAL AND
SOUTH NEW GUINEA

Sembakung = Simbakong. Bolongan D.→
NORTHWEST AUSTRONESIAN

Sembla. Samo D.→MANDE

Seme→GUR

SEMELAIC→SAKAI

Semi Gallian = Zemgalian→BALTIC

Semigae. Andoa Tr.→ANDEAN

SEMITIC see article

Semnani. Persian D.→IRANIAN

Semobi. Puyuma D.→FORMOSAN AUS-
TRONESIAN

Semou = Samo→MANDE

Sempan→ASMAT

Semu = Samo→MANDE

Sena→CENTRAL EASTERN BANTU

Senadi = Senari→GUR
SENAGI→NORTH NEW GUINEA
Senagi→NORTH NEW GUINEA
Senahu. Tala D.→EAST INDONESIAN
Senaki. Zan D.→CAUCASIAN
Senar. Senari D.→GUR
Senari→GUR
Sendal = Tzeltal→MAYAN
Sene→HUON-FINISTERRE
Sene = Gola→WEST ATLANTIC
Seneca→IROQUOIS
Seneca = Cayuga. Seneca Tr.→IROQUOIS
Senecka = Seneca. Seneca Tr.→IROQUOIS
Sened→BERBER
SENEGAL→WEST ATLANTIC
Senegal→ROMANCE
Senegele→NORTH WESTERN BANTU
Senga. Tumbuka D.→CENTRAL EASTERN
    BANTU
Senga = Nsenga→CENTRAL EASTERN
    BANTU
Sengan→NORTH WESTERN AND CENTRAL
    SOLOMONS
SENGA-SENA→CENTRAL EASTERN BAN-
    TU
Sengeju = Daiso→NORTH EASTERN
    BANTU
Sengga = Sengan→NORTHWESTERN AND
    CENTRAL SOLOMONS
Sengmai→BURMESE-LOLO
Senhaja De Srair. Riff D.→BERBER
Senje = Gola→WEST ATLANTIC
SENOIC = SAKAI
Sensi. Conibo D.→PANO
Sentah. Land Dayak D.→WEST INDONESIAN
SENTANI→NORTH PAPUAN
Sentani→NORTH PAPUAN
Senthang→NAGA-KUKI-CHIN
SENUFO→GUR
Sepa→EAST INDONESIAN
Sepa. Manam D.→NORTHEAST NEW GUIN-
    EA AUSTRONESIAN
se-Pedi = Pedi = Northern Sotho→SOUTH
    EASTERN BANTU
Sepen→BOGIA
SEPIK see article
Sepohskanumakahkee = Mandan→SIOUAN
Sepous = Tuxis. Mohegan Tr.→ALGON-
    QUIAN
Seputan = Sabutan. Land Dayak D.→WEST
    INDONESIAN
Sera. Fordat D.→MOLUCCAN
Serahuli. Soninke Tr.→MANDE
Serambau. Land Dayak D.→WEST INDONE-
SIAN
Serambo = Serambau. Land Dayak D.→WEST
    INDONESIAN
Seramina→KOIARI
Seran→EAST INDONESIAN
Serano Huilche. Araucanian D.→PENUTIAN
Serau. Central Sakai D.→SAKAI
Sera-Yogur. Pao-an D.→MONGOLIAN
Serbocroatian→SLAVIC
Serbodjadi. Gayo D.→WEST INDONESIAN
Sere→EASTERN
Serer→WEST ATLANTIC
Serer None = Non→WEST ATLANTIC
Serer Sin = Sin. Serer D.→WEST ATLANTIC
Serere = Serer→WEST ATLANTIC
Serhta. Rawang D.→BODO-NAGA-KACHIN
Seri→HOKAN
Seria = Selya. Nyakyusa D.→CENTRAL
    EASTERN BANTU
Serian = Sadong. Land Dayak D.→WEST IN-
    DONESIAN
Sering. Land Dayak D.→WEST INDONESIAN
Sermah. Land Dayak D.→WEST INDONE-
    SIAN
Sermata. Leti D.→MOLUCCAN
Seroa→KHOISAN
Serrano→UTO-AZTECAN
Serrano. Seri Tr.→HOKAN
Serrer = Serer→WEST ATLANTIC
Serting. Southeastern Sakai D.→SAKAI
Serua→EAST INDONESIAN
Seruawan→EAST INDONESIAN
Serui. Japen D.→MOLUCCAN
Serwang. Rawang D.→BODO-NAGA-KA-
    CHIN
Sesa→EAST NEW GUINEA HIGHLANDS
Sesake. Tongoa D.→EASTERN OCEANIC
Sese→NORTH EASTERN BANTU
Sese. Gumuz D.→KOMAN
Sese = Bira→NORTH EASTERN BANTU
Seshalt = Seshelt→SALISH
Seshelt→SALISH
se-Sotho = Southern Sotho→SOUTH EAST-
    ERN BANTU
Seta→TUPI
Seta→TORRICELLI
Setaman→OK
Setauket. Mohegan Tr.→ALGONQUIAN
Setebo. Conibo D.→PANO
Setenggau Jagio. Land Dayak D.→WEST IN-
    DONESIAN
Seti→TORRICELLI
Seti→EAST INDONESIAN
Setiali→SEPIK

Setibo = Setebo. Conibo D.→PANO
Setiit = Setit. Kunama D.→CHARI-NILE
Setit. Kunama D.→CHARI-NILE
se-Tswana = Tswana→SOUTH EASTERN
    BANTU
Sewa. Mende D.→MANDE
Sewa = Seba→CENTRAL EASTERN BANTU
Sewacu→ARAWAKAN
Sewa-Mende = Sewa. Mende D.→MANDE
Sewe→ADAMAWA
Sənoi. Central Sakai D.→SAKAI
Səru-viri. Askun D.→NURISTANI
Sgaw→KAREN
Sha = Shan→KAM-TAI
Shaale = Shale. Tama D.→EASTERN SU-
    DANIC
Shacriaba = Chacriaba→GE
Shadal. Mankanya D.→WEST ATLANTIC
Shadar = Shadal. Mankanya D.→WEST AT-
    LANTIC
Shahaptin = Sahaptin→SAHAPTIN-NEZ
    PERCE
Shahari. Modern South Arabic D.→SEMITIC
Shaho = Saho. Afar-Saho D.→CUSHITIC
Shahrudi. Persian D.→IRANIAN
Shai. Adangme D.→GA-ADANGME
Shaiab. Beja Tr.→CUSHITIC
SHAKA = CHAGA→NORTH EASTERN
    BANTU
Shaka = Caga→NORTH EASTERN BANTU
Shake = Kota→NORTH WESTERN BANTU
Shakiri = Gudur. Sukur D.→CHADIC
Shakko = Sheko→OMOTIC
Shako = Sheko→OMOTIC
Shal→PLATEAU BENUE-CONGO
Shale. Tama D.→EASTERN SUDANIC
Shalgno = Central Tibetan→TIBETAN
Shalkandu = Chalkandu. Northern Altai D.→
    TURKIC
Sham. West Tibetan D.→TIBETAN
Shamaitish. Lithuanian D.→BALTIC
Shamatari. Waica D.→WAICAN
SHAMBAA = SHAMBALA→CENTRAL
    EASTERN BANTU
Shambaa→CENTRAL EASTERN BANTU
SHAMBALA→CENTRAL EASTERN BAN-
    TU
Shambala = Shambaa→CENTRAL EASTERN
    BANTU
Shamishuna. Puri D.→PURI
Shan→KAM-TAI
Shan = Khamti→KAM-TAI
Shan, Twelve Districts = Yunnan Shant'ou→
    KAM-TAI

Shandu→NAGA-KUKI-CHIN
Shanga. Shona D.→SOUTH EASTERN
    BANTU
Shanga = Busa→MANDE
Shangaan = Hlanganu. Tsonga D.→SOUTH
    EASTERN BANTU
Shangaan = Tsonga→SOUTH EASTERN
    BANTU
Shangalla = Shogale. Berta D.→CHARI-NILE
Shangawa = Busa→MANDE
Shango = Sangu→NORTH WESTERN
    BANTU
Shangwe. Shona D.→SOUTH EASTERN
    BANTU
Shanjo→SOUTH WESTERN BANTU
Shankadi = Samba→CENTRAL WESTERN
    BANTU
Shankillinya = Ari→OMOTIC
Shankillinya = Gumuz→KOMAN
Shant'ou, Yunnan→KAM-TAI
SHANTOU YEHJEN = KACHIN→BODO-
    NAGA-KACHIN
Shaŋwe = Shangwe. Shona D.→SOUTH
    EASTERN BANTU
Shao = Thao→FORMOSAN AUSTRONE-
    SIAN
Shapra. Candoshi D.→JIVAROAN
Shapsug. Circassian D.→CAUCASIAN
Shari = Chari→MON-KHMER
Sharpa. Central Tibetan D.→TIBETAN
Shashatapoosh = Montagnais. Cree D.→AL-
    GONQUIAN
Shashatapooshoish = Montagnais. Cree D.→
    ALGONQUIAN
SHASTAN→HOKAN
Shat = Shinasha→OMOTIC
Shateras = Tutelo→SIOUAN
Shati = Koasati→MUSKOGEAN
Shatt→EASTERN SUDANIC
Shavannice = Shawnee→ALGONQUIAN
Shavante = Chavante→GE
Shavante = Oti→MACRO-GE
Shavaye = Javahe→CARAJA
Shawan = Shawnee→ALGONQUIAN
Shawanawa. Catuquina D.→PANO
Shawanee = Shawnee→ALGONQUIAN
Shawanese = Shawnee→ALGONQUIAN
Shawann = Shawnee→ALGONQUIAN
Shawannee = Shawnee→ALGONQUIAN
Shawanno = Shawnee→ALGONQUIAN
Shawano = Shawnee→ALGONQUIAN
Shawanoe = Shawnee→ALGONQUIAN
Shawanoese = Shawnee→ALGONQUIAN
Shawanose = Shawnee→ALGONQUIAN

Shawasha. Shona D.→SOUTH EASTERN
BANTU
Shawi. Kotoko D.→CHADIC
Shawnee→ALGONQUIAN
Shawnese = Shawnee→ALGONQUIAN
Shawni = Shawnee→ALGONQUIAN
Shawnoe = Shawnee→ALGONQUIAN
She→OMOTIC
Shebayo→MAIPURAN
Shede = Cheke→CHADIC
Shedekka = Seediq→FORMOSAN AUSTRO-
NESIAN
Sheetswa = Tswa→SOUTH EASTERN
BANTU
Sheikhan. Zaza D.→IRANIAN
Sheke = Sekiyani→NORTH WESTERN
BANTU
Shekiri = Itsekiri. Yoruba D.→YORUBA
Shekka = Mocho→OMOTIC
Sheko→OMOTIC
Shelknam. Ona D.→ANDEAN
Shelkota. Midob Tr.→EASTERN SUDANIC
Shellengcha = Kanakuru→CHADIC
Sheminawa. Cashinwa D.→PANO
Shendu = Shandu→NAGA-KUKI-CHIN
Sheneiab. Beja Tr.→CUSHITIC
Shenge Sherbro. Southern Bullom D.→WEST
ATLANTIC
Shengwe = Tonga→SOUTH EASTERN
BANTU
Sheni→PLATEAU BENUE-CONGO
Shepalu = Lwo→EASTERN SUDANIC
Sherafada = Sherfada. Tebu Tr.→SAHARAN
Sherbro = Southern Bullom→WEST
ATLANTIC
Sherente = Cherente→GE
Sherfada. Tebu Tr.→SAHARAN
Sheshapotosh = Montagnais. Cree D.→AL-
GONQUIAN
Sheshatapoosh = Montagnais. Cree D.→AL-
GONQUIAN
Sheta = Seta→TUPI
Shete Tsere = Tsh'iti. Shua D.→KHOISAN
Shetimasha = Chitamacha→MACRO-ALGON-
QUIAN
Sheva = Cewa. Nyanja D.→CENTRAL
EASTERN BANTU
Shewa = Tulema. Galla D.→CUSHITIC
Sheyenne = Cheyenne→ALGONQUIAN
Shi. Havu D.→NORTH EASTERN BANTU
Shiba = Southern Bullom→WEST ATLANTIC
shi-Chopi = Chopi→SOUTH EASTERN
BANTU
shi-Copi = Chopi→SOUTH EASTERN
BANTU
Shidishana. Waica Tr.→WAICAN
Shienne = Cheyenne→ALGONQUIAN
Shifalu = Lwo→EASTERN SUDANIC
Shighni = Shughni→IRANIAN
Shino = Saho. Afar-Saho D.→CUSHITIC
Shikalu = Nkoya→CENTRAL WESTERN
BANTU
Shikiana→CARIB
Shikotan. Ainu D.
Shila. Taabwa D.→CENTRAL EASTERN
BANTU
shi-Laŋganu = Hlanganu. Tsonga D.→SOUTH
EASTERN BANTU
shi-Leŋgwe = Hlengwe. Tswa D.→SOUTH
EASTERN BANTU
Shilha→BERBER
Shilluk→EASTERN SUDANIC
shi-Mbwera = Mbwera→CENTRAL WEST-
ERN BANTU
Shimigae = Semigae. Andoa Tr.→ANDEAN
Shimopaiwan. Paiwan D.→FORMOSAN AUS-
TRONESIAN
SHIMRIN→NAGA-KUKI-CHIN
Shina. Rutul D.→CAUCASIAN
Shinasha→OMOTIC
Shinca = Xinca→MACRO-CHIBCHAN
Shingi→CENTRAL WESTERN BANTU
Shingini = Kamabari→PLATEAU BENUE-
CONGO
Shinji = Shingi→CENTRAL WESTERN
BANTU
Shinkoya = Nkoya→CENTRAL WESTERN
BANTU
Shinnecock. Mohegan Tr.→ALGONQUIAN
Shinumo = Hopi→UTO-AZTECAN
shi-ŋwaluŋgu = Ngwalungu. Tsonga D.→
SOUTH EASTERN BANTU
Shioko = Ciokwe→SOUTH WESTERN
BANTU
Ship. Albanian D.
Shiparicot = Xiparicot→CARIB
Shipibo. Conibo D.→PANO
Shir = Mondari. Bari D.→EASTERN SUDAN-
IC
Shira. Caga D.→NORTH EASTERN BANTU
Shira = Sira→NORTH WESTERN BANTU
SHIRA-PUNU→NORTH WESTERN BANTU
Shirawa→CHADIC
Shirazi. Persian D.→IRANIAN
Shiriana. Waica D.→WAICAN
SHIRINAN = WAICAN
Shirino = Xirino. Cashibo D.→PANO
Shirishana→WAICAN

Shirishiana = Shirishana→WAICAN
shi-Ronga = Ronga→SOUTH EASTERN BANTU
Shirri = Shurri. Northern Mao D.→KOMAN
Shishi = Seba→CENTRAL EASTERN BANTU
Shishiatl = Seshelt→SALISH
shi-Tsonga = Tsonga→SOUTH EASTERN BANTU
shi-Tswa = Tswa→SOUTH EASTERN BANTU
Shiyan = Cheyenne→ALGONQUIAN
Shi-zang = Siyin→NAGA-KUKI-CHIN
Sho = Aso→NAGA-KUKI-CHIN
Shoa = Aso→NAGA-KUKI-CHIN
Shoa = Tulema. Galla D.→CUSHITIC
Shoba = Pianga. Busooŋ Tr.→NORTH WESTERN BANTU
Shobwa = Pianga. Busooŋ Tr.→NORTH WESTERN BANTU
Shobyo. Ruanda D.→NORTH EASTERN BANTU
Shocleng. Seta D.→TUPI
Shoe = Shawi. Kotoko D.→CHADIC
Shogale. Berta D.→CHARI-NILE
Shoho = Saho. Afar-Saho D.→CUSHITIC
Shom Pen→NICOBARESE
Shom Peng = Shom Pen→NICOBARESE
Shomo = Chomo→JUKUNOID
SHONA→SOUTH EASTERN BANTU
Shona→SOUTH EASTERN BANTU
Shong = Chong→MON-KHMER
Shongo = Busooŋ→NORTH WESTERN BANTU
Shongu→NORTHEASTERN NEW GUINEA
Shonshe = Sonse→NAGA-KUKI-CHIN
Shooswaap = Shuswap→SALISH
Shooswap = Shuswap→SALISH
Shor→TURKIC
Shor. Khakas D.→TURKIC
Shosho = Birom→PLATEAU BENUE-CONGO
SHOSHONEAN, PLATEAU = NUMIC→UTO-AZTECAN
SHOSHONEAN, SOUTHERN CALIFORNIAN = TAKIC→UTO-AZTECAN
Shoshonee = Shoshoni→UTO-AZTECAN
Shoshoni→UTO-AZTECAN
Shoshonie = Shoshoni→UTO-AZTECAN
Shqip = Albanian
Shqiperi = Albanian
Shqipni = Albanian
Shu. Ndandi D.→NORTH EASTERN BANTU

Shu = Pho→KAREN
Shua→KHOISAN
Shuakhwe = Shua→KHOISAN
Shuakwe = Shua→KHOISAN
Shuara = Jivaro→JIVAROAN
Shubi = Subi→NORTH EASTERN BANTU
Shughni→IRANIAN
Shui = Sui→KAM-TAI
Shukaali = Shu. Ndandi D.→NORTH EASTERN BANTU
Shukulumbwe = Ila→CENTRAL EASTERN BANTU
Shulanin. Avar D.→CAUCASIAN
Shuli = Akoli→EASTERN SUDANIC
Shunkla = Tashon→NAGA-KUKI-CHIN
Shupaman = Bamoun→BANTOID
Shuri = Suri. Tirma D.→EASTERN SUDANIC
Shuro = Mekan→EASTERN SUDANIC
Shurri. Northern Mao D.→KOMAN
Shuru = Bats. Berta D.→CHARI-NILE
Shushtar-Dizfali. Persian D.→IRANIAN
Shushwapumsh = Shuswap→SALISH
Shuswap→SALISH
Shuway = Shwai→KORDOFANIAN
Shwai→KORDOFANIAN
Shwoyelpi = Colville. Okanogan D.→SALISH
Shyenne = Cheyenne→ALGONQUIAN
Si Djundjung. Minangkabau D.→WEST INDONESIAN
Sia = Sya→MANDE
Siacuas = Magach. Mbaya-Guaicuru Tr.→GUAYCURU
Sialum→HUON-FINISTERRE
Siama. Loma D.→MANDE
Siamese→KAM-TAI
SIANE→EAST NEW GUINEA HIGHLANDS
Siane→EAST NEW GUINEA HIGHLANDS
Siar→BISMARCK ARCHIPELAGO
Siati see CHIMBU→EAST NEW GUINEA HIGHLANDS
Siaute→NORTH NEW GUINEA
Siaviri = Gae. Andoa Tr.→ANDEAN
Sibbe = Nagovisi→BOUGAINVILLE
Sibil→OK
Sibo. Manchu D.→TUNGUS
Sibop→WEST INDONESIAN
Sibu. Melanau D.→WEST INDONESIAN
Sibucoon. Puyuma D.→FORMOSAN AUSTRONESIAN
Sibuguey. Subanun D.→NORTHWEST AUSTRONESIAN
Sibuku = Sivukun. Bunun D.→FORMOSAN AUSTRONESIAN
Sicacao. Mape D.→CARIB

Sicatl = Seshelt→SALISH
Sicel→ITALIC
Sichule→WEST INDONESIAN
Sickenames = Pequot. Mohegan D.→ALGON-
    QUIAN
Sidak. Ingassana Tr.→CHARI-NILE
Sidama = Sidamo→CUSHITIC
Sidaminya = Sidamo→CUSHITIC
SIDAMO→CUSHITIC
Sidamo→CUSHITIC
Sidamonya = Sidamo→CUSHITIC
Sideia = Siraya→FORMOSAN AUSTRONE-
    NESIAN
Sideis = Siraya→FORMOSAN AUSTRONE-
    SIAN
Sidetic see article
Sidianka = Sidya. Malinka D.→MANDE
Sidin. Land Dayak D.→WEST INDONESIAN
Siding = Sidin. Land Dayak D.→WEST INDO-
    NESIAN
Sidjuai→MOMBERAMO RIVER
Sidondo. Palu D.→CENTRAL AND SOUTH-
    ERN CELEBES
Siduan. Melanau D.→WEST INDONESIAN
Siduani = Siduan. Melanau D.→WEST INDO-
    NESIAN
Sidya. Malinka D.→MANDE
Sidyanka = Sidya. Malinka D.→MANDE
Sie. Eromanga D.→SOUTHERN NEW HEB-
    RIDES
Sierra Popoluca→MIXE-ZOQUE
Sigala-Tɔdala. Dyimini D.→GUR
Siggoyo = Northern Mao→KOMAN
Sigi. Palu D.→CENTRAL AND SOUTHERN
    CELEBES
Sigila→CHADIC
Sigisigero = Baitsi→BOUGAINVILLE
Sihanaka. Malagasy D.→WEST INDONESIAN
Sihia→BURMESE-LOLO
Sihong. Maanyan D.→WEST INDONESIAN
Siis = Yu. Manjaku D.→WEST ATLANTIC
Sikaiana. Luangiua D.→POLYNESIAN
Sikayana = Sikaiana. Luangiua D.→POLY-
    NESIAN
Sikiana = Sikaiana. Luangiua D.→POLYNE-
    SIAN
Sikirari. Maasai Tr.→EASTERN SUDANIC
Sikka→MOLUCCAN
Sikkamese = Da-njong-ka. Central Tibetan D.→
    TIBETAN
SIKKIC→MOLUCCAN
Sikkim. Central Tibetan D.→TIBETAN
Siksika = Blackfoot→ALGONQUIAN
Sikube→GOILALA

Sikule = Sichule→WEST INDONESIAN
Silabu. Mentawai D.→WEST INDONESIAN
Siladja = Selajar. Makasarese D.→CENTRAL
    AND SOUTHERN CELEBES
Silajara = Selajar. Makasarese D.→CENTRAL
    AND SOUTHERN CELEBES
Silam. Sumo Tr.→MISUMALPAN
Silanganen. Tagbanua D.→NORTHWEST
    AUSTRONESIAN
Silen→EAST INDONESIAN
Siletz. Tillamook D.→SALISH
Sili = Tsh'iti. Shua D.→KHOISAN
Siliama→TACANA
Silipan. Ifugao D.→NORTHWEST AUSTRO-
    NESIAN
Siliput→TORRICELLI
si-Lozi = Lozi→SOUTH WESTERN BANTU
Silti = Inneqor. East Gurage D.→SEMITIC
Simaa→SOUTH WESTERN BANTU
Simacu→ANDEAN
Simajek — Iseimajek. Tatog Tr.→EASTERN
    SUDANIC
Simalegi. Mentawai D.→WEST INDONESIAN
Simalungun→WEST INDONESIAN
Simalur→WEST INDONESIAN
Simba = Cimba. Herero D.→SOUTH WEST-
    ERN BANTU
Simbakong. Bolongan D.→NORTHWEST
    AUSTRONESIAN
Simbari→KUKUKUKU
Simbiti. Koria D.→NORTH EASTERN
    BANTU
Simeku→BOUGAINVILLE
Simelungan = Simalungun→WEST INDONE-
    SIAN
SIMEN GURAGINYA = NORTH GURAGE
    →SEMITIC
Simeuloe = Simalur→WEST INDONESIAN
Simi→NAGA-KUKI-CHIN
Similaton. Lenca D.→MACRO-CHIBCHAN
Simirinch. Piro D.→MAIPURAN
Simityek = Iseimajek. Tatog Tr.→EASTERN
    SUDANIC
Simog→NORTH PAPUAN
Simolul. Sichule D.→WEST INDONESIAN
Simori. Kapauku D.→WEST NEW GUINEA
    HIGHLANDS
Simpi = Age→BANTOID
Simulul = Simalur→WEST INDONESIAN
Sin. Serer D.→WEST ATLANTIC
SINA→INDIC
Sina→INDIC
Sinabo→PANO
Sinabo. Conibo D.→PANO

Sinagen = Galu→TORRICELLI
Sinaki→PAPUA AUSTRONESIAN
Sinaloa. Cahita D.→UTO-AZTECAN
Sinalua = Sinaloa. Cahita D.→UTO-AZTECAN
Sinan. Land Dayak D.→WEST INDONESIAN
Sinasina. Chimbu D.→EAST NEW GUINEA HIGHLANDS
Sinaugoro→PAPUA AUSTRONESIAN
Sinca = Xinca→MACRO-CHIBCHAN
Sindagua→BARBACOAN
Sindamon→HUON-FINISTERRE
Sindangan. Subanun D.→NORTHWEST AUSTRONESIAN
Sindhi→INDIC
Sinding. Land Dayak D.→WEST INDONESIAN
Sindjai. Buginese D.→CENTRAL AND SOUTHERN CELEBES
Sinesine = Sinasina. Chimbu D.→EAST NEW GUINEA HIGHLANDS
Sinesip→NORTHWESTERN NEW HEBRIDES
Singa→NORTH EASTERN BANTU
Singasinga = Vasengasenga→NORTHWESTERN AND CENTRAL SOLOMONS
Singgi. Land Dayak D.→WEST INDONESIAN
Singhalese = Sinhalese→INDIC
Singhi = Singgi. Land Dayak D.→WEST INDONESIAN
Singhpo = Chingpaw→BODO-NAGA-KACHIN
Singkarak. Minangkabau D.→WEST INDONESIAN
Sinhalese→INDIC
Sinhmaw. Bwe D.→KAREN
Sini→GOILALA
Sinicker = Seneca →IROQUOIS
Sinimiut = Netsilik. Inuit D.→ESKIMO-ALEUT
Sinipe = Chunupi. Vilela Tr.→LULE-VILELA-CHARRUA
SINITIC see SINO-TIBETAN
Sinja = Subi→NORTH EASTERN BANTU
Sinkan. Siraya D.→FORMOSAN AUSTRONESIAN
Sinkat Keinab. Beja Tr.→CUSHITIC
Sinkat Kenab = Sinkat Keinab. Beja Tr.→ CUSHITIC
Sinkiuse = Columbian→SALISH
Sinkiuse-Columbia = Columbian→SALISH
Sinkyone. Nongatl D.→ATHAPASCAN-EYAK
Sinohoan→CENTRAL AND SOUTHERN CELEBES
Sinolon. Tagabili D.→NORTHWEST AUSTRONESIAN
Sinongko. Mori D.→CENTRAL AND SOUTHERN CELEBES
SINO-TIBETAN see article
Sinsiga→CHIBCHAN
Sinsin. Bwe D.→KAREN
Sinsin = Sin. Serer D.→WEST ATLANTIC
Siokun. Subanun D.→NORTHWEST AUSTRONESIAN
Sioni. Pioje-Sioni Tr.→MACRO-TUCANOAN
Siora. Zanaki D.→NORTH EASTERN BANTU
SIOUAN see article
SIOUAN, MACRO- see article
Sioux = Dakota→SIOUAN
Sipaya→TUPI
Sipo→ARAWAKAN
Sipolilo. Shona D.→SOUTH EASTERN BANTU
Siquisaye. Cuica D.→EQUATORIAL
Sira→NORTH WESTERN BANTU
Sira. Ndrosun D.→ADMIRALTY-WESTERN ISLANDS
Siraiki. Sindhi D.→INDIC
Sirawa→CHADIC
Siraya→FORMOSAN AUSTRONESIAN
Sirenik→ESKIMO-ALEUT
Sirhe→NEW CALEDONIA
Siria. Maasai Tr.→EASTERN SUDANIC
Sirimeri→MAIPURAN
Siringol. Pao-an D.→MONGOLIAN
Siriono→TUPI
Siripuria. Bengali D.→INDIC
Sirmauri. Western Pahari D.→INDIC
Siroi = Pasa. Ganglau D.→INDO-PACIFIC
Sirunki. Enga D.→EAST NEW GUINEA HIGHLANDS
Sirxin. Dargwa D.→CAUCASIAN
Sisai = Sisala→GUR
Sisala→GUR
Sisano→NORTHEAST NEW GUINEA AUSTRONESIAN
Sisiaini. Bamu Kiwai D.→CENTRAL AND SOUTH NEW GUINEA
Sisingga = Sensan→NORTHWESTERN AND CENTRAL SOLOMONS
Sisiulu. Tala D.→EAST INDONESIAN
Siska = Tonga→CENTRAL EASTERN BANTU
Sisya = Tonga→CENTRAL EASTERN BANTU
Sisyaban = Saaroa→FORMOSAN AUSTRONESIAN
Siti = Vagala→GUR
Sitia Sherbro. Southern Bullom D.→WEST

ATLANTIC
Sitigo = Vagala→GUR
Siu. Swahili D.→CENTRAL EASTERN BANTU
Siuci→NORTHERN UMAIPRAN
Siusi = Siuci→NORTHERN MAIPURAN
Siuslaw→YAKONAN
Sivukun. Bunun D.→FORMOSAN AUSTRO-NESIAN
Siwa→BERBER
Siwai→BOUGAINVILLE
Siwu = Akpafu→CENTRAL TOGO
Siwuri = Bowili→CENTRAL TOGO
Siya = Avatime→CENTRAL TOGO
Siyang = Siyin→NAGA-KUKI-CHIN
Siyase = Avatime→CENTRAL TOGO
Siyin→NAGA-KUKI-CHIN
Siyu = Siu. Swahili D.→CENTRAL EAST-ERN BANTU
Sizang = Siyin→NAGA-KUKI-CHIN
Sjiagha = Syiagha→AWYU
Skagit. Puget Sound Salish D.→SALISH
Skalza = Kutenai
Skalzi = Kutenai
Skay-wa-mish = Squamish→SALISH
Skeena Indians = Tsimshian→PENUTIAN
Skidegate. Haida D.→NA-DENE
Skidi Pawnee. Pawnee D.→CADDOAN
Skip = Albanian
Skiri Pawnee = Skidi Pawnee. Pawnee D.→CADDOAN
Skitsamish = Coeur d'Alene→SALISH
Skitsuish = Coeur d'Alene→SALISH
Skitswish = Coeur d'Alene→SALISH
Skittagetan = Haida→NA-DENE
Sklallam = Clallam→SALISH
SKO→NORTH PAPUAN
Sko→NORTH PAPUAN
Skoffi = Naskapi. Cree D.→ALGONQUIAN
Skoffie = Naskapi. Cree D.→ALGONQUIAN
SKOFRO→NORTH PAPUAN
Skofro→NORTH PAPUAN
Skokomish = Twana→SALISH
Skolt Lapp→URALIC
Skoyelpi = Colville. Okanogan D.→SALISH
S'lai = Li→KAM-TAI
Slave. Chipewyan Tr.→ATHAPASCAN-EYAK
Slavey = Slave. Chipewyan Tr.→ATHAPAS-CAN-EYAK
SLAVIC see article
Slavic, Old Church = Slavonic, Old Church→SLAVIC
Slavonian. Serbocroatian D.→SLAVIC
Slavonic, Old Church→SLAVIC

SLAVONIC = SLAVIC
Sliammon. Comox D.→SALISH
Slim. Central Sakai D.→SAKAI
Slovak→SLAVIC
Slovene→SLAVIC
Slovenian = Slovene→SLAVIC
Slovincian. Kashubian D.→SLAVIC
Snabi Watubela. Geser D.→EAST INDONE-SIAN
Snake. Northern Paiute D.→UTO-AZTECAN
Snake = Shoshoni→UTO-AZTECAN
Snohomish. Puget Sound Salish D.→SALISH
Snoqualmie. Puget Sound Salish D.→SALISH
So→NORTH WESTERN BANTU
So→MON-KHMER
So = Aso→NAGA-KUKI-CHIN
Soahuwe = Uli. Tala D.→EAST INDONESIAN
Sobei→SARMIC
SOBEIC→SARMIC
Sobiobo. Pichobo D.→PANO
Sobo = Urhobo→EDO
Sobojo→MOLUCCAN
Sochile = Nyakyusa→CENTRAL EASTERN BANTU
Sock = Sooke. Northern Straits Salish D.→SALISH
Socunusca = Tapachultec→MIXE-ZOQUE
Soddo→SEMITIC
Sodia = Gudwa. Gutob D.→MUNDA
Sofala = Ndau. Shona D.→SOUTH EASTERN BANTU
Soga→NORTH EASTERN BANTU
Sogadas. Kunama D.→CHARI-NILE
Sogdian→IRANIAN
Sogero. Wabuda D.→CENTRAL AND SOUTH NEW GUINEA
Sogha = Dyula. Dyula Tr.→MANDE
Sogore = Mekan→EASTERN SUDANIC
Sohur = Yaqay→MARIND
Sok→MON-KHMER
Soke = Zoque→MIXE-ZOQUE
Sokile = Nyakyusa→CENTRAL EASTERN BANTU
Sokili = Nyakyusa→CENTRAL EASTERN BANTU
Soko. Ntombo-Bolia Tr.→NORTH WESTERN BANTU
Soko = So→NORTH WESTERN BANTU
SOKO-KELE→NORTH WESTERN BANTU
Sokoro→CHADIC
SOKORO-MUBI→CHADIC
Sokotri. Modern South Arabic D.→SEMITIC
Sokte→NAGA-KUKI-CHIN
Sokue = Zoque→MIXE-ZOQUE

Sokwele. Bete Tr.→KRU
Sokya = Sokwele. Bete Tr.→KRU
Solamba = Soruba-Kuyobe→GUR
Soledad. Southern Costanoan D.→MIWOK-
  COSTANOAN
Soledad Mission = Esselen→HOKAN
Soli→CENTRAL EASTERN BANTU
SOLOMONS, CENTRAL→CENTRAL MELA-
  NESIAN
SOLOMONS, NORTHWESTERN AND CEN-
  TRAL see article
Solon→TUNGUS
Solongo. Kongo D.→CENTRAL WESTERN
  BANTU
Solor→MOLUCCAN
Soloto→EQUATORIAL
Solowat→WESTERN NEW GUINEA
Som→HUON-FINISTERRE
Soma = Somba→GUR
Somali→CUSHITIC
Somalinya = Somali→CUSHITIC
Somba→GUR
Some = Somba→GUR
Somo. Gbaya Tr.→EASTERN
Somono. Bambara D.→MANDE
SOMRAI→CHADIC
Somrai→CHADIC
SOMRAI-SOKORO→CHADIC
Somray = Somrai→CHADIC
Somre = Somrai→CHADIC
Somrei = Somrai→CHADIC
Son. Wa D.→PALAUNG-WA
Sonay = Songhai→NILO-SAHARAN
Sonder. Tontemboan D.→NORTHERN CELE-
  BES
SONGE→CENTRAL WESTERN BANTU
Songe→CENTRAL WESTERN BANTU
Songhai→NILO-SAHARAN
Songhees = Songish. Northern Straits Salish
  D.→SALISH
Songi = Songe→CENTRAL WESTERN BAN-
  TU
Songish. Northern Straits Salish D.→SALISH
Songo→CENTRAL WESTERN BANTU
Songola→NORTH EASTERN BANTU
Songola = Ombo→NORTH WESTERN BAN-
  TU
Songomeno→NORTH WESTERN BANTU
Songoora. Ndandi D.→NORTH EASTERN
  BANTU
Sonilu. Ndrosun D.→ADMIRALTY-WEST-
  ERN ISLANDS
Soninke→MANDE
Sonjo→NORTH EASTERN BANTU

SONORAN→UTO-AZTECAN
Sonrai = Songhai→NILO-SAHARAN
Sonse→NAGA-KUKI-CHIN
Sonsoral. Ulithian D.→MICRONESIAN
Sonyo = Sonjo→NORTH EASTERN BANTU
Sooke. Northern Straits Salish D.→SALISH
Soonde→CENTRAL WESTERN BANTU
Sooso = Soso. Kongo D.→CENTRAL WEST-
  ERN BANTU
Soow Huhelia→EAST INDONESIAN
Sopi. 'Beli D.→CENTRAL SUDANIC
Sopocnovskij. Kamchadal D.→CHUKCHEE-
  KAMCHATKAN
Sopvoma. Simi D.→NAGA-KUKI-CHIN
Soqotri = Sokotri. Modern South Arabic D.→
  SEMITIC
Sor. Biak D.→MOLUCCAN
Sor = Ngaing→HUON-FINISTERRE
Sora→MUNDA
Sorathi. Gujarati D.→INDIC
Sorbian = Lusatian→SLAVIC
Sore = Kipsorai. Nandi D.→EASTERN SU-
  DANIC
Sorendidori. Biak D.→MOLUCCAN
Sori→ADMIRALTY-WESTERN ISLANDS
Sorko = Bozo. Soninke D.→MANDE
Soroako. Mori D.→CENTRAL AND SOUTH-
  ERN CELEBES
Sorogo = Bozo. Soninke D.→MANDE
Sorol. Ulithian D.→MICRONESIAN
Sorora = Opata→UTO-AZTECAN
Sorrido. Biak D.→MOLUCCAN
Soruba-Kuyobe→GUR
Sorung = Sie. Eromanga D.→SOUTHERN
  NEW HEBRIDES
Soso. Kongo D.→CENTRAL WESTERN
  BANTU
Soso = Susu→MANDE
Sosso = Tsotso. Hungu D.→CENTRAL WEST-
  ERN BANTU
Sotati-po. Central Tibetan D.→TIBETAN
Soteomellos = Wappo→YUKI
Sotho, Northern→SOUTH EASTERN BANTU
Sotho, Southern→SOUTH EASTERN BANTU
Sotho = Southern Sotho→SOUTH EASTERN
  BANTU
Sotho, Transvaal = Northern Sotho→SOUTH
  EASTERN BANTU
SOTHO-TSWANA→SOUTH EASTERN BAN-
  TU
Sotiagay = Ashushlay→MATACO
Sotomieyos = Wappo→YUKI
Sou = Suq→MON-KHMER
Soubiya = Subia→SOUTH WESTERN BANTU

Souei = Soui→MON-KHMER
Souhegan. Massachussett Tr.→ALGONQUIAN
Soui→MON-KHMER
Souk = Sok→MON-KHMER
Sourikwos = Micmac→ALGONQUIAN
Souriquois = Micmac→ALGONQUIAN
Soussou = Susu→MANDE
South River→MOMBERAMO RIVER
Sowanda→NORTH PAPUAN
Sowek. Biak D.→MOLUCCAN
Soyboibo = Sobiobo. Pichobo D.→PANO
Soyod = Tuva→TURKIC
Soyon = Tuva→TURKIC
Soyopas = Mohave. River Yuman D.→
    YUMAN
Soyot. Sayan Samoyed D.→URALIC
Spanish→ROMANCE
Speng. Ba Mali D.→WEST INDONESIAN
Spiti. Central Tibetan D.→TIBETAN
Spokan = Spokane. Kalispel D.→SALISH
Spokane. Kalispel D.→SALISH
Spuch'-æ-lotz — Tsimshian—·PENUTIAN
Sqolyek. Atayal D.→FORMOSAN AUSTRO-
    NESIAN
Squamish→SALISH
Squawmish = Squamish—·SALISH
Sranan→GERMANIC
Sranan Tongo=Sranan→GERMANIC
Sre. Koho D.→MON-KHMER
Srem. Albanian D.
Srubu = Surubu→PLATEAU BENUE-CONGO
Ssu Ghassi = Dzu/'oasi. Kung D.→KHOISAN
Ssuga = Suga. Bute D.→BANTOID
Ssugur = Sukur→CHADIC
St. Philip's Bay→NORTHWESTERN NEW
    HEBRIDES
St. Francis = Abnaki. Penobscot D.→ALGON-
    QUIAN
St. Jean = Malecite. Passamaquoddy D.→AL-
    GONQUIAN
St. Jean Baptiste = Onandaga. Seneca Tr.→
    IROQUOIS
St. John = Abnaki. Penobscot D.→ALGON-
    QUIAN
St. John = Malecite. Passamaquoddy D.→
    ALGONQUIAN
St. Regis = Mohawk→IROQUOIS
St. Xavier = Oneida→IROQUOIS
Staly. Lezghian D.→CAUCASIAN
Stang. Land Dayak D.→WEST INDONESIAN
Stelatin. Carrier Tr.→ATHAPASCAN-EYAK
Stieng→MON-KHMER
Stockbridge = Mohegan→ALGONQUIAN
Stokavian. Serbocroatian D.→SLAVIC

Stoney = Assiniboin. Dakota D.→SIOUAN
Stonies = Stone Chilcotin. Chilcotin Tr.→
    ATHAPASCAN-EYAK
Stony = Assiniboin. Dakota D.→SIOUAN
Straits Salish, Northern→SALISH
Strieng = Trieng→MON-KHMER
Su→NORTH WESTERN BANTU
Su = Sok→MON-KHMER
Sua. Chuave D.→EAST NEW GUINEA HIGH-
    LANDS
Sua = Mansoanka→WEST ATLANTIC
Suaheli = Swahili→CENTRAL   EASTERN
    BANTU
Suahili = Swahili→CENTRAL   EASTERN
    BANTU
Suain→NORTHEAST NEW GUINEA AUS-
    TRONESIAN
Suam→NORTHEAST NEW GUINEA AUS-
    TRONESIAN
Suambe→KOIARI
Suamle. Kweni D.→MANDE
Suaru→BOGIA
Suau→PAPUA AUSTRONESIAN
Subah = Limbu→GYARUNG-MISHMI
Sub-Akhmimic = Asyutic. Coptic D.→AFRO-
    ASIATIC
Subano = Subanun→NORTHWEST   AUS-
    TRONESIAN
Subanu = Subanun→NORTHWEST   AUS-
    TRONESIAN
Subanun→NORTHWEST AUSTRONESIAN
Subi→NORTHWESTERN AND CENTRAL
    SOLOMONS
Subi→NORTH EASTERN BANTU
Subia→SOUTH WESTERN BANTU
Subinha-Solomec. Kanjobal D.→MAYAN
SUBIYA→SOUTH WESTERN BANTU
Subiya = Subia→SOUTH WESTERN BANTU
Subtiaba→TLAPANECAN
SUBTIABA-TLAPANEC = TLAPANECAN
SUBTIABA-TLAPANEC-YOPI = TLAPA-
    NECAN
Subu = Su—NORTH WESTERN BANTU
Subya = Subia·→SOUTH WESTERN BANTU
Sucuriyu = Moriuene→NORTHERN MAI-
    PURAN
SUDANIC see NIGER-CONGO
SUDANIC, CENTRAL see article
SUDANIC, EASTERN see article
SUDANIC, MACRO- = CHARI-NILE
SUDANIC, WEST see NIGER-CONGO
Sudest = Tagula→PAPUA AUSTRONESIAN
Sudfluss = South River→MOMBERAMO
    RIVER

Suduvian = Jatvian→BALTIC
Sue = Suq→MON-KHMER
Suena→BINANDERE
Suerre→CHIBCHAN
Suffah = Limbu→GYARUNG-MISHMÍ
Suga. Bute D.→BANTOID
Suganga = Wagarabai→OK
Sugbuanon = Sebuano→NORTHWEST AUS-
    TRONESIAN
Sugbuhanon = Sebuano→NORTHWEST AUS-
    TRONESIAN
Sugu→EASTERN OCEANIC
Sugur = Sukur→CHADIC
Suhu = Sugu→EASTERN OCEANIC
Sui→KAM-TAI
Sui. Kol. D.→NEW BRITAIN
Sui. Southern Kiwai D.→CENTRAL AND
    SOUTH NEW GUINEA
Sui Ai. Sui D.→KAM-TAI
Sui Li. Sui D.→KAM-TAI
Sui-P'o. Sui D.→KAM-TAI
Suisun — Patwin→WINTUN
Suk = Polot→EASTERN SUDANIC
Suk = Sok→MON-KHMER
Sukhutix. Pawnee D.→CADDOAN
Suki→MARIND
Suku→CENTRAL WESTERN BANTU
Suku→KOIARI
Sukulumbwe = Ila→CENTRAL EASTERN
    BANTU
Sukuma→NORTH EASTERN BANTU
SUKUMA-NYAMWEZI→NORTH EASTERN
    BANTU
Sukur→CHADIC
Sula = Palmar. Jicaque D.→HOKAN
Sulamata→NORTHWEST AUSTRONESIAN
Suleimaniyi. Kermanji D.→IRANIAN
SULIC→NORTHWEST AUSTRONESIAN
Sulka→NEW BRITAIN
Sulu = Taw Sug→NORTHWEST AUSTRO-
    NESIAN
Sum. Pasai D.→INDIC
Sumadel. Kalinga D.→NORTHWEST AUS-
    TRONESIAN
Sumariup→SEPIK
Sumas. Halkomelem D.→SALISH
Sumasti→INDIC
Sumau→BOGIA
Sumba→MOLUCCAN
Sumbawa→WEST INDONESIAN
Sumburu=Bira→NORTH EASTERN BANTU
Sumbwa→NORTH EASTERN BANTU
Sumbwa = Mweri. Nyamwesi D.→NORTH
    EASTERN BANTU

Sumerian see article
Sumite. Tala D.→EAST INDONESIAN
Sumo→MISUMALPAN
Sumoun→NORTHWESTERN AND CEN-
    TRAL SOLOMONS
Sumpo. Land Dayak D.→WEST INDONESIAN
Sumtsu. Thebor D.→GYARUNG-MISHMI
Sumu = Sumo→MISUMALPAN
Sundanese→WEST INDONESIAN
Sundei. Biak D.→MOLUCCAN
Sundi. Oriya D.→INDIC
SUNDIC→WEST INDONESIAN
Sungai Piah. Northern Sakai D.→SAKAI
Sungai Raya. Central Sakai D.→SAKAI
Sunggari. Gold D.→TUNGUS
Sunggum→INDO-PACIFIC
Sungkai. Central Sakai D.→SAKAI
Sungnam. Thebor D.→GYARUNG-MISHMI
Sungor→EASTERN SUDANIC
Sungu = Songo→CENTRAL WESTERN BAN-
    TU
Sungu = Tetela→NORTH WESTERN BANTU
Sungum = Sungumana→NORTHEASTERN
    NEW GUINEA
Sungumana→NORTHEASTERN NEW GUI-
    NEA
Sunit. Ordos D.→MONGOLIAN
Sunuwar = Sunwari→GYARUNG-MISHMI
Sunwar = Sunwari→GYARUNG-MISHMI
Sunwari→GYARUNG-MISHMI
SUOY see MON-KHMER
SUPANEC = TLAPANECAN
SUPANECAN = TLAPANECAN
Supe = Samo→PARE-SAMO-BEAMI-BOSAVI
Supi = Sopi. 'Beli D.→CENTRAL SUDANIC
Sup'ide = Suppire→GUR
Supiori. Biak D.→MOLUCCAN
Suppire→GUR
Suq→MON-KHMER
Suquamish = Squamish. Puget Sound Salish
    D.→SALISH
Sura→CHADIC
Surati. Gujarati D.→INDIC
Surbm = Mekan→EASTERN SUDANIC
Surci. Kermanji D.→IRANIAN
Surguch. Balkan Gagauz Turkish D.→TURKIC
Suri. Tirma D.→EASTERN SUDANIC
Suri = Batangan→NORTHWEST AUSTRO-
    NESIAN
Surigao. Sebuano D.→NORTHWEST AUS-
    TRONESIAN
Surigaonon. Sebuano D.→NORTHWEST AUS-
    TRONESIAN
SURINAM = GUSAP-MOT→HUON-FINIS-

TERRE
Suri-Tirma-Tid = Tirma→EASTERN SUDAN-
IC
SURMA = BEIER-DIDINGA→EASTERN
SUDANIC
Surma = Mekan→EASTERN SUDANIC
Surma = Suri. Tirma D.→EASTERN SUDAN-
IC
Suro = Mekan→EASTERN SUDANIC
Surubu→PLATEAU BENUE-CONGO
Susee = Sarsi→ATHAPASCAN-EYAK
Susian = Elamite
Susquehannock→IROQUOIS
Sussekoon = Sarsi→ATHAPASCAN-EYAK
Sussu = Susu→MANDE
Susu→MANDE
Susulu→NORTHWESTERN AND CENTRAL
SOLOMONS
Suthu = Southern Sotho→SOUTH EASTERN
BANTU
Suto = Southern Sotho→SOUTH EASTERN
BANTU
Sutu = Ngoni→CENTRAL EASTERN
BANTU
Suwa. Amba D.→NORTH EASTERN BANTU
Suwaira. Tairora D.→EAST NEW GUINEA
HIGHLANDS
Suwal. Kwalhioqua D.→ATHAPASCAN-
EYAK
Suwawa→NORTHWEST AUSTRONESIAN
Suwawa-Bunda = Suwawa→NORTHWEST
AUSTRONESIAN
Suya→GE
Svan→CAUCASIAN
Swaga. Ndandi D.→NORTH EASTERN
BANTU
SWAHILI→CENTRAL EASTERN BANTU
Swahili→CENTRAL EASTERN BANTU
Swaka→CENTRAL EASTERN BANTU
Swase. Mbo D.→NORTH WESTERN BANTU
Swati. Nguni D.→SOUTH EASTERN BANTU
Swazi = Swati. Nguni D.→SOUTH EASTERN
BANTU
Swedish. Continental Scandinavian D.→GER-
MANIC
Sweta. Koria D.→NORTH EASTERN BANTU
Swit→NORTHEAST NEW GUINEA AUS-
TRONESIAN
Swosə = Swase. Mbo D.→NORTH WESTERN
BANTU
Sya→MANDE
Syaka. Enga D.→EAST NEW GUINEA HIGH-
LANDS
Syan→NORTH EASTERN BANTU

Syenere = Senari→GUR
Syer. Karaboro D.→GUR
Syiagha→AWYU
Sylhet. Khasi D.→MON-KHMER
Synteng. Khasi D.→MON-KHMER
Syriac. East Aramaic D.→SEMITIC
Szi = Tsaiwa→BODO-NAGA-KACHIN
Szu-i. Cantonese D.→CHINESE

T

TAA→KHOISAN
Taa. Bare'e D.→CENTRAL AND SOUTHERN
CELEBES
Ta'a Doe = Dolage. Sausu D.→CENTRAL
AND SOUTHERN CELEBES
Ta'a Dolo = Sausu→CENTRAL AND
SOUTHERN CELEBES
Taabwa→CENTRAL EASTERN BANTU
Ta'adjio = Kasimbar→NORTHERN CELEBES
Ta'am. Kei D.→MOLUCCAN
TA-ARAWAKAN→NORTHERN MAIPUR-
AN
Taataal. Gula D.→ADAMAWA
Taba = Ligbi→MANDE
Tabar→BISMARCK ARCHIPELAGO
Tabara. Shona D.→SOUTH EASTERN
BANTU
Tabare-Dom = Dom. Chimbu D.→EAST NEW
GUINEA HIGHLANDS
Tabaru→NORTH HALMAHERA
Tabasaran→CAUCASIAN
Tabataba = Tambatamba→NORTHWESTERN
AND CENTRAL SOLOMONS
Tabele = Ndebele→SOUTH EASTERN BAN-
TU
Tabenu. Timorese D.→EAST INDONESIAN
Tabetouo = Tabetuo. Bakwe Tr.→KRU
Tabetuo. Bakwe Tr.→KRU
Tabi = Ingassana→CHARI-NILE
Tabiica. Penyoqui D.→CHIQUITO
Tableng = Angwanku. Tangsa D.→BODO-
NAGA-KACHIN
Tabojan = Tabuyan. Lawangan D.→WEST
INDONESIAN
Tabojan Tongka = Tabuyan. Lawangan D.→
WEST INDONESIAN
Tabriak→NORTH NEW GUINEA
Tabu→NORTH PAPUAN
Tabukan. Sangir D.→HESPERONESIAN
Tabulaga. Logo Tr.→CENTRAL SUDANIC
Tabulahan. Pitu-ulunna-salu D.→CENTRAL
AND SOUTHERN CELEBES

Tabuloba = Tabulaga. Logo Tr.→CENTRAL SUDANIC

Tabun. Sarawak Murut D.→WEST INDO-NESIAN

Tabuyan. Lawangan D.→WEST INDONESIAN

Tabwa = Taabwa→CENTRAL EASTERN BANTU

Tacana. Mam D.→MAYAN

TACANA see article

Tacaneco = Tacana. Mam D.→MAYAN

Tac-cui = Tong-luang→KHMUIC

Tachaban. Paiwan D.→FORMOSAN AUSTRO-NESIAN

Tachi. Valley Yokuts D.→YOKUTS

Tacho. Moro Hills Tr.→KORDOFANIAN

Taconi. Luhya D.→NORTH EASTERN BANTU

Tacumbu = Magach. Mbaya-Guaicuru Tr.→ GUAYCURU

Tadermanji = Thaua→YUIN-KURIC

Tadianan = Tadyawan→NORTHWEST AUS-TRONESIAN

Tadje = Petapa→NORTHERN CELEBES

Tadjik = Tajik. Persian D.→IRANIAN

Tadjio = Kasimbar→NORTHERN CELEBES

Tadjoni = Taconi. Luhya D.→NORTH EAST-ERN BANTU

Tado. Southern Epera D.→CHOCO

Tado = Lindu. Kulawi D.→CENTRAL AND SOUTHERN CELEBES

Tadyawan→NORTHWEST AUSTRONESIAN

Tadzhik = Tajik. Persian D.→IRANIAN

Tadzik = Tajik. Persian D.→IRANIAN

Tae' = Balangnipa. Mandarese D.→CENTRAL AND SOUTHERN CELEBES

Tae' = Binuang. Mandarese D.→CENTRAL AND SOUTHERN CELEBES

Taemi = Tami→NORTHEAST NEW GUINEA AUSTRONESIAN

Taena = Makasarese→CENTRAL AND SOUTHERN CELEBES

Taensa. Natchez D.→MACRO-ALGON-QUIAN

Tafi. Nyangbo D.→CENTRAL TOGO

Tafile = Tafire. Tagbana D.→GUR

Tafire. Tagbana D.→GUR

Tafiri = Tafire. Tagbana D.→GUR

Tagabelies = Tagabili→NORTHWEST AUS-TRONESIAN

Tagabili→NORTHWEST AUSTRONESIAN

Tagacola = Tagakaolo→NORTHWEST AUS-TRONESIAN

Tagaidan = Tadyawan→NORTHWEST AUS-TRONESIAN

Taga-kaliwa = Nauhan→NORTHWEST AUS-TRONESIAN

Tagakaolo→NORTHWEST AUSTRONESIAN

Tagakolu = Tagakaolo→NORTHWEST AUS-TRONESIAN

Tagal. Murut D.→NORTHWEST AUSTRO-NESIAN

Tagal = Tagalog→NORTHWEST AUSTRO-NESIAN

Tagala = Tagalog→NORTHWEST AUSTRO-NESIAN

Tagalag. Ilba D.→PAMA-MARIC

Tagalagad = Bilaan→NORTHWEST AUS-TRONESIAN

Tagali→KORDOFANIAN

TAGALIC→NORTHWEST AUSTRONESIAN

Tagalo = Tagalog→NORTHWEST AUSTRO-NESIAN

Tagalog→NORTHWEST AUSTRONESIAN

Tagara. Senari D.→GUR

Tagara = Parji→DRAVIDIAN

Tagare. Chayma D.→CARIB

Tagaur = Iron. Ossetic D.→IRANIAN

Tagaydan = Tadyawan→NORTHWEST AUS-TRONESIAN

Tagba = Suppire→GUR

Tagba = Tagbu→EASTERN

Tagbana→GUR

Tagbanua→NORTHWEST AUSTRONESIAN

Tagbanuwa = Tagbanua→NORTHWEST AUS-TRONESIAN

Tagbari. Senari D.→GUR

Tagbo = Mambila→BANTOID

Tagbo = Tagbu→EASTERN

Tagbo = Togbo. Banda D.→EASTERN

Tagbona = Tagbana→GUR

Tagbu→EASTERN

Tagbwali. Banda D.→EASTERN

Tagdapaya = Obo. Bagobo D.→NORTH-WEST AUSTRONESIAN

Tage = Creye→GE

Tagen. Dafla D.→GYARUNG-MISHMI

Taghdansh = Azer. Soninke D.→MANDE

Tagish. Tahltan D.→ATHAPASCAN-EYAK

Tagnani. Southwest Nambicuara D.→NAMBI-CUARA

Tagoi→KORDOFANIAN

Tagota→CENTRAL AND SOUTH NEW GUINEA

Tagouana = Tagbana→GUR

Tagoy = Tagoi→KORDOFANIAN

Taguaca = Twahka. Sumo Tr.→MISUMAL-PAN

Tagula→PAPUA AUSTRONESIAN

Taguniourung = Tangurong→KULINIC
Tagwana = Tagbana→GUR
Tagwenda. Nyankole D.→NORTH EASTERN BANTU
Tahami. Cenu D.→CARIB
Tahari→BINANDERE
Tahitian→POLYNESIAN
TAHITIC→POLYNESIAN
Tahltan→ATHAPASCAN-EYAK
Tahoi = Taoih→MON-KHMER
Tahu. Bakwe Tr.→KRU
Tahue. Cahita D.→UTO-AZTECAN
Tahueco = Tahue. Cahita D.→UTO-AZTECAN
Tahuru-ina. Iranche D.→MAIPURAN
TAI→KAM-TAI
Tai, Red→KAM-TAI
Tai, Black = Tai Noir→KAM-TAI
Tai, White = Tai Blanc→KAM-TAI
Tai Blanc→KAM-TAI
Tai Lu = Lu→KAM-TAI
Tai Noir→KAM-TAI
TAI, NORTHERN = DIOI→KAM-TAI
Taiai. Saisiyat D.→FORMOSAN AUSTRONESIAN
Taifasy. Malagasy D.→WEST INDONESIAN
Taigi. Sayan Samoyed D.→URALIC
Taih-long = Teressa→NICOBARESE
Taihyo. Atayal D.→FORMOSAN AUSTRONESIAN
Taikaku. Mentawai D.→WEST INDONESIAN
Tailoi. Wa D.→PALAUNG-WA
Tailoi = Monglwe. Angku D.→PALAUNG-WA
Taimanambondro. Malagasy D.→WEST INDONESIAN
Taimani. Persian D.→IRANIAN
Taimoro. Malagasy D.→WEST INDONESIAN
Taimouri = Timuri. Persian D.→IRANIAN
Tain→GE
Tainbour = Thany Bur. Rek D.→EASTERN SUDANIC
Tain-daware = Ambasi→BINANDERE
Taino→ARAWAKAN
Taiobe. Tupi Tr.→TUPI
Taiof→NORTHWESTERN AND CENTRAL SOLOMONS
Taior→PAMA-MARIC
Taipechiche = Tapechiche. Kawaib Tr.→TUPI
TAIRORA→EAST NEW GUINEA HIGHLANDS
Tairora→EAST NEW GUINEA HIGHLANDS
Taisaka. Malagasy D.→WEST INDONESIAN
Tait. Halkomelem D.→SALISH
Taita→NORTH EASTERN BANTU

Taiyal = Atayal→FORMOSAN AUSTRONESIAN
Tajik. Persian D.→IRANIAN
Tak Bai. Southern Thai D.→KAM-TAI
Taka. Solor D.→MOLUCCAN
Takalak = Tagalag. Ilba D.→PAMA-MARIC
Takalako = Kalamai→MIRNINY
Takama. Nyamwesi D.→NORTH EASTERN BANTU
Takamakau = Taramakau. Rukai D.→FORMOSAN AUSTRONESIAN
Takamanda→BANTOID
TAKANA = TACANA
Takelma→PENUTIAN
Takemba→GUR
Takete. Vilela Tr.→LULE-VILELA-CHARRUA
Takfwelottine. Dogrib Tr.→ATHAPASCAN-EYAK
Takhtan = Serrano→UTO-AZTECAN
TAKIC→UTO-AZTECAN
Takilma = Takelma→PENUTIAN
Taki-Taki = Sranan→GERMANIC
Takon. Han Tr.→ATHAPASCAN-EYAK
Takonan. Atayal D.→FORMOSAN AUSTRONESIAN
Takpa. Central Tibetan D.→TIBETAN
Takpasyeeri. Senari D.→GUR
Takponin = Tagbana→GUR
Taku = Takuu. Luangiua D.→POLYNESIAN
Takua→MON-KHMER
Takum. Jukun D.→JUKUNOID
Takuna = Tucano→MACRO-TUCANOAN
Takunape→TUPI
Takurda. Malgana D.→KARDU
Takuu. Luangiua D.→POLYNESIAN
Takwa→EASTERN OCEANIC
Takwenda = Tagwenda. Nyankole D.→NORTH EASTERN BANTU
Tal→CHADIC
Tala→EAST INDONESIAN
Tala. Koho D.→MON-KHMER
Tala = Tarascan
Talagit. Altai D.→TURKIC
Talagit-Tolos. Altai D.→TURKIC
Talahundra. Shona D.→SOUTH EASTERN BANTU
Talaindji = Talandji→KANYARA
Talaing = Mon→MON-KHMER
Talamakau = Taramakau. Rukai D.→FORMOSAN AUSTRONESIAN
TALAMANCA→CHIBCHAN
Talamoh = Tillamook→SALISH
Talandji→KANYARA
Talang. Kerintji D.→WEST INDONESIAN

Talanjee = Talandji→KANYARA
Talanji = Talandji→KANYARA
Talansi = Talensi→GUR
Talassa. Tumtum Tr.→KORDOFANIAN
Talau = Tallau. Liguri D.→EASTERN SU-
DANIC
Talaud→HESPERONESIAN
Tale = Tali. Kari D.→ADAMAWA
Taleni = Talensi→GUR
Talensi→GUR
Tali→BURMESE-LOLO
Tali. Kari D.→ADAMAWA
Taliang. Hre D.→MON-KHMER
Talieng = Kasseng→MON-KHMER
Talisi→EASTERN OCEANIC
Talkee Talkee = Krio→GERMANIC
Tallainga = Talandji→KANYARA
Tallainji = Talandji→KANYARA
Tallan = Sec→ANDEAN
Tallau. Liguri D.→EASTERN SUDANIC
Tallensi→GUR
Talligewi = Cherokee→IROQUOIS
Tallion Nation = Bella Coola→SALISH
Talni = Talensi→GUR
Talo→EAST INDONESIAN
Talo = Tallau. Liguri D.→EASTERN SUDAN-
IC
TALODI→KORDOFANIAN
Talodi→KORDOFANIAN
TALODI-MASAKIN = TALODI→KORDO-
FANIAN
Taloinga = Talandji→KANYARA
Taloka = Daloka. Masakin Tr.→KORDO-
FANIAN
Taltaltepec. Chatino D.→ZAPOTECAN
Taltushtuntude = Galice→ATHAPASCAN-
EYAK
Taluche = Taluhet. Araucanian D.→PENU-
TIAN
Taluhet. Araucanian D.→PENUTIAN
Talumpa. Mamudju D.→CENTRAL AND
SOUTHERN CELEBES
Taluti→EAST INDONESIAN
Taluy. Kantu D.→MON-KHMER
Talysh→IRANIAN
TAMA→EASTERN SUDANIC
TAMA→SEPIK
Tama→EASTERN SUDANIC
Tama. Correguaje D.→MACRO-TUCANOAN
Tama = Dama. Nama D.→KHOISAN
Tama = Masongo→EASTERN SUDANIC
Tamado'wan = Tamaroan. Bunun D.→FOR-
MOSAN AUSTRONESIAN
Tamaha = Tsamai→CUSHITIC

Tamainde. Southwest Nambicuara D.→NAM-
BICUARA
Tamakwa = Dama. Nama D.→KHOISAN
Tamala. Malgana D.→KARDU
Tamalu. Rawang D.→BODO-NAGA-KACHIN
Taman→BURMESE-LOLO
Taman = Toman→NORTHWESTERN NEW
HEBRIDES
Tamana. Patangoro D.→CARIB
Tamang = Murmi→GYARUNG-MISHMI
Tamanik Lomuriki = Tima→KORDOFANIAN
Tamari→GUR
Tamari. Paiwan D.→FORMOSAN AUSTRO-
NESIAN
Tamarkholea. Limbu D.→GYARUNG-
MISHMI
Tamaroa = Illinois. Miami D.→ALGON-
QUIAN
Tamaroan. Bunun D.→FORMOSAN AUS-
TRONESIAN
Tamaroau = Tamaroan. Bunun D.→FOR-
MOSAN AUSTRONESIAN
Tamarois = Illinois. Miami D.→ALGON-
QUIAN
Tamaulipeco→UTO-AZTECAN
Tamazight→BERBER
TAMAZIGHT-RIFF-KABYLE→BERBER
Tamazulaxa. Mixtec D.→MIXTECAN
Tambaggo. Banda D.→EASTERN
Tambago. Banda D.→EASTERN
Tambaro = Kabena. Alaba D.→CUSHITIC
T'ambaro = Kabena. Alaba D.→CUSHITIC
Tambatamba→NORTHWESTERN AND CEN-
TRAL SOLOMONS
Tambe'e. Mori D.→CENTRAL AND SOUTH-
ERN CELEBES
Tamberma = Somba→GUR
Tambo→CENTRAL EASTERN BANTU
Tamboki. Mekongka D.→CENTRAL AND
SOUTHERN CELEBES
Tambuka = Tumbuka→CENTRAL EASTERN
BANTU
Tambunan. Dusun D.→NORTHWEST AUS-
TRONESIAN
Tambuoki = Laiwui→CENTRAL AND
SOUTHERN CELEBES
Tame = Tunebo→CHIBCHAN
Tamezret→BERBER
TAMI→NORTH PAPUAN
Tami→NORTHEAST NEW GUINEA AUS-
TRONESIAN
Tami, Upper→NORTH PAPUAN
Tamian. Lettish D.→BALTIC
Tamil→DRAVIDIAN

Tamlu = Tsingmegnu. Tangsa D.→BODO-NAGA-KACHIN

Tamma = Dama. Nama D.→KHOISAN

Tamoia. Tupi Tr.→TUPI

Tamoio. Tupi Tr.→TUPI

Tamok = Tama→EASTERN SUDANIC

Tamongobo = Tama→EASTERN SUDANIC

Tamot = Tama→EASTERN SUDANIC

Tampa. Campa D.→MAIPURAN

Tampahoaka. Malagasy D.→WEST INDONE-SIAN

Tampele = Tamprusi→GUR

Tampole = Tamprusi→GUR

Tampolem = Tamprusi→GUR

Tampolense = Tamprusi→GUR

Tamprun. Coroado D.→PURI

Tamprusi→GUR

Tampulma→GUR

Tampur. Gayo D.→WEST INDONESIAN

Tamsui. Siraya D.→FORMOSAN AUSTRO-NESIAN

Tamun = Chrau→MON-KHMER

Tamungkolowi→CENTRAL AND SOUTH-ERN CELEBES

Tan = Tang. Nsungli D.→BANTOID

Tana. Vale D.→CENTRAL SUDANIC

Tanabili = Atago→SANTA CRUZ AUSTRO-NESIAN

Tanah. Minangkabau D.→WEST INDONE-SIAN

Tanah Kumu. Endeh D.→MOLUCCAN

Tanah Merah = Tanamerah→WESTERN NEW GUINEA

Tanahana. Malagasy D.→WEST INDONE-SIAN

Tanahmerah = Tanamerah→WESTERN NEW GUINEA

Tanah-Merah = Tanamerah→NORTH PA-PUAN

Tanaina→ATHAPASCAN-EYAK

Tanala. Malagasy D.→WEST INDONESIAN

Tanamerah→NORTH PAPUAN

Tanana→ATHAPASCAN-EYAK

Tanana, Upper→ATHAPASCAN-EYAK

Tanang. Dafla D.→GYARUNG-MISHMI

Tanctonai. Dakota D.→SIOUAN

Tanda Basari = Basari→WEST ATLANTIC

Tande. Shona D.→SOUTH EASTERN BANTU

Tandjo'u = Togia. Bare'e D.→CENTRAL AND SOUTHERN CELEBES

Tandroy. Malagasy D.→WEST INDONESIAN

Tane = Tana. Vale D.→CENTRAL SUDANIC

Tang. Nsungli D.→BANTOID

Tanga→BISMARCK ARCHIPELAGO

Tanga = Batanga→NORTH WESTERN BANTU

Tanganalum = Tanganekald→NARRINYE-RIC

Tangane = Tanganekald→NARRINYERIC

Tanganekald→NARRINYERIC

Tangao. Seediq D.→FORMOSAN AUSTRO-NESIAN

Tangara = Antakirinya. Kardutjara D.→WATI

Tangdulanen. Tagbanua D.→NORTHWEST AUSTRONESIAN

Tangetti = Dainggati. Ngamba D.→YUIN-KURIC

Tanggu = Tanggum→BOGIA

TANGGUM→BOGIA

Tanggum→BOGIA

Tangi. Ndandi D.→NORTH EASTERN BANTU

TANGIC = TANGKIC

TANGKIC see article

Tangkul→NAGA-KUKI-CHIN

Tangole→CHADIC

Tangpril. Kantu D.→MON-KHMER

TANGSA = NAGA→BODO-NAGA-KA-CHIN

Tangsa→BODO-NAGA-KACHIN

Tangsarr→BODO-NAGA-KACHIN

Tangu = Tanggum→BOGIA

Tanguat→BOGIA

Tangural. Marengar D.→DALY

Tani→BOGIA

Tanjong. Melanau D.→WEST INDONESIAN

Tanjong Rambutan. Northern Sakai D.→SAKAI

Tankamba = Takemba→GUR

Tanna→SOUTHERN NEW HEBRIDES

Tannu-Tuva = Tuva→TURKIC

TANO→VOLTA-COMOE

TANOAN see article

Tanoriki = Maewo→EASTERN OCEANIC

Tanosy. Malagasy D.→WEST INDONESIAN

Tanotenne. Carrier Tr.→ATHAPASCAN-EYAK

Tantawaits = Chemehuevi. Southern Paiute D.→UTO-AZTECAN

Ta'n-ta'wats = Chemehuevi. Southern Paiute D.→UTO-AZTECAN

Tanygua. Tupi Tr.→TUPI

Tao. Paraujano D.→NORTHERN MAIPURAN

Tao. Penyoqui D.→CHIQUITO

Taoih→MON-KHMER

Ta-oih = Taoih→MON-KHMER

Taokas→FORMOSAN AUSTRONESIAN

Taolende. More D.→GUR

Taos. Tiwa D.→TANOAN
Taoujjout→BERBER
Taowa = Tewa→TANOAN
Tapachula = Tapachultec→MIXE-ZOQUE
Tapachultec→MIXE-ZOQUE
Tapachulteca = Tapachultec→MIXE-ZOQUE
Tapacua = Chavante→GE
Tapacura = Chapacura→CHAPACURA-WAN-HAMAN
Tapage = Pitahauerat. Pawnee D.→CADDOAN
Tapah. Central Sakai D.→SAKAI
Tapah. Sichule D.→WEST INDONESIAN
Tapahue. Cahita D.→UTO-AZTECAN
Tapangu. Tsou D.→FORMOSAN AUSTRONESIAN
Tapanhuna = Tepanhuna. Apiaka D.→TUPI
Tapanoan. Timote D.→EQUATORIAL
Tapanta. Abxazo D.→CAUCASIAN
Tapapi→CENTRAL AND SOUTH NEW GUINEA
Tapari = Tapapi→CENTRAL AND SOUTH NEW GUINEA
Taparita. Otamaco D.→EQUATORIAL
Taparito→CARIB
Taparito = Taparita. Otamaco D.→EQUATORIAL
Taparon. Ami D.→FORMOSAN AUSTRONESIAN
Tapas = Colima. Carare D.→CARIB
Tapechiche. Kawaib Tr.→TUPI
Tapessi = Tiapi. Landuma D.→WEST ATLANTIC
Tapiete. Tupi D.→TUPI
Tapiete = Ashushlay→MATACO
Tapii→BORORO
Tapiitin. Apiaka D.→TUPI
Tapijualapane-Mixe = Mixe→MIXE-ZOQUE
Tapijulapa = Tapixulapan→MIXE-ZOQUE
Tapijulapan = Tapixulapan→MIXE-ZOQUE
Tapirape→TUPI
Tapiraua. Tenetehara Tr.→TUPI
Tapixulapan→MIXE-ZOQUE
Taposa = Toposo→EASTERN SUDANIC
Taquial. Mam D.→MAYAN
Tar Bagrimma = Bagirmi→CENTRAL SUDANIC
Tar Barma = Bagirmi→CENTRALS UDANIC
Tara→CENTRAL AND SOUTHERN CELEBES
Tara = Bobo Wule. Bobo D.→GUR
Tara Baaka = Baka→CENTRAL SUDANIC
Taracahitan. Cahita D.→UTO-AZTECAN
TARACAHITIC→UTO-AZTECAN

Tarahumar = Tarahumara→UTO-AZTECAN
Tarahumara→UTO-AZTECAN
Tarahumare = Tarahumara→UTO-AZTECAN
Taraika. Ainu D.
Tarakan→NORTHWEST AUSTRONESIAN
Taram→ADAMAWA
Taramakau. Rukai D.→FORMOSAN AUSTRONESIAN
Taranchi = Ili. Uighur D.→TURKIC
Tarangap. Oksapmin D.→CENTRAL AND SOUTH NEW GUINEA
Tarao→NAGA-KUKI-CHIN
Tarapecosi = Chiquito→CHIQUITO
Tarascan see article
Tarasco = Tarascan
Tarase = Bobo Wule. Bobo D.→GUR
Tarasken = Tarascan
Tarat = Kurmuk. Burun Tr.→EASTERN SUDANIC
Tarauhmarice = Tarahumara→UTO-AZTECAN
Taraumara = Tarahumara→UTO-AZTECAN
Tarbanawalun = Ramindjeri. Tanganekald D.→NARRINYERIC
Tare'e = Taa. Bare'e D.→CENTRAL AND SOUTHERN CELEBES
Tarera→SOUTH HALMAHERA AUSTRONESIAN
Tarfia = Tarpia→SARMIC
Targalag = Tagalag. Ilba D.→PAMA-MARIC
Targari = Thargari→MANTHARDA
Targoodi = Targudi. Kardutjara D.→WATI
Targudi. Kardutjara D.→WATI
Tari→PLATEAU BENUE-CONGO
Tariaca. Bribri D.→CHIBCHAN
Tariana→NORTHERN MAIPURAN
TARIANAN→NORTHERN MAIPURAN
Taribelang = Taribeleng→WAKA-KABIC
Taribeleng→WAKA-KABIC
Tarikukuri = Tambatamba→NORTH WESTERN AND CENTRAL SOLOMONS
Tarimuki. Gujarati D.→INDIC
Tarkarri = Thargari→MANTHARDA
Taro. Enga D.→EAST NEW GUINEA HIGHLANDS
Tarof→WESTERN NEW GUINEA
Taroko. Atayal D.→FORMOSAN AUSTRONESIAN
Taroko. Seediq D.→FORMOSAN AUSTRONESIAN
Taromak = Dainan. Rukai D.→FORMOSAN AUSTRONESIAN
Taromaki = Dainan. Rukai D.→FORMOSAN AUSTRONESIAN
Taron = Rawang→BODO-NAGA-KACHIN

Tarpia→SARMIC
TARPIC→SARMIC
Tarpuntjari. Kardutjara D.→WATI
Tarqum. East Aramaic D.→SEMITIC
Tarrahumara = Tarahumara→UTO-AZTECAN
Tarratine = Abnaki. Penobscot D.→ALGON-
    QUIAN
Tarrawarrachal = Bratauolung→PAMA-
    NYUNGAN
Tarrawarracka = Bratauolung→PAMA-
    NYUNGAN
Tarribelung = Taribeleng→WAKA-KABIC
Taru = Taungyo. Burmese D.→BURMESE-
    LOLO
Tarua. Enga D.→EAST NEW GUINEA HIGH-
    LANDS
Taruma→GE-PANO-CARIB
Taruma. Tupi Tr.→TUPI
Tarumbal = Darambal→WAKA-KABIC
Tarumbul = Darambal→WAKA-KABIC
Tarunggare→MOMBERAMO RIVER
Tarute. Southwest Nambicuara D.→NAMBI-
    CUARA
Taruw = Danu. Burmese D.→BURMESE-
    LOLO
Tashon→NAGA-KUKI-CHIN
Tashuite. Southwest Nambicuara D.→NAMBI-
    CUARA
Tasiko→EASTERN OCEANIC
Tasing = Tjampalagian. Mandarese D.→
    CENTRAL AND SOUTHERN CELE-
    BES
Tasiriki. Tasiko D.→EASTERN OCEANIC
Tasman = Nukumanu. Luangiua D.→POLY-
    NESIAN
TASMANIAN see article
Tasmate→EASTERN OCEANIC
Tasobi→NORTHWESTERN AND CENTRAL
    SOLOMONS
Tat→IRANIAN
Tatar→TURKIC
Tatar, Crimean = Crimean Turkish→TURKIC
Tataru = Tatog→EASTERN SUDANIC
Tatche = Tachi. Valley Yokuts D.→YOKUTS
Tate→INDO-PACIFIC
Tateburra = Iningai. Mandandanji D.→PAMA-
    MARIC
Tati = G//abake→KHOISAN
Tati = Tate→INDO-PACIFIC
Tati Bushman = G//abake→KHOISAN
Tatiara = Potaruwutj. Djadjala D.→KULINIC
Tatimolo. Totonac D.→TOTONACAN
Tatiquilhati. Totonac D.→TOTONACAN
Tatitati = Wathiwathi. Djadjala D.→KULINIC

Tatog→EASTERN SUDANIC
Tatoga = Tatog→EASTERN SUDANIC
Tatoongolong = Tatungalung. Bratauolung D.→
    PAMA-NYUNGAN
Tatsanottine = Yellow-knife. Chipewyan Tr.→
    ATHAPASCAN-EYAK
Tatshiautin. Carrier Tr.→ATHAPASCAN-
    EYAK
Tatshikotin. Carrier Tr.→ATHAPASCAN-
    EYAK
Tatsienlu = Dartsemdo. Central Tibetan D.→
    TIBETAN
Tatsoni = Taconi. Luhya D.→NORTH EAST-
    ERN BANTU
Tattayarra = Potaruwutj. Djadjala D.→KULI-
    NIC
Tatu = Adzaneni→NORTHERN MAIPURAN
Ta-T'ung. Mongour D.→MONGOLIAN
Tatunga = Tatungalung. Bratauolung D.→
    PAMA-NYUNGAN
Tatungalung. Bratauolung D.→PAMA-NYUN-
    GAN
Tatungolung = Tatungalung. Bratauolung D.→
    PAMA-NYUNGAN
Taʔu = Takuu. Luangiua D.→POLYNESIAN
Tauada = Kambesi→GOILALA
Tauade→GOILALA
Tauahca = Twahka. Sumo Tr.→MISUMAL-
    PAN
Tauaira = Thaua→YUIN-KURIC
Tauare→MACRO-TUCANOAN
Tauata = Tauade→GOILALA
Tauira = Tawira. Miskito D.→MISUMAL-
    PAN
Tauit = Itawi→NORTHWEST AUSTRONE-
    SIAN
Tauite. Southwest Nambicuara D.→NAMBI-
    CUARA
Taulil→NEW BRITAIN
Taulipang. Arecuna D.→CARIB
Taumako. Pileni D.→POLYNESIAN
Tauna. Awa D.→EAST NEW GUINEA HIGH-
    LANDS
Taung. Southern Sotho D.→SOUTH EASTERN
    BANTU
Taungtha→NAGA-KUKI-CHIN
Taungthu→KAREN
Taungurong→KULINIC
Taungyo. Burmese D.→BURMESE-LOLO
Taupota. Wedauan D.→PAPUA AUSTRO-
    NESIAN
Taura→NORTHWESTERN AND CENTRAL
    SOLOMONS
Taura. Tebu Tr.→SAHARAN

Tauran. Ami D.→FORMOSAN AUSTRO-NESIAN

Taurawa→PLATEAU BENUE-CONGO

Taurepan = Taulipang. Arecuna D.→CARIB

Tausug = Taw Sug→NORTHWEST AUSTRO-NESIAN

Tautin. Carrier Tr.→ATHAPASCAN-EYAK

Tauu = Takuu. Luangiua D.→POLYNESIAN

Ta'uushn = Teuex. Chon D.→ANDEAN

Taux = Nanticoke. Mohegan D.→ALGON-QUIAN

Tava = Rabah. Hre D.→MON-KHMER

Tavaik. Southeast Ambryn D.→EASTERN OCEANIC

Tavalavola. Omba D.→EASTERN OCEANIC

Tavalon = Taparon. Ami D.→FORMOSAN AUSTRONESIAN

Tavara→PAPUA AUSTRONESIAN

Tavara = Tabara. Shona D.→SOUTH EAST-ERN BANTU

TAVEN→GE

Taveta = Tubeta→CENTRAL EASTERN BANTU

Tavgy→URALIC

Tavhatsindi. Vende D.→SOUTH EASTERN BANTU

Tavola = Vagua→NORTHWESTERN AND CENTRAL SOLOMONS

Tavoyan. Burmese D.→BURMESE-LOLO

Tavula = Vagua→NORTHWESTERN AND CENTRAL SOLOMONS

Taw Sug→NORTHWEST AUSTRONESIAN

Tawa = Ottawa. Ojibwa D.→ALGONQUIAN

Tawaelia→CENTRAL AND SOUTHERN CELEBES

Tawaili→CENTRAL AND SOUTHERN CELEBES

Tawana = Nwato. Tswana D.→SOUTH EAST-ERN BANTU

Tawarafa. Kahua D.→EASTERN OCEANIC

Taware = Tarare→MACRO-TUCANOAN

Tawas. Alabama D.→MUSKOGEAN

Tawasa. Timucua D.

Tawatawas = Miami→ALGONQUIAN

Tawgi Samoyed = Tavgy→URALIC

Tawi→ADMIRALTY-WESTERN ISLANDS

Tawi Island. Mok D.→ADMIRALTY-WEST-ERN ISLANDS

Tawira. Miskito D.→MISUMALPAN

Tawit = Itawi→NORTHWEST AUSTRONE-SIAN

Tawka = Paya→MACRO-CHIBCHAN

Tawr→NAGA-KUKI-CHIN

Tay→KAM-TAI

Tay Nua→KAM-TAI

Tay Poong. Muong D.→VIET-MUONG

Taya = Paya→MACRO-CHIBCHAN

Tayaga. Achagua D.→NORTHERN MAI-PURAN

Tayagua. Achagua D.→NORTHERN MAI-PURAN

Tayakou→GUR

Tayaku = Tayakou→GUR

Tayal = Atayal→FORMOSAN AUSTRONE-SIAN

Tayhat→KHMUIC

Tayhay = Khang. Khmu' D.→KHMUIC

Taying = Digaru Mishmi→GYARUNG-MISHMI

Tayok = Yunnan Shant'ou→KAM-TAI

Taz. Ostyak Samoyed D.→URALIC

Taze = Crenge→GE

Tazlina = Chitina. Ahtena D.→ATHAPAS-CAN-EYAK

Tcaiti = Tsh'iti. Shua D.→KHOISAN

Tcalke = Cherokee→IROQUOIS

Tcengui = Tsaangi→NORTH WESTERN BANTU

Tcerokieco = Cherokee→IROQUOIS

Tchaga = Enga→EAST NEW GUINEA HIGH-LANDS

Tchak = Syaka. Enga D.→EAST NEW GUINEA HIGHLANDS

Tchalagi = Cherokee→IROQUOIS

Tchangui = Tsaangi→NORTH WESTERN BANTU

Tchien. Krahn Tr.→KRU

Tchikai = Barera→BURERAN

Tchinoque = Lower Chinook→CHINOOKAN

Tchinouc = Lower Chinook→CHINOOKAN

Tcholo = Tsoko→BURMESE-LOLO

Tco'ko = Sarsi→ATHAPASCAN-EYAK

Tdama = Masongo→EASTERN SUDANIC

Te = Twabo. Krahn Tr.→KRU

Teacuacitzia = Cora→UTO-AZTECAN

Teacaueitzica = Cora→UTO-AZTECAN

Tebaca. Cahita D.→UTO-AZTECAN

Tebakang = Sadong. Land Dayak D.→WEST INDONESIAN

Tebe = Teve. Shona D.→SOUTH EASTERN BANTU

Tebele = Ndebele→SOUTH EASTERN BANTU

Tebia. Tebu Tr.→SAHARAN

Tebu→SAHARAN

TECANA = TACANA

Tecaya. Cahita D.→UTO-AZTECAN

Techbi. Terraba D.→CHIBCHAN

Teco→MAYAN
Tecua→NORTHERN MAIPURAN
Tecual = Pinome→UTO-AZTECAN
Teda→SAHARAN
Tedi, Eastern→OK
Tedi, Upper→OK
Teduray = Tiruray→NORTHWEST AUSTRO-
NESIAN
Tee = Gola→WEST ATLANTIC
TEGALI→KORDOFANIAN
TEGALI-TAGOL = TEGALI→KORDOFA-
NIAN
Tege = Gola→WEST ATLANTIC
Tege = Tege-kali. North Teke D.→NORTH
WESTERN BANTU
Tege-kali. North Teke D.→NORTH WEST-
ERN BANTU
Tegele = Tagali→KORDOFANIAN
Tegesye. Kulango D.→GUR
Tegua = Tewa→TANOAN
Tegue = Tege-kali. North Teke D.→NORTH
WESTERN BANTU
Teguima = Opata→UTO-AZTECAN
Teguray = Tiruray→NORTHWEST AUSTRO-
NESIAN
Tehama = Nomlaki→WINTUN
Tehema = Nomlaki→WINTUN
Tehit→WESTERN NEW GUINEA
Tehnu = Katchal. Central Nicobarese D.→
NICOBARESE
Tehua = Tewa→TANOAN
Tehuelche = Chon→ANDEAN
Tehuelche, Northern = Puelche→ANDEAN
Teita = Taita→NORTH EASTERN BANTU
Teixeira Pinto = Bok. Manjaku D.→WEST
ATLANTIC
Tejano = Coahuilteco→HOKAN
TEKE→NORTH WESTERN BANTU
Teke. Turkmen D.→TURKIC
Teke = North Teke→NORTH WESTERN
BANTU
Teke, Central→NORTH WESTERN BANTU
Teke, East→NORTH WESTERN BANTU
Teke, North→NORTH WESTERN BANTU
Teke, North East→NORTH WESTERN
BANTU
Teke, South→NORTH WESTERN BANTU
Teke, South West = West Teke→NORTH
WESTERN BANTU
Teke, West→NORTH WESTERN BANTU
Tekeim. Lafofa D.→KORDOFANIAN
Tekel→EASTERN OCEANIC
Tekela = Swati. Nguni D.→SOUTH EASTERN
BANTU

Tekeze = Swati. Nguni D.→SOUTH EASTERN
BANTU
Tekin. Oksapmin D.→CENTRAL AND
SOUTH NEW GUINEA
Tela'a. Leti D.→MOLUCCAN
Telame = Tachi. Valley Yokuts D.→YOKUTS
Telami = Tachi. Valley Yokuts D.→YOKUTS
Tele = Tana. Vale D.→CENTRAL SUDANIC
Teleefool = Telefol→OK
Telefol→OK
Telefomin = Telefol→OK
Telefool = Telefol→OK
Telei = Buin→BOUGAINVILLE
Telengut = Teleut. Altai D.→TURKIC
Teleut. Altai D.→TURKIC
Teliang. Pangan D.→SEMANG
Telma = Tewa→TANOAN
Teltal = Afar. Afar-Saho D.→CUSHITIC
T'elt'al = Afar. Afar-Saho D.→CUSHITIC
Telugu→DRAVIDIAN
TEM = EASTERN GRUSI→GUR
Tem→GUR
Temacin. Ouargla D.→BERBER
Tembagla. Medlpa D.→EAST NEW GUINEA
HIGHLANDS
Tembe?. Northern Sakai D.→SAKAI
Tembe. Tenetehara D.→TUPI
Tembeta = Ciriguano. Tupi D.→TUPI
Tembi = Tembe?. Northern Sakai D.→SAKAI
Tembo→CENTRAL WESTERN BANTU
Tembo→NORTH WESTERN BANTU
Tembo = Nyabungu→NORTH EASTERN
BANTU
Tembo = Tambo→CENTRAL EASTERN
BANTU
Teme→ADAMAWA
TEMEIN→EASTERN SUDANIC
Temein→EASTERN SUDANIC
Temiar = Northern Sakai→SAKAI
Temne→WEST ATLANTIC
Temogun = Timugan. Murut D.→NORTH-
WEST AUSTRONESIAN
Temomeyeme = Guinao→NORTHERN MAI-
PURAN
Temomoyamo = Guinao→NORTHERN MAI-
PURAN
Tempasuk. Dusun D.→NORTHWEST AUS-
TRONESIAN
Tempuen = Campuon→MON-KHMER
T'en→KAM-TAI
Tena = Makasarese→CENTRAL AND
SOUTHERN CELEBES
Tenae = Hruso→GYARUNG-MISHMI
Tenda see WEST ATLANTIC

Tenda Duka = Konyagi→WEST ATLANTIC
Tendanke = Bedik→WEST ATLANTIC
Tende = Koria→NORTH EASTERN BANTU
Tende = Tiini→NORTH WESTERN BANTU
Tende Bande = Bedik→WEST ATLANTIC
TENDE-YANZI→NORTH WESTERN BANTU
Tenere. Senari D.→GUR
Tenetehara→TUPI
Teng = Khang. Khmu' D.→KHMUIC
Tengara. Murut D.→NORTHWEST AUSTRONESIAN
Tengganu = Krau of Ketiar. Eastern Sakai D.→SAKAI
Tenggi = Tanganekald→NARRINYERIC
Tengiela = Kandere. Senari D.→GUR
Tengima. Angami D.→NAGA-KUKI-CHIN
Tenh = Khang. Khmu' D.→KHMUIC
Tenino = Columbia River. Sahaptin D.→SAHAPTIN-NEZ PERCE
Tenma→MANTHARDA
Tensa→NAGA-KUKI-CHIN
Tenteria = Talumpa. Mamudju D.→CENTRAL AND SOUTHERN CELEBES
Tenyer. Karaboro D.→GUR
Teo = Bali→NORTH WESTERN BANTU
Teop→NORTHWESTERN AND CENTRAL SOLOMONS
TEOPIC→NORTHWESTERN AND CENTRAL SOLOMONS
Tepa. Leti D.→MOLUCCAN
Tepanhuna. Apiaka D.→TUPI
Tepda = Kiowa→TANOAN
Tepecano. Tepehuan D.→UTO-AZTECAN
Tepegua = Tepehuan→UTO-AZTECAN
Tepeguan = Tepehuan→UTO-AZTECAN
Tepeguana = Tepehuan→UTO-AZTECAN
Tepehua = Tepehuan→UTO-AZTECAN
Tepehuan→UTO-AZTECAN
Tepehuana = Tepehuan→UTO-AZTECAN
Tepehuane = Tepehuan→UTO-AZTECAN
Tepehuano = Tepehuan→UTO-AZTECAN
Tepes→EASTERN SUDANIC
Tepeth = Tepes→EASTERN SUDANIC
Tepkinago = Kiowa→TANOAN
Tepo = Tewi. Grebo Tr.→KRU
Tepo = Twabo. Krahn Tr.→KRU
Tepocas. Seri Tr.→HOKAN
Teptyar. Tatar D.→TURKIC
Tepuzculano. Mixtec D.→MIXTECAN
Teqel = Tekel→EASTERN OCEANIC
TEQUISTLATECAN see article
Tequistlateco, Mountain→TEQUISTLATECAN
TERA→CHADIC

Tera→CHADIC
Tera = Chara→PLATEAU BENUE-CONGO
Terawa = Tera→CHADIC
Terawia = Bideyat. Zaghawa D.→SAHARAN
Terea = Chara→PLATEAU BENUE-CONGO
Terebendyuke = Vai→MANDE
Terebu→NORTHEAST NEW GUINEA AUSTRONESIAN
Tereila. Punthamara D.→DIERIC
Terena = Tereno→MAIPURAN
Tereno→MAIPURAN
Terenoke. Tupi Tr.→TUPI
Teressa→NICOBARESE
Teri = Sagala. Taita D.→NORTH EASTERN BANTU
Teria = Chara→PLATEAU BENUE-CONGO
Terik. Nandi D.→EASTERN SUDANIC
Teri-Kawalsch→FREDERIK HENDRIK IS AND SE WEST IRIAN
Termanu. Roti D.→EAST INDONESIAN
Ternate→NORTH HALMAHERA
Ternateno→ROMANCE
Terraba→CHIBCHAN
Terria = Chara→PLATEAU BENUE-CONGO
Teshbi = Techbi. Terraba D.→CHIBCHAN
Teshina = Mekan→EASTERN SUDANIC
TESO→EASTERN SUDANIC
Teso→EASTERN SUDANIC
Tesuque. Tewa D.→TANOAN
Teta = Nyungwe→CENTRAL EASTERN BANTU
Tete = Deti→KHOISAN
Tete = Nyungwe→CENTRAL EASTERN BANTU
TETELA→NORTH WESTERN BANTU
Tetela→NORTH WESTERN BANTU
Tetelcinco. Nahua D.→UTO-AZTECAN
Tetepari→NORTHWESTERN AND CENTRAL SOLOMONS
Tetes De Boule = Cree→ALGONQUIAN
Teton. Dakota D.→SIOUAN
Tettum→MOLUCCAN
Tetum = Tettum→MOLUCCAN
Teu = Katu→MON-KHMER
Teueia = Macushi→CARIB
Teuesh = Teuex. Chon D.→ANDEAN
Teuex. Chon D.→ANDEAN
Te'un→EAST INDONESIAN
TEUSO→EASTERN SUDANIC
Teuso→EASTERN SUDANIC
Teuth = Teuso→EASTERN SUDANIC
Teve. Shona D.→SOUTH EASTERN BANTU
Tevi→DAGA
Tew = Tumbuka→CENTRAL EASTERN

BANTU
Tewa→TANOAN
Tewa, Arizona = Hano. Tewa D.→TANOAN
Tewara. Dobu D.→PAPUA AUSTRONESIAN
Tewelche = Chon→ANDEAN
Teweya = Macushi→CARIB
Tewi. Grebo Tr.→KRU
Texas = Coahuilteco→HOKAN
Texistepec = Texixtepec→MIXE-ZOQUE
Texixtepec→MIXE-ZOQUE
Tez. Oroc D.→TUNGUS
Tezuque = Tesuque. Tewa D.→TANOAN
Tətet = Chowra→NICOBARESE
Tfalati→KALAPUYA
Tfuea. Tsou D.→FORMOSAN AUSTRONE-
SIAN
Tfuya = Tfuea. Tsou D.→FORMOSAN AUS-
TRONESIAN
Thado→NAGA-KUKI-CHIN
Thado-pao = Thado→NAGA-KUKI-CHIN
Thagunworong = Taungurong→KULINIC
Thaguwurru = Taungurong→KULINIC
Thai, Northern→KAM-TAI
Thai, Southern→KAM-TAI
Thai = Siamese→KAM-TAI
Thai, Central = Siamese→KAM-TAI
Thai, Standard = Siamese→KAM-TAI
Thai Che = Yunnan Shant'ou→KAM-TAI
Thai Khe = Yunnan Shant'ou→KAM-TAI
Thai Miao = Yi. Miao D.→MIAO-YAO
Thai Yai = Shan→KAM-TAI
Thai Yuan = Yuan→KAM-TAI
Thakara = Parji→DRAVIDIAN
Thaksya→GYARUNG-MISHMI
Thali. Lahnda D.→INDIC
Thami→GYARUNG-MISHMI
Thaminyi = Dair. Kordofanian Nubian Tr.→
EASTERN SUDANIC
Thaminyini Be = Dair. Kordofanian Nubian
Tr.→EASTERN SUDANIC
THAN→WAKA-KABIC
Thangatti = Dainggati. Ngamba D.→YUIN-
KURIC
Thangatty = Dainggati. Ngamba D.→YUIN-
KURIC
Thany = Aliab. Agar D.→EASTERN SU-
DANIC
Thany Bur. Rek D.→EASTERN SUDANIC
Thao→FORMOSAN AUSTRONESIAN
Thap = Katu→MON-KHMER
Tharaka→NORTH EASTERN BANTU
Tharamirttong = Jaitmathang→PAMA-
NYUNGAN
Thararrabura = Iningai. Mandandanji D.→

PAMA-MARIC
Tharawal = Thurawal→YUIN-KURIC
Thareli. Sindhi D.→INDIC
Thargari→MANTHARDA
Tharu. Bihari D.→INDIC
Tharumba = Walbanga. Thaua D.→YUIN-
KURIC
Tharumbal = Darambal→WAKA-KABIC
That = Sak→BURMESE-LOLO
Thaua→YUIN-KURIC
Thauaira = Thaua→YUIN-KURIC
Thawa = Thaua→YUIN-KURIC
Thayetmyo. Aso Tr.→NAGA-KUKI-CHIN
Thebor→GYARUNG-MISHMI
Theddora = Jaitmathang→PAMA-NYUNGAN
Theddoramittung = Jaitmathang→PAMA-
NYUNGAN
Thehuoco = Tahue. Cahita D.→UTO-AZTE-
CAN
Theinbaw = Chingpaw→BODO-NAGA-
KACHIN
The-ke-ne = Sekani. Sekani D.→ATHAPAS-
CAN-EYAK
Themne = Temne→WEST ATLANTIC
Theng = Pheng→KHMUIC
Thet = Sak→BURMESE-LOLO
Thiang. Nuer D.→EASTERN SUDANIC
Thilanottine. Chipewyan Tr.→ATHAPSCAN-
EYAK
Thio = Haragure→NEW CALEDONIA
thi-Phalaburwa = Phalaburwa. Northern Sotho
D.→SOUTH EASTERN BANTU
Thiralla = Tereila. Punthamara D.→DIERIC
Thiro = Tira→KORDOFANIAN
Thlaping. Tswana D.→SOUTH EASTERN
BANTU
Thlapiŋ = Thlaping. Tswana D.→SOUTH
EASTERN BANTU
Thlaro. Tswana D.→SOUTH EASTERN
BANTU
Thlaru = Thlaro. Tswana D.→SOUTH EAST-
ERN BANTU
Thlingchadinne = Dogrib→ATHAPASCAN-
EYAK
Tho→KAM-TAI
Thochu = Thotsu→SINO-TIBETAN
Thog Naath = Nuer→EASTERN SUDANIC
Thoi. Padang D.→EASTERN SUDANIC
Tholomeo. Yarigui D.→CARIB
Thompson→SALISH
Thon. Rek D.→EASTERN SUDANIC
Thonga = Tsonga→SOUTH EASTERN
BANTU
Thongho→BURMESE-LOLO

Thoorga = Thaua→YUIN-KURIC
Thoorga = Walbanga. Thaua D.→YUIN-KURIC
Thotsu→SINO-TIBETAN
Thracian→INDO-EUROPEAN
Thu = Kelao→KAM-TAI
Thu = Tho→KAM-TAI
Thuak = Suri. Tirma D.→EASTERN SUDAN-IC
Thuanga→NEW CALEDONIA
THUANGIC→NEW CALEDONIA
Thukumi→NAGA-KUKI-CHIN
Thulishi = Tulishi→KORDOFANIAN
Thulung→GYARUNG-MISHMI
Thunga = Tanganekald→NARRINYERIC
Thungah = Tanganekald→NARRINYERIC
Thurawal→YUIN-KURIC
Thurga = Thaua→YUIN-KURIC
Thurga = Walbanga. Thaua D.→YUIN-KURIC
Thuri→EASTERN SUDANIC
Thurrawal = Thurawal→YUIN-KURIC
Ti. Roti D.→EAST INDONESIAN
Tiadje = Tomini→NORTHERN CELEBES
Tiala. Gula D.→ADAMAWA
Tialo = Tomini→NORTHERN CELEBES
Tiamus. Maasai D.→EASTERN SUDANIC
Tiapaneco = Tlapanec→TLAPANECAN
Tiapi. Landuma D.→WEST ATLANTIC
Ti'ara = Bada'→CENTRAL AND SOUTH-ERN CELEBES
TIATINAGUA→TACANA
Tibas Skadd = Kanawari→GYARUNG-MISHMI
Tibbu = Tebu→SAHARAN
TIBETAN see article
TIBETO-BURMAN see article
Tibolal. Puyuma D.→FORMOSAN AUSTRO-NESIAN
Tibu. Bangba D.→EASTERN
Tiburon. Seri Tr.→HOKAN
Tiburon = Seri→HOKAN
Tiche = Qiche→MAYAN
Tid. Tirma D.→EASTERN SUDANIC
Tidda = Midob→EASTERN SUDANIC
Tideing = Kiowa→TANOAN
Tidi = Tid. Tirma D.→EASTERN SUDANIC
Tidikelt→BERBER
Tidore→NORTH HALMAHERA
TIDUNG→NORTHWEST AUSTRONESIAN
Tie = Tchien. Krahn Tr.→KRU
Tiebala = Tyebala. Senari D.→GUR
Tiefo→GUR
Tien-chow→KAM-TAI

Tiene = Tiini→NORTH WESTERN BANTU
T'ien-pa→KAM-TAI
Tien-pao→KAM-TAI
T'ien-pao = Tien-pao→KAM-TAI
T'ien-yu. Mongour D.→MONGOLIAN
Tifal→OK
Tigak = Omo→BISMARCK ARCHIPELAGO
TIGON = MBEMBE→JUKUNOID
TIGONG = MBEMBE→JUKUNOID
Tigong = Bitare→BANTOID
Tigray = Tigrinya→SEMITIC
Tigre→SEMITIC
Tigrigna = Tigrinya→SEMITIC
Tigrina = Tigrinya→SEMITIC
Tigrinya→SEMITIC
Tigua = Tewa→TANOAN
TIGUM = MBEMBE→JUKUNOID
Tihoru→EAST INDONESIAN
Tiika = Tika. Kunama D.→CHARI-NILE
Tiini→NORTH WESTERN BANTU
Tiitaal. Gula D.→ADAMAWA
Tika. Kunama D.→CHARI-NILE
Tika = Tikar→BANTOID
Tikali = Tikar→BANTOID
Tikar→BANTOID
Tikare = Tikar→BANTOID
Tikari = Tikar→BANTOID
Tike. Peri D.→NORTH EASTERN BANTU
Tiker = Tikar→BANTOID
Tikhak. Tangsa D.→BODO-NAGA-KACHIN
Tikie. Macu D.→MACRO-TUCANOAN
Tikopia→POLYNESIAN
Tikulu = Tikuu→CENTRAL EASTERN BANTU
Tikuu→CENTRAL EASTERN BANTU
Tilamuk = Tillamook→SALISH
Tilamuta→NORTHWEST AUSTRONESIAN
Tillamook→SALISH
Tim = Tem→GUR
Tima→KORDOFANIAN
Timalatia. Iranche D.→MAIPURAN
Timba→CHIBCHAN
Timbara = Kabena. Alaba D.→CUSHITIC
Timbaro = Kabena. Alaba D.→CUSHITIC
Timbe→HUON-FINISTERRE
Timbira→GE
Timbira, West = Apinage→GE
TIMBIRA, EAST→GE
Timbuka = Tumbuka→CENTRAL EASTERN BANTU
Timene = Temne→WEST ATLANTIC
Timimino. Tupi Tr.→TUPI
Timirem→CARIB
Timmanne = Temne→WEST ATLANTIC

Timne = Temne→WEST ATLANTIC
Timol = Vaikenu→EAST INDONESIAN
Timor Pidgin→ROMANCE
TIMOR-ALOR see article
Timorese→EAST INDONESIAN
TIMOTE→EQUATORIAL
Timote→EQUATORIAL
Timputs→NORTHWESTERN AND CEN-
TRAL SOLOMONS
Timu. Havunese D.→MOLUCCAN
Timu = Pidie. Achinese D.→WEST INDO-
NESIAN
Timu = Tem→GUR
Timucua see article
Timucuana = Timucua
Timugan. Murut D.→NORTHWEST AUS-
TRONESIAN
Timuquan = Timucua
Timuquana = Timucua
Timuri. Persian D.→IRANIAN
T'in→KHMUIC
Tina = Tino. Sambali D.→NORTHWEST
AUSTRONESIAN
Tinan = Rangloi. Manchati D.→GYARUNG-
MISHMI
Tinata Tuna = Gunantuna→BISMARCK AR-
CHIPELAGO
Tindi→CAUCASIAN
Tindi = Xaayo. Luhya D.→NORTH EAST-
ERN BANTU
Tindiga = Hatsa→KHOISAN
Tingal→KORDOFANIAN
Tingelin. Fali D.→ADAMAWA
Tinggian→NORTHWEST AUSTRONESIAN
Tinglayan. Bontok D.→NORTHWEST AUS-
TRONESIAN
Tingou. Buyang D.→ADMIRALTY-WEST-
ERN ISLANDS
Tinguian = Tinggian→NORTHWEST AUS-
TRONESIAN
Tinigua→EQUATORIAL
Tinitianes = Babuyan→NORTHWEST AUS-
TRONESIAN
Tinjar Sibop. Sibop D.→WEST INDONESIAN
Tino. Sambali D.→NORTHWEST AUSTRO-
NESIAN
Tinombo→NORTHERN CELEBES
Tio = Bali→NORTH WESTERN BANTU
Tiokossi = Chakosi→VOLTA-COMOE
Tionontati. Wyandot D.→IROQUOIS
Tio'or. Geser D.→EAST INDONESIAN
Tiopane. Karankawa Tr.
Tipai. Diegueno D.→YUMAN
Tipasaka = Kiposaka→NORTHWESTERN

AND CENTRAL SOLOMONS
Tipri→MON-KHMER
Tipun = Chipon. Puyuma D.→FORMOSAN
AUSTRONESIAN
Tira→KORDOFANIAN
Tira Dagig = Tira El Akhdar. Tira Tr.→
KORDOFANIAN
Tira El Akhdar. Tira Tr.→KORDOFANIAN
Tira Lumun. Tira Tr.→KORDOFANIAN
Tira Mandi. Tira Tr.→KORDOFANIAN
Tirahi→INDIC
Tirahutia = Maithili. Bihari D.→INDIC
Tirari. Dieri D.→DIERIC
Tiribi = Terraba→CHIBCHAN
Tiriki. Luhya D.→NORTH EASTERN BANTU
Tirima = Tirma→EASTERN SUDANIC
Tirinie. Siriono D.→TUPI
TIRIO→CENTRAL AND SOUTH NEW
GUINEA
Tirio→CENTRAL AND SOUTH NEW
GUINEA
Tirma→EASTERN SUDANIC
Tiro→CENTRAL AND SOUTHERN CELE-
BES
Tiron = Batangan→NORTHWEST AUSTRO-
NESIAN
Tirribi = Terraba→CHIBCHAN
Tirtalowakani = Brabralung. Bratauolung D.→
PAMA-NYUNGAN
Tirthung = Brabralung. Bratauolung D.→
PAMA-NYUNGAN
Tirumbae = Tapiete. Tupi D.→TUPI
Tirurai = Tiruray→NORTHWEST AUSTRO-
NESIAN
Tiruray→NORTHWEST AUSTRONESIAN
Tishana = Mekan→EASTERN SUDANIC
Tishena = Mekan→EASTERN SUDANIC
Tita→CROSS RIVER BENUE-CONGO
Titchaat = Kachichere. Katab D.→PLATEAU
BENUE-CONGO
Titin. Askun D.→NURISTANI
Titu = South Nkundo. Mongo-Nkundo D.→
NORTH WESTERN BANTU
TIV→BANTOID
Tiv→BANTOID
Tivativa = Warao→MACRO-CHIBCHAN
Tivericoto→CARIB
Tivi = Tiv→BANTOID
Tiwa→TANOAN
Tiwa. Tebu Tr.→SAHARAN
Tiwi→AUSTRALIAN MACRO-PHYLUM
Tiwi = Tiv→BANTOID
Tiwirkum = Widekum→BANTOID
Tjabogaitjandki = Djabugay. Wakaman D.→

PAMA-MARIC
Tjabogaitjanji = Djabugay. Wakaman D.→
PAMA-MARIC
Tjakulprap = Ngarkat. Djadjala D.→KULINIC
Tjalkadjara. Kardutjara D.→WATI
Tjam = Cham→WEST INDONESIAN
Tjaminjun = Djamindjung→DJAMINDJUN-
GAN
Tjampalagian. Mandarese D.→CENTRAL AND
SOUTHERN CELEBES
Tjanngayth. Awngthim D.→PAMA-MARIC
Tjapalulu. Mangole D.→EAST INDONESIAN
Tjapukai = Djabugay. Wakaman D.→PAMA-
MARIC
Tjapukandi = Djabugay. Wakaman D.→
PAMA-MARIC
Tjapukanja = Djabugay.   Wakaman   D.→
PAMA-MARIC
Tjapwurong→KULINIC
Tjawen = Djauan→GUNWINGGUAN
Tjenrana. Mandarese D.→CENTRAL AND
SOUTHERN CELEBES
Tjeraridjal. Kardutjara D.→WATI
Tjimba = Cimba. Herero D.→SOUTH WEST-
ERN BANTU
Tjimundo =   Angoram→NORTH   NEW
GUINEA
Tjinggili = Tjingilu→TJINGILI-WAMBAYAN
TJINGILI-WAMBAYAN see article
Tjingilu→TJINGILI-WAMBAYAN
Tjirbal = Djirbal. Wakaman D.→PAMA-
MARIC
Tjirerau→SOUTH HALMAHERA AUSTRO-
NESIAN
Tjitijamba =   Tjitiyamba. Kardutjara D.→
WATI
Tjitiyamba. Kardutjara D.→WATI
Tjiwarlin→NGUMBIN
Tjuave =   Chuave→EAST NEW GUINEA
HIGHLANDS
Tjuroro. Binigura D.→NGAYARDA
Tjururu = Tjuroro. Binigura D.→NGAYARDA
Tlamelula→TEQUISTLATECAN
Tlantlang =   Klang-Klang→NAGA-KUKI-
CHIN
TLAPANECAN see article
Tlapaneco = Tlapanec→TLAPANECAN
Tlapi = Thlaping. Tswana D.→SOUTH EAST-
ERN BANTU
Tlappenac = Tlapanec→TLAPANECAN
Tlathenkotin. Chilcotin Tr.→ATHAPASCAN-
EYAK
Tlatman. Mam D.→MAYAN
Tlatskanai. Kwalhioqua D.→ATHAPASCAN-

EYAK
Tlatsop =   Clatsop. Lower Chinook D.→
CHINOOKAN
Tlaxiaco. Mixtec D.→MIXTECAN
Tleskotin.   Chilcotin   Tr.→ATHAPASCAN-
EYAK
Tletle = Deti→KHOISAN
Tlingit→NA-DENE
Tlokeang = Kato→ATHAPASCAN-EYAK
Tlokoa = Tlokwa. Northern Sotho D.→SOUTH
EASTERN BANTU
Tlokwa. Northern Sotho D.→SOUTH EAST-
ERN BANTU
Tlongsai. Mara D.→NAGA-KUKI-CHIN
tloue = //xegwe→KHOISAN
tloutle = //xegwe→KHOISAN
Tlukko =   Iboho. Seediq D.→FORMOSAN
AUSTRONESIAN
Tmagourt→BERBER
Toa = Loma→MANDE
To?abaita = Toqabaita→EASTERN OCEAN-
IC
Toags =   Nanticoke. Mohegan D.→ALGON-
QUIAN
Toala→CENTRAL   AND   SOUTHERN
CELEBES
Toale = Loma→MANDE
Toali = Loma→MANDE
Toanhooch = Twana→SALISH
Toanhuch = Twana→SALISH
TOARIPI see article
Toba→GUAYCURU
Toba→WEST INDONESIAN
Tobacco =   Tionontati. Wyandot D.→IRO-
QUOIS
Tobajara. Tupi Tr.→TUPI
Tobaku→CENTRAL   AND   SOUTHERN
CELEBES
Tobati→SOUTH HALMAHERA AUSTRO-
NESIAN
Tobatin. Tupi Tr.→TUPI
Tobelo→NORTH HALMAHERA
Tobi. Ulithian D.→MICRONESIAN
Tobikhar = Gabrieleno→UTO-AZTECAN
Tobiri = Gosisi→KOIARI
Tobo→HUON-FINISTERRE
Tobote→GUR
Tobur = Labwor→EASTERN SUDANIC
TOCHARIAN see article
Toche. Pijao D.→CARIB
Tocobaga. Timucua D.
Tocoshina. Waica Tr.→WAICAN
Toda→DRAVIDIAN
Toda = Teda→SAHARAN

Todrah→MON-KHMER
Tofa→TURKIC
Tofoke = Poke→NORTH WESTERN BANTU
Toga. Torres D.→EASTERN OCEANIC
Togbo. Banda D.→EASTERN
Togia. Bare'e D.→CENTRAL AND SOUTH-
ERN CELEBES
Togla→EASTERN OCEANIC
TOGO, CENTRAL see article
Togole = Tagali→KORDOFANIAN
TOGORESTSPRACHEN = CENTRAL TOGO
Togoyo→EASTERN
Tohawi = Djaui. Nyulnyul D.→NYULNYUL-
AN
Toholabal = Tojolabal→MAYAN
Toi = Didinga→EASTERN SUDANIC
Toicho = Tacho. Moro Hills Tr.→KORDO-
FANIAN
Tojar. Terraba D.→CHIBCHAN
Tojolabal→MAYAN
Toka. Tomga D.→CENTRAL EASTERN BAN-
TU
Tokelauan. Ellicean D.→POLYNESIAN
Tokistine. Lule Tr.→LULE-VILELA-CHAR-
RUA
Tokita. Karata D.→CAUCASIAN
Tokovul = Tokubun. Paiwan D.→FORMOSAN
AUSTRONESIAN
Tokubun. Paiwan D.→FORMOSAN AUSTRO-
NESIAN
Tokukan-Asin. Ifugao D.→NORTHWEST
AUSTRONESIAN
Tokunu→PAPUA AUSTRONESIAN
Tokuvul = Tokubun. Paiwan D.→FORMOSAN
AUSTRONESIAN
Tokwa = Tlokwa. Northern Sotho D.→SOUTH
EASTERN BANTU
Tolay→EASTERN OCEANIC
Toldil = Gola→WEST ATLANTIC
Tole'e. Pipikoro D.→CENTRAL AND SOUTH-
ERN CELEBES
Tolitoli = Tontoli→NORTHERN CELEBES
Tolo. Bahnar D.→MON-KHMER
Tolo = Talisi→EASTERN OCEANIC
Tololiku. Pagu D.→NORTH HALMAHERA
Tolou = Tondano→NORTHERN CELEBES
Tolour = Tondano→NORTHERN CELEBES
Tolowa. Chasta Costa D.→ATHAPASCAN-
EYAK
Toloweri. Bima D.→EAST INDONESIAN
Toltec-Chichimec. Pipil D.→UTO-AZTECAN
Toltichi. Foothill North Yokuts D.→YOKUTS
Toma = Loma→MANDE
Tomagera. Teda Tr.→SAHARAN

Toman→NORTHWESTERN NEW HEB-
RIDES
Tombaggo = Tambago. Banda D.→EASTERN
Tombenam→NORTHEASTERN NEW GUI-
NEA
Tombo. Dogon D.→GUR
Tombucas = Tumbuka→CENTRAL EAST-
ERN BANTU
Tombulion. Dusun D.→NORTHWEST AUS-
TRONESIAN
Tombulu→NORTHERN CELEBES
TOMINI→NORTHERN CELEBES
Tomini→NORTHERN CELEBES
Tom-Kuznets Tatar = Shor→TURKIC
Tomoip→BISMARCK ARCHIPELAGO
Tomonok. Bari Tr.→EASTERN SUDANIC
Tomoyp = Tomoip→BISMARCK ARCHI-
PELAGO
Tompakewa = Tontemboan→NORTHERN
CELEBES
Tompaso. Tontemboan D.→NORTHERN
CELEBES
Tomuala. Tala D.→EAST INDONESIAN
TON = MINHASA→NORTHERN CELEBES
Tona. Rukai D.→FORMOSAN AUSTRONE-
SIAN
Tonaca = Totonac→TOTONACAN
Tonbakai. Soninke Tr.→MANDE
Tondano→NORTHERN CELEBES
Tong→MON-KHMER
Tong. Pak D.→ADMIRALTY-WESTERN
ISLANDS
Tong = Kam→KAM-TAI
Tonga→CENTRAL EASTERN BANTU
Tonga→SOUTH EASTERN BANTU
Tonga. Mbo D.→CENTRAL EASTERN BAN-
TU
Tonga. Shona D.→SOUTH EASTERN BANTU
Tonga = Tsonga→SOUTH EASTERN BANTU
Tonga, Plateau = Tonga→CENTRAL EAST-
ERN BANTU
Tonga, Southern = Toka. Tonga D.→CEN-
TRAL EASTERN BANTU
Tonga, Valley = We. Tonga D.→CENTRAL
EASTERN BANTU
Tongan→POLYNESIAN
Tongaranka = Danggali. Kula D.→PAMA-
NYUNGAN
Tongareva = Penrhyn→POLYNESIAN
Tongbo = Mambila→BANTOID
TONGIC→POLYNESIAN
Tong-luang→KHMUIC
Tongo→ADMIRALTY-WESTERN ISLANDS
Tongoa→EASTERN OCEANIC

TONGWE→NORTH EASTERN BANTU
Tongwe→NORTH EASTERN BANTU
Tonkawa→MACRO-ALGONQUIAN
Tonkawe = Tonkawa→ MACRO-ALGON-
QUIAN
TONKIN = EAST LOLO→BURMESE-LOLO
Tonko. Limba D.→WEST ATLANTIC
Tonko = Maban→EASTERN SUDANIC
Tonsawang→NORTHERN CELEBES
Tonsea'→NORTHERN CELEBES
Tonsina = Chitina. Ahtena D.→ATHAPAS-
CAN-EYAK
Tontemboan→NORTHERN CELEBES
Tonthain. Makasarese D.→CENTRAL AND
SOUTHERN CELEBES
Tonto. Navajo Tr.→ATHAPASCAN-EYAK
Tonto = Havasupai. Upland Yuman D.→YU-
MAN
Tonto = Yavapai. Upland Yuman D.→YU-
MAN
Tonto = Yuma. River Yuman D.→YUMAN
Tontoli→NORTHERN CELEBES
Toode-nunjer = Balardong. Juat D.→
SOUTHWEST PAMA-NYUNGAN
Toodii = Gola→WEST ATLANTIC
Tooma = Loma→MANDE
Tooro = Toro→NORTH EASTERN BANTU
Toosey. Chilcotin Tr.→ATHAPASCAN-EYAK
Topia = Taracahitan. Cahita D.→UTO-AZTEC-
AN
Topocoro. Yarigui D.→CARIB
Topoke = Poke→NORTH WESTERN BANTU
Toposa = Toposo→EASTERN SUDANIC
Toposo→EASTERN SUDANIC
Topotha = Toposo→EASTERN SUDANIC
Topoyo. Yarigui D.→CARIB
Toqabaita→EASTERN OCEANIC
Toquequa. Chol D.→MAYAN
Tora→CHAPACURA-WANHAMAN
TORADJA→CENTRAL AND SOUTHERN
CELEBES
Toradja→ CENTRAL AND SOUTHERN
CELEBES
Torah = Yergham→PLATEAU BENUE-
CONGO
Torai. Tawaili D.→CENTRAL AND SOUTH-
ERN CELEBES
Toram. Mubi D.→CHADIC
Torau→NORTHWESTERN AND CENTRAL
SOLOMONS
Toraz = Tora→CHAPACURA-WANHAMAN
Torbi = Mambila→BANTOID
Tordukana = Maga. Rukai D.→FORMOSAN
AUSTRONESIAN

Torgon. Gold D.→TUNGUS
Torgut. Oirat D.→MONGOLIAN
Tori→MOMBERAMO RIVER
Tori Aikwakai = Tori Aikwawakai→MOMBE-
RAMO RIVER
Tori Aikwawakai→MOMBERAMO RIVER
Toriko = Liko→NORTH EASTERN BANTU
Torlakian. Serbocroatian D.→SLAVIC
Toro→NORTH EASTERN BANTU
Toro→FREDERIK HENDRIK IS AND SE
WEST IRIAN
Toro. Bambara D.→MANDE
Toro Ga = Toro. Bambara D.→MANDE
Toro Ke = Toro. Bambara D.→MANDE
Torobo = Dorobo. Nandi D.→EASTERN SU-
DANIC
Toromona = Turamona→TACANA
Torona. Moro Hills Tr.→KORDOFANIAN
Torondoyan = Mocochi. Timote D.→EQUA-
TORIAL
Torres→EASTERN OCEANIC
TORRICELLI see article
Torti. Midob Tr.→EASTERN SUDANIC
Torwali→INDIC
Tosauwihi = Shoshoni→UTO-AZTECAN
Tosk. Albanian D.
Tosque = Tosk. Albanian D.
Tostoan. Cuica D.→EQUATORIAL
Totela→SOUTH WESTERN BANTU
Toto→GYARUNG-MISHMI
Totoguani. Pima D.→UTO-AZTECAN
Totolaca = Totonac→TOTONACAN
Totonac→TOTONACAN
Totonaca = Totonac→TOTONACAN
TOTONACAN see article
Totonacca = Totonac→TOTONACAN
Totonaco = Totonac→TOTONACAN
Totonak = Totonac→TOTONACAN
Totonaka = Totonac→TOTONACAN
Totonaken = Totonac→TOTONACAN
Totonaquae = Totonac→TOTONACAN
Totonaque = Totonac→TOTONACAN
Totonicapan = Totonac→TOTONACAN
Totonoco = Totonac→TOTONACAN
Totorame = Pinome→UTO-AZTECAN
Totore→BINANDERE
Totoro→INTER-ANDINE
Toubau = Tebu→SAHARAN
Toubouri = Tupuri→ADAMAWA
Toucouleur = Ful→WEST ATLANTIC
Touggourt. Ouargla D.→BERBER
Toughnowawmish = Puget Sound Salish→
SALISH
Toumak = Tumak→CHADIC

Tounia = Tunya→CHADIC
Tourouka = Turuka→GUR
Touscarora = Tuscarora→IROQUOIS
Toussia = Win→GUR
Towa→TANOAN
Towahi = Djaui. Nyulnyul D.→NYULNYUL-AN
Toweahge = Pawnee→CADDOAN
Toxrica = Bura→CHADIC
Toyo. Bakwe Tr.→KRU
Tozluk Turks. Balkan Gagauz Turkish D.→ TURKIC
Trakiri. Ijo D.→IJO
Tramalhys = Trumai→EQUATORIAL
Trangan→EAST INDONESIAN
TRANS-FLY, EASTERN = ORIOMO RIVER
Traw = Cua→MON-KHMER
Tregami→NURISTANI
Treng. Sarawak Murut D.→WEST INDONE-SIAN
Tri. Bru D.→MON-KHMER
Tri = Bru→MON-KHMER
Tribu = Delo→GUR
Trieng→MON-KHMER
Trike = Trique→MIXTECAN
Trimitarios. Moxo D.→MAIPURAN
Tring. Koho D.→MON-KHMER
Tringgus. Land Dayak D.→WEST INDONE-SIAN
Trinity = Wintu→WINTUN
Trinity Indians = Hupa→ATHAPASCAN-EYAK
Trinkat = Trinkut. Central Nicobarese D.→ NICOBARESE
Trinkut. Central Nicobarese D.→NICOBARESE
Trio→CARIB
Trique→MIXTECAN
Triton Bay→SOUTH HALMAHERA AUS-TRONESIAN
Troc = Zoque→MIXE-ZOQUE
Tromawa = Groma. Central Tibetan D.→ TIBETAN
Truj = El Kebira. Tulishi D.→KORDO-FANIAN
Trukese→MICRONESIAN
Trukhmen. Turkmen D.→TURKIC
TRUKIC→MICRONESIAN
Trumai→EQUATORIAL
Trusan. Sarawak Murut D.→WEST INDO-NESIAN
Tsa Khmu = Khmu'→KHMUIC
Tsaan = Bok. Manjaku D.→WEST ATLANTIC
Tsaan = Samba→CENTRAL WESTERN BAN-TU

Tsaanba = Samba→CENTRAL WESTERN BANTU
Tsaangi→NORTH WESTERN BANTU
Tsaayi. West Teke D.→NORTH WESTERN BANTU
Tsaba = Kanakuru→CHADIC
Tsaconia = Tsakonian→GREEK
Tsaga = Enga→EAST NEW GUINEA HIGH-LANDS
Tsahatsaha. Carijona D.→CARIB
Tsaina. Buhagana Tr.→MACRO-TUCANOAN
Tsaiwa→BODO-NAGA-KACHIN
Tsakaitsitlin = Spokane. Kalispel D.→SALISH
Tsakhur = Tsaxur→CAUCASIAN
Tsakonian→GREEK
Tsakrima→NAGA-KUKI-CHIN
Tsala?'avus = Raisha. Paiwan D.→FORMO-SAN AUSTRONESIAN
Tsalisen = Rukai→FORMOSAN AUSTRO-NESIAN
Tsam. Nkom D.→BANTOID
Tsamai→CUSHITIC
Tsamako = Tsamai→CUSHITIC
Tsamba = Chamba→ADAMAWA
Tsamphung→NAGA-KUKI-CHIN
Tsana = Chana→LULE-VILELA-CHARRUA
Tsang = Chang. Tangsa D.→BODO-NAGA-KACHIN
Tsangi = Tsaangi→NORTH WESTERN BAN-TU
Tsanki = Changki. Ao D.→NAGA-KUKI-CHIN
Tsantieottine. Dogrib Tr.→ATHAPASCAN-EYAK
Tsao-min. Mien D.→MIAO-YAO
Tsaovali = Tamari. Paiwan D.→FORMOSAN AUSTRONESIAN
Tsa'ova'ovul = Naibun. Paiwan D.→FORMO-SAN AUSTRONESIAN
Tsa'ovo'ovol = Naibun. Paiwan D.→FORMO-SAN AUSTRONESIAN
Tsarisen = Rukai→FORMOSAN AUSTRO-NESIAN
Tsarrua = Charrua→LULE-VILELA-CHAR-RUA
Tsaso = Babadjou→BANTOID
Tsattine = Beaver. Sekani D.→ATHAPASCAN-EYAK
Tsaudangsi = Chaudangsi→ GYARUNG-MISHMI
Tsaukwe. Naron D.→KHOISAN
Tsaukwe = n/ /hai→KHOISAN
Tsaurasya = Chaurasya→ GYARUNG-MISH-MI

Tsaxur→CAUCASIAN

Tsaye = Tsaayi. West Teke D.→NORTH WEST-
ERN BANTU

Tsayi = Tsaayi. West Teke D.→NORTH WEST-
ERN BANTU

Tschako = Sheko→OMOTIC

Tschama = Conibo→PANO

Tschamina = Tobote→GUR

Tschana = Chana→LULE-VILELA-CHAR-
RUA

Tscherokese = Cherokee→IROQUOIS

Tschiboko = Coikwe→SOUTH WESTERN
BANTU

Tschintsche = Ntem→BANTOID

Tschokwe = Ciokwe→SOUTH WESTERN
BANTU

Tschopi = Chopi→SOUTH EASTERN BAN-
TU

Tschwa = Cwa. Nancere D.→CHADIC

Ts'e-heng→KAM-TAI

Tsekani. Sekani D.→ATHAPASCAN-EYAK

Tsekenne = Sekani. Sekani D.→ATHAPAS-
CAN-EYAK

Tseku. Central Tibetan D.→TIBETAN

Tselogi = Cherokee→IROQUOIS

Tseloni. Sekani D.→ATHAPASCAN-EYAK

Tseloni = Sekani. Sekani D.→ATHAPASCAN-
EYAK

Tseottine. Dogrib Tr.→ATHAPASCAN-EYAK

Tsepang = Chepang→GYARUNG-MISHMI

Tserekwe. Naron D.→KHOISAN

Tsetsaut→ATHAPASCAN-EYAK

Ts'exa = Handa→KHOISAN

Tsez = Dido→CAUCASIAN

Tshairel→NAGA-KUKI-CHIN

Tshala = Cala→GUR

Tshamberi = Chambri→NORTH NEW GUIN-
EA

Tshere = Gabri→CHADIC

Tsh'erekhwe. Deti Tr.→KHOISAN

Tshi = Twi. Akan D.→VOLTA-COMOE

Tshiga. Ruanda D.→NORTH EASTERN BAN-
TU

Tshiluba = Luba-Lulua→CENTRAL WEST-
ERN BANTU

Tshim'-chæ-an' = Tsimshian→PENUTIAN

Tshimiang. Dari D.→CHADIC

Tshimshean = Tsimshian→PENUTIAN

Tshimshian = Tsimshian→PENUTIAN

Tshimsian = Tsimshian→PENUTIAN

Tshingtang = Lambichhong→GYARUNG-
MISHMI

Tshinook = Lower Chinook→CHINOOKAN

Tshinuk = Lower Chinook→CHINOOKAN

Tshiok = Ciokwe→SOUTH WESTERN BAN-
TU

Tshirambo→BANTOID

Tshiri = Gabri→CHADIC

tshi-sala-Mpasu = Salampasu→ CENTRAL
WESTERN BANTU

tsh'iti. Shua D.→KHOISAN

tshi-Venda = Vende→SOUTH EASTERN
BANTU

Tshobwa = Pianga. Busooŋ Tr.→NORTH
WESTERN BANTU

TSHU-KHWE→KHOISAN

Tshuma→KHOISAN

Tshumakwe = Shua→KHOISAN

Tshuwau = Hiotshuwau→KHOISAN

Tshwosh = Sawos→SEPIK

Tsia = Zia→BINANDERE

Tsikhuli→GYARUNG-MISHMI

Tsilkotin = Chilcotin→ATHAPASCAN-EYAK

Tsilmano = Zelmamu→EASTERN SUDANIC

Tsimihety. Malagasy D.→WEST INDONESIAN

Tsimshian→PENUTIAN

Tsimsian = Tsimshian→PENUTIAN

Tsinbok = Chinbok→NAGA-KUKI-CHIN

Tsingmegnu. Tangsa D.→BODO-NAGA-KA-
CHIN

Tsinuk = Lower Chinook→CHINOOKAN

Tsinyaji→EAST NEW GUINEA HIGHLANDS

Tsiracua. Northern Zamucoan Tr.→EQUA-
TORIAL

Tsiri = Gabri→CHADIC

TSIRIBA = CHIRIGUA→TACANA

TSIRIGUA = CHIRIGUA→TACANA

Tsiru = Chiru→NAGA-KUKI-CHIN

Tsishaath. Nootka D.→WAKASHAN

Tsitsikhar. Dagur D.→MONGOLIAN

Ts'ixa = Handa→KHOISAN

Tsmak = Maidu→MAIDU

Tsoa-qatsilai = Kachirai. Paiwan D.→FORMO-
SAN AUSTRONESIAN

Tsogap = Bagam→BANTOID

TSOGO→NORTH WESTERN BANTU

Tsogo→NORTH WESTERN BANTU

Tsogo. Ruanda D.→NORTH EASTERN BAN-
TU

Tsohke = Sooke. Northern Straits Salish D.→
SALISH

Tsoko→BURMESE-LOLO

Tsola. Tucano Tr.→MACRO-TUCANOAN

Tsoloa. Buhagana Tr.→MACRO-TUCANOAN

Tsong = Limbu→GYARUNG-MISHMI

TSONGA = TSWA-RONGA→SOUTH EAST-
ERN BANTU

Tsonga→SOUTH EASTERN BANTU

Tsongol. Buryat D.→MONGOLIAN

Tsontsu = Hlota→NAGA-KUKI-CHIN

Tsoo = Tsou→FORMOSAN AUSTRONE-
SIAN

Tsootso. Luhya D.→NORTH EASTERN BAN-
TU

Tso-Ottine = Sarsi→ATHAPASCAN-EYAK

Tsorokwe. Naron D.→KHOISAN

Tsotso. Hungu D.→CENTRAL WESTERN
BANTU

Tsotso = Tsootso. Luhya D.→NORTH EAST-
ERN BANTU

Tsou→FORMOSAN AUSTRONESIAN

Tsou, Northern = Tsou→FORMOSAN AUS-
TRONESIAN

Tsou, Southern = Kanakanabu→FORMOSAN
AUSTRONESIAN

Tsou, Southern = Saaroa→FORMOSAN AUS-
TRONESIAN

TSOUIC→FORMOSAN AUSTRONESIAN

Tsudakhar = Cudaxar.' Dargwa D.→CAUCA-
SIAN

Tsugurti. Kanuri Tr.→SAHARAN

Tsuihwan. Bunun D.→FORMOSAN AUS-
TRONESIAN

Tsuihwan = Tfuea. Tsou D.→FORMOSAN
AUSTRONESIAN

Tsulu-la = Chilula. Hupa D.→ATHAPASCAN-
EYAK

Tsumada. Chamalal D.→CAUCASIAN

Tsumada-Urukh. Chamalal D.→CAUCASIAN

Tsunga. Shona D.→SOUTH EASTERN BAN-
TU

Tsungli = Chungli. Ao D.→NAGA-KUKI-
CHIN

Ts'un-lao→KAM-TAI

Tsuŋga = Tsunga. Shona D.→SOUTH EAST-
ERN BANTU

Tsuou = Tsou→ FORMOSAN AUSTRONE-
SIAN

Tsureshe = Reshe→PLATEAU BENUE-CON-
GO

Tsu-u = Tsou→FORMOSAN AUSTRO-
NESIAN

Tsu'u = Tsou→FORMOSAN AUSTRONE-
SIAN

Tswa→SOUTH EASTERN BANTU

Tswana→SOUTH EASTERN BANTU

TSWA-RONGA→SOUTH EASTERN BANTU

Tswene = Koni. Northern Sotho D.→SOUTH
EASTERN BANTU

Tsweni = Koni. Northern Sotho D.→SOUTH
EASTERN BANTU

Ttama = Masongo→EASTERN SUDANIC

Ttzae = Maya→MAYAN

T'u = Tho→KAM-TAI

Tua. Teda Tr.→SAHARAN

Tuadhu = Twana→SALISH

Tual. Ossetic D.→IRANIAN

Tualati = Tfalati→KALAPUYA

Tualatims = Tfalati→KALAPUYA

Tualatin = Tfalati→KALAPUYA

Tuam→NORTHEAST NEW GUINEA AUS-
TRONESIAN

Tuamotuan→POLYNESIAN

Tuaran. Dusun D.→NORTHWEST AUSTRO-
NESIAN

Tuareg→BERBER

Tuba. Northern Altai D.→TURKIC

Tuba = Tuva→TURKIC

Tubatulabal→UTO-AZTECAN

Tubbia. Land Dayak D.→WEST INDONESIAN

Tubeta→CENTRAL EASTERN BANTU

Tubetube→PAPUA AUSTRONESIAN

Tubi. Piti-ulunna-salu D.→CENTRAL AND
SOUTHERN CELEBES

Tubu = Tebu→SAHARAN

Tubuai. Tahitian D.→POLYNESIAN

Tuburi→CHADIC

Tuburi = Tupuri→ADAMAWA

TUCANA = TACANA→TACANA

Tucano→MACRO-TUCANOAN

Tucano Dyapa = Tucundiapa→MACRO-TU-
CANOAN

TUCANOAN→MACRO-TUCANOAN

TUCANOAN, MACRO- see article

Tuchinaua. Jurua-Purus Tr.→PANO

Tucuco. Chake D.→CARIB

Tucuco. Mape D.→CARIB

Tucun Dyapa = Tucundiapa→MACRO-TUCA-
NOAN

Tucuna→MACRO-TUCANOAN

Tucundiapa→MACRO-TUCANOAN

Tucupi. Moseten D.→MACRO-PANOAN

Tucurrike→CHIBCHAN

Tucurrique = Tucurrike→CHIBCHAN

Tucurrique-Orisa = Suerre→CHIBCHAN

Tucururu. Timucua D.

Tuda = Teda→SAHARAN

Tudaga = Teda→SAHARAN

Tudza→BURMESE-LOLO

Tuey = Sabela→ANDEAN

Tufuja = Tfuea. Tsou D.→FORMOSAN AUS-
TRONESIAN

Tuga = Gubinengo→NORTHWESTERN AND
CENTRAL SOLOMONS

Tugara = Parji→DRAVIDIAN

Tugauanon = Tugauanum. Ata D.→NORTH-

WEST AUSTRONESIAN
Tugauanum. Ata D.→NORTHWEST AUS-
TRONESIAN
Tugen = Tuken. Nandi D.→EASTERN SU-
DANIC
Tugeri = Marind→MARIND
Tugin = Tuken. Nandi D.→EASTERN SU-
DANIC
TUGONG = MBEMBE→JUKUNOID
Tugu→ROMANCE
TUGUN = MBEMBE→JUKUNOID
Tugurimba = Arakwal. Kitabal D.→BAN-
DJALANGIC
Tugutil. Tobelo D.→NORTH HALMAHERA
Tuholi. Foothill South Yokuts D.→YOKUTS
Tuhwalati = Tfalati→KALAPUYA
Tuic. Rek D.→EASTERN SUDANIC
Tujetge = Machicui. Mascoy D.→MACRO-
PANOAN
Tukam = Tukum→KORDOFANIAN
Tukana = Tucano→MACRO-TUCANOAN
Tukangbesi→CENTRAL AND SOUTHERN
CELEBES
Tukatuk. Pawnee D.→CADDOAN
Tuke-Kaweah. Foothill North Yokuts D.→
YOKUTS
Tuken. Nandi D.→EASTERN SUDANIC
Tukin = Tuken. Nandi D.→EASTERN SU-
DANIC
Tukiumu. Rawang D.→BODO-NAGA-KA-
CHIN
Tukkongo = Wongo→NORTH WESTERN
BANTU
Tukolor = Ful→WEST ATLANTIC
Tukongo = Wongo→NORTH WESTERN
BANTU
Tukpa→GYARUNG-MISHMI
Tukstanu. Pawnee D.→CADDOAN
Tukudede→EAST INDONESIAN
Tukulu = Tikuu→CENTRAL EASTERN
BANTU
Tukum→KORDOFANIAN
TUKUM = MBEMBE→JUKUNOID
Tukungo = Wongo→NORTH WESTERN
BANTU
Tukuran. Subanun D.→NORTHWEST AUS-
TRONESIAN
Tula→ADAMAWA
Tulama = Tulema. Galla D.→CUSHITIC
Tulambatu. Bungku D.→CENTRAL AND
SOUTHERN CELEBES
Tulamni. Foothill South Yokuts D.→YOKUTS
Tul'bush = Mattole→ATHAPASCAN-EYAK
Tulema. Galla D.→CUSHITIC

Tulesh = Tulishi→KORDOFANIAN
Tulishi→KORDOFANIAN
Tulkepa = Yavapai. Upland Yuman D.→YU-
MAN
Tulkepaia = Yavapai. Upland Yuman D.→
YUMAN
Tulu→DRAVIDIAN
Tulu→ADMIRALTY-WESTERN ISLANDS
Tulua. Taribeleng D.→WAKA-KABIC
Tuluva = Tulu→DRAVIDIAN
Tum = Kaninkwom→PLATEAU BENUE-
CONGO
Tumak→CHADIC
Tumale. Tagoi D.→KORDOFANIAN
Tumanao = Balud. Bilaan D.→NORTHWEST
AUSTRONESIAN
Tumapasa→TACANA
Tumara = Tumaru→NORTH NEW GUINEA
Tumaru→NORTH NEW GUINEA
Tumba. Mbo D.→CENTRAL EASTERN BAN-
TU
Tumbatu. Pemba D.→CENTRAL EASTERN
BANTU
Tumbez→MACRO-CHIBCHAN
Tumboka = Tumbuka→CENTRAL EASTERN
BANTU
Tumbuka→CENTRAL EASTERN BANTU
Tumbwe. Lega D.→NORTH EASTERN BAN-
TU
Tumereha. Southern Zamucoan Tr.→EQUA-
TORIAL
Tumet. Ordos D.→MONGOLIAN
Tumleo→NORTHEAST NEW GUINEA AUS-
TRONESIAN
Tumma→KORDOFANIAN
Tummok = Tumak→CHADIC
Tumok = Tumak→CHADIC
TUMTUM→KORDOFANIAN
Tumtum→KORDOFANIAN
Tumu = Dumu→KIKORI RIVER
Tumu = Tikar→BANTOID
Tumuip = Tomoip→BISMARCK ARCHI-
PELAGO
Tuna = Gunantuna→BISMARCK ARCHI-
PELAGO
Tunacho. Southern Zamucoan Tr.→EQUA-
TORIAL
Tunbe = Tegesye. Kulango D.→GUR
Tunebo→CHIBCHAN
Tung = Kam→KAM-TAI
Tunga = Tanganekald→NARRINYERIC
Tungan = Maban→EASTERN SUDANIC
Tungarlee = Danggali. Kula D.→PAMA-
NYUNGAN

Tung-hsiang. Pao-an D.→MONGOLIAN
Tungistani. Persian D.→IRANIAN
Tungsen. Ao D.→NAGA-KUKI-CHIN
Tungu = Angba→NORTH WESTERN BAN-
TU
Tungui = Tunki. Sumo Tr.→MISUMALPAN
TUNGUS see article
Tung-yen. Pao-an D.→MONGOLIAN
Tunia = Tunya→CHADIC
Tunica→MACRO-ALGONQUIAN
Tunjuamu→CENTRAL AND SOUTH NEW
GUINEA
Tunjur. Sokoro D.→CHADIC
Tunka. Buryat D.→MONGOLIAN
Tunki. Sumo Tr.→MISUMALPAN
Tunli. Ao D.→NAGA-KUKI-CHIN
Tunni. Somali D.→CUSHITIC
Tunong. Achinese D.→WEST INDONESIAN
Tunuermiut = Iglulik. Inuit D.→ESKIMO-
ALEUT
Tunya→ADAMAWA
Tunya→CHADIC
Tuopo. Bakwe Tr.→KRU
Tupadidi = Ngamai-iki→AGOB
Tupancal. Mam D.→MAYAN
TUPARI→TUPI
Tupari→TUPI
TUPI see article
TUPI-GUARANI→TUPI
Tupina. Tupi Tr.→TUPI
Tupinamba. Tupi D.→TUPI
Tupiniquin. Tupi Tr.→TUPI
Tups. Karankawa Tr.
Tupuri→ADAMAWA
Tupuri = Tuburi→CHADIC
Tur. Woga D.→CHADIC
Tura. Kweni D.→MANDE
Turamona→TACANA
Turatea = Turateya. Makasarese D.→CEN-
TRAL AND SOUTHERN CELEBES
Turateya. Makasarese D.→CENTRAL AND
SOUTHERN CELEBES
Tureture = Turituri. Southern Kiwai D.→CEN-
TRAL AND SOUTH NEW GUINEA
Turituri. Southern Kiwai D.→CENTRAL AND
SOUTH NEW GUINEA
Turiuara = Turiwara. Tenetehara D.→TUPI
Turiwara. Tenetehara D.→TUPI
Turka = Turuka→GUR
Turkana→EASTERN SUDANIC
TURKIC see article
Turkish→TURKIC
Turkmen→TURKIC
Turra = Narangga. Jadliaura D.→YURA

Turrubul = Jagara→DURUBULIC
Turrubul = Thurawal→YUIN-KURIC
Turu = Remi→NORTH EASTERN BANTU
Turu = Tur. Woga D.→CHADIC
Turucaca. Boruca D.→CHIBCHAN
Turuj = El Kebira. Tulishi D.→KORDOFA-
NIAN
Turuka→GUR
Turum→KORDOFANIAN
Turumbu = Lombo→NORTH WESTERN
BANTU
Turupu = Terebu→NORTHEAST NEW
GUINEA AUSTRONESIAN
Turuwul = Thurawal→YUIN-KURIC
Turuwull = Thurawal→YUIN-KURIC
Tuscarora→IROQUOIS
Tush. Georgian D.→CAUCASIAN
Tushan→KAM-TAI
Tu-shan = Tushan→KAM-TAI
Tusi = Tutsi. Ruanda D.→NORTH EASTERN
BANTU
Tusia = Win→GUR
Tuskara = Tuscarora→IROQUOIS
Tuskarora = Tuscarora→IROQUOIS
Tuskegee. Alabama D.→MUSKOGEAN
Tuskeruru = Tuscarora→IROQUOIS
Tussi = Tutsi. Ruanda D.→NORTH EASTERN
BANTU
Tutchone→ATHAPASCAN-EYAK
Tutelo→SIOUAN
Tutong. Narom D.→WEST INDONESIAN
Tutsi. Ruanda D.→NORTH EASTERN BAN-
TU
Tutu. Kaurareg D.→MABUIAGIC
Tutuapa. Mam D.→MAYAN
Tutunohan→EAST INDONESIAN
Tututni. Chasta Costa D.→ATHAPASCAN-
EYAK
Tuva→TURKIC
Tuwang. Lawangan D.→WEST INDONESIAN
Tuwari→LEONARD SCHULTZE
Tuxis. Mohegan Tr.→ALGONQUIAN
Tuy. Bakwe Tr.→KRU
Tuyo = Toyo. Bakwe Tr.→KRU
Tuyoneri = Tuyuneri→EQUATORIAL
Tuyuca. Tucano Tr.→MACRO-TUCANOAN
Tuyuneri→EQUATORIAL
T-Valley = Naltje→CENTRAL AND SOUTH
NEW GUINEA
Tver. Karelian D.→URALIC
Twa. Lenje D.→CENTRAL EASTERN BAN-
TU
Twa. Ruanda D.→NORTH EASTERN BANTU
Twabo. Krahn Tr.→KRU

Twahca = Twahka. Sumo Tr.→MISUMAL-
PAN
Twahka. Sumo Tr.→MISUMALPAN
Twakwama = North Koma. Koma D.→KO-
MAN
Twana→SALISH
Twi. Akan D.→VOLTA-COMOE
Twi. Bor D.→EASTERN SUDANIC
Twic = Tuic. Rek D.→EASTERN SUDANIC
Twich = Tuic. Rek D.→EASTERN SUDANIC
Twi-Fante = Akan→VOLTA-COMOE
Twightwees = Miami→ALGONQUIAN
Twij = Tuic. Rek D.→EASTERN SUDANIC
Twoyu = Maji→OMOTIC
Txapacura = Urupa→CHAPACURA-WAN-
HAMAN
Tyaman = Kyama→LAGOON
Tyamuhi = Camuhi→NEW CALEDONIA
Tyan = Bobo Gbe. Bobo D.→GUR
Tyanse = Bobo Gbe. Bobo D.→GUR
Tyap = Katab→PLATEAU BENUE-CONGO
Tyapi = Tiapi. Landuma D.→WEST ATLAN-
TIC
Tyatyalli = Potaruwutj. Djadjala D.→KULI-
NIC
Tye = Kaba Tie. Kaba Dunjo D.→CENTRAL
SUDANIC
Tyebala. Senari D.→GUR
Tyebali = Tyebala. Senari D.→GUR
Tyebara. Senari D.→GUR
Tyeddyuwurru = Potaruwutj. Djadjala D.→
KULINIC
Tyefo = Tiefo→GUR
Tyeforo = Tiefo→GUR
Tyeliri→GUR
Tyemeri. Nangumiri D.→DALY
Tyenga = Busa→MANDE
Tygh Valley = Columbia River. Sahaptin D.→
SAHAPTIN-NEZ PERCE
Tym = Ket. Ostyak Samoyed D.→URALIC
Tyo = Bali→NORTH WESTERN BANTU
Typawurru = Tjapwurong→KULINIC
Tyrrhenian see article
Tyura = Nukuna. Jadliaura D.→YURA
Tyurama→GUR
Tzeltal→MAYAN
TZELTALAN→MAYAN
TZELTALOID = TZELTALAN→MAYAN
Tzendal = Tzeltal→MAYAN
Tzental = Tzeltal→MAYAN
Tzinanteco = Tzotzil→MAYAN
Tzoc = Zoque→MIXE-ZOQUE
Tzotzil→MAYAN
TZOTZILAN = TZELTALAN→MAYAN

Tzutohile = Tzutuhil→MAYAN
Tzutuchil = Tzutuhil→MAYAN
Tzutuchile = Tzutuhil→MAYAN
Tzutuhil→MAYAN
Tzutujil = Tzutuhil→MAYAN

θ

θegiha = Dhegiha→SIOUAN
θuanga = Thuanga→NEW CALEDONIA

U

U = Lhasa. Central Tibetan D.→TIBETAN
Uabari→KOIARI
Uadioparanindiapa. Tauare D.→MACRO-TU-
CANOAN
Uadzoli. Carutana D.→NORTHERN MAI-
PURAN
Uaiai = Paumari. Purupuru D.→ARAWAKAN
Uaiana = Oyana→CARIB
Uaiana = Waina. Tucano Tr.→MACRO-
TUCANOAN
Uaica→CARIB
UAICAN = WAICAN
Uaicana. Tucano Tr.→MACRO-TUCANOAN
Uaieue = Waiwai→CARIB
Uaimare. Cachiniti D.→MAIPURAN
Uaimiri→CARIB
Uainamari→MAIPURAN
Uainana. Tucano Tr.→MACRO-TUCANOAN
Uaintazu. Southwest Nambicuara D.→NAMBI-
CUARA
Uainuma→NORTHERN MAIPURAN
Uaiora = Wayoro→TUPI
Uaiquiare = Wokiare. Yabarana D.→CARIB
Uaiuai = Waiwai→CARIB
Uaiumare = Wayumara→CARIB
Ualari = Yualyai→WIRADJURIC
Uanana = Wanana. Tucano Tr.→MACRO-
TUCANOAN
Uanham→CHAPACURA-WANHAMAN
UANHAM = WANHAM→CHAPACURA-
WANHAMAN
Uapichana→MAIPURAN
Uaraicu→MAIPURAN
Uardai. Galla D.→CUSHITIC
Uaripi. Toaripi D.→TOARIPI
Uariquena = Arequena→NORTHERN MAI-
PURAN
Uarow = Warao→MACRO-CHIBCHAN
Uasi→NEW BRITAIN

Uasona = Wasona. Tucano Tr.→MACRO-TU-CANOAN
Uaura→MAIPURAN
Uba. Walamo Tr.→OMOTIC
Ubach = Jawe. Nemi D.→NEW CALEDONIA
Ubamer. Ari Tr.→OMOTIC
Ubang→CROSS RIVER BENUE-CONGO
UBANGIAN = EASTERN
Ubba = Uba. Walamo Tr.→OMOTIC
Ubegua. Tupi D.→TUPI
Uberi→KOIARI
Ubian Banadan→NORTHWEST AUSTRO-NESIAN
Ubina. Aymara Tr.→ANDEAN
Ubir→PAPUA AUSTRONESIAN
U-boi = Kobiana→WEST ATLANTIC
Uboi = Kobiana→WEST ATLANTIC
Ubulgara→MURNGIC
Ubykh = Ubyx→CAUCASIAN
Ubyx→CAUCASIAN
Uche = Yuchi→MACRO-SIOUAN
Uchee = Yuchi→MACRO-SIOUAN
Uchi = Yuchi→MACRO-SIOUAN
Uchicrin→GE
Uchita. Waicuru Tr.→WAICURIAN
Uchumi = Uru→CHIPAYAN
Uchupiamona→TACANA
Ucuelet. Nootka D.→WAKASHAN
Ucumble = Jukambal→YUIN-KURIC
Udai = Mamudju→CENTRAL AND SOUTH-ERN CELEBES
Udekama = Degema→EDO
Udi→CAUCASIAN
UDIHE→TUNGUS
Udihe→TUNGUS
Udjir→EAST INDONESIAN
Udmurt = Votyak→URALIC
U:dom = Nde→BANTOID
Uduk→KOMAN
/u/ /ein = ŋ/u//en.   ŋ/amani D.→KHOISAN
Uellenskij. Chukchee D.→CHUKCHEE-KAM-CHATKAN
Uen. Kwenyi D.→NEW CALEDONIA
//u//en = ŋ/u/ /en.   ŋ/amani D.→KHOISAN
Ufia. Oring D.→CROSS RIVER BENUE-CONGO
Ufien→BOGIA
Ufim→HUON-FINISTERRE
Ufiom. Oring D.→CROSS RIVER BENUE-CONGO
Ugalachmut = Eyak→ATHAPASCAN-EYAK
Ugalakmiut = Eyak→ATHAPASCAN-EYAK
Ugalense = Eyak→ATHAPASCAN-EYAK
Ugalenzisch = Eyak→ATHAPASCAN-EYAK

Ugana. Kulube D.→BISMARCK ARCHI-PELAGO
Ugaritic→SEMITIC
Uge = Gayi→CROSS-RIVER BENUE-CON-GO
Ugele→NORTHWESTERN AND CENTRAL SOLOMONS
Ughelli. Urhobo D.→EDO
Ughienvwe. Urhobo D.→EDO
Ugi→EASTERN OCEANIC
Ugie = Ngi→BANTOID
UGRIC→URALIC
Ugunichiri. Campa D.→MAIPURAN
Uhami→EDO
Uhei Kachlakin→EAST INDONESIAN
Uhunduni→WEST NEW GUINEA HIGH-LANDS
Uighur→TURKIC
Uighur, Yellow→TURKIC
Uina Tupuyo. Tucano D.→MACRO-TUCA-NOAN
Uirafed = Wirafed. Kawaib D.→TUPI
Uiridiapa→MACRO-TUCANOAN
Uirina→NORTHERN MAIPURAN
Uitai→BOUGAINVILLE
Ujang = Masongo→EASTERN SUDANIC
Ujumcin. Ordos D.→MONGOLIAN
Ukaan = Kakumo→CENTRAL AKOKO
Ukele = Kukele→CROSS RIVER BENUE-CONGO
Ukelle = Kukele→CROSS RIVER BENUE-CONGO
Ukfwo→BANTOID
Ukit. Punan Ba D.→WEST INDONESIAN
Ukiuvak = Ukiuvangmiut. Inuit D.→ESKIMO-ALEUT
Ukiuvangmiut. Inuit D.→ESKIMO-ALEUT
Ukkia = Wakaya→WAKAYA-WARLUWA-RIC
Ukpe→CROSS RIVER BENUE-CONGO
Ukrainian→SLAVIC
Ukrul. Tangkul D.→NAGA-KUKI-CHIN
Ukue→EDO
Ukumbil = Jukambal→YUIN-KURIC
Ukwese. Boki Tr.→CROSS-RIVER BENUE-CONGO
Ukwese = Kwese→CENTRAL WESTERN BANTU
Ulad Amian = Yenoa. Tebu Tr.→SAHARAN
Ulaolinya→PITTAPITTIC
Ulau-Suein = Suain → NORTHEAST NEW GUINEA AUSTRONESIAN
Ulbarag = Urbarag. East Gurage D.→SEMIT-IC

Uldrau. Tawi D.→ADMIRALTY-WESTERN ISLANDS
Ule = Bobo Wule. Bobo D.→GUR
Uled Djemma. Maba Tr.→MABAN
Uled Jemaa = Uled Djemma. Maba Tr.→ MABAN
Ulfola. Mangole D.→EAST INDONESIAN
Uli. Tala D.→EAST INDONESIAN
Ulingan→BOGIA
Ulithian→MICRONESIAN
Ulkulu = Uwokol. Kundjen D.→PAMA-MARIC
Ulrata→EASTERN OCEANIC
Ultateca = Qiche→MAYAN
Ultatecat = Qiche→MAYAN
Ultateco = Qiche→MAYAN
Ulu→BURMESE-LOLO
Ulu. Kerintji D.→WEST INDONESIAN
Ulu. Minangkabau D.→WEST INDONESIAN
Ulu. Pangan D.→SEMANG
Ulu Aring. Pangan D.→SEMANG
Ulu Ceres. Eastern Sakai D.→SAKAI
Ulu Gedang. Central Sakai D.→SAKAI
Ulu Indau. Southeastern Sakai D.→SAKAI
Ulu Kampar. Central Sakai D.→SAKAI
Ulu Kəlantan. Pangan D.→SEMANG
Ulu Kinta. Northern Sakai D.→SAKAI
Ulu Palong. Southeastern Sakai D.→SAKAI
Ulu Səlama. Semang Proper D.→SEMANG
Ulu Tembeling. Eastern Sakai D.→SAKAI
Ulua = Ulva. Sumo Tr.→MISUMALPAN
ulu-Bukusu = Bukusu. Masaba D.→NORTH EASTERN BANTU
ulu-Buya = Buya. Masaba D.→NORTH EASTERN BANTU
ulu-Dadiri = Central Masaba. Masaba D.→ NORTH EASTERN BANTU
Uludri. Low Lugbara D.→CENTRAL SUDANIC
ulu-Gishu = Masaba→NORTH EASTERN BANTU
Uluwa→EASTERN OCEANIC
Ulva. Sumo Tr.→MISUMALPAN
Ulwa = Ulva. Sumo Tr.→MISUMALPAN
Uma. Kposo D.→CENTRAL TOGO
Uma. Pipikoro D.→CENTRAL AND SOUTHERN CELEBES
Uma Aria = Pipikoro→CENTRAL AND SOUTHERN CELEBES
Uma Baloi. Kayan D.→WEST INDONESIAN
Uma Blubo. Kayan D.→WEST INDONESIAN
Uma Poh. Kayan D.→WEST INDONESIAN
Umairof→SEPIK
Umaisha Igbira = Igbira-Panda. Igbira. D.→ NUPE-GBARI
Umalasa→NORTHERN CELEBES
Umana-Kaina→INDO-PACIFIC
Umar. Wandamen D.→MOLUCCAN
Umatilla = Columbia River. Sahaptin D.→ SAHAPTIN-NEZ PERCE
Umawa = Carijona→CARIB
Umbaia = Wambaya→TJINGILI-WAMBAYAN
Umbertana = Adnyamathana. Wailpi D.→ YURA
Umboi→NORTHEAST NEW GUINEA AUSTRONESIAN
Umboi = Kovai→HUON-FINISTERRE
Umbrak-Aiku = Aiku→TORRICELLI
Umbrian→ITALIC
UMBRO-SABELLIAN→ITALIC
UMBUNDU→SOUTH WESTERN BANTU
u-Mbundu = Mbundu→SOUTH WESTERN BANTU
Ume. Urhobo D.→EDO
Ume Lapp→URALIC
Umida→WORORAN
Uminnie = Ngameni. Dieri D.→DIERIC
Umm Durein. Moro D.→KORDOFANIAN
Umm Gabralla. Moro D.→KORDOFANIAN
Umnak = Eastern Aleut. Aleut D.→ESKIMO-ALEUT
Umon→CROSS RIVER BENUE-CONGO
Umotina→BORORO
Umpai. Lawa D.→PALAUNG-WA
ʔumpila = Ombila→PAMA-MARIC
Umpila = Ombila→PAMA-MARIC
Umpilo = Ombila→PAMA-MARIC
Umpqua, Lower. Siuslaw D.→YAKONAN
Umpqua, Upper→ATHAPASCAN-EYAK
Umuapa = Omoampa. Vilela Tr.→LULE-VILELA-CHARRUA
Unachog = Montauk. Mohegan D.→ALGONQUIAN
Unachog = Patchogue. Mohegan Tr.→ALGONQUIAN
Unalachtigo. Delaware D.→ALGONQUIAN
Unalachtigo = Nanticoke. Mohegan D.→ALGONQUIAN
Unalaska = Eastern Aleut. Aleut D.→ESKIMO-ALEUT
Unale. Roti D.→EAST INDONESIAN
Unalla = Iwaidji→IWAIDJAN
Unamara = Wanamara→MAYAPIC
Unambal = Wunambal→WORORAN
Unami. Delaware D.→ALGONQUIAN
Unar = Beseme→CHADIC
Una-Una = Togia. Bare'e D.→CENTRAL

AND SOUTHERN CELEBES
Unchechauge = Passamaquoddy→ALGONQUIAN
Unconino = Autaniri. Campa D.→MAIPURAN
Unde = Lore→CENTRAL AND SOUTHERN CELEBES
Unde'e = Lala'eo. Bare'e D.→CENTRAL AND SOUTHERN CELEBES
Underkerebina = Andakerebina. Iliaura D.→ARANDIC
Unechtgo = Nanticoke. Mohegan D.→ALGONQUIAN
Unelgo = Naualko. Kula D.→PAMA-NYUNGAN
Uneme→EDO
Ungami = Unggumi→WORORAN
Ungarinjin = Ungarinyin→WORORAN
Ungarinyin→WORORAN
UNGARINYINIC→WORORAN
Unggarangi→WORORAN
Unggumi→WORORAN
Ungieskie = Pomo→POMO
Ungin. Buryat D.→MONGOLIAN
Ungorri = Kunggara→PAMA-MARIC
Ungorri = Kunggari. Mandandanji D.→PAMA-MARIC
Ungourra = Nguru. Banda D.→EASTERN
Unguja. Swahili D.→CENTRAL EASTERN BANTU
Unietti = Afitti→EASTERN SUDANIC
Uningangk→MANGERIAN
Unini. Campa D.→MAIPURAN
Univitza. Pichobo D.→PANO
Unkia→OK
Unkpapa. Dakota D.→SIOUAN
Unmatjera = Anmatjera. Iliaura D.→ARANDIC
Unquachog = Montauk. Mohegan D.→ALGONQUIAN
Unquachog = Patchogue. Mohegan Tr.→ALGONQUIAN
Unquechauge = Passamaquoddy→ALGONQUIAN
Unterrgerrie = Antakirinya. Kardutjara D.→WATI
Untib. Avar D.→CAUCASIAN
Unua = Onua→NORTHWESTERN NEW HEBRIDES
Unyama. Shona D.→SOUTH EASTERN BANTU
Unymootha = Adnyamathana. Wailpi D.→YURA
Unza = Rengma→NAGA-KUKI-CHIN
Uollaroi = Juwalarai. Yualyai D.→WIRADJURIC

Uom→NORTHEASTERN NEW GUINEA
Upale = Nuangeya→EASTERN SUDANIC
Upanguayma. Seri Tr.→HOKAN
Upe = Pokot→EASTERN SUDANIC
UPPER TOR→NORTH PAPUAN
Upsaroka = Crow→SIOUAN
Upsaropa = Crow→SIOUAN
Upunuhu = Mantauran. Rukai D.→FORMOSAN AUSTRONESIAN
Upurui = Oyana→CARIB
Ura→PLATEAU BENUE-CONGO
Ura→SOUTHERN NEW HEBRIDES
Urabuna = Arabana→PAMA-NYUNGAN
Urabunna = Arabana→PAMA-NYUNGAN
Uradhi = Otati→PAMA-MARIC
Uraguassu = Araguaju. Oyampi D.→TUPI
Uraicu = Uaraicu→MAIPURAN
Urakin = Urat→TORRICELLI
URAL-ALTAIC see article
URALIAN→TURKIC
URALIC see article
Urama. Northern Kiwai D.→CENTRAL AND SOUTH NEW GUINEA
Urapuna = Arabana→PAMA-NYUNGAN
Urarina. Simacu D.→ANDEAN
Urartaean→HURRIAN
Urat→TORRICELLI
Urat. Ordos D.→MONGOLIAN
Uraxa-Urkarax. Dargwa D.→CAUCASIAN
Urbarag = Urbareg. East Gurage D.→SEMITIC
Urbareg. East Gurage D.→SEMITIC
Urdu = Western Hindi→INDIC
Ure = Opata→UTO-AZTECAN
Uren. Terraba D.→CHIBCHAN
Ureparapara, East→EASTERN OCEANIC
Urepo. Bakwe Tr.→KRU
Urhobo→EDO
Uri→HUON-FINISTERRE
Uria→NORTH PAPUAN
Uriangkhai. Oirat D.→MONGOLIAN
Uriangkhai = Tuva→TURKIC
Urigina→BOGIA
Urim = Kalp→TORRICELLI
Urimo→NORTH NEW GUINEA
Urinama Valiente. Bribri D.→CHIBCHAN
Uripiv→NORTHWESTERN NEW HEBRIDES
Uriya = Oriya→INDIC
Urmitchee = Anmatjera. Iliaura D.→ARANDIC
Uro = Uru→CHIPAYAN
Urocolla = Uru→CHIPAYAN
Uroko. Bakwe Tr.→KRU
Uroquilla = Uru→CHIPAYAN

Urrti. Midob Tr.→EASTERN SUDANIC
Uru→CHIPAYAN
Uru. Kwaio D.→EASTERN OCEANIC
Uruaguacu = Araguaju. Oyampi D.→TUPI
Uruaguassu = Araguaju. Oyampi D.→TUPI
Uruangnirin→EAST INDONESIAN
Uruava→NORTHWESTERN AND CENTRAL
   SOLOMONS
Urubu. Carutana D.→NORTHERN MAI-
   PURAN
Urubu. Tenetehara D.→TUPI
Urubus = Urubu. Tenetehara D.→TUPI
Urucena = Urucuiana. Oyana D.→CARIB
URU-CHIPAYAN = CHIPAYAN
Urucoto = Purucoto→CARIB
Urucuena→CARIB
Urucuiana. Oyana D.→CARIB
uru-Kiga = Tshiga. Ruanda D.→NORTH
   EASTERN BANTU
Uruku→TUPI
Uruleba = High Lugbara→CENTRAL SU-
   DANIC
Uruleba-ti = High Lugbara→CENTRAL SU-
   DANIC
Urulera = Lera. Ruanda D.→NORTH EAST-
   ERN BANTU
Urumi→TUPI
Urunamacan = Urunumacan→CHAPACURA-
   WANHAMAN
Urundi = Rundi→NORTH EASTERN BAN-
   TU
Urungwe. Shona D.→SOUTH EASTERN BAN-
   TU
Urunumacan→CHAPACURA-WANHAMAN
Urunyarwanda = Ruanda→NORTH EAST-
   ERN BANTU
Urupa→CHAPACURA-WANHAMAN
Urupaya = Arupai. Manitsawa D.→TUPI
Ururagwe = Karagwe. Nyambo D.→NORTH
   EASTERN BANTU
Ururudiapa→MACRO-TUCANOAN
Ururu-Dyapa = Ururudiapa→MACRO-TUCA-
   NOAN
uru-Subi = Subi→NORTH EASTERN BANTU
u-Ruund = Luwunda→CENTRAL WESTERN
   BANTU
URUWA→HUON-FINISTERRE
u-Samba = Samba→CENTRAL WESTERN
   BANTU
Ushery = Catawba→MACRO-SIOUAN
Ushi = Aushi→CENTRAL EASTERN BANTU
Ushicring = Uchicrin→GE
Ushpee = Ofo→SIOUAN
Usi = Aushi→CENTRAL EASTERN BANTU

Usilele = Lele→NORTH WESTERN BANTU
Using. Ordos D.→MONGOLIAN
Usino→BOGIA
Uskara = Basque
Usokun. Degema D.→EDO
Uspa. Omurano Tr.→ANDEAN
Uspantec→MAYAN
Uspanteca = Uspantec→MAYAN
Uspanteco = Uspantec→MAYAN
Ussuri. Gold D.→TUNGUS
Usumutong. Kohumono D.→CROSS-RIVER
   BENUE-CONGO
Usuri = Kuseri. Kotoko D.→CHADIC
Usurufa. Auyana D.→EAST NEW GUINEA
   HIGHLANDS
Uta' = Menemo→BANTOID
Uta = Ute. Southern Paiute D.→UTO-AZTEC-
   AN
Utah = Ute. Southern Paiute D.→UTO-AZ-
   TECAN
Utaha = Ifo. Eromanga D.→SOUTHERN
   NEW HEBRIDES
Utang. Boki Tr.→CROSS-RIVER BENUE-
   CONGO
Utchee = Yuchi→MACRO-SIOUAN
Utchitie = Uchita. Waicuru Tr.→WAICURIAN
Utciti = Uchita. Waicuru Tr.→WAICURIAN
Ute. Southern Paiute D.→UTO-AZTECAN
Utina. Timucua D.
Utkali = Oriya→INDIC
Utkuhigjalingmiut = Netsilik. Inuit D.→ESKI-
   MO-ALEUT
UTO-AZTECAN see article
Utonkon. Oring D.→CROSS RIVER BENUE-
   CONGO
Utu→BOGIA
Uturupa = Usurufa. Auyana D.→EAST NEW
   GUINEA HIGHLANDS
Uvea, West→POLYNESIAN
Uvea, East = Uvean. Tongan D.→POLYNE-
   SIAN
Uvean. Tongan D.→POLYNESIAN
Uvol→BISMARCK ARCHIPELAGO
Uwassi = Alawa→CUSHITIC
Uwayan. Kundjen D.→PAMA-MARIC
Uwet = Bakpinka→CROSS RIVER BENUE-
   CONGO
Uwheron. Urhobo D.→EDO
Uwi = Iwi. Kposo D.→CENTRAL TOGO
Uwinkan. Kundjen D.→PAMA-MARIC
Uwolkol. Kundjen D.→PAMA-MARIC
Uyanga→CROSS RIVER BENUE-CONGO
Uzbek→TURKIC
Uzere. Urhobo D.→EDO

Uzhil = Aushi→CENTRAL EASTERN BANTU

Uzokpo = Ebom. Kohumono D.→CROSS RIVER BENUE-CONGO

Uzokpo = Ebom. Kohumono D.→CROSS RIVER BENUE-CONGO

V

Vaalpens = Xatia. ŋ/amani D.→KHOISAN

Vacaa. Vilela Tr.→LULE-VILELA-CHARRUA

Vacoreque. Cahita D.→UTO-AZTECAN

Vadi = Wadi. Zumu D.→CHADIC

Vadorari. Gujarati D.→INDIC

Vaedda = Veda→INDIC

Vagala→GUR

Vagena→NORTHWESTERN AND CENTRAL SOLOMONS

Vagua→NORTHWESTERN AND CENTRAL SOLOMONS

Vai→MANDE

Vaicura = Waicuru→WAICURIAN

Vaicura = Waicuru→WAICURIAN

Vaikenu→EAST INDONESIAN

Vailala→TOARIPI

Vakuise = Kwise. Kwadi Tr.→KHOISAN

va-Kwachikwakwa = Kwachikwakwa. Shona D.→SOUTH EASTERN BANTU

va-Kwazwimba = Kwazimba. Shona D.→SOUTH EASTERN BANTU

Vakwengo = Hukwe→KHOISAN

Vale→CENTRAL SUDANIC

Valiente = Bribri→CHIBCHAN

Valiente = Move. Guaymi D.→CHIBCHAN

Valiperi = Waliperi. Siuci D.→NORTHERN MAIPURAN

Valman→TORRICELLI

Valpay→NORTHWESTERN NEW HEBRIDES

Valscian→ITALIC

Valuga = Volow→EASTERN OCEANIC

Valuva = Volow→EASTERN OCEANIC

Va-Ma'a = Mbugu→CUSHITIC

Vamtu→NAGA-KUKI-CHIN

Van Kieu, Huu River = Phuang→MON-KHMER

Van Kieu, Quangtri = Bru→MON-KHMER

Van Kieu, River = Pacoh→MON-KHMER

Van Kieu, Ta River = Katu→MON-KHMER

Vandals. Burgundian D.→GERMANIC

Vanikoro→SANTA CRUZ AUSTRONESIAN

Vanimo→NORTH PAPUAN

Vannic Haldean = Urartaean→HURRIAN

Vanuma = Bvanuma. Huku D.→NORTH EASTERN BANTU

Vanyume. Serrano D.→UTO-AZTECAN

Vao→NORTHWESTERN NEW HEBRIDES

Vapidiana = Uapichana→MAIPURAN

Varai. Tupi Tr.→TUPI

Varhadi-Nagpuri Marathi. Marathi D.→INDIC

Varisi→NORTHWESTERN AND CENTRAL SOLOMONS

Varjan-ala. Kalasa-ala D.→NURISTANI

Vartashen. Udi D.→CAUCASIAN

Vasengasenga→ NORTHWESTERN AND CENTRAL SOLOMONS

Vasorontu = Zorotua. Kwadi Tr.→KHOISAN

Vatrat→EASTERN OCEANIC

Vaturanga→EASTERN OCEANIC

Vaygal. Kalasa-ala D.→NURISTANI

Vayu→GYARUNG-MISHMI

Vazama = Hukwe→KHOISAN

Veda→INDIC

Vedda = Veda→INDIC

Veddah = Veda→INDIC

Veddha = Veda→INDIC

Vegliot = Vegliotic. Dalmato-Romanic D.→ROMANCE

Vegliotic. Dalmato-Romanic D.→ROMANCE

Veh→MON-KHMER

Vei = Vai→MANDE

Veiao = Yao→SOUTH EASTERN BANTU

VEJNAX→CAUCASIAN

Vejoz. Mataguayo Tr.→MATACO

Velaviuru→NORTHWESTERN AND CENTRAL SOLOMONS

Vele Uasi→BISMARCK ARCHIPELAGO

Veliche = Huiliche. Araucanian D.→PENUTIAN

Veligal. Kalasa-ala D.→NURISTANI

Vemgo. Woga D.→CHADIC

Venaambakaia = Pomo→POMO

Venambakaiia = Pomo→POMO

Venda = Vende→SOUTH EASTERN BANTU

Vende→SOUTH EASTERN BANTU

Venetic→ITALIC

Ventureno = Emigdiano. CHUMASH TR.→HOKAN

Vepsian→URALIC

Veracruzano. Huastec D.→MAYAN

Vere→ADAMAWA

Veron = Wasi-weri→NURISTANI

Verre→ADAMAWA

Vestinian→ITALIC

Vetere = Metyibo→VOLTA-COMOE

Vetre = Metyibo→VOLTA-COMOE

Veverau→EASTERN OCEANIC

Vezo. Malagasy D.→WEST INDONESIAN

Viard = Wiyok→MACRO-ALGONQUIAN

Viatin. Tupi Tr.→TUPI

Vice-Arxava. Zan D.→CAUCASIAN

Vicholo. Sindhi D.→INDIC

Vicol = Bikol→NORTHWEST AUSTRONE-
SIAN

Vicxin. Lak D.→CAUCASIAN

Vidri = Mvedere. Banda D.→EASTERN

Vidunda→CENTRAL EASTERN BANTU

Vientiene. Lao D.→KAM-TAI

VIET-MUONG see article

Vietnamese→VIET-MUONG

VIETNAMUONG = VIET-MUONG

Vige→GUR

Vigue = Vige→GUR

Vigye = Vige→GUR

Vikhlin = Vixlin. Lak D.→CAUCASIAN

Vila = Bila. Tsonga D.→SOUTH EASTERN
BANTU

Vilela→LULE-VILELA-CHARRUA

Vili→CENTRAL WESTERN BANTU

Vili→NORTH WESTERN BANTU

Vilimuluche = Moluche. Araucanian D.→
PENUTIAN

Vinza→NORTH EASTERN BANTU

Vira. Zyoba D.→NORTH EASTERN BANTU

Viru→NORTHWESTERN AND CENTRAL
SOLOMONS

Virulata→NORTHWESTERN AND CEN-
TRAL SOLOMONS

Viryal. Chuvash D.→TURKIC

Visigoth. Gothic D.→GERMANIC

Vitre = Metyibo→VOLTA-COMOE

Vitse-Arkhava = Vice-Arxava. Zan D.→CAU-
CASIAN

Vitskhin = Vicxin. Lak D.→CAUCASIAN

Vitu→NORTHEAST NEW GUINEA AUS-
TRONESIAN

Viwivakeu. Amahuaca D.→PANO

Vixlin. Lak D.→CAUCASIAN

Vizik. Woga D.→CHADIC

Vodere = Mvedere. Banda D.→EASTERN

Vogul→URALIC

Voko = Woko→ADAMAWA

VOLGAIC→URALIC

Vollamo = Walamo→OMOTIC

Volof = Wolof→WEST ATLANTIC

Volow→EASTERN OCEANIC

VOLTA-COMOE see article

VOLTAIC = GUR

Vonkutu. Mamvu-Efe D.→CENTRAL SU-
DANIC

Vonum = Bunun→FORMOSAN AUSTRO-
NESIAN

Vora. Banda D.→EASTERN

Vorohio. Cahita D.→UTO-AZTECAN

Votic→URALIC

Voto→CHIBCHAN

Votyak→URALIC

Vu. Wa D.→PALAUNG-WA

Vuela = Huela→MANDE

Vuite→NAGA-KUKI-CHIN

Vulava. Bogotu D.→NORTHWESTERN AND
CENTRAL SOLOMONS

Vulum. Musgu D.→CHADIC

Vuma. Sese D.→NORTH EASTERN BANTU

Vumba. Swahili D.→CENTRAL EASTERN
BANTU

Vungunya. Kongo D.→CENTRAL WESTERN
BANTU

Vunjo. Caga D.→NORTH EASTERN BANTU

Vunmarana = Lamalanga → EASTERN
OCEANIC

Vunun = Bunun→FORMOSAN AUSTRO-
NESIAN

Vuras→EASTERN OCEANIC

Vureas = Vuras→EASTERN OCEANIC

Vute = Bute→BANTOID

Vuture = Bute→BANTOID

Vwela = Huela→MANDE

Vy = Vai→MANDE

W

Wa→PALAUNG-WA

Wa. Nsungli D.→BANTOID

Wa = Dyula. Dyula Tr.→MANDE

Wa = Wakawaka. Dungidjau D.→WAKA-
KABIC

Wa Maathi = Mbugu→CUSHITIC

Waa = Bobwa. Bete D.→KRU

Waagai = Wakaya→WAKAYA-WARLUWA
RIC

Waagi = Wakaya→WAKAYA-WARLUWA-
RIC

Waamba = Wembawemba. Djadjala D.→
KULINIC

Waana. 'Bidyo D.→CHADIC

Wab→INDO-PACIFIC

Wabag = Mae. Enga D.→EAST NEW
GUINEA HIGHLANDS

Wabi = Huave→PENUTIAN

Wabuda→CENTRAL AND SOUTH NEW
GUINEA

Wabudori. Biak D.→MOLUCCAN

Wachipairi = Huachipairi. Masco D.→MAI-

PURAN

Wada. Banda D.→EASTERN

Wada Thuri = Thuri→EASTERN SUDANIC

Wadaginam→BOGIA

Wadai = Uardai. Galla D.→CUSHITIC

Wadai-Bergit. Mubi D.→CHADIC

Wadaman = Wardaman→GUNWINGGUAN

Wadamkong. Rawang D.→BODO-NAGA-KACHIN

Wadarandee = Wardandi. Juat D.→SOUTH-WEST PAMA-NYUNGAN

Wa-dashi. Berta D.→CHARI-NILE

Wadega = Jumjum. Maban D.→EASTERN SUDANIC

Waderman = Wardaman→GUNWINGGUAN

Wa'di. Moru D.→CENTRAL SUDANIC

Wadi. Zumu D.→CHADIC

Wadibu. Biak D.→MOLUCCAN

Wadigali = Wadikali. Karenggapa D.→DIERIC

Wadikali. Karenggapa D.→DIERIC

Wa'di-ti = Wa'di. Moru D.→CENTRAL SUDANIC

Wadiwadi = Wodiwodi. Thurawal D.→YUIN-KURIC

Wadiwangga→KANYARA

Wadja→WAKA-KABIC

Wadjabangai. Mandandanji D.→PAMA-MARIC

Wadjainggo = Wadja→WAKA-KABIC

Wadjalang = Wadjelang. Mandandanji D.→ PAMA-MARIC

Wadjari = Wudjari. Juat D.→SOUTHWEST PAMA NYUNGAN

Wadjelang. Mandandanji D.→PAMA-MARIC

Wadjeri→KARDU

Wadjiginy.→DALY

Wadjuk. Juat D.→SOUTHWEST PAMA-NYUNGAN

Wadthaurung = Wathurung. Kurung D.→ KULINIC

Waduman = Wardaman→GUNWINGGUAN

Wadye = Bobwa. Bete D.→KRU

Wadyo-Paranin-Dyapa = Uadioparanindiapa. Tauare D.→MACRO-TUCANOAN

Wadzoli = Uadzoli. Carutana D.→NORTH-ERN MAIPURAN

Waelulu→EAST INDONESIAN

Waesama→EAST INDONESIAN

Waesisi = Nupuanmen. Tanna D.→SOUTH-ERN NEW HEBRIDES

Waffa→EAST NEW GUINEA HIGHLANDS

Wafordori. Biak D.→MOLUCCAN

Waga = Bobwa. Bete D.→KRU

Wagai = Wakaya→WAKAYA-WARLUWA-RIC

Wagait see DALY

Wagaitj = Wogait see DALY

Wagap = Camuhi→NEW CALEDONIA

Wagarabai→OK

Wagarindem→NORTH PAPUAN

Wagatsch = Wogait see DALY

Wagawaga→PAPUA AUSTRONESIAN

Wa-Gaya = Luo→EASTERN SUDANIC

Wageman→GUNWINGGUAN

wa-Genia = Ena→NORTH EASTERN BANTU

Waggaia = Wakaya→WAKAYA-WARLU-WARIC

Waggait = Wogait see DALY

Waggate = Wogait see DALY

Waggote = Wogait see DALY

Wagilag→MURNGIC

Wagimuda→BOGIA

Wagoman = Wageman→GUNWINGGUAN

Wahai→EAST INDONESIAN

Wahema = 'Bahema. Lendu D.→CENTRAL SUDANIC

Waherama. Wahai D.→EAST INDONESIAN

Wahgi→EAST NEW GUINEA HIGHLANDS

Wahibo = Guahibo→EQUATORIAL

Wahke. Rawang D.→BODO-NAGA-KACHIN

Wahtani = Mandan→SIOUAN

Wai = Houailou→NEW CALEDONIA

Wai = Waioli→NORTH HALMAHERA

Wai-ala = Kalasa-ala→NURISTANI

Waiangara = Waringari. Djaru D.→NGUMBIN

Waianwonga = Wadjeri→KARDU

Waibron Bano-Demenggong = Mekwei→ NORTH PAPUAN

Waibry = Walbiri→NGARGA

Waica→WAICAN

Waica = Uaica→CARIB

WAICAN see article

WAICURIAN see article

Waicuru→WAICURIAN

WAICURU = GUAYCURU

Waidjelu. Sumba D.→MOLUCCAN

Waigali = Kalasa-ala→NURISTANI

Waigan. Hanunoo D.→NORTHWEST AUS-TRONESIAN

Waigeli = Kalasa-ala→NURISTANI

Waigeo→SOUTH HALMAHERA AUSTRO-NESIAN

Waiiemi→KIKORI RIVER

WAIKAN = WAICAN

Waikeri. Warao D.→MACRO-CHIBCHAN

Waikur = Waicuru→WAICURIAN

Waikuri = Waicuru→WAICURIAN

Waikurio = Waicuru→WAICURIAN
Waikuru = Waicuru→WAICURIAN
Waikywaiky = Warkawarka. Djadjala D.→
 KULINIC
Wailaki→ATHAPASCAN-EYAK
WAILATPUAN see PENUTIAN
Wailbri = Walbiri→NGARGA
Wailetpu = Cayuse→PENUTIAN
WAILIC→NEW CALEDONIA
Wailpi→YURA
Wailu = Houailou→NEW CALEDONIA
Waimaha→EAST INDONESIAN
Waimare = Uaimare. Cachiniti D.→MAI-
 PURAN
Waimbo = Mararba. Gobabingo D.→MURN-
 GIC
Waimbo = Maraura→NARRINYERIC
Waimdra→ADMIRALTY-WESTERN IS-
 LANDS
Waimiry = Uaimiri→CARIB
Wain = Nabak→HUON-FINISTERRE
Waina. Tucano Tr.→MACRO-TUCANOAN
Wainamari = Uainamari→MAIPURAN
Wainawonga = Madoitja. Kardutjara D.→
 WATI
Waindjago = Wadja→WAKA-KABIC
Wainggo = Wadja→WAKA-KABIC
Wainuma = Uainuma→NORTHERN MAI-
 PURAN
Wainungomo = Decuana. Maquiritare D.→
 CARIB
Waioli→NORTH HALMAHERA
Waipu = Moi→WESTERN NEW GUINEA
Waisera→INDO-PACIFIC
Waitina. Mangole D.→EAST INDONESIAN
Waiwai→CARIB
Waja→ADAMAWA
Wajamli. Buli D.→SOUTH HALMAHERA
 AUSTRONESIAN
Wajao = Yao→SOUTH EASTERN BANTU
Wajari = Wardal. Muliara D.→KARDU
Wajaru = Wayoro→TUPI
Wajeri = Wadjeri→KARDU
Wajewa. Sumba D.→MOLUCCAN
Wajgaj. Sanana D.→EAST INDONESIAN
Wajokeso→KUKUKUKU
Waka→ADAMAWA
Waka. Enga D.→EAST NEW GUINEA HIGH-
 LANDS
Waka = Wakawaka. Dungidjau D.→WAKA-
 KABIC
Wakaja = Wakaya→WAKAYA-WARLUWA-
 RIC
WAKA-KABIC see article

Wakaman→PAMA-MARIC
Wakamara = Nenium→CENTRAL AND
 SOUTH NEW GUINEA
Wakari = Wapan. Jukun D.→JUKUNOID
WAKASHAN see article
Wakasihu. Ambonese D.→MOLUCCAN
Wakawaka. Dungidjau D.→WAKA-KABIC
WAKAYA-WARLUWARIC see article
Wakde = Moar→SARMIC
Wakelbara = Jagalingu. Mandandanji D.→
 PAMA-MARIC
Wakhi→IRANIAN
Wakindiga = Hatsa→KHOISAN
Wakkawakka = Wakawaka. Dungidjau D.→
 WAKA-KABIC
Wakolo-Patahue. Sapolewa D.→EAST INDO-
 NESIAN
Wakosho. Berta D.→CHARI-NILE
Wakove. Soninke Tr.→MANDE
Wa-kut = Tailoi. Wa D.→PALAUNG-WA
Wakwafi = Maasai→EASTERN SUDANIC
Wakwavi = Maasai→EASTERN SUDANIC
Wakynakane = Okanogan→SALISH
Wala→NORTHWESTERN NEW HEBRIDES
Wala = Wali. Dagari D.→GUR
Walachian. Rumanian D.→ROMANCE
Walad Dulla. Sungor Tr.→EASTERN
 SUDANIC
Waladjangari. Wolyamidi D.→WORORAN
Walaf = Wolof→WEST ATLANTIC
Walai = Masa→CHADIC
Walaita = Walamo→OMOTIC
Walaitta = Walamo→OMOTIC
Walamin = Agwamin. Wakaman D.→PAMA-
 MARIC
Walamo→OMOTIC
Walangama→PAMA-NYUNGAN
Walani. East Gurage D.→SEMITIC
Walapai. Upland Yuman D.→YUMAN
Walar. Wolyamidi D.→WORORAN
Walari = Wali. Kordofanian Nubian Tr.→
 EASTERN SUDANIC
Walarishe = Wali. Kordofanian Nubian Tr.→
 EASTERN SUDANIC
Walaro = Weraeria. Bigumbil D.→WIRA-
 DJURIC
Walbanga. Thaua D.→YUIN-KURIC
Walbiri→NGARGA
Wale. Enga D.→EAST NEW GUINEA HIGH-
 LANDS
Walega = Lendu→CENTRAL SUDANIC
Walese = Lese. Mamvu-Efe D.→CENTRAL
 SUDANIC
Walgalu = Wolgal. Ngarigo D.→YUIN-

KURIC
Wali. Dagari D.→GUR
Wali. Kordofanian Nubian Tr.→EASTERN SUDANIC
Wali Banuah = Sichule→WEST INDONESIAN
Waliem→WESTERN NEW GUINEA
Waling→GYARUNG-MISHMI
Walio→LEONARD SCHULTZE
Waliperi. Siuci D.→NORTHERN MAIPURAN
Waljbiri = Walbiri→NGARGA
Waljen = Walyen. Kardutjara D.→WATI
Waljuk = Balardong. Juat D.→SOUTHWEST PAMA-NYUNGAN
Waljwan = Walyen. Kardutjara D.→WATI
Walla Walla = Wanapam. Sahaptin D.→ SAHAPTIN-NEZ PERCE
Wallaroi = Waraeria. Bigumbal D.→WIRA-DJURIC
Walmadjari = Wolmeri. Tjiwarlin D.→NGUM-BIN
Walmaharri – Wolmeri. Tjiwarlin D.→NGUM-BIN
Walmala – Walmanba→NGARGA
Walmanba→NGARGA
Walookera = Warluwara→WAKAYA-WAR-LUWARIC
Walpari = Walbiri→NGARGA
Walpiri = Walbiri→NGARGA
Walu = Ngizim→CHADIC
Walurigi = Omba→EASTERN OCEANIC
Walwallie = Andakerebina. Iliaura D.→ARAN-DIC
Walyen. Kardutjara D.→WATI
Walywan = Weilwan. Wongaibon D.→ WIRADJURIC
Wam→TORRICELLI
Wamai→KOIARI
Wamai = Sɔru-Viri. Askun D.→NURISTANI
Wamalca. Vilela Tr.→LULE-VILELA-CHAR-RUA
Wamalca = Yooc. Vilela Tr.→LULA-VILELA-CHARRUA
Wamar→EAST INDONESIAN
Wamas→BOGIA
WAMATE = OMETO→OMOTIC
Wambaia = Wambaya→TJINGILI-WAM-BAYAN
Wambawamba = Wembawemba. Djadjala D.→ KULINIC
Wambaya→TJINGILI-WAMBAYAN
WAMBAYIC→TJINGILI-WAMBAYAN
Wambisa = Huambisa. Jivaro D.→JIVAROAN
Wambon→AWYU
Wambori. Puri D.→PURI

Wa-Mbulu = Iraqw→CUSHITIC
Wambutu = Mangbutu→CENTRAL SU-DANIC
Wameni = Nadubea→NEW CALEDONIA
Wamesit. Massachusett Tr.→ALGONQUIAN
Wamia = Teso→EASTERN SUDANIC
Wamin = Agwamin. Wakaman D.→PAMA-MARIC
Wamoang→NEW CALEDONIA
Wamola = Wamora. Kate D.→HUON-FINISTERRE
Wamora. Kate D.→HUON-FINISTERRE
Wampanoag. Massachusett D.→ALGON-QUIAN
Wampur→NORTHEAST NEW GUINEA AUSTRONESIAN
Wana. Bare'e D.→CENTRAL AND SOUTH-ERN CELEBES
Wanac. Kate D.→HUON-FINISTERRE
Wanakald – Ngaralta. Tanganekald D.→ NARRINYERIC
Wanam–CENTRAL AND SOUTH NEW GUINEA
Wanamara–MAYAPIC
WANAMARIC = MAYAPIC
Wanambere→BOGIA
Wanami. Manam D.→NORTHEAST NEW GUINEA AUSTRONESIAN
Wanana. Tucano Tr.→MACRO-TUCANOAN
WANANG→BOGIA
Wanang→BODO-NAGA-KACHIN
Wanap = Kayik→TORRICELLI
Wanapam. Sahaptin D.→SAHAPTIN-NEZ PERCE
Wanarua→YUIN-KURIC
Wanat = Wyandot→IROQUOIS
Wanaulum = Ngaralta. Tanganekald D.→ NARRINYERIC
Wanawana→NORTHWESTERN AND CEN-TRAL SOLOMONS
Wanayaga→NGARGA
Wanbarda = Ngarla→NGAYARDA
Wanbiri = Mirning→MIRNINY
Wancavilca = Huancavilca→MACRO-CHIB-CHAN
Wanda→CENTRAL EASTERN BANTU
Wandala = Mandara→CHADIC
Wandala = Wannala. Tebu Tr.→SAHARAN
Wandalla = Wannala. Tebu Tr.→SAHARAN
Wandamen→MOLUCCAN
WANDAMIC→MOLUCCAN
Wandanian = Walbanga. Thaua D.→YUIN-KURIC
Wandara = Mandara→CHADIC

Wandaran→MARAN
Wandarang = Wandaran→MARAN
Wandatokwe→CENTRAL AND SOUTH NEW GUINEA
Wandia = Wanda→CENTRAL EASTERN BANTU
Wandji→NORTH WESTERN BANTU
Wandjira. Djaru D.→NGUMBIN
Wandjiwalku. Kula D.→PAMA-NYUNGAN
Wandot = Wyandot→IROQUOIS
Wanee = Wanji→KARWAN
Wang. Ordos D.→MONGOLIAN
Wangan. Mandandanji D.→PAMA-MARIC
Wangarabana = Arabana→PAMA-NYUNGAN
Wangarabunna = Arabana→PAMA-NYUNGAN
Wangarainbula = Peramangk. Tanganekald D.→NARRINYERIC
Wangata. Mongo-Nkundo D.→NORTH WESTERN BANTU
Wanggadjaga. Arabana D.→PAMA-NYUNGAN
Wanggom→AWYU
Wangkadjera→PITTAPITTIC
Wangkamala = Wongkamala. Arabana D.→PAMA-NYUNGAN
Wangkanguru = Wongkanguru. Arabana D.→PAMA-NYUNGAN
Wangki = Wanki. Miskito D.→MISUMALPAN
Wango. Arosi D.→EASTERN OCEANIC
Wan?guri→MURNGIC
WANHAM→CHAPACURA-WANHAMAN
Wanja = Wanya→NORTH PAPUAN
Wanjakalde = Ngaralta. Tanganekald D.→NARRINYERIC
Wanji→CENTRAL EASTERN BANTU
Wanji→KARWAN
Wanjiwalku = Wandjiwalku. Kula D.→PAMA-NYUNGAN
Wanjur. Yirgay D.→PAMA-MARIC
Wankara = Dyula. Dyula Tr.→MANDE
Wankgumara = Wongkumara. Punthamara D.→DIERIC
Wanki. Miskito D.→MISUMALPAN
Wanman→WATI
Wanmaraing = Mirning→MIRNINY
Wannala. Tebu Tr.→SAHARAN
Wannerawa = Wanarua→YUIN-KURIC
Wano→WEST NEW GUINEA HIGHLANDS
Wanoni. Kahua D.→EASTERN OCEANIC
Wansum = Pahi→SEPIK
Wantakia. Barua D.→KUKUKUKU

Wante = Wanti. Ntem D.→BANTOID
Wanti. Ntem D.→BANTOID
Wantji. Tukangbesi D.→CENTRAL AND SOUTHERN CELEBES
WANTOAT→HUON-FINISTERRE
Wantoat→HUON-FINISTERRE
Wanukaka. Sumba D.→MOLUCCAN
Wanuma→BOGIA
Wanya→NORTH PAPUAN
Wanyabalku = Wandjiwalku. Kula D.→PAMA-NYUNGAN
Wanyakalde = Ngaralta. Tanganekald D.→NARRINYERIC
WANYAM = WANHAM→CHAPACURA-WANHAMAN
Wanyam = Uanham→CHAPACURA-WANHAMAN
Wanyaturu = Remi→NORTH EASTERN BANTU
Wanyee = Wanji→KARWAN
Wanyi = Wanji→KARWAN
Wanyoro. Alur Tr.→EASTERN SUDANIC
Wanyuwalgu = Wandjiwalku. Kula D.→PAMA-NYUNGAN
Waogatsch = Wogait see DALY
Wapa = Wapan. Jukun D.→JUKUNOID
Wapan. Jukun D.→JUKUNOID
Wapatu = Santiam→KALAPUYA
Wapatu = Tfalati→KALAPUYA
Wape. Enga D.→EAST NEW GUINEA HIGHLANDS
Wape = Olo→TORRICELLI
WAPEI→TORRICELLI
WAPEI, WEST→TORRICELLI
WAPEI-PALEI = TORRICELLI
Wapeto = Tfalati→KALAPUYA
Wapi→INDO-PACIFIC
Wapi. Enga D.→EAST NEW GUINEA HIGHLANDS
Wapi = Olo→TORRICELLI
Wapishana = Uapichana→MAIPURAN
WAPISHANAN→MAIPURAN
Wapitxano = Uapichana→MAIPURAN
Wappatoo = Tfalati→KALAPUYA
Wappatu = Tfalati→KALAPUYA
Wappinger. Mohegan D.→ALGONQUIAN
Wappo→YUKI
Wapto = Tfalati→KALAPUYA
Wapumni = Southern Maidu→MAIDU
War. Khasi D.→MON-KHMER
War. Nsungli D.→BANTOID
Wara. Palara D.→GUR
Warabba = Worabba. Tebu Tr.→SAHARAN
Warabei. Tongo D.→ADMIRALTY-WEST-

ERN ISLANDS

Waramanga = Warumungu→PAMA-NYUN-
GAN

Warameri. Riraidjango D.→MURNGIC

Waramiri = Warameri. Riraidjango D.→
MURNGIC

Waramungu — Warumungu→PAMA-NYUN-
GAN

Warangoo = Wudjari. Juat D.→SOUTHWEST
PAMA-NYUNGAN

Warao→MACRO-CHIBCHAN

Warapiche = Chayma→CARIB

Warasai. Mayo D.→SEPIK

Warat→DALY

Warawalde = Portaulun. Tanganekald D.→
NARRINYERIC

Warawara. Limba D.→WEST ATLANTIC

Waray→NORTHWEST AUSTRONESIAN

Waray-Waray = Waray→NORTHWEST AUS-
TRONESIAN

Waraywaray = Waray→NORTHWEST AUS-
TRONESIAN

Warburton Ranges. Kardutjara D.→WATI

Wardal. Muliara D.→KARDU

Wardaman→GUNWINGGUAN

Wardandi. Juat D.→SOUTHWEST PAMA-
NYUNGAN

Wardandie = Wardandi. Juat D.→SOUTH-
WEST PAMA-NYUNGAN

Warday = Uardai. Galla D.→CUSHITIC

Wardo. Biak D.→MOLUCCAN

Warduman = Wardaman→GUNWINGGUAN

Ware→NORTH EASTERN BANTU

Ware = Wari→PAPUA AUSTRONESIAN

Warekena = Arequena→NORTHERN MAI-
PURAN

Warembori→MOMBERAMO RIVER

Wargamy. Wakaman D.→PAMA-MARIC

Wargbi = Iwaidji→IWAIDJAN

Wari→PAPUA AUSTRONESIAN

Wari. Biak D.→MOLUCCAN

Warianga = Warienga→MANTHARDA

Waribu = Alibu→PARE-SAMO-BEAMI-
BOSAVI

Warienga→MANTHARDA

Warilau→EAST INDONESIAN

Warimai = Worimi→YUIN-KURIC

Waringari. Djaru D.→NGUMBIN

WARIS→NORTH PAPUAN

Waris→NORTH PAPUAN

Wariwonga = Wagienga→MANTHARDA

Warjawa→CHADIC

Warkamai = Wargamy. Wakaman D.→PAMA-
MARIC

Warkaman = Wakaman→PAMA-MARIC

Warkamin = Wakaman→PAMA-MARIC

Warkawarka. Djadjala D.→KULINIC

Warkeeman = Wakaman→PAMA-MARIC

Warkeemon = Wakaman→PAMA-MARIC

Warkend = Warki. Tanganekald D.→NARRIN-
YERIC

Warki. Tanganekald D.→NARRINYERIC

Warki = Dilling. Kordofanian Nubian Tr.
→EASTERN SUDANIC

Warkim Be = Dilling. Kordofanian Nubian
Tr.→EASTERN SUDANIC

Warkya = Wakaya→WAKAYA-WARLU-
WARIC

Warluwara→WAKAYA-WARLUWARIC

Warmala = Wolmeri. Tjiwarlin D.→NGUMBIN

Warmawa. Kermanji D.→IRANIAN

Warnabinnie = Mirning→MIRNINY

Warnabirrie = Mirning→MIRNINY

Warnman = Wanman→WATI

Waropen→MOLUCCAN

Waropen of Wandamen Bay = Ambumi.
Wandamen D.→MOLUCCAN

Waropu = Arop→NORTHEAST NEW GUIN-
EA AUSTRONESIAN

Warra = Nukuna. Jadliaura D.→YURA

Warrai→AUSTRALIAN MACRO-PHYLUM

Warranger = Wudjari. Juat D.→SOUTHWEST
PAMA-NYUNGAN

Warrangle = Wudjari. Juat D.→SOUTHWEST
PAMA-NYUNGAN

Warrangoo = Wirangu→SOUTHWEST
PAMA-NYUNGAN

Warraw = Warao→MACRO-CHIBCHAN

Warrimee = Worimi→YUIN-KURIC

Warrimi = Worimi→YUIN-KURIC

Warriwonga = Warienga→MANTHARDA

Warrwai = Warwa→NYULNYULAN

Warsa. Biak D.→MOLUCCAN

Wartaman = Wardaman→GUNWINGGUAN

Waru. Laki D.→CENTRAL AND SOUTHERN
CELEBES

Warumungu→PAMA-NYUNGAN

Waruna→CENTRAL AND SOUTH NEW
GUINEA

Warungu. Wakaman D.→PAMA-MARIC

WARUP→HUON-FINISTERRE

Warwa→NYULNYULAN

Warwai = Warwa→NYULNYULAN

Wasa. Banda D.→EASTERN

Wasabane. Sumo Tr.→MISUMALPAN

Wa-sanye = Sanye→CUSHITIC

Wasare = Kapriman→SEPIK

Wasco. Upper Chinook D.→CHINOOKAN

Wase. Jukun D.→JUKUNOID
Wasepnau = Urat→TORRICELLI
Washkuk = Kwoma→SEPIK
Washo→HOKAN
Wasi = Alawa→CUSHITIC
Wasi = Uasi→NEW BRITAIN
Wasia. Tala D.→EAST INDONESIAN
Wasin Gishu = Wuasinkishu. Maasai Tr.→
    EASTERN SUDANIC
Wasi-weri→NURISTANI
Waskia→BOGIA
Wasona. Tucano Tr.→MACRO-TUCANOAN
Wassi = Alawa→CUSHITIC
Wassisi = Nupuanmen. Tanna D.→SOUTH-
    ERN NEW HEBRIDES
Wassu. Gyarung D.→GYARUNG-MISHMI
Wasuai. Nimo D.→LEFT MAY
Wasulu. Malinka D.→MANDE
Watakataui→SEPIK
Watalu = Namie→SEPIK
Watam→BOGIA
Watao = Adai→CADDOAN
Watawit. Berta D.→CHARI-NILE
Watchandi = Watjandi. Malgana D.→KARDU
Watchee = Badjelang. Kitabal D.→BAN-
    DJALANGIC
Wathaurung = Wathurung. Kurung D.→
    KULINIC
Wathiwathi. Djadjala D.→KULINIC
Wathurung. Kurung D.→KULINIC
WATI see article
Watindiga = Hatsa→KHOISAN
Watjandi. Malgana D.→KARDU
Watta = Sanye→CUSHITIC
Watthiwatthi = Wathiwathi. Djadjala D.→
    KULINIC
Wattywatty = Wathiwathi. Djadjala D.→KULI-
    NIC
Watu. Bungku D.→CENTRAL AND SOUTH-
    ERN CELEBES
Watulai→EAST INDONESIAN
Watyi. Ewe D.→EWE
Waula. Kardutjara D.→WATI
Waumin = Agwamin. Wakaman D.→PAMA-
    MARIC
Waunana→CHOCO
Waura = Uaura→MAIPURAN
Wa-Vu = Vu. Wa D.→PALAUNG-WA
Wawan. Hanunoo D.→NORTHWEST AUS-
    TRONESIAN
Wawayachtonoc. Mohegan Tr.→ALGON-
    QUIAN
Wawenoc = Abnaki. Penobscot D.→ALGON-
    QUIAN

Wawi = Dida. Bete D.→KRU
Wawmin = Agwamin. Wakaman D.→PAMA-
    MARIC
Wawoni = Wowoni. Bungku D.→CENTRAL
    AND SOUTHERN CELEBES
Wawoorong = Wurundjeri. Taungurong D.→
    KULINIC
Wawurong = Wurundjeri. Taungurong D.→
    KULINIC
Wawyukma = Wanapam. Sahaptin D.→
    SAHAPTIN-NEZ PERCE
Waya = Bobwa. Bete D.→KRU
Wayana = Oyana→CARIB
Wayoro→TUPI
Wayumara→CARIB
Wazaizara = Guaja. Tenetehara D.→TUPI
Wazire = Werize. Gawwada D.→CUSHITIC
We→BANTOID
We. Tonga D.→CENTRAL EASTERN
    BANTU
Wea = Miami→ALGONQUIAN
Weal = Wiilman. Juat D.→SOUTHWEST
    PAMA-NYUNGAN
Weasisi = Nupuanmen. Tanna D.→SOUTH-
    ERN NEW HEBRIDES
Webanaki = Delaware→ALGONQUIAN
Weda→SOUTH HALMAHERA AUSTRO-
    NESIAN
Weda = Veda→INDIC
Wedauan→PAPUA AUSTRONESIAN
WEDAUIC→PAPUA AUSTRONESIAN
Wedda = Veda→INDIC
Weddo = Veda→INDIC
Weedokarry = Widugari. Nyamal D.→NGAY-
    ARDA
Weedookarry = Widugari. Nyamal D.→
    NGAYARDA
Weel = Wiilman. Juat D.→SOUTHWEST
    PAMA-NYUNGAN
Weeyot = Wiyok→MACRO-ALGONQUIAN
Weh = We→BANTOID
Weidyenye = Munduruku→TUPI
Weil = Wiilman. Juat D.→SOUTHWEST
    PAMA-NYUNGAN
Weilwan. Wongaibon D.→WIRADJURIC
Weima. Loma D.→MANDE
Weima = Siama. Loma D.→MANDE
Weima Buzi = Weima. Loma D.→MANDE
Weining→BURMESE-LOLO
Weinondot = Wyandot→IROQUOIS
Weithspek = Yurok → MACRO - ALGON-
    QUIAN
Weitspeh = Yurok→MACRO-ALGONQUIAN
Weiyot = Wiyok→MACRO-ALGONQUIAN

Wekiweki = Warkawarka. Djadjala D.→KULI-
NIC
Wela'pakote'li. Kwalhioqua D.→ATHAPAS-
CAN-EYAK
Wele = Were→GOILALA
Welemur→EAST INDONESIAN
Wellega = Mecha. Galla D.→CUSHITIC
Wello. Galla D.→CUSHITIC
Welsh→CELTIC
Wemale = Tala→EAST INDONESIAN
Wemba = Bemba→CENTRAL EASTERN
BANTU
Wembawemba. Djadjala D.→KULINIC
Wembi→NORTH PAPUAN
Wemo. Kate D.→HUON-FINISTERRE
Wen Yai = Iai→LOYALTY ISLANDS
Wenatchee. Columbian D.→SALISH
Wenatchi-Columbia = Columbian→SALISH
Wendish = Lusatian→SLAVIC
Wengbit. Oksapmin D.→CENTRAL AND
SOUTH NEW GUINEA
Wenke→NORTHWESTERN NEW GUINEA
Wepulprap = Potaruwutj. Djadjala D.→KULI-
NIC
Weraeria. Bigumbil D.→WIRADJURIC
Werang = Kurung→KULINIC
Werchikwar. Burushaski D.
Were→GOILALA
Were = Vere→ADAMAWA
Were = Weda→SOUTH HALMAHERA AUS-
TRONESIAN
Werekatyalli = Potaruwutj. Djadjala D.→KULI-
NIC
Weriagar. Kampong Baru D.→WESTERN
NEW GUINEA
Werize. Gawwada D.→CUSHITIC
WERIZOID→CUSHITIC
Werna = Werni. Fungor Tr.→KORDOFANI-
AN
Werni. Fungor Tr.→KORDOFANIAN
Werogery = Wiradjuri→WIRADJURIC
Werowocomoco. Powhatan Tr.→ALGON-
QUIAN
Wescos→GERMANIC
Wesi. Geser D.→EAST INDONESIAN
Westenhuck. Mohegan Tr.→ALGONQUIAN
WESTERN DESERT = WATI
Wetan→EAST INDONESIAN
Wetawit = Watawit. Berta D.→CHARI-NILE
Wetere = Bute→BANTOID
Wetoki. Leti D.→MOLUCCAN
Wetu. 'Beli D.→CENTRAL SUDANIC
Weumba = Wembawemba. Djadjala D.→KULI-
NIC

Wewaw→KAREN
Wewenoc = Abnaki. Penobscot D.→ALGON-
QUIAN
Wewewa. Sumba D.→MOLUCCAN
Weyneubulkoo = Wandjiwalku. Kula D.→
PAMA-NYUNGAN
Whadjuk = Wadjuk. Juat D.→SOUTHWEST
PAMA-NYUNGAN
Whajook = Wadjuk. Juat D.→SOUTHWEST
PAMA-NYUNGAN
Wheelman = Wiilman. Juat D.→SOUTHWEST
PAMA-NYUNGAN
Whe-el-po = Colville. Okanogan D.→SALISH
Whilkut. Hupa D.→ATHAPASCAN-EYAK
!WI→KHOISAN
Wiakei = Wiaki→TORRICELLI
Wiaki→TORRICELLI
Wichita→CADDOAN
Wicocomoco. Powhatan Tr.→ALGONQUIAN
Widagaree = Widugari. Nyamal D.→NGA-
YARDA
Widagari = Widugari. Nyamal D.→NGA-
YARDA
Widekum→BANTOID
Widi. Muliara D.→KARDU
Widi = Wiri. Mandandanji D.→PAMA-MARIC
Widjabal. Kitabal D.→BANDJALANGIC
Widjara = Wudjari. Juat D.→SOUTHWEST
PAMA-NYUNGAN
Widninga = Kaurna. Jadliaura D.→YURA
Widugari. Nyamal D.→NGAYARDA
Wiekagjok. Mohegan Tr.→ALGONQUIAN
Wierdi = Wiri. Mandandanji D.→PAMA-
MARIC
Wihinasht = Shoshoni→UTO-AZTECAN
Wiilman. Juat D.→SOUTHWEST PAMA-
NYUNGAN
Wiinza-Baali. Ngombe D.→NORTH WEST-
ERN BANTU
Wiiyahuurong = Wathurung. Kurung D.→
KULINIC
Wik Alkan = Wikngatara→PAMA-MARIC
Wik Epa = Wikepa→PAMA-MARIC
Wik Mean = Wikmean→PAMA-MARIC
Wik Me?nh = Wikmean→PAMA-MARIC
Wik Muminh→PAMA-MARIC
Wik Mungkan = Wikmunkan→PAMA-MARIC
Wik Munkan = Wikmunkan→PAMA-MARIC
Wik Ngandjara. Wikngatara D.→PAMA-MA-
RIC
Wik Ngatara = Wikngatara→PAMA-MARIC
Wik Ngathara = Wikngatara→PAMA-MARIC
Wik?ep = Wikepa→PAMA-MARIC
Wikepa→PAMA-MARIC

Wikmean→PAMA-MARIC
Wikmunkan→PAMA-MARIC
Wikngatara→PAMA-MARIC
Wilawila. Ungarinyin D.→WORORAN
Wild Rice Men = Menomini→ALGONQUIAN
Wiliche = Huiliche. Araucanian D.→PENU-
    TIAN
Wiljagali = Wiljakali. Kula D.→PAMA-
    NYUNGAN
Wiljakali. Kula D.→PAMA-NYUNGAN
Will = Wiilman. Juat D.→SOUTHWEST
    PAMA-NYUNGAN
Willamot = Santiam→KALAPUYA
WILLAUMEZ→NORTHEAST NEW GUIN-
    EA AUSTRONESIAN
Williams River→INDO-PACIFIC
Williwille = Andakerebina. Iliaura D.→ARAN-
    DIC
Willo = Wiljakali. Kula D.→PAMA-NYUN-
    GAN
Wilya = Wiljakali. Kula D.→PAMA-NYUN-
    GAN
Wilyakali = Wiljakali. Kula D.→PAMA-
    NYUNGAN
Wimbun = Nsungli→BANTOID
Win→GUR
Wina = Wanya→NORTH PAPUAN
Winantu-Gimpu. Pipikoro D.→CENTRAL
    AND SOUTHERN CELEBES
Windesi = Wandamen→MOLUCCAN
Windessi = Wandamen→MOLUCCAN
Winebago = Winnebago→SIOUAN
Winiv→NORTHWESTERN NEW HEBRIDES
Winnaynie = Kaurna. Jadliaura D.→YURA
Winnebago→SIOUAN
Winnipesaukee. Massachusett Tr.→ALGON-
    QUIAN
WINTOON = WINTUN
WINTUN see article
Wipie = Wailpi→YURA
Wipsi-ni→PLATEAU BENUE-CONGO
Wira. Morokodo D.→CENTRAL SUDANIC
Wira-Athorree = Wiradjuri→WIRADJURIC
Wiradhari = Wiradjuri→WIRADJURIC
Wiradhuri = Wiradjuri→WIRADJURIC
Wiradjeri = Wiradjuri→WIRADJURIC
WIRADJURIC see article
Wiraduri = Wiradjuri→WIRADJURIC
Wirafed. Kawaib D.→TUPI
Wirairai = Weraeria. Bigumbil D.→WIRA-
    DJURIC
Wirajeree = Wiradjuri→WIRADJURIC
Wiram = Suki→MARIND
Wiramaya = Ngadjuri. Jadliaura D.→YURA

Wirameju = Ngadjuri. Jadliaura D.→YURA
Wirameyu = Ngadjuri. Jadliaura D.→YURA
Wirangu→SOUTHWEST PAMA-NYUNGAN
Wirashuri = Wiradjuri→WIRADJURIC
Wiratheri = Wiradjuri→WIRADJURIC
Wirdinja = Wirdinya. Kardutjara D.→WATI
Wirdinya. Kardutjara D.→WATI
Wiri. Mandandanji D.→PAMA-MARIC
Wiri-Dyapa = Uiridiapa→MACRO-TUCA-
    NOAN
Wirigirek = Potaruwutj. Djadjala D.→KULI-
    NIC
Wirina = Uirina→NORTHERN MAIPURAN
Wiriwiri→WIRADJURIC
Wirracharee = Wiradjuri→WIRADJURIC
Wirraidyuri = Wiradjuri→WIRADJURIC
Wirraiyarrai = Wiradjuri→WIRADJURIC
Wirramaya = Ngadjuri. Jadliaura D.→YURA
Wirramayo = Ngadjuri. Jadliaura D.→YURA
Wirrameyu = Ngadjuri. Jadliaura D.→YURA
Wirrung = Wirangu→SOUTHWEST PAMA-
    NYUNGAN
Wirrunga = Wirangu→SOUTHWEST PAMA-
    NYUNGAN
Wirtjapokandja = Jangkundjara. Kardutjara
    D.→WATI
Wiru→EAST NEW GUINEA HIGHLANDS
Wisa = Biisa→CENTRAL EASTERN BANTU
Wischosk = Wiyok→MACRO-ALGONQUIAN
Wishram. Upper Chinook D.→CHINOOKAN
WISSEL   LAKES - KEMANDOGA→WEST
    NEW GUINEA HIGHLANDS
Witawurong = Wathurung. Kurung D.→KULI-
    NIC
Witji = Gunwiggu→GUNWINGGUAN
Witoto→WITOTOAN
WITOTOAN see Article
Witoura = Wathurung. Kurung D.→KULINIC
Witowro = Wathurung. Kurung D.→KULINIC
Witowurrong = Wathurung. Kurung D.→
    KULINIC
Witowurung = Wathurung. Kurung D.→KULI-
    NIC
Witshita = Wichita→CADDOAN
Wiwash = Nanticoke. Mohegan D.→ALGON-
    QUIAN
Wiwi Rano. Laki D.→CENTRAL AND
    SOUTHERN CELEBES
Wiya. Nsungli D.→BANTOID
Wiyap = Jiru→JUKUNOID
Wiyok→MACRO-ALGONQUIAN
Wiyot = Wiyok→MACRO-ALGONQUIAN
Wlastukweek = Malecite. Passamaquoddy D.→
    ALGONQUIAN

Wlookera = Warluwara→WAKAYA-WARLU-WARIC

Wo = Basari→WEST ATLANTIC

Wobe = Bobwa. Bete D.→KRU

Woccon→MACRO-SIOUAN

Woda = Wolani→WEST NEW GUINEA HIGHLANDS

Wodani = Wolani→WEST NEW GUINEA HIGHLANDS

Wodiwodi. Thurawal D.→YUIN-KURIC

Woeewoorong = Wurundjeri. Taungurong D.→ Kulinic

Woeworung = Wurundjeri. Taungurong D.→ KULINIC

Woga→CHADIC

Woga = Wakawaka. Dungidjau D.→WAKA-KABIC

WOGAITY→DALY

Wogamusin→SEPIK

Wogatj - Wogait see DALY

Wogco→NORTHEAST NEW GUINEA AUSTRONESIAN

Wogga = Wakawaka. Dungidjau D.→WAKA-KABIC

Wogu = Bahinemo→SEPIK

Wohia. Tobelo D.→NORTH HALMAHERA

Woiworung = Wurundjeri. Taungurong D.→ KULINIC

Woiwurru = Wurundjeri. Taungurong D.→ KULINIC

Woiwurung = Wurundjeri. Taungurong D.→ KULINIC

Wokiare. Yabarana D.→CARIB

Wokka = Taribeleng→WAKA-KABIC

Wokka = Wakawaka. Dungidjau D.→WAKA-KABIC

Wokkari = Wakawaka. Dungidjau D.→WAKA-KABIC

Woko→ADAMAWA

Wolaitsa = Walamo→OMOTIC

Wolamo = Walamo→OMOTIC

Wolane = Walani. East Gurage D.→SEMITIC

Wolani→WEST NEW GUINEA HIGHLANDS

Wolaroi = Weraeria. Bigumbil D.→WIRADJURIC

Wolataita = Walamo→OMOTIC

Woleai. Ulithian D.→MICRONESIAN

Wolga = Warluwara→WAKAYA-WARLU-WARIC

Wolgai. Ngarigo D.→YUIN-KURIC

Wolio→CENTRAL AND SOUTHERN CELEBES

Woljamidi = Wolyamidi→WORORAN

Wollaminya = Walamo→OMOTIC

Wollega = Mecha. Galla D.→CUSHITIC

Wollegara = Warluwara→WAKAYA-WARLU-WARIC

Wollo = Wello. Galla D.→CUSHITIC

Wolmaharry = Wolmeri. Tjiwarlin D.→NGUMBIN

Wolmera = Wolmeri. Tjiwarlin D.→NGUMBIN

Wolmeri. Tjiwarlin D.→NGUMBIN

Wolof→WEST ATLANTIC

Wolperi = Walbiri→NGARGA

Wolpirra = Walbiri→NGARGA

Wolroi = Weraeria. Bigumbil D.→WIRADJURIC

Wolyamidi→WORORAN

Wolyamini = Wolyamidi→WORORAN

Wom→ADAMAWA

Wom = Wam→TORRICELLI

Womba = Wembawemba. Djadjala D.→KULINIC

Wombelbara - Giramay. Wakaman D.→ PAMA-MARIC

Wombungee = Wongaibon→WIRADJURIC

Wom-by-a = Wambaya→TJINGILI-WAMBAYAN

Wombya = Wambaya→TJINGILI-WAMBAYAN

Wommin = Agwamin. Wakaman D.→PAMA-MARIC

Womsak = Seim→SEPIK

Wonarua = Wanarua→YUIN-KURIC

Wondama = Wandamen→MOLUCCAN

Woneiga = Wanayaga→NGARGA

Wongagibun = Wongaibon→WIRADJURIC

Wongaibon→WIRADJURIC

Wongaidya = Nukuna. Jadliaura D.→YURA

Wongamusin = Wogamusin→SEPIK

Wongapitcha = Pitjantjatjara. Kardutjara D.→ WATI

Wongapitjira = Pitjantjatjara. Kardutjara D.→ WATI

Wongbo = Wanti. Ntem D.→BANTOID

Wonggai = Pindiini. Kardutjara D.→WATI

Wonggongaru = Wongkanguru. Arabana D.→ PAMA-NYUNGAN

Wonghi = Wongaibon→WIRADJURIC

Wonghibon = Wongaibon→WIRADJURIC

Wongkamala. Arabana D.→PAMA-NYUNGAN

Wongkami = Unggumi→WORORAN

Wongkanguru. Arabana D.→PAMA-NYUNGAN

Wongkongaru = Wongkanguru. Arabana D.→ PAMA-NYUNGAN

Wongkumara. Punthamara D.→DIERIC

Wongkurapuna = Arabana→PAMA-NYUN-GAN

Wongo→NORTH WESTERN BANTU

Wongonooroo = Wongkanguru. Arabana D.→PAMA-NYUNGAN

Woni→BURMESE-LOLO

Wonipalku = Wandjiwalku. Kula D.→PAMA-NYUNGAN

Wonjimalku = Wandjiwalku. Kula D.→PAMA-NYUNGAN

Wonkagnurra = Wongkanguru. Arabana D.→PAMA-NYUNGAN

Wonkamara = Wongkumara. Punthamara D.→DIERIC

Wonkamarra = Wongkumara. Punthamara D.→DIERIC

Wonkamudla = Wongkamala. Arabana D.→PAMA-NYUNGAN

Wonkamura = Wongkumara. Punthamara D.→DIERIC

Wonkamurra = Wongkumara. Punthamara D.→DIERIC

Wonkanguru = Wongkanguru. Arabana D.→PAMA-NYUNGAN

Wonkaoora = Wongkanguru. Arabana D.→PAMA-NYUNGAN

Wonkaooroo = Wongkanguru. Arabana D.→PAMA-NYUNGAN

Wonkomarra = Wongkumara. Punthamara D.→DIERIC

Wonkongaru = Wongkanguru. Arabana D.→PAMA-NYUNGAN

Wonkongnuru = Wongkanguru. Arabana D.→PAMA-NYUNGAN

Wonkonguru = Wonkanguru. Arabana D.→PAMA-NYUNGAN

Wonkubara = Wongkumara. Punthamara D.→DIERIC

Wonnarua = Wanarua→YUIN-KURIC

Wonoka = Jadliaura→YURA

Wooeewoorong = Wathurung. Kurung D.→KULINIC

Wo'oi. Japen D.→MOLUCCAN

Woonamurra = Wanamara→MAYAPIC

Woordinya = Wirdinya. Kardutjara D.→WATI

Woorenga = Warienga→MANTHARDA

Woorienga = Warienga→MANTHARDA

Worabba. Tebu Tr.→SAHARAN

Woradjera = Wiradjuri→WIRADJURIC

Wordaman = Wardaman→GUNWINGGUAN

Wordjerg = Wiradjuri→WIRADJURIC

Worgai = Wakaya→WAKAYA-WARLUWA-RIC

Worgaia = Djadjala→KULINIC

Worgaia = Wakaya→WAKAYA-WARLUWA-RIC

Worgait = Wogait see DALY

Worgite = Wogait see DALY

Worimi→YUIN-KURIC

Worin→HUON-FINISTERRE

Workai→EAST INDONESIAN

Workia = Wakaya→WAKAYA-WARLUWA-RIC

Woro. Kresh D.→CENTRAL SUDANIC

Worom = Birom→PLATEAU BENUE-CON-GO

Worora→WORORAN

WORORAN see article

WORORIC→WORORAN

Wororra = Worora→WORORAN

Worugi = Ro→EAST NEW GUINEA HIGH-LANDS

Wosera. Abelam D.→SEPIK

Wotadi = Otati→PAMA-MARIC

Wotapuri-Katarqalai→INDIC

Wotati = Otati→PAMA-MARIC

Wotjobaluk. Djadjala D.→KULINIC

Wottowotti = Wathiwathi. Djadjala D.→KULINIC

Wotu→CENTRAL AND SOUTHERN CELE-BES

Wouri = Oli→NORTH WESTERN BANTU

Wovanga = Wowonga→KOIARI

Wovea = Bobea→NORTH WESTERN BAN-TU

Wowonga→KOIARI

Wowoni. Bungku D.→CENTRAL AND SOUTHERN CELEBES

Woychibirik = Potaruwutj. Djadjala D.→KULINIC

Woyo = Ngoyo. Ndingi D.→CENTRAL WESTERN BANTU

Wragarite = Ngarkat. Djadjala D.→KULINIC

Wrangell. Tlingit D.→NA-DENE

Wu→CHINESE

Wu. Seediq D.→FORMOSAN AUSTRONE-SIAN

Wuasinkishu. Maasai Tr.→EASTERN SUDAN-IC

Wuboma. Loma D.→MANDE

Wuddyawurru = Wathurung. Kurung D.→KULINIC

Wuding = Kilba→CHADIC

Wudir = Woga→CHADIC

Wudjar. Wakaman D.→PAMA-MARIC

Wudjari. Juat D.→SOUTHWEST PAMA-NYUNGAN

Wudjawuru→KULINIC

Wudjawurung = Wathurung. Kurung D.→ KULINIC

Wukan. Jukun D.→JUKUNOID

Wukchamni. Foothill North Yokuts D.→ YOKUTS

Wulaki = Jandjinung→MURNGIC

Wulane = Walani. East Gurage D.→SEMITIC

Wulgurukaba. Ilba D.→PAMA-MARIC

Wuli→NORTHWESTERN AND CENTRAL SOLOMONS

Wulima. Lala D.→CENTRAL EASTERN BAN-TU

Wulisi = Kasem→GUR

Wullaroi = Weraeria. Bigumbil D.→WIRA-DJURIC

Wulpura. Koko Jelandji D.→PAMA-MARIC

Wulua→NORTHWESTERN NEW HEBRIDES

Wululi. Abui D.→TIMOR-ALOR

Wulumari = Wolmeri. Tjiwarlin D.→NGUM-BIN

Wulwa = Ulva. Sumo Tr.→MISUMALPAN

Wum→BANTOID

Wumbu = Wuumu→NORTH WESTERN BANTU

Wumbvu→NORTH WESTERN BANTU

Wu-ming→KAM-TAI

Wummabel = Wunambal→WORORAN

Wun Anei = Anei. Rek D.→EASTERN SU-DANIC

Wuna→LARAKIAN

Wu-nai. Punu D.→MIAO-YAO

Wunamara = Wanamara→MAYAPIC

Wunambal→WORORAN

WUNAMBALIC→WORORAN

Wunambullu = Wunambal→WORORAN

Wunci = Ghulfan. Kordofanian Nubian Tr.→ EASTERN SUDANIC

Wuncim Be = Ghulfan. Kordofanian Nubian Tr.→EASTERN SUDANIC

Wundat = Wyandot→IROQUOIS

Wunjo = Vunjo. Caga D.→NORTH EASTERN BANTU

Wunuk = Tiwi→AUSTRALIAN MACRO-PHYLUM

Wunumara = Wanamara→MAYAPIC

Wunyakalde = Ngaralta. Tanganekald D.→ NARRINYERIC

Wuo = Kwe. West Teke D.→NORTH WEST-ERN BANTU

Wuong→NORTHEASTERN NEW GUINEA

Wurara = Worora→WORORAN

Wurbereq = Urbareg. East Gurage D.→SEMIT-IC

WURBO→JUKUNOID

Wuri = Oli→NORTH WESTERN BANTU

Wurkum = Kulung→BANTOID

Wurrunjeri = Wurundjeri. Taungurong D.→ KULINIC

Wurundjeri. Taungurong D.→KULINIC

Wurunjeri = Wurundjeri. Taungurong D.→ KULINIC

Wutati = Otati→PAMA-MARIC

Wute = Bute→BANTOID

Wutong→NORTH PAPUAN

Wuumu→NORTH WESTERN BANTU

Wuvulu → ADMIRALTY-WESTERN IS-LANDS

Wu-yang-pu. Mongour D.→MONGOLIAN

Wuyar = Jiru→JUKUNOID

Wyandot→IROQUOIS

Wyandote = Wyandot→IROQUOIS

Wyandott = Wyandot→IROQUOIS

Wyandotte = Wyandot→IROQUOIS

Wychinga = Wongkanguru. Arabana D.→ PAMA-NYUNGAN

Wymar Bouzie = Weima. Loma D.→MANDE

X

Xa = Khang. Khmu' D.→KHMUIC

Xa Cau = Khang. Khmu' D.→KHMUIC

Xa Khao = Khang. Khmu' D.→KHMUIC

Xaayo. Luhya D.→NORTH EASTERN BAN-TU

Xagua→JIRARAN

Xajdak = Kajtak. Dargwa D.→CAUCASIAN

Xajrjuzovskij. Kamchadal D.→CHUKCHEE-KAMCHATKAN

Xatepec. Mixtec D.→MIXTECAN

/xam→KHOISAN

Xamir = Khamir→CUSHITIC

/xam-ka-!k'e = Xam→KHOISAN

Xamta = Khamta. Khamir D.→CUSHITIC

Xamtanga = Khamir→CUSHITIC

Xananwa. Northern Sotho D.→SOUTH EAST-ERN BANTU

Xanti = Ostyak→URALIC

Xaput. Kryts D.→CAUCASIAN

Xarbuk. Dargwa D.→CAUCASIAN

Xaroxa = Didinga→EASTERN SUDANIC

Xasouke = Khasonke→MANDE

Xassa = Tigre→SEMITIC

Xatia. ŋ/amani D.→KHOISAN

Xatyrskij. Chukchee D.→CHUKCHEE-KAM-CHATKAN

Xatyrskij. Kerek D.→CHUKCHEE-KAM-

CHATKAN
/ /xegwe→KHOISAN
/ /xegwi = / /xegwe→KHOISAN
Xesiba. Nguni D.→SOUTH EASTERN BAN-
TU
Xeta = Seta→TUPI
Xevero = Chebero→ANDEAN
Xevsur. Georgian D.→CAUCASIAN
Xhosa. Nguni D.→SOUTH EASTERN BAN-
TU
Xibba = Kilba→CHADIC
Xibitaona. Kokama D.→TUPI
Xibito→ANDEAN
XIBITO-CHOLON→ANDEAN
Xicaque = Jicaque→HOKAN
Xihuila = Chebero→ANDEAN
Xikongo = Southern Kongo. Kongo D.→
CENTRAL WESTERN BANTU
Ximbioa = Chamboa→CARAJA
Xinalug→CAUCASIAN
Xinca→MACRO-CHIBCHAN
XINGU→MAIPURAN
Xingu Caiapo = Gorotire→GE
Xinji = Shingi→CENTRAL WESTERN BAN-
TU
Xiparicot→CARIB
Xipaya = Sipaya→TUPI
Xirikwa = Grikwa→KHOISAN
Xirino. Cashibo D.→PANO
Xirixana = Shirishana→WAICAN
Xitswa = Tswa→SOUTH EASTERN BANTU
Xivaro = Jivaro→JIVAROAN
Xixime. Cahita D.→UTO-AZTECAN
Xojalee = Shogale. Berta D.→CHARI-NILE
Xokleng = Xokreng. Caingang D.→GE
Xokreng. Caingang D.→GE
Xolota = Choroti→MATACO
!Xon = ≠Hua→KHOISAN
Xong = Chong→MON-KHMER
!Xoŋ = ≠Hua→KHOISAN
Xopa. Zan D.→CAUCASIAN
Xorrhue = Corrhue. Cabecar D.→CHIBCHAN
Xosa = Xhosa. Nguni D.→SOUTH EASTERN
BANTU
Xosnaw. Kermanji D.→IRANIAN
Xrikwa = Grikwa→KHOISAN
XU = NORTHERN S. AFRICAN KHOI-
SAN→KHOISAN
Xu = Hukwe→KHOISAN
!Xu = Kung→KHOISAN
Xukhwe = Hukwe→KHOISAN
Xukuchi. Circassian D.→CAUCASIAN
Xunzax. Avar D.→CAUCASIAN
Xvarshi→CAUCASIAN

Y

Ya→KAM-TAI
Yaa. West Teke D.→NORTH WESTERN
BANTU
Yaakoyaako = Mararba. Gobabingo D.→
MURNGIC
Yaakoyaako = Maraura→NARRINYERIC
Yaamba. Mbole D.→NORTH EASTERN BAN-
TU
Yaara = Jaara. Djadjala D.→KULINIC
Yaba. Buhagana Tr.→MACRO-TUCANOAN
Yabaana = Jabaana→NORTHERN MAI-
PURAN
Yaban = Kampong Baru→WESTERN NEW
GUINEA
Yabarana→CARIB
Yabasi. Basa Tr.→NORTH WESTERN BAN-
TU
Yabaypura→TACANA
Yabein. Burmese D.→BURMESE-LOLO
Yabem = Yabim→NORTHEAST NEW GUIN-
EA AUSTRONESIAN
Yaben→BOGIA
Yabi = Jabi. Kapauku D.→WEST NEW
GUINEA HIGHLANDS
Yabim→NORTHEAST NEW GUINEA AUS-
TRONESIAN
Yabio→LEONARD SCHULTZE
Yabiyufa→EAST NEW GUINEA HIGH-
LANDS
Yabue. Bakwe Tr.→KRU
Yabura. Bauwaki D.→MAILU
Yacanes = Yakan→NORTHWEST AUSTRO-
NESIAN
Yacaoyana. Carijona D.→CARIB
Yache→IDOMA
Yachumi→NAGA-KUKI-CHIN
Yackarabul = Jagara→DURUBULIC
Yacoua = Yakpa. Banda D.→EASTERN
Yadliura = Jadliaura→YURA
Yadre. More D.→GUR
Yaeyama. Southern Ryukyuan D.→JAPANESE
Yafera. Timucua D.
Yaganon→INDO-PACIFIC
Yagara = Jagara→DURUBULIC
Yagaria. Keigana D.→EAST NEW GUINEA
HIGHLANDS
Yagawak→HUON-FINISTERRE
Yagba. Yoruba D.→YORUBA
Yaghnobi→IRANIAN
Yagoua. Masa D.→CHADIC
Yagoua. Tuburi D.→CHADIC
Yagoua. Tupuri D.→ADAMAWA

Yaguai. Achagua D.→NORTHERN MAI-PURAN
Yagua→PEBA-YAGUAN
YAGUAN = PEBA-YAGUAN
Yagwoia→KUKUKUKU
Yahadian→WESTERN NEW GUINEA
Yahang→TORRICELLI
Yahgan→ANDEAN
Yahi→YANAN
Yahow = Zahao→NAGA-KUKI-CHIN
Yahua = Yagua→PEBA-YAGUAN
Yahuna→MACRO-TUCANOAN
Yaikole. Mbole D.→NORTH EASTERN BANTU
Yairy-yairy = Jarijari. Djadjala D.→KULINIC
Yaisu. Mbole D.→NORTH EASTERN BANTU
Yaitepec. Chatino D.→ZAPOTECAN
Yaitmathang = Jaimathang→PAMA-NYUN-GAN
Yajima = Yalima. Mongo-Nkundo D.→ NORTH WESTERN BANTU
Yaka→CENTRAL WESTERN BANTU
Yaka = Kako→NORTH WESTERN BANTU
Yaka = Yaa. West Teke D.→NORTH WEST-ERN BANTU
Yakamul→NORTHEAST NEW GUINEA AUSTRONESIAN
Yakan→NORTHWEST AUSTRONESIAN
Yakə = Yakurr→CROSS RIVER BENUE-CONGO
Yakha→GYARUNG-MISHMI
Yakiba→BOGIA
Yakima. Sahaptin D.→SAHAPTIN-NEZ PERCE
Yako = Yakurr→CROSS RIVER BENUE-CONGO
Yakoma→EASTERN
Yakon = Yaquina. Alsea D.→YAKONAN
Yakona = Yaquina. Alsea D.→YAKONAN
YAKONAN see article
Yakoro. Bekwarra D.→CROSS RIVER BE-NUE-CONGO
Yakpa. Banda D.→EASTERN
Yakpwa = Yakpa. Banda D.→EASTERN
Yakthomba = Yakha→GYARUNG-MISHMI
Yakthungba = Limbu→GYARUNG-MISHMI
Yakuba = Dan→MANDE
Yakurr→CROSS RIVER BENUE-CONGO
Yakut→TURKIC
Yakutat. Tlingit D.→NA-DENE
Yakwa = Yakpa. Banda D.→EASTERN
Yakwina = Yaquina. Alsea D.→YAKONAN
Yala→IDOMA
Yalach = Lach. Czech D.→SLAVIC

Yalalag. Zapotec D.→ZAPOTECAN
Yalarnnga = Jalanga→PAMA-NYUNGAN
Yalasu. Nenema D.→NEW CALEDONIA
Yalikoka. Kele Tr.→NORTH WESTERN BAN-TU
Yalima. Mongo-Nkundo D.→NORTH WEST-ERN BANTU
Yallof = Wolof→WEST ATLANTIC
Yalunka. Susu D.→MANDE
Yalunke = Yalunka. Susu D.→MANDE
Yalyi = Karenggapa→DIERIC
Yam = Jam. Kaurareg D.→MABUIAGIC
Yamai→NORTHEAST NEW GUINEA AUS-TRONESIAN
Yamaluba→TACANA
Yamamadi→ARAWAKAN
Yamandil = Wolyamidi→WORORAN
Yamarikuma→CARIB
Yamas→NORTHEAST NEW GUINEA AUS-TRONESIAN
Yamba = Wembawemba. Djadjala D.→KULI-NIC
Yambasa→NORTH WESTERN BANTU
Yambayamba = Wembawemba. Djadjala D.→ KULINIC
Yambeena = Jambina. Mandandanji D.→ PAMA-MARIC
Yambes→TORRICELLI
Yambeta. Banen Tr.→NORTH WESTERN BANTU
Yambeta. Mandi D.→NORTH WESTERN BANTU
Yambo = Anuak→EASTERN SUDANIC
Yameci→CHIBCHAN
Yamegi = Kara→CENTRAL SUDANIC
Yameo→PEBA-YAGUAN
Yami→NORTHWEST AUSTRONESIAN
Yamiaca. Atsahuaca D.→PANO
Yaminawa = Jaminaua. Jurua-Purus Tr.→ PANO
Yamma = Janjero→OMOTIC
YAMMADI→ARAWAKAN
Yamna = Janjero→OMOTIC
Yamongiri. Buja D.→NORTH WESTERN BANTU
Yamorai. Chayahuita D.→ANDEAN
Yampai = Yavapai. Upland Yuman D.→ YUMAN
Yampio = Yavapai. Upland Yuman D.→ YUMAN
Yamu. Guahibo D.→EQUATORIAL
Yana→YANAN
Yanaigua = Tapiete. Tupi D.→TUPI
Yanam→WAICAN

YANAN see article
Yanbye. Burmese D.→BURMESE-LOLO
Yanda = Janda→PAMA-NYUNGAN
Yandairunga. = Antakirinya. Kardutjara D.→ WATI
Yandapu. Enga D.→EAST NEW GUINEA HIGHLANDS
Yanderawartha = Jandruwanta. Dieri D.→ DIERIC
Yanderika = Indri→EASTERN
Yandijinang = Jandjinung→MURNGIC
Yandirika = Indri→EASTERN
Yandjinung = Jandjinung→MURNGIC
Yandrawontha = Jandruwanta. Dieri D.→ DIERIC
Yandruwunta = Jandruwanta. Dieri D.→ DIERIC
Yanduwulda = Jandruwanta. Dieri D.→DIERIC
Yang Huang = T'en→KAM-TAI
Yang Sek = Riang-lang→PALAUNG-WA
Yang Wan Kun = Riang-lang→PALAUNG-WA
Yanga. More D.→GUR
Yangafek. Ewondo D.→NORTH WESTERN BANTU
Yangafuk' = Yangafek. Ewondo D.→NORTH WESTERN BANTU
Yangaro = Janjero→OMOTIC
Yangeberra = Kuungkari. Mandandanji D.→ PAMA-MARIC
Yangele. Gbaya Tr.→EASTERN
Yangere. Banda D.→EASTERN
Yanggal = Njangga. Gayardilt D.→TANGKIC
Yanghuang = T'en→KAM-TAI
Yangman = Jungman→GUNWINGGUAN
YANGMANIC→GUNWINGGUAN
Yangonda. Mbole D.→NORTH EASTERN BANTU
Yangoru = Yengoru. Boiken D.→SEPIK
Yanhuitlan. Mixtec D.→MIXTECAN
Yanindo = Andakerebina. Iliaura D.→ARANDIC
Yankibura = Kuungkari. Mandandanji D.→ PAMA-MARIC
Yankton. Dakota D.→SIOUAN
Yano→GYARUNG-MISHMI
Yanoama = Yanomani. Waica Tr.→WAICAN
YANOMAMA = WAICAN
Yanoman→WAICAN
Yanomani→WAICAN
Yanomani. Waica Tr.→WAICAN
Yans = Yanzi→NORTH WESTERN BANTU
Yansi = Yadre. More D.→GUR
Yansi = Yanzi→NORTH WESTERN BANTU

Yantruwunta = Jandruwanta. Dieri D.→ DIERIC
Yanzi→NORTH WESTERN BANTU
YAO→SOUTH EASTERN BANTU
Yao→SOUTH EASTERN BANTU
Yao = Mien→MIAO-YAO
Yaokandja. Kele Tr.→NORTH WESTERN BANTU
Yapese→MICRONESIAN
Yapooa. Macu D.→MACRO-TUCANOAN
Yapua. Desana D.→MACRO-TUCANOAN
Yapunda→TORRICELLI
YAPURA→NORTHERN MAIPURAN
Yaqay→MARIND
YAQAY-MARIND-BOAZI = MARIND
Yaquina. Alsea D.→YAKONAN
YARA→PAMA-MARIC
Yaraikana = Jathaikana. Otati D.→PAMA-MARIC
Yaralde = Jarildekald. Tanganekald D.→ NARRINYERIC
Yaran = Potaruwutj. Djadjala D.→KULINIC
Yarda. Tebu Tr.→SAHARAN
Yardwa-tyalli = Jardwa. Djadjala D.→KULI-NIC
YAREBA→MAILU
Yareba→MAILU
Yarigui→CARIB
Yarikiluk = Jarijari. Djadjala D.→KULINIC
Yarilde = Jarildekald. Tanganekald D.→ NARRINYERIC
Yariyari = Jarijari. Djadjala D.→KULINIC
Yarleeyandee = Jeljendi. Dieri D.→DIERIC
Yarnango = Jarnango→MURNGIC
Yaro = Chana→LULE-VILELA-CHARRUA
Yaroinga = Jaroinga. Iliaura D.→ARANDIC
Yarr = Ngunawal→YUIN-KURIC
Yarrapo. Yameo D.→PEBA-YAGUAN
Yarrawaurka = Jauraworka→DIERIC
Yarreyarre = Jarijari. Djadjala D.→KULINIC
Yarrildie = Jarildekald. Tanganekald D.→ NARRINYERIC
Yarroinga = Jaroinga. Iliaura D.→ARANDIC
Yarrowin = Jaroinga. Iliaura D.→ARANDIC
Yaruma→CARIB
Yaruro→JIVAROAN
Yasa→NORTH WESTERN BANTU
Yasa. Mape D.→CARIB
Yasem. Ewondo D.→NORTH WESTERN BANTU
Yasgua = Yeskwa→PLATEAU BENUE-CON-GO
Yashi→PLATEAU BENUE-CONGO
Yasica. Sumo Tr.→MISUMALPAN

Yasing→ADAMAWA
Yassing = Yasing→ADAMAWA
Yatasi, Upper. Caddo Tr.→CADDOAN
Yate. Keigana D.→EAST NEW GUINEA HIGHLANDS
Yatsam→NAGA-KUKI-CHIN
Yatsumi = Yachumi→NAGA-KUKI-CHIN
Yau→TORRICELLI
Yauagepa→NORTH NEW GUINEA
Yauaperi = Jauaperi→CARIB
Yauavo = Jauavo. Jurua-Purus Tr.→PANO
Yaudi. Phoenician D.→SEMITIC
Yauelmani. Valley Yokuts D.→YOKUTS
Yauera = Jauor→NYULNYULAN
Yaugang→INDO-PACIFIC
Yaukaniga = Mapenuss. Abipon Tr.→GUAY-CURU
Yaulapiti = Jaulapiti→MAIPURAN
Yaunde = Ewondo→NORTH WESTERN BANTU
YAUNDE-FANG→NORTH WESTERN BANTU
Ya'unk = Yahang→TORRICELLI
Yauor = Jauor→NYULNYULAN
Yaura = Jaara. Djadjala D.→KULINIC
Yaurawakka = Jauraworka→DIERIC
Yauri = Kambari→PLATEAU BENUE-CONGO
Yaurorka = Jauraworka→DIERIC
Yauroworka = Jauraworka→DIERIC
Yauungillam = Taungurong→KULINIC
YAVA→WESTERN NEW GUINEA
Yavahe = Javahe→CARAJA
Yavanai = Javahe→CARAJA
Yavapai. Upland Yuman D.→YUMAN
Yavape = Yavapai. Upland Yuman D.→YUMAN
Yavepe Kutcan = Yavapai. Upland Yuman D.→YUMAN
Yavipai = Yavapai. Upland Yuman D.→YUMAN
Yavitero→MAIPURAN
Yaviyufa = Yabiyufa→EAST NEW GUINEA HIGHLANDS
Yaw. Burmese D.→BURMESE-LOLO
Yaw = Nanda→KARDU
Yawa Ziru = Gbandi. Mende D.→MANDE
Yawaim = Taribeleng→WAKA-KABIC
Yawanawa = Jauanaua. Jurua-Purus Tr.→PANO
Yawangillam = Taungurong→KULINIC
Yawarete Tapuya = Jauarete. Carutana D.→NORTHERN MAIPURAN
Yawdanchi. Foothill North Yokuts D.→YOKUTS
Yawdwin. Chinbok D.→NAGA-KUKI-CHIN
Yawelmani = Yauelmani. Valley Yokuts D.→YOKUTS
Yawembe. Kele Tr.→NORTH WESTERN BANTU
Yay→KAM-TAI
Yayauring = Jaara. Djadjala D.→KULINIC
Yayeyama = Yaeyama. Southern Ryukyuan D.→JAPANESE
Yazdi. Persian D.→IRANIAN
Yazva. Zyrian D.→URALIC
Ye = Mon Nya. Mon D.→MON-KHMER
Ye Jein = Chingpaw→BODO-NAGA-KACHIN
Ye Yeh = Chingpaw→BODO-NAGA-KACHIN
Yecoanita. Vilela Tr. → LULE - VILELA-CHARRUA
Yecauna = Mayongong. Maquiritare D.→CARIB
Yecunampa = Yocomoampa. Vilela Tr.→LULE-VILELA-CHARRUA
Yedina = Buduma→CHADIC
Yeei. Yanzi D.→NORTH WESTERN BANTU
Yeei = Yeye→SOUTH WESTERN BANTU
Yega→BINANDERE
Yega of Gona→BINANDERE
Yeghuye = Yagwoia→KUKUKUKU
Yegir→KUMBAINGGARIC
Yegua = Yagua→PEBA-YAGUAN
Yeh = Jeh→MON-KHMER
Yehen = Poai. Nemi D.→NEW CALEDONIA
Yei = Yeye→SOUTH WESTERN BANTU
Yeico = Jeico→GE
Yeinbaw = Yinbaw. Bwe D.→KAREN
Yeji→VOLTA-COMOE
Yekinawe = Yequinahue. Alacaluf D.→ANDEAN
Yekora→BINANDERE
Yela→NORTH WESTERN BANTU
Yele→INDO-PACIFIC
Yelina = Jalanga→PAMA-NYUNGAN
Yelinda. Bulu Tr.→NORTH WESTERN BANTU
Yellanga = Jalanga→PAMA-NYUNGAN
Yellow-knife. Chipewyan Tr.→ATHAPASCAN-EYAK
Yelmana. Tebu Tr.→SAHARAN
Yelmek→FREDERIK HENDRIK IS AND SE WEST IRIAN
Yelogu→SEPIK
Yelyayendi = Jeljendi. Dieri D.→DIERIC
Yema = Suena→BINANDERE
Yema-Yarawe = Suena→BINANDERE
Yembama. Bulu Tr.→NORTH WESTERN

BANTU
Yembe. Hungu D.→CENTRAL WESTERN
BANTU
Yembe = Songe→CENTRAL WESTERN
BANTU
Yemchidi = Djamchidi. Persian D.→IRANIAN
Yemma = Janjero→OMOTIC
Yemna = Janjero→OMOTIC
Yemsa = Janjero→OMOTIC
Yenava = Erukala. Tamil D.→DRAVIDIAN
Yendang→ADAMAWA
Yenets = Yenisei Samoyed→URALIC
Yengen = Poai. Nemi D.→NEW CALEDONIA
Yengi Hissar. Uighur D.→TURKIC
Yengono. Bulu Tr.→NORTH WESTERN
BANTU
Yengoru. Boiken D.→SEPIK
Yenimu = Oser→AWYU
Yenisei Samoyed→URALIC
Yenisei Tatars = Khakas→TURKIC
Yenisei Turks = Khakas→TURKIC
YENISEIAN see article
YENISEI-OSTYAK→YENISEIAN
Yenisei-Ostyak = Ket→YENISEIAN
Yenoa. Tebu Tr.→SAHARAN
Yequinahue. Alacaluf D.→ANDEAN
Yerakai→INDO-PACIFIC
Yerava. Malayalam D.→DRAVIDIAN
Yerawaka = Jauraworka→DIERIC
Yere = Vere→ADAMAWA
Yerewa = Jeru. Great Andamanese D.→
ANDAMANESE
Yergam = Yergham→PLATEAU BENUE-
CONGO
Yergham→PLATEAU BENUE-CONGO
Yergum = Yergham→PLATEAU BENUE-
CONGO
Yeripa→KUKUKUKU
Yerraleroi = Juwalarai. Yualyai D.→WIRA-
DJURIC
Yerraruck = Erawirung. Nganguruku D.→
NARRINYERIC
Yerreyerre = Jarijari. Djadjala D.→KULINIC
Yerriyerri = Jarijari. Djadjala D.→KULINIC
Yerrunthully = Jirandali. Mandandanji D.→
PAMA-MARIC
Yerukala = Erukala. Tamil D.→DRAVIDIAN
Yesan-Mayo = Mayo→SEPIK
Yeshkun = Burushaski
Yeskwa→PLATEAU BENUE-CONGO
Yesoum = Mvele. Ewondo D.→NORTH
WESTERN BANTU
Yeti = Wembi→NORTH PAPUAN
Yettimaralla = Kabelbara. Mandandanji D.→
PAMA-MARIC
Yewa→NORTH WESTERN BANTU
Yey→FREDERIK HENDRIK IS AND SE
WEST IRIAN
Yey = Yeei. Yanzi D.→NORTH WESTERN
BANTU
Yeye→SOUTH WESTERN BANTU
Yeyi = Yeye→SOUTH WESTERN BANTU
Yezo = Ezo. Ainu D.
Yezum = Mvele. Ewondo D.→NORTH WEST-
ERN BANTU
Yi. Miao D.→MIAO-YAO
Yibiwan = Wardaman→GUNWINGGUAN
Yibwa Lomuriki = Tima→KORDOFANIAN
Yidda = Mada→PLATEAU BENUE-CONGO
Yiddish. Netherlandic-German D.→GERMAN-
IC
Yidena = Buduma→CHADIC
Yidi = Kwegu→EASTERN SUDANIC
Yidin. Wakaman D.→PAMA-MARIC
Yidinich = Kwegu→EASTERN SUDANIC
Yiegera = Yegir→KUMBAINGGARIC
Yigha = Leyigha→CROSS RIVER BENUE-
CONGO
Yiilima = Ngunawal→YUIN-KURIC
Yil→TORRICELLI
Yillaro = Laro→KORDOFANIAN
Yimas→NORTH NEW GUINEA
Yimbe = Limba→WEST ATLANTIC
Yimtsurr = Yachumi→NAGA-KUKI-CHIN
Yinbaw. Bwe D.→KAREN
Yindi. Khami D.→NAGA-KUKI-CHIN
Yindu = Yindi. Khami D.→NAGA-KUKI-
CHIN
Ying = Amangu. Nanda D.→KARDU
Yingiebandie = Jindjibandi. Kurama D.→
NGAYARDA
Yinoa = Yenoa. Tebu Tr.→SAHARAN
Yintale. Bwe D.→KAREN
Yinwum = Jinwun→PAMA-MARIC
yi-Nzebi = Nzebi→NORTH WESTERN BAN-
TU
Yiporok→BOTOCUDO
yi-Punu = Punu→NORTH WESTERN BANTU
Yir Thangedl. Koko Mindjan D.→PAMA-
MARIC
Yir Tjutjam. Koko Mindjan D.→PAMA-
MARIC
Yir? Yoront = Jir Joront. Koko Mindjan D.→
PAMA-MARIC
Yira. Ndandi D.→NORTH EASTERN BANTU
Yiran = Erawirung. Nganguruku D.→NAR-
RINYERIC
Yirau = Erawirung. Nganguruku D.→NAR-

RINYERIC
Yirgay→PAMA-MARIC
Yiri. Tulu D.→ADMIRALTY-WESTERN
ISLANDS
Yiri = Iria. Tebu Tr.→SAHARAN
Yiringo. Tongo D.→ADMIRALTY-WEST-
ERN ISLANDS
Yiriw. Ndrosun D.→ADMIRALTY-WEST-
ERN ISLANDS
Yirkla = Mirning→MIRNINY
Yis→TORRICELLI
yi-Sangu = Sangu→NORTH WESTERN
BANTU
Yitha = Jitajita. Djadjala D.→KULINIC
Yiti·nyti = Yidin. Wakaman D.→PAMA-
MARIC
Yitsa = Jitajita. Djadjala D.→KULINIC
Ylinesa = Illinois. Miami D.→ALGONQUIAN
Ynezeno = Barbareno. CHUMASH TR.→
HOKAN
Yo. Lao D.→KAM-TAI
Yo = Yos→NAGA-KUKI-CHIN
Yoabu. Somba D.→GUR
Yoadabe-Watoare = Maring→EAST NEW
GUINEA HIGHLANDS
Yoangen. Kube D.→HUON-FINISTERRE
Yoconoampa. Vilela Tr.→LULE-VILELA-
CHARRUA
Yoda→BINANDERE
Yofo = Kumba→ADAMAWA
Yofuaha = Choroti→MATACO
Yogad→NORTHWEST AUSTRONESIAN
Yogli. Tangsa D.→BODO-NAGA-KACHIN
Yohoraa. Tucano D.→MACRO-TUCANOAN
Yoidik→BOGIA
Yokaia = Pomo→POMO
Yoko. Bete Tr.→KRU
Yokod. Foothill North Yokuts D.→YOKUTS
Yokogbo. Bete Tr.→KRU
Yoku. Eromanga D.→SOUTHERN NEW HEB-
RIDES
YOKUTS see article
Yokwa→NAGA-KUKI-CHIN
Yola = Diola→WEST ATLANTIC
Yolo→CHIBCHAN
Yolox→CHINANTECAN
Yom = Pila→GUR
Yombe. Kongo D.→CENTRAL WESTERN
BANTU
Yombe. Tumbuka D.→CENTRAL EASTERN
BANTU
Yombe Classique = Vungunya. Kongo D.→
CENTRAL WESTERN BANTU
Yomkallie = Yonkalla→KALAPUYA

Yomud. Turkmen D.→TURKIC
Yon. Boki Tr.→CROSS-RIVER BENUE-
CONGO
Yon = Yuan→KAM-TAI
Yoncalla = Yonkalla→KALAPUYA
Yonggom→OK
Yongo. Mbangala D.→CENTRAL WESTERN
BANTU
Yoni. Temne D.→WEST ATLANTIC
Yonkalla→KALAPUYA
Yoo = Yooc. Vilela Tr.→LULE-VILELA-
CHARRUA
Yooadda = Wadjuk. Juat D.→SOUTHWEST
PAMA-NYUNGAN
Yooard = Wadjuk. Juat D.→SOUTHWEST
PAMA-NYUNGAN
Yooc. Vilela Tr.→LULE-VILELA-CHARRUA
Yookambul = Jukambal→YUIN-KURIC
Yookumbil = Jukambal→YUIN-KURIC
Yookumble = Jukambal→YUIN-KURIC
Yoolanlanya = Ulaolinya→PITTAPITTIC
Yope = Yopi→TLAPANECAN
Yopi→TLAPANECAN
Yoppi = Yopi→TLAPANECAN
Yora. Jicaque D.→HOKAN
Yorda. Tebu Tr.→SAHARAN
Yoria→NORTHEAST NEW GUINEA AUS-
TRONESIAN
Yorrowinga = Jaroinga. Iliaura D.→ARANDIC
Yoruba see article
Yos→NAGA-KUKI-CHIN
Yotafa = Tobati→SOUTH HALMAHERA
AUSTRONESIAN
Yotayota = Jotijota→YOTAYOTIC
YOTAYOTIC see article
Youchee = Yuchi→MACRO-SIOUAN
Yowangillam = Taungurong→KULINIC
Yowerawarrika = Jauraworka→DIERIC
Yowerawoolka = Jauraworka→DIERIC
Yoza. Ziba D.→NORTH EASTERN BANTU
Ysa = Catawba→MACRO-SIOUAN
Ysletta = Isleta. Tiwa D.→TANOAN
Yu. Manjaku D.→WEST ATLANTIC
Yualai = Yaulyai→WIRADJURIC
Yualarai = Juwalarai. Yualyai D.→WIRA-
DJURIC
Yualyai→WIRADJURIC
Yuan→KAM-TAI
Yuanga = Thuanga→NEW CALEDONIA
Yuba = Maidu→MAIDU
Yubamona→TACANA
Yuberi→ARAWAKAN
Yucatan = Maya→MAYAN
Yucatana = Maya→MAYAN

Yucatanice = Maya→MAYAN
Yucatano = Maya→MAYAN
Yucatec = Maya→MAYAN
Yucateca = Maya→MAYAN
Yucateco = Maya→MAYAN
Yucateque = Maya→MAYAN
Yucatese = Maya→MAYAN
Yuchi→MACRO-SIOUAN
Yucuna→NORTHERN MAIPURAN
Yue = Cantonese→CHINESE
Yueh = Cantonese→CHINESE
Yueh Hai. Cantonese D.→CHINESE
Yugambe→BANDJALANGIC
Yugumbal = Yugambe→BANDJALANGIC
Yugumbil = Jukambal→YUIN-KURIC
YUIN-KURIC see article
YUKAGHIR see article
Yukai = Yuki→YUKI
Yukaliwa = Kiliwa→YUMAN
Yukambal = Jukambal→YUIN-KURIC
Yukambil = Jukambal→YUIN-KURIC
Yukan. Atayal D.→FORMOSAN AUSTRONE-
   SIAN
Yuke = Yuki→YUKI
Yukeh = Yuki→YUKI
YUKI see article
YUKIAN = YUKI
Yukkaburra = Ilba→PAMA-MARIC
Yukkaburra = Yidin. Wakaman D.→PAMA-
   MARIC
Yukuben = Boritsu→JUKUNOID
YUKUBEN-KUTEP→JUKUNOID
Yukutare = Bitare→BANTOID
Yulaparitya = Yulbaridja. Kardutjara D.→
   WATI
Yulbaridja. Kardutjara D.→WATI
Yule = Kasem→GUR
Yulngi = Djinba→MURNGIC
Yulngo = Jarnango→MURNGIC
YULNGU→MURNGIC
Yulu. Yulu-Binga D.→CENTRAL SUDANIC
Yulu-Binga→CENTRAL SUDANIC
Yum = Wum→BANTOID
Yuma. River Yuman D.→YUMAN
Yuma = Juma
Yuma Apache = Yavapai. Upland Yuman D.→
   YUMAN
YUMAN see article
Yumana = Jumana→NORTHERN MAI-
   PURAN
Yumaya = Yuma. River Yuman D.→YUMAN
Yumbri→KHMUIC
Yumpia = Wambaya→TJINGILI-WAMBA-
   YAN

Yunca→CHIPAYAN
Yuncarirx = Chiquito→CHIQUITO
Yunga = Wudjari. Juat D.→SOUTHWEST
   PAMA-NYUNGAN
Yunga = Yunca→CHIPAYAN
Yung-ch'eng. Pao-an D.→MONGOLIAN
Yung-ching. Mongour D.→MONGOLIAN
Yung-chu'un→KAM-TAI
Yunger→ADAMAWA
Yunggor→DALY
Yungman = Jungman→GUNWINGGUAN
Yungmanni = Jungman→GUNWINGGUAN
Yungmun = Jungman→GUNWINGGUAN
Yungmunee = Jungman→GUNWINGGUAN
Yungmunnee = Jungman→GUNWINGGUAN
Yungmunni = Jungman→GUNWINGGUAN
Yungo = Shingi→CENTRAL WESTERN
   BANTU
Yung-shun = Yung-chu'un→KAM-TAI
Yungur = Wadjuk. Juat D.→SOUTHWEST
   PAMA-NYUNGAN
Yunka = Yunca→CHIPAYAN
Yunnalinka = Warluwara→WAKAYA-WAR-
   LUWARIC
Yu-no. Punu D.→MIAO-YAO
Yuon = Yuan→KAM-TAI
Yupik, Central Alaskan→ESKIMO-ALEUT
Yupik, Pacific Gulf→ESKIMO-ALEUT
Yupik, St. Lawrence Island→ESKIMO-ALEUT
YUPNA→HUON-FINISTERRE
Yupu = Maipu→MAIDU
YURA see article
Yuracare = Uru→CHIPAYAN
Yuracare, Eastern = Soloto→EQUATORIAL
Yuracare, Western = Mansinyo→EQUATO-
   RIAL
YURACAREAN→EQUATORIAL
Yurak Samoyed→URALIC
Yuri→MACRO-TUCANOAN
Yuri→NORTH NEW GUINEA
Yurimbil = Jukambal→YUIN-KURIC
Yurmaty. Bashkir D.→TURKIC
Yuroa = Yuruwa. Tebu Tr.→SAHARAN
Yurok→MACRO-ALGONQUIAN
Yuron = Tunica→MACRO-ALGONQUIAN
Yurquin = Zhorquin. Terraba D.→CHIBCHAN
Yurra Yurra = Jarijari. Djadjala D.→KULINIC
Yuruk. Balkan Gagauz Turkish D.→TURKIC
YURUNA→TUPI
Yuruna→TUPI
Yurupari Tapuya = Jurupari. Carutana D.→
   NORTHERN MAIPURAN
Yuruwa. Tebu Tr.→SAHARAN
Yusku. Sumo Tr.→MISUMALPAN

Yuta = Ute. Southern Paiute D.→UTO-AZTECAN
Yutah = Ute. Southern Paiute D.→UTO-AZTECAN
Yutuwichan. Sekani D.→ATHAPASCAN-EYAK
Yvytigua. Tupi Tr.→TUPI

Z

Zabana→NORTHWESTERN AND CENTRAL SOLOMONS
Zacapoaxtla. Nahua D.→UTO-AZTECAN
Zacapula = Tzutuhil→MAYAN
Zacatula = Tzutuhil→MAYAN
Zadu. Lendu D.→CENTRAL SUDANIC
Zagai = Wom→ADAMAWA
Zagaoua = Zaghawa→SAHARAN
Zaghawa→SAHARAN
Zahao→NAGA-KUKI-CHIN
Zakara = Nzakara→EASTERN
Zakataly. Avar D.→CAUCASIAN
Zakho. Zaza D.→IRANIAN
Zaki = Lui. High Lugbara D.→CENTRAL SUDANIC
Zaklapahkap = Mam→MAYAN
Zaklohpakap = Mam→MAYAN
Zaklopacap = Mam→MAYAN
Zaklopahkap = Mam→MAYAN
Zala. Walamo D.→OMOTIC
Zama = Hukwe→KHOISAN
Zaman. Bulu Tr.→NORTH WESTERN BANTU
Zamana. Patangoro D.→CARIB
Zamangon = Kamantan→PLATEAU BENUE-CONGO
Zamboangueno→ROMANCE
ZAMUCOAN→EQUATORIAL
Zamucoan, Northern→EQUATORIAL
Zamucoan, Southern→EQUATORIAL
Zan→CAUCASIAN
Zan. Gula D.→ADAMAWA
Zan = Kanuri→SAHARAN
Zanaki→NORTH EASTERN BANTU
Zande→EASTERN
Zandeh = Sandeh→EASTERN
Zanga. Dya D.→GUR
Zangram. Thebor D.→GYARUNG-MISHMI
Zani = Njai→CHADIC
Zanniat→NAGA-KUKI-CHIN
Zany = Njai→CHADIC
Zanzibari. Arabic D.→SEMITIC
Zan-zun→TIBETAN

Zao = Mara→NAGA-KUKI-CHIN
Zapa. Omurano Tr.→ANDEAN
Zapaluta = Tojolabal→MAYAN
Zapara→CARIB
Zaparo→ANDEAN
ZAPAROAN→ANDEAN
Zapateco = Zapotec→ZAPOTECAN
Zapotec→ZAPOTECAN
ZAPOTECAN see article
Zara = Sankura. Bobo D.→GUR
Zaramo→CENTRAL EASTERN BANTU
Zarandi. Persian D.→IRANIAN
Zarma. Songhai D.→NILO-SAHARAN
Zatieno = Satienyo. Northern Zamucoan Tr.→EQUATORIAL
Zavaze = Javahe→CARAJA
Zayahueco. Cora Tr.→UTO-AZTECAN
Zayein. Bwe D.→KAREN
Zayse→OMOTIC
Zaysinya = Zayse→OMOTIC
Zaysse = Zayse→OMOTIC
Zaza→IRANIAN
Zazere = Kulango→GUR
Zazing = Yasing→ADAMAWA
ZE = GE
Zegbe = Kwaya. Bete D.→KRU
Zeguha = Zigula→CENTRAL EASTERN BANTU
Zelmamo = Zelmamu→EASTERN SUDANIC
Zelmamu→EASTERN SUDANIC
Zelmogbo. Bete Tr.→KRU
Zemaiciai = Shamaitish. Lithuanian D.→BALTIC
Zemaitis = Shamaitish. Lithuanian D.→BALTIC
Zemaitish = Shamaitish. Lithuanian D.→BALTIC
Zemgalian→BALTIC
Zenaga→BERBER
ZENATI→BERBER
Zenu = Cenu→CARIB
Zenu = Cenu→CHOCO
Zenzontepec. Chatino D.→ZAPOTECAN
Zergulla. Zayse D.→OMOTIC
Zergullinya. Zayse D.→OMOTIC
Zeri = Seri→HOKAN
Zet = Shinasha→OMOTIC
Zeuhnang→NAGA-KUKI-CHIN
Zezeru. Shona D.→SOUTH EASTERN BANTU
Zezuru = Zezeru. Shona D.→SOUTH EASTERN BANTU
Zhgabe = Albanian
Zhimomi = Zumoni→NAGA-KUKI-CHIN
Zhorquin. Terraba D.→CHIBCHAN

Zhu/oase = Dzu/'oasi. Kung D.→KHOISAN
Zia→BINANDERE
Zia. Keres D.
Ziba→NORTH EASTERN BANTU
Ziba. Havu D.→NORTH EASTERN BANTU
Ziba = Dzindza→NORTH EASTERN BANTU
Zigua = Zigula→CENTRAL EASTERN BANTU
Zigula→CENTRAL EASTERN BANTU
ZIGULA-ZARABO→CENTRAL EASTERN BANTU
Ziida = 'Bahema. Lendu D.→CENTRAL SUDANIC
Zilmamo = Zelmamu→EASTERN SUDANIC
Zilo. Andi D.→CAUCASIAN
Zimakani→MARIND
Zimba→NORTH EASTERN BANTU
Zimba = Kwazwimba. Shona D.→SOUTH EASTERN BANTU
Zimba = Nzema→VOLTA-COMOE
Zimbabwe→KHOISAN
Zimu = Njem. Njem-Bajue Tr.→NORTH WESTERN BANTU
Zincanteco. Tzotzil D.→MAYAN
Zingero = Janjero→OMOTIC
Zinja = Dzindża→NORTH EASTERN BANTU
Zinza = Dzindza→NORTH EASTERN BANTU
Zirizan. Waica Tr.→WAICAN
Zithung→BODO-NAGA-KACHIN
Zitung = Zithung→BODO-NAGA-KACHIN
Ziwe. Ono D.→HUON-FINISTERRE
Zlogba. Mandara Tr.→CHADIC
Znedal = Tzeltal→MAYAN
Zo = Yos→NAGA-KUKI-CHIN
Zoc = Zoque→MIXE-ZOQUE
Zoke = Zoque→MIXE-ZOQUE
Zokhaoh→NAGA-KUKI-CHIN
Zombo. Kongo D.→CENTRAL WESTERN BANTU
Zomo = Zumu→CHADIC
Zomper = Zumper→JUKUNOID
Zompere = Zumper→JUKUNOID
Zoncigal. Kalasa-ala D.→NURISTANI
Zoombo = Zombo. Kongo D.→CENTRAL WESTERN BANTU
Zoque→MIXE-ZOQUE
ZOQUEAN = MIXE-ZOQUE
Zorotua. Kwadi Tr.→KHOISAN
Zorquin = Zhorquin. Terraba D.→CHIBCHAN
Zotung→NAGA-KUKI-CHIN
Zotzil = Tzotzil→MAYAN
Zotzlem = Tzotzil→MAYAN
Zozil = Tzotzil→MAYAN
Zuak = Suri. Tirma D.→EASTERN SUDANIC
Zuande = Bitare→BANTOID
Zuaque. Cahita D.→UTO-AZTECAN
Zuaque = Tahue. Cahita D.→UTO-AZTECAN
Zugweya = Busa→MANDE
Zulmamu = Zelmamu→EASTERN SUDANIC
Zulu. Nguni D.→SOUTH EASTERN BANTU
Zumoni→NAGA-KUKI-CHIN
Zumper→JUKUNOID
Zumperi = Zumper→JUKUNOID
Zumpes = Zumper→JUKUNOID
Zumu→CHADIC
Zunda = Zulu. Nguni D.→SOUTH EASTERN BANTU
Zungle = Nsungli→BANTOID
Zuni→PENUTIAN
Zurina→PANO
Zusu = Wipsi-ni→PLATEAU BENUE-CONGO
Zutugil = Tzutuhil→MAYAN
Zutuhil = Tzutuhil→MAYAN
Zuwarah. Jabal Nafusah D.→BERBER
Zway. East Gurage D.→SEMITIC
Zyoba→NORTH EASTERN BANTU
Zyrian→URALIC